# The Canterbury Book of Spiritual Quotations

William Sykes recently retired as Chaplain of University College, Oxford. For over twenty-five years he ran Reflection Groups for undergraduates and post-graduate students using his ever-expanding collection of quotations from the Bible and from spiritual writers through the ages as a basis for quiet meditation and discussion. *The Canterbury Book of Spiritual Quotations* is drawn from this vast treasure store.

# The Canterbury Book of Spiritual Quotations

*Compiled by*
William Sykes

CANTERBURY
PRESS
Norwich

First published in 2002 under the title *The Eternal Vision*
by the Canterbury Press Norwich
(a publishing imprint of Hymns Ancient & Modern Limited,
a registered charity)
St Mary's Works, St Mary's Plain,
Norwich, Norfolk, NR3 3BH

www.scm-canterburypress.co.uk

This paperback edition published in 2007



British Library Cataloguing in Publication data

A catalogue record for this book is available
from the British Library



ISBN 978 1 85311 827 2

Typeset by Regent Typesetting
Printed and bound by
Biddles Ltd, King's Lynn, Norfolk

# CONTENTS

Introduction vii

Themes:

Acceptance 1
Action 4
Adoration 8
Anxiety 12
Art 16
Aspiration 20
Awareness 24
Beauty 27
Belief 31
Blessedness 35
Character 39
Cheerfulness 43
Christian 46
Church 50
Commitment 54
Compassion 58
Contemplation 62
Contentment 66
Courage 70
Cross 74
Death 78
Depression 82
Discipleship 86
Divinity 90
Doubt 94
Education 98
Eternal Life 102
Experience 106
Faith 110
Finding God 114
Freedom 118
Friendship 122
Fulfilment 126
Glory 130
God 134
Goodness 138
Grace 142
Greatness 146
Grief 150
Growing 154
Guidance 158
Happiness 162
Healing 166
Holiness 170
Holy Spirit 173
Hope 177
Humility 181
Ideals 185
Image of God 189
Imagination 193
Incarnation 197
Influence 201
Inner Life 205

CONTENTS


Inspiration 209
Integrity 213
Intellect 217
Jesus Christ 221
Joy 225
Kindness 229
Kingdom of God 233
Knowledge 237
Leadership 241
Life 245
Light 249
Listening 253
Literature 257
Loneliness 261
Longing 265
Love 269
Marriage 273
Meditation 277
Mind 281
Money 285
Morals 289
Music 293
Mystics 297
Neighbour 301
Obedience 305
Other Faiths 309
Patience 313
Peace 317
Perseverance 321
Philosophy 325
Poetry 329
Power 333
Prayer 337
Presence 341
Pride 345
Progress 349
Purpose 353
Quietness 357
Relationships 361
Resurrection 365
Revelation 369
Saints 373
Salvation 377
Science and Religion 381
Seeking 385
Self 389
Selfishness 392
Serenity 396
Service 400
Sin 404
Soul 408
Suffering 412
Temptation 416
Thanksgiving 420
Thinking 424
Time 428
Transformation 432
Trust 436
Truth 440
Understanding 444
Vision 448
Vocation 452
Wholeness 456
Will 460
Wisdom 464
Wonder 468
Work 472
Worldliness 476
Worship 480

Notes 484
Acknowledgements 547
Index of Authors 553

# INTRODUCTION

*The underlying vision of this anthology*

At the age of thirty, having just completed a busy four-year curacy at Bradford Cathedral, I became aware of being spiritually bankrupt. In my next appointment I was fortunate in being appointed chaplain to University College, London, which gave me an opportunity for renewal. Shortly after arriving in my new location someone put me in touch with two anthologies: *A Year of Grace* and *From Darkness to Light* – both from the publisher Victor Gollancz. I found these books enormously helpful.

On another visit to what was now my favourite bookshop, I jocularly asked the elderly shop assistant which, in her opinion, was the best book in the shop. She immediately said the book she would recommend was out of stock, but would I like to borrow her own copy? I declined as I did not know her very well, but asked if I could order a copy? 'Yes,' she said, 'provided you are prepared to wait for six weeks. This book is an American publication. We shall have to import it.' As it happened I was due to go to New York soon and she gave me the address of a bookshop where I might find a copy of *The Choice Is Always Ours* by Dorothy Berkley Phillips.

As soon as I opened it I realized I had been looking for this book unconsciously for ten years. Pondering over its contents led to the emergence of an underlying framework of faith. The starting-point is the Genesis story of the creation of humankind. In this story God is depicted as fashioning and shaping humankind in his own image and likeness, and the last thing he does is breathe into 'man/woman', and 'man' becomes a living being. I took this to mean that God breathed something of his own Spirit into 'man', giving him something akin to a divine potential. The phrase 'Let us make man in our image' suggests that the divine inbreathing is the Spirit of the Father, Son and Holy Spirit.

The other truth which comes out of this story is that which was fashioned and shaped in the image and likeness of God was taken from the dust of the earth, so that as well as our having something akin to a divine potential we are at one and the same time earthy and creaturely. I would like to add 'and rightly so' as I see a value in the earthy and creaturely as a potential source of energy and dynamism.

If we want to see this framework of faith fully worked out in a life we go to the Gospels – to the person of Jesus Christ. As he went through life he discovered something of the presence of the Father in the depths of himself. After his baptism and the coming of the Holy Spirit into his life, the Gospels reveal he discovered in himself the full range of the gifts of the Holy Spirit: wisdom, counsel (guidance), understanding, knowledge, fear (in the sense of awe and reverence), power and the Spirit of the Lord. This in turn led to the full development of the fruits of the Spirit: love, joy, peace, patience, kindness, goodness, faithfulness, gentleness and self-control. We can also find divine attributes in his personality, such as his life, light, truth, hope, grace and glory.

Lastly he brought about an inner integration of the divine with the earthy and creaturely, becoming 'very God and very man.' Later he was acknowledged to be 'the image of the invisible God', and 'the second Adam'.

We find in the epistles a valuable insight coming from the pen of St Paul. He discovered that what Christ had experienced in his life, we can also experience in some measure in our lives. This comes out in a powerful passage in his letter to the Ephesians:

> For this reason I bow my knees before the Father, from whom every family in heaven and on earth takes its name. I pray that, according to the riches of his glory, he may grant you to be strengthened in your inner being with power through his Spirit, and that Christ may dwell in your hearts through faith, as you are being rooted and grounded in love. I pray that you may have power to comprehend, with all the saints, what is the breadth and length and height and depth, and to know the love of Christ which surpasses knowledge, so that you may be filled with all the fullness of God. Ephesians 3.14–19

Note well this final phrase! This includes the gifts and fruits of the Holy Spirit as well as those divine attributes – life, light, truth, hope, grace and glory. We can now see that this outline of faith is deeply rooted in both the Old and the New Testaments, and in the depths of ourselves.

This outline of faith expands enormously when we consider the spiritual experience of the last two thousand years. We move on to the works of those people we normally consider to have been 'inspired' – i.e. 'breathed into' – as in the Genesis story of the creation of humankind. This opens up our framework of faith to the spiritual experience and insight of many poets, playwrights, novelists; philosophers, theologians, scientists, historians, politicians, economists, artists, musicians, psychologists and statesmen. In the last thirty years I have had an exciting time rounding up insights, thoughts and experiences from the writings of these 'inspired' men and women. Over a period of time I have arranged these findings in 220 topics. Many of these have been published in six collections: *Visions of Faith*, *Visions of Hope*, *Visions of Love*, *Visions of Grace* and *Visions of Glory* and *The Eternal Vision*, here reissued with a new title: *The Canterbury Book of Spiritual Quotations*. Of *Visions of Grace*, a critic wrote rather amusingly: 'If there is a shortage of wisdom in the world it is because . . . Bill Sykes has used it all up in this book.'

## *Using this anthology*

How can we best use the material in this anthology? The quotations are arranged by subject and so are readily accessible illustrations for preaching, teaching and writing. First and foremost I use this book for personal growth and in moving towards becoming a whole person. The underlying practice for this is reflection – a simple form of meditation and contemplation. Reflection involves pondering, mulling over, and 'chewing' the quotations in this anthology, trying to extract all possible value from them.

In reflection we are encouraged to think with our minds as far as they will go. We also use our instincts and intuition (feelings), by looking carefully at the quotations and working out what the feelings they evoke tell us. We make full use of our imaginations and our experiences of life so far. A good description of reflection comes from the Book of Common Prayer, from a Collect intended for the scriptures, but also relevant here:

> Grant that we may in such wise hear them, read, mark, learn, and inwardly digest them.

In reflection great use is made of silence, making way for a listening form of prayer.

Reflecting on the contents of this anthology is an excellent way of fostering spiritual growth and so maybe a valuable follow-up after confirmation. There is enough material here (and in my other publications) to last a lifetime.

Twenty-nine years ago I was elected Chaplain Fellow of University College, Oxford – having been chaplain to University College London, for nine years. Since coming to Oxford, I have been running Reflection Groups in college for well over twenty-five years. These Reflection Groups have been remarkably successful. They have been voluntary and at times I have had thirty different groups meeting each week during term-time.

A typical Reflection Group had up to four or five members who met for an hour a week in my rooms. On arrival each member of the group was offered a cup of tea, coffee, hot chocolate (a great favourite in winter months) or orange juice. There was also an inviting and open tin of biscuits on hand.

A list of 120 topics was then circulated and each member was invited to choose a topic they would like to reflect on. After three or four minutes we shared the titles of potential topics put forward and selected one by consensus. Clipboards and pens were made available for those who wanted to use them.

After a twenty-five minute period of silent reflection on the contents of the chosen topic, I, as the facilitator, would ask the person who chose the topic if there was a reason for his or her choice. The follow-up question usually was, 'Did you find anything helpful?' This question usually started us off on a positive note. We then shared our insights about the topic, with me asking further questions if necessary. However, having reflected on the same material for twenty-five minutes conversation came relatively easily. We ended promptly on the hour.

Participants came from a wide variety of backgrounds. In the groups we had Roman Catholics, Anglicans, Methodists, United Reformed Church members, some members of the Christian Union, Jews, Hindus, Buddhists, atheists and agnostics, and a wide variety of undergraduates and graduates of no fixed allegiance. The groups varied a great deal. At one time we had a group of brilliant sportsmen, most of whom had represented their countries at an international level. There was another group in which each member went on to get a First Class degree. On the other hand a Reflection Group could be just one person and myself, and that person might be going through a difficult time and often the material helped someone to connect with their inner resources.

This pattern of Reflection Group seemed to work well in a college setting. Sometimes the pattern varied and different patterns may develop in other locations. These are to be welcomed and encouraged.

Three reactions were most common from our undergraduates and graduates. Firstly, for many, the Reflection Group was their most enjoyable and valuable hour of the week. Secondly, many said 'These groups really made me think.' Thirdly, 'being a member of a Reflection Group was the most valuable thing I did in Oxford.'

I hope you enjoy the contents of this anthology. If used well, the book acts as a skeleton or framework of faith. Lots of clues are given but it allows the person reflecting the freedom to put his or her own flesh and blood on that skeleton or framework of faith. This is an attempt to get to the heart and core of spirituality, making it readily available for a wide variety of people at the beginning of the twenty-first century.

William Sykes
Oxford 2007

# I

# ACCEPTANCE

## *Acceptance – favourable reception, approval, belief*

At the age of ten I had a firm conviction that there was one job I would never do – that of being a priest. In my teens, in the midst of a very active life, I became aware of a growing faith. This led to a commitment in my early twenties and a conviction that from now on, whatever happened, I was going to lead a Christian life. What particularly stimulated me was a quiet but encouraging awareness of the Holy Spirit. At the time I was wrestling with what to do in life. While pondering over various possibilities I was suddenly challenged by the thought that if my Christian faith was so important to me, perhaps instead of just living it I ought to be actively engaged in spreading it? A chord had been struck and a state of acceptance reached. Over the years I have also been aware of another area of acceptance. At one level there is an acceptance of the worst life can throw at you, and at another level, facing disaster in the most creative way possible. Another form of acceptance is being accepted by God and by other people. There are, therefore, several sides to acceptance.

The beloved of the Lord rests in safety – the High God surrounds him all day long – the beloved rests between his shoulders.

Deuteronomy 33.12

But to all who received him, who believed in his name, he gave power to become children of God.

John 1.12

It is so, it cannot be otherwise.

Anon

We must accept finite disappointment, but we must never lose infinite hope.

Martin Luther King, in Coretta Scott King, *The Words of Martin Luther King*

The will of God . . . cannot be simply that we accept the situations of life but must be rather that we go through them and emerge from them.

John S. Dunne, *The Reasons of the Heart*

You often try to run away from your life, but you're wasting your time. If you sincerely believe that your life is worthwhile and necessary, then you will have accepted it.

Michel Quoist, *With Open Heart*

He who is in a state of rebellion cannot receive grace, to use the phrase of which the Church is so fond – so rightly fond, I dare say – for in life as in art the mood of rebellion closes up the channels of the soul, and shuts out the airs of heaven.

Oscar Wilde, *De Profundis*

The self-accepting person has a realistic appraisal of his resources combined with appreciation of his own worth; assurance about standards and convictions of his own without being a slave to the opinions of others; and realistic assessment of limitations without irrational self-reproach.

Arthur T. Jersild, *The Psychology of Adolescence*

To accept a person does not mean that I deny his defects, that I gloss over them or try to explain them away. Neither does acceptance mean to say that everything the person does is beautiful and fine. Just the opposite is true. When I deny the defects of the person, then I certainly do not accept him. I have not touched the depth of that person. Only when I accept a person can I truly face his defects . . .

Peter G. van Breemen SJ, *As Bread that Is Broken*

There liveth no man on earth who may always have rest and peace without troubles and crosses, with whom things always go according to his will; there is always something to be suffered here, turn which way you will. And as soon as you are quit of one assault, perhaps two will come in its place. Wherefore yield thyself willingly to them, and seek only that true peace of the heart, which none can take away from thee, that thou mayest overcome all assaults.

*Theologia Germanica*

I am accepted by God as I am – *as I am*, and not as I should be . . . He loves me with my ideals and disappointments, my sacrifices and my joys, my successes and my failures. God is himself the deepest Ground of my being. It is one thing to know I am accepted and quite another thing to realize it. It is not enough to have but just once touched the love of God. There is more required to build one's life on God's love. It takes a long time to believe that I am accepted by God as I am.

Peter G. van Breemen SJ, *As Bread that Is Broken*

Out of evil, much good has come to me. By keeping quiet, repressing nothing, remaining attentive, and by accepting reality – taking things as they are, and not as I wanted them to be – by doing all this, unusual knowledge has come to me, and unusual powers as well, such as I could never have imagined before. I always thought that when we accepted things they overpowered us in some way or other. This turns out not to be true at all, and it is only by accepting them that one can assume an attitude toward them.

Richard Wilhelm and C.G. Jung (extract from a former patient), *The Secret of the Golden Flower*

One of the deepest needs of the human heart is the need to be appreciated. Every human being wants to be valued . . . Every human being craves to be accepted, accepted for what he is . . . When I am not accepted, then something in me is broken . . . Acceptance means that the people with whom I live give me a feeling of self-respect, a feeling that I am worthwhile.

They are happy that I am who I am. Acceptance means that I am welcome to be myself. Acceptance means that though there is need for growth, I am not forced. I do not have to be the person I am not!

Peter G. van Breemen SJ, *As Bread that Is Broken*

Sometimes . . . a wave of light breaks into our darkness, and it is as though a voice were saying: 'You are accepted.' *You are accepted*, accepted by that which is greater than you, and the name of which we do not know. Do not ask for the name now; perhaps you will find it later. Do not try to do anything now; perhaps later you will do much. Do not seek for anything; do not perform anything; do not intend anything. *Simply accept the fact that you are accepted!* If that happens to us, we experience grace.

Paul Tillich, *The Shaking of the Foundations*

Each one of us is born with many potentialities. But unless they are drawn out by the warm touch of another's acceptance, they will remain dormant. Acceptance liberates everything that is in me. Only when I am loved in that deep sense of complete acceptance can I become myself. The love, the acceptance of other persons, makes me the unique person that I am meant to be. When a person is appreciated for what he *does*, he is not unique; someone else can do the same work perhaps better than the other. But when a person is loved for what he *is*, then he becomes a unique and irreplaceable personality.

Peter G. van Breemen SJ, *As Bread that Is Broken*

**See also** Contentment, Freedom, Obedience, Patience, Understanding

2

# ACTION

*Action – process of acting, exertion, of energy or influence, as men of action, thing done, act*

In *The Devils of Loudun*, Aldous Huxley comes out with this challenging sentence: 'A man of prayer can do more in a single year than another can accomplish in a whole lifetime.' In retrospect, the early years of my life were taken up in action. I loved all sorts of sport – rugby, hockey, cricket and golf – and played them to the full. In my late teens I was called up for National Service and commissioned into the Gurkhas. After 'Malaya' I went to Balliol for three years, ending with a university expedition to Nepal, followed by training at theological college, and a four-year curacy in Bradford. By the time I was thirty I was feeling the strain. Fortunately I had a colleague – Father Simon Holden of the Community of the Resurrection, Mirfield – who introduced me to the passive side of life, to the life of prayer. The result has been an emergence of a balance between the active life and the passive life.

Now begin the work, and the Lord be with you.
  1 Chronicles 22.16

So let us not grow weary in doing what is right, for we will reap at harvest time, if we do not give up.
  Galatians 6.9

What you theoretically know, vividly realize.
  Francis Thompson, 'Shelley'

Perform every action as though it were your last.
  Marcus Aurelius, *The Meditations of Marcus Aurelius*

Pray, with *humility*; and do, with *diligence*.
  Benjamin Whichcote, *Moral and Religious Aphorisms*

Action springs not from thought, but from a readiness for responsibility.
Dietrich Bonhoeffer, *Letters and Papers from Prison*

There is nothing like active work for relieving and steadying the mind.
A.C. Benson, *Letters of Dr A.C. Benson to M.E.A.*

In our era, the road to holiness necessarily passes through the world of action.
Dag Hammarskjöld, *Markings*

No man can read the Gospels without being impressed with the immense activity of Christ.
Henry Ward Beecher, *Proverbs from Plymouth Pulpit*

Christians are living in this sinful world and must bear its burden, they may not steal away from the battlefield.
Nicolas Berdyaev, *Christianity and Class War*

The worst of partialities is to withhold oneself, the worst ignorance is not to act, the worst lie is to steal away.
Charles Péguy, *Basic Verities*

Enlarging insight depends on expansion due to exercise; vision on action, on acting up to the limit of what has been glimpsed.
Anon

He who is morally active does not exert himself in vain, for much more of the seed falls on fertile ground than the Gospel all too modestly estimates in the parable of the sower.
Johann Wolfgang von Goethe, in Ludwig Curtius, *Wisdom and Experience*

Why stand we here trembling around
Calling on God for help, and not ourselves, in whom God dwells
Stretching a hand to save the falling Man?
William Blake, 'Jerusalem'

All passion becomes strength when it has an outlet from the narrow limits of our personal lot in the labour of our right arm, the cunning of our right hand, or the still, creative activity of our thought.
George Eliot, *Adam Bede*

No one need search for a programme of action or a crusade. The world and suffering humanity create the agenda for those who have eyes for human misery, ears for the stories of oppression and degradation and hearts to respond to the distress of our human family.

Basil Hume OSB, *To Be a Pilgrim*

'Tis God gives skill,
But not without men's hands: He could not make
Antonio Stradivari's violins
Without Antonio.

George Eliot, 'Stradivarius'

These two lives, action and contemplation, instead of excluding each other, call for each other's help, implement and complete each other. Action, to be productive, has need of contemplation. The latter, when it gets to a certain degree of intensity, diffuses some of its excess on the first. By contemplation the soul draws directly from the heart of God the graces which the active life distributes.

Mother Teresa, in Brother Angelo Devananda, *Jesus, the Word to Be Spoken*

He would have urged all Christians to fulfil their duties in a world that still belongs to God despite its sin and shame. But equally firmly he would have declared that no scheme for social betterment, no international organization, no political or ecclesiastical reform can in themselves heal the wounds of humanity. In one way only can men be saved, by ridding their hearts of the selfishness that hides from them the knowledge of the love of God.

Florence Higham, said of F.D. Maurice, in *Frederick Denison Maurice*

Seen with the eyes of the social historian, this three years' activity as a social revolutionary is the life of Jesus in its impact upon human history. What makes it unique is the scope of the vision which it embodies, and his profound insight into the conditions demanded for its accomplishment. The teaching of Jesus is not something separable from his life; it is the expression of the understanding which grew out of his life. Theory and practice are there completely unified. The one interprets and expounds the other. It is the fusion of insight and action that makes the life of Jesus the religious life *par excellence* . . .

John Macmurray, *Creative Society*

Two methods exist, of aiming at human improvement, – by adjusting circumstances without and by addressing the affections within; by creating facilities of position, or by developing force of character; by mechanism or by mind. The one institutional and systematic, operating on a large scale; reaching individuals circuitously and at last; the other is personal and moral, the influence of soul on soul, life creating life, beginning in the regeneration of the individual and spreading thence over communities; the one, in short, reforming from the circumference to the centre, the other from the centre to the circumference. And in comparing these it is not difficult to show the superior triumphs of the latter, which was the method of Christ and Christianity.

James Martineau, *Endeavours After the Christian Life: Discourses*

**See also** Discipleship, Kingdom of God, Progress, Service, Work

# 3

# ADORATION

*Adoration – regarding with the utmost respect and affection: worshipping as a deity; reverence*

We had a tragedy in college. One of our retired Fellows had a daughter with a tumour on the brain. She was married with a two-year-old son. The surgeon had operated on her several times, but was unable to remove the roots of the tumour. He feared he might irretrievably damage her speech and eyesight, some considerable time before she died, which sadly seemed inevitable. I was visiting her in hospital after one of these operations. I had only been there a short time when there was a knock on the door and in came her son – along with other members of the family. He quickly made his way to her bedside and looked adoringly into her eyes. Contact was made and suddenly they gave each other a look of sheer delight and wonder – the look reserved for a person greatly loved and adored. This was one of the most beautiful sights I have ever seen, and gave me a valuable insight into adoration.

O come, let us worship and bow down, let us kneel before the Lord, our Maker!
Psalm 95.6

And all of us, with unveiled faces, seeing the glory of the Lord as though reflected in a mirror, are being transformed into the same image from one degree of glory to another; for this comes from the Lord, the Spirit.
2 Corinthians 3.18

We adore in order to love, to absorb into our own beings the being of God.
Kenneth Leech, *True Prayer*

This is adoration: not a difficult religious exercise, but an attitude of the soul.
Evelyn Underhill, *The Love of God*

If we would understand Divine things, we must cultivate an attitude of humble adoration. Whoever does not begin by kneeling down, runs every possible risk.

Ernest Hello, *Life, Science, and Art*

Nothing is more needed by humanity today, and by the church in particular, than the recovery of a sense of 'beyondness' in the whole of life to revive the springs of wonder and adoration.

John V. Taylor, *The Go-Between God*

It is a beauteous evening, calm and free,
The holy time is quiet as a Nun
Breathless with adoration.

William Wordsworth, 'It is a Beauteous Evening'

Man is most truly himself, as the Eastern Church well knows, not when he toils but when he adores. And we are learning more and more that all innocent joy in life may be a form of adoration.

Vida D. Scudder, *The Privilege of Age*

What I cry out for, like every being, with my whole life and all my earthly passions, is something very different from an equal to cherish: it is for a God to adore . . .

The more man becomes man, the more will he become prey to a need, a need that is always more explicit, more subtle and more magnificent, the need to adore.

Pierre Teilhard de Chardin, *Le Milieu Divin*

But 'to adore' (Lat: ad-orare) is 'to pray toward . . .'. It is to go out of oneself, to commune with a Reality larger, deeper, purer than one's own being. Adoration is an enhancement of one's being, though paradoxically this comes about through going out of oneself.

John Macquarrie, *Paths in Spirituality*

To adore . . . means to lose oneself in the unfathomable, to plunge into the inexhaustible, to find peace in the incorruptible, to be absorbed in defined immensity, to offer oneself to the fire and the transparency, to annihilate oneself in proportion as one becomes more deliberately conscious of oneself, and to give one's deepest to that whose depth has no end.

Pierre Teilhard de Chardin, *Le Milieu Divin*

To worship is to quicken the conscience by the holiness of God, to feed the mind with the truth of God, to purge the imagination by the beauty of God, to open the heart to the love of God, to devote the will to the purpose of God. All this is gathered up in that emotion which most cleanses us from selfishness because it is the most selfless of all emotions – adoration.

William Temple, *The Hope of a New World*

Adoration is a rejoicing in what we believe God is in himself, in the more that he must be that we cannot understand; it is reaching out to this in love and longing, wanting to know and prove as much of this as is permitted here on earth, going to that rim of experience where something tells you to turn back to life because this is as far as you can go in wonder at the devastating richness of life. The rest we may hope to know after death, but it is not for now.

J. Neville Ward, *The Use of Praying*

Worship is essentially an act of adoration, adoration of the one true God in whom we live and move and have our being. Forgetting our little selves, our petty ambitions, our puny triumphs, our foolish cares and fretful anxieties, we reach out towards the beauty and majesty of God. The religious life is not a dull, grim drive towards moral virtues, but a response to a vision of greatness . . . The pattern prayer given by our Lord offers us the clue to right worship. It begins and ends with words of adoration.

Thomas F. Green, *Preparation for Worship*

Adoration is the first and greatest of life's responses to its spiritual environment; the first and most fundamental of spirit's movements towards Spirit, the seed from which all other prayer must spring. It is among the most powerful of the educative forces which purify the understanding, form and develop the spiritual life. As we can never know the secret of great art or music until we have learned to look and listen with a self-oblivious reverence, acknowledging a beauty that is beyond our grasp – so the claim and loveliness remain unrealized, till we have learned to look, to listen, to adore.

Evelyn Underhill, *The Golden Sequence*

The essence of adoration . . . is something far deeper and more demanding than the most ardent praise. It asks for our whole being; and it is rooted in the will. In the words of a French writer: 'you must be convinced that you go to adoration not to receive but to give, and, further, to give often without seeing what you are giving. You go to this act of worship to give your whole being to God in the dark.

And you need to realize what these words mean of obscure faith, sometimes of suffering, and always of love.'

Olive Wyon, *On the Way*

For Christian experience, the life and person of Christ stand apart as the greatness of these self-revelations; the perfect self-expression of the Holy in human terms, and the supreme school and focus of man's adoring prayer. For here the Invisible God, by the most wonderful of His condescensions, discloses His beauty and attraction – the brightness of His glory and the express image of His person – in a way that is mercifully adapted to our limitations, and meets us on our own ground. Therefore the events of Christ's life – alike the most strange and the most homely – are truly 'mysteries'. They contain far more than they reveal.

Evelyn Underhill, *The Golden Sequence*

**See also** Love, Music, Transformation, Wonder, Worship

## 4

# ANXIETY

*Anxiety – uneasiness, concern, solicitous desire (for a thing, to do)*

When I was young I went through several periods of anxiety. A close friend recommended a book to me by Dale Carnegie. The title of this book was *How to Stop Worrying and Start Living.* He observed far too many people lived in the future and were caught up in fears and anxieties. He drew our attention to the design of a modern liner. Many of these were now equipped with heavy steel partition doors. If a liner was holed, the doors could seal off the damaged part and enable the liner to stay afloat. He suggested we discipline ourselves to live 'in watertight compartments'. I also read *The Power of Positive Thinking* by Norman Vincent Peale. I used to have a problem with anxiety in taking exams. In revision time fear would set in and I would almost talk myself into failure. Having read this book, I suddenly realized it was possible to adopt a more positive approach and gently talk myself in to passing exams. Later I found 'positive thinking' a valuable help in all areas of life and an antidote to anxiety. Somewhere in my reading I have picked up the phrase 'wise forethought' as a help in facing anxiety. Writing out solutions to problems and anxieties has also been a great help. The daily time of quiet has proved invaluable.

Cast your burden on the Lord, and he will sustain you.

Psalm 55.22

Humble yourselves therefore under the mighty hand of God, so that he may exalt you in due time. Cast all your anxieties on him, because he cares for you.

1 Peter 5.6–7

Cast all your cares on God; that anchor holds.

Alfred, Lord Tennyson, 'Enoch Arden'

He has not learned the lesson of life who does not every day surmount a fear.

Ralph Waldo Emerson, *Letters and Social Aims, Addresses*

It is a help to have something to do, and not to creep about in a dim fatiguing dream of anxiety.

A.C. Benson, *Extracts from the Letters of Dr A.C. Benson to M.E.A.*

Anxiety, fear, ill-fated desire are signatures on the human face. Suffering and anxious care are written there.

Henry Ward Beecher, *Proverbs from Plymouth Pulpit*

I know well the feeling of being all tense with business and worry. The only cure is the old one – 'whenever you have too much to do, don't do it'.

A.C. Benson, *Extracts from the Letters of Dr A.C. Benson to M.E.A.*

Anxiety is the rust of life, destroying its brightness and weakening its powers. A childlike and abiding trust in Providence is its best preventive and remedy.

Author unknown

Anxiety usually comes from strain, and strain is caused by too complete a dependence on ourselves, on our own devices, our own plans, our own idea of what we are able to do.

Thomas Merton, *No Man Is an Island*

The peril of certain troubles is that although they prevent consecutive thinking, they stimulate a tumultuous activity round a fixed point. Then ensues rapid, monstrous diseased growth.

Mark Rutherford, *Last Pages from a Journal*

If what we have we receive as a gift, and if what we have is to be cared for by God, and if what we have is available to others, then we will possess freedom from anxiety.

Richard Foster, *The Celebration of Discipline*

If we are relieved from serious care we are not necessarily relieved from cares. A crowd of small, impertinent worries torment me which I should not notice if I were in real trouble.

Mark Rutherford, *Last Pages from a Journal*

In our age everything has to be a 'problem'. Ours is a time of anxiety because we have willed it to be so. Our anxiety is not imposed on us by force from outside. We impose it on our world and upon one another from within ourselves.

Thomas Merton, *Thoughts in Solitude*

Let us put all our worries to God, squarely, and then, having told him everything, so that he should know them from us, we should drop them, leave them to him. Now that he is in the know, it is no longer any of our concern: we can freely think of him.

Anthony Bloom, *The Essence of Prayer*

This bewilderment – this confusion as to who we are and what we should do – is the most painful thing about anxiety. But the positive and hopeful side is that just as anxiety destroys our self-awareness, so awareness of ourselves can destroy anxiety. That is to say, the stronger our consciousness of ourselves, the more we can take a stand against and overcome anxiety.

Rollo May, *Man's Search for Himself*

The release of anxiety is to turn cares into prayers. If we feel anxious about somebody, ill or in danger or need, that anxiety does no good to us or to them. But if that anxiety is turned into a prayer, it widens and enriches our spiritual life, it turns a thought which is depressing into a thought which is uplifting, and it helps the person we are praying for.

Geoffrey Harding, in George Appleton, *Journey for a Soul*

. . . if God has you, then He has your yesterdays and your tomorrows. He has your yesterdays and forgives all that has been amiss in them; He has your tomorrows and will provide grace and power to meet them. But only as they come. He will not provide for what is not yet here. His grace is like manna – when kept over for the next day, it spoiled. It had to be eaten day by day.

E. Stanley Jones, *Growing Spiritually*

While there is always need of wise forethought and due reference to the demands of the future, these have yet nothing in common with mere anxieties and worries which are disintegrating and fret away all the pure gold in life. Worry is simply lack of faith in God. 'For your heavenly Father knoweth what things ye have need of before ye ask Him.' Only in peace of spirit can any true achievement be won.

Lilian Whiting, *Lilies of Eternal Peace*

Annihilation of this swarm of petty invading cares by adoration! They possess and distract, not by their inherent strength but through the absence of a dominant power. The lover is absorbed in the desire to be with his mistress and keeps his appointment with her, breaking all hindrances like threads. Who shall deliver me from the body of this death? The answer was not difficult to St Paul, but how is it with me?

Mark Rutherford, *Last Pages from a Journal*

'Anxiety and misgiving,' wrote Fénelon, 'proceed solely from love of self. The love of God accomplishes all things quietly and completely; it is not anxious or uncertain. The spirit of God rests continually in quietness. Perfect love casteth out fear. It is in forgetfulness of self that we find peace. Happy is he who yields himself completely, unconsciously, and finally to God. Listen to the inward whisper of His Spirit and follow it – that is enough; but to listen one must be silent, and to follow one must yield.'

Lilian Whiting, *The Life Radiant*

**See also** Courage, Faith, Grace, Hope, Trust

# 5

# ART

*Art – skill applied to imitation and design, as in painting, etc., of artistic design, etc., thing in which skill may be exercised*

At theological college, we were each assigned a pastoral task. I was a member of a team which went to an experimental boarding school for boys with problems. We used to go there twice a week – on a Wednesday evening and a Sunday morning. The school had a mid-term break. There was one boy who had no home to go to so we invited him to come and stay in college. As you can imagine, he was soon bored stiff. One of our team knew he had an artistic streak so bought him brushes and paints, and offered him a wall in his room, for a mural. For the next forty-eight hours this fourteen-year-old boy was thoroughly engrossed. When we were eventually allowed in we were completely taken aback by what we saw. What he had produced was a magnificent picture of the nativity. It was the work of a genius. Where had this artistic 'gift' come from? Is this another consequence of the 'divine inbreathing' of the Genesis story of the creation of human beings? Some of the quotations are suggesting this.

I have filled him with divine spirit, with ability, intelligence, and knowledge in every kind of craft, to devise artistic designs, to work in gold, silver, and bronze, in cutting stones for setting, and in carving wood, in every kind of craft.

Exodus 31.3–5

. . . and there are varieties of activities, but it is the same God who activates all of them in everyone.

1 Corinthians 12.6

Nature is a revelation of God; Art a revelation of man.

Henry Wadsworth Longfellow, 'Hyperion'

Fine art is that in which the hand, the head, and the *heart* of man go together.

John Ruskin, *The Two Paths*

Every artist dips his brush in his own soul, and paints his own nature into his pictures.

Henry Ward Beecher, *Proverbs from Plymouth Pulpit*

The Fine Arts once divorcing themselves from *truth*, are quite certain to fall mad, if they do not die.

Thomas Carlyle, *Latter-Day Pamphlets*

True art, is the desire of a man to express himself, to record the reactions of his personality to the world he lives in.

Amy Lowell, *Tendencies in Modern American Poetry*

The art which is grand and yet simple is that which presupposes the greatest elevation both in artist and in public.

Henri Frédéric Amiel, *Amiel's Journal*

The artist, of whatever kind, is a man so much aware of the beauty of the universe that he must impart the same beauty to whatever he makes.

A. Clutton Brock, *The Ultimate Belief*

All true Art is the expression of the soul. The outward forms have value only in so far as they are the expression of the inner spirit of man.

Mohandas K. Gandhi, in C.F. Andrews, *Mahatma Gandhi's Ideas*

Painting is an art, and art is not vague production, transitory and isolated, but a power which must be directed to the improvement and refinement of the human soul.

Wassily Kandinsky, *Concerning the Spiritual in Art*

To draw a moral, to preach a doctrine, is like shouting at the north star. Life is a vast and awful business. The great artist sets down his vision of it and is silent.

Ludwig Lewisohn, *The Modern Drama*

All great art is the work of the whole living creature, body and soul, and chiefly of the soul. But it is not only *the work* of the whole creature, it likewise *addresses* the whole creature.

John Ruskin, *The Stones of Venice*

The man who has honesty, integrity, the love of inquiry, the desire to see beyond, is ready to appreciate good art. He needs no one to give him an art education; he is already qualified.

Robert Henri, *The Art Spirit*

Art is the gift of God, and must be used
Unto His glory. That in Art is highest
Which aims at this.

Henry Wadsworth Longfellow, 'Michel Angelo'

Not everything has a name. Some things lead us into a realm beyond words. Art thaws even the frozen, darkened soul, opening it to lofty spiritual experience. Through Art we are sometimes sent – indistinctly, briefly – revelations not to be achieved by rational thought.

Alexander Solzhenitsyn, *One Word of Truth: The Nobel Speech in Literature*

A picture, however admirable the painter's art, and wonderful his power, requires of the spectator a surrender of himself, in due proportion with the miracle which has been wrought. Let the canvas glow as it may, you must love with the eye of faith, or its highest excellence escapes you.

Nathaniel Hawthorne, *The Marble Faun*

Art is the true and happy science of the soul,
exploring nature for spiritual influences,
as doth physical science for comforting powers,
advancing so to a sure knowledge with life progress.

Robert Bridges, 'The Testament of Beauty'

But the artist appeals to that part of our being which is not dependent on wisdom; to that in us which is a gift and not an acquisition – and, therefore more permanently enduring. He speaks to our capacity for delight and wonder, to the sense of mystery surrounding our lives; to our sense of pity, and beauty, and pain.

Joseph Conrad, *The Nigger of the 'Narcissus'*

When the artist is alive in any person, whatever his kind of work may be, he becomes an inventive, searching, daring, self-expressing creature. He becomes interesting to other people. He disturbs, upsets, enlightens, and he opens ways for a better understanding. Where those who are not artists are trying to close the book, he opens it, shows there are still more pages possible.

Robert Henri, *The Art Spirit*

Upon the whole it seems to me, that the object and intention of all the Arts is to supply the natural imperfection of things, and often to gratify the mind by realizing and embodying what never existed but in the imagination.

It is allowed on all hands, that facts, and events, however they may bind the historian, have no dominion over the poet or the painter. With us, history is made to bend and conform to this great idea of art. And why? Because these arts, in their highest province, are not addressed to the gross senses; but to the desires of the mind, to that spark of divinity which we have within . . .

Sir Joshua Reynolds, *Sir Joshua Reynolds' Discourses*

**See also** Beauty, Literature, Music, Poetry, Truth

## 6

# ASPIRATION

*Aspiration – drawing of breath; desiring earnestly – for or after*

I think I have always been susceptible to aspiration. A special time of aspiration was a visit to Oxford at the age of fifteen. On looking at the colleges and the university buildings I was suddenly fired with a burning desire to study in Oxford. From then onwards I worked hard at my studies, and was delighted some years later to get a place at Balliol. A smaller aspiration, which bore fruit later, was watching the coronation on television, and seeing the Gurkhas for the first time. Later I saw them again, taking part in an Edinburgh Tattoo. When I came to do National Service, I soon became aware of a burning desire to serve with them, and was greatly privileged to be with them in Singapore. What is the difference between inspiration and aspiration? Inspiration is an inward influence, a divine inbreathing – as in the Genesis story of the creation. Aspiration is more of an outward influence, as in the two instances cited above.

How lovely is your dwelling-place, O Lord of hosts! My soul longs, indeed faints for the courts of the Lord; my heart and my flesh sing for joy to the living God.

Psalm 84.1–2

. . . he breathed on them, and said to them, 'Receive the Holy Spirit.'

John 20.22

My . . . aspirations are my only friends.

Henry Wadsworth Longfellow, 'The Masque of Pandora'

Thou, who canst *think* as well as *feel.*
Mount from the earth. aspire! aspire!

William Wordsworth, 'Devotional Incitements'

By aspiring to a similitude of God in goodness or love, neither man nor angel ever transgressed, or shall transgress.

Francis Bacon, *The Advancement of Learning*

A good man, through obscurest aspiration,
Has still an instinct of the one true way.

Johann Wolfgang von Goethe, *Faust*

It's not a matter of chasing sensations, but welcoming those which come to us legitimately, and directing them towards the goals we aspire to.

Michel Quoist, *With Open Heart*

And thou my mind aspire to higher things:
Grow rich in that which never taketh rust.

Sir Philip Sidney, 'Leave Me, O Love'

An aspiration is a joy for ever, a possession as solid as a landed estate, a fortune which we can never exhaust and which gives year by year a revenue of pleasurable activity.

Robert Louis Stevenson, *Familiar Studies of Men and Books, Virginibus Puerisque, Selected Poems*

Enflam'd with the study of learning, and the admiration of virtue; stirr'd up with high hopes of living to be brave men, and worthy patriots, dear to God, and famous to all ages.

John Milton, *Of Education*

By the word soul, or psyche, I mean that inner consciousness which aspires. By prayer I do not mean a request for anything preferred to a deity; I mean soul-emotion, intense aspiration.

Richard Jefferies, *The Story of My Heart*

The sensual man is at home in worldliness because he has no higher aspiration. The spiritual man, however much attracted to worldliness, cannot be at home in the world of sense because he is groping towards the world of spirit.

Hubert van Zeller, *Considerations*

It is true, no doubt . . . that many persons 'go through life' without being consciously aware of their high endowment, they accumulate 'things', live in their outside world, 'make good' . . . but . . . the *push for the beyond* is always there in us . . .

Rufus M. Jones, in H. Loukes, *The Quaker Contribution*

But I do hold to a something more, far higher than the actual human, something to which it is human to aspire and to seek to translate into life individual and communal; this something translates itself to me best as the Holy Spirit.

Stephen MacKenna, *Journal and Letters*

For rigorous teachers seized my youth,
And purged its faith, and trimmed its fire,
Showed me the high, white star to Truth,
There bade me gaze, and there aspire.

Matthew Arnold, 'Stanzas from the Grande Chartreuse'

It was my duty to have loved the highest:
It surely was my profit had I known:
It would have been my pleasure had I seen.
We needs must love the highest when we see it.

Alfred, Lord Tennyson, 'Idylls of the King, Guinevere'

The religious spirit is in us. It preceded the religions, and their task as well as that of the prophets, of the initiated, consists in releasing, directing, and developing it. This mystical aspiration is an essentially human trait. It slumbers at the bottom of our souls awaiting the event, or the man capable, in the manner of an enzyme, of transforming it into true mysticism, into faith.

Lecomte du Nöuy, *Human Destiny*

All religions, arts and sciences are branches of the same tree. All these aspirations are directed toward ennobling man's life, lifting it from the sphere of mere physical existence and leading the individual toward freedom. It is no mere chance that our older universities have developed from clerical schools. Both churches and universities – insofar as they live up to their true function – serve the ennoblement of the individual. They seek to fulfil this great task by spreading moral and cultural understanding, renouncing the use of brute force.

Albert Einstein, *Out of My Later Years*

No aspiring soul, . . . has not at some time bowed in worship before the wonder, mystery and beauty of the world. The glorious forms and colours of sunset and dawn; the ripple of moonlight on the surface of some quiet lake; the majesty of mountain peaks; and the quaintly flowing music of mountain streams, remind every lover of Nature that God is not apart from His world, but can be found hidden there as the very Spirit of it all – 'Beauty Itself among beautiful things'. The beauty is there for all to see, but men dwell in the shadows of their own creation and their eyes are blind to it.

Raynor C. Johnson, *A Pool of Reflections*

**See also** Experience, Inspiration, Revelation, Vision, Wonder

# 7

# AWARENESS

*Awareness – a condition of knowing*

In the latter reaches of a nine-year period as chaplain to University College London, I was invited to join a group consisting of the Director of the Health Centre (a psychiatrist), two GPs from the health centre, and the student counsellor. We met once a fortnight. We took it in turns to present a student problem. If it was my turn I would put before the others all the material facts about the student and the problem, except his or her name – observing confidentiality. We would then try to solve the problem using our different skills and experience. At the end of the hour's session, I would leave the health centre, feeling my awareness had increased fourfold. As a consequence there was now a real possibility of solving the problem. Reflection Groups and using this anthology on an individual basis, work on the same principle, with the aim of increasing our awareness.

O Lord, you have searched me and known me. You know when I sit down and when I rise up; you discern my thoughts from far away.

Psalm 139.1

Be alert at all times.

Luke 21.36

The seership of a poet's heart, the insight that is given to faith.

Edward Bellamy, *Looking Backwards*

How another sees you depends on how you see him. Respect him, and he will respect you.

Michel Quoist, *With Open Heart*

The only way to get our values right is to see, not the beginning, but the end of the way, to see things, not only in the light of time, but in the light of eternity.

William Barclay, *The Gospel of Matthew*

The inability to see into ourselves often manifests itself in a certain coarseness and clumsiness. One can be brazen, rude and even dishonest without being aware of it.

Eric Hoffer, *The Passionate State of Mind*

Be quite sure that you will never have the unclouded vision of God here in this life. But you may have the awareness of him, if he is willing by his grace to give it you.

*The Cloud of Unknowing*

He [Jesus] was not concerned with advice about conduct, but with the exposure of motive, penetrating the inner heart's secrets with the two-edged sword of his inescapable insight.

F.R. Barry, *The Relevance of Christianity*

When thou lookest upon the Imperfections of others, allow one Eye for what is Laudable in them, and the balance they have from some excellency, which may render them considerable.

Sir Thomas Browne, *Christian Morals*

If we had a keen vision and feeling of all ordinary human life, it would be like hearing the grass grow and the squirrel's heart beat, and we should die of that roar which lies on the other side of silence. As it is, the quickest of us walk about well wadded with stupidity.

George Eliot, *Middlemarch*

Another lesson I learned was that the intensity of prayer is not measured by time, but by the reality and depth of one's awareness of unity with God. I learned to look on prayer not as a means of influencing the Creator in my favour, but as an awareness of the presence of God – everywhere.

Margaret Bondfield, *What Life Has Taught Me*

If we do not understand our fellow creatures we shall never love them. And it is equally true, that if we do not love them we shall never understand them. Want of charity, want of sympathy, want of good feeling and fellow-feeling – what does it, what can it breed but endless mistakes and ignorances, both of men's characters and men's circumstances.

Charles Kingsley, *Daily Thoughts*

The person who never notices the person next to him can never move beyond and see the 'incognito' Christ in him. Busyness can lead pastors to miss seeing those they meet: people can be a hindrance in a carefully-planned schedule for the day, since they are so unpredictable and time-consuming. And simply to be noticed, recognized as a person, transforms the day for many people.

Frank Wright, *The Pastoral Nature of the Ministry*

Whoever really loves will use a magnifying glass to see the small and hidden details of another's need. I will be able to see that he has cold feet and I can move him nearer the fire; that he is deaf and I must speak closer to his ear; that a secret anxiety torments him; that he longs for a good word; and many more such things which usually lie, seemingly hidden, under the surface of our lives.

Helmut Thielicke, *I Believe – The Christian's Creed*

While we are immersed in our own thoughts we cannot recognize the reality of other people's needs, we do not see the other person at all as he is; all we see is a being who is or is not meeting our requirements. For this reason most domestic dissension is a battle between ghosts. Neither husband nor wife is loving or hating the real other, only an illusion, a projection of his or her personal wishes or resentments. J. Neville Ward, *The Use of Praying*

I learned . . . that to condemn others is a grave mistake, since hatred, and even the wrong kind of criticism, is an evil which recoils upon its author and poisons every human relationship.

That does not mean we should be blind to the weaknesses or wickedness of others, any more than to our own, but that we should learn to look at them as the limitations of birth and circumstance, limitations which it is our duty to help them to rise above. In this I have found that example and service are more helpful than advice or preaching. Margaret Bondfield, *What Life Has Taught Me*

Our most important task is to become aware of the fact that our new consciousness of space no longer admits the traditional imagery by which we represent to ourselves our encounter with God. At the same time, we must also recognize that this traditional imagery *was never essential to Christianity*. We must recover the New Testament awareness that our God does not need a temple (Acts 7.47–53) or even a cathedral. The New Testament teaches in fact that God has one indestructible temple: which is man himself (1 Cor. 3.17). To understand that God is present in the world in man is in fact no new or radical idea. It is, on the contrary, one of the most elementary teachings in the New Testament.

Thomas Merton, *Conjectures of a Guilty Bystander*

**See also** Belief, Education, Listening, Understanding

# 8

# BEAUTY

*Beauty – combination of qualities, as shape, proportion, colour, in human face or form, or in other objects, that delight the sight; combined qualities, delighting the other senses, the moral sense, or the intellect*

I have been conscious of beauty as far back as I can remember. In childhood I quickly discovered the beauty of nature in a garden – in the flowers, the trees, and the shrubs. After this I became aware of the beauty of the seasons – snow in winter, crocuses and daffodils in springtime, the sun, sea and sky in summer, and the rich hues of autumn. Travel opened up fresh vistas of beauty, especially in the mountains of the Himalayas, Africa and the Alps. Dawn and dusk are also constant reminders of the beauty of the world. For many people today, beauty is seen as something outside us, not only in nature, but in music, poetry and art, and in the beauty of another person. However, we seem to have lost the awareness of beauty present in the depths of our being, and rarely do we become the beauty we feel after and long for.

And let the beauty of the Lord our God be upon us.

Psalm 90.17 (AV)

Finally, beloved, whatever is true, whatever is honourable, whatever is just, whatever is pure, whatever is pleasing, whatever is commendable, if there is any excellence and if there is anything worthy of praise, think about these things.

Philippians 4.8

He has a daily beauty in his life.

William Shakespeare, *Othello*

Beauty may be said to be God's trade mark in creation.

Henry Ward Beecher, *Proverbs from Plymouth Pulpit*

Nothing in human life, least of all religion, is ever right until it is beautiful.
Harry Emerson Fosdick, *As I See Religion*

This world is the world of wild storm kept tame with the music of beauty.
Rabindranath Tagore, *Stray Birds*

The hours when the mind is absorbed by beauty are the only hours when we really live.
Richard Jefferies, *Pageant of Summer*

I want to help you to grow as beautiful as God meant you to be when he thought of you first.
George Macdonald, *The Marquis of Lossie*

Though we travel the world over to find the beautiful, we must carry it with us, or we find it not.
Ralph Waldo Emerson, *Essays and Representative Men*

When you reach the heart of life you shall find beauty in all things, even in the eyes that are blind to beauty.
Kahlil Gibran, *Sand and Foam*

It is part and parcel of every man's life to develop beauty in himself. All perfect things have in them an element of beauty.
Henry Ward Beecher, *Proverbs from Plymouth Pulpit*

Every bit of beauty in this world, the beauty of man, of nature, of a work of art, is a partial transfiguration of this world, a creative break-through to another.
Nicolas Berdyaev, *Christian Existentialism*

Flowers, shade, a fine view, a sunset sky, joy, grace, feeling, abundance, and serenity, tenderness, and song, – here you have the element of beauty.
Henri Frédéric Amiel, *Amiel's Journal*

Physical beauty is the sign of an interior beauty, a spiritual and moral beauty which is the basis, the principle, and the unity of the beautiful.
Friedrich Schiller, *Essays, Aesthetical and Philosophical*

I feel more and more that the instinct for beauty (spiritual and moral as well as natural) is the most trustworthy of all instincts, and the surest sign of the nearness of God.
A.C. Benson, *Extracts from the Letters of Dr A.C. Benson to M.E.A.*

Spirit of BEAUTY, that dost consecrate
With thine own hues all thou dost shine upon
Of human thought or form – where art thou gone?
Percy Bysshe Shelley, 'Hymn to Intellectual Beauty'

Man comes into life to seek and find his sufficient beauty, to serve it, to win and increase it, to fight for it, to face anything and dare anything for it, counting death as nothing so long as the dying eyes still turn to it.
H.G. Wells, *The History of Mr Polly*

There comes a moment in life . . . when moral beauty seems more urgent, more penetrating, than intellectual beauty; when all that the mind has treasured must be bathed in the greatness of soul, lest it perish in the sandy desert, forlorn as the river that seeks in vain for the sea.
Maurice Maeterlinck, *Wisdom and Destiny*

But a celestial brightness – a more ethereal beauty –
Shone on her face and encircled her form, when, after confession,
Homeward serenely she walked with God's benediction upon her.
When she had passed, it seemed like the ceasing of exquisite music.
Henry Wadsworth Longfellow, 'Evangeline, Part the First'

Man is so inclined to concern himself with the most ordinary things, while his mind and senses are so easily blunted against impressions of beauty and perfection, that we should use all means to preserve the capacity of feeling them . . . Each day we should at least hear one little song, read one good poem, see one first-rate picture, and if it can be arranged, utter some sensible remarks.
Johann Wolfgang von Goethe, *Wilhelm Meister's Year of Apprenticeship*

Spirit of Beauty, whose sweet impulses,
Flung like the rose of dawn across the sea,
Alone can flush the exalted consciousness
With shafts of sensible divinity –
Light of the World, essential loveliness.
Alan Seeger, 'An Ode to Natural Beauty'

I believe that there is nothing lovelier, deeper, more sympathetic, more rational, more manly, and more perfect than the Saviour; I say to myself with jealous love that not only is there no one else like Him, but that there could be no one. I would say even more: If anyone could prove to me that Christ is outside the truth, and if the truth really did exclude Christ, I should prefer to stay with Christ and not with truth . . . There is in the world only one figure of absolute beauty: Christ. That infinitely lovely figure, is as a matter of course, an infinite marvel.

Fyodor Dostoyevsky, *Letters of Fyodor Michailovitch Dostoyevsky to His Family and Friends*

**See also** Art, Literature, Music, Poetry, Truth

# 9

# BELIEF

*Belief – trust or confidence (in); acceptance of Christian theology; thing believed, religion, opinion, intuition*

Mark Rutherford, in this section, encourages us to struggle earnestly to increase our beliefs. 'Every addition to these', he writes, 'is an extension of life both in breadth and depth.' My belief started off as a belief in God the creator. In my teens I went one stage further and found I could assent to a belief in the contents of a creed. In my early twenties belief focused mainly on the person of Jesus Christ and the Holy Spirit. At the age of thirty a big step forward was taken when I came to believe in 'the God within' – something of the Father, Son, and the gifts and fruits of the Holy Spirit. A constant unfolding of belief has led to an extension of life both in breadth and depth. The results are to be found in this anthology. *The Eternal Vision* acts as a skeleton or framework of belief, but enables us to put our own flesh and blood on them through the practice of reflection.

Believe in the Lord your God and you will be established; believe his prophets

2 Chronicles 20.20

I believe; help my unbelief!

Mark 9.24

Belief makes the mind abundant.

W.B. Yeats, in Samuel H. Miller, *The Great Realities*

He does not believe, that does not live according to his Belief.

Thomas Fuller, *Gnomologia*

When I believe, I am no longer a mere man, I am already a son of God.

Carlo Carretto, *Summoned by Love*

Believe that life *is* worth living, and your belief will help create the fact.

William James, *The Will to Believe*

In the world of today the crisis of Christianity is essentially a crisis of belief.

F.R. Barry, *Secular and Supernatural*

Belief consists in accepting the affirmations of the soul; unbelief, in denying them.

Ralph Waldo Emerson, *Essays and Representative Men*

But we ought to struggle earnestly to increase our beliefs. Every addition to these is an extension of life both in breadth and depth.

Mark Rutherford, *Last Pages from a Journal*

So, once again, you chose for yourself – and opened the door to chaos. The chaos you become whenever God's hand does not rest upon your head.

Dag Hammarskjöld, *Markings*

Firstly I believe in the reality of God as the centre of human aspiration and history. What I believe about man, made in the image of God, derives first and foremost from what I believe about God.

David Sheppard, *Bias to the Poor*

That all things are possible to him who *believes*, that they are less difficult to him who *hopes*, they are more easy to him who *loves*, and still more easy to him who perseveres in the practice of these three virtues.

Brother Lawrence, *The Practice of the Presence of God*

I believe in Jesus Christ, in whom I get a picture of God within the limits of my comprehension. Upon Him rests the whole fabric of my life. He alone holds it together in form and purpose, and without Him it would disintegrate.

Hugh Redwood, *Residue of Days*

We all know people who tell us they cannot believe what cannot be proved. Of course it is not true. Of course they do in fact believe a great deal that they cannot prove – concerning the trustworthiness of their friends, for example.

William Temple, *The Hope of a New World*

We have only to believe. And the more threatening and irreducible reality appears, the more firmly and desperately must we believe. Then, little by little, we shall see the universal horror unbend, and then smile upon us, and then take us in its more than human arms.

Pierre Teilhard de Chardin, *Le Milieu Divin*

There comes a time when we have to believe where we cannot prove, and to accept where we cannot understand. If, even in the darkest hour, we believe that somehow there is a purpose in life, and that somehow that purpose is love, then even the unbearable becomes bearable, and even in the darkness there is still a glimmer of light.

William Barclay, *The Gospel of John*

There is nothing that so sanctifies the heart of man, that keeps us in such habitual love, prayer and delight in God: nothing that so kills all the roots of evil in our nature, that so renews and perfects all our virtues, that fills us with so much love, goodness, and good wishes to every creature as this faith that God is always present in us with His Light and Holy Spirit.

William Law, in Stephen Hobhouse, *Selected Mystical Writings of William Law*

One thing, however, which the apologist must always have in mind is that the debate between belief and unbelief is by no means merely a debate between himself who believes and another who disbelieves. It is also in large part a debate within himself, who both believes and disbelieves, and who must ever continue to pray humbly, 'Lord, I believe; help thou mine unbelief.'

John Baillie, *Invitation to Pilgrimage*

And so I accept God, and I accept him not only without reluctance, but, what's more, I accept his divine wisdom and purpose – which are completely beyond our comprehension. I believe in the underlying order and meaning of life. I believe in the eternal harmony into which we are all supposed to merge one day. I believe in the Word to which the universe is striving, and which itself was 'with God' and which was God, and, well, so on and so forth, *ad infinitum.*

Fyodor Dostoyevsky, *The Brothers Karamazov*

As one who has put God to the test in peace and war, who has let himself go on Jesus, who has tried the way of love and the path of prayer, I am not the less definite here. I believe in God. I believe in the love of God. I believe He lived, and died, and rose again. I believe in mercy, I believe in judgement.

These are not opinions with me. These are convictions. By these I steer. Respecting this chart, I am confident of coming in safety to the haven under the hill.

W.E. Sangster, *These Things Abide*

I believe in one God, the creator of the universe. That he governs it by his Providence. That he ought to be worshipped. That the most acceptable service we can render to him is doing good to his other children. That the soul of man is immortal, and will be treated with justice in another life respecting its conduct in this. These I take to be the fundamental points in all sound religion, and I regard them as you do in whatever sect I meet with them. As to Jesus of Nazareth, my opinion of whom you particularly desire, I think the system of morals and his religion as he left them to us, the best the world saw or is like to see.

Benjamin Franklin, *The Private Correspondence of B. Franklin 1753–90*

**See also** Acceptance, Commitment, Faith, Obedience, Trust

10

# BLESSEDNESS

*Blessedness – happiness, enjoyment of divine favours*

It took me some thirty-six years to understand the mystery of blessedness. The insight came through a rereading of the Genesis story of the creation of humanity. In that story God is depicted as fashioning and shaping Adam in his own image and likeness, and the last thing he did was breathe into Adam and for him to become a living being. I have taken this to mean that all of us have an enormous source of life in the depths of ourselves. If we want to see this fully worked out in a life we can go to the person of Jesus Christ – recognized in scripture as 'the image of the invisible God'. During his life he found something of the 'Father's' presence in the depths of himself – as well as the gifts and fruits of the Holy Spirit. In this he experienced blessedness and discovered true 'happiness; enjoyment of divine favours'. We too can find this source of happiness and divine favour in ourselves through reflection, meditation and contemplation.

The Lord bless you and keep you; the Lord make his face to shine upon you, and be gracious to you; the Lord lift up his countenance upon you, and give you peace.

Numbers 6.24–26

And God is able to provide you with every blessing in abundance, so that by always having enough of everything, you may share abundantly in every good work.

2 Corinthians 9.8

Blessed is he who has found his work; let him ask no other blessedness.

Thomas Carlyle, *Past and Present*

There is in man a HIGHER than Love of Happiness: he can do without Happiness, and instead thereof find Blessedness.

Thomas Carlyle, *Sartor Resartus*

He is blessed who is assured that the animal is dying out in him day by day, and the divine being established.

Henry David Thoreau, *Walden*

Amid my list of blessings infinite,
Stand this the foremost, 'That my heart has bled.'

Edward Young, *Night Thoughts*

But blessedness comes to the man who, in spite of failures and failings, still clutches to him the passionate love of the highest.

William Barclay, *The Gospel of Matthew*

The soul of man can by recognizing God draw Him into its narrow boundaries, but also by love to Him itself expand into the Infinite – and this is blessedness on earth.

John Burchhardt, *The Civilization of the Renaissance in Italy*

There is nothing that is a greater blessing in a community than a man who is known to be an honest, truth-speaking man, and who is kind and genial and cheerful everywhere and at all times.

Henry Ward Beecher, *Proverbs from Plymouth Pulpit*

Blessings, we enjoy daily. And for most of them, because they be so common, most men forget to pay their praises: but let not us; because it is a sacrifice so pleasing to Him that made that sun and us, and still protects us, and gives us flowers, and showers, and stomachs, and meat, and content, and leisure.

Izaak Walton, *The Compleat Angler*

God is present in a silent way always. A certain hidden element or hiding element then is in the Divine Mind. God's blessings steal into life noiselessly. They are neither self-proclaiming nor even self-announcing.

Henry Ward Beecher, *Proverbs from Plymouth Pulpit*

All the great works and wonders that God has ever wrought or shall ever work in or through the creatures, or even God Himself with all His goodness, so far as these things exist or are done outside of me, can never make me blessed, but only in so far as they exist and are done and loved, known, tasted and felt within me.

*Theologia Germanica*

The first Beatitude is very properly first. 'Blessed are the poor in spirit'. This means: Blessed is he who knows that he is not wise and good and strong enough to make himself good, and who therefore relies wholly upon God to give him that positive righteousness which alone is sufficient. The man in Christ is not distinguished by the absence of evil in him, but by the dominant and overmastering presence in him of the good which comes from God.

Carroll E. Simcox, *The Promises of God*

The Spirit of Love, wherever it is, is its own Blessing and Happiness, because it is the Truth and Reality of God in the Soul; and therefore is in the same Joy of Life, and is the same Good to itself, everywhere, and on every Occasion . . .

Would you know the Blessing of all Blessings, it is this God of Love dwelling in your Soul, and killing every Root of Bitterness, which is the Pain and Torment of every earthly selfish Love.

William Law, *The Spirit of Love and the Spirit of Prayer*

Life indeed must be measured by thought and action, not by time. It certainly may be, and ought to be, bright, interesting, and happy; and, according to the Italian proverb, 'if all cannot live on the Piazza, everyone may yet feel the sun'.

If we do our best; if we do not magnify trifling troubles; if we look resolutely, I do not say at the bright side of things, but at things as they really are; if we avail ourselves of the manifold blessings which surround us; we cannot but feel that life is indeed a glorious inheritance.

Sir John Lubbock, *The Pleasures of Life*

Magnificent weather. The morning seems bathed in happy peace, and a heavenly fragrance rises from mountain and shore; it is as though a benediction were laid upon us . . . One might believe oneself in a church – a vast temple in which every being and every natural beauty has its place. I dare not breathe for fear of putting the dream to flight, – a dream traversed by angels . . . In these heavenly moments the cry of Pauline rises to one's lips. 'I feel! I believe! I see!' All the miseries, the cares, the vexations of life, are forgotten; the universal joy absorbs us; we enter into the divine order, and into the blessedness of the Lord.

Henri Frédéric Amiel, *Amiel's Journal*

Things worth remembering:
The value of time,
The success of perseverance,
The pleasure of working,
The dignity of simplicity,
The worth of character,
The improvement of talent,
The influence of example,
The obligation of duty,
The wisdom of economy,
The virtue of patience,
The joy of originating,
The power of kindness.
Anon

**See also** Grace, Fulfilment, Happiness, Joy, Serenity

11

# CHARACTER

*Character – moral strength, back-bone; reputation, good reputation; description of person's qualities*

I have always been influenced by people of character. Two biographies, both by George Seaver, have been about men of character, and have influenced me a great deal. The first was *Edward Wilson of the Antarctic* – the life story of the doctor, zoologist and artist, on Scott's expedition to the Antarctic. Although Scott was the official leader, the qualities of Edward Wilson's character exercised a quiet but decisive influence on the members of the expedition. The second was *Albert Schweitzer: The Man and His Mind.* Here was portrayed the character of a man with four doctorates, in philosophy, theology, music and medicine, who went on to found and run a mission hospital in a remote part of equatorial West Africa. He was described as a man of moral strength, with impressive qualities. Character continues to be an important influence in our day and age.

For as he thinketh in his heart, so is he.
Proverbs 23.7 (AV)

Do you not know that you are God's temple and that God's Spirit dwells in you?
1 Corinthians 3.16

This above all: to thine own self be true.
William Shakespeare, *Hamlet*

An honest man's the noblest work of God.
Alexander Pope, *An Essay on Man*

Happiness is not the end of life, character is.
Henry Ward Beecher, *Life Thoughts*

A talent is formed in stillness, a character in the world's torrent.
Johann Wolfgang von Goethe, *Torquato Tasso*

Character is higher than intellect . . . A great soul will be strong to live, as well as strong to think.
Ralph Waldo Emerson, *Society and Solitude: Letters and Social Aims: Addresses*

Religion is only another word for character, and it is developed in man. Religious education is a growth, and requires time.
Henry Ward Beecher, *Proverbs from Plymouth Pulpit*

Let us be true: this is the highest maxim of art and of life, the secret of eloquence and of virtue, and of all moral authority.
Henri Frédéric Amiel, *Amiel's Journal*

[Jesus] – the most innocent, the most benevolent, the most eloquent and sublime character that ever has been exhibited to man.
Thomas Jefferson, *The Writings of Thomas Jefferson*

In Christ was comprehended the fullest conception of greatness and nobleness of character. Every idea of true manhood is in Him.
Henry Ward Beecher, *Proverbs from Plymouth Pulpit*

Friends, suffering, marriage, environment, study and recreation are influences which shape character. The strongest influence, if you are generous enough to yield to it, is the grace of God.
Hubert van Zeller, *Considerations*

There is no sight more beautiful than a character which has been steadfastly growing in every direction, and has come to old age rich and ripe.
Henry Ward Beecher, *Proverbs from Plymouth Pulpit*

Character cannot be developed in ease and quiet. Only through experiences of trial and suffering can the soul be strengthened, vision cleared, ambition inspired and success achieved.
Helen Keller, *Helen Keller's Journal*

There is no point so critical of Christian character as the power to maintain love toward all men – not a love of personal attraction, but a love of benevolence, that begets a willingness to bear with them and work for them.
Henry Ward Beecher, *Proverbs from Plymouth Pulpit*

The character I admire is a character that is a rod of iron to itself and a wellspring of tenderness and pity for others; a character that forces itself to be happy in itself, blames no one but itself, and compels itself to clear away obstacles from the path to happiness for every organism it encounters.

John Cowper Powys, *Autobiography*

People's characters are tested in three ways: by the circumstances in which they live, by the people whom they meet, and by the experience of their own failure. Their characters are tested by the degree in which these things draw forth from them love and not bitterness, a humble penitence and dependence upon God and not despair.

Father Andrew SDC, *A Gift of Light*

Our characters are shaped by our companions and by the objects to which we give most of our thoughts and with which we fill our imaginations. We cannot always be thinking even about Christ, but we can refuse to dwell on any thoughts which are out of tune with Him. We can, above all, quite deliberately turn our minds towards Him at any time when those thoughts come in.

William Temple, *Christian Faith and Life*

Supreme and tremendous energy and positiveness enter into the spiritual delineation of Christian character. Intense virtues and self-denials, bearing yokes, bearing the cross, sacrificing, crucifying, are enjoined.

Henry Ward Beecher, *Proverbs from Plymouth Pulpit*

It is the character only of a good man to be able to deny and disown himself, and to make a full surrender of himself unto God; forgetting himself, and minding nothing but the will of his Creator; triumphing in nothing more than in his own nothingness, and in the allness of the Divinity. But indeed this, his being nothing, is the only way to be all things; this, his having nothing, the truest way of possessing all things.

John Smith the Platonist, *Select Discourses*

Now these mental and moral possessions are their own reward. They cannot, like earthly possessions, be taken away from us. For those who know what they are worth, the world is a much brighter place than for those who think that a man's life consisteth in the abundance of the things which he possesseth. The man whose 'mind to him a kingdom is' does not complain much of the injustices of life. Still less does the true Christian complain. He has found the joy that no man taketh from him. This world is not a bad place in his eyes, because he finds it full of love and beauty and wisdom.

W.R. Inge, *Personal Religion and the Life of Devotion*

The crown and glory of life is character. It is the noblest possession of a man, constituting a rank in itself, and an estate in the general good-will; dignifying every station, and exalting every position in society. It exercises a greater power than wealth, and secures all the honour without the jealousies of fame. It carries with it an influence which always tells; for it is the result of proved honour, rectitude, and consistency – qualities which, perhaps more than any other, command the general confidence and respect of mankind. Character is human nature in its best form. It is moral order embodied in the individual.

Samuel Smiles, *Self-Help*

**See also** Friendship, Integrity, Mystics, Saints, Wholeness

## 12

# CHEERFULNESS

*Cheerfulness – being contented, in good spirits, hopeful, animating, pleasant; being willing, not reluctant*

The Gurkhas are noted for their cheerfulness. On jungle patrols my platoon sergeant, Sgt Nandaraj, would come and see me shortly after we had bivouacked for the night. With nostrils twitching and eyes twinkling, he would give me his latest *sungur* (wild pig) report. He had just reconnoitred the area, and knew exactly where the wild pigs were. He was extremely keen to ambush them and supplement our basic army rations. On another occasion we were by the sea, and manoeuvres were over by 4 pm. The Gurkhas went off crabbing, again to supplement their *bhat* (curry). That night Sgt Major Kabiram dug his fingers into the curry, and pulled out a huge crab's claw. In broken English he said, 'Ah, this afternoon, you ate me; now, I eat you.' With that he stuffed the claw into his mouth, crunched the contents and scoffed the lot. With the Gurkhas, cheerfulness, linked with loyalty, made them excellent soldiers and companions.

A cheerful heart is a good medicine, but a downcast spirit dries up the bones.
Proverbs 17.22

I have said this to you, so that in me you may have peace. In the world you face persecution. But take courage; I have conquered the world!
John 16.33

Continual cheerfulness is a sign of wisdom.
Thomas Fuller, *Gnomologia*

That which befits us . . . is cheerfulness and courage.
Ralph Waldo Emerson, *Essays and Representative Men*

Health and cheerfulness mutually beget each other.

Joseph Addison, *The Works of Joseph Addison*

And so of cheerfulness, or a good temper – the more it is spent, the more of it remains.

Ralph Waldo Emerson, *The Conduct of Life, Nature, and Other Essays*

A happy, joyful spirit spreads joy everywhere; a fretful spirit is a trouble to ourselves and to all around us.

Anon

A merry heart goes all the day,
Your sad tires in a mile-a.

William Shakespeare, *The Winter's Tale*

A cheerful temper, joined with innocence, will make beauty attractive, knowledge delightful, and wit good-natured.

Joseph Addison, *The Works of Joseph Addison*

In my long illness, the people who helped me most were those who took for granted that I should behave with apparent cheerfulness and courage.

A.C. Benson, *Extracts from the Letters of Dr A.C. Benson to M.E.A.*

Cheerfulness, it would appear, is a matter which depends fully as much as on the state of things within, as on the state of things without, and around us.

Charlotte Brontë, *Shirley*

Good nature is worth more than knowledge, more than money, more than honour, to the persons who possess it, and certainly to everybody who dwells with them, in so far as mere happiness is concerned.

Henry Ward Beecher, *Proverbs from Plymouth Pulpit*

Mirth is like a flash of lightning, that breaks through in a gloom of clouds and glitters for a moment; cheerfulness keeps up a kind of day-light in the mind, and fills it with a steady and perpetual serenity.

Joseph Addison, *The Works of Joseph Addison*

Cheered by the presence of God, I will do at the moment, without anxiety, according to the strength which he shall give me, the work that his providence assigns me. I will leave the rest; it is not my affair.

François de la M. Fénelon, in Mrs Follen, *Extracts from the Writings of Fénelon*

The men whom I have seen succeed best in life have always been cheerful and hopeful men, who went about their business with a smile on their faces, and took the changes and chances of this mortal life like men, facing rough and smooth alike as it came, and so found the truth of the old proverb 'that good times and bad times and all times pass over'.

Charles Kingsley, *Daily Thoughts*

Use your sense of humour. Laugh about things. Laugh at the absurdities of life. Laugh about yourself and about your own absurdity.

We are all of us infinitesimally small and ludicrous creatures within God's universe. You have to be serious, but never be solemn, because if you are solemn about anything there is the risk of you becoming solemn about yourself.

Michael Ramsey, in Margaret Duggan, *Through the Year with Michael Ramsey*

Thy soul was like a Star, and dwelt apart:
Thou hadst a voice whose sound was like the sea:
Pure as the naked heavens, majestic, free,
So didst thou travel on life's common way,
In cheerful godliness.

William Wordsworth, 'London'

Be brave! Let us remain aware of our task and not grumble, a solution will come . . . I know what I want, I have a goal, an opinion, I have a religion and love. Let me be myself, and then I am satisfied. I know that I'm a woman with inward strength and plenty of courage.

If God lets me live . . . I shall not remain insignificant, I shall work in the world and for mankind!

And now I know that first and foremost I shall require courage and cheerfulness!

Anne Frank, *The Diary of Anne Frank*

I believe that God will help us to forget things, the memory of which would do us harm, or rather that He will enable us to remember only so much of them as will be for our good, and we, ourselves, not emotionally overwhelmed . . .

The pain endured. The lesson learned. Let it now be forgotten! Face the future with courage, cheerfulness, and hope. Give God the chance and He will make you forget all that it would be harmful to remember.

W.E. Sangster, *Westminster Sermons*

**See also** Happiness, Holiness, Joy, Kindness, Thanksgiving

# 13

# CHRISTIAN

*Christian – an adherent of Christianity*

I grew up thinking I was a Christian because I had been baptized as an infant and confirmed at the age of sixteen. Within a few weeks of arriving in Oxford I burnt my boats and made a firm commitment to the person of Jesus Christ. I now felt that in following Christ lay the very essence of being a Christian. Six busy years passed by and I found myself in a crisis. Intuitively I felt something was radically wrong. It was at this stage I discovered the book *The Choice Is Always Ours*, by Dorothy Berkley Phillips. This brilliant anthology enabled me to find 'the God within' – that in the depths of our being we can discover something of the presence of the Father, the Son, and the gifts and fruits of the Holy Spirit. At last I had found what I had been looking for. I now think of a Christian as a person who experiences the richness of divine life in the depths of his or her being and lives by it.

You are the salt of the earth.

Matthew 5.13

Yet if any one of you suffers as a Christian, do not consider it a disgrace, but glorify God because you bear this name.

1 Peter 4.16

A Christian is the highest style of man.

Edward Young, *Night Thoughts*

O noble testimony of the soul by nature Christian!

Tertullian, *The Writings of Tertullian*

Those who reject Christian beliefs, cannot count on keeping Christian morals.

Sir Richard Livingstone, *On Education*

If a man cannot be a Christian in the place where he is, he cannot be a Christian anywhere.

Henry Ward Beecher, *Life Thoughts*

The greatest of all blessings, as it is the most ennobling of all privileges, is to be indeed a Christian.

Samuel Taylor Coleridge, *Letters of Samuel Taylor Coleridge*

It doesn't take much of a person to be a Christian, but it takes all there is of him – person and possessions.

E. Stanley Jones, *Growing Spiritually*

The only absolute for the Christian is love, and on *that* you have got to be prepared to take *unconditional* stands and say, 'Here I stand, I can no other' (sic).

John A.T. Robinson, *The Roots of a Radical*

The ultimate criterion of a person's Christian spirit is not theory but practice: not how he thinks of teachings, dogmas, interpretations, but how he acts in ordinary life.

Hans Küng, *On Being a Christian*

The life of every Christian on earth has in it much that is mysterious. It is aiming at an awful grandeur which has never been unveiled. God carries in His bosom the full ideal. We know it not.

Henry Ward Beecher, *Proverbs from Plymouth Pulpit*

When the imitation of Christ does not mean to live a life like Christ, but to live your life authentically as Christ lived his, then there are many ways and forms in which a man can be a Christian.

Henri J.M. Nouwen, *The Wounded Healer*

. . . That simplicity which was usually found in the primitive Christians, who were (as most Anglers are) quiet men, and followers of peace; men that were so simply-wise, as not to sell their Consciences to buy riches.

Izaak Walton, *The Compleat Angler*

To live Christ is not to screw oneself up to great heights of moral endeavour and self-sacrifice. It is to accept, to accept what God says is possible for us. This is the achievement, the only achievement for a Christian, to become open to what God offers and what God can do.

Henry McKeating, *God and the Future*

Not only do I leave the door open for the Christian message, but I consider it of central importance for Western man. It needs, however, to be seen in a new light, in accordance with the changes wrought by the contemporary spirit. Otherwise, it stands apart from the times, and has no effect on man's wholeness.

C.G. Jung, *Memories, Dreams, Reflections*

He only is a Christian in fact in whom Christ dwelleth, liveth and hath His being, in whom Christ hath arisen as the eternal ground of the soul. He only is a Christian who has this high title in himself, and has entered with mind and soul into that Eternal Word which has manifested itself as the life of our humanity.

Rufus M. Jones, *Spiritual Reformers in the 16th and 17th Centuries*

What originality Christianity admits! A man may be a Christian and yet lose nothing of that which is truly original in him. Nay, more, it provokes originality, just as the polishing of a pebble brings out the beauty and definiteness of its structure. I can call to mind people whom I knew forty or fifty years ago . . . who had become *individual* through their religion.

Mark Rutherford, *Last Pages from a Journal*

He [Sebastian Franck] is especially interesting and important as an exponent and interpreter of a religion based on inward authority because he unites, in an unusual manner, the intellectual ideals of the Humanist with the experience and attitude of the Mystic. In him we have a Christian thinker who is able to detach himself from the theological formulations of his own and of earlier times, and who could draw, with a breadth of mind and depth of insight, from the wells of the great original thinkers of all ages, and who, besides, in his own deep and serious soul could feel the inner flow of central realities.

Rufus M. Jones, *Spiritual Reformers in the 16th and 17th Centuries*

Christians are, or should be, the pioneers of the new humanity which God is bringing into being through Christ, for they are already experiencing in themselves the renewal which God intends for all his creation. Christ is not only 'the first born among a large family of brothers', but he is also in relation to mankind as a whole 'a second Adam'. In Christ, God made a new and fresh beginning and its success is assured by the victory which Christ, 'the second

Adam', achieved over evil. Those who are inspired by his spirit and live in his way are the prototype of a new re-ordered humanity.

David Brown, *God's Tomorrow*

**See also** Acceptance, Commitment, Compassion, Love, Service

# 14

# CHURCH

*Church – building for public Christian worship; body of all Christians, organized Christian society, clergy or clerical profession*

I was listening recently to an American at a summer school in Oxford. He was telling me that although he had a spiritual awareness he found organized religion boring. As far as I could tell he was being thoroughly honest and voicing what a large number of people felt. I remember trying to tackle this problem in my early twenties. A group of us got together and used to meet for an hour a week, trying to work out the aim and the function of the church. We were greatly helped by Ernest Southcott's book *The Parish Comes Alive*. The author, a parish priest, recorded his experiences at Halton, Leeds. As I recall it, when he first went there he found the church services, dull, boring and sterile. He felt the congregation was going through the motions of worship with little inner conviction. He tackled this at two levels. First, he formed a number of house churches which used to meet in the parish during the week. Second, the life generated by these house churches was fed into the corporate life of the church. Inner conviction was rediscovered and the parish did indeed come alive.

Unless the Lord builds the house, those who build it labour in vain.

Psalm 127.1

. . . strive to excel in them for building up the church.

1 Corinthians 14.12

The maintenance of powerful benevolence is more vital to the Christian church than dogmatic systems.

Henry Ward Beecher, *Proverbs from Plymouth Pulpit*

... the church is itself a mystery which opens on to the 'ineffable riches of Christ', which we must accept in their totality.

Cardinal Suenens, *A New Pentecost?*

A humiliated and defenceless church must go out into a hostile world to rediscover the God-man in the least of his brethren.

Paul Oestreicher, Introduction to Hans Jürgen Schultz, *Conversion to the World*

There must be vitality, elasticity, variety, and liberty in church life, or it will fail for the most part in the great ends for which it was established.

Henry Ward Beecher, *Proverbs from Plymouth Pulpit*

. . . it belongs to the very life of the people of God that it must accept again and again to have its life renewed by a new confrontation with its Lord and his holy will.

W.A. Visser 'T Hooft, *The Renewal of the Church*

The church exists to proclaim the good news of where true humanity is to be found and to exemplify in the midst of this present world what growth towards maturity in Christ means.

Daniel Jenkins, *Christian Maturity and the Theology of Success*

Jesus never required membership of a church as a condition of entry into God's kingdom. The obedient acceptance of his message and the immediate and radical submission to God's will sufficed.

Hans Küng, *On Being a Christian*

The Church has a right to edify itself by the gifts of all its members. Nothing is more striking than the latent and undeveloped power in the Church to-day.

Henry Ward Beecher, *Proverbs from Plymouth Pulpit*

The Church is most true to its own nature when it seeks nothing for itself, renounces power, humbly bears witness to the truth but makes no claim to be the *possessor* of truth, and is continually dying in order that it may live.

J.H. Oldham, *Life Is Commitment*

A Church without hope has nothing to offer anyone. It is just a collection of demoralized individuals so concerned about their own survival that they haven't the freedom to offer society the Gospel in its power and comprehensiveness.

Colin Morris, *The Hammer of the Lord*

The great problem of the Church (and therefore of its theologians) is to establish or re-establish some kind of vital contact with that enormous majority of human beings for whom the Christian faith is not so much unlikely as irrelevant and uninteresting.

H.E. Root, in A.R. Vidler, *Soundings*

It is not permissable to designate as 'unchurched' those who have become alienated from organized denominations and traditional creeds. In living among these groups for half a generation I learned how much of the latent Church there is within them.

Paul Tillich, *On the Boundary*

The Church must take care that in trying to build bridges across to the secularized modern world, it does not abandon the bridgehead on the Christian side and find itself left with nothing to communicate and nothing distinctively Christian to contribute.

F.R. Barry, *Secular and Supernatural*

Without contemplation and interior prayer the Church cannot fulfil her mission to transform and save mankind. Without contemplation, she will be reduced to being the servant of cynical and worldly powers, no matter how hard her faithful may protest that they are fighting for the Kingdom of God.

Thomas Merton, *Contemplative Prayer*

It is the Church of the saints and martyrs and prophets, who have been the lights of the world in their several generations, that has the demand upon your allegiance – not the Church which has been corrupted by wealth and worldly power. But the true Church is embedded in the existing Churches – you will not find it elsewhere.

Alec R. Vidler, *God's Demand and Man's Response*

If we manage to be clever and busy about all else – contemporary problems and contemporary tasks, even the meeting of other great and real human ends, but are silent or ineffective about the mystery of the soul's communion with God, then the greatest riches offered to the Church are lost and its ultimate distinctiveness from all other associations has gone.

Norman Goodall, *The Local Church*

The Church is the community of the Spirit, not as having a monopoly of the Spirit, but as having been called into existence by God and entrusted with the word and the sacraments. In the Church there should be going on in a concentrated way the work of the Spirit, which in a diffuse way is going on throughout creation. When the Church is truly the Church it is introducing a new dimension into the social situation, thus giving hope for an eventual transformation.

George Appleton, *Journey for a Soul*

Within the strange, sprawling, quarrelling mass of the churches, within their stifling narrowness, their ignorance, their insensitivity, their stupidity, their fear of the senses and of truth, I perceive another Church, one which really is Christ at work in the world. To this Church men seem to be admitted as much as by a baptism of the heart as of the body, and they know more of intellectual charity, of vulnerability, of love, of joy, of peace, than most of the rest of us. They have learned to live with few defences and so conquered the isolation which torments us. They do not judge, especially morally; their own relationships make it possible for others to grow.

Monica Furlong, *With Love to the Church*

**See also** God, Holy Spirit, Jesus Christ, Kingdom of God, Saints

# 15

# COMMITMENT

*Commitment – act of committing or being committed; dedication or obligation to particular action or cause, etc.*

I can remember my initial act of commitment very clearly. The occasion was a Sunday morning in Oxford during my first year as an undergraduate. I went along to a church service, little knowing what lay in store for me that day. The preacher was Cuthbert Bardsley, the then Bishop of Coventry. I remember very little of the sermon, but what impressed me was the man himself. Here was someone vitally alive and radiant, living the Christian life in the power of the Spirit. This was the quality of life I had unconsciously been looking for. At the end of the service I went forward, along with a few others, to take a step of commitment. The bishop then spoke to us gently and gave us his blessing. I remember feeling at the time a vital step had been taken in life, and was now looking forward to the future with a mixture of feelings, of awe and excitement, and of fear and trepidation.

Commit your way to the Lord; trust in him, and he will act.
Psalm 37.5

And every one who has left houses or brothers or sisters or father or mother or children or lands, for my name's sake, will receive a hundredfold, and inherit eternal life.
Matthew 19.29

The words he spoke, the deeds he performed, the demands he raised confronted people with a final decision. Jesus left no one neutral. He himself had become the great question.
Hans Küng, *On Being a Christian*

If we are to be in Christ new creatures, we must show that we are so, by having new ways of living in the world. If we are to follow Christ, it must be in our common way of spending every day.

William Law, *A Serious Call to a Devout and Holy Life*

The most sovereign act of an independent person is to give the one thing he owns – himself. Then God gives the most precious thing He owns – Himself. Then we are filled with the Holy Spirit.

E. Stanley Jones, *Mastery*

. . . the self is not lost when it is surrendered to Christ. It is lost in a higher will, redeemed from a self-centred will, and found again in obedience to that higher will. So it all ends in self-affirmation. The self is not cancelled – it is heightened.

E. Stanley Jones, *The Word Became Flesh*

I leaped headlong into the Sea, and thereby have become better acquainted with the Soundings, the quicksands, & the rocks, than if I had stayed upon the green shore, and piped a silly pipe, and took tea & comfortable advice.

John Keats, *The Letters of John Keats*

The death by which we enter into life is not an escape from reality but a complete gift of ourselves which involves a total commitment to reality. It begins by renouncing the illusory reality which created things acquire when they are seen only in their relation to our own selfish interests.

Thomas Merton, *Thoughts in Solitude*

He [Jesus] provoked a final *decision*, but not a yes or no to a particular title, to a particular dignity, a particular office, or even to a particular dogma, rite or law. His message and community raised the question of the aim and purpose to which a man will ultimately direct his life. Jesus demanded a final decision for God's cause and man's.

Hans Küng, *On Being a Christian*

Either we must confess our blindness and seek the opening of our eyes; or else we must accept the light and walk by it. What we may not do, yet all strive to do, is to keep our eyes half open and live by half the light. That kind of sight holds us to our sin and our sin to us. But the only way of avoiding it is to look with eyes wide open upon ourselves and the world as the full light reveals it; but this is the surrender of faith, and pride resists it.

William Temple, *Readings in St John's Gospel*

The one thing he [Jesus] seems to have condemned utterly was evasion of choice. The man in the parable who was afraid to risk his bag of gold and brought it back uninvested and uncommitted was flung out into the dark. To choose is to commit yourself. To commit yourself is to run the risk of failure, the risk of sin, the risk of betrayal. Jesus can deal with all those, for forgiveness is his métier. The only thing he can do nothing with is the refusal to be committed. Even Judas should do quickly whatever he chooses to do and be responsible.

John V. Taylor, *The Go-Between God*

There are some commitments that need a lifetime to be fulfilled. The commitment of baptism, which is simply the special Christian expression of the general commitment to become a truly human person along the way of transcendence; to be a loyal and reliable friend, in season and out of season; to be a good husband or wife, father or mother, to make a success of marriage and family; to be devoted to a vocation, whether it be that of priest or scientist or nurse or farmer; these all need a lifetime, and even at the end of a lifetime there is more to be done.

John Macquarrie, *In Search of Humanity*

Father Raymond tells the charming story of a little child whose mother was teaching him to pray. When he got to the part, 'Lord, I surrender everything to thee, everything I own,' he abruptly broke off and whispered to himself, 'except my baby rabbit.'

All of us have our baby rabbits. Sometimes it is an ugly thing, sometimes beautiful, sometimes large, sometimes small; but we are more attached to it than to anything else. But this is the thing that God asks of us and that he touches upon when we sincerely ask guidance of him. God does not, however, ask us to seek out our neighbour's little rabbits.

Paul Tournier, *Escape from Loneliness*

The terrible thing, the almost impossible thing is to hand over your whole self – all your wishes and precautions – to Christ. But it is far easier than what we are all trying to do instead. For what we are trying to do is to remain what we call 'ourselves', to keep personal happiness as our great aim in life, and yet at the same time to be 'good'. We are all trying to let our mind and heart go their own way – centred on money or pleasure or ambition – and hoping, in spite of this, to behave honestly and chastely and humbly. And that is exactly what Christ warned us you could not do. As He said, a thistle cannot produce figs. If I am a field that contains nothing but grass-seed, I cannot produce wheat . . . If I want to produce wheat, the change must go deeper than the surface. I must be ploughed up and re-sown.

C.S. Lewis, *Mere Christianity*

I had gone a-begging from door to door in the village path, when thy golden chariot appeared in the distance like a gorgeous dream and I wondered who was this King of all kings! . . . The chariot stopped where I stood. Thy glance fell on me and thou camest down with a smile. I felt that the luck of my life had come at last. Then of a sudden thou didst hold out thy right hand and say, 'What hast thou to give me?' Ah, what a kingly jest was it to open thy palm to a beggar to beg! I was confused and stood undecided, and then from my wallet I slowly took out the least little grain of corn and gave it thee.

But how great my surprise when at the day's end I emptied my bag on the floor to find a least little grain of gold among the poor heap. I bitterly wept and wished that I had had the heart to give thee my all.

Rabindranath Tagore, *Gitanjali*

**See also** Belief, Cross, Faith, Obedience, Trust

# 16

# COMPASSION

*Compassion – pity inclining one to spare or help*

I was in my chaplain's office in London. The phone rang one Sunday morning – after the early service. It was a student asking for help. He had come across a young man in a semi-conscious state, suffering from drug abuse. Could I come over and lend a hand? I drove over to where he was – in Holborn. Initial fears were quickly confirmed. We were both out of our depth! Fortunately I knew an Anglican priest nearby, an unusual man – a qualified psychiatric nurse, with a specialized knowledge of drugs. He was free to come and lend a hand. From the moment he arrived I saw 'compassion' in action. The young man quickly realized he was in the presence of an expert. Communication immediately took place. The names and quantities of drugs were taken and noted. An atmosphere of pity and sympathy predominated. The priest then showed the depth of his compassion by taking him to his home and looking after him there.

The Lord is good to all, and his compassion is over all he has made.

Psalm 145.9

As God's chosen ones, holy and beloved, clothe yourselves with compassion, kindness, lowliness, meekness, and patience. Bear with one another and, if one has a complaint against another, forgiving each other; as the Lord has forgiven you, so you also must forgive.

Colossians 3.12–13

What value has compassion that does not take its object in its arms?

Antoine de Saint-Exupéry, *The Wisdom of the Sands*

Christianity taught us to care. Caring is the greatest thing, caring matters most.

Baron Friedrich von Hügel, *Letters to a Niece*

Compassion was the chief and, perhaps, the only law of all human existence.

Fyodor Dostoyevsky, *The Idiot*

Jesus does not regard in Judas his enmity, but the order of God, which He loves, and admits, since He calls him friend.

Blaise Pascal, *Pensées*

Our tragedy is not that we suffer but that we waste suffering. We waste the opportunity of growing into compassion.

Mary Craig, *Blessings*

Compassion is born when we discover in the centre of our own existence not only that God is God and man is man, but also that our neighbour is really our fellow man.

Henri J.M. Nouwen, *The Wounded Healer*

Jesus *found him*. The man did not find Jesus; Jesus found him. That is the deepest truth of Christian faith; Jesus found me. Our fellowship with Him is rooted in His compassion.

William Temple, *Readings in St John's Gospel*

Compassion is not a simple feeling-state but a complex emotional attitude toward another, characteristically involving imaginative dwelling on the condition of the other person, an active regard for his good, a view of him as a fellow human being, and emotional responses of a certain degree of intensity.

L. Blum, in James F. Childress and John Macquarrie, *A New Dictionary of Christian Ethics*

Let us not underestimate how hard it is to be compassionate. Compassion is hard because it requires the inner disposition to go with others to the place where they are weak, vulnerable, lonely, and broken. But this is not our spontaneous response to suffering. What we desire most is to do away with suffering by fleeing from it or finding a quick cure for it.

Henri J.M. Nouwen, *The Way of the Heart*

Compassion is one of the emotions or attitudes with an emotional component, that are altruistic or other regarding. Compassion presupposes sympathy, is close to both pity and mercy, and leads to acts of beneficence – the Samaritan 'showed mercy on' the victim and 'took care of him'. Compassion is often an expression of love or *agape*.

James F. Childress, in James F. Childress and John Macquarrie, *A New Dictionary of Christian Ethics*

The root of the matter is a very simple and old-fashioned thing, a thing so simple that I am almost ashamed to mention it, for fear of the derisive smile with which wise cynics will greet my words. The thing I mean – please forgive me for mentioning it – is love, Christian love, or compassion. If you feel like this, you have a motive for existence, a guide in action, a reason for courage, an imperative necessity for intellectual honesty.

Bertrand Russell, *The Impact of Science on Society*

The Son of God was seen
Most glorious, in him all his Father shone
Substantially express'd, and in his face
Divine compassion visibly appear'd.
Love without end, and without measure Grace.

John Milton, 'Paradise Lost'

Compassion is probably the only antitoxin of the soul. Where there is compassion even the most poisonous impulses are relatively harmless. One would rather see the world run by men who set their hearts on toys but are accessible to pity than by men animated by lofty ideals whose dedication makes them ruthless. In the chemistry of man's soul, almost all noble qualities – courage, honour, hope, faith, duty, loyalty, etc. – can be transmuted into ruthlessness. Compassion alone stands apart from the continuous traffic between good and evil proceeding within us.

Eric Hoffer, *The Passionate State of Mind*

But to share with Christ his passion, his crucifixion, his death, means to accept unreservedly all these events, in the same spirit as he did, that is, to accept them in an act of free will, to suffer together with the man of sorrows, to be there in silence, the very silence of Christ, interrupted only by a few decisive words, the silence of real communion; not just the silence of pity, but of compassion, which allows us to grow into complete oneness with the other so that there is no longer one and the other, but only one life and one death.

Anthony Bloom, *Living Prayer*

I don't know what has caused me to read so many articles lately on the subject of 'compassion', but I think we, as Co-workers, are faced with compassion when we are with the poor and the lonely and the dying. Compassion asks us to go where it hurts, to enter into places of pain, to share in brokenness, fear, confusion and anguish. Compassion challenges us to cry out with those in misery, to mourn with those who are lonely, to weep with those in tears. Compassion requires us to be weak with the weak, vulnerable with the vulnerable, and powerless with the powerless. Compassion means full immersion in the conditions of being human. When we look at compassion in this way, it becomes clear that something more is involved than a general kindness.

A co-worker, in Kathryn Spink, *A Chain of Love*

**See also** Awareness, Kindness, Love, Saints, Understanding

# 17

# CONTEMPLATION

*Contemplation – gazing upon; viewing mentally*

As far back as I can remember I have always had a contemplative side to my nature. When I was nearing the end of National Service I took some leave and spent a quiet day on the beach at Port Dixon, near Penang, northern Malaya (as it was then). I took very little with me – a swimming costume, a towel and some food – and finding a secluded spot, spent the whole day on the beach, doing absolutely nothing at all. At first numerous thoughts and feelings came to the surface. I listened to the ebbing of the sea, and began to muse over the early part of my life. Precious truths and insights came to the surface. New ideas took root. I felt this was my first real experience of contemplation. Now I try to spend a day on the beach every year, and contemplate.

Be still, and know that I am God!
Psalm 46.10

Pray in the Spirit at all times in every prayer and supplication.
Ephesians 6.18

Contemplatives are not useful, they are only indispensable.
Ernest Dimnet, *What We Live By*

What we plant in the soil of contemplation we shall reap in the harvest of action.
Meister Eckhart, in Franz Pfeiffer, *Meister Eckhart*

Mystical theology, the secret science of God, which spiritual men call contemplation.
St John of the Cross, *The Complete Works of St John of the Cross*

All civil mankind have agreed in leaving one day for contemplation against six for practice.

Ralph Waldo Emerson, *Miscellaneous Pieces*

The peace of the contemplative is at once the most beautiful and the most fruitful act of man.

Stephen MacKenna, *Journal and Letters*

A Church which starves itself and its members in the contemplative life deserves whatever spiritual leanness it may experience.

Michael Ramsey, *Canterbury Pilgrim*

When Contemplation, like the night-calm felt
Through earth and sky, spreads widely, and sends deep
Into the soul its tranquillizing power.

William Wordsworth, 'Prelude'

More than anything else, it is the loving contemplation of its Maker that causes the soul to realize its own insignificance, and fills it with holy fear and true humility, and with abundant love to our fellow Christians.

Lady Julian of Norwich, *Revelations of Divine Love*

Contemplation means rest, suspension of activity, withdrawal into the mysterious interior solitude in which the soul is absorbed in the immense and fruitful silence of God and learns something of the secret of His perfections less by seeing than by fruitful love.

Thomas Merton, *Elected Silence*

In popular usage the word can indicate either thinking about some object or gazing upon some object. In Christian spirituality it is the latter meaning that is uppermost: thinking about God gives place to a simple, loving, looking towards him, and this is contemplation.

Richard Harries, in Alan Richardson and John Bowden, *A New Dictionary of Christian Theology*

All contemplative life on earth implies penance as well as prayer, because in contemplation there are always two aspects: the positive one, by which we are united to God in love, and the negative one, by which we are detached and separated from everything that is not God. Without both these elements there is no real contemplation.

Thomas Merton, *The Waters of Silence*

I think there is a place both inside and outside of religion for a sort of contemplation of the Good, not just by dedicated experts but by ordinary people: an attention which is not just the planning of particular good actions but an attempt to look right away from self towards a distant transcendent perfection, a source of uncontaminated energy, a source of *new* and quite undreamt-of-virtue.

Iris Murdoch, *The Sovereignty of Good Over Other Concepts*

For not, surely, by deliberate effort of thought does a man grow wise. The truths of life are not discovered by us. At moments unforeseen, some gracious influence descends upon the soul, touching it to an emotion which, we know not how, the mind transmutes into thought. This can happen only in a calm of the senses, a surrender of the whole being to passionless contemplation. I understand, now, the intellectual mood of the quietist.

George Gissing, *The Private Papers of Henry Rycroft*

Contemplation is the state of union with the divine Ground of all being. The highest prayer is the most passive. Inevitably; for the less there is of self, the more there is of God. That is why the path to passive or infused contemplation is so hard, and, for many, so painful – a passage through successive or simultaneous Dark Nights, in which the pilgrim must die to the life of sense as an end in itself, to the life of private and even of traditionally hallowed thinking and believing, and finally to the deep source of all ignorance and evil, the life of the separate, individualized will.

Aldous Huxley, *The Perennial Philosophy*

Contemplation is the highest expression of man's intellectual and spiritual life. It is that life itself, fully awake, fully active, fully aware that it is alive. It is spiritual wonder. It is spontaneous awe at the sacredness of life, of being. It is gratitude for life, for awareness and for being. It is a vivid realization of the fact that life and being in us proceed from an invisible, transcendent and infinitely abundant Source. Contemplation is, above all, awareness of the reality of that Source. It *knows* the Source, obscurely, inexplicably, but with a certitude that goes both beyond reason and beyond simple faith. For contemplation is a kind of spiritual vision to which both reason and faith aspire, by their very nature, because without it they must always remain incomplete.

Thomas Merton, *New Seeds of Contemplation*

The contemplation of God – and contemplative prayer is, I believe, not necessarily an advanced state but something accessible to us very backward Christians – the waiting upon God in quietness can be our greatest service to the world if in our apartness the love for people is on our heart. As Aaron went into the holy of holies wearing a breastplate with jewels representing the twelve tribes upon it, so the Christian puts himself deliberately into the presence of God with the needs and sorrows of humanity upon his heart. And he does this best not by the vocal skill with which he informs the Deity about the world's needs but by the simplicity of his own exposure to God's greatness and the world's need.

Michael Ramsey, 'The Idea of the Holy and the World Today' in *Spirituality for Today*

Poetry, music and art have something in common with the contemplative experience. But contemplation is beyond aesthetic intuition, beyond art, beyond poetry. Indeed, it is beyond philosophy, beyond speculative theology. It resumes, transcends and fulfils them all, and yet at the same time it seems, in a certain way, to supersede and to deny them all. Contemplation is always beyond our own knowledge, beyond our own light, beyond systems, beyond explanations, beyond discourse, beyond dialogue, beyond our own self. To enter into the realm of contemplation one must in a certain sense die: but this death is in fact the entrance into a higher life. It is a death for the sake of life, which leaves behind all that we can know or treasure as life, as thought, as experience, as joy, as being.

Thomas Merton, *New Seeds of Contemplation*

**See also** Listening, Meditation, Prayer, Thinking, Wonder

# 18

# CONTENTMENT

*Contentment – being in a state of satisfaction, well pleased – originally it meant, bounded (in desires by what one has)*

I had the good fortune to go to Kenya to stay with some friends during a summer vacation. We went to stay on a farm on the slopes of Mount Kenya. The farm was vast, specializing in the cultivation of wheat. The farmhouse, built to overlook the farm included a magnificent view of Mount Kenya. This alone was impressive. What was more striking was the farmer, his wife and family. They all had about them an air of contentment. Here they were, living in the heart of Africa, at an altitude of 8,000 feet. The climate was well-nigh perfect. All the time they were close to nature, living an outdoor life. Here was a contentment rarely to be found elsewhere. How do we find contentment?

The lines have fallen for me in pleasant places; yea, I have a goodly heritage.
Psalm 16.6

. . . for I have learned to be content with whatever I have. I know what it is to have little, and I know what it is to have plenty. In any and all circumstances I have learned the secret of being well-fed and of going hungry, of having plenty and of being in need. I can do all things through him who strengthens me.
Philippians 4.11–13

A contented mind is a continual feast.
English proverb

The noblest mind the best contentment has.
Edmund Spenser, 'The Faerie Queene'

A mind content, both Crown and Kingdom is.
Robert Greene, 'Farewell to Folly'

Great wealth and content seldom live together.
Thomas Fuller, *Gnomologia*

Content will never dwell but in a meek and quiet soul.
Izaak Walton, *The Compleat Angler*

We only see in a lifetime a dozen faces marked with the peace of a contented spirit.
Henry Ward Beecher, *Proverbs from Plymouth Pulpit*

How seldom a face in repose is a face of serene content.
W.E. Sangster, *The Secret of Radiant Life*

To be content with little is difficult; to be content with much, impossible.
Old proverb

The rarest feeling that ever lights the human face is the contentment of a loving soul.
Henry Ward Beecher, *Proverbs from Plymouth Pulpit*

Content is Wealth, the Riches of the Mind;
And happy He who can that Treasure find.
John Dryden, 'The Wife of Bath, Her Tale'

. . . nobody who gets enough food and clothing in a world where most are hungry and cold has any business to talk about 'misery' . . .
C.S. Lewis, *They Stand Together*

In order to be content men must also have the possibility of developing their intellectual and artistic powers to whatever extent accord with their personal characteristics and abilities.
Albert Einstein, *Out of My Later Years*

Those who face that which is actually before them, unburdened by the past, undistracted by the future, these are they who live, who make the best use of their lives; these are those who have found the secret of contentment.
Alban Goodier SJ, *The School of Love*

To be content with a little is greater than to possess the world, which a man may possess without being so. Lay up my treasure! What matters where a man's treasure is whose heart is in the Scriptures? There is the treasure of the Christian.

Henry Fielding, *Joseph Andrews*

My crown is in my heart, not on my head;
Not deck'd with diamonds and Indian stones,
Nor to be seen: my crown is call'd content;
A crown it is that seldom kings enjoy.

William Shakespeare, *King Henry VI*

Content and discontent should run in and out of each other in every true man's life. Every man should have a generous discontent with what he has attained, and strive to go upward; and yet every one should be so much the master of himself as to refuse to be disquieted by his environments.

Henry Ward Beecher, *Proverbs from Plymouth Pulpit*

For not that, which men covet most, is best,
Nor that thing worst, which men do most refuse;
But fittest is, that all contented rest
With that they hold: each hath his fortune in his brest.

Edmund Spenser, 'The Faerie Queene'

How calm and quiet a delight
It is alone, to read, and meditate, and write,
By none offended, nor offending none;
To walk, ride, sit, or sleep at one's own ease,
And pleasing a man's self, none other to displease!

Charles Cotton, 'The Retirement'

To live content with small means; to seek elegance rather than luxury, and refinement rather than fashion; to be worthy, not respectable, and wealthy, not rich; to study hard, to think quietly, talk gently, act frankly; to listen to stars and birds, to babes and sages, with open heart; to bear all cheerfully, do all bravely, await occasions, hurry never. In a word, to let the spiritual, unbidden and unconscious, grow up through the common. This is to be my symphony.

William E. Channing, *A Series of Miscellaneous Illustrated Cards*

Let us be contented with what has happened to us and thankful for all we have been spared. Let us accept the natural order in which we move. Let us reconcile ourselves to the mysterious rhythm of our destinies, such as they must be in this world of space and time. Let us treasure our joys but not bewail our sorrows. The glory of light cannot exist without its shadows. Life is a whole, and good and ill must be accepted together. The journey has been enjoyable and well worth making – once.

Winston S. Churchill, *Thoughts and Adventures*

**See also** Joy, Peace, Serenity, Thanksgiving, Trust

# 19

# COURAGE

*Courage – bravery, boldness, ability to nerve oneself to a venture*

In recent years we have had several physically handicapped undergraduates in college. All of them have had something in common, namely, a quiet courageous approach to life. This has caused me to think about the nature of their courage. I found some clues in the words of Cardinal Manning. He wrote in *Pastime Papers*: 'the Italians call it *Coraggio*, or greatness of heart; the Spaniards, *Corage*; the French, *Courage*, from whom we have borrowed it. And we understand it to mean manliness, bravery, boldness, fearlessness, springing not from a sense of physical power, or from insensibility to danger or pain, but from the moral habit of self-command, with deliberation, fully weighing present dangers, and clearly foreseeing future consequences, and yet in the path of duty advancing unmoved to its execution.' This fits in roughly with my observations. Somehow they have found an inner strength which carries them beyond their various disabilities.

Be strong and of good courage; be not frightened, neither be dismayed; for the Lord your God is with you wherever you go.

Joshua 1.9

Keep alert, stand firm in your faith, be courageous, be strong. Let all that you do be done in love.

1 Corinthians 16.13–14

Great things are done more through courage than through wisdom.

German proverb

. . . but there is a higher sort of courage, the bravery of self-control.

Thomas Bailey Aldrich, *The Stillwater Tragedy*

It requires moral courage to grieve; it requires religious courage to rejoice.

Søren Kierkegaard, *The Journals of Søren Kierkegaard*

Courage is the basic virtue for everyone so long as he continues to grow, to move ahead.

Rollo May, *Man's Search for Himself*

The Courage we desire and prize is not the Courage to die decently, but to live manfully.

Thomas Carlyle, *Boswell's Life of Johnson*

Courage is sustained, not only by prayer, but by calling up anew the vision of the goal.

A.D. Sertillanges OP, *The Intellectual Life*

The greatest virtue in life is real courage, that knows how to face facts and live beyond them.

D.H. Lawrence, *The Selected Letters of D.H. Lawrence*

Courage is what it takes to stand up and speak; courage is also what it takes to sit down, and listen.

Anon

The most precious thing about Jesus is the fact that he is not the great discourager, but the great encourager.

William Barclay, *The Gospel of Matthew*

One has to be courageous not to let oneself be carried along by the world's march; one needs faith and will-power to go cross-current.

Carlo Carretto, *Letters from the Desert*

Courage is not simply *one* of the virtues but the form of every virtue at the testing point, which means at the point of highest reality.

C.S. Lewis, in Cyril Connelly, *The Unquiet Grave*

The stout heart is also a warm and kind one. Affection dwells with Danger, all the holier and lovelier for such stern environment.

Thomas Carlyle, *Corn-Law Rhymes*

People talk about the courage of condemned men walking to the place of execution: sometimes it needs as much courage to walk with any kind of bearing towards another person's habitual misery.

Graham Greene, *The Heart of the Matter*

Courage is required not only in a person's occasional crucial decision for his own freedom, but in the little hour-to-hour decisions which place the bricks in the structure of his building of himself into a person who acts with freedom and responsibility.

Rollo May, *Man's Search for Himself*

Life, willing to surpass itself, is the good life, and the good life is courageous life. It is the life of the 'powerful soul' and their 'triumphant body' whose self-enjoyment is virtue. Such a soul banishes everything cowardly; it says: 'bad – that is cowardly'.

Paul Tillich, *The Courage to Be*

The world seems somehow so made as to suit best the adventurous and courageous, the men who, like Nelson, wear all their stars, like Napoleon's marshals their most splendid uniforms, not that they may be less but more conspicuous and incur greater dangers than their fellows.

W. MacNeile Dixon, *The Human Situation*

We must accept our existence as far as it is possible; everything, even the unheard of, must be possible there. That is fundamentally the only courage which is demanded of us; to be brave in the face of the strangest, most singular and most inexplicable things that can befall us.

Rainer Maria Rilke, *Letters to a Young Poet*

The affirmation of one's essential being in spite of desires and anxieties creates joy . . . it is the happiness of a soul which is 'lifted above every circumstance'. Joy accompanies the self-affirmation of our essential being in spite of the inhibitions coming from the accidental elements in us. Joy is the emotional expression of the courageous Yes to one's own being.

Paul Tillich, *The Courage to Be*

Courage is far more common than is commonly supposed, and it belongs as much, and more, to the ordinary events of life than to the spectacular. Every man who lives in intimate contact with other people, especially the unprivileged people, is amazed at the quiet bravery of obscure folk. To those who have eyes to see, there is evidence of courage on every hand.

W.E. Sangster, *These Things Abide*

Strange is the vigour of a brave man's soul. The strength of his spirit and his irresistible power, the greatness of his heart and the height of his condition, his mighty confidence and contempt of danger, his true security and repose in himself, his liberty to dare and do what he pleaseth, his alacrity in the midst of fears, his invincible temper, are advantages which make him master of fortune. His courage fits him for all attempts, renders him serviceable to God and man, and makes him the bulwark and defence of his king and country.

Thomas Traherne, *The Way to Blessedness*

**See also** Aspiration, Cheerfulness, Commitment, Faith, Ideals

## 20

# CROSS

*Cross – stake (usually with traverse bar) used by the ancients for crucifixion, especially that on which Christ was crucified; Christian religion; trial, affliction, annoyance*

I wonder if we place too much emphasis on the historical cross of Christ, and not enough on taking up our cross daily and following Christ I am fond of Jesus' teaching, that unless a grain of wheat falls into the earth and dies, it remains alone; but if it dies it bears much fruit. This parable contains a vital truth for understanding one of the mysteries of the cross. The grain of wheat, of course, does not wholly die when sown. The outer case perishes, but this lets in the nutrients of the soil, stimulating growth from the centre. Roots grow downward and the stem grows upwards, seeking sun, warmth and rain. Growth continues until the grain is ripe – and plentiful. Apply this parable now to the human scene. Our self-centredness, like the outer case of the grain of wheat, has to perish in order for the divine in the depths of our being to grow and flourish. This is what I mean by taking up our cross daily and following Christ. It is a painful process, but in it lies the secret of life.

Then Jesus told his disciples, 'If any want to become my followers, let them deny themselves and take up their cross and follow me. For those who want to save their life will lose it, and those who lose their life for my sake will find it.'

Matthew 16.24–25

I have been crucified with Christ; and it is no longer I who live, but it is Christ who lives in me. And the life I now live in the flesh I live by faith in the Son of God, who loved me and gave himself for me.

Galatians 2.20

It is the crushed grape that yields the wine.

Anon

The way to God is the way of the Cross. Christ Himself is the pattern and His way of Life is the typical way for all who would find God.

Rufus M. Jones, *Spiritual Reformers in the 16th and 17th Centuries*

All the activity of man in the works of self-denial has no good in itself, but is only an entrance for the one only Good, the light of God, to operate upon us.

William Law, in Stephen Hobhouse, *Selected Mystical Writings of William Law*

It is the triumph over one's own nature that means full victory; for when a man has himself under control so that every desire submits to reason and reason submits to me, then he is really victorious over self, and is master of the world.

Thomas à Kempis, *The Imitation of Christ*

Except the seed die . . . It has to die in order to liberate the energy it bears within it so that with this energy new forms may be developed. So we have to die in order to liberate a *tied up* energy, in order to possess an energy which is free and capable of understanding the true relationship of things.

Simone Weil, *Gravity and Grace*

The Way of the Cross winds through our towns and cities, our hospitals and factories, and through our battlefields; it takes the road of poverty and suffering in every form. It is in front of these new Stations of the Cross that we must stop and meditate and pray to the suffering Christ for strength to love him enough to act.

Michel Quoist, *Prayers of Life*

'Our kingdom go' is the necessary and unavoidable corollary of 'Thy Kingdom come'. For the more there is of self, the less there is of God. The divine fullness of life can be gained only by those who have deliberately lost the partial, separative life of craving and self-interest, of egocentric thinking, feeling, wishing, and acting.

Aldous Huxley, *The Perennial Philosophy*

[How could Christ die for our sins?] This is the hardest thing for people to realize intellectually. You can tell them about it, but I believe the experience of Christ's death, the freedom from sin, can only be experienced personally. You can hear about it and know about it, but I think this is the gap across which a person has to leap by experience or by faith.

George Reindorp, in Gerald Priestland, *Priestland's Progress*

Batter my heart, three-person'd God; for you
As yet but knocke, breathe, shine, and seeke to mend;
That I may rise, and stand, o'erthrowe mee, and bend
Your force, to breake, blowe, burn and make me new.

John Donne, 'Holy Sonnets, XIV'

Therefore we should make ourselves poor, that we may fundamentally die, and in this dying be made alive again. Therefore Christ said, 'Unless the grain of corn fall into the ground and die it cannot bring forth fruit. But if it die it bringeth forth much fruit.' So also is it in truth. Whoso wisheth to have all the fruit of life must suffer all manner of death . . . And whoso doth not entirely die cannot either fully live.

John Tauler, *The Following of Christ*

The Cross was not a transaction. It was the culmination of this mighty Love, for 'here on the cross hung God and man' – God's Love springing forth in a soul strong enough to show it in its full scope. But let no person think he can 'cover himself with the purple mantle of Christ's sufferings and death', and so win his salvation: 'Thou thyself', he says, 'must go through Christ's whole journey, and enter wholly into His process.'

Rufus M. Jones, *Spiritual Reformers in the 16th and 17th Centuries*

The Christ of God was not then first crucified when the Jews brought him to the Cross; but Adam and Eve were his first real Murderers; for the Death which happened to them, in the Day that they did eat of the earthly Tree, was the Death of the Christ of God, or the Divine Life in their Souls. For Christ had never come into the World as a Second Adam to redeem it, had he not been originally the Life and Perfection, and Glory of the First Adam.

William Law, in Sidney Spencer, *The Spirit of Prayer and the Spirit of Love*

We Christians often use the words 'Christ died to save us from our sins'. He shows us the limitless measure of God's love and that draws our hearts to him. He makes known to us God's forgiveness, not only in his teaching, but by the fact of his own forgiveness of those who brought him to the cross. There is something more which it is difficult to describe – he works within us, assuring us of God's forgiveness, changing our hearts towards sin and selfishness, and sharing his risen life so that sin, though it may attack us, need find no entry.

George Appleton, *Journey for a Soul*

Are you willing to be sponged out, erased, cancelled, made nothing?
Are you willing to be made nothing, dipped into oblivion?
If not, you will never really change. The phoenix renews her youth only when she is burnt,
burnt alive, burnt down to hot and flocculent ash.
Then the small stirring of a new and small bub in the nest with strands of down like floating ash
Shows us that she is renewing her youth like the eagle, immortal bird.

D.H. Lawrence, 'Phoenix'

**See also** Humility, Selfishness, Suffering, Temptation, Transformation

## 21

# DEATH

*Death – dying, end of life, ceasing to be, annihilation, want of spiritual life*

I remember a teacher at primary school telling us time was valuable. 'Every minute of your life is precious,' she said. 'One day you will die, so never waste time. Make the most of your life, and then you will be happy.' She had such a determined look in her eyes I took these words to heart and have lived by them ever since. My teenage years were very full as a consequence. I had also taken on board some advice from my parents that you only get out of life what you are prepared to put into it. I was still not satisfied. Something vital was missing. A book by Ralph Waldo Trine, *In Tune with the Infinite*, opened my eyes to the spiritual dimension. Through reflection I began to discover a new quality and value of life. From time to time I was given brief moments of 'eternal life'. In them I experienced feelings of joy, freedom, harmony and wholeness. The fear of death was transcended. When I die, I hope to enter more fully a dimension I have already experienced. Death is then seen as a culmination, not an annihilation.

By the sweat of your face you shall eat bread until you return to the ground, for out of it you were taken; you are dust, and to dust you shall return.

Genesis 3.19

In my Father's house there are many dwelling-places. If it were not so, would I have told you that I go to prepare a place for you? And if I go and prepare a place for you, I will come again and will take you to myself, so that where I am, there you may be also.

John 14.2–3

A good life has a peaceful death.

French Proverb

As a well-spent day brings happy sleep, so life well used brings happy death.

Leonardo da Vinci, *The Notebooks of Leonardo da Vinci*

Death helps us to see what is worth trusting and loving and what is a waste of time.

J. Neville Ward, *Five for Sorrow, Ten for Joy*

To die is poignantly bitter, but the idea of having to die without having lived is unbearable.

Erich Fromm, *Man for Himself*

Do not seek death. Death will find you. But seek the road which makes death a fulfilment.

Dag Hammarskjöld, *Markings*

Death's stamp gives value to the coin of life; making it possible to buy with life what is truly precious.

Rabindranath Tagore, *Stray Birds*

Walking with God . . . means walking through death. It means living with death behind one rather than ahead of one.

John S. Dunne, *The Reasons of the Heart*

People who love life and love giving to it and receiving from it do not find themselves particularly perturbed about death.

J. Neville Ward, *Friday Afternoon*

The only religious way to think of death is as part and parcel of life; to regard it, with the understanding and with the emotions, as the inviolable condition of life.

Thomas Mann, *The Magic Mountain*

I have a feeling that there probably is some fellowship and communion of like-minded people beyond death, which can begin here – and that our jealous and exclusive friendships and alliances rather hinder it. But it is all a very big subject!

A.C. Benson, *Extracts from the Letters of Dr A.C. Benson to M.E.A.*

It makes it possible for us to rest in the certainty that the end of life on earth is not the end of life, that the haunting fragility of things has a meaning, that love is given for eternity, that no accident in these dimensions of time and space can prevent the accomplishment of the ends for which men and women with minds and hearts have come into existence

Norman Goodall, *The Local Church*

On the day when death will knock at thy door what wilt thou offer to him? Oh, I will set before my guest the full vessel of my life – I will never let him go with empty hands.

All the sweet vintage of all my autumn days and summer nights, all the earnings and gleanings of my busy life will I place before him at the close of my days when death will knock at my door.

Rabindranath Tagore, *Gitanjali*

The Lord does not promise that anyone who keeps His word shall avoid the physical incident called death; but that if his mind is turned towards that word it will not pay any attention to death; death will be to it irrelevant. It may truly be said that such a man will not 'experience' death, because, though it will happen to him, it will matter to him no more than the fall of a leaf from a tree under which he might be reading a book.

William Temple, *Readings in St John's Gospel*

Our attitude to all men would be Christian if we regarded them as though they were dying, and determined our relation to them in the light of death, both of their death and our own. A person who is dying calls forth a special kind of feeling. Our attitude to him is at once softened and lifted on to a higher plane. We then can feel compassion for people whom we did not love. But every man is dying. I too am dying and must never forget about death.

Nicolas Berdyaev, *The Destiny of Man*

People who believe that death is part of God's purpose, one of the forms of his caring, can take their time over life. There being a message of beginning or deepening in every ending, their sufferings are worth working through with considerable care. They are not going to miss or lose anything that matters. And there is never any reason for ceasing to love, even for loving less, since every moment, every experience, brings God with it and the possibility of deeper communion with life.

J. Neville Ward, *Friday Afternoon*

It was not physical life and physical death of which Jesus was thinking. He meant that, for the man who fully accepted Him, there is no such thing as death. Death had lost its finality. The man who enters into fellowship with Jesus has entered into a fellowship which is independent of time. The man who accepts Jesus has entered into a relationship with God which neither time nor eternity can sever. Such a man goes, not from life to death, but from life to life. Death is only the introduction to the nearer presence of God.

William Barclay, *The Gospel of John*

The death of someone we love is always shattering. To love is to carry another within oneself, to keep a special place in one's heart for him or her. This spiritual space is nourished by a physical presence; death, then, tears out a part of our own heart. Those who deny the suffering of death have never truly loved; they live in a spiritual illusion.

To celebrate death, then, is not to deny this laceration and the grief it involves, it is to give space to live it, to speak about it, and even to sing of it. It is to give mutual support, looking the reality in the face and placing all in the Heart of God in deep trust.

Jean Vanier, *Man and Woman He Made Them*

**See also** Anxiety, Depression, Doubt, Grief, Loneliness, Resurrection

## 22

# DEPRESSION

*Depression – a psychological state of extreme low spirits characterized by a sense of hopelessness and despair*

A medical student dropped in to see me. He was normally a bright and cheerful person, competent in his studies and a gifted musician but now he was going through a period of depression. I listened to him carefully, gave him a short quotation, and suggested he get a pen and paper, and write down all his thoughts as he pondered over these words. He was to come and see me in an hour's time. Two hours went by and then he returned, back to his usual cheerful self. 'Do you know,' he exclaimed, 'I have just had my very first thoughts ever! For a long time I have been learning facts and more facts. I reckon that is what has been depressing me. But today, for the very first time in my life, I've discovered I have a mind that can think. I got so absorbed I forgot about the time. Now at least I can live.' How often external pressures depress us, and dampen down our precious inner resources.

Why are you cast down, O my soul, and why are you disquieted within me? Hope in God; for I shall again praise him, my help and my God.

Psalm 43.5

. . . God, who consoles the downcast.

2 Corinthians 7.6

Despair gives courage.

Sir Walter Scott, *The Heart of Midlothian*

Darkness is more productive of sublime ideas than light.

Edmund Burke, *Burke's Works*

Half the spiritual difficulties that men and women suffer arise from a morbid state of health.

Henry Ward Beecher, *Proverbs from Plymouth Pulpit*

Into each life some rain must fall,
Some days must be dark and dreary.

Henry Wadsworth Longfellow, 'The Rainy Day'

I believe there is a way out of dark experiences though one cannot see it, and that all the suffering does not come in vain.

A.C. Benson, *Extracts from the Letters of Dr A.C. Benson to M.E.A.*

Resolve to be thyself; and know that he,
Who finds himself, loses his misery!

Matthew Arnold, 'Self-Dependence'

More people are destroyed by unhappiness than by drink, drugs, disease, or even failure. There must be something about sadness which attracts or people would not accept it so readily into their lives.

Hubert van Zeller, *Considerations*

For there is no despair so absolute as that which comes with the first moments of our first great sorrow, when we have not yet known what it is to have suffered and be healed, to have despaired and to have recovered hope.

George Eliot, *Adam Bede*

The severely self-rejecting adolescent is his own enemy. He has taken unto himself all the unkindness of his heredity and all the harshness of his environment, and then has added something more: everything is his fault and he is no good.

Arthur T. Jersild, *The Psychology of Adolescence*

The human being cannot live in a condition of emptiness for very long: if he is not growing *toward* something, he does not merely stagnate; the pent-up potentialities turn into morbidity and despair, and eventually into destructive activities.

Rollo May, *Man's Search for Himself*

It is one of the secrets of Nature in its mood of mockery that fine weather lays a heavier weight on the minds and hearts of the depressed and the inwardly tormented than does a really bad day with the dark rain snivelling continuously and sympathetically from a dirty sky.

Muriel Spark, *Territorial Rights*

Then black despair,
The shadows of a starless night, was thrown
Over the world in which I moved alone.

Percy Bysshe Shelley, 'The Revolt of Islam: Dedication: To Mary'

That Jesus fought despair and triumphed we know from his prayers on the cross which began with 'My God, why have you forsaken me?' and ended with 'Into your hand, Lord, I commend my spirit.' However near we come to despair, we have this precedent to refer to.

Hubert van Zeller, *Considerations*

I can enjoy feeling melancholy, and there is a good deal of satisfaction about being thoroughly miserable, but nobody likes a fit of the blues. Nevertheless, everybody has them; notwithstanding which, nobody can tell why. There is no accounting for them. You are just as likely to have one on the day after you have come into a large fortune, as on the day after you have left your new silk umbrella in the train.

Jerome K. Jerome, *Idle Thoughts of an Idle Fellow*

Sometimes I battle with depression. I never know all the reasons for this 'dark pit', as it seems to me. Some of it may be hurt pride. Sometimes it is obviously exhaustion, physical, mental, emotional and spiritual. At times, when I am tired and strained, I can get angry over an incident that may be quite trivial in itself; and then I get angry with myself for getting angry. As I suppress both forms of anger, depression is the result. I am then even more difficult to live with than usual. I do not want people to get too near to me, but I hope very much that they will not go too far away either.

David Watson, *You Are My God*

When the heart is hard and parched up, come upon me with a shower of mercy.
When grace is lost from life, come with a burst of song.
When tumultuous work raises its din on all sides shutting me out from beyond, come to me, my lord of silence, with thy peace and rest.
When my beggarly heart sits crouched, shut up in a corner, break open the door, my king, and come with the ceremony of a king.
When desire blinds the mind with delusion and dust, O thou holy one, thou wakeful, come with thy light and thy thunder.

Rabindranath Tagore, *Gitanjali*

A vague feeling of anguish is prowling around in me like a caged beast, immobilizing my energies and concentration. The feeling has no shape and I don't know what to call it. I am its prisoner. I've got to shake it off. I need all my energy at the moment, at every moment, if I'm to live my life in its fullness. But I won't be free of it until I've let the bad feeling wash over me, then faced it without fear, grabbed it with both hands and offered it to God who can bring new life out of sin.

I can understand the awful pain of those who are suffering from depression. It's a paralysing of one's whole being, while others whisper: He should pull up his socks! Control himself! But the trouble is *he can't*. It's an ordeal, one of the worst. He needs drugs, perhaps. But he also needs someone always to be there, patient, sensitive, to help him set free the little pieces of life which are stagnating in him, polluting his source.

Michel Quoist, *With Open Heart*

**See also** Healing, Loneliness, Perseverance, Suffering, Transformation

## 23

# DISCIPLESHIP

*Discipleship – one who attends upon another for the purpose of learning from him/her – includes practice as well as theory; learning by doing*

When I first went to Bradford Cathedral as a curate I had a brief chat with one of my colleagues. I was keen to find out how best to operate in this new environment. His advice was: observe the provost closely and learn all you can from him. He likened this to an apprenticeship, in which one learned from an experienced old hand. At theological college the emphasis had been mainly on theory, on the academic side of things. In that rarefied atmosphere we had studied the Bible, doctrine, church history, ethics and worship. Now the time had come for practical application, under the watchful eye of the provost. I did as he suggested. Looking back over the four-year curacy, the 'apprenticeship' was in reality a valuable period of discipleship. Theory and practice were carefully brought together.

You shall speak to him and put the words in his mouth; and I will be with your mouth and with his mouth, and will teach you what you shall do.

Exodus 4.15

Come to me, all you that are weary and are carrying heavy burdens, and I will give you rest. Take my yoke upon you, and learn from me; for I am gentle and humble in heart, and you will find rest for your souls. For my yoke is easy, and my burden is light.

Matthew 11.28–30

When the body is most disciplined, the mental and the spiritual faculties are most alert.

William Barclay, *The Gospel of Matthew*

The commandment of absolute truthfulness is really only another name for the fulness of discipleship.

Dietrich Bonhoeffer, *The Cost of Discipleship*

Christ cannot be followed unless a man gives the benefit of his gifts and attainments to the whole community.

Henry Ward Beecher, *Proverbs from Plymouth Pulpit*

We are called to represent Christ spontaneously and with incalculable consequences in the pedestrian obscurity of everyday life.

Hans Jürgen Schultz, *Conversion to the World*

In dealing with ourselves inner genuineness, with our fellows utter goodwill, with God perfect confidence – that, in brief, is discipleship to Jesus.

Harry Emerson Fosdick, *The Hope of a New World*

For though our Saviour's passion is over, his compassion is not. That never fails his humble sincere disciples. In him they find more than all they lose in the world.

William Penn, *Fruits of Solitude*

When we fail in our discipleship it is always for one of two reasons; either we are not trying to be loyal, or else we are trying in our own strength and find that it is not enough.

William Temple, *Readings in St John's Gospel*

We know by doing. Take up thy cross, lift it up yourself on your own shoulder, stagger under it, go on with it, and your intellect will be enriched with what no books could give.

Mark Rutherford, *Last Pages from a Journal*

God in Jesus Christ enters the human battles for existence and wholeness, and exerts his power to redeem men. The disciple is called to enter into this decisive issue – not merely 'decide' about it, but participate in it.

John J. Vincent, *Secular Christ*

On one occasion three would-be disciples came to Jesus and offered their discipleship with reservations or delays. He warned them that discipleship involved hardship, with total, immediate and life-long commitment (Luke 9.57–62). When we begin to follow we shall soon realize that more is needed, and if we are honest enough or rash enough to ask 'What do I still lack?' he will unerringly put his finger on the one thing we are least ready to surrender.

George Appleton, *Journey for a Soul*

There is a kind of Church-worker for whom our age even more urgently calls, and on whom the life and example of Christ set more immediately the seal of discipleship – the man who, to the glory of God and for the good of his fellows, does honest work of the everyday sort.

Archibald C. Craig, *University Sermons*

He prepared His disciples for a change after the critical moment was passed; with the Cross and Resurrection His Kingdom would have come with power, and they were no longer to be apart from the world, bringing to it *ab extra* the divine act of redemption which is itself the revelation of God, but were to carry its power into the world as leaven that should leaven the whole lump.

William Temple, *Citizen and Churchman*

The Christian who reads, in these verses (Luke 14.25–35), of the price of discipleship will see that, if he is to take the divine words seriously, he must learn not to be too much 'entangled in the affairs of this life', whether human affairs or relationships, or personal and material things. He must learn to think of these as things that he can do without, including life itself. No one knows what he may be called upon one day to face or to do in loyalty to his profession as a Christian disciple – especially in a world as dangerous and uncertain as that in which our lives are cast. The man who is bogged down by worldly ties and considerations will find obedience much harder if God should call him one day to do some sacrificial act.

J.R.H. Moorman, *The Path to Glory*

Every disciple knows that the aim of his life is to grow like his Lord. To achieve this he will study the earliest records of the divine life lived among men. He will want to get back behind the words to their meaning, behind the actions to the mind and character which inspired those actions. He will be eager to enter into intimate touch with him who promised to be with men and to live within the inmost being of each man. So with the outer study and the inner communion he will come to understand and acquire something of the mind of Christ.

George Appleton, *Journey for a Soul*

We are summoned to a new level of identification. We are summoned to be disciples, and so to a discipline. A disciple is a learner and his discipline is the training whereby he learns. To learn the way of the cross is the hardest thing of all, and the training by which we are to advance in this learning is provided for us by the discipline of prayer and worship. Those who disparage prayer and worship and imagine that without these one can achieve some kind of instant Christianity do not know what they are talking about. They understand neither the weakness of our humanity nor the depth of the richness of the spiritual maturity into which Christ is calling us.

John Macquarrie, *Paths in Spirituality*

The price of discipleship, . . . is to be willing to give up everything if occasion should demand it, and, in the meanwhile, to live as men 'looking for their Lord', with loins girt and lamps burning, ready for action when the word is given. Discipleship, is, or may be, a very costly thing. It may cost us all we have. In this passage [Luke 14.25–35] therefore, Jesus introduces a fourth condition, and that is that we should not go into it except with our eyes wide open. He does this in the form of three little parables, those of the tower builder who carefully surveys his material; the warrior-king who closely considers his chances of success; and the salt, which, if it cannot last out, goes bad.

Jesus bids us count the cost of discipleship. Can we face it? Is it going to be too much for us? Dare we risk failure and be cast out?

J.R.H. Moorman, *The Path to Glory*

**See also** Action, Christian, Growing, Obedience, Service

# 24

# DIVINITY

*Divinity – theology; being divine, Godhood*

One of our undergraduates was helped in her understanding of the Christian faith by some words of Meister Eckhart in this section. 'The seed of God is in us. Given an intelligent farmer and a diligent fieldhand, it will thrive and grow up to God whose seed it is, and accordingly its fruit will be God-nature. Pear seeds grow into pear trees; nut seeds into nut trees, and God-seed into God!' Through these words she was able to understand baptism (and confirmation) as a cleansing and *a spiritual rebirth*. She then considered the words of the confirmation service; that 'she may . . . daily increase in your Holy Spirit more and more, until she comes to your everlasting Kingdom'. She worked out spiritual rebirth, initiated in baptism and confirmation, needed to grow in prayer, as in reflection. She now came to understand divinity as a 'divine life', rather than 'a divine science', and she was gradually changed by it.

His divine power has given us everything needed for life and godliness, through the knowledge of him who called us by his own glory and goodness. Thus he has given us, through these things, his precious and very great promises, so that through them you may escape from the corruption that is in the world because of lust, and may become participants in the divine nature. For this very reason, you must make every effort to support your faith with goodness, and goodness with knowledge, and knowledge with self-control, and self-control with endurance, and endurance with godliness, and godliness with mutual affection, and mutual affection with love.

2 Peter 1.3–7

We know that we are God's children.

1 John 5.19

The mystery of a Person, indeed, is ever divine, to him that has a sense for the Godlike.

Thomas Carlyle, *Sartor Resartus*

There's a divinity that shapes our ends,
Rough-hew them how we will.

William Shakespeare, *Hamlet*

The essential truth . . . is that man is under an absolute mandate to express divinity in his own nature and in his whole life.

F. Ernest Johnson, *The Social Gospel Re-Examined*

The seeds of godlike power are in us still;
Gods we are, bards, saints, heroes, if we will!

Matthew Arnold, *Written in Emerson's Essays*

He is divinely favoured who may trace a silver vein in all the affairs of life, see sparkles of light in the gloomiest scenes, and absolute radiance in those which are bright.

Henry Ward Beecher, *Proverbs from Plymouth Pulpit*

Were I indeed to define divinity, I should rather call it a *divine life*, rather than a *divine science*; it being something rather to be understood by a spiritual sensation, than by any verbal description.

John Smith the Platonist, *Select Discourses*

There is a power in the soul untouched by time and flesh, flowing from the Spirit, remaining in the Spirit, altogether spiritual. In this power is God, ever verdant, flowering in all the joy and glory of his actual self.

Meister Eckhart, in Franz Pfeiffer, *Meister Eckhart,* translated by C. de B. Evans

That only which we have within, can we see without. If we meet no gods, it is because we harbour none. If there is grandeur in you, you will find grandeur in porters and sweeps. He only is rightly immortal, to whom all things are immortal.

Ralph Waldo Emerson, *The Conduct of Life, Nature and Other Essays*

Divinity is essentially the first of the professions, because it is necessary for all at all times; law and physic are only necessary for some at some times. I speak of them, of course, not in their abstract existence, but in their applicability to man.

Samuel Taylor Coleridge, *Table Talk of Samuel Taylor Coleridge*

The soul may rise through all earthly influences into such a susceptible spiritual condition that the throb and impulse of the Divine nature shall fall upon our souls and give us an abiding state of wisdom, of peace, of rest, and of joy in the Holy Ghost.

Henry Ward Beecher, *Proverbs from Plymouth Pulpit*

To the poet, to the philosopher, to the saint, all things are friendly and sacred, all events profitable, all days holy, all men divine. For the eye is fastened on the life, and slights the circumstance. Every chemical substance, every plant, every animal in its growth, teaches the unity of cause, the variety of appearance.

Ralph Waldo Emerson, *Essay on History*

. . . it takes a divine man to exhibit anything divine, Socrates, Alfred, Columbus, Wordsworth, or any other brave preferrer of the still small voice within to the roar of the populace – a thing very easy to speak and very hard to do for twenty-four hours. The rest are men potentially, not actually, now only pupas or tadpoles – say rather quarries of souls, heroes that shall be, seeds of gods.

Ralph Waldo Emerson, *Journals*

'All divinity is love, or wonder', John Donne wrote in one of his poems. No phrase could better express the intense religious life of the group of spiritual poets in England who interpreted in beautiful, often immortal, form this religion of the spirit, this glowing consciousness that the world and all its fulness is God's and that eternity is set within the soul of man, who never is himself until he finds his Life in God.

Rufus M. Jones, *Spiritual Reformers in the 16th and 17th Centuries*

I think it might be said not (with Voltaire) that we invent our gods, but that we carry them with us and inside us.

Cutting across the differences in doctrines between the great world religions – of Moses and Jesus, of Lao-tzu and Buddha, of Confucius and Mohammed – there remains the truth that God is what man finds that is divine in himself. God is the best way man can behave in the ordinary occasions of life, and the farthest point to which man can stretch himself.

Max Lerner, *The Unfinished Country*

The Scriptures say of human beings that there is an outward man and, along with him, an inner man. To the outward man belong those things that depend on the soul but are connected with the flesh and blended with it, and the co-operative functions of the several members such as the eye, the ear, the tongue, the hand, and so on. The Scripture speaks of all this as the old man, the earthy man, the outward person, the enemy, the servant. Within us all is the other person, the inner man, whom the Scripture calls the new man, the heavenly man, the young person, a friend, the aristocrat . . .The seed of God is in us. Given an intelligent farmer and a diligent fieldhand, it will thrive and grow up to God whose seed it is, and accordingly its fruit will be God-nature. Pear seeds grow into pear trees; nut seeds into nut trees, and God-seed into God!

Meister Eckhart, *Meister Eckhart*, translated by Raymond B. Blakney

**See also** God, Holy Spirit, Incarnation, Jesus Christ, Mystics

# 25

# DOUBT

*Doubt – feeling of uncertainty about something, undecided state of mind, inclination to disbelieve; uncertain state of things, lack of full proof or clear indication*

At theological college we had a quiet day taken by the then Archbishop of York, Stuart Blanch. He was giving us some advice about coping with doubt, and told us of a recent experience. It was summertime. In the evening he was taking his dog for a walk in his grounds, and they came across a hedgehog on the lawn. The dog had never seen a hedgehog before and joyfully bounded up to explore. The hedgehog, sensing danger, curled itself into a ball, and the dog got its nose badly pricked. With a great howl of pain the dog tucked its tail between its legs and headed off for the security of the bushes. The next evening there was a repeat performance. This time the dog was more circumspect. He approached the hedgehog slowly, stopping six feet in front of it, observing it carefully. After a while he turned on his heels, tail high, and bounded off to the bushes. The archbishop made the point the dog was unable to understand the hedgehog but felt he could still enjoy life, not knowing all the answers. He wondered if this had something to tell us about living creatively with doubt.

Among those nations you shall find no ease, no resting-place for the sole of your foot. There the Lord will give you a trembling heart, failing eyes, and a languishing spirit. Your life shall hang in doubt before you; night and day you shall be in dread, with no assurance of your life.

Deuteronomy 28.65–66

So the other disciples told him, 'We have seen the Lord.' But he said to them, 'Unless I see the mark of the nails in his hands, and put my finger in the mark of the nails, and my hand in his side, I will not believe.'

John 20.25

Honest doubt is suspended judgment.
A.R. Orage, *On Love*

Feed your faith, and your doubts will starve to death.
Anon

All fanaticism is a strategy to prevent doubt from becoming conscious.
H.A. Williams CR, *The True Wilderness*

If we are sensible, we will not doubt God, we will doubt our world and we will doubt ourselves.
Agnes Sanford, *The Healing Light*

Modest doubt is call'd
The beacon of the wise.
William Shakespeare, *Troilus and Cressida*

To doubt is to live, to struggle, to struggle for life and to live by struggle . . . A faith which does not continue to doubt is a dead faith.
Miguel de Unamuno, *The Agony of Christianity*

When we say: 'Yes, I doubt, but I do believe in God's love more than I trust my own doubts', it becomes possible for God to act.
Anthony Bloom, *The Essence of Prayer*

If Christ has grappled our hearts to Himself at all, then it were surely wise to trust His certainties and not our own doubts, however persistent.
Herbert H. Farmer, *The Healing Cross*

I refused to allow myself to accept any of it in my heart, because I was afraid of a headlong fall, but I was hanging in suspense which was more likely to be fatal than a fall.
St Augustine, *Confessions*

If a man will begin in certainties, he shall end in doubts; but if he will be content to begin with doubts, he shall end in certainties.
Francis Bacon, *The Advancement of Learning*

There are the shadows of doubts and uncertainties. Sometimes the way ahead is far from being clear. Sometimes we feel like people groping among the shadows with nothing firm to cling to.

William Barclay, *The Gospel of John*

Our doubts are traitors,
And make us lose the good we oft might win,
By fearing to attempt.

William Shakespeare, *Measure for Measure*

Enthusiasm for the universe, in knowing as well as in creating, also answers the question of doubt and meaning. Doubt is the necessary tool of knowledge. And meaninglessness is no threat so long as enthusiasm for the universe and for man as its centre is alive.

Paul Tillich, *The Courage to Be*

For nothing worthy proving can be proven,
Nor yet disproven: wherefore thou be wise,
Cleave ever to the sunnier side of doubt,
And cleave to Faith beyond the forms of Faith!

Alfred, Lord Tennyson, 'The Ancient Sage'

But this is an age not of faith, but of cathartic doubt, and unless everything can, potentially at least, be questioned, then there is a kind of betrayal of the spirit of the times. It seems possible that doubt *is* our search for meaning, and that whatever refuses this painful path has cut itself off from our search for life.

Monica Furlong, *The End of Our Exploring*

There is an increasing number of people to whom everything they are doing seems futile. They are still under the spell of the slogans which preach faith in the secular paradise of success and glamour. But doubt, the fertile condition of all progress, has begun to beset them and has made them ready to ask what their real self-interest as human beings is.

Eric Fromm, *Man for Himself*

Doubt and perplexity will often be the lot of travellers on this life's journey. Beyond the questions arising in our daily thought and conduct are those greater difficulties which seem to stop our progress and to render existence an insoluble riddle. Doubt has many sources. It may be true that some could find the origin of their doubts in an unwillingness to face their moral condition and obey the demands of duty. But at the present day, doubt frequently arises from a sense that received dogmas do not correspond with the facts of life or with the moral values which our truest insight reveals. In other cases there may be not so much perplexity and doubt as an exhilarating spirit of inquiry and exploration driving a man forward on the quest for truth for himself and all men.

*Christian Faith and Practice in the Experience of the Society of Friends*

**See also** Faith, Growing, Guidance, Hope, Thinking

## 26

# EDUCATION

*Education – bringing up (young persons); giving intellectual and moral training; development of character or mental powers*

A quotation about higher education suggests we are in danger of producing intellectual giants who remain spiritual and emotional pygmies. Over the years I have been impressed with the intellectual qualities of our fellows, postgraduates, and undergraduates. However I sometimes wonder if we are too one-sided in our system of education. The emphasis tends to be mainly on developing critical and analytical skills, and the power of reason and the intellect. Reflection Groups are an attempt to educate the 'whole' person. They are based on the original meaning of the Latin word *educere* – to draw out, lead out – and concentrate on developing latent gifts and talents. A typical Reflection Group meets for an hour a week, chooses a topic, mulls over the contents in silence and then talks it through. Much is learned from the other members of the group. The intellectual content is still present, but the spiritual and moral contents are also there, and development of character takes place unconsciously. The Reflection Group thus makes its contribution in the academic institution aiming to educate the whole person, body, mind and spirit.

I will instruct you and teach you the way you should go; I will counsel you with my eye upon you.
Psalm 32.8

About the middle of the festival Jesus went up into the temple and began to teach. The Jews were astonished at it, saying, 'How does this man have such learning, when he has never been taught?'
John 7.14–15

Learning is its own exceeding great reward.
William Hazlitt, *The Plain Speaker*

Deep verst in books and shallow in himself.

John Milton, *Paradise Regain'd*

Education has for a chief object the formation of character.

Herbert Spencer, *Social Statics*

The direction in which education starts a man will determine his future life.

Plato, *The Republic of Plato*

To be what we are, and to become what we are capable of becoming, is the only end of life.

Robert Louis Stevenson, *Familiar Studies of Men and Books, Virginibus Puerisque*

. . . he is perfectly educated who is taught all the will of God concerning him, and enabled, through life, to execute it.

Thomas Arnold, *Sermons*

Finally, education, alone, can conduct us to that enjoyment which is, at once, best in quality and infinite in quantity.

Horace Mann, *Lectures and Reports on Education*

A child is not educated who has not physical education, social education, intellectual education, industrial education, professional education, spiritual education.

Henry Ward Beecher, *Proverbs from Plymouth Pulpit*

The task of religious education is to fashion a religious lifestyle, and to nurture in people that creative spirit of love that will help them to grow up and live wisely without a rule-book.

Roy Stevens, *On Education and the Death of Love*

*Education*: by that I understand not merely the imparting of knowledge, but the drawing out of the powers of the mind, spirit, and body; the evoking of a reverence for the truth, and the use of the imagination in its pursuit.

Michael Ramsey, in Margaret Duggan, *Through the Year with Michael Ramsey*

Education . . . is the leading of human souls to what is best, and making what is best out of them; and these two objects are always attainable together, and by the same means; the training which makes men happiest in themselves, also makes them most serviceable to others.

John Ruskin, *The Stones of Venice*

Education ought to teach how to be in love always and what to be in love with. The great things of history have been done by the great lovers, by the saints and men of science and artists; and the problem of civilization is to give every man a chance of being a saint, a man of science, or an artist.

A. Clutton Brock, *The Ultimate Belief*

An education which is not religious is atheistic; there is no middle way. If you give to children an account of the world from which God is left out, you are teaching them to understand the world without reference to God. If He is then introduced, He is an excrescence. He becomes an appendix to His own creation.

William Temple, *The Hope of a New World*

One person who has mastered life is better than a thousand persons who have mastered only the contents of books, but no one can get anything out of life without God. If I were looking for a master of learning, I should go to Paris to the colleges where the higher studies are pursued, but if I wanted to know about the perfection of life, they could not tell me there.

Meister Eckhart, *Meister Eckhart*, translated by Raymond B. Blakney

. . . the modern educationalist is forever pointing out that *educere* means to lead forth, or to draw out, a student's potentiality, as opposed to the old-style education that was content to stuff a head full of presumed facts. If there is any analogy with spiritual direction, then it is very up-to-date indeed, for this has always been its aim; to develop innate gifts and graces.

Martin Thornton, *Spiritual Direction*

Ordinary, secular education, as it deals only with the comprehensible, puts the pupil in a wrong position. He has to do with nothing which may not be mastered, and becomes insensible to that which is beyond. Worse – he is affected only by reasons which appeal to his understanding, by what is immediate, and his conduct is not governed, as it so often should be, by that which is intangible, shadowy, and remote.

Mark Rutherford, *Last Pages from a Journal*

The development of general ability for independent thinking and judgment should always be placed foremost, not the acquisition of special knowledge. If a person masters the fundamentals of his subject and has learnt to think and work independently, he will surely find his way and besides will be better able to adapt himself to progress and changes than the person whose training principally consists in the acquiring of detailed knowledge.

Albert Einstein, *Out of My Later Years*

Most people live, whether physically, intellectually, or morally, in a very restricted circle of their potential being. They *make use* of a very small portion of their possible consciousness, and of their soul's resources in general, much like a man who, out of his whole bodily organism, should get into the habit of using and moving only his little finger. Great emergencies and crises show us how much greater our vital resources are than we had supposed.

William James, *The Letters of William James*

**See also** Growing, Intellect, Knowledge, Mind, Thinking

## 27

# ETERNAL LIFE

*Eternal life – existing always, without end or usually beginning; a quality and value of life; endless life after death; being eternal*

I once had the good fortune to meet George Appleton in his home in Oxford, where he had settled down in retirement. His writings had always appealed to me; that is why so many of them have been included. One of his contributions on eternal life has been particularly helpful. He describes eternal life as 'a quality of life, the kind of life which Jesus had, human life permeated by the grace and love of God . . . Jesus taught his disciples they could have eternal life now, the perfection of which will come in the dimension beyond death.' I feel he gets right to the heart of the matter in these few words. If we want to know more about this quality of life we can go to the Gospels, and see for ourselves a life permeated by the grace and love of God. As we read, we might become aware of this grace and love of God welling up inside us, and experience eternal life for ourselves. One of the great joys of Christianity is to experience moments of eternal life in this present life, and thus have an assurance of eternal life in the future.

The eternal God is a dwelling-place, and underneath are the everlasting arms.

Deuteronomy 33.27

But those who drink of the water that I will give them will never be thirsty. The water that I will give will become in them a spring of water gushing up to eternal life.

John 4.14

We feel and know that we are eternal.

Benedict Spinoza, *Spinoza's Ethics and De Intellectus Emendatione*

Time is eternity; and we live in eternity now.

Herman Melville, *Mardi*

The truest end of life is to know the life that never ends.

William Penn, *Fruits of Solitude*

The noise of the moment scoffs at the music of the Eternal.

Rabindranath Tagore, *Stray Birds*

To have the sense of the eternal in life is a short flight for the soul. To have had it, is the soul's vitality.

George Meredith, *Diana of the Crossways*

But felt through all this fleshly dresse
Bright *shoots* of everlastingnesse.

Henry Vaughan, *Silex Scintillans*

Every creative act of ours in relation to other people – an act of love, of pity, of help, of peacemaking – not merely has a future but is eternal.

Nicolas Berdyaev, *The Destiny of Man*

If there is a God and a future life, then there is truth and goodness, and man's highest happiness consists in striving to attain them.

Leo Tolstoy, *War and Peace*

Eternal life is the life of God, and to have eternal life is to share the life of God. Here we are at the very heart of the matter. Eternal life is nothing less than God's life.

William Barclay, *The Plain Man Looks at the Apostles' Creed*

It is eternity now. I am in the midst of it. It is about me in the sunshine; I am in it, as the butterfly floats in the light-laden air. Nothing has to come: it is now. Now is eternity; now is the immortal life.

Richard Jefferies, *The Story of My Heart*

Any one who feels the full significance of what is involved in knowing the *truth* has a coercive feeling that Eternity has been set within us, that our finite life is deeply rooted in the all-pervading Infinite.

Rufus M. Jones, *Spiritual Reformers in the 16th and 17th Centuries*

Eternal life is not a gift as something out of the hand of God, like a sceptre, or like a coronet. It is a gift as education is; something wrought patiently and long in a man. It is a gift as the sunlight is to the flowers – an influence which enters into them and fashions them.

Henry Ward Beecher, *Proverbs from Plymouth Pulpit*

If a man once knows the Spirit within him, the source of all his aspiration after holiness, as indeed the Spirit of Jesus Christ, and if he knows this Spirit of Jesus Christ within himself as none other than the Spirit of the Eternal and Almighty God, what more can he want? *This is the eternal life.*

William Temple, *Readings in St John's Gospel*

The eternal life is not the future life; it is life in harmony with the true order of things, – life in God. We must learn to look upon time as a movement of eternity, as an undulation in the ocean of being. To live, so as to keep this consciousness of ours in perpetual relation with the eternal, is to be wise; to live, so as to personify and embody the eternal, is to be religious.

Henri Frédéric Amiel, *Amiel's Journal*

Jesus did not promise to men simply life after death, but a quality of life now. He promised us eternal life, the sharing of God's life, participation in his own risen life. He said that he had come to give men abundant life – sufficient to keep the body in health and strength, to illuminate and guide the mind, to bring peace to the heart. If we have that life within us now, we shall not worry about our last migration into the spiritual world, for we shall know a good deal about it already.

George Appleton, *Journey for a Soul*

Religion, in its fullest development, essentially requires, not only this our little span of earthly years, but a life beyond. Neither an Eternal Life that is already fully achieved here below, nor an Eternal Life already to be begun and known solely in the beyond, satisfies these requirements. Only an Eternal Life already begun and truly known in part here, though fully to be achieved and completely to be understood hereafter, corresponds to the deepest longings of man's spirit as touched by the prevenient Spirit, God.

Friedrich von Hügel, *Eternal Life*

Now there are some things we all know, but we don't take'm out and look at'm very often. We all know that *something* is eternal. And it ain't houses and it ain't names, and it ain't earth, and it ain't even the stars . . . everybody knows in their bones that *something* is eternal, and that something has to do with human beings. All the greatest people ever lived have been telling us that for five thousand years, and yet you'd be surprised how people are always losing hold of it. There's something way down deep that's eternal about every human being.

Thornton Wilder, *Our Town*

Now let us take the idea of *eternal life*. It is far better to speak of *eternal* life than to speak of *everlasting* life. The main idea behind eternal life is not simply that of duration. It is quite clear that a life which went on for ever could just as easily be hell as heaven. The idea behind eternal life is the idea of a certain quality of life, a certain kind of life. What kind of life? There is only one person who can properly be described by this adjective eternal (*aionios*) and that one person is God. Eternal life is the kind of life that God lives; it is God's life.

William Barclay, *The Gospel of John*

**See also** Awareness, Freedom, Hope, Life, Time

# 28

# EXPERIENCE

*Experience – personal observation of or involvement with fact, event, etc.; knowledge of skill based on this; event that affects one*

This topic is not about experience of life in general but of experience of 'God' in particular. I am very fond of St Augustine's 'experience' of God, recorded in his *Confessions*. He writes of Beauty – 'at once so ancient and so new' – and after a long search discovers this Beauty as something within himself. It takes him many years to find this Beauty, as he was outside himself, searching elsewhere. He concludes, 'You were with me, but I was not with you.' His experience of Beauty was deeply convincing. With me the penny finally dropped when I discovered Beauty in the depths of myself, and was able to experience this at first hand. Beauty, of course, is only one aspect of this 'inner presence'. There are many others – Father, Son, Holy Spirit and the gifts and fruits of the Holy Spirit. Experience of this kind is crucial in our quest for faith. Through it we reach an inner conviction of mind, heart and spirit, at one with our deepest intuitions and instincts.

I have acquired great wisdom . . . and my mind has had great experience of wisdom and knowledge.

Ecclesiastes 1.16

. . . though indeed he is not far from each one of us. For 'In him we live and move and have our being.'

Acts 17.27–28

Never, 'for the sake of peace and quiet', deny your own experience or convictions.

Dag Hammarskjöld, *Markings*

So much of the Gospel as has been reproduced in a living form in Christian people's experience is what the world needs more than almost anything else.

Henry Ward Beecher, *Proverbs from Plymouth Pulpit*

All authentic religion originates with mystical experience, be it the experience of Jesus, of the Buddha, or Mohammed, of the seers and prophets of the *Upanishads.*

William Johnston, *The Inner Eye of Love*

The notes of religious experience that ring out of the soul are notes gladder than marriage-bells. Religion is real if it is experimental. Religion is glorious, and experimental religion is the most glorious of all.

Henry Ward Beecher, *Proverbs from Plymouth Pulpit*

His emphasis is always . . . upon the native divine possibilities of the soul, upon the fact of a spiritual environment in immediate correspondence and co-operation with the soul, and upon the necessity of personal and inward experience as the key to every gate of life.

Rufus M. Jones, *Spiritual Reformers in the 16th and 17th Centuries*

By religious experience we ought to mean an experience which is religious through and through – an experiencing of all things in the light of the knowledge of God. It is this, and not any moment of illumination, of which we may say that it is self-authenticating; for in such an experience all things increasingly fit together in a single intelligible whole.

William Temple, *Thoughts on Some Problems of the Day*

He who receives Christ *experiences* something, but he hardly notices it. The wonder of the new life, the joy of forgiveness, and the liberation from fear keep him looking constantly to this figure from whom streams of living water flow into his life, reclaiming the desert of his lost heart and working the miracle of a new beginning.

Helmut Thielicke, *I Believe: The Christian's Creed*

A creed is always the result and fruit of many minds and many centuries, purified from all the oddities, shortcomings, and flaws of individual experience. But for all that, the individual experience, with its very poverty, is immediate life, it is the warm red blood pulsating today. It is more convincing to a seeker after truth than the best tradition.

C.G. Jung, in Jolande Jacobi, *Psychological Reflections*

The significant features of the experience are the consciousness of fresh springs of life, the release of new energies, the inner integration and unification of personality, the inauguration of a sense of mission, the flooding of the life with hope and gladness, and the conviction, amounting in the mind of the recipient to certainty, that God is found as an environing and vitalizing presence.

Rufus M. Jones, *Spiritual Reformers in the 16th and 17th Centuries*

. . . strain every nerve in every possible way to know and experience yourself as you really are. It will not be long, I suspect, before you have a real knowledge and experience of God as he is. Not as he is in himself, of course, for that is impossible to any save God; and not as you will in Heaven, both in body and soul. But as much as is now possible for a humble soul in a mortal body to know and experience him . . . and as much as he will permit.

*The Cloud of Unknowing*

He comes to us as One unknown, without a name, as of old, by the lake-side, He came to those men who knew Him not. He speaks to us the same word: 'Follow thou me!' and sets us to the tasks which He has to fulfil for our time. He commands. And to those who obey Him, whether they be wise or simple, He will reveal Himself in the toils, the conflicts, the sufferings which they shall pass through in His fellowship, and, as an ineffable mystery, they shall learn in their own experience Who He is.

Albert Schweitzer, *The Quest of the Historical Jesus*

People today are not prepared to take their faith from the tradition in which they were born, nor from other people. They want to deduce it from their own experience of life. They do not need theories, but the experience which will be the source of their own interpretation. They are suspicious of anything which seems to escape from life into theory, from experience into doctrine, or from the thing itself into talk about it. The method they want to follow is the inductive one rather than the deductive.

George Appleton, *Journey for a Soul*

Science has never discovered any 'God', epistemological criticism proves the impossibility of knowing God, but the psyche comes forward with the assertion of the experience of God. God is a psychic fact of immediate experience, otherwise there would never have been any talk of God. The fact is valid in itself, requiring no non-psychological proof and inaccessible to any form of non-psychological criticism. It can be the most immediate and hence the most real of experiences, which can be neither ridiculed nor disproved. Only people with a poorly developed sense of fact, or who are obstinately superstitious, could deny this truth.

C.G. Jung, *The Structure and Dynamics of the Psyche*

Religious experience is absolute. It is indisputable. You can only say that you have never had such an experience, and your opponent will say: 'Sorry, I have.' And there your discussion will come to an end. No matter what the world thinks about religious experience, the one who has it possesses the great treasure of a thing that has provided him with a source of life, meaning and beauty and that has given him a new splendour, to the world and to mankind. He has *pistis* and peace. Where is the criterium by which you could say that such a life is not legitimate, that such experience is not valid and thus such *pistis* is mere illusion? Is there, as a matter of fact, any better truth about ultimate things than the one that helps you to live?

C.G. Jung, *Psychology and Religion*

**See also** Finding God, Fulfilment, Inner Life, Presence, Revelation

# 29

# FAITH

*Faith – strong belief, especially in the Christian faith; things believed; loyalty, trustworthiness*

When I was ordained, I had a fear about the future. I would be keen and enthusiastic for the first years of ministry and then would end up going through the motions. As it happened my faith came to a grinding halt after only four years. A new way beckoned forward through the discovery of *The Choice Is Always Ours* – an anthology compiled by Dorothy Berkley Phillips. This remarkable book opened up to me a new vision of faith of enormous dimensions. At first I had to be content with a skeleton of faith, but for the last twenty-five years I have been collecting material and putting flesh and blood on it. This vision of faith is founded on the Bible and the writings of many theologians, but includes the insights from poets, novelists, playwrights, philosophers, historians, scientists, politicians, economists, statesmen, psychologists, artists and musicians. With this vision of faith goes the practice of reflection. In reflection we mull over the contents of this anthology. After thirty-seven years of ministry I am still keen and enthusiastic about faith, learning something new day by day.

Though they do not see me with bodily eyes, yet with the spirit they will believe the things I have said.

2 Esdras 1.37

For we walk by faith, not by sight.

2 Corinthians 5.7

*Reason* saw not till *Faith* sprung the Light.

John Dryden, 'Religio Laici'

We live in an age which asks for faith, pure faith, naked faith, mystical faith.

William Johnston, *The Inner Eye of Love*

Relying on God has to begin all over again every day as if nothing had yet been done.

C.S. Lewis, *Letters of C.S. Lewis*

Faith is kept alive in us, and gathers strength, from practice more than from speculation.

Joseph Addison, *The Works of Joseph Addison*

To abandon religion for science is merely to fly from one region of faith to another.

Giles and Melville Harcourt, *Short Prayers for the Long Day*

Faith is a kind of winged intellect. The great workmen of history have been men who believed like giants.

Charles H. Parkhurst, *The Pattern and the Mount and Other Sermons*

It is neither *necessary*, nor indeed *possible*, to understand any matter of Faith; farther than it is Revealed.

Benjamin Whichcote, *Moral and Religious Aphorisms*

Faith in Christ was not primarily a matter of doctrinal or intellectual belief, but a way of life, a following, an allegiance.

Said of Edward Wilson, in George Seaver, *Edward Wilson of the Antarctic*

The life of faith is a continually renewed victory over doubt, a continually renewed grasp of meaning in the midst of meaninglessness.

Lesslie Newbigin, *Honest Religion for Secular Man*

It is faith that is expected of you and honest living, not profound understanding and deep knowledge of the mysteries of God.

Thomas à Kempis, *The Imitation of Christ*

Faith is a certitude without proofs . . . Faith is a sentiment, for it is a hope, it is an instinct, for it precedes all outward instruction.

Henri Frédéric Amiel, *Amiel's Journal*

Nothing in life is more wonderful than faith – the one great moving force which we can neither weigh in the balance nor test in the crucible.

Sir William Osler, *Aphorisms from His Bedside Teachings and Writings*

Religious faith does not consist in supposing that there is a God. It consists in personal trust in God rising to personal fellowship with God.

William Temple, *Basic Convictions*

The only faith that wears well and holds its colour in all weathers is that which is woven of conviction and set with the sharp mordant of experience.

J.R. Lowell, *My Study Windows*

Like all human knowledge, the knowledge of faith is also fragmentary. Only when faith remains aware of this does it remain free from arrogance, intolerance and false zeal.

Hans Küng, *On Being a Christian*

To have faith is to meet the world with the conviction that in spite of all its ambiguities and its downright evils, there can be discerned in it the reality of love and a ground of hope.

John Macquarrie, *Paths in Spirituality*

Proofs are the last thing looked for by a truly religious mind which feels the imaginative fitness of its faith and knows instinctively that, in such a manner, imaginative fitness is all that can be required.

George Santayana, *Interpretations of Poetry and Religion*

One in whom persuasion and belief
Had ripened into faith, and faith become
A passionate intuition.

William Wordsworth, 'The Excursion'

That man is perfect in faith who can come to God in the utter dearth of his feelings and his desires, without a glow or an inspiration, with the weight of low thoughts, failures, neglects, and wandering forgetfulness, and say to him, 'Thou art my refuge, because thou art my home.'

George Macdonald, *Unspoken Sermons*

How do we stand in respect of our use of the watch-tower of Faith? Are we so busy on the ground floor that we take it for granted, and seldom go upstairs? It is true that those stairs are dark and steep; but if we never make the effort, never ascend to the soul's summit, we remain something less than human.

Evelyn Underhill, in John Stobbart, *The Wisdom of Evelyn Underhill*

The creeds are not objects of faith; they are expressions of a faith of which Christ is the object, and in regard to all such personal relationships there is scope for at least a great width of intellectual movement as we seek more and more perfectly to understand and to interpret the character with which we are confronted.

William Temple, *The Preacher's Theme Today*

. . . it is only by living completely in this world that one learns to believe . . . This is what I mean by worldliness – taking life in one's stride, with all its duties and problems, its successes and failures, its experiences and helplessness. It is in such a life that we throw ourselves utterly into the arms of God and participate in his sufferings in the world and watch with Christ in Gethsemane. That is faith, that is *metanoia*, and that is what makes a man and a Christian.

Dietrich Bonhoeffer, *Letters and Papers from Prison*

**See also** Belief, Commitment, Experience, Mystics, Trust

30

# FINDING GOD

*Finding God – the search, discovery and coming to a personal knowledge of God*

William Law wrote one of the greatest religious treatises in the English language – *The Spirit of Prayer*. In this book he encourages us to find God by searching the deepest and most central part of our souls. There we shall discover the Light and Spirit of God, and so come to a personal knowledge of God. This approach rings true to my own experience. Early in life, I discerned something of God the creator in the creation. Several years later in the Gospels I was confronted by the person of Jesus Christ. In my early twenties I experienced something of the Holy Spirit. However these manifestations were mainly seen to be outside myself, and so lacked conviction. What ultimately proved decisive was the search suggested by William Law which led to the discovery of the Light and Spirit of God within me, and so to a personal knowledge of God. Reflecting on this material may help us to find God. We put ourselves in a position where God can find us, and expose ourselves to 'the gift of faith'.

O that I knew where I might find him, that I might come even to his dwelling!
Job 23.3

Search, and you will find.
Matthew 7.7

Humble recognition of what your nature is will lead more surely to God than profound searching for knowledge.
Thomas à Kempis, *The Imitation of Christ*

People are generally better persuaded by the reasons which they have themselves discovered than by those which have come into the mind of others.
Blaise Pascal, *Pensées*

None of the formal arguments for the existence of God really convince. The proof lies in hints and dreams which are not expressible by human language.

Mark Rutherford, *Last Pages from a Journal*

There is only one 'place' to look for God and that is in one's own soul, there is only one 'region' in which to find heaven or hell, and that is in the nature and character of the person's own desire and will.

Rufus M. Jones, *Spiritual Reformers in the 16th and 17th Centuries*

I found Him in the shining of the stars,
I marked Him in the flowering of His fields
But in His ways with men I find Him not.

Alfred, Lord Tennyson, 'The Passing of Arthur'

To discover God is not to discover an idea but to discover oneself. It is to awake to that part of one's existence which has been hidden from sight and which one has refused to recognize. The discovery may be very painful; it is like going through a kind of death. But it is the one thing which makes life worth living.

Bede Griffiths OSB, *The Golden String*

Thy hand be on the latch to open the door at his first knock.

Shouldst thou open the door and not see him, do not say he did not knock, but understand that he is there, and wants thee to go out to him. It may be he has something for thee to do for him. Go and do it, and perhaps thou wilt return with a new prayer, to find a new window in thy soul.

George Macdonald, *Unspoken Sermons*

The French religious writer Père Jean de Caussade insisted, in one of his discussions of Christian prayer, that we are to find God 'in the sacrament of the present moment'. That is, we are to find him when we are confronted with the demands of life, given the opportunity to make our response to those demands, and enabled to labour responsibly for God in the place where we are.

Norman Pittenger, *The Christian Situation Today*

The longer one travels toward the city he seeks the nearer and nearer he comes to the goal of his journey; exactly so is it with the soul that is seeking God. If he will travel away from himself and away from the world and seek only God as the precious pearl of his soul, he will come steadily nearer to God, until he becomes one spirit with God the Spirit; but let him not be afraid of mountains and valleys on the way, and let him not give up because he is tired and weary, *for he who seeks finds.*

Rufus M. Jones, *Spiritual Reformers in the 16th and 17th Centuries*

. . . How did I come to Him? He alone knows. I groped for Him and could not find Him. I prayed to Him unknown and He did not answer . . . Then, one day, He was there again . . . It should be an occasion, I knew. One should be able to say: 'This was the time, the place, the manner of it. This was my conversion to religion. A good man spoke to me and I became good. I saw creation in the face of a child and I believed.' It was not like that at all. He was there. I knew He was there, and that He made me and that He still loved me . . . I never understood till this moment the meaning of the words 'The gift of faith'.

Morris West, *The Devil's Advocate*

For this turning to the Light and Spirit of God within Thee, is thy *only true* turning unto God, there is no other way of finding Him but in that Place where he dwelleth in Thee. For though God be everywhere present, yet He is only present to Thee in the deepest, and most central Part of thy Soul. Thy natural *Senses* cannot possess God, or unite Thee to Him, nay thy inward Faculties of *Understanding, Will,* and *Memory*, can only reach after God, but cannot be the *Place* of his Habitation in Thee. But there is a *Root*, or *Depth* in Thee, from whence all these Faculties come forth, as Lines from a *Centre*, or as Branches from the Body of the Tree.

William Law, in Sidney Spencer, *The Spirit of Prayer*

Experiencing God. An indescribable embrace, dazzling, breathtaking. A certainty, a sureness that wipes out months and years of searching, thinking, doubts and discussion. Oh, yes, you can reason on the subject of God, but 'knowing' him (being born to him) is a different matter altogether!

I need to write down these moments of life – real life, not the superficial daily spectacle that passes for life. I'm trembling. I fear that words may turn out to be obstacles.

A few minutes, and I'm drunk with light. I don't know anything any more. I just feel very peaceful.

Michel Quoist, *With Open Heart*

Many persons, Christians and non-Christians, whose thought has been influenced by a particular philosophy and by modern scientific attitudes, profess themselves no longer able to admit the concept of God as presented by the Church. Any facet of the human personality that has been projected upon this concept, must, they feel, be stripped away. They go so far as to speak of idols. Others even maintain that we can neither say anything nor can we know anything about God. Now in so far as this demand to clarify and advance in the knowledge of God is legitimate and possible, it must be recognized that the contemplatives who have been able to translate their experiences of the divine into human language, give us the loftiest and the purest possible concept of God.

René Voillaume, *The Need for Contemplation*

**See also** Divinity, Experience, God, Holy Spirit, Jesus Christ

## 31

# FREEDOM

*Freedom – personal liberty, non-slavery; independence; liberty of action, right to do; power of self-determination, independence of fate or necessity, freedom of speech and religion, from fear and want*

It was two o'clock on a Monday afternoon. I began my weekly visiting on the wards of the Bradford Royal Infirmary. The man in the first bed was rather anxious about a pending operation. We chatted briefly about his condition, the doctors and nurses on the ward, and the likely outcome of the operation. I tried to give him some reassurance and moved on to the next patient. Here was a man of a very different disposition – blunt and direct – a typical Yorkshireman. 'They are not very intelligent in here, padre,' he started off apologetically, 'take, for instance, the man you have just been talking to. He came in yesterday, and tried to make conversation with me. 'I've worked for thirty-five years for such-and-such a firm,' he said. 'Really,' I replied, 'you might just as well have been a cabbage.' He hasn't spoken to me since. He was proud of the fact that he had worked so long for one firm. I don't think of it in that way at all. With those sort of people there is no get-up-and-go, no initiative, and certainly no freedom.' I wonder if most of us settle down too quickly – in our work, in getting married, and in having families – at the cost of our freedom.

Out of my distress I called on the Lord; the Lord answered me and set me in a broad place.

Psalm 118.5

And you will know the truth, and the truth will make you free.

John 8.32

So free we seem, so fettered fast we are!

Robert Browning, 'Andrea del Sarto'

Anything is free when it spontaneously expresses its own nature to the full in activity.

John Macmurray, *Freedom in the Modern World*

Christianity promises to make men free; it never promises to make them independent.

W.R. Inge, *The Philosophy of Plotinus*

Every man has freedom to do all that he wills, provided he infringes not the equal freedom of any other man.

Herbert Spencer, *Social Statics*

Freedom has always been an expensive thing. History is fit testimony to the fact that freedom is rarely gained without sacrifice and self-denial.

Martin Luther King, in Coretta Scott King, *The Words of Martin Luther King*

The freedom of the heart from all that is other than God is needful if it is to be preoccupied with the love of Him and the direct experience of Him.

Al-Ghazali, *Al-Ghazali, The Mystic*

The hope of the world is still in dedicated minorities. The trailblazers in human, academic, scientific, and religious freedom have always been in the minority.

Martin Luther King, in Coretta Scott King, *The Words of Martin Luther King*

God has laid upon man the duty of being free, of safeguarding freedom of spirit, no matter how difficult that may be, or how much sacrifice and suffering it may require.

Nicolas Berdyaev, *The Fate of Man in the Modern World*

All creation is for [God] a communication of his very being, that is, he can only create free beings. He can only call into existence beings that he calls upon to make themselves.

Louis Lavelle, in Paul Foulquié, *Existentialism*

When freedom is not an inner idea which imparts strength to our activities and breadth to our creations, when it is merely a thing of external circumstance, it is like an open space to one who is blindfolded.

Rabindranath Tagore, *Creative Unity*

If we would have a living thing, we must give that thing some degree of liberty – even though liberty brings with it risk. If we would debar all liberty and all risk, then we can have only the mummy and the dead husk of the thing.

Edward Carpenter, *Love's Coming-of-Age*

Men were invited to hear; but none was compelled to listen or to respond. For that is the law of the New Birth. Initiation is free from constraint, because freedom is of the essence of the Spirit-begotten life and the faith which accompanies it.

L.S. Thornton CR, *The Common Life in the Body of Christ*

The coming of the Son of God and the Messiah in His power and glory as the King of the world and as a conqueror would have been the end of the freedom of the human spirit and the realization of the Kingdom of God by means of necessity and compulsion.

Nicolas Berdyaev, *Freedom and the Spirit*

The price of freedom for all musicians, both composers and interpreters, is tremendous control, discipline and patience; but perhaps not only for musicians. Do we not all find freedom to improvise, in all art, in all life, along the guiding lines of discipline?

Yehudi Menuhin, *Theme and Variations*

You shall be free indeed when your days are not without a care and your nights without a want and a grief.

But rather when these things girdle your life and yet you rise above them named and unbound.

Kahlil Gibran, *The Prophet*

Yes! To this thought I hold with firm persistence;
The final word of all that's wise and true:
He only earns his freedom and existence,
Who daily conquers them anew.

Johann Wolfgang von Goethe, *Faust*

Be sure that if you offer your freedom to God – whether it is a question of time or affection or place or anything else – He will take it, He will take it, and you will no longer be free *in the same way*. But He will give you a far greater liberty instead. You will be free with the liberty of the children of God.

Hubert van Zeller, *Praying while You Work*

Freedom in Christ is not freedom to do what I like, but freedom to be what I am meant to be. It is freedom from all the chains which hold me back from being my true self. It is freedom from all imposed limitations and external pressures. It is to share in Christ's freedom to do God's will, and then to help others find a similar freedom.

George Appleton, *Journey for a Soul*

It may now be very easily conceived what is human freedom, which I define to be this: it is, namely, a firm reality which our understanding acquires through direct union with God, so that it can bring forth ideas in itself, and effects outside itself, in complete harmony with its nature; without, however, its effects being subjected to any external causes, so as to be capable of being changed or transformed by them.

Benedict Spinoza, *Short Treatise on God, Man, and His Well-Being*

**See also** Eternal Life, Grace, Joy, Power, Presence

## 32

# FRIENDSHIP

*Friendship – the state of being a friend; association of persons as friends; a friendly intimacy, conformity, affinity, correspondence, aptness to unite*

Friendship is very important in all stages of life but particularly so with young people. At the beginning of an academic year with a fresh intake there is always a frenetic rush to make new friends. For some undergraduates this is their first time away from home. A few suffer acutely from homesickness and it takes them time to settle down in a new environment. Most experience bouts of loneliness during their three or four years at university. The learning process involves hours and hours of reading on one's own, and this inevitably cuts people off from one another. Stress and strain inevitably take their toll. Friendship is thus extremely important in this situation. In this arena I have found some words of Ralph Waldo Emerson helpful: 'The only way to have a friend is to be one.'

Faithful friends are a sturdy shelter: whoever finds one has found a treasure.
 Ecclesiasticus 6.14

I do not call you servants any longer, because the servant does not know what the master is doing; but I have called you friends, because I have made known to you everything that I have heard from my Father.
 John 15.15

I am wealthy in my friends.
 William Shakespeare, *Timon of Athens*

Be a friend to thy self, and others will be so too.
 Thomas Fuller, *Gnomologia*

A friend may well be reckoned the masterpiece of nature.
Ralph Waldo Emerson, *Essays*

To be a strong hand in the dark to another in the time of need.
Hugh Black, *Friendship*

The essence of friendship is entireness, a total magnanimity and trust.
Ralph Waldo Emerson, *Essays*

Friendship . . . is an union of spirits, a marriage of hearts, and the bond thereof virtue.
William Penn, *Reflections and Maxims, Relating to, the Conduct of Human Life*

Friendship requires great communication between friends. Otherwise, it can neither be born nor exist.
St Francis de Sales, *Introduction to the Devout Life*

To experience God's presence in earthly friendship and to be friendliness oneself – that is the dialectic which rules the good man's life.
Ladislaus Boros, *Hidden God*

Nor do I question for a moment that Affection is responsible for nine-tenths of whatever solid and durable happiness there is in our natural lives.
C.S. Lewis, *The Four Loves*

A true friend unbosoms freely, advises justly, assists readily, adventures boldly, takes all patiently, defends courageously, and continues a friend unchangeably.
William Penn, *Reflections and Maxims, Relating to, the Conduct of Human Life*

Fortunate people manage to gather two or three friends on their journey through life. Others speak loosely of having hosts of friends, but what they mean is that they have a lot of pleasant acquaintances.
Robert Standish, *The Big One Got Away*

That friendship may be at once fond and lasting, there must not only be equal virtue on each part, but virtue of the same kind; not only the same end must be proposed, but the same means must be approved by both.
Samuel Johnson, *The Rambler*

Like everyone else I feel the need of relations and friendship, of affection, of friendly intercourse, and I am not made of stone or iron, so I cannot miss these things without feeling, as does any other intelligent and honest man, a void and deep need. I tell you this to let you know how much good your visit has done me.

Vincent van Gogh, *Dear Theo: An Autobiography of Vincent van Gogh*

To be honest, to be kind – to earn a little, and to spend a little less, to make upon the whole a family happier for his presence, to renounce when that shall be necessary and not be embittered, to keep a few friends, but these without capitulation – above all, on the same grim condition, to keep friends with himself – here is a task for all that a man has of fortitude and delicacy.

Robert Louis Stevenson, *Across the Plains*

We pine for a friend to whom we can unbosom our thoughts and emotions and we are disappointed. We think only of ourselves in our discontent. Ought we not to think a little of others and allow some small consideration to the possibility of doing good? The friendship which proceeds from unselfishness will be firmer and more intimate than that which is, after all, mere selfishness refined.

Mark Rutherford, *Last Pages from a Journal*

I dream'd in a dream I saw a city invincible to the attacks
of the whole of the rest of the earth,
I dream'd that was the new city of Friends,
Nothing was greater there than the quality of robust love, it led the rest,
It was seen every hour in the actions of the men of that city,
And in all their looks and words.

Walt Whitman, 'I Dream'd in a Dream'

The end of friendship is a commerce the most strict and homely that can be joined; more strict than any of which we have experience. It is for aid and comfort through all the relations and passages of life and death. It is fit for serene days, and graceful gifts, and country rambles, but also for rough road, and hard fare, shipwreck, poverty and persecution. It keeps company with the sallies of the wit and the trances of religion. We are to dignify to each other the daily needs and offices of man's life, and embellish it by courage, wisdom and unity.

Ralph Waldo Emerson, *Essay on Friendship*

The truest kind of friendship is what we call spiritual friendship. We should desire it for its own intrinsic worth and for the way it reaches into the human heart, rather than for any external reason or because it might bring any worldly advantage.

The spiritual friendship that exists between people of integrity springs out of their common attitude to life, their shared moral outlook and the kind of activities they engage in – in other words, it consists of mutual agreement in matters human and divine, combined with goodwill and practical loving concern.

Aelred of Rievaulx, *De spiritu amicitia*

**See also** Character, Kindness, Relationships, Trust, Understanding

# 33

# FULFILMENT

## *Fulfilment – develop fully one's gifts and character*

This may seem far-fetched but a key to an understanding of fulfilment lies in some words of Etty Hillesum: 'I thank You for the sense of fulfilment I sometimes have; that fulfilment is after all nothing but being filled with You.' This fits in with the vision behind this book. As a consequence of the divine inbreathing in the Genesis story of the creation of humans, and the life of Christ, we are able to find something of this divine life in the depths of our being – Father, Son, Holy Spirit – and the gifts and fruits of the Holy Spirit. Seen from this perspective the parables of the pearl of great price, the treasure buried in a field, and faith as a grain of mustard seed begin to make sense. How then do we develop fully our gifts and character and feel a sense of fulfilment? I have found the practice of reflection helpful. In reflection we draw to the surface something of that rich resource of divine life from the depths of our being. The outcome is an experience of fulfilment.

He died at a good old age, full of days, riches, and honour.

1 Chronicles 29.28

For this reason I bow my knees before the Father, from whom every family in heaven and on earth takes its name. I pray that, according to the riches of his glory, he may grant that you may be strengthened in your inner being with power through his Spirit, and that Christ may dwell in your hearts through faith, as you are being rooted and grounded in love. I pray that you may have the power to comprehend, with all the saints, what is the breadth and length and height and depth, and to know the love of Christ that surpasses knowledge, so that you may be filled with all the fullness of God.

Ephesians 3.14–19

None save God can fill the perfect whole.
P.J. Bailey, *Festus*

Happiness lies in the fulfilment of the spirit through the body.
Cyril Connolly, *The Unquiet Grave*

Thou crossest desert lands of barren years to reach the moment of fulfilment.
Rabindranath Tagore, *Stray Birds*

We must make the choices that enable us to fulfil the deepest capacities of our real selves.
Thomas Merton, *No Man Is an Island*

It is by losing himself in the objective, in inquiry, creation and craft, that a man becomes something.
Paul Goodman, *The Community of Scholars*

The moment one is on the side of life 'peace and security' drop out of consciousness. The only peace, the only security, is in fulfilment.
Henry Miller, *The Wisdom of the Heart*

When we rejoice in our fullness, then we can part with our fruits with joy.
Rabindranath Tagore, *Stray Birds*

The truth is that all of us attain the greatest success and happiness possible in this life whenever we use our native capacities to their fullest extent.
Smiley Blanton, *Love or Perish*

Nothing is unthinkable, nothing impossible to the balanced person, provided it arises out of the needs of life and is dedicated to life's furthest developments.
Lewis Mumford, *The Conduct of Life*

To me there is something completely and satisfyingly restful in that stretch of sea and sand, sea and sand and sky – complete peace, complete fulfillment.
Anne Morrow Lindbergh, *Bring Me a Unicorn*

God is good, and He wishes a fulfilment for beings in the universe that they may also enjoy bliss and become Sons – that they may enter into the psychology of the Being who created the World.
A.R. Orage, *On Love*

I think people ought to fulfil sacredly their desires. And this means fulfilling the deepest desire, which is a desire to live unhampered by things which are extraneous, a desire for pure relationships and living truth.

D.H. Lawrence, *Letter to Catherine Caswell*

In order to reach the deepest levels of relationship to God one has to put imagination to work and to start upon the daring venture of seeking a God who is loving beyond any experience we have and fulfilling in a way that few of us have ever dreamed of.

Morton T. Kelsey, *The Other Side of Silence*

To be capable of giving and receiving mature love is as sound a criterion as we have for the fulfilled personality. But by that very token it is a goal gained only in proportion to how much one has fulfilled the prior condition of becoming a person in one's own right.

Rollo May, *Man's Search for Himself*

The greatness of the work of the fulfiller, as compared with the work of the destroyer, is indicated by the faculties and qualities which it requires. Destruction calls for nothing but hatred and vigour. Fulfilment calls for sympathy, intelligence, patience and hope.

Phillips Brooks, *Twenty Sermons*

As long as anyone believes that his ideal and purpose is outside him, that it is above the clouds, in the past or in the future, he will go outside himself and seek fulfillment where it can not be found. He will look for solutions and answers at every point except the one where they can be found – in himself.

Erich Fromm, *Man for Himself*

We and God have business with each other; and in opening ourselves to his influence our deepest destiny is fulfilled. The universe, at those parts of which our personal being constitutes, takes a turn genuinely for the worse or for better in proportion as each one of us fulfils or evades God's demands.

William James, *The Varieties of Religious Experience*

The social, friendly honest man,
Whate'er he be,
'Tis he, fulfils great Nature's plan,
And none but *he*.

Robert Burns, 'Second Epistle to J. Lapraik'

Give me fulness of life like to the sea and the sun, to the earth and the air; give me fulness of physical life, mind equal and beyond their fulness; give me a greatness and perfection of soul higher than all things; give me my inexpressible desire which swells in me like a tide – give it to me with all the force of the sea.

My heart has been lifted the higher towards perfection of soul . . . Fulness of physical life ever brings to me a more eager desire of soul-life.

Richard Jefferies, *The Story of My Heart*

**See also** Blessedness, Ideals, Joy, Love, Wholeness

# 34

# GLORY

*Glory – exalted renown, honourable fame; resplendent majesty, beauty, or magnificence, imagined unearthly beauty; state of exaltation, prosperity, etc.; circle of light round head or figure of deity or saint, aureole, halo*

I have a firm conviction that the divine glory first and foremost can be found in ourselves. If we want to see this fully worked out in a life, we go to the Gospels – to the person of Jesus Christ. In the Prologue of John's Gospel we find the words: 'And the Word became flesh and lived among us, and we have seen his glory, the glory as of a father's son, full of grace and truth.' Jesus went one stage further and spelt out the implications of this verse in a crucial passage later on in John's Gospel: 'The glory that you have given me I have given them, so that they may be one as we are one, I in them and you in me, that they may become completely one.' In my early twenties I came across someone who had entered into this heritage, and whose features radiated the glory of God. This meeting with glory was to change the whole course of my life.

The heavens are telling the glory of God; and the firmament proclaims his handiwork.

Psalm 19.1

For it is the God who said, 'Let light shine out of darkness', who has shone in our hearts to give the light of the knowledge of the glory of God in the face of Christ. But we have this treasure in clay jars.

2 Corinthians 4.6

God! glory in His goodness.

Henry Ward Beecher, *Proverbs from Plymouth Pulpit*

The glory of God is a living Man (i.e. a man fully alive).

St Irenaeus, *Five Books of St Irenaeus Against Heresies*

That is what gives Him the greatest glory – the achieving of great things through the weakest and most improbable means.

Thomas Merton, *The Sign of Jonas*

When one candle is lighted . . . we light many by it, and when God hath kindled the Life of His glory in one man's Heart he often enkindles many by the flame of that.

Rufus M. Jones, *Spiritual Reformers in the 16th and 17th Centuries*

What is the freedom of the godly man? Being absolutely nothing to and wanting absolutely nothing for himself but only the glory of God in all his works.

Meister Eckhart, in Franz Pfeiffer, *Meister Eckhart*, translated by C. de B. Evans

To live and work for the glory of God cannot remain an idea about which we think once in a while. It must become an interior, unceasing doxology.

Henri J.M. Nouwen, *The Way of the Heart*

There is the supreme truth that the glory of God lies in His compassion, and that God never so fully reveals His glory as when He reveals His pity.

William Barclay, *The Gospel of John*

The glory of love is its unaccountability: it is not something rendered proportionately – such and such an excellence, so much regard for it – but is rather a divine overflow.

Mark Rutherford, *Last Pages from a Journal*

God does all for his *own* glory, by communicating good out of himself; *not* by looking for anything from his creatures; our duty is not for His sake: our duty is our perfection and happiness.

Benjamin Whichcote, *Moral and Religious Aphorisms*

Every energetic person wants something they can count as 'glory'. There are those who get it – film stars, famous athletes, military commanders, and even some few politicians, but they are a small minority, and the rest are left to day dreams.

Bertrand Russell, *Authority and the Individual*

Sound, sound the clarion, fill the fife!
To all the sensual world proclaim,
One crowded hour of glorious life
Is worth an age without a name.

Anon in Sir Walter Scott, *Old Mortality*

It is to God that all glory must be referred. This glory is the end of the Divine work . . . If God adopts us as His children; if He realizes this adoption through the grace of which the plenitude is in His Son Jesus, if He wills to make us partakers in Christ's eternal inheritance, it is for the exaltation of His glory.

D. Columba Marmion, *Christ the Life of the Soul*

The principle that governs the universe 'became flesh and dwelt among us and we beheld His glory', and the impression was as of something that shone through Him from beyond – 'glory as of an Only Begotten Son from a Father'; of One who perfectly represented something and who is perfectly united with it.

William Temple, *Christian Faith and Life*

As we become forgetful of ourselves and entirely filled with His glory, the glory of His righteousness and love, we become transformed into His image . . . from glory to glory and because we are more like Him, we shall do something that is far more truly His will than what we might have planned out for ourselves in an eager and perhaps impatient generosity.

William Temple, *Basic Convictions*

I believe God gives a glory to every period of life. I believe that the people who are wise – the people who live with Him – learn now to take the glory from each succeeding age. If you ask those people – those who have really learned the secret – at any stage of their life, 'What is the most glorious period of their life?' they will always say: 'Now! Now!'

W.E. Sangster, *Westminster Sermons*

To God be the glory. Think how Jesus lived, prayed, worked, suffered, all to the *greater* glory of God. He sought always the Father's glory. His pure ambition was the glory of God and the Kingdom of God. Pre-eminently Jesus could have said: 'to thee, O Father, be the glory for ever and ever: Amen.' 'I seek not mine own glory, but the glory of him that sent me.' All was done to the Father's greater glory.

Eric Symes Abbott, *The Compassion of God and the Passion of Christ*

A man does not direct all his actions to the glory of God by forming a conception in his mind, or stirring up a strong imagination upon any action, that that must be for the glory of God: it is not thinking of God's glory that is glorifying of Him . . .

We rather glorify God by entertaining the impressions of His glory upon us, than by communicating any kind of glory to Him. Then does a good man become the tabernacle of God, wherein the divine Shechinah does rest, and which the Divine glory fills, when the frame of his mind and life is wholly according to that idea and pattern which he receives from the mount.

John Smith the Platonist, *Select Discourses*

**See also** Grace, Light, Presence, Saints, Transformation

## 35

# GOD

*God – Supreme Being, Creator and Ruler of the universe, often the Lord God, Almighty God, God the Father, Son, Holy Ghost, Persons of the Trinity*

I think I have always had an intuitive awareness of God. As a child I was most acutely aware of this while gardening or out at play in the woods and fields. At university I went through a phase where I came to believe all we can know about God is to be found in the person of Jesus Christ. Three books, *A Year of Grace, From Darkness to Light* (both by Victor Gollancz) and *The Choice Is Always Ours* by Dorothy Berkley Phillips, revealed to me something of the breadth and length, and height and depth of God. These books directed my gaze beyond the historical Jesus, to the experiences of God enjoyed by many people down the ages. From there I was encouraged to look within – for the presence of God in my own soul. The penny dropped. The wealth I found is beyond description. To 'know' God we have to experience him in ourselves. Some form of contemplation is crucial.

God said to Moses, 'I AM WHO I AM.'

Exodus 3.14

And I heard a loud voice from the throne saying, 'See, the home of God is among mortals. He will dwell with them; they will be his peoples, and God himself will be with them.'

Revelation 21.3

God isn't a think; He's a feel.

Joyce Grenfell, *In Pleasant Places*

God is not an optional extra, He's an absolute must.

A girl of fourteen

God! Thou art love! I build my faith on that.
Robert Browning, 'Paracelsus V'

The Divine Essence itself is Love and Wisdom.
Emanuel Swedenborg, *The Divine Love and Wisdom*

The Father is our ground and origin, in which we begin our being and our life.
John of Ruysbroeck, *The Adornment of Spiritual Marriage*

[God is] . . . someone present in the quick of being . . . in existence as it exists, in the fibre, in the pulse of the world.
Dennis Potter, *The Other Side of the Dark*

Our best conceptions, our truest ideals, our highest moods – even these interpret God but imperfectly to us. We see through a glass darkly.
Henry Ward Beecher, *Proverbs from Plymouth Pulpit*

I will tell you, Scholar, I have heard a grave Divine say, that God has two dwellings; one in heaven, and the other in a meek and thankful heart.
Izaak Walton, *The Compleat Angler*

. . . there is still a way in which God can be called 'transcendent'. It is not that God is beyond all human experience. It is, rather, that the experience is inexhaustible, that further insight is always possible.
John S. Dunne, *The Reasons of the Heart*

True Religion never finds itself out of the Infinite Sphere of Divinity and wherever it finds Beauty, Harmony, Goodness, Love, Ingenuity, Wisdom, Holiness, Justice, and the like, it is ready to say: *Here is God*.
Rufus M. Jones, *Spiritual Reformers in the 16th and 17th Centuries*

I should like to speak of God not only on the borders of life but at its centre, not in weakness but in strength, not, therefore, in man's suffering and death but in his life and prosperity . . . God is the beyond in the midst of life.
Dietrich Bonhoeffer, *Letters and Papers from Prison*

. . . an inner flooding of the life with a consciousness of God, a rational apprehension of the soul's inherent relation to the Divine, and a transforming discovery of the meaning of life through the revelation in Christ, which sets all one's being athrob with love and wonder.
Rufus M. Jones, *Spiritual Reformers in the 16th and 17th Centuries*

. . . to say that God is Love is to say that God is the living, active, dynamic, ceaselessly desiring reality who will not let go until he has won the free response of his creation – and won this response, not by the employment of methods other than love, but by the indefatigable quality of his loving.

Norman Pittenger, *Christology Reconsidered*

Every man, though he realizes that he was conceived by a bodily father in his mother's womb, is conscious also that he has within him a spirit that is free, intelligent, and independent of the body. That eternal spirit proceeding from the infinite, is the origin of all and is what we call God.

Leo Tolstoy, *A Confession, the Gospel in Brief, and what I Believe*

We know that God is everywhere; but certainly we feel His presence most when His works are on the grandest scale spread before us; and it is the unclouded night-sky, where His worlds wheel their silent course, that we read clearest His infinitude, His omnipotence, His omniscience.

Charlotte Brontë, *Jane Eyre*

There is something in men which compels them instinctively to rebel against an irrational universe and which will not allow them to conceive of a Divine Being except as One who is the sum total, and much more, of everything they, in their highest moments, feel to be most beautiful and good and true.

F.C. Happold, *Mysticism*

A voice is in the wind I do not know;
A meaning on the face of the high hills,
Whose utterance I cannot comprehend.
A something is behind them: that is God.

George Macdonald, 'Without and Within'

The Word 'God' is used in most cases as by no means a term of science or exact knowledge, but a term of poetry and eloquence, a term *thrown out*, so to speak, at a not fully grasped object of the speaker's consciousness, a *literary* term, in short; and mankind mean different things by it as their consciousness differs.

Matthew Arnold, *Literature and Dogma*

We can never know God by seeking to grasp and manipulate him, but only by letting him grasp us. We know him not by taking him into our possession (which is absurd) but by letting ourselves be possessed by him, by becoming open to his infinite being which is within us and above us and around us.

John Macquarrie, *Paths in Spirituality*

As yet, no race has been discovered without some word for what is not-visible, not-finite, not-human, for something super human and divine . . . To my mind the historical proof of the existence of God, which is supplied to us by the history of the religions of the world, has never been refuted, and cannot be refuted.

F. Max Muller, *Anthropological Religion*

**See also** Divinity, Finding God, Holy Spirit, Incarnation, Jesus Christ

36

# GOODNESS

*Goodness – virtue; positive or comparative excellence; benevolence, kindness, generosity; what is good in a thing, its essence or strength*

John's Gospel gives a clue on the nature of 'good' and 'goodness'. In a certain passage Jesus described himself as 'the good shepherd'. The good shepherd was a tough character, carrying a heavy burden of responsibility. He spent endless days in the mountains looking after the village flock. Often this involved sleepless nights, keeping a vigilant eye on the sheep, protecting them from wild animals, thieves and robbers, sometimes laying down his life for the sheep. For Jesus 'good' and 'goodness' were not passive concepts, but meant activity and costly involvement, right in the thick of life. As followers we are expected to live in like manner: 'The good man out of the treasure of his heart produces good.' Perhaps this is another consequence of the divine inbreathing of the Genesis story of the creation of humanity.

God saw everything that he had made, and indeed, it was very good.
  Genesis 1.31

I am the good shepherd. The good shepherd lays down his life for the sheep.
  John 10.11

Be good yourself, and the world will be good.
  Hindu proverb

Nature meant me to be, on the whole, a good man.
  Charlotte Brontë, *Jane Eyre*

To be good is to be in harmony with one's self.

Oscar Wilde, *The Picture of Dorian Gray*

Good nature is one of the richest fruits of Christianity.

Henry Ward Beecher, *Proverbs from Plymouth Pulpit*

Goodness is a special kind of truth and beauty. It is truth and beauty in human behaviour.

H.A. Overstreet, *The Enduring Quest*

[Goodness] needeth not to enter into the soul, for it is there already, only it is unperceived.

*Theologia Germanica*

Goodness is something so simple: always to live for others, never to seek one's own advantage.

Dag Hammarskjöld, *Markings*

I am larger, better than I thought,
I did not know I held so much goodness.

Walt Whitman, 'Song of the Open Road'

Loving-kindness is the better part of goodness. It lends grace to the sterner qualities of which this consists.

W. Somerset Maugham, *The Summing Up*

Look around the Habitable World, how few
Know their own Good; or knowing it, pursue.

John Dryden, 'The Satires of Juvenal'

Good in a strong many-compounded nature is of slower growth than any other mortal thing, and must not be forced.

George Meredith, *The Ordeal of Richard Feverel*

Good is no good, but if it be spend:
God giveth good for none other end.

Edmund Spenser, 'The Shepherd's Calendar: May'

In his love he clothes us, enfolds and embraces us; that tender love completely surrounds us, never to leave us. As I saw it he is everything that is good.

Lady Julian of Norwich, *Revelation of Divine Love*

How God is a true, simple, perfect Good, and how He is a Light and a Reason and all virtues, and how what is highest and best, that is, God, ought to be most loved by us.

*Theologia Germanica*

Good, the more
Communicated, more abundant grows.

John Milton, 'Paradise Lost'

Anyone who proposes to do good must not expect people to roll stones out of his way, but must accept his lot calmly if they even roll a few more upon it.

Albert Schweitzer, *Out of My Life and Thought*

Goodness as a fruit of the Divine Spirit is raining satisfaction and happiness upon all around us, not studying our own welfare; a fountain out of which all the time flow streams of delight for others.

Henry Ward Beecher, *Proverbs from Plymouth Pulpit*

There is but one unconditional commandment, which is that we should seek incessantly, with fear and trembling, so to vote and to act as to bring about the very largest total universe of good which we can see.

William James, *The Will to Believe*

By desiring what is perfectly good, even when we don't quite know what it is and cannot do what we would, we are part of the divine power against evil – widening the skirts of light and making the struggle with darkness narrower.

George Eliot, *Middlemarch*

But my life now, my whole life, independently of anything that can happen to me, every minute of it is no longer meaningless as it was before, but has a positive meaning of goodness with which I have power to invest it.

Leo Tolstoy, *Anna Karenina*

Good men are not those who now and then do a good act, but men who join one good act to another. It is men, the whole tendency of whose lives is the production of good things, kind things, right things.

Henry Ward Beecher, *Proverbs from Plymouth Pulpit*

It should be part of our private ritual to devote a quarter of an hour every day to the concentration of the good qualities of our friends. When we are not *active*, we fall back idly upon defects, even of those whom we most love.

Mark Rutherford, *Last Pages from a Journal*

He [John Smith the Platonist] lived in a continuous enjoyment of God and perpetually drew nearer to the Centre of his soul's rest and always stayed God's time of advancement. His spirit was absorbed in the business and employment of becoming perfect in his art and profession – which was the art *of being a good man.*

Rufus M. Jones, *Spiritual Reformers in the 16th and 17th Centuries*

**See also** Holiness, Integrity, Kindness, Mystics, Saints

# 37

# GRACE

*Grace – unmerited favour of God, divine regenerating, inspiring and strengthening influence, condition (also state of grace) of being so influenced; divinely given talent*

Once a year the Gurkhas celebrate a big religious festival called Dashera. On the final night the whole battalion gathers together and there is feasting, singing, dancing, sketches and role playing, throughout the night. At ten o'clock the following morning the battalion's weapons are assembled, and a specially selected Gurkha officer (noted for his strength) beheads a bullock – usually in one stroke of a double-handed kukri. The blood of the bullock is then sprinkled over the weapons – a blessing for the coming year. I arrived at the battalion during Dashera, and was intrigued by this ceremony. I particularly enjoyed watching one of the Gurkha dancers. He was brilliant. His sense of rhythm and timing was perfect, and he made it look so easy. The only word to describe his dancing was *graceful*. I can still see him dancing in my mind's eye, forty years after the event. This is only one manifestation of *grace* and there are many others. I still value the simple definition of grace I learnt as a child – 'God's love in action.' The older I get the more I value God's grace.

The Lord make his face to shine upon you, and be gracious to you.
 Numbers 6.25

From his fullness we have all received, grace upon grace.
 John 1.16

. . . God gives us grace, but leaves it to us to become new creatures.
 Anthony Bloom, *The Essence of Prayer*

God gives His gifts where He finds the vessel empty enough to receive them.
 C.S. Lewis, *Williams and the Arthuriad*

The greater the perfection to which a soul aspires, the more dependent it is upon divine grace.

Brother Lawrence, *The Practice of the Presence of God*

Christian graces are natural faculties which have blossomed under the influence of divine love.

Henry Ward Beecher, *Proverbs from Plymouth Pulpit*

Grace was in all her steps, Heav'n in her Eye,
In every gesture dignitie and love.

John Milton, 'Paradise Lost'

. . . he discovered the central significance of the new birth through a creative work of Grace within.

Rufus M. Jones, *Spiritual Reformers in the 16th and 17th Centuries*

And when grace comes and your soul is penetrated by the spirit, you shouldn't pray or exert yourself, but remain passive.

John Osborne, *Luther*

The chief characteristic of the new people of God gathered together by Jesus is their awareness of the boundlessness of God's grace.

Joachim Jeremias, *New Testament Theology*

. . . it clearly seems that man by grace is made like unto God, and a partaker in His divinity, and that without grace he is like unto the brute beasts.

Blaise Pascal, *Pensées*

The power of grace always remains God's power but it becomes operative in man and thus fulfils, sustains, and renews human nature.

Daniel D. Williams, in James F. Childress and John Macquarrie, *A New Dictionary of Christian Ethics*

It is not only through the qualities of native strength that God can work. Quite equally and more conspicuously He can make our weakness the opportunity of His grace.

William Temple, *Readings in St John's Gospel*

Grace is not something other than God, imparted by Him; it is the very Love of God (which is Himself) approaching and seeking entry to the soul of man.

William Temple, *Nature, Man and God*

If you knew how to annihilate self-interest and cast out all affection for the created world, then I would come, and my grace would well up abundantly within you.

Thomas à Kempis, *The Imitation of Christ*

This gift is from God and not of man's deserving. But certainly no one ever receives such a great grace without tremendous labour and burning desire.

Richard of Saint-Victor, *Selected Writings on Contemplation*

Do you know that sentence from a prayer – 'Give us grace to bear both our joys and our sorrows lightly'? It is so perfectly true and brave and sensible, and is often in my mind.

A.C. Benson, *Extracts from the Letters of Dr A.C. Benson to M.E.A.*

Let nobody presume upon his own powers for such exaltation or uplifting of the heart or ascribe it to his own merits. For it is certain that this comes not from human deserving but is a divine gift.

Richard of Saint-Victor, *Selected Writings on Contemplation*

Grace strikes us when we are in great pain and restlessness. It strikes us when we walk through the dark valley of a meaningless and empty life. It strikes us when we feel that our separation is deeper than usual.

Paul Tillich, *The Shaking of the Foundations*

Grace, *charis*, in its Greek religious usage means 'divine gift' or 'favour'. Thus a 'grace' was a quality or power usually bestowed by the gods, a quality that could be exhibited by a mortal. The English word 'graceful' reflects this meaning.

Daniel D. Williams, in James F. Childress and John Macquarrie, *A New Dictionary of Christian Ethics*

O Lord, I need your grace so much if I am to start anything good, or go on with it, or bring it to completion. Without grace, I have no power to do anything – but nothing is beyond my powers, if your grace gives strength to me.

Thomas à Kempis, *The Imitation of Christ*

No one is suddenly endowed with all graces, but when God, the source of all grace, helps and teaches a soul, it can attain this state by sustained spiritual exercises and wisely ordered activity. For without His especial help and inner guidance no soul can reach a state of perfection.

Walter Hilton, *The Ladder of Perfection*

If and when a horror turns up you will then be given Grace to help you. I don't think one is usually given it in advance. 'Give us our daily bread' (not an annuity for life) applies to spiritual gifts too; the little *daily* support for the *daily* trial. Life has to be taken day by day and hour by hour.

C.S. Lewis, *Letters of C.S. Lewis*

By 'grace' we do not mean some magical power of God forcibly intervening in the events of history or in the inner life of man. We mean rather a humble presence. Grace is God's presence and solidarity with his creatures in their strivings. God is not a distant figure presiding in the skies, but one who stands with his creation, to strengthen and encourage whatever is affirmative in it.

John Macquarrie, *The Humility of God*

**See also** Contemplation, Contentment, Divinity, Freedom, Serenity

# 38

# GREATNESS

*Greatness – of remarkable ability, genius, intellectual or practical qualities, loftiness or integrity of character*

At school we undertook a study of Napoleon. Recently I came across a record of Napoleon's 'Conversation with General Bertrand at St Helena'. To my delight I discovered Napoleon himself had made some interesting remarks on greatness. He is recorded as having said several great men: 'Alexander, Caesar, Charlemagne and myself founded empires. But on what did we rest the creations of our genius? Upon force. Jesus Christ alone founded his empire upon love; and at this hour, millions of men would die for him.' He added: 'everything in Christ astonishes me. His spirit overawes me, and his will confounds me . . . the nearer I approach, the more carefully I examine, everything is above me; everything remains grand, – of a grandeur which overpowers'. In the life of Jesus we find all the qualities mentioned in the dictionary definition of greatness – remarkable ability, genius, intellectual and practical qualities, and a loftiness or integrity of character. His greatness continues to inspire those of us who worship him.

Look, the Lord our God has shown us his glory and greatness.
Deuteronomy 5.24

I pray that the God of our Lord Jesus Christ, the Father of glory, may give you a spirit of wisdom and revelation as you come to know him, so that, with the eyes of your heart enlightened, you may know what is the hope to which he has called you, what are the riches of his glorious inheritance among the saints, and what is the immeasurable greatness of his power for us who believe, according to the working of his great power.
Ephesians 1.17–19

Great Hopes make great Men.
Thomas Fuller, *Gnomologia*

Great souls care only for what is great.
Henri Frédéric Amiel, *Amiel's Journal*

It is a rough road that leads to the heights of greatness.
Seneca, *Epistulae Morales*

Great men are the guide-posts and landmarks in the state.
Edmund Burke, *Speeches and Letters on American Affairs*

Nothing great or new can be done without enthusiasm.
Dr Harvey Cushing, in *Dialogues of Alfred North Whitehead*

All great gifts are one-sided and pretty well exclude the others.
Theodor Haecker, *Journal in the Night*

There is never any easy way to greatness; greatness is always the product of toil.
William Barclay, *The Gospel of Matthew*

[Jesus] was clear that He had come 'not to make life easy, but to make men great'.
William Barclay, *The Gospel of Matthew*

No great man lives in vain. The History of the world is but the Biography of great men.
Thomas Carlyle, *Sartor Resartus*

Some are born great, some achieve greatness,
And some have greatness thrust upon 'em.
William Shakespeare, *Twelfth Night*

There is a great man who makes every man feel small. But the real great man is the man who makes every man feel great.
G.K. Chesterton, *Charles Dickens*

Very rarely something may emerge complete and perfect in a flash, but far oftener greatness is the result of long labour and constant attention to detail.
William Barclay, *The Gospel of Matthew*

Great truths are portions of the soul of man;
Great souls are portions of Eternity.

J.R. Lowell, 'Sonnet No. 6'

Man's Unhappiness, as I construe, comes of his Greatness; it is because there is an Infinite in him, which with all his cunning he cannot quite bury under the Finite.

Thomas Carlyle, *Sartor Resartus*

Greatness after all, in spite of its name, appears to be not so much a certain size as a certain quality in human lives. It may be present in lives whose range is very small.

Phillips Brooks, *Sermons*

And I smiled to think God's greatness flowed around our incompleteness, –
Round our restlessness, His rest.

E.B. Browning, 'Rhyme of the Duchess May'

Greatness is a spiritual condition worthy to excite love, interest, and admiration and the outward proof of possessing greatness is that we excite love, interest, and admiration.

Matthew Arnold, *Sweetness and Light*

If a man is great in the spiritual elements, he is great everywhere else; but if he is small there, he is small everywhere else. Not animalhood, but manhood, must be measured.

Henry Ward Beecher, *Proverbs from Plymouth Pulpit*

Great men are the true men, the men in whom Nature has succeeded. They are not extraordinary – they are in the true order. It is the other species of men who are not what they ought to be.

Henri Frédéric Amiel, *Amiel's Journal*

All things that we see standing accomplished in the world are properly the outer material result, the practical realization and embodiment, of Thoughts that dwelt in the Great Men sent into the world.

Thomas Carlyle, *Sartor Resartus*

The heights by great men reached and kept
Were not attained by sudden flight,
But they, while their companions slept,
Were toiling upward in the night.
Henry Wadsworth Longfellow, 'The Ladder of St Augustine'

**See also** Courage, Inspiration, Integrity, Jesus Christ, Saints

# 39

# GRIEF

*Grief – deep or violent sorrow caused by loss or trouble; keen or bitter regret or remorse*

As a college chaplain I have come across a special form of grief, caused by the untimely death of young people. This leaves me feeling deeply upset and sorrowful. Sometimes I feel guilty and regret not having cared enough for that person when alive. Often I experience a sense of injustice, and feel angry the young person in question never had a chance to find fulfilment in life. I also experience feelings of inadequacy in dealing with grief-stricken parents. Keeping busy and occupied helps us cope with grief, provided we don't overdo it. Talking about feelings with relatives and friends acts as a valuable safety-valve. A good aid is a Cruse publication entitled *All in the End Is Harvest*, edited by Agnes Whitaker. This book contains experiences of those who have known grief at first hand, and helps us in our time of sorrow. (Cruse is a national organization for the bereaved and their children.)

Be gracious to me, O Lord, for I am in distress; my eye wastes away from grief, my soul and body also.

Psalm 31.9

Blessed are those who mourn, for they will be comforted.

Matthew 5.4

Grief is itself a med'cine.

William Cowper, 'Charity'

See how Time makes all griefs decay.

Adelaide Anne Proctor, *Life in Death and Death in Life*

To weep is to make less the depth of grief.
William Shakespeare, *King Henry VI*

Time and thinking tame the strongest grief.
English proverb

Those who have known real grief seldom seem sad.
Benjamin Disraeli, *Endymion*

For grief once told brings somewhat back of peace.
William Morris, 'Prologue, The Wanderers'

In mourning let grief suffice as its highest expression.
Confucius, *The Analects of Confucius*

Someone has called bereavement 'loving in a new key'.
J. Neville Ward, *Friday Afternoon*

Every man is a solitary in his griefs. One soon finds that out.
Norman Douglas, *An Almanac*

Passionate grief does not link us with the dead but cuts us off from them.
C.S. Lewis, *A Grief Observed*

In the great complication or grief, only the saint can 'see life steadily and see it whole'.
J. Neville Ward, *Friday Afternoon*

It is dangerous to abandon oneself to the luxury of grief; it deprives one of courage, and even the wish for recovery.
Henri Frédéric Amiel, *Amiel's Journal*

You cannot prevent the birds of sorrow from flying over your head, but you can prevent them from building nests in your hair.
Chinese proverb

When we lose one we love, our bitterest tears are called forth by the memory of hours when we loved not enough.
Maurice Maeterlinck, *Wisdom and Destiny*

Grief is near-sighted, and holds its trouble close up; but love is long-sighted, and looks at them in all points of view.

Henry Ward Beecher, *Proverbs from Plymouth Pulpit*

One must go on living, in spite of anything tragic that may happen – and it's useless to break one's heart over troubles.

A.C. Benson, *Extracts from the Letters of Dr A.C. Benson to M.E.A*

To spare oneself from grief at all cost can be achieved only at the price of total detachment, which excludes the ability to experience happiness.

Erich Fromm, *Man for Himself*

I value sympathy in bereavement, because it seems – I won't say to *replace* the affection taken away, but to remind one that love is still there.

A.C. Benson, *Extracts from the Letters of Dr A.C. Benson to M.E.A*

No bond
In closer union knits two human hearts
Than fellowship in grief.

Robert Southey, *Joan of Arc and Minor Poems*

Grief is beautiful, as in winter ice-clad trees are beautiful when the sun shines upon them, but it is dangerous. Ice breaks many a branch, and so many persons are bowed down and crushed by their afflictions.

Henry Ward Beecher, *Proverbs from Plymouth Pulpit*

Do you imagine that it is in a fit of absent-mindedness that God has afflicted you? We have so much to learn, and grief must be our master. It is only through suffering that we can hope to come to self-knowledge.

Mary Craig, *Blessings*

But grief should be the instructor of the wise;
Sorrow is knowledge: they who know the most
Must mourn the deepest.

Lord Byron, *Manfred*

The thought of death leaves me perfectly calm for I am fully convinced that our spirit is absolutely indestructible: it is something that works on from eternity to eternity, it is like the sun which only seems to sink judged by our earthly eyes and in reality never sinks at all but shines without ceasing.

Johann Wolfgang von Goethe, *To Eckermann*

People often say, 'My mother was such a good woman: why should she have suffered?' or 'My boy was such a fine boy: why should he have died?' It is a very natural thing to say, but when we find ourselves saying it we should look at Jesus crowned with thorns, holiest of all, loveliest of all, and yet suffering more than all. His whole life, as He lived it amongst the people of His time, was a beauty and a glory, a flame of love passing by, and yet He was crucified.

Father Andrew SDC, *A Gift of Light*

**See also** Compassion, Cross, Death, Depression, Suffering

## 40

# GROWING

*Growth – increasing in size, height, quality, degree, power etc., advancing to maturity, reaching full size*

When I was being prepared for confirmation at the age of sixteen, the school chaplain told us our main aim in life was 'to glorify God and enjoy him for ever'. This did not mean much to me at the time. God was somehow put over as being 'out there' miles away beyond the clouds. 'Glorifying God' suggested an attitude of worship, with hands upraised towards the heavens. I was somehow meant to enjoy this for ever, but I was unable to enjoy it at all.

Years later I was trying to work out what our main aim in life is, in a practical and realistic way. I remember looking at a flower, observing it carefully, and suddenly realizing that if it unfolded, blossomed, bloomed, flourished and then died, nobody would be particularly upset because it had achieved in what it set out to do. It had actually succeeded in growing to its highest level of development and expression. I wondered if there was a lesson here for human life. Could it be that our main aim in life is to grow a soul (a character or a personality) which is us at our highest level of development and expression – so that we become most truly and fully ourselves? But do not most of us get stunted in our growing and never reach our wholeness?

Happy are those whose strength is in you . . . They go from strength to strength.

Psalm 84.5, 7

The kingdom of heaven is like a mustard seed that someone took and sowed in his field; it is the smallest of all the seeds, but when it has grown it is the greatest of shrubs and becomes a tree.

Matthew 13.31–32

Big oaks from little acorns grow.

Anon

Why stay we on the earth unless to grow?

Robert Browning, 'Cleon'

If only I may grow: firmer, simpler – quieter, warmer.

Dag Hammarskjöld, *Markings*

No life is spoiled but one whose growth is arrested.

Oscar Wilde, *The Picture of Dorian Gray*

Men never grow up into manhood as an acorn grows into an oak-tree. Men come to it by re-birth in every faculty, again, and again, and again.

Henry Ward Beecher, *Proverbs from Plymouth Pulpit*

All growth that is not towards God
Is growing to decay.

George Macdonald, 'Within and Without'

Only love enables humanity to grow, because love engenders life and it is the only form of energy that lasts forever.

Michel Quoist, *With Open Heart*

There is in the universe a provision by which men are helped by the Divine Spirit. God inspires us to the Christian life, and helps to the development of its graces.

Henry Ward Beecher, *Proverbs from Plymouth Pulpit*

There is little hope for us until we become tough-minded enough to break loose from the shackles of prejudice, half-truths, and downright ignorance.

Martin Luther King, in Coretta Scott King, *The Words of Martin Luther King*

To regret one's own experience is to arrest one's own development. To deny one's own experience is to put a lie into the lips of one's own life. It is no less than a denial of the soul.

Oscar Wilde, *De Profundis*

I never allow principles to carry me far enough. I do not think that in this I am peculiar. I notice that in the gardens of most men are nothing but arrested buds. How rare it is to see the fully developed flower!

Mark Rutherford, *Last Pages from a Journal*

If your roots are firmly planted, be sure you know what you're doing before pulling them up and moving on. A plant always suffers when transplanted; it needs time to grow more roots and time to develop before it can bear any fruit.

Michel Quoist, *With Open Heart*

A child-like man is not a man whose development has been arrested; on the contrary, he is a man who has given himself a chance of continuing to develop long after most adults have muffled themselves in the cocoon of middle-aged habit and convention.

Aldous Huxley, *Music at Night*

Omnipotence as a divine attribute comes to meaning in organic growth. The tree does not develop first at this point, and then at the other. *All over* it proceeds to perfection. So should the growth of character be, and so it is when it is divinely prompted.

Mark Rutherford, *Last Pages from a Journal*

. . . we need some means by which in time the Eternal grows real, the invisible shines through the seen, God becomes a speaking Presence, conscience is quickened, resources are deepened and hope is renewed, until one hears the trumpets of the soul again and is adequate for life!

Harry Emerson Fosdick, *Successful Christian Living*

To grow is to emerge gradually from a land where our vision is limited, where we are seeking and governed by egotistical pleasure, by our sympathies and antipathies, to a land of unlimited horizons and universal love, where we will be open to every person and desire their happiness.

Jean Vanier, *Community and Growth*

I would finally just like to advise you to grow through your development quietly and seriously; you can interrupt it in no more violent manner than by looking outwards, and expecting answer from outside to questions which perhaps only your innermost feeling in your most silent hour can answer.

Rainer Maria Rilke, *Letters to a Young Poet*

The hope is not in our own efforts to love. It is not in psychoanalysis which tries to throw light on the knots and blocks of our life, nor in a more equitable reorganization of the political and economic structures which have their effects on our personal lives. All this is perhaps necessary. But true growth comes from God, when we cry to him from the depths of the abyss to let his Spirit penetrate us. Growth in love is a growth in the Spirit. The stages through which we must pass in order to grow in love are the stages through which we must pass to become more totally united to God.

Jean Vanier, *Community and Growth*

**See also** Contemplation, Holy Spirit, Ideals, Meditation, Transformation

# 41

# GUIDANCE

*Guidance – guiding, being guided, advice on problems*

I was greatly helped on guidance by Edward Wilson, the doctor on Scott's expedition to the Antarctic. In George Seaver's book, *Edward Wilson of the Antarctic*, the biographer describes how Wilson kept a journal. His practice was to go through the Gospels over a period of years. Often the meaning was obvious, but when this was not so, he would work out his own interpretations and record these in his 'spiritual diary'. Over the years he was conscious of being guided. This practice appealed to me so I started keeping a journal. Following Edward Wilson, I began with the Gospels, and later moved on to the material in this compilation. What evolved was a listening form of prayer out of which came guidance. The rationale is that if God is within us, he might want to guide us. So I look carefully at the material and listen, with a pen in my hand, recording what is presented to me in the journal. Sometimes we need to be reminded that counsel (guidance) is one of the gifts of the Holy Spirit.

I will put my law within them, and I will write it on their hearts; and I will be their God, and they shall be my people.

Jeremiah 31.33

If you love me, you will keep my commandments. And I will ask the Father, and he will give you another Advocate, to be with you for ever. This is the Spirit of truth, whom the world cannot receive, because it neither sees him nor knows him. You know him, because he abides with you, and he will be in you.

John 14.15–17

Let me think that there is one among those stars that guides my life through the dark unknown.

Rabindranath Tagore, *Stray Birds*

We are not meant to live solely by intellectual convictions, we are meant more and more to open ourselves to the Spirit.

Basil Hume OSB, *Searching for God*

God shall be my hope,
My stay, my guide, and lantern to my feet.

William Shakespeare, *King Henry VI*

There is a spirit that works within us, and develops a power in us that teaches us how to accomplish what we will, and guides us by its inspiration to successful results.

Henry Ward Beecher, *Proverbs from Plymouth Pulpit*

Guidance does not end when calamity begins. In every situation He meets us and out of every situation He can lead us to a greener pasture and a sphere of wider use.

W.E. Sangster, *God Does Guide Us*

From thee, great God, we spring, to thee we tend,
Path, motive, guide, original and end.

Samuel Johnson, Motto for *The Rambler*

I don't think some decisions are made by the reasoning faculties, but by some instinct. One *knows* what one can do and what one cannot do, when the time arrives.

A.C. Benson, *Extracts from the Letters of Dr A.C. Benson to M.E.A.*

For a time will come when your innermost voice will speak to you, saying: 'This is *my* path; here I shall find peace. I will pursue this path, come what may.'

Grace Cooke, *Spiritual Unfoldment*

God is not a Person of caprice. If we can venture at all on belief in His detailed guidance, we can believe also that the conditions of our life are known to Him, and that He will direct us in such circumstances as we find ourselves.

W.E. Sangster, *God Does Guide Us*

And I will place within them as a guide,
My umpire *Conscience*, who if they will hear,
Light after light well us'd they shall attain,
And to the end persisting, safe arrive.

John Milton, 'Paradise Lost'

We do not need to be very old to look back on life and see that things that we thought were disasters worked out to our good; things that we thought were disappointments worked out to greater blessings. We can look back, and we can see a guiding and a directing hand in it and through it all.

William Barclay, *The Letter to the Romans*

If I am to learn to want what God wants, the way to do it is not to disown the inmost desires of my heart, but rather deliberately to spread them out before God – to face with all the honesty I can achieve the real truth about my desires, to wrestle with the sham of professing desires which are not really mine, and *then* to pray.

John Burnaby, in A.R. Vidler, *Soundings*

I give you the end of a golden string:
Only wind it into a ball,
It will lead you in at Heaven's Gate
Built in Jerusalem's wall.

William Blake, *Epigrams, Verses, and Fragments for the Note Book*

Over and over again it will happen that if a man, having thought out such a problem to the best of his ability, will then lay the whole matter in the hands of God, and genuinely desire that God's Will shall be done in his life and not his own, he will become perfectly clear what that will is. Over and over again that happens.

William Temple, *Christian Faith and Life*

It is the chief object of prayer and of a seclusion of heart from outward things, that we should be brought to attend to the guidance of this tender Guide, and be wholly in His power, and according to His will. No human plans or forms can help in this matter – they only hinder. The soul must be as the clay – formless and passive in the hand of the potter. This Hand of love forms us according to His own heart.

Gerhard Tersteegen, in Frances Bevan, *Sketches of the Great in the Land*

Jesus promised that his Spirit would guide his disciples into all truth, both truth of mind and direction of life. There can be no hesitation in the choice between what is good and what is evil, what is loving and what is selfish, what is true and what is false. Sometimes, however, the choice is between two goods or between two paths neither of which is completely good. How do we seek the Spirit's guidance?

George Appleton, *Journey for a Soul*

I have nothing to say at the finish except that if one wants a permanent rock in life and goes deep enough for it, it is difficult for historical events to shake it. There are times when we can never meet the future with sufficient elasticity of mind, especially if we are locked in the contemporary systems of thought. We can do worse than remember a principle which both gives us a firm Rock and leaves us with the maximum elasticity for our minds: the principle: Hold to Christ, and for the rest remain totally uncommitted.

Herbert Butterfield, *Christianity and History*

**See also** Holy Spirit, Listening, Obedience, Prayer, Thinking

# 42

# HAPPINESS

*Happiness – (of person or circumstance) lucky, fortunate, contented with one's lot*

When I was young, the one thing I wanted out of life was happiness. At school, happiness came by way of achievement, getting through exams, involvement in sport, and friendships. In National Service, happiness came through a sense of adventure, an involvement with the Gurkhas, and travel. There was the long sea voyage in the troopship the *Empire Fowey* via Gibraltar, the Suez Canal, Aden (now South Yemen), Ceylon (Sri Lanka), and finally Singapore. This led to new experiences in Malaya (Malaysia), Hong Kong and Sarawak. At university, happiness came primarily through being in Oxford with many opportunities for learning, sport and friendship. I began to realize how lucky and fortunate I had been so far in life. I then did a lot of thinking about the future. I was not going to pursue happiness as an end in itself, but fulfilment. There have been many ups and downs working as a priest but also precious moments of happiness and fulfilment.

Happy is everyone who fears the Lord, who walk in his ways. You shall eat the fruit of the labour of your hands; you shall be happy, and it shall go well with you.

Psalm 128.1–2

Happiness lies more in giving than in receiving.

Acts 20.35 (NEB)

There is no duty we so much underrate as the duty of being happy.

Robert Louis Stevenson, *Virginibus Puerisque*

The happy person is he who is striving to actualize his potentialities.

A.R. Orage, *On Love*

Happiness is more than anything that serene, secure, happy freedom from guilt.

Henrik Ibsen, *Rosmersholm*

Happiness is neither without us nor within us. It is in God, both without us and within us.

Blaise Pascal, *Pensées*

Happiness . . . must be something solid and permanent, without fear and without uncertainty.

Samuel Johnson, *The History of Rasselas*

In every part and corner of our life, to lose oneself is to be gainer; to forget oneself is to be happy.

Robert Louis Stevenson, *Memories and Portraits*

Look inwards, for you have a lasting fountain of happiness at home that will always bubble up if you will but dig for it.

Marcus Aurelius, *The Meditations of Marcus Aurelius*

The happy people are those who are producing something; the bored people are those who are consuming much and producing nothing.

W.R. Inge, in Sir James Marchant, *The Wit and Wisdom of Dean Inge*

We are to give our heart to God that he may make it happy, with a happiness which stretches its capacity to the full.

Gordon S. Wakefield, in *A Dictionary of Christian Spirituality*

The largest proportion of the happiness experienced among men on earth has been derived from social relationships.

Henry Ward Beecher, *Proverbs from Plymouth Pulpit*

I have come to know happy individuals, by the way, who are happy only because they are whole. Even the lowliest, provided he is whole, can be happy and in his own way perfect.

Johann Wolfgang von Goethe, *Wisdom and Experience*

. . . there is a secret belief amongst some men that God is displeased with man's happiness; and in consequence they slink about creation, ashamed and afraid to enjoy themselves.

Arthur Helps, *Companions of My Solitude*

If you will be true to the best of yourself, fearing and desiring nothing, but living up to your nature, standing boldly by the truth of your word, and satisfied therewith, then you will be a happy man.

Marcus Aurelius, *The Meditations of Marcus Aurelius*

There is certainly no greater happiness, than to be able to look back on a life usefully and virtuously employed, to trace our own progress in existence, by such tokens as excite neither shame nor sorrow.

Samuel Johnson, *The Rambler*

The monastery is a school – a school in which we learn from God how to be happy. Our happiness consists in sharing the happiness of God, the perfection of His unlimited freedom, the perfection of His love.

Thomas Merton, *Elected Silence*

A loving heart, a genuine sympathy, a pure, unadulterated taste, a life that is not scorched by dissipation or wasted by untimely hours, a good, sound body and a clear conscience, ought to make any man happy.

Henry Ward Beecher, *Proverbs from Plymouth Pulpit*

It is not our level of prosperity that makes for happiness but the kinship of heart to heart and the way we look at the world. Both attitudes lie within our power, so that a man is happy so long as he chooses to be happy and no one can stop him.

Alexander Solzhenitsyn, *Cancer Ward*

And happiness . . . what is it? I say it is neither virtue nor pleasure nor this thing nor that, but simply *growth*. We are happy when we are growing. It is this primal law of all nature and the universe, and literature and art are the cosmic movements in the conscious mind.

J.B. Yeats, *Letters to His Son, W.B. Yeats and Others*

If we were to ask the question: 'What is human life's chief concern?' one of the answers we should receive would be: 'It is happiness.' How to gain, how to keep, how to recover happiness, is in fact for most men at all times the secret motive of all they do, and of all they are willing to endure.

William James, *The Varieties of Religious Experience*

Is not making others happy the best happiness? To illuminate for an instant the depths of a deep soul . . . is to me a blessing and a precious privilege. There is a sort of religious joy in helping to renew the strength and courage of noble minds. We are surprised to find ourselves the possessors of a power of which we are not worthy, and we long to exercise it purely and seriously.

Henri Frédéric Amiel, *Amiel's Journal*

When I looked outside right into the depth of nature and God, then I was happy, really happy . . . so long as I have that happiness here, the joy in nature, health and a lot more besides, all the while one has that, one can always recapture happiness.

Riches can all be lost, but that happiness in your own heart can only be veiled, and it will still bring you happiness again, as long as you live. As long as you can look fearlessly up into the heavens, as long as you know that you are pure within and that you will still find happiness.

Anne Frank, *The Diary of Anne Frank*

**See also** Blessedness, Cheerfulness, Contentment, Fulfilment, Joy

# 43

# HEALING

*Healing – restoring (person, wound), to health, cure (person of disease); (of wound) become sound or whole; health-giving; conducive to moral or spiritual welfare*

An experience of 'healing' affected me greatly. It occurred in a hospital in Bradford, West Yorkshire, while visiting as a part-time hospital chaplain. I knocked on the door of a single room and got a rather feeble 'come in'. I found 'Douglas' in an extremely weak condition. He had just undergone major surgery, in which his bowels had been removed, and a catheter fitted. He was in pain and weary, and just wanted to die. The meeting was short. He asked me: 'Do you believe in faith healing?' I told him I did when I felt the circumstances were right. 'Could you please lay hands on me and pray?' I did so, and then took my leave as he was in such a weak condition. The next day he seemed a little stronger and we had a five minute conversation ending with the laying on of hands. I saw him regularly during the next few weeks, and he made a remarkable recovery. On my last visit he said: 'Do you realize you've got the gift of healing in your hands? Whenever you lay hands on my head and pray it is as if an electric shock goes right through my body. I'm convinced it has played a major part in healing me.' From time to time we need to be reminded that Jesus 'healed' people, and still does so, through others gifted in this way.

. . . for I am the Lord who heals you.

Exodus 15.26

Jesus went throughout Galilee, teaching in their synagogues and proclaiming the good news of the kingdom and curing every disease and every sickness among the people.

Matthew 4.23

Stress has replaced disease as the problem of the day.

GP in Birmingham, in *Faith in the City*

The crickets sing, and man's o'er-labour'd sense
Repairs itself by rest.
William Shakespeare, *Cymboline*

God is Himself a vast medicine for man. It is the heart of God that carries restoration, inspiration, aspiration, and final victory.
Henry Ward Beecher, *Proverbs from Plymouth Pulpit*

A bodily disease, which we look upon as whole and entire within itself, may, after all, be but a symptom of some ailment in the spiritual part.
Nathaniel Hawthorne, *The Scarlet Letter*

. . . it remains eternally true that we can never be right physically until we are right spiritually, that health in body and peace with God go hand in hand.
William Barclay, *The Gospel of Matthew*

Psychosomatic illnesses are illnesses of the soul transmitted to the body; a sick spirit and a healthy body inevitably come into conflict and finally break down.
Michel Quoist, *With Open Heart*

There is a healing curative nature forever outworking from the Divine Mind upon ours, although we may not co-operate voluntarily upon His will.
Henry Ward Beecher, *Proverbs from Plymouth Pulpit*

The exercise of prayer, in those who habitually exert it, must be regarded by us doctors as the most adequate and normal of all the pacifiers of the mind and calmers of the nerves.
William James, *On Faith and Morals*

It is the infinite, overflowing, swelling impulse of the Divine nature to cure souls of their diseases; to augment that which is good in them; to develop them; to equip them; to perfect them.
Henry Ward Beecher, *Proverbs from Plymouth Pulpit*

Look to your health: and if you have it, praise God, and value it next to a good conscience; for health is the second blessing that we mortals are capable of; a blessing that money cannot buy; and therefore value it, and be thankful for it.
Izaak Walton, *The Compleat Angler*

The basic idea of inner healing is simply this: that Jesus, who is the same yesterday, today, and forever, can take the memories of our past and (1) *Heal* them from the wounds that still remain and affect our present lives; and (2) *Fill* with his love all these places in us that have been empty for so long, once they have been healed and drained of the poison of past hurts and resentment.

Francis MacNutt, *Healing*

I find great occasion for alarm in very much of that modern practice of psychotherapy from which no doubt we are also going to gain great benefits. But in some of this practice there is a strong suggestion that all we have to do is somehow to become at peace with ourselves, to restore an internal harmony, to become, as they like to say, fully integrated. And I want to ask, about what centre? – with what manner of self is my whole being to be harmonized?

William Temple, *The Preacher's Theme Today*

I am not a mechanism, an assembly of various sections.
And it is not because the mechanism is working wrongly, that I am ill.
I am ill because of wounds to the soul, to the deeper emotional self
and the wounds to the soul take a long, long time, only time can help
and patience, and a certain difficult repentance
long, difficult repentance, realization of life's mistake, and freeing oneself
from the endless repetition of the mistake
which mankind at large has chosen to sanctify.

D.H. Lawrence, 'Healing'

The paralysed man (Mark 2.1–12) could not get free from a feeling of guilt and was healed by the word of forgiveness. The paralysed man at the Sheep Gate (John 5.2–9) was asked 'Do you want to be healed?' inferring that he preferred to escape from the responsibilities of daily life. The man who called himself Legion (Mark 5.1–20) had his many divisions unified in the acceptance of Christ's authority and encouragement. Many of our troubles are spiritual and will not be healed by treating the physical symptoms but only by tackling the spiritual causes – fear of failure, fear of ridicule, anxiety, frustrated irritation, escapism, inner division, feelings of guilt for which we are not humble enough or wise enough to accept God's forgiveness.

George Appleton, *Journey for a Soul*

Let us open ourselves to the healing, forgiving Spirit of Jesus. Let us open up all the pains of the past, the wounds that came from the moment of conception –

wanted or unwanted – and from the months we were carried in our mother's womb; the wounds from our early childhood when we felt rejected or stifled, unloved in our being and unrecognized in our gifts; the wounds coming from all the failures of the past; our incapacity to love and give life, the people we have hurt because of our sinfulness, pride or fears, and the barriers we have built around our vulnerability.

Let us allow the healing, forgiving Spirit of Jesus to penetrate our whole being, and lead us to wholeness. Then will rise from that very darkness a new understanding of others.

Jean Vanier, *The Broken Body*

**See also** Acceptance, Grace, Holiness, Salvation, Wholeness

# 44

# HOLINESS

*Holiness – consecrated, sacred; belonging to, commissioned by, devoted to, God; of high moral excellence*

One of my earliest childhood memories was being taken to a church by my godmother. It must have been just before Christmas, for we went off to see the baby Jesus in the crib. I remember it was dark inside the church and she hushed me to be quiet. In a spirit of awe and reverence we peeped into the manger. A light shone on the baby Jesus. There was a quiet atmosphere of holiness about the whole scene. It made a deep impression on me. Years later I remember the same feeling of holiness listening to a sermon, preached by a bishop. I can't remember a word he said now, but I can remember his face. It was radiant and energetic. There was something sacred permeating his being. I was never argued into accepting the Christian faith but I was won over by the sight of holiness.

Worship the Lord in holy splendour.

1 Chronicles 16.29

. . . and be renewed in the spirit of your minds, and clothe yourselves with the new self, created according to the likeness of God in true righteousness and holiness.

Ephesians 4.23–24

There is no true Holiness, without Humility

Thomas Fuller, *Gnomologia*

Real holiness has a fragrance about it which is its own advertisement.

Father Andrew SDC, *The Way of Victory*

There is nothing holier, in this life of ours, than the first consciousness of love, – the first fluttering of its silken wings.

Henry Wadsworth Longfellow, 'Hyperion'

That the Inward man by the Light of Grace, through possession and practice of a holy life, is to be acknowledged and live in us.

Rufus M. Jones, *Spiritual Reformers in the 16th and 17th Centuries*

A true love to God must begin with a delight in his holiness, and not with a delight in any other attribute: for no other attribute is truly lovely without this.

Jonathan Edwards, *A Treatise Concerning Religious Affections*

Let the remembrance of all the glory wherein I was created make me more serious and humble, more deep and penitent, more pure and holy before Thee.

Thomas Traherne, *Centuries*

Holiness means living within the divine perspective. It comes from attention to God – on your knees in prayer; and it comes from obedience to God – on your feet in action.

Hugh Montefiore, *Sermons from Great St Mary's*

Jesus wants us to be holy as his Father is. We can become very great saints if we only want to. Holiness in not the luxury of the few, but a simple duty for you and for me.

Mother Teresa, in Brother Angelo Devanando, *Jesus, the Word to Be Spoken*

We cannot reach our Saviour's puritie,
Yet are we bid, *Be holy e'en as He.*
In both let's do our best.

George Herbert, 'Lent'

No one can resist the argument of holiness, brought in a personified form before him, in its gentleness, in its sweetness, in its aspiration, in its love, in all its blossoms and fruits of peace and joy.

Henry Ward Beecher, *Proverbs from Plymouth Pulpit*

*Holiness* . . . in men, is their dei-formity; likeness to God in goodness, righteousness, and truth. Such real holiness sanctifies the subject by its presence: and where that is, the person is made pure, good, righteous.

Benjamin Whichcote, *Moral and Religious Aphorisms*

The way of holiness was by the gift of the Holy Spirit, and the common use of the word 'saint' waited on the outpouring of the Spirit. The outpouring of the Spirit was the Birthday of the Christian Church.

W.E. Sangster, *The Pure in Heart*

The measure of your holiness is proportionate to the goodness of your will. Consider then how good your will is, and the degree of your holiness will be clear to you. For every one is as holy, as he is good of heart.

John of Ruysbroeck, *The Seven Steps of the Ladder of Spiritual Love*

Holiness is the goal of every Christian. 'Holy' means 'set apart for God'. A holy person is not gloomy and unnatural, but 'whole' and therefore happy. That is why holiness, whenever we see it in others, is always attractive.

Hugh Montefiore, *Confirmation Notebook*

He that sees the beauty of holiness, or true moral good, sees the greatest and most important thing in the world, which is the fulness of all things, without which all the world is empty . . . Unless this is seen, nothing is seen that is worth the seeing; for there is no other true excellency or beauty.

Jonathan Edwards, *A Treatise Concerning Religious Affections*

It doesn't matter, he is holy, his heart contains the secret of a renewal for all, the power which will finally establish truth on earth, and all will be holy, and will love each other, and there will be no more rich nor poor, exalted nor humbled, but all men will be as the children of God and the real kingdom of Christ will come.

Fyodor Dostoyevsky, *The Brothers Karamazov*

All human love is a holy thing, the holiest thing in our experience. It is the chief mode of initiation into the mysteries of the divine life, the most direct point of contact with the nature of the Creator. 'He prayeth best who loveth best.' Pure affection 'abides' in a sense in which nothing else abides. It is rooted in the eternal, and cannot be destroyed by any of the changes and chances of mortal life.

W.R. Inge, *Speculum Animae*

It is not to the clever folk, nor even to the scientific folk, that the empire over souls belongs, but to those who impress us as having conquered nature by grace, as having passed through the burning bush, and as speaking, not the language of human wisdom, but that of the divine will. In religious matters it is holiness which gives authority; it is love, or the power of devotion and sacrifice, which goes to the heart, which moves and persuades.

Henri Frédéric Amiel, *Amiel's Journal*

**See also** Beauty, Blessedness, Healing, Saints, Wholeness

# 45

# HOLY SPIRIT

*Holy Spirit – third Person of the Trinity, God as spiritually active, sevenfold gift of the Spirit: counsel, wisdom, understanding, knowledge, fear (awe, reverence), might (power) and the spirit of the Lord. Also the fruits of the Spirit – love, joy, peace, patience, kindness, goodness, faithfulness, gentleness, self-control*

In my last year as an undergraduate I was trying to work out what to do in life. A friend had given me a book for a birthday present, *Margaret* by James Davidson Ross. I remember reading this book on a train journey from the West Country to London. Margaret was a teenage girl. She was smitten by cancer. The way she faced up to her ordeal, dying at such a young age, convinced me of the reality of the Holy Spirit. In her short life there was ample evidence of God spiritually alive and active. My feelings at the time were summed up by the words of Goethe in this section: 'The spirit, alive and gifted, focusing with practical intent on the most immediate concerns, is the finest thing on earth.' The way ahead opened up. I wanted to dedicate myself to the finest things on earth, to the work of the Holy Spirit. The gifts and fruits of the Holy Spirit are open to all and our spiritual heritage.

I will put my spirit within you, and you shall live.

Ezekiel 37.14

When he had said this, he breathed on them and said to them, 'Receive the Holy Spirit.'

John 20.22

The simple fact is that the world is too busy to give the Holy Spirit a chance to enter in.

William Barclay, *The Gospel of John*

Spiritual experience is the supreme reality in man's life: in it the divine is not proven, it is simply shown.

Nicolas Berdyaev, *Christian Existentialism*

The Divine Spirit works along the line of a man's own thinking power, along the channel of a man's own motive power, and wakes up in the man that which was in him.

Henry Ward Beecher, *Proverbs from Plymouth Pulpit*

He was an ideal pastor and true shepherd of his flock – loving them and being beloved by them. His ministry was fresh and vital, and made his hearers *feel* the presence and power of the Spirit of God.

Rufus M. Jones, *Spiritual Reformers in the 16th and 17th Centuries*

A spiritual life is simply a life in which all that we do comes from the centre, where we are anchored in God: a life soaked through and through by a sense of His reality and claim, and self-given to the great movement of His will.

Evelyn Underhill, in John Stobbart, *The Wisdom of Evelyn Underhill*

. . . the Church's real business is the nurture of men and women in life's final meaning, the provision – the mediation – of resources for living in the power and grace and serenity (serenity amidst toil and sacrifice) of the Holy Spirit of God.

Norman Goodall, *The Local Church*

Spirit is no less real than matter, and the spiritual values of truth, goodness, and beauty no mere creations of finite minds, but abiding characteristics of that reality in the apprehension of which all minds capable of apprehending it find their satisfaction.

C.G.J. Webb, *Religious Experience*

The true goal of the spiritual life is such a oneness with God that He is in us and we in Him, so that the inner joy and power take our outer life captive and draw us away from the world and its 'pictures' and make it a heartfelt delight to do all His commandments and to suffer anything for Him.

Rufus M. Jones, *Spiritual Reformers in the 16th and 17th Centuries*

. . . spirituality is the basis and foundation of human life . . . It must underlie everything. To put it briefly, man is a spiritual being, and the proper work of his mind is to interpret the world according to his higher nature, and to conquer the material aspects of the world so as to bring them into subjection to the spirit.

Robert Bridges, *The Spirit of Man*

Holy Spirit . . . was hardly recognized as distinct from the Word until the Word was uttered in a new fullness of expression, as Christians believe, in the historical Person, Jesus of Nazareth. That fuller objective self-manifestation of the divine called forth a new potency of responsive aspiration to which, as an experienced fact, was given the name Holy Spirit.

William Temple, *Nature, Man and God*

From the beginning, the Spirit of God has been understood as God in the midst of men, God present and active in the world, God in his closeness to us as a dynamic reality shaping the lives and histories of men. The Spirit, in this sense, is not something other than God, but God in that manner of the divine Being in which he comes closest, dwells with us, acts upon us.

John Macquarrie, *Paths in Spirituality*

The Holy Ghost is . . . the manifest Energy of God in the world. He is, moreover, the indwelling Strengthener who enables man to live righteously in God's sight; the Guide who leads us into truth; the Revealer of the truths of God; the Consoler in our distresses; the Encourager in our tribulations. Our Lord in His promise of the special coming of the Spirit stresses His personal and loving attributes.

Carroll Simcox, *Living the Creed*

My own attempt to understand the Holy Spirit has convinced me He is active in precisely those experiences that are very common – experiences of recognition, sudden insight, an influx of awareness when you wake up and become alive to something. It may be another person, or a scientific problem, and suddenly the penny drops. Every time a human being cries 'Ah! I see it now!', that's what I mean by the Holy Spirit.

John V. Taylor, in Gerald Priestland, *Priestland's Progress*

But if a man here on earth is enlightened with the Holy Ghost from the fountain of Jesus Christ, so that the spirits of nature, which signify the Father, are kindled in him, then there ariseth such a joy in his heart, and it goeth forth into all his veins, so that the whole body trembleth, and the soulish animal spirit triumpheth, as if it were in the holy Trinity, which is understood only by those who have been its guests in that place.

Jacob Boehme, *The Aurora*

No person will ever reach a stage of earthly life in which the spur of the flesh is eradicated, and so no person can be infallibly certain that he is beyond sin, but when Christ is inwardly united to the soul and His Spirit dwells in us and reigns in us and we are risen in soul, spirit, and mind with Him, then we no longer live after the flesh, or according to its thrust and push, and share His life and partake of the conquering power of His Spirit.

Rufus M. Jones, *Spiritual Reformers in the 16th and 17th Centuries*

Spirituality of life is an achievement as well as a gift. It is not a mere negation, a sentimental attitude that ignores and eludes all the just claims of the great realities of human existence, but it is intellectual and moral energy raised to the highest degree; it is an absolute persistence in well-doing; it is justice and gentleness; it is consideration and good judgment and discriminating appreciation and love.

Spirituality of life is, indeed, life raised to the highest power.

Lilian Whiting, *Lilies of Eternal Peace*

**See also** Divinity, God, Jesus Christ, Mystics, Presence

## 46

# HOPE

*Hope – expectation and desire combined (of thing, of doing, that); feeling of trust*

I remember a programme on TV. A young woman, whose baby son had disappeared some years ago while they were on holiday on a Greek island, was being interviewed. She still hoped he would be found and that they would be reunited. There was something inside her which gave her hope. An important verse of scripture is: 'May the God of hope fill you with all joy and peace in believing, so that you may abound in hope by the power of the Holy Spirit.' One of God's attributes is 'hope'. As a consequence of the divine inbreathing a seed or a spark of this 'God of hope' resides in the depths of our being. This can be catalysed and brought to life. When we reflect and contemplate on the contents of this topic the source of hope already in us can come alive so that 'by the power of the Holy Spirit we may abound in hope'. The odds were stacked against Jesus, but he was rooted and grounded in hope, and went out to transform the world. His work continues, and we are invited to play our part – in hope.

Let your steadfast love, O Lord, be upon us, even as we hope in you.
Psalm 33.22

Blessed be the God and Father of our Lord Jesus Christ! By his great mercy he has given us a new birth into a living hope through the resurrection of Jesus Christ from the dead, and into an inheritance that is imperishable, undefiled, and unfading, kept in heaven for you.
1 Peter 1.3–4

. . . entertain him with hope . . .
William Shakespeare, *The Merry Wives of Windsor*

Hope in action is charity, and beauty in action is goodness.
Miguel de Unamuno, *The Tragic Sense of Life in Men and in Peoples*

The ability to hope is the greatest gift that God could make to man.
Carlo Carretto, *Summoned by Love*

Hope is itself a species of happiness, and, perhaps, the chief happiness which this world affords.
Samuel Johnson, *Boswell's Life of Johnson*

Ah! If man would but see that hope is from within and not from without – that he himself must work out his own salvation.
H. Rider Haggard, *She*

Optimism means faith in men, in the human potentiality; hope means faith in God in His omnipotence.
Carlo Carretto, *The Desert in the City*

To hope till Hope creates
From its own wreck the thing it contemplates.
Percy Bysshe Shelley, 'Prometheus Unbound'

Hope is the best possession. None are completely wretched but those who are without hope; and few are reduced so low as that.
William Hazlitt, *Characteristics*

The virtue of hope is an orientation of the soul towards a transformation after which it will be wholly and exclusively love.
Simone Weil, *Gateway to God*

Hope is lived, and it comes alive, when we go outside of ourselves and, in joy and pain take part in the lives of others. It becomes concrete in open community with others.
Jürgen Moltmann, *The Open Church*

Hope springs eternal in the human breast:
Man never is, but always to be blest.
Alexander Pope, 'An Essay on Man'

Anything that is found to stimulate hope should be seized upon and made to serve. This applies to a book, a film, a broadcast, or a conversation with someone who can impart it.

Hubert van Zeller, *Considerations*

Christian Hope is the consecration of desire, and desire is the hardest thing of all to consecrate. That will only happen as you begin to think how lovely the life according to Christ is.

William Temple, *Christian Faith and Life*

'Hope', says St Thomas Aquinas, 'is a divinely infused quality of the soul, whereby with certain trust we expect those good things of the life eternal which are to be attained by the grace of God.'

W.R. Inge, *Personal Religion and the Life of Devotion*

He is a God who does not make empty promises for the hereafter nor trivilize the present darkness, futility and meaninglessness, but who himself in the midst of darkness, futility and meaninglessness invites us to the venture of hope.

Hans Küng, *On Being a Christian*

Oh, how good a thing it is that the great God who has placed us in this world – where amid so much that is beautiful, there still exists vast bestowal among men of grief, disappointment, and agony – has planted in our bosoms the great sheet-anchor, Hope.

Walt Whitman, *The Early Poems and the Fiction*

Hope to the last . . . Always hope; . . . Never leave off hoping; . . . Don't leave a stone unturned. It's always something to know you've done the most you could. But don't leave off hoping, or it's no use doing anything. Hope, hope, to the last!

Charles Dickens, *Nicholas Nickleby*

Hope is a completely confident expectation; that sureness and certitude with which the awakened soul aims at God and rests in God. It is the source of that living peace, that zest and alertness, that power of carrying on, which gives its special colour to the genuine Christian life.

Evelyn Underhill, in John Stobbart, *The Wisdom of Evelyn Underhill*

For if you find hope in the ground of history, you are united with the great prophets who were able to look into the depth of their times, who tried to escape it, because they could not stand the horror of their visions, and who yet had the strength to look to an even deeper level and there to discover hope.

Paul Tillich, *The Shaking of the Foundations*

Every blade of grass, each leaf, each separate floret and petal, is an inscription of hope. Consider the grasses and the oaks, the swallows, the sweet blue butterfly – they are one and all a sign and token showing before our eyes earth made into life . . . my hope becomes as broad as the horizon afar, reiterated by every leaf, sung on every bough, reflected in the gleam of every flower. There is so much for us yet to come, as much to be gathered, and enjoyed. Not for you or me, now, but for our race, who will ultimately use this magical secret for their happiness.

Richard Jefferies, *The Pageant of Summer*

**See also** Faith, Grace, Ideals, Inner Life, Kingdom of God

# 47

# HUMILITY

*Humility – the faculty of being humble, or having a lowly opinion of oneself; meekness, lowliness, humbleness; the opposite of pride or haughtiness*

William Temple once wrote: 'The source of humility . . . is the habit of realizing the presence of God.' We have a good illustration of this in the experience of John the Baptist. When Jesus started baptizing people, John's disciples questioned his authority which led John to say: 'He must increase, I must decrease.' We, too, in our day, must develop a habit of realizing the presence of God in our lives, and in humility adopt John the Baptist's words. To the outsider this looks ridiculous, but to the adherent humility is the gateway to that more abundant life Jesus came to bring.

He leads the humble in what is right, and teaches the humble his way.
Psalm 25.9

. . . unless you change and become like children, you will never enter the kingdom of heaven. Whoever becomes humble like this child is the greatest in the kingdom of heaven.
Matthew 18.3–4

True humility is contentment.
Henri Frédéric Amiel, *Amiel's Journal*

Show yourselves humble in all things.
Thomas à Kempis, *The Imitation of Christ*

Humility like darkness reveals the heavenly lights.
Henry David Thoreau, *Walden*

An humble able man is a jewel worth a kingdom.
William Penn, *Fruits of Solitude*

Humility . . . is the groundwork of Christian virtues.
Charlotte Brontë, *Jane Eyre*

The Churches must learn humility as well as teach it.
George Bernard Shaw, *The Complete Bernard Shaw Prefaces*

All paths open up before me because I walk in humility.
Johann Wolfgang von Goethe, *Wisdom and Experience*

The humble man, because he sees himself as nothing, can see other things as they are.
Iris Murdoch, *The Sovereignty of Good Over Other Concepts*

In itself, humility is nothing else but a true knowledge and awareness of oneself as one really is.
*The Cloud of Unknowing*

We must learn to detach ourselves from all that is capable of being lost, to bind ourselves absolutely only to what is absolute and eternal.
Henri Frédéric Amiel, *Amiel's Journal*

He that is humble, ever shall
Have God to be his Guide.
John Bunyan, *The Pilgrim's Progress*

There must be feelings of humility, not from nature, but from penitence, not to rest in them, but to go on to greatness.
Blaise Pascal, *Pensées*

True humility,
The highest virtue, mother of them all.
Alfred, Lord Tennyson, 'The Holy Grail'

You will find Angling to be like the virtue of humility, which has a calmness of spirit, and a world of other blessings attending upon it.
Izaak Walton, *The Compleat Angler*

The Holy Ghost flows into the soul as fast as she is poured forth in humility and so far as she has gotten the capacity. He fills all the room he can find.

Meister Eckhart, in Franz Pfeiffer, *Meister Eckhart*, translated by C. de B. Evans

The humble are not those who are most troubled by their own defects and dwell upon them. True humility is begotten by the worship of superiority, and chiefly by the worship of God.

Mark Rutherford, *Last Pages from a Journal*

Humility is a head-on quality – not a dragging, miserable, mean feeling. It is not mortified pride. It is one of the noblest and one of the most resplendent of all the experiences of the soul.

Henry Ward Beecher, *Proverbs from Plymouth Pulpit*

Fast and pray,
That so perchance the vision may be seen
By thee and those, and all the world be heal'd.

Alfred, Lord Tennyson, 'The Holy Grail'

Let us acquiesce. Let us take our bloated nothingness out of the path of the divine circuits. Let us unlearn our wisdom of the world. Let us lie low in the Lord's power, and learn that truth alone makes rich and great.

Ralph Waldo Emerson, *Spiritual Laws*

Now I find hidden somewhere away in my nature something that tells me that nothing in the whole world is meaningless, and suffering least of all. That something hidden away in my nature, like a treasure in a field, is Humility.

Oscar Wilde, *De Profundis*

I shall recommend humility to you, as highly proper to be made the constant subject of your devotions . . . earnestly desiring you to think no day safe, or likely to end well, in which you have not . . . called upon God to carry you through the day, in the exercise of a meek and lowly spirit.

William Law, *A Serious Call to a Devout and Holy Life*

If thou wouldst become a pilgrim on the path
Of love
The first condition is
That thou become as humble as dust
And ashes.

Al-Ansari, 'The Invocations of Sheikh Abdullah Ansari of Herat'

I believe the first test of a truly great man is his humility. I do not mean, by humility, doubt of his own power, or hesitation in speaking his opinions; but a right understanding of the relation between what *he* can do and say and the rest of the world's sayings and doings. All the great men not only know their business, but usually know that they know it, and are not only right in their main opinions, but usually know that they are right in them; only, they do not think much of themselves on that account.

John Ruskin, *Modern Painters*

**See also** Acceptance, Cross, Guidance, Obedience, Salvation

# 48

# IDEALS

*Ideals – one's highest conceptions; things embodying an idea; things existing only in idea; the visionary, relating to, consisting of, ideas; perfect types; actual things as standards for imitation*

My ideals are in this book and have been collected from a wide variety of sources. The foundation is made up of many verses from the Bible, culminating in the Gospels and Epistles. To these have been added ideals coming from poets, playwrights, novelists, philosophers, theologians, historians, scientists, artists, musicians, statesmen, politicians, economists, and psychologists. Albert Schweitzer advises us: 'Grow into your ideals, so that life can never rob you of them. If all of us could become what we were at fourteen, what a different place the world would be!' In the practice of reflection, meditation and contemplation we mull over the contents of this book and grow into our ideals.

Mark the blameless, and behold the upright, for there is posterity for the peaceable.

Psalm 37.37

The kingdom of heaven is like treasure hidden in a field, which someone found and hid; then in his joy he goes and sells all that he has and buys that field. Again, the kingdom of heaven is like a merchant in search of fine pearls; on finding one pearl of great value, he went and sold all that he had and bought it.

Matthew 13.44–46

An ideal is often but a flaming vision of reality.

Joseph Conrad, *Chance*

To be happy one must have an ideal and strive to live up to it.

George Moore, *Evelyn Innes*

The Christian ideal has not been tried and found wanting. It has been found difficult; and left untried.

G.K. Chesterton, *What's Wrong with the World*

The Ideal is in thyself, the Impediment too is in thyself: thy condition is but the stuff thou art to shape that same Ideal out of.

Thomas Carlyle, *Sartor Resartus*

Even a rich man is sad if he has no ideals. He may try to hide his sadness from himself and from others, but his efforts only make him sadder still.

Yevgeny Yevtushenko, *A Precocious Autobiography*

It is hard for a man to take the ideals of honour, and truth, and rectitude, and plough through life with them. It breeds conflicts with himself and with all others.

Henry Ward Beecher, *Proverbs from Plymouth Pulpit*

The highest flights of charity, devotion, trust, patience, bravery to which the wings of human nature have spread themselves have been flown for religious ideals.

William James, *The Varieties of Religious Experience*

It is the very ideal of true manhood not to be suppressed. A man should lay it down in his mind, when he begins life, 'I am, and I will be, superior to my circumstances.'

Henry Ward Beecher, *Proverbs from Plymouth Pulpit*

If one advances confidently in the direction of his dreams, and endeavours to live the life which he has imagined, he will meet with a success unexpected in common hours.

Henry David Thoreau, *Walden*

The most consummate ideal that men have ever known, or felt, or thought, is the ideal of one who is supreme and sovereign, guiding nature and in it Providence.

Henry Ward Beecher, *Proverbs from Plymouth Pulpit*

For the idealist living wholly with people occupied with the concrete, existence is not merely lonely, but fatiguing. It is as though he or she were for ever talking a foreign language.

L. Falconer, in M.G. Ostle, *The Note Books of a Woman Alone*

Christ's ideal of manhood is power in the head, and power in the heart, and art in the hand, with the humiliation of love, and carried down to the lowest and meanest, if thereby they may be helped.

Henry Ward Beecher, *Proverbs from Plymouth Pulpit*

Every ideal affirms that, in some sense, our supernatural environment is more truly active than the world of our apprehension, and is always offering itself as a world to be possessed and not to be created.

John Oman, *The Natural and the Supernatural*

The ideal, after all, is truer than the real: for the ideal is the eternal element in perishable things: it is their type, their sum, their *raison d'etre*, their formula in the book of the Creator, and therefore at once the most exact and most condensed expression of them.

Henri Frédéric Amiel, *Amiel's Journal*

'The kingdom of heaven is like a merchant seeking precious pearls.' Yes, we have promised great things but greater things are promised us. Be faithful to Christ and pray for perseverance. Remember to say to yourself, 'I have been created for greater things.' Never stoop lower than the ideal. Let nothing satisfy you but God.

Mother Teresa, in Brother Angelo Devananda, *Jesus, the Word to Be Spoken*

Religion cannot remain on the level of ideas alone. Religion must be an expression. It must be an incarnation in the real world of an ideal that is of supreme import to the individual of belief. Religion not only has to be worth living for, it has to be worth living. Faith on a theoretical level is a fossilized faith if it only remains on that level.

Harry James Cargas, *Encountering Myself*

In reverence for life my knowledge passes into existence . . . My life carries its own meaning in itself. This meaning lies in my living out the highest idea which shows itself in my will-to-live, the idea of reverence for life. With that as a starting-point I give value to my own life and to all the will-to-live which surrounds me, I persevere in activity, and I produce values.

Albert Schweitzer, *The Philosophy of Civilization*

The ideals which have lighted my way, and time after time have given me new courage to face life cheerfully, have been Kindness, Beauty, and Truth. Without the sense of kinship with men of like mind, without the occupation with the objective world, the eternally unattainable in the field of art and scientific endeavour, life would have seemed to me empty. The trite objects of human efforts – possessions, outward success, luxury – have always seemed to me contemptible.

Albert Einstein, *Ideas and Opinions*

There is something more in man than is apparent in his ordinary consciousness, something which frames ideals and thoughts, a finer spiritual presence, which makes him dissatisfied with mere earthly pursuits. The one doctrine that has the longest intellectual ancestry is the belief that the ordinary condition of man is not his ultimate being, that he has in him a deeper self, call it breath or ghost, soul or spirit. In each being dwells a light which no power can extinguish, an immortal spirit, benign and tolerant, the silent witness in his heart. The greatest thinkers of the world unite in asking us to know the self.

Sir Sarvepalli Radhakrishnan, *Eastern Religions and Western Thought*

**See also** Beauty, Character, Goodness, Integrity, Truth

# 49

# IMAGE OF GOD

*Image of God – man's original nature, made in the image and likeness of God, fully worked out in the life of Christ*

In the second chapter of the book of Genesis we read that God formed the first human of dust from the ground, and breathed into his nostrils the breath of life; and Adam became a living being. Initially the man of dust was earthy and creaturely, but once God breathed into his nostrils the breath of life, this man had also something akin to a divine potential. If we wish to see this fully worked out in a life we go to the Gospels, to the person of Jesus Christ. As he went through life he discovered something of the Father in himself, as well as the full range of the gifts and fruits of the Holy Spirit. At the same time he accepted the earthy and creaturely side of his nature, bringing about an inner integration, and thereby becoming a whole person. Paul acknowledged Jesus as the image of the invisible God and recognized the implications for us: 'Just as we have born the image of the man of dust, so shall we also bear the image of the man of heaven.'

– then the Lord God formed man from the dust of the ground, and breathed into his nostrils the breath of life; and the man became a living being.

Genesis 2.7

And all of us, with unveiled faces, seeing the glory of the Lord as though reflected in a mirror, are being transformed into the same image from one degree of glory to another; for this comes from the Lord, the Spirit.

2 Corinthians 3.18

When God made man the innermost heart of the Godhead was put into man.

Meister Eckhart, in Franz Pfeiffer, *Meister Eckhart*, translated by C. de B. Evans

You never know yourself till you know more than your body. The Image of God is not seated in the features of your face, but in the lineaments of your Soul.

Thomas Traherne, *Centuries*

The God-image in man was not destroyed by the Fall but was only damaged and corrupted ('deformed'), and can be restored through God's grace.

C.G. Jung, *Aion*

If we take Adam as a type of the natural man, and ask in whose image he was created, we are told that it was in God's image. Man alone has mind, intelligence, reason, and a nature destined to be ennobled through the Incarnation.

Father Andrew SDC, *Meditations for Every Day*

. . . 'moulded into the image of his Son' (Romans 8.29). Let us gaze upon this adorable Image, remain always with His radiance, that He may impress Himself upon us. Then let us do everything in the same disposition as our Holy Master.

Sister Elizabeth of the Trinity, *Spiritual Writings*

The greatest of painters only once painted a mysteriously divine child; he couldn't have told how he did it, and we can't tell why we feel it to be divine. I think there are stores laid up in our human nature that our understandings can make no complete inventory of.

George Eliot, *Mill on the Floss*

. . . they all proclaimed that deep in the central nature of man – an inalienable part of Reason – there was a Light, a Word, an Image of God, something permanent, reliable, universal, and unsundered from God himself. They all knew that man is vastly more than 'mere man'.

Rufus M. Jones, *Spiritual Reformers in the 16th and 17th Centuries*

. . . 'Honour all men'. Every man should be honoured as God's image, in the sense in which Novalis says – that we touch Heaven when we lay our hand on a human body! . . . The old Homeric Greeks I think, felt that, and acted up to it, more than any nation. The Patriarchs too seem to have had the same feeling . . .

Charles Kingsley, *Daily Thoughts*

The Difference then of a good and a bad Man does not lie in this, that the one wills that which is good, and the other does not, but solely in this, that the one concurs with the living inspiring Spirit of God within him, and the other resists it, and is and can be *only chargeable* with Evil, because he resists it.

William Law, *The Spirit of Love*

'Let us make man in OUR image.' Such is man's height and depth and breadth and mystery. He has not come from one principle or distinction of the Divine Nature, but out of all principles. Man is the image of the whole Deity. There is in him a sanctuary, for the Father, and for the Son, and for the Holy Ghost. 'We will make our abode with him.'

John Pulsford, *Quiet Hours*

I have often said before that there is an agent in the soul, untouched by time and flesh, which proceeds out of the Spirit, and which remains forever in the Spirit and is completely spiritual. In this agent God is perpetually verdant and flowering with all the joy and glory that is in him. Here is joy so hearty, such inconceivably great joy that no one can ever fully tell it . . . God glows and burns without ceasing, in all his fullness, sweetness, and rapture.

Meister Eckhart, *Meister Eckhart*, translated by Raymond B. Blakney

The image of God in man is the conformity of the human soul, understanding, spirit, mind, will, and all internal and external bodily and spiritual powers with God and the Holy Trinity and with all divine qualities, virtues, wills, and characteristics. This is indicated in the decision of the Holy Trinity: Let us make man in our image after our likeness; and let him have dominion over the fish of the sea, and over the birds of the air, and over the cattle, and over all the earth (Gen. 1.26).

Johann Arndt, *True Christianity*

How do we detect this spark within us? I imagine that it is different in each person, which would not be surprising since every person is unique. I think it has something to do with a longing deep down within us. We long to know and possess the good, or the good that we see in a great number of persons and objects which fall within our experience. In the end we discover that the pursuit of truth and goodness leads us to long for truth and goodness in their absolute form. This absolute truth and this absolute goodness we call God.

Basil Hume OSB, *To Be a Pilgrim*

. . . the secret impulse out of which kindness acts is an instinct which is the noblest part of ourselves, the most undoubted remnant of the image of God, which was given us at the first. We must therefore never think of kindness as being a common growth of our nature, common in the sense of being of little value. It is the nobility of man. In all its modifications it reflects a heavenly type. It runs up into one, and it is human because it springs from the soul of man just at the point of where the divine image was graven deepest.

F.W. Faber, *Spiritual Writings*

**See also** Divinity, Holy Spirit, Imagination, Jesus Christ, Presence

## 50

# IMAGINATION

*Imagination – imagining, mental faculty forming images of external objects not present to the senses; creative faculty of the mind*

Late one evening an undergraduate popped in to see me. He was looking shaken. He had been to see a film called *The Shining* and it had affected him greatly. I listened carefully and promised to go and see the film with him the following evening. The film was absorbing. We returned to my rooms to talk it through. I knew my undergraduate friend was reputed to have 'a Rolls Royce mind', but now I witnessed a powerful imagination in action. He quickly revealed to me the underlying plot, not immediately obvious to a casual film-goer like myself. He then slipped his imagination into top gear and made scores and scores of connections. We must have gone on for two or three hours – an exciting and stimulating experience. Not surprisingly he went into television when he graduated. In the many programmes he has produced, he has continued to make excellent use of his imagination.

For God speaks in one way, and in two, though people do not perceive it. In a dream, in a vision of the night, when deep sleep falls on mortals, while they slumber on their beds, then he opens their ears.

Job 33.14–16

Do not be conformed to this world, but be transformed by the renewing of your minds, so that you may discern what is the will of God – what is good and acceptable and perfect.

Romans 12.2

Imagination is the eye of the soul.

Joseph Joubert, *Pensées and Letters*

There is no power on earth like imagination . . .

Laurens van der Post, *Venture to the Interior*

The great instrument of moral good is the imagination.

Percy Bysshe Shelley, *A Defence of Poetry*

Faith means a sanctified imagination, or the imagination applied to spiritual things.

Henry Ward Beecher, *Proverbs from Plymouth Pulpit*

There are no days in life so memorable as those which vibrated to some stroke of the imagination.

Ralph Waldo Emerson, *The Conduct of Life, Nature, and Other Essays*

It is the marriage of the soul with Nature that makes the intellect fruitful, that gives birth to imagination.

Henry David Thoreau, *The Journal of Henry D. Thoreau*

Imagination grows by exercise and contrary to common belief is more powerful in the mature than in the young.

W. Somerset Maugham, *The Summing Up*

Meditation, experience of life, hope, charity, and all the emotions – out of these the imaginative reason speaks.

J.B. Yeats, *Letters to His Son, W.B. Yeats and Others*

For God hath made you able to create worlds in your own mind which are more precious unto Him than those which He created.

Thomas Traherne, *Centuries*

Only in men's imagination does every truth find an effective and undeniable existence. Imagination, not invention, is the supreme master of art as of life.

Joseph Conrad, *A Personal Record*

What is it that we ask of our ideal audience? It is imagination. And is not all our writing a profession of belief in the powers of the imagination?

Katherine Mansfield, in Anthony Alpers, *Katherine Mansfield*

The imagination is the secret and marrow of civilization. It is the very eye of faith. The soul without imagination is what an observatory would be without a telescope.

Henry Ward Beecher, *Proverbs from Plymouth Pulpit*

'What is imagination?' asks Rider Haggard in the midst of his narratives. And he answers: 'Perhaps it is a shadow of the intangible truth, perhaps it is the soul's thought!'

Henry Miller, *The Books in My Life*

But how entirely I live in my imagination; how completely depend upon spurts of thought, coming as I walk, as I sit; things churning up in my mind and so making a perpetual pageant, which is to be my happiness.

Virginia Woolf, *A Writer's Diary*

When the pioneer in science sends forth the groping fingers of his thoughts, he must have a vivid intuitive imagination, for new ideas are not generated by deduction, but by an artistically creative imagination.

Max Planck, in F.C. Happold, *Religious Faith and Twentieth-Century Man*

He realized in the entire sphere of human relations that imaginative sympathy which in the Sphere of Art is the sole secret of creation. He understood the leprosy of the leper, the darkness of the blind, the fierce misery of those who live for pleasure, the strange poverty of the rich.

Oscar Wilde, *De Profundis*

. . . I cannot tell you how strongly I feel that the kind of imagination which the gods have given me is more than imagination! In fact almost all the power we call 'imagination' may come from an actual tapping of some great reservoir of planetary, if not cosmic, experience.

John Cowper Powys, *Autobiography*

Imagination is distinct from the mere dry faculty of reasoning. Imagination is creative – it is an immediate intuition; not a logical analysis – we call it popularly a kind of inspiration. Now imagination is a power of the heart: – Great thoughts originate from a large heart: – a man must have a heart, or he never could create.

F.W. Robertson, *Sermons*

If I were asked what has been the most powerful force in the making of history, you would probably adjudge of unbalanced mind were I to answer, as I should have to answer, metaphor figurative expression. It is by imagination that men have lived; imagination rules all our lives. The human mind is not, as philosophers would have you think, a debating hall, but a picture gallery. Around it hang our similes, our concepts.

W. MacNeile Dixon, *The Human Situation*

The imagination – the divinest of mental faculties – is God's self in the soul. All our other faculties seem to me to have the brown touch of earth on them but this one carries the very livery of heaven. It is God's most supernal faculty, interpreting to us the difference between the material and the immaterial, and the difference between the visible and the invisible; teaching us how to take material and visible things and carry them up into the realm of the invisible and the immaterial, and how to bring down immaterial and invisible things, and embody them in visible and material symbols; – and so being God's messenger and prophet, standing between our soul and God's.

Henry Ward Beecher, *Royal Truths*

**See also** Aspiration, Experience, Image of God, Inspiration, Vision

## 51

# INCARNATION

*Incarnation – embodiment in flesh, especially in human form; living type (of quality); the incarnation of God in Christ*

For many years I have been going to Mürren, a village high up in the Swiss Alps, to take services at the 'English Church' during the Christmas and New Year period. One of the main services is Midnight Communion on Christmas Eve. In the short address I usually speak about the mystery of the incarnation. At one level we are celebrating the historical birth of Jesus at Bethlehem. At another level we are celebrating a birth at the present time. A way of understanding this comes through some words of Angelus Silesius:

Christ could be born  
A thousand times in Galilee –  
But all in vain  
Until he is born in me.

Discovering this simple verse led me to a deeper understanding of Christmas and the mystery of the incarnation. There is a line in the carol 'O Little Town of Bethlehem' which almost makes the same point 'Be born in us today.' How important the incarnation is, both historically and today.

In the beginning was the Word, and the Word was with God, and the Word was God . . . And the Word became flesh and lived among us, and we have seen his glory, the glory as of a father's only son, full of grace and truth.

John 1.1, 14

Those who love me will keep my word, and my Father will love them, and we will come to them and make our home with them.

John 14.23

By virtue of the Creation and still more, of the Incarnation, *nothing* here below is *profane* for those who know how to see.

Pierre Teilhard de Chardin, *Le Milieu Divin*

God became man to turn creatures into sons: not simply to produce better men of the old kind but to produce a new kind of man.

C.S. Lewis, *Mere Christianity*

Everyone has, inside himself . . . what shall I call it? A piece of good news! Everyone is . . . a very great, very important character.

Ugo Betti, *The Burnt Flower-Bed*

The Word of God, Jesus Christ our Lord: Who for His immense love's sake was made that which we are, in order that He might perfect us to be what He is.

St Irenaeus, *Five Books of St Irenaeus*

God so united Himself to us and us to Him, that the descent of God to the human level was at the same time the ascent of man to the divine level.

St Leo, in F.C. Happold, *Religious Faith and Twentieth-Century Man*

Christianity does mean getting down to actual ordinary life as the medium of the Incarnation, doesn't it, and our lessons in that get sterner, not more elegant as times goes on.

Evelyn Underhill, *The Letters of Evelyn Underhill*

God incarnated himself in Jesus Christ. Many people spend their time denying his incarnation. They search the sky and miss him right here on earth, where he is to be found in their daily lives.

Michel Quoist, *With Open Heart*

At this time . . . the renewal of Christianity depends solely on accepting the Incarnation in all its fulness. For without the realization of God's love for the world, we can love neither the world nor God.

Alan W. Watts, *Behold the Spirit*

As it is, there is one road, and one only, well secured against all possibility of going astray and this road is provided by one who is himself both God and man. As God, he is the goal; as man, he is the way.

St Augustine, *City of God*

Prayer then is the interiorizing of the Incarnation. The Word is to become enfleshed in me. Bethlehem is here. So Christmas Day is to become all days, and the adoration of Emmanuel, God with us, must be a daily and continuous event.

Kenneth Leech, *True Prayer*

The real difficulty which prevents people from believing in the Virgin Birth is not want of evidence, but belief in a 'closed universe', and the impossibility of miracles. But he who believes this, cannot believe in the Incarnation, and therefore cannot be a Christian at all.

C.B. Moss, *The Christian Faith*

The soul of a monk is a Bethlehem where Christ comes to be born – in the sense that Christ is born where His likeness is re-formed by grace, and where His Divinity lives, in a special manner, with His Father and His Holy Spirit, by charity, in this 'new incarnation', this 'other Christ'.

Thomas Merton, *Elected Silence*

True religion . . . is a reception and assimilation of the Life of God within the soul of man which is predisposed by its fundamental nature to the influx and formative influence of the Spirit of God, who is the environing Life and inner atmosphere of all human spirits; '*Spiritual Life comes from God's breath within us and from the formation of Christ within the soul.*'

Rufus M. Jones, *Spiritual Reformers in the 16th and 17th Centuries*

'Man is the true Shekinah' – the visible presence, that is to say, of the divine. We are far too apt to limit and mechanize the great doctrine of the Incarnation which forms the centre of the Christian faith. Whatever it may mean, it means at least this – that in the conditions of the highest human life we have access, as nowhere else, to the inmost nature of the divine.

A.S. Pringle-Pattison, *The Idea of God*

Once the Creator Spirit became involved in matter and in developing life, once the spirit of man was created in the likeness of the divine Spirit, it would seem natural that he should become fully incarnate in a person, not only to manifest the divine life but also to be the prototype of human life. The union of the divine and human in Jesus speaks of the hope of man sharing in the divine life.

George Appleton, *Journey for a Soul*

The incarnation is a proclamation that 'the All-great is the All-loving too' – a doctrine which few, I think, accept who do not believe in the Incarnation of the Son of God in Christ.

And if, with the Church of the Creeds and Fathers, we accept something like the Logos-doctrine already held by St Paul and briefly summarized by St John, we have the most inspiring thought that the laws of the universe, in their deepest meaning, are the expression of the character of the creating and sustaining Word who became flesh and tabernacled among us in the person of Jesus of Nazareth. I need not dwell on the consecration of the whole of nature which follows from this belief . . .

W.R. Inge, *Speculum Animae*

The Incarnation was not an isolated event, wonderful though it would have been if it was that and nothing more. It was the beginning of something new, perhaps rather the manifestation of something which had never been recognized, but which could now happen in a fully conscious and effective way. The Spirit of God, incarnate fully and supremely in Jesus, wishes to indwell every man, not only as an immanent force, but as an invited, personal guest.

George Appleton, *Journey for a Soul*

**See also** Divinity, Inner Life, Jesus Christ, Presence, Transformation

52

# INFLUENCE

*Influence – affecting character and destiny of persons; action insensibly exercised upon, ascendancy, moral power (over, with persons, etc.); thing, person, exercising power*

There are certainly some very important institutional influences at work in our lives – home, school, higher education, state, Church, work, marriage, the media, and so on. Looking back over my life, I can see there have been many institutional forces at work which have helped to mould and fashion me. These institutions, however, are made up of vast numbers of individual people, and I know that hundreds of men, women, and children, have influenced me at various stages of my life. Books have exerted an incalculable influence on me; so have the difficulties and tragedies I have been through. Other people's experiences of life have been invaluable. Lastly the grace of God has influenced me. This sometimes comes to me in quiet times of reflection and exercises an influence over the whole of life.

O Lord, the God of Abraham, Isaac, and Israel, our ancestors, keep for ever such purposes and thoughts in the hearts of your people, and direct their hearts towards you.

1 Chronicles 29.18

. . . he died, but through his faith he still speaks.

Hebrews 11.4

In every relationship lies a possibility of influence.

André Gide, *The Journals of André Gide*

Your influence, your life, your all, depends on prayer.

Forbes Robinson, *Letters to His Friends*

Every throb of our spirit that answers to spiritual things is caused by the influence of God.

Henry Ward Beecher, *Proverbs from Plymouth Pulpit*

Blessed influence of one true loving human soul on another!

George Eliot, *Scenes of Clerical Life, Janet's Repentance*

A teacher affects eternity; he can never tell where his influence stops.

Henry Adams, *The Education of Henry Adams*

God must act and pour in as soon as he finds that you are ready.

Meister Eckhart, *Meister Eckhart*, translated by Raymond B. Blakney

The very point of power in the church of Christ is the personal influence of Christian lives.

Henry Ward Beecher, *Proverbs from Plymouth Pulpit*

It is certain, that either wise bearing or ignorant carriage is caught, as men take diseases, one of another, therefore, let men take heed of their company.

William Shakespeare, *II King Henry IV*

The secret of his influence lay in a self-discipline that was as habitual as most men's habits are, an inner culture of mind and heart and will that gave his life a poise, so that he could not be untrue either to himself or his fellow-men.

George Seaver (said of Edward Wilson) in *Edward Wilson of the Antarctic*

Except by the personal influence of God's nature on ours, we cannot reach our higher manhood.

Henry Ward Beecher, *Proverbs from Plymouth Pulpit*

When we think about the people who have given us hope and have increased the strength of our soul, we might discover that they were not the advice givers, warners or moralists, but the few who were able to articulate in words and actions the human condition in which we participate and who encouraged us to face the realities of life.

Henri J.M. Nouwen, *Reaching Out*

The older we grow, the more we understand our own lives and histories, the more we shall see that the spirit of wisdom is the spirit of love, that the true way to gain influence over our fellow-men is to have charity towards them. That is a hard lesson to learn; and all those who learn it generally learn it late; almost . . . too late!

Charles Kingsley, *Daily Thoughts*

'Tis the same with human beings as with books. All of us encounter, at least once in our life, some individual who utters words that make us think for ever. There are men whose phrases are oracles; who condense in a sentence the secrets of life; who blurt out an aphorism that forms a character or illustrates an existence. A great thing is a great book; but greater than all is the talk of a great man.

Benjamin Disraeli, *Coningsby*

Certainly religion has lost its extensive control over other fields: it has less and less direct influence – on science, education, politics, law, medicine, social service. But can we conclude from all this that the influence of religion on the life of the individual and of society as a whole has declined? Instead of the former extensive control and guardianship, it may now have a more extensive and indirect moral influence.

Hans Küng, *On Being a Christian*

Any man or woman, in any age and under any circumstances, who will, can live the heroic life and exercise heroic influences.

It is of the essence of self-sacrifice, and therefore of heroism, that it should be voluntary; a work of supererogation, at least, towards society and man; an act to which the hero or heroine is not bound by duty, but which is above though not against duty.

Charles Kingsley, *Daily Thoughts*

If the sublime fire of infused love burns in your soul, it will inevitably send forth throughout the Church and the world an influence more tremendous than could be estimated by the radius reached by words or by example. St John of the Cross writes: 'A very little of this pure love is more precious in the sight of God and of greater profit to the Church, even though the soul appear to be doing nothing, than are all other works put together.'

Thomas Merton, *Elected Silence*

The spirit and character which is already advanced in constant creativeness, in wide compassion and unceasing illumination, knowing what life means and how to attain that meaning – such a spirit not only influences those among whom it is – but its influence spreads radioactively, telepathetically, and the limits of its force cannot be set, because the source on which it is drawing is itself illimitable. Being, therefore, is all, and doing merely the symptom and sign of being, as body is the appearance of spirit.

Anon

We can influence and direct others as we desire their good, but only when they are convinced, with the shrewd sense that all creatures have, that our motives are clean, our statements true, that we do seek their good, and not our advancement and elevation as their essential benefactors. All of us are individual spirits created to evolve into a common union. If we have made ourselves to grow, so that we are advanced some stages beyond the average intensity of individualism, we can directly influence those who wish to grow, and who are feeling the natural need to grow, in that direction.

Anon

**See also** Character, Greatness, Integrity, Power, Service

53

# INNER LIFE

*Inner life – interior, internal, humanity's soul or mind, spirit*

After I had taken a step of faith in my early twenties I began to keep a 'quiet time' each day. In the evening, just before going to bed, I would read a passage of scripture, and think it through with the aid of a pen and paper. Shortly afterwards I began collecting verses from the Bible and short phrases from elsewhere, to be used as a resource for the quiet time. One of these phrases from the Psalms became a great favourite: 'Be still, and know that I am God'. I would spend a few minutes mulling over this phrase, so that it became a part of my inner life. In retrospect the practice of a quiet time was invaluable and formed the basis of my inner life. Later on I collected material on a larger scale, and this eventually led to the forming of this compilation. The contents of this book are mainly about the inner life. With the practice of reflection, this material can be used to foster the 'quiet time' and so promote the growth of the inner life.

I have heard of you that a spirit of the gods is in you, and that enlightenment, understanding, and excellent wisdom are found in you.

Daniel 5.14

I pray that, according to the riches of his glory, he may grant that you may be strengthened in your inner being with power through his Spirit, and that Christ may dwell in your hearts through faith . . .

Ephesians 3.16

The man who has no inner life is the slave of his surroundings.

Henri Frédéric Amiel, *Amiel's Journal*

It is wonderful how a time away, especially abroad, changes all one's views of life from within.

A.C. Benson, *Extracts from the Letters of Dr A.C. Benson to M.E.A.*

. . . the inner life is the only means whereby we may oppose a profitable resistance to circumstance.

Henri Frédéric Amiel, *Amiel's Journal*

The important matter was the increase of this inward life, the silent growth of this kingdom of God in the hearts of men, the spread of this invisible Church.

Rufus M. Jones, *Spiritual Reformers in the 16th and 17th Centuries*

We must revolutionize this system of life, that is based on *outside* things, money, property, and establish a system of life which is based on *inside* things.

D.H. Lawrence, *The Letters of D.H. Lawrence*

God does not die on the day when we cease to believe in a personal deity, but we die on the day when our lives cease to be illumined by the steady radiance, renewed daily, of a wonder, the source of which is beyond all reason.

Dag Hammarskjöld, *Markings*

. . . he turned more and more, as time went on, toward interior religion, the cultivation of an inner sanctuary, the deepening of the mystical roots of his life, and the perfection of a religion of inner and spiritual life.

Rufus M. Jones, *Spiritual Reformers in the 16th and 17th Centuries*

There is in most of us a lyric germ or nucleus which deserves respect; it bids a man ponder, or create; and in this dim corner of himself he can take refuge and find consolations which the society of his fellow-creatures does not provide.

Norman Douglas, *An Almanac*

The life of Jesus was a calm. It was a life of marvellous composure. The storms were all about it, tumult and tempest, tempest and tumult, waves breaking over Him all the time . . . But the inner life was a sea of glass. It was a life of perfect composure . . . the great calm is there.

Henry Drummond, *The Greatest Thing in the World*

Part of the discipline of the Christian's spiritual life is designed to bring the insights and the inspiration of the inner life to bear on his conduct in the outer life, in his relations with his fellows and his responsibilities towards his family and his country.

Christopher Bryant SSJE, *Jung and the Christian Way*

He, within,
Took measure of his soul, and knew its strength,
And by that silent knowledge, day by day,
Was calmed, ennobled, comforted, sustained.

Matthew Arnold, 'Mycerinus'

Such practice of inward orientation, of inward worship and listening, is no mere counsel for special religious groups, for small religious orders, for special 'interior souls,' for monks retired in cloisters. This practice is the heart of religion. It is the secret, I am persuaded, of the inner life of the Master of Galilee. He expected this secret to be freshly discovered in everyone who would be his follower.

Thomas Kelly, *A Testament of Devotion*

He that thus seeks shall find; he shall live in truth, and that shall live in him; it shall be like a stream of living waters issuing out of his own soul; he shall drink of the waters of his own cistern, and be satisfied; he shall every morning find this heavenly manna lying upon the top of his own soul, and be fed with it to eternal life; he will find satisfaction within, feeling himself in conjunction with truth, though all the world should dispute against him.

John Smith the Platonist, *Select Discourses*

I have nothing to give to another; but I have a duty to open him to his own life, to allow him to be himself – infinitely richer and more beautiful than he could ever be if I tried to enrich and shape him only from the outside. All is *within* him because the source lies in his heart of hearts. But so many obstacles prevent it from surfacing! I must be the one to help it spring forth and smash the concrete around him, and in him. I must be the one to help him dig and search, and dig some more, to find the source. And from that source, life will spring.

Michel Quoist, *With Open Heart*

The divine mystery of this infinite God is revealed and discovered in the hearts of the sons of men, whom He hath chosen: and He hath given us, to enjoy and possess in us a measure of that fulness that is in Himself, even a measure of the same Love and Life, of the same Mercy and Power, and of the same divine Nature . . . These things ye know, if ye be born from above, and if the immortal birth live in you, and you be constant in the faith, then are you heirs through it, of the everlasting inheritance of eternal life . . . and all are yours, because you are Christ's, and he is God's, and you have the Father and the Son.

Edward Burroughs, *The Memorable Works of a Son of Thunder and Consolation*

And many a man carries within him an inheritance of incalculable worth, who is not aware of his immense resources. The richest things are ever hidden from common gaze. The things of God are neither entrusted to the brute, nor to 'the brutish man.' The sensual man can have very little perception of the soul's immortality, for the life to which he has abandoned himself is not immortal. His is the false life, the life that is not lawful *for a man* to live, and there is no eternity which will be any comfort to him. Eternity will most rigorously punish him. But there is no man who reverently, wisely, and perseveringly cultivates his own spiritual life, who is not rewarded far beyond his thoughts.

John Pulsford, *Quiet Hours*

**See also** Blessedness, Grace, Inspiration, Mystics, Presence

# 54

# INSPIRATION

*Inspiration – drawing in of breath; divine influence, sudden happy idea; inspiring principle*

In the Genesis story of the creation of humanity, God is depicted as fashioning and shaping humans in his own image and likeness, and the last thing he does is breathe into humans and they become living beings – that is, fundamentally 'inspired'. Consider for a moment those we think of being inspired – William Shakespeare, Mozart, Shelley and the scientist Marie Curie. What were the sources of their inspiration? Was it environment, hereditary, or something deeper – a gift of God perhaps? I came across an interesting observation of inspiration some years ago. An American, a former member of University College came to visit me. In the conversation which followed he said, 'You know, Bill, I have come to realize Oxford is a very spiritual place. I think *the Spirit is in the walls*.' I knew exactly what he meant. Oxford is an inspirational place. The Spirit is, indeed, in the walls.

But truly it is the spirit in a mortal, the breath of the Almighty, that makes for understanding. It is not the old that are wise, nor the aged that understand what is right. Therefore I say, 'Listen to me; let me also declare my opinion.'

Job 32.8–10

Now we have received not the spirit of the world, but the Spirit that is from God, so that we may understand the gifts bestowed on us by God. And we speak of these things in words not taught by human wisdom but taught by the Spirit, interpreting spiritual things to those who are spiritual.

1 Corinthians 2.12–13

When a man has given up the one fact of the inspiration of the Scriptures, he has given up the whole foundation of revealed religion.

Henry Ward Beecher, *Proverbs from Plymouth Pulpit*

Inspiration will always sing; inspiration will never explain.
Kahlil Gibran, *Sand and Foam*

Spirit gives meaning to his [man's] life, and the possibility of the greatest development.
C.G. Jung, in Jolande Jacobi, *Psychological Reflections*

The soul may be so inspired by the Divine Spirit as to be certified of its relationship to God.
Henry Ward Beecher, *Proverbs from Plymouth Pulpit*

An inspiration – a long deep breath of the pure air of thought – could alone give health to the heart.
Richard Jefferies, *The Story of My Heart*

Christ reformed man by inspiring the love of goodness, as well as by hatred of evil. He controlled the passions by the inspiration of the moral sentiments.
Henry Ward Beecher, *Proverbs from Plymouth Pulpit*

Perpetual Inspiration, therefore, is in the Nature of the Thing as necessary to a Life of Goodness, Holiness, and Happiness, as perpetual Respiration of the Air is necessary to animal life.
William Law, *The Spirit of Love*

It is the man who puts the vigour and enthusiasm which God inspires into the life that now is who will be fitted for the world that is to come. 'Having done all, stand.'
Henry Ward Beecher, *Proverbs from Plymouth Pulpit*

The authority of the inspired scriptures resides, not in an intrusive control of the writing process, nor in an error-free presentation, but in a reliable expression of the faith in the unique period of its earliest gestation.
James Tunstead Burtchaell CSC, in Alan Richardson and John Bowden, *A New Dictionary of Christian Theology*

There is in human life very little spiritual inspiration; very little that men can get from each other; very little that they can get from society; very little that they can get from laws and institutions. Its source is above us.
Henry Ward Beecher, *Proverbs from Plymouth Pulpit*

And do we not all agree to call rapid thought and noble impulse by the name of inspiration? After our subtlest analysis of the mental process, we will still say . . . that our highest thoughts and our best deeds are all given to us.

George Eliot, *Adam Bede*

Those divinely possessed and inspired have at least the knowledge that they hold some greater thing within them though they cannot tell what it is; from the movements that stir them and the utterances that come from them they perceive the power, not themselves, that moves them.

Plotinus, *The Enneads*

God should be in the Christian's soul, in his living consciousness, vital, active, fiery. He should inspire him and fill him with admiration. His God should be one that loves him, inspires him, rebukes him, punishes him, wounds him, heals him, and rejoices him – one whose arms and whose bosom he feels.

Henry Ward Beecher, *Proverbs from Plymouth Pulpit*

To dare to listen to that inspiration from within which voices the ultimate reality of one's own being requires an act of faith which is rare indeed. When the conviction is borne in upon one that anything which is put together, or made up, has no ultimate reality and so is certain to disintegrate, one turns to one's own final reality in the faith that it and it alone can have any virtue or any value.

Esther Harding, *Women's Mysteries*

The artist's inspiration may be either a human or a spiritual grace, or a mixture of both. High artistic achievement is impossible without at least those forms of intellectual, emotional and physical mortification appropriate to the kind of art which is being practised. Over and above this course of what may be called professional mortification, some artists have practised the kind of self-naughting which is the indispensable pre-condition of the unitive knowledge of the divine Ground. Fra Angelico, for example, prepared himself for this work by means of prayer and meditation.

Aldous Huxley, *The Perennial Philosophy*

The uninitiated imagine one must await inspiration in order to create. That is a mistake. I am far from saying that there is no such thing as inspiration; quite the opposite. It is found as a driving force in every kind of human activity, and is in no wise peculiar to artists. But that force is only brought into action by an effort, and that effort is work. Just as appetite comes by eating, so work brings inspiration, if inspiration is not discernible at the beginning. But it is not simply inspiration that counts; it is the result of inspiration – that is, the composition.

Igor Stravinsky, *An Autobiography*

It is by long obedience and hard work that the artist comes to unforced spontaneity and consummate mastery. Knowing that he can never create anything on his own account, out of the top layers, so to speak, of his personal consciousness, he submits obediently to the workings of 'inspiration'; and knowing that the medium in which he works has its own self-nature, which must not be ignored or violently overridden, he makes himself its patient servant and, in this way, achieves freedom of expression. But life is also an art, and the man who would become a consummate artist in living must follow, on all the levels of his being, the same procedure as that by which the painter or the sculptor or any other craftsman comes to his own more limited perfection.

Aldous Huxley, *The Perennial Philosophy*

**See also** Art, Aspiration, Literature, Music, Poetry

# 55

# INTEGRITY

*Integrity – wholeness; soundness; uprightness, honesty, purity*

Shortly after returning from our expedition to Nepal someone recommended a book entitled *Edward Wilson of the Antarctic* by George Seaver. Edward Wilson was the doctor on Scott's expedition to the Antarctic in 1910. He was a man of deep religious convictions. He had an intense love of the countryside and was a sensitive artist, committing to paper what he observed in nature. In the pages of this book I was confronted with the finest character I have ever come across. Throughout his life he was solid and dependable. Scott wrote of him as being shrewdly practical, intensely loyal and quite unselfish. He knew and understood people, more deeply than most. He had a quiet sense of humour and was modest and unassuming in his relationships. Always discreet and tactful, he was also kind and friendly. He was a man of many parts – a skilful doctor as well as a zoologist. His courage and bravery were outstanding features of his character. In short, he was a man of the utmost integrity.

The integrity of the upright guides them.

Proverbs 11.3

. . . by purity, knowledge, patience, kindness, holiness of spirit, genuine love, truthful speech, and the power of God; with the weapons of righteousness for the right hand and for the left; in honour and dishonour, in ill repute and good repute. We are treated as impostors, and yet are true.

2 Corinthians 6.6–8

Integrity is the noblest possession.

Latin proverb

Nothing endures but personal qualities.
Walt Whitman, 'Song of the Broad-Axe'

What stronger breastplate than a heart untainted!
William Shakespeare, *II King Henry VI*

Rather than love, than money, than fame, give me truth.
Henry David Thoreau, *Walden*

Each man needs to develop the sides of his personality which he has neglected.
Alexis Carrel, *Reflections on Life*

Man's main task in life is to give birth to himself, to become what he potentially is. The most important product of his efforts is his own personality.
Erich Fromm, *Man for Himself*

. . . the individual needs to be in constant struggle with his environment if he is to develop to his highest capacity. Hard conditions of life are indispensable to bringing out the best in human personality.
Alexis Carrel, *Reflections on Life*

A cultivation of the powers of one's own personality is one of the greatest needs of life, too little realized even in these assertive days, and the exercise of the personality makes for its most durable satisfactions.
Randolph Bourne, *Youth and Life*

One whose greatest power lay in unfolding the love of God by speech and action, and in helping individual men and women to find the meaning and the glory, the purpose and the joy of life, in that surrender to the all-pervading presence of God which for him gave each the character of heaven.
G.A. Studdert Kennedy, *By His Friends*

The only drama that really interests me and that I should always be willing to depict anew is the debate of the individual with whatever keeps him from being authentic, with whatever is opposed to his integrity, to his integration. Most often the obstacle is within him. And all the rest is merely accidental.
André Gide, *The Journals of André Gide*

One person with integrity, even living the most private life, affects the entire behaviour of the universe. That is God's promise, and it is among modern psychology's great lessons. But the converse is also true. So with each of us empowered with this awesome ability, will we dare be less than as fully Christians as we can?

Harry James Cargas, *Encountering Myself*

The present state of the world calls for a moral and spiritual revolution, revolution in the name of personality, of man, of every single person. This revolution should restore the hierarchy or values, now quite shattered, and place the value of human personality above the idols of production, technics, the state, the race or nationality, the collective.

Nicolas Berdyaev, *The Fate of Man in the Modern World*

Integrity originally means wholeness. The leader who can attain within himself a unity or wholeness of drive and outlook will possess integrity. The acquiring of this quality is thus no little thing, and the process requires no minor adjustments. It is a major problem of the whole life philosophy and character of the individual. It is a question of the leader's capacity to be loyal to the basic demand for loyalty itself.

Ordway Tead, *The Art of Leadership*

If we could adapt ourselves more to the life of God within us we would be more able to adapt ourselves to the will of God as expressed all about us. We are unyielding in outward things only because we have not fully yielded to inward ones. The integrated soul, the man who has broken down the barriers of selfishness and is detached from his own will, is ready to meet every circumstance however suddenly presented and however apparently destructive, fortuitous, unreasonable, and mad.

Hubert van Zeller, *Leave Your Life Alone*

By integrity I do not mean simply sincerity or honesty; integrity rather according to the meaning of the word as its derivation interprets it – entireness – wholeness – soundness: that which Christ means when He says, 'If thine eye be single or sound, thy whole body shall be full of light.'

This integrity extends through the entireness or wholeness of the character. It is found in small matters as well as great; for the allegiance of the soul to truth is tested by small things rather than by those which are more important.

F.W. Robertson, *Sermons*

Let your actions speak; your face ought to vouch for your speech. I would have virtue look out of the eye, no less apparently than love does in the sight of the beloved. I would have honesty and sincerity so incorporated with the constitution, that it should be discoverable by the senses, and as easily distinguished as a strong breath, so that a man must be forced to find it out whether he would or no . . . In short, a man of integrity, sincerity, and good-nature can never be concealed, for his character is wrought into his countenance.

Marcus Aurelius, *The Meditations of Marcus Aurelius*

What do we mean when we speak of a man of integrity? One who will be true to the highest he knows; who will never betray the truth or trifle with it; one who will never make a decision from self-regarding motives; one who will never yield to the persuasion of friends or the pressure of critics unless either conforms to his own standards of right and wrong; one who will face the consequences of his attitudes, decisions and actions, however costly they may be; one who will not be loud in self-justification, but quietly confident and humbly ready to explain.

George Appleton, *Journey for a Soul*

**See also** Character, Relationships, Saints, Truth, Wholeness

# 56

# INTELLECT

*Intellect – faculty of knowing and reasoning; understanding; persons collectively, of good understanding*

While chaplain to University College, London, I was fortunate in being a member of a group that went on a tour of the east coast of America. Several of us had a special interest in student counselling and took every opportunity to meet experts in this field. At Baltimore we visited a downtown hospital. This hospital was going through a difficult time, financially and administratively, and had just called in a 'high-flyer' from Harvard to sort out these problems. We met him for a few minutes and he gave a brief analysis of the situation. He then went on to give an outline of the proposals to rescue the hospital. He was brilliant – a man of enormous intellect. His clear lucid mind had immediately identified the causes of the problems. Not only did he understand them in full, but at one and the same time, thought out practical ways to resolve them – a true intellectual in action.

Wise warriors are mightier than strong ones, and those who have knowledge than those who have strength.

Proverbs 24.5

Therefore prepare your minds for action.

1 Peter 1.13

But only to our intellect is he incomprehensible: not to our love.

*The Cloud of Unknowing*

Logic does not help you to appreciate York Minister, or Botticelli's Primavera, and mathematics give no useful hints to lovers.

W. MacNeile Dixon, *The Human Situation*

The greater intellect one has, the more originality one finds in men. Ordinary persons find no difference between men.

Blaise Pascal, *Pensées*

It is always the task of the intellectual to 'think otherwise'. This is not just a perverse idiosyncrasy. It is an absolutely essential feature of a society.

Harvey Cox, *The Secular City*

When Man has arrived at a certain ripeness of intellect any one grand and spiritual passage serves him as a starting-post towards all 'the two-and-thirty Palaces'.

John Keats, *Letter to J.H. Reynolds*

The mind will never unveil God to man. God is only found at a certain point on the road of experience. He speaks to man through his heart and when that happens man knows, and he never again questions the love of God.

Grace Cooke, *Spiritual Unfoldment*

We must shut the eye of sense, and open that brighter eye of our understandings, that other eye of the soul, (as the philosopher calls our intellectual faculty,) . . . which indeed all have, but few make use of.

John Smith the Platonist, *Select Discourses*

How often does the weak will obscure the clear call of conscience by resort to intellectual 'difficulties'! Some of these are real enough but some are sheer self-protection against the exacting claim of the holy love of God.

William Temple, *Readings in St John's Gospel*

The uncertainty, however, lies always in the intellectual region, never in the practical. What Paul cares about is plain enough to the true heart, however far from plain to the man whose desire to understand goes ahead of his obedience.

George Macdonald, *Unspoken Sermons*

There is a moral faith which is a virtue – faith in a friend, for example. Is there not an intellectual faith which is a virtue, which holds fast when proof fails? I believe there is such an intellectual faith and that it is a sign of strength.

Mark Rutherford, *Last Pages from a Journal*

We should not pretend to understand the world only by the intellect; we apprehend it just as much by feeling. Therefore the judgement of the intellect is, at best, only the half of truth, and must, if it be honest, also come to an understanding of its inadequacy.

C.G. Jung, *Psychological Types*

To cultivate the man of intellect is not enough, for stillness is a quality of the whole man . . . Each man must discover the perfect tension of his being – in action or solitude, in love or asceticism, in philosophy or faith – by continual adjustments of thought and experience.

Charles Morgan, *The Fountain*

All these intellectual attitudes would have short shrift if Christianity had remained what it was, a communion, if Christianity had remained what it was, a religion of the heart. This is one of the reasons why modern people understand nothing of true, real Christianity, of the true, real history of Christianity and what Christendom really was.

Charles Péguy, *Basic Verities*

But intellectual acceptance even of correct doctrine is not by itself vital religion; orthodoxy is not identical with the fear or the love of God. This fact of the inadequacy of the truest doctrine is a warning that to argue syllogistically from doctrinal formula is to court disaster. The formula may be the best possible; yet it is only a label used to designate a living thing.

William Temple, *Nature, Man and God*

The longest way to God
the indirect
lies through the intellect
Here is my journey's end
and here its start.

Angelus Silesius, 'Of the Inner Light and Enlightenment'

The intellectual is constantly betrayed by his own vanity. God-like, he blandly assumes that he can express everything in words; whereas the things one loves, lives, and dies for are not, in the last analysis, completely expressible in words. To write or to speak is almost inevitably to lie a little. It is an attempt to clothe an intangible in a tangible form; to compress an immeasurable into a mold. And in the act of compression, how Truth is mangled and torn.

Anne Morrow Lindbergh, *The Wave of the Future*

Western civilization is distinguished by its worship of the intellect. Yet there is no reason to give intellect pride of place over feeling. It is obviously wrong to classify young people by examinations in which the moral and organic values have no place. To make thought itself the goal of thought is a kind of mental perversion. Intellect and sexual activity alike should be exercised in a natural way. The function of the intellect is not to satisfy itself but to contribute, along with the other organic and mental functions, to the satisfaction of the individual's total needs.

Alexis Carrel, *Reflections on Life*

**See also** Education, Knowledge, Mind, Philosophy, Thinking

57

# JESUS CHRIST

*Jesus Christ – the name Jesus refers to the person Jesus of Nazareth as known from historical research; Christ refers to the 'Messiah', or 'Lord's anointed' of Jewish prophecy, now applied to Jesus as fulfilling this prophecy; image or picture of Jesus*

Jesus Christ is important to me because he worked out in his person what is meant by humanity being made in the image and likeness of God. As he went through life he discovered the presence of the Father in himself. At the height of his ministry he was able to say to his disciples: 'Whoever has seen me has seen the Father . . . Do you not believe that I am in the Father and the Father in me?' He also discovered in himself the full range of the gifts and fruits of the Holy Spirit. In the epistles, the apostle Paul recognized that what Christ had experienced we can all in some measure also experience. He points out that 'in him the whole fullness of deity dwells bodily', and states what this means for us 'and you have come to fullness in him'. I like J.S. Whale's observation: 'the man Christ Jesus has the decisive place in man's ageless relationship with God. He is what God means by "Man". He is what man means by "God".'

'If you know me, you will know my Father also; from now on you do know him and have seen him.' Philip said to him, 'Lord, show us the Father, and we will be satisfied.' Jesus said to him, 'Have I been with you all this time Philip, and you still do not know me? Whoever has seen me has seen the Father. How can you say, "Show us the Father?" Do you not believe that I am in the Father and the Father is in me? The words that I say to you I do not speak on my own; but the Father who dwells in me does his works. Believe me that I am in the Father and the Father is in me; but if you do not, then believe me because of the works themselves.'

John 14.7–11

. . . that is, Christ himself, in whom are hidden all the treasures of wisdom and knowledge.

Colossians 2.2–3

Jesus is not a figure in a book; He is a living presence.

William Barclay, *The Gospel of Matthew*

Jesus did not come into the world to make life easy; he came to make men great.

Anon

As Man alone, Jesus could not have saved us; as God alone, he would not; Incarnate, he could and did.

Malcolm Muggeridge, *Jesus, the Man who Lives*

We need the personal allegiance of love to Christ – such a presentation of Him through the imagination of our minds as will draw forth the soul's enthusiasm and secret life.

Henry Ward Beecher, *Proverbs from Plymouth Pulpit*

If we refuse the invitation of Christ, some day our greatest pain will be, not in the things we suffer, but in the realization of the precious things we have missed, and of which we have cheated ourselves.

William Barclay, *The Gospel of Matthew*

He does not say 'No man knoweth God save the Son'. That would be to deny the truth of the Old Testament revelation. What he does say is that He alone has a deeper secret, the essential Fatherhood of the Sovereign Power.

D.S. Cairns, *The Riddle of the World*

Two thousand years ago, there was One here on this earth who lived the grandest life that ever has been lived yet, a life that every thinking man, with deeper or shallower meaning, has agreed to call Divine.

F.W. Robertson, *Lectures and Addresses*

When criticism has done its worst, the words and acts of our Lord which remain are *not* those of 'a good and heroic man', but of one deliberately claiming unique authority and insight, and conscious of a unique destiny.

Evelyn Underhill, *The Letters of Evelyn Underhill*

Christ in us and we in Him! Why should the activity of God and the presence of the Son of Man within us not be real and observable? Every day I am thankful to God that I have been allowed to experience the reality of the Divine Image within me.

C.G. Jung, in F.C. Happold, *Religious Faith and Twentieth-Century Man*

His is easily the dominant figure in history . . . A historian without any theological bias whatever should find that he simply cannot portray the progress of humanity honestly without giving a foremost place to a penniless teacher from Nazareth.

H.G. Wells, in William Barclay, *The Gospel of Matthew*

Look on our divinest Symbol: on Jesus of Nazareth, and his Life . . . and what followed therefrom. Higher has the human Thought not yet reached . . . a Symbol of quite perennial infinite character; whose significance will ever demand to be anew inquired into, and anew made manifest.

Thomas Carlyle, *Sartor Resartus*

But the Wind of heav'n
bloweth where it listeth, and Christ yet walketh the earth,
and talketh still as with those two disciples once
on the road to Emmaus.

Robert Bridges, 'The Testament of Beauty'

If you accept that Jesus is the revelation and manifestation of the Father, then you are a follower of Christ and so a Christian. If you move from that to asking in what sense is Christ God, then I would think you have to come in the end to making that act of faith which is recorded of St Thomas the Doubtful: 'My Lord and my God'.

Basil Hume OSB, in Gerald Priestland, *Priestland's Progress*

What was Christ's life? Not one of deep speculations, quiet thoughts, and bright visions, but a life of fighting against evil; earnest, awful prayers and struggles within, continued labour of body and mind without; insult, and danger, and confusion, and violent exertion, and bitter sorrow. This was Christ's life. This was St Peter's, and St James's, and St John's life afterwards.

Charles Kingsley, *Daily Thoughts*

Christ's communion with His Father was the life-centre, the point of contact with Eternity, whence radiated the joy and power of the primitive Christian flock: the classic example of a corporate spiritual life. When the young man with great possessions asked Jesus, 'What shall I do to be saved?' Jesus replied in effect, 'Put aside all lesser interests, strip off unrealities, and come, give yourself the chance of catching the infection of holiness from Me!'

Evelyn Underhill, in John Stobbart, *The Wisdom of Evelyn Underhill*

Unless we know Christ experimentally so that 'He lives within us spiritually, and so that all which is known of Him in the Letter and Historically is truly done and acted in our souls – until we experimentally verify all we read of Him – the Gospel is a mere tale to us.' It is not saving knowledge to know that Christ is born in Bethlehem but to know that He is born in us. It is vastly more important to know experimentally that we are crucified with Christ than to know historically that He died in Jerusalem many years ago, and to feel Jesus Christ risen again within you is far more operative than to have 'a notional knowledge' that He rose on the third day . . . here is a Christ indeed, a real Christ who will do thee some good.

Rufus M. Jones, *Spiritual Reformers in the 16th and 17th Centuries*

**See also** Character, Divinity, God, Holy Spirit, Image of God

# 58

# JOY

*Joy – pleasurable emotion due to well-being or satisfaction; the feeling or state of being highly pleased; exultation of spirit, gladness, delight*

I wonder if joy can be seen as another illustration of the Genesis story of the creation of humanity. In that story a seed or a spark of the divine joy is 'breathed into' human beings. Jesus was no stranger to joy. He found joy in the depths of his own being and wished to extend this to his disciples. In John's Gospel he is recorded as having said to them: 'I have said these things to you so that my joy may be in you, and that your joy may be complete.' We remember the 'good and faithful servant' was bidden to 'enter into the joy of your master'. Joy has not been a stranger to our experience during the last two thousand years. Many of us are able to sympathize with those words of Samuel Taylor Coleridge: 'Joy rises in me, like a summer's morn.'

You show me the path of life. In your presence there is fullness of joy; in your right hand are pleasures for evermore.

Psalm 16.11

But now I am coming to you, and I speak these things in the world so that they may have my joy made complete in themselves.

John 17.13

Joy rises in me, like a summer's morn.

Samuel Taylor Coleridge, 'A Christmas Carol'

But the fulness of joy is in God's immediate presence.

Richard Baxter, *The Saints' Everlasting Rest*

Every joy, great or small, is akin and always a refreshment.

Johann Wolfgang von Goethe, *The Practical Wisdom of Goethe*

Life in the dimension of Spirit is a mystery rooted in the joy of being.

John Main OSB, in Clare Hallward, *The Joy of Being*

These little thoughts are the rustle of leaves: they have their whisper of joy in my mind.

Rabindranath Tagore, *Stray Birds*

The joy which a man finds in his work and which transforms the tears and sweat of it into happiness and delight – that joy is God.

Harry Williams CR, *The True Wilderness*

Joy is prayer – Joy is strength – Joy is love . . . A joyful heart is the normal result of a heart burning with love.

Mother Teresa, in Malcolm Muggeridge, *Something Beautiful for God*

How good is man's life, the mere living! how fit to employ
All the heart and soul and the senses for ever in joy!

Robert Browning, 'Saul'

This glory and honour wherewith man is crowned ought to affect every person that is grateful, with celestial joy: and so much the rather because it is every man's proper end and sole inheritance.

Thomas Traherne, *Centuries*

Joy is the sentiment that is born in a soul, conscious of the good it possesses. The good of our intelligence is truth; the more this truth is abundant and luminous, the deeper is our inward joy.

D. Columba Marmion, *Christ in His Mysteries*

The Christian joy and hope do not arise from an ignoring of the evil in the world, but from facing it at its worst. The light that shines for ever in the Church breaks out of the veriest pit of gloom.

William Temple, *Readings in St John's Gospel*

Our faith is faith in what the synoptic gospels call 'the Kingdom of God' and the Kingdom of God is simply God's power enthroned in our hearts. This is what makes us light of heart and it is what Christian joy is all about.

John Main OSB, *Moment of Christ*

If a man has sought first and chiefly the soul's treasure – goodness, kindness, gentleness, devoutness, cheerfulness, hope, faith, and love – he will extract more joy from the poorest furniture and outfitting of life than otherwise he would get from the whole world.

Henry Ward Beecher, *Proverbs from Plymouth Pulpit*

'To be a joy-bearer and a joy-giver says everything,' she wrote, 'for in our life, if one is joyful it means that one is faithfully living for God, and that *nothing else counts*; and if one gives joy to others one is doing God's work; with joy without and joy within, all is well . . . I can conceive no higher way.'

Janet Erskine Stuart, in Maud Monahan, *Life and Letters of Janet Erskine Stuart*

At first the Lark, when she means to rejoice, to cheer herself and those that hear her; she then quits the earth, and sings as she ascends higher into the air, and having ended her heavenly employment, grows then mute, and sad, to think she must descend to the dull earth, which she could not touch, but for necessity.

Izaak Walton, *The Compleat Angler*

Joy is the affect which comes when we use our powers. Joy, rather than happiness, is the goal of life, for joy is the emotion which accompanies our fulfilling our natures as human beings. It is based on the experience of one's identity as a being of worth and dignity, who is able to affirm his being, if need be, against all other beings and the whole organic world.

Rollo May, *Man's Search for Himself*

'The fruit of the spirit is love – joy.' So the opaque Christian is a slander on God. The thing which the church has been so much afraid of – joy, cheerfulness, hopefulness, gentleness, sweetness, overflowing manhood – this is one of the fruits of the Spirit. Love and joy are put first.

Henry Ward Beecher, *Proverbs from Plymouth Pulpit*

*Joy*; the Greek word is *chara*, and the characteristic of this word is that it most often describes that joy which has a basis in religion, and whose real foundation is God . . . It is not the joy that comes from earthly things or cheap triumphs; still less is it the joy that comes from triumphing over someone else in rivalry or competition. It is a joy whose basis is God.

William Barclay, *The Letters to the Galatians and Ephesians*

There are some people who have the quality of richness and joy in them and they communicate it to everything they touch. It is first of all a physical quality; then it is a quality of spirit. With such people it makes no difference if they are rich or poor; they are really always rich because they have such wealth and vital power within them that they give everything interest, dignity, and a warm colour.

Thomas Wolfe, *The Web and the Rock*

**See also** Cheerfulness, Freedom, Fulfilment, Happiness, Transformation

# 59

# KINDNESS

*Kindness – the quality or habit of being kind; kind feeling; affection, love*

If someone were to ask me what has been the greatest influence in my life, I would have to say – kindness. When I went into the army to do National Service, we were first of all put through basic training. Towards the end of this I was recommended to attend a WOSB – a War Office Selection Board. If I passed this hurdle I would go to Mons Officer Cadet School in Aldershot for four months' training. After that, all being well, I would be commissioned. I remember going to a very cold barracks in a remote part of Hampshire. For three days we were put through a series of tests. I was then summoned to see the colonel. My papers were laid out before him. 'I notice your eyesight is not A1. Regulations restrict you to the Pay Corps or the Pioneer Corps.' He looked at me intently. 'How keen are you to go into the infantry?' I looked him straight in the eye and said, 'Very keen, Sir.' He said, 'Okay, we'll see what we can do.' His act of kindness changed the whole course of my life. I ended up in the 2nd Gurkhas.

Blessed be the Lord: for he has wondrously shown his steadfast love to me.

Psalm 31.21

But love your enemies, do good, and lend, expecting nothing in return. Your reward will be great, and you will be children of the Most High; for he is kind to the ungrateful and the wicked.

Luke 6.35

A kind word is like a spring day.

Russian proverb

Kind hearts are more than coronets.

Alfred, Lord Tennyson, 'Lady Clara Vere de Vere'

Kindnesses, like grain, grow by sowing.
Proverb

Kindliness in judgement is nothing less than a sacred duty.
William Barclay, *The Gospel of Matthew*

What wisdom can you find that is greater than kindness?
Jean Jacques Rousseau, *Emile or Education*

There is a grace of kind listening, as well as a grace of kind speaking.
F.W. Faber, *Spiritual Conferences*

Kindness is the principle of tact, and respect for others the first condition of *savoir-vivre*. Henri Frédéric Amiel, *Amiel's Journal*

The heart benevolent and kind
The most resembles GOD.
Robert Burns, 'A Winter Night'

Gentleness as the fruit of the Spirit is a strong man's treating all men with lenity, and kindness, and forbearance, and patience.
Henry Ward Beecher, *Proverbs from Plymouth Pulpit*

My feeling is that there is nothing in life but refraining from hurting others, and comforting those that are sad.
Olive Schreiner, *The Letters of Olive Schreiner*

Life is short, and we have never too much time for gladdening the hearts of those who are travelling the dark journey with us. Oh, be swift to love, make haste to be kind!
Henri Frédéric Amiel, *Amiel's Journal*

On that best portion of a good man's life,
His little, nameless, unremembered, acts
Of kindness and of love.
William Wordsworth, 'Lines Composed a few Miles Above Tintern Abbey'

I have had that curiously *symbolic* and reassuring pleasure, of being entertained with overflowing and simple kindness by a family of totally unknown people – an adventure which always brings home to me the goodwill of the world.
A.C. Benson, *Extracts from the Letters of Dr A.C. Benson to M.E.A.*

True kindness presupposes the faculty of imagining as one's own the suffering and joy of others. Without imagination, there can be weakness, theoretical or practical philanthropy, but not true kindness.

André Gide, *Pretexts, Reflections on Literature and Morality*

I expect to pass through this world but once; any good thing therefore that I can do, or any kindness that I can show to any fellow-creature, let me do it now; let me not defer or neglect it, for I shall not pass this way again.

Attributed to Stephen Grellet

Kind thoughts are rarer than either kind words or kind deeds. They imply a great deal of thinking about others. This in itself is rare. But they imply also a great deal of thinking about others without the thoughts being criticisms. This is rarer still.

F.W. Faber, *Spiritual Conferences*

Let the weakest remember – let the humblest . . . remember, that in his daily course he can, if he will, shed around him almost a heaven. Kindly words, sympathizing attentions, watchfulness against wounding men's sensitiveness – these cost very little, but they are priceless in their value. Are they not . . . almost the stable of our daily happiness? From hour to hour, from moment to moment, we are supported, blest, by small kindnesses.

F.W. Robertson, *Sermons*

Be kind and merciful. Let no one ever come to you without leaving better and happier. Be the living expression of God's kindness – kindness in your face, kindness in your eyes, kindness in your smile, kindness in your warm greeting. In the slums we are the light of God's kindness to the poor. To children, to the poor, all who suffer and are lonely, give always a happy smile. Give them not only your care but also your heart. Because of God's goodness and love every moment of our life can be the beginning of great things. Be open, ready to receive and you will find him everywhere. Every work of love brings a person face to face with God.

Mother Teresa, in Kathryn Spink, *In the Silence of the Heart*

And it is here that the saints serve us yet again. Kindness recovers all its apostolic quality in them. In the saint it is never sentimental; never divorced from reality; never undisciplined; never evasive. On the other hand, it is ever-present: never excluded by their concern for God's holiness; never driven away by any pride in their own virtue. The cheapening of the word in the world, and the neglect of this grace in the sanctuary, are both corrected in the saint. He reveals kindness *as a fruit of the Spirit*. He shows it grounded in the nature of God. It flows directly from his faith. It is supernatural love disclosing itself in costly affection towards his fellow-men . . . That is why it has a robustness and pertinacity unknown to the sentimental kindness of the world . . .

W.E. Sangster, *The Pure in Heart*

**See also** Awareness, Compassion, Grace, Love, Neighbour

# 60

# KINGDOM OF GOD

*Kingdom of God – the central theme of the teaching of Jesus, involving an understanding of his own person and work*

In the process of growing in faith, I have come to discover something of the kingdom of God in the depths of my being. At one level this has come through baptism, with the spiritual rebirth of the Father, the Son and the Holy Spirit. In the course of prayer one has become aware of the 'presence' of the gifts and fruits of the Holy Spirit. I have also been greatly helped by commentators who point out 'the kingdom of God is within you' can also mean 'the kingdom of God is among you'. My experience has been that when the kingdom of God 'within you' becomes a living reality, it is as though scales are removed from our eyes, and we are able to see the kingdom of God 'among you' – in other people, in the processes of nature and creation, in other faiths, in work, and in the international scene as a whole. It is then that a phrase of the Lord's Prayer not only enables us to understand the person and work of Jesus, but calls us, too, to the kingdom of God – 'Thy kingdom come . . . on earth as it is in heaven.'

But strive first for the kingdom of God and his righteousness, and all these things will be given to you as well.

Matthew 6.33

The time is fulfilled, and the kingdom of God has come near; repent, and believe in the good news.

Mark 1.15

This life, this kingdom of God, this simplicity of absolute existence, is hard to enter. How hard? As hard as the Master of salvation could find words to express the hardness.

George Macdonald, *Unspoken Sermons*

To keep alive the sense of wonder, to live in unquestioning trust, instinctively to obey, to forgive and forget – that is the childlike spirit, and that is the passport to the Kingdom of God.

William Barclay, *The Gospel of Luke*

The outer world, with all its phenomena, is filled with divine splendour, but we must have experienced the divine within ourselves, before we can hope to discover it in our environment.

Rudolf Steiner, *Knowledge of the Higher Worlds*

This Kingdom of God is now within us. The Grace of the Holy Spirit likewise shines forth and warms us, distils a multitude of fragrances in the air around us, and pervades our senses with heavenly delight, flooding our hearts with inexpressible joy.

Seraphim of Sarov, in G.P. Fedotov, *A Treasury of Russian Spirituality*

'The Kingdom of God is within you' – it is written in the very constitution of our being. The laws of the Kingdom are the laws of our being, stamped within our very selves, therefore inescapable. When you revolt against them, you revolt against yourself.

E. Stanley Jones, *Mastery*

As a matter of fact, that is the one business of man on earth – to co-operate with the divine power. All the activities of life – commercial, industrial, economic, social, political – should be, in their real nature, this co-operation with the divine power for the advancement of humanity.

Lilian Whiting, *Lilies of Eternal Peace*

The kingdom of God, which the Christian wishes to share with others, involves the individual and the community of faith in a process of looking back to the life and ministry of Jesus, in a deep commitment to the present where the kingdom is to be more clearly recognized and established, and in a longing for the future when all obstacles to the kingdom have been removed and the beauty and perfection of God's love is experienced in all its glory.

Trevor Beeson, *An Eye for an Ear*

The Kingdom of God is something within you which has the power of growth like a seed; something that you discover almost accidentally; something that you are searching for, and of whose value you become more confident and excited as the search proceeds, and you discover truer, lovelier things which are constantly being surpassed; something for which you have to give everything you have, no less yet no more, including the earlier finds with which you were once so completely delighted.

George Appleton, *Journey for a Soul*

We are at the beginning of the end of the human race. The question now before it is whether it will use for beneficial purposes or for purposes of destruction the power which modern science has placed in its hands. So long as its capacity for destruction was limited, it was possible to hope that reason would set a limit to disaster. Such an illusion is impossible today, when its power is illimitable. Our only hope is that the Spirit of God will strive with the spirit of the world and will prevail.

Albert Schweitzer, in E.N. Mozley, *The Theology of Albert Schweitzer*

To discover the Kingdom of God exclusively within oneself is easier than to discover it, not only there, but also in the outer world of minds and things and living creatures. It is easier because the heights within reveal themselves to those who are ready to exclude from their purview all that lies without. And though this exclusion may be a painful and mortificatory process, the fact remains that it is less arduous than the process of inclusion, by which we come to know the fullness as well as the heights of spiritual life.

Aldous Huxley, *The Perennial Philosophy*

Modern faith finds the beginning of the Kingdom of God in Jesus and in the Spirit which came into the world with him. We no longer leave the fate of mankind to be decided at the end of the world. The time in which we live summons us to new faith in the Kingdom of God.

We are no longer content, like the generations before us, to believe in the Kingdom that comes of itself at the end of time. Mankind today must either realize the Kingdom of God or perish. The very tragedy of our present situation compels us to devote ourselves in faith to its realization.

Albert Schweitzer, in E.N. Mozley, *The Theology of Albert Schweitzer*

The Kingdom of God was the main subject of the early preaching of Jesus. He claimed that in himself the Kingdom had drawn near, was in operation, and he called to men to accept this fact in faith and to change their attitudes, behaviour and world view. Many of his parables dealt with the meaning of the Kingdom, as if he were wanting to ensure that those who could not at first understand would remember one vivid human story, and that one day the penny would drop. He wanted everyone to share the treasure that he had brought.

George Appleton, *Journey for a Soul*

The miracle must happen in us before it can happen in the world. We dare not set our hope on our own efforts to create the conditions of God's Kingdom in the world. We must indeed labour for its realization. But there can be no Kingdom of God in the world without the Kingdom of God in our hearts. The starting-point is our determined effort to bring every thought and action under the sway of the Kingdom of God. Nothing can be achieved without inwardness. The Spirit of God will only strive against the spirit of the world when it has won its victory over that spirit in our hearts.

Albert Schweitzer, in E.N. Mozley, *The Theology of Albert Schweitzer*

Why did the idea of the Kingdom of God have no significance in the early church? It was closely connected with the expectation of the end of the world. And when hope of the coming of the end of the world had faded, the idea of the Kingdom of God lost its force as well. So it came about that the creeds were not at the same time preoccupied with the idea of redemption. Only after the reformation did the idea gradually arise that we men and women in our own age must so understand the religion of Jesus that we endeavour to make the Kingdom of God a reality in this world. It is only through the idea of the Kingdom of God that religion enters into relationship with civilization.

Albert Schweitzer, in Charles H. Joy, *An Anthology*

**See also** Church, Incarnation, Inner Life, Presence, Transformation

## 61

# KNOWLEDGE

*Knowledge – the sum of what is known, as every branch of knowledge, personal knowledge, knowledge of God*

Last week I went into All Souls for lunch, and spotted the portrait of one of my heroes – Sir Sarvepalli Radhakrishnan. He has been a Fellow of All Souls, but more importantly was at one time President of India. In this introductory paragraph, I include a short passage from his book, *Indian Philosophy*, as it has something important to say about knowledge. 'Knowledge,' he wrote, 'is not something to be packed away in some corner of our brain, but what enters into our being, colours our emotion; haunts our soul, and is as close to us as life itself. It is the overmastering power which through the intellect moulds the whole personality, trains the emotions and disciplines the will.'

Wise words indeed. However nowadays we tend to concentrate on the first phrase of his passage, and pack away the contents of a degree course in some corner of our brain. By and large we ignore that overmastering power which through the intellect moulds the whole personality, trains the emotions and disciplines the will. Who would see to this in a modern-day university anyway? So, for some students, a university education is a disappointment and produces low performance.

Talk no more so very proudly, let not arrogance come from your mouth; for the Lord is a God of knowledge . . .

1 Samuel 2.3

I want their hearts to be encouraged and united in love, so that they may have all the riches of assured understanding and have the knowledge of God's mystery, that is, Christ himself, in whom are hidden all the treasures of wisdom and knowledge.

Colossians 2.2–3

Knowledge is the action of the soul.
Ben Jonson, *Explorata: or, Discoveries*

Knowledge comes, but wisdom lingers.
Alfred, Lord Tennyson, 'Locksley Hall'

To know is not to prove, nor to explain. It is to accede to vision.
Antonio de Saint-Exupéry, *Flight to Arras*

To know yourself is to realize that you're at once unique and multiple.
Michel Quoist, *With Open Heart*

But those who know do not theorize, they merely bear witness to what they have seen and experienced.
Kathleen Raine, *Defending Ancient Springs*

Knowledge is proud that he has learn'd so much;
Wisdom is humble that he knows no more.
William Cowper, 'The Task'

To *know*, to get into the truth of anything, is ever a mystic act, – of which the best Logics can but babble on the surface.
Thomas Carlyle, *Sartor Resartus*

I see more and more that the knowledge of one human being, such as love alone can give, and the apprehension of our own private duties and relations, is worth more than all the book learning in the world.
Charles Kingsley, *Daily Thoughts*

What then can give rise to a true spirit of peace on earth? Not commandments and not practical experience. Like all human progress, the love of peace must come from knowledge. All living knowledge as opposed to academic knowledge can have but one object. This knowledge may be seen and formulated by thousands in a thousand different ways, but it must always embody one truth. It is the knowledge of the living substance in us, in each of us, in you and me, of the secret magic, the secret godliness that each of us bears within him.
Hermann Hesse, *If the War Goes on*

We do well to gather in every available fact which biology or anthropology or psychology can give us that throws light on human behaviour, or on primitive cults, or on the richer subjective and social religious functions of full-grown men. But the interior insight got from religion itself, the rich wholeness of religious experience, the discovery within us of an inner nature which defies description and baffles all plumb-lines, and which *can draw out of itself more than it contains,* indicate that we here have dealings with a type of reality which demands for adequate treatment other methods of comprehension than those available to science.

Rufus M. Jones, *Spiritual Reformers in the 16th and 17th Centuries*

The Indian mind has never been content to know 'about God'; it has always sought to know God. And here there is no separation between subject and object. To 'realize' God is to experience his presence, not in the imagination or in the intellect but in the ground of the soul from which all human faculties spring. This is the knowledge which the Upanishads were intended to impart, the knowledge of the Self, the Knower, which is the subject not the object of thought, the ground alike of being and of thought. To realize God in this way is to discover one's true self.

Bede Griffiths OSB, in Peter Spink, *The Universal Christ*

There has long been a distinction between two types of knowledge. There is the knowledge of things created, and this exerts a proper attraction on most of us. There is, more importantly, self-knowledge which, unfortunately, does not attract us nearly as much. Knowledge of that which is outside ourselves is very important and becomes a problem only when we make that the goal of our journey in life. It complements, in a very important way, self-knowledge but must be held in balance so as not to crowd out our search for the true interior of our beings. For it is deep within ourselves that the meaning of the universe is to be found.

Harry James Cargas, *Encountering Myself*

But the greatest error . . . is the mistaking or misplacing of the last or furthest end of knowledge. For men have entered into a desire of learning and knowledge, sometimes upon a natural curiosity and inquisitive appetite; sometimes to entertain their minds with variety and delight; sometimes for ornament and reputation; and sometimes to enable them to victory of wit and contradiction; and most times for lucre and profession; and seldom sincerely to give a true account of their gift of reason to the benefit and use of men: as if there were sought in knowledge a couch whereupon to rest a searching and restless spirit; or a terrace for a wandering and variable mind to walk up and down with a fair prospect; . . . and not a rich storehouse for the glory of the Creator and the relief of man's estate.

Francis Bacon, *The Advancement of Learning*

The message the mystics have for us is that while there is indeed a very real world 'out there', there is a more real world within each of us. What the meaning of this cosmic centre is, each must learn, individually. I am the living text for me and the only text. I cannot learn the lesson from what another has experienced or has written. Some can help me on the periphery, but the heart of the matter is in the heart of my soul. To ignore the truth from the Messenger is to put ourselves outside the *community of individuals* who are the true seekers, who are willing to wrestle and struggle with the difficulties that self-knowledge implies to gain the freedom and light that self-knowledge promises.

Harry James Cargas, *Encountering Myself*

**See also** Education, Listening, Meditation, Thinking, Wisdom

62

# LEADERSHIP

*Leadership – direction given by going in front, example, encouragement by doing thing*

During my time of National Service we were given some training on 'leadership' at Mons Officer Cadet School in Aldershot. Here we were given a technique for exercising leadership in the field. First of all we had to 'make an appreciation of the situation'. This enabled us to identify our aim and objective. We then considered factors to be taken into account. Having made an appreciation of the situation, identified our aim and objective, and worked out our strategy, we were now be in a position to give clear, concise orders, and take group action. We were then able to exercise effective practical leadership. Leadership is costly. Leadership skills are increasingly needed in modern society.

You should also look for able men among all the people, men who fear God, are trustworthy, and hate dishonest gain.

Exodus 18.21

. . . the greatest among you must become like the youngest, and the leader like one who serves. For who is greater, the one who is at table, or the one who serves it? Is it not the one at the table? But I am among you as one who serves.

Luke 22.26–27

A leader must have but one passion: for his work and his profession.

André Maurois, *The Art of Living*

The real leader has no need to lead – he is content to point the way.

Henry Miller, *The Wisdom of the Heart*

In the simplest terms, a leader is one who knows where he wants to go, and gets up and goes.

John Erskine, *The Complete Life*

Many leaders are in the first instance executives whose primary duty is to direct some enterprise or one of its departments or sub-units . . .

It remains true that in every leadership situation the leader has to possess enough grasp of the ways and means, the technology and processes by means of which the purposes are being realized, to give wise guidance to the directive effort *as a whole* . . .

Ordway Tead, *The Art of Leadership*

There are men, who, by their sympathetic attractions, carry nations with them, and lead the activity of the human race.

Ralph Waldo Emerson, *The Conduct of Life, Nature, and Other Essays*

He that would govern others, first should be
The master of himself.

Philip Massinger, *The Bondman*

No man is great enough or wise enough for any of us to surrender our destiny to. The only way in which any one can lead us is to restore to us the belief in our own guidance.

Henry Miller, *The Wisdom of the Heart*

In general the principle underlying success at the co-ordinative task has been found to be that *every special and different point of view in the group affected* by the major executive decisions should *be fully represented by its own exponents when decisions are being reached.* These special points of view are inevitably created by the differing outlooks which different jobs or functions inevitably foster. The more the leader can know at first hand about the technique employed by all his group, the wiser will be his grasp of all his problems . . .

Ordway Tead, *The Art of Leadership*

People think of leaders as men devoted to service, and by service they mean that these men serve their followers . . . The real leader serves truth, not people.

J.B. Yeats, *Letters to His Son, W.B. Yeats and Others*

Good leaders are aware of both their strengths and weaknesses. They are not afraid to admit to the latter. They know how to find support and are humble enough to ask for it. There is no perfect leader who has all the gifts necessary for good leadership.

Jean Vanier, *Community and Growth*

However dedicated men may be, the success of their work inevitably depends on the quality of their leaders. I am convinced that the key to leadership lies in the principle: 'He that is greatest among you, let him be as the younger and he that is chief, as he that doth serve.' Leadership should not bring privileges, but duties.

Sir John Glubb, *The Fate of Empires and Search for Survival*

We that had loved him so, followed him, honoured him,
Lived in his mild and magnificent eye,
Learned his great language, caught his clear accents,
Made him our pattern to live and to die!

Robert Browning, 'The Lost Leader'

Leaders must take great care of those who have been given responsibility in the community and who for one reason or another (health, tiredness, lack of certain qualities, etc.) cannot exercise it well. Sometimes they must be relieved of their responsibility; in other cases, the leader must be more demanding and encourage them to do better. Much wisdom is needed here.

Jean Vanier, *Community and Growth*

The leader also must recognize that his job is more demanding than the average. Strength literally goes out from him. Leading is hard work. It usually requires more average working hours than are given by others. It often requires sustained, concentrated effort; it requires occasional emergency demands which must be able to draw on physical reserves of strength and endurance. By his enthusiasm the leader makes unusual demands upon himself. Leading means a generous lavishing of energy which is abnormally taxing.

Ordway Tead, *The Art of Leadership*

A leader of his people, unsupported by any outward authority; a politician whose success rests neither upon craft nor the mastery of technical devices, but simply on the convincing power of his personality; a victorious fighter who has always scorned the use of force; a man of wisdom and humility, armed with resolve and inflexible consistency, who has devoted all his strength to the uplifting of his people and the betterment of their lot; a man who has confronted the brutality of Europe with the dignity of the simple human being, and thus at all times risen superior. Generations to come, it may be, will scarce believe that such a one as this ever in flesh and blood walked upon this earth.

Albert Einstein (written of Mahatma Gandhi), *Ideas and Opinions*

Organizations tend to put a premium upon a display of sheer activity or busyness and upon constant physical presence on the job. Yet the values which leadership peculiarly demands are not cultivated by a flurry of constant action. More thoughtfulness, more chance for meditation, for serenity, for using one's imagination, for developing one's total personal effectiveness and poise, for being more straightforwardly human with one's associates – these are required. And these values flourish where there is physical well-being. People who are going to lead have to be rested and fresh; they need time to think about the aims and the problems of their organization. And their working schedules should allow for this.

Ordway Tead, *The Art of Leadership*

**See also** Awareness, Character, Influence, Integrity, Power

# 63

# LIFE

*Life – period from birth to death, birth to the present time, or present time to death; energy, liveliness, vivacity, animation; vivifying influence, active part of existence*

At the age of twenty-four I was at the crossroads of life. I was soon to sit 'Schools' (the Oxford name for Finals) for a law degree, and make a choice of career. I thought carefully about going into the family firm of lawyers. The material rewards were promising. As I was musing over this possibility, I discerned a certain selfishness of outlook. I was thinking primarily of myself and my own comfort and security. About this time I made a spiritual commitment – to live the Christian *life* at all costs. I had just come to see the spiritual dimension as the most important thing in life. Before long an inner voice challenged my integrity: 'Come on, Bill, if living this Christian spiritual life is so important to you, shouldn't you be actively engaged in spreading it?' A vital question had been asked. Money, comfort and status were set aside as I made a bid for life itself.

– then the Lord God formed man from the dust of the ground, and breathed into his nostrils the breath of life; and the man became a living being.

Genesis 2.7

Let anyone who is thirsty come to me, and let the one who believes in me drink. As the scripture has said, 'Out of the believer's heart shall flow rivers of living water.'

John 7.38

Creative life is always on the yonder side of convention.

C.G. Jung, in Jolande Jacobi, *Psychological Reflections*

The secret of life is to be found in life itself; in the full organic, intellectual and spiritual activities of our body.

Alexis Carrel, *Reflections on Life*

Is life so wretched? Isn't it rather your hands which are too small, your vision which is muddied? You are the one who must grow up.

Dag Hammarskjöld, *Markings*

To live as fully, as completely as possible, to be happy and again to be happy is the true aim and end of life. 'Ripeness is all.'

Llewelyn Powys, *Impassioned Clay*

After all it is those who have a deep and real inner life who are best able to deal with the 'irritating details of outer life'.

Evelyn Underhill, *The Letters of Evelyn Underhill*

What makes our lives worthwhile is stretching towards God who is love and truth. That we reach out beyond our capacity is at once our pain, our adventure, our hope.

Hubert van Zeller, *Considerations*

Life, as Christianity has always taught, as all clear-eyed observers have known, is a perilous adventure, and a perilous adventure for men and nations it will, I fear and believe, remain.

W. MacNeile Dixon, *The Human Situation*

The web of our life is of a mingled yarn, good and ill together; our virtues would be proud if our faults whipp'd them not, and our crimes would despair if they were not cherish'd by our virtues.

William Shakespeare, *All's Well that Ends Well*

The true spiritual goal of life is the formation of a rightly fashioned will, the creation of a controlling personal love, the experience of a guiding inward Spirit, which keep the awakened soul steadily approximating the perfect Life which Christ has revealed.

Rufus M. Jones, *Spiritual Reformers in the 16th and 17th Centuries*

People are always blaming their circumstances for what they are. I don't believe in circumstances. The people who get on in this world are the people who get up and look for the circumstances they want, and, if they can't find them, make them.

George Bernard Shaw, *Mrs Warren's Profession*

You have striven so hard, and so long, to *compel* life. Can't you slowly change, and let life slowly drift into you. Surely it is even a greater mystery and preoccupation even than willing, to let the invisible life steal into you and slowly possess you.

D.H. Lawrence, *The Selected Letters of D.H. Lawrence*

A woman . . . recalls on one occasion when, as a girl, she complained of her hardships, and her mother, who was of pioneer stock, turned on her. 'See here,' said the mother, 'I have given you life; that is about all I will ever be able to give you – life. Now stop complaining and do something with it.'

Harry Emerson Fosdick, *On Being a Real Person*

Human life is the expression of a spiritual existence, which we know has its glory in spiritual values and in spiritual beauty. 'In the way of righteousness is life', not in the way of riches or prosperity or health or happiness, but in the way of righteousness which is revealed to be nothing else than the purity of love.

Father Andrew SDC, *The Way of Victory*

Not a May-Game is this man's life; but a battle and a march, a warfare with principalities and powers. No idle promenade through fragrant orange-groves and green flowery spaces, waited on by coral Muses and rosy Hours: it is a stern pilgrimage through burning sandy solitudes, through regions of thick-ribbed ice.

Thomas Carlyle, *Past and Present*

If you don't know what man was made for, neither do you know what man can do. You don't know the heights to which he can rise, the fullness of living of which he is capable or the happiness which can come his way. The whole thing means a tremendous difference here and now, the difference of knowing what life really can be.

R.L. Smith, 'Life Made Possible by the Gospel' in Paul Rowntree Clifford, *Man's Dilemma and God's Answer*

I want to prepare you, to organize you for life, for illness, for crisis, and death . . . Live all you can – as complete and full a life as you can find – do as much as you can for others. Read, work, enjoy – love and help as many souls – do all this. Yes – but remember: Be alone, be remote, be away from the world, be desolate. Then you will be near God.

Frederick von Hügel, *Letters to a Niece*

We come fully to life only in meeting one another . . . and because we do come fully to life in that meeting we appear to have met not only one another but also

God. We appear to have met God in one another, to have addressed God, to have been stirred with a breath of God. Yet that breath is not a breath of immortality but a breath of eternal life.

John S. Dunne, *The Reasons of the Heart*

A man contains all that is needful to his government within himself. He is made a law unto himself. All real good or evil that can befall him must be from himself . . . The purpose of life seems to be to acquaint a man with himself. He is not to live to the future as described to him, but to live to the real future by living the real present. The highest revelation is that God is in every man.

Ralph Waldo Emerson, *The Heart of Emerson's Journals*

**See also** Blessedness, Eternal Life, Fulfilment, Love, Wholeness

# 64

# LIGHT

*Light – mental illumination, elucidation, enlightenment, vivacity in a person's face, especially the eyes, illumination of the soul by divine truth*

At Bradford Cathedral we devised a special service for the feast of the Epiphany. The format consisted of lessons, carols and anthems, celebrating the manifestation of Christ (the light of the world) to the Gentiles. Once everyone was in place, all the lights were switched off and the service started in darkness – symbolic of a world without the light of Christ. Gradually as the service progressed, lights were switched on. By the end of the service the cathedral was bathed in light. As I recall there was a particular sequence in the readings. The service began with the three wise men seeking the baby Jesus – a light to lighten the Gentiles. The main focus then was on Christ 'the Light of the World'. More lights were switched on, with the words: 'You are the light of the world.' When all the lights had been switched on, we were dismissed with the words: 'Let your light shine before others, so that they may see your good works and give glory to your Father who is in heaven.' The sequence of the service mirrored my own journey of faith – of finding light through the person of Jesus Christ.

Indeed, you are my lamp, O Lord, the Lord lightens my darkness.
  2 Samuel 22.29

I am the light of the world. Whoever follows me will never walk in darkness but will have the light of life.
  John 8.12

Open your heart to the influence of the light, which, from time to time, breaks in upon you.
  Samuel Johnson, *The History of Rasselas*

Of the great world of light that lies
Behind all human destinies.
Henry Wadsworth Longfellow, 'To a Child'

A man should learn to detect and watch that gleam of light which flashes across his mind from within, more than the lustre of the firmament of bards and sages.
Ralph Waldo Emerson, *Self-Reliance*

I am aware of something in myself *whose shine is my reason.* I see clearly that something is there, but what it is I cannot understand. But it seems to me, that, if I could grasp it, I should know all truth.
Meister Eckhart, *Meister Eckhart*, translated by Raymond B. Blakney

The 'Depth of God within the Soul', the Inner Light, is the precious Pearl, the never-failing Comfort, the Panacea for all diseases, the sure Antidote even against death itself, the unfailing Guide and Way of all Wisdom.
Rufus M. Jones, *Spiritual Reformers in the 16th and 17th Centuries*

What is that light whose gentle beams now and again strike through to my heart, causing me to shudder in awe yet firing me with their warmth? I shudder to feel how different I am from it; yet in so far as I am like it, I am aglow with its fire.
St Augustine, *Confessions*

Hast never come to thee an hour,
A sudden gleam divine, precipitating, bursting all these bubbles,
fashions, wealth?
These eager business aims – books, politics, art, amours,
To utter nothingness?
Walt Whitman, 'Hast Never Come to Thee an Hour'

. . . I thought the Light of Heaven was in this world: I saw it possible, and very probable, that I was infinitely beloved of Almighty God, the delights of Paradise were round about me, Heaven and earth were open to me, all riches were little things; this one pleasure being so great that it exceeded all the joys of Eden.
Thomas Traherne, *Centuries*

And I said to the man who stood at the gate of the year:
'Give me a light that I may tread safely into the unknown.'
And he replied: 'Go out into the darkness and put your hand into
the hand of God.
That shall be to you better than light and safer than a known way.'
Louise M. Haskins, 'God Knows'

There is a light in man which shines into his darkness, reveals his condition to him, makes him aware of evil and checks him when he is in the pursuit of it; gives him a vision of righteousness, attracts him towards goodness, and points him infallibly toward Christ from whom the Light shines. The light is pure, immediate, and spiritual. It is of God, in fact it is God immanently revealed.

Rufus M. Jones, *Spiritual Reformers in the 16th and 17th Centuries*

The doctrine of Christ in every man, as the indwelling Word of God, the Light who lights every one who comes into the world, is no peculiar tenet of the Quakers, but one which runs through the whole of the Old and New Testaments, and without which they would both be unintelligible, just as the same doctrine runs through the whole history of the Early Church for the first two centuries, and is the only explanation of them.

Charles Kingsley, *Daily Thoughts*

The world may be in darkness but this should not upset us. Christ is the light of the world. If we bring this truth into the context of our own experience we must know that light inaccessible has invited us to enter into this light. He has asked us not merely to reflect it but to *be* it. Otherwise his words 'you are the light of the world, the city seated on a hill, the salt of the earth' are no more than an oratorical flourish. Jesus did not go in for oratorical flourishes.

Hubert van Zeller, *Consideratiions*

The supreme experience of his life – and one of the most remarkable instances of 'illumination' in the large literature of mystical experiences – occurred when Boehme was twenty-five years of age, some time in the year 1600. His eye fell by chance upon the surface of a polished pewter dish which reflected the bright sunlight, when suddenly he felt himself environed and penetrated by the Light of God, and admitted into the innermost ground and centre of the universe. His experience, instead of waning as he came back to normal consciousness, on the contrary deepened.

Rufus M. Jones, *Spiritual Reformers in the 16th and 17th Centuries*

Jesus said: 'He who follows me will not walk in darkness, but he will have the light of life.' The phrase *the light of life* means two things. In the Greek it can mean, either, the light which issues from the source of life, or, the light which gives life to men. In this passage it means both things. Jesus is the very light of God come among men; and Jesus is the light which gives men life. Just as the flower can never blossom when it never sees the sunlight, so our lives can never flower with the grace and beauty they ought to have until they are irradiated with the light and presence of Jesus Christ.

William Barclay, *The Gospel of John*

I do not believe that we can put into anyone ideas which are not in him already. As a rule there are in everyone all sorts of good ideas, ready like tinder. But much of this tinder catches fire, or catches it successfully, only when it meets some flame or spark from outside, i.e., from some other person. Often, too, our own light goes out, and is rekindled by some experience we go through with a fellow-man. Thus we have each of us cause to think with deep gratitude of those who have lighted the flames within us. If we had before us those who have thus been a blessing to us, and could tell them how it came about, they would be amazed to learn what had passed over from their life into ours.

Albert Schweitzer, *Memoirs of Childhood and Youth*

**See also** Beauty, Grace, Inspiration, Revelation, Vision

## 65

# LISTENING

*Listening – make effort to hear something, hear person speaking with attention; give ear to or now usually to (person or sound or story)*

I was prepared for confirmation by our school chaplain. As part of our preparation we were taught how to say our prayers. I used his method for several years, until I gradually became aware of the importance of *listening*. I realized that in my prayer-life I was doing all the talking, almost telling God what to do. If God was indeed, in some mysterious way, in the depths of my being, then perhaps I ought to be taking a humbler approach and listen to him instead of speaking. It was just possible he might have something important to say to me. So I started *listening*. At first I found it very difficult. I would sit down in my room in a comfortable chair and try to listen. Soon I would get very restless and fidgety. A breakthrough came when I took up a pen and paper, and started writing – eventually leading to keeping a spiritual diary. I now go through the contents of *The Eternal Vision*, *listening* carefully, and recording insights which come to me in times of quiet. The emerging form of *listening prayer* has become a vital source of guidance. This book can be used to encourage the practice of *listening*.

Incline your ear, and come to me; listen, so that you may live.

Isaiah 55.3

Then a cloud overshadowed them, and from the cloud there came a voice. 'This is my Son, the Beloved; listen to him!'

Mark 9.7

Give us grace to listen well.

John Keble, *The Christian Year*

Listen for the meaning beneath the words.

Anon

He [God] cannot be seen, but he can be listened to.

Martin Buber, *I and Thou*

By listening it is possible to bring a man's soul into being.

Anon, heard on the radio

Listen, my heart, to the whispers of the world with which it makes love to you.

Rabindranath Tagore, *Stray Birds*

The more faithfully you listen to the voice within you, the better you will hear what is sounding outside.

Dag Hammarskjöld, *Markings*

Difficult as it is really to listen to someone in affliction, it is just as difficult for him to know that compassion is listening to him.

Simone Weil, *Waiting on God*

Basically the answer is simple, very simple. We need only listen to what Jesus has told us. It's enough to listen to the Gospel and put into practice what it tells us.

Carlo Carretto, *Letters from the Desert*

How can you expect to keep your powers of hearing when you never want to listen? That God should have time for you, you seem to take as much for granted as that you cannot have time for Him.

Dag Hammarskjöld, *Markings*

I've become, re-become, a sceptic: with however a deepened spiritual sense, more of a Listener, a deeper sense of the possibilities of something stirring, emerging, from There Back-of-things.

Stephen MacKenna, *Journal and Letters*

Before we can hear the Divine Voice we must shut out all other voices, so that we may be able to listen, to discern its faintest whisper. The most precious messages are those which are whispered.

Mark Rutherford, *More Pages from a Journal*

If we knew how to listen to God, we should hear him speaking to us. For God does speak. He speaks in his Gospel; he speaks also through life – that new Gospel to which we ourselves add a page each day.

Michel Quoist, *Prayers of Life*

The boy Samuel was told by Heli to pray: 'Speak, Lord, for your servant listens.' He was not instructed to say: 'Listen, Lord, for your servant speaks.' If we listened more we would learn more about spirit and truth . . . and in turn would be better able to worship in spirit and in truth.

Hubert van Zeller, *Considerations*

And when, as happens more and more here, people bring their problems to me, I know that that is no compliment to my learning. It is better than that. It is a recognition on their part that I am free to listen to them, that I am open to them, that I am in some sort a free man.

Dan Billany and David Dowie, *The Cage*

Most of us in our praying, devote far less time and attention to 'waiting upon God' – to the listening side of prayer – than we devote to the incessantly active and vocal form of praying that most of us indulge in. We ought . . . to give more time to listening to God than we do to speaking to Him.

Dr Cyril H. Powell, *Secrets of Answered Prayer*

There are different kinds of listening. There is the listening of criticism; there is the listening of resentment. There is the listening of superiority; there is the listening of indifference. There is the listening of the man who only listens because for the moment he cannot get the chance to speak. The only listening that is worth while is the listening which listens and learns. There is no other way to listen to God.

William Barclay, *The Gospel of John*

If he didn't tell you what was on his mind it was because he didn't feel he could.

You think he was afraid. In a way that's true, but if he was afraid, it was because you weren't really inviting, you weren't 'empty' enough, loving enough, to receive him. Listening isn't easy! And yet, I'm fairly sure that people are overflowing with words, and in allowing them to express themselves, we allow them a measure of release, and a chance to become themselves again.

Michel Quoist, *With Open Heart*

Listening to oneself is so difficult because this art requires another ability, rare in modern man: that of being alone with oneself . . .

Listening to the feeble and indistinct voice of our conscience is difficult also because it does not speak to us directly but indirectly and because we are often not aware that it is our conscience which disturbs us. We may feel only anxious (or even sick) for a number of reasons which have no apparent connection with our conscience.

Erich Fromm, *Man for Himself*

The most difficult and decisive part of prayer is acquiring this ability to listen. Listening is no passive affair, a space when we happen not to be doing or speaking. Inactivity and superficial silence do not necessarily mean that we are in a position to listen. Listening is a conscious, willed action, requiring alertness and vigilance, by which our whole attention is focused and controlled. Listening is in this sense a difficult thing. And it is decisive because it is the beginning of our entry into a personal and unique relationship with God, in which we hear the call of our own special responsibilities for which God has intended us. Listening is the aspect of silence in which we receive the commission of God.

Mother Mary Clare SLG, *Encountering the Depths*

**See also** Awareness, Contemplation, Guidance, Meditation, Prayer

# 66

# LITERATURE

*Literature – literary culture; realm of letters, writings of country or period; writings whose value lies in beauty of form or emotional effect*

I once went on a camping holiday with my young sister on the continent. Our ultimate destination was a beach in what was then Yugoslavia but we planned to take our time over the journey, visit places of interest en route, and read as we went along. We crossed the Channel and soon got into a leisurely routine. We enjoyed a brief sojourn in Paris. In Switzerland we camped in the Lauterbrunnen valley and visited the high-altitude village of Mürren. By now we were both deeply absorbed in novels and for me Tolstoy's *Anna Karenina* was compulsive reading. Various times during the day were set aside for books. As we approached Venice we faced a mini-crisis. We had read all our books. Luck was on our side and we replenished our supplies in Venice. After a couple of days we moved on to Yugoslavia and camped near a beach. The next few days were spent sun-bathing, swimming and reading. On this holiday I discovered something of the truth of Carlyle's words: 'Literature is the Thought of thinking Souls.'

Seek and read from the book of the Lord.

Isaiah 34.16

But as for you, continue in what you have learned and firmly believed, knowing from whom you learned it, and how from childhood you have known the sacred writings that are able to instruct you for salvation through faith in Christ Jesus.

2 Timothy 3.14–15

Works of fiction are just as wholesome as anything else, if they are read wholesomely.

Henry Ward Beecher, *Proverbs from Plymouth Pulpit*

Great literature is simply language charged with meaning to the utmost possible degree.

Ezra Pound, *How to Read*

. . . something that was greater than Jefferies's books – the spirit that led Jefferies to write them.

E.M. Forster, *Howard's End*

The Bible stands alone in human literature in its elevated conception of manhood, in character and conduct.

Henry Ward Beecher, *Proverbs from Plymouth Pulpit*

Can anything be called a book unless it forces the reader by one method or another, by contrast or sympathy, to discover himself?

Norman Douglas, *An Almanac*

. . . a true work of art . . . is an analysis of experience and a synthesis of the findings into a unity that excites the reader.

Rebecca West, *Ending in Earnest*

Literature is rather an image of the spiritual world, than of the physical, is it not? – of the internal, rather than the external.

Henry Wadsworth Longfellow, *Kavanagh*

He [Shakespeare] was the man who of all Modern, and perhaps Ancient Poets, had the largest and most comprehensive soul.

John Dryden, *Essay of Dramatic Poesy*

I tell him prose and verse are alike in one thing – the best is that to which went the hardest thoughts. This also is the secret of originality, also the secret of sincerity.

J.B. Yeats, *Letters to His Son, W.B. Yeats and Others*

Those writers are to be valued above all others who lay hold of us and gently transform us into a new world, closing communication with the world in which we live.

Mark Rutherford, *Last Pages from a Journal*

Books are the treasured wealth of the world and the fit inheritance of generations and nations . . . Their authors are a natural and irresistible aristocracy in every society, and, more than kings or emperors, exert an influence on mankind!

Henry David Thoreau, *Walden*

Of all literary pleasures, the reading of a poem is the highest and purest. Only pure lyric poetry can sometimes achieve the perfection, the ideal form wholly permeated by life and feeling, that is otherwise the secret of music.

Hermann Hesse, in Volker Michels, *Reflections*

It is a marvel of literature that the most profound conceptions of the sin and guilt of mankind are the subject matters of a sacred literature more cheerful and hopeful, more invigorating and comforting, than any that has ever existed.

Henry Ward Beecher, *Proverbs from Plymouth Pulpit*

It is chiefly through books that we enjoy intercourse with superior minds, and these invaluable means of communication are in the reach of all. In the best books, great men talk to us, give us their most precious thoughts, and pour their souls into ours. God be thanked for books. They are the voices of the distant and the dead, and make us heirs of the spiritual life of past ages. Books are the true levellers. They give to all, who will faithfully use them, the society, the spiritual presence of the best and greatest of our race.

William E. Channing, *Self-Culture*

There are some books, when we close them; one or two in the course of our life, difficult as it may be to analyse or ascertain the cause: our minds seem to have made a great leap. A thousand obscure things receive light; a multitude of indefinite feelings are determined. Our intellect grasps and grapples with all subjects with a capacity, a flexibility and a vigour before unknown to us. It masters questions hitherto perplexing, which are not even touched or referred to in the volume just closed. What is this magic? It is the spirit of the supreme author, by a magnetic influence blending with our sympathising intelligence, that directs and inspires it.

Benjamin Disraeli, *Coningsby*

Just as words have two functions – information and creation – so each human mind has two personalities, one on the surface, one deeper down. The upper personality has a name. It is called S.T. Coleridge, or William Shakespeare, or Mrs Humphry Ward. It is conscious and alert, it does things like dining out, answering letters, etc., and it differs vividly and amusingly from other personalities. The lower personality is a very queer affair. In many ways it is a perfect fool, but without it there is no literature, because, unless a man dips a bucket down into it occasionally he cannot produce first-class work. There is something general about it. Although it is inside S.T. Coleridge, it cannot be labelled with his name. It has something in common with all other deeper personalities, and the mystic will assert that the common quality is God, and that here, in the obscure recesses of our being, we near the gates of the Divine . . . What is so wonderful about great literature is that it transforms the man who reads it towards the condition of the man who wrote, and brings to birth in us also the creative impulse. Lost in the beauty where he was lost, we find more than we ever threw away, we reach what seems to be our spiritual home, and remember that it was not the speaker who was in the beginning but the Word.

E.M. Forster, *Anonymity, An Enquiry*

**See also** Imagination, Revelation, Thinking, Understanding, Wisdom

# 67

# LONELINESS

*Loneliness – dejection at the consciousness of being alone; having a feeling of solitariness, dreariness*

Some years ago I went on sabbatical leave. A friend kindly lent me a farmhouse cottage in a remote hamlet on the Cumbrian fells. The nearest village was three miles away. At first I greatly enjoyed the peace and quiet, and being able to work without anyone making demands on me was a great privilege. After a few weeks a feeling of loneliness crept up on me, and I was missing people. I was feeling extremely isolated and dejected. I remember one morning bemoaning the fact I had a voice and no one to talk to, eyes and no one to look at, only scores of sheep in the surrounding fields. Loneliness is a great source of human suffering today and afflicts both young and old alike. The breakdown of society and the competitive nature of living bring about feelings of isolation difficult to combat. One antidote to loneliness is an acquisition of wholeness in which we become happy in ourselves, and learn to relate well with those around us.

Turn to me, and be gracious to me, for I am lonely and afflicted. Relieve the troubles of my heart, and bring me out of my distress.

Psalm 25.16–17

In the morning, while it was still very dark, he got up and went out to a deserted place, and there he prayed.

Mark 1.35

The quiet and exalted thoughts
Of loneliness.

William Wordsworth, 'Prelude'

Pray that your loneliness may spur you into finding something to live for, great enough to die for.

Dag Hammarskjöld, *Markings*

The deepest need of man . . . is the need to overcome his separateness, to leave the prison of his aloneness.

Erich Fromm, *The Art of Loving*

When one does give one's heart over to the loneliness of God . . . one does actually experience a transformation of loneliness into love.

John S. Dunne, *The Reasons of the Heart*

Does not all creativity ask for a certain encounter with our loneliness, and does not the fear of this encounter severely limit our possible self-expression.

Henri J.M. Nouwen, *Reaching Out*

And lifting up my eyes, I found myself
Alone, and in a land of sand and thorns.

Alfred, Lord Tennyson, 'The Holy Grail'

Loneliness is bred of a mind that has grown earthbound. For the spirit has its homeland, which is the realm of the meaning of all things.

Antoine de Saint-Exupéry, *The Wisdom of the Sands*

We are born helpless. As soon as we are fully conscious we discover loneliness. We need others physically, emotionally, intellectually; we need them if we are to know anything, even ourselves.

C.S. Lewis, *The Four Loves*

Our language has wisely sensed those two sides of man's being alone. It has created the word 'loneliness' to express the pain of being alone. And it has created the word 'solitude' to express the glory of being alone.

Paul Tillich, *The Eternal Now*

The knowledge of the ever-present Christ can reach down into the hidden depths and assure lonely modern man that he is not alone. More than that; it can draw him out of his loneliness to the rediscovery of the human race.

Stephen Neill, *The Church and Christian Union*

It is true, 'loneliness is not the sickness unto death', but when there is no passing over, no entering into the lives of others, then the longing in loneliness becomes something dark at work in our lives, something 'evil and lonely', a nightmare of soul, a 'heart of darkness'.

John S. Dunne, *The Church of the Poor Devil*

Children, adolescents, adults, and old people are in growing degree exposed to the contagious disease of loneliness in a world in which a competitive individualism tries to reconcile itself with a culture that speaks about togetherness, unity, and community as the ideals to strive for . . .

Henri J.M. Nouwen, in Robert Durback, *Seeds of Hope*

When loneliness is haunting me with its possibility of being a threshold instead of a dead end, a new creation instead of a grave, a meeting place instead of an abyss, then time loses its desperate clutch on me. Then I no longer have to live in a frenzy of activity, overwhelmed and afraid for the missed opportunity.

Henri J.M. Nouwen, *Reaching Out*

I never know what people mean when they complain of loneliness.

To be alone is one of life's greatest delights, thinking one's own thoughts, doing one's own little jobs, seeing the world beyond and feeling oneself uninterrupted in the rooted connection with the centre of all things.

D.H. Lawrence, *Loneliness*

The roots of loneliness are very deep and cannot be touched by optimistic advertisement, substitute love images, or social togetherness. They find their food in the suspicion that there is no one who cares and offers love without conditions, and no place where we can be vulnerable without being used.

Henri J.M. Nouwen, in Robert Durback, *Seeds of Hope*

We are always being told that no man is an island, but are not most of us islands? Desert islands at that. Each man has his empty shore of sand, his jungle thicket, his struggle for survival. Left to himself he deals with whatever habitation there is as best he can. But the point is that if he has faith in the presence and providence of God he is not left to himself.

Hubert van Zeller, *Considerations*

*Lonely* is not a synonym for *alone*. The word *lonely* connotes isolation and dejection, a missed absence of companions when it is applied to persons. The root of *alone*, however, is in two words: *all one*. This means the opposite of isolation and dejection. The emphasis is not on the *one* but on the *wholly one*. It means complete by oneself.

Harry James Cargas, *Encountering Myself*

Essentially loneliness is the knowledge that one's fellow human beings are incapable of understanding one's condition and therefore are incapable of bringing the help most needed. It is not a question of companionship – many are ready to offer this and companionship is certainly not to be despised – but rather one of strictly sharing, of identifying. No two human beings can manage this, so to a varying extent loneliness at times is the lot of all.

Hubert van Zeller, *Considerations*

**See also** Inner Life, Longing, Presence, Transformation, Wholeness

# 68

# LONGING

*Longing – yearn, wish vehemently, for thing to do*

Kenya is a beautiful country. On a short visit I went to Treetops, and stayed up all night to watch wild animals come to the salt lick and waterhole. After dusk the area around Treetops is spotlighted, so there is an excellent view of animals coming to seek refreshment. During the night a number of gazelles came to drink water, and I was reminded of the words of the psalmist: 'As a deer longs for flowing streams, so my soul longs for you, O God.'

This set me off thinking about longing. I recalled to mind my youth. I saw this as a time of life of intense longing – for meaning, for purpose, for companionship, for a spouse, for sporting achievement, for success, for a career, for money, for security – for God perhaps? St Augustine took me one stage further in: 'You have made us for yourself and our hearts find no peace until they rest in you.' I wonder if we have something akin to a homesickness, namely 'a God-sickness', in our longing. This I take to be a longing for the divine, best satisfied by experiencing the presence of God.

As a deer longs for flowing streams, so my soul longs for you, O God.
Psalm 42.1

For the creation waits with eager longing for the revealing of the children of God.
Romans 8.19

This longing is for the one who is felt in the dark, but not seen in the day.
Rabindranath Tagore, *Stray Birds*

In every man's bosom there is that which at times longs for something better and purer than he is.
Henry Ward Beecher, *Proverbs from Plymouth Pulpit*

> The thing we long for, that we are
> For one transcendent moment.
>
> J.R. Lowell, 'Longing'

But it [longing] is also there, playing its part in the despair and the sorrowing and the regrets and the remorse. Sadly it seems that this yearning can become misdirected into channels which lead to drugs or drink or other excesses for excitement to assuage the longing when it has not been recognized for what it is.

There are countless ways in which the longing can be expressed, by poets and painters, musicians and dancers, and by so many of those whose talent is for living and loving in awe and worship.

Perhaps the whole of life is concerned with this yearning. Nothing can be left out, but it carries us on into death and beyond when we dare hope that we shall come face to face with the source of all our longing.

Elizabeth Bassett, *The Bridge Is Love*

> None but God can satisfy the longings of an immortal soul;
> that, as the heart was made for Him, so He only, can fill it.
>
> Richard Chevenix Trench, *Notes on the Parables of Our Lord*

Men turn to prayer in the extremity of their fears, or anxieties, or helplessness before the perils of their day, and of all human existence. But they also turn to prayer because of the almost universal and unquenchable yearning they have for God, and for that fullness of life to be found in knowing, loving and serving Him.

John L. Casteel, *Rediscovering Prayer*

He found God in solitude, 'the source and reason of all joy', but he still felt, even after he had found God, an unfulfilled longing for intimacy. It was an undifferentiated longing that did not know whether it longed for God or for a human being. It was dark and unknowing like the heart of a leopard, fierce and violent like the heart of a lion, cold and unloving like the heart of a wolf.

John S. Dunne, *The Reasons of the Heart*

I once heard Professor Jung say: 'Always follow your longing and it will lead you to God, even if at the beginning it seems to turn another way.' I followed this principle with my patients and it has proved sound. If I follow a person's deepest longing, although it may seem to lead to human love, to amusement, or to other things, as we go deeper, following the thread of that longing, we come to the inner life, to the sanctuary of the Divine.

Anon

This longing, this love has, we believe, undoubtedly been implanted in us by God; and as the eye naturally demands light and vision and our body by its nature desires food and drink, so our mind cherishes a natural and appropriate longing to know God's truth and to learn the causes of things.

Now we have not received this longing from God on the condition that it should not or could not ever be satisfied; for in that case the 'love of truth' would appear to have been implanted in our mind by God the Creator to no purpose, if its gratification is never to be accomplished

Origen, in G.W. Butterworth, *Origen on First Principles*

The promise of it [of longing] is there in our love for another person. In the glory of a sunrise or sunset, the silver path of the moon on the sea, the sad haunting cry of sea-birds, the touching protective courage of a wild thing for its young or its mate. In the mountains and the streams, in the flowers and the forests, in the suffering and sorrows of mankind as well as in the joys and the laughter. This longing is all bound up with memories too, it carries its light like a will-o-the-wisp through the scents and sounds and sights which suddenly bring back to us the magical moments when we were very young and in love with life.

Elizabeth Basset, *The Bridge Is Love*

In saying: 'I know who I am' Don Quixote said: 'I know what I will be!' That is the hinge of all human life: to know what one wills to be. Little ought you to care who you are; the urgent thing is what you will to be. The being that you are is but an unstable, perishable being, which eats of the earth and which the earth some day will eat; what you will to be is the idea of you in God, the Consciousness of the universe; it is the divine idea of which you are the manifestation in time and space. And your longing impulse toward the one you will to be is only homesickness drawing toward your divine home. Man is complete and upstanding only when he would be more than man.

Miguel de Cervantes Saavedra, *The Life of Don Quixote and Sancho*

Life is a search for this 'something', a search for something or someone to give meaning to our lives, to answer the question, who am I, why am I here, what is the purpose of my life?

I believe that this great need we all feel is caused by a longing which cannot be satisfied by the usual goals we set ourselves in this journey of life. Even when they have been achieved they so often fall short of our hopes and expectations. The longed-for objective is not something which can be possessed, it cannot be held or kept, can only be fleetingly glimpsed as it comes and goes.

It can only be hinted at, referred to obliquely, indescribable in words, it can only be felt, and all we know of it is that it is what we are looking for.

Elizabeth Bassett, *The Bridge Is Love*

If there was one that I could trust and love and be so bound up with that he or she could share with me and understand my joys and my love, and my passion for beauty, for colour, for form, for pure joy in nature, – if he or she could enter into my thoughts and feel with me, – if my sorrow, my pain, my doubts, my unspoken thoughts and hopes and fancies and longings – my life and my love – if only – If I could find such a one, shouldn't I bring every joy, every delight, every pain, every sorrow, every passion, every love to be shared and to open the whole before that one: I know that I should: but there exists not the person on earth with whom lies the power of even to a small extent feeling with me in one of the smallest of my joys. Now and again one can truly say that one has felt with another, in joy or pain, in love or sorrow. But it is only now and again, and for years the heart hungers in between.

Edward Wilson, in George Seaver, *Edward Wilson of the Antarctic*

**See also** Aspiration, Eternal Life, Finding God, Love, Relationships

## 69

# LOVE

*Love – warm affection, attachment, liking, or fondness. In its deepest expression, a self-sacrificial form of love as exemplified in the life of Christ*

If we want to see 'Love' fully worked out in a life we can go to the person of Jesus Christ. At the height of his ministry he came out with his greatest command: 'You shall love the Lord your God with all your heart, and with all your soul, and with all your mind, and with all your strength . . . You shall love your neighbour as yourself.' I imagine Jesus was speaking out of his own experience. Here was someone who was prepared to love God with all his inner being: heart, soul, mind and strength. This was to be balanced with an outer love to neighbour (which included everyone in the immediate vicinity) and was further balanced by a true and genuine love of himself. In John's Gospel he confirmed the source of his love: 'As the Father has loved me, so have I loved you; abide in my love. If you keep my commandments, you will abide in my love, just as I have kept my Father's commandments and abide in his love.' The two commandments were simplified into one: 'I give you a new commandment that you love one another. Just as I have loved you, you also should love one another.' Jesus lived out this 'new commandment' to the very end.

. . . you shall love your neighbour as yourself.

Leviticus 19.18

I give you a new commandment, that you love one another. Just as I have loved you, you also should love one another.

John 13.34

Whoever lives true life, will love true love.

E R. Browning, 'Aurora Leigh'

By love may He be gotten and holden; but by thought never.
*The Cloud of Unknowing*

We are all born for love . . . It is the principle of existence and its only end.
Benjamin Disraeli, *Sybil or the Two Nations*

The great tragedy of life is not that men perish, but that they cease to love.
W. Somerset Maugham, *The Summing Up*

The highest love of all finds its fulfilment not in what it keeps, but in what it gives.
Father Andrew SDC, *Seven Words from the Cross*

You give but little when you give of your possessions.
It is when you give of yourself that you truly give.
Kahlil Gibran, *The Prophet*

The greatest thing that can happen to any human soul is to become utterly filled with love; and self-sacrifice is love's natural expression.
William Temple, *Christian Faith and Life*

For even as love crowns you so shall he crucify you. Even as he is for your growth so is he for your pruning.
Kahlil Gibran, *The Prophet*

There is no surprise more magical than the surprise of being loved; it is God's finger on man's shoulder.
Charles Morgan, *The Fountain*

We should take pains to be polite to those whom we love. Politeness preserves love, is a kind of sheath to it.
Mark Rutherford, *More Pages from a Journal*

Love it is – not conscious – that is God's regent in the human soul, because it can govern the soul as nothing else can.
Henry Ward Beecher, *Proverbs from Plymouth Pulpit*

Nothing is sweeter than love, nothing stronger, nothing higher, nothing broader; nothing is more lovely, nothing richer, nothing better in heaven or in earth.
Thomas à Kempis, *The Imitation of Christ*

Love to God is the slowest development to mature in the soul. No man ever learned to love God with all his heart, and his neighbour as himself, in a day.

Henry Ward Beecher, *Proverbs from Plymouth Pulpit*

All noble qualities feed and exalt Love. They in turn are by Love fed and exalted. Love, even as a *passion*, derives singular strength from its alliance with them.

Mark Rutherford, *Last Pages from a Journal*

When you love you should not say, 'God is in my heart', but rather, 'I am in the heart of God.' And think not you can direct the course of love, for love, if it finds you worthy, directs your course.

Kahlil Gibran, *The Prophet*

Love . . . is the supreme badge of any true Christianity, and the traits of the beatitudes in a person's life are a surer evidence that he belongs in Christ's family, than is the fact that he holds current opinions on obscure questions of belief.

Rufus M. Jones, *Spiritual Reformers in 16th and 17th Centuries*

Love is eager, sincere and kind; it is glad and lovely; it is strong, patient and faithful; wise, long-suffering and resolute; and it never seeks its own ends, for where a man seeks his own ends, he at once falls out of love.

Thomas à Kempis, *The Imitation of Christ*

Would'st thou learn thy Lord's meaning in these things? Learn it well: Love was His meaning. Who shewed it thee? Love. What shewed He thee? Love. Wherefore shewed it He? For Love. Hold thee therein and thou shalt learn and know more in the same.

Lady Julian of Norwich, *Revelations of Divine Love*

Love all God's creation, the whole of it and every grain of sand. Love every leaf, every ray of God's light! Love the animals, love the plants, love everything. If you love everything, you will perceive the divine mystery in things. And once you have perceived it, you will begin to comprehend it ceaselessly more and more every day.

Fyodor Dostoyevsky, *The Brothers Karamazov*

To make Love the ruling power of my life, the only power. To be kind, gentle, considerate and unselfish, to let nothing stand in the way of doing everyone a good turn, never to consider myself and my own feelings, but only other people's.

To put myself out to any extent for the sake of others, especially for the sake of those who are not attractive.

Edward Wilson, in George Seaver, *The Faith of Edward Wilson*

Existence will remain meaningless for you if you yourself do not penetrate into it with active love and if you do not in this way discover its meaning for yourself. Everything is waiting to be hallowed by you; it is waiting for this meaning to be disclosed and to be realized by you . . . Meet the world with the fullness of your being and you shall meet God. If you wish to believe, love!

Martin Buber, in Aubrey Hodes, *Encounter with Martin Buber*

**See also** Friendship, Longing, Marriage, Relationships, Saints

70

# MARRIAGE

*Marriage – the relation between married persons – intimate union*

A young couple came to see me for marriage preparation. At the time I prepared couples for marriage by going through the wedding service, drawing out the meaning in considerable detail. On this particular occasion we were still on the first page when a terrific row broke out between the couple. A fundamental difference had surfaced which resulted in the 'bride' storming out of the room, and their relationship was at an end. Fortunately there was a happy outcome – both married different spouses later on. As a result of this experience I changed my way of preparing couples for marriage. I now lend them a copy of about fifty quotations on my 'Marriage material' and encourage them to reflect on 'Marriage' in their own time. In this way they can share their hopes and aspirations on marriage, and develop their unique relationship. My hope is having reflected on 'Marriage' they will continue the practice of reflection on other topics and deepen and widen their relationship.

It is not good that the man should be alone; I will make a helper as his partner.
Genesis 2.18

But from the beginning of creation, 'God made them male and female.' 'For this reason a man shall leave his father and mother and be joined to his wife, and the two shall become one flesh.' So they are no longer two, but one flesh. Therefore what God has joined together, let no one separate.
Mark 10.6–9

Never marry but for love; but see that thou lovest what is lovely.
William Penn, *Fruits of Solitude*

None can be eternally united who have not died for each other.

Coventry Patmore, *The Rod, the Root and the Flower*

Being married is something that takes everything you've got.

Henry Ibsen, *The League of Youth*

Love is a glass which shatters if you hold it too tightly or too loosely.

Russian proverb

But the highest form of affection is based on full sincerity on both sides.

Thomas Hardy, *Jude the Obscure*

Love does not cause suffering: what causes it is the sense of ownership, which is love's opposite.

Antoine de Saint-Exupéry, *The Wisdom of the Sands*

Suitability helps the security of a marriage, but spirituality, by calling for mutual self-sacrifice, ensures it.

Hubert van Zeller, *Considerations*

Life has taught us that love does not consist in gazing at each other but in looking outward together in the same direction.

Antoine de Saint-Exupéry, *Wind, Sand and Stars*

It is an essential condition for the proper choice of partners that both should be on the same plane of existence.

Count Hermann Keyserling, *The Book of Marriage*

Love is a recent discovery and requires a new law. Easy divorce is the vulgar solution. The true solution is some undiscovered security for true marriage.

Coventry Patmore, *The Rod, the Root and the Flower*

Seldom, or perhaps never, does a marriage develop into an individual relationship smoothly and without crises; there is no coming to consciousness without pain.

C.G. Jung, *Contributions to Analytical Psychology*

The most precious gift that marriage gave me was this constant impact of something very close and intimate yet all the time unmistakably other, resistant – in a word, real.

C.S. Lewis, *A Grief Observed*

Unless marriage is thought of in terms of supernatural vocation even the natural side of it will be incomplete. The material and physical will outweigh the natural and spiritual.

Hubert van Zeller, *Considerations*

For the rest let him attend to his work, be glad in it, love his wife, be glad in her, bring up his children with joyfulness, love his fellow men, rejoice in life.

Søren Kierkegaard, *Training in Christianity*

If love be not thy chiefest motive, thou will soon grow weary of a married state, and stray from thy promise, to search out thy pleasures in forbidden places.

William Penn, *Fruits of Solitude*

As man is essentially a dynamic, aspiring, evolutionary being, marriage can bring fulfilment only inasmuch as it intensifies life. Wherever it causes diminution it fails in its purpose.

Count Hermann Keyserling, *The Book of Marriage*

Marriage is a terrifying responsibility. Marriage is a unique wholeness and completeness and having a best friend to confide in, to hurt, a friend who will understand, argue, fight, but still make love and be friends.

A young housewife

Love is not getting, but giving; not a wild dream of pleasure, and a madness of desire – oh, no, love is not that – it is goodness, and honour, and peace, and pure living – yes, love is that; and it is the best thing in the world, and the thing that lives longest.

Henry Van Dyke, *Little Rivers*

The fulfilment of marriage is that joy in which each lover's true being is flowering because its growth is being welcomed and unconsciously encouraged by the other in the infinite series of daily decisions which is their life together.

J. Neville Ward, *Five for Sorrow, Ten for Joy*

Affection, companionship, common interests, mutual respect and enduring devotion: these are the temporal elements in a good marriage. Temporal elements have their eternal dimension.

Hubert van Zeller, *Considerations*

The joy of going through life hand in hand with the comrade of one's choice, sharing one another's burdens, stimulating one another's courage, doubling one another's sagacity, buckling on one another's armour, wearing one another's laurels and easing one another's pain.

W.C. Willoughby, *Race Problems in the New Africa*

The essence of a good marriage is respect for each other's personality combined with that deep intimacy, physical, mental, and spiritual, which makes a serious love between man and woman the most fructifying of all human experiences. Such love, like everything else that is great and precious, demands its own morality, and frequently entails a sacrifice of the less to the greater, but such sacrifice must be voluntary, for where it is not, it will destroy the very basis of the love for the sake of which it is made.

Bertrand Russell, *Marriage and Morals*

**See also** Friendship, Kindness, Love, Relationships, Trust

# 71

# MEDITATION

*Meditation – the verb means to plan mentally, design; exercise the mind in contemplation on (upon) a subject, thinking about or reflecting on something spiritual or religious*

I began meditation at theological college. We had an official quiet time each day, before breakfast, lasting for half an hour. When the weather was fine I used to go to the nearby university parks and walk down to the river. I used sentences from the psalms such as – 'Be still and know that I am God!' – and repeated this phrase quietly to myself as I strolled around the parks. The beauty of nature added another dimension to the meditation. When the weather was bad I stayed in my room, and carried out the same exercise, seated in a chair. My practice of meditation developed slowly. I carefully searched the scriptures and noted suitable phrases for meditation. Later I made a collection of short phrases and sentences from a wide selection of sources. I then began to keep a spiritual diary or journal. With the aid of a pen and clipboard I would write out thoughts and feelings that came to the surface in meditation. My hope is others will benefit from the valuable practice of meditation.

I will meditate on your precepts, and fix my eyes on your ways.

Psalm 119.15

The good person out of the good treasure of the heart produces good . . . for it is out of the abundance of the heart that the mouth speaks.

Luke 6.45

Our duty is not primarily to strive and to brace up our wills, but primarily to fasten our attention upon the divine love, that it may do its own work upon us and within us.

William Temple, *The Preacher's Theme Today*

The art of meditation may be exercised at all hours, and in all places, and men of genius, in their walks, at table, and amidst assemblies, turning the eye of the mind upwards, can form an artificial solitude; retired amidst a crowd, calm amidst distraction, and wise amidst folly.

Isaac Disraeli, *Literary Character of Men of Genius*

A man will be effective to the degree that he is able to concentrate! Concentration is not basically a mode of *doing* but above all a mode of being.

We meditate to find, to recover, to come back to something of ourselves we once dimly and unknowingly had and have lost without knowing what it was or where or when we lost it.

Lawrence LeShan, *How to Meditate*

In meditative prayer, one thinks and speaks not only with the mind and lips, but in a certain sense with one's *whole being*. Prayer is not then just a formula of words or a series of desires springing up in the heart – it is the orientation of our whole body, mind and spirit to God in silence, attention, and adoration. All good meditative prayer is a *conversion of our entire self to God.*

Thomas Merton, *Thoughts in Solitude*

Mental prayer, by way of meditation, is very easy, even to the meanest capacities; it requires nothing but a good will, a sincere desire of conversing with God, by thinking of him, and loving him. In effect, the great business of mental prayer is *thinking* and *loving*; and who is there that can even live without *thinking* and *loving*?

Richard Challenor, in Gordon S. Wakefield, *A Dictionary of Christian Spirituality*

After having placed yourself in the presence of God, by an act of loving faith, you must read something which is substantial, and stop gently upon it; not that you may reason, but only to fix your mind, remembering that the principal exercise ought to be the [practice of the presence] of God, and that the subject should serve more to stay your mind than to employ your reason.

Madame Guyon, *A Method of Prayer*

The purpose of meditation is not to achieve an academic exercise in thinking; it is not meant to be a purely intellectual performance, nor a beautiful piece of thinking without further consequences; it is meant to be a piece of straight thinking under God's guidance and Godwards, and should lead us to draw conclusions about how to live.

Anthony Bloom, *Living Prayer*

Unless one takes time to turn inward and be silent, meditation and the spiritual quest will not get very far. We seldom find God in a hurry, or in bits and pieces of reflection on a day of busy activity. I am told that Dr Jung once remarked: 'Hurry is not *of* the Devil, it *is* the Devil.' There is simply no better way to keep ourselves out of relationship with God than by simply having no time for Him, having no time to look within in meditation.

Morton T. Kelsey, *The Other Side of Silence*

People need to discover their own self-identity. Many go to drugs, not to forget the miseries of life, but to discover its secrets, to explore an inner life of identity, liberation and happiness. The mystics tell us that this experience can be gained from some discipline of meditation, entering into silence, stilling the activity of the mind, allowing feelings and intuitions to rise from the depths of our being.

George Appleton, *Journey for a Soul*

Meditative prayer is not an intellectual exercise in which we reflect about theological propositions. In meditation we are not *thinking* about God at all, nor are we thinking of His Son, Jesus, nor of the Holy Spirit. In meditation we seek to do something immeasurably greater; we seek to *be with* God, to *be with* Jesus, to *be with* his Holy Spirit, not merely to think about them.

John Main OSB, in Clare Hallward, *The Joy of Being*

Living things need an appropriate climate in order to grow and bear fruit. If they are to develop to completion, they require an environment that allows their potential to be realized. The seed will not grow unless there is soil that can feed it, light to draw it from, warmth to nurture and moisture that unlocks its vitality. Time is also required for its growth to unfold . . .

Meditation is the attempt to provide the soul with a proper environment in which to grow and to become.

Morton T. Kelsey, *The Other Side of Silence*

Meditation is a way of liberation from all fear. Fear is the greatest impediment to fullness of life. The wonder of the vision proclaimed by Jesus is that the great power of love which dispels fear is the power that we make contact with in the depths of our own being. The power of love is the energy that sweeps all before it. What we need to understand and what we need to proclaim if we are going to proclaim the Christian message to the world is that in prayer we begin to live fully from the life force that is set free in our inmost being and that life force is love because it is God.

John Main OSB, *Moment of Christ*

Meditation is a channel for the continuous reconstitution of the self, to prepare it that it may move into the new . . . The entire nervous system and the vital processes rest as in deep sleep, while there is a condition of alert attention in the mind, a listening to the world of being. We are then open to the qualities of the Higher Self, which essentially are peace, love, gentleness, courage and joy.

While these fill the soul, there is simply no room for the negative qualities of the lower self, which include remorse, regret, disappointment, anger, resentment for things past, and fear, anxiety and doubt about the future. These negative emotions cannot enter, any more than darkness can remain in a room when we switch on the light.

George Trevelyan, *A Vision of the Aquarian Age*

One of the main purposes of meditation is to expose us to the reality of the Father in such a way that we can become the kind of people who are able to love. His life radiating through us cleanses, heals and transforms us. Then we can truly love in the way that Jesus asked of us. He did not tell us that we are His followers when we are great at meditating and religious activities, but only when we love one another as He loved us. This is the ultimate criterion of our lives, which can be fully realized only as we turn inward and open ourselves to God.

Morton T. Kelsey, *The Other Side of Silence*

**See also** Contemplation, Guidance, Listening, Revelation, Transformation

# 72

# MIND

*Mind – direction of thoughts or desires; way of thinking and feeling, seat of consciousness; thought, volition, and feeling; person as embodying mental qualities*

I was delighted with my rooms at Balliol. There were old and had a medieval feel about them. Sadly, they no longer exist. I had only been in residence a few days when I learnt they had once been occupied by a famous person – William Temple, a former Archbishop of Canterbury. Here was a man who impressed me with the sheer quality of his mind. He went on to be a lecturer in philosophy at Queen's College, Oxford, and wrote a major work, *The Creative Mind*. Later he combined his philosophy with theology, and became one of the most influential thinkers in the Church of England in recent times. 'You shall love the Lord your God . . . with all your mind'. What a challenge for us to use our minds. 'Let the same mind be in you that was in Christ Jesus'. What a command. 'Be transformed by the renewal of your minds'. What potential. The quotations which follow have been gathered from great minds of earlier generations. Reflection is a way to develop our minds on these lines.

For the human heart and mind are deep.

Psalm 64.6

You shall love the Lord your God . . . with all your mind.

Mark 12.30

But the essential thing is to put oneself in a frame of mind which is close to that of prayer.

Henri Matisse, in Françoise Gilot and Carlton Lake, *Life with Picasso*

The centre of nature is in the human mind. The meaning of the outward world is not in itself but in us.

Henry Ward Beecher, *Proverbs from Plymouth Pulpit*

The mind of man is capable of anything – because everything is in it, all the past as well as all the future.

Joseph Conrad, *Heart of Darkness*

The mind grows always by intercourse with a mind more mature than itself. That is the secret of all teaching.

William Temple, *Christian Faith and Life*

It is the mind that maketh good or ill,
That maketh wretch or happy, rich or poor.

Edmund Spenser, 'The Faerie Queene'

The Divine Mind does not think for us, or in spite of us, but works in us to think, and to will, and to do.

Henry Ward Beecher, *Proverbs from Plymouth Pulpit*

Thinkers sometimes look on doers with pity. Things are always easier and more attractive in the mind . . .

Michel Quoist, *With Open Heart*

Few of us . . . make the most of our minds. The body ceases to grow in a few years; but the mind, if we will let it, may grow almost as long as life lasts.

Sir John Lubbock, *The Pleasures of Life*

Our minds are finite, and yet even in these circumstances of finitude we are surrounded by possibilities that are infinite, and the purpose of human life is to grasp as much as we can out of that infinitude.

Alfred North Whitehead, in Lucien Price, *Dialogues of Alfred North Whitehead*

Christ presents to the mind a better, wider, deeper, and more correct theory and conception of what God is than can be derived from nature or philosophy or any of the analogies of human life or human experience.

Henry Ward Beecher, *Proverbs from Plymouth Pulpit*

The truth of things is what they are in the mind of God, and it is only when we act according to the mind of God that we are acting in accordance with the truth, in accordance with reality. Everything else is making a mistake.

William Temple, *Basic Convictions*

The life of Christ is not simply a thing written. It is a thing lived. My sanctification lies in re-living this life in the context of my own life. It lies in identifying myself with the mind of Christ which is primarily the mind of love.

Hubert van Zeller, *Considerations*

Man is distinguished from the animals by possessing, among other things, a conscious mind, with the ability to think, reason, remember, imagine, understand and express himself. He is not just mind, nor is mind just a machine that he uses. It is a vital part of man's personality but not the whole of it. It needs to be brought under the inspiration and guidance of God.

George Appleton, *Journey for a Soul*

No man is changed till his mind is changed. We do most of our living within. Our deeds express our thoughts. It is into our minds that Christ must come if He is to come into our lives. From our minds, He will shape our character, discipline our will and control our bodies.

W.E. Sangster, *The Secret of Radiant Life*

It is a hard thing for a man to take such an instrument as the human mind and keep it in tune with itself, and also keep it in accord with other minds, with their different temperaments, and in all their varying moods, and under all their trials and swayings, and warpings and biasings.

Henry Ward Beecher, *Proverbs from Plymouth Pulpit*

There is a certain paradox in the human situation. God gave man a mind, and it is man's duty to use that mind to think to the very limits of human thought. But it is also true that there are times when that mind can only go so far, and, when that limit is reached, all that is left is to accept and to adore.

William Barclay, *The Letter to the Romans*

This is a plea for the use of the whole mind, intellectual and emotional, detached and involved; for only when the whole mind is alive can imagination work and creatively operate. And the trouble is that so many institutions formally connected with education and with morality behave as if they had, at best, only half a mind.

Roy Stevens, *Education and the Death of Love*

The mind of man is meant to be a microcosm of the mind of God. This was shown supremely, in terms of a human life, in Jesus Christ. We therefore need to study the records of that divine and human life, recognizing the faith of the writers but reaching back as far as possible to the life itself. Also, by communion with the ever-living, ever-present Christ, we can experience direct, intuitive contact and illumination.

George Appleton, *Journey for a Soul*

**See also** Intellect, Knowledge, Thinking, Truth, Wisdom

# 73

# MONEY

*Money – current coin; property viewed as convertible into money; coin in reference to its purchasing power*

I remember reading a book – *Miracle on the River Kwai*. This book was a grim account of life in a prisoner of war camp in the Second World War. When POWs were dying (of wounds, fever, dysentery, malnutrition and the like) they were moved to a special hut and left to die. There were hardly any survivors. A Scottish minister, the author of the book, rounded up some able-bodied men and began to care for the sick and the dying. With the help of prayer, nursing and friendship, lives were saved. For those caught up in this healing work this was the *Miracle on the River Kwai*. The author, encouraged by what he had experienced, went home at the end of the war with high hopes for the future. Soon, however, he saw a return to the conditions which had existed before the war. He came to see men were separated by *economic competition*. He recognized the love of money was indeed a root of all evil. Is this still true today?

The lover of money will not be satisfied with money; nor the lover of wealth, with gain. This also is vanity.

Ecclesiastes 5.10

But those who want to be rich fall into temptation and are trapped by many senseless and harmful desires that plunge people into ruin and destruction. For the love of money is a root of all kinds of evil, and in their eagerness to be rich some have wandered away from the faith and pierced themselves with many pains.

1 Timothy 6.9–10

To have money is a fear, not to have it a grief.
George Herbert, *Outlandish Proverbs*

Great Wealth and Content seldom live together.
Thomas Fuller, *Gnomologia*

The dangers gather as the treasures rise.
Samuel Johnson, *The Vanity of Human Wishes*

He who multiplies Riches multiplies Cares.
Benjamin Franklin, *Poor Richard's Almanack*

Riches are gotten with pain, kept with care, and lost with grief.
Thomas Fuller, *Gnomologia*

Money – money, like everything else – is a deception and a disappointment.
H.G. Wells, *Kipps*

There is nothing that makes men rich and strong but that which they carry inside of them.
Henry Ward Beecher, *Proverbs from Plymouth Pulpit*

Is there no prosperity other than commercial? It is surely time to have done with this utilitarian nonsense.
Norman Douglas, *An Almanac*

Ill fares the land, to hastening ills a prey,
Where wealth accumulates, and men decay.
Oliver Goldsmith, 'The Deserted Village'

The commerce of the world is conducted by the strong; and usually it operates against the weak.
Henry Ward Beecher, *Proverbs from Plymouth Pulpit*

Whenever money is the principal object of life with either man or nation, it is both got ill, and spent ill; and does harm both in the getting and spending.
John Ruskin, *The Crown of Wild Olives*

We can hardly respect money enough for the blood and toil it represents. Money is frightening. It can serve or destroy man.
Michel Quoist, *Prayers of Life*

Money is human happiness in the abstract: he, then, who is no longer capable of enjoying human happiness in the concrete devotes himself utterly to money.

Arthur Schopenhauer, in W.H. Auden, *A Certain World*

We are prone to judge success by the index of our salaries or the size of our automobiles, rather than by the quality of our service and our relationship to humanity.

Martin Luther King, in Coretta Scott King, *The Words of Martin Luther King*

. . . money-getting men, men that spend all their time first in getting, and next in anxious care to keep it; men that are condemned to be rich, and then always busy or discontented.

Izaak Walton, *The Compleat Angler*

I saw that . . . where the heart was set on greatness, success in business did not satisfy the craving; but that commonly with an increase of wealth, the desire of wealth increased.

John Woolman, *The Journal of John Woolman*

Strong as is money and invincible, yet, in the long run, ideas are mightier than money. Tyrannies are overthrown by ideas. Armies are defeated by ideas. Nations, and Time itself, are overmatched by ideas.

Henry Ward Beecher, *Proverbs from Plymouth Pulpit*

Riches are a slow poison, which strikes almost imperceptibly, paralyzing the soul at the moment when it seems healthiest. They are thorns which grow with the grain and suffocate it right at the moment when corn is beginning to shoot up.

Carlo Carretto, *Letters from the Desert*

For forty years he had fought against economic fatality. It was the central ill of humanity, the cancer which was eating into its entrails. It was there that one must operate; the rest of the healing process would follow.

Arthur Koestler, *Darkness at Noon*

Money as money is not evil. It speeds on errands of mercy, and lends itself to a thousand philanthropies. It feeds the hungry, clothes the naked, and succours men who are tempted to suicide. It is the insensate love of riches which is the perilous thing.

W.E. Sangster, *He Is Able*

The two things which, of all others, most want to be under a strict rule, and which are the greatest blessings both to ourselves and others, when they are rightly used, are our time and our money. These talents are continual means and opportunities of doing good.

William Law, *A Serious Call to a Devout and Holy Life*

We have not driven home upon men His clear intuition that though, if wealth comes, it ought to be accepted and used as an opportunity, yet it must be recognized as rather a snare to the spiritual life than an aim which the Christian may legitimately set before himself to pursue.

William Temple, *Christian Faith and Life*

**See also** Happiness, Freedom, Pride, Temptation, Worldliness

# 74

# MORALS

*Morals – concerned with the distinction between right and wrong*

I have tried to work out why I behave the way I do. Looking back, I am aware of several strands which have influenced me in my behaviour. First of all, there is home, and the upbringing of one's parents. Second, there is school, and for me, National Service and going to university. In these institutions I reached important stages of life – working out my own values – and conscious of coming into being as a person in my own right. Third, there has been the influence of the media. However, the most important influence for me has been an evolving Christian faith. As a foundation there is the Bible and the person of Jesus Christ. Then there are the findings of theology, broadly construed, and the tradition of the church down the ages. An important influence here has been the recorded experience of the saints over the last two thousand years, still being collected, and the object of reflection. And lastly there is conscience, in constant need of education for fresh truth. And dare one end this section without mentioning the influence of 'grace' and the Holy Spirit?

Do what is right and good in the sight of the Lord, so that it may go well with you . . .

Deuteronomy 6.18

Blessed are those who hunger and thirst after righteousness, for they will be filled.

Matthew 5.6

Men are great in proportion as they are moral.

Henry David Thoreau, *The Journal of Henry D. Thoreau*

Morality is often grace working out into a noble life-form.

Henry Ward Beecher, *Proverbs from Plymouth Pulpit*

Morality, when vigorously alive, sees farther than intellect.
J.A. Froude, *Short Stories on Great Subjects*

Conduct is three-fourths of our life and its largest concern.
Matthew Arnold, *Literature and Dogma*

If your morals make you dreary, depend upon it they are wrong.
Robert Louis Stevenson, *Across the Plains*

Half at least of all morality is negative and consists in keeping out of mischief.
Aldous Huxley, *The Doors of Perception*

A right moralist is a great and good man; but, for that reason, he is rarely to be found.
William Penn, *Fruits of Solitude*

Morality without spirituality has no roots. It becomes a thing of custom, transient, and optional.
Henry Ward Beecher, *Proverbs from Plymouth Pulpit*

Without civic morality communities perish; without personal morality their survival has no value.
Bertrand Russell, *Authority and the Individual*

His [Jesus'] system of morality was the most benevolent and sublime probably that has been ever taught.
Thomas Jefferson, *The Writings of Thomas Jefferson*

The moral man is he that loves God above all, and his neighbour as himself: which fulfils both tables at once.
William Penn, *Fruits of Solitude*

The whole spectrum about morality is an effort to find a way of living which men who live it will instinctively feel is good.
Walter Lippman, *A Preface to Politics*

So far, about morals, I know only that what is moral is what you feel good after and what is immoral is what you feel bad after . . .
Ernest Hemingway, *Death in the Afternoon*

The ultimate foundation for morality is that immorality doesn't work, it doesn't pay off. It doesn't lighten the burden of living. It increases it.

Norman Vincent Peale, *Man, Morals and Maturity*

The Christian moral standard is, after all, not a code which has to be defended against the attacks of a forward generation: it is an insight to be achieved.

F.R. Barry, *The Relevance of Christianity*

The real immorality, as far as I can see it
Lies in forcing yourself or somebody else
Against all your deeper instincts and your intuition.

D.H. Lawrence, 'Immorality'

Jesus Christ takes as man a place alike in the realms of ethics and of faith. He gives to us the moral standard of life, the ethical ideal; He discloses the culminating power of the religious consciousness, for He is, in the deep harmony of his relationship with God, the mystic ideal also.

William Boyd Carpenter, *The Witness to the Influence of Christ*

The great secret of morals is love; or a going out of our own nature, and an identification of ourselves with the beautiful which exists in thought, action, or person, not our own. A man, to be greatly good, must imagine intensely and comprehensively; he must put himself in the place of another and of many others; the pains and pleasures of his species must become his own.

Percy Bysshe Shelley, *A Defence of Poetry*

We can offer this summary of moral obligation: Your being is personal; live as a person in fellow-membership with all others who, being personal, are your fellow-members in the community of persons. Strive to grow in fullness of personality, in width and depth of fellowship; and seek to draw the energy for this from that to which you and all things owe their origin, the Personal Love which is Creator and Sustainer of the world.

William Temple, *Nature, Man and God*

The standard of morals is the mind of Christ; that is our great principle if we are Christian. It will not help you at once to solve each particular problem; it will give you a touchstone. As you seek to live in the constant companionship of Christ, you will find yourself knowing ever more fully what your duty is in accordance with His mind. Your moral authority is not a principle, but a Person. It is the mind of Christ.

William Temple, *Christian Faith and Life*

The things that will destroy us are:
Politics without principle;
Pleasure without conscience;
Wealth without work;
Knowledge without character;
Business without morality;
Science without humanity;
and Worship without sacrifice.
Anon

**See also** Awareness, Life, Neighbour, Relationships, Selfishness

## 75

# MUSIC

*Music – art of combining sounds with a view to beauty of form and expression of emotion; sounds so produced*

I wonder if in *music* we can see another variant and consequence of what it means to be made in the image and likeness of God, and of the divine inbreathing. A seed or a spark of the divine is planted in the depths of our being. Some people, with a sensitive and intuitive ear for sound, might experience this as music. Take, for instance, a composer such as Beethoven. In the depths of the night, or out for a walk in the forest he becomes aware of a tune or harmony. Slowly a symphony takes form. Later a conductor comes along with an orchestra (whose members are also made in the image and likeness of God) and they put on a concert. The audience, with a feel for music, enjoy the performance. Dare we say – that something akin to a divine performance has taken place? It is no accident that music plays such an important part in worship in a church. But why restrict it to a church building? Music is everywhere.

It is good to give thanks to the Lord, to sing praises to your name, O Most High; to declare your steadfast love in the morning, and your faithfulness by night, to the music of the lute and the harp, to the melody of the lyre.

Psalm 92.1–3

. . . but be filled with the Spirit, as you sing psalms and hymns and spiritual songs among yourselves, singing and making melody to the Lord in your hearts.

Ephesians 5.18–19

Organ playing . . . is the manifestation of a will fitted with a vision of eternity.

C.M. Widor, in Charles R. Joy, *Music in the Life of Albert Schweitzer*

Who hears music, feels his solitude
People at once.

Robert Browning, 'Balaustion's Adventure'

The soul continues as an instrument of God's harmony, a tuned instrument of divine joy for the Spirit to strike on.

William Law, in Stephen Hobhouse, *Selected Mystical Writings of William Law*

See deep enough, and you see musically; the heart of Nature *being* everywhere music, if you can only reach it.

Thomas Carlyle, *Sartor Resartus*

. . . music is a higher revelation than all wisdom and philosophy, the wine which inspires one to new generative processes.

Ludwig von Beethoven in *Thayer's Life of Beethoven*

The language of tones belongs equally to all men, and that melody is the absolute language in which a musician addresses every heart.

Richard Wagner, *Beethoven*

God makes every man happy who knows how to play upon himself. Every man is full music; but it is not every man who knows how to bring it out.

Henry Ward Beecher, *Proverbs from Plymouth Pulpit*

When music sounds, gone is the earth I know,
And all her lovely things even lovelier grow.

Walter de la Mare, 'Music'

There was no instrument that was ever struck that has such music as every faculty of the human soul has in it. God never makes anything else so beautiful as man.

Henry Ward Beecher, *Proverbs from Plymouth Pulpit*

Who is there that, in logical words, can express the effect music has on us? A kind of inarticulate unfathomable speech, which leads us to the edge of the Infinite, and lets us for moments gaze into that!

Thomas Carlyle, *Sartor Resartus*

For even that vulgar and Taverne Musicke, which makes one merry, another mad, strikes me into a deepe fit of devotion, and a profound contemplation of the first Composer; there is something in it of Divinity more than the eare discovers.

Sir Thomas Browne, *Religio Medici*

I lost myself in a Schubert Quartet at the end of a Crowndale Road concert, partly by ceasing all striving to understand the music, partly by driving off intruding thoughts, partly feeling the music coming up inside me, myself a hollow vessel filled with sound.

Joanna Field, *A Life of One's Own*

[Music] is a principal means of glorifying our merciful Creator, it heightens our devotion, it gives delight and ease to our travails, it expelleth sadness and heaviness of spirit, preserveth people in concord and amity, allayeth fierceness and anger; and lastly, is the best physic for many melancholy diseases.

Henry Peacham, *The Compleat Gentleman*

Musical training is a more potent instrument than any other, because rhythm and harmony find their way into the secret places of the soul, on which they mightily fasten, imparting grace, and making the soul graceful of him who is rightly educated, or ungraceful of him who is ill-educated.

Plato, *The Republic of Plato*

. . . I came gradually to see that music and poetry were perhaps closer kin than I had at first realized. I came gradually to see that beyond the music of both arts there is an essence that joins them – an area where the meanings behind the notes and the meaning beyond the words spring from some common source.

Aaron Copeland, *Music and Imagination*

For his part, Henri Bergson was interested in Casals' subjective reactions to music – what did he feel when he was playing the music of Bach or Beethoven? Casals tried to explain that if he was satisfied after a good performance . . . he had a special feeling, an almost physical sensation that could be likened to carrying inside himself a weight of gold.

H.L. Kirk, *Pablo Casals. A Biography*

Now, what is music? This question occupied me for hours before I fell asleep last night. Music is a strange thing. I would almost say it is a miracle. For it stands halfway between thought and phenomenon, between spirit and matter, a sort of nebulous mediator, like and unlike each of the things it mediates – spirit that requires manifestation in time, and matter that can do without space. We do not know what music is.

Heinrich Heine, in Jacques Barzun, *Pleasures of Music*

A patient once said to S., 'I sometimes have the feeling that God is right inside me, for instance when I hear the St Matthew Passion.' And S. said something like: 'At such moments you are completely at one with the creative and cosmic forces that are at work in every human being.' And these creative forces are ultimately part of God, but you need courage to put that into words.

Etty Hillesum, *A Diary, 1941–43*

**See also** Art, Beauty, Literature, Poetry, Wonder

# 76

# MYSTICS

*Mystics, mysticism – a type of religion which puts the emphasis on immediate awareness of relation with God, on direct and immediate awareness of divine presence; religion in its most acute, intense and living stage*

I like this definition of mystics and mysticism. The words have given me an insight into the character and personality of Jesus Christ. I now feel to be in a much better position to understand his life and work. The same applies to St Paul. Many people down the ages have spoken of an immediate awareness of relation with God. In prayer and contemplation they found rich resources of divine life welling up in themselves. The great mystical poets George Herbert and John Donne found their inspiration in a direct and immediate consciousness of the divine. The composer, Ralph Vaughan Williams, was influenced by the mystics and mysticism. The artist Fra Angelico used to meditate before painting, and attributed his genius to a divine source. According to our definition, mysticism is religion in its most acute, intense and living stage. Long ago, Henri Frédéric Amiel claimed we had lost the mystical sense. Perhaps this helps us to understand why today the church is struggling in our day and age. A rediscovery of mysticism might well bring about a much-needed regeneration.

Now there was a great wind, so strong that it was splitting the mountains and breaking rocks in pieces before the Lord, but the Lord was not in the wind; and after the wind an earthquake, but the Lord was not in the earthquake; and after the earthquake a fire, but the Lord was not in the fire; and after the fire a sound of sheer silence.

1 Kings 19.11–12

I became its servant according to God's commission that was given to me for you, to make the word of God fully known, the mystery that has been hidden throughout the ages and generations but has now been revealed to his saints.

Colossians 1.25–26

We have lost the mystical sense, and what is religion without mysticism?

Henri Frédéric Amiel, *Amiel's Journal*

The ultimate gift of conscious life is a sense of the mystery that encompasses it.

Lewis Mumford, *The Conduct of Life*

... mysticism is wisdom and knowledge that is found through love; it is loving knowledge.

William Johnston, *The Inner Eye of Love*

For the mystics, the great aim of all religious experience is the vision of God and union with him.

William Barclay, *The Letters to the Corinthians*

The mystics are not only themselves an incarnation of beauty, but they reflect beauty on all who with understanding approach them.

Havelock Ellis, *Selected Essays*

'Mysticism' ... the simple childlike intercourse of the believing soul with God, by no effort of the mind, but by the working of the Holy Spirit.

Gerhard Tersteegen, in Frances Bevan, *Sketches of the Quiet in the Land*

... by love, by the willing loss of self, we realize our true nature and become partakers in the being of God. The ego may be said to represent a stage in a spiritual process. By breaking out of its shell we can be born again, into a boundless freedom. That is the doctrine implied in all mystical philosophy.

Gerald Bullett, *The English Mystics*

Other faiths have their mystics but only in Jesus, I believe, can we find such spontaneous and personal communion with God combined with such a passionate ethical concern for humanity. Both awareness of God and awareness of the world attain their zenith in him.

John V. Taylor, *The Go-Between God*

The typical mystic is the person who has a certain first-hand experience and knowledge of God through Love; and the literature of mysticism tells us, or tries to tell us, what the finite human spirit has come to know through love of the relation between the little half-made spirit of man and the Infinite Spirit of God.

Evelyn Underhill, in John Stobbart, *The Wisdom of Evelyn Underhill*

The highest thought . . . is ineffable; it must be felt from one person to another but cannot be articulated. All the most essential and thinking part of thought is done without words. It is not till doubt and consciousness enter that words become possible. Our profoundest and most important convictions are unspeakable.

Samuel Butler, in Gerald Bullett, *The English Mystics*

The problem of mysticism is to endow the mind and will of man with a supernatural experience of God as He is in Himself and, ultimately, to transform a human soul into God by a union of love. This is something that no human agency can perform or merit or even conceive by itself. This work can be done only by the direct intervention of God.

Thomas Merton, *The Waters of Silence*

'In the time of the philosophers,' he [Al-Ghazzali] writes, 'as at every period, there existed some of these fervent mystics. God does not deprive this world of them, for they are its sustainers.' It is they who, dying to themselves, become capable of perpetual inspiration and so are made the instruments through which divine grace is mediated to those whose unregenerated nature is impervious to the delicate touches of the Spirit.

Aldous Huxley, *The Perennial Philosophy*

That which makes Christian mysticism so rich, deep, life-giving, and beautiful is the Christian doctrine of the nature and action of God. It is different because it is based upon the Incarnation, the redemptive self-giving of the Eternal Charity. The Christian mystic tries to continue in his own life Christ's balanced life of ceaseless communion with the Father and the lonely service to the crowd.

Evelyn Underhill, in John Stobbart, *The Wisdom of Evelyn Underhill*

It is a central idea of mysticism that there is a way to God through the human soul. The gate to Heaven is thus kept, not by St Peter or by any other saint of the calendar; it is kept by each individual person himself as he opens or closes within himself the spiritual circuit of connection with God. The door into the Eternal swings within the circle of our own inner life, and all things are ours if we learn how to use the key that opens, for 'to open' and 'to find God' are one and the same thing.

Rufus M. Jones, *Spiritual Reformers in the 16th and 17th Centuries*

The most beautiful and most profound emotion we can experience is the sensation of the mystical. It is the sower of all true science. He to whom this emotion is a stranger, who can no longer wonder and stand wrapt in awe, is as good as dead. To know that what is impenetrable to us really exists, manifesting itself as the highest wisdom and the most radiant beauty which our dull faculties can comprehend only in their most primitive forms – this knowledge, this feeling is at the centre of true religiousness.

Albert Einstein, in Lincoln Barnett, *The Universe and Dr Einstein*

Mysticism keeps men sane. As long as you have mystery you have health; when you destroy mystery you create morbidity. The ordinary man has always been sane because the ordinary man has always been a mystic. He has permitted the twilight. He has always had one foot in earth and the other in fairyland. He has always left himself free to doubt his gods; but (unlike the agnostic of to-day) free also to believe in them. He has always cared more for truth than for consistency. If he saw two truths that seemed to contradict each other, he would take the two truths and the contradiction along with them.

G.K. Chesterton, *Orthodoxy*

**See also** Divinity, Holiness, Holy Spirit, Inner Life, Saints

# 77

# NEIGHBOUR

*Neighbour – dweller in the same street or district, or one having claims on others' friendliness*

Somewhere I have come across a description of a neighbour as 'anyone close by in need'. Within half an hour of being ordained there was a knock on the clergy house door, and there was a young woman with a baby in her lap, 'close by in need' – of money and food.

This was the start of coming close to hundreds of people in need during the last thirty-seven years of ministry. Some have been destitute men and women in need of food and sustenance. Others have been sick, physically, mentally and spiritually, in need of healing. Another group have been the elderly and the infirm, in need of care. I also have taken on individuals with special needs. I remember trying to help a young 'drop-out' over a three-year period, and he was followed by another man, with serious psychological problems, whom I saw regularly for fifteen years. As a college chaplain I have been confronted by almost every student problem imaginable. Being resident in college means being exposed and vulnerable throughout a term to neighbours – i.e. 'anyone close by in need'.

Do not plan harm against your neighbour who lives trustingly beside you.
Proverbs 3.29

In everything do to others as you would have them do to you; for this is the law and the prophets.
Matthew 7.12

You cannot love a fellow-creature fully till you love God.
C.S. Lewis, *The Great Divorce*

All is well with him, who is beloved of his neighbours.
George Herbert, *Outlandish Proverbs*

The love of our neighbour is the only door out of the dungeon of self.

George Macdonald, *Unspoken Sermons*

We are made *one for another*; and each is to be a Supply to his Neighbour.

Benjamin Whichcote, *Morals and Religious Aphorisms*

Those who are all things to their neighbours cease to be anything to themselves.

Norman Douglas, *An Almanac*

The good neighbour looks beyond the external accidents and discerns those inner qualities that make all men human, and therefore, brothers.

Martin Luther King, *Strength to Love*

We cannot be sure if we are loving God, although we may have good reasons for believing that we are, but we can know quite well if we are loving our neighbour.

St Teresa of Avila, *Interior Castle*

Each man can learn something from his neighbour; at least he can learn this – to have patience with his neighbour, to live and let live.

Charles Kingsley, *Daily Thoughts*

A man must not choose his neighbour; he must take the neighbour that God sends him . . . The neighbour is just the man who is next to you at the moment, the man with whom any business has brought you into contact.

George Macdonald, *Unspoken Sermons*

But it is His long-term policy, I fear, to restore to them a new kind of self-love – a charity and gratitude for all selves, including their own; when they have really learned to love their neighbours as themselves, they will be allowed to love themselves as their neighbours.

C.S. Lewis, *The Screwtape Letters*

Jesus, however, is not interested in universal, theoretical or poetical love . . . It is a love, not of man in general, of someone remote, with whom we are not personally involved, but quite concretely love of one's immediate neighbour . . . *anyone who wants me here and now.*

Hans Küng, *On Being a Christian*

We must . . . not mix ourselves up uninvited in other people's business. On the other hand we must not forget the danger lurking in the reserve which our practical daily life forces upon us. We cannot possibly let ourselves get frozen into regarding everyone we do not know as an absolute stranger.

Albert Schweitzer, *Memoirs of Childhood and Youth*

The ultimate measure of a man is not where he stands in moments of comfort and convenience, but where he stands at times of challenge and controversy. The true neighbour will risk his position, his prestige, and even his life for the welfare of others. In dangerous valleys and hazardous pathways, he will lift some bruised and beaten brother to a higher and more noble life.

Martin Luther King, in Coretta Scott King, *The Words of Martin Luther King*

Strive to love your neighbours actively and indefatigably. And the nearer you come to achieving this love, the more convinced you will become of the existence of God and the immortality of your soul. If you reach the point of complete selflessness in your love of your neighbours, you will most certainly regain your faith and no doubt can possibly enter your soul. This has been proved. This is certain.

Fyodor Dostoyevsky, *The Brothers Karamozov*

The remarkable thing is that we really love our neighbour as ourselves: we do unto others as we do unto ourselves. We hate others when we hate ourselves. We are tolerant towards others when we tolerate ourselves. We forgive others when we forgive ourselves. We are prone to sacrifice others when we are ready to sacrifice ourselves.

It is not love of self but hatred of self which is at the root of all the troubles that afflict the world.

Eric Hoffer, *The Passionate State of Mind*

True neighbourliness must begin within our own psychological attitudes. I must accept my neighbour for what he is, I must let him be himself, respect his 'isness' and self-understanding. I must not impose my pattern on him or exploit him for my own purposes. I must be interested in him as a person, so that our relationship will encourage mutual development in maturity. I must be ready to take initiatives, to engage in adventures of understanding and friendship.

George Appleton, *Journey for a Soul*

Today there is an inescapable duty to make ourselves the neighbour of every man, no matter who he is, and if we meet him, to come to his aid in a positive way, whether he is an aged person abandoned by all, a foreign worker despised without reason, a refugee, an illegitimate child wrongly suffering for a sin he did not commit, or a starving human being who awakens our conscience by calling to mind the words of Christ: 'As you did it to one of the least of these my brothers, you did it to me' (Mt 25.40).

Vatican Council II, *The Conciliar and Post Conciliar Documents*

**See also** Friendship, Image of God, Other Faiths, Relationships, Self

# 78

# OBEDIENCE

*Obedience – obeying the will of God; doing God's will rather than doing one's own*

One of the authors who has helped me to understand 'obedience' is Victor Gollancz. In an excerpt in *From Darkness to Light* he wrote: 'I dislike talk about obeying God, as if he were some Stalin or Hitler; I cannot think that he wants me to obey him; what he wants, I think, is that I should learn to cooperate, quietly and in complete freedom, with his blessed and blessing will, that will of his which I discover deep in my own heart as my will also – as the best, essential me – and which, discovering it also deep in the heart of everything else, I find to be not only vaster, but also saner and more fruitful of life and peace and joy, than the self-regarding wilfulness that would deceive me with its appearance of leading me to my goal, but would in fact cut me off, if it had its way, from my birthright of unity with all things.' I have quoted this almost verbatim as it coincides with what I have experienced. I don't think God wants me to obey him as some Stalin or Hitler – but prefers quiet cooperation.

Teach me your way, O Lord.
Psalm 27.11

Everyone then who hears these words of mine and acts on them will be like a wise man who built his house on rock. The rain fell, the floods came, and the winds blew and beat on that house, but it did not fall, because it had been founded on rock.
Matthew 7.24–25

Obedience is the key to every door.
George Macdonald, *The Marquis of Lossie*

If within us we find nothing over us we succumb to what is around us.

P.T. Forsyth, *Positive Preaching and the Modern Mind*

The 'obedience' of Jesus is not simply submission, but real striving, cooperation, activity.

John J. Vincent, *Secular Christ*

God does not desire that we should abound in spiritual lights, but that in all things we should submit to His will.

Henry Suso, in St Alphonus de Liguori, *On Conformity with the Will of God*

Had he done as the Master told him, he would soon have come to understand. Obedience is the opener of eyes.

George Macdonald, *Unspoken Sermons*

Men should find their hearts with a sense of fidelity, of generosity, and of obedience to God, and then let God take care of the result.

Henry Ward Beecher, *Proverbs from Plymouth Pulpit*

We can only have power if we are obedient. If we are disobedient, all power falls from us, because we are living in our own strength, in our own way.

Father Andrew SDC, *A Gift of Light*

. . . there are various paths to Christian obedience. The essential point, however, is that this obedience can only be measured by its commitment to the world.

Paul Oestreicher, in Hans Jürgen Schultz, *Conversion to the World*

There is but one single faculty in the whole roll of the soul's faculties to which every one in the nature of man consents to be obedient. This is the faculty of LOVE.

Henry Ward Beecher, *Proverbs from Plymouth Pulpit*

If a man does not keep pace with his companions, perhaps it is because he hears a different drummer. Let him step to the music which he hears, however measured or far away.

Henry David Thoreau, *Walden*

In practical terms obedience is in line with the very root of the word which suggests 'listening to' – listening to the will of God by listening *to* each other and listening *with* each other to its varied manifestations.

Sister Madeleine OSA, *Solitary Refinement*

'If,' said a Celtic saint of the ninth century, 'If a man does his own will he walks with a shadow on the heart, but if with Christ's power in thee, thou doest God's will, thou shalt walk in a circle of light.'

Alistair MacLean, *The Quiet Heart*

So many people need to learn that Obedience must often come before Faith; that it is by going on patiently obeying the commandments of God and the teaching of Christ that faith will come to them; that faith is neither something to which they are entitled nor something which is either given or withheld, but something which has to be earned by a life of discipline and obedience. It is really no good saying: 'I find it so difficult to believe' when we are doing little or nothing to build up faith by using the means of grace which God has provided for us and by bringing our lives under the control of his will.

J.R.H. Moorman, *The Path to Glory*

Jesus lays hold on the individual and summons him to *obedience to God,* who is to embrace his whole life. These are simple, transparent, liberating appeals, dispensing with arguments from authority or tradition but providing examples, signs, tokens, for transforming one's life.

Hans Küng, *On Being a Christian*

Obedience is a complicated act of virtue, and many graces are exercised in one act of obedience. It is an act of humility, of mortification and self-denial, of charity to God, of care of the public, of order and charity to ourselves and all our society, and a great instance of a victory over the most refractory and unruly passions.

Jeremy Taylor, *Holy Living*

God . . . lays claim not to half the will, but the whole. He demands not only external acts which can be observed and controlled, but also internal responses which cannot be controlled or checked. He demands man's heart. He wants not only good fruits, but the good tree: not only action but being; not something, but myself – and myself wholly and entirely.

Hans Küng, *On Being a Christian*

We have no code of rules that can only be obeyed in the circumstances of their origin, no scheme of thought which can only be understood in the terms in which it was first conceived, but a Person to whom we can be loyal in all circumstances whatever, with that infinite flexibility and delicacy of adjustment which are compatible with a loyalty that remains absolute and unalterable.

William Temple, *Thoughts on Some Problems of the Day*

And if we are to practise obedience we can scarcely do better than begin with the three commands which Jesus gave to Peter in the boat. 'Thrust out a little from the land'; do not allow yourself to become earthbound, your life dominated by things of this world; . . . And then 'launch out into the deep' and explore the depths of God's love; consider his nature, his goodness, his strength; let the thought of his majesty and of his tender mercy and compassion flow into your heart; learn to be alone with him in the deep. And then 'Let down your nets for a draught'; learn to accept what God gives of his grace, his peace, his strength; spread your nets wide for that miraculous draught of all that your soul can need.

J.R.H. Moorman, *The Path to Glory*

**See also** Belief, Commitment, Discipleship, Guidance, Humility

# 79

# OTHER FAITHS

*Other faiths – the relationship of Christianity to Judaism, Islam, Buddhism, Hinduism, etc.*

Three things have altered the way I look at people of other faiths. The first is the Genesis story of the creation of humanity. In this story God is depicted as fashioning and shaping humans in his own image and likeness, and the last thing he does is breathe into the first man, and he becomes a living being. This means all men and women, irrespective of race, creed, caste and colour, have something of the divine latent in them. The second is a passage by William Barclay: 'There are many ways to God. God has His own secret stairway into every heart. God fulfils Himself in many ways; and no man, and no Church, has a monopoly of the truth of God.' The third is a passage by Mahatma Gandhi: 'After long study and experience I have come to these conclusions that: 1) all religions are true; 2) all religions have some error in them; 3) all religions are almost as dear to me as my own Hinduism. My veneration for other faiths is the same as for my own faith. Consequently, the thought of conversion is impossible . . . Our prayer for others ought never to be: "God! give them the light thou has given to me!" But: "Give them all the light and truth they need for their highest development."' My attitude is to be loyal to the truths of Christ, and open to truths of God to be found in people of other faiths, and from different backgrounds.

I have other sheep that do not belong to this fold.
John 10.16

Now among those who went up to worship at the festival were some Greeks. They came to Philip, who was from Bethsaida in Galilee, and said to him, 'Sir, we wish to see Jesus.'
John 12.20–21

As all men are alike (tho' infinitely various),
So all Religions &, as all similars, have one source,
The true Man is the source, he being the Poetic Genius.
William Blake, 'All Religions Are One'

. . . we believe we may speak not only of the unknown God of the Greeks but also of the *hidden Christ of Hinduism* – hidden and unknown and yet present and at work because he is not far from any one of us.

Raimundo Panikkar, *The Unknown Christ of Hinduism*

The humble, meek, merciful, just, pious, and devout souls, are everywhere of one religion; and when death has taken off the mask, they will know one another, though the diverse liveries they wear have made them strangers.

William Penn, *Fruits of Solitude*

The Church has never declared that the Judeo-Christian religion was alone in possessing revealed Scriptures, sacraments, and supernatural knowledge about God. It has never declared that there was no affinity at all between Christianity and the mystical traditions of countries other than Israel.

Simone Weil, *Gateway to God*

If we believe in God as Creator we must surely think of him as wanting to make an impact on all, through their history, their experience, their prophets. We believe that he is the source of all truth, goodness and love, so where we see signs of these we must surely believe that he has been active.

George Appleton, *Journey for a Soul*

In Jesus we see mirrored and perfectly revealed the Cosmic Being, the principle of the Godhead active in all history.

The Cosmic Christ may be seen working in and through the Israelites and speaking through the patriarchs and prophets. In like manner the same Cosmic Being may be seen moving in and through all the great religions in every age.

Bede Griffiths OSB, in Peter Spink, *The Universal Christ*

'But the Jews, the Mohammedans, the Confucians, the Buddhists – what of them?' he put to himself the dilemma that had threatened him before. 'Can those hundreds of millions of human beings be deprived of that greatest of blessings without which life has no meaning?' he pondered, but immediately pulled himself up. 'But what is it that I want to know?' he said to himself. 'I am asking about the relation to the Deity of all the different religions of mankind.'

Leo Tolstoy, *Anna Karenina*

Our purpose is to take God and his love to the poorest of the poor, irrespective of their ethnical origin or the faith that they profess. Our discernment of all is not the belief but the necessity. We never try to convert those who receive to Christianity but in our work we bear witness to the love of God's presence and if Catholics, Protestants, Buddhists or agnostics become for this better men – simply better – we will be satisfied. Growing up in love they will be nearer to God and will find him in his goodness.

Mother Teresa, in Kathryn Spink, *In the Silence of the Heart*

Once some blind men chanced to come near an animal that someone had told them was an elephant. They were asked what the elephant was like. The blind men began to feel its body. One of them said the elephant was like a pillar; he had touched only its leg. Another said it was like a winnowing-fan; he had touched only its ear. In this way the others, having touched its tail or belly, gave their different versions of the elephant. Just so, a man who has seen only one aspect of God limits God to that alone. It is his conviction that God cannot be anything else.

Sri Ramakrishna, *Ramakrishna: Prophet of New India*

People of other faiths are our spiritual neighbours in the journey of life and in the search for spiritual dimensions and values. The outgoing Christian mission has made them neighbours and has stimulated them to examine their own religious traditions. The ease of travel and the development of trade brings them to our countries, so they are now physical as well as spiritual neighbours. Their presence makes them our neighbours, as well as their interest in religious questions. We have to interpret the second great commandment in our attitude towards them.

George Appleton, *Journey for a Soul*

The Holy Spirit is at work in all creation and within all humanity, drawing all men and all things to unity in Christ, that is, into his mystical Body.

The realization of this unity begins within ourselves. From the depths of our being we learn with Christ to say 'Abba, Father'. It is there that we touch the source from which all life flows.

At the surface level of the various religions there are great diversity, differences and separation to unity, from contradiction to oneness and from diversity to convergence. In every human being the Holy Spirit is present and at work. Even when ignored or denied the Spirit is moving, and drawing towards unity in Christ.

Bede Griffiths OSB, in Peter Spink, *The Universal Christ*

There have been times when the Christian Church has rightly claimed to have an exclusive role. This was particularly so in its beginnings. If Christianity had not claimed to be the final and only true revelation in its own Mediterranean world and refused to become merely one of the many religions of that world, it could never have become the inspiration of European civilization. Those days are now past. The Spirit of God is moving in the world, leading men into a wider vision, which does not destroy but fulfils and is in part contained within all the earlier partial visions. Christianity, and this is true of all higher religions, is now called upon, within the divine economy, to become universal, not by each religion ceasing to be itself, or watering down its own particular revelation, not by an attempt to iron out differences at the intellectual level, so that all may be lost in some nebulous World Faith, but by each seeing itself within the other, by each becoming incarnate within the other.

F.C. Happold, *The Journey Inwards*

**See also** Awareness, Humility, Listening, Love, Neighbour

# 80

# PATIENCE

*Patience – calm endurance of pain or any provocation; perseverance*

In 1968 I went to Nigeria for six months, looking after All Saints Church, Jericho, Ibadan. I soon discovered Nigerians have a different concept of time from ours. This came home to me officiating at a wedding. The service was scheduled to start at 11.00am. At 10.55am hardly anyone had arrived. At 12.00 noon about half the guests had arrived and I was beginning to get impatient. At 1.00pm the bride and her father arrived, as did the bridegroom and the best man. The bridesmaids, however, were still not to be seen. I started the wedding at 1.30pm and the service ended an hour later. While the couple were proceeding down the aisle after the final blessing, six beautifully dressed bridesmaids arrived – supposedly for the start of the service. Amidst much laughter and hilarity we set off for the reception. I learnt a great deal about patience in my six months in Nigeria. As I have gone through life I value more and more my 'apprenticeship' in patience.

Be still before the Lord, and wait patiently for him.
Psalm 37.7

But as for that in the good soil, these are the ones who, when they hear the word, hold it fast in an honest and good heart, and bear fruit with patient endurance.
Luke 8.15

Possess your soul with patience.
John Dryden, 'The Hind and the Panther'

Calumnies are answer'd best with silence.
Ben Jonson, *Volpone*

One of the principal parts of faith is patience.
George Macdonald, *Weighed and Wanting*

Patience and application will carry us through.
Thomas Fuller, *Gnomologia*

I worked with patience, which means almost power.
E.B. Browning, 'Aurora Leigh'

Endurance is nobler than strength, and patience than beauty.
John Ruskin, *The Two Paths*

Sorrow and silence are strong, and patient endurance is godlike.
Henry Wadsworth Longfellow, 'Evangeline'

This impatience or strenuousness is the white man's characteristic, and his curse.
Norman Douglas, *An Almanac*

Patience is not passive; on the contrary, it is active; it is concentrated strength.
Anon

Endurance is the crowning quality,
And patience all the passion of great hearts.
J.R. Lowell, 'Columbus'

One moment of patience may ward off great disaster, one moment of impatience may ruin a whole life.
Chinese proverb

I know how unbearable is suspense of mind, to have to face a situation which one cannot alter or even affect, and have to wait.
A.C. Benson, *Extracts from the Letters of Dr A.C. Benson to M.E.A.*

People are always talking of perseverance, and courage, and fortitude, but patience is the first and worthiest part of fortitude – and the rarest too.
John Ruskin, *Ethics of the Dust*

I can see that patience is essential in this life, for there is much that goes against the grain. Whatever I do to ensure my peace, I find that fighting and suffering are inevitable.
Thomas à Kempis, *The Imitation of Christ*

To be silent, to suffer, to pray, when there is no room for outward action, is an acceptable offering to God. A disappointment, a contradiction, an injury received and endured for God's sake, are of as such value as a long prayer.

François de la M. Fénelon, *Spiritual Thoughts for Busy People*

Let patience have her perfect work. Statue under the chisel of the sculptor, stand steady to the blows of his mallet. Clay on the wheel, let the fingers of the divine potter model you at their will. Obey the Father's lightest word; hear the Brother who knows you, and died for you.

George Macdonald, *Unspoken Sermons*

I do oppose
My patience to his fury, and am armed
To suffer with a quietness of spirit
The very tyranny and rage of his.

William Shakespeare, *The Merchant of Venice*

Patience and diligence, like faith, remove mountains. Never give out while there is hope; but hope not beyond reason, for that shows more desire than judgment. It is a profitable wisdom, to know when we have done enough; much time and pains are spared, in not flattering ourselves against probabilities.

William Penn, *Fruits of Solitude*

Someone has said that the secret of patience is 'doing something else in the meantime'. The 'something else' the saints do is to dwell on the use God can make even now of the trials which beset them. 'Let me receive them with patient meekness' they seem to say 'and perhaps by this means, God will polish His Jewel.'

W.E. Sangster, *The Pure in Heart*

Patience is the most difficult thing of all and the only thing that is worth learning. All nature, all growth, all peace, everything that flowers and is beautiful in the world depends on patience, requires time, silence, trust, and faith in long-term processes which far exceed any single lifetime, which are accessible to the insight of no one person, and which in their totality can be experienced only by peoples and epochs, not by individuals.

Hermann Hesse, in Volker Michels, *Reflections*

We must wait for God, long, meekly, in the wind and wet, in the thunder and the lightning, in the cold and the dark. Wait, and He will come. He never comes to those who do not wait. He does not go their road. When He comes, go with Him, but go slowly, fall a little behind; when He quickens His pace, be sure of it, before you quicken yours. But when He slackens, slacken at once. And do not be slow only, but silent, very silent, for He is God.

F.W. Faber, *Growth in Holiness*

**See also** Acceptance, Hope, Kindness, Obedience, Perseverance

# 81

# PEACE

*Peace – freedom from, cessation of war, freedom from civil disorder, quiet tranquillity, mental calm, bring person, oneself, back into friendly relations*

I can clearly remember the end of the Second World War. For the first time for several years we experienced peace. There was an immediate lessening of tension everywhere and a great communal sense of relief. At last we could relax and start enjoying life again. At a more personal level, twenty years later, I recall a visit to the Bradford Royal Infirmary. There I met a man in one of the wards. He was dying of cancer and knew it. I was struck by his appearance. He had a calm, serene disposition and quiet demeanour. He had come to terms with the fact that he was shortly to die, and I was impressed by his faith and peace of mind. He was troubled by a row in the ward between a patient and a nurse. This had somehow tarnished the atmosphere, so he went to considerable trouble to sort it out. He was delighted with the outcome, especially as the peaceful atmosphere of the ward was restored. Peace is supremely important and many of us can be instruments of peace, wherever we are. Peace is one of the fruits of the Spirit, and is its own reward.

Those of steadfast mind you keep in peace – in peace because they trust in you.
  Isaiah 26.3

Peace I leave with you, my peace I give to you. I do not give to you as the world gives. Do not let not your hearts be troubled, and do not let them be afraid.
  John 14.27

Peace is always beautiful.
  Walt Whitman, 'The Sleepers'

Where there is peace, God is.

George Herbert, *Outlandish Proverbs*

You touched me, and I am inflamed with love of your peace.

St Augustine, *Confessions*

Peace,
The central feeling of all happiness.

William Wordsworth, 'The Excursion'

Peace comes not by establishing a calm outward setting so much as by inwardly surrendering to whatever the setting.

Hubert van Zeller, *Leave Your Life Alone*

Live in peace yourself and then you can bring peace to others – a peaceable man does more good than a learned one.

Thomas à Kempis, *The Imitation of Christ*

I am a child of peace and am resolved to keep the peace for ever and ever, with the whole world, inasmuch as I have concluded it at last with my own self.

Johann Wolfgang von Goethe, *Wisdom and Experience*

People are always expecting to get peace in heaven; but you know whatever peace they get there will be ready made. Whatever making of peace *they* can be blest for, must be on earth here.

John Ruskin, *The Eagle's Nest*

The more a man gives up his heart to God, to his vocation and to men, forgetful of himself and of that which belongs to him – the greater poise he will acquire, until he reaches peace, quiet, joy – the apanage of simple and humble souls.

Father Yelchaninov, in G.P. Fedotov, *A Treasury of Russian Spirituality*

A soul divided against itself can never find peace. Peace cannot exist where there are contrary loyalties. For true peace there has to be psychological and moral harmony. Conscience must be at rest.

Hubert van Zeller, *Considerations*

When people are praying for peace, the cause of peace is being strengthened by their very act of prayer, for they are themselves becoming immersed in the spirit of peace, and committed to the cause of peace.

John Macquarrie, *The Concept of Peace*

To thee, O God, we turn for peace . . . but grant us too the blessed assurance that nothing shall deprive us of that peace, neither *ourselves*, nor our foolish, earthly desires, nor my wild longings, nor the anxious craving of my heart.

Søren Kierkegaard, *The Journals of Søren Kierkegaard*

In India the great example of the power of peace was seen in Mahatma Gandhi whose inner peace influenced the whole nation. Work for peace must first of all be a work within ourselves.

Bede Griffiths OSB, in Peter Spink, *The Universal Christ*

Calm soul of things! make it mine
To feel amid the city's jar,
That there abides a peace of thine,
Man did not make and cannot mar!

Matthew Arnold, 'In Kensington Gardens'

No man has touched the essential characteristics of Christianity, and no man has entered into the interior spirit of Christianity, who has not reached to a certain extent that peace which Christ said He gave to His disciples, and which at times they declared to be past all understanding.

Henry Ward Beecher, *Proverbs from Plymouth Pulpit*

Children, that peace which is found in the spirit and inner life is well worth our care, for in that peace lies the satisfaction of all our wants. In it the Kingdom of God is discovered and His righteousness is found. This peace a man should allow nothing to take from him, whatever betide, come weal or woe, honour or shame.

John Tauler, *The History and Life of the Reverend Doctor John Tauler*

There is an experience of being in pure consciousness which gives lasting peace to the soul. It is an experience of the Ground or Depth of being in the Centre of the soul, an awareness of the mystery of being beyond sense and thought, which gives a sense of fulfilment, of finality, of absolute truth.

Bede Griffiths OSB, *Return to the Centre*

In the Bible the word *peace*, *shalom*, never simply means the absence of trouble. Peace means everything which makes for our highest good. The peace which the world offers us is the peace of escape, the peace which comes from the avoidance of trouble, the peace which comes from refusing to face things. The peace which Jesus offers us is the peace of conquest. It is the peace which no experience in life can ever take from us. It is the peace which no sorrow, no danger, no suffering can make less. It is the peace which is independent of outward circumstances.

William Barclay, *The Gospel of John*

**See also** Acceptance, Contemplation, Contentment, Grace, Presence

# 82

# PERSEVERANCE

*Perseverance – a steadfast pursuit of an aim, constant persistence*

I met a young disabled woman. She had come to University College, London, to do a postgraduate degree in librarianship. After a week or so she told me about herself. She had been born with cerebral palsy. Her father had left home when she was very young and had not been seen by her since. She decided to get stuck into life, and got through her O and A levels at school. She made a successful application to Exeter University and managed to get an honours degree. Disaster struck again. In her early twenties she was involved in a serious car accident, which left her more disabled than ever. Life then became a constant struggle to survive. She had now arrived in London to get a further qualification. She was not finding it easy. London provided her with peculiar problems of its own. The course was academic and demanding. It required all her powers of perseverance. She was involved in another car crash. Her persistence was rewarded when she got her qualification and a job as a librarian. She has persisted in her job ever since, but recently has had to take early retirement. Perseverance and endurance have definitely played an important part in her life.

The way of the Lord is a stronghold for the upright.

Proverbs 10.29

Pray in the Spirit at all times in every prayer and supplication. To that end keep alert and always persevere . . .

Ephesians 6.18

Some strains are bearable and even bracing, but others are deadly.

A.C. Benson, *Extracts from the Letters of Dr A.C. Benson to M.E.A*

No great cause is ever lost or ever won. The battle must always be renewed and the creed restated.

John Buchan, *Montrose*

Perseverance, dear my lord,
Keeps honour bright.

William Shakespeare, *Troilus and Cressida*

Life should be a voluntary overcoming of difficulties, those met with and those voluntarily created, otherwise it is just a dice-game.

A.R. Orage, *On Love*

Attempt the end, and never stand to doubt;
Nothing's so hard, but search will find it out.

Robert Herrick, 'Hesperides: Seek and Find'

I often wish there were some index or inward monitor showing me when I had not reached the limit of my power of resistance and endurance in trouble. Sometimes, I dare say, I fancy I can hold out no longer when, in reality, I am nowhere near falling.

Mark Rutherford, *Last Pages from a Journal*

To endure is greater than to dare; to tire out hostile fortune; to be daunted by no difficulty; to keep heart when all have lost it; to go through intrigue spotless; to forego even ambition when the end is gained – who can say this is not greatness?

William Makepeace Thackeray, *The Virginians*

There remain times when one can only endure. One lives on, one doesn't die, and the only thing that one can do, is to fill one's mind and time as far as possible with the concerns of other people. It doesn't bring immediate peace, but it brings the dawn nearer.

A.C. Benson, *Extracts from the Letters of Dr A.C. Benson to M.E.A.*

For me at least there came moments when faith wavered. But there is the great lesson and the great triumph if you keep the fire burning until, by and by, out of the mass of sordid details there comes some result, be it some new generalization or be it a transcending spiritual repose.

Oliver Wendell Holmes, in Max Lerner, *The Mind and Faith of Justice Holmes*

The years should temper a man like steel, so that he can bear more and more and emerge more and more the conqueror over life. In the nature of things we must grow weaker in body, but in the divine nature of things we must grow ever stronger in the faith which can endure the slings and arrows of life, and not fail.

William Barclay, *The Letters to Timothy and Titus*

Exasperation at not being able to do a thing *uninterruptedly*; and I am more and more convinced that nothing good is achieved without a long perseverance, without applying one's effort for some time in the same direction. It is a matter of patient selection, analogous to that exercised by good horticulturalists.

André Gide, *The Journals of André Gide*

We live in a very beautiful world; but few good things are to be had in it without hard work. It is not a world in which any one can expect to be prosperous if he is easily discouraged. Perseverance – earnest, steady perseverance – is necessary to success. This is no drawback. Good, solid work is as necessary to peace of mind as it is for the health of the body; in fact the two are inseparable.

Right Hon. Lord Avebury, *Essays and Addresses*

The value of such moral teaching lies in a man learning what others have experienced and what he too may expect of life. Whatever happens to him, he will realize that he is meeting the common lot of mankind and not a peculiar fate, fortunate or unfortunate. Even if this knowledge does not help us to escape sorrows, it shows us how to endure them and, perhaps, how to conquer them.

Johann Wolfgang von Goethe, in Emil Ludwig, *The Practical Wisdom of Goethe*

Life makes many an attempt to take away our faith. Things happen to us and to others which baffle our understanding; life has its problems to which there seems no solution and its questions to which there seems no answer; life has its dark places where there seems to be nothing to do but hold on. Faith is always a *victory*, the victory of the soul which tenaciously maintains its clutch on God.

William Barclay, *The Letters to the Corinthians*

Disraeli the elder held that the secret of all success consisted in being master of your subject, such mastery being attainable only through continuous application and study. Hence it happens that the men who have most moved the world have been not so much men of genius, strictly so called, as men of intense mediocre abilities, untiring workers, persevering, self-reliant and indefatigable; not so often the gifted, of naturally bright and shining qualities, as those who have applied themselves diligently to their work, in whatever line that might lie.

Samuel Smiles, *Self-Help*

He [Paul] begins with one triumphant word of the Christian life – *endurance (hupomone)*. It is untranslatable. It does not describe the frame of mind which can sit down with folded hands and bowed head and let a torrent of troubles sweep over it in passive resignation. It describes the ability to bear things in such a triumphant way that it transfigures them . . . It is the courageous and triumphant ability to pass the breaking-point and not to break and always to greet the unseen with a cheer. It is the alchemy which transmutes tribulation into strength and glory.

William Barclay, *The Letters to the Corinthians*

Another important value in an abundance of energy should be mentioned. The *ability to persevere* in the face of discouragement and disappointment and the possession of *courage* to face strong opposition are both qualities which mark successful leaders. And both of these qualities are fed at their roots by an endowment of energy. Probably no single corroding influence eats away perseverance and courage so much as fatigue and bodily unfitness. Both the buoyancy of the outlook and the constancy of the effort of all of us derive from forces not primarily of the mind but of the body.

Ordway Tead, *The Art of Leadership*

**See also** Action, Courage, Discipleship, Hope, Patience

83

# PHILOSOPHY

*Philosophy – love of wisdom or knowledge, especially that which deals with ultimate reality, or with the most general causes – principles of things, study of principles of human action or conduct; system of conduct of life*

At university the study of philosophy has become a very exacting academic discipline, far removed from the ordinary person. I have been greatly helped by some words of Lord Byron which he wrote in his poem, 'Childe Harold's Pilgrimage', of 'that untaught innate philosophy'. This was fortified in turn by some words of a former Dean of St Paul's – W.R. Inge. In his book *Outspoken Essays* he wrote that 'philosophy means thinking things out for oneself'. I wonder if we can make yet another link here with the Genesis story of the creation of humanity and of the divine inbreathing; that as a natural consequence of this we have inside us something of 'that untaught innate philo-sophy'. If ordinary people can get hold of this, then they may be given confi-dence to go one stage further and 'think things out for themselves'. We might then get an increase in the 'love of wisdom or knowledge', and an enrichment of our corporate life. *The Eternal Vision* provides us with some thought-provoking material and the practice of reflection, whether in groups or on an individual basis, a way in which we too can think things out for ourselves.

Can you find out the deep things of God? Can you find out the limit of the Almighty?

Job 11.7

My speech and my proclamation were not with plausible words of wisdom, but with a demonstration of the Spirit and of power.

1 Corinthians 2.4

The example of good men is visible philosophy.
English proverb

Any genuine philosophy leads to action and from action back again to wonder, to the enduring fact of mystery.
Henry Miller, *The Wisdom of the Heart*

Philosophical knowledge is a spiritual act, where not only the intellect is active, but the whole of man's spiritual power, his emotions and his will.
Nicolas Berdyaev, *Christian Existentialism*

For philosophy is the study of wisdom, and wisdom is the knowledge of things divine and human; and their causes. Wisdom is therefore queen of philosophy.
Clement of Alexandria, *The Miscellanies*

The maxims and statements of Christ were the very roots of philosophy. We have never, under any moral philosophy, come up to the maxims and root-teachings of the Lord Jesus Christ.
Henry Ward Beecher, *Proverbs from Plymouth Pulpit*

The philosophy of six thousand years has not searched the chambers and magazines of the soul. In its experiments, there has always remained, in the last analysis, a residium it could not resolve.
Ralph Waldo Emerson, *Essays and Representative Men*

Philosophies of life, when they are widely believed, also have a very great influence on the vitality of a community. The most widely accepted philosophy of life at present is that what matters most to a man's happiness is his income. This philosophy, apart from other demerits, is harmful because it leads men to aim at a result rather than an activity, an enjoyment of material goods in which men are not differentiated, rather than a creative impulse which embodies each man's individuality . . .
Bertrand Russell, *Principles of Social Reconstruction*

To be a philosopher is not merely to have subtle thoughts, nor even to found a school, but so to love wisdom as to live according to its dictates, a life of simplicity, independence, magnanimity, and trust.
Henry David Thoreau, *Walden*

'Come unto me . . . and I will give you rest'; it is not Philosophy that can estimate the right of the Speaker to issue that invitation or to make that promise; that right can be proved or disproved only by the experiment of life.

William Temple, *Nature, Man and God*

The philosophy which is so important in each of us is not a technical matter; it is our more or less dumb sense of what life honestly and deeply means. It is only partly got from books; it is our individual way of just seeing and feeling the total push and pressure of the cosmos.

William James, *Pragmatism*

Theology, which is the science of Religion, starts from the Supreme Spirit and explains the world by reference to Him. Philosophy starts from the detailed experience of men, and seeks to build up its understanding of that experience by reference to that experience alone.

William Temple, *Nature, Man and God*

Most people in England think of a philosopher as one who talks in a difficult language about matters which are of interest only to philosophers. But Philosophy is concerned with what must interest every human being, with the nature of man and the nature of the universe. Every man is born a philosopher, but often the philosopher is suppressed in him by the hand-to-mouth thinking needed for the struggle for life.

A. Clutton Brock, *The Ultimate Belief*

The world has need of a philosophy, or a religion, which will promote life. But in order to promote life it is necessary to value something other than mere life. Life devoted only to life is animal, and without any real human value, incapable of preserving men permanently from weariness and the feeling that all is vanity. If life is to be fully human it must serve some end which seems, in some sense, outside human life, some end which is personal and above mankind, such as God or truth or beauty.

Bertrand Russell, *Principles of Social Reconstruction*

The highest triumphs of philosophy are possible only to those who have achieved in themselves a purity of soul. This purity is based upon a profound acceptance of experience, realized only when some point of hidden strength within man, from which he can not only inspect but comprehend life, is found. From this inner source the philosopher reveals to us the truth of life, a truth which mere intellect is unable to discover. The vision is produced almost as naturally as a fruit from a flower out of the mysterious centre, where all experience is reconciled.

Sir Sarvepalli Radhakrishnan, *Indian Philosophy*

Those who best promote life do not have life for their purpose. They aim rather at what seems like a gradual incarnation, a bringing into our human existence of something eternal, something that appears to imagination to live in a heaven remote from strife and failure and the devouring jaws of Time. Contact with this eternal world – even if it be only a world of our imagining – brings a strength and a fundamental peace which cannot be wholly destroyed by the struggles and apparent failures of our temporal life. It is this happy contemplation of what is eternal that Spinoza calls the intellectual love of God. To those who have once known it, it is the key of wisdom.

Bertrand Russell, *Principles of Social Reconstruction*

**See also** Intellect, Mind, Thinking, Truth, Wisdom

# 84

# POETRY

*Poetry – art, work, of the poet; elevated expression of elevated thought or feeling in metrical form; quality (in any thing) that calls for poetical expression*

I was intrigued to see a young poet in action. He was a student at University College, London, and lived in our chaplaincy house. From time to time he would stay up late at night. This was when he was feeling lucid and receptive. He found his best poems came in the early hours of the morning, when it was quiet and there were no distractions. It seemed as though the source of his inspiration was in the deep centre of his being, though he did have a finely-tuned mind and a vivid imagination. All these faculties were used in the writing of his poems. The cost was great. I would see him the following morning, ashen white, haggard, and exhausted, though there was usually a twinkle in his eyes. I wonder if the poet taps into the same reservoir of 'inspiration' as the artist, musician, playwright, etc., but it comes out in a unique form of expression.

My heart overflows with a goodly theme; I address my verses to the king; my tongue is like the pen of a ready scribe.

Psalm 45.1

. . . so that they would search for God and perhaps grope for him and find him – though indeed he is not far from each one of us. For 'In him we live and move and have our being'; as even some of your own poets have said, 'For we too are his offspring.'

Acts 17.27–28

The true poet is a solitary, as is man in his great moments.

J.B. Yeats, *Letters to His Son, W.B. Yeats and Others*

Poetry is the record of the best and happiest moments of the happiest and best minds.

Percy Bysshe Shelley, *A Defence of Poetry*

Poetry, therefore, we will call *musical Thought*. The Poet is he who *thinks* in that manner.

Thomas Carlyle, *Sartor Resartus*

Poetry is divine because it is the voice of the personality – this poor captive caged behind the bars.

J.B. Yeats, *Letters to His Son, W.B. Yeats and Others*

Let us therefore deem the glorious art of Poetry a kind of medicine divinely bestowed upon man.

John Keble, *Lectures on Poetry*

All that is best in the great poets of all countries is not what is national in them, but what is universal.

Henry Wadsworth Longfellow, *Kavanagh*

Poets deal with what I call ultimate human nature – descending into the depths.

J.B. Yeats, *Letters to His Son, W.B. Yeats and Others*

The poet enters into himself in order to create. The contemplative enters into God in order to be created.

Thomas Merton, *New Seeds of Contemplation*

Most people do not believe in anything very much and our greatest poetry is given us by those who do.

Cyril Connolly, in Stephen Spender, *The Making of a Poem*

[Poetry] was ever thought to have some participation of divineness, because it doth raise and erect the mind.

Francis Bacon, *The Advancement of Learning*

Poetry should be great and unobtrusive, a thing which enters into one's soul, and does not startle it or amaze it with itself, but with its subject.

John Keats, *Letter to J.H. Reynolds*

I had said of Christ that he ranks with the poets. That is true. Shelley and Sophocles are his company. But his entire life also is the most wonderful of poems.

Oscar Wilde, *De Profundis*

Poetry should be vital – either stirring our blood by its divine movement, or snatching our breath by its divine perfection. To do both is supreme glory; to do either is enduring fame.

Augustine Birrell, *Obiter Dicta, Mr Browning's Poetry*

The essence of all poetry is to be found, not in high-wrought subtlety of thought, nor in pointed cleverness of phrase, but in the depths of the heart and the most sacred feelings of the men who write.

John Keble, *Keble's Lectures on Poetry*

The touchstone of genuine poetry is that it has the ability, as a secular gospel, to liberate us from the weight of our earthly burden by an inner serenity and an outward sense of well-being.

Johann Wolfgang von Goethe, in Herman J. Weigand, *Wisdom and Experience*

When a poet takes words as his instruments . . . the very sound of the words is now part of the meaning; that meaning can never be apprehended or recovered except by re-hearing physically or in imagination the actual sound of the words . . . Here we are near to a sacrament.

William Temple, *Nature, Man and God*

A poem is the image of life expressed in its eternal truth. There is this difference between a story and a poem, that a story is a catalogue of detached facts, which have no other bond of connexion than time, place, circumstance, cause and effect; the other is the creation of actions according to the unchangeable forms of human nature, as existing in the mind of the creator, which is itself the image of all other minds.

Percy Bysshe Shelley, *Prose, A Defence of Poetry*

The most beautiful poem there is, is life – life which discerns its own story in the making, in which inspiration and self-consciousness go together and help each other, life which knows itself to be the world in little, a repetition in miniature of the divine universal poem. Yes, be man; that is to say, be nature, be spirit, be the image of God, be what is greatest, most beautiful, most lofty in all the spheres of being, be infinite will and idea, a reproduction of the great whole.

Henri Frédéric Amiel, *Amiel's Journal*

What is a Poet? To whom does he address himself? And what language is to be expected from him? – He is a man speaking to men: a man, it is true, endowed with more lively sensibility, more enthusiasm and tenderness, who has a greater knowledge of human nature, and a more comprehensive soul, than are supposed to be common among mankind; a man pleased with his own passions and volitions, and who rejoices more than other men in the spirit of life that is in him . . .

William Wordsworth, *Lyrical Ballads*

**See also** Art, Beauty, Literature, Music, Wonder

# 85

# POWER

*Power – ability to do or act; particular faculty of body or mind, vigour, energy; influential person, body or thing*

In the Wisdom of Solomon we read of 'the One who shaped him, who breathed an active soul into him, and inspired a living spirit'. Writers, such as Meister Eckhart, believe we are born with a seed or spark of the divine power in the depths of ourselves. An awareness of this power was experienced by the prophets. Micah, for instance, acknowledged he was 'filled with power, with the Spirit of the Lord, and with justice and might'. In the Gospels, we recall the claim of Jesus: 'All authority in heaven and on earth has been given me.' Paul prays for the members of the early church: 'May you be made strong with all the strength that comes from his glorious power, and may you be prepared to endure everything with patience while joyfully giving thanks to the Father, who has enabled you to share in the inheritance of the saints in the light.' Today we have lost sight of the divine power to be found in ourselves. We need to return to that source for a richer experience of life.

. . . he gives power and strength to his people.

Psalm 68.35

I pray that the God of our Lord Jesus Christ, the Father of glory, may give you a spirit of wisdom and of revelation as you come to know him, so that, with the eyes of your heart enlightened, you may know what is the hope to which he has called you, what are the riches of his glorious inheritance among the saints, and what is the immeasurable greatness of his power for us who believe, according to the working of his great power.

Ephesians 1.17–19

Energy is Eternal Delight.

William Blake, 'The Marriage of Heaven and Hell'

Patience and Gentleness is Power.
Leigh Hunt, 'On a Lock of Milton's Hair'

The power of God is the worship He inspires.
Alfred North Whitehead, *Science and the Modern World*

Man is a born child, his power is the power of growth.
Rabindranath Tagore, *Stray Birds*

The strongest man in the world is the man who stands alone.
Henrik Ibsen, *An Enemy of the People*

Right and Truth are greater than any *Power*, and all Power is limited by Right.
Benjamin Whichcote, *Moral and Religious Aphorisms*

Life engenders life. Energy creates energy. It is by spending oneself that one becomes rich.
Sarah Bernhardt, in Cornelia Otis Skinner, *Madam Sarah*

Self-reverence, self-knowledge, self-control,
These three alone lead life to sovereign power.
Alfred, Lord Tennyson, 'Oenone'

From the summit of power men no longer turn their eyes upward, but begin to look about them.
J.R. Lowell, *New England Two Centuries Ago*

Concentration is the secret of strength in politics, in war, in trade, in short, in all management of human affairs.
Ralph Waldo Emerson, *The Conduct of Life, Nature and Other Essays*

To know the pains of power, we must go to those who have it; to know its pleasures, we must go to those who are seeking it: the pains of power are real, its pleasures imaginary.
C.C. Colton, *Lacon*

We are the wire, God is the current. Our only power is to let the current pass through us. Of course, we have the power to interrupt it and say 'no'. But nothing more.
Carlo Carretto, *Letters from the Desert*

A non-violent revolution is not a programme of 'seizure of power'. It is a programme of transformation of relationships ending in a peaceful transfer of power.

Mohandas K. Gandhi, *Non-Violence in Peace and War*

Justice without might is helpless; might without justice is tyrannical . . . We must then combine justice and might, and for this end make what is just strong, or what is strong just.

Blaise Pascal, *Pensées*

He [Christ] stimulates us, as other great men stimulate us, but we find a power coming from Him into our lives that enables us to respond. That is the experience that proves Him to be the universal Spirit. It does not happen with others.

William Temple, *Christian Faith and Life*

His power [that of Kahlil Gibran] came from some great reservoir of spiritual life else it could not have been so universal and so potent, but the majesty and beauty of the language with which he clothed it were all his own.

Claude Bragdon, in Kahlil Gibran, *The Prophet*

There is a power which lapses into the human soul, and by that divine power all the faculties of man become competent to do or to be what they cannot do or be when they are left to the laws of society or to the laws of nature.

Henry Ward Beecher, *Proverbs from Plymouth Pulpit*

You have lost the knack of drawing strength from God, and vain strivings after communion of the *solitude à deux* will do nothing for you at this point. Seek contact with Him now in the goodness and splendour which is in other people, in *all* people, for those who have the art to find it.

Evelyn Underhill, *The Letters of Evelyn Underhill*

For man, discovering that knowledge is power, uses that power to dominate. The power within him is not the power of a great personality, the power which is sure and strong and is therefore able to be gentle and tolerant. This is the true power of God, the power of an infinite understanding, and it can only exist in a context of eternity.

Stuart B. Jackman, *The Numbered Days*

Christianity is not, as it is sometimes presented and sometimes practised, an additional burden of observances and obligations to weigh down and increase the already heavy load, or to multiply the already paralysing ties of our life in society. It is, in fact, a soul of immense power which bestows significance, beauty and a new lightness on what we are already doing.

Pierre Teilhard de Chardin, *Le Milieu Divin*

It was at the baptism that the Spirit came upon Jesus with power . . . The Jewish word for Spirit is *ruach*, which is the word which means *wind*. To the Jew there was always three basic ideas of Spirit. The Spirit was *power*, power like a mighty rushing wind; the Spirit was *life*, the very centre and soul and essence of life, the very dynamic of the existence of man; the Spirit was *God*; the power and the life of the Spirit were beyond mere human achievement and attainment. The coming of the Spirit into a man's life was the coming of God.

William Barclay, *The Gospel of John*

**See also** Influence, Inner Life, Leadership, Presence, Wholeness

# 86

# PRAYER

*Prayer – solemn request to God or object of worship; formula used in praying, practice of prayer; entreaty to a person; thing prayed for*

I was taught to say my prayers by our school chaplain. He gave us a simple technique in preparing us for confirmation. We were to say our prayers at night, just before going to bed. First we were to start with thanksgiving, giving thanks for the many blessings we enjoyed. Second, we were to move on to confession, owning up to all that had gone wrong in our lives – in thought, word, deed, and omission – ending with an acceptance of God's forgiveness. Third, we were to say the Lord's Prayer. Fourth, we were to pray for other people, especially those who were in any kind of need. Finally we were to pray for ourselves and for our own particular needs. I used this technique for several years, until the time came for a change. Instead of doing all the talking I had to learn to keep quiet and listen. I found this difficult at first. Keeping a journal was a help. Gradually I learnt to reflect, meditate and contemplate.

. . . then you will delight in the Almighty, and lift up your face to God. You will pray to him, and he will hear you.

Job 22.26–27

In the morning, while it was still very dark, he got up and went out to a deserted place, and there he prayed.

Mark 1.35

Prayer takes place in the heart, not in the head.

Carlo Carretto, *The Desert in the City*

Prayer is the Divine in us appealing to the Divine above us.

C.H. Dodd, in William Barclay, *The Letter to the Romans*

Prayer is the nearest approach to God, and the highest enjoyment of Him, that we are capable of in this life.

William Law, *A Serious Call to a Devout and Holy Life*

Prayer is not an old woman's idle amusement. Properly understood and applied, it is the most potent instrument of action.

Mohandas K. Gandhi, *Non-Violence in Peace and War*

You pray in your distress and in your need; would that you might pray also in the fullness of your joy and in your days of abundance.

Kahlil Gibran, *The Prophet*

Prayer, crystallized in words, assigns a permanent wavelength on which the dialogue has to be continued, even when our mind is occupied with other matters.

Dag Hammarskjöld, *Markings*

So true prayer demands that we be more passive than active; it requires more silence than words, more adoration than study, more concentration than rushing about, more faith than reason.

Carlo Carretto, *Letters from the Desert*

Prayer is the responsibility to meet others with *all* that I have, to be ready to encourage the unconditional in the conditional, to expect to meet God in the way, not to turn aside from the way.

John Robinson, *Honest to God*

You pray best when the mirror of your soul is empty of every image except the image of the invisible Father. This image is the Wisdom of the Father, the Word of the Father . . . the glory of the Father.

Thomas Merton, *Thoughts in Solitude*

Lift up your heart to Him, sometimes even at your meals and when you are in company; the least little remembrance will always be acceptable to Him. You need not cry very loud; He is nearer to us than we are aware of.

Brother Lawrence, *The Practice of the Presence of God*

In our Lord's teaching about petitionary prayer there are three main principles. The first is confidence, the second is perseverance and the third, for lack of a better word, I will call correspondence with Christ.

William Temple, *Christian Faith and Life*

Prayer should never be regarded as a science or reduced to a system – that ruins it, because it is essentially a living and personal relationship, which tends to become more personal and also more simple, as one goes on.

Evelyn Underhill, in Charles Williams, *The Letters of Evelyn Underhill*

Prayer places our understanding in the divine brightness and light and exposes our will to the warmth of heavenly love. There is nothing that so effectually purges our understanding of its ignorance and our will of its depraved affections.

St Francis de Sales, *Introduction to the Devout Life*

Do not forget to say your prayers. If your prayer is sincere, there will be every time you pray a new feeling containing an idea in it, an idea you did not know before, which will give you fresh courage; you will then understand that prayer is education.

Fyodor Dostoyevsky, *The Brothers Karamazov*

The Lord's prayer is the prayer above all prayers, a prayer which the most high Master taught us, wherein are comprehended all spiritual and temporal blessings, and the strongest comforts in all trials, temptations, and troubles, even in the hour of death.

Martin Luther, *Table-Talk*

Believe and trust that as it is easy for you to breathe the air and live by it, or to eat and drink, so it is easy and even still easier for your faith to receive all spiritual gifts from the Lord. Prayer is the breathing of the soul; prayer is our spiritual food and drink.

John of Cronstadt, in G.P. Fedatov, *A Treasury of Russian Spirituality*

Prayer is a fundamental style of thinking, passionate and compassionate, responsible and thankful, that is deeply rooted in our humanity and that manifests itself not only among believers but also among serious-minded people who do not profess any religious faith.

John Macquarrie, *Paths in Spirituality*

Love to pray – feel the need to pray often during the day and take the trouble to pray. If you want to pray better, you must pray more. Prayer enlarges the heart until it is capable of containing God's gift of himself. Ask and seek and your heart will grow big enough to receive him and keep him as your own.

Mother Teresa, in Kathryn Spink, *In the Silence of the Heart*

God will always answer our prayers; *but He will answer them in His way*, and His way will be the way of perfect wisdom and of perfect love. Often if He answered our prayers as we at the moment desire, it would be the worst thing possible for us, for in our ignorance we often ask for gifts which would be our ruin.

William Barclay, *The Gospel of Matthew*

**See also** Action, Adoration, Contemplation, Listening, Meditation

# 87

# PRESENCE

*Presence – being present; real presence, place where person is*

There was a time when I tended to think of God miles above the sky and therefore absent from everyday living. Christ was seen primarily as someone who lived nearly two thousand years ago and distanced from us by time. My eyes were opened to the presence of God by an experience recorded by Joseph Estlin Carpenter. One afternoon he went for a walk in the country. He had not gone far before he became conscious of the presence of someone else. He was unable to describe it. He felt he had as direct a perception of the being of God all about him, as if he were with a friend. For him, it was an act of spiritual apprehension. This experience never happened to him again but the effects never left him. The sense of a direct relation to God then generated in his soul became a part of his habitual thought and feeling. I am also indebted to Brother Lawrence, a Carmelite lay brother of the seventeenth century. He developed a form of prayer called *The Practice of the Presence of God*. Perhaps we should take a leaf out of his book and learn to practise the presence of God.

My presence will go with you, and I will give you rest.
Exodus 33.14

I am with you always, to the end of the age.
Matthew 28.20

Faith is the realization of an invisible presence of truth.
Henry Ward Beecher, *Proverbs from Plymouth Pulpit*

Though God be everywhere present, yet He is only present to Thee in the deepest, and most central Part of thy Soul.
William Law, *The Spirit of Prayer*

Drench your spirit in the palpitating consciousness of the Presence! Then let an astonished world behold the resultant change.

F.W. Boreham, *A Late Lark Singing*

> Speak to Him thou for He hears, and Spirit with Spirit can meet –
> Closer is He than breathing, and nearer than hands and feet.
>
> Alfred, Lord Tennyson, 'The Higher Pantheism'

The doctrine of the presence of God, to be realized here and now, should give to the habitually unhappy both the light to see what Christian hope is all about and the grace to act upon this light.

Hubert van Zeller, *Considerations*

The time of business does not with me differ from the time of prayer; and in the noise and clatter of my kitchen, while several persons are at the same time calling for different things, I possess God in as great tranquillity as if I were upon my knees at the Blessed Sacrament.

Brother Lawrence, *The Practice of the Presence of God*

It is easier to attain knowledge of this presence by personal experience, than by reading books, for it is life and love, strength and light, joy and peace to a chosen soul. A soul that has once experienced it cannot therefore lose it without pain; it cannot cease to desire it, because it is so good in itself, and brings such comfort.

Walter Hilton, *The Ladder of Perfection*

The presence of God which sanctifies our souls is the indwelling of the Blessed Trinity, who take up their abode in the depths of our hearts when we submit to the divine will; for the presence of God that results from contemplation effects this intimate union in us only in the same way as other things which are part of God's design.

Jean-Pierre de Caussade SJ, *Self-Abandonment to the Divine Providence*

The practice of the presence of God may involve very many hours of hard work; but the reward is great; for this is the joy that no man can take from us; this is the faith which is the human side of divine grace, an experiment which is becoming an experience, a foretaste and assurance of the rest remaineth for the people of God.

W.R. Inge, *Personal Religion and the Life of Devotion*

Practise . . . the presence of God . . . Let us thus think often that our only business in this life is to please God, that perhaps all besides is but folly and vanity . . . Let us think of Him perpetually. Let us put all our trust in Him . . . We cannot have too much in so good and faithful a Friend, Who will never fail us in this world or in the next.

Brother Lawrence, *The Practice of the Presence of God*

What Christians claim in 'Christian experience' is not to pick up a body of wrought-out knowledge on the cheap, and to have a pat reply to all the mysteries of the universe, but to be aware of a Presence . . . As the Christian responds to the Presence and ventures forward, he becomes acquainted with a Person – holy, loving and merciful, and One who proves His personal care over all who turn to Him in trust.

W.E. Sangster, *Give God a Chance*

At the same time they became conscious by degrees of an usual yearning of the soul for stillness and solitude, and for a rest and quietness in which all the natural powers are hushed and silent. And their hearts seem to them to be drawn away into a region where all external things become distasteful, and pass into forgetfulness. And they are drawn sweetly and gently in the hidden power of love, to God Himself, and *awaken to a sense of His presence.*

Gerhard Tersteegen, in Frances Bevan, *Sketches of the Quiet of the Land*

. . . to live in the Presence of God is the way to perfection. We never depart from that way, but by losing sight of God, and forgetting our dependence upon Him. God is the Light by which we see, and the end at which we should aim. In all the business and events of life we should consider only the order of His Providence, and we shall maintain a sense of His Presence in the midst of our business, as long as we have no other intention in performing it, but purely that of obeying Him.

François de la M. Fénelon, *Spiritual Thoughts for Busy People*

It is the presence of God which makes anywhere heaven or hell or what we call purgatory. The presence of God is the heaven of those who love His presence; the presence of God is the hell of those who do not love His presence; and the presence of God is the sweet purification of the penitent who longs to be worthy of His presence. The presence of God is everywhere, and it is our reaction to it which makes us either good or peaceful people, or rebellious, defiant people, or penitent, learning people.

Father Andrew SDC, *The Symbolism of the Sanctuary*

In those rare glimpses of Christ's own life and prayer which the Gospels vouchsafe for us, we always notice the perpetual reference to the unseen Father; so much more vividly present to Him than anything that is seen. Behind that daily life into which He entered so generously, filled as it was with constant appeals to His practical pity and help, there is ever the sense of that strong and tranquil Presence, ordering all things and bringing them to their appointed end; not with a rigid and mechanical precision, but with the freedom of a living, creative, cherishing thought and love.

Evelyn Underhill, *Abba*

What if it be true that the key to the correct understanding of the Second Coming is indeed to be found in John's Gospel in the words which tell how Father and Son will come and make their dwelling in the loving and obedient heart? (John 14.23). The cosmic upheaval may well stand for the destruction of the old life and the creation of the new when Christ enters into life. The judgement may well stand for the confrontation of the soul with Christ. The blessedness may well stand for the new life which is the life lived in Christ.

William Barclay, *The Plain Man Looks at the Apostles' Creed*

**See also** Divinity, Experience, Glory, Inner Life, Power

# 88

# PRIDE

*Pride – overweening opinion of one's own qualities, merits etc; arrogant bearing or conduct; exalted position, consciousness of this, arrogance; also proper pride – a sense of what befits one's position, preventing one from doing an unworthy thing*

The Gurkhas are a good illustration of a proper sense of pride. They have an honourable outlook on life and an infectious enthusiasm for their work. They are reputed to be the smartest soldiers in the world, both on and off parade. They have a well-deserved reputation for loyalty, cheerfulness and bravery. I remember an occasion when a rifleman was picked up for a fault in his arms drill. Late that evening he was hard at work, ironing out the fault. He, like the others, had a proper sense of pride which insisted on doing a good job and producing top quality work. I was very privileged to serve with them. We all know of instances of the other kind of pride. For the writer of Ecclesiasticus, the beginning of human pride is to forsake the Lord, and to turn one's heart away from one's Maker. We then tend to get caught up in an inordinate self-love, and we succumb to pride.

The beginning of human pride is to forsake the Lord; the heart has withdrawn from its Maker.

Ecclesiasticus 10.12

. . . he has scattered the proud in the thoughts of their hearts. He has brought down the powerful from their thrones.

Luke 1.51–52

His own opinion was his law.

William Shakespeare, *Henry VIII*

Self-blinded are you by your pride.
Alfred, Lord Tennyson, 'The Two Voices'

The whole trouble is that we won't let God help us.
George Macdonald, *The Marquis of Lossie*

Pride is over-estimation of oneself by reason of self-love.
Benedict Spinoza, *Spinoza's Ethics and de Intellectus Emendatione*

Evil can have no beginning, but from pride; nor any end, but from humility.
William Law, in Stephen Hobhouse, *Selected Mystical Writings of William Law*

Pride is therefore pleasure arising from a man's thinking too highly of himself.
Benedict Spinoza, *Spinoza's Ethics and de Intellectus Emendatione*

A *Proud* man hath no *God*: for he hath put God down, and set Himself up.
Benjamin Whichcote, *Moral and Religious Aphorisms*

Pride: ignorant presumption that the qualities and status of the organism are due to merit.
A.R. Orage, *On Love*

Intellectual pride inflicts itself upon everybody. Where it dwells there can be no other opinion in the house.
Cardinal Manning, *Pastime Papers*

Pride, like the magnet, constantly points to one object, self; but, unlike the magnet, it has no attractive pole, but at all points repels.
C. C. Colton, *Lacon*

Perverted pride is a great misfortune in men; but pride in its original function, for which God created it, is indispensable to a proper manhood.
Henry Ward Beecher, *Proverbs from Plymouth Pulpit*

There are two states or conditions of pride. The first is one of self-approval, the second one of self-contempt. Pride is seen probably at its purest in the last.
Henri Frédéric Amiel, *Amiel's Journal*

Every good thought that we have, every good *action* that we do, lays us open to pride, and exposes us to the assaults of vanity and self-satisfaction.
William Law, *A Serious Call to a Devout and Holy Life*

He that is proud eats up himself: pride is his own glass, his own trumpet, his own chronicle and whatever praises itself, but in the deed, devours the deed in the praise.

William Shakespeare, *Troilus and Cressida*

Now, if this thought that you deliberately conjure up, or harbour, and dwell lovingly upon, is natural worth or knowledge, charm or station, favour or beauty – then it is *Pride*.

*The Cloud of Unknowing*

As all things are God's, so all things are to be used and regarded as the things of God. For men to abuse things on earth, and live to themselves, is the same rebellion against God, as for angels to abuse things in Heaven; because God is just the same Lord of all on earth, as He is the Lord of all in Heaven.

William Law, *A Serious Call to a Devout and Holy Life*

We need to avoid pride. Pride destroys everything. That's why Jesus told his disciples to be meek and humble. He didn't say contemplation is a big thing – but being meek and humble with one another. If you understand that, you understand your vocation. To live his way is the key to being meek and humble.

Mother Teresa, in Brother Angelo Devananda, *Jesus, the Word to Be Spoken*

Of all Causes which conspire to blind
Man's erring Judgement, and misguide the Mind,
What the weak Head with strongest Byass rules,
Is *Pride*, the *never-failing Vice of Fools*.

Alexander Pope, 'An Essay on Criticism'

The self-centred or self-concerned soul, making itself the object of its contemplation, and seeing all else as related to itself, is trying to feed upon itself. The food may be congenial, but the process is inevitably one of wastage. Such a soul must shrink and shrivel, suffering at last both the pain of unsatisfied hunger and the pain of contraction.

William Temple, *Nature, Man and God*

Nothing hath separated us from God but our own will, or rather our own will is our separation from God . . . The fall of man brought forth the kingdom of this world; sin in all shapes is nothing else but the will of man driving on in a state of self-motion and self-government, following the workings of a nature broken off from its dependency upon, and union with, the divine will. All the evil and misery in the creation arises only and solely from this one cause.

William Law, in Stephen Hobhouse, *Selected Mystical Writings of William Law*

In the last resort there are only two pivots about which human life can revolve, and we are always organizing society and ourselves about one or other of them. They are self and God. In the great book with which the Bible closes, these two principles are set before us under the symbolical figures of the 'Lamb standing, as it had been slain' – the symbol of love that uses sacrifice as its instrument – and the great wild beast, the symbol of self-will or pride, whose instrument is force.

William Temple, *Christian Faith and Life*

**See also** Doubt, Loneliness, Selfishness, Sin, Worldliness

# 89

# PROGRESS

*Progress – forward or onward movement in space, advance, development*

Martin Luther King put his finger on a crucial point when he wrote we must work passionately and indefatigably to bridge the gulf between our scientific progress and our moral progress. He went on to add one of the great problems of humanity is that we suffer from a poverty of spirit which stands in glaring contrast to our scientific and technological abundance. The scientific and technological revolutions have been truly impressive, and we have witnessed awe-inspiring progress in both these spheres in the twentieth century. This form of progress can be seen in every technical area of life, but for some reason similar progress has not been forthcoming in the spiritual and moral spheres of life. What I think is now needed is a spiritual and moral revolution, similar to the one we have experienced in science and technology, coming to us through meditation and contemplation.

But the path of the righteous is like the light of dawn, which shines brighter and brighter until full day.

Proverbs 4.18

I press on towards the goal for the prize of the heavenly call of God in Christ Jesus.

Philippians 3.14

There's a back'ard current in the world, and we must do our utmost to advance in order just to bide where we be.

Thomas Hardy, *Desperate Remedies*

Progress in the spiritual life comes from climbing a ladder of which the rungs are made alternately of belief and doubt.

Edward Patey, *Christian Life Style*

I consider that the way of life in urbanized, rich countries, as it exists today, and as it is likely to go on developing, is probably the most degraded and unillumined ever to come to pass on earth.

Malcolm Muggeridge, *Jesus Rediscovered*

So long as all the increased wealth which modern progress brings goes but to build up great fortunes, to increase luxury and make sharper the contrast between the House of Have and the House of Want, progress is not real and cannot be permanent.

Henry George, *Progress and Poverty*

His test of progress – of the moral worth of his own or any other age – was the *men* it produced. He admired most of all things in this world single-minded and sincere people, who believed honestly what they professed to believe, and lived it out in their actions.

James A. Froude, *Thomas Carlyle*

The whole process of social and civic development is the parallel growth of two things: richness of individual personality with completeness of social intercourse. The development of personality in fellowship is no bad definition of what we mean by progress.

William Temple, *Christian Faith and Life*

Life has lost its controlling unity. The idea of progress has been dissociated from the inspiration of faith. The subsidence of the ancient framework has brought down the overarching roof of certainty that God is regnant in the universe which, for the men of an earlier generation, gave life shelter and significance.

F.R. Barry, *The Relevance of Christianity*

. . . the heart of moral improvement, the heart of moral progress, therefore also of social progress, and the amelioration of this world's bitter condition, is always to be found in worship, worship which is the opening of the heart to the love of God and the exposure of the conscience to be quickened by it.

William Temple, *The Preacher's Theme Today*

We must work passionately and indefatigably to bridge the gulf between our scientific progress and our moral progress. One of the great problems of mankind is that we suffer from a poverty of the spirit which stands in glaring contrast to our scientific and technological abundance. The richer we have become materially, the poorer we have become morally and spiritually.

Martin Luther King, in Coretta Scott King, *The Words of Martin Luther King*

In the great mystics we see the highest and widest development of that consciousness to which the human race has yet attained. We see its growth exhibited to us on a grand scale, perceptible to all men . . . The germ of that same transcendent life, the spring of the amazing energy which enables the great mystic to rise to freedom and dominate his world, is latent in all of us; an integral part of our humanity.

Evelyn Underhill, *Mysticism*

Progress, however, of the best kind, is comparatively slow. Great results cannot be achieved at once; and we must be satisfied to advance in life as we walk, step by step . . . 'to know *how to wait* is the great secret of success'. We must sow before we can reap, and often have to wait long, content meanwhile to look patiently forward in hope; the fruit best worth waiting for often ripening the slowest. But 'time and patience', says the Eastern proverb, 'change the mulberry leaf to satin'.

Samuel Smiles, *Self-Help*

Human progress is neither automatic nor inevitable. Even a superficial look at history reveals that no social advance rolls in on the wheels of inevitability. Every step toward the goal of justice requires sacrifice, suffering, and struggle; the tireless exertions and passionate concern of dedicated individuals. Without persistent effort, time itself becomes an ally of the insurgent and primitive forces of irrational emotionalism and social destruction. This is no time for apathy or complacency. This is a time for vigorous and positive action.

Martin Luther King, in Coretta Scott King, *The Words of Martin Luther King*

Just as it was thought that developing science and technology would bring happiness and progress, there are people today who think that building just, social, economic and political structures will bring happiness and progress.

It is true that better conditions help, but it's illusory to believe that they alone are sufficient. Man doesn't change anything – unless *man himself takes part in these changes* for himself and his brothers. What changes him then is his commitment, his dedication to others. It becomes a spiritual mission at the core of which the believer recognizes the presence of God.

Michel Quoist, *With Open Heart*

A man's ability to be a pioneer of progress, that is, to understand what civilization is and to work for it, depends, therefore, on his being a thinker and on his being free. He must be the former if he is to be capable of comprehending his ideals and putting them into shape. He must be free in order to be in a position to launch his ideals out into the general life. The more completely his activities are taken up in any way by the struggle for existence, the more strongly will the impulse to improve his own condition find expression in the ideals of his thought. Ideals of self-interest then get mixed up with and spoil his ideals of civilization. Material and spiritual freedom are closely bound up with one another. Civilization presupposes free men, for only by free men can it be thought out and brought to realization.

Albert Schweitzer, *The Philosophy of Civilization, The Decay and Restoration of Civilization*

**See also** Action, Blessedness, Fulfilment, Growing, Transformation

# 90

# PURPOSE

*Purpose – object, thing intended; fact, faculty, of resolving on something; design or intention*

Louis Lavelle wrote that the object of life is the discovery (by a deepening of the self) of the centre of the self that constitutes our unique and personal essence. He went on to add that most of us miss this by remaining on the surface of things, thinking only in terms of self-aggrandizement. In retrospect, I realize that I lived very much on the surface of things for the first twenty years of my life. At school I worked away to get through 'O' levels, and then specialized in three subjects for 'A' levels. In other areas of life my interest was mainly on sporting achievement. It was only later that I realized this was superficial. Self-aggrandizement was the order of the day. I would do National Service, go to university, get a well-paid job, buy a house and a car, have a family, and so on. I thought this must surely be right because everyone else was doing it. In my twenties I had a change of priorities, due to an evolving Christian faith. Eventually I discovered a real sense of purpose, which has been with me ever since.

I cry to God Most High, to God who fulfils his purpose for me.
Psalm 57.2

With all wisdom and insight he has made known to us the mystery of his will, according to his good pleasure that he set forth in Christ, as a plan for the fullness of time.
Ephesians 1.9–10

What makes life dreary is the want of motive.
George Eliot, *Daniel Deronda*

Purpose is what gives life a meaning . . . A drifting boat always drifts downstream.
Charles H. Parkhurst, *The Pattern in the Mount and Other Sermons*

Man is never happy until his own vague striving has found and fixed its goal.
Johann Wolfgang von Goethe, *Wilhelm Meister's Apprenticeship*

God has a purpose and it is the function of normal beings to try to comprehend that purpose.
A.R. Orage, *On Love*

Make me useful, positive, appreciative, generous.
Make me live.
Norman W. Goodacre, 'Layman's Lent'

As individuals, we should sometimes pause and ask ourselves: what is our aim in life? Have we got one at all?
William Barclay, *The Letters to Timothy and Titus*

Decide who and what you want to be; then pursue your purpose with total concentration until you become what you wish to be.
Anon

Deeply the Christian believes that beneath all the flux and change of this mortal life, God is seeking to work out a profound purpose.
W.E. Sangster, *God Does Guide Us*

Continuity of purpose is one of the most essential ingredients of happiness in the long run, and for most men this comes chiefly through their work.
Bertrand Russell, *The Conquest of Happiness*

We need God, not in order to understand the why, but in order to feel and sustain the ultimate wherefore, to give a meaning to the Universe.
Miguel de Unamuno, *The Tragic Sense of Life*

How could there be any question of acquiring or possessing, when the one thing needful for man is to *become* – to *be* at last, and to die in the fullness of his being.
Antoine de Saint-Exupéry, *The Wisdom of the Sands*

Many persons have a wrong idea of what constitutes true happiness. It is not attained through self-gratification but through fidelity to a worthy purpose.
Helen Keller, *Helen Keller's Journal*

The end of life is not profit, amusement, philosophy, science or religion. It is not even happiness: it is life itself. Life consists in the plenitude of all the organic and mental activities of the body.

Alexis Carrel, *Reflections on Life*

The need for devotion to something outside ourselves is even more profound than the need for companionship. If we are not to go to pieces or wither away, we must all have some purpose in life; for no man can live for himself alone.

Ross Parmenter, *The Plant in My Window*

The man who consecrates his hours
By vig'rous effort and honest aim,
At once he draws the sting of life and death.

Edward Young, *Night Thoughts*

What is the meaning of human life, or, for that matter, of the life of any creature? To know an answer to this question means to be religious. You ask: Does it make any sense, then, to pose this question? I answer: The man who regards his own life and that of his fellow-creatures as meaningless is not merely unhappy but hardly fit for life.

Albert Einstein, *Ideas and Opinions*

This is the true joy in life, the being used for a purpose, recognized by yourself as a mighty one; the being thoroughly worn out before you are thrown on the scrap heap; the being a force of Nature instead of a feverish selfish little clod of ailments and grievances complaining that the world will not devote itself to making you happy.

George Bernard Shaw, *The Complete Bernard Shaw Prefaces*

But it is not the place where you are that is the important thing. It is the intensity of your presence there. It is not the situation that counts. What counts is that you are fully alive in any situation. It is this that puts down roots and then flowers in your life. Availability: that is obedience. That, and looking hard at the place where you are, instead of wanting to work wonders somewhere else.

Neville Cryer, *Michel Quoist*

To accomplish anything you need an interest, a motive, a centre for your thought. You need a star to steer by, a cause, a creed, an idea, a passionate attachment. Men have followed many guiding lights. They have followed Christ, Mahomet,

Napoleon. Something must beckon you or nothing is done, something about which you ask no questions. Thought needs a fulcrum for its lever, effort demands an incentive or an aim.

W. MacNeile Dixon, *The Human Situation*

Life does not need comfort, when it can be offered meaning, nor pleasure, when it can be shown purpose. Reveal what is the purpose of existence and how he may attain it – the steps he must take – and man will go forward again hardily, happily, knowing that he has found what he must have – intentional living – and knowing that an effort, which takes all his energy because it is worth his full and constant concentration, is the only life deserving the devotion, satisfying the nature and developing the potentialities of a self-conscious being.

Anon

**See also** Commitment, Fulfilment, Hope, Life, Transformation

# 91

# QUIETNESS

*Quietness – silence, stillness; being free from disturbance or agitation or urgent tasks; rest, repose; peace of mind*

Ambrose Bierce in his book, *The Devil's Dictionary*, defined noise as a 'stench in the ear'. Noise has become one of the great pollutions of modern time. I know this only too well having spent the last thirty-seven years in the centre of cities. I am also fond of the phrase 'oases of quiet' – those times when we can withdraw, perhaps, from the thick of things, and find moments of quiet to get a sense of perspective and proportion. I have had a busy and active ministry, but have been able to balance this by observing times of quietness. The practice started as an undergraduate. For many years now, I have kept a journal or what might be called a spiritual diary. I regard this as the most valuable thing I have done in my life. I have found it possible to have 'oases of quiet' on a daily basis, on a Sunday and on holiday. In the summer I love to go to an isolated part of the coast and have an extended time of quietness which sets me up for the following year. Through this practice it is possible to experience that rare commodity, quiet, and peace of mind.

In returning and rest you shall be saved; in quietness and in trust shall be your strength.

Isaiah 30.15

. . . let your adornment be the inner self with the lasting beauty of a gentle and quiet spirit, which is very precious in God's sight.

1 Peter 3.4

I am come by a hard way to the quiet of God.

Alistair MacLean, *The Quiet Heart*

Think glorious thoughts of God and serve with a quiet mind.

Charles Duthrie, *God in His World*

In silence alone does a man's truth bind itself together and strike root.

Antoine de Saint-Exupéry, *The Wisdom of the Sands*

A happy life must be to a great extent a quiet life, for it is only in an atmosphere of quiet that true joy can live.

Bertrand Russell, *The Conquest of Happiness*

Tranquillity! Thou better name
Than all the family of Fame.

Samuel Taylor Coleridge, 'Ode to Tranquillity'

I have discovered that all the unhappiness of men arises from one single fact, that they cannot stay quietly in their own chamber.

Blaise Pascal, *Pensées*

To go up alone into the mountain and come back as an ambassador to the world, has ever been the method of humanity's best friends.

Evelyn Underhill, *Mysticism*

The quiet of quiet places is made quieter by natural sounds. In a wood on a still day the quiet is increased by the whisper of the trees.

Mark Rutherford, *Last Pages from a Journal*

Altogether it will be found that a quiet life is characteristic of great men, and that their pleasures have not been of the sort that would look exciting to the outward eye.

Bertrand Russell, *The Conquest of Happiness*

Unhappy, unfulfilled people, who find it difficult to care, are going to be the people interested in wars, fast cars, consumer fads in ridiculous variety, in conflict and in competition and in all the hectic and feverish pursuit of a lost security – not in those things which make for quietness of heart and mind.

Roy Stevens, *Education and the Death of Love*

Christ's existence was ruled by a great silence. His soul was 'listening'. It was given over to the needs of others. In his innermost being he was silent, not asserting himself, detached. He did not grasp at anything in the world. Thus he overcame in his life the power of habit and daily routine, of dullness and fatigue, and created within himself a carefree tranquillity, a place for every encounter.

Ladislaus Boros, *In Time of Temptation*

Drop thy still dews of quietness,
Till all our strivings cease;
Take from our souls the strain and stress,
And let our ordered lives confess
The beauty of thy peace.

John Greenleaf Whittier, 'The Brewing of Soma'

Violence is not strength, noisiness is not earnestness. Noise is a sign of want of faith, and violence is a sign of weakness.

By quiet, modest, silent, private influence we shall win. 'Neither strive nor cry nor let your voice be heard in the streets', was good advice of old, and is still. I have seen many a movement tried by other method of striving and crying and making a noise in the streets, but I have never seen one succeed thereby, and never shall.

Charles Kingsley, *Daily Thoughts*

Many people today look for silence, solitude and peace. They dream of places where they can rest, away from the daily hassles of living which tear them apart, exhaust them and leave them dissatisfied, wounded and bleeding – and always alone.

But they won't necessarily find peace and quiet waiting for them in other places. There is a place within us where quiet reigns – the centre, our heart of hearts. There we can find him who is the plenitude of silence. But who will guide us there? We must learn the way.

Michel Quoist, *With Open Heart*

. . . we simply need quiet time in the presence of God. Although we want to make all our time for God, we will never succeed if we do not reserve a minute, an hour, a morning, a day, a week, a month, or whatever period of time for God and God alone.

This asks for much discipline and risk-taking because we always seem to have something more urgent to do and 'just sitting there' and 'doing nothing' often disturbs us more than it helps. But there is no way around this. Being useless and silent in the presence of our God belongs to the core of all prayer.

Henri J.M. Nouwen, in Robert Durback, *Seeds of Hope*

God is a Being, still, and peaceful, dwelling in the still eternity. Therefore should your mind be as a still, clear mountain tarn, reflecting the glory of God as in a mirror, where the image is unbroken and perfect. Avoid, therefore, all that would needlessly disturb or confuse or stir up your natural mind, from without or from within. Nothing in the whole world is worth being disturbed about . . . God is in His holy temple. Let all that is in you keep silence before Him – silence of the mouth, silence of all desires and all thoughts, silence of labour and toil. Oh, how precious and how useful is a still and quiet spirit in the eyes of God.

Gerhard Tersteegen, in Frances Bevan, *Sketches of the Quiet in the Land*

**See also** Contemplation, Contentment, Meditation, Peace, Serenity

# 92

# RELATIONSHIPS

*Relationships – what one person or thing has to do with another, way in which one stands or is related to another*

The Swiss psychologist C.G. Jung once wrote the love problem is part of humanity's heavy toll of suffering, and nobody should be ashamed that he must pay his tribute. Over the years I have found Jung's words helpful, especially in the wake of broken relationships. I have also been helped in my understanding of the nature of relationships by some words of R.E.C. Browne. In *The Ministry of the Word* he wrote in the sphere of human relationships there are no rules to be found for knowing the appropriate behaviour in a particular situation. Perhaps this helps us to understand why relationships are so difficult. No fixed guidance to follow. One thing I am learning from my experience of relationships is to be honest, in thoughts and in feelings. This is difficult, and sometimes painful, but it can prevent much stress and strain later on in our relationships.

Set me as a seal upon your heart, as a seal upon your arm; for love is strong as death . . . Many waters cannot quench love, neither can floods drown it. If one offered for love all the wealth of one's house, it would be utterly scorned.

Song of Solomon 8.6–7

Love is patient; love is kind; love is not envious or arrogant or rude. It does not insist on its own way; it is not irritable or resentful; it does not rejoice in wrongdoing, but rejoices in the truth. It bears all things, believes all things, hopes all things, endures all things. Love never ends.

1 Corinthians 13.4–8

The emotionally crippled person is always the produce of a love gone wrong.

Michel Quoist, *With Open Heart*

An intimate relationship between people not only asks for mutual openness, but also for mutual respectful protection of each other's uniqueness.

Henri J.M. Nouwen, *Reaching Out*

A man needs something which is more than friendship and yet is not love as it is generally understood. This something nevertheless a woman only can give.

Mark Rutherford, *Last Pages from a Journal*

Good judgment in our dealings with others consists not in seeing through deceptions and evil intentions but in being able to waken the decency dormant in every person.

Eric Hoffer, *The Passionate State of Mind*

When a person loves, all that is in his power is invested with a sense of purpose, as available for the other, or becomes a cause or occasion of gratitude, as received as gift from the other.

W.H. Vanstone, *Love's Endeavour, Love's Expense*

I like direct and simple relations with people, and dread complex, subtle, intricate relations – and above all *claims*. One gives, and does the best one can, but the moment that *claims* come in, the atmosphere is uneasy.

A.C. Benson, *Extracts from the Letters of Dr A.C. Benson to M.E.A.*

> Talk not of wasted affection, affection never was wasted;
> If it enrich not the heart of another, its waters, returning
> Back to their springs, like the rain, shall fill them full of refreshment.
>
> Henry Wadsworth Longfellow, 'Evangeline'

I have often wondered why it is that men should be so fearful of new ventures in social relationships . . . Most of us fear, actually fear, people who differ from ourselves, either up or down the scale.

David Grayson, *The Friendly Road*

There is hardly anything that can make one happier than to feel that one counts for something with other people. What matters here is not numbers, but intensity. In the long run, human relationships are the most important thing in life.

Dietrich Bonhoeffer, *Letters and Papers from Prison*

We discover, perhaps to our astonishment, that our greatest moments come when we find that we are not unique, when we come upon another self that is very like our own. The discovery of a continent is mere idle folly compared with this discovery of a sympathetic other-self, a friend or a lover.

J.B. Priestley, *All About Ourselves and Other Essays*

The woman is increasingly aware that love alone can give her her full stature, just as the man begins to discern that spirit alone can endow his life with its highest meaning. Fundamentally, therefore, both seek a psychic relation one to the other; because love needs the spirit, and the spirit, love, for their fulfilment.

C.G. Jung, *Contributions to Analytical Psychology*

True relationship with others involves humility of attitude, refusal to treat others as things or slaves, refusal to pass judgement upon them, acceptance of their limitations and culpability, readiness to welcome and to listen to what they have to say, respect for their uniqueness, progressive understanding of their mystery, trust in what they can become, stimulation of their spiritual progress, appreciation of both the value and insufficiency of ethical norms and moral virtues.

Emil Rideau, in George Appleton, *Journey for a Soul*

The first [danger] is that a man lives for himself alone, deciding everything in the light of his own advantage, disregarding the rights and needs of his fellow-men. The second [danger] is that we should think of people impersonally, in the mass, with numbers rather than names, thinking of them as cast in the same mould, with no individuality of their own. Each man wants value in himself, thinking of others in the same way. Neither individualism or collectivism is the right way of human relationships.

George Appleton, *Journey for a Soul*

The sexual act is not a mere pleasure of the body, a purely carnal act, but is a means by which love is expressed and life perpetuated. It becomes evil, if it harms others or if it interferes with a person's spiritual development, but neither of these conditions is inherent in the act itself. The act by which we live, by which love is expressed and the race continued is not an act of shame or sin. But when the masters of spiritual life insist on celibacy, they demand that we should preserve singleness of mind from destruction by bodily desires.

Sir Sarvepalli Radhakrishnan, *Mahatma Gandhi*

If we think about it, we find our life *consists* in this achieving of a pure relationship between ourselves and the living universe about us. This is how I 'save my soul' by accomplishing a pure relationship between me and another person, me and other people, me and a nation, me and a race of men, me and the animals, me and the trees or flowers, me and the earth, me and the skies and sun and stars, me and the moon: an infinity of pure relations, big and little, like the stars of the sky: that makes our eternity, for each one of us, me and the timber I am sawing, the lines of force I follow; and the dough I knead for bread, me and the very motion with which I write, me and the bit of gold I have got.

D.H. Lawrence, *The Phoenix*

To drive home the close parallel between the sexual act and the mystical union with God may seem blasphemous today. Yet the blasphemy is not in the comparison, but in the degrading of the one act of which man is capable that makes him like God both in the intensity of his union with his partner and in the fact that by this union he is a co-creator with God. All the higher religions recognize the sexual act as something holy; hence the condemnation of adultery and fornication under all circumstances. These acts are not forbidden because they are demonstrably injurious on rational grounds; they are forbidden because they are a desecration of a holy thing, they are a misuse of what is most godlike in man.

R.C. Zaehner, *Mysticism Sacred and Profane*

**See also** Acceptance, Awareness, Character, Compassion, Friendship

# 93

# RESURRECTION

*Resurrection – rising from the dead, especially the resurrection of Christ; rising again of people at the last day; revival from disuse of inactivity*

Three observations have helped me to believe in the resurrection of Christ. The first comes from some words of Martin Luther, writing about nature: 'Our Lord has written the promise of the resurrection, not in books alone, but in every leaf in springtime.' The second comes from some words of Emil Brunner, the Swiss theologian: 'You believe in the Resurrection, not because it is reported by the Apostles but because the Resurrected One Himself encounters you in a living way.' I would like to link this statement with the experience of Archbishop Anthony Bloom, recorded in the last quotation of this section. The third follows on from the Genesis story of the creation of humanity, and the life of Christ. When we are open and receptive to the grace of God it is possible to experience a 'resurrection', a *re-surrection* – a rising of the divine from the depths of ourselves. These observations have helped me to a belief in the historic resurrection.

For I know that my Redeemer lives, and that at the last he will stand upon the earth; and after my skin has been thus destroyed, then in my flesh I shall see God.

Job 19.25–26

Were not our hearts burning within us while he was talking to us on the road, while he was opening the scriptures to us?

Luke 24.32

Christian theology has never suggested that the 'fact' of Christ's resurrection could be known apart from faith.

Alan Richardson, *History Sacred and Profane*

Jesus' resurrection makes it impossible for man's story to end in chaos – it has to move inexorably towards light, towards life, towards love.

Carlo Carretto, *The Desert in the City*

The Resurrection is not a miracle like any other. It is a unique manifestation within this world of the transition God makes for us out of this way of being into another.

Austin Farrer, *Saving Belief*

What is more difficult, to be born or to rise again; that what has never been should be, or that what has been should be again? Is it more difficult to come into existence than to return to it?

Blaise Pascal, *Pensées*

The Christian doctrine is a doctrine not of immortality but of Resurrection. The difference is profound. The method of all non-Christian systems is to seek an escape from the evils and misery of life. Christianity seeks no escape, but accepts these at their worst, and makes them the material of its triumphant joy. That is the special significance in this connection of the Cross and Resurrection of Jesus Christ.

William Temple, *Nature, Man and God*

You ask, 'What is the Good?' I suppose God Himself is the Good; and it is this, in addition to a thousand things, which makes me feel the absolute certainty of a resurrection, and a hope that this, our present life, instead of being an ultimate one, which is to decide our fate for ever, in which man's faculties are so narrow and cramped, his chances (I speak of millions, not of units) of knowing the Good so few, that he may have chances hereafter, perhaps continually fresh ones, to all eternity.

Charles Kingsley, *Daily Thoughts*

The New Testament promises us that our physical body shall be transmuted into a spiritualized body, like the body of the risen Christ, released from the domination of the material, the spatial and the temporal. Yet in some mysterious way it will be recognizable perhaps with its most significant features, as the nail-marks and the spear-wound on our Lord's resurrection body. We may think of the body as a life-long comrade, who will survive death and in some spiritualized form be our comrade still.

George Appleton, *Journey for a Soul*

The Christian belief is that after death individuality will survive, that you will still be you and I will still be I. Beside that we have to set another immense fact. To the Greek the body could not be consecrated. It was matter, the source of all evil, the prison-house of the soul. But to the Christian the body is not evil. Jesus, the Son of God, has taken this human body upon him and therefore it is not contemptible because it has been inhabited by God. To the Christian, therefore, the life to come involves the total man, body and soul.

William Barclay, *The Letters to the Corinthians*

Without the Resurrection the Christian movement would have petered out in ignominy, and there would have been no Christianity. It is not too much to say that without the Resurrection the phenomenon of Christianity in the apostolic age and since is scientifically unaccountable. It is also true to say that without the Resurrection Christianity would not be itself, as the distinctiveness of Christianity is not its adherence to a teacher who lived long ago but its belief that 'Jesus is Lord' for every generation through the centuries.

Michael Ramsey, in Margaret Duggan, *Through the Year with Michael Ramsey*

Jesus revealed God to them and became so utterly the central form that they were clinging to Him. But that could not go on for ever. They had to make a painful transition to a new relationship in which they clung to Him as something within their own lives, and not just as a nostalgic kind of thing. The great story that marks this transition is that of Jesus saying to Mary Magdalen on the Resurrection Day: 'Do not cling to Me, as in the past. It really is Me, but you and my other followers are passing on to a new relationship of a very tremendous kind.'

Michael Ramsey, in Gerald Priestland, *Priestland's Progress*

The friends of Jesus saw him and heard him only a few times after that Easter morning, but their lives were completely changed. What seemed to be the end proved to be the beginning; what seemed to be a cause for fear proved to be a cause for courage; what seemed to be defeat proved to be victory; and what seemed to be the basis for despair proved to be the basis for hope. Suddenly a wall becomes a gate, and although we are not able to say with much clarity or precision what lies beyond the gate, the tone of all that we do and say on our way to the gate changes drastically.

Henri J.M. Nouwen, in Robert Durback, *Seeds of Hope*

. . . Paul never said that we would rise with the body with which we died. He insisted that we would have a spiritual body. What he really meant was that a man's *personality* would survive. It is almost impossible to conceive of personality without a body, because it is through the body that the personality expresses itself. What Paul is contending for is that after death the individual remains. He did not inherit the Greek contempt of the body but believed in the resurrection of the whole man. He will still be himself, he will survive as a person.

William Barclay, *The Letters to the Corinthians*

While I was reading the beginning of St Mark's Gospel, before I reached the third chapter, I suddenly became aware that on the other side of my desk there was a presence. And the certainty was so strong that it was Christ standing there that it has never left me. This was the real turning-point. Because Christ was alive and I had been in his presence I could say with certainty that what the Gospel said about the crucifixion of the prophet of Galilee was true, and the centurion was right when he said 'Truly he is the Son of God' . . . I became absolutely certain within myself that Christ is alive and that certain things existed. I didn't have all the answers, but having touched that experience, I was certain that ahead of me there were answers, visions, possibilities.

Anthony Bloom, *School for Prayer*

**See also** Cross, Experience, Grace, Hope, Presence

# 94

# REVELATION

*Revelation – disclosing of knowledge, to man by divine or supernatural agency; knowledge so disclosed*

In the opening verses of the Bible we read of God creating 'the heavens and the earth . . . and the Spirit of God was moving over the face of the waters'. As a result of these words I expect to see some evidence of the creator in the creation. Consequently nature has always been an important source of revelation for me. The opening words of John's Gospel point us to a revelation in the person of Jesus Christ: 'In the beginning was the Word, and the Word was with God, and the Word was God . . . And the Word became flesh and dwelt among us, full of grace and truth; we have beheld his glory, glory as of the only Son from the Father.' Consequently the Gospels have always been for me an important media of revelation. I have also found the saints an important source of revelation of God as experienced in their lives. Close allies are other people, and art, music, poetry, literature, drama, philosophy, science, etc. All these are potential sources of revelation. Mention must also be made of worship, the sacraments, and an open and receptive form of prayer.

In the beginning when God created the heavens and the earth, the earth was a formless void and darkness covered the face of the deep, while a wind from God swept over the face of the waters.

Genesis 1.1–2

They who have my commandments and keep them are those who love me; and those who love me will be loved by my Father, and I will love them and reveal myself to them.

John 14.21

The world is charged with the grandeur of God.

Gerard Manley Hopkins, 'God's Grandeur'

Man is the revelation of the Infinite, and it does not become finite in him. It remains the Infinite.

Mark Rutherford, *More Pages from a Journal*

If you only say, you have a Revelation from God; I must have a Revelation from God too, before I can believe you.

Benjamin Whichcote, *Moral and Religious Aphorisms*

The one obvious, unmistakable manifestation of the Deity is the law of good and evil disclosed to men by revelation.

Leo Tolstoy, *Anna Karenina*

Instead of complaining that God had hidden Himself, you will give Him thanks for having revealed so much of Himself.

Blaise Pascal, *Pensées*

For each truth revealed by grace, and received with inward delight and joy, is a secret murmur of God in the ear of a pure soul.

Walter Hilton, *The Ladder of Perfection*

The first and most important fact that we can know about God is ever this: *we* know nothing of Him, except what He Himself has revealed to us.

Emil Brunner, *Our Faith*

That which we really know about God, is not what we have been clever enough to find out, but what the Divine Charity has secretly revealed.

Evelyn Underhill, *The School of Charity*

My own mind is the direct revelation which I have from God and far least liable to mistake in telling his will of any revelation.

Ralph Waldo Emerson, *The Heart of Emerson's Journals*

The knowledge of man is as the waters, some descending from above, and some springing from beneath: the one informed by the light of nature, the other inspired by divine revelation.

Francis Bacon, *The Advancement of Learning*

God is revealed as the God of love, and henceforth every morally good act, that is, every act formed by charity, is a revelation of God. Every word of truth and love, every hand extended in kindness, echoes the inner life of the Trinity.

Gabriel Moran FSC, *Theology of Revelation*

One of the mistakes which men sometimes make is to identify God's revelation *solely* with the Bible. That would be to say that since about AD 120, when the latest book in the New Testament was written, God has ceased to speak, that since then there has been no more revelation from God. God's Spirit is *always* revealing Himself. It is true that God's supreme and unsurpassable revelation came in Jesus Christ; but Jesus is not a figure in a book. He is a living person, and in Him God's revelation goes on. God is still leading us into a greater and greater realization of what Jesus means . . .

William Barclay, *The Gospel of John*

In nature we find God; we do not infer from Nature what God must be like, but when we see Nature truly, we see God self-manifested in and through it. Yet the self-revelation so given is incomplete and inadequate. Personality can only reveal itself in persons. Consequently it is specially in Human Nature – in men and women – that we see God.

William Temple, *Nature, Man and God*

Love, whether in its most exalted form as the love between husband and wife, or in the less ardent experience of affection and sympathy, unlocks the doors of our prison-house and reveals to us something of the breadth and length and depth and height of the spiritual world which surrounds us. In various degrees, all cordial human intercourse is a liberation and an enhancement of our personality; it is a channel of revelation.

W.R. Inge, *Personal Religion and the Life of Devotion*

For two reasons the event in which the fullness of revelation is given must be the life of a Person: the first is that the revelation is to persons who can fully understand only what is personal; the second is that the revelation is of a personal Being, who accordingly cannot be adequately revealed in anything other than personality. Moreover, if the Person who is Himself the revelation is to be truly adequate to that function, He must be one in essence with the Being whom He reveals.

William Temple, *Nature, Man and God*

It is quite wrong to think of God's revelation as being confined to what we might call theological truth. The theologians and the preachers are not the only persons who are inspired . . . When a great poet delivers to men a great message in words which defy time, he is inspired . . . A great musician is inspired . . . When a scientist discovers something which will help the world's toil and make life better for men, when a surgeon discovers a new technique which will save men's lives and ease their pain, when someone discovers a new treatment, a new drug, which will bring life and hope to suffering humanity, that is a revelation from God. It actually happens in a way that we can see.

William Barclay, *The Gospel of John*

**See also** Aspiration, Holy Spirit, Inspiration, Jesus Christ, Light

# 95

# SAINTS

## *Saints – the holy people of God*

I grew up with a rather jaundiced view of saints. I spotted a few of them in stained-glass windows in churches. They looked cold and severe in demeanour, and thin and emaciated in body. The turning-point came in meeting a real live saint. I was surprised to be confronted by a warm and loving person. He was outgoing and fully alive. His disposition was kindly and sympathetic. His bright shining eyes were evidence of an inner energy and enthusiasm. He was radiant. I wonder how he got to be like that? Something of the divine in him coming alive, nurtured by prayer and worship, and finding an outlet in service? I began to look around and discovered several more. I came to call them my 'heroes' and 'heroines'. Indirectly they have been an enormous help to me. In times of difficulty, I have thought about my 'heroes' and 'heroines' and immediately felt much better. Whatever else was happening in the world, they were quietly getting on with things – their lives giving ample evidence of God. The experience of the saints has also provided me with an invaluable source of inspiration.

As for the holy ones in the land, they are the noble, in whom is all my delight.
  Psalm 16.3

. . . called to be saints, together with all those who in every place call on the name of our Lord Jesus Christ, both their Lord and ours.
  1 Corinthians 1.2

To pray is to open oneself to the possibility of sainthood, to the possibility of becoming set on fire by the Spirit.
  Kenneth Leech, *True Prayer*

The holiness of the saints is the restored image of God in them.

Benedicta Ward, in Alan Richardson and John Bowden, *A New Dictionary of Christian Theology*

The heroes, the saints and sages – they are those who face the world alone.

Norman Douglas, *An Almanac*

Grace is indeed needed to turn a man into a saint, and he who doubts it does not know what a saint or a man is.

Blaise Pascal, *Pensées*

The saint is essentially someone who communicates and radiates the character of God, his love, his joy, his peace.

Kenneth Leech, *True Prayer*

The loving acceptance of the saints is never mistaken by sinners as condoning their sins. Rather it lifts them to new aspirations.

Anon

God creates out of *nothing*, wonderful, you say: yes, to be sure, but he does what is still more wonderful: he makes saints out of sinners.

Søren Kierkegaard, *The Journals of Søren Kierkegaard*

They may have had their trials too – failing health, declining years, the ingratitude of men – but they have endured as seeing Him who is invisible.

Benjamin Jowett, *College Sermons*

The power of the Soul for good is in proportion to the strength of its passions. Sanctity is not the negation of passion but its order . . . Hence great Saints have often been great sinners.

Coventry Patmore, *The Rod, the Root and the Flower*

They were men of intense religious faith, of marked mystical type, characterized by interior depth of experience, but at the same time they were men of scholarship, breadth and balance.

Rufus M. Jones, *Spiritual Reformers in the 16th and 17th Centuries*

We may allow that the saints are specialists, but they are specialists in a career to which all Christians are called. The difference between them and us is a difference in degree, not in kind.

Evelyn Underhill, in John Stobbart, *The Wisdom of Evelyn Underhill*

This man is known by five signs. First, he never complains. Next, he never makes excuses: when accused, he leaves the facts to vindicate him. Thirdly, there is nothing he wants in earth or heaven but what God wills himself. Fourthly, he is not moved in time. Fifthly, he is never rejoiced: he is joy itself.

Meister Eckhart, in Franz Pfeiffer, *Meister Eckhart*, translated by C. de B. Evans

The saint is God's greatest work. All the world's 'great' men seem small beside the saint. The great statesman, the great writer, the great soldier may be far above us, but he remains altogether of our world. The great saint fills us with awe and seems at times almost a visitor from another sphere.

W.E. Sangster, *The Pure in Heart*

I have met in my life two persons, one a man, the other a woman, who convinced me that they were persons of sanctity. Utterly different in character, upbringing and interests as they were, their affect on me was the same. In their presence I felt myself to be ten times as nice, ten times as intelligent, ten times as good-looking as I really am.

W.H. Auden, *A Certain World*

The eyes of the saint make all beauty holy and the hands of the saint consecrate everything they touch to the glory of God, and the saint is never offended by anything and judges no man's sin because he does not know sin. He knows the mercy of God. He knows that his own mission on earth is to bring that mercy to all men.

Thomas Merton, *Seeds of Contemplation*

The saints are men and women of prayer to whom we owe our deepest revelations of the Supernatural – those who give us real news about God – are never untrained amateurs or prodigies. Such men and women as Paul, Augustine, Catherine, Julian, Ruysbroeck, are genuine artists of eternal life. They have accepted and not scorned the teachings of tradition: and humbly trained and disciplined their God-given genius for ultimates.

Evelyn Underhill, *Man and the Supernatural*

There is after all something in Christian saintliness which eludes analysis. For saintliness is the partial expression, the reflection in the external life, of the hidden man of the heart, who is not fully known even to the saint himself; and it is always imperfect, because it is always going on to perfection. I will not have my portrait painted, said a holy man; for which man do you want to paint? One of them is not worth painting, and the other is not finished yet.

W.R. Inge, *Types of Christian Saintliness*

A saint is not so much a man who realizes that he possesses virtues and sanctity as one who is overwhelmed by the sanctity of God. God is holiness. And therefore things are holy in proportion as they share what He is. All creatures are holy insofar as they share in His being, but men are called to be holy, in a far superior way – by somehow sharing His transcendence and rising above the level of everything that is not God.

Thomas Merton, *The Sign of Jonas*

A saint is a human creature devoured and transformed by love: a love that has dissolved and burnt out those instinctive passions – acquisitive and combative, proud and greedy – which commonly rule the lives of men.

Evelyn Underhill, in John Stobbart, *The Wisdom of Evelyn Underhill*

**See also** Character, Holiness, Holy Spirit, Love, Mystics

# 96

# SALVATION

*Salvation – saving of the soul; deliverance from sin and its consequences and admission to heaven brought about by Christ; acquisition of holiness*

William Law gave me a valuable insight into the meaning of salvation: 'There is but one salvation for all mankind,' he wrote, 'and that is the life of God in the soul.' He added that God's intent is to 'introduce or generate His own life, light, and Spirit in them, that all may be so many images, temples and habitations of the Holy Trinity'. Baptism is about cleansing and the birth of the life of God in the soul. We are baptized in the name (nature of) the Father, the Son and the Holy Spirit. The seed or spark of God already in us is triggered off and catalysed. The gifts of the Holy Spirit, latent within us, are brought to life and activated. As we grow and develop we experience the presence of the fruits of the Spirit in our lives. Through prayer and sacrament, our bodies become temples and habitations of the Holy Trinity. I have mentioned previously the presence of the earthly and creaturely in our lives. In the process of salvation, the life of God thus generated in the soul accepts the earthly and creaturely and brings about an integration. A valuable part of our nature, thought to be fallen, is redeemed and salvation – the acquisition of wholeness – gets under way.

The Lord is my strength and my might, and he has become my salvation.
   Exodus 15.2

For you were going astray like sheep, but now you have returned to the shepherd and guardian of your souls.
   1 Peter 2.25

What is most contrary to salvation is not sin but habit.
   Charles Péguy, *Basic Verities*

Our salvation, thank God! depends much more on His love of us than of our love of Him.

Father Andrew SDC, *Meditations for Every Day*

. . . the man who is saved, made whole, is the man who responds to a vision of God's life in Christ.

Frank Wright, *The Pastoral Nature of the Ministry*

God both represents to us what we are to become and shows us both the way to become it. Union with God is the goal and the love of God is the way.

Don Cupitt, *Taking Leave of God*

Man needs, above all else, salvation. He needs to turn round and see that God is standing there with a rope ready to throw to him if only he will catch it and attach it to himself. Then life can start all over again for him.

Norman W. Goodacre, *Laymen's Lent*

Salvation does not come from not going along, or running away. Nor does it come from letting oneself be carried along without willing. Salvation comes from complete self-surrender, and one's gaze must be directed upon a centre.

C.G. Jung, *The Integration of the Personality*

Christ died to save us, not from suffering, but from ourselves; not from injustice, far less from justice, but from being unjust. He died that we might live – but live as he lives, by dying as he died who died to himself that he might live unto God.

George Macdonald, *Unspoken Sermons*

The believer is one who places a particular kind of interpretation on his past – he sees it as salvation. And he does this, not by selecting from it what suits him; not by ignoring the less pleasant bits. He ignores nothing. He accepts it *all* as the way God brought him; learns from it all, but is bowed down by none of it. His past becomes not the history of failure, but the history of what God has done to him, and for him, and with him.

Henry McKeating, *God and the Future*

It was something in which they were *being saved*. It is interesting to note that in the Greek this is a present tense, and not past. It would be strictly correct to translate it not, 'in which you have been saved', but 'in which you are being saved'. Salvation goes from glory to glory. It is not something which is ever completed in this world. There are many things in this life which we can exhaust, but the meaning of salvation is something which a man can never exhaust.

William Barclay, *The Letters to the Corinthians*

There is but one salvation for all mankind, and that is the life of God in the soul. God has but one design or intent towards all mankind and that is to introduce or generate His own life, light, and Spirit in them, that all may be as so many images, temples and habitations of the Holy Spirit . . . There is not one for the Jew, another for a Christian, and a third for the heathen. No; God is one, human nature is one, salvation is one, and the way to it is one; and that is, the desire of the soul turned to God.

William Law, in Stephen Hobhouse, *Selected Mystical Writings of William Law*

Those who are in the Universities and Churches of men have Christ in their mouths, and they have a measuring-reed by their side – the inhabitants of God's Church on the other hand have the Life of Christ and the testing-standing within themselves. Those who are 'nominal professors' hang salvation on a literal knowledge of the merit secured by Christ's death; the true believer knows that salvation is never a purchase, is never outwardly effected, but is a new self, a new spirit, a new relation to God: 'Man must cease to be what he is before he can come to be another kind of person.'

Rufus M. Jones, *Spiritual Reformers in the 16th and 17th Centuries*

The true aim of the soul is not its own salvation; to make that the chief aim is to ensure its perdition ('Whosoever would save his soul shall lose it' – St Matthew 16.25); for it is to fix the soul on itself as centre. The true aim of the soul is to glorify God; in pursuing that aim it will attain to salvation unawares. No one who is convinced of his own salvation is as yet even safe, let alone 'saved'. Salvation is the state of him who has ceased to be interested whether he is saved or not, provided that what takes the place of that supreme self-interest is not a lower form of self-interest but the glory of God.

William Temple, *Nature, Man and God*

Consider yourself a refractory pupil for whom you are responsible as mentor and tutor. To sanctify sinful nature, by bringing it gradually under control of the angel within us, by the help of a holy God, is really the whole of Christian pedagogy and of religious morals. Our work – my work – consists in taming, subduing, evangelizing and *angelizing* the evil self and in restoring harmony with the good self. Salvation lies in abandoning the evil self in principle, and in taking refuge with the other, the divine self, – in accepting with courage and prayer the task of living with one's own demon, and making it into a less and less rebellious instrument of good.

Henri Frédéric Amiel, *Amiel's Journal*

What every man looks for in life is his own salvation and the salvation of the men he lives with. By salvation I mean first of all the full discovery of who he himself really is. Then I mean something of the fulfilment of his own God-given powers, in the love of others and of God. I mean also the discovery that he cannot find himself in himself alone, but that he must find himself in and through others. Ultimately, these propositions are summed up in two lines of the Gospel: 'If any man would save his life, he must lose it,' and, 'Love one another as I have loved you.' It is also contained in another saying from St Paul: 'We are members one of another.'

Thomas Merton, *No Man Is an Island*

When, therefore, the first spark of a desire after God arises in thy soul, cherish it with all thy care, give all thy heart into it, it is nothing less than a touch of the divine loadstone that is to draw thee out of the vanity of time into the riches of eternity. Get up, therefore, and follow it gladly as the Wise men of the East followed the star from Heaven that appeared before them. It will do for thee as the star did for them: it will lead thee to the birth of Jesus, not in a stable in Bethlehem in Judea, but to the birth of Jesus in the dark centre of thy own fallen soul.

William Law, in Stephen Hobhouse, *Selected Mystical Writings of William Law*

**See also** Finding God, Freedom, Healing, Transformation, Wholeness

# 97

# SCIENCE AND RELIGION

*Science – branch of knowledge; organized body of knowledge that has been accumulated on a subject; one dealing with material phenomena and based mainly on observation, experiment, and induction, as chemistry, biology*

Professor Coulson in his book *Science and Christian Belief* wrote: 'To the question, 'What is a primrose?' several valid answers may be given. One person says:

*A primrose by the river's brim*
*A yellow primrose was to him,*
*And it was nothing more*.

'Just that, and no more'. Another person, the scientist, says, 'a primrose is a delicately balanced biochemical mechanism, requiring potash, phosphates, nitrogen and water in definite proportions'. A third person says, 'a primrose is God's promise of spring'. All three definitions are correct. We see here three different approaches to truth – that of the poet, scientist and theologian.' Add to this some words of William Temple, and we have an understanding of the relationship of science and religion. In *Nature, Man and God*, he wrote 'the theologian who quarrels with science on its own ground is but a presumptuous fool. But the scientist who quarrels with theology on its own grounds is no better. If there is mutual respect and common reverence for truth in all its forms there may still be divergence and even what we have called tension; but there will be no quarrel.'

For it is he who gave me unerring knowledge of what exists, to know the structure of the world and the activity of the elements; the beginning and end and middle of times, the alternations of the solstices and the changes of the seasons, the cycles of the year and the constellations of the stars, the natures of animals and the tempers of wild animals, the powers of spirits and the thoughts of human beings, the varieties of plants and the virtues of roots.

Wisdom of Solomon 7.17–20

. . . for 'the earth and its fullness is the Lord's'.
1 Corinthians 10.26

Science without religion is lame, religion without science is blind.
Albert Einstein, *Out of My Later Years*

Science cannot supply faith in a loving God, and a God whom we can love.
Henry Ward Beecher, *Proverbs from Plymouth Pulpit*

Perhaps some day science can explain the world, but it can never explain its meaning.
Michel Quoist, *With Open Heart*

[Evolution] has for many taken the place of God Himself, and bowed Him calmly out of His Own Universe.
G.A. Studdert Kennedy, *Food for the Fed-Up*

Science may have found a cure for most evils; but it has found no remedy for the worst of them all – the apathy of human beings.
Helen Keller, *My Religion*

Science sees everything mechanically, through part of the moving-instinctive centre. It has no answer to human needs in a crisis.
A.R. Orage, *On Love*

Scientists are attempting to come to God head-first. They must come to Him heart-first. Then let their heads interpret what they have found.
Henry Ward Beecher, *Proverbs from Plymouth Pulpit*

The means by which we live have outdistanced the ends for which we live. Our scientific power has outrun our spiritual power. We have guided missiles and misguided man.
Martin Luther King, *Strength to Love*

Anybody who has been seriously engaged in scientific work of any kind realizes that over the entrance to the gates of the temple of science are written the words: *Ye must have faith*. It is a quality which the scientist cannot dispense with.
Max Planck, *Where is Science Going?*

But to the great man of science, science is an art, and he himself is an artist. And his creation is not the less a work of art because it is but a faint and imperfect copy of another – of the supreme work of art which is nature itself.

J.W.N. Sullivan, *Limitations of Science*

It may be that in the practice of religion men have real evidence of the Being of God. If that is so, it is merely fallacious to refuse consideration of this evidence because no similar evidence is forthcoming from the study of physics, astronomy or biology.

William Temple, *Nature, Man and God*

Science cannot solve the ultimate mystery of nature. And that is because, in the last analysis, we ourselves are part of nature and therefore part of the mystery that we are trying to solve. Music and art are, to an extent, also attempts to solve or at least express the mystery. But to my mind the more we progress with either the more we are brought into harmony with all nature itself. And that is one of the great services of science to the individual.

Max Planck, *Where is Science Going?*

Science investigates; religion interprets. Science gives man knowledge which is power; religion gives man wisdom which is control. Science deals mainly with facts; religion deals mainly with values. The two are not rivals. They are complementary. Science keeps religion from sinking into the valley of crippling irrationalism and paralyzing obscurantism. Religion prevents science from falling into the marsh of obsolete materialism and moral nihilism.

Martin Luther King, in Coretta Scott King, *The Words of Martin Luther King*

All science has God as its author and giver. Much is heard of the conflict between science and religion, and of the contrast between sacred and secular. There may be aspects of truth to which religion is the gate, as indeed there are aspects of truth to which particular sciences are the gate. But if there be a Creator, and if truth be one of his attributes, then everything that is true can claim his authorship, and every search for truth can claim his authority.

Michael Ramsey, in Margaret Duggan, *Through the Year with Michael Ramsey*

The simple and plain fact is that the scientific method wins its success by ignoring parts of reality as given in experience; it is perfectly right to do this for its own purposes; but it must not be permitted by a kind of bluff to create the impression that what it ignores is non-existent.

William Temple, *Nature, Man and God*

You will hardly find one among the profounder sort of scientific minds without a religious feeling of his own . . . His religious feeling takes the form of a rapturous amazement at the harmony of natural law, which reveals an intelligence of such superiority that, compared with it, all systematic thinking and acting of human beings is an utterly insignificant reflection. This feeling is the guiding principle of his life and work, in so far as he succeeds in keeping himself from the shackles of selfish desire. It is beyond question closely akin to that which has possessed the religious geniuses of all ages.

Albert Einstein, *Ideas and Opinions*

**See also** Awareness, Education, Humility, Truth, Wonder

# 98

# SEEKING

*Seeking – making search or inquiry for; anxious to find or get; asking (thing or person) for advice*

Several years ago I was on a chalet reading party in the French Alps with a dozen undergraduates. One of our Junior Research Fellows dropped in for a couple of days. He wanted to see as much of Mont Blanc as possible in the limited time available; so the two of us went for a walk by the Bionnassay glacier, up to a place called Le Nid d'Aigle, and back. We had not gone very far before he made a direct request. 'Bill, tell me, what do you believe in?' 'Oh, gosh,' I thought to myself, 'he's so bright, he is never going to believe this.' Anyway I gave him an outline of my vision of faith; of the divine inbreathing of the Genesis story of the creation of humanity; of this being fully worked out in the life of Jesus Christ; of St Paul realizing what Christ had experienced we can all in some measure also experience – something of the presence of the Father in ourselves, the Son, the gifts and fruits of the Holy Spirit. This seemed to strike a chord in him. To my great surprise he found what he had been seeking on our walk in the French Alps. Shortly after this he was baptized and confirmed.

. . . and those who seek me diligently find me.

Proverbs 8.17

. . . search, and you will find.

Matthew 7.7

Prayer has much more to do with God's search for us than our search for him.

Christopher Bryant SSJE, *Jung and the Christian Way*

A man travels the world over in search of what he needs and returns home to find it.

George Moore, *The Brook Kerith*

The search for meaning is richly rewarded when an adolescent can find something that deeply absorbs the talents of his mind and his emotional resources. He then has a passion for life.

Arthur T. Jersild, *The Psychology of Adolescence*

The way to know God is not by mental search, but by giving attention to Jesus Christ. The search for God can end in the contemplation of Jesus Christ, for in Him we see what God is like.

William Barclay, *The Gospel of Matthew*

The Kingdom of God is in you and he who searches for it outside himself will never find it, for *apart from God no one can either seek or find God, for he who seeks God, already in truth has Him.*

Rufus M. Jones, *Spiritual Reformers in the 16th and 17th Centuries*

My only task is to be what I am, a man seeking God in silence and solitude, with deep respect for the demands and realities of his own vocation, and fully aware that others too are seeking the truth in their own way.

Thomas Merton, *Contemplation in a World of Action*

Know that, by nature, every creature seeks to become like God . . . Nature's intent is neither food nor drink, nor clothing, nor comfort, nor anything else in which God is left out. Covertly, nature seeks, hunts, tries to ferret out the track on which God may be found.

Meister Eckhart, *Meister Eckhart*, translated by Raymond B. Blakney

Even in the midst of the lowest pleasures, the most abandoned voluptuary is still seeking God; nay more, as far as regards what is positive in his acts, that is to say in all that makes them an analogue of the true Love, it is God Himself Who, in him and for him, seeks Himself.

Etienne Gilson, *The Spirit of Medieval Philosophy*

I veritably believe that the Religion of the future will be something like this, an awed seeking, an orientation towards the superhuman, the Power behind all; with no permanent dogma, but the use of any and every dogma, when, if only for a day that dogma appears to be either true or a bridgeway towards truth or towards spiritual value, spiritual beauty.

Stephen MacKenna, *Journal and Letters*

There seem times when one can neither help oneself nor anyone else to find what we are all in search of, and it seems impossible to submit or acquiesce. I, as you know, have been in this frame of mind, and can only say that one does go on, though it seems impossible. The only way I think, is to do whatever comes to one, as quietly and fully as one can.

A.C. Benson, *Extracts from the Letters to Dr A.C. Benson*

Hold fast to God and he will add every good thing. Seek God and you shall find him and all good with him . . . To the man who cleaves to God, God cleaves and adds virtue. Thus, what you have sought before, now seeks you; what you once pursued, now pursues you; what once you fled, now flees you. Everything comes to him who truly comes to God, bringing all divinity with it, while all that is strange and alien flies away.

Meister Eckhart, *Meister Eckhart*, translated by Raymond B. Blakney

. . . Seek God and discover Him and make Him a power in your life. Without Him all of our efforts turn to ashes and our sunrises into darker nights. Without Him, life is a meaningless drama with the decisive scenes missing. But with Him we are able to rise from the fatigue of despair to the buoyancy of hope. With Him we are able to rise from the midnight of desperation to the daybreak of joy. St Augustine was right – we were made for God and we will be restless until we find our rest in Him.

Martin Luther King, in Coretta Scott King, *The Words of Martin Luther King*

We must learn to realize that the love of God seeks us in every situation, and seeks our good. His inscrutable love seeks our awakening. True, since this awakening implies a kind of death to our exterior self, we will dread His coming in proportion as we are identified with this exterior self and attached to it. But when we understand the dialectic of life and death we will learn to take risks implied by faith, to make the choices that deliver us from the routine self and open to us the door of a new being, a new reality.

Thomas Merton, *New Seeds of Contemplation*

When is the Search ended? In one sense, it is finished when our hand, stretched out to God in the name of His anointed mediator Jesus Christ, feels an answering grasp and knows that He is there. But in another sense the searching never ends, for the first discovery is quickly follow by another, and that by another, and so it goes on.

To find *that* He is, is the mere starting-point of our search. We are lured on to explore *what* He is, and that search is never finished, and it grows more thrilling the farther one proceeds.

Isobel Kuhn, *By Searching*

If we seek God earnestly, we shall find him – or – rather he will find us. If we ask God humbly to come into our lives, he will indeed come. And he will not do with us what we had expected – still less what we had 'hoped'. We shall find, to our dismay as natural men, that the God whose assistance we remotely invoked is already here, within us, speaking, even commanding; his presence manifested in an immediate and imperative revealing of duty and obligation. We asked him to advise, to help, to strengthen, from afar. He comes to indwell, command, and direct, within.

Harry Blamires, *The Will and the Way*

**See also** Experience, Finding God, Listening, Meditation, Presence

99

# SELF

*Self – person's or thing's own individuality or essence, person or thing as object of introspection or reflexive action*

Some writers in previous generations have made a distinction between the false self and the real self. The false self is usually made up of a number of elements. First, self-centredness or selfishness, often cunningly disguised. Second, a single-minded pursuit of wealth and what money can buy. Third, a striving for status and success; i.e. an ego trip. Fourth, a quest for happiness and pleasure, often with sexual connotations. In brief, the false self is completely taken up with the 'earthy and creaturely'. The real self is rather different. In this section W.R. Inge enables us to understand the nature of the real self: 'We are potentially all things; our personality is what we are able to realize of the infinite wealth which our divine–human nature contains hidden in its depths.' The real self discovers the 'infinite wealth' of our 'divine–human nature'. This is integrated with the 'earthy–creaturely' and leads to wholeness, at ease with oneself, and with other people. There is now no longer any need for pretence and cut-throat competition.

Keep your heart with all vigilance, for from it flow the springs of life.

Proverbs 4.23

But we have this treasure in clay jars, so that it may be made clear that this extraordinary power belongs to God and does not come from us.

2 Corinthians 4.7

Very often a change of self is needed more than a change of scene.

A.C. Benson, *Extracts from the Letters of Dr A.C. Benson to M.E.A*

He, that has no government of himself, has no Enjoyment of himself.

Benjamin Whichcote, *Moral and Religious Aphorisms*

My business is not to remake myself,
But make the absolute best of what God made.
Robert Browning, 'Bishop Blougram's Apology'

Self-knowledge comes to us only in the dark times, when we are stripped of illusion and naked to truth.
Mary Craig, *Blessings*

Resolve to be thyself; and know that he,
Who finds himself, loses his misery!
Matthew Arnold, 'Self-Dependence'

*The true value of a human being* is determined primarily by the measure and the sense in which he has attained liberation from the self.
Albert Einstein, *Ideas and Opinions*

Man is made 'in God's image'. God is a 'subsequent relation'. Within this relationship, man is made; through it, he becomes what he is. Out of it, he falls apart.
Michel Quoist, *With Open Heart*

The living self has one purpose only: to come into its own fullness of being, as a tree comes into full blossom, or a bird into spring beauty, or a tiger into lustre.
D.H. Lawrence, *The Phoenix*

Remember that there is but one man in the world, with whom you are to have perpetual contention, and be always striving to exceed him, and that is yourself.
William Law, *A Serious Call to a Devout and Holy Life*

We are potentially all things; our personality is what we are able to realize of the infinite wealth which our divine–human nature contains hidden in its depths.
W.R. Inge, *The Philosophy of Plotinus*

Not in the clamour of the crowded street,
Not in the shouts and plaudits of the throng,
But in ourselves, are triumph and defeat.
Henry Wadsworth Longfellow, 'The Poems'

Learning to know oneself is not just an affair of private introspection. It is also an affair of seeing how others behave and of recognizing and identifying feelings of theirs with feelings of one's own. Each is indispensable to the other.
John S. Brubacher, *Modern Philosophies of Education*

For it is precisely when all the bogus protective structures have collapsed, when the soul is 'pulverized' or nihilated, when it cries out, as the soul of Jesus did, in its helplessness and pain – it is precisely then that God is discovered in the darkness and love shapes itself in the world. David Anderson, *Simone Weil*

Love of self is the basic sin, from which all others flow. The moment a man makes his own will the centre of life, divine and human relationships are destroyed, obedience to God and charity to men both become impossible. The essence of Christianity is not the enthronement but the obliteration of self.

William Barclay, *The Letters to Timothy, Titus and Philemon*

Begin to search and dig in thine own Field for this *Pearl of Eternity*, that lies hidden in it; it cannot cost Thee too much, nor canst thou buy it too dear, for it is *All*, and when thou hast found it, thou wilt know, that all which thou hast sold or given away for it, is as mere a Nothing, as a Bubble upon the Water.

William Law, *The Spirit of Prayer*

But can one actually find oneself in someone else? In someone else's love? Or even in the mirror someone else holds up for one? I believe that true identity is found, as Eckhart once said, by 'going into one's own ground and knowing oneself'. It is found in creative activity springing from within. It is found, paradoxically, when one loses oneself. One must lose one's life to find it.

Anne Morrow Lindbergh, *Gift from the Sea*

The more man goes out from himself or goes beyond himself, the more the spiritual dimension of his life is deepened, the more he becomes truly man, the more also he grows in likeness to God, who is Spirit. On the other hand, the more he turns inward and encloses himself in self-interest, the less human does he become. This is the strange paradox of spiritual being – that precisely by going out and spending itself, it realizes itself.

John Macquarrie, *Paths in Spirituality*

Just as we say that we must look at ourselves both as members of the entire world body and in individuals, so, too, I must seek universal truth as well as my own personal truth. These are not contradictory or exclusive truths, they are in harmony. Yet the part of the great truth which is my very own truth is unique to me. My task then is to search for that truth which is mine – which is me, really – find it, and then seize it, make it so conscious a part of my existence that it informs everything that I do. Harry James Cargas, *Encountering Myself*

**See also** Acceptance, Image of God, Incarnation, Inner Life, Jesus Christ

## 100

# SELFISHNESS

*Selfishness – deficient in consideration for others, alive chiefly to personal profit or pleasure, actuated by self-interest, that pursuit of pleasure of one kind or another is the ultimate aim of every action*

There is a vital point we often miss in reading the Genesis story of the creation of man and woman. It comes out in the sentence: 'That which was fashioned and shaped in the image and likeness of God *was taken from the dust of the earth*'. Interpreted, this means although we have an enormous potential of divine life in the depths of our being, we are at one and the same time earthy and creaturely, and rightly so. This earthy and creaturely side is a valuable source of power and energy. What is needed is an inner integration of these two sides of our nature, leading to a full-blooded person, as worked out in the life of Jesus Christ. This is wholeness – salvation. We have forgotten this and by and large centre ourselves on our earthy and creaturely side and end up in selfishness. The cost is, we dampen down the enormous potential of divine life in the depths of ourselves, and greatly restrict our lives and relationships with others.

And you, do you seek great things for yourself? Do not seek them.
Jeremiah 45.5

All of them are seeking their own interests.
Philippians 2.21

One suffers most who is most selfish.
Taoist saying

The selfish heart deserves the pain it feels.
Edward Young, *Night Thoughts*

No man is more cheated than the selfish man.
  Henry Ward Beecher, *Proverbs from Plymouth Pulpit*

Man seeks his own good at the whole world's cost.
  Robert Browning, 'Luria'

The more selfish you are, the more involved life becomes.
  Thomas Merton, *The Sign of Jonas*

Perhaps one should not think so much of oneself, though it is an interesting subject.
  Norman Douglas, *An Almanac*

Selfish prosperity makes a man a vortex rather than a fountain; instead of throwing out, he learns only to draw in.
  Henry Ward Beecher, *Proverbs from Plymouth Pulpit*

Egoism: measuring others by our likes and dislikes – not by their needs but by our preferences.
  A.R. Orage, *On Love*

Selfish persons are incapable of loving others, but they are not capable of loving themselves either.
  Erich Fromm, *Man for Himself*

Selfish man, who does not want to be selfish – that aspiration for something better, is of God. Worldly man, conscious of spiritual things – that consciousness is of God.
  Henry Ward Beecher, *Proverbs from Plymouth Pulpit*

Selfish men may possess the earth, but it is the meek who inherit it, and enjoy it as an inheritance from their heavenly Father, free from all the defilements and perplexities of unrighteousness.
  John Woolman, *The Journal of John Woolman*

Every man must decide whether he will walk in the light of creative altruism or the darkness of destructive selfishness. This is the judgment. Life's most persistent and urgent question is, What are you doing for others?
  Martin Luther King, in Coretta Scott King, *The Words of Martin Luther King*

I may say that the growth has all been upward toward the elimination of selfishness. I do not mean simply the grosser, more sensual forms, but those subtler and generally unrecognized kinds, such as express themselves in sorrow, grief, regret, envy, etc.

William James, *The Varieties of Religious Experience*

If a man is centred upon himself, the smallest risk is too great for him, because both success and failure can destroy him. If he is centred upon God, then no risk is too great because success is already guaranteed – the successful union of Creator and creature beside which everything else is meaningless.

Morris West, *The Shoes of the Fisherman*

In your excessive self-love you are like a molecule closed in upon itself and incapable of entering easily into any new combination. God looks to you to be more open and more pliant. If you are to enter into him you need to be freer and more eager. Have done, then, with your egoism and your fear of suffering.

Pierre Teilhard de Chardin, *Let Me Explain*

It seems to me that nothing is so important from the point of view of Christianizing society as to recognize that competition is not a thing limited to business. It is a thing that pervades the whole of our life. It is simply organized selfishness, and, as things stand, from the moment we become conscious, almost throughout our lives, the whole influence of our environment is competitive, and suggests that our business is to do the utmost for ourselves in the struggle against other people.

William Temple, *The Kingdom of God*

The great evils of society do not result from the startling and appalling wickedness of some few individuals; they are the result of a few million people like ourselves living together; and if anyone wants to see the picture of his sin, let him look at slums, and wars, and the like. These things have their origin in characters like ours, ready, no doubt, to be generous with superfluities, but in the last resort self-centred with alike that defensiveness and aggressiveness that go with that self-centredness.

William Temple, *The Preacher's Theme Today*

For the self-centred spirit there can be no eternal life. Even if it should exist for ever, its existence could only be an ever deepening chill of death. Because it seeks its satisfaction in itself, where none is to be found, it must suffer an always intenser pang of spiritual hunger, which cannot be allayed until that spirit turns to another source of satisfaction. In the self which it contemplates there can only be successive states. The self is not sufficient to inspire a dedication such as brings purposive unity into life.

William Temple, *Nature, Man and God*

Anyone who from time to time will sit quiet with himself and survey his life and present state will be conscious of failure. He will remember things of which he is now ashamed. He will see his secret selfishness, his carefully controlled ambitions, his secret lusts. He will know the power of temptations – from without and from within. He will recognize times of wilful choice of wrong attitudes and deeds. When he compares himself with the perfection of Jesus, he will realize his need of forgiveness, a fresh start and continuing grace.

George Appleton, *Journey for a Soul*

**See also** Cross, Loneliness, Pride, Sin, Suffering

## 101

# SERENITY

*Serenity – calmness, placidity, tranquillity, unperturbed*

C.S. Duthrie, in his book *God in His World*, wrote: 'The serenity relevant for our time is a serenity that does not bypass the turmoil and torment of the atomic age but sends its roots down through the agonies to the life and power of God.' I find this sentence helpful because it fits in with the vision of faith which has evolved for me during the last twenty-five years. Most of us experience elements of turmoil, torment and agonies in everyday life. If we balance this by developing an inner life, we become rooted in the life and power of God, and at times experience serenity. I am very fond of my set of rooms in University College, Oxford. Sometimes I feel surrounded by turmoil, torment and agonies towards the end of a term when people are tired, and yet in spite of this there is an atmosphere of peace in my sitting-room. In these surroundings I can cope with stress and strain provided I tap into my inner resources. In this way I can keep things in perspective. St Augustine wrote: 'You have made us for yourself and our hearts find no peace until they rest in you.' This is what serenity means to me.

. . . he made the storm be still, and the waves of the sea were hushed. Then they were glad because they had quiet, and he brought them to their desired haven.

Psalm 107.29–30

We call those happy who were steadfast.

James 5.11 (RSV)

No one can achieve Serenity until the glare of passion is past the meridian.

Cyril Connolly, *The Unquiet Grave*

All men who live with any degree of serenity live by some assurance of grace.

Reinhold Niebuhr, *Reflections on the End of an Era*

Serenity of Mind, and Calmness of Thought are a better Enjoyment; than any thing without us.

Benjamin Whichcote, *Moral and Religious Aphorisms*

Serene but strong, majestic yet sedate,
Swift without violence, without terror great.

Matthew Prior, 'Carmen Seculare for the Year MDCC'

In Jesus there is the quiet, strong serenity of one who seeks to conquer by love, and not by strife of words.

William Barclay, *The Gospel of Matthew*

We have yet to learn that strength is shown at least as well as by serenity and poise as in strenuous action.

Odell Shepard, *The Joys of Forgetting*

There is certainly something in angling . . . that tends to produce a gentleness of spirit, and a pure serenity of mind.

Washington Irving, *The Sketch-Book*

True contemplative grace gently tranquillizes the personality, giving a wonderful serenity and a calm self-dominion.

William Johnston, *The Mysticism of the Cloud of Unknowing*

An old age, serene and bright
And lovely as a Lapland night.

William Wordsworth, in W.E. Sangster, *The Secret of Radiant Life*

Only a soul full of despair can ever attain serenity and, to be in despair, you must have loved a good deal and still love the world.

Henry Miller, *The Books in My Life*

Whatever helps a person to use his resources productively and reduces his need to live up to a false image of strength and perfection is likely to add to his serenity and freedom from fear.

Arthur T. Jersild, in *Educational Psychology*

A sense of rest, of deep quiet even. Silence within and without. A quietly burning fire. A sense of comfort . . . I am not dazed or stupid, but only happy in this peaceful morning. Whatever may be the charm of emotion, I do not know whether it equals the sweetness of those hours of silent meditation, in which we have a glimpse and foretaste of the contemplative joys of Paradise. Desire and fear, sadness and care, are done away. Existence is reduced to the simplest form, the most ethereal mode of being, that is, to pure self-consciousness. It is a state of harmony, without tension and without disturbance, the dominical state of the soul, perhaps the state which awaits it beyond the grave.

Henri Frédéric Amiel, *Amiel's Journal*

I am serene because I know thou lovest me.
Because thou lovest me, naught can move me from my peace. Because thou lovest me, I am as one to whom all good has come.

Alistair Maclean, in *God in Our Midst*

Serene will be our days and bright,
And happy will our nature be,
When love is an unerring light,
And joy its own security.

William Wordsworth, 'Ode to Duty'

It was one of those moments of total serenity which the spiritual part of me, always aspiring to the heights of philosophical detachment, so often compelled me to seek in the days of my meditative youth; one of those moments when all the materialistic and cynical views of life collapse like pathetic fabrications before the sovereign evidence of life's beauty, meaning and wisdom, and when every man experiences the triumphant feeling of an artist of genius who has just entirely expressed himself.

Romain Gary, *Promise at Dawn*

Sometimes we meet a person who has a quiet serenity of spirit of which we become quickly conscious; who seems to be unhurried and unworried; uncomplaining about the past, content with the present, unafraid of the future; one who seems to live in another tempo of life, with a stillness that is not a technique but comes from a centre of stillness within himself; one who is relaxed and restful, unself-assertive; whose 'isness' says more than his words, and will validate his words when he speaks of what he has discovered.

George Appleton, *Journey for a Soul*

It is clear that the western nations . . . know very little of this state of feeling [serenity]. For them life is devouring and incessant activity. They are eager for gold, for power, for dominion; their aim is to crush men and to enslave nature. They show an obstinate interest in means, and have not a thought for the end. They confound being with individual being, and the expansion of the self with happiness, – that is to say, they do not live by the soul; they ignore the unchangeable and the eternal; they live at the periphery of their being, because they are unable to penetrate to its axis. They are excited, ardent, positive, because they are superficial. Why so much effort, noise, struggle, and greed? – it is all a mere stunning and deafening of the self.

Henri Frédéric Amiel, *Amiel's Journal*

**See also** Acceptance, Contentment, Joy, Peace, Quietness

## 102

# SERVICE

*Service – doing of work, or work done, for another or for a community, etc.; assistance or benefit given to someone, readiness to perform this*

One of my duties in Nigeria was to teach in a local school – The Good Samaritan School for Handicapped Children. This unique school had been founded, a few years previously, by an elderly missionary couple, Mr and Mrs Patey. The pupils were small in number, but because of their physical and mental disabilities required a great deal of attention. I was impressed by Mr and Mrs Patey. They accommodated the children in their own home, looked after them, fed them, taught them and nursed them, and were on call twenty-four hours a day. Somehow, in spite of all the demands on their time and energy, they remained cheerful and produced a happy atmosphere. A warm friendly spirit pervaded the school – a consequence of costly service. In the end the cost proved to be too great and their health broke down and eventually they had to return to England. Jesus realized the importance of service. He said of himself: 'I am among you as one who serves.' He was also aware of the demands of service and warned his disciples to count the cost beforehand. Even the Good Samaritan needed to share the burden of service with the innkeeper.

Here is my servant, whom I uphold, my chosen, in whom my soul delights; I have put my spirit upon him.

Isaiah 42.1

Worship the Lord your God, and serve him only.

Matthew 4.10

Be useful where thou livest.

George Herbert, 'The Church Porch'

Life is given to us, we earn it by giving it.
Rabindranath Tagore, *Stray Birds*

They also serve who only stand and wait.
John Milton, 'Sonnet on His Blindness'

In Jesus the service of God and the service of the least of the brethren were one.
Dietrich Bonhoeffer, *The Cost of Discipleship*

Great works, do not always lie in our way, but every moment we may do little ones excellently, that is, with great love.
St Francis de Sales, *On the Love of God*

You have not done enough, you have never done enough, so long as it is still possible that you have something of value to contribute.
Dag Hammarskjöld, *Markings*

The service of the fruit is precious, the service of the flower is sweet, but let my service be the service of the leaves in its shade of humble devotion.
Rabindranath Tagore, *Stray Birds*

Nothing I can do, even if I do my best, can be good. As Jesus said, 'We are unprofitable servants, we have done our duty.' Therefore I shall strive to do my best.
A.R. Orage, *On Love*

Service of man . . . does not replace service of God. But the service of God never excuses from service of man: it is in service to man that service to God is proved.
Hans Küng, *On Being a Christian*

The giving of self to the service of God is not like making a single offer, handing over a single gift, receiving a single acknowledgement. It is a continued action, renewed all the time.
Hubert van Zeller, *Considerations*

*Abide in me and I in you . . .* All truth and depth of devotion, all effectiveness in service springs from this. It is not a theme for words, but for the deeper apprehensions of silence.
William Temple, *Readings in St John's Gospel*

When a man turns to Him, desiring to serve Him, God directs his attention to the world and its need. It is His will that our service of Him should be expressed as our service to the world, through Him, and for His sake.

Emil Brunner, *The Divine Imperative*

An act of prayer at the heart of every act of service – a self-offering to His purpose so that the action may be His and not our own. That, in its perfection, is the secret of the saints. *I live – yet not I*! Christ is the boundless source of energy and love.

Evelyn Underhill, *The Light of Christ*

The lives of the saints have always been for Christians the reminder that in this life men and women of all kinds, temperaments and cultures have touched the heights of Christian experience and have committed themselves utterly to the service of their fellows.

E.G. Rupp, in Alan Richardson and John Bowden, *A New Dictionary of Christian Theology*

There came to me, as I awoke, the thought that I must not accept this happiness as a matter of course, but must give something in return for it . . . I settled with myself before I got up, that I would consider myself justified in living till I was thirty for science and art, in order to devote myself from that time forward to the direct service of humanity.

Albert Schweitzer, *My Life and Thought*

Everybody can be great. Because anybody can serve. You don't have to have a college degree to serve. You don't have to make your subject and your verb agree to serve. You don't have to know about Plato and Aristotle to serve. You don't have to know Einstein's theory of relativity to serve. You don't have to know the second theory of thermo-dynamics in physics to serve. You only need a heart full of grace. A soul generated by love.

Martin Luther King, in Coretta Scott King, *The Words of Martin Luther King*

What, then, is the service rendered to the world by Christianity? The proclamation of 'good news'. And what is this 'good news'? The pardon of sin. The God of holiness loving the world and reconciling it to Himself by Jesus, in order to establish the kingdom of God, the city of souls, the life of heaven on earth, – here you have the whole of it, but in this is revolution. 'Love one another, as I have loved you'; 'Be ye one with me, as I am one with the Father', for this is life eternal, here is perfection, salvation, joy.

Henri Frédéric Amiel, *Amiel's Journal*

Ah yes, men must learn to serve
not for money, but for life.
Ah yes, men must learn to obey
not a boss, but the gleam of life on the face of a man
who has looked into the eyes of the gods.
Man is only perfectly human
when he looks beyond humanity.

D.H. Lawrence, 'Service'

**See also** Commitment, Discipleship, Leadership, Neighbour, Work

# 103

# SIN

*Sin – transgression, a transgression against the divine law of principles of morality*

Father Andrew has written, 'Sin is that condition in which a man makes himself the centre of his own life, and either ignores God or pushes Him on to the circumference. Fallen human nature is self-centred human nature.' Seen in the context of the Genesis story of the creation of humanity, humans choose to centre themselves on the earthy and creaturely, and ignore the fact they are made in the image and likeness of God. The divine life, latent in the depths of their being, is ignored altogether or pushed out on to the circumference of life. The outcome is a serious condition called sin. This leads to the commission of sins, and to a deadening of real life. Father Andrew goes on to point out: 'The human nature Christ brought to earth is God-centred.' Looking at the life of Christ as revealed in the Gospels we notice he centred his life on God, and brought about an integration of the earthy and creaturely. The outcome was wholeness or salvation. We need to centre our lives on God in like manner, integrating the earthy and creaturely.

. . . and be sure your sin will find you out.
Numbers 32.23

. . . since all have sinned and fall short of the glory of God; they are now justified by his grace as a gift, through the redemption that is in Christ Jesus.
Romans 3.23–24

You have ordained and so it is with us, that every soul that sins brings its own punishment upon itself.
St Augustine, *Confessions*

. . . The principle of sin which is man's self-centred desire to secure his independence against God.

G.W.H. Lampe, in A.R. Vidler, *Soundings*

Know this, O man, the sole root of sin in thee
Is not to know thine own divinity!

James Rhoades, in Ralph Waldo Trine, *My Philosophy and My Religion*

The worst sin towards our fellow creatures is not to hate them, but to be indifferent to them, that's the essence of inhumanity.

George Bernard Shaw, *The Devil's Disciple*

The appalling thing about sin is that man does not appear to be able to create in that realm, it is always the same old thing man has been doing all along.

J. Neville Ward, *The Use of Praying*

The safest road to Hell is the gradual one – the gentle slope, soft underfoot, without sudden turnings, without milestones, without signposts.

C.S. Lewis, *The Screwtape Letters*

Original sin? It is probably the malice that is ever flickering within us. Seen thus, it is a grievous error for those who manage human affairs not to take original sin into account.

Eric Hoffer, *The Passionate State of Mind*

One shall not kill 'the evil impulse', the passion, in oneself, but one shall serve God *with it*; it is the power which is destined to receive its direction from man.

Martin Buber, *Hasidism*

Sin is something inside our fallen selves trying to come out and be free to hurt. The evil outside ourselves in the fallen world is something which is trying to come in – also to hurt.

Hubert van Zeller, *Considerations*

. . . means the determined or lackadaisical refusal to live up to one's essential humanity. It is the torpid unwillingness to revel in the delights or to share in the responsibilities of being fully human.

Harvey Cox, *God's Revolution and Man's Responsibility*

Whenever you fight against the root of sin in general or any sin in particular, hold fast to this desire, and fix your mind upon Jesus Christ for whom you long rather than upon the sin which you are fighting.

Walter Hilton, *The Ladder of Perfection*

St Paul says that the wages of sin is death, not that God condemns us to death for our sins, but that sin kills the life of the spirit. Sin is a sickness that leads to spiritual death unless it is cured by forgiveness and the soul kept healthy by grace.

George Appleton, *Journey for a Soul*

Sin has always been an ugly word, but it has been made so in a new sense over the last half-century. It has been made not only ugly, but passé. People are no longer sinful, they are only immature or underprivileged or frightened or, more particularly, sick.

Phyllis McGinley, *The Province of the Heart*

The smallest atom of good realized and applied to life, a single vivid experience of love, will advance us much further, will far more surely protect our souls from evil, than the most arduous *struggle* against sin, than the resistance to sin by the severest ascetic methods of chaining the dark passions within us.

Father Yelchaninov, in G.P. Fedotov, *A Treasury of Russian Spirituality*

Over and over again, as we break some rule which seems rather arbitrary and meaningless, we discover the principle which had dictated it. We set in motion the causes and effects from which we understand, for the first time, why there had ever been that prohibition; then it is too late. The discovery is called the Fall of Man.

William Temple, *Christian Faith and Life*

Sin is the putting of self in the centre where God alone should be. Sin is acting from the self instead of from God. It is falling short of the will and glory of God. Often it is more than that – it is setting one's will against God's will, consciously (where guilt is involved) or unconsciously (when the sinful consequences are equally disastrous).

George Appleton, *Journey for a Soul*

I'm very much of a Jungian, and I feel Jung's concept of the dark side in all of us is very near the truth. If we equate that dark side with the Devil, we are not far wrong in our understanding of what the Devil is up to. The interesting thing about the dark side, or the Devil, is that he was a fallen angel – he belongs to God really – and our problem is to reconcile the dark side and make use of its energy. It's always recognized that the Devil is walking up and down the earth, full of energy. In education I used to find the apparently wicked boy was full of it. You've got to understand it, come to terms with it and make use of it. In other words, bring the Devil back into God's Kingdom.

Kenneth Barnes, in Gerald Priestland, *Priestland's Progress*

Eden is on no map, and Adam's fall fits no historical calendar. Moses is not nearer the Fall than we are, because he lived three thousand years before our time. The Fall refers not to some datable aboriginal calamity in the historic past of humanity, but to a dimension of human experience which is always present – namely, that we who have been created for fellowship with God repudiate it continually; and that the whole of mankind does this along with us. Every man is his own 'Adam', and all men are solidarily 'Adam'. Thus, Paradise before the Fall, the *status perfectionis*, is not a period of history, but our 'memory' of a divinely intended quality of life, given to us along with our consciousness of guilt.

J.S. Whale, *Christian Doctrine*

**See also** Anxiety, Cross, Loneliness, Pride, Selfishness

# 104

# SOUL

*Soul – the spiritual or immaterial part of humans, often regarded as immortal; the moral or emotional or intellectual nature of a person; the meeting-place of God in a person*

The Authorized Version of the Bible uses a different terminology in the Genesis story of the creation of humanity from the one we have been using. Genesis 2.7 reads: 'And the Lord God formed man of the dust of the ground, and breathed into his nostrils the breath of life; and man became a living soul.' This was the beginning of the meeting-place of God in humans, fully worked out in the life of our Lord. The lives of the saints, prophets and martyrs testify to the reality of the soul, and are examples of this way of life.

Non-biblical language may help us to understand more about the nature of the soul. Richard Jefferies in *The Story of My Heart*, wrote of a desire for 'a greatness of soul, an irradiance of mind, a deeper insight, a broader hope . . . By the word soul, or psyche, I mean an inner consciousness which aspires.' For Henry Ward Beecher, 'The human soul is God's treasury, out of which He coins unspeakable riches.' This insight points to the role of the priest and the 'cure of souls', enabling people to come to wholeness by drawing out the divine in them. We have now largely abandoned this role through ignorance and unbelief.

. . . the one who formed them and inspired them with active souls and breathed a living spirit into them.

Wisdom of Solomon 15.11

For what will it profit them to gain the whole world and forfeit their life? Indeed, what can they give in return for their life?

Mark 8.36–37

What is a soul? The thing that keeps the body alive.

James A. Froude, *Thomas Carlyle*

And it is with the soul that we grasp the essence of another human being, not with the mind, not even with the heart.

Henry Miller, *The Books in My Life*

There is a direct in-shining, a direct in-breathing, a direct in-reaching of the Divine Soul upon the human soul.

Henry Ward Beecher, *Proverbs from Plymouth Pulpit*

We shall know some day that death can never rob us of that which our soul has gained, for her gains are one with herself.

Rabindranath Tagore, *Stray Birds*

When he is in possession of his soul, then will man be fully alive, caring nothing for immortality and knowing nothing of death.

Henry Miller, *The Books in My Life*

The sphere that is deepest, most unexplored, and most unfathomable, the wonder and the glory of God's thought and head, is our own souls!

Henry Ward Beecher, *Proverbs from Plymouth Pulpit*

Love unites the soul with God, and, the more degrees of love the soul has, the more profoundly does it enter into God and the more it is centred in Him.

St John of the Cross, *Living Flame of Love*

I desire a greatness of soul, an irradiance of mind, a deeper insight, a broader hope. Give me power of soul, so that I may actually effect by its will that which I strive for.

Richard Jefferies, *The Story of My Heart*

The soul is a temple; and God is silently building it, by night and by day. Precious thoughts are building it; disinterested love is building it; all-penetrating faith is building it.

Henry Ward Beecher, *Proverbs from Plymouth Pulpit*

God's designs, God's good pleasure, the will of God, the action of God and his grace are all one and the same thing in life. They are God's working in the soul to make it like himself.

Jean-Pierre de Caussade SJ, *Self-Abandonment to Divine Providence*

But with Western man the value of the self sinks to zero. Hence the universal depreciation of the soul in the West. Whoever speaks of the reality of the soul or psyche is accused of 'psychologism'.

C.G. Jung, *The Collected Works of C.G. Jung*

The human soul is God's treasury, out of which He coins unspeakable riches. Thoughts and feelings, desires and yearnings, faith and hope – these are the most precious things which God finds in us.

Henry Ward Beecher, *Proverbs from Plymouth Pulpit*

By the word soul, or psyche, I mean that inner consciousness which aspires. By prayer I do not mean a request for anything preferred to a deity; I mean intense soul-emotion, intense aspiration.

Richard Jefferies, *The Story of My Heart*

By nature the core of the soul is sensitive to nothing but the divine Being, unmediated. Here God enters the soul with all he has and not in part. He enters the soul through the core and nothing may touch that core except God himself.

Meister Eckhart, *Meister Eckhart*, translated by Raymond B. Blakney

And see all sights from pole to pole,
And glance, and nod, and bustle by,
And never once possess our soul
Before we die.

Matthew Arnold, 'A Southern Night'

It is man's soul that Christ is always looking for. He calls it 'God's Kingdom', and finds it in every one. He compares it to little things, to a tiny seed, to a handful of leaven, to a pearl. That is because one realizes one's soul only by getting rid of all alien passions, all acquired culture, and all external possessions, be they good or evil.

Oscar Wilde, *De Profundis*

Either we have an immortal soul, or we have not. If we have not, we are beasts; the first and wisest of beasts, it may be; but still true beasts. We shall only differ in degree, and not in kind; just as the elephant differs from the slug. But by the concession of all the materialists of all the schools, or almost all, we are not of the same kind as beasts – and this also we say from our own consciousness. Therefore, methinks, it must be the possession of a soul within us that makes the difference.

Samuel Taylor Coleridge, *Table Talk of Samuel Taylor Coleridge*

If we wish to respect men we must forget what they are, and think of the ideal which they carry hidden within them, of the just man and the noble, the man of intelligence and goodness, inspiration and creative force, who is loyal and true, faithful and trustworthy, of the higher man, in short, and that divine thing we call a soul. The only men who deserve the name are the heroes, the geniuses, the saints, the harmonious, puissant, and perfect samples of the race.

Henri Frédéric Amiel, *Amiel's Journal*

**See also** Character, Eternal Life, Holy Spirit, Inner Life, Wholeness

# 105

# SUFFERING

*Suffering – undergoing pain, loss, grief, defeat, disablement, change, punishment, wrong, etc.*

I have been thinking about the carnage of the two World Wars recently. Most forms of suffering pale into insignificance in comparison, except when we ourselves have suffered directly, or have witnessed suffering in another, close by. In the small ways in which I have suffered, I have stopped asking the question, 'Why has this happened to me?' This seems to be the wrong sort of question. The thing has already happened, and that's that. The important question now is: 'How am I going to respond to this suffering, and is it possible to make a creative use of it?' While out in Singapore during National Service I went down with a severe dose of prickly heat, so much so that I was nearly invalided back to England. However the doctor put me on a new, possibly dangerous drug, and ordered me to bed for several days, lying down on my back and keeping perfectly still. I was bored stiff, but learnt important lessons. My mind took over and sorted out a great deal of dross. I was able to return to duties a wiser person.

The Lord is near to the broken-hearted, and saves the crushed in spirit.

Psalm 34.18

And after you have suffered for a little while, the God of all grace, who has called you to his eternal glory in Christ, will himself restore, support, strengthen and establish you.

1 Peter 5.10

He who suffers much will know much.

Greek proverb

In time of sickness the soul collects itself anew.

Latin proverb

We must somehow believe that unearned suffering is redemptive.

Martin Luther King, in Coretta Scott King, *The Words of Martin Luther King*

Although the world is full of suffering, it is full also of the overcoming of it.

Helen Keller, *Optimism*

Deep, unspeakable suffering may well be called a baptism, a regeneration, the initiation into a new state.

George Eliot, *Adam Bede*

Know how sublime a thing it is
To suffer and be strong.

Henry Wadsworth Longfellow, 'The Light of Stars'

Understood in its deepest sense, being Christ's follower means suffering that is unendurable to the great majority of mankind.

C.G. Jung, *Psychology and Alchemy*

I wonder why we suffer so strangely – to bring out something in us, I try to believe, which can't be brought out in any other way.

A.C. Benson, *Extracts from the Letters of Dr A.C. Benson to M.E.A.*

Shut out suffering, and you see only one side of this strange and fearful thing, the life of man. Brightness, and happiness, and rest – that is not life. It is only one side of life: Christ saw both sides.

F.W. Robertson, *Sermons*

There are powerful kinds of good that can come into life only where something has gone terribly wrong. That does not justify even the smallest area of life going wrong; it just happens to be one aspect of the composition of things.

J. Neville Ward, *Friday Afternoon*

. . . The bad things that happen to us in our lives do not have a meaning when they happen. But we can redeem these tragedies from senselessness by imposing meaning on them. In the final analysis, the question is not why bad things happen to good people, but how we respond when such things happen.

Rabbi H. Kushner, *When Bad Things Happen to Good People*

The mark of the spiritually mature man is that he can endure sorrow without bitterness, bewilderment without fuss, loss without envy or recrimination or self-pity. Above all, whatever the set-backs and misunderstandings, public and private, that he maintains a belief in the essential goodness of mankind.

Hubert van Zeller, *Considerations*

Only by saying 'Amen' ('So be it') explicitly or implicitly – despite everything – can suffering be endured if not explained. Saying 'Amen' is the translation of the Old Testament noun 'belief' (*heemen*). The world with its enigma, its evil and suffering, can be affirmed because of God. Not otherwise. The mystery of the Incomprehensible in his goodness embraces also the misery of our suffering.

Hans Küng, *On Being a Christian*

When trouble hits us we can react to it in a variety of ways. We can let it knock us out, so that we lose all hope and stamina. We can rebel and refuse to accept the rightness or merit of it. We can fill our lives with feverish activity so that we have no time to think about it. Or we can accept it – without defeat, rebellion, or evasion – trusting that God will make clear tomorrow what is so difficult to understand today.

George Appleton, *Journey for a Soul*

Job never found an answer to the problem of unmerited suffering. The problem remained insoluble, but in it he met God. That is where man always meets God. That is where man most frequently meets his fellows. For he is so constituted that he needs problems more than solutions. His soul thrives on questions but grows sickly on answers – especially answers served up by others and, most of all, answers laid down by authority.

John V. Taylor, *The Go-Between God*

Creative suffering – and this alone is real suffering – is positively non-resistant. It is a spiritual act, not a physical or mental reaction. And we cannot truly perform it until we wholly consent to the situation in which we find ourselves, however painful or disconcerting it may be, regarding it as the price we must pay for spiritual growth. By thus consenting to suffer we learn how to live by dying, how to surrender our existence to our being, until it is informed, more and more, by the eternal light of our essence.

Hugh L'Anson Fausset, *Fruits of Silence*

Sooner or later suffering, misfortune, trouble come to every life. Some of it comes from our own ignorance, some from our own mistakes, some is a consequence of our own sin. But in almost every life there is a residue which seems inexplicable.

Our Christian faith does not completely explain the mystery of suffering. It teaches us how to deal with suffering. It assures us that God does not will suffering, but he is in it, to redeem it and to turn it into good and blessing. Let us also remember that the perfect life was not exempt from suffering.

George Appleton, *Journey for a Soul*

**See also** Anxiety, Cross, Death, Depression, Grief

106

# TEMPTATION

*Temptation – tempting or being tempted, incitement especially to wrongdoing; attractive thing or course of action; archaic putting to the test*

While chaplain to University College, London, I went through a testing time and was tempted to leave the ordained ministry. I looked around for openings elsewhere, and was attracted to student counselling, or some form of psychotherapy. Fortunately providence came to my rescue and took me on a three-week tour to America, organized by the London University Church of Christ the King. We began with a week in New York. At the first opportunity I nipped off to a certain bookshop, to buy a copy of *The Choice Is Always Ours*, by Dorothy Berkley Phillips – a book which had been highly recommended to me. Back at the hotel, I quickly realized I had been looking for this book for ten years. By the time we landed at Gatwick, I was back on course with an outline of a new vision of faith. As I look back I value that initial period of testing and temptation. Without that I would never have come across *The Choice Is Always Ours* which has changed the whole course of my life.

My child, when you come to serve the Lord, prepare yourself for testing. Set your heart right and be steadfast, and do not be impetuous in time of calamity. Cling to him and do not depart, so that your last days may be prosperous. Accept whatever befalls you, and in times of humiliation be patient. For gold is tested in the fire, and those found acceptable, in the furnace of humiliation. Trust in him, and he will help you; make your ways straight, and hope in him.

Ecclesiasticus 2.1–6

Stay awake and pray that you may not come into the time of trial; the spirit indeed is willing, but the flesh is weak.

Matthew 26.41

All temptations are founded either in hope or fear.
Thomas Fuller, *Gnomologia*

Every evil to which we do not succumb is a benefactor.
Ralph Waldo Emerson, *Essays*

Subdue your appetites . . . and you've conquered human nature.
Charles Dickens, *Nicholas Nickleby*

Yet temptations often bring great benefits, even if they are disagreeable and a great burden; for in temptation a man is humbled, purified and disciplined.
Thomas à Kempis, *The Imitation of Christ*

He did not say, 'You will never have a rough passage, you will never be over-strained, you will never feel uncomfortable', but he *did* say 'You will never be overcome.'
Lady Julian of Norwich, *Revelations of Divine Love*

No man is tempted so, but may o'ercome,
If that he has a will to Masterdome.
Robert Herrick, 'Temptations'

The habitual conviction of the Presence of God is the sovereign remedy; it supports, it consoles, it calms us. We must not be surprised that we are tempted. We are placed here to be proved by temptation. Everything is temptation to us.
F. de la M. Fénelon, in B.W. Randolph, *Letters and Reflections*

The story of the Temptations is, of course, a parable of His spiritual wrestlings, told by Himself to His disciples. It represents the rejection, under three typical forms, of all existing conceptions of the Messianic task, which was to inaugurate the Kingdom of God.
William Temple, *Readings in St John's Gospel*

*Temptation* in the New Testament means any testing situation. It includes far more than the mere seduction to sin; it covers every situation which is a challenge to and a test of a person's manhood and integrity and fidelity. We cannot escape it, but we can meet it with God.
William Barclay, *The Gospel of Luke*

Thou know'st that Thou hast formed me,
With Passions wild and strong;
And list'ning to their witching voice
Has often led me wrong.

Robert Burns, 'A Prayer in the Prospect of Death'

Man is not entirely safe from temptation as long as he is alive, because the source of temptation lies within us – we are born in concupiscence. When one trial or temptation leaves us, another takes its place, and we will always have something to endure, because we have lost the blessing of human happiness.

Thomas à Kempis, *The Imitation of Christ*

Ay me, how many perils doe enfold
The righteous man, to make him daily fall?
Were not, that heavenly grace doth him uphold,
And stedfast truth acquit him out of all.

Edmund Spenser, 'The Faerie Queene'

The drunken Rip Van Winkle in Jefferson's play excuses himself for every fresh dereliction by saying, 'I won't count this time!' Well, he may not count it, and a kind Heaven may not count it, but it is being counted none the less. Down among his nerve-cells and fibres the molecules are counting it, registering and storing it up to be used against him when the next temptation comes.

William James, *The Principles of Psychology*

Some of the most difficult and perplexing experiences in life come to us in temptation. We have given ourselves to God; we have begun to pray in earnest; we are trying to order our lives – so far as we can – in accordance with the will of God. And then, when we think that we have made a good start . . . we are suddenly overwhelmed by a storm of temptations. Sins we thought we had overcome renew their attacks, and a host of new and bewildering temptations come upon us. This is both painful and bewildering . . .

Olive Wyon, *On the Way*

In the very overcoming of temptation . . . we may draw out a hidden spiritual sweetness, as the bees suck honey from the thorn-bushes as well as from all other flowers. He who has not been tempted, knows nothing, nor lives as yet, say the wise man Solomon, and the holy teacher St Bernard. We find more than a thousand testimonies in Scripture to the great profit of temptation; for it is the special sign of the love of God towards a man for him to be tempted and yet kept from falling; for thus he must and shall of a certainty receive the crown.

John Tauler, *The History and Life of the Reverend Doctor John Tauler*

There are but two things that we can do against temptations. The first is to be faithful to the light within us, in avoiding all exposure to temptation, which we are at liberty to avoid. I say, all that we are at liberty to avoid, because it does not always depend upon ourselves, whether we shall escape occasions of sin. Those that belong to the situation in life in which Providence has placed us, are not under our control. The other is to turn our eyes to God in moments of temptation, to throw ourselves immediately upon the protection of heaven, as a child, when in danger, flies to the arms of its parent.

F. de la M. Fénelon, in B.W. Randolph, *Letters and Reflections of Fénelon*

**See also** Anxiety, Doubt, Pride, Sin, Worldliness

## 107

# THANKSGIVING

*Thanksgiving – expression of gratitude, especially to God*

I shall always remember a sermon preached on the phrase – 'Learn to count your blessings, name them one by one.' I have tried to put this into practice on a daily basis ever since. The first few weeks of being a part-time hospital chaplain at the Bradford Royal Infirmary were particularly difficult and demanding. At the beginning of each week I would visit a hundred sick people and spend a few minutes with each patient. At the end of each session I was physically and mentally exhausted – mainly through concentration. On the way back to the cathedral clergy house I would 'count my blessings'. I would go over the session in the wards. For instance, I had met a man about to have his leg amputated. How thankful I was having both legs functioning properly, and able to walk and run. I had spent a few minutes with a woman who had a constriction in her throat. She had been fed solely on liquids for the last two months. How thankful I was, able to eat solid foods. By the time I had reached home I was well on the road to recovery. William Law has some good advice: 'If anyone would tell you the shortest, surest way to all happiness, and all perfection, he must tell you to make a rule to yourself, to thank and praise God for everything that happens to you.'

But I am like a green olive tree in the house of God. I trust in the steadfast love of God for ever and ever. I will thank you for ever, because of what you have done. In the presence of the faithful I will proclaim your name, for it is good.

Psalm 52.8–9

Thanks be to God for his indescribable gift!

2 Corinthians 9.15

Joy untouched by thankfulness is always suspect.

Theodor Haecker, *Journal in the Night*

Gratitude is a fruit of great cultivation; you do not find it among gross people.
Samuel Johnson, *Boswell's Life of Johnson*

To wake at dawn with a winged heart and give thanks for another day of loving.
Kahlil Gibran, *The Prophet*

Let us, therefore, be thankful for health and a competence; and above all, for a quiet conscience.
Izaak Walton, *The Compleat Angler*

Let never day nor night unhallow'd pass,
But still remember what the Lord hath done.
William Shakespeare, *II King Henry VI*

... the chief idea of my life ... the doctrine I should always have liked to teach. That is the idea of taking things with gratitude, and not taking things for granted.
G.K. Chesterton, *Autobiography*

Gratitude was surely implanted in our hearts by our great Creator, and to fail in its observance, is acting against the dictates of conscience and humanity.
Elizabeth Helme, *St Margaret's Cave; or, The Nun's Story*

Thank God, carefully and wonderingly, for your continuing privileges, and for every experience of his goodness. Thankfulness is a soil in which pride does not easily grow.
Michael Ramsey, in Margaret Duggan, *Through the Year with Michael Ramsey*

Cultivate the thankful spirit – it will be to thee a perpetual feast. There is, or ought to be, no such things as small mercies. A really thankful heart will extract motive for gratitude from everything, making the most even of scanty blessings.
Anon

Thank God that those times which strain faith so hard come only occasionally in life. For the most part we travel a sunlit road, and when we are unaware of the love of God it is often because we have not looked for it. To see the evidence of God's mercies you have only to look.
W.E. Sangster, *Westminster Sermons*

... I will thank and praise God for the strength of my body enabling me to work, for the refreshment of sleep, for my daily bread, for the days of painless health, for the gift of my mind and the gift of my conscience, for His loving guidance of my mind ever since it first began to think, and of my heart ever since I first began to love.

Edward King, *Sermons and Addresses*

Thank God every morning, when you get up, that you have something to do that day which must be done, whether you like it or not. Being forced to work, and forced to do your best, will breed in you temperance and self-control, diligence and strength of will, cheerfulness and content and a hundred virtues which the idle man never knows.

Charles Kingsley, *Town and Country Sermons*

Would you know who is the greatest saint in the world? It is not he who prays most or fasts most; it is not he who gives most alms, or is most eminent for temperance, chastity or justice; but it is he who is always thankful to God who wills everything that God willeth, who receives everything as an instance of God's goodness, and has a heart always ready to praise God for it . . .

William Law, *A Serious Call to a Devout and Holy Life*

Certainly a marked feature of Christ's character was his perennial gratefulness of spirit. Run through His prayers and you will be surprised how large a place thanksgiving holds in them, how often He gave eager praise for what would have soured you and me, and made us feel quite certain that God had forgotten to be gracious. Did He not take the cup, that awful symbol of things so near and so fearsome, and even then give thanks?

A.J. Gossip, *From the Edge of the Crowd*

If anyone would tell you the shortest, surest way to all happiness, and all perfection, he must tell you to make a rule to yourself, to thank and praise God for everything that happens to you. For it is certain that whatever seeming calamity happens to you, if you thank and praise God for it, you turn it into a blessing. Could you therefore work miracles, you could not do more for yourself than by this thankful spirit; for it heals with a word speaking and turns all that it touches into happiness.

William Law, *A Serious Call to a Devout and Holy Life*

I will thank Him for the pleasures given me through my senses, for the glory of the thunder, for the mystery of music, the singing of birds and the laughter of children. I will thank Him for the pleasures of seeing, for the delights through colour, for the awe of the sunset, the beauty of flowers, the smile of friendship and the look of love; for the changing beauty of the clouds, for the wild roses in the hedges, for the form and beauty of birds, for the leaves on the trees in spring and autumn, for the witness of the leafless trees through the winter, teaching us that death is sleep and not destruction, for the sweetness of flowers and the scent of hay. Truly, O Lord, the earth is full of thy riches!

Edward King, *Sermons and Addresses*

**See also** Adoration, Contentment, Fulfilment, Happiness, Prayer

# 108

# THINKING

*Thinking – considering; being of opinion; forming conception of; exercising the mind otherwise than by passive reception of another's idea, imagining*

D.H. Lawrence opens up thinking in his poem on 'Thought':

> Thought is the welling up of unknown life into consciousness,
> Thought is the testing of statements on the touchstone of the conscience,
> Thought is gazing onto the face of life, and reading what can be read,
> Thought is pondering over experience, and coming to a conclusion.
> Thought is not a trick, or an exercise, or a set of dodges,
> Thought is a man in his wholeness wholly attending.

All this sounds rather like reflection. In reflection full use is made of our minds, as in the poem above. Full use is also made of our hearts, meaning our feelings and emotions, our instinct and intuition. Full use is made too of our imagination, and our experience of life. More importantly we open ourselves to what D.H. Lawrence described as 'the welling up of unknown life into consciousness'. Seen this way, thinking can be a great adventure. Let D.H. Lawrence have the final word: 'Thought is a man in his wholeness wholly attending.'

We ponder your steadfast love, O God, in the midst of your temple.
Psalm 48.9

What do you think of the Messiah?
Matthew 22.42

One thought fills immensity.
William Blake, 'Proverbs of Hell'

What is the hardest task in the world? To think.

Ralph Waldo Emerson, *Essays*

Thought feeds itself with its own words and grows.

Rabindranath Tagore, *Stray Birds*

It is wonderful what a breadth of life can be encompassed in a moment's thought.

O.T. Beard, *Bristling with Thorns*

Christianity has need of thought that it may come to the consciousness of its real self.

Albert Schweitzer, *Out of My Life and Thought*

It is thoughts of God's thinking which we need to set us right, and remember, they are not as our thoughts.

W.M. Macgregor, *Jesus Christ the Son of God*

My own thoughts
Are my companions.

Henry Wadsworth Longfellow, 'The Masque of Pandora'

Thought that can emerge wholly into feeling, feeling that can merge wholly into thought – these are the artist's highest joy.

Thomas Mann, *Death in Venice*

. . . We must recognize that the whole world is ruled in a wrong spirit, and that a change of spirit will not come from one day to the next. Our expectations must not be for tomorrow, but for the time when what is thought now by a few shall have become the common thought of many. If we have courage and patience, we can think the thought and feel the hopes by which, sooner or later, men will be inspired, and weariness and discouragement will be turned into energy and ardour. For this reason, the first thing we have to do is to be clear in our own minds as to the kind of life we think good and the kind of change that we desire in the world.

Bertrand Russell, *Principles of Social Reconstruction*

As soon as man does not take his existence for granted, but beholds it as something unfathomably mysterious, thought begins.

Albert Schweitzer, *The Teaching of Reverence for Life*

'A' thinks much, but it is always something to be done. The thinking in the Old Testament and the Gospels is of this type.

Mark Rutherford, *Last Pages from a Journal*

No one can fail of the regenerative influence of optimistic thinking, pertinaciously pursued. Every man owns indefeasibly this inlet to the divine.

William James, *The Varieties of Religious Experience*

When we ask the ultimate questions, whether about the direction of our own lives or about the meaning of existence, the outcome of thinking is not an answer but a transformed way of thinking, not propositions to assent to but heightened power of apprehension.

Helen Merry Lynd, *On Shame and the Search for Identity*

I began to think, and to think is one real advance from hell to heaven. All that hellish, hardened state and temper of soul, which I have said so much of before, is but a deprivation of thought; he that is restored to his power of thinking, is restored to himself.

Daniel Defoe, *Moll Flanders*

Elemental thinking is that which starts from the fundamental questions about the relations of man in the universe, about the meaning of life, and about the nature of goodness. It stands in the most immediate connexion with the thinking which impulse stirs in everyone. It enters into that thinking, widening and deepening it.

Albert Schweitzer, *My Life and Thought*

The powers of thought, the vast regions which it can master, the much more vast regions which it can only dimly suggest to imagination, to those whose minds have travelled beyond the daily round an amazing richness of material, an escape from the triviality and wearisomeness of familiar routine, by which the whole of life is filled with interest, and the prison walls of the commonplace are broken down.

Bertand Russell, *Principles of Social Reconstruction*

And, too, Jesus appeals to the mind. Again and again he challenges his hearers to think. He doesn't reveal the truth to them in a kind of tabloid packet to be swallowed whole – 'Shut your eyes and swallow'. No, Jesus challenges his hearers, sowing seeds of truth in their minds and consciences, and then urging them to think out the meaning of it.

Think it out, think it out. It is in this process of thinking it out – together with the love and the will and the imagination – that Jesus and his message are made known.

Michael Ramsey, in Margaret Duggan, *Through the Year with Michael Ramsey*

But those who wish to gain the world by thought must be content to lose it as a support in the present. Most men go through life without much questioning, accepting the beliefs and practices which they find current, feeling that the world will be their ally if they do not put themselves in opposition to it. New thought about the world is incompatible with this comfortable acquiescence; it requires a certain intellectual detachment, a certain solitary energy, a power of inwardly dominating the world and the outlook that the world engenders. Without some willingness to be lonely new thought cannot be achieved. And it will not be achieved to any purpose if the loneliness is accompanied by aloofness, so that the wish for union with others dies, or if intellectual detachment leads to contempt. It is because the state of mind required is subtle and difficult, because it is hard to be intellectually detached yet not aloof, that fruitful thought on human affairs is not common, and that most theorists are conventional or sterile.

Bertrand Russell, *Principles of Social Reconstruction*

**See also** Intellect, Knowledge, Meditation, Mind, Wisdom

# 109

# TIME

*Time – duration; continued existence; progress of this viewed as affecting person or things, past, present and future*

When I was at theological college I went through a minor crisis, and it was to do with 'time'. I had taken on too many commitments, and suddenly everything seemed to go wrong, and my little world collapsed. In trying to rescue the situation, I came across a book written by Max Warren, called *The Master of Time*, and found it helpful. According to him, the 'mastery of time' depended on putting into practice the two main commandments, to love the Lord your God with heart, soul, mind and strength, and to love your neighbour as yourself. Easy to state, but difficult to do, even in a theological college. I put his recommendations into practice, and drastically reduced my commitments. It turned out to be a valuable exercise. Even now I stand back from time to time and prune my activities. We tend to waste so much time in trivia and superficialities.

Remember the sabbath day, and keep it holy. For six days you shall labour and do all your work. But the seventh day is a sabbath to the Lord your God; you shall not do any work.

Exodus 20.8

. . . because we look not at what can be seen but at what cannot be seen; for what can be seen is temporary, but what cannot be seen is eternal.

2 Corinthians 4.18

Time is the great physician.

Benjamin Disraeli, *Henrietta Temple*

Let every man be master of his time.

William Shakespeare, *Macbeth*

The day is of infinite length for him who knows how to appreciate and use it.

Johann Wolfgang von Goethe, in Ludwig Curtius, *Wisdom and Experience*

We must use time creatively, in the knowledge that the time is always ripe to do right.

Martin Luther King, in Coretta Scott King, *The Words of Martin Luther King*

Life must be measured rather by depth than by length, by thought and action rather than by time.

Sir John Lubbock, *The Pleasures of Life*

The more a person is able to direct his life consciously, the more he can use time for constructive benefit.

Rollo May, *Man's Search for Himself*

Time is lost when we have not lived a full human life, time unenriched by experience, creative endeavour, enjoyment and suffering.

Dietrich Bonhoeffer, *Letters and Papers from Prison*

If time is not to be either hoarded or pressed out of existence it must be spent as possessions are spent; not solely for personal use but for others.

Hubert van Zeller, *Considerations*

Love Jesus, and everything he has is yours. Because he is God, he is maker and giver of time. Because he is Man, he has given true heed to time. Because he is both God and Man he is the best judge of the spending of time.

*The Cloud of Unknowing*

Man's greatest disease is the consciousness of transience. Nothing is so likely to produce despair as the awareness of the contingency and vanity of life. A powerful and time-honoured cure is to seek a perception of eternity.

Peter Munz, *Problems of Religious Knowledge*

I think I have learned a new view of time – one that brings freedom from many useless anxieties, as Jesus said it would. As the horizon of the future contracts, the importance of 'now' is so much clearer than when there always seemed to be time in hand.

Leslie J. Tizard, *Facing Life and Death*

Time . . . is what keeps the light from reaching us. There is no greater obstacle to God than time. He means not time alone but temporalities: not only temporal things but temporal affections; not only temporal affections but the very taint and aroma of time.

Meister Eckhart, in Franz Pfeiffer, *Meister Eckhart*, translated by C. de B. Evans

All men complain that they haven't enough time. It's because they look at their lives from too human a point of view. There's always time to do what God wants us to do, but we must put ourselves completely into each moment that he offers us.

Michel Quoist, *Prayers of Life*

What is Time? The shadow on the dial, the striking of the clock, the running of the sand, day and night, summer and winter, months, years, centuries – these are but arbitrary and outward signs, the measure of Time, not Time itself. Time is the Life of the soul. If not this, then tell me, what is Time?

Henry Wadsworth Longfellow, 'Hyperion'

Everything is in the mind; time and beyond time, hell and heaven, death and life. The key to understanding is awareness in the now. But awareness of the moment is not a state that comes naturally to man. Usually, if at all, it comes and goes, elusively, with happiness or suffering; it comes with the creative urge, in abstract thought, through the love of God, or the love of creatures.

Anon (on T.S. Eliot's 'Four Quartets')

I don't have the time! We don't have the time!

It's not time. We don't *take* the time. We let life gnaw away at our time, stealing it from us bit by bit. We're slaves, not masters. We must be masters of our time. I must control my life – and the obligations it imposes on me – not the other way round.

Michel Quoist, *With Open Heart*

Today we have no time even to look at each other, to talk to each other, to enjoy each other, and still less to be what our children expect from us, what the husband expects from the wife, what the wife expects from her husband. And so less and less we are in touch with each other. The world is lost for want of sweetness and kindness. People are starving for love because everybody is in such a great rush.

Mother Teresa, in Kathryn Spink, *The Silence of the Heart*

The word 'time' is used in two ways in the New Testament. The first is in the sense of duration, time by the clock or the calendar, a purely impersonal, chronological idea. The second is judged by rightness, ripeness, achievement of purpose, which is determined by reference to God, in his goodwill, in his love and patience. Those who believe in God try to live their lives in chronological time with ever-deepening understanding of God's purpose, God's timelessness and their own keen eye for opportunity.

George Appleton, *Journey for a Soul*

**See also** Awareness, Eternal Life, Love, Mystics, Worldliness

# 110

# TRANSFORMATION

*Transformation – transforming, being transformed, as having undergone a great transformation; change of character, outward appearance*

I love the story of the transfiguration – of Jesus going up the mountain with his inner core of disciples, and of being transformed before them. His face, we are told 'shone like the sun'. While an undergraduate I was confronted with something similar. I came across someone transfigured, whose face also 'shone like the sun'. The occasion was a Sunday morning in a church in Oxford. A visiting bishop had come to preach. As soon as I saw him I was taken aback by his appearance. It was as though light were radiating from him. He was vibrantly alive, a picture of health, and full of energy. I listened carefully to what he had to say, but cannot now remember a word he said. The important thing was him – transfigured and transformed – and I knew I wanted to be like that. I took a step of faith. I was never argued into faith but won over at the sight of someone transformed.

Look to him, and be radiant.
  Psalm 34.5

And all of us, with unveiled faces, seeing the glory of the Lord as though reflected in a mirror, are being transformed into the same image from one degree of glory to another; for this comes from the Lord, the Spirit.
  2 Corinthians 3.18

The central idea in Christianity is not justification, but transfiguration.
  Nicolas Berdyaev, in Donald A. Lowrie, *Christian Existentialism*

Love is the only force capable of transforming an enemy into a friend.
  Martin Luther King, in Coretta Scott King, *The Words of Martin Luther King*

Human souls, transformed by the Spirit of God till they live in the highest qualities, must form a public sentiment that is to be the transforming power among men.

Henry Ward Beecher, *Proverbs from Plymouth Pulpit*

The process of transforming our inner lives must be expressed in the transformation of our outer life, of the life of the individual as well as that of the community.

Martin Buber, in Aubrey Hodes, *Encounter with Martin Buber*

The highest degree, which the mystics call the transformation or essential and immediate union with God, is the reality of pure love in which there is no self-interest.

François de la M. Fénelon, in B.W. Randolph, *Maxims of the Mystics*

It is far more important that one's life should be perceived than that it should be transformed; for no sooner has it been perceived, than it transforms itself of its own accord.

Maurice Maeterlinck, *The Treasure of the Humble*

Our day-to-day life is of vital importance as the mystery of transformation is worked out in us and through us by the power of Christ. No detail is insignificant because the reassimilation of all creation in Christ is to be complete.

John Main OSB, in Clare Hallward, *The Joy of Being*

But once a man accepts Christ, he has accepted an entirely new set of standards; he is committed to an entirely new kind of life at his work, in his personal relationships, in his pleasure, in his conduct, in his speech, in the things which he allows himself to do.

William Barclay, *The Letters to Timothy and Titus*

The harvest of suffering cannot be reaped until it has been eaten, burnt, digested. If the suffering is accepted and lived through, not fought against and refused, then it is completed and becomes transmuted. It is absorbed, and having accomplished its work, it ceases to exist as suffering, and becomes part of our growing self.

E. Graham Howe and L. Le Mesurier, *The Open Way*

It is one of the most moving experiences of life to watch a bewildered frightened human being, starved of friendship and hardly daring to be expectant of it, blossom out into a happy, trustful and confident personal life as the result of being so welcomed and received. It is of the essence of the Gospel that we are so received in Christ, that His Yes to men is pronounced in such directly personal terms.

Alan Ecclestone, *Yes to God*

Life should be a giving birth to the soul, the development of a higher mode of reality. The animal must be humanized: flesh must be made spirit; physiological activity must be transmuted into intellect and conscience, into reason, justice, and generosity, as the torch is transmuted into life and warmth. The blind, greedy selfish nature of man must put on beauty and nobleness. This heavenly alchemy is what justifies our presence on the earth; it is our mission and our glory.

Henri Frédéric Amiel, *Amiel's Journal*

In his love for someone he brought out that which was peculiar to a person's life, even though it lay hidden under layers of dirt; he loved it out. Therefore many who knew that he saw them and loved them became new persons and experienced the great transformation. His love was not simply a reaction to something lovable, as our love is. His love was creative. It called a 'new creature' into existence.

Helmut Thielicke, *I Believe – The Christian's Creed*

The mainspring of life is in the heart. Joy is the vital air of the soul . . . To make anyone happy, then, is strictly to augment his store of being, to double the intensity of his life, to reveal him to himself, to ennoble him and transfigure him. Happiness does away with ugliness, and even makes the beauty of beauty. The man who doubts it, can never have watched the first gleam of tenderness dawning in the clear eyes of one who loves; – sunrise itself is a lesser marvel.

Henri Frédéric Amiel, *Amiel's Journal*

If the soul is transformed by participation in the divine nature so also must the body be and with the body the whole material universe. God in Christ becomes what we are in order that we might become his 'body'. This transformation of man by the divine life begins even now on earth, but it is only completed when man's body is also transformed by the resurrection.

Bede Griffiths OSB, in Peter Spink, *The Universal Christ*

A fundamental transformation is expected: something like a new birth of man himself, which can be understood only by one who actively takes part in it. It is therefore a transformation which does not come about merely through progress in right thinking for the sake of right action . . . or through the education of man who is fundamentally good . . . Nor is it a transformation through enlightenment . . . According to Jesus, a fundamental transformation is achieved through a man's surrender to God's will.

Hans Küng, *On Being a Christian*

One morning when I was in the wood something happened which was nothing less than a transformation of myself and the world, although I 'believed' nothing new. I was looking at a great, spreading, bursting oak. The first tinge from the greenish-yellow buds was just visible. It seemed to be no longer a tree away from me and apart from me. The enclosing barriers of consciousness were removed and the text came into my mind, *Thou in me and I in thee*. The distinction of self and not-self was an illusion. I could feel the rising sap; in me also sprang the fountain of life uprushing from its roots, and the joy of its outbreak at the extremity of each twig right up to the summit was my own: that which kept me apart was nothing.

Mark Rutherford, *More Pages from a Journal*

**See also** Fulfilment, Glory, Grace, Healing, Wholeness

III

# TRUST

*Trust – firm belief in the honesty, veracity, justice, strength, etc., of a person or thing – as our trust is in God*

In my early twenties I came to trust in God, and took a simple step of faith. I accepted the contents of the Gospels as substantially true, and the person they revealed – Jesus Christ. In the next two years I put down some roots to fortify this trust. The next major step taken on trust was ordination. The last thirty-six years of ministry have been lived in a background of trust, but what crevasses, hurricanes and minefields. The quotation on trust I most clearly identify with comes from *Mister God, This is Anna*: 'And what a word that is! Define it how you like and I bet you'll miss the main point! It's more than confidence, more than security; it doesn't belong to ignorance or, for that matter, to knowledge either. It is simply the ability to move out of the, "I'm the centre of all things" and to let something or someone take over.' This fits in well with the underlying vision of faith in *The Eternal Vision*. I have consistently pointed out that God in the first instance is a 'presence' to be found in the depths of ourselves. Somehow we have to let go of the insistent claims of the ego for predominance and let this 'something or someone' take over. To this end, this book acts as a skeleton or framework of faith, designed to undergird trust. The practice of reflection can be used as an aid to let Anna's 'something or someone' take over, and to foster a spirit of trust.

Those of steadfast mind you keep in peace – in peace because they trust in you.
Isaiah 26.3

See, I am sending you out like sheep into the midst of wolves; so be wise as serpents and innocent as doves.
Matthew 10.16

God provides for him that trusteth.
George Herbert, *Outlandish Proverbs*

Let this be my last word, that I trust in thy love.
Rabindranath Tagore, *Stray Birds*

The recurrent needs of every day are all known to God. A full reliance can be put upon all His promises.
W.E. Sangster, *He Is Able*

You can trust and rest in God simply because He has said, you may and you must.
Henry Ward Beecher, *Proverbs from Plymouth Pulpit*

When we trust as far as we can, we often find ourselves able to trust at least a little further.
Mark Gibbard, *Jesus, Liberation and Love*

The whole of God's being cannot be understood, but enough of it can be understood to trust it.
Henry Ward Beecher, *Proverbs from Plymouth Pulpit*

We have reached that stage in human development when we are able to ask the questions, but are not always able to understand the answers. God expects us to trust His Love.
W.E. Sangster, *He Is Able*

Trust men, and they will be true to you; treat them greatly, and they will show themselves great, though they make an exception in your favour to all their rules of trade.
Ralph Waldo Emerson, *Essays and Representative Men*

In such a world as this, with such ugly possibilities hanging over us all, there is but one anchor which will hold, and that is utter trust in God; let us keep that, and we may yet get to our graves without *misery* though not without *sorrow*.
Charles Kingsley, *Daily Thoughts*

We can trust Him wholly with His world. We can trust Him with ourselves. We are sure He cares far more to make the best of us, and to do the most through us, than we have ever cared ourselves. He is ever trying to make us understand that He yearns to be to us more than aught in the universe besides. That He really wants us, and needs us, is the wonder and strength of our life.
A.W. Robinson, *The Personal Life of the Clergy*

Trust, which is always on the way to being love, must be spontaneous or non-existent. It grows of itself within our hearts as we come to appreciate the character and wisdom of someone whose record we know; and it grows more surely when we come to know personally in actual companionship someone who, the more we know him, inspires in us more trust and confidence in his character and wisdom.

William Temple, *The Hope of a New World*

In simple trust like theirs who heard
Beside the Syrian sea
The gracious calling of the Lord,
Let us, like them, without a word,
Rise up and follow thee.

John Greenleaf Whittier, 'The Brewing of Soma'

If you have doubts about the existence of God or misgivings as to the kind of God He is, I do not think your need will be met by argument. It will be met only by an act of trust on your part. You must be willing to be found by the pursuing love of God which will not let you go; to face the challenge which is relentless; to move out fearlessly from your narrow self-centred life into a new, wide, spacious life with Christ at the centre – trusting not in yourself but in the all-sufficient love and power of God.

Leslie J. Tizard, *Facing Life and Death*

Trust thyself: every heart vibrates to that iron string. Accept the place the divine providence has found for you, the society of your contemporaries, the connection of events. Great men have always done so, and confided themselves childlike to the genius of their age, betraying their perception that the absolutely trustworthy was seated at their heart, working through their hands, predominating in all their being. And we are now men, and must accept in the highest mind the same transcendent dignity; and not minors and invalids in a protected corner, not cowards fleeing before a revolution, but guides, redeemers, and benefactors, obeying the Almighty effort, and advancing on Chaos and the Dark.

Ralph Waldo Emerson, *Self-Reliance*

If the universe was created by God and human life planned by God, then we should see principles of goodness and wisdom embedded in both. The writer of the book of Genesis pictures God looking at his creation and finding it good. He is emphatic that man is akin to God, made in the divine image. He is conscious of man's ignorance, foolishness and wilfulness, but never does he think of man as being so depraved as not to be able to hear God speaking within himself. There may be a lot of original sin but there is also original goodness to which God and men can appeal. In spite of occasional natural catastrophes, for most of the time we think life is good. So we can trust life, both empirically from experience, and also because we trust the Creator.

George Appleton, *Journey for a Soul*

Over the greater part of the so-called civilized world is spreading a deep distrust, a deep irreverence of every man towards his neighbour, and a practical unbelief in every man whom you do see, atones for itself by a theoretical belief in an ideal human nature which you do not see. Such a temper of mind, unless it be checked by that which alone can check it, namely, the grace of God, must lead towards sheer anarchy. There is a deeper and uglier anarchy. There is a deeper and uglier anarchy than any mere political anarchy – which the abuse of the critical spirit leads to – the anarchy of society and of the family, the anarchy of the head and of the heart, which leaves poor human beings as orphans in the wilderness to cry in vain, 'What can I know? What can I love?'

Charles Kingsley, *Daily Thoughts*

**See also** Belief, Commitment, Faith, Hope, Joy

112

# TRUTH

*Truth – quality or state of being true or faithful*

Having spent over thirty years in a university setting I have come across many different kinds of truth – both in the arts and sciences. Our definition above speaks of personal truth. F.W. Robertson, in his *Sermons*, wrote: 'Truth lies in character. Christ did not simply *speak* truth; He was truth: true through and through; for truth is a thing, not of words, but of Life and Being.' The psalmist thought of God desiring truth in the inward being and requested to be taught wisdom in his secret heart. According to the writer of John's Gospel, truth came through Jesus Christ, and his promise was: 'You will know the truth, and the truth will set you free.' A modern writer, Rufus Jones, concisely sums all this up in these marvellous words: 'To find Truth . . . we must break through the outward shell of words and phrases which house it, and by *experience and practice* discover the "inward beauty, life and loveliness of Truth".'

You desire truth in the inward being; therefore teach me wisdom in my secret heart.

Psalm 51.6

The law indeed was given through Moses; grace and truth came through Jesus Christ. No one has ever seen God. It is God the only Son, who is close to the Father's heart, who has made him known.

John 1.17–18

Truth . . . loves to be centrally located.

Herman Melville, *Typee*

Truth is the highest thing that men may keep.

Geoffrey Chaucer, *The Franklin's Tale*

In the usefulness of truth lies the hope of humanity.
Norman Douglas, *An Almanac*

Rather than love, than money, than fame, give me truth.
Henry David Thoreau, *Walden*

The friend of Truth obeys not the multitude *but the Truth.*
Rufus M. Jones, *Spiritual Reformers in the 16th and 17th Centuries*

Say not, 'I have found the truth', but rather, 'I have found a truth.'
Kahlil Gibran, *The Prophet*

But it is not enough to possess a truth; it is essential that the truth should possess us.
Maurice Maeterlinck, *The Treasure of the Humble*

Truth is given, not to be contemplated, but to be done. Life is an action – not a thought.
F.W. Robertson, *Sermons*

Love of truth asserts itself in the ability to find and appreciate what is good wherever it be.
Johann Wolfgang von Goethe, in Herman J. Weigand, *Wisdom and Experience*

Truth does not lie beyond humanity, but is one of the products of the human mind and feeling.
D.H. Lawrence, *The Rainbow*

I think the most important quality in a person connected with religion is absolute devotion to the truth.
Albert Schweitzer, *Out of My Life and Thought*

I thirst for truth,
But shall not drink it till I reach the source.
Robert Browning, 'The Ring and the Book'

Ethical axioms are found and tested not very differently from the axioms of science. Truth is what stands the test of experience.
Albert Einstein, *Out of My Later Years*

'I cannot hear what you say for listening to what you are.' Truth and preaching are both 'truth through personality'.

William Barclay, *The Gospel of Luke*

Truth lies in character. Christ did not simply *speak* truth: He *was* truth: true through and through; for truth is a thing, not of words, but of Life and Being.

F.W. Robertson, *Sermons*

The gospel story, whether historically true or not, could still be regarded as a parable; that is, as a working model, cast in fictitious form, of the way things really are.

Sydney Carter, *Dance in the Dark*

The arrogance of supposing that, what could not be clearly expressed could be cheerfully discarded, has impoverished religion and made lonely men of its mystics and seers.

W.E. Sangster, *The Pure in Heart*

Truth, in a word, is whatever cleanses you. Truth is whatever delights the higher you in you. Truth is whatever summons your spirit to do battle in her service. Truth is whatever makes you or me one with the mind of God.

Alistair MacLean, *The Happy Finder*

When man is, with his whole nature, loving and willing the truth, he is then a live truth. But this he has not originated in himself. He has seen it and striven for it, but not originated it. The one originating, living, visible truth, embracing all truths in all relations, is Jesus Christ. He is true; he is the live Truth.

George Macdonald, *Unspoken Sermons*

Truth is the perfect correlation of mind and reality; and this is actualized in the Lord's Person. If the Gospel is true and God is, as the Bible declares, a Living God, the ultimate truth is not a system of propositions grasped by a perfect intelligence, but is a Personal Being apprehended in the only way in which persons are ever fully apprehended, that is, by love.

William Temple, *Readings in St John's Gospel*

From my youth I have held the conviction that all religious truth must in the end be capable of being grasped as something that stands to reason. I, therefore, believe that Christianity, in the contest with philosophy and with other religions, should not ask for exceptional treatment, but should be in the thick of the battle of ideas, relying solely on the power of its own inherent truth.

Albert Schweitzer, *Christianity and the Religions of the World*

. . . the truth which Jesus brings to us shows us the real values of life. The fundamental question to which every man has consciously or unconsciously to give an answer is: 'To what am I to give my life?' 'Am I to give it to a career? Am I to give it to the amassing of material possessions? Am I to give it to pleasure? Am I to give it to the obedience and to the service of God?' The truth which Jesus brings enables us to get our scale of values right; it is in His truth that we see what things are really important and what things are not.

William Barclay, *The Gospel of John*

**See also** Character, Experience, Integrity, Mind, Wisdom

## 113

# UNDERSTANDING

*Understanding – comprehending, perceiving the meaning of, grasping mentally, perceiving the significance or explanation or cause or nature of, knowing how to deal with, having insight*

One of our undergraduates was reputed to be a very brilliant geologist. I was curious to know what constituted his brilliance, so asked his tutor about him. He paused for a moment and recalled the experience of a recent tutorial. He had been teaching him a new area of study. The undergraduate was not only able to understand it completely first time round, but was two steps ahead of the tutor in the course of his instruction. It was as if he had an intuitive knowledge of the entire subject, the tutor merely confirming what he already knew. This was one area of his brightness, the ability to assimilate new material quickly. The other was his capacity to understand the significance of what he had learnt and to make imaginative leaps. These two areas of understanding, working together, constituted his brilliance. So much for understanding an academic discipline, but what about something even more complex – understanding oneself and other people.

. . . I will light in your heart the lamp of understanding, which shall not be put out.

2 Esdras 14.25

I want their hearts to be encouraged and united in love, so that they may have all the riches of assured understanding and have the knowledge of God's mystery, that is, Christ himself, in whom are hidden all the treasures of wisdom and knowledge.

Colossians 2.2–3

What one has not experienced, one will never understand in print.

Isadora Duncan, *My Life*

The highest of all is not to understand the highest but to act upon it.
Søren Kierkegaard, in Harold Loukes, *The Quaker Contribution*

The real thing is to understand, and love that you may understand.
J.B. Yeats, *Letters to His Son, W.B. Yeats and Others*

All the glory of greatness has no lustre for people who are in search of understanding.
Blaise Pascal, *Pensées*

A clear understanding of God makes one want to follow the direction of things, the direction of oneself.
André Gide, *The Journals of André Gide*

To understand a matter properly, a man must dominate it, instead of allowing it to dominate him.
Ernest Hello, *Life, Science, and Art*

That which enables us to know and understand aright in the things of God, must be a living principle of holiness within us.
John Smith the Platonist, *Select Discourses*

If one is master of one thing and understands one thing well, one has at the same time insight into and understanding of many things.
Vincent van Gogh, *Dear Theo: An Autobiography of Vincent van Gogh*

You never really understand a person until you consider things from his point of view . . . until you climb into his skin and walk around in it.
Harper Lee, *To Kill a Mockingbird*

Understanding a person does not mean condoning; it only means that one does not accuse him as if one were God or a judge placed above him.
Erich Fromm, *Man for Himself*

We are apt to outgrow our teachers in wisdom, but whoever has helped us to a larger understanding is entitled to our gratitude for all time.
Norman Douglas, *An Almanac*

Of course, *understanding* of our fellow-beings is important. But this understanding becomes fruitful only when it is sustained by sympathetic feeling in joy and sorrow.
Albert Einstein, *Ideas and Opinions*

The language of the mystics cannot, of course, match that of science or reason. Yet, in a world craving for evidence from real life, it will remain one of the means through which our contemporaries can find God.

René Voillaume, *The Need for Contemplation*

I want, by understanding myself, to understand others. I want to be all that I am capable of becoming . . . This all sounds very strenuous and serious. But now that I have wrestled with it, it's no longer so. I feel happy – deep down. *All is well.*

Katherine Mansfield, *Journal of Katherine Mansfield*

Actually, of course, few people in this world see what is going on about them. Nobody really sees until he understands, until he can create a pattern into which the helter-skelter of passing events fits and makes a significance. And for this sort of vision a personal death is required . . . Nobody sees with his eyes alone; we see with our souls.

Henry Miller, *The Cosmological Eye*

For the rights of understanding to be valid one must venture out into life, out on the sea and lift up one's voice, even though God hears it not, and not stand on the shore and watch others fighting and struggling – only then does understanding acquire its *official sanction*, for to stand on one leg and prove God's existence is a very different thing from going on one's knees and thanking him.

Søren Kierkegaard, *The Journals of Kierkegaard*

The greatest gift that any human being can give to another is the gift of understanding and of peace. To have someone to whom we can go at any time, and know that they will not laugh at our dreams, or misunderstand our confidences is a most wonderful thing. To have somewhere to go to where the tensions of life are relaxed in peace is a lovely thing. It is open to us all to make our own homes like that. This is something which does not cost money, and which does not need lavish and costly hospitality. It costs only the understanding heart.

William Barclay, *The Gospel of John*

The comprehension of life, of its living flow is beyond conceptual thought, which, in the very effort to comprehend, arrests, divides and falsifies it. Life can be understood only by living. To understand any living thing you must, so to say, creep within; and feel the beating of its heart. Every creature knows at least enough about the world to support its own existence there. The intellect seems to stand in its own light, reducing all it contemplates to the shadowiness of its self-chosen concepts, and by its own confession we can know nothing more than these, its peculiar creation. Life lies too deep to be penetrated by them. It is an island fortress. You cannot march into it on your two feet of logic and mathematics.

W. MacNeile Dixon, *The Human Situation*

**See also** Acceptance, Awareness, Compassion, Faith, Truth

# 114

# VISION

*Vision – act of faculty of seeing, things seen in dream or trance; thing seen in the imagination, imaginative insight; statesmanlike foresight*

I have never seen a vision in a dream or in a trance. My visions have been more down-to-earth, involving the imagination and imaginative insight. Thomas Traherne once wrote: 'And thus you have a Gate, in the prospect even of this world, whereby you may see into God's Kingdom.' In one sense these words could have been written of *The Eternal Vision*. This book acts as a gate through which one can 'see' a prospect (of a vision) of this world, and of God's kingdom. In mulling over the contents of this compilation the imagination is stimulated, and through imaginative insight we 'see' things not previously 'seen'. We discover the main part of the vision in the lives and writings of poets, novelists, playwrights, philosophers, theologians, artists, musicians, historians, scientists, psychologists, statesmen, etc. up to the present day. We bring reflection into play and open up a 'prospect even of this world', whereby we 'may see into God's Kingdom'.

. . . the oracle of one who hears the words of God, and knows the knowledge of the Most High, who sees the vision of the Almighty.

Numbers 24.15–16

. . . I was not disobedient to the heavenly vision.

Acts 26.19

And thus you have a Gate, in the prospect even of this world, whereby you may see into God's Kingdom.

Thomas Traherne, *Centuries*

The true poet is all the time a visionary and whether with friends or not, as much alone as a man on his death bed . . .

J.B. Yeats, *Letters to His Son, W.B. Yeats and Others*

Golden hours of vision come to us in this present life, when we are at our best, and our faculties work together in harmony.

Charles Fletcher Dole, *The Hope of Immortality*

The simple vision of pure love, which is marvellously penetrating, does not stop at the outer husk of creation; it penetrates to the divinity which is hidden within.

Malaval, in Evelyn Underhill, *Mysticism*

An eternal trait of men is the need for vision and the readiness to follow it; and if men are not given the right vision, they will follow wandering fires.

Sir Richard Livingstone, *On Education*

A mere dream, a vague hope may be more potent than certainty in a lesser matter. The faintest vision of God is more determinative of life than a gross earthly certainty.

Mark Rutherford, *More Pages from a Journal*

The spirit of the world, the great calm presence of the Creator, comes not forth to the sorceries of opium or of wine. The sublime vision comes to the pure and simple souls in a clear and chaste body.

Ralph Waldo Emerson, *The Poet, from Essays and Representative Men*

I have seen the vision,
the vision of mine own revealing itself,
coming out from within me.

Rabindranath Tagore, *The Religion of Man*

This made it more likely that he had seen a vision; for instead of making common things look commonplace, as a false vision would have done, it had made common things disclose the wonderful that was in them.

George Macdonald, *Cross Purposes and the Shadows*

Now, this state of 'spiritual unrest' can never bring you to a state of vision, of which the essential is peace. And struggling to see does not help one to see. The light comes, when it does come, rather suddenly and strangely I think. It is just like falling in love; a thing that never happens to those who are always trying to do it.

Evelyn Underhill, edited by Charles Williams, *The Letters of Evelyn Underhill*

The normal limits of the human vision are not the limits of the universe. There are other worlds than that which our senses reveal to us, other senses than those which we share with the lower animals, other forces than those of material nature. If we have faith in the soul, then the supernatural is also a part of the natural.

Sir Sarvepalli Radhakrishnan, *Indian Philosophy*

Religion is the vision of something which stands beyond, behind, and within, the passing flux of immediate things; something which is real, and yet waiting to be realized; something which is a remote possibility, and yet the greatest of present facts; something that gives meaning to all that passes, and yet eludes apprehension; something whose possession is the final good, and yet is beyond all reach; something which is the ultimate ideal, and the hopeless quest. The immediate reaction of human nature to the religious vision is worship.

Alfred North Whitehead, *Science and the Modern World*

The nature of the mind is such that the sinner who repents and makes an act of faith in a higher power is more likely to have a blissful visionary experience than is the self-satisfied pillar of society with his righteous indignations, his anxiety about possessions and pretensions, his ingrained habits of blaming, despising and condemning.

Aldous Huxley, *Heaven and Hell*

Most of us go through life with eyes half shut and with dull minds and heavy hearts, and even the few who have had those rare moments of vision and awakening fall back quickly into somnolence. It is good to know that the ancient thinkers required us to realize the possibilities of the soul in solitude and silence and transform the flashing and fading moments of vision into a steady light which could illumine the long years of life.

Sir Sarvepalli Radhakrishnan, *Indian Philosophy*

There are analagous moments when one suddenly sees the glory of people. On some unforgettable evening one's friend is suddenly seen as the unique, irreplaceable, and utterly delightful being that he is. It is as if he had been freshly created. One is no longer concerned with his relations to oneself, with his *pragmatic* value. He exists wholly in his own right; his significance is eternal, and the essential mystery of his being is as fathomless as that of God Himself.

J.W.N. Sullivan, *But for the Grace of God*

Religion has emerged into human experience mixed with the crudest fancies of barbaric imagination. Gradually, slowly, steadily the vision recurs in history under nobler form and with clearer expression. It is the one element in human experience which persistently shows an upward trend. It fades and then recurs. But when it renews its force, it recurs with an added richness and purity of content. The fact of the religious vision, and its history of persistent expansion, is our one ground for optimism. Apart from it, human life is a flash of occasional enjoyments lighting up a mass of pain and misery, a bagatelle of transient experience.

Alfred North Whitehead, *Science and the Modern World*

**See also** Aspiration, Imagination, Inspiration, Kingdom of God, Light

## 115

# VOCATION

*Vocation – divine call to, or sense of fitness for a career or occupation; employment, trade, profession*

Occasionally people ask me – why did I become ordained? My answer is that in my early twenties, I took a step of faith and made a commitment. Two years later, I went on a long train journey and read a book entitled *Margaret* by James Davidson Ross. 'Margaret' was a fifteen-year-old schoolgirl, the life and soul of the party, and a person of faith. She came home one day not feeling very well. At first she was thought to be suffering from flu, but eventually an aggressive cancer was diagnosed, and she had not long to live. I was very moved by the way Margaret faced up to her ordeal. She accepted it all in faith. Visitors who came to cheer her up found the roles reversed and she was cheering them up. As I read the book I became convinced the Holy Spirit was at work in her life, and that she was 'living in the power of the resurrection'. By the time the train reached Paddington I had already decided to live my life in like manner. After a few days I became aware of a little voice inside me asking, 'If this is so important to you, shouldn't you be actively engaged in spreading this, rather than just living it for yourself?' I was unable to avoid this searching challenge, and shortly afterwards offered myself for ordination.

Before I formed you in the womb I knew you, and before you were born I consecrated you; I appointed you a prophet to the nations.
  Jeremiah 1.5

You did not choose me but I chose you. And I appointed you to go and bear fruit, fruit that would last.
  John 15.16

The test of a vocation is the love of the drudgery it involves.
  Logan Pearsall Smith, *Afterthoughts*

God has a task for every one of us, which is made to measure for us.

William Barclay, *The Gospel of Matthew*

There is a specialty of work in the world for each man. But man must search for it, for it will not hunt the man.

Henry Ward Beecher, *Proverbs from Plymouth Pulpit*

Vocation is not the exceptional prerogative of a few specially good or gifted people . . . All men and women are called to serve God.

F.R. Barry, *Vocation and Ministry*

Do not despise your situation; in it you must act, suffer, and conquer. From every point on earth we are equally near to heaven and to the infinite.

Henri Frédéric Amiel, *Amiel's Journal*

All things are produced plentifully and easily and of a better quality when one man does one thing which is natural to him and at the right time, and leaves other things.

Plato, *The Republic of Plato*

If a man could take his choice of all the lives that are possible on earth, there is none so much to be desired for its joy-producing quality as a truly self-denying, consecrated Christian life.

Henry Ward Beecher, *Proverbs from Plymouth Pulpit*

Whatever work you do for a living, it must be a form of service of some kind, for no one will pay you for your work if he does not want it done. What makes all the difference is what you are thinking of first and foremost, as you consider the spirit and temper in which you carry out your work. Is it your livelihood, or is it God's service? The work in itself is both. But which do you think of first? Nothing would bring nearer the promised day of God than that all Christian people should enter on their profession in the spirit of those who regard it as their chief sphere of serving God.

William Temple, *Christian Faith and Life*

God's principal job is *to make man*: 'Let us make man in our image.' So, to work at 'making man' – developing, helping and protecting him – is to join God in his essential plan, working to realize his project.

Michel Quoist, *With Open Heart*

Vocation today means also to understand the hard but stupendous mission of the church, now more than ever engaged in teaching man his true nature, his end, his fate, and in revealing to the faithful the immense riches of the charity of Christ.

Mother Teresa, in Brother Angelo Devananda, *Jesus, the Word to Be Spoken*

His vocation is to become fully human himself by helping others to achieve a deeper, fuller, humanity by all means available. This is what Christians are for, and at this time perhaps we are able to see our vocation as part of the universal striving towards a more complete understanding and living of human life.

Rosemary Haughton, *On Trying to Be Human*

There are so few people who become what they have it in them to be. It may be through lethargy and laziness, it may be through timidity and cowardice, it may be through lack of discipline and self-indulgence, it may be through the involvement in second-bests and byways. The world is full of people who have never realized the possibilities which are in them.

William Barclay, *The Gospel of John*

Each man has his own vocation. The talent is the call. There is one direction in which all space is open to him. He has faculties silently inviting him thither to endless exertion. He is like a ship in a river: he runs against obstructions on every side but one; on that side all obstruction is taken away, and he sweeps serenely over a deepening channel into an infinite sea.

Ralph Waldo Emerson, *Spiritual Laws*

What are you going to do with your lives? To choose your career for selfish reasons is a worse sin, than, let us say, committing adultery, for it is the withdrawal of the greater part of your time and energy from the service of God. Of course you are not going to be turned out of a club for doing it, but you will turn yourself out of the fellowship of Christ by doing it.

William Temple, *Christian Faith and Life*

There is a will for career as well as for character. There is a will for *where* – in what place, viz., in this town or another town – I am to become like God, as well as *that* I am to become like God. There is a will for where I am to be, and what I am to be, and what I am to do to-morrow. There is a will for what scheme I am to take up, and what work I am to do for Christ, and what business arrangements to make, and what money to give away. This is God's private will for me, for every step I take, for the path of life along which He points my way: God's will for my *career*.

Henry Drummond, *The Greatest Thing in the World*

But if you are in doubt how you may best lay out your life, and if you are quite clear in your acceptance of Jesus Christ as your Saviour and your God, then the mere circumstances of the time constitute a call to the Church's direct service in its ministry which you must face; for there is no sphere of life in which a man can more certainly lay out all talents in the service of God. It will call for every capacity; it will bring you into touch with human beings in every conceivable relation. There is no life so rich or so full of all those joys which come from serving people at the point of their greatest need.

William Temple, *Christian Faith and Life*

**See also** Commitment, Discipleship, Listening, Obedience, Service

# 116

# WHOLENESS

*Wholeness – in good health, in sound condition, intact; thing complete in itself, organic unity, complete system, total make up of parts*

A few years ago I was leading a morning session, and one of the participants asked me what I was trying to do in my work. I said in reply I was trying to bring about some form of wholeness unique to each individual person. The emphasis of my work is on the 'God within' seen primarily as Father, Son, and the gifts and fruits of the Holy Spirit. Reflection is rather like 'practising the presence of God' to quote a phrase used by Brother Lawrence, a seventeenth-century Carmelite lay brother. In silent reflection we open ourselves to experiencing something of the presence of God. Some find it helpful to think of reflection as a listening form of prayer, in which great use is made of the mind and heart (feelings), as well as intuition and imagination. Reflection is mainly about the cure of souls, enabling people to come to wholeness through the releasing of the divine in them. As D.H. Lawrence wrote in *The Phoenix*: 'To be alive, to be man alive, to be whole man alive: that is the point.'

I will give thanks to you, O Lord my God, with my whole heart, and I will glorify your name for ever.

Psalm 86.12

Your faith has made you well.

Matthew 9.22

When we rejoice in our fulness, then we can part with our fruits with joy.

Rabindranath Tagore, *Stray Birds*

Wholeness demands relationship – with man or with God, and often with both together.

Monica Furlong, *Travelling In*

I wished for all things that I might enjoy life, and was granted life that I might enjoy all things.

Anon

'Holy', 'Healthy', 'Whole' – they all come from the same root and carry different overtones of the same meaning.

Aldous Huxley, *Island*

There is no such thing as an immortal work of art. There is one art – the greatest of all, the art of making a complete human being of oneself.

A.R. Orage, *On Love*

But this work may not be accomplished in one moment of conversion; it is not the work of one day, but of much time, much sweat, much labour, according to the grace of God that pitieth and the zeal of man that willeth and runneth.

William of St Thierry, *The Golden Epistles of Abbot William of St Thierry*

The cure for all the illness of life is stored in the inner depth of life itself, the access to which becomes possible when we are alone. This solitude is a world in itself, full of wonders and resources unthought of. It is so absurdly near, yet so unapproachably distant.

Rabindranath Tagore, *Letters to a Friend*

I keep on saying Our Lord was the first psychiatrist, with a penetrating awareness of human beings ten times better than psychological theory. And finally, what He did on the Cross was to take all the human ingredients and transform them into both a human wholeness and a divine wholeness. Only Christ could achieve that. What our Lord could do was to take the fulness of being divine and transform it in terms which we could understand.

Jack Dominion, in Gerald Priestland, *Priestland's Progress*

Above all, the individual should aim at fullness and wholeness of development. Every human being is confronted with the task of growing up, of building a personality out of the raw materials of his infant self. A rich and full personality, in moral and spiritual harmony with itself and with its destiny, one whose talents are not buried and whose wholeness transcends its conflicts, is the highest creation of which we have knowledge, and in its attainment the individual possibilities of the evolutionary process are brought to supreme fruition.

Sir Julian Huxley, *Religion Without Revelation*

Many of us do not grow an inner health and maturity as we grow in bodily health, mental ability and control over outside things. Few of us devote to the study of God and his will the same time and application that we give to worldly studies and professional training. The writers of the New Testament frequently lament the lack of maturity in the Christians for whom they are writing. That spiritual maturity is essential for inner health, right attitudes and right decisions and is creative for a dimension of life beyond the physical and the material

George Appleton, *Journey for a Soul*

Faith is not just conformity. It is *life*. It embraces all the realms of life, penetrating into the most mysterious and inaccessible depths not only of our unknown spiritual being but even of God's own hidden essence and love. Faith, then, is the only way of opening up the true depths of reality, even of our own reality. Until a man yields himself to God in the consent of total belief, he must inevitably remain a stranger to himself, an exile from himself, because he is excluded from the most meaningful depths of his own being: those which remain obscure and unknown because they are too simple and too deep to be attained by reason.

Thomas Merton, *New Seeds of Contemplation*

Yesterday I met a whole man. It is a rare experience but always an illuminating and ennobling one. It costs so much to be a full human being that there are very few who have the enlightenment or the courage to pay the price . . . One has to abandon altogether the search for security, and reach out to the risk of living with both arms. One has to embrace the world like a lover, and yet demand no easy return of love. One has to accept pain as a condition of existence. One has to court doubt and darkness as the cost of knowing. One needs a will stubborn in conflict, but apt always to the total acceptance of every consequence of living and dying.

Morris West, *The Shoes of the Fishermen*

When scientific specialization has almost reached the point where a different surgeon is required to remove each tonsil, a key question hangs in the air of our time. When the specialists have taken Man apart, who is to put him together again? Who will see him steadily and whole as a person who lives, loves, sins and dies? I would contend that it is the preacher and only the preacher who addresses Man in his wholeness, the totality of his being. In this world of specialists, the preacher is an unashamed generalizer. With breathtaking audacity, he states truths which are cosmic in sweep and yet apply to any individual, anywhere at any time.

Colin Morris, *The Word and the Words*

When a man ignores the 'spiritual life' it means that, however brilliant, well-intentioned, decent, a man may be, he is really only half-alive; his life is incomplete, unfulfilled; for he has not found the clue to the meaning of life. He is unaware of the need for 'wholeness' or 'integration' which is felt by so many people, even without any reference to what they would call 'religion' . . .

It is our conviction, as Christians, that man was made for 'wholeness' – that every part of his nature is so ordered that it cannot find fulfilment unless all is co-ordinated and integrated into a whole; this can only happen – even in a very general and imperfect way – as the whole personality is unified to serve *one* end: 'Who keeps one end in view, makes all things serve.' In other words: we have been created for God, and we are lost, empty and restless until we come to our senses, and come home to our Father.

Olive Wyon, *On the Way*

**See also** Fulfilment, Healing, Holiness, Presence, Salvation

# 117

# WILL

*Will – faculty by which a person decides to conceive himself as deciding upon and initiating action; power of determining one's choice of action independently of causation, doing the will of God, God's will*

When I was a teenager at school, sometimes I would get up early and go to a communion service in the Lady Chapel. In those days we used the Book of Common Prayer, and one of the offertory sentences which registered with me was: 'Not every one that saith unto me, Lord, Lord, shall enter into the kingdom of heaven, but he that doeth the will of my Father which is in heaven.' When I took a deeper step of commitment in my early twenties these words challenged me even more forcibly, and brought about a determination to do 'the will of my Father' at all costs. In retrospect this developing attitude of 'all or nothing' influenced me in going forward to ordination. Some of William Barclay's words put over my feelings at the time concisely: 'The one great principle was that in all things a man must seek God's will and that, when he knows it, he must dedicate his whole life to the obeying it.' Well, the step to ordination was taken, but how difficult it has been to do God's will in the succeeding years. Help has been found in these words of Jesus: 'Anyone who resolves to do the will of God will know whether the teaching is from God, or whether I am speaking on my own.'

I delight to do your will, O my God; your law is within my heart.

Psalm 40.8

. . . not my will, but yours be done.

Luke 22.42

In His will is our peace.

Dante Alighieri, *The Divine Comedy*

The unconquerable Will.

John Milton, 'Paradise Lost'

Today, more than ever, we need to pray for the light to know the will of God, for the love to accept the will of God, for the way to do the will of God.

Mother Teresa, in Brother Angelo Devananda, *Jesus, the Word to Be Spoken*

The one great principle was that in all things a man must seek God's will and that, when he knows it, he must dedicate his whole life to the obeying it.

William Barclay, *The Gospel of Matthew*

Great things are not done by impulse, but by a series of small things brought together. And great things are not something accidental, but must certainly be *willed*.

Vincent van Gogh, *Dear Theo: An Autobiography of Vincent van Gogh*

He [Christ] hangs all true acquaintance with divinity upon the doing of God's will: 'If any man will do His will, he shall know of the doctrine, whether it be of God' (John 7.17).

John Smith the Platonist, *Select Discourses*

He gave man the power to thwart his will, that, by means of that same power, he might come at last to do his will in a higher kind and way than would otherwise have been possible.

George Macdonald, *Unspoken Sermons*

This is certain, that there is no peace but in the will of God. God's will is our peace and there is no other peace. God's peace is perfect freedom and there is no other freedom.

Father Andrew SDC, *The Life and Letters of Fr Andrew SDC*

. . . the will of God cannot be simply read off from facts or events but must be discerned, must be found through insight, through the kindling of the heart and the illumining of the mind that occur on the spiritual adventure.

John S. Dunne, *The Reasons of the Heart*

The one complete cure for the sense of frustration and futility is to know and do the will of God. Everyone to whom this becomes a reality is at once supplied with a purpose in life and one which covers the whole of life.

William Temple, *The Hope of a New World*

God's will does not waver. Nor can it be manipulated. From all that we have said hitherto, from the concrete requirements of Jesus himself, it should already have become clear that God wills nothing for himself, nothing for his own advantage, for his greater glory. God wills nothing but man's advantage, man's true greatness and his ultimate dignity. This then is God's will: *man's well-being.*

Hans Küng, *On Being a Christian*

The night of prayer which preceded Jesus's selection of the twelve apostles was focussed, we must surely believe, upon the kingdom and the power and the glory of God rather than on any short-list of candidates. It was communion and submission and adoration, renewing and clarifying the human body and mind and soul of Christ, which led, quite incidentally, to that sure knowledge of the next step he had to take in doing his Father's will.

John V. Taylor, *The Go-Between God*

The spiritual life, the Christian life does not consist in developing a strong will capable of compelling us to do what we do not want. In a sense, of course, it is an achievement to do the right things when we really wish to do the wrong ones, but it remains a small achievement. A mature spiritual life implies that our conscious will is in accordance with the words of God and has remoulded, transformed our nature so deeply, with the help of God's grace, that the totality of our human person is only one will.

Anthony Bloom, *The Essence of Prayer*

There is a clue in the Gospel of John in the saying of Jesus, 'I have food to eat which you do not know' . . . 'My food is to do the will of him who sent me, and to accomplish his work.' There is a sense here of relating to other human beings out of a fullness rather than an emptiness . . . As one passes from the languishing to the love it becomes possible to relate to others out of a fullness. The will of God is no longer what happens to one but is something to be done, as is this saying of Jesus, something to be accomplished.

John S. Dunne, *The Reasons of the Heart*

God's will is not just goodwill towards men in the sense of a benevolent disposition, though it is certainly that. It is a determined, dynamic force, working to achieve his purpose, ceaselessly opposed to evil, constantly countering the mistaken or sinful moves of men, always ready to guide those who take his will as the purpose of their lives, immediately generous to supply more than abundant grace to carry it out. 'Thy will be done!' is a cry of glad acceptance of the rightness, goodness and love of God. 'Thy will be done' is an equally joyful conviction.

George Appleton, *Journey for a Soul*

'I will arise and go to my Father', and so develop in itself the highest *Divine* of which it is capable – the will for the good against the evil – the will to be one with the life whence it has come, and in which it still is – the will to close the round of its procession in its return, so working the perfection of reunion – to shape in its own life the ring of eternity – to live immediately, consciously, and active-willingly from its source, from its own very life – to restore to the beginning the end that comes of that beginning – to be the thing the maker thought of when he willed, ere he began to work its being.

George Macdonald, *Unspoken Sermons*

**See also** Commitment, Contemplation, Love, Meditation, Obedience

## 118

# WISDOM

*Wisdom – being wise, (possession of) experience and knowledge together with the power of applying them critically or practically, sagacity, prudence, common sense*

'For wisdom will come into your heart'. So wrote the author of the book of Proverbs on the source of wisdom. If we want to see this fully worked out in a life we can go to the New Testament. In the Gospels some of those who heard our Lord's teaching were astonished, saying, 'Where did this man get all this? What is the wisdom given to him?' A modern writer, Christopher Bryant, wrote: 'It is part of the Christian spiritual tradition that God dwells in the centre of every man, an unseen, largely unknown Strength and Wisdom, moving him to be human, to grow and to expand his humanity to the utmost of its capacity.' We have found that being open and receptive in reflection is one of the best ways of growing in wisdom. In reflection we use the mind as far as it will go. We also use the 'heart' – our feelings and emotions, our instinct and intuition. Great use is also made of the imagination, and our experience of life. A full use can also be made of these quotations.

My mouth shall speak wisdom; the meditation of my heart shall be understanding.
Psalm 49.3

Who is wise and understanding among you? Show by your good life that your works are done with gentleness born of wisdom.
James 3.13

Wisdom cometh by suffering.
Aeschylus, *Agamemnon*

God waits for man to regain his childhood in wisdom.
Rabindranath Tagore, *Stray Birds*

The wisdom of the wise is an uncommon degree of common sense.
W.R. Inge, in Sir James Marchant, *Wit and Wisdom of Dean Inge*

Wisdom lies more in – affection and sincerity – than people are apt to imagine.
George Eliot, *Middlemarch*

Only when we offer our minds to God do we receive the illumination of his wisdom.
Bede Griffiths OSB, in Peter Spink, *The Universal Christ*

There is a deep wisdom inaccessible to the wise and prudent but disclosed to babes.
Christopher Bryant SSJE, *The Heart in Pilgrimage*

Some hold . . . that there is a wisdom of the Head, and that there is a wisdom of the Heart.
Charles Dickens, *Hard Times*

Common sense mellowed and experienced is wisdom; and wisdom in its ripeness is beauty.
A.R. Orage, *On Love*

The true sage is not he who sees, but he who, seeing the furthest, has the deepest love for mankind.
Maurice Maeterlinck, *Wisdom and Destiny*

Wisdom is oftimes nearer when we stoop
Than when we soar.
William Wordsworth, 'The Excursion'

Accumulated knowledge does not make a wise man. Knowledgeable people are found everywhere, but we are cruelly short of wise people.
Michel Quoist, *With Open Heart*

Wisdom is the knowledge of truth in its inmost reality, expression of truth, arrived at through the rectitudes of our own soul. Wisdom knows God in ourselves and ourselves in God.
Thomas Merton, *Thoughts in Solitude*

And we shall be truly wise if we be made content; content, too, not only with what we can understand, but, content with what we do not understand – the habit of mind which theologians call – and rightly – faith in God.

Charles Kingsley, *Health and Education*

By 'a new nativity' – initiated by obedient response to the inward Light . . . of God the indwelling Spirit – he may put on the new man, created after the likeness of God, and become the recipient of heavenly Wisdom springing up within him from the Life of the Spirit.

Rufus M. Jones, *Spiritual Reformers in the 16th and 17th Centuries*

The Wisdom of God is working through all created life, and far and wide is the sustainer and the inspirer of the thought and the endeavour of men. The Church will therefore reverence every honest activity of the minds of men; it will perceive that therein the Spirit of God is moving, and it will tremble lest by denying this, in word or in action, it blaspheme the Spirit of God.

Michael Ramsey, *The Gospel and the Catholic Church*

Aristotle defined *sophia*, wisdom, as knowledge of the most precious things. Cicero defined it as knowledge of things both human and divine. *Sophia* was a thing of the searching intellect, of the questing mind, of the reaches of the thoughts of men. *Sophia* is the answer to the eternal problems of life and death, and God and man, and time and eternity.

William Barclay, *The Letters to the Galatians and Ephesians*

Here is the test of wisdom,
Wisdom is not finally tested in schools,
Wisdom cannot be pass'd from one having it to another not having it,
Wisdom is of the soul, is not susceptible of proof, is its own proof.

Walt Whitman, 'Song of the Open Road'

What is the price of Experience? do men buy it for a song?
Or wisdom for a dance in the street? No, it is bought, with the price
Of all that a man hath, his house, his wife, his children.
Wisdom is sold in the desolate market place where none come to buy,
And in the wither'd field where the farmer ploughs for bread in vain.

William Blake, 'Vale or the Four Zoas'

The whole secret of remaining young in spite of years, and even of gray hairs, is to cherish enthusiasm in oneself, by poetry, by contemplation, by charity, – that is, in fewer words, by the maintenance of harmony in the soul. When everything is in its right place within us, we ourselves are in equilibrium with the whole work of God. Deep and grave enthusiasm for the eternal beauty and the eternal order, reason touched with emotion and a serene tenderness of heart – these surely are the foundations of wisdom.

Henri Frédéric Amiel, *Amiel's Journal*

Wisdom is not cheaply won. It is achieved through hard sacrifice and discipline, through the endurance of conflict and pain. It is the perfection of human living, the ceaseless straining of the human soul to pierce through the crushing body, the distracting intellect, the selfish will, and to apprehend the unsheathed spirit. It is intent living, the most fruitful act of man by which he tries to reach reality behind the restless stream of nature and his own feelings and desires. The destiny of the human soul is to realize its oneness with the supreme.

Sir Sarvepalli Radhakrishnan, *Eastern Religions and Western Thought*

**See also** Intellect, Knowledge, Mind, Thinking, Truth

# 119

# WONDER

*Wonder – emotion excited by what surpasses expectation or experience or seems inexplicable, surprise mingled with admiration or curiosity or bewilderment*

One morning I went into University College, London (where I used to work) and was hailed excitedly by one of our postgraduates. 'Hey, Bill, have you got a moment? Come and look at this.' I was ushered into his laboratory and invited to look down a microscope. What I saw was what I took to be a shell of the most perfect proportions – something of real beauty. I responded enthusiastically, 'Yes,' he said, 'it is wonderful, isn't it. But do you know what it is?' 'Well, it looks to be a rather lovely shell.' 'Yes, you are partly right, but last week we took it to be merely a grain of sand which we've dredged up from the North Sea. Under the microscope, we've discovered it's a shell. That's very significant, isn't it. Maybe there is something to be said for your Creator God after all.' I left his laboratory feeling rather excited. Even in that microscopic shell there was a sense of order and design. Nature still remains a great source of wonder to me.

For it was you who formed my inward parts; you knit me together in my mother's womb. I praise you, for I am fearfully and wonderfully made. Wonderful are your works; that I know very well.

Psalm 139.13–14

And all spoke well of him, and were amazed at the gracious words that came from his mouth.

Luke 4.22

To be surprised, to wonder, is to begin to understand.

José Ortega Y Gasset, *The Revolt of the Masses*

The idea of God that man has in his being is the wonder of all wonders.

Rabindranath Tagore, *Sadhana*

Worship is transcendent wonder; wonder for which there is no limit or measure.

Thomas Carlyle, *Heroes and Hero-Worship*

Philosophy begins in wonder. And, at the end, when philosophic thought has done its best, the wonder remains.

Alfred North Whitehead, *Modes of Thought*

Truth sees God: wisdom gazes on God. And these produce a third, a holy, wondering delight in God, which is love.

Lady Julian of Norwich, *Revelations of Divine Love*

Wonder and love are caught, not taught; and to catch them we must be in an atmosphere where we are sure to find the germs.

Evelyn Underhill, in John Stobbart, *The Wisdom of Evelyn Underhill*

The wonder and curiosity which welcomes what is new and regards it not as threatening but enriching life – that wonder and curiosity is God.

H.A. Williams CR, *The True Wilderness*

There is nothing that is so wonderfully created as the human soul. There is something of God in it. We are infinite in the future, though we are finite in the past.

Henry Ward Beecher, *Proverbs from Plymouth Pulpit*

Wonder is the highest thing in man, and if the ultimate phenomenon sets him wondering he should be content: he can be aware of nothing higher and he should seek nothing beyond: here is the limit.

Johann Wolfgang von Goethe, in Emil Ludwig, *The Practical Wisdom of Goethe*

Wonder . . . is essentially an 'opening' attitude – an awareness that there is more to life than one has yet fathomed, an experience of new vistas in life to be explored as well as new profundities to be plumbed.

Rollo May, *Man's Search for Himself*

The first and fundamental wonder is existence itself. That I should be alive, conscious, a person, a part of the whole, that I should have emerged out of nothingness, that the Void should have given birth, not merely to things, but to me.

W. MacNeile Dixon, *The Human Situation*

It is wonder that prompts the mind to examine its environment – and at first the elementary wonder how to make the best of it; but the enquiry ends in the wonder of awe, before that which, the more it is understood, by so much the more transcends our understanding.

William Temple, *Nature, Man and God*

Then there is the appeal of Jesus to the imagination, to the sense of wonder. How often we read in the gospel story that the people wondered at what Jesus did and said! They marvelled – the wondering imagination.

Jesus evokes that sense of wonder, and isn't it perhaps that sense of wonder which is a large part of what we call worship, and which really makes the difference between what is only an ethical allegiance, and what is religion?

Michael Ramsey, in Margaret Duggan, *Through the Year with Michael Ramsey*

The most beautiful experience we can have is the mysterious. It is the fundamental emotion which stands at the cradle of true art and science. Whoever does not know it and can no longer wonder, no longer marvel, is as good as dead, and his eyes are dimmed. It was the experience of mystery – even if mixed with fear – that engendered religion. A knowledge of the existence of something we cannot penetrate, our perceptions of the profoundest reason and the most radiant beauty, which only in their most primitive forms are accessible to our minds – it is this knowledge and this emotion that constitutes true religiosity.

Albert Einstein, *Ideas and Opinions*

No man or woman begins to live a full life until they realize they live in the presence of something greater, outside and beyond themselves. Self-consciousness truly means that you are standing over against that other than yourself and you cannot be living in truth. Wonder is at the base of true living, and wonder leads to worship and after that the great other than self; it is yet kin to you, you are one with it. Then you begin to live more completely and realize the kinship between you and nature, that out of nature you came and are part and parcel with it, this brings nearer faith which is self-conscious life (opposed to birds, trees, etc.), reaching out to perfection.

G.A. Studdert Kennedy, *The New Man in Christ*

And when the wonder has gone out of a man he is dead . . . When all comes to all, the most precious element in life is wonder. Love is a great emotion, and power is power. But both love and power are based on wonder. Love without wonder is a sensational affair, and power without wonder is mere force and compulsion.

The one universal element in consciousness which is fundamental to life is the element of wonder . . .

Plant consciousness, insect consciousness, fish consciousness, all are related by one permanent element, which we may call the religious element inherent in all life, even in a flea: the sense of wonder. That is our sixth sense. And it is the *natural* religious sense.

D.H. Lawrence, *Phoenix II*

**See also** Adoration, Freedom, Imagination, Joy, Worship

## 120

# WORK

*Work – expenditure of energy, striving, application of effort to some purpose; task to be undertaken; employment, especially of earning money by labour; laborious occupation*

'Work hard, play hard, pray hard, and then you will be happy.' This was the advice I was given on arriving at school. For the next seven years I put these words into practice, and found I was very happy. My first work experience was in the army, while doing National Service. As a private soldier the advice I received was somewhat different from the advice received at school. On the first day we were taught by the corporals never to volunteer for anything, and the next day we received instructions from them on the gentle art of skiving. While at university I had some valuable work experience in a bacon factory during a long vacation. The pigs were slaughtered at one end of a production line, and I was at the far end of the production line, stacking sides of bacon into a huge refrigerator, and doing something (I've forgotten precisely what) with the heads of pigs. I was incredibly bored as the job made no demands on my mind whatsoever. After a few weeks I came to the conclusion the secret of work was interest in the job – and enjoyment while doing it

The Lord God took the man and put him in the garden of Eden to till it and keep it.

Genesis 2.15

We must work the works of him who sent me.

John 9.4

Work is not the curse, but drudgery is.

Henry Ward Beecher, *Proverbs from Plymouth Pulpit*

The real essence of work is concentrated energy.
Walter Bagehot, *Biographical Studies*

A man can be so busy making a living that he forgets to make a life.
William Barclay, *The Gospel of Matthew*

It is a good sign where a man is proud of his work or his calling.
Henry Ward Beecher, *Proverbs from Plymouth Pulpit*

Certainly work is not always required of a man. There is such a thing as a sacred idleness, the cultivation of which is now fearfully neglected.
George Macdonald, *Wilfred Cumbermede*

Blessed be the man whose work drives him. Something must drive men; and if it is wholesome industry, they have no time for a thousand torments and temptations.
Henry Ward Beecher, *Proverbs from Plymouth Pulpit*

The most important motive for work in the school and in life is the pleasure of work, pleasure in its results and the knowledge of the value of the result to the community.
Albert Einstein, *Out of My Later Years*

I don't like work – no man does – but I like what is in the work, – the chance to find yourself. Your own reality – for yourself, not for others – what no other man can ever know.
Joseph Conrad, *Heart of Darkness, in Youth, a Narrative and Two Other Stories*

There is no right more universal and more sacred, because lying so near to the root of existence, than the right of men to their own labour.
Henry Ward Beecher, *Proverbs from Plymouth Pulpit*

Every citizen should have a voice in the conduct of the business or industry which is carried on by means of his labour, and the satisfaction of knowing that his labour is directed to the well-being of the community.
William Temple, *Christianity and the Social Order*

Love work: for if thou dost not want it for food, thou mayst for physic. It is wholesome for thy body, and good for thy mind. It prevents the fruits of idleness, which many times come of nothing to do, and leads too many to do what is worse than nothing.

William Penn, *Fruits of Solitude*

The world demands work. Work is needed for the mere maintenance of life; more work is needed for the maintenance of a particular level of civilization; still more work is needed if we look to the future and aim at giving later generations better chances of fuller life.

Sir Julian Huxley, *Religion Without Revelation*

The story is relevant here of the somewhat pompous parson leaning over the gate with the farmer, viewing a fine crop of barley. 'It is wonderful,' said the parson, 'what can be done when you and God get together.' 'Aye,' said the farmer, 'but you should have seen this field last year when God had it all to Himself.'

George Macleod, *Only One Way Left*

Capitalism is an evil thing, because it is based on what is called enlightened self-interest, and that is a baptismal name for selfishness. Poverty is a crime. The Church has been very specific on other matters. It hasn't hesitated to speak arbitrarily on most intimate affairs like sex. I don't see why it should restrict its particularity to those and not extend them to the world of the unemployed.

Lord Soper, in Gerald Priestland, *Priestland's Progress*

The problem set before us is to bring our daily task into the temple of contemplation and ply it there, to act as in the presence of God, to interfuse one's little part with religion. So only can we inform the detail of life, all that is passing, temporary, and insignificant, with beauty and nobility. So may we dignify and consecrate our meanest of occupations. So may we feel that we are paying our tribute to the universal work and the eternal will. So are we reconciled with life and delivered from the fear of death. So we are in order and in peace.

Henri Frédéric Amiel, *Amiel's Journal*

Commitment does not stop with contemplation. It seeks issue at work. For the God discovered thus is a God at work, reconciling the world to Himself. And those who worship in spirit and truth find themselves called to a ministry of reconciliation. A world unfinished and broken is to be made whole. Ultimately, it is God, not we, who must heal it, but in our small measure, we may be co-labourers with God. That is our calling. Worship sends us out to work. But work in turn, through frustration or consummation, may continually tend again toward worship, wherein illumination and renewal are to be found. Such, in part, is man's way toward God.

Robert Lowry Calhoun, *God and the Common Life*

No work done by any man, however great, will really prosper unless it has a distinct religious backing. But what is Religion? I for one would answer: 'Not the Religion you will get after reading all the scriptures of the world. Religion is not really grasped by the brain, but a heart grasp.'

Religion is a thing not alien to us. It has to be evolved out of us. It is always within us: with some, consciously so; with others, quite unconsciously. But it is always there. And whether we wake up this religious instinct in us through outside assistance or by inward growth, no matter how it is done, it has got to be done, if we want to do anything in the right manner, or to achieve anything that is going to persist.

Mohandas K. Gandhi, in C.F. Andrews, *Mahatma Gandhi's Ideas*

**See also** Action, Discipleship, Kingdom of God, Progress, Service

## 121

# WORLDLINESS

*Worldliness – temporal, earthly, exclusively or preponderantly concerned with or devoted to the affairs of this life, especially the pursuit of wealth or pleasure, prudence in advancing one's own interests*

I wonder if I am correct in discerning three forms of worldliness in our day and age. First, there is material wealth. Money and what money can buy seem to be crucially important for most people. Second, there is success and status. Our sense of identity often comes by having made it to the top. Third, there are relationships, with sex having a high profile. I would counter these forms of worldliness by regarding women and men as made primarily in the image and likeness of God.

Three consequences seem to follow from this. First, there is wealth. This is not to be found primarily in cash, but in the human personality, and in realizing one's gifts and talents. Second, there is success and status. Our sense of identity would come primarily in realizing our status as a child of God, and not just in having made it to the top. Third, there are relationships. First get our inner relatedness with God established, and then our outer relationships will naturally follow, with sex finding its rightful, valuable place. There will then be no need to worship it to excess, and exploit people. We shall be in the world, but not of it.

He will judge the world with righteousness, and the peoples with his truth.

Psalm 96.13

For what will it profit them if they gain the whole world and forfeit their life?

Matthew 16.26

The kingdom of this world is 'human society as it organizes itself apart from God'.

Leslie J. Tizard, *Facing Life and Death*

Those who set out to serve both God and Mammon soon discover that there is no God.

Logan Pearsall Smith, *Afterthoughts*

Where wealth and freedom reign contentment fails,
And honour sinks where commerce long prevails.

Oliver Goldsmith, 'The Traveller'

The character of worldly men is shaped by the influence of the love of property, of power, of influence, of praise, and the love of animal indulgence – not by the right, the true, the noble.

Henry Ward Beecher, *Proverbs from Plymouth Pulpit*

This secular world – formerly regarded as 'this' world, the wicked world *par excellence*, a neopagan world – today is not only taken into account in Christendom, but largely consciously approved and assisted in its development.

Hans Küng, *On Being a Christian*

The world expresses itself in magnificence, the spirit in magnanimity. The one means making big, inflating. The other means greatness (or openness) of mind, heart, soul. It is the difference between false and true generosity.

Hubert van Zeller, *Considerations*

Most people are kept from a true sense and taste of religion, by a regular kind of sensuality and indulgence, than by gross drunkenness. More men live regardless of the great duties of piety, through too great a concern for worldly goods, than through direct injustice.

William Law, *A Serious Call to a Devout and Holy Life*

The things which most often happen in life and are esteemed as the greatest good of all, as may be gathered from their works, can be reduced to these three headings: to wit, Riches, Fame, and Pleasure. With these three the mind is so engrossed that it cannot scarcely think of any other good.

Benedict Spinoza, *Spinoza's Ethics and De Intellectus Emendatione*

The world is too much with us; late and soon,
Getting and spending, we lay waste our powers:
Little we see in Nature that is ours;
We have given our hearts away, a sordid boon!

William Wordsworth, 'The World Is too much with Us'

The so-called 'real world'; the world which psychiatrists and social scientists and tycoons in advertising firms want us to adjust to and be at home in. That world saps our integrity and eats up our whole personality, giving us not freedom to do what we really want to do but a whole set of false wants and artificial and quite unnecessary 'needs'.

Geoffrey Preston OP, *Hallowing the Time*

*The world* [is] the sum of created being, which belongs to the sphere of human life as an ordered whole, considered apart from God, and in its moral aspect represented by humanity . . . It is easy to see how the thought of an ordered whole relative to man and considered *apart* from God passes into that of the ordered whole *separated* from God.

B.F. Westcott, *The Gospel According to St John*

The 'worldly' man is not necessarily the depraved man. He is the man who is misled into treating the world's goods as absorbing ends in themselves, and so misses the awareness of meaning and purpose beyond them.

The 'unworldly' man is not necessarily the devout man, or the man with conscious concern for God or for heaven. He is the man who is not absorbed in the world's goods or dominated by them, for there is in him an imagination or a simplicity or a humility or a care for persons which hints at something beyond. His unworldliness is properly seen not in any neglect of the world, but in the nature of his care for it.

Michael Ramsey, in Margaret Duggan, *Through the Year with Michael Ramsey*

There is so much frustration in the world because we have relied on gods rather than God. We have genuflected before the god of science only to find that it has given us the atomic bomb, producing fears and anxieties that science can never mitigate. We have worshipped the god of pleasure only to discover that thrills play out and sensations are short-lived. We have bowed before the god of money only to learn that there are such things as love and friendship that money cannot buy and that in a world of possible depressions, stock market crashes, and bad business investments, money is a rather uncertain deity. These transitory gods are not able to save or bring happiness to the human heart. Only God is able. It is faith in Him that we must rediscover.

Martin Luther King, in Coretta Scott King, *The Words of Martin Luther King*

The world . . . is a co-operative society with limited liability, existing for purely secular and chiefly selfish ends, some of which can only be realized by combined action, preying on the weakness of others, and exploiting their moral as well as physical and economic weakness. If its victims are trampled on, or if they are tempted to take part in iniquities the guilt of which is spread and distributed over a large number of persons, the world disclaims all responsibility. Like the Chief Priests to the remorseful Judas, it says, 'What is that to us? See thou to that.' All who take part in practical work, especially in political or semi-political work, but also in business or commerce, know how extremely difficult it is not to be caught in the toils of this ubiquitous and intricate machinery; they know how difficult it is to win any sort of success without soiling our hands and straining our consciences.

W.R. Inge, *Personal Religion and the Life of Devotion*

**See also** Anxiety, Power, Pride, Selfishness, Temptation

# 122

# WORSHIP

*Worship – reverent homage or service paid to God; acts, rites or ceremonies of honour and respect, adoration and devotion*

Over the years I have greatly enjoyed church music, and listening to anthems, feel to be close to the spirit of worship. For the most part I find formal worship difficult, and was greatly helped in my understanding by a sentence from J. Neville Ward's book, *Five for Sorrow, Ten for Joy*. In this book he wrote: 'Institutional religion will always exasperate us because it is carried on in the words and deeds of inadequate and sinful human beings.' Anthony Bloom has also enabled me to understand another difficulty with formal worship. In *Living Prayer*, he wrote: 'One of the reasons why communal worship or private prayer seems to be so dead or so conventional, is that the act of worship, which takes place in the heart, communicating with God, is too often missing. Every expression, either verbal or in action, may help, but they are only expressions of what is essential, namely, a deep silence of communion . . . If we want to worship God, we must first of all learn to feel happy, being silent together with him.' In the silence of reflection we try to worship God in spirit and truth.

O come, let us worship and bow down, let us kneel before the Lord our Maker! For he is our God.

Psalm 95.6–7

But the hour is coming, and is now here, when the true worshippers will worship the Father in spirit and truth, for the Father seeks such as these to worship him. God is spirit, and those who worship him must worship in spirit and truth.

John 4.23–24

Wonder . . . is the basis of Worship.

Thomas Carlyle, *Sartor Resartus*

We *Worship* God best; when we Resemble Him most.

Benjamin Whichcote, *Moral and Religious Aphorisms*

Without worship you shrink; it's as brutal as that . . .

Peter Shaffer, *Equus*

But the purpose of all worship is the same: to offer praise to God for his grace and glory.

Alan Richardson, in Alan Richardson and John Bowden, *A New Dictionary of Christian Theology*

So long as the letter is the servant of the spirit and not its master, the spirit gives life to the letter. Hence public worship. Hence vocal prayer.

Hubert van Zeller, *Considerations*

. . . worship is a communing, the opening of human life to God, the response to grace, the growing up into union with God, who has made us for himself.

John Macquarrie, *Paths in Spirituality*

This alone is true worship – the giving to God of body, soul and spirit ('ourselves, our souls and bodies') with all that they need for their full development, so that He may take and use them for His purpose.

William Temple, *Citizen and Churchman*

When our Lord told the Samaritan woman that worship of the Father should be in spirit and in truth he was not ruling out considerations of place, ceremonial, formulas. He was saying that these factors were useless unless animated by spirit and truth.

Hubert van Zeller, *Considerations*

. . . a spiritual discipline must be freely accepted and embraced if it is to be fully effective . . . worship must be a free response of love rather than a homage exacted.

John Macquarrie, *Paths in Spirituality*

What else can a lame old man as I am do but chant the praise of God? If, indeed, I were a nightingale I should sing as a nightingale, if a swan, as a swan; but as I am a rational creature I must praise God. This is my task, and I do it: and I will not abandon this duty, so long as it is given me; and I invite you all to join in this same song.

Epictetus, in Witney J. Oates, *The Stoic and Epicurean Philosophers*

For worship is the submission of all our nature to God. It is the quickening of the conscience by His holiness; the nourishment of mind with His truth; the purifying of imagination by His beauty; the opening of the heart to His love; the surrender of will to His purpose – and all of this gathered up in adoration, the most selfless emotion of which our nature is capable.

William Temple, *Readings in St John's Gospel*

The true worship, the really spiritual worship, is the offering of one's body, and all that one does every day with it, to God. Real worship is not the offering of elaborate prayers to God; it is not the offering to God of a liturgy, however noble, and a ritual, however magnificent. *Real worship is the offering of everyday life to God.* Real worship is not something which is transacted in a church; real worship is something which sees the whole world as the temple of the living God, and every common deed an act of worship.

William Barclay, *The Letter to the Romans*

The word 'worship' comes from an old English word meaning worthship – giving to God his true worth as Creator, Redeemer, and indwelling Spirit. Worship is man's response to these divine activities. As we realize the greatness, the goodness and the 'allness' of God, we forget ourselves and our hearts break forth in praise. Yet worship is not just an expression in words or music of feeling, but the outgoing of our hearts and the acceptance of God as the governing reality of our lives. He becomes our chiefest good and our lives are henceforth offered to him in loving obedience.

George Appleton, *Journey for a Soul*

*Abide in me, and I in you.* The whole phrase has an imperative tone: let there be mutual indwelling. *Abide in me*, of which the consequence will be that I shall abide in you . . .

All forms of Christian worship, all forms of Christian discipline, have this as their object. Whatever leads to this is good; whatever hinders this is bad; whatever does not bear on this is futile. This is the life of the Christian: *Abide in me and I in you.* All truth and depth of devotion, all effectiveness in service spring from this. It is not a theme for words but for the deeper apprehensions of silence.

William Temple, *Readings in St John's Gospel*

The worship of God is itself the inner core of Christian spirituality: the heart, the mind, and the will, directed towards the glory of God as man's goal. Every time that a Christian lifts up his soul to God in desire towards him he is, however faintly, realizing that fellowship with the Creator for which he was created, and he is, in a tiny and yet significant way, anticipating the goal of heaven. Thus regarded, spirituality is no escape from the world. It is lived out in all the complexities of our social life, in family, city, country, industry, culture, joy, sorrow, for it is the spirituality of a man, and a man is involved in all these things. It is inseparable from service, love, duty, the moulding of the common-life. Yet in deep-down essence it is the spirit of worship.

Michael Ramsey, in Margaret Duggan, *Through the Year with Michael Ramsey*

. . . worship can be a continuously creative thing. It means coming from the world, from the squalor, the hunger, the misery, the heartbreak, for the act of acknowledging again the love and kingship of God. It means ascending the hill of the Lord to receive again His pardon, to receive again the bread and wine of life, to offer obedience again and find the strength for it, to bring all that has been learned and suffered at the crossroads of life to God for His dealing. But it does not mean a permanent lodging in the cathedrals and churches where worship in community is offered. It means going back from the hour of worship to the arena of the world's life and the place of man's need only to discover that God to whom the worship was offered is the contemporary friend and partner to farmer and healer, teacher and preacher and all others who for the love of God and man seek to meet man's need.

Leonard Hurst, *Hungry Men*

**See also** Adoration, Church, Contemplation, Meditation, Thanksgiving

# NOTES

*Acceptance*

1. NRSV.
2. NRSV.
3. Anon.
4. Martin Luther King, in Coretta Scott King, *The Words of Martin Luther King*, William Collins Sons and Co. 1986, p. 25.
5. John S. Dunne, *The Reasons of the Heart*, SCM Press 1978, p. 26.
6. Michel Quoist, *With Open Heart*, translated by Colette Copeland, Gill and Macmillan 1983, p. 183.
7. Oscar Wilde, *De Profundis, The Works of Oscar Wilde*, edited by G.F. Maine, William Collins Sons and Co. 1948, p. 866.
8. Arthur T. Jersild, *The Psychology of Adolescence*, The Macmillan Co. 1963, p. 34.
9. Peter G. van Breemen SJ, *As Bread that Is Broken*, Dimension Books 1978, p. 9.
10. *Theologia Germanica*, translated by Susanna Winkworth, Stuart and Watkins 1966, p. 53.
11. van Breemen, *As Bread that Is Broken*, p. 9.
12. Richard Wilhelm and C.G. Jung, *The Secret of the Golden Flower*, Routledge and Kegan Paul 1972, p. 126.
13. van Breemen, *As Bread that Is Broken*, p. 9.
14. Paul Tillich, *The Shaking of the Foundations*, SCM Press 1949, p. 162.
15. van Breemen, *As Bread that Is Broken*, p. 9.

*Action*

1. NRSV.
2. NRSV.
3. Francis Thompson, '*Shelley*', *The Works of Francis Thompson*, Burns and Oates 1913, vol. III, p. 2.
4. Marcus Aurelius, *The Meditations of Marcus Aurelius*, translated by Jeremy Collier, Walter Scott n.d., p. 25.
5. Benjamin Whichcote, *Moral and Religious Aphorisms*, century X, no. 912, Elkin Mathews and Marrot 1930.
6. Dietrich Bonhoeffer, *Letters and Papers from Prison*, William Collins Sons and Co. 1963, p. 158.
7. A.C. Benson, *Extracts from the Letters of Dr A.C. Benson to M.E.A.*, Jarrold Publishing 1927, p. 6.
8. Dag Hammarskjöld, *Markings*, translated by Leif Sjoberg and W.H. Auden, Faber and Faber 1964, p. 108.
9. Henry Ward Beecher, *Proverbs from Plymouth Pulpit*, Charles Burnet and Co. 1887, p. 151.
10. Nicolas Berdyaev, *Christianity and Class War*, translated by Donald Attwater, Sheed and Ward 1933, p. 50.
11. Charles Péguy, *Basic Verities*, translated by Ann and Julian Green, Kegan Paul, Trench, Trubner and Co. 1943, p. 51.

12. Anon.
13. Johann Wolfgang von Goethe, in Ludwig Curtius, *Wisdom and Experience*, translated by Hermann J. Weigand, Routledge and Kegan Paul 1949, p. 210.
14. William Blake, 'Jerusalem', *The Complete Writings of William Blake*, edited by Geoffrey Keynes, Oxford University Press 1974, p. 672.
15. George Eliot, *Adam Bede*, Virtue and Co. 1908, vol. 1, p. 318.
16. Basil Hume OSB, *To Be a Pilgrim*, St Paul Publications 1984, p. 157.
17. George Eliot, 'Stradivarius', *The Works of George Eliot*, Virtue and Co. 1913, vol. XVIII, *Jubal and Other Poems*, p. 218.
18. Mother Teresa, in Brother Angelo Devananda, *Jesus, the Word to Be Spoken*, William Collins Sons and Co. 1990, p. 8.
19. Florence Higham, said of F.D. Maurice, in *Frederick Denison Maurice*, SCM Press 1947, p. 126.
20. John Macmurray, *Creative Society*, SCM Press 1935, p. 88.
21. James Martineau, *Endeavours after the Christian Life: Discourses*, Longmans, Green, Reader and Dyer 1876, p. 90.

## *Adoration*

1. NRSV.
2. NRSV.
3. Kenneth Leech, *True Prayer*, Sheldon Press 1980, p. 119.
4. Evelyn Underhill, *The Love of God*, Mowbray 1953, p. 136.
5. Ernest Hello, *Life, Science, and Art,* R. and T. Washbourne 1913, p. 158.
6. John V. Taylor, *The Go-Between God*, SCM Press 1973, p. 45.
7. William Wordsworth, 'It is a Beauteous Evening', *The Poetical Works of William Wordsworth*, edited by E. de Selincourt and Helen Darbishire, Oxford at the Clarendon Press 1954, vol. III, *Miscellaneous Sonnets*, p. 17.
8. Vida D. Scudder, *The Privilege of Age*, J.M. Dent and Sons 1939, p. 30.
9. Pierre Teilhard de Chardin, *Le Milieu Divin*, William Collins Sons and Co. 1960, p. 117.
10. John Macquarrie, *Paths in Spirituality*, SCM Press 1972, p. 6.
11. de Chardin, *Le Milieu Divin*, p. 188.
12. William Temple, *The Hope of a New World*, SCM Press 1940, p. 30.
13. J. Neville Ward, *The Use of Praying*, Epworth Press 1967, p. 28.
14. Thomas F. Green, *Preparation for Worship*, (Swarthmore Lecture), George Allen and Unwin Publishers 1952, p. 17.
15. Evelyn Underhill, *The Golden Sequence*, Methuen and Co. 1932, p. 162.
16. Olive Wyon, *On the Way*, SCM Press 1958, p. 101.
17. Underhill, *The Golden Sequence*, p. 165.

## *Anxiety*

1. NRSV.
2. NRSV.
3. Alfred, Lord Tennyson, 'Enoch Arden', *The Works of Alfred Lord Tennyson*, Macmillan Publishers 1898, p. 128.
4. Ralph Waldo Emerson, *Letters and Social Aims, Addresses, The Works of Ralph Waldo Emerson, vol. III, Society and Solitude,* edited by George Sampson, George Bell and Sons 1906, p. 147.
5. A.C. Benson, *Extracts from the Letters of Dr A.C. Benson to M.E.A.*, Jarrold Publishing 1927, p. 69.
6. Henry Ward Beecher, *Proverbs from Plymouth Pulpit*, Charles Burnet and Co. 1887, p. 18.
7. Benson, *Extracts from the Letters of Dr A.C. Benson to M.E.A.*, p. 60.
8. Author unknown.
9. Thomas Merton, *No Man Is an Island*, Burns and Oates 1974, p. 197.
10. Mark Rutherford, *Last Pages from a Journal*, Oxford University Press 1915, p. 257.
11. Richard Foster, *The Celebration of Discipline*, Hodder and Stoughton 1982, p. 77.
12. Rutherford, *Last Pages from a Journal*, p. 308.

13. Thomas Merton, *Thoughts in Solitude*, Burns and Oates 1958, p. 71.
14. Anthony Bloom, *The Essence of Prayer*, Darton, Longman and Todd 1989, p. 116.
15. Rollo May, *Man's Search for Himself*, George Allen and Unwin 1953, p. 44.
16. Geoffrey Harding, in George Appleton, *Journey for a Soul*, William Collins Sons and Co. 1976, p. 114.
17. E. Stanley Jones, *Growing Spiritually*, Hodder and Stoughton 1954, p. 45.
18. Lilian Whiting, *Lilies of Eternal Peace*, Gay and Hancock 1908, p. 17.
19. Rutherford, *Last Pages from a Journal*, p. 290.
20. Lilian Whiting, *The Life Radiant*, Gay and Bird 1904, p. 320.

## *Art*

1. NRSV.
2. NRSV.
3. Henry Wadsworth Longfellow, 'Hyperion', George Routledge and Sons 1887, p. 196.
4. John Ruskin, *The Two Paths*, George Allen 1905, p. 57.
5. Henry Ward Beecher, *Proverbs from Plymouth Pulpit*, Charles Burnet and Co. 1887, p. 223.
6. Thomas Carlyle, *Latter-Day Pamphlets*, Chapman and Hall 1899, p. 271.
7. Amy Lowell, *Tendencies in Modern American Poetry*, The Macmillan Co. 1917, p. 7.
8. Henri Frédéric Amiel, *Amiel's Journal*, translated by Mrs Humphry Ward, Macmillan and Co. 1918, p. 249.
9. A. Clutton Brock, *The Ultimate Belief*, Constable and Co. 1916, p. 101.
10. Mohandas K. Gandhi, in C.F. Andrews, *Mahatma Gandhi's Ideas*, George Allen and Unwin 1929, p. 332.
11. Wassily Kandinsky, *Concerning the Spiritual in Art*, translated by M.T.H. Sadler, Dover Publications 1977, p. 54.
12. Ludwig Lewisohn, *The Modern Drama*, B.W. Huebsch 1915, p. 109.
13. John Ruskin, *The Stones of Venice*, edited by Jan Morris, Faber and Faber 1981, p. 233.
14. Robert Henri, *The Art Spirit*, compiled by Margery A. Ryerson, J.B. Lippincott and Co. 1960, p. 66.
15. Henry Wadsworth Longfellow, 'Michel Angelo', *The Poetical Works of Longfellow*, Humphrey Milford, Oxford University Press 1913, part 1, section 3, p. 793.
16. Alexander Solzhenitsyn, *One Word of Truth: The Nobel Speech in Literature*, The Bodley Head 1970, p. 5.
17. Nathaniel Hawthorne, *The Marble Faun*, The Bobbs-Merrill Co. 1971, p. 324.
18. Robert Bridges, The Testament of Beauty', Oxford at the Clarendon Press, iii. 1058, p. 126.
19. Joseph Conrad, *The Nigger of the 'Narcissus'*, J.M. Dent and Sons 1929, p. viii.
20. Henri, *The Art Spirit*, p. 15.
21. Sir Joshua Reynolds, *Sir Joshua Reynolds' Discourses*, Kegan Paul, Trench and Co. 1883, p. 247.

## *Aspiration*

1. NRSV.
2. NRSV.
3. Henry Wadsworth Longfellow, 'The Masque of Pandora', *The Poetical Works of Longfellow*, Humphrey Milford, Oxford University Press 1913, p. 688.
4. William Wordsworth, 'Devotional Incitements', 'Poems of the Imagination', no. XLVI, *The Poetical Works of William Wordsworth*, edited by E. de Selincourt, Oxford at the Clarendon Press 1944, vol. II, p. 313.
5. Francis Bacon, *The Advancement of Learning*, Cassell and Co. 1905, p. 156.
6. Johann Wolfgang von Goethe, *Faust*, translated by Bayard Taylor, Sphere Books 1974, part 1, 'Prologue in Heaven', l.328.
7. Michel Quoist, *With Open Heart*, translated by Colette Copeland, Gill and Macmillan 1983, p. 66.
8. Sir Philip Sidney, 'Leave Me, O Love', *The Poems of Sir Philip Sidney*, edited by William A. Ringler, Jr, Oxford at the Clarendon Press 1962, p. 161.

9. Robert Louis Stevenson, *Familiar Studies of Men and Books, Virginibus Puerisque, Selected Poems*, William Collins Sons and Co. 1956, p. 293.
10. John Milton, *Of Education, Complete Works of John Milton*, Oxford University Press 1959, vol. 11, p. 385.
11. Richard Jefferies, *The Story of My Heart*, Macmillan and Co. 1968, p. 142.
12. Hubert van Zeller, *Considerations*, Sheed and Ward 1974, p. 84.
13. Rufus M. Jones, in H. Loukes, *The Quaker Contribution*, SCM Press 1965, p. 91.
14. Stephen MacKenna, *Journal and Letters*, Constable and Co. 1936, p. 276.
15. Matthew Arnold, 'Stanzas from the Grande Chartreuse', *The Poems of Matthew Arnold*, edited by Kenneth Allott, Longmans, Green and Co. 1965, xii.67, p. 288.
16. Alfred, Lord Tennyson, 'Idylls of the King, Guinevere', *The Poems of Tennyson*, edited by Christopher Ricks, Longmans, Green and Co. 1969, No. 474, l.652, p. 1741.
17. Lecomte du Nöuy, *Human Destiny*, Longmans, Green and Co. 1947, p. 178.
18. Albert Einstein, *Out of My Later Years*, Thames and Hudson 1950, p. 9.
19. Raynor C. Johnson, *A Pool of Reflections*, Hodder and Stoughton 1975, p. 143.

## *Awareness*

1. NRSV.
2. NRSV.
3. Edward Bellamy, *Looking Backwards*, Alvin Redman 1948, p. 111.
4. Michel Quoist, *With Open Heart*, translated by Colette Copeland, Gill and Macmillan 1983, p. 168.
5. William Barclay, *The Gospel of Matthew*, The Saint Andrew Press 1987, vol. 1, p. 280.
6. Eric Hoffer, *The Passionate State of Mind*, Martin Secker and Warburg 1956, p. 76.
7. *The Cloud of Unknowing*, translated by Clifton Wolters, Penguin Books 1971, p. 66.
8. F.R. Barry, *The Relevance of Christianity*, James Nisbet and Co. 1932, p. 75.
9. Sir Thomas Browne, *Christian Morals, The Works of Sir Thomas Browne*, edited in 4 volumes by Geoffrey Keynes, Faber and Faber 1964, vol. 1, p. 254.
10. George Eliot, *Middlemarch*, Penguin Books 1985, p. 226.
11. Margaret Bondfield, *What Life Has Taught Me*, edited by Sir James Marchant, Odhams Press 1948, p. 27.
12. Charles Kingsley, *Daily Thoughts*, Macmillan Publishers 1884, p. 103.
13. Frank Wright, *The Pastoral Nature of the Ministry*, SCM Press 1980, p. 34.
14. Helmut Thielicke, *I Believe – The Christian's Creed*, translated by John W. Doberstein and M. George Anderson, William Collins Sons and Co. 1969, p. 35.
15. J. Neville Ward, *The Use of Praying*, Epworth Press 1967, p. 25.
16. Bondfield, *What Life Has Taught Me*, p. 27.
17. Thomas Merton, *Conjectures of a Guilty Bystander*, Burns and Oates 1968, p. 274.

## *Beauty*

1. AV.
2. NRSV.
3. William Shakespeare, *Othello*, act V.i.19.
4. Henry Ward Beecher, *Proverbs from Plymouth Pulpit*, Charles Burnet and Co. 1887, p. 101.
5. Harry Emerson Fosdick, *As I See Religion*, SCM Press, 1932, p. 128.
6. Rabindranth Tagore, *Stray Birds, Collected Poems and Plays of Rabindranath Tagore*, Macmillan and Co. 1936, CXCV, p. 312.
7. Richard Jefferies, *Pageant of Summer*, Chatto and Windus 1911, p. 39.
8. George Macdonald, *The Marquis of Lossie*, Everett and Co. 1912, p. 68.
9. Ralph Waldo Emerson, *Essays and Representative Men, The Works of Ralph Waldo Emerson*, edited by George Sampson, George Bell and Sons 1906, vol. 1, p. 191.
10. Kahlil Gibran, *Sand and Foam*, William Heineman 1927, p. 23.
11. Beecher, *Proverbs from Plymouth Pulpit*, p. 187.
12. Nicolas Berdyaev, *Christian Existentialism*, selected and translated by Donald A. Lowrie, George Allen and Unwin 1965, p. 323.

13. Henri Frédéric Amiel, *Amiel's Journal*, translated by Mrs Humphry Ward, Macmillan and Co. 1918, p. 68.
14. Friedrich Schiller, *Essays, Aesthetical and Philosophical*, George Bell and Sons 1875, p. 4.
15. A.C. Benson, *Extracts from the Letters of Dr A.C. Benson to M.E.A.*, Jarrold Publishing 1927, p. 77.
16. Percy Bysshe Shelley, 'Hymn to Intellectual Beauty', *The Complete Poems of Percy Bysshe Shelley*, Oxford University Press 1935, verse 11, p. 526.
17. H.G. Wells, *The History of Mr Polly*, Thomas Nelson and Sons 1910, p. 321.
18. Maurice Maeterlinck, *Wisdom and Destiny*, translated by A. Sutro, George Allen 1898, p. xiii.
19. Henry Wadsworth Longfellow, 'Evangeline, Part the First', *The Poetical Works of Longfellow*, Humphrey Milford, Oxford University Press 1913, p. 144, l.59.
20. Johann Wolfgang von Goethe, *Wilhelm Meister's Year of Apprenticeship*, translated by H.M. Waidson, John Calder (Publishers) 1978, vol. II, p. 74.
21. Alan Seeger, 'An Ode to Natural Beauty', *Poems*, Constable and Co. 1917, p. 4.
22. Fyodor Dostoyevsky, *Letters of Fyodor Michailovitch Dostoyevsky to His Family and Friends*, translated by Ethel Colburn Mayne, Peter Owen, pp. 71 and 142.

## *Belief*

1. NRSV.
2. NRSV.
3. W.B. Yeats, in Samuel H. Miller, *The Great Realities*, Longmans, Green and Co. 1956, p. 112.
4. Thomas Fuller, *Gnomologia*, Stearne Brock 1773, p. 71.
5. Carlo Carretto, *Summoned by Love*, translated by Alan Neame, Darton, Longman and Todd 1977, p. 35.
6. William James, *The Will to Believe*, Longmans, Green and Co. 1904, p. 62.
7. F.R. Barry, *Secular and Supernatural*, SCM Press 1969, p. 36.
8. Ralph Waldo Emerson, *Essays and Representative Men, The Works of Ralph Waldo Emerson*, edited by George Sampson, George Bell and Sons 1906, vol. 1, p. 453.
9. Mark Rutherford, *Last Pages from a Journal*, Oxford University Press 1915, p. 318.
10. Dag Hammarskjöld, *Markings*, translated by Leif Sjoberg and W.H. Auden, Faber and Faber 1964, p. 95.
11. David Sheppard, *Bias to the Poor*, Hodder and Stoughton 1983, p. 151.
12. Brother Lawrence, *The Practice of the Presence of God*, A.R. Mowbray and Co. 1977, p. 19.
13. Hugh Redwood, *Residue of Days*, Hodder and Stoughton 1958, p. 20.
14. William Temple, *The Hope of a New World*, SCM Press 1940, p. 107.
15. Pierre Teilhard de Chardin, *Le Milieu Divin*, William Collins Sons and Co. 1960, p. 129.
16. William Barclay, *The Gospel of John*, The Saint Andrew Press 1965, vol. 2, p. 177.
17. William Law, in Stephen Hobhouse, *Selected Mystical Writings of William Law*, Rockliff 1948, p. 32.
18. John Baillie, *Invitation to Pilgrimage*, Oxford University Press 1942, p. 18.
19. Fyodor Dostoyevsky, *The Brothers Karamazov*, translated by David Magarshack, Penguin Books 1963, vol. 1, p. 275.
20. W.E. Sangster, *These Things Abide*, Hodder and Stoughton 1939, p. 78.
21. Benjamin Franklin, *The Private Correspondence of B. Franklin*, printed for Henry Colburn 1817, p. 131.

## *Blessedness*

1. NRSV.
2. NRSV.
3. Thomas Carlyle, *Past and Present*, Ward, Lock and Co., lxxx, p. 136.
4. Thomas Carlyle, *Sartor Resartus*, Ward, Lock and Co., lxxx, p. 128.
5. Henry David Thoreau, *Walden*, The New American Library of World Literature Inc 1960, p. 149.
6. Edward Young, *Night Thoughts*, Thomas Nelson 1841, p. 210.

7. William Barclay, *The Gospel of Matthew*, The Saint Andrew Press 1987, vol. 1, p. 100.
8. John Burchhardt, *The Civilization of the Renaissance in Italy*, Harper and Brothers, Publishers, 1958, p. 516.
9. Henry Ward Beecher, *Proverbs from Plymouth Pulpit*, Charles Burnet and Co. 1887, p. 170.
10. Izaak Walton, *The Compleat Angler*, Macmillan and Co. 1906, p. 174.
11. Beecher, *Proverbs from Plymouth Pulpit*, p. 136.
12. *Theologia Germanica*, translated by Susanna Winkworth, Stuart and Watkins 1966, p. 48.
13. Carroll E. Simcox, *The Promises of God*, Dacre Press, A. and C. Black 1958, p. 91.
14. William Law, *The Spirit of Love and the Spirit of Prayer*, edited by Sidney Spencer, James Clarke and Co. 1969, p. 165.
15. Sir John Lubbock, *The Pleasures of Life*, Macmillan Publishers 1891, p. 5.
16. Henri Frédéric Amiel, *Amiel's Journal*, translated by Mrs Humphry Ward, Macmillan and Co. 1918, p. 188.
17. Anon.

## *Character*

1. AV.
2. NRSV.
3. William Shakespeare, *Hamlet*, act I.iii.78.
4. Alexander Pope, *An Essay on Man*, Cassell and Co. 1905, 'Epistle IV', p. 52.
5. Henry Ward Beecher, *Life Thoughts*, Alexander Strahan and Co. 1895, p. 95.
6. Johann Wolfgang von Goethe, *Torquato Tasso,* 1709, act I. ii. 66.
7. Ralph Waldo Emerson, *Society and Solitude: Letters and Social Aims: Addresses*, *The Works of Ralph Waldo Emerson*, edited by George Sampson, George Bell and Sons, vol. III 1906, p. 381.
8. Henry Ward Beecher, *Proverbs from Plymouth Pulpit*, Charles Burnet and Co. 1887, p. 122.
9. Henri Frédéric Amiel, *Amiel's Journal*, translated by Mrs Humphry Ward, Macmillan and Co. 1918, p. 47.
10. Thomas Jefferson, *The Writings of Thomas Jefferson*, Taylor and Maury 1854, vol. IV, p. 476.
11. Beecher, *Proverbs from Plymouth Pulpit*, p. 150.
12. Hubert van Zeller, *Considerations*, Sheed and Ward 1974, p. 13.
13. Beecher, *Proverbs from Plymouth Pulpit*, p. 43.
14. Helen Keller, *Helen Keller's Journal*, Michael Joseph 1938, p. 66.
15. Beecher, *Proverbs from Plymouth Pulpit*, p. 164.
16. John Cowper Powys, *Autobiography*, Macdonald and Co. 1967, p. 376.
17. Father Andrew SDC, *A Gift of Light*, elected and edited by Harry C. Griffith, A.R. Mowbray and Co. 1968, p. 84.
18. William Temple, *Christian Faith and Life*, SCM Press 1963, p. 43.
19. Beecher, *Proverbs from Plymouth Pulpit*, p. 166.
20. John Smith the Platonist, *Select Discourses*, Cambridge at the University Press 1859, p. 401.
21. W.R. Inge, *Personal Religion and the Life of Devotion*, Longmans, Green and Co. 1924, p. 59.
22. Samuel Smiles, *Self-Help*, S.W. Partridge and Co. 1912, p. 285.

## *Cheerfulness*

1. NRSV.
2. NRSV.
3. Thomas Fuller, *Gnomologia*, Stearne Brock 1733, p. 43.
4. Ralph Waldo Emerson, *Essays and Representative Men, The Works of Ralph Waldo Emerson*, edited by George Sampson, George Bell and Sons, vol. 1, 1906, p. 353.
5. Joseph Addison, *The Works of Joseph Addison*, edited and published by Henry G. Bohn 1856, vol. III, p. 363.
6. Ralph Waldo Emerson, *The Conduct of Life, Nature, and Other Essays*, J.M. Dent and Sons 1911, p. 279.
7. Anon.
8. William Shakespeare, *The Winter's Tale*, act IV.iii.125.

9. Addison, *The Works of Joseph Addison*, vol. II, p. 153.
10. A.C. Benson, *Extracts from the Letters of Dr A.C. Benson to M.E.A.*, Jarrold Publishing 1927, p. 19.
11. Charlotte Brontë, *Shirley*, Clarendon Press 1979, p. 43.
12. Henry Ward Beecher, *Proverbs from Plymouth Pulpit*, Charles Burnet and Co. 1887, p. 20.
13. Addison, *The Works of Joseph Addison*, vol. III, p. 356.
14. Francois de la M. Fénelon, in Mrs Follen, *Extracts from the Writings of Fénelon*, Edward T. Whitfield 1850, p. 233.
15. Charles Kingsley, *Daily Thoughts*, Macmillan Publishers 1884, p. 227.
16. Michael Ramsey, in Margaret Duggan, *Through the Year with Michael Ramsey*, Hodder and Stoughton 1975, p. 81.
17. William Wordsworth, 'London, 1802', l.9, 'Poems Dedicated to National Independence and Liberty', no. XIV, *The Poetical Works of William Wordsworth*, edited by E. de Selincourt, Oxford at the Clarendon Press 1954, vol. III, p. 131.
18. Anne Frank, *The Diary of Anne Frank*, Pan Books 1954, p. 175.
19. W.E. Sangster, *Westminster Sermons*, Epworth Press 1960, vol. 1, *At Morning Worship*, p. 4.

## *Christian*

1. NRSV.
2. NRSV.
3. Edward Young, *Night Thoughts*, Thomas Nelson 1841, p. 64.
4. Tertullian, *The Writings of Tertullian*, Hamilton and Co. 1869, vol. 1, Apology no.17, p. 87.
5. Sir Richard Livingstone, *On Education*, Cambridge at the University Press 1954, p. 133.
6. Henry Ward Beecher, *Life Thoughts*, Alexander Strahan and Co. 1859, p. 135.
7. Samuel Taylor Coleridge, *Letters of Samuel Taylor Coleridge*, edited by Ernest Hartley Coleridge, William Heineman 1895, vol. 11, Letter No. 209, p. 775.
8. E. Stanley Jones, *Growing Spiritually*, Hodder and Stoughton 1954, p. 188.
9. John A.T. Robinson, *The Roots of a Radical*, SCM Press 1980, p. 55.
10. Hans Küng, *On Being a Christian*, translated by Edward Quinn, William Collins Sons and Co. 1977, p. 380.
11. Henry Ward Beecher, *Proverbs from Plymouth Pulpit*, Charles Burnet and Co. 1887, p. 171.
12. Henri J.M. Nouwen, *The Wounded Healer*, Doubleday 1979, p. 99.
13. Izaak Walton, *The Compleat Angler*, The Nonesuch Press 1929, p. 18.
14. Henry McKeating, *God and the Future*, SCM Press 1974, p. 58.
15. C.G. Jung, *Memories, Dreams, Reflections*, William Collins Sons and Co. 1971, p. 236.
16. Rufus M. Jones, *Spiritual Reformers in the 16th and 17th Centuries*, Macmillan and Co. 1914, p. 170.
17. Mark Rutherford, *Last Pages from a Journal*, Oxford University Press 1915, p. 266.
18. Jones, *Spiritual Reformers in the 16th and 17th Centuries*, p. 46.
19. David Brown, *God's Tomorrow*, SCM Press 1977, p. 55.

## *Church*

1. NRSV.
2. NRSV.
3. Henry Ward Beecher, *Proverbs from Plymouth Pulpit*, Charles Burnet and Co. 1887, p. 109.
4. Cardinal Leon Joseph Suenens, *A New Pentecost?*, translated by Francis Martin, Darton, Longman and Todd 1975, p. 1.
5. Paul Oestreicher, in Hans Jurgen Schultz, *Conversion to the World*, SCM Press 1967, p. 32.
6. Henry Ward Beecher, *Proverbs from Plymouth Pulpit*, Charles Burnet and Co. 1887, p. 200.
7. W.A. Visser 'T Hooft, *The Renewal of the Church*, SCM Press 1956, p. 23.
8. Daniel Jenkins, *Christian Maturity and the Theology of Success*, SCM Press 1976, p. 67.
9. Hans Küng, *On Being a Christian*, translated by Edward Quinn, William Collins Sons and Co. 1977, p. 285.
10. Beecher, *Proverbs from Plymouth Pulpit*, p. 198.

11. J.H. Oldham, *Life is Commitment*, SCM Press 1953, p. 95.
12. Colin Morris, *The Hammer of the Lord*, Epworth Press 1973, p. 10.
13. H.E. Root, in A.R. Vidler, *Soundings*, Cambridge at the University Press 1962, p. 6.
14. Paul Tillich, *On the Boundary*, William Collins Sons and Co. 1967, p. 67.
15. F.R. Barry, *Secular and Supernatural*, SCM Press 1969, p. 33.
16. Thomas Merton, *Contemplative Prayer*, Darton, Longman and Todd 1973, p. 144.
17. Alec R. Vidler, *God's Demand and Man's Response*, John Hermitage, The Unicorn Press 1938, p. 102.
18. Norman Goodall, *The Local Church*, Hodder and Stoughton 1966, p. 28.
19. George Appleton, *Journey for a Soul*, William Collins Sons and Co. 1976, p. 166.
20. Monica Furlong, *With Love to the Church*, Hodder and Stoughton 1965, p. 22.

## *Commitment*

1. NRSV.
2. NRSV.
3. Hans Küng, *On Being a Christian*, translated by Edward Quinn, William Collins Sons and Co. 1977, p. 286.
4. William Law, *A Serious Call to a Devout and Holy Life*, J.M. Dent and Co. 1898, p. 8.
5. E. Stanley Jones, *Mastery*, Hodder and Stoughton 1956, p. 45.
6. E. Stanley Jones, *The Word Became Flesh*, Hodder and Stoughton 1964, p. 343.
7. John Keats, *The Letters of John Keats*, Oxford University Press, 'To James Augustus Hessey, Friday 9th Oct. 1818', editor, Maurice Buxton Forman, number 90, 1952, p. 221.
8. Thomas Merton, *Thoughts in Solitude*, Burns and Oates 1958, p. 17.
9. Küng, *On Being a Christian*, p. 291.
10. William Temple, *Readings in St John's Gospel*, first and second series, Macmillan and Co. 1947, p. 161.
11. John V. Taylor, *The Go-Between God*, SCM Press 1973, p. 98.
12. John Macquarrie, *In Search of Humanity*, SCM Press 1982, p. 157.
13. Paul Tournier, *Escape from Loneliness*, translated by John S. Gilmour, SCM Press 1962, p. 111.
14. C.S. Lewis, *Mere Christianity*, William Collins Sons and Co. 1961, p. 164.
15. Rabindranath Tagore, *Gitanjali*, Macmillan and Co. 1971, p. 42.

## *Compassion*

1. NRSV.
2. NRSV.
3. Antoine de Saint-Exupéry, *The Wisdom of the Sands*, translated by Stuart Gilbert, Hollis and Carter, 1952, p. 98.
4. Baron Friedrich von Hügel, *Letters to a Niece*, J.M. Dent and Sons 1929, p. xiv.
5. Fyodor Dostoyevsky, *The Idiot*, translated by David Magarshack, Penguin Books 1983, p. 248.
6. Blaise Pascal, *Pensées*, translated by W.F. Trotter, Random House, Inc. 1941, p. 176.
7. Mary Craig, *Blessings*, Hodder and Stoughton 1979, p. 61.
8. Henri J.M. Nouwen, *The Wounded Healer*, Doubleday 1979, p. 41.
9. William Temple, *Readings in St John's Gospel*, first and second series, Macmillan and Co. 1947, p. 160.
10. L. Blum, in James F. Childress and John Macquarrie, *A New Dictionary of Christian Ethics*, SCM Press 1986, p. 109.
11. Henri J.M. Nouwen, *The Way of the Heart*, Darton, Longman and Todd 1981, p. 34.
12. James F. Childress, in Childress and Macquarrie, *A New Dictionary of Christian Ethics*, p. 109.
13. Bertrand Russell, *The Impact of Science on Society*, George Allen and Unwin 1968, p. 84.
14. John Milton, 'Paradise Lost', *The Poems of John Milton*, Clarendon Press 1900, book III, l.138, p. 231.
15. Eric Hoffer, *The Passionate State of Mind*, Martin Secker and Warburg 1956, p. 69.
16. Anthony Bloom, *Living Prayer*, Darton, Longman and Todd 1966, p. 16.
17. A co-worker, in Kathryn Spink, *A Chain of Love*, SPCK 1984, p. 113.

## Contemplation

1. NRSV.
2. NRSV.
3. Ernest Dimnet, *What We Live By*, Jonathan Cape 1932, p. 195.
4. Meister Eckhart, in Franz Pfeiffer, *Meister Eckhart*, translated by Raymond B. Blakney, Harper and Row, 1941, p. 111.
5. St John of the Cross, *The Complete Works of Saint John of the Cross*, translated and edited by E. Allison Peers, Burns, Oates and Washbourne 1953, vol. II, 27,5, p. 326.
6. Ralph Waldo Emerson, *Miscellaneous Pieces, The Works of Ralph Waldo Emerson*, edited by George Sampson, George Bell and Sons Ltd 1906, vol. IV, p. 431.
7. Stephen MacKenna, *Journal and Letters*, Constable and Co. 1936, p. 120.
8. Michael Ramsey, *Canterbury Pilgrim*, SPCK 1974, p. 60.
9. William Wordsworth, 'Prelude', Book Fifth, l.3.
10. Lady Julian of Norwich, *Revelations of Divine Love*, Penguin Books 1976, p. 71.
11. Thomas Merton, *Elected Silence*, Hollis and Carter 1949, p. 368.
12. Richard Harries, in Alan Richardson and John Bowden, *A New Dictionary of Christian Theology*, SCM Press 1985, p. 121.
13. Thomas Merton, *The Waters of Silence*, Hollis and Carter 1950, p. 14.
14. Iris Murdoch, *The Sovereignty of Good Over Other Concepts*, Cambridge University Press 1967, p. 34.
15. George Gissing, *The Private Papers of Henry Rycroft*, J.M. Dent and Sons 1964, p. 134.
16. Aldous Huxley, *The Perennial Philosophy*, Chatto and Windus 1974, p. 259.
17. Thomas Merton, *New Seeds of Contemplation*, Burns and Oates 1962, p. 1.
18. Michael Ramsey, in *Spirituality for Today*, edited by Eric James, SCM Press 1968, p. 139.
19. Merton, *New Seeds of Contemplation*, p. 1.

## Contentment

1. NRSV.
2. NRSV.
3. English proverb.
4. Edmund Spenser, 'The Faerie Queene', edited by J.C. Smith, Oxford at the Clarendon Press 1964, book 1, canto 1, st.xxxv, l.4, p. 13.
5. Robert Greene, 'Farewell to Folly' 1587, st.ii, l.12
6. Thomas Fuller, *Gnomologia*, Stearne Brock 1733, p. 68.
7. Izaak Walton, *The Compleat Angler*, The Nonesuch Press 1929, p. 191.
8. Henry Ward Beecher, *Proverbs from Plymouth Pulpit*, Charles Burnet and Co. 1887, p. 178.
9. W.E. Sangster, *The Secret of Radiant Life*, Hodder and Stoughton 1957, p. 19.
10. Old proverb.
11. Beecher, *Proverbs from Plymouth Pulpit*, p. 26.
12. John Dryden, 'The Wife of Bath, Her Tale', *The Poems of John Dryden*, edited by James Kinsley, Oxford at the Clarendon Press 1958, vol. IV, l.466, p. 1715.
13. C.S. Lewis, *They Stand Together*, The Letters of C.S. Lewis, to Arthur Greeves (1914–63), edited by Walter Hooper, William Collins Sons and Co. 1979, p. 161.
14. Albert Einstein, *Out of My Later Years*, Thames and Hudson 1950, p. 12.
15. Alban Goodier SJ, *The School of Love*, Burns and Oates and Washbourne 1920, p. 68.
16. Henry Fielding, *Joseph Andrews*, J.M. Dent and Sons 1910, p. 173.
17. William Shakespeare, *King Henry VI*, part III, act III.i.62.
18. Beecher, *Proverbs from Plymouth Pulpit*, p. 224.
19. Spenser, 'The Faerie Queene', book VI canto IX, st.xxix, l.6.
20. Charles Cotton, 'The Retirement', *Poems*, chosen and edited by J.R. Tutin, published by the editor 1903, p. 16.
21. William E. Channing, 'My Symphony', *A Series of Miscellaneous Illustrated Cards* 1902, p. 37.
22. Winston S. Churchill, *Thoughts and Adventures*, Thornton Butterworth 1932, p. 19.

## *Courage*

1. NRSV.
2. NRSV.
3. German proverb.
4. Thomas Bailey Aldrich, *The Stillwater Tragedy*, David Douglas 1886, vol. 1, p. 172.
5. Søren Kierkegaard, *The Journals of Søren Kierkegaard*, a selection edited and translated by Alexander Dru, Oxford University Press 1938, p. 87.
6. Rollo May, *Man's Search for Himself*, George Allen and Unwin 1953, p. 224.
7. Thomas Carlyle, *Boswell's Life of Johnson, The Works of Thomas Carlyle*, Chapman and Hall 1899, *Critical and Miscellaneous Essays*, vol. III, p. 123.
8. A.D. Sertillanges OP, *The Intellectual Life*, translated by Mary Ryan, The Mercier Press 1948, p. 157.
9. D.H. Lawrence, *The Selected Letters of D.H. Lawrence*, edited by Diana Trilling, Farrar, Straus and Cudahy 1958, p. 243.
10. Anon.
11. William Barclay, *The Gospel of Matthew*, The Saint Andrew Press 1975, vol. II, p. 37.
12. Carlo Carretto, *Letters from the Desert*, translated by Rose Mary Hancock, Darton, Longman and Todd 1972, p. 130.
13. C.S. Lewis, in Cyril Connelly, *The Unquiet Grave*, Hamish Hamilton 1945, p. 75.
14. Thomas Carlyle, *Corn-Law Rhymes, The Works of Thomas Carlyle*, Chapman and Hall 1899, *Critical and Miscellaneous Essays*, vol. III, p. 147.
15. Graham Greene, *The Heart of the Matter*, William Heinemann 1959, p. 61.
16. Rollo May, *Man's Search for Himself*, George Allen and Unwin 1953, p. 229.
17. Paul Tillich, *The Courage to Be*, Nisbet and Co. 1952, p. 28.
18. W. MacNeile Dixon, *The Human Situation*, Edward Arnold and Co. 1937, p. 89.
19. Rainer Maria Rilke, *Letters to a Young Poet*, translated by Reginald Snell, Sidgwick and Jackson 1945, p. 38.
20. Tillich, *The Courage to Be*, 1952, p. 14.
21. W.E. Sangster, *These Things Abide*, Hodder and Stoughton 1939, p. 157.
22. Thomas Traherne, *The Way to Blessedness*, the spelling and punctuation by Margaret Bottrall, The Faith Press 1962, p. 178.

## *Cross*

1. NRSV.
2. NRSV.
3. Anon.
4. Rufus M. Jones, *Spiritual Reformers in the 16th and 17th Centuries*, Macmillan and Co. 1914, p. 250.
5. William Law, in Stephen Hobhouse, *Selected Mystical Writings of William Law*, Rockliff 1948, p. 99.
6. Thomas à Kempis, *The Imitation of Christ*, translated by Betty I. Knott, William Collins Sons and Co. 1979, p. 196.
7. Simone Weil, *Gravity and Grace*, Routledge and Kegan Paul 1972, p. 30.
8. Michel Quoist, *Prayers of Life*, translated by Anne Marie de Commaile and Agnes Mitchell Forsyth, Gill and Macmillan 1963, p. 5.
9. Aldous Huxley, *The Perennial Philosophy*, Chatto and Windus 1974, p. 113.
10. George Reindorp, in Gerald Priestland, *Priestland's Progress*, BBC Worldwide 1982, p. 79.
11. John Donne, 'Holy Sonnets, XIV', *Poetical Works*, edited by Sir Herbert Grierson, Oxford University Press 1977, xiv, p. 299.
12. John Tauler, *The Following of Christ*, translated by J.R. Morell, Burns and Oates 1886, p. 175.
13. Jones, *Spiritual Reformers in the 16th and 17th Centuries*, p. 194.
14. William Law, in Sidney Spencer, *The Spirit of Prayer and the Spirit of Love*, James Clarke and Co. 1969, p. 167.
15. George Appleton, *Journey for a Soul*, William Collins Sons and Co. 1976, p. 178.

16. D.H. Lawrence, 'Pheonix', *The Complete Poems of D.H. Lawrence*, edited by Vivian de Sola Pinto and Warren Roberts, William Heinemann 1967, vol. 2, p. 728.

## *Death*

1. NRSV.
2. NRSV.
3. French proverb.
4. Leonardo da Vinci, *The Notebooks of Leonardo da Vinci*, edited by Edward McCurdy, vol. 1, Jonathan Cape 1977, p. 65.
5. J. Neville Ward, *Five for Sorrow, Ten for Joy*, Epworth Press 1971, p. 83.
6. Erich Fromm, *Man for Himself*, Routledge and Kegan Paul 1975, p. 162.
7. Dag Hammarskjöld, *Markings*, translated by Leif Sjoberg and W.H. Auden, Faber and Faber 1964, p. 136.
8. Rabindrananth Tagore, *Stray Birds, Collected Poems and Plays of Rabindranath Tagore*, Macmillan and Co. 1936, xcix, p. 299.
9. John S. Dunne, *The Reasons of the Heart*, SCM Press 1978, p. 61.
10. J. Neville Ward, *Friday Afternoon*, Epworth Press 1982, p. 131.
11. Thomas Mann, *The Magic Mountain*, translated by H.T. Lowe-Porter, Penguin Books 1983, p. 200.
12. A.C. Benson, *Extracts from the Letters of Dr A.C. Benson to M.E.A.*, Jarrold Publishing 1927, p. 22.
13. Norman Goodall, *The Local Church*, Hodder and Stoughton 1966, p. 18.
14. Rabindranath Tagore, *Gitanjali*, Macmillan and Co. 1971, p. 83.
15. William Temple, *Readings in St John's Gospel*, first and second series, Macmillan and Co. 1947, p. 147.
16. Nicolas Berdyaev, *The Destiny of Man*, translated by Natalie Duddington, Geoffrey Bles: The Centenary Press 1937, p. 156.
17. J. Neville Ward, *Friday Afternoon*, Epworth Press 1982, p. 103.
18. William Barclay, *The Gospel of John*, The Saint Andrew Press 1965, vol. 2, p. 38.
19. Jean Vanier, *Man and Woman He Made Them*, Darton, Longman and Todd 1985, p. 149.

## *Depression*

1. NRSV.
2. NRSV.
3. Sir Walter Scott, *The Heart of Midlothian*, Oxford University Press 1912, p. 581.
4. Edmund Burke, *Burke's Works*, printed for J. Dodsley, vol. 1, 'Light: On the Sublime and Beautiful', l.17, p. 145.
5. Henry Ward Beecher, *Proverbs from Plymouth Pulpit*, Charles Burnet and Co. 1887, p. 163.
6. Henry Wadsworth Longfellow, 'The Rainy Day', *The Poetical Works of Longfellow*, Humphrey Milford, Oxford University Press 1913, st.iii, l.44, p. 63.
7. A.C. Benson, *Extracts from the Letters of Dr A.C. Benson to M.E.A.*, Jarrold Publishing 1927, p. 14.
8. Matthew Arnold, 'Self-Dependence', *The Poems of Matthew Arnold*, edited by Kenneth Allott, Longmans, Green and Co. 1965, l.31, p. 144.
9. Hubert van Zeller, *Considerations*, Sheed and Ward 1974, p. 25.
10. George Eliot, *Adam Bede*, Virtue and Co. 1908, vol. II, p. 68.
11. Arthur T. Jersild, *The Psychology of Adolescence*, Macmillan Publishers 1963, p. 35.
12. Rollo May, *Man's Search for Himself*, Souvenir Press 1975, p. 24.
13. Murial Spark, *Territorial Rights*, Macmillan Publishers 1979, p. 51.
14. Percy Bysshe Shelley, 'The Revolt of Islam: Dedication: To Mary', *The Complete Poetical Works of Percy Bysshe Shelley*, edited by Thomas Hutchinson, Oxford University Press 1935, st.6, p. 39.
15. van Zeller, *Considerations*, p. 76.
16. Jerome K. Jerome, *Idle Thoughts of an Idle Fellow*, J.M. Dent and Sons 1983, p. 21.

17. David Watson, *You Are My God*, Hodder and Stoughton 1983, p. 190.
18. Rabindranath Tagore, *Gitanjali*, Macmillan Publishers 1971, p. 30.
19. Michel Quoist, *With Open Heart*, translated by Colette Copeland, Gill and Macmillan 1983, p. 173.

## *Discipleship*

1. NRSV.
2. NRSV.
3. William Barclay, *The Gospel of* Matthew, The Saint Andrew Press 1987, vol. 1, p. 234.
4. Dietrich Bonhoeffer, *The Cost of Discipleship*, translated by R.H. Fuller, SCM Press 1956, p. 119.
5. Henry Ward Beecher, *Proverbs from Plymouth Pulpit*, Charles Burnet and Co. 1887, p. 161.
6. Hans Jürgen Schultz, *Conversion to the World*, SCM Press 1967, p. 100.
7. Harry Emerson Fosdick, *The Hope of a New World*, SCM Press 1933, p. 179.
8. William Penn, *The Fruits of Solitude*, A.W. Bennett 1863, p. 13.
9. William Temple, *Readings in St John's Gospel*, first and second series, Macmillan and Co. 1947, p. 225.
10. Mark Rutherford, *Last Pages from a Journal*, Oxford University Press 1915, p. 303.
11. John J. Vincent, *Secular Christ*, Lutterworth Press 1968, p. 77.
12. George Appleton, *Journey for a Soul*, William Collins Sons and Co. 1976, p. 188.
13. Archibald C. Craig, *University Sermons*, James Clarke and Co. 1937, p. 147.
14. William Temple, *Citizen And Churchman*, Eyre and Spottiswoode 1941, p. 65.
15. J.R.H. Moorman, *The Path to Glory*, SPCK and Seabury Press 1960, p. 182.
16. Appleton, *Journey for a Soul*, p. 157.
17. John Macquarrie, *Paths in Spirituality*, SCM Press 1972, p. 116.
18. Moorman, *The Path to Glory*, p. 182.

## *Divinity*

1. NRSV.
2. NRSV
3. Thomas Carlyle, *Sartor Resartus*, Ward, Lock and Co., p. 92.
4. William Shakespeare, *Hamlet*, act V.ii.10.
5. F. Ernest Johnson, *The Social Gospel Re-Examined*, James Clarke and Co. 1942, p. 50.
6. Matthew Arnold, *Written in Emerson's Essays*, *The Poems of Matthew Arnold*, edited by Kenneth Allott, Longmans, Green and Co. 1965, l.11, p. 53.
7. Henry Ward Beecher, *Proverbs from Plymouth Pulpit*, Charles Burnet and Co. 1887, p. 116.
8. John Smith the Platonist, *Select Discourses*, Cambridge at the University Press 1859, p. 1.
9. Meister Eckhart, in Franz Pfeiffer, *Meister Eckhart*, translated by C. de B. Evans, John M. Watkins 1956, vol. 1, p. 36.
10. Ralph Waldo Emerson, *The Conduct of Life, Nature and Other Essays*, J.M. Dent and Sons 1911, p. 262.
11. Samuel Taylor Coleridge, *Table Talk of Samuel Taylor Coleridge*, George Routledge and Sons, 1884, p. 186.
12. Beecher, *Proverbs from Plymouth Pulpit*, p. 155.
13. Ralph Waldo Emerson, *Essay on History, The Works of Ralph Waldo Emerson*, George Bell and Sons 1960, vol. 1, *Essays and Representative Men*, p. 6.
14. Ralph Waldo Emerson, *Journals*, Constable and Co. 1910, vol. 3, p. 14.
15. Rufus M. Jones, *Spiritual Reformers in the 16th and 17th Centuries*, Macmillan and Co. 1914, p. 322.
16. Max Lerner, *The Unfinished Country*, Simon and Schuster 1959, p. 724.
17. Meister Eckhart, *Meister Eckhart*, translated by Raymond B. Blakney, Harper and Row 1941, p. 74.

## *Doubt*

1. NRSV.
2. NRSV.
3. A.R. Orage, *On Love*, The Janus Press 1957, p. 60.
4. Anon.
5. H.A. Williams CR, *The True Wilderness*, William Collins Sons and Co. 1983, p. 49.
6. Agnes Sanford, *The Healing Light*, Arthur James 1949, p. 52.
7. William Shakespeare, *Troilus and Cressida*, act II.ii.15.
8. Miguel de Unamuno, *The Agony of Christianity*, Payson and Clarke 1928, p. 27.
9. Anthony Bloom, *The Essence of Prayer*, Darton, Longman and Todd 1989, p. 69.
10. Herbert H. Farmer,*The Healing Cross*, Nisbet and Co. 1938, p. 208.
11. St Augustine of Hippo, *Confessions*, translated by R.S. Pine-Coffin, Penguin Books 1964, p. 116.
12. Francis Bacon, *The Advancement of Learning*, Cassell and Co. 1905, p. 38.
13. William Barclay, *The Gospel of John*, The Saint Andrew Press 1965, vol. 2, p. 151.
14. William Shakespeare, *Measure for Measure*, act I.v.78.
15. Paul Tillich, *The Courage to Be*, Nisbet and Co. 1952, p. 115.
16. Alfred, Lord Tennyson, 'The Ancient Sage', *The Poems of Tennyson*, edited by Christopher Ricks, Longmans, Green and Co. 1969, p. 1351.
17. Monica Furlong, *The End of Our Exploring*, Hodder and Stoughton 1973, p. 16.
18. Erich Fromm, *Man for Himself*, Routledge and Kegan Paul 1975, p. 140.
19. *Christian Faith and Practice in the Experience of the Society of Friends*, London Yearly Meeting of the Religious Society of Friends, 1972, number 119, 1911; 1925.

## *Education*

1. NRSV.
2. NRSV.
3. William Hazlitt, *The Plain Speaker*, *The Collected Works of William Hazlitt*, J.M. Dent and Co. 1903, vol. VII, p. 320.
4. John Milton, *Paradise Regain'd*, *The Poetical Works of Milton*, edited by Revd. H.C. Beeching, Oxford at the Clarendon Press 1900, p. 495, Book IV, l.327.
5. Herbert Spencer, *Social Statics*, Williams and Norgate 1892, p. 81.
6. Plato, *The Republic of Plato*, translated by B. Jowett, Oxford at the Clarendon Press 1881, p. 110, book IV, 425B.
7. Robert Louis Stevenson, *Familiar Studies of Men and Books, Virginibus Puerisque*, William Collins Sons and Co. 1956, p. 112.
8. Thomas Arnold, *Sermons*, Longmans, Green, and Co. 1878, vol. III, xvi, p. 131.
9. Horace Mann, *Lectures and Reports on Education*, Cambridge, published for the editor 1867, p. 84.
10. Henry Ward Beecher, *Proverbs from Plymouth Pulpit*, Charles Burnet and Co. 1887, p. 76.
11. Roy Stevens, *On Education and the Death of Love*, Epworth Press 1978, p. 136.
12. Michael Ramsey, in Margaret Duggan, *Through the Year with Michael Ramsey*, Hodder and Stoughton 1975, p. 215.
13. John Ruskin, *The Stones of Venice*, edited by Ernest Rhys, J.M. Dent and Co. 1907, vol. III, p. 197.
14. A. Clutton, Brock, *The Ultimate Belief*, Constable and Co. 1916, p. 99.
15. William Temple, *The Hope of a New World*, SCM Press 1940, p. 12.
16. Meister Eckhart, *Meister Eckhart*, translated by Raymond B. Blakney, Harper and Row 1941, p. 236.
17. Martin Thornton, *Spiritual Direction*, SPCK 1984, p. 11.
18. Mark Rutherford, *Last Pages from a Journal*, Oxford University Press 1915, p. 279.
19. Albert Einstein, *Out of My Later Years*, Thames and Hudson 1950, p. 36.
20. William James, *The Letters of William James*, edited by Henry James, Longmans, Green and Co. 1926, p. 253.

## *Eternal Life*

1. NRSV.
2. NRSV.
3. Benedict Spinoza, *Spinoza's Ethics and De Intellectus Emendatione*, J.M. Dent and Sons 1955, p. 214.
4. Herman Melville, *Mardi*, The New American Library of World Literature 1964, p. 516.
5. William Penn, *Fruits of Solitude*, A.W. Bennett 1863, p. 60.
6. Rabindranath Tagore, *Stray Birds, Collected Poems and Plays of Rabindranath Tagore*, Macmillan and Co. 1936, xcvi, p. 299.
7. George Meredith, *Diana of the Crossways*, Archibald Constable and Co. 1909, p. 11.
8. Henry Vaughan, *Silex Scintillans, The Works of Henry Vaughan*, edited by L.C. Martin, Oxford at the Clarendon Press 1957, p. 419.
9. Nicolas Berdyaev, *The Destiny of Man*, translated by Natalie Duddington, Geoffrey Bles: The Centenary Press 1937, p. 189.
10. Leo Tolstoy, *War and Peace*, translated by Rosemary Edmonds, Penguin Books 1969, vol. 1, p. 455.
11. William Barclay, *The Plain Man Looks at the Apostles' Creed*, William Collins Sons and Co. 1967, p. 374.
12. Richard Jefferies, *The Story of My Heart*, Duckworth and Co. 1923, p. 30.
13. Rufus M. Jones, *Spiritual Reformers in the 16th and 17th Centuries*, Macmillan and Co. 1914, p. xxxiv.
14. Henry Ward Beecher, *Proverbs from Plymouth Pulpit*, Charles Burnet and Co. 1887, p. 168.
15. William Temple, *Readings in St John's Gospel*, first and second series, Macmillan and Co. 1947, p. 310.
16. Henri Frédéric Amiel, *Amiel's Journal*, translated by Mrs Humphry Ward, Macmillan and Co. 1918, p. 96.
17. George Appleton, *Journey for a Soul*, William Collins Sons and Co. 1976, p. 212.
18. Friedrich von Hügel, *Eternal Life*, T. and T. Clarke 1913, p. 396.
19. Thornton Wilder, *Our Town*, Longmans, Green and Co. 1964, act III, p. 93.
20. William Barclay, *The Gospel of John*, The Saint Andrew Press 1965, vol. 1, p. 118.

## *Experience*

1. NRSV.
2. NRSV.
3. Dag Hammarskjöld, *Markings*, translated by Leif Sjoberg and W.H. Auden, Faber and Faber 1964, p. 85.
4. Henry Ward Beecher, *Proverbs from Plymouth Pulpit*, Charles Burnet and Co. 1887, p. 173.
5. William Johnston, *The Inner Eye of Love*, William Collins Sons and Co. 1978, p. 81.
6. Beecher, *Proverbs from Plymouth Pulpit*, p. 163.
7. Rufus M. Jones, *Spiritual Reformers in the 16th and 17th Centuries*, Macmillan and Co. 1914, p. 190.
8. William Temple, *Thoughts on Some Problems of the Day*, Macmillan and Co. 1931, p. 25.
9. Helmet Thielicke, *I Believe: The Christian's Creed*, translated by John W. Doberstein and H. George Anderson, William Collins Sons and Co. 1969, p. 11.
10. C.G. Jung, in Jolande Jacobi, *Psychological Reflections*, Routledge and Kegan Paul 1953, p. 322.
11. Jones, *Spiritual Reformers in the 16th and 17th Centuries*, p. xxi.
12. *The Cloud of Unknowing*, translated by Clifton Wolters, Penguin Books 1971, p. 71.
13. Albert Schweitzer, *The Quest of the Historical Jesus*, A. and C. Black 1954, p. 401.
14. George Appleton, *Journey for a Soul*, William Collins Sons and Co. 1976, p. 37.
15. C.G. Jung, *The Stucture and Dynamics of the Psyche, The Collected Works of C.G. Jung*, vol. 8, translated by R.F.C. Hull, Routledge and Kegan Paul 1969, p. 328.
16. C.G. Jung, *Psychology and Religion*, Yale University Press 1960, p. 113.

## *Faith*

1. NRSV.
2. NRSV.
3. John Dryden, 'Religio Laici', *The Poems of John Dryden*, edited by James Kinsley, Oxford at the Clarendon Press 1958, vol. 1, p. 313.
4. William Johnston, *The Inner Eye of Love*, William Collins Sons and Co. 1978, p. 85.
5. C.S. Lewis, *Letters of C.S. Lewis*, edited by W. H. Lewis, Geoffrey Bles 1966, p. 220.
6. Joseph Addison, *The Works of Joseph Addison*, edited and published by Henry G. Bohn 1856, vol. III, p. 484.
7. Giles and Melville Harcourt, *Short Prayers for the Long Day*, William Collins Sons and Co. 1978, p. 18.
8. Charles Parkhurst, *The Pattern and the Mount and Other Sermons*, R.D. Dickinson 1890, p. 57.
9. Benjamin Whichcote, *Moral and Religious Aphorisms*, century XII, no. 1168, Elkin, Mathews and Marrot 1930, p. 136.
10. Said of Edward Wilson, in George Seaver, *Edward Wilson of the Antarctic*, John Murray 1935, p. 104.
11. Lesslie Newbigin, *Honest Religion for Secular Man*, SCM Press 1966, p. 98.
12. Thomas à Kempis, *The Imitation of Christ*, translated by Betty I. Knott, William Collins Sons and Co. 1979, p. 249.
13. Henri Frédéric Amiel, *Amiel's Journal*, translated by Mrs Humphry Ward, Macmillan and Co. 1918, p. 192.
14. Sir William Osler, *Aphorisms from His Bedside Teachings and Writings*, collected by Robert Bennett Bean, edited by William Bennett Bean, Charles C. Thomas 1961, p. 102.
15. William Temple, *Basic Convctions*, Hamish Hamilton 1937, p. 16.
16. J.R. Lowell, *My Study Windows*, George Routledge and Sons 1905, p. 142.
17. Hans Küng, *On Being a Christian*, translated by Edward Quinn, William Collins Sons and Co. 1977, p. 159.
18. John Macquarrie, *Paths in Spirituality*, SCM Press 1972, p. 33.
19. George Santayana, *Interpretations of Poetry and Religion,* Charles Scribner's Sons 1916, p. 95.
20. William Wordsworth, 'The Excursion', *The Poetical Works of William Wordsworth*, vol. V, edited by E. de Selincourt and Helen Darbishire, Oxford at the Clarendon Press, 1959, iv. 1294, p. 150.
21. George Macdonald, *Unspoken Sermons*, first series, Alexander Strahan 1867, p. 25.
22. Evelyn Underhill, in John Stobbart, *The Wisdom of Evelyn Underhill*, A.R. Mowbray and Co. 1951, p. 18.
23. William Temple, *The Preacher's Theme Today*, SPCK 1936, p. 31.
24. Dietrich Bonhoeffer, *Letters and Papers from Prison*, William Collins Sons and Co. 1963, p. 125.

## *Finding God*

1. NRSV.
2. NRSV.
3. Thomas à Kempis, *The Imitation of Christ*, translated by Betty I. Knott, William Collins Sons and Co. 1979, p. 41.
4. Blaise Pascal, *Pensées*, translated by W.F. Trotter, Random House 1941, p. 7.
5. Mark Rutherford, *Last Pages from a Journal*, Oxford University Press 1915, p. 274.
6. Rufus M. Jones, *Spiritual Reformers in the 16th and 17th Centuries*, Macmillan and Co. 1914, p. 187.
7. Alfred, Lord Tennyson, 'The Passing of Arthur', *The Works of Alfred Lord Tennyson*, Macmillan and Co. 1898, p. 467.
8. Bede Griffiths OSB, *The Golden String*, The Harvill Press 1954, p. 12.
9. George Macdonald, *Unspoken Sermons*, third series, Longmans, Green and Co. 1889, p. 227.
10. Norman Pittenger, *The Christian Situation Today*, Epworth Press 1969, p. 116.
11. Jones, *Spiritual Reformers in the 16th and 17th Centuries*, p. 52.
12. Morris West, *The Devil's Advocate*, Heinemann/Octopus 1977, p. 168.

13. William Law, in Sidney Spencer, *The Spirit of Prayer*, James Clarke and Co. 1969, p. 44.
14. Michel Quoist, *With Open Heart*, translated by Colette Copeland, Gill and Macmillan 1983, p. 180.
15. René Voillaume, *The Need for Contemplation*, translated by Elizabeth Hamilton, Darton, Longman and Todd 1972, p. 57.

## *Freedom*

1. NRSV.
2. NRSV.
3. Robert Browning, 'Andrea del Sarto', *The Poetical Works of Robert Browning*, Smith, Elder and Co. 1899, vol. 1, l.51, p. 524.
4. John Macmurray, *Freedom in the Modern World*, Faber and Faber 1935, p. 101.
5. W.R. Inge, *The Philosophy of Plotinus*, Longmans, Green and Co. 1948, vol. II, p. 192.
6. Herbert Spencer, *Social Statics*, Williams and Norgate 1892, p. 54.
7. Martin Luther King, in Coretta Scott King, *The Words of Martin Luther King*, William Collins Sons and Co. 1986, p. 51.
8. Al-Ghazali, *Al-Ghazali, The Mystic*, Margaret Smith, Luzac and Co. 1944, p. 106.
9. King, *The Words of Martin Luther King*, p. 58.
10. Nicolas Berdyaev, *The Fate of Man in the Modern World*, translated by Donald A. Lowrie, SCM Press 1935, p. 44.
11. Louis Lavelle, in Paul Foulquié, *Existentialism*, translated by Kathleen Raine, Dennis Dobson 1947, p. 113.
12. Rabindranath Tagore, *Creative Unity*, Macmillan and Co. 1922, p. 133.
13. Edward Carpenter, *Love's Coming-of-Age*, George Allen and Unwin 1923, p. 108.
14. L.S. Thornton CR, *The Common Life of the Body of Christ*, Dacre Press: A. and C. Black 1950, p. 242.
15. Nicolas Berdyaev, *Freedom and the Spirit*, Geoffrey Bles, The Centenary Press 1935, p. 140.
16. Yehudi Menuhin, *Theme and Variations*, William Heinemann 1972, p. 46.
17. Kahlil Gibran, *The Prophet*, Sheldon Press 1970, p. 56.
18. Johann Wolfgang von Goethe, *Faust*, translated by Bayard Taylor, Sphere Books 1974, part 2, act V. vi. 1573, p. 424.
19. Hubert van Zeller, *Praying While You Work*, Burns, Oates and Washbourne 1951, p. 48.
20. George Appleton, *Journey for a Soul*, William Collins Sons and Co. 1976, p. 181.
21. Benedict Spinoza, *Short Treatise on God, Man, and His Well-Being*, translated by A. Wolf, Adam and Charles Black 1910, p. 148.

## *Friendship*

1. NRSV.
2. NRSV.
3. William Shakespeare, *Timon of Athens*, act II.ii.189.
4. Thomas Fuller, *Gnomologia*, Stearne Brock 1733, p. 31.
5. Ralph Waldo Emerson, *Essays*, Bernhard Tauchnitz Edition 1915, p. 147.
6. Hugh Black, *Friendship*, Hodder and Stoughton 1897, p. 43.
7. Emerson, *Essays*, p. 156.
8. William Penn, *Reflections and Maxims, Relating to, the Conduct of Human Life*, A.W. Bennett 1863, p. 23.
9. St Francis de Sales, *Introduction to the Devout Life*, translated and edited by John K. Ryan, Longmans, Green and Co. 1962, p. 186.
10. Ladislaus Boros, *Hidden God*, translated by Erika Young, Search Press 1973, p. 62.
11. C.S. Lewis, *The Four Loves*, William Collins Sons and Co. 1981, p. 52.
12. Penn, *Reflections and Maxims, Relating to, the Conduct of Human Life*, p. 24.
13. Robert Standish, *The Big One Got Away*, Peter Davies 1960, p. 217.
14. Samuel Johnson, *The Rambler*, *The Yale Edition of the Works of Samuel Johnson*, edited by W.J. Bate and Albrecht B. Strauss, Yale University Press 1969, vol. III, no. 64, p. 341.

15. Vincent van Gogh, *Dear Theo: An Autobiography of Vincent van Gogh*, edited by Irving Stone, Constable and Co. 1937, p. 39.
16. Robert Louis Stevenson, *Across the Plains*, T. Nelson and Sons 1892, p. 274.
17. Mark Rutherford, *Last Pages from a Journal*, Oxford University Press 1915, p. 304.
18. Walt Whitman, 'I Dream'd in a Dream', *The Complete Poems*, edited by Francis Murphy, Penguin Books 1982, l.1, p. 164.
19. Ralph Waldo Emerson, *Essay on Friendship*, Roycrofters 1899, p. 34.
20. Aelred of Rievaux, *De spiritu amicitia* 1:45 (adapted).

## *Fulfilment*

1. NRSV.
2. NRSV.
3. P.J. Bailey, *Festus*, William Pickering 1839, p. 51.
4. Cyril Connolly, *The Unquiet Grave*, Hamish Hamilton 1945, p. 26.
5. Rabindranath Tagore, *Stray Birds, Collected Poems and Plays of Rabindranath Tagore*, Macmillan and Co. 1936, ccciii, p. 326.
6. Thomas Merton, *No Man Is an Island*, Burns and Oates 1974, p. 20.
7. Paul Goodman, *The Community of Scholars*, Random House 1962, p. 175.
8. Henry Miller, *The Wisdom of the Heart*, New Directions Books 1941, p. 87.
9. Tagore, *Stray Birds, Collected Poems and Plays of Rabindranath Tagore*, clix, p. 307.
10. Smiley Blanton, *Love or Perish*, The World's Work (1913) 1957, p. 132.
11. Lewis Mumford, *The Conduct of Life*, Secker and Warburg 1952, p. 291.
12. Anne Morrow Lindbergh, *Bring Me a Unicorn*, A Helen and Kurt Wolff Book 1972, p. 38.
13. A.R. Orage, *On Love*, The Janus Press 1957, p. 54.
14. D.H. Lawrence, *Letter to Catherine Caswell, The Letters of D.H. Lawrence*, edited by George J. Zytaruk and James T. Boulton, Cambridge University Press 1981, vol. 2, 1913–16, 16 July 1916, p. 633.
15. Morton T. Kelsey, *The Other Side of Silence*, SPCK 1977, p. 61.
16. Rollo May, *Man's Search for Himself*, Souvenir Press 1975, p. 238.
17. Phillips Brooks, *Twenty Sermons*, Macmillan and Co. 1897, p. 216.
18. Erich Fromm, *Man For Himself*, Routledge and Kegan Paul 1975, p. 249.
19. William James, *The Varieties of Religious Experience*, William Collins Sons and Co. 1974, p. 491.
20. Robert Burns, 'Second Epistle to J. Lapraik', *The Poems and Songs of Robert Burns*, edited by James Kinsley, Oxford at the Clarendon Press 1968, vol. 1, p. 92.
21. Richard Jefferies, *The Story of My Heart*, Duckworth and Co. 1923, pp. 79 and 86.

## *Glory*

1. NRSV.
2. NRSV.
3. Henry Ward Beecher, *Proverbs from Plymouth Pulpit*, Charles Burnet and Co. 1887, p. 141.
4. St Irenaeus, *Five Books of St Irenaeus Against Heresies*, translated by the Rev. John Keble, James Parker and Co. 1872, book IV, p. 369.
5. Thomas Merton, *The Sign of Jonas*, Sheldon Press 1976, p. 76.
6. Rufus M. Jones, *Spiritual Reformers in the 16th and 17th Centuries*, Macmillan and Co. 1914, p. 287.
7. Meister Eckhart, in Franz Pfeiffer, *Meister Eckhart*, translated by C. de B. Evans, John M. Watkins 1956, vol. 1, p. 287.
8. Henri J.M. Nouwen, *The Way of the Heart*, Darton, Longman and Todd 1981, p. 86.
9. William Barclay, *The Gospel of John*, The Saint Andrew Press 1965, vol. 2, p. 46.
10. Mark Rutherford, *Last Pages from a Journal*, Oxford University Press 1915, p. 263.
11. Benjamin Whichcote, *Moral and Religious Aphorisms*, Elkin, Mathews and Marrot 1930, iv. 321.
12. Bertrand Russell, *Authority and the Individual*, Unwin Paperbacks 1977, p. 21.
13. Anon. In Sir Walter Scott, *Old Mortality*, Oxford University Press 1912, p. 316.

14. D. Columba Marmion, *Christ the Life of the Soul*, Sands and Co. 1922, p. 24.
15. William Temple, *Christian Faith and Life*, SCM Press 1963, p. 34.
16. William Temple, *Basic Convictions*, Hamish Hamilton 1937, p. 29.
17. W.E. Sangster, *Westminster Sermons*, Epworth Press 1961, vol. 2, *At Fast and Festival*, p. 20.
18. Eric Symes Abbott, *The Compassion of God and the Passion of* Christ, Geoffrey Bles 1963, p. 92.
19. John Smith the Platonist, *Select Discourses*, Cambridge at the University Press 1859, p. 417.

## *God*

1. NRSV.
2. NRSV.
3. Joyce Grenfell, *In Pleasant Places*, Macmillan General Books 1983, p. 161.
4. A girl of fourteen.
5. Robert Browning, 'Paracelsus V', *The Poetical Works of Robert Browning*, vol. 1, Smith, Elder, and Co. 1899, p. 61.
6. Emanuel Swedenborg, *The Divine Love and Wisdom*, J.M. Dent and Sons 1914, p. 12.
7. John of Ruysbroeck, *The Adornment of Spiritual Marriage*, translated by C.A. Wynschenk Dom, edited by Evelyn Underhill, John M. Watkins 1951, p. 173.
8. Dennis Potter, *A Lent Talk, The Other Side of the Dark*, Radio 4, March 1978, in Mary Craig, *Blessings*, Hodder and Stoughton 1979, p. 121.
9. Henry Ward Beecher, *Proverbs from Plymouth Pulpit*, Charles Burnet and Co. 1887, p. 142.
10. Izaak Walton, *The Compleat Angler*, Macmillan and Co. 1906, p. 175.
11. John S. Dunne, *The Reasons of the Heart*, SCM Press 1978, p. 24.
12. Rufus M. Jones, *Spiritual Reformers in the 16th and 17th Centuries*, Macmillan and Co. 1914, p. 315.
13. Dietrich Bonhoeffer, *Letters and Papers from Prison*, William Collins Sons and Co. 1963, p. 93.
14. Rufus M. Jones, *Spiritual Reformers in the 16th and 17th Centuries*, Macmillan and Co. 1914, p. 323.
15. Norman Pittenger, *Christology Reconsidered*, SCM Press 1970, p. 21.
16. Leo Tolstoy, *A Confession, the Gospel in Brief, and What I Believe*, translated by Aylmer Maude, Oxford University Press 1940, p. 267.
17. Charlotte Brontë, *Jane Eyre*, Oxford at the Clarendon Press 1969, p. 414.
18. F.C. Happold, *Mysticism*, Penguin Books 1981, p. 65.
19. George Macdonald, 'Without and Within', Longman, Brown, Green and Longman 1855, p. 9.
20. Matthew Arnold, *Literature and Dogma,The Complete Prose Works of Matthew Arnold*, vol. VI, *Dissent and Dogma*, edited by R.H. Super, The University of Michigan Press 1968, p. 171.
21. John Macquarrie, *Paths in Spirituality*, SCM Press 1972, p. 55.
22. F. Max Muller, *Anthropological Religion*, Longmans, Green, and Co. 1892, p. 90.

## *Goodness*

1. NRSV.
2. NRSV.
3. Hindu proverb.
4. Charlotte Brontë, *Jane Eyre*, Oxford at the Clarendon Press 1969, p. 166.
5. Oscar Wilde, *The Picture of Dorian Gray*, Chivers Press 1979, p. 128.
6. Henry Ward Beecher, *Proverbs from Plymouth Pulpit*, Charles Burnet and Co. 1887, p. 107.
7. H.A. Overstreet, *The Enduring Quest*, Jonathan Cape 1931, p. 174.
8. *Theologia Germanica*, translated by Susanna Winkworth, Stuart and Watkins 1966, p. 48.
9. Dag Hammarskjöld, *Markings*, translated by Leif Sjoberg and W.H. Auden, Faber and Faber 1964, p. 87.
10. Walt Whitman, 'Song of the Open Road', *The Complete Poems*, edited by Francis Murphy, Penguin Books 1982, section 5, l.60, p. 181.
11. W. Somerset Maugham, *The Summing Up*, Bernhard Tauchnitz 1938, p. 242.
12. John Dryden, 'The Satires of Juvenal', *The Poems of John Dryden*, Oxford at the Clarendon Press 1958, vol. II, p. 720, 'The Tenth Satyr', l.1.

13. George Meredith, *The Ordeal of Richard Feverel*, The Times Book Club 1912, p. 210.
14. Edmund Spenser, 'The Shepherd's Calendar: May', *Spenser Poetical Works*, edited by J.C. Smith and E. de Selincourt, Oxford University Press 1943, p. 436.
15. Lady Julian of Norwich, *Revelations of Divine Love*, Penguin Books 1976, p. 67.
16. *Theologia Germanica*, translated by Susanna Winkworth, Stuart and Watkins 1966, p. 84.
17. John Milton, 'Paradise Lost', *The Poetical Works of John Milton*, edited by the Rev. H.C. Beeching, Oxford at the Clarendon Press 1900, Book V, l.71, p. 274.
18. Albert Schweitzer, *Out of My Life and Thought*, Henry Holt and Co. 1949, p. 92.
19. Beecher, *Proverbs from Plymouth Pulpit*, p. 154.
20. William James, *The Will to Believe*, Longmans, Green and Co. 1904, p. 209.
21. George Eliot, *Middlemarch*, edited by W.J. Harvey, Penguin Books 1985, p. 427.
22. Beecher, *Proverbs from Plymouth Pulpit*, p. 96.
23. Leo Tolstoy, *Anna Karenina*, translated by Rosemary Edmonds, Penguin Books 1983, p. 853.
24. Mark Rutherford, *Last Pages from a Journal*, Oxford University Press 1915, p. 319.
25. Rufus M. Jones, *Spiritual Reformers in the 16th and 17th Centuries*, Macmillan and Co. 1914, p. 308.

## *Grace*

1. NRSV.
2. NRSV.
3. Anthony Bloom, *The Essence of Prayer*, Darton, Longman and Todd 1989, p. 25.
4. C.S. Lewis, *Williams and the Arthuriad*, Oxford University Press 1948, p. 156.
5. Brother Lawrence, *The Practice of the Presence of God*, introduction by Dorothy Day, Burns and Oates 1977, p. 51.
6. Henry Ward Beecher, *Proverbs from Plymouth Pulpit*, Charles Burnet and Co. 1887, p. 176.
7. John Milton, 'Paradise Lost', *The Poetical Works of John Milton*, edited by H.C. Beeching, Oxford at the Clarendon Press 1900, viii.488.
8. Rufus M. Jones, *Spiritual Reformers in the 16th and 17th Centuries*, Macmillan and Co. 1914, p. 154.
9. John Osborne, *Luther*, Faber and Faber 1961, 11.ii., p. 56.
10. Joachim Jeremias, *New Testament Theology*, SCM Press 1971, vol. 1, p. 178.
11. Blaise Pascal, *Pensées*, translated by W.F. Trotter, Random House 1941, p. 145.
12. Daniel D. Williams, in James F. Childress and John Macquarrie, *A New Dictionary of Christian Ethics*, SCM Press 1986, p. 139.
13. William Temple, *Readings in St John's Gosepl*, First and Second Series, Macmillan and Co. 1957, p. 29.
14. William Temple, *Nature, Man and God*, Macmillan and Co. 1934, p. 485.
15. Thomas à Kempis, *The Imitation of Christ*, translated by Betty I. Knott, William Collins Sons and Co. 1979, p. 175.
16. Richard of Saint-Victor, *Selected Writings on Contemplation*, translated by Clare Kirchberger, Faber and Faber 1957, p. 111.
17. A.C. Benson, *Extracts from the Letters of Dr A.C. Benson to M.E.A.*, Jarrold Publishing 1927, p. 60.
18. Richard of Saint-Victor, *Selected Writings on Contemplation*, p. 205.
19. Paul Tillich, *The Shaking of the Foundations*, Penguin Books 1962, p. 163.
20. Williams, in Childress and Macquarrie, *A New Dictionary of Christian Ethics*, p. 254.
21. Thomas à Kempis, *The Imitation of Christ*, p. 202.
22. Walter Hilton, *The Ladder of Perfection*, translated by Leo Sherley-Price, Penguin Books 1957, p. 146.
23. C.S. Lewis, *Letters of C.S. Lewis*, edited by W. H. Lewis, Geoffrey Bles 1966, p. 250.
24. John Macquarrie, *The Humility of God*, SCM Press 1978, p. 9.

## Greatness

1. NRSV.
2. NRSV.
3. Thomas Fuller, *Gnomologia*, Dublin 1732, No. 1759, p. 67.
4. Henri Frédéric Amiel, *Amiel's Journal*, translated by Mrs Humphry Ward, Macmillan and Co. 1918, p. 137.
5. Seneca, *Epistulae Morales*, Richard M. Gummere, William Heinemann, vol. II, p. 285.
6. Edmund Burke, *Speeches and Letters on American Affairs*, J.M. Dent and Sons 1961, p. 51.
7. Dr Harvey Cushing, in *Dialogues of Alfred North Whitehead*, recorded by Lucien Price, Max Reinhardt 1954, p. 47.
8. Theodor Haecker, *Journal in the Night*, translated by Alexander Dru, Harvill Press 1950, p. 37.
9. William Barclay, *The Gospel of Matthew*, The Saint Andrew Press 1987, vol. 1, p. 278.
10. Barclay, *The Gospel of Matthew*, vol. 1, p. 111.
11. Thomas Carlyle, *Sartor Resartus*, Chapman and Hall 1840, 'Lectures on Heroes', p. 206.
12. William Shakespeare, *Twelfth Night*, act II.v.48.
13. G.K. Chesterton, *Charles Dickens*, Methuen and Co. 1906, p. 8.
14. Barclay, *The Gospel of Matthew*, vol. 1, p. 279.
15. J.R. Lowell, 'Sonnet No. 6', *The Poetical Works of James Russell Lowell*, Ward, Lock and Co. 1911, p. 110.
16. Carlyle, *Sartor Resartus*, p. 127.
17. Phillips Brooks, *Sermons*, Richard D. Dickinson 1879, p. 14.
18. E.B. Browning, 'Rhyme of the Duchess May', *Elizabeth Barrett Browning's Poetical Works*, Smith, Elder, and Co. 1875, vol. 2, st. xi, p. 82.
19. Matthew Arnold, *Sweetness and Light*, *The Complete Prose Works of Matthew Arnold*, vol. V, *Culture and Anarchy*, edited by R.H. Super, Ann Arbor, The University of Michigan Press 1965, p. 96.
20. Henry Ward Beecher, *Proverbs from Plymouth Pulpit*, Charles Burnet and Co. 1887, p. 16.
21. Henri Frédéric Amiel, *Amiel's Journal*, translated by Mrs Humphry Ward, Macmillan and Co. 1918, p. 112.
22. Carlyle, 'Lectures on Heroes', p. 185.
23. Henry Wadsworth Longfellow, 'The Ladder of St Augustine', *The Poetical Works of Longfellow*, Humphrey Milford, Oxford University Press 1858, st.x, l.1, p. 299.

## Grief

1. NRSV.
2. NRSV.
3. William Cowper, 'Charity', *The Poetical Works of Cowper*, edited by H.S. Milford, Oxford University Press 1950, p. 79.
4. Adelaide Anne Proctor, *Life in Death and Death in Life,* The Complete Works of Adelaide Anne Proctor, George Bell and Sons 1905, p. 169.
5. William Shakespeare, *King Henry VI*, part III, act II.i.85.
6. English proverb.
7. Benjamin Disraeli, *Endymion*, Longmans, Green, and Co. 1880, p. 42.
8. William Morris, 'Prologue, The Wanderers', *The Earthly Paradise*, vol. 1, Reeves and Turner 1896, p. 5.
9. Confucius, *The Analects of Confucius*, translated by William Edward Soothill, edited by Lady Hosie, Oxford University Press 1937, p. 213.
10. J. Neville Ward, *Friday Afternoon*, Epworth Press 1982, p. 101.
11. Norman Douglas, *An Almanac*, Chatto and Windus in association with Martin Secker and Warburg 1945, p. 11.
12. C.S. Lewis, *A Grief Observed*, Faber and Faber 1961, p. 44.
13. Ward, *Friday Afternoon*, p. 97.
14. Henri Frédéric Amiel, *Amiel's Journal*, translated by Mrs Humphry Ward, Macmillan and Co. 1918, p. 192.

15. Chinese proverb.
16. Maurice Maeterlinck, *Wisdom and Destiny*, translated by Alfred Sutro, George Allen and Sons 1898, p. 113.
17. Henry Ward Beecher, *Proverbs from Plymouth Pulpit*, Charles Burnet and Co. 1887, p. 202.
18. A.C. Benson, *Extracts from the Letters of Dr A.C. Benson to M.E.A.*, Jarrold Publishing 1927, p. 19.
19. Erich Fromm, *Man for Himself*, Routledge and Kegan Paul 1975, p. 190.
20. Benson, *Extracts from the Letters of Dr A.C. Benson to M.E.A.*, p. 18.
21. Robert Southey, *Joan of Arc and Minor Poems*, George Routledge and Co. 1854, p. 9.
22. Beecher, *Proverbs from Plymouth Pulpit*, p. 209.
23. Mary Craig, *Blessings*, Hodder and Stoughton 1979, p. 63.
24. Lord Byron, *Manfred*, *The Complete Poetical Works*, edited by Jerome J.McGann, Clarendon Press 1986, vol. IV, act 1. sc.i. l.9, p. 53.
25. Johann Wilhelm von Goethe, *To Eckerman*, *The Practical Wisdom of Goethe*, chosen by Emil Ludwig, George Allen and Unwin Publishers 1933, p. 75.
26. Father Andrew SDC, *A Gift of Light*, selected and edited by Harry C. Griffith, Mowbray 1968, p. 31.

## *Growing*

1. NRSV.
2. NRSV.
3. Anon.
4. Robert Browning, 'Cleon', *The Poetical Works of Robert Browning*, Smith, Elder and Co. 1899, vol. 1, *Men and Women*, l.114, p. 543.
5. Dag Hammarksjöld, *Markings*, translated by Leif Sjoberg and W.H. Auden, Faber and Faber 1964, p. 89.
6. Oscar Wilde, *The Picture of Dorian Gray*, Chivers Press 1979, p. 122.
7. Henry Ward Beecher, *Proverbs from Plymouth Pulpit*, Charles Burnet and Co. 1887, p. 8.
8. George Macdonald, 'Within and Without', Longman, Brown, Green, and Longman 1855, p. 16.
9. Michel Quoist, *With Open Heart*, translated by Colette Copeland, Gill and Macmillan 1983, p. 202.
10. Beecher, *Proverbs from Plymouth Pulpit*, p. 180.
11. Martin Luther King, in Coretta Scott King, *The Words of Martin Luther King*, William Collins Sons and Co. 1986, p. 30.
12. Oscar Wilde, *De Profundis*, *The Works of Oscar Wilde*, edited by G.F. Maine, William Collins Sons and Co. 1948, p. 860.
13. Mark Rutherford, *Last Pages from a Journal*, Oxford University Press 1915, p. 280.
14. Quoist, *With Open Heart*, p. 133.
15. Aldous Huxley, *Music at Night*, Chatto and Windus 1970, p. 332.
16. Rutherford, *Last Pages from a Journal*, p. 256.
17. Harry Emerson Fosdick, *Successful Christian Living*, SCM Press 1938, p. 16.
18. Jean Vanier, *Community and Growth*, Darton, Longman and Todd 1991, p. 105.
19. Rainer Maria Rilke, *Letters to a Young Poet*, translation and commentary by Reginald Snell, Sidgwick and Jackson 1945, p. 13.
20. Vanier, *Community and Growth*, p. 133.

## *Guidance*

1. NRSV.
2. NRSV.
3. Rabindranath Tagore, *Stray Birds*, *Collected Poems and Plays of Rabindranath Tagore*, Macmillan and Co. 1936, cxlii, p. 305.
4. Basil Hume OSB, *Searching for God*, Hodder and Stoughton 1977, p. 54.
5. William Shakespeare, *King Henry VI*, part II, act II.iii.24.
6. Henry Ward Beecher, *Proverbs from Plymouth Pulpit*, Charles Burnet and Co. 1887, p. 154.

7. W.E. Sangster, *God Does Guide Us*, Hodder and Stoughton 1934, p. 144.
8. Samuel Johnson, Motto for *The Rambler*, *The Yale Edition of the Works of Samuel Johnson*, vol. III, edited by W.J. Bate and Albrecht B. Strauss, Yale University Press 1969, p. 36.
9. A.C. Benson, *Extracts from the Letters of Dr A.C. Benson to M.E.A*, Jarrold Publishing 1927, p. 7.
10. Grace Cooke, *Spiritual Unfoldment*, The White Eagle Publishing Trust 1961, p. 13.
11. Sangster, *God Does Guide Us*, p. 190.
12. John Milton, 'Paradise Lost', *The Works of John Milton*, Columbia University Press 1931, vol. 2, part 1, iii 194, p. 84.
13. William Barclay, *The Letter to the Romans*, The Saint Andrew Press 1969, p. 117.
14. John Burnaby, in A.R. Vidler, *Soundings*, Cambridge at the University Press 1962, p. 235.
15. William Blake, *Epigrams, Verses, and Fragments for the Note Book*, *The Complete Writings of William Blake*, edited by Geoffrey Keynes, Oxford University Press 1974, p. 551.
16. William Temple, *Christian Faith and Life*, SCM Press 1963, p. 57.
17. Gerhard Tersteegen, in Francis Bevan, *Sketches of the Great in the Land*, John F. Shaw and Co. 1891, p. 390.
18. George Appleton, *Journey for a Soul*, William Collins Sons and Co. 1976, p. 207.
19. Herbert Butterfield, *Christianity and History*, George Bell and Sons 1949, p. 145.

## *Happiness*

1. NRSV.
2. NEB.
3. Robert Louis Stevenson, *Virginibus Puerisque*, Chatto and Windus 1906, p. 80.
4. A.R. Orage, *On Love*, The Janus Press 1957, p. 61.
5. Henrik Ibsen, *Rosmersholm*, translated and edited by James Walter McFarlane, Oxford University Press 1960, vol. VI, act III, p. 349.
6. Blaise Pascal, *Pensées*, translated by W.F. Trotter, Random House 1941, p. 154.
7. Samuel Johnson, *The History of Rasselas*, Oxford University Press 1971, p. 48.
8. Robert Louis Stevenson, *Memories and Portraits*, Chatto and Windus 1887, p. 48.
9. Marcus Aurelius, *The Meditations of Marcus Aurelius*, translated by Jeremy Collier, Walter Scott, p. 116.
10. W.R. Inge, in Sir James Marchant, *The Wit and Wisdom of Dean Inge*, Longmans, Green and Co. 1927, p. 55.
11. Gordon S. Wakefield, in *A Dictionary of Christian Spirituality*, SCM Press 1986, p. 68.
12. Henry Ward Beecher, *Proverbs from Plymouth Pulpit*, Charles Burnet and Co. 1887, p. 186.
13. Johann Wolfgang von Goethe, *Wisdom and Experience*, selections by Ludwig Curtius, translated and edited by Hermann J. Weigand, Routledge and Kegan Paul 1949, p. 213.
14. Arthur Helps, *Companions of My Solitude*, George Routledge and Sons 1907, p. 20.
15. Marcus Aurelius, *The Meditations of Marcus Aurelius*, p. 42.
16. Samuel Johnson, *The Rambler*, *The Yale Edition of the Works of Samuel Johnson*, edited by W.J. Bate and Albrecht B. Strauss, Yale University Press 1969, vol. III, p. 225.
17. Thomas Merton, *Elected Silence*, Hollis and Carter 1949, p. 332.
18. Henry Ward Beecher, *Proverbs from Plymouth Pulpit*, Charles Burnet and Co. 1887, p. 22.
19. Alexander Solzhenitsyn, *Cancer Ward*, translated by Nicholas Bethell and David Burg, Penguin Books 1972, p. 290.
20. J.B. Yeats, *Letters to His Son, W.B. Yeats and Others*, Faber and Faber 1944, p. 121.
21. William James, *The Varieties of Religious Experience*, William Collins Sons and Co. 1974, p. 92.
22. Henri Frédéric Amiel, *Amiel's Journal*, translated by Mrs Humphry Ward, Macmillan and Co. 1918, p. 239.
23. Anne Frank, *The Diary of Anne Frank*, Pan Books 1954, p. 137.

## Healing

1. NRSV.
2. NRSV.
3. GP in Birmingham, in *Faith in the City*, Church House Publishing 1985, p. 265.
4. William Shakespeare, *Cymboline* act II.ii.11.
5. Henry Ward Beecher, *Proverbs from Plymouth Pulpit*, Charles Burnet and Co. 1887, p. 137.
6. Nathaniel Hawthorne, *The Scarlet Letter*, The Gresham Publishing Co. 1900, p. 90.
7. William Barclay, *The Gospel of Matthew*, The Saint Andrew Press 1987, vol. 1, p. 328.
8. Michel Quoist, *With Open Heart*, translated by Colette Copeland, Gill and Macmillan 1983, p. 66.
9. Beecher, *Proverbs from Plymouth Pulpit*, p. 153.
10. William James, *Essays on Faith and Morals*, Longmans, Green and Co. 1943, p. 235.
11. Beecher, *Proverbs from Plymouth Pulpit*, p. 138.
12. Izaak Walton, *The Compleat Angler*, The Nonesuch Press 1929, p. 193.
13. Francis MacNutt, *Healing*, Ave Maria Press 1977, p. 164.
14. William Temple, *The Preacher's Theme Today*, SPCK 1936, p. 53.
15. D.H.Lawrence, 'Healing', *The Complete Poems of D.H. Lawrence*, edited by Vivian de Sola Pinto and Warren Roberts, William Heinemann 1967, p. 620.
16. George Appleton, *Journey for a Soul*, William Collins Sons and Co. 1976, p. 185.
17. Jean Vanier, *The Broken Body*, Darton, Longman and Todd 1988, p. 135.

## Holiness

1. NRSV.
2. NRSV.
3. Thomas Fuller, *Gnomologia*, 1732 Dublin, no. 4924, p. 214.
4. Father Andrew SDC, *The Way of Victory*, A.R. Mowbray and Co. 1938, p. 12.
5. Henry Wadsworth Longfellow, 'Hyperion', George Routledge and Sons 1887, p. 215.
6. Rufus M. Jones, *Spiritual Reformers in the 16th and 17th Centuries*, Macmillan and Co. 1914, p. 148.
7. Jonathan Edwards, *A Treatise Concerning Religious Affections*, Chalmers and Collins 1825, p. 323.
8. Thomas Traherne, *Centuries*, The Faith Press 1969, p. 39.
9. Hugh Montefiore, *Sermons from Great St Mary's*, William Collins Sons and Co. 1968, p. 16.
10. Mother Teresa, in Brother Angelo Devananda, *Jesus, the Word to be Spoken*, William Collins Sons and Co. 1990, p. 49.
11. George Herbert, 'Lent', *The Works of George Herbert*, edited by F.E. Hutchinson, Oxford at the Clarendon Press 1953, p. 87.
12. Henry Ward Beecher, *Proverbs from Plymouth Pulpit*, Charles Burnet and Co. 1887, p. 171.
13. Benjamin Whichcote, *Moral and Religious Aphorisms*, century iii, no. 262, Elkin Mathews and Marrot 1930, p. 32.
14. W.E. Sangster, *The Pure in Heart*, Epworth Press 1954, p. 28.
15. John of Ruysbroeck, *The Seven Steps of the Ladder of Spiritual Love*, translated by F. Sherwood Taylor, Dacre Press 1942, p. 15.
16. Hugh Montefiore, *Confirmation Notebook*, Fifth Edition, SPCK 1985, p. 39.
17. Jonathan Edwards, *A Treatise Concerning Religious Affections*, Chalmers and Collins 1825, p. 349.
18. Fyodor Dostoyevsky, *The Brothers Karamazov*, translated by David Magarshack, Penguin Books 1962, vol. 1, p. 32.
19. W.R. Inge, *Speculum Animae*, Longmans, Green and Co. 1911, p. 50.
20. Henri Frédéric Amiel, *Amiel's Journal*, translated by Mrs Humphry Ward, Macmillan and Co. 1918, p. 155.

## Holy Spirit

1. NRSV.
2. NRSV.
3. William Barclay, *The Gospel of John*,The Saint Andrew Press 1965, vol. 2, p. 195.
4. Nicolas Berdyaev, *Christian Existentialism*, selected and translated by Donald A. Lowrie, George Allen and Unwin 1965, p. 39.
5. Henry Ward Beecher, *Proverbs from Plymouth Pulpit*, Charles Burnet and Co. 1887, p. 152.
6. Rufus M. Jones, *Spiritual Reformers in the 16th and 17th Centuries*, Macmillan and Co. 1914, p. 139.
7. Evelyn Underhill, in John Stobbart, *The Wisdom of Evelyn Underhill*, A.R. Mowbray and Co. 1951, p. 8.
8. Norman Goodall, *The Local Church*, Hodder and Stoughton 1966, p. 33.
9. C.C.J. Webb, *Religious Experience*, Oxford University Press 1945, p. 35.
10. Jones, *Spiritual Reformers in the 16th and 17th Centuries*, p. 43.
11. Robert Bridges, *The Spirit of Man*, Longmans, Green and Co. 1973, p. 1.
12. William Temple, *Nature, Man and God*, Macmillan and Co. 1934, p. 446.
13. John Macquarrie, *Paths in Spirituality*, second edition, SCM Press 1992, p. 42.
14. Carroll E. Simcox, *Living the Creed*, Dacre Press: A. and C. Black 1954, p. 116.
15. John V. Taylor, in Gerald Priestland, *Priestland's Progress*, BBC Worldwide 1982, p. 108.
16. Jacob Boehme, *The Aurora*, translated by John Sparrow, John M. Watkins 1914, p. 72.
17. Jones, *Spiritual Reformers in the 16th and 17th Centuries*, p. 217.
18. Lilian Whiting, *Lilies of Eternal Peace*, Gay and Hancock 1908, p. 26.

## Hope

1. NRSV.
2. NRSV.
3. William Shakespeare, *The Merry Wives of Windsor*, act II.i.58.
4. Miguel de Unamuno, *The Tragic Sense of Life in Men and in Peoples*, Macmillan and Co. 1921, p. 203.
5. Carlo Carretto, *Summoned by Love*, translated by Alan Neame, Darton, Longman and Todd 1977, p. 116.
6. Samuel Johnson, *Boswell's Life of Johnson*, edited by G.B. Hill, revised by L.F. Powell, Oxford at the Clarendon Press 1934, vol. 1, p. 368.
7. H. Rider Haggard, *She*, William Collins Sons and Co. 1957, p. 199.
8. Carlo Carretto, *The Desert in the City*, translated by Barbara Wall, William Collins Sons and Co. 1983, p. 90.
9. Percy Bysshe Shelley, 'Prometheus Unbound', *The Poetical Works of Percy Bysshe Shelley*, edited by H. Buxton Forman, George Bell and Sons 1892, vol. III, act IV, l.573, p. 257.
10. William Hazlitt, *Characteristics*, *The Collected Works of William Hazlitt*, J.M. Dent and Co. 1902, vol. II, XXXIV, p. 359.
11. Simone Weil, *Gateway to God*, edited by David Raper, with the collaboration of Malcolm Muggeridge and Vernon Sproxton, William Collins Sons and Co. 1974, p. 131.
12. Jürgen Moltmann, *The Open Church*, SCM Press 1978, p. 35.
13. Alexander Pope, 'An Essay on Man', introduction by Henry Morley, Cassell and Co. 1905, epistle 1, p. 18.
14. Hubert van Zeller, *Considerations*, Sheed and Ward 1974, p. 100.
15. William Temple, *Christian Faith and Life*, SCM Press 1963, p. 44.
16. W.R. Inge, *Personal Religion and the Life of Devotion*, Longmans, Green and Co. 1924, p. 54.
17. Hans Küng, *On Being a Christian*, translated by Edward Quinn, William Collins Sons and Co. 1977, p. 311.
18. Walt Whitman, *The Early Poems and the Fiction*, *The Collected Writings of Walt Whitman*, edited by Thomas L. Brasher, New York University Press, Franklin Evans 1963, vol. VI, p. 148.
19. Charles Dickens, *Nicholas Nickleby*, The Gresham Publishing Co. 1904, p. 528.

20. Evelyn Underhill, in John Stobbart, *The Wisdom of Evelyn Underhill*, A.R. Mowbray and Co. 1951, p. 21.
21. Paul Tillich, *The Shaking of the Foundations*, SCM Press 1949, p. 59.
22. Richard Jefferies, *The Pageant of Summer*, Chatto and Windus 1911, p. 10.

## *Humility*

1. NRSV.
2. NRSV.
3. Henri Frédéric Amiel, *Amiel's Journal*, translated by Mrs Humphry Ward, Macmillan and Co. 1918, p. 46.
4. Thomas à Kempis, *The Imitation of Christ*, translated by Betty I. Knott, William Collins Sons and Co. 1979, p. 150.
5. Henry David Thoreau, *Walden*, The New American Library of World Literature 1960, p. 218.
6. William Penn, *Fruits of Solitude*, A.W. Bennett 1863, p. 92.
7. Charlotte Brontë, *Jane Eyre*, Clarendon Press 1969, p. 514.
8. George Bernard Shaw, *The Complete Bernard Shaw Prefaces*, Paul Hamlyn 1965, *St Joan*, p. 622.
9. Johann Wolfgang von Goethe, *Wisdom and Experience*, selected by Ludwig Curtius, translated and edited by Hermann J. Weigand, Routledge and Kegan Paul 1949, p. 189.
10. Iris Murdoch, *The Sovereignty of Good Over Other Concepts*, Routledge and Kegan Paul 1970, p. 103.
11. *The Cloud of Unknowing*, translated by Clifton Wolters, Penguin Books 1971, p. 70.
12. Amiel, *Amiel's Journal*, p. 1.
13. John Bunyan, *The Pilgrim's Progress*, J.M. Dent and Sons 1964, p. 237.
14. Blaise Pascal, *Pensées*, translated by W.F. Trotter, Random House 1941, p. 169.
15. Alfred, Lord Tennyson, 'The Holy Grail', *The Poems of Tennyson*, edited by Christopher Ricks, Longmans, Green and Co. 1969, no. 471, l.445, p. 1674.
16. Izaak Walton, *The Compleat Angler*, Macmillan and Co. 1906, p. 37.
17. Meister Eckhart, in Franz Pfeiffer, *Meister Eckhart*, translated by C. de B. Evans, John M. Watkins 1956, vol. 1, p. 158.
18. Mark Rutherford, *Last Pages from a Journal*, Oxford University Press 1915, p. 301.
19. Henry Ward Beecher, *Proverbs from Plymouth Pulpit*, Charles Burnet and Co. 1887, p. 175.
20. Alfred, Lord Tennyson, 'The Holy Grail', p. 420.
21. Ralph Waldo Emerson, *Spiritual Laws*, *The Works of Ralph Waldo Emerson*, George Bell and Sons 1906, vol.1, *Essays and Representative Men*, p. 87.
22. Oscar Wilde, *De Profundis*, *The Works of Oscar Wilde*, William Collins Sons and Co. 1948, p. 858.
23. William Law, *A Serious Call to a Devout and Holy Life*, J.M. Dent and Sons 1898, p. 245.
24. Al-Ansari, 'The Invocations of Sheikh Abdullah Ansari of Herat', *The Persian Mystics*, translated by Sardar Sir Jogendra Sing, John Murray 1939, p. 39.
25. John Ruskin, *Modern Painters*, George Allen and Sons 1910, vol. III, p. 276.

## *Ideals*

1. NRSV.
2. NRSV.
3. Joseph Conrad, *Chance*, J.M. Dent and Sons 1949, p. 262.
4. George Moore, *Evelyn Innes*, Bernhard Tauchnitz 1898, vol. II, p. 103.
5. G.K. Chesterton, *What's Wrong with the World*, Bernhard Tauchnitz 1910, p. 43.
6. Thomas Carlyle, *Sartor Resartus*, Ward, Lock and Co., p. 131.
7. Yevgeny Yevtushenko, *A Precocious Autobiography*, translated by Andrew H. MacAndrew, Collins and Harvill Press 1963, p. 39.
8. Henry Ward Beecher, *Proverbs from Plymouth Pulpit*, Charles Burnet and Co. 1887, p. 54.
9. William James, *The Varieties of Religious Experience*, William Collins Sons and Co. 1974, p. 258.
10. Beecher, *Proverbs from Plymouth Pulpit*, p. 22.

11. Henry David Thoreau, *Walden*, The New American Library of World Literature, 1960, p. 215.
12. Beecher, *Proverbs from Plymouth Pulpit*, p. 127.
13. L. Falconer, in M.G. Ostle, *The Note Books of a Woman Alone*, J.M. Dent and Sons 1935, p. 228.
14. Beecher, *Proverbs from Plymouth Pulpit*, p. 23.
15. John Oman, *The Natural and the Supernatural*, Cambridge at the University Press 1931, p. 329.
16. Henri Frédéric Amiel, *Amiel's Journal*, translated by Mrs Humphry Ward, Macmillan and Co. 1918, p. 105.
17. Mother Teresa, in Brother Angelo Devananda, *Jesus, the Word to be Spoken*, William Collins Sons and Co. 1990, p. 42.
18. Harry James Cargas, *Encountering Myself*, SPCK 1978, p. 54.
19. Albert Schweitzer, *The Philosophy of Civilization*, Part II, *Civilization and Ethics*, translated by C.T. Campion, A. and C. Black, third English edition, revised by Mrs C.E.B. Russell 1946, p. xvii.
20. Albert Einstein, *Ideas and Opinions*, Souvenir Press (Educational and Academic) 1973, p. 9.
21. Sir Sarvepalli Radhakrishnan, *Eastern Religions and Western Thought*, Oxford University Press 1940, p. 25.

## *Image Of God*

1. NRSV.
2. NRSV.
3. Meister Eckhart, in Franz Pfeiffer, *Meister Eckhart*, vol. 1, translated by C. de B. Evans, John M. Watkins 1956, p. 436.
4. Thomas Traherne, *Centuries*, The Faith Press 1969, p. 9.
5. C.G. Jung, *Aion*, *The Collected Works of C.G. Jung*, translated by R.F.C. Hull, Routledge and Kegan Paul 1959, vol. 9, part 2, p. 39.
6. Father Andrew SDC, *Meditations for Every Day*, A.R. Mowbray and Co. 1941, p. 352.
7. Sister Elizabeth of the Trinity, *Spiritual Writings*, Geoffrey Chapman 1962, p. 147.
8. George Eliot, *Mill on the Floss*, Virtue and Co. 1908, vol. 2, p. 58.
9. Rufus M. Jones, *Spiritual Reformers in the 16th and 17th Centuries,* Macmillan and Co. 1914, p. xxx.
10. Charles Kingsley, *Daily Thoughts*, Macmillan and Co. 1884, p. 229.
11. William Law, *The Spirit of Love*, edited by Sidney Spencer, James Clarke and Co. 1969, p. 207.
12. John Pulsford, *Quiet Hours*, James Nisbet and Co. 1857, p. 75.
13. Meister Eckhart, *Meister Eckhart*, translated by Raymond B. Blakney, Harper and Row 1941, p. 209.
14. Johann Arndt, *True Christianity*, translated by Peter Erb, SPCK 1979, p. 29.
15. Basil Hume OSB, *To Be a Pilgrim*, St Paul Publications 1984, p. 66.
16. F.W. Faber, *Spiritual Writings*, Thomas Richardson and Son 1859, p. 2.

## *Imagination*

1. NRSV.
2. NRSV.
3. Joseph Joubert, *Pensées and Letters*, George Routledge and Sons 1928, p. 48.
4. Laurens van der Post, *Venture to the Interior*, Penguin Books 1968, p. 26.
5. Percy Bysshe Shelley, *A Defence of Poetry*, *The Prose Works of Percy Bysshe Shelley*, edited by H. Buxton Forman, Reeves and Turner 1880, vol. III, p. 111.
6. Henry Ward Beecher, *Proverbs from Plymouth Pulpit*, Charles Burnet and Co. 1887, p. 183.
7. Ralph Waldo Emerson, *The Conduct of Life, Nature, and Other Essays*, J.M. Dent and Sons, 1911, p. 298.
8. Henry David Thoreau, *The Journal of Henry D. Thoreau*, edited by Bradford Torrey and Francis H. Allen, Houghton Mifflin Co., Boston, The Riverside Press 1949, vol. II, p. 413.
9. W. Somerset Maugham, *The Summing Up*, Bernhard Tauchnitz 1938, p. 131.
10. J.B. Yeats, *Letters to His Son, W.B. Yeats and Others*, Faber and Faber 1944, p. 87.
11. Thomas Traherne, *Centuries*, The Faith Press 1969, p. 90.

12. Joseph Conrad, *A Personal Record*, J.M. Dent and Sons 1923, p. 25.
13. Katherine Mansfield, in Antony Alpers, *Katherine Mansfield*, Jonathan Cape 1954, p. 296.
14. Beecher, *Proverbs from Plymouth Pulpit*, p. 25.
15. Henry Miller, *The Books in My Life*, Village Press 1974, p. 84.
16. Virginia Woolf, *A Writer's Diary*, edited by Leonard Woolf, The Hogarth Press 1953, p. 67.
17. Max Planck, in F.C. Happold, *Religious Faith and Twentieth-Century Man*, Darton, Longman and Todd 1980, p. 41.
18. Oscar Wilde, *De Profundis*, *The Works of Oscar Wilde*, edited by G.F. Maine, William Collins Sons and Co. 1948, p. 867.
19. John Cowper Powys, *Autobiography*, Macdonald and Co. 1967, p. 436.
20. F.W. Robertson, *Sermons*, Kegan Paul, Trench, Trubner and Co. 1907, First Series, p. 8.
21. W. MacNeile Dixon, *The Human Situation*, Edward Arnold and Co. 1937, p. 65.
22. Henry Ward Beecher, *Royal Truths*, Alexander Strahan and Co. 1862, p. 47.

## *Incarnation*

1. NRSV.
2. NRSV.
3. Pierre Teilhard de Chardin, *Le Milieu Divin*, William Collins Sons and Co. 1960, p. 38.
4. C.S. Lewis, *Mere Christianity*, William Collins Sons and Co. 1961, p. 179.
5. Ugo Betti, *The Burnt Flower-Bed*, Three Plays by Ugo Betti, translated by Henry Read, Victor Gollancz 1956, act II, p. 151.
6. St Irenaeus, *Five Books of St Irenaeus*, translated by the Rev. John Keble, James Parker and Co. 1872, p. 449.
7. St Leo, in F.C. Happold, *Religious Faith and Twentieth-Century Man*, Darton, Longman and Todd 1980, p. 145.
8. Evelyn Underhill, *The Letters of Evelyn Underhill*, edited by Charles Williams, Longmans, Green and Co. 1947, p. 259.
9. Michel Quoist, *With Open Heart*, translated by Colette Copeland, Gill and Macmillan 1983, p. 147.
10. Alan Watts, *Behold the Spirit*, John Murray 1947, p. 244.
11. St Augustine, *City of God*, translated by Henry Bettenson, edited by David Knowles, Penguin Books 1972, p. 431.
12. Kenneth Leech, *True Prayer*, Sheldon Press 1980, p. 13.
13. C.B. Moss, *The Christian Faith*, SPCK 1944, p. 115.
14. Thomas Merton, *Elected Silence*, Hollis and Carter 1949, p. 332.
15. Rufus M. Jones, *Spiritual Reformers in the 16th and 17th Centuries*, Macmillan and Co. 1914, p. 310.
16. A.S. Pringle-Pattison, *The Idea of God*, Oxford University Press 1920, p. 157.
17. George Appleton, *Journey for a Soul*, William Collins Sons and Co. 1976, p. 135.
18. W.R. Inge, *Speculum Animae*, Longmans, Green and Co. 1911, p. 19.
19. Appleton, *Journey for a Soul*, p. 138.

## *Influence*

1. NRSV.
2. NRSV.
3. André Gide, *The Journals of André Gide*, translated by Justin O'Brien, Secker and Warburg 1947, p. 42.
4. Forbes Robinson, *Letters to His Friends*, Spottiswoode and Co. 1904, p. 165.
5. Henry Ward Beecher, *Proverbs from Plymouth Pulpit*, Charles Burnet and Co. 1887, p. 153.
6. George Eliot, *Scenes of Clerical Life, Janet's Repentance*, Oxford University Press 1909, p. 369.
7. Henry Adams, *The Education of Henry Adams*, Constable and Co. 1919, p. 300.
8. Meister Eckhart, *Meister Eckhart*, translated by Raymond B. Blakney, Harper and Row 1941, p. 121.

9. Beecher, *Proverbs from Plymouth Pulpit*, p. 161.
10. William Shakespeare *II King Henry IV*, act V.ii.76.
11. George Seaver (said of Edward Wilson) in *Edward Wilson of the Antarctic*, John Murray 1935, p. 104.
12. Beecher, *Proverbs from Plymouth Pulpit*, p. 153.
13. Henri J.M. Nouwen, *Reaching Out*, William Collins Sons and Co. 1980, p. 59.
14. Charles Kingsley, *Daily Thoughts*, Macmillan and Co. 1884, p. 37.
15. Benjamin Disraeli, *Coningsby*, Peter Davies 1927, p. 129.
16. Hans Küng, *On Being a Christian*, translated by Edward Quinn, William Collins Sons and Co. 1977, p. 63.
17. Charles Kingsley, *Daily Thoughts*, Macmillan and Co. 1884, p. 71.
18. Thomas Merton, *Elected Silence*, Hollis and Carter 1949, p. 371.
19. Anon.
20. Anon.

## *Inner Life*

1. NRSV.
2. NRSV.
3. Henri Frédéric Amiel, *Amiel's Journal*, translated by Mrs Humphry Ward, Macmillan and Co. 1918, p. 114.
4. A.C. Benson, *Extracts from the Letteers of Dr A.C. Benson to M.E.A.*, Jarrold Publishing 1927, p. 67.
5. Amiel, *Amiel's Journal*, p. 114.
6. Rufus M. Jones, *Spiritual Reformers in the 16th and 17th Centuries*, Macmillan and Co. 1914, p. 85.
7. D.H. Lawrence, *The Letters of D.H. Lawrence*, edited by George T. Zytaruk and James T. Boulton, Cambridge University Press, vol. II, 1981, p. 280.
8. Dag Hammarskjöld, *Markings*, translated by Leif Sjoberg and W.H. Auden, Faber and Faber 1964, p. 64.
9. Jones, *Spiritual Reformers in the 16th and 17th Centuries*, p. 97.
10. Norman Douglas, *An Almanac*, Chatto and Windus in association with Martin Secker and Warburg, 1945, p. 59.
11. Henry Drummond, *The Greatest Thing in the World*, William Collins Sons and Co. 1978, p. 169.
12. Christopher Bryant SSJE, *Jung and the Christian Way*, Darton, Longman and Todd 1983, p. 103.
13. Matthew Arnold, 'Mycerinus', *The Poems of Matthew Arnold*, Longmans, Green and Co. 1965, l.108, p. 31.
14. Thomas Kelly, *A Testament of Devotion*, Hodder and Stoughton 1943, p. 31.
15. John Smith the Platonist, *Select Discourses*, Cambridge at the University Press 1859, p. 13.
16. Michel Quoist, *With Open Heart*, translated by Colette Copeland, Gill and Macmillan 1983, p. 31.
17. Edward Burroughs, *The Memorable Works of a Son of Thunder and Consolation* 1672, p. 698.
18. John Pulsford, *Quiet Hours*, James Nisbet and Co. 1857, p. 216.

## *Inspiration*

1. NRSV.
2. NRSV.
3. Henry Ward Beecher, *Proverbs from Plymouth Pulpit*, Charles Burnet and Co. 1887, p. 132.
4. Kahlil Gibran, *Sand and Foam*, William Heinemann 1927, p. 21.
5. C.G. Jung, in Jolandi Jacobi, *Psychological Reflections*, Routledge and Kegan Paul 1953, p. 239.
6. Beecher, *Proverbs from Plymouth Pulpit*, p. 168.
7. Richard Jefferies, *The Story of My Heart*, Macmillan and Co. 1968, p. 1.
8. Beecher, *Proverbs from Plymouth Pulpit*, p. 132.
9. William Law, *The Spirit of Love*, by Sidney Spencer, full text, James Clarke and Co. 1969, p. 206.
10. Beecher, *Proverbs from Plymouth Pulpit*, p. 150.

11. James Tunstead, Burtchaell CSC, in Alan Richardson and John Bowden, *A New Dictionary of Christian Theology*, SCM Press 1985, p. 304.
12. Beecher, *Proverbs from Plymouth Pulpit*, p. 54.
13. George Eliot, *Adam Bede*, Virtue and Co. 1908, vol. 1, p. 168.
14. Plotinus, *The Enneads*, translated by Stephen Mackenna, Faber and Faber 1956, p. 396.
15. Beecher, *Proverbs from Plymouth Pulpit*, p. 170.
16. Esther Harding, *Women's Mysteries*, Pantheon Books 1955, p. 232.
17. Aldous Huxley, *The Perennial Philosophy*, Chatto and Windus 1974, p. 196.
18. Igor Stravinsky, *An Autobiography*, Calder and Boyars 1975, p. 174.
19. Huxley, *The Perennial Philosophy*, p. 135.

## *Integrity*

1. NRSV.
2. NRSV.
3. Latin proverb.
4. Walt Whitman, 'Song of the Broad-Axe', *The Complete Poems*, edited by Francis Murphy, Penguin Books 1982, iv.99, p. 218.
5. William Shakespeare *II King Henry VI*, act III.ii.232.
6. Henry David Thoreau, *Walden*, The New American Library of World Literature 1960, p. 219.
7. Alexis Carrel, *Reflections on Life*, Hamish Hamilton 1952, p. 183.
8. Erich Fromm, *Man for Himself*, Routledge and Kegan Paul 1975, p. 237.
9. Carrel, *Reflections on Life*, p. 41.
10. Randolph Bourne, *Youth and Life*, Constable and Co. 1913, p. 181.
11. G.A. Studdert Kennedy, *By His Friends*, Hodder and Stoughton 1929, p. 63.
12. André Gide, *The Journals of André Gide*, translated by Justin O'Brien, Secker and Warburg 1947, p. 116.
13. Harry James Cargas, *Encountering Myself*, SPCK 1978, p. 67.
14. Nicolas Berdyaev, *The Fate of Man in the Modern World*, translated by Donald A. Lowrie, SCM Press 1935, p. 83.
15. Ordway Tead, *The Art of Leadership*, McGraw-Hill Book Co. 1935, p. 111.
16. Hubert van Zeller, *Leave Your Life Alone*, Sheed and Ward 1973, p. 109.
17. F.W. Robertson, *Sermons*, Kegan Paul, Trench, Trubner and Co. 1907, first series, p. 286.
18. Marcus Aurelius, *The Meditations of Marcus Aurelius*, translated by Jeremy Collier, Walter Scott, p. 186.
19. George Appleton, *Journey for a Soul*, William Collins Sons and Co. 1976, p. 96.

## *Intellect*

1. NRSV.
2. NRSV.
3. *The Cloud of Unknowing*, translated by Clifton Wolters, Penguin Books 1961, p. 55.
4. W. MacNeile Dixon, *The Human Situation*, Edward Arnold and Co. 1937, p. 64.
5. Blaise Pascal, *Pensées*, translated by W.F. Trotter, Random House 1941, p. 6.
6. Harvey Cox, *The Secular City*, SCM Press 1967, p. 228.
7. John Keats, *Letter to J.H. Reynolds*, *The Works of John Keats*, edited by H. Buxton Forman, Reeves and Turner 1883, vol. III, p. 117.
8. Grace Cooke, *Spiritual Unfoldment*, The White Eagle Publishing Trust 1961, p. 113.
9. John Smith the Platonist, *Select Discourses*, Cambridge at the University Press 1859, p. 16.
10. William Temple, *Readings in St John's Gospel*, first and second series, Macmillan and Co. 1947, p. 68.
11. George Macdonald, *Unspoken Sermons*, third series, Longmans, Green and Co. 1889, p. 43.
12. Mark Rutherford, *Last Pages from a Journal*, Oxford University Press 1915, p. 311.
13. C.G. Jung, *Psychological Types*, translated by H. Godwin Baynes, Kegan Paul, Trench, Trubner and Co. 1946, p. 628.
14. Charles Morgan, *The Fountain*, Macmillan and Co. 1932, p. 58.

15. Charles Péguy, *Basic Verities*, translated by Ann and Julian Green, Kegan Paul, Trench, Trubner and Co. 1943, p. 115.
16. William Temple, *Nature, Man and God*, Macmillan and Co. 1934, p. 379.
17. Angelus Silesius, 'Of the Inner Light and Enlightenment', translated by Frederick Franck, Wildwood House 1976, p. 104.
18. Anne Morrow Lindbergh, *The Wave of the Future*, Harcourt, Brace and Co. 1940, p. 6.
19. Alexis Carrel, *Reflections on Life*, Hamish Hamilton 1952, p. 33.

## *Jesus Christ*

1. NRSV.
2. NRSV.
3. William Barclay, *The Gospel of Matthew*, The Saint Andrew Press 1965, vol. 1, p. 234.
4. Anon.
5. Malcolm Muggeridge, *Jesus, the Man who Lives*, William Collins Sons and Co. 1981, p. 31.
6. Henry Ward Beecher, *Proverbs from Plymouth Pulpit*, Charles Burnet and Co. 1887, p. 148.
7. William Barclay, *The Gospel of Matthew*, The Saint Andrew Press 1975, vol. 2, p. 296.
8. D.S. Cairns, *The Riddle of the World*, SCM Press 1937, p. 321.
9. F.W.Robertson, *Lectures and Addresses*, Smith, Elder and Co. 1858, p. 77.
10. Evelyn Underhill, *The Letters of Evelyn Underhill*, edited by Charles Williams, Longmans, Green and Co. 1947, p. 217.
11. C.G. Jung, in F.C. Happold, *Religious Faith and Twentieth-Century Man*, Darton, Longman and Todd 1980, p. 71.
12. H.G. Wells, in Barclay, *The Gospel of Matthew*, vol. 1, p. 87.
13. Thomas Carlyle, *Sartor Resartus*, Ward, Lock and Co., p. 148.
14. Robert Bridges, 'The Testament of Beauty', Oxford at the Clarendon Press 1930, iv. 1399, p. 190.
15. Basil Hume OSB, in Gerald Priestland, *Priestland's Progress*, BBC Worldwide 1982, p. 41.
16. Charles Kingsley, *Daily Thoughts*, Macmillan and Co. 1884, p. 45.
17. Evelyn Underhill, in John Stobbart, *The Wisdom of Evelyn Underhill*, edited by John Stobbart, A.R. Mowbray and Co. 1951, p. 15.
18. Rufus M. Jones, *Spiritual Reformers in the 16th and 17th Centuries*, Macmillan and Co. 1914, p. 244.

## *Joy*

1. NRSV.
2. NRSV.
3. Samuel Taylor Coleridge, 'A Christmas Carol', *Coleridge's Poetical Works*, edited by Ernest Hartley Coleridge, Oxford University Press 1978, st.viii, l.47, p. 340.
4. Richard Baxter, *The Saints' Everlasting Rest*, Blackie and Son 1817, p. 16.
5. Johann Wolfgang von Goethe, *The Practical Wisdom of Goethe*, chosen by Emil Ludwig, Martin Secker and Warburg 1933, *Travels in Italy*, p. 26.
6. John Main OSB, in Clare Hallward, *The Joy of Being*, Darton, Longman and Todd 1989, p. 42.
7. Rabindranath Tagore, *Stray Birds, Collected Poems and Plays of Rabindranath Tagore*, Macmillan and Co. 1936, XVII, p. 289.
8. Harry Williams CR, *The True Wilderness*, William Collins Sons and Co. 1983, p. 111.
9. Mother Teresa, in Malcolm Muggeridge, *Something Beautiful for God*, William Collins Sons and Co. 1983, p. 68.
10. Robert Browning, 'Saul', *The Poetical Works of Robert Browning*, Smith, Elder and Co. 1899, vol. 1, st.ix, l.21, p. 275.
11. Thomas Traherne, *Centuries*, The Faith Press 1969, p. 150.
12. D. Columba Marmion, *Christ in His Mysteries*, Sands and Co. 1924, p. 9.
13. William Temple, *Readings in St John's Gospel*, first and second series, Macmillan 1947, p. 295.
14. John Main OSB, *Moment of Christ*, Darton, Longman and Todd 1984, p. 80.
15. Henry Ward Beecher, *Proverbs from Plymouth Pulpit*, Charles Burnet and Co. 1887, p. 185.

16. Beecher, *Proverbs from Plymouth Pulpit*, p. 170.
17. Janet Erskine Stuart, in Maud Monahan, *Life and Letters of Janet Erskine Stuart*, Longmans, Green and Co. 1922, p. 88.
18. Izaak Walton, *The Compleat Angler*, Macmillan and Co. 1906, p. 15.
19. Rollo May, *Man's Search for Himself*, Souvenir Press 1975, p. 96.
20. William Barclay, *The Letters to the Galations and Ephesians*, The Saint Andrew Press 1958, p. 55.
21. Thomas Wolfe, *The Web and the Rock*, The Sun Dial Press 1940, p. 377.

## *Kindness*

1. NRSV.
2. NRSV.
3. Russian proverb.
4. Alfred, Lord Tennyson, 'Lady Clara Vere de Vere', *The Complete Works of Alfred Lord Tennyson*, Macmillan 1898, p. 49.
5. Proverb.
6. William Barclay, *The Gospel of Matthew*, The Saint Andrew Press 1987, vol. 1, p. 262.
7. Jean Jacques Rousseau, *Emile or Education*, translated by Barbara Foxley, J.M. Dent and Sons 1911, p. 43.
8. F.W. Faber, *Spiritual Conferences*, Thomas Richardson and Son 1859, p. 40.
9. Henri Frédéric Amiel, *Amiel's Journal*, translated by Mrs Humphry Ward, Macmillan and Co. 1918, p. 16.
10. Robert Burns, 'A Winter's Night', *The Poems and Songs of Robert Burns*, edited by James Kinsley, Clarendon Press 1968, vol. 1, l.95, p. 305.
11. Henry Ward Beecher, *Proverbs from Plymouth Pulpit*, Charles Burnet and Co. 1887, p. 154.
12. Olive Schreiner, *The Letters of Olive Schreiner*, edited by S.C. Cronwright-Schreiner, T. Fisher Unwin 1924, p. 48.
13. Amiel, *Amiel's Journal*, p. 146.
14. William Wordsworth, 'Lines Composed a few Miles Above Tintern Abbey', *The Poetical Works of William Wordsworth*, edited by E. de Selincourt, Oxford at the Clarendon Press 1944, vol. II, l.33, p. 260.
15. A.C. Benson, *Extracts from the Letters of Dr A.C. Benson to M.E.A.*, Jarrold Publishing 1927, p. 40.
16. André Gide, *Pretexts, Reflections on Literature and Morality*, selected by Justin O'Brien, Martin Secker and Warburg 1960, p. 313.
17. Attributed to Stephen Grellet.
18. F.W. Faber, *Spiritual Conferences*, Thomas Richardson and Son 1859, p. 22.
19. F.W. Robertson, *Sermons*, Kegan Paul, Trench, Trubner and Co. 1897, second series, p. 293.
20. Mother Teresa, in Kathryn Spink, *In the Silence of the Heart*, SPCK 1983 p. 42.
21. W.E. Sangster, *The Pure in Heart*, Epworth Press 1954, p. 136.

## *Kingdom Of God*

1. NRSV.
2. NRSV.
3. George Macdonald, *Unspoken Sermons*, Longmans, Green and Co., second series 1885, p. 38.
4. William Barclay, *The Gospel of Luke*, The Saint Andrew Press 1964, p. 236.
5. Rudolf Steiner, *Knowledge of the Higher Worlds*, Rudolf Steiner Press 1963, p. 22.
6. Seraphim of Sarov, in G.P. Fedatov, *A Treasury of Russian Spirituality*, Sheed and Ward 1977, p. 277.
7. E. Stanley Jones, *Mastery*, Hodder and Stoughton 1956, p. 199.
8. Lilian Whiting, *Lilies of Eternal Peace*, Gay and Hancock 1908, p. 34.
9. Trevor Beeson, *An Eye for an Ear*, SCM Press 1972, p. 28.
10. George Appleton, *Journey for a Soul*, William Collins Sons and Co. 1976, p. 160.
11. Albert Schweitzer, in E.N. Mozley, *The Theology of Albert Schweitzer*, 'Epilogue: The Conception

of the Kingdom of God in the Transformation of Eschatology', translated by J.R. Coates, A. and C. Black 1950, p. 106.

12. Aldous Huxley, *The Perennial Philosophy*, Chatto and Windus 1974, p. 74.
13. Schweitzer, in Mozley, *The Theology of Albert Schweitzer*, p. 106.
14. George Appleton, *Journey for a Soul*, William Collins Sons and Co. 1976, p. 159.
15. Schweitzer, in Mozley, *The Theology of Albert Schweitzer*, p. 106.
16. Albert Schweitzer, in Charles H. Joy, *An Anthology*, A. and C. Black 1955, p. 110.

## *Knowledge*

1. NRSV.
2. NRSV.
3. Ben Jonson, *Explorata: or, Discoveries*, in Ben Jonson, *The Poems, The Prose Works*, vol. VIII, edited by C.H. Herford, Percy and Evelyn Simpson, Oxford at the Clarendon Press 1947, p. 588.
4. Alfred, Lord Tennyson, 'Locksley Hall', *The Poems of Tennyson*, edited by Christopher Ricks, Longmans, Green and Co. 1969, p. 697.
5. Antoine de Saint-Exupéry, *Flight to Arras*, translated by Lewis Galantiere, William Heinemann 1942, p. 33.
6. Michel Quoist, *With Open Heart*, translated by Colette Copeland, Gill and Macmillan 1983, p. 40.
7. Kathleen Raine, *Defending Ancient Spings*, Oxford University Press 1967, p. 118.
8. William Cowper, 'The Task', *The Poetical Works of Cowper*, edited by H.S. Milford, Oxford University Press 1950, p. 221.
9. Thomas Carlyle, *Sartor Resartus*, 'Lectures on Heroes', Chapman and Hall 1840, p. 227.
10. Charles Kingsley, *Daily Thoughts*, Macmillan and Co. 1884, p. 151.
11. Hermann Hesse, *If the War Goes on*, translated by Ralph Manheim, Pan Books 1974, p. 54.
12. Rufus M. Jones, *Spiritual Reformers in the 16th and 17th Centuries*, Macmillan and Co. 1914, p. xviii.
13. Bede Griffiths OSB, in Peter Spink, *The Universal Christ*, Darton, Longman and Todd 1990, p. 44.
14. Harry James Cargas, *Encountering Myself*, SPCK 1978, p. 120.
15. Francis Bacon, *The Advancement of Learning*, Cassell and Co. 1905, p. 38.
16. Cargas, *Encountering Myself*, p. 120.

## *Leadership*

1. NRSV.
2. NRSV.
3. André Maurois, *The Art of Living*, The English Universities Press 1940, p. 160.
4. Henry Miller, *The Wisdom of the Heart*, New Directions Books 1941, p. 46.
5. John Eskine, *The Complete Life*, Andrew Melrose 1945, p. 134.
6. Ordway Tead, *The Art of Leadership*, McGraw-Hill Book Co. 1935, p. 98.
7. Ralph Waldo Emerson, *The Conduct of Life, Nature, and Other Essays*, J.M. Dent and Sons 1911, p. 175.
8. Philip Massinger, *The Bondman*, *The Plays of Massinger*, Alfred Thomas Crocker 1868, act 1. sc.iii, p. 102.
9. Henry Miller, *The Wisdom of the Heart*, New Directions Books 1941, p. 122.
10. Tead, *The Art of Leadership*, p. 115.
11. J.B. Yeats, *Letters to His Son, W.B. Yeats and Others*, Faber and Faber 1944, p. 218.
12. Jean Vanier, *Community and Growth*, Darton, Longman and Todd 1991, p. 220.
13. Sir John Glubb, *The Fate of Empires and Search for Survival*, William Blackwood and Sons 1978, p. 39.
14. Robert Browning, 'The Lost Leader', *The Poetical Works of Robert Browning*, Smith, Elder and Co. 1899, vol. 1, st.i, l.12, p. 249.
15. Vanier, *Community and Growth*, p. 219.
16. Tead, *The Art of Leadership*, p. 115.

17. Albert Einstein, (written of Mahatma Gandhi), *Ideas and Opinions*, Souvenir Press (Educational and Academic) 1973, p. 7.
18. Tead, *The Art of Leadership*, p. 87.

## *Life*

1. NRSV.
2. NRSV.
3. C.G. Jung, in Jolande Jacobi, *Psychological Reflections*, Routledge and Kegan Paul 1953, p. 185.
4. Alexis Carrel, *Reflections on Life*, translated by Antonia White, Hamish Hamilton 1952, p. 76.
5. Dag Hammarskjöld, *Markings*, translated by Leif Sjoberg and W.H. Auden, Faber and Faber 1964, p. 63.
6. Llewelyn Powys, *Impassioned Clay*, Longmans, Green and Co. 1931, p. 94.
7. Evelyn Underhill, *The Letters of Evelyn Underhill*, edited by Charles Williams, Longmans, Green and Co. 1947, p. 219.
8. Hubert van Zeller, *Considerations*, Sheed and Ward 1974, p. 69.
9. W. MacNeile Dixon, *The Human Situation*, Edward Arnold and Co. 1937, p. 50.
10. William Shakespeare, *All's Well that Ends Well*, act IV.iii.68.
11. Rufus M. Jones, *Spiritual Reformers in the 16th and 17th Centuries*, Macmillan and Co. 1914, p. 38.
12. George Bernard Shaw, *Mrs Warren's Profession*, *The Complete Plays of Bernard Shaw*, Paul Hamlyn 1965, Act 11, p. 75.
13. D.H. Lawrence, *The Selected Letters of D.H. Lawrence*, edited by Diana Trilling, Farrar, Straus and Cudahy 1958, p. 210.
14. Harry Emerson Foskick, *On Being a Real Person*, Harper and Row 1943, p. 77.
15. Father Andrew SDC, *The Way of Victory*, A.R. Mowbray and Co. 1938, p. 146.
16. Thomas Carlyle, *Past and Present*, Ward, Lock and Co., p. 198.
17. R.L. Smith, in Paul Rowntree Clifford, *Man's Dilemma and God's Answer*, Broadcast talks, SCM Press 1964, p. 73.
18. Frederick von Hugel, *Letters to a Niece*, J.M. Dent and Sons 1929, p. xi.
19. John S. Dunne, *The Reasons of the Heart*, SCM Press 1978, p. 123.
20. Ralph Waldo Emerson, *The Heart of Emerson's Journals*, edited by Bliss Perry, Constable and Co. 1927, p. 79.

## *Light*

1. NRSV.
2. NRSV.
3. Samuel Johnson, *The History of Rasselas*, Oxford University Press 1971, p. 124.
4. Henry Wadsworth Longfellow, 'To a Child', *The Poetical Works of Longfellow*, Oxford University Press 1913, p. 126.
5. Ralph Waldo Emerson, *Self-Reliance*, *The Works of Ralph Waldo Emerson*, George Bell and Sons 1906, vol. 1, *Essays and Representative Men*, p. 23.
6. Meister Eckhart, *Meister Eckhart*, translated by Raymond B. Blakney, Harper and Row 1941, p. 101.
7. Rufus M. Jones, *Spiritual Reformers in the 16th and 17th Centuries*, Macmillan and Co. 1914, p. 219.
8. St Augustine, *Confessions*, translated by R.S. Pine-Coffin, Penguin Books 1964, p. 260.
9. Walt Whitman, 'Hast Never Come to Thee an Hour', *The Complete Poems*, edited by Francis Murphy, Penguin Books 1982, p. 303.
10. Thomas Traherne, *Centuries*, The Faith Press 1969, p. 129.
11. Louise M. Haskins, 'God Knows', quoted by King George VI in a Christmas Broadcast, 25 December 1939.
12. Jones, *Spiritual Reformers in the 16th and 17th Centuries*, p. 345.
13. Charles Kingsley, *Daily Thoughts*, Macmillan and Co. 1884, p. 259.
14. Hubert van Zeller, *Considerations*, Sheed and Ward 1974, p. 51.

15. Jones, *Spiritual Reformers in the 16th and 17th Centuries*, p. 159.
16. William Barclay, *The Gospel of John*, The Saint Andrew Press 1965, vol. 2, p. 13.
17. Albert Schweitzer, *Memoirs of Childhood and Youth*, translated by C.T. Campion, George Allen and Unwin 1924, p. 90.

## *Listening*

1. NRSV.
2. NRSV.
3. John Keble, *The Christian Year*, edited by Ernest Rhys, J.M. Dent and Sons 1914, p. 72.
4. Anon.
5. Martin Buber, *I and Thou*, translated by Walter Kaufman, T. and T. Clark 1971, p. 26.
6. Anon, heard on the radio.
7. Rabindranath Tagore, *Stray Birds*, *Collected Poems and Plays of Rabindranath Tagore*, Macmillan and Co. 1936, p. 288.
8. Dag Hammarskjöld, *Markings*, translated by Leif Sjoberg and W.H. Auden, Faber and Faber 1964, p. 35.
9. Simone Weil, *Waiting on God*, translated by Emma Craufurd, William Collins Sons and Co. 1974, p. 106.
10. Carlo Carretto, *Letters from the Desert*, translated by Rose Mary Hancock, Darton, Longman and Todd, Orbis Books 1972, p. 40.
11. Hammarskjöld, *Markings*, p. 34.
12. Stephen MacKenna, *Journal and Letters*, Constable and Co. 1936, p. 260.
13. Mark Rutherford, *More Pages from a Journal*, Oxford University Press 1910, p. 223.
14. Michel Quoist, *With Open Heart*, translated by Anne Marie de Commaile and Agnes Mitchell Forsyth, Gill and Macmillan 1963, p. 2.
15. Hubert van Zeller, *Considerations*, Sheed and Ward 1974, p. 88.
16. Dan Billany and David Dowie, *The Cage*, Longmans, Green and Co. 1949, p. 158.
17. Dr Cyril H. Powell, *Secrets of Answered Prayer*, Arthur James 1858, p. 123.
18. William Barclay, *The Gospel of John*, The Saint Andrew Press 1974, vol. 1, p. 225.
19. Quoist, *With Open Heart*, p. 159.
20. Erich Fromm, *Man for Himself*, Routledge and Kegan Paul 1975, p. 161.
21. Mother Mary Clare SLG, *Encountering the Depths*, Darton, Longman and Todd 1981, p. 33.

## *Literature*

1. NRSV.
2. NRSV.
3. Henry Ward Beecher, *Proverbs from Plymouth Pulpit*, Charles Burnet and Co. 1887, p. 102.
4. Erza Pound, *How to Read*, Desmond Harmsworth 1931, p. 21.
5. E.M. Forster, *Howard's End*, Penguin Books 1981, p. 127.
6. Beecher, *Proverbs from Plymouth Pulpit*, p. 129.
7. Norman Douglas, *An Almanac*, Chatto and Windus in association with Secker and Warburg 1945, p. 31.
8. Rebecca West, *Ending in Earnest*, Doubleday, Doran and Co. 1931, p. 77.
9. Henry Wadsworth Longfellow, *Kavanagh*, *The Writings of Henry Wadsworth Longfellow*, George Routledge and Sons, vol. II, p. 366.
10. John Dryden, *Essay on Dramatic Poesy*, *The Works of John Dryden*, general editor, H.T. Swedenberg, Jr, University of California Press 1971, vol. XVII, *Prose 1668–1691*, l.20, p. 55.
11. J.B. Yeats, *Letters to His Son, W.B. Yeats and Others*, Faber and Faber 1944, p. 53.
12. Mark Rutherford, *Last Pages from a Journal*, Oxford University Press 1915, p. 280.
13. Henry David Thoreau, *Walden*, The New American Library of World Literature 1960, p. 74.
14. Hermann Hesse, in Volker Michels, *Reflections*, translated by Ralph Manheim, Jonathan Cape 1977, p. 109.
15. Beecher, *Proverbs from Plymouth Pulpit*, p. 128.
16. William E. Channing, *Self-Culture*, Dutton and Wentworth, 1838, p. 40.

17. Benjamin Disraeli, *Coningsby*, Peter Davies 1927, p. 129.
18. E.M. Forster, *Anonymity, An Enquiry*, Leonard and Virginia Woolf at the Hogarth Press 1925, p. 16.

## *Loneliness*

1. NRSV.
2. NRSV.
3. William Wordsworth, 'Prelude', book third, l.210.
4. Dag Hammarskjöld, *Markings*, translated by Leif Sjoberg and W.H. Auden, Faber and Faber 1964, p. 85.
5. Erich Fromm, *The Art of Loving*, George Allen and Unwin 1974, p. 14.
6. John S. Dunne, *The Reasons of the Heart*, SCM Press 1978, p. 50.
7. Henri J.M. Nouwen, *Reaching Out*, William Collins Sons and Co. 1980, p. 29.
8. Alfred, Lord Tennyson, 'The Holy Grail', *The Poems of Tennyson*, edited by Christopher Ricks, Longmans, Green and Co. 1969, *The Idylls of the King*, no. 471, p. 1673.
9. Antoine de Saint-Exupéry, *The Wisdom of the Sands*, translated by Stuart Gilbert, Hollis and Carter 1952, p. 224.
10. C.S. Lewis, *The Four Loves*, William Collins Sons and Co. 1960, p. 7.
11. Paul Tillich, *The Eternal Now*, SCM Press 1963, p. 11.
12. Stephen Neill, *The Church and Christian Union*, Oxford University Press 1968, p. 279.
13. John S. Dunne, *The Church of the Poor Devil*, SCM Press 1983, p. 18.
14. Henri J.M. Nouwen, in Robert Durback, *Seeds of Hope*, Darton, Longman and Todd 1989, p. 12.
15. Nouwen, *Reaching Out*, 1980, p. 35.
16. D.H. Lawrence, *Loneliness*, *The Complete Poems of D.H. Lawrence*, edited by Vivian de Sola Pinto and Warren Roberts, William Heinemann 1967, vol. II, p. 610.
17. Nouwen, in Durback, *Seeds of Hope*, p. 12.
18. Hubert van Zeller, *Considerations*, Sheed and Ward 1974, p. 23.
19. Harry James Cargas, *Encountering Myself*, SPCK 1978, p. 108.
20. van Zeller, *Considerations*, p. 18.

## *Longing*

1. NRSV.
2. NRSV.
3. Rabindranath Tagore, *Stray Birds*, *Collected Poems and Plays of Rabindranath Tagore*, Macmillan and Co. 1936, LXXXVIII, p. 298.
4. Henry Ward Beecher, *Proverbs from Plymouth Pulpit*, Charles Burnet and Co. 1887, p. 116.
5. J.R.Lowell, 'Longing', *The Poetical Works of James Russell Lowell*, Ward, Lock and Co. 1911, p. 94.
6. Elizabeth Bassett, *The Bridge is Love*, Darton, Longman and Todd 1981, p. 31.
7. Richard Chevenix Trench, *Notes on the Parables of Our Lord*, Pickering and Inglis 1953, p. 400.
8. John L. Casteel, *Rediscovering Prayer*, Hodder and Stoughton 1955, p. 13.
9. John S. Dunne, *The Reasons of the Heart*, SCM Press 1978, p. 112.
10. Anon.
11. Origen, in G.W. Butterworth, *Origen on First Principles*, SPCK 1936, p. 149.
12. Elizabeth Bassett, *The Bridge is Love*, Darton, Longman and Todd 1981, p. 31.
13. Miguel de Cervantes Saavedra, *The Life of Don Quixote and Sancho*, translated by Homer P. Earle, Alfred A. Knopf 1927, p. 33.
14. Bassett, *The Bridge is Love*, p. 31.
15. Edward Wilson, in George Seaver, *Edward Wilson of the Antarctic*, John Murray 1935, p. 46.

## *Love*

1. NRSV.
2. NRSV.
3. E.B. Browning, 'Aurora Leigh', *Elizabeth Barrett Browing's Poetical Works*, Smith, Elder and Co. 1873, vol. V, first book, p. 39.
4. *The Cloud of Unknowing*, John M. Watkins 1956, p. 77.
5. Benjamin Disraeli, *Sybil or the Two Nations*, Peter Davies 1927, p. 354.
6. W. Somerset Maugham, *The Summing Up*, Bernhard Tauchnitz 1938, p. 312.
7. Father Andrew SDC, *Seven Words from the Cross*, A.R. Mowbray and Co. 1954, p. 32.
8. Kahlil Gibran, *The Prophet*, William Heinemann 1970, p. 24.
9. William Temple, *Christian Faith and Life*, SCM Press 1963, p. 106.
10. Gibran, *The Prophet*, p. 11.
11. Charles Morgan, *The Fountain*, Macmillan 1932, p. 211.
12. Mark Rutherford, *More Pages from a Journal*, Oxford University Press 1910, p. 244.
13. Henry Ward Beecher, *Proverbs from Plymouth Pulpit*, Charles Burnet and Co. 1887, p. 106.
14. Thomas à Kempis, *The Imitation of Christ*, translated by Betty I. Knott, William Collins Sons and Co. 1963, p. 117.
15. Beecher, *Proverbs from Plymouth Pulpit*, p. 180.
16. Mark Rutherford, *Last Pages from a Journal*, Oxford University Press 1915, p. 283.
17. Gibran, *The Prophet*, p. 12.
18. Rufus M. Jones, *Spiritual Reformers in the 16th and 17th Centuries*, Macmillan and Co. 1914, p. 96.
19. Thomas à Kempis, *The Imitation of Christ*, p. 118.
20. Lady Julian of Norwich, *Revelations of Divine Love*, edited by Grace Warrack, Methuen and Co. 1949, p. 202.
21. Fyodor Dostoyevsky, *The Brothers Karamazov*, translated by David Magarshack, Penguin Books 1963, vol. 1, p. 375.
22. Edward Wilson, in George Seaver, *The Faith of Edward Wilson*, John Murray 1949, p. 15.
23. Martin Buber, in Aubrey Hodes, *Encounter with Martin Buber*, Allen Lane, The Penguin Press 1972, p. 66.

## *Marriage*

1. NRSV.
2. NRSV.
3. William Penn, *Fruits of Solitude*, A.W. Bennett 1863, part 1, no. 79, p. 19.
4. Coventry Patmore, *The Rod, the Root and the Flower*, The Grey Walls Press 1950, p. 215.
5. Henrik Ibsen, *The League of Youth*, edited and translated by James Walter McFarlane and Graham Orton, Oxford University Press 1963, vol. IV, act IV, p. 99.
6. Russian proverb.
7. Thomas Hardy, *Jude the Obscure*, Macmillan Publishers, 1924, p. 325.
8. Antoine de Saint-Exupéry, *The Wisdom of the Sands*, translated by Stuart Gilbert, Hollis and Carter 1952, p. 152.
9. Hubert van Zeller, *Considerations*, Sheed and Ward 1974, p. 94.
10. Antoine de Saint-Exupéry, *Wind, Sand and Stars*, translated by Lewis Galantiere, William Heinemann 1939, p. 268.
11. Count Hermann Keyserling, *The Book of Marriage*, Harcourt, Brace and Co. 1926, p. 286.
12. Patmore, *The Rod, the Root and the Flower*, 'Aurea Dicta', cxxxv, p. 51.
13. C.G. Jung, *Contributions to Analytical Psychology*, translated by H.G. and Cary F. Baynes, Kegan Paul, Trench, Trubner and Co. 1928, p. 193.
14. C.S. Lewis, *A Grief Observed*, Faber and Faber 1961, p. 18.
15. van Zeller, *Considerations*, p. 93.
16. Søren Kierkegaard, *Training in Christianity*, translated by Walter Lowrie, Princeton University Press 1942, p. 71.
17. Penn, *Fruits of Solitude*, p. 19.

18. Keyserling, *The Book of Marriage*, p. 290.
19. A young housewife.
20. Henry Van Dyke, *Little Rivers*, David Nutt 1903, p. 132.
21. J. Neville Ward, *Five for Sorrow, Ten for Joy*, Epworth Press 1971, p. 17.
22. van Zeller, *Considerations*, p. 94.
23. W.C. Willoughby, *Race Problems in the New Africa*, Clarendon Press 1923, p. 104.
24. Bertrand Russell, *Marriage and Morals*, George Allen and Unwin 1976, p. 203.

## *Meditation*

1. NRSV.
2. NRSV.
3. William Temple, *The Preacher's Theme Today*, SPCK 1936, p. 60.
4. Isaac Disraeli, *Literary Character of Men of Genius*, edited by The Earl of Beaconsfield, Frederick Warne and Co. 1881, p. 131.
5. Lawrence LeShan, *How to Meditate*, Turnstone Press 1983, p. 9.
6. Thomas Merton, *Thoughts in Solitude*, Burns and Oates 1958, p. 41.
7. Richard Challoner, in Gordon Wakefield, *A Dictionary of Christian Spirituality*, SCM Press 1986, p. 85.
8. Madam Guyon, *A Method of Prayer*, James Clarke and Co. 1902, p. 9.
9. Anthony Bloom, *Living Prayer*, Darton, Longman and Todd 1966, p. 52.
10. Morton T. Kelsey, *The Other Side of Silence*, SPCK 1977, p. 83.
11. George Appleton, *Journey for a Soul*, William Collins Sons and Co. 1976, p. 38.
12. John Main OSB, in Clare Hallward, *The Joy of Being*, Darton, Longman and Todd 1989, p. 26.
13. Kelsey, *The Other Side of Silence*, p. 31.
14. John Main OSB, *Moment of Christ*, Darton, Longman and Todd 1984, p. 31.
15. George Trevelyan, *A Vision of an Aquarian Age*, Coverture 1977, p. 87.
16. Kelsey, *The Other Side of Silence*, p. 65.

## *Mind*

1. NRSV.
2. NRSV.
3. Henri Matisse, in Francoise Gilot and Carlton Lake, *Life with Picasso*, Thomas Nelson and Sons 1965, p. 245.
4. Henry Ward Beecher, *Proverbs from Plymouth Pulpit*, Charles Burnet and Co. 1887, p. 26.
5. Joseph Conrad, *Heart of Darkness*, J.M. Dent and Sons 1923, p. 96.
6. William Temple, *Christian Faith and Life*, SCM Press 1963, p. 36.
7. Edmund Spenser, 'The Faerie Queene', *The Works of Edmund Spenser*, The Johns Hopkins Press, 1961, book VI, XI. xxx.1, p. 109.
8. Beecher, *Proverbs from Plymouth Pulpit*, p. 153.
9. Michel Quoist, *With Open Heart*, translated by Colette Copeland, Gill and Macmillan 1983, p. 135.
10. Sir John Lubbock, *The Pleasures of Life*, Macmillan and Co. 1904, part II, p. 250.
11. Alfred North Whitehead, in Lucien Price, *Dialogues of Alfred North Whitehead*, recorded by Lucien Price, Max Reinhardt 1954, p. 160.
12. Beecher, *Proverbs from Plymouth Pulpit*, p. 147.
13. William Temple, *Basic Convictions*, Hamish Hamilton 1937, p. 78.
14. Hubert van Zeller, *Considerations*, Sheed and Ward 1974, p. 67.
15. George Appleton, *Journey for a Soul*, William Collins Sons and Co. 1976, p. 18.
16. W.E. Sangster, *The Secret of Radiant Life*, Hodder and Stoughton 1957, p. 174.
17. Beecher, *Proverbs from Plymouth Pulpit*, p. 30.
18. William Barclay, *The Letter to the Romans*, The Saint Andrew Press 1969, p. 167.
19. Roy Stevens, *Education and the Death of Love*, Epworth Press 1978, p. 138.
20. Appleton, *Journey for a Soul*, p. 19.

## *Money*

1. NRSV.
2. NRSV.
3. George Herbert, *Outlandish Proverbs, The Works of George Herbert*, edited by F.E. Hutchinson, Oxford at the Clarendon Press 1945, no. 591, p. 341
4. Thomas Fuller, *Gnomologia*, published in Dublin 1732, p. 68.
5. Samuel Johnson, *The Vanity of Human Wishes*, The Yale Edition of the Works of Samuel Johnson, Yale University Press 1964, volume VI, 'Poems', p. 92.
6. Benjamin Franklin, *Poor Richard's Almanack,*Taurus Press 1962, p. 4.
7. Thomas Fuller, *Gnomologia*, Stearne Brock 1733, p. 172.
8. H.G. Wells, *Kipps*, Thomas Nelson and Sons 1909, p. 260.
9. Henry Ward Beecher, *Proverbs from Plymouth Pulpit*, Charles Burnet and Co. 1887, p. 8.
10. Norman Douglas, *An Almanac*, Chatto and Windus in association with Secker and Warburg 1945, p. 2.
11. Oliver Goldsmith, 'The Deserted Village', *Collected Works of Oliver Goldsmith*, edited by Arthur Friedman, Oxford at the Clarendon Press 1966, vol. IV, l.51, p. 289.
12. Beecher, *Proverbs from Plymouth Pulpit*, p. 36.
13. John Ruskin, *The Crown of Wild Olives*, George Allen and Sons 1910, p. 46.
14. Michel Quoist, *Prayers of Life*, translated by Anne Marie de Commaile and Agnes Mitchell Forsyth, Gill and Macmillan 1963, p. 23.
15. Arthur Schopenhauer, in W.H. Auden, *A Certain World*, Faber and Faber 1971, p. 266.
16. Martin Luther King, in Coretta Scott King, *The Words of Martin Luther King*, William Collins Sons and Co. 1986, p. 21.
17. Izaak Walton, *The Compleat Angler*, The Nonesuch Press 1929, p. 17.
18. John Woolman, *The Journal of John Woolman*, Edward Marsh 1857, p. 16.
19. Beecher, *Proverbs from Plymouth Pulpit*, p. 27.
20. Carlo Carretto, *Letters from the Desert*, translated by Rose Mary Hancock, Darton, Longman and Todd 1972, p. 81.
21. Arthur Koestler, *Darkness at Noon*, translated by Daphne Hardy, Jonathan Cape 1980, p. 257.
22. W.E. Sangster, *He Is Able*, Hodder and Stoughton 1936, p. 124.
23. William Law, *A Serious Call to a Devout and Holy Life*, J.M. Dent and Co. 1898, p. 88.
24. William Temple, *Christian Faith and Life*, SCM Press 1963, p. 131.

## *Morals*

1. NRSV.
2. NRSV.
3. Henry David Thoreau, *The Journal of Henry D. Thoreau*, vol. IV, edited by Bradford Torrey and Francis H. Allen, Houghton Mifflin Co., Boston, The Riverside Press 1949, p. 128.
4. Henry Ward Beecher, *Proverbs from Plymouth Pulpit*, Charles Burnet and Co. 1887, p. 96.
5. J.A. Froude, *Short Stories on Great Subjects*, Longmans, Green and Co. 1907, vol. IV, p. 265.
6. Matthew Arnold, *Literature and Dogma, The Complete Prose Works of Matthew Arnold*, vol. VI, *Dissent and Dogma*, edited by R.H. Super, The University of Michigan Press 1968, p. 180.
7. Robert Louis Stevenson, *Across the Plains*, T. Nelson and Sons 1892, p. 276.
8. Aldous Huxley, *The Doors of Perception*, Harper and Row 1970, p. 43.
9. William Penn, *Fruits of Solitude*, A.W. Bennett 1863, p. 67.
10. Beecher, *Proverbs from Plymouth Pulpit*, p. 97.
11. Bertrand Russell, *Authority and the Individual*, George Allen and Unwin Publishers 1949, p. 111.
12. Thomas Jefferson, *The Writings of Thomas Jefferson*, Taylor and Maury 1854, vol. IV, p. 476.
13. William Penn, *Fruits of Solitude*, A.W. Bennett 1863, p. 68.
14. Walter Lippman, *A Preface to Politics*, Ann Arbor Publications 1962, p. 152.
15. Ernest Hemingway, *Death in the Afternoon*, Jonathan Cape 1968, p. 11.
16. Norman Vincent Peale, *Man, Morals and Maturity*, World's Work 1970, p. 77.
17. F.R. Barry, *The Relevance of Christianity*, James Nisbet and Co. 1932, p. 8.

18. D.H. Lawrence, 'Immorality', *The Complete Poems of D.H. Lawrence*, edited by Vivian de Sola Pinto and Warren Roberts, William Heinemann 1967, vol. II, p. 836.
19. William Boyd Carpenter, *The Witness to the Influence of Christ*, Constable and Co. 1905, p. 59.
20. Percy Bysshe Shelley, *A Defence of Poetry*, *The Prose Works of Percy Bysshe Shelley*, vol. III, edited by H. Buxton Forman, Reeves and Turner 1880, p. 111.
21. William Temple, *Nature, Man and God*, Macmillan 1934, p. 196.
22. William Temple, *Christian Faith and Life*, SCM Press 1963, p. 60.
23. Anon.

### *Music*

1. NRSV.
2. NRSV.
3. C.M. Widor, in Charles R. Joy, *Music in the Life of Albert Schweitzer*, selections from his writings translated and edited by Charles R. Joy, A. and C. Black 1953, p. 157.
4. Robert Browning, 'Balaustion's Adventure', *The Poetical Works of Robert Browning*, Smith, Elder and Co. 1899, vol. 1, p. 631.
5. William Law, in Stephen Hobhouse, *Selected Mystical Writings of William Law*, Rockliff 1948, p. 631.
6. Thomas Carlyle, *Sartor Resartus*, 'Lectures on Heroes', Chapman and Hall 1840, p. 246.
7. Ludwig von Beethoven, in *Thayer's Life of Beethoven*, revised and edited by Elliot Forbes, Princeton University Press 1970, p. 494.
8. Richard Wagner, *Beethoven*, translated by Edward Dannreuther, William Reeves 1880, p. 1.
9. Henry Ward Beecher, *Proverbs from Plymouth Pulpit*, Charles Burnet and Co. 1887, p. 11.
10. Walter de la Mare, 'Music', *The Complete Poems of Walter de la Mare*, Faber and Faber 1969, p. 199.
11. Beecher, *Proverbs from Plymouth Pulpit*, p. 28.
12. Carlyle, *Sartor Resartus*, 'Lectures on Heroes', p. 247.
13. Sir Thomas Browne, *Religio Medici*, *The Works of Sir Thomas Browne*, edited by Geoffrey Keynes, Faber and Faber 1964, vol. 1, p. 84.
14. Joanna Field, *A Life of One's Own*, Chatto and Windus 1934, p. 29.
15. Henry Peacham, *The Compleat Gentleman*, Da Capo Press, Theatrum Orbis Terrarum 1968, p. 104.
16. Plato, *The Republic of Plato*, translated by B. Jowett, Oxford at the Clarendon Press 1881, book III, 401D, p. 85.
17. Aaron Copeland, *Music and Imagination*, Harvard University Press 1977, p. 1.
18. H.L. Kirk, *Pablo Casals: A Biography*, Hutchinson and Co. 1974, p. 187.
19. Heinrich Heine, in Jacques Barzun, *Pleasures of Music*, Michael Joseph 1952, p. 268.
20. Etty Hillesum, *A Diary 1941–43*, translated by Arnold J. Pomerans, Jonathan Cape 1983, p. 62.

### *Mystics*

1. NRSV.
2. NRSV.
3. Henri Frédéric Amiel, *Amiel's Journal*, translated by Mrs Humphry Ward, Macmillan and Co. 1918, p. 80.
4. Lewis Mumford, *The Conduct of Life*, Secker and Warburg 1952, p. 57.
5. William Johnston, *The Inner Eye of Love*, William Collins Sons and Co. 1978, p. 20.
6. William Barclay, *The Letters to the Corinthians*, The Saint Andrew Press 1988, p. 256.
7. Havelock Ellis, *Selected Essays*, J.M. Dent and Sons 1936, p. 186.
8. Gerhard Tersteegen, in Frances Bevan, *Sketches of the Quiet in the Land*, John F. Shaw and Co. 1891, p. 396.
9. Gerald Bullett, *The English Mystics*, Michael Joseph 1950, p. 17.
10. John V. Taylor, *The Go-Between God*, SCM Press 1973, p. 225.
11. Evelyn Underhill, in John Stobbart, *The Wisdom of Evelyn Underhill*, A.R. Mowbray and Co. 1951, p. 22.

12. Samuel Butler, in Gerald Bullett, *The English Mystics*, Michael Joseph 1950, p. 227.
13. Thomas Merton, *The Waters of Silence*, Hollis and Carter 1950, p. 20.
14. Aldous Huxley, *The Perennial Philosophy*, Chatto and Windus 1974, p. 345.
15. Underhill in Stobbart, *The Wisdom of Evelyn Underhill*, p. 23.
16. Rufus M. Jones, *Spiritual Reformers in the 16th and 17th Centuries*, Macmillan and Co. 1914, p. 133.
17. Albert Einstein, in Lincoln Barnett, *The Universe and Dr Einstein*, Victor Gollancz 1949, p. 95.
18. C.K. Chesterton, *Orthodoxy*, The Bodley Head 1935, p. 46.

## *Neighbour*

1. NRSV.
2. NRSV.
3. C.S. Lewis, *The Great Divorce*, William Collins Sons and Co. 1982, p. 84.
4. George Herbert, *Outlandish Proverbs*, *The Works of George Herbert*, edited by F.E. Hutchinson, Oxford at the Clarendon Press 1972, no.10, p. 321.
5. George Macdonald, *Unspoken Sermons*, first series, Alexander Strahan 1867, p. 214.
6. Benjamin Whichcote, *Morals and Religious Aphorisms* 1930, century II, no.122, p. 16.
7. Norman Douglas, *An Almanac*, Chatto and Windus in association with Martin Secker and Warburg 1945, p. 10.
8. Martin Luther King, *Strength to Love*, William Collins Sons and Co. 1980, p. 29.
9. St Teresa of Avila, *Interior Castle*, *Complete Works of St Teresa of Jesus*, translated by E. Allison Peers, Sheed and Ward 1978, p. 261.
10. Charles Kingsley, *Daily Thoughts*, Macmillan Publishers 1884, p. 59.
11. Macdonald, *Unspoken Sermons*, p. 210.
12. C.S. Lewis, *The Screwtape Letters*, Chivers Press 1983, p. 58.
13. Hans Küng, *On Being a Christian*, translated by Edward Quinn, William Collins Sons and Co. 1977, p. 256.
14. Albert Schweitzer, *Memoirs of Childhood and Youth*, translated by C.T. Campion, George Allen and Unwin 1924, p. 95.
15. Martin Luther King, in Coretta Scott King, *The Words of Martin Luther King*, William Collins Sons and Co. 1986, p. 24.
16. Fyodor Dostoyevsky, *The Brothers Karamazov*, translated by David Magarshack, Penguin Books 1963, vol. 1, p. 61.
17. Eric Hoffer, *The Passionate State of Mind*, Martin Secker and Warburg 1956, p. 54.
18. George Appleton, *Journey for a Soul*, William Collins Sons and Co. 1976, p. 60.
19. Vatican Council II, *The Conciliar and Post Conciliar Documents*, 1981 edition, General Editor, Austin Flannery OP, Fowler Wright Books, p. 928.

## *Obedience*

1. NRSV.
2. NRSV.
3. George Macdonald, *The Marquis of Lossie*, Everett and Co. 1912, p. 207.
4. P.T. Forsyth, *Positive Preaching and the Modern Mind*, Independent Press 1949, p. 32.
5. John J. Vincent, *Secular Christ*, Lutterworth Press 1968, p. 199.
6. Henry Suso, in St Alphonsus de Liguori, *On Conformity with the Will of God*, translated by the Rev. James Jones, Catholic Truth Society 1892, p. 7.
7. George Macdonald, *Unspoken Sermons*, second series, Longmans, Green and Co. 1885, p. 22.
8. Henry Ward Beecher, *Proverbs from Plymouth Pulpit*, Charles Burnet and Co. 1887, p. 179.
9. Father Andrew SDC, *A Gift of Light*, selected and edited by Harry C. Griffith, A.R. Mowbray and Co. 1968, p. 89.
10. Paul Oestreicher, in Hans Jürgen Schultz, *Conversion to the World*, SCM Press 1967, p. 12.
11. Beecher, *Proverbs from Plymouth Pulpit*, p. 206.
12. Henry David Thoreau, *Walden*, The New American Library of World Literature 1960, p. 216.
13. Sister Madeleine OSA, *Solitary Refinement*, SCM Press 1972, p. 49.

14. Alistair MacLean, *The Quiet Heart*, Allenson and Co. 1940, p. 186.
15. J.R.H. Moorman, *The Path to Glory*, SPCK 1960, p. 54.
16. Hans Küng, *On Being a Christian*, translated by Edward Quinn, William Collins Sons and Co. 1977, p. 244.
17. Jeremy Taylor, *Holy Living*, abridged by Anne Lamb, The Langford Press 1970, p. 85.
18. Küng, *On Being a Christian*, p. 246.
19. William Temple, *Thoughts on Some Problems of the Day*, Macmillan and Co. 1931, p. 28.
20. Moorman, *The Path to Glory*, p. 54.

## *Other Faiths*

1. NRSV.
2. NRSV.
3. William Blake, 'All Religions Are One', *Complete Writings*, edited by Geoffrey Keynes, Oxford University Press 1974, p. 98.
4. Raimundo Panikkar, *The Unknown Christ of Hinduism*, Darton, Longman and Todd 1981, p. 168.
5. William Penn, *Fruits of Solitude*, A.W. Bennett 1863, p. 63.
6. Simone Weil, *Gateway to God*, William Collins Sons and Co. 1974, p. 147.
7. George Appleton, *Journey for a Soul*, William Collins Sons and Co. 1976, p. 71.
8. Bede Griffiths OSB, in Peter Spink, *The Universal Christ*, Darton, Longman and Todd 1990, p. 10.
9. Leo Tolstoy, *Anna Karenina*, translated by Rosemary Edmonds, Penguin Books 1983, p. 851.
10. Mother Teresa, in Kathryn Spink, *In the Silence of the Heart*, SPCK 1983, p. 81.
11. Sri Ramakrishna, *Ramakrishna: Prophet of New India*, translated by Swami Nikhilananda, Rider and Co. 1951, p. 163.
12. Appleton, *Journey for a Soul*, p. 70.
13. Griffiths in Spink, *The Universal Christ*, p. 33.
14. F.C. Happold, *The Journey Inwards*, Darton, Longman and Todd 1974, p. 128.

## *Patience*

1. NRSV.
2. NRSV.
3. John Dryden, 'The Hind and the Panther', *The Poems of John Dryden*, edited by James Kinsley, Oxford at the Clarendon Press 1958, vol. II, *The Third Part*, l.839, p. 525.
4. Ben Johnson, *Volpone*, edited by C.H. Herford and Percy Simpson, Oxford at the Clarendon Press 1965, vol. V, act II, sc.ii, p. 50.
5. George Macdonald, *Weighed and Wanting*, Sampson Low, Marston, Searle and Rivington 1882, vol. III, p. 191.
6. Thomas Fuller, *Gnomologia*, Stearne Brock 1733, p. 164.
7. E B. Browning, 'Aurora Leigh', *Elizabeth Barrett Browning's Poetical Works*, Smith, Elder, and Co. 1873, vol. V, *Third Book*, p. 96.
8. John Ruskin, *The Two Paths*, George Allen 1905, p. 179.
9. Henry Wadsworth Longfellow, 'Evangeline', *The Poetical Works of Longfellow*, Humphrey Milford, Oxford University Press 1913, *Part the Second*, l.160, p. 156.
10. Norman Douglas, *An Almanac*, Chatto and Windus in association with Martin Secker and Warburg 1945, p. 26.
11. Anon.
12. J.R. Lowell, 'Columbus', *The Poetical Works of James Russell Lowell*, Ward, Lock and Co. 1911, p. 58.
13. Anon.
14. A.C. Benson, *Extracts from the Letters of Dr A.C. Benson to M.E.A*, Jarrold Publishing 1927, p. 7.
15. John Ruskin, *Ethics of the Dust*, George Allen and Sons 1907, p. 61.
16. Thomas à Kempis, *The Imitation of Christ*, translated by Betty I. Knott, William Collins Sons and Co. 1979, p. 129.

17. Francois de la M. Fénelon, *Spiritual Thoughts for Busy People*, SPCK 1894, p. 80.
18. George Macdonald, *Unspoken Sermons*, third series, Longmans, Green and Co. 1889, p. 227.
19. William Shakespeare, *The Merchant of Venice*, act IV.i.9.
20. William Penn, *Fruits of Solitude*, A.W. Bennett 1863, p. 36.
21. W.E. Sangster, *The Pure in Heart*, Epworth Press 1954, p. 129.
22. Hermann Hesse, in Volker Michels, *Reflections*, translated by Ralph Manheim, Jonathan Cape 1977, p. 58.
23. F.W. Faber, *Growth in Holiness*, Thomas Richardson and Son 1855, p. 148.

## *Peace*

1. NRSV.
2. NRSV.
3. Walt Whitman, 'The Sleepers', *The Complete Poems*, edited by Francis Murphy, Penguin Books 1982, l.147, p. 447.
4. George Herbert, *Outlandish Poems*, *The Works of George Herbert*, edited by F.E. Hutchinson, Oxford at the Clarendon Press 1972, no.733, p. 345.
5. St Augustine, *Confessions*, translated by R.S. Pine-Coffin, Penguin Books 1964, p. 232.
6. William Wordsworth, 'The Excursion', book III, l.382, *The Poetical Works of William Wordsworth*, edited by E. de Selincourt, Oxford at the Clarendon Press 1959, vol. IV, p. 861.
7. Hubert van Zeller, *Leave Your Life Alone*, Sheed and Ward 1973, p. 103.
8. Thomas à Kempis, *The Imitation of Christ*, translated by Betty I. Knott, William Collins Sons and Co. 1979, p. 87.
9. Johann Wolfgang von Goethe, *Wisdom and Experience*, selected by Ludwig Curtius, translated and edited by Herman J. Weigand, Routledge and Kegan Paul 1949, p. 295.
10. John Ruskin, *The Eagle's Nest*, George Allen and Sons 1910, p. 222.
11. Father Yelchaninov, in G.P. Fedatov, *A Treasury of Russian Spirituality*, Sheed and Ward 1977, p. 445.
12. Hubert van Zeller, *Considerations*, Sheed and Ward 1974, p. 43.
13. John Macquarrie, *The Concept of Peace*, SCM Press 1973, p. 81.
14. Søren Kierkegaard, *The Journals of Søren Kierkegaard*, selected, edited and translated by Alexander Dru, Oxford University Press 1938, p. 85.
15. Bede Griffiths OSB, in Peter Spink, *The Universal Christ*, Darton, Longman and Todd 1993, p. 25.
16. Matthew Arnold, 'Lines written in Kensington Gardens', l.37, *The Poems of Matthew Arnold*, edited by Kenneth Allott, Longmans, Green and Co. 1965, p. 257.
17. Henry Ward Beecher, *Proverbs from Plymouth Pulpit*, Charles Burnet and Co. 1887, p. 169.
18. John Tauler, *The History and Life of the Reverend Doctor John Tauler*, translated by Susanna Winkworth, Smith, Elder and Co. 1857, p. 381.
19. Bede Griffiths OSB, *Return to the Centre*, William Collins Sons and Co. 1976, p. 136.
20. William Barclay, *The Gospel of John*, The Saint Andrew Press 1974, vol. 2, p. 199.

## *Perseverance*

1. NRSV.
2. NRSV.
3. A.C. Benson, *Extracts from the Letters of Dr A.C.Benson to M.E.A.*, Jarrold Publishing 1927, p. 41.
4. John Buchan, *Montrose*, Oxford University Press 1957, p. 423.
5. William Shakespeace, *Troilus and Cressida*, act III.iii.150.
6. A.R. Orage, *On Love*, The Janus Press 1957, p. 61.
7. Robert Herrick, 'Hesperides: Seek and Find', *The Poetical Works of Robert Herrick*, Oxford University Press 1915, p. 311.
8. Mark Rutherford, *Last Pages from a Journal*, Oxford University Press 1915, p. 316.
9. William Makepeace Thackeray, *The Virginians*, Smith, Elder, and Co. 1894, p. 761.
10. Benson, *Extracts from the Letters of Dr A.C. Benson to M.E.A.*, p. 14.
11. Oliver Wendell Holmes, in Max Lerner, *The Mind and Faith of Justice Holmes*, Little, Brown and Co. 1945, p. 425.

12. William Barclay, *The Letters to Timothy and Titus*, The Saint Andrew Press 1965, p. 283.
13. André Gide, *The Journals of André Gide*, translated by Justin O'Brien, Secker and Warburg 1929, vol. IV, p. 71.
14. Right Hon. Lord Avebury, *Essays and Addresses*, Macmillan and Co. 1903, p. 276.
15. Johann Wolfgang von Goethe, in Emil Ludwig, *The Practical Wisdom of Goethe*, George Allen and Unwin 1933, p. 159.
16. William Barclay, *The Letters to the Corinthians*, The Saint Andrew Press 1988, p. 143.
17. Samuel Smiles, *Self-Help*, S.W. Partridge and Co. 1912, p. 53.
18. Barclay, *The Letters to the Corinthians*, p. 212.
19. Ordway Tead, *The Art of Leadership*, McGraw-Hill Book Co. 1935, p. 92.

## *Philosophy*

1. NRSV.
2. NRSV.
3. English proverb.
4. Henry Miller, *The Wisdom of the Heart*, New Directions Books 1941, p. 93.
5. Nicolas Berdyaev, *Christian Existentialism*, selected and translated by Donald A. Lowrie, George Allen and Unwin 1965, p. 119.
6. Clement of Alexandria, *The Miscellanies*, *The Writings of Clement of Alexandria*, translated by the Rev. William Wilson, T. and T. Clark 1867, p. 368.
7. Henry Ward Beecher, *Proverbs from Plymouth Pulpit*, Charles Burnet and Co. 1887, p. 152.
8. Ralph Waldo Emerson, *The Works of Ralph Waldo Emerson*, George Bell and Sons 1906, vol. 1, *Essays and Representative Men*, 'Essay on the Over-Soul', p. 143.
9. Bertrand Russell, *Principles of Social Reconstruction*, George Allen and Unwin 1971, p. 168.
10. Henry David Thoreau, *Walden*, The New American Library of World Literature 1960, p. 15.
11. William Temple, *Nature, Man and God*, Macmillan and Co. 1934, p. 520.
12. William James, *Prgamatism*, Longmans, Green and Co. 1943, p. 4.
13. Temple, *Nature, Man and God*, p. 45.
14. A. Clutton Brock, *The Ultimate Belief*, Constable and Co. 1916, p. 9.
15. Russell, *Principles of Social Reconstruction*, p. 168.
16. Sir Sarvepalli Radhakrishnan, *Indian Philosophy*, George Allen and Unwin 1923, p. 44.
17. Russell, *Principles of Social Reconstruction*, p. 168.

## *Poetry*

1. NRSV.
2. NRSV.
3. J.B. Yeats, *Letters to His Son, W.B. Yeats and Others,* Faber and Faber 1944, p. 105.
4. Percy Bysshe Shelley, *A Defence of Poetry*, *The Prose Works of Percy Bysshe Shelley*, edited by H. Buxton Forman, Reeves and Turner 1880, vol. III, p. 138.
5. Thomas Carlyle, *Sartor Resartus*, 'Lectures on Heroes', Chapman and Hall 1840, p. 247.
6. Yeats, *Letters to His Son, W.B. Yeats and Others*, p. 150.
7. John Keble, *Lectures on Poetry*, vol. 1, lecture 1, Oxford at the Clarendon Press, p. 22.
8. Henry Wadsworth Longfellow, *Kavanagh*, *The Writings of Henry Wadsworth Longfellow*, George Routledge and Sons, vol. II, p. 367.
9. Yeats, *Letters to His Son, W.B. Yeats and Others*, p. 212.
10. Thomas Merton, *New Seeds of Contemplation*, Burns and Oates 1962, p. 85.
11. Cyril Connolly, in Stephen Spender, *The Making of a Poem*, Hamish Hamilton 1955, in a review of Keats' Collected Letters, p. 26.
12. Francis Bacon, *The Advancement of Learning*, Cassell and Co. 1905, p. 79.
13. John Keats, *Letter to J.H. Reynolds*, *The Works of John Keats*, edited by H. Buxton Forman, Reeves and Turner 1883, vol. III, p. 113.
14. Oscar Wilde, *De Profundis*, *The Works of Oscar Wilde*, William Collins Sons and Co. 1948, p. 868.
15. Augustine Birrell, *Obiter Dicta*, *Mr Browning's Poetry*, Elliot Stock 1884, p. 92.

16. John Keble, *Keble's Lectures on Poetry*, translated by E.K. Francis, Oxford at the Clarendon Press 1912, vol. II, p. 201.
17. Johann Wolfgang von Goethe, in Ludwig Curtius, *Wisdom and Experience*, translated and edited by Hermann J. Weigand, Routledge and Kegan Paul 1949, p. 246.
18. William Temple, *Nature, Man and God*, Macmillan and Co. 1934, p. 484.
19. Percy Bysshe Shelley, *Prose, A Defence of Poetry*, *The Works of Percy Bysshe Shelley*, edited by Roger Ingpen and Walter E. Peck, Ernest Benn 1930, vol. VII, p. 115.
20. Henri Frédéric Amiel, *Amiel's Journal*, translated by Mrs Humphry Ward, Macmillan and Co. 1918, p. 28.
21. William Wordsworth, *Lyrical Ballads, The Poems of William Wordsworth*, edited by Nowell Charles Smith, Methuen and Co. 1908, vol. III, Preface to the second edition of *Lyrical Ballads*, p. 490.

## *Power*

1. NRSV.
2. NRSV.
3. William Blake, 'The Marriage of Heaven and Hell', *The Complete Writings of William Blake*, edited by Geoffrey Keynes, Oxford University Press 1974, p. 149.
4. Leigh Hunt, 'On a Lock of Milton's Hair', *The Poetical Works of Leigh Hunt*, edited by H.S. Milford, Oxford University Press 1923, p. 247.
5. Alfred North Whitehead, *Science and the Modern World*, The New American Library 1964, p. 172.
6. Rabindranath Tagore, *Stray Birds*, *Collected Poems and Plays of Rabindranath Tagore*, Macmillan and Co. 1936, p. 290.
7. Henrik Ibsen, *An Enemy of the People*, translated and edited by James Walter McFarlane, Oxford University Press 1960, vol. VI, p. 126.
8. Benjamin Whichcote, *Moral and Religious Aphorisms*, Elkin, Mathews and Marrot 1930, no.34, p. 5.
9. Sarah Bernhardt, in Cornelia Otis Skinner, *Madam Sarah*, Michael Joseph 1967, p. xvi.
10. Alfred, Lord Tennyson, 'Oenone', *The Poems of Tennyson*, edited by Christopher Ricks, Longmans, Green and Co. 1969, p. 392.
11. J.R. Lowell, *New England Two Centuries Ago*, in *Among My Books*, J.M. Dent and Sons 1914, p. 182.
12. Ralph Waldo Emerson, *The Conduct of Life, Nature and Other Essays*, J.M. Dent and Sons 1911, p. 186.
13. C.C. Colton, *Lacon*, William Tegg 1866, p. 243.
14. Carlo Carretto, *Letters from the Desert*, translated by Rose Mary Hancock, Darton, Longman and Todd 1972, p. 19.
15. Mohandas K. Gandhi, *Non-Violence in Peace and War*, Navajivan Publishing House, vol. II, 1949, p. 8.
16. Blaise Pascal, *Pensées*, translated by W.F. Trotter, Random House 1941, p. 103.
17. William Temple, *Christian Faith and Life*, SCM Press 1963, p. 45.
18. Claude Bragdon, in Kahlil Gibran, *The Prophet*, William Heinemann 1923, introduction.
19. Henry Ward Beecher, *Proverbs from Plymouth Pulpit*, Charles Burnet and Co. 1887, p. 155.
20. Evelyn Underhill, *The Letters of Evelyn Underhill*, edited by Charles Williams, Longmans, Green and Co. 1947, p. 98.
21. Stuart B. Jackman, *The Numbered Days*, SCM Press 1954, p. 31.
22. Pierre Teilhard de Chardin, *Le Milieu Divin*, William Collins Sons and Co. 1960, p. 43.
23. William Barclay, *The Gospel of John*, The Saint Andrew Press 1965, vol. 1, p. 66.

## *Prayer*

1. NRSV.
2. NRSV.
3. Carlo Carretto, *The Desert in the City*, translated by Barbara Wall, William Collins Sons and Co. 1983, p. 23.

4. C.H. Dodd, in William Barclay, *The Letter to the Romans*, The Saint Andrew Press 1969, p. 116.
5. William Law, *A Serious Call to a Devout and Holy Life*, J.M. Dent and Co. 1898, p. 78.
6. Mohandas K. Gandhi, *Non-Violence in Peace and War*, Navajivan Publishing House 1949, vol. II, p. 77.
7. Kahlil Gibran, *The Prophet*, William Heinemann 1970, p. 78.
8. Dag Hammarskjöld, *Markings*, translated by Leif Sjoberg and W.H. Auden, Faber and Faber 1964, p. 97.
9. Carlo Carretto, *Letters from the Desert*, translated by Rose Mary Hancock, Darton, Longman and Todd 1972, p. 55.
10. John Robinson, *Honest to God*, SCM Press 1963, p. 100.
11. Thomas Merton, *Thoughts in Solitude*, Burns and Oates 1958, p. 91.
12. Brother Lawrence, *The Practice of the Presence of God*, A.R. Mowbray and Co. 1977, p. 47.
13. William Temple, *Christian Faith and Life*, SCM Press 1963, p. 115.
14. Evelyn Underhill, in Charles Williams, *The Letters of Evelyn Underhill*, Longmans, Green and Co. 1947, p. 271.
15. St Francis de Sales, *Introduction to the Devout Life*, Longmans, Green and Co. 1962, p. 54.
16. Fyodor Dostoyevsky, *The Brothers Karamazov*, translated by David Magarshack, Penguin Books 1963, vol. 1, p. 375.
17. Martin Luther, *Table-Talk*, translated and edited by William Hazlitt, George Bell and Sons 1895, p. 125.
18. John of Cronstadt, in G.P. Fedatov, Sheed and Ward 1977, p. 354.
19. John Macquarrie, *Paths in Spirituality*, SCM Press, 1992, second edition, p. 30.
20. Mother Teresa, in Kathryn Spink, *In the Silence of the Heart*, SPCK 1983, p. 17.
21. William Barclay, *The Gospel of Matthew*, The Saint Andrew Press 1965, vol. 1, p. 275.

## *Presence*

1. NRSV.
2. NRSV.
3. Henry Ward Beecher, *Proverbs from Plymouth Pulpit*, Charles Burnet and Co. 1887, p. 183.
4. William Law, *The Spirit of Prayer*, edited by Sidney Spencer, full text, James Clarke and Co., 1969, p. 44.
5. F.W. Boreham, *A Late Lark Singing*, Epworth Press 1945, p. 160.
6. Alfred, Lord Tennyson, 'The Higher Pantheism', *The Poems of Tennyson*, edited by Christopher Ricks, Longmans, Green and Co. 1969, no. 353, l.11, p. 1205.
7. Hubert van Zeller, *Considerations*, Sheed and Ward 1974, p. 100.
8. Brother Lawrence, *The Practice of the Presence of God*, A.R. Mowbray and Co. 1977, p. 23.
9. Walter Hilton, *The Ladder of Perfection*, translated by Leo Sherley-Price, Penguin Books 1957, p. 233.
10. Jean-Pierre de Caussade SJ, *Self-Abandonment to the Divine Providence*, William Collins Sons and Co. 1972, p. 42.
11. W.R. Inge, *Personal Religion and the Life of Devotion*, Longmans, Green and Co. 1924, p. 32.
12. Brother Lawrence, *The Practice of the Presence of God*, p. 50.
13. W.E. Sangster, *Give God a Chance*, Epworth Press 1968, p. 104.
14. Gerhard Tersteegen, in Frances Bevan, *Sketches of the Quiet of the Land*, John F. Shaw and Co. 1891, p. 384.
15. Francois de la M. Fénelon, *Spiritual Thoughts for Busy People*, SPCK 1894, p. 85.
16. Father Andrew SDC, *The Symbolism of the Sanctuary*, A.R. Mowbray and Co. 1927, p. 18.
17. Evelyn Underhill, *Abba*, Longmans, Green and Co. 1940, p. 12.
18. William Barclay, *The Plain Man Looks at the Apostles' Creed*, William Collins Sons and Co. 1967, p. 197.

## Pride

1. NRSV.
2. NRSV.
3. William Shakespeare, *Henry VII*, act IV.ii.37.
4. Alfred, Lord Tennyson, 'The Two Voices', *The Works of Alfred Lord Tennyson*, Macmillan and Co. 1898, p. 31.
5. George Macdonald, *The Marquis of Lossie*, Everett and Co. 1912, p. 91.
6. Benedict Spinoza, *Spinoza's Ethics and de Intellectus Emendatione*, J.M. Dent and Sons 1955, p. 134.
7. William Law, in Stephen Hobhouse, *Selected Mystical Writings of William Law*, Rockliff 1948, p. 107.
8. Spinoza, *Spinoza's Ethics and de Intellectus Emendatione*, p. 102.
9. Benjamin Whichcote, *Moral and Religious Aphorisms*, Elkin, Mathews and Marrot 1930, ix, 801, p. 90.
10. A.R. Orage, *On Love*, The Janus Press 1957, p. 60.
11. Cardinal Manning, *Pastime Papers*, Burns and Oates 1892, p. 27.
12. C.C. Colton, *Lacon*, William Tegg 1866, p. 248.
13. Henry Ward Beecher, *Proverbs from Plymouth Pulpit*, Charles Burnett and Co. 1887, p. 26.
14. Henri Frédéric Amiel, *Amiel's Journal*, translated by Mrs Humphry Ward, Macmillan and Co. 1918, p. 45.
15. William Law, *A Serious Call to a Devout and Holy Life*, J.M. Dent and Co. 1898, p. 246.
16. William Shakespeare, *Troilus and Cressida*, act II.iii.156.
17. *The Cloud of Unknowing*, translated by Clifton Wolters, Penguin Books 1971, p. 68.
18. Law, *A Serious Call to a Devout and Holy Life*, p. 39.
19. Mother Teresa, in Brother Angelo Devananda, *Jesus, the Word to Be Spoken*, William Collins Sons and Co. 1990, p. 20.
20. Alexander Pope, 'An Essay on Criticism', *The Poems of Alexander Pope*, vol. 1, *Pastoral Poetry and An Essay on Criticism*, edited by E. Audra and Aubrey Williams, Methuen and Co. 1961, p. 263.
21. William Temple, *Nature, Man and God*, Macmillan and Co. 1934, p. 421.
22. Law in Hobhouse, *Selected Mystical Writings of William Law*, pp. 25 and 29.
23. William Temple, *Christian Faith and Life*, SCM Press 1963, p. 132.

## Progress

1. NRSV.
2. NRSV.
3. Thomas Hardy, *Desperate Remedies*, Macmillan and Co. 1918, p. 450.
4. Edward Patey, *Christian Life Style*, A.R. Mowbray and Co. 1976, p. 113.
5. Malcolm Muggeridge, *Jesus Rediscovered*, William Collins Sons and Co. 1982, p. 52.
6. Henry George, *Progress and Poverty*, Kegan Paul and Co. 1881, p. 9.
7. James A. Froude, *Thomas Carlyle*, Longmans, Green and Co. 1884, vol. II, p. 77.
8. William Temple, *Christian Faith and Life*, SCM Press 1963, p. 96.
9. F.R. Barry, *The Relevance of Christianity*, Nisbet and Co. 1932, p. 14.
10. William Temple, *The Preacher's Theme Today*, SPCK 1936, p. 60.
11. Martin Luther King, in Coretta Scott King, *The Words of Martin Luther King*, William Collins Sons and Co. 1986, p. 67.
12. Evelyn Underhill, *Mysticism*, Methuen and Co. 1912, p. 532.
13. Samuel Smiles, *Self-Help*, S.W. Partridge and Co. 1912, p. 54.
14. King, *The Words of Martin Luther King*, 1986, p. 59.
15. Michel Quoist, *With Open Heart*, translated by Colette Copeland, Gill and Macmillan 1983, p. 186.
16. Albert Schweitzer, *The Philosophy of Civilization, The Decay and Restoration of Civilization*, translated by C.T. Campion, A. and C. Black 1932, p. 16.

## *Purpose*

1. NRSV.
2. NRSV.
3. George Eliot, *Daniel Deronda*, J.M. Dent and Sons 1964, vol. II, p. 580.
4. Charles H. Parkhurst, *The Pattern in the Mount*, R.D. Dickinson 1890, p. 8.
5. Johann Wolfgang von Goethe, *Wilhelm Meister's Apprenticeship*, *The Practical Wisdom of Goethe*, chosen by Emil Ludwig, Secker and Warburg 1933, p. 26.
6. A.R. Orage, *On Love*, The Janus Press 1957, p. 54.
7. Norman W. Goodacre, 'Laymen's Lent', A.R. Mowbray and Co. 1969, p. 33.
8. William Barclay, *The Letters to Timothy and Titus*, The Saint Andrew Press 1965, p. 225.
9. Anon.
10. W.E. Sangster, *God Does Guide Us*, Hodder and Stoughton 1934, p. 30.
11. Bertrand Russell, *The Conquest of Happiness*, George Allen and Unwin 1984, p. 48.
12. Miguel de Unamuno, *The Tragic Sense of Life*, Macmillan and Co. 1921, p. 152.
13. Antoine de Saint-Exupéry, *The Wisdom of the Sands*, translated by Stuart Gilbert, Hollis and Carter 1952, p. 127.
14. Helen Keller, *Helen Keller's Journal*, Michael Joseph 1938, p. 64.
15. Alexis Carrel, *Reflections on Life*, Hamish Hamilton 1952, p. 131.
16. Ross Parmenter, *The Plant in My Window*, Geoffrey Bles 1951, p. 39.
17. Edward Young, *Night Thoughts*, Thomas Nelson 1841, p. 17.
18. Albert Einstein, *Ideas and Opinions*, Souvenir Press (Educational and Academic) 1973, p. 11.
19. George Bernard Shaw, *The Complete Bernard Shaw Prefaces*, Paul Hamlyn 1965, p. 163.
20. Neville Cryer, *Michel Quoist*, Hodder and Stoughton 1977, p. 53.
21. W. MacNeile Dixon, *The Human Situation*, Edward Arnold and Co. 1937, p. 34.
22. Anon.

## *Quietness*

1. NRSV.
2. NRSV.
3. Alistair MacLean, *The Quiet Heart*, Allenson and Co. 1940, p. 25.
4. Charles Guthrie, *God in His World*, Independent Press 1955, p. 43.
5. Antoine de Saint-Exupéry, *The Wisdom of the Sands*, translated by Stuart Gilbert, Hollis and Carter 1952, p. 45.
6. Bertrand Russell, *The Conquest of Happiness*, George Allen and Unwin 1984, p. 52.
7. Samuel Taylor Coleridge, 'Ode to Tranquillity', *Coleridge's Poetical Works*, edited by Ernest Hartley Coleridge, Oxford University Press 1978, p. 360.
8. Blaise Pascal, *Pensées*, translated by W.F. Trotter, Random House 1941, p. 48.
9. Evelyn Underhill, *Mysticism*, Methuen and Co. 1912, p. 210.
10. Mark Rutherford, *Last Pages from a Journal*, Oxford University Press 1915, p. 273.
11. Russell, *The Conquest of Happiness*, p. 49.
12. Roy Stevens, *Education and the Death of Love*, Epworth Press 1978, p. 127.
13. Ladislaus Boros, *In Time of Temptation*, translated by Simon and Erika Young, Burns and Oates 1968, p. 18.
14. John Greenleaf Whittier, 'The Brewing of Soma', *The Poetical Works of John Greenleaf Whittier*, Macmillan and Co. 1874, p. 457.
15. Charles Kingsley, *Daily Thoughts*, Macmillan and Co. 1884, p. 139.
16. Michel Quoist, *With Open Heart*, translated by Colette Copeland, Gill and Macmillan 1983, p. 65.
17. Henri J.M. Nouwen, in Robert Durback, *Seeds of Hope*, Darton, Longman and Todd 1989, p. 70.
18. Gerhard Tersteegen, in Frances Bevan, *Sketches of the Quiet in the Land*, John F. Shaw and Co. 1891, p. 400.

## *Relationships*

1. NRSV.
2. NRSV.
3. Michel Quoist, *With Open Heart,* translated by Colette Copeland, Gill and Macmillan 1983, p. 36.
4. Henri J.M. Nouwen, *Reaching Out*, William Collins Sons and Co. 1980, p. 32.
5. Mark Rutherford, *Last Pages from a Journal*, Oxford University Press 1915, p. 261.
6. Eric Hoffer, *The Passionate State of Mind*, Martin Secker and Warburg 1956, p. 70.
7. W.H. Vanstone, *Love's Endeavour, Love's Expense*, Darton, Longman and Todd 1978, p. 45.
8. A.C. Benson, *Extracts from the Letters of Dr A.C. Benson to M.E.A.*, Jarrold Publishing 1927, p. 12.
9. Henry Wadsworth Longfellow, 'Evangeline', *The Poetical Works of Longfellow*, Humphrey Milford, Oxford University Press 1913, 'Part the Second', l.55, p. 158.
10. David Grayson, *The Friendly Road*, Andrew Melrose 1946, p. 117.
11. Dietrich Bonhoeffer, *Letters and Papers from Prison*, edited by Eberhard Bethge, translated by R.H. Fuller, SCM Press 1967, second revised edition, p. 212.
12. J.B. Priestley, *All About Ourselves and Other Essays*, William Heinemann 1956, p. 232.
13. C.G. Jung, *Contributions to Analytical Psychology*, translated by H.G. and Cary F. Baynes, Kegan Paul, Trench, Trubner and Co. 1928, p. 185.
14. Emid Rideau, in George Appleton, *Journey for a Soul*, William Collins Sons and Co. 1976, p. 26.
15. Appleton, *Journey for a Soul*, 1976, p. 27.
16. Sir Sarvepalli Radhakrishnan, *Mahatma Gandhi*, George Allen and Unwin 1949, p. 18.
17. D.H. Lawrence, *The Phoenix*, edited by Edward D. McDonald, William Heinemann 1936, p. 528.
18. R.C. Zaehner, *Mysticism Sacred and Profance*, Oxford University Press 1967, p. 152.

## *Resurrection*

1. NRSV.
2. NRSV.
3. Alan Richardson, *History Sacred and Profane*, SCM Press 1964, p. 206.
4. Carlo Carretto, *The Desert in the City*, translated by Barbara Wall, William Collins Sons and Co. 1983, p. 103.
5. Austin Farrer, *Saving Belief*, Hodder and Stoughton 1964, p. 83.
6. Blaise Pascal, *Pensées*, translated by W.F. Trotter, Random House 1941, p. 77.
7. William Temple, *Nature, Man and God*, Macmillan and Co. 1934, p. 461.
8. Charles Kingsley, *Daily Thoughts*, Macmillan and Co. 1884, p. 171.
9. George Appleton, *Journey for a Soul*, William Collins Sons and Co. 1976, p. 16.
10. William Barclay, *The Letters to the Corinthians*, The Saint Andrew Press 1988, p. 141.
11. Michael Ramsey, in Margaret Duggan, *Through the Year with Michael Ramsey*, Hodder and Stoughton 1975, p. 71.
12. Michael Ramsey, in Gerald Priestland, *Priestland's Progress*, BBC Worldwide 1982, p. 111.
13. Henri J.M. Nouwen, in Robert Durback, *Seeds of Hope*, Darton, Longman and Todd 1989, p. 137.
14. Barclay, *The Letters to the Corinthians*, p. 141.
15. Anthony Bloom, *School for Prayer*, Darton, Longman and Todd 1970, p. xi.

## *Revelation*

1. NRSV.
2. NRSV.
3. Gerard Manley Hopkins, 'God's Grandeur', *The Poems of Gerard Manley Hopkins*, Oxford University Press 1967, p. 66.
4. Mark Rutherford, *More Pages from a Journal*, Oxford University Press 1910, p. 251.
5. Benjamin Whichcote, *Moral and Religious Aphorisms*, Elkin Mathews and Marrot 1930, p. 51.
6. Leo Tolstoy, *Anna Karenina*, translated by Rosemary Edmonds, Penguin Books 1983, p. 851.

7. Blaise Pascal, *Pensées*, translated by W.F. Trotter, Random House 1941, p. 98.
8. Walter Hilton, *The Ladder of Perfection*, translated by Leo Sherley-Price, Penguin Books 1957, p. 252.
9. Emil Brunner, *Our Faith*, translated by John W. Rilling, Charles Scribner's Sons 1936, p. 11.
10. Evelyn Underhill, *The School of Charity*, Longmans, Green and Co. 1956, p. 12.
11. Ralph Waldo Emerson, *The Heart of Emerson's Journals*, edited by Bliss Perry, Constable and Co. 1927, p. 53.
12. Francis Bacon, *The Advancement of Learning*, Cassell and Co. 1905, p. 81.
13. Gabriel Moran FSC, *Theology of Revelation*, Burns and Oates 1967, p. 127.
14. William Barclay, *The Gospel of John*, The Saint Andrew Press 1974, vol. II, p. 227.
15. William Temple, *Nature, Man and God*, Macmillan and Co. 1934, p. 266.
16. W.R. Inge, *Personal Religion and the Life of Devotion*, Longmans, Green and Co. 1924, p. 16.
17. Temple, *Nature, Man and God*, 1934, p. 319.
18. Barclay, *The Gospel of John*, vol. II, p. 227.

## *Saints*

1. NRSV.
2. NRSV.
3. Kenneth Leech, *True Prayer*, Sheldon Press 1980, p. 36.
4. Benedicta Ward, in Alan Richardson and John Bowden, *A New Dictionary of Christian Theology*, SCM Press 1985, p. 518.
5. Norman Douglas, *An Almanac*, Chatto and Windus in association with Martin Secker and Warburg 1945, p. 13.
6. Blaise Pascal, *Pensées*, translated by W.F. Trotter, Random House 1941, p. 165.
7. Kenneth Leech, *True Prayer*, Sheldon Press 1980, p. 36.
8. Anon.
9. Søren Kierkegaard, *The Journals of Søren Kierkegaard*, edited and translated by Alexander Dru, Oxford University Press 1938, p. 59.
10. Benjamin Jowett, *College Sermons*, edited by W.H. Fremantle, John Murray 1895, p. 317.
11. Coventry Patmore, *The Rod, the Root and the Flower*, 'Aurea Dicta', Grey Walls Press 1950, p. 51.
12. Rufus M. Jones, *Spiritual Reformers in the 16th and 17th Centuries*, Macmillan and Co. 1914, p. 336.
13. Evelyn Underhill, in John Stobbart, *The Wisdom of Evelyn Underhill*, Mowbray 1951, p. 30.
14. Meister Eckhart, in Franz Pfeiffer, *Meister Eckhart*, vol. 1, translated by C. de B. Evans, John M. Watkins 1956, p. 327.
15. W.E. Sangster, *The Pure in Heart*, Epworth Press 1954, p. 96.
16. W.H. Auden, *A Certain World*, Faber and Faber 1971, p. 331.
17. Thomas Merton, *Seeds of Contemplation*, Anthony Clarke Books 1972, p. 20.
18. Evelyn Underhill, *Man and the Supernatural*, Methuen and Co. 1927, p. 211.
19. W.R. Inge, *Types of Christian Saintliness*, Longmans, Green and Co. 1915, p. 92.
20. Thomas Merton, *The Sign of Jonas*, Sheldon Press 1976, p. 262.
21. Underhill in Stobbart, *The Wisdom of Evelyn Underhill*, p. 30.

## *Salvation*

1. NRSV.
2. NRSV.
3. Charles Péguy, *Basic Verities*, translated by Ann and Julian Green, Kegan Paul, Trench, Trubner and Co. 1943, p. 181.
4. Father Andrew SDC, *Meditations for Every Day*, A.R. Mowbray and Co. 1941, p. 164.
5. Frank Wright, *The Pastoral Nature of the Ministry*, SCM Press 1980, p. 16.
6. Don Cupitt, *Taking Leave of God*, SCM Press 1980, p. 9.
7. Norman W. Goodacre, *Laymen's Lent*, A.R. Mowbray and Co. 1969, p. 31.

8. C.G. Jung, *The Integration of the Personality*, Kegan Paul, Trench, Trubner and Co. 1941, p. 158.
9. George Macdonald, *Unspoken Sermons*, Longmans, Green and Co. 1889, Third Series, p. 96.
10. Henry McKeating, *God and the Future*, SCM Press 1974, p. 8.
11. William Barclay, *The Letters to the Corinthians*, The Saint Andrew Press 1988, p. 143.
12. William Law, in Stephen Hobhouse, *Selected Mystical Writings of William Law*, Rockliff 1948, p. 102.
13. Rufus M. Jones, *Spiritual Reformers in the 16th and 17th Centuries*, Macmillan and Co. 1914, p. 147.
14. William Temple, *Nature, Man and God*, Macmillan and Co. 1934, p. 390.
15. Henri Frédéric Amiel, *Amiel's Journal*, translated by Mrs Humphry Ward, Macmillan and Co. 1918, p. 70.
16. Thomas Merton, *No Man Is an Island*, Burns and Oates 1974, p. xiv.
17. Law in Hobhouse, *Selected Mystical Writings of William Law*, p. 102.

## *Science And Religion*

1. NRSV.
2. NRSV.
3. Albert Einstein, *Out of My Later Years*, Thames and Hudson 1950, p. 26.
4. Henry Ward Beecher, *Proverbs from Plymouth Pulpit*, Charles Burnet and Co. 1887, p. 118.
5. Michel Quoist, *With Open Heart*, translated by Colette Copeland, Gill and Macmillan 1983, p. 196.
6. G.A. Studdert Kennedy, *Food for the Fed-Up*, Hodder and Stoughton 1921, p. 34.
7. Helen Keller, *My Religion*, Hodder and Stoughton 1927, p. 162.
8. A.R. Orage, *On Love*, The Janus Press 1957, p. 57.
9. Henry Ward Beecher, *Proverbs from Plymouth Pulpit*, Charles Burnet and Co. 1887, p. 138.
10. Martin Luther King, *Strength to Love*, William Collins Sons and Co. 1980, p. 74.
11. Max Planck, *Where is Science Going?*, translated and edited by James Murphy, George Allen and Unwin 1933, p. 214.
12. J.W.N. Sullivan, *Limitations of Science*, Chatto and Windus 1933, p. 266.
13. William Temple, *Nature, Man and God*, Macmillan and Co. 1934, p. 11.
14. Planck, *Where is Science Going?*, p. 217.
15. Martin Luther King, in Coretta Scott King, *The Words of Martin Luther King*, William Collins Sons and Co. 1986, p. 63.
16. Michael Ramsey, in Margaret Duggan, *Through the Year with Michael Ramsey*, Hodder and Stoughton 1975, p. 147.
17. Temple, *Nature, Man and God*, p. 216.
18. Albert Einstein, *Ideas and Opinions*, Souvenir Press (Educational and Academic) 1973, p. 40.

## *Seeking*

1. NRSV.
2. NRSV.
3. Christopher Bryant SSJE, *Jung and the Christian Way*, Darton, Longman and Todd 1983, p. 105.
4. George Moore, *The Brook Kerith*, William Heinemann 1927, p. 121.
5. Arthur T. Jersild, *The Psychology of Adolescence*, The Macmillan Co. 1963, p. 10.
6. William Barclay, *The Gospel of Matthew*, The Saint Andrew Press 1975, vol. II, p. 17.
7. Rufus M. Jones, *Spiritual Reformers in the 16th and 17th Centuries*, Macmillan and Co. 1914, p. 24.
8. Thomas Merton, *Contemplation in a World of Action*, Unwin Paperbacks 1980, p. 231.
9. Meister Eckhart, *Meister Eckhart*, translated by Raymond B. Blakney, Harper and Row 1941, p. 167.
10. Etienne Gilson, *The Spirit of Medieval Philosophy*, translated by A.H.C. Downes, Sheed and Ward 1950, p. 274.
11. Stephen MacKenna, *Journal and Letters*, Constable and Co. 1936, p. 206.
12. A.C. Benson, *Extracts from the Letters of Dr A.C. Benson to M.E.A.*, Jarrold Publishing 1927, p. 15.

13. Eckhart, *Meister Eckhart*, p. 7.
14. Martin Luther King, in Coretta Scott King, *The Words of Martin Luther King*, William Collins Sons and Co. 1986, p. 64.
15. Thomas Merton, *New Seeds of Contemplation*, Burns and Oates 1962, p. 13.
16. Isobel Kuhn, *By Searching*, Overseas Missionary Fellowship (IHQ) 1990, p. 93.
17. Harry Blamires, *The Will and the Way*, SPCK 1957, p. x.

## *Self*

1. NRSV.
2. NRSV.
3. A.C. Benson, *Extracts from the Letters of Dr A.C. Benson to M.E.A.*, Jarrold Publishing 1927, p. 64.
4. Benjamin Whichcote, *Moral and Religious Aphorisms*, Elkin Mathews and Marrot 1930, p. 30.
5. Robert Browing, 'Bishop Blougram's Apology', *The Poetical Works of Robert Browning*, Smith, Elder, and Co. 1897, vol. 1, p. 533.
6. Mary Craig, *Blessings*, Hodder and Stoughton 1979, p. 104.
7. Matthew Arnold, 'Self-Dependence', edited by Kenneth Allott, Longmans, Green and Co. 1965, l.31, p. 144.
8. Albert Eistein, *Ideas and Opinions*, Souvenir Press (Educational and Academic) 1973, p. 12.
9. Michel Quoist, *With Open Heart*, translated by Colette Copeland, Gill and Macmillan 1983, p. 41.
10. D.H. Lawrence, *The Phoenix*, edited by Edward D. McDonald, William Heinemann 1936, p. 714.
11. William Law, *A Serious Call to a Devout and Holy Life*, J.M. Dent and Sons 1898, p. 288.
12. W.R. Inge, *The Philosophy of Plotinus*, Longmans, Green and Co. 1918, vol. 1, p. 248.
13. Henry Wadsworth Longfellow, 'The Poems', *The Poetical Works of Longfellow*, Humphrey Milford, Oxford University Press 1913, p. 717.
14. John S. Brubacher, *Modern Philosophies of Education,* McGraw-Hill Book Co. 1969, p. 9.
15. David Anderson, *Simone Weil*, SCM Press 1971, p. 61.
16. William Barclay, *The Letters to Timothy, Titus and Philemon*, The Saint Andrew Press 1987, p. 184.
17. William Law, *The Spirit of Prayer*, full text, edited by Sidney Spencer, James Clarke and Co. 1969, p. 44.
18. Anne Morrow Lindbergh, *Gift from the Sea*, Chatto and Windus 1974, p. 68.
19. John Macquarrie, *Paths in Spirituality*, SCM Press 1972, p. 45.
20. Harry James Cargas, *Encountering Myself*, SPCK 1978, p. 14.

## *Selfishness*

1. NRSV.
2. NRSV.
3. Taoist saying.
4. Edward Young, *Night Thoughts*, Thomas Nelson 1841, p. 8.
5. Henry Ward Beecher, *Proverbs from Plymouth Pulpit*, Charles Burnet and Co. 1887, p. 191.
6. Robert Browning, 'Luria', *The Poetical Works of Robert Browning*, vol. 1, Smith, Elder and Co. 1899, act 1, p. 441.
7. Thomas Merton, *The Sign of Jonas*, Sheldon Press 1976, p. 102.
8. Norman Douglas, *An Almanac*, Chatto and Windus in association with Martin Secker and Warburg 1945, p. 60.
9. Henry Ward Beecher, *Proverbs from Plymouth Pulpit*, Charles Burnet and Co. 1887, p. 49.
10. A.R. Orage, *On Love*, The Janus Press 1957, p. 60.
11. Erich Fromm, *Man for Himself*, Routledge and Kegan Paul 1975, p. 131.
12. Beecher, *Proverbs from Plymouth Pulpit*, p. 154.
13. John Woolman, *The Journal of John Woolman*, Edward Marsh 1857, p. 311.
14. Martin Luther King, in Coretta Scott King, *The Words of Martin Luther King*, William Collins Sons and Co. 1986, p. 17.

15. William James, *The Varieties of Religious Experience*, William Collins Sons and Co. 1974, p. 136.
16. Morris West, *The Shoes of the Fisherman*, William Heinemann 1963, p. 296.
17. Pierre Teilhard de Chardin, *Let Me Explain*, William Collins Sons and Co. 1970, p. 137.
18. William Temple, *The Kingdom of God*, Macmillan Publishers 1912, p. 96.
19. William Temple, *The Preacher's Theme Today*, SPCK 1936, p. 52.
20. William Temple, *Nature, Man and God*, Macmillan and Co. 1934, p. 424.
21. George Appleton, *Journey for a Soul*, William Collins Sons and Co. 1976, p. 121.

## *Serenity*

1. NRSV.
2. RSV.
3. Cyril Connolly, *The Unquiet Grave*, Hamish Hamilton 1945, p. 13.
4. Reinhold Niebuhr, *Reflections on the End of an Era*, Charles Scribner's Sons 1936, p. 284.
5. Benjamin Whichcote, *Moral and Religious Aphorisms* 1930, century III, no.280.
6. Matthew Prior, 'Carmen Seculare for the Year MDCC', *The Poetical Works of Matthew Prior*, edited by Charles Cowden Clarke, William P. Nimmo 1868, p. 116.
7. William Barclay, *The Gospel of Matthew*, The Saint Andrew Press 1975, vol. II, p. 37.
8. Odell Shepard, *The Joys of Forgetting*, George Allen and Unwin 1928, p. 22.
9. Washington Irving, *The Sketch-Book*, George Newnes 1902, vol. 11, p. 226.
10. William Johnston, *The Mysticism of the Cloud of Unknowing*, Anthony Clarke Books 1978, p 265.
11. William Wordsworth, in W.E. Sangster, *The Secret of Radiant Life*, Hodder and Stoughton 1957, p. 14.
12. Henry Miller, *The Books in My Life*, Village Press 1974, p. 59.
13. Arthur T. Jersild, in *Educational Psychology*, edited by Charles E. Skinner, Staples Press 1952, p. 93.
14. Henri Frédéric Amiel, *Amiel's Journal*, translated by Mrs Humphry Ward, Macmillan and Co., p. 263.
15. Alistair Maclean, in *God in Our Midst*, Triangle/SPCK 1989, p. 27.
16. William Wordsworth, 'Ode to Duty', *The Poetical Works of William Wordsworth*, edited by E. de Selincourt and Helen Darbishire, Oxford at the Clarendon Press 1958, vol. IV, p. 84.
17. Romain Gary, *Promise at Dawn*, Michael Joseph 1962, p. 26.
18. George Appleton, *Journey for a Soul*, William Collins Sons and Co. 1976, p. 99.
19. Amiel, *Amiel's Journal*, p. 263.

## *Service*

1. NRSV.
2. NRSV.
3. George Herbert, 'The Church Porch', *The Works of George Herbert*, edited by F.E. Hutchinson, Oxford at the Clarendon Press 1972, p. 19.
4. Rabindranath Tagore, *Stray Birds*, *Collected Poems and Plays of Rabindranath Tagore*, Macmillan and Co. 1936, lvi, p. 294.
5. John Milton, 'Sonnet on His Blindness', *John Milton: Complete Shorter Poems*, edited by John Carey, Longmans Group 1971, 83, Sonnet XVI, l.14, p. 328.
6. Dietrich Bonhoeffer, *The Cost of Discipleship*, revised and abridged edition, SCM Press 1959, p. 118.
7. St Francis de Sales, *On the Love of God*, Methuen and Co. 1902, p. 94.
8. Dag Hammarskjöld, *Markings*, translated by Leif Sjoberg and W.H. Auden, Faber and Faber 1964, p. 135.
9. Rabindranath Tagore, *Stray Birds*, *Collected Poems and Plays of Rabindranath Tagore*, Macmillan and Co. 1936, ccxvii, p. 315.
10. A.R. Orage, *On Love*, The Janus Press 1957, p. 61.
11. Hans Küng, *On Being a Christian*, translated by Edward Quinn, William Collins Sons and Co. 1977, p. 253.

12. Hubert van Zeller, *Considerations*, Sheed and Ward 1974, p. 124.
13. William Temple, *Readings in St John's Gospel*, first and second series, Macmillan and Co. 1947, p. 258.
14. Emil Brunner, *The Divine Imperative*, translated by Olive Wyon, Lutterworth Press 1942, p. 189.
15. Evelyn Underhill, *The Light of Christ*, Longmans, Green and Co. 1944, p. 94.
16. E.G. Rupp, in Alan Richardson and John Bowden, *A New Dictionary of Christian Theology*, SCM Press 1985, p. 441.
17. Albert Schweitzer, *My Life and Thought*, translated by C.T. Campion, George Allen and Unwin 1933, p. 103.
18. Martin Luther King, in Coretta Scott King, *The Words of Martin Luther King*, William Collins Sons and Co. 1986, p. 17.
19. Henri Frédéric Amiel, *Amiel's Journal*, translated by Mrs Humphry Ward, Macmillan and Co. 1918, p 147.
20. D.H. Lawrence, 'Service', *The Complete Poems of D.H. Lawrence*, edited by Vivian de Sola Pinto and Warren Roberts, William Heinemann 1967, vol. II, p. 650.

## *Sin*

1. NRSV.
2. NRSV.
3. St Augustine, *Confessions*, translated by R.S. Pine-Coffin, Penguin Books 1964, p. 33.
4. G.W.H. Lampe, in A.R. Vidler, *Soundings*, Cambridge at the University Press 1962, p. 186.
5. James Rhoades, in Ralph Waldo Trine, *My Philosophy and My Relgion*, George Bell and Sons 1926, p. 27.
6. George Bernard Shaw, *The Devil's Disciple*, *The Complete Plays of Bernard Shaw*, Paul Hamlyn 1965, act II, p. 230.
7. J. Neville Ward, *The Use of Praying*, Epworth Press 1967, p. 45.
8. C.S. Lewis, *The Screwtape Letters*, William Collins Sons and Co. 1960, p. 65.
9. Eric Hoffer, *The Passionate State of Mind*, Secker and Warburg 1956, p. 70.
10. Martin Buber, *Hasidism*, The Philosophical Library 1948, p. 71.
11. Hubert van Zeller, *Considerations*, Sheed and Ward 1974, p. 49.
12. Harvey Cox, *God's Revolution and Man's Responsibility*, SCM Press 1969, p. 40.
13. Walter Hilton, *The Ladder of Perfection*, translated by Leo Sherley-Price, Penguin Books 1957, p. 109.
14. George Appleton, *Journey for a Soul*, William Collins Sons and Co. 1976, p. 122.
15. Phyllis McGinley, *The Province of the Heart*, The World's Work (1913) 1962, p. 35.
16. Father Yelchaninov, in G.P. Fedotov, *A Treasury of Russian Spirituality*, Sheed and Ward 1977, p. 461.
17. William Temple, *Christian Faith and Life*, SCM Press 1963, p. 65.
18. Appleton, *Journey for a Soul*, p. 122.
19. Kenneth Barnes, in Gerald Priestland, *Priestland's Progress*, BBC Worldwide 1982, p. 72.
20. J.S. Whale, *Christian Doctrine*, Cambridge University Press 1942, p. 52.

## *Soul*

1. NRSV.
2. NRSV.
3. James A. Froude, *Thomas Carlyle*, Longmans, Green, and Co. 1884, vol. 2, p. 35.
4. Henry Miller, *The Books in My Life*, Village Press 1974, p. 212.
5. Henry Ward Beecher, *Proverbs from Plymouth Pulpit*, Charles Burnet and Co. 1887, p. 153.
6. Rabindranath Tagore, *Stray Birds*, *Collected Poems and Plays of Rabindranath Tagore*, Macmillan and Co. 1936, cccxii, p. 327.
7. Miller, *The Books in My Life*, p. 193.
8. Beecher, *Proverbs from Plymouth Pulpit*, p. 27.
9. St John of the Cross, *Living Flame of Love*, translated by E. Allison Peers, Image Books 1962, p. 40.

10. Richard Jefferies, *The Story of My Heart*, Macmillan and Co. 1968, p. 8.
11. Henry Ward Beecher, *Proverbs from Plymouth Pulpit*, Charles Burnet and Co. 1887, p. 31.
12. Jean-Pierre de Caussade SJ, *Self-Abandonment to Divine Providence*, translated by Algar Thorold, William Collins Sons and Co. 1972, p. 37.
13. C.G. Jung, *The Collected Works of C.G. Jung*, translated by R.F.C. Hull, Routledge and Kegan Paul 1953, vol. XII, p. 8.
14. Beecher, *Proverbs from Plymouth Pulpit*, p. 31.
15. Richard Jefferies, *The Story of My Heart*, Duckworth and Co. 1923, p. 143.
16. Meister Eckhart, *Meister Eckhart*, translated by Raymond B. Blakney, Harper and Row 1941, p. 97.
17. Matthew Arnold, 'A Southern Night', *The Poems of Matthew Arnold*, edited by Kenneth Allott, Longmans, Green and Co. 1965, p. 460.
18. Oscar Wilde, *De Profundis*, *The Works of Oscar Wilde*, William Collins Sons and Co. 1948, p. 870.
19. Samuel Taylor Coleridge, *Table Talk of Samuel Taylor Coleridge*, George Routledge and Sons 1884, p. 33.
20. Henri Frédéric Amiel, *Amiel's Journal*, translated by Mrs Humphry Ward, Macmillan and Co. 1918, p. 247.

## *Suffering*

1. NRSV.
2. NRSV.
3. Greek proverb.
4. Latin proverb.
5. Martin Luther King, in Coretta Scott King, *The Words of Martin Luther King*, William Collins Sons and Co. 1986, p. 67.
6. Helen Keller, *Optimism*, George G. Harrop 1903, p. 17.
7. George Eliot, *Adam Bede*, J.M. Dent and Sons 1960, p. 409.
8. Henry Wadsworth Longfellow, 'The Light of Stars', *The Poetical Works of Longfellow*, edited by Humphrey Milford, Oxford University Press 1913, p. 4.
9. C.G. Jung, *Psychology and Alchemy*, *The Collected Works of C.G. Jung*, vol. XII, translated by R.F.C. Hull, Routledge and Kegan Paul 1953, p. 22.
10. A.C. Benson, *Extracts from the Letters of Dr A.C. Benson to M.E.A.*, Jarrold Publishing 1927, p. 13.
11. F.W. Robertson, *Sermons*, fifth series, Kegan Paul, Trench, Trubner and Co. 1890, p. 17.
12. J. Neville Ward, *Friday Afternoon*, Epworth Press 1982, p. 97.
13. Rabbi H. Kushner, *When Bad Things Happen to Good People*, Pan Books 1982, p. 142.
14. Hubert van Zeller, *Considerations*, Sheed and Ward 1974, p. 122.
15. Hans Küng, *On Being a Christian*, translated by Edward Quinn, William Collins Sons and Co. 1977, p. 299.
16. George Appleton, *Journey for a Soul*, William Collins Sons and Co. 1976, p. 51.
17. John V. Taylor, *The Go-Between God*, SCM Press 1973, p. 146.
18. Hugh L'Anson Fausset, *Fruits of Silence*, Abelard-Schuman 1963, p. 197.
19. Appleton, *Journey for a Soul*, p. 50.

## *Temptation*

1. NRSV.
2. NRSV.
3. Thomas Fuller, *Gnomologia*, Stearne Brock 1733, p. 21.
4. Ralph Waldo Emerson, 'Compensation', *Essays*, Bernhard Tauchnitz 1915, p. 84.
5. Charles Dickens, *Nicholas Nickleby*, The Gresham Publishing Co. 1904, p. 36.
6. Thomas à Kempis, *The Imitation of Christ*, translated by Betty I. Knott, William Collins Sons and Co. 1979, p. 53.
7. Lady Julian of Norwich, *Revelations of Divine Love*, translated by Clifton Wolters, Penguin Books 1976, p. 185.

8. Robert Herrick, 'Temptations', *The Poetical Works of Robert Herrick*, edited by F.W. Moorman, Oxford at the Clarendon Press 1915, p. 389.
9. F. de la M. Fénelon, in B.W. Randolph, *Letters and Reflections of Fénelon*, A.R. Mowbray and Co. 1906, p. 93.
10. William Temple, *Readings in St John's Gospel*, first and second series, Macmillan and Co. 1947, p. xxvi.
11. William Barclay, *The Gospel of Luke*, The Saint Andrew Press 1965, p. 146.
12. Robert Burns, 'A Prayer in the Prospect of Death', edited by James Kinsley, *The Poems and Songs of Robert Burns*, Oxford at the Clarendon Press 1968, vol. 1, p. 20.
13. Thomas à Kempis, *The Imitation of Christ*, p. 53.
14. Edmund Spenser, 'The Faerie Queene', edited by J.C. Smith, Oxford at the Clarendon Press 1964, p. 95.
15. William James, *The Principles of Psychology*, Macmillan and Co. 1890, vol. 1, p. 127.
16. Olive Wyon, *On the Way*, SCM Press 1958, p. 55.
17. John Tauler, *The History and Life of the Reverend Doctor John Tauler*, translated by Susanna Winkworth, Smith, Elder and Co. 1857, p. 404.
18. Fénelon in Randolph, *Letters and Reflections of Fénelon*, p. 93.

## *Thanksgiving*

1. NRSV.
2. NRSV.
3. Theodor Haecker, *Journal in the Night*, translated by Alexander Dru, The Harvill Press 1950, p. 1.
4. Samuel Johnson, *Boswell's Life of Johnson*, vol. V, edited by G.B. Hill, revised by L.F. Powell, Oxford at the Clarendon Press 1950, p. 232.
5. Kahlil Gibran, *The Prophet*, William Heinemann 1970, p. 15.
6. Izaak Walton, *The Compleat Angler*, Macmillan and Co. 1906, p. 172.
7. William Shakespeare, *II King Henry VI*, act II.i.85.
8. G.K. Chesterton, *Autobiography*, Hutchinson and Co. 1969, p. 330.
9. Elizabeth Helme, *St Margaret's Cave; or, The Nun's Story*, printed for Earle and Hemet 1801, vol. 2, p. 141.
10. Michael Ramsey, in Margaret Duggan, *Through the Year with Michael Ramsey*, Hodder and Stoughton 1975, p. 82.
11. Anon.
12. W.E. Sangster, *Westminster Sermons*, Epworth Press 1961, vol. 2, *At Fast and Festival*, p. 140.
13. Edward King, *Sermons and Addresses*, Longmans, Green and Co. 1911, p. 37.
14. Charles Kingsley, *Town and Country Sermons*, Macmillan and Co. 1868, p. 99.
15. William Law, *A Serious Call to a Devout and Holy Life*, J.M. Dent and Co. 1898, p. 231.
16. A.J. Gossip, *From the Edge of the Crowd*, T. and T. Clark 1925, p. 37.
17. Law, *A Serious Call to a Devout and Holy Life*, p. 231.
18. Edward King, *Sermons and Addresses*, Longmans, Green and Co. 1911, p. 37.

## *Thinking*

1. NRSV.
2. NRSV.
3. William Blake, 'Proverbs of Hell', *The Complete Writings of William Blake*, edited by Geoffrey Keynes, Oxford University Press 1974, p. 151.
4. Ralph Waldo Emerson, 'Intellect', *Essays*, Bernhard Tauchnitz Edition 1915, p. 191.
5. Rabindranath Tagore, *Stray Birds*, *Collected Poems and Plays of Rabindranath Tagore*, Macmillan and Co. 1936, clxix, p. 308.
6. O.T. Beard, *Bristling with Thorns*, The Gregg Press 1968, p. 400.
7. Albert Schweitzer, *Out of My Life and Thought*, Henry Holt and Co. 1949, p. 236.
8. W.A. Macgregor, *Jesus Christ the Son of God*, T. and T. Clark 1907, p. 99.
9. Henry Wadsworth Longfellow, 'The Masque of Pandora', *The Poetical Works of Longfellow*, Humphrey Milford, Oxford University Press 1913, p. 688.

10. Thomas Mann, *Death in Venice*, translated by H.T. Lowe-Porter, Penguin Books 1978, p. 52.
11. Bertrand Russell, *Principles of Social Reconstruction*, George Allen and Unwin 1971, p. 155.
12. Albert Schweitzer, *The Teaching of Reverence for Life*, Peter Owen 1965, p. 33.
13. Mark Rutherford, *Last Pages from a Journal*, Oxford University Press 1915, p. 272.
14. William James, *The Varieties of Religious Experience*, William Collins Sons and Co. 1974, p. 119.
15. Helen Merry Lynd, *On Shame and the Search for Identity*, Routledge and Kegan Paul 1958, p. 251.
16. Daniel Defoe, *Moll Flanders*, Arandar Books 1946, p. 245.
17. Albert Schweitzer, *My Life and Thought*, translated by C.T. Campion, George Allen and Unwin 1933, p. 260.
18. Bertrand Russell, *Principles of Social Reconstruction*, George Allen and Unwin 1971, p. 114.
19. Michael Ramsey, in Margaret Duggan, *Through the Year with Michael Ramsey*, Hodder and Stoughton 1975, p. 24.
20. Russell, *Principles of Social Reconstruction*, p. 155.

## *Time*

1. NRSV.
2. NRSV.
3. Benjamin Disraeli, *Henrietta Temple*, John Lane, The Bodley Head 1906, p. 430.
4. William Shakespeare, *Macbeth*, act III.i.48.
5. Johann Wolfgang von Goethe, in Ludwig Curtius, *Wisdom and Experience*, translated and edited by Hermann J. Weigand, Routledge and Kegan Paul 1949, p. 216.
6. Martin Luther King, in Coretta Scott King, *The Words of Martin Luther King*, William Collins Sons and Co. 1986, p. 33.
7. Sir John Lubbock, *The Pleasures of Life*, Macmillan and Co. 1881, p. 109.
8. Rollo May, *Man's Search for Himself*, George Allen and Unwin 1953, p. 259.
9. Dietrich Bonhoeffer, *Letters and Papers from Prison*, William Collins Sons and Co. 1963, p. 134.
10. Hubert van Zeller, *Considerations*, Sheed and Ward 1974, p. 60.
11. *The Cloud of Unknowing*, translated by Clifton Wolters, Penguin Books 1971, p. 56.
12. Peter Munz, *Problems of Religious Knowledge*, SCM Press 1959, p. 129.
13. Leslie J. Tizard, *Facing Life and Death*, George Allen and Unwin 1959, p. 162.
14. Meister Eckhard, in Franz Pfeiffer, *Meister Eckhart*, translated by C. de B. Evans, John M. Watkins 1956, vol. 1, p. 237.
15. Michel Quoist, *Prayers of Life*, translated by Anne Marie de Commaile and Agnes Mitchell Forsyth, Gill and Macmillan 1963, p. 76.
16. Henry Wadsworth Longfellow, 'Hyperion', George Routledge and Sons 1887, p. 123.
17. Anon. (on T.S. Eliot's 'Four Quartets').
18. Michel Quoist, *With Open Heart*, translated by Colette Copeland, Gill and Macmillan 1983, p. 137.
19. Mother Teresa, in Kathryn Spink, *In the Silence of the Heart*, SPCK 1983, p. 42.
20. George Appleton, *Journey for a Soul*, William Collins Sons and Co. 1976, p. 221.

## *Transformation*

1. NRSV.
2. NRSV.
3. Nicolas Berdyaev, in Donald A. Lowrie, *Christian Existentialism*, George Allen and Unwin 1965, p. 248.
4. Martin Luther King, in Coretta Scott King, *The Words of Martin Luther King*, William Collins Sons and Co. 1986, p. 18.
5. Henry Ward Beecher, *Proverbs from Plymouth Pulpit*, Charles Burnet and Co. 1887, p. 161.
6. Martin Buber, in Aubrey Hodes, *Encounter with Martin Buber*, Allen Lane, The Penguin Press 1972, p. 83.
7. Francois de la M. Fénelon, in B.W. Randolph, *Maxims of the Mystics*, translated by W.W. Williams, A.R. Mowbray and Co. 1909, p. 104.

8. Maurice Maeterlinck, *The Treasure of the Humble*, translated by Alfred Sutro, George Allen, 1897, p. 185.
9. John Main OSB, in Clare Hallward, *The Joy of Being*, Darton, Longman and Todd 1989, p. 9.
10. William Barclay, *The Letters to Timothy and Titus*, The Saint Andrew Press 1965, p. 245.
11. E.Graham Howe and L. le Mesurier, *The Open Way*, Methuen and Co. 1939, p. 180.
12. Alan Ecclestone, *Yes to God*, Darton, Longman and Todd 1975, p. 116.
13. Henri Frédéric Amiel, *Amiel's Journal*, translated by Mrs Humphry Ward, Macmillan and Co. 1918, p. 285.
14. Helmut Thielicke, *I Believe – The Christian's Creed*, translated by John W. Doberstein and H. George Anderson, William Collins Sons and Co. 1969, p. 90.
15. Amiel, *Amiel's Journal*, p. 104.
16. Bede Griffiths OSB, in Peter Spink, *The Universal Christ*, Darton, Longman and Todd 1990, p. 27.
17. Hans Küng, *On Being a Christian*, translated by Edward Quinn, William Collins Sons and Co. 1977, p. 249.
18. Mark Rutherford, *More Pages from a Journal*, Oxford University Press 1910, p. 182.

## *Trust*

1. NRSV.
2. NRSV.
3. George Herbert, *Outlandish Proverbs*, *The Works of George Herbert*, edited by F.E. Hutchinson, Oxford at the Clarendon Press 1972, p. 345.
4. Rabindranath Tagore, *Stray Birds*, *Collected Poems and Plays of Rabindranath Tagore*, Macmillan and Co. 1936, cccxxv, p. 329.
5. W.E. Sangster, *He is Able*, Hodder and Stoughton 1936, p. 42.
6. Henry Ward Beecher, *Proverbs from Plymouth Pulpit*, Charles Burnet and Co. 1887, p. 173.
7. Mark Gibbard, *Jesus, Liberation and Love*, A.R. Mowbray and Co. 1982, p. 55.
8. Beecher, *Proverbs from Plymouth Pulpit*, p. 145.
9. W.E. Sangster, *He Is Able*, Hodder and Stoughton 1936, p. 23.
10. Ralph Waldo Emerson, *Essays and Representative Men*, *The Works of Ralph Waldo Emerson*, edited by George Sampson, George Bell and Sons 1906, vol. 1, p. 128.
11. Charles Kingsley, *Daily Thoughts*, Macmillan and Co. 1884, p. 239.
12. A.W. Robinson, *The Personal Life of the Clergy*, Longmans, Green and Co. 1902, p. 157.
13. William Temple, *The Hope of a New World*, SCM Press 1940, p. 28.
14. John Greenleaf Whittier, 'The Brewing of Soma', *The Poetical Works of John Greenleaf Whittier*, Macmillan and Co. 1874, p. 457.
15. Leslie Tizard, *Facing Life and Death*, George Allen and Unwin 1959, p. 73.
16. Ralph Waldo Emerson, *Self-Reliance*, *The Works of Ralph Waldo Emerson*, George Bell and Sons 1906, vol. 1, *Essays and Representative Men*, p. 24.
17. George Appleton, *The Journey of a Soul*, William Collins Sons and Co. 1976, p. 84.
18. Kingsley, *Daily Thoughts*, p. 165.

## *Truth*

1. NRSV.
2. NRSV.
3. Herman Melville, *Typee*, Heron Books 1968, p. 203.
4. Geoffrey Chaucer, *The Franklin's Tale*, G. Routledge and Co. 1838, p. 319.
5. Norman Douglas, *An Almanac*, Chatto and Windus in association with Martin Secker and Warburg, 1945, p. 37.
6. Henry David Thoreau, *Walden*, The New American Library of World Literature 1960, p. 219.
7. Rufus M. Jones, *Spiritual Reformers in the 16th and 17th Centuries*, Macmillan and Co. 1914, p. 90.
8. Kahlil Gibran, *The Prophet*, William Heinemann 1970, p. 66.
9. Maurice Maeterlinck, *The Treasure of the Humble*, translated by Alfred Sutro, George Allen 1897, p. 187.

10. F.W. Robertson, *Sermons,* first series, Kegan Paul, Trench, Trubner and Co. 1893, p. 289.
11. Johann Wolfgang von Goethe, in Ludwig Curtius, *Wisdom and Experience*, translated and edited by Hermann J. Weigang, Routledge and Kegan Paul 1949, p. 212.
12. D.H. Lawrence, *The Rainbow*, Cambridge University Press 1989, p. 317.
13. Albert Schweitzer, *Out of My Life and Thought*, translated by C.T. Campion, Henry Holt and Co. 1949, p. 249.
14. Robert Browning, 'The Ring and the Book', *The Complete Poetical Works of Robert Browning*, Ohio University Press 1988, vol. 8, vi. 2038, p. 156.
15. Albert Einstein, *Out of My Later Years*, Thames and Hudson 1950, p. 115.
16. William Barclay, *The Gospel of Luke*, The Saint Andrew Press 1964, p. 79.
17. Robertson, *Sermons*, p. 286.
18. Sydney Carter, *Dance in the Dark*, William Collins Sons and Co. 1980, p. 26.
19. W.E. Sangster, *The Pure in Heart*, Epworth Press 1954, p. 3.
20. Alistair MacLean, *The Happy Finder*, Allenson and Co. 1949, p. 71.
21. George Macdonald, *Unspoken Sermons*, third series, Longmans, Green and Co. 1889, p. 79.
22. William Temple, *Readings in St John's Gospel*, first and second series, Macmillan and Co. 1947, p. 230.
23. Albert Schweizer, *Christianity and the Religions of the World*, translated by Joanna Powers, George Allen and Unwin 1924, p. 18.
24. William Barclay, *The Gospel of John*, The Saint Andrew Press 1965, vol. 2, p. 25.

## *Understanding*

1. NRSV.
2. NRSV.
3. Isadora Duncan, *My Life*, Sphere Books 1968, p. 60.
4. Søren Kierkegaard, in Harold Loukes, *The Quaker Contribution*, SCM Press 1965, p. 9.
5. J.B. Yeats, *Letters to His Son, W.B. Yeats and Others*, Faber and Faber 1944, p. 136.
6. Blaise Pascal, *Pensées*, translated by W.F. Trotter, Random House 1941, p. 277.
7. Andre Gidé, *The Journals of André Gide* 1894, translated by Justin O'Brien, Martin Secker and Warburg 1947, p. 41.
8. Ernest Hello, *Life, Science, and Art*, R. and T. Washbourne 1913, p. 106.
9. John Smith the Platonist, *Select Discourses*, Cambridge at the University Press 1859, p. 3.
10. Vincent van Gogh, *Dear Theo: An Autobiography of Vincent van Gogh*, edited by Irving Stone, Constable and Co. 1937, p. 28.
11. Harper Lee, *To Kill a Mockingbird*, Pan Books 1981, p. 35.
12. Erich Fromm, *Man for Himself*, Routledge and Kegan Paul 1975, p. 237.
13. Norman Douglas, *An Almanac*, Chatto and Windus in association with Martin Secker and Warburg 1945, p. 82.
14. Albert Einstein, *Ideas and Opinions*, Souvenir Press (Educational and Academic) 1973, p. 53.
15. René Voillaume, *The Need for Contemplation*, translated by Elizabeth Hamilton, Darton, Longman and Todd 1972, p. 58.
16. Katherine Mansfield, *Journal of Katherine Mansfield*, edited by John Middleton Murry, Constable and Co. 1927, p. 251.
17. Henry Miller, *The Cosmological Eye*, New Directions 1939, p. 282.
18. Søren Kierkegaard, *The Journals of Kierkegaard*, Harper and Row 1959, p. 68.
19. William Barclay, *The Gospel of John*, The Saint Andrew Press 1974, vol. 2, p. 93.
20. W. MacNeile Dixon, *The Human Situation*, Edward Arnold 1937, p. 64.

## *Vision*

1. NRSV.
2. NRSV.
3. Thomas Traherne, *Centuries*, The Faith Press 1969, p. 71.
4. J.B. Yeats, *Letters to His Son, W.B. Yeats and Others*, Faber and Faber 1944, p. 179.

5. Charles Fletcher Dole, *The Hope of Immortality*, Houghton Mifflin Co., The Riverside Press 1906, p. 59.
6. Malaval, in Evelyn Underhill, *Mysticism*, Methuen and Co. 1912, p. 305.
7. Sir Richard Livingston, *On Education*, Cambridge at the University Press 1954, p. 151.
8. Mark Rutherford, *More Pages from a Journal*, Oxford University Press 1910, p. 220.
9. Ralph Waldo Emerson, *The Poet,* from *Essays and Representative Men*, *The Works of Ralph Waldo Emerson*, George Bell and Sons 1906, vol. 1, p. 213.
10. Rabindranath Tagore, *The Religion of Man*, George Allen and Unwin 1931, p. 117.
11. George Macdonald, *Cross Purposes and the Shadows*, Blackie and Son, 1891, p. 62.
12. Evelyn Underhill, edited by Charles Williams, *The Letters of Evelyn Underhill*, Longmans, Green and Co. 1947, p. 51.
13. Sir Sarvepalli Radhakrishnan, *Indian Philosophy*, George Allen and Unwin 1931, vol. II, p. 373.
14. Alfred North Whitehead, *Science and the Modern World*, Cambridge at the University Press 1932, p. 238.
15. Aldous Huxley, *Heaven and Hell*, Chatto and Windus 1956, p. 52.
16. Radhakrishnan, *Indian Philosophy*, p. 373.
17. J.W.N. Sullivan, *But for the Grace of God*, Jonathan Cape 1932, p. 133.
18. Alfred North Whitehead, *Science and the Modern World*, Cambridge at the University Press 1932, p. 238.

## *Vocation*

1. NRSV.
2. NRSV.
3. Logan Pearsall Smith, *Afterthoughts*, Constable and Co. 1931, p. 54.
4. William Barclay, *The Gospel of Matthew*, The Saint Andrew Press 1965, vol. 2, p. 19.
5. Henry Ward Beecher, *Proverbs from Plymouth Pulpit*, Charles Burnet and Co. 1887, p. 48.
6. F.R. Barry, *Vocation and Ministry*, James Nisbet and Co. 1958, p. 8.
7. Henri Frédéric Amiel, *Amiel's Journal*, translated by Mrs Humphry Ward, Macmillan and Co. 1918, p. 45.
8. Plato, *The Republic of Plato*, translated by B. Jowett, Oxford at the Clarendon Press 1881, p. 49.
9. Beecher, *Proverbs from Plymouth Pulpit*, p. 165.
10. William Temple, *Christian Faith and Life*, SCM Press 1963, p. 107.
11. Michel Quoist, *With Open Heart*, translated by Colette Copeland, Gill and Macmillan 1983, p. 49.
12. Mother Teresa, in Brother Angelo Devananda, *Jesus, the Word to Be Spoken*, William Collins Sons and Co. 1990, p. 89.
13. Rosemay Haughton, *On Trying to Be Human*, Geoffrey Chapman 1966, p. 33.
14. William Barclay, *The Gospel of John*, The Saint Andrew Press 1965, vol. 1, p. 40.
15. Ralph Waldo Emerson, *Spiritual Laws*, *Essays*, Bernhard Tauchnitz 1915, p. 120.
16. Temple, *Christian Faith and Life*, p. 44.
17. Henry Drummond, *The Greatest Thing in the World*, William Collins Sons and Co. 1978, p. 291.
18. Temple, *Christian Faith and Life*, p. 139.

## *Wholeness*

1. NRSV.
2. NRSV.
3. Rabindranath Tagore, *Stray Birds*, Indian edition, Macmillan and Co. 1941, p. 42.
4. Monica Furlong, *Travelling In*, Hodder and Stoughton 1971, p. 64.
5. Anon.
6. Aldous Huxley, *Island*, Chatto and Windus 1962, p. 92.
7. A.R. Orage, *On Love*, The Janus Press 1957, p. 59.
8. William of St Thierry, *The Golden Epistles of Abbot William of St Thierry*, Sheed and Ward 1930, p. 45.

9. Rabindranath Tagore, *Letters to a Friend*, George Allen and Unwin 1928, p. 55.
10. Jack Dominion, in Gerald Priestland, *Priestland's Progress*, BBC Worldwide 1982, p. 82.
11. Sir Julian Huxley, *Religion Without Revelation*, C.A. Watts and Co. 1967, p. 168.
12. George Appleton, *Journey for a Soul*, William Collins Sons and Co. 1976, p. 110.
13. Thomas Merton, *New Seeds of Contemplation*, Burns and Oates 1962, p. 106.
14. Morris West, *The Shoes of the Fisherman*, William Heinemann 1983, p. 204.
15. Colin Morris, *The Word and the Words*, Epworth Press 1975, p. 15.
16. Olive Wyon, *On the Way*, SCM Press 1958, p. 30.

## *Will*

1. NRSV.
2. NRSV.
3. Dante Alighieri, *The Divine Comedy*, translated by Charles S. Singleton, Princeton University Press, Bollingen Series, LXXX 1977, vol. 1, 'Paradisio', iii.85.
4. John Milton, 'Paradise Lost', *The Poetical Works of John Milton*, edited by the Rev. H.C. Beeching, Oxford at the Clarendon Press 1900, book 1, p. 184.
5. Mother Teresa, in Brother Angelo Devananda, *Jesus, the Word to Be Spoken*, William Collins Sons and Co. 1990, p. 98.
6. William Barclay, *The Gospel of Matthew*, The Saint Andrew Press 1965, vol. 1, p. 127.
7. Vincent van Gogh, *Dear Theo: An Autobiography*, edited by Irving Stone, Constable and Co. 1937, p. 187.
8. John Smith the Platonist, *Select Discourses*, Cambridge at the University Press 1859, p. 9.
9. George Macdonald, *Unspoken Sermons*, Third Series, Longmans, Green and Co. 1889, p. 229.
10. Father Andrew SDC, *The Life and Letters of Fr Andrew SDC*, Mowbray 1948, p. 121.
11. John S. Dunne, *The Reasons of the Heart*, SCM Press 1978, p. 21.
12. William Temple, *The Hope of a New World*, SCM Press 1940, p. 114.
13. Hans Küng, *On Being a Christian*, translated by Edward Quinn, William Collins Sons and Co. 1977, p. 251.
14. John V. Taylor, *The Go-Between God*, SCM Press 1973, p. 231.
15. Anthony Bloom, *The Essence of Prayer*, Darton, Longman and Todd 1989, p. 61.
16. John S. Dunne, *The Reasons of the Heart*, SCM Press 1978, p. 13.
17. George Appleton, *Journey for a Soul*, William Collins Sons and Co. 1976, p. 234.
18. George Macdonald, *Unspoken Sermons*, Second Series, Longmans, Green and Co. 1885, p. 168.

## *Wisdom*

1. NRSV.
2. NRSV.
3. Aeschylus, *Agamemnon*, translated by Herbert Weir Smyth, William Heinemann 1952, p. 19.
4. Rabindranath Tagore, *Stray Birds, Collected Poems and Plays of Rabindranath Tagore*, Macmillan and Co. 1936, ccxciv, p. 325.
5. W.R. Inge, in Sir James Marchant, *Wit and Wisdom of Dean Inge*, selected and arranged by Sir James Marchant, Longmans, Green and Co. 1927, p. 112.
6. George Eliot, *Middlemarch*, J. M. Dent and Sons 1959, vol. 2, p. 77.
7. Bede Griffiths OSB, in Peter Spink, *The Universal Christ*, Darton, Longman and Todd 1990, p. 7.
8. Christopher Bryant SSJE, *The Heart in Pilgrimage*, Darton, Longman and Todd 1980, p. 98.
9. Charles Dickens, *Hard Times*, The Gresham Publishing Co. 1904, p. 155.
10. A.R. Orage, *On Love*, The Janus Press 1957, p. 60.
11. Maurice Maeterlinck, *Wisdom and Destiny*, translated by Alfred Sutro, George Allen 1898, p. 38.
12. William Wordsworth, 'The Excursion', *The Poetical Works of William Wordsworth*, edited by E. de Selincourt and Helen Darbishire, Oxford at the Clarendon Press 1959, vol. V, book III, l.231, p. 82.
13. Michel Quoist, *With Open Heart*, translated by Colette Copeland, Gill and Macmillan 1983, p. 50.
14. Thomas Merton, *Thoughts in Solitude*, Burns and Oates 1958, p. 64.

15. Charles Kingsley, *Health and Education*, W. Isbister and Co. 1874, p. 194.
16. Rufus M. Jones, *Spiritual Reformers in the 16th and 17th Centuries*, Macmillan and Co. 1914, p. 150.
17. Michael Ramsey, *The Gospel and the Catholic Church*, Longmans, Green and Co. 1936, p. 125.
18. William Barclay, *The Letters to the Galatians and Ephesians*, The Saint Andrew Press 1958, p. 95.
19. Walt Whitman, 'Song of the Open Road', *The Complete Poems*, edited by Francis Murphy, Penguin Books 1982, section 6, l.77, p. 182.
20. William Blake, 'Vale or the Four Zoas', *The Complete Writings of William Blake*, edited by Geoffrey Keynes, Oxford University Press 1974, p. 290.
21. Henri Frédéric Amiel, *Amiel's Journal*, translated by Mrs Humphry Ward, Macmillan and Co. 1918, p. 95.
22. Sir Sarvepalli Radhakrishna, *Eastern Religions and Western Thought*, Oxford University Press 1940, p. 96.

## *Wonder*

1. NRSV.
2. NRSV.
3. José Ortega Y Gasset, *The Revolt of the Masses*, George Allen and Unwin 1932, p. 12.
4. Rabindranath Tagore, *Sadhana*, Macmillan Publishers 1930, p. 48.
5. Thomas Carlyle, *Heroes and Hero-Worship*, Ward, Lock 1841, p. 8.
6. Alfred North Whitehead, *Modes of Thought*, Cambridge University Press 1938, p. 232.
7. Lady Julian of Norwich, *Revelations of Divine Love*, Penguin Books 1976, p. 130.
8. Evelyn Underhill, in John Stobbart, *The Wisdom of Evelyn Underhill,* Mowbray 1951, p. 11.
9. H.A. Williams CR, *The True Wilderness*, William Collins Sons and Co. 1983, p. 111.
10. Henry Ward Beecher, *Proverbs from Plymouth Pulpit*, Charles Burnet and Co. 1887, p. 31.
11. Johann Wolfgang von Goethe, in Emil Ludwig, *The Practical Wisdom of Goethe*, George Allen and Unwin Publishers 1933, *To Ekermann* 1829, p. 91.
12. Rollo May, *Man's Search for Himself*, George Allen and Unwin 1953, p. 212.
13. W. MacNeile Dixon, *The Human Situation*, Edward Arnold 1937, p. 75.
14. William Temple, *Nature, Man and God*, Macmillan Publishers 1934, p. 156.
15. Michael Ramsey, in Margaret Duggan, *Through the Year with Michael Ramsey*, Hodder and Stoughton 1975, p. 24.
16. Albert Einstein, *Ideas and Opinions*, Souvenir Press (Educational and Academic) 1973, p. 11.
17. G.A. Studdert Kennedy, *The New Man in Christ*, edited by the Dean of Worcester, Hodder and Stoughton 1932, p. 132.
18. D.H. Lawrence, *Phoenix II*, William Heinemann 1968, p. 598.

## *Work*

1. NRSV.
2. NRSV.
3. Henry Ward Beecher, *Proverbs from Plymouth Pulpit*, Charles Burnet and Co. 1887, p. 37.
4. Walter Bagehot, *Biographical Studies*, edited by Richard Holt Hutton, Longmans, Green, and Co. 1907, p. 370.
5. William Barclay, *The Gospel of Matthew*, The Saint Andrew Press 1976, vol. 11, p. 296.
6. Beecher, *Proverbs from Plymouth Pulpit*, p. 36.
7. George Macdonald, *Wilfred Cumbermede*, Hurst and Blackett, 1872, vol. III, p. 169.
8. Beecher, *Proverbs from Plymouth Pulpit*, p. 58.
9. Albert Einstein, *Out of My Later Years*, Thames and Hudson 1950, p. 35.
10. Joseph Conrad, *Heart of Darkness, in Youth, a Narrative and Two Other Stories*, J.M. Dent and Sons 1923, p. 37.
11. Beecher, *Proverbs from Plymouth Pulpit*, p. 37.
12. William Temple, *Christianity and the Social Order*, Penguin Books 1942, p. 73.

13. William Penn, *Fruits of Solitude*, A.W. Bennett 1863, p. 16.
14. Sir Julian Huxley, *Religion without Revelation*, C.A. Watts and Co. 1967, p. 140.
15. George Macleod, *Only One Way Left*, The Iona Community 1956, p. 29.
16. Lord Soper, in Gerald Priestland, *Priestland's Progress*, BBC Worldwide 1982, p. 54.
17. Henri Frédéric Amiel, *Amiel's Journal*, translated by Mrs Humphry Ward, Macmillan and Co. 1918, p. 224.
18. Robert Lowry Calhoun, *God and the Common Life*, The Shoe String Press 1954, p. 240.
19. Mohandas K. Gandhi, in C.F. Andrews, *Mahatma Gandhi's Ideas*, George Allen and Unwin 1929, p. 101.

## *Worldliness*

1. NRSV.
2. NRSV.
3. Leslie J. Tizard, *Facing Life and Death*, George Allen and Unwin 1959, p. 111.
4. Logan Pearsall Smith, *Afterthoughts*, Constable and Co. 1931, p. 29.
5. Oliver Goldsmith, 'The Traveller', *Collected Works of Oliver Goldsmith*, vol. IV, edited by Arthur Friedman, Oxford at the Clarendon Press 1966, p. 252.
6. Henry Ward Beecher, *Proverbs from Plymouth Pulpit*, Charles Burnet and Co. 1887, p. 44.
7. Hans Küng, *On Being a Christian*, translated by Edward Quinn, William Collins Sons and Co. 1977, p. 28.
8. Hubert van Zeller, *Considerations*, Sheed and Ward 1974, p. 10.
9. William Law, *A Serious Call to a Devout and Holy Life*, J.M. Dent and Co. 1898, p. 85.
10. Benedict Spinoza, *Spinoza's Ethics and De Intellectus Emendatione*, J.M. Dent and Sons 1955, p. 227.
11. William Wordsworth, 'The World Is too much with Us', *The Poetical Works of William Wordsworth*, edited by E. de Selincourt and Helen Darbishire, Oxford at the Clarendon Press 1954, vol. III, p. 16.
12. Geoffrey Preston OP, *Hallowing the Time*, Darton, Longman and Todd 1980, p. 32.
13. B.F. Westcott, *The Gospel According to St John*, John Murray 1908, vol. 1, pp. 14 and 64.
14. Michael Ramsey, in Margaret Duggan, *Through the Year with Michael Ramsey*, Hodder and Stoughton 1975, p. 123.
15. Martin Luther King, in Coretta Scott King, *The Words of Martin Luther King*, William Collins Sons and Co. 1986, p. 63.
16. W.R. Inge, *Personal Religion and the Life of Devotion*, Longmans, Green and Co. 1924, p. 79.

## *Worship*

1. NRSV.
2. NRSV.
3. Thomas Carlyle, *Sartor Resartus*, Ward, Lock and Co., p. 52.
4. Benjamin Whichcote, *Moral and Religious Aphorisms*, Number 248, Elkin, Mathews and Marrot 1930.
5. Peter Shaffer, *Equus*, Longman 1983, II.xxv, p. 67.
6. Alan Richardson, in Alan Richardson and John Bowden, *A New Dictionary of Christian Theology*, SCM Press 1985, p. 605.
7. Hubert van Zeller, *Considerations*, Sheed and Ward 1974, p. 86.
8. John Macquarrie, *Paths in Spirituality*, SCM Press 1972, p. 21.
9. William Temple, *Citizen and Churchman*, Eyre and Spottiswoode 1941, p. 43.
10. van Zeller, *Considerations*, p. 87.
11. Macquarrie, *Paths in Spirituality*, p. 20.
12. Epictetus, in Witney J. Oates, *The Stoic and Epicurean Philosophers*, Random House 1940, p 253.
13. William Temple, *Readings in St John's Gospel*, first and second series, Macmillan and Co. 1947, p. 68.
14. William Barclay, *The Letter to the Romans*, The Saint Andrew Press 1969, p. 169.

15. George Appleton, *Journey for a Soul*, William Collins Sons and Co. 1976, p. 215.
16. Temple, *Readings in St John's Gospel*, p. 258.
17. Michael Ramsey, in Margaret Duggan, *Through the Year with Michael Ramsey*, Hodder and Stoughton 1975, p. 75.
18. Leonard Hurst, *Hungry Men*, The Livingstone Press 1955, p. 107.

# ACKNOWLEDGEMENTS

We would like to thank all those who have given us permission to reproduce extracts from publications in this book, as indicated in the list below. Every effort has been made to trace copyright ownership. The publisher would be grateful to be informed of any omissions.

Michel Quoist, *With Open Heart*, 1983, translated by Colette Copeland, by permission of the publishers, Gill and Macmillan Ltd. Michel Quoist, *Prayers of Life*, 1963, translated by Anne Marie de Commaile and Agnes Mitchell Forsyth, Gill and Macmillan Ltd. Basil Hume OSB, *To Be a Pilgrim*, 1984, by permission of St Pauls Press (formerly St Paul Publications). Albert Schweitzer, *The Teaching of Reverence for Life*, 1965, Peter Owen Ltd, London. Sir Sarvepalli Radhakrishnan, *Eastern and Western Thought*, 1940, reprinted by permission of Oxford University Press. Andrew Seth Pringle-Pattison, *The Idea of God in the Light of Recent Philosophy*, 1917, reprinted by permission of Oxford University Press. John Baillie, *Invitation to Pilgrimage*, 1942, reprinted by permission of Oxford University Press. Stephen Neill, *The Church and Christian Union*, 1968, reprinted by permission of Oxford University Press. R.C. Zaehner, *Mysticism Sacred and Profane*, 1957, reprinted by permission of Oxford University Press. Iris Murdoch, *The Sovereignty of Good Over Other Concepts*, 1967, reprinted by permission of Cambridge University Press. John Oman, *The Natural and the Supernatural*, 1931, Cambridge at the University Press, permission granted by Cambridge University Press. Sir Richard Livingstone, *On Education*, 1954, Cambridge at the University Press, permission granted by Cambridge University Press. J.H. Whale, *Christian Doctrine*, 1942, Cambridge University Press, permission granted by Cambridge University Press. Alfred North Whitehead, *Modes of Thought*, 1938, Cambridge University Press, permission granted by them. Alfred North Whitehead, *Science and the Modern World*, 1932, The New American Library, 1964, permission granted by Cambridge University Press. A.R. Vidler, *Soundings*, 1962, Cambridge at the University Press, permission granted by Cambridge University Press. Cyril H. Powell, *Secrets of Answered Prayer*, 1958, Arthur James Ltd. Agnes Sanford, *The Healing Light*, 1949, Arthur James Ltd. Alan Watts, *Behold the Spirit*, 1947, John Murray (Publishers) Ltd. C.S. Lewis, *The Screwtape Letters*, © C.S. Lewis Pte, Ltd. 1942. C.S. Lewis, *Mere Christianity*, © C.S. Lewis Pte, Ltd. 1942, 1943, 1944, 1952. C.S. Lewis, *They Stand Together*, © C.S. Lewis Pte, Ltd. 1979. C.S. Lewis, *The Four Loves*, © C.S. Lewis Pte. Ltd, 1960. C.S. Lewis, *The Great Divorce*, © C.S. Lewis, 1946. Extracts reprinted by permission. Rosemary Haughton, *On Trying to Be Human*, Geoffrey Chapman, 1966, by permission of The Continuum International Publishing Group Ltd. Sister Elizabeth of the Trinity, *Spiritual Writings*, 1962, Geoffrey Chapman, by permission of The Continuum International Publishing Group Ltd. Martin Buber, *I and Thou*, translated by Walter Kaufman, 1971, T&T Clark, by permission of The Continuum International Publishing Group Ltd. W.M. Macgregor, *Jesus Christ the Son of God*, 1907, T&T Clark, by permission of The Continuum International Publishing Group Ltd. A.J. Gossip, *From the Edge of the Crowd*, 1925, T&T Clark, by permission of The Continuum International Publishing Group Ltd. Mark Gibbard, *Liberation and Love*, 1982, A.R. Mowbray and Co., by permission of The Continuum International Publishing Group Ltd. Father Andrew SDC, *The Life and Letters of Fr Andrew* SDC, 1948, A.R. Mowbray and Co., by permission of The Continuum International Publishing Group Ltd. Father Andrew SDC, *A Gift of Light*, selected and edited by Harry C. Griffith, 1968, A.R. Mowbray and Co., by permission of The Continuum International Publishing Group Ltd. Father Andrew SDC, *The Symbolism of the Sanctuary*, 1927, A.R. Mowbray and Co., by permission of The Continuum International Publishing Group Ltd. Father Andrew SDC, *The Seven Words from the Cross*, 1954, A.R. Mowbray and Co., by permission of The Continuum International Publishing Group Ltd. Father Andrew SDC, *The Way of Victory*, 1938, A.R. Mowbray and Co., by permission of The Continuum International Publishing Group Ltd. Father Andrew SDC, *Meditations for Every Day*, 1941, A.R.

Mowbray and Co., by permission of The Continuum International Publishing Group Ltd. Evelyn Underhill, *The Love of God*, 1953, A.R. Mowbray and Co., by permission of The Continuum International Publishing Group Ltd. Evelyn Underhill, in John Stobbart, editor, *The Wisdom of Evelyn Underhill*, 1951, A.R. Mowbray and Co., by permission of The Continuum International Publishing Group Ltd. Edward Patey, *Christian Life Style*, 1976, A.R. Mowbray and Co., by permission of The Continuum International Publishing Group Ltd. Norman W. Goodacre, *Laymen's Lent*, 1969, A.R. Mowbray and Co., by permission of The Continuum International Publishing Group Ltd. Rabindranath Tagore, *Letters to a Friend*, © 1928, George Allen and Unwin, permission given by HarperCollins Publishers Ltd. Rabindranath Tagore, *The Religion of Man*, © 1931, George Allen and Unwin, permission given by HarperCollins Publishers Ltd. Norman Pittenger, *The Christian Situation Today*, © Epworth Press, used by permission of Methodist Publishing House. W.E. Sangster, *The Pure in Heart*, © Epworth Press, used by permission of Methodist Publishing House. W.E. Sangster, *Westminster Sermons*, Volume 1, 1960, and Volume 2, 1962, © Epworth Press, used by permission of Methodist Publishing House. J. Neville Ward, *The Use of Praying*, 1967, © Epworth Press, used by permission of Methodist Publishing House. J. Neville Ward, *Five for Sorrow, Ten for Joy*, 1971, © Epworth Press, used by permission of Methodist Publishing House. J. Neville Ward, *Friday Afternoon*, 1982, © Epworth Press, used by permission of Methodist Publishing House. W.E. Sangster, *Give God a Chance*, 1968, © Epworth Press, used by permission of Methodist Publishing House. F.W. Boreham, *A Late Lark Singing*, 1945, © Epworth Press, used by permission of Methodist Publishing House. Roy Stevens, *Education and the Death of Love*, 1978, © Epworth Press, used by permission of Methodist Publishing House. Colin Morris, *The Hammer of the Lord*, Epworth Press, 1973, © Epworth Press, used by permission of Methodist Publishing House. Colin Morris, *The Word and the Words*, 1975, © Epworth Press, used by permission of Methodist Publishing House. Henri J.M. Nouwen, *Reaching Out*, William Collins Sons and Co., © 1880, reprinted by permission of HarperCollins Publishers Ltd. Albert Schweitzer, *Christianity and the Religions of the World*, 1924, translated by Joanna Powers, George Allen and Unwin, permission granted by HarperCollins Publishers Ltd. Leslie J. Tizard, *Facing Life and Death*, 1959, George Allen and Unwin, permission granted by HarperCollins Publishers Ltd. Sir Sarvepalli Radhakrishnan, *Mahatma Gandhi: Essays and Reflections*, 1949, George Allen and Unwin Publishers Ltd, permission granted by HarperCollins Publishers Ltd. Joseph Joubert, *Pensées and Letters*, 1928, George Routledge and Sons Ltd, permission granted by Thomson Publishing Services, North Way, Andover, Hants, SP10 5BE. Richard Wilhelm and C.G. Jung, *The Secret of the Golden Flower*, (extract from a former patient), 1972, Routledge and Kegan Paul, permission granted by Thomson Publishing Services. C.G. Jung, *The Collected Works of C.G. Jung*, Volume 12, 1953, translated by R.F.C. Hull, Routledge and Kegan Paul, permission granted by Thomson Publishing Services. C.G. Jung, *The Structure and Dynamics of the Psyche, The Collected Works of C.G. Jung*, Volume 8, 1969, translated by R.F.C. Hull, Routledge and Kegan Paul, permission granted by Thomson Publishing Services. C.G. Jung, *Psychological Reflections*, 1953, Routledge and Kegan Paul Ltd, permission granted by Thomson Publishing Services. C.G. Jung, *Aion, The Collected Works of C.G. Jung*, Volume 9, Part 2, 1959, translated by R.F.C. Hull, Routledge and Kegan Paul, permission granted by Thomson Publishing Services. C.G. Jung, *Psychology and Alchemy, The Collected Works of C.G. Jung*, 1953,Volume 12, translated by R.F.C. Hull, Routledge and Kegan Paul, permission granted by Thomson Publishing Services. Simon Weil, *Gravity and Grace*, 1972, Routledge and Kegan Paul, permission granted by Thomson Publishing Services. Helen Mary Lynd, *On Shame and Search for Identity*, 1958, Routledge and Kegan Paul Ltd, permission granted by Thomson Publishing Services. Erich Fromm, *Man for Himself*, 1975, Routledge and Kegan Paul, permission granted by Thomson Publishing Services. Ernest Hemingway, *Death in the Afternoon*, 1968, Jonathan Cape Ltd, reprinted by permission of The Random House Group Ltd. Arthur Koestler, *Darkness at Noon*, 1980, Jonathan Cape, reprinted by permission of The Random House Group Ltd. Thomas Merton, *Contemplative Prayer*, 1973, Darton Longman and Todd, permission granted by the publisher. Alan Ecclestone, *Yes to God*, 1975, Darton, Longman and Todd, permission granted by the publisher. Anthony Bloom, *School for Prayer*, 1970, Darton, Longman and Todd, permission granted by the publisher. Anthony Book, *The Essence of Prayer*, 1989, Darton, Longman and Todd, permission granted by the publisher. John Main OSB, *The Joy of Being*, selection by Clare Hallward, 1989, Darton, Longman and Todd, permission granted by the publisher. John Main OSB, *Moment of Christ*, 1984, Darton, Longman and Todd, permission granted by the publisher. Carlo Corretto, *Letters from the Desert*, 1972, translated by Rose Mary Hancock, Darton, Longman and Todd, permission granted by the publisher. Henri J.M. Nouwen, *The Way of the Heart*, 1981, Darton, Longman and Todd Ltd, permission granted by the publisher. Henri J.M. Nouwen, *Seeds of Hope*, 1989, edited by Robert Durback, Darton, Longman and Todd Ltd, permission granted by the publisher. Hubert van Zeller, *Praying While You Work*, 1951, Burns, Oates and Washbourne, permission granted by The Continuum International Publishing Group Ltd. Thomas Merton, *Conjectures of a Guilty Bystander*, 1968, Burns and Oates Ltd, permission granted by The Continuum International Publishing Group Ltd. Thomas Merton, *No Man Is an Island*, 1974, Burns and Oates, permission granted by The Continuum International Publishing Group Ltd. Thomas Merton, *Thoughts in Solitude*, 1958, Burns and Oates, permission granted by The Continuum International Publishing Group Ltd. Thomas Merton, *New Seeds of Contemplation*, 1962, Burns and Oates Ltd, permission granted by The Continuum International Publishing Group Ltd. Alban Goodier SJ, *The School of Love*, 1920, Burns and Oates and Washbourne, permission granted by The Continuum International Publishing Group Ltd. Ladislaus Boros, *In Time of Temptation*, 1968, translated by Simon and Erika Young, Burns and Oates Ltd, permission granted by The Continuum International Publishing Group Ltd. Gabriel Moran FSC, *The Theology of Revelation*, 1967, Burns and Oates, permission granted by The Continuum International Publishing Group Ltd. Lewis Mumford, *The Conduct of Life*, 1952, Secker and Warburg, used by permission of The Random House Group Limited. André Gide, *The Journals of André Gide*, 1894, translated by Justin O'Brien, Secker and Warburg, 1947, used by permission of The Random House Group Limited. Virginia Woolf, *A Writer's Diary*, 1953, edited by Leonard Woolf, The Hogarth Press, used by permission of the executors of the Virginia Woolf Estate and The Random House Group Limited. Yevgeny Yevtushenko, *A Precocious Autobiography*, 1963, translated by Andrew R. MacAndrew, Collins and Harvill Press, used by permission of The Random House Group Limited. A.D. Sertillanges OP, *The Intellectual Life*, 1948, translated by Mary Ryan, The Mercier Press, permission granted by The Mercier Press. Wassily Kandinsky, *Concerning the Spiritual in Art*, 1977, translated by M.T.H, Sadler, Dover Publications, permission given by Dover Publications. William Barclay, *The Plain Man Looks at the Apostles Creed*, 1967, William Collins Sons and Co. Ltd, permission given by The Estate of William Barclay. C.G. Jung, *Memories, Dreams, Reflections*, 1971, William Collins Sons and Co., permission granted by HarperCollins Publishers Ltd. Sydney Carter, *Dance in the Dark* (originally *Rock of Doubt*) 1980, William Collins Sons and Co., permission granted by HarperCollins Publishers Ltd. William Johnston, *The Inner Eye of Love*, 1978, William Collins Sons and Co., permission granted by HarperCollins Publishers Ltd. Giles and Melville Harcourt/Hugh Montefiore, *Short Prayers for the Long Day/Sermons from Great St. Mary's*, 1978, William Collins Sons and Co., permission granted by HarperCollins Publishers Ltd. Rabbi H. Kushner, *When Bad Things Happen to Good People*, 1982, Pan Books, permission granted by Pan Macmillan. Stephen MacKenna, *Journal and Letters*, 1936, Constable and Co. Ltd, reproduced by kind permission of Constable and Robinson Publishing Ltd. Logan Pearsall Smith, *Afterthoughts*, 1931, Constable and Co. Ltd, reproduced by kind permission of Constable and Robinson Publishing Ltd. A. Clutton Brock, *The Ultimate Belief*, 1916, Constable and Company, reproduced by kind permission of Constable and Robinson Publishing Ltd. F.R. Barry, *Vocation and Ministry*, James Nisbet and Co. Ltd, 1958. F.R. Barry, *The Relevance of Christianity*, James Nisbet and Co. Ltd, 1932. Paul Tillich, *The Courage To Be*, James Nisbet and Co. Ltd, 1952. Herbert Farmer, *The Healing Cross*, James Nisbet and Co. Ltd, 1938. C.M. Vidor, in Charles R. Joy, *Music in the Life of Albert Schweitzer, Selections from His Writings*, translated and edited by Charles R. Joy, 1953, A. and C. Black, by kind permission of A. and C. Black (Publishers) Ltd. Norman Goodall, *The Local Church*, Hodder and Stoughton, 1960, reproduced by permission of Hodder and Stoughton Limited. Mary Craig, *Blessings*, Hodder and Stoughton, 1979, reproduced by permission of Hodder and Stoughton Limited. David Watson, *You Are My God*, Hodder and Stoughton, 1983, reproduced by permission of Hodder and Stoughton Limited. Raynor C. Johnson, *A Pool of Reflections*, Hodder and Stoughton, 1983, reproduced by permission of Hodder and Stoughton Limited. Richard Foster, *The Celebration of Discipline*, Hodder and Stoughton, 1982, reproduced by permission of Hodder and Stoughton Limited. Neville Cryer, *Michel Quoist*, Hodder and Stoughton, 1977, reproduced by permission of Hodder and Stoughton Limited. Austin Farrer, *Saving Belief*, Hodder and Stoughton, 1964, reproduced by permission of Hodder and Stoughton Limited. W.E. Sangster, *He Is Able*, Hodder and Stoughton, 1936, permission granted for this and the next three books, by Dr Paul Sangster. W.E. Sangster, *God Does Guide Us*, Hodder and Stoughton, 1934. W.E. Sangster, *These Things Abide*, Hodder and Stoughton, 1939. W.E. Sangster, *The Secret of Radiant Life*, Hodder and Stoughton, 1957. Hugh Redwood, *Residue of Days*, Hodder and Stoughton, 1958, reproduced by permission of Hodder and Stoughton Limited. David Sheppard, *Bias to the Poor*, Hodder and Stoughton, 1983, reproduced by permission of Hodder and Stoughton Limited. Norman

Goodall, *The Local Church*, Hodder and Stoughton, 1966, reproduced by permission of Hodder and Stoughton Limitied. W. MacNeile Dixon, *The Human Situation*, Edward Arnold (Publishers) Ltd, 1937. Lesslie Newbigin, *Honest Religion for Secular Man*, SCM Press, 1966, this and the next 48 entries, reproduced by permission from SCM Press. Peter Munz, *Problems of Religious Knowledge*, SCM Press, 1959. Florence Higham, said of F.D. Maurice, in *Frederick Denison Maurice*, SCM Press, 1947. John Macmurray, *Creative Society*, SCM Press, 1935. Olive Wyon, *On The Way*, SCM Press, 1958. F.R. Barry, *Secular and Supernatural*, SCM Press, 1969. Frank Wright, *The Pastoral Nature of the Ministry*, SCM Press, 1980. Harry Emerson Fosdick, *As I See Religion*, SCM Press, 1932. Harry Emerson Fosdick, *Successful Christian Living*, SCM Press, 1938. Harry Emerson Fosdick, *The Hope of a New World*, SCM Press, 1933. D.S. Cairns, *The Riddle of the World*, SCM Press, 1937. Trevor Beeson, *An Eye for an Ear*, SCM Press, 1972. R.L. Smith, *Life Made Possible by the Gospel*, in Paul Rowntree Clifford, *Man's Dilemma and God's Answer*, Broadcast Series, SCM Press, 1944. Sister Madeleine OSA, *Solitary Refinement*, SCM Press, 1972. Stuart B. Jackman, *The Numbered Days*, SCM Press, 1954. Alan Richardson, *History Sacred and Profane*, SCM Press, 1964. Don Cupitt, *Taking Leave of God*, SCM Press, 1980. David Anderson, *Simone Weil*, SCM Press, 1971. John Macquarrie, *The Humility of God*, SCM Press, 1978. William Temple, *Christian Faith and Life*, SCM Press (1931), reissued 1963. Norman Pittenger, *Christology Reconsidered*, SCM Press, 1970. Joachim Jeremias, *New Testament Theology*, Volume 1, SCM Press, 1971. Jürgen Moltmann, *The Open Church*, SCM Press, 1978. Harvey Cox, *God's Revolution and Man's Responsibility*, SCM Press, 1969. Harvey Cox, *The Secular City*, SCM Press, 1967. William Temple, *The Hope of a New World*, SCM Press, 1940. John S. Dunne, *The Reasons of the Heart*, SCM Press, 1978. John S. Dunne, *The Church of the Poor Devil*, SCM Press, 1983. John Macquarrie, *Paths in Spirituality*, SCM Press, 1972. John Macquarrie, *The Concept of Peace*, SCM Press, 1973. John Macquarrie, *In Search of Humanity*, SCM Press, 1982. John V. Taylor, *The Go-Between God*, SCM Press, 1973. Paul Tillich, *The Shaking of the Foundations*, SCM Press, 1949. Paul Tillich, *The Eternal Now*, SCM Press, 1963. Dietrich Bonhoeffer, *Letters and Papers from Prison*, The Enlarged Edition, SCM Press, 1971. Dietrich Bonhoeffer, *The Cost of Discipleship*, translated by R.H. Fuller, SCM Press, 1959. Nicolas Berdyaev, *The Fate of Man in the Modern World*, translated by Donald A. Lowrie, SCM Press, 1935. John A.T. Robinson, *The Roots of a Radical*, SCM Press, 1980. Henry McKeating, *God and the Future*, SCM Press, 1974. David Brown, *God's Tomorrow*, SCM Press, 1977. Paul Oestreicher, Introduction to Hans Jürgen Schultz, *Conversion to the World*, SCM Press, 1967. W.A. Visser't Hooft, *The Renewal of the Church*, SCM Press, 1956. Daniel Jenkins, *Christian Maturity and the Theology of Success*, SCM Press, 1976. J.H. Oldham, *Life is Commitment*, SCM Press, 1953. Hans Jürgen Schultz, *Conversion to the World*, SCM Press. Paul Tournier, *Escape from Loneliness*, translated by John S. Gilmour, SCM Press, 1962. Michael Ramsey, *The Idea of the Holy and the World Today*, in *Spirituality for Today*, edited by Eric James, SCM Press, 1968. Alan Richardson and John Bowden, *A New Dictionary of Christian Theology*, SCM Press, 1983. James F. Childress, in *A New Dictionary of Christian Ethics*, James F. Childress and John Macquarrie, SCM Press, 1986. Gordon S. Wakefield in *A Dictionary of Christian Spirituality*, edited by Gordon S. Wakefield, SCM Press, 1986. Harry Williams CR, *The True Wilderness*, William Collins Sons and Co. Ltd, 1983, reprinted by permission of Constable and Robinson Ltd. Graham Greene, *The Heart of the Matter*, William Heinemann, 1959, by permission of David Higham Associates Limited. Hubert van Zeller, *Leave Your Life Alone*, Sheed and Ward, 1973, permission granted by The Continuum International Publishing Group Ltd. Hubert van Zeller, *Considerations*, Sheed and Ward, 1974, permission granted by The Continuum International Publishing Group Ltd. Nicolas Berdyaev, *Christianity and Class War*, translated by Donald Attwater, Sheed and Ward, 1933, permission granted by The Continuum International Publishing Group Ltd. Etienne Gilson, *The Spirit of Medieval Philosophy*, translated by A.H.C. Downes, Sheed and Ward, 1950, permission granted by The Continuum International Publishing Group Ltd. G.P. Fedatov, *A Treasury of Russian Spirituality*, Sheed and Ward, 1977, permission granted by The Continuum International Publishing Group Ltd. G.K. Chesterton, *Charles Dickens*, Methuen and Co., 1906, permission given by A.P. Watt Ltd on behalf of the Royal Literary Fund. J.B. Priestley, *All About Ourselves and Other Essays*, William Heinemann Ltd, 1956 (© J.B. Priestly 1956) by permission of PFD on behalf of the Estate of J.B. Priestley. Malcolm Muggeridge, *Jesus Rediscoved*, William Collins Sons and Co. Ltd, 1982, by permission of David Higham Associates Ltd. Carroll E. Simcox, *Living the Creed*, Dacre Press/ A. and C. Black, 1954, permission given by A. and C. Black Publishers Ltd. Carroll E. Simcox, *The Promises of God*, Dacre Press/ A. and C. Black, 1958, permission given by A. and C. Black Publishers Ltd. Albert Schweitzer, *The Quest of the Historical Jesus*, A. and C. Black, 1954, permission given by A. and C. Black Publishers Ltd. Albert Schweitzer, in E.N. Mozley, *The Theology of Albert Schweitzer*, translated by J.R. Coates, A. and C. Black, 1950, permission given by A. and C. Black Publishers Ltd. Albert Schweitzer, *The Philosophy of Civilization, Part II, Civilization and Ethics*, translated by C.T. Campion, Third English Edition, revised by Mrs C.E.B. Russell, 1946, permission given by A. and C. Black Publishers Ltd. Albert Schweitzer in Charles H. Joy, *An Anthology*, A. and C. Black, 1955, permission given by A. and C. Black Publishers Ltd. L.S. Thorton CR, *The Common Life in the Body of Christ*, Dacre Press/ A. and C. Black, 1950, permission given by A. and C. Black Publishers Ltd. Thomas Kelly, *A Testament of Devotion*, Hodder and Stoughton, 1943, reproduced by permission of William Neill-Hall Ltd. Anne Morrow Lindbergh, *Gift from the Sea*, Chatto and Windus Ltd, 1974, used by permission of The Random House Group Limited. John Macquarrie, *Paths in Spirituality*, SCM Press, 1972, 1992, reprinted with permission by Morehouse Publishing, Harrisburg Pennsylvania. Bede Griffiths, *Return to the Center*, Templegate Publishers (templegate.com) 1977. Hermann Hesse, in Volker Michels, *Reflections*, translated by Ralph Manheim, Jonathan Cape, 1977, © Suhrkamp Verlag, permission granted by them. Mother Teresa, *Jesus, The Word to Be Spoken*, compiled by Fr. Angelo Devananda Scolozzi M.C.III.O. – William Collins Sons and Co. Ltd, 1990 – permission sentence from *Jesus, The Word to Be Spoken*, Mother Teresa, compiled by Fr Angelo Devanande Scolozzi M.C.III.O © 1998 by Servant Publications. Published by Servant Publications, P.O. Box 8617, Ann Arbor, Michigan, 48107. Used with permission. Aaron Copeland, *Music and Imagination*, Harvard University Press, 1977, reprinted by the permission of the publisher from *Music and Imagination: The Charles Eliot Norton Lectures 1951–1952* by Aaron Copeland, Cambridge, Mass.: Harvard University Press, © 1952 by the President and Fellows of Harvard College, © renewed 1980 by Aaron Copeland. George Moore, *Evelyn Innes*, Volume II, Bernhard Tauchnitz, 1898. Hans Küng, *On Being a Christian*, translated by Edward Quinn, William Collins Sons and Co., 1977, permission granted by Professor Dr Hans Küng. André Gide, *The Journals of André Gide*, translated by Justin O'Brien, Secker and Warburg, 1947. Dag Hammarskjöld, *Markings*, translated by Leif Sjöberg and W.H. Auden, Faber and Faber, 1964, permission granted by Faber and Faber Ltd. C.S. Lewis, *A Grief Observed*, Faber and Faber, 1961, permission granted by Faber and Faber Ltd. W.H. Auden, *A Certain World*, Faber and Faber, 1971, permission granted by Faber and Faber Ltd. André Maurois, *The Art of Living*, The English Universities Press, 1940, permission granted 'L'Art de Vivre' © Heritiers André Maurois – Paris. W. Somerset Maugham, *The Summing Up*, Bernhard Tauchnitz, 1938, permission granted by A.P. Watt Ltd on behalf of the Royal Literary Fund. G.K. Chesterton, *Orthodoxy*, 1935, The Bodley Head, permission granted by A.P. Watt Ltd on behalf of the Royal Literary Fund. G.K. Chesterton, *What's Wrong with the World*, Bernhard Tauchnitz, 1910, permission granted by A.P. Watt Ltd on behalf of the Royal Literary Fund. Bertrand Russell, *Principles of Social Reconstruction*, George Allen and Unwin, 1971, permission granted by Taylor and Francis Books (Unwin Hyman). Bertrand Russell, *The Conquest of Happiness*, 1984, George Allen and Unwin Ltd, 1984, permission granted by Taylor and Francis Books (Unwin Hyman). Bertrand Russell, *The Impact of Science*, George Allen and Unwin Publishers Ltd, 1968, permission granted by Taylor and Francis Books (Unwin Hyman). Bertrand Russell, *Authority and the Individual*, Unwin Paperbacks, 1977, permission granted by Taylor and Francis Books (Unwin Hyman). Bertrand Russell, *Marriage and Morals*, George Allen and Unwin Publishers Ltd, 1976, permission granted by Taylor and Francis Books (Unwin Hyman). John Cowper Powys, *Autobiography*, Macdonald and Co., (Publishers), 1967, by permission of the Estate of John Cowper Powys. Henri J.M. Nouwen, *Seeds of Hope*, edited by Robert Durback, Darton, Longman and Todd, 1989, permission is granted by Doubleday, a division of Random House Inc. Norman Douglas, *An Almanac*, Chatto and Windus in association with Martin Secker and Warburg Ltd, 1945, permission granted by The Society of Authors as the Literary Representative of the Estate of Norman Douglas. Arthur Koestler, *Darkness at Noon*, translated by Daphne Hardy, Jonathan Cape, 1980, USA, English language right granted by Peters Fraser and Dunlop Ltd, on behalf of the Estate of Arthur Koestler. John C. Vincent, *Secular Press*, Lutterworth Press, 1968, permission granted by James Clarke and Co. Ltd. Emil Brunner, *The Divine Imperative*, translated by Olive Wyon, Lutterworth Press, 1942, permission granted by James Clarke and Co. Ltd. Ernest Johnson, *The Social Gospel Re-Examined*, James Clarke and Co. Ltd, 1942, permission granted by James Clarke and Co. Ltd. Thomas Merton, *Seeds of Contemplation*, Anthony Clarke Books, 1972, permission granted by The Merton Legacy Trust. Yehudi Menuhin, *Theme and Variations*, William Heinemann, 1972, permission given by The Estate of Yehudi Menuhin. Malcolm Muggeridge, Mother Teresa in, *Something Beautiful for God*, William Collins Sons and Co. Ltd, 1983, permission granted by The Zondervan Corporation.

# ACKNOWLEDGEMENTS

Albert Schweitzer, *Out of My Life and Thought: An Autobiography*, translated by C.T. Campion, Henry Holt and Co., 1949. H.L. Kirk, *Pablo Casals: A Biography*, Hutchinson and Co. (Publishers), 1974, © H.L. Kirk, permission granted by A.M. Heath and Co. Ltd. Eric Hoffer, *The Passionate State of Mind*, Martin Secker and Warburg Ltd, © 1956, reprinted by permission of Curtis Brown, Ltd. Monica Furlong, *Travelling In*, Hodder and Stoughton Ltd, © 1971, permission granted by Sheil L and Associates Ltd. Monica Furlong, *The End of Our Exploring*, Hodder and Stoughton, © 1973, permission granted by Sheil Land Associates Ltd. André Gide, *Pretexts, Reflections on Literature and Morality*, selected by Justin O'Brien, Martin Secker and Warburg Ltd, 1960, permission granted. English translation © 1959 by Meridian Books, Inc. Originally published in French as *Pretextes and Nouveaux Pretextes* by Mercure de France. Reprinted by permission of Georges Borchardt, Inc., for Mecure de France. Anne Morrow Lindbergh, *Gift from the Sea*, Chatto and Windus Ltd, 1974, permission credit line – from *Gift from the Sea*, by Anne Morrow Lindbergh, © 1955, 1975, renewed 1983, used by permission of Pantheon Books, a division of Random House, Inc. E. Stanley Jones, *The Word Became Flesh*, Hodder and Stoughton, 1964, © 1963, Abington Press – used by permission. Thomas Merton, *Contemplation in a World of Action*, George Allen and Unwin Ltd, 1971, permission granted by Thomson Publishing Services – on behalf of Taylor and Francis Books (publisher). *Christian Faith and Practice in the Experience of the Society of Friends*, Yearly Meeting of the Religious Society of Friends in Britain, 1972, Number 119, 1911: 1925, permission granted by The Religious Society of Friends in Britain. George Trevelyan, *A Vision of the Aquarian Age*, Coverture, 1977, by permission of Catriona Tyson. Winston S. Churchill, *Thoughts and Adventures*, Thornton Butterworth Ltd, 1932, reproduced with permission of Curtis Brown Ltd, London on behalf of Winston S. Churchill, © Winston S. Churchill 1932. William Barclay, *New Testament Daily Bible Study Commentaries*, The Saint Andrew Press, permission given by the estate of William Barclay. Ezra Pound, 'How to Read' from *The Literary Essays of Ezra Pound*, © Ezra Pound 1935, reprinted by permission of New Directions Publishing Corp. Excerpt from Lewis Mumford, *The Conduct of Life*, © 1951 and renewed 1979, reprinted by permission of Harcourt Inc. Excerpt from Virginia Woolf, *A Writer's Diary*, © 1954 Leonard Woolf and renewed 1982 by Quentin Bell and Angelica Garnett, reprinted by permission of Harcourt Inc. Excerpt from C.S. Lewis, *The Four Loves*, © 1960 Helen Joy Lewis and renewed Arthur Owen Barfield, reprinted by permission of Harcourt Inc. Excerpt from Antoine de Saint-Exupéry, *Wind, Sand and Stars*, © renewed 1967 by Lewis Galantiere, reprinted by permission of Harcourt Inc. Pierre Tielard de Chardin, *Le Milieu Divin*, William Collins Sons and Co. © 1960, by permission of Editions du Seuil. W.R. Inge, *The Philosophy of Plotinus*, Longmans, Green and Co., 1948, permission granted by Pearson Education Ltd. W.R. Inge, *Personal Religion and the Life of Devotion*, Longmans, Green and Co., 1924, permission granted by Pearson Education Ltd. W.R. Inge, *Types of Christian Saintliness*, Longmans, Green and Co., 1915, permission granted by Pearson Education Ltd. W.R. Inge, *Speculum Animae*, Longmans, Green and Co., 1911, permission granted by Pearson Education Ltd. W.R. Inge, *The Wit and Wisdom of Dean Inge*, compiled by Sir James Marchant, Longmans, Green and Co.,1927, permission granted by Pearson Education Ltd. Lecomte du Nöuy, *Human Destiny*, Longmans, Green and Co., 1947, permission granted by Pearson Education Ltd. Evelyn Underhill, *The Light of Christ*, Longmans, Green and Co., 1944, permission granted by Pearson Education Ltd. Evelyn Underhill, *The School of Charity*, Longmans, Green and Co., 1956, permission granted by Pearson Education Ltd. Evelyn Underhill, *The Letters of Evelyn Underhill*, edited by Charles Williams, Longmans, Green and Co., 1947, permission granted by Pearson Education Ltd. Evelyn Underhill, *Abba*, Longmans, Green and Co., 1940, permission granted by Pearson Education Ltd. Janet Erskine Stuart, in Maud Monahan, *Life and Letters of Janet Erskine Stuart*, Longmans, Green and Co., 1922, permission granted by Pearson Education Ltd. Llewelyn Powys, *Impassioned Clay*, Longmans, Green and Co., 1931, permission granted by Pearson Education Ltd. Dan Billany and David Dowie, *The Cage*, Longmans, Green and Co., 1949, permission granted by Pearson Education Ltd. W.B. Yeats, in Samuel H. Miller, *The Great Realities*, Longmans, Green and Co., 1956, permission granted by Pearson Education Ltd. Thornton Wilder, *Our Town*, Longmans, Green and Co., 1964, permission granted by Pearson Education Ltd. Michael Ramsey, *The Gospel and the Catholic Church*, Longmans, Green and Co., 1936, permission granted by Pearson Education Ltd. Peter Shaffer, *Equus*, Longmans, Green and Co., 1983, permission granted by Pearson Education Ltd. Ordway Tead, *The Art of Leadership*, McGraw-Hill Book Co., 1935, permission granted by McGraw-Hill Education. Clement G.J. Webb, *Religious Experience*, Oxford University Press, 1944, with permission.

# INDEX OF AUTHORS


Abbott, Eric Symes 132
Adams, Henry 202
Addison, Joseph 44, 111
Aelred of Rievaulx 124
Aeschylus 464
A girl of fourteen 134
Al-Ansari 183
Aldrich, Thomas Bailey 70
Al-Ghazali 119
Alighieri, Dante 460
Amiel, Henri Frédéric 17, 28, 37, 40, 104, 111, 147, 148, 151, 164, 172, 181, 182, 187, 205, 206, 230, 298, 331, 346, 379, 397, 398, 402, 411, 434, 453, 466, 474
Anderson, David 391
Andrew SDC, Father 41, 153, 170, 190, 247, 270, 306, 343, 378, 461
Anon., 1, 5, 38, 44, 71, 74, 95, 132, 154, 203, 204, 222, 254, 266, 292, 314, 354, 356, 374, 421, 430, 457
Appleton, George 52, 76, 87, 88, 104, 108, 121, 160, 168, 199, 200, 216, 234, 235, 279, 283, 303, 310, 311, 363, 366, 395, 398, 406, 414, 431, 438, 458, 462, 482
Arndt, Johann 191
Arnold, Matthew 22, 83, 91, 136, 148, 207, 290, 319, 390, 410
Arnold, Thomas 99
Auden, W.H. 375
Augustine, St 95, 198, 250, 318, 404
Aurelius, Marcus 4, 163, 164, 215
Avebury, Right Hon. Lord 323
A young housewife 275

Bacon, Francis 21, 95, 239, 330, 370
Bagehot, Walter 473
Bailey, P.J. 127
Baillie, John 33
Barclay, William 25, 33, 36, 71, 80, 86, 96, 103, 105, 131, 147, 160, 167, 173, 222, 227, 230, 234, 251, 255, 283, 298, 319, 323, 324, 336, 340, 344, 354, 367, 371, 378, 386, 391, 397, 417, 433, 442, 443, 446, 453, 454, 461, 466, 473, 482
Barnes, Kenneth 406
Barry, F.R. 25, 32, 52, 291, 350, 453
Bassett, Elizabeth 266, 267
Baxter, Richard 225
Beard, O.T. 425
Beecher, Henry Ward 5, 13, 17, 27, 28, 36, 39, 40, 41, 44, 47, 47, 50, 51, 67, 68, 83, 87, 91, 92, 99, 103, 107, 130, 135, 139, 140, 143, 148, 152, 155, 159, 163, 164, 167, 171, 174, 183, 186, 187, 194, 196, 202, 209, 210, 211, 222, 227, 230, 257, 258, 259, 265, 270, 271, 281, 282, 283, 286, 287, 289, 290, 294, 306, 319, 326, 335, 341, 346, 382, 386, 393, 409, 410, 433, 437, 453, 469, 472, 473, 477
Beeson, Trevor 234
Beethoven, Ludwig von 294
Bellamy, Edward 24
Benson, A.C. 5, 13, 13, 28, 44, 79, 83, 144, 152, 159, 205, 230, 314, 321, 322, 362, 387, 389, 413
Berdyaev, Nicolas 5, 28, 80, 103, 119, 120, 174, 215, 326, 432
Bernhardt, Sarah 334
Betti, Ugo 198
Billany, Dan, and Dowie, David 255
Birrell, Augustine 331
Black, Hugh 123
Blake, William 5, 160, 310, 333, 424, 466
Blamires, Harry 388
Blanton, Smiley 127
Bloom, Anthony 14, 60, 95, 142, 278, 368, 462
Blum, L. 59
Boehme, Jacob 175
Bondfield, Margaret 25, 26
Bonhoeffer, Dietrich 5, 87, 113, 135, 362, 401, 429
Boreham, F.W. 342
Boros, Ladislaus 123, 358
Bourne, Randolph 214
Boyd Carpenter, William 291

Bragdon, Claude 335
Breemen SJ, Peter G. van 2, 3
Bridges, Robert 18, 174, 223
Brontë, Charlotte 44, 136, 138, 182
Brooks, Phillips 128, 148
Brown, David 48
Browne, Sir Thomas 25, 294
Browning, E.B. 148, 269, 314
Browning, Robert 118, 135, 155, 226, 243, 294, 390, 393, 441
Brubacker, John S. 390
Brunner, Emil 370, 402
Bryant SSJE, Christopher 206, 385, 465
Buber, Martin 254, 272, 405, 433
Buchan, John 322
Bullett, Gerald 298
Bunyan, John 182
Burchhardt, John 36
Burke, Edmund 82, 147
Burnaby, John 160
Burns, Robert 128, 230, 418
Burroughs, Edward 207
Burtchaell CSC, James Tunstead 210
Butler, Samuel 299
Butterfield, Herbert 161
Byron, Lord 152

Cairns, D.S. 222
Calhoun, Robert Lowry 474
Cargas, Harry James 187, 214, 239, 240, 263, 391
Carlyle, Thomas 17, 35, 36, 71, 91, 147, 148, 186, 223, 238, 247, 294, 330, 469, 480
Carpenter, Edward 120
Carrel, Alexis 214, 214, 220, 245, 355
Carretto, Carlo 31, 71, 178, 178, 254, 287, 334, 337, 338, 366
Carter, Sydney 442
Casteel, John L. 266
Caussade SJ, Jean-Pierre de 342, 409
Challenor, Richard 278
Channing, William E 68, 259
Chardin, Pierre Teilhard de 9, 32, 198, 335, 394
Chaucer, Geoffrey 440
Chesterton, G.K. 147, 186, 300, 421
Childress, F. 59
Chinese proverb 151, 314
Christian Faith and Practice in the Experience of the Society of Friends 96
Churchill, Winston S. 68
Clare SLG, Mother Mary 256
Clement of Alexandria 326
*Cloud of Unknowing, The* 25, 108, 182, 217, 270, 347, 429
Clutton Brock, A. 17, 100, 327
Coleridge, Samuel Taylor 47, 91, 225, 358, 410
Colton, C.C. 334, 346
Confucius 151
Connolly, Cyril 127, 330, 396
Conrad, Joseph 18, 185, 194, 282, 473
Cooke, Grace 159, 218
Copeland, Aaron 295
Cotton, Charles 68
Co-worker 60
Cowper, William 150, 238
Cox, Harvey 218, 405
Craig, Archibald, C. 88
Craig, Mary 59, 152, 390
Cryer, Neville 355
Cupitt, Don 378
Cushing, Harvey, Dr 147

Defoe, Daniel 426
Dickens, Charles 179, 417, 465
Dimnet, Ernest 62
Disraeli, Benjamin 151, 203, 259, 270, 428
Disraeli, Isaac 278
Dodd, C.H. 337
Dole, Charles Fletcher 449
Dominion, Jack 457
Donne, John 76
Dostoyevsky, Fyodor 29, 33, 59, 172, 271, 303, 339
Douglas, Norman 151, 206, 258, 286, 302, 314, 374, 393, 441, 445
Drummond, Henry 206, 454
Dryden, John 67, 110, 139, 258, 313
Duncan, Isadora 444
Dunne, John S. 2, 79, 135, 247, 262, 263, 266, 461, 462
Duthrie, Charles 358
Dyke, Henry Van 275

Ecclestone, Alan 433
Eckhart, Meister 62, 91, 92, 100, 131, 183, 189, 191, 202, 250, 375, 386, 387, 410, 430
Edwards, Jonathan 171, 172
Einstein, Albert 22, 67, 100, 187, 243, 299, 355, 382, 384, 390, 441, 445, 470, 473
Eliot, George 5, 6, 25, 83, 140, 190, 202, 211, 353, 413, 465
Elizabeth, Sister, of the Trinity 190
Ellis, Havelock 298
Emerson, Ralph Waldo 13, 28, 32, 40, 43, 44, 63, 91, 92, 123, 124, 183, 194, 242, 248, 250, 326, 334, 370, 417, 425, 437, 438, 449, 454
English proverb 66, 151, 326
Epictetus 481
Erskine, John 242

Faber, F.W. 192, 230, 231, 315
Falconer, L. 186
Farmer, H.H. 95
Farrer, Austin 366
Fausset, Hugh L'Anson 414
Fénelon, F. de la M. 44, 315, 343, 417, 419, 433
Field, Joanna 295
Fielding, Henry 68
Forster, E.M. 258, 259
Forsyth, P.T. 306
Fosdick, Harry Emerson 28, 87, 156, 247
Foster, Richard 13
Francis de Sales, St 123, 339, 401
Frank, Anne 45, 165
Franklin, Benjamin 34, 286
French proverb 78
Fromm, Erich 79, 96, 128, 152, 214, 256, 262, 393, 445
Froude, James A. 290, 350, 409
Fuller, Thomas 31, 43, 67, 122, 147, 170, 286, 286, 314, 417
Furlong, Monica 53, 96, 456

Gandhi, Mohandas K. 17, 335, 338, 475
Gary, Romain 398
Gasset, José Ortega Y. 468
George, Henry 350
German proverb 70
Gibbard, Mark 437
Gibran, Kahlil 28, 120, 210, 270, 271, 338, 421, 441
Gide, André 201, 214, 231, 323, 445
Gilson, Etienne 386
Gissing, George 64
Glubb, Sir John 243
Goethe, Johann Wolfgang von 5, 21, 29, 40, 120, 152, 163, 182, 226, 318, 323, 331, 354, 429, 441, 469
Gogh, Vincent van 124, 445, 461
Goldsmith, Oliver 286, 477
Goodacre, Norman W. 354, 378
Goodall, Norman 52, 79, 174
Goodier SJ, Alban 67
Goodman, Paul 127
GP in Birmingham 166
Gossip, A.J. 422
Grayson, David 362
Greek proverb 412
Green, Thomas F. 10
Greene, Graham 72
Greene, Robert 67
Grellet, Stephen 231
Grenfell, Joyce 134
Griffiths OSB, Bede 115, 239, 310, 311, 319, 434, 465
Guyon, Madame 278

Haecker, Theodor 147, 420
Haggard, H. Rider 178
Hammarskjöld, Dag 5, 32, 79, 106, 139, 155, 206, 246, 254, 262, 338, 401
Happold, F.C. 136, 312
Harcourt, Giles and Melville 111
Harding, Esther 211
Harding, Geoffrey 14
Hardy, Thomas 274, 349
Harries, Richard 63
Haskins, Louise M. 250
Haughton, Rosemary 454
Hawthorne, Nathaniel 18, 167
Hazlitt, William 98, 178
Heine, Heinrich, 295
Hello, Ernest 9, 445
Helme, Elizabeth 421
Helps, Arthur 163
Hemingway, Ernest 290
Henri, Robert 17, 18
Herbert, George 171, 286, 301, 318, 400, 436
Herrick, Robert 322, 417
Hesse, Hermann 238, 259, 315
Higham, Florence 6
Hillesum, Etty 295
Hilton, Walter 144, 342, 370, 406
Hindu proverb 138
Hoffer, Eric 25, 60, 303, 362, 405
Holmes, Oliver Wendell 322
Hopkins, Gerard Manley 369
Howe, E. Graham and Le Mesurier, L. 433
Hugel, Baron Friedrich von 58, 104, 247
Hume OSB, Basil 6, 159, 191, 223
Hunt, Leigh 334
Hurst, Leonard 483
Huxley, Aldous 64, 75, 156, 211, 212, 235, 290, 299, 450, 457
Huxley, Sir Julian 457, 474

Ibsen, Henrik 163, 274, 334
Inge, W.R. 41, 119, 163, 172, 179, 200, 342, 371, 375, 390, 465, 478
Irenaeus, St 131, 198
Irving, Washington 397

Jackman, Stuart, B. 335
James, William 32, 101, 128, 140, 164, 167, 186, 327, 394, 418, 426
Jefferies, Richard 21, 28, 103, 129, 180, 210, 409, 410
Jefferson, Thomas 40, 290
Jenkins, Daniel 51
Jeremias, Joachim 143
Jerome, Jerome K. 84

Jersild, Arthur T. 2, 83, 386, 397
John of the Cross, St 62, 409
John of Cronstadt 339
Johnson, Ernest F. 91
Johnson, Raynor C. 22
Johnson, Samuel 123, 159, 163, 164, 178, 249, 286, 421
Johnston, William 107, 110, 298, 397
Jones, Stanley E. 14, 47, 55, 234
Jones, Rufus M. 21, 48, 48, 75, 76, 92, 103, 107, 108, 115, 131, 135, 141, 143, 171, 174, 175, 190, 199, 206, 224, 238, 246, 250, 251, 271, 299, 374, 379, 386, 441, 466
Jonson, Ben 238, 313
Joubert, Joseph 193
Jowett, Benjamin 374
Julian of Norwich, Lady 63, 139, 271, 417, 469
Jung, C.G. 3, 48, 107, 108, 190, 210, 218, 223, 245, 274, 363, 378, 410, 413

Kandinsky, Wassily 17
Keats, John 55, 218, 330
Keble, John 253, 330, 331
Keller, Helen 40, 354, 382, 413
Kelly, Thomas 207
Kelsey, Morton T. 128, 279, 280
Kempis, Thomas à 75, 111, 114, 144, 181, 270, 271, 314, 318, 417, 418
Kennedy, G.A. Studdert 214, 382, 470
Kerseyling, Count Hermann 274, 275
Kierkegaard, Søren 71, 275, 319, 374, 445, 446
King, Edward 421
King, Martin Luther 1, 119, 155, 287, 302, 303, 350, 351, 382, 383, 387, 393, 402, 413, 429, 432, 478
Kingsley, Charles 25, 45, 190, 202, 203, 223, 238, 251, 302, 359, 366, 422, 437, 439, 466
Kirk, H.L. 295
Koestler, Arthur 287
Kuhn, Isobel 387
Küng, Hans 47, 51, 54, 55, 112, 179, 203, 302, 307, 401, 414, 434, 462, 477
Kushner, Rabbi H. 413

Lampe, G.W.H. 405
Latin proverb 213, 412
Lavelle, Louis 119
Law, William 33, 37, 55, 75, 76, 116, 183, 191, 210, 288, 294, 338, 341, 346, 347, 379, 380, 390, 391, 422, 477
Lawrence, Brother 32, 143, 338, 342, 343
Lawrence, D.H. 71, 77, 128, 168, 206, 247, 263, 291, 363, 390, 403, 424, 441, 470
Lee, Harper 445
Leech, Kenneth 8, 199, 373, 374
Leo, St 198
Lerner, Max 92
LeShan, Lawrence 278
Lewis, C.S. 56, 67, 71, 111, 123, 142, 145, 151, 198, 262, 274, 301, 302, 405
Lewisohn, Ludwig 17
Lindbergh, Anne Morrow 127, 219, 391
Lippmann, Walter 290
Livingstone, Sir Richard 47, 449
Longfellow, Henry Wadsworth 16, 18, 20, 29, 83, 149, 170, 250, 258, 314, 330, 362, 390, 413, 425, 430
Lowell, Amy 17
Lowell, J.R. 112, 148, 266, 314, 334
Lubbock, Sir John 37, 282, 429
Luther, Martin 339
Lynd, Helen Merrell 426

Macdonald, George 28, 112, 115, 136, 155, 218, 233, 302, 305, 306, 314, 315, 346, 378, 442, 449, 461, 463, 473
Macgregor, W.M. 425
MacKenna, Stephen 22, 63, 254, 386
MacLean, Alistair 307, 357, 398, 442,
Macleod, George 474
Macmurray, John 6, 119
MacNeile Dixon, W. 72, 195, 217, 246, 355, 446, 469
MacNutt, Francis 168
Macquarrie, John 9, 56, 88, 112, 136, 145, 175, 318, 339, 391, 481,
McGinley, Phyllis 406
McKeating, Henry 47, 378
Madeleine OSA, Sister 306
Maeterlinck, Maurice 29, 151, 433, 441, 465
Main OSB, John 226, 279, 433
Malaval 449
Mann, Horace 99
Mann, Thomas 79, 425
Manning, Cardinal 346
Mansfield, Katherine 194, 446
Marmion, D. Columba 132, 226
Martineau, James 6
Massinger, Philip 242
Matisse, Henri 281
Maugham, W. Somerset 139, 194, 270
Maurois, André 241
May, Rollo 14, 71, 72, 83, 128, 227, 429, 469
Melville, Herman 102, 440
Menuhin, Yehudi 120
Meredith, George 103, 139
Merton, Thomas 13, 14, 26, 52, 55, 63, 64, 65, 127, 131, 164, 199, 203, 278, 299, 330, 338, 375, 376, 380, 386, 387, 393, 458, 465
Miller, Henry 127, 195, 241, 242, 326, 397, 409, 446

Milton, John 21, 60, 99, 140, 143, 159, 401, 461
Moltmann, Jürgen 178
Montefiore, Hugh 171, 172
Moore, George 185, 385
Moorman, J.R.H. 88, 89, 307, 308
Moran FSC, Gabriel 370
Morgan, Charles 219, 270
Morris, Colin 51, 458
Morris, William 151
Moss, C.B. 199
Muggeridge, Malcolm 222, 350
Muller, F. Max 137
Mumford, Lewis 127, 298
Munz, Peter 429
Murdoch, Iris 64, 182

Neill, Stephen 262
Newbigin, Lesslie 111
Niebuhr, Reinhold 396
Nouwen, Henri J.M. 47, 59, 131, 202, 262, 263, 359, 362, 367
Nöuy, Lecomte du 22

Oestreicher, Paul 51, 306
Oldham, J.H. 51
Old proverb 67
Olser, Sir William 111
Oman, John 187
Orage, A.R. 95, 127, 162, 322, 346, 354, 382, 393, 401, 457, 465
Origen 267
Osborne, John 143
Overstreet, H.A. 139

Panikkar, Raimundo 310
Parkhurst, Charles H. 111, 353
Parmenter, Ross 355
Pascal, Blaise 59, 114, 143, 163, 182, 218, 335, 358, 366, 370, 374, 445
Patey, Edward 349
Patmore, Coventry 274, 374
Peacham, Henry 295
Peale, Norman, Vincent 291
Péguy, Charles 5, 219, 377
Penn, William 87, 103, 123, 182, 273, 275, 290, 310, 315, 473
Pittenger, Norman 115, 136
Planck, Max 195, 382, 383
Plato 99, 295, 453
Plotinus 211
Pope, Alexander 39, 178, 347
Post, Laurens van der 194
Potter, Dennis 135
Pound, Ezra 258
Proverb 230
Powell, Dr Cyril H. 255
Powys, John Cowper 41, 195
Powys, Llewelyn 246
Preston OP, Geoffrey 478
Priestley, J.B. 363
Pringle-Patterson, A.S. 199
Prior, Matthew 397
Procter, Adelaide Anne 150
Pulsford, John 191, 208

Quoist, Michel 2, 21, 24, 75, 85, 116, 155, 156, 167, 198, 207, 238, 255, 282, 286, 351, 359, 361, 382, 390, 430, 453, 465

Radhakrishnan, Sir Sarvepalli 188, 327, 363, 450, 467
Raine, Kathleen 238
Ramakrishna, Sri 311
Ramsey, Michael 45, 63, 64, 99, 367, 383, 421, 426, 466, 470, 478, 482
Redwood, Hugh 32
Reindorp, George 75
Reynolds, Sir Joshua 18
Rhoades, James 405
Richard of Saint-Victor 144
Richardson, Alan 365, 481
Rideau, Emil 363
Rilke, Rainer Maria 72, 156
Robertson, F.W. 195, 215, 222, 231, 413, 441, 442
Robinson, A.W. 437
Robinson, Forbes 201
Robinson, John A.T. 47, 338
Root, H.E. 52
Rousseau, Jean Jacques 230
Rupp, E.G. 402
Ruskin, John 16, 17, 99, 184, 286, 314, 318
Russell, Bertrand 60, 131, 276, 290, 326, 327, 328, 354, 358, 425, 426, 427
Russian proverb 229, 274
Rutherford, Mark 13, 15, 32, 48, 87, 100, 115, 124, 131, 141, 155, 156, 183, 218, 254, 258, 270, 271, 322, 358, 362, 370, 426, 435, 449
Ruysbroeck, John of 135, 172

Saint-Exupéry, Antoine de 58, 238, 262, 274, 354, 358
Sanford, Agnes 95
Sangster, W.E. 33, 45, 67, 72, 132, 159, 171, 231, 283, 287, 315, 343, 354, 375, 421, 437, 437, 442
Santayana, George 112
Schiller, Friedrich 28
Schopenhauer, Arthur 287
Schreiner, Olive 230
Schultz, Hans Jürgen 87

Schweitzer, Albert 108, 140, 187, 235, 236, 252, 302, 351, 402, 425, 426, 441, 442
Scott, Sir Walter 82
Scudder, Vida, D. 9
Seaver, George 111, 202
Seeger, Alan 29
Seneca 147
Seraphim of Sarov 234
Sertillanges, A.D. 71
Shaffer, Peter 481
Shakespeare, William 27, 39, 44, 68, 91, 95, 96, 122, 147, 151, 159, 167, 177, 202, 214, 246, 315, 322, 345, 347, 421, 428
Shaw, George Bernard 182, 246, 355, 405
Shelley, Percy Bysshe 29, 84, 178, 194, 291, 330, 331
Shepard, Odell 397
Sheppard, David 32
Sidney, Sir Philip 21
Silesius, Angelus 219
Simcox, Carroll E. 37, 175
Smiles, Samuel 42, 323, 351
Smith, John, the Platonist 41, 91, 133, 207, 218, 445, 461
Smith, Logan Pearsall 452, 477
Smith, R.L. 247
Solzhenitsyn, Alexander 18, 164
Soper, Lord 474
Southey, Robert 152
Spark, Muriel 83
Spencer, Herbert 99, 119
Spenser, Edmund, 66, 68, 139, 282, 418
Spinoza, Benedict 102, 121, 346, 477
Standish, Robert 123
Steiner, Rudolf 234
Stevens, Roy 99, 283, 358
Stevenson, Robert Louis 21, 99, 124, 162, 163, 290
Stravinsky, Igor 211
Stuart, Janet Erskine 227
Suenens, Cardinal 51
Sullivan, J.W.N. 383, 450
Suso, Henry 306
Swedenborg, Emanuel 135

Tagore, Rabindranath 28, 57, 79, 80, 84, 103, 119, 127, 127, 158, 226, 254, 265, 334, 401, 409, 425, 437, 449, 456, 457, 464, 469
Taoist saying 392
Tauler, John 76, 319, 418
Taylor, Jeremy 307
Taylor, John V. 9, 56, 175, 298, 414, 462
Tead, Ordway 215, 242, 243, 244, 324
Temple, William 10, 32, 41, 55, 59, 80, 87, 88, 100, 104, 107, 112, 113, 132, 143, 160, 168, 175, 179, 218, 219, 226, 270, 277, 282, 288, 291, 307, 327, 331, 335, 338, 347, 348, 350, 366, 371, 379, 383, 394, 401, 406, 417, 438, 442, 453, 454, 455, 461, 470, 473, 481, 482
Tennyson, Alfred Lord 12, 22, 96, 115, 182, 183, 229, 238, 262, 334, 342, 346
Teresa, St of Avila 302
Teresa of Calcutta, Mother 6, 171, 187, 226, 231, 311, 339, 347, 430, 454, 461
Tersteegen, Gerhard 160, 298, 343, 360
Tertullian 46
Thackeray, William Makepeace 322
*Theologia Germanica* 2, 36, 139, 140
Thielicke, Helmut 26, 107, 434
Thompson, Francis 4
Thoreau, Henry David 36, 181, 186, 194, 214, 258, 289, 306, 326, 441
Thornton CR, L.S. 120
Thornton, Martin 100
Tillich, Paul 3, 52, 72, 72, 96, 144, 179, 262
Tizard, Leslie J. 429, 438, 476
Tolstoy, Leo 103, 136, 140, 190, 310, 370
Tournier, Paul 56
Traherne, Thomas 73, 171, 190, 194, 226, 250, 448
Trench, Richard Chevenix 266
Trevelyan, George 280

Unamuno, Miguel de 95, 178, 354
Underhill, Evelyn 8, 10, 11, 112, 174, 179, 198, 222, 223, 246, 298, 299, 335, 339, 344, 351, 358, 370, 374, 375, 376, 402, 449, 469

Vanier, Jean 81, 156, 168, 242, 243
Vanstone, W.H. 362
Vatican II Council 303
Vaughan, Henry 103
Vidler, Alec R. 52
Vincent, John J. 87, 306
Vinci, Leonardo da 79
Visser 'T Hooft, W.A. 51
Voillaume, René 116, 446

Wagner, Richard 294
Wakefield, Gordon, S. 163
Walton, Izaak 36, 47, 67, 135, 167, 182, 227, 287, 421
Ward, Benedicta 374
Ward, J. Neville 10, 26, 79, 79, 80, 151, 275, 405, 413
Watson, David 84
Watts, Alan W. 198
Webb, C.G.J. 174
Weil, Simone 75, 178, 254, 310
Wells, H.G. 29, 223, 286
West, Morris 116, 394, 458

West, Rebecca 258
Westcott, B.F. 478
Whale, J.S. 407
Whichcote, Benjamin 4, 111, 131, 171, 302, 334, 346, 370, 389, 397, 481
Whitehead, Alfred North 282, 334, 450, 451, 469
Whiting, Lilian 14, 15, 176, 234
Whitman, Walt 124, 139, 179, 214, 250, 317, 466
Whittier, John Greenleaf 359, 438
Widor, C.M. 293
Wilde, Oscar 2, 138, 155, 183, 195, 331, 410
Wilder, Thornton 104
Wilhelm, Richard 3
William of St Thierry 457
Williams, Daniel D. 143, 144
Williams CR, H.A. 95, 226, 469
Willoughby, W.C. 276
Wilson, Edward 268, 271
Wolfe, Thomas 227
Woolf, Virginia 195
Woolman, John 287, 393
Wordsworth, William 9, 20, 45, 63, 112, 230, 261, 318, 332, 397, 398, 465, 477
Wright, Frank 26, 378
Wyon, Olive 10, 418, 459

Yeats, J.B. 164, 194, 242, 258, 329, 330, 445, 449
Yeats, W.B. 31
Yelchaninov, Father 318, 406
Yevgeny, Yevtushenko 186
Young, Edward, 36, 46, 355, 392

Zaehner, R.C. 364
Zeller, Hubert van 21, 40, 83, 84, 120, 179, 215, 246, 251, 255, 263, 264, 274, 275, 283, 318, 342, 401, 405, 413, 429, 477, 481

## Images and activities

The book contains many carefully selected photographs. Photographs bring the real wor... show the relevance of sociology to today's society. There are also specially drawn cartoons in chapters 3 and 5. They provide entertaining and memorable snapshots of key ideas.

Each cartoon and photograph is accompanied by an activity – one or more questions which ask you to think about and comment on the picture with reference to the preceding text. These activities give you the opportunity to apply what you've just learned.

### Activity

*Take Back the Workplace and #MeToo survivors march, November 2017.*

Why does Higgins describe the fourth wave of feminism as digital feminism?

### Activity

*Language difficulties may result in incomplete questionnaires, group efforts to complete them and low response rates.*

Special thanks to Matt Timson for the excellent cartoons.

## Contemporary issues

*Contemporary issues* are short international case studies with activities asking you to apply sociological ideas to issues of the day from societies around the world. This shows the relevance of sociology to you and the society you live in. For example, do you live in a fair and just society? Is there equality of opportunity? Does everybody have an equal chance to succeed in the education system? These are fundamental questions which we hope will stay with you long after your A Level exams.

### Contemporary issues: Fake news

*US presidential candidates Hillary Clinton and Donald Trump debating before the election in 2016.*

The Macedonian town of Veles in Eastern Europe has launched over 140 United States political news websites. Almost all support Donald Trump, mostly with fake news stories. Here are a couple of false news stories for Trump supporters about Hillary Clinton, his opponent for the presidency.

**A 'quote' from Hillary Clinton** Hillary Clinton is falsely quoted on one website as saying, in 2013, 'I would like to see people like Donald Trump running for office. They're honest and can't be bought and sold.' In its first week on Facebook, this post had 480 000 shares, reactions and comments.

Source: Buzzfeed News online.

**'Your Prayers Have Been Answered'** Under this headline, the article claimed that Hillary Clinton would be indicted and tried in 2017 for crimes related to her supposed misuse of her personal email. This fake news produced 140 000 shares, reactions and comments on Facebook.

#### Questions

1. Why is it important to study fake news?
2. Should fake news be censored? Think about freedom of expression in your answer.
3. How might fake news have influenced the US presidential election in 2016?

## Then and now

This is a feature which revisits ground-breaking sociological studies from the last 50 years. Usually written by the original authors, from Paul Willis to Carol Smart, *Then and now* features assess the significance of these classic studies to today's society. They also give you an insight into how sociologists think and carry out their research.

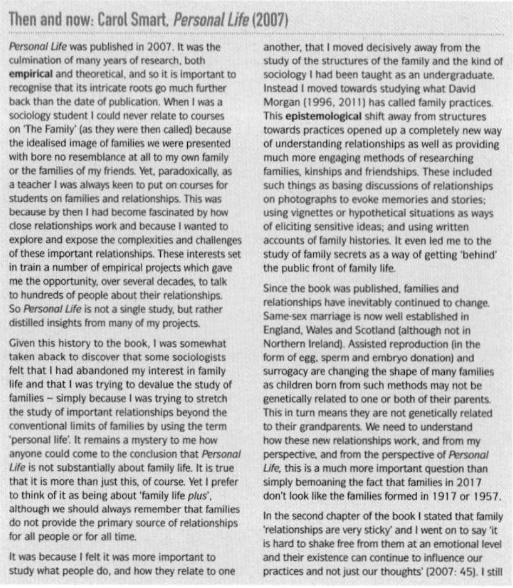

**Then and now: Carol Smart, *Personal Life* (2007)**

*Personal Life* was published in 2007. It was the culmination of many years of research, both **empirical** and theoretical, and so it is important to recognise that its intricate roots go much further back than the date of publication. When I was a sociology student I could never relate to courses on 'The Family' (as they were then called) because the idealised image of families we were presented with bore no resemblance at all to my own family or the families of my friends. Yet, paradoxically, as a teacher I was always keen to put on courses for students on families and relationships. This was because by then I had become fascinated by how close relationships work and because I wanted to explore and expose the complexities and challenges of these important relationships. These interests set in train a number of empirical projects which gave me the opportunity, over several decades, to talk to hundreds of people about their relationships. So *Personal Life* is not a single study, but rather distilled insights from many of my projects.

Given this history to the book, I was somewhat taken aback to discover that some sociologists felt that I had abandoned my interest in family life and that I was trying to devalue the study of families – simply because I was trying to stretch the study of important relationships beyond the conventional limits of families by using the term 'personal life'. It remains a mystery to me how anyone could come to the conclusion that *Personal Life* is not substantially about family life. It is true that it is more than just this, of course. Yet I prefer to think of it as being about 'family life *plus*', although we should always remember that families do not provide the primary source of relationships for all people or for all time.

It was because I felt it was more important to study what people do, and how they relate to one another, that I moved decisively away from the study of the structures of the family and the kind of sociology I had been taught as an undergraduate. Instead I moved towards studying what David Morgan (1996, 2011) has called family practices. This **epistemological** shift away from structures towards practices opened up a completely new way of understanding relationships as well as providing much more engaging methods of researching families, kinships and friendships. These included such things as basing discussions of relationships on photographs to evoke memories and stories; using vignettes or hypothetical situations as ways of eliciting sensitive ideas; and using written accounts of family histories. It even led me to the study of family secrets as a way of getting 'behind' the public front of family life.

Since the book was published, families and relationships have inevitably continued to change. Same-sex marriage is now well established in England, Wales and Scotland (although not in Northern Ireland). Assisted reproduction (in the form of egg, sperm and embryo donation) and surrogacy are changing the shape of many families as children born from such methods may not be genetically related to one or both of their parents. This in turn means they are not genetically related to their grandparents. We need to understand how these new relationships work, and from my perspective, and from the perspective of *Personal Life*, this is a much more important question than simply bemoaning the fact that families in 2017 don't look like the families formed in 1917 or 1957.

In the second chapter of the book I stated that family 'relationships are very sticky' and I went on to say 'it is hard to shake free from them at an emotional level and their existence can continue to influence our practices and not just our thoughts' (2007: 45). I still

With many thanks to the following sociologists for contributing a 'Then and now' feature:

- Professor Becky Francis, University College London
- Professor Carol Smart, University of Manchester
- Professor Rebecca Dobash, University of Manchester
- Professor Russell Dobash, University of Manchester
- Professor Paul Willis, Beijing Normal University (retired)
- Glasgow University Media Group, University of Glasgow.

## Exam preparation

Each chapter ends with exam-style practice questions. In the final chapter, these questions are explored in detail with annotated sample responses at different levels to help you evaluate your own work and to show you how to improve. These questions, responses and the accompanying commentaries have been written by our team of authors, not by Cambridge Assessment International Education.

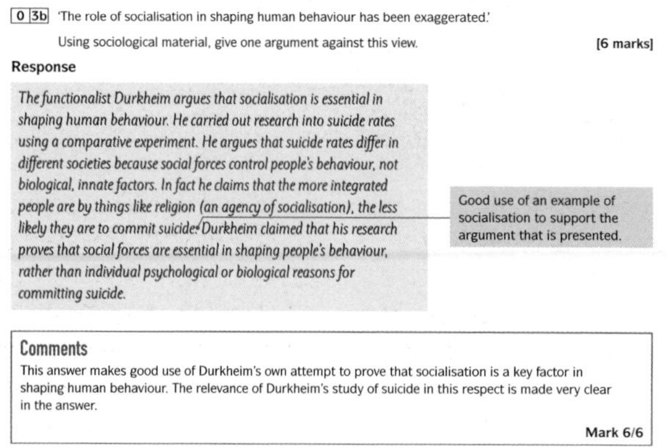

0 3b 'The role of socialisation in shaping human behaviour has been exaggerated.'

Using sociological material, give one argument against this view. **[6 marks]**

**Response**

*The functionalist Durkheim argues that socialisation is essential in shaping human behaviour. He carried out research into suicide rates using a comparative experiment. He argues that suicide rates differ in different societies because social forces control people's behaviour, not biological, innate factors. In fact he claims that the more integrated people are by things like religion (an agency of socialisation), the less likely they are to commit suicide. Durkheim claimed that his research proves that social forces are essential in shaping people's behaviour, rather than individual psychological or biological reasons for committing suicide.*

Good use of an example of socialisation to support the argument that is presented.

**Comments**

This answer makes good use of Durkheim's own attempt to prove that socialisation is a key factor in shaping human behaviour. The relevance of Durkheim's study of suicide in this respect is made very clear in the answer.

**Mark 6/6**

## Teacher resource

A free, editable resource for teachers is available on the Collins website www.collins.co.uk/cambridge-international-downloads.

We hope you enjoy using the book.

Collins

# Cambridge International AS & A Level Sociology

## STUDENT'S BOOK

**Series consultant:** Michael Kirby
**Authors:** Michael Haralambos, Martin Holborn,
Steve Chapman, Tim Davies, Pauline Wilson and Laura Pountney

William Collins' dream of knowledge for all began with the publication of his first book in 1819.

A self-educated mill worker, he not only enriched millions of lives, but also founded a flourishing publishing house. Today, staying true to this spirit, Collins books are packed with inspiration, innovation and practical expertise. They place you at the centre of a world of possibility and give you exactly what you need to explore it.

Collins. Freedom to teach.

Published by Collins

An imprint of HarperCollins*Publishers*
The News Building
1 London Bridge Street
London
SE1 9GF

HarperCollins Publishers
1st Floor
Watermarque Building
Ringsend Road
Dublin 4
Ireland

Browse the complete Collins catalogue at **www.collins.co.uk**



10 9 8 7 6 5 4 3 2

ISBN 978-0-00-828762-7



British Library Cataloguing-in-Publication Data

A catalogue record for this publication is available from the British Library.

Authors: Michael Haralambos, Martin Holborn, Steve Chapman, Tim Davies, Pauline Wilson and Laura Pountney
Contributing author: Natalie Meadows
Series consultant: Michael Kirby
Development editor and project manager: Hetty Marx
Commissioning editor: Catherine Martin
In-house editor: Natasha Paul
Copyeditor: Kim Vernon
Proofreader: Nikky Twyman
Image permissions researcher: Alison Prior
Text permissions researcher: Rachel Thorne
Cover designers: Kevin Robbins and Gordon MacGilp
Cover illustrator: Maria Herbert-Liew
Typesetter: Jouve India Private Limited
Production controller: Sarah Burke
Printed and bound by: Grafica Veneta SpA in Italy

With thanks to Dr Sarah Burch, Professor Paul Trowler and Steve Chapman for their contributions to the chapter of *Sociology: Themes and Perspectives* (8th Edition) by Michael Haralambos and Martin Holborn on which Chapter 6 The media has drawn.

**MIX**
**Paper from responsible sources**
**FSC® C007454**

This book is produced from independently certified FSC™ paper to ensure responsible forest management.

For more information visit:
**www.harpercollins.co.uk/green**

Exam-style questions and sample answers have been written by the authors. References to assessment and/or assessment preparation are the publisher's interpretation of the syllabus requirements and may not fully reflect the approach of Cambridge Assessment International Education. Cambridge International recommends that teachers consider using a range of teaching and learning resources in preparing learners for assessment, based on their own professional judgement of their students' needs.

With thanks to the following teachers for reviewing the manuscript in development:

- Matthew Wilkin, Bellerbys College, Brighton, UK and formerly Braeburn School, Nairobi, Kenya
- Raluca Stoenoiu, Transylvania College, Cluj-Napoca, Romania
- Batool Ahmed, Karachi Grammar School, Karachi, Pakistan.

# TABLE OF CONTENTS

How to use this book iv

## Chapter 1 Introduction 1
(Michael Kirby and Steve Chapman)

## Chapter 2 Socialisation and identity 24
(Steve Chapman)

**Section A Socialisation and the creation of social identity**
Part 1 The process of learning and socialisation 26
Part 2 Social control, conformity and resistance 42
Part 3 Social identity and change 53
Exam-style practice questions 73

## Chapter 3 Research methods 74
(Michael Haralambos and Pauline Wilson)

**Section A Research methods, approaches and issues**
Part 1 Types of data, methods and research design 76
Part 2 Approaches to sociological research 112
Part 3 Research issues 132
Exam-style practice questions 141

## Chapter 4 The family 142
(Steve Chapman)

**Section A Theories of the family and social change**
Part 1 Perspectives on the role of the family 144
Part 2 Diversity and social change 157
**Section B Family roles and changing relationships**
Part 3 Gender equality and experiences of family life 178
Part 4 Age and family life 203
Exam-style practice questions 225

## Chapter 5 Education 226
(Michael Haralambos and Pauline Wilson)

**Section A Education and society**
Part 1 Theories about the role of education 228
Part 2 Education and social mobility 247
Part 3 Influences on the curriculum 259
**Section B Education and inequality**
Part 4 Intelligence and educational attainment 271
Part 5 Social class and educational attainment 277
Part 6 Ethnicity and educational attainment 301
Part 7 Gender and educational attainment 307
Exam-style practice questions 323

## Chapter 6 The media 324
(Tim Davies)

**Section A Ownership and control of the media**
Part 1 The media in global perspective 326
Part 2 Theories of the media and influences on media content 336
Part 3 The impact of the new media 350
**Section B Media representation and effects**
Part 4 Media representations 366
Part 5 Media effects 381
Exam-style practice questions 391

## Chapter 7 Religion 392
(Martin Holborn, Pauline Wilson and Laura Pountney)

**Section A Religion and social order**
Part 1 Religion and society 394
Part 2 Religion and social order 414
Part 3 Gender, feminism and religion 421
Part 4 Religion as a source of social change 429
**Section B The influence of religion**
Part 5 The secularisation debate 440
Part 6 Religion and postmodernity 454
Exam-style practice questions 461

## Chapter 8 Globalisation 462
(Steve Chapman)

**Section A Key debates, concepts and perspectives**
Part 1 Perspectives on globalisation 464
Part 2 Globalisation and identity 477
Part 3 Globalisation, power and politics 494
**Section B Contemporary issues**
Part 4 Globalisation, poverty and inequality 519
Part 5 Globalisation and migration 534
Part 6 Globalisation and crime 559
Exam-style practice questions 581

## Chapter 9 Preparing for examinations 582

**Glossary of key terms 622**
**References 653**
**Index 664**
**Permissions acknowledgements 673**

# HOW TO USE THIS BOOK

Welcome to sociology and welcome to this book. Sociology is about you and the society you live in. As such it is important and exciting – and it can also be fun. This book is full of interesting international case studies reflecting issues of the day – 'fake news' and the 2016 US election, the #MeToo campaign, debates about 'toxic masculinity', and moral panics over migration.

The book has been specially written for Cambridge International AS & A Level Sociology and contains a chapter on exam preparation. However, there's a lot more to sociology than passing exams. If we've done our job properly, sociology will open your eyes to all sorts of new ideas. It will help you to see the world and yourself from a variety of different perspectives, and to understand and respect the ideas and views of others. It will encourage you to question everything you're told.

The book contains a number of features to help you to understand and enjoy sociology and to develop your skills in interpretation, application, analysis and evaluation. They include the following.

## Section openers

The opening page for each section of the book outlines how the Key Concepts from the syllabus will be explored in the pages that follow.

5 EDUCATION

SECTION A
EDUCATION AND SOCIETY

## Key terms and summary boxes

Each chapter is divided into sections, parts and units. Each unit ends with a *Key terms* box, which defines the key terms used in the unit, and a *Summary*, which recaps the main points covered in the unit. The *Summary* boxes provide short and straightforward outlines, which are ideal for revision. The key terms are also collated into a full *Glossary of key terms* at the end of the book.

### Key terms

**Marketisation** The process in which organisations compete in the market.

**Performativity** How well an individual or organisation performs.

**Vocationalism** Education and training designed to prepare young people for employment and to teach work skills to meet the needs of industry.

**Multinational education businesses** Private education companies which have branches in two or more countries.

**Attainment gap** A difference in achievements between groups which is based, for example, on class, gender or ethnicity.

### Summary

1. Culture is a crucial component of a society because it provides a template that most members of a society share and follow, in terms of what they should believe, what they should value and how they should behave in any given social context.
2. Cultures are relative. They are unique to specific societies and historical periods.
3. Social groups living within the same society may share cultural values and norms, but regard particular aspects of culture – high, folk and popular – as more worthy of their attention.

# 1 INTRODUCTION

Sociology is the systematic study of society, patterns of social relationships, social interaction and **culture.** Sociologists use a variety of research methods to study the behaviour and experiences of people in social groups. The information collected from these studies is termed 'research data'. To help interpret and explain their research findings, sociologists have developed a range of concepts and theories. In this chapter, you are introduced to five Key Concepts that have an important influence on the way that sociologists think about the social world and construct their theories and explanations. These concepts are: inequality and opportunity; power, control, and resistance; social change and development; socialisation, culture and identity; structure and human agency. Each of the Key Concepts are explained using relevant examples and there are related activities and questions to help develop your understanding of the terms. The chapter also considers the origins of sociology as an academic subject and highlights some of the main issues and debates that define the work of the sociologist.

# Unit 1.1.1 What is sociology?

The origins of sociology as an academic subject can be traced to Europe in the early 19th century. This was a time of great **social change** brought about by the transition from traditional society based on an agricultural economy to a world shaped by the industrial revolution and the associated growth in towns and cities. Early sociological thinkers such as Henri de Saint-Simon (1760–1825) and Auguste Comte (1798–1857) wanted to study the society of that time because they were unsure how industrialisation would affect people's lives and whether it would be a positive **development**. Comte advocated a scientific approach to social inquiry and this idea was developed in more detail by a later thinker, Émile Durkheim (1858–1917). Durkheim is credited with being one of the founding fathers of sociology and his work contributed greatly to the development of the functionalist perspective that you will read more about in subsequent sections of this book. Durkheim's ambition to establish a science of society was taken further in the 20th century when sociology became an accepted university subject and academic studies of different aspects of society were undertaken by sociologists from all parts of the world. In the current century, sociologists have continued to identify fresh topics to research, including the impact of new technology on our cultures and communities and the social significance of global forces (often referred to as **globalisation**) that are transforming the way we live.

From the outset, sociologists have found the social world to be one of deep complexity and fascinating contrasts. At one level, people working together in society can achieve the most amazing things, such as the construction of beautiful buildings, the discovery of new medical treatments, space exploration, and the protection of endangered habitats. Yet the opposite is also true, as some forms of social behaviour can be destructive and troubling. Examples of this include gang violence, warfare, racial and sexual discrimination, and pollution of the environment. That humans as a species are capable of such extremes of behaviour can seem almost incomprehensible, particularly when reflecting on the contrasts between magnificent social achievements that benefit humanity immensely and the horrible atrocities and mistreatment of people that, sadly, is also a feature of many societies. However, sociologists would argue that even the most extreme examples of human group behaviour can be explained through a study of social relationships and interaction.

Another sharp contrast in society is between those aspects of life that seem ordinary and familiar and those which we experience as different and unusual. Much of our social behaviour is quite routine: for example, getting up in the morning, going to school, talking with friends, following teacher instructions, doing homework – these are things that you may be familiar with as part of your ordinary, everyday life. But now imagine you are taken out of this familiar world and find you are living in a society where young people have no access to education and must work to earn an income in a harsh environment, such as a coal mine or a textile factory. That way of life would seem quite strange and challenging. How to make sense of a social world that can seem both familiar and unfamiliar, and which also incorporates so many diverse forms of behaviour and relations between people, is the intellectual challenge that defines the work of the sociologist and which you, as a student of sociology, will also investigate.

## Activity

*Coal-burning power station.*

How might sociologists explain the failure of societies to prevent pollution of the environment?

## Activity

Think about your personal experience of society: what does it feel like to be a member of a social group and to live in a world where people are expected to work together and follow common rules and ways of behaving? Choose some words that describe your feelings about being part of society and explain your choices.

Now make a list of some good things that are achieved by people working together in society. Consider what factors make these achievements possible. How important are each of the following factors?

- leadership
- hierarchy
- shared values
- mutual cooperation
- organisation
- education
- spiritual belief

## Key concepts

To help make sense of our complex social world, sociologists have developed a set of concepts and theories which you will learn about in this textbook. The most important of these concepts and theoretical insights have been identified in the Cambridge International AS & A Level syllabus as 'Key Concepts'. Broadly, a Key Concept is one that is used throughout a subject to help link ideas together and to provide an explanatory framework for making sense of the topics that are being studied. The Key Concepts in sociology are as follows:

- Inequality and opportunity
- Power, control and resistance
- Social change and development
- Socialisation, culture and identity
- Structure and human agency.

### Inequality and opportunity

**Inequality** is the situation where some people have more **opportunities** and resources than other people in a society. Sociologists seek to understand why inequality exists and how it affects different sections of society. Poverty is an extreme form of inequality. The poor have low incomes and may struggle to afford the basic necessities of life, such as food, adequate shelter and healthcare. By contrast, there are rich people who have more than enough income to live on and are able to buy luxury items as well, such as expensive cars, houses, holidays and jewellery. Sociologists have noted that children born into poverty tend to remain in poverty throughout their life, whereas the children of the rich continue to enjoy the same privileges and wealth as their parents. This implies that there is a pattern to inequality whereby some sections of society are positioned more favourably than others in terms of what sociologists call 'life chances'. Life chances are the opportunities each individual has to improve their quality of life.

How does this inequality come about and why are some groups more privileged than others? These are issues that will be explored at frequent points in your study of sociology. You will examine different types of inequality, such as those based on age, gender, class and ethnicity. Evidence about the extent of inequality in particular societies will be considered and there will also be a chance to reflect on the wider issue of differences in the distribution of wealth between countries. The complex ways in which different forms of inequality are often interlinked will be explored, and you

## Activity

*Inequality of income.*

Suggest reasons why some social groups live in poverty, while other people enjoy great wealth.

will be introduced to the major theories that have been put forward to explain inequality. A further dimension will involve studying the opportunities available to people to improve their quality of life by, for example, achieving educational qualifications, obtaining a better job or finding a nice place to live.

## Power, control and resistance

**Power** is the ability to direct or influence the behaviour of others. Sociologists are interested in how power is distributed in society and what forms it takes. Why do some groups have more power than others, for example, and for what purposes is power used? One use of power is to maintain **social control**. Social control refers to the many ways in which our behaviour, thoughts and appearance are regulated by the norms, rules and laws of society. A police officer using her powers to prevent someone breaking the law would be an example of social control. Another example would be the pressure people often feel to fit in with social expectations about matters such as how to dress and what foods to eat.

Without social control, there would be no structure governing the way people behave and interact with each other. Each person would be free to act as they pleased and it would be the individual's responsibility to decide what is appropriate behaviour. A society without social control is likely to be chaotic, with many conflicts between people and no recognised way of settling disputes. The English philosopher Thomas Hobbes (1588–1679) used the phrase 'the war of all against all' to describe this type of situation where there is complete disorder and lawlessness. Fortunately, societies rarely descend into such a disorganised state. The norm is much more one of social order, where people mostly accept and follow a given way of life which ensures that behaviour patterns are similar and mutually understood. Conflicts between people may still arise, but processes exist to help reduce the tensions and find solutions. The law, for example, is an institutional arrangement that helps people to resolve disputes about matters such as marital breakdown, family inheritance, business transactions and claims of libel and slander.

To have an orderly, well-regulated society in some ways is clearly desirable. But what if the arrangements for ensuring social control favour the interests of some groups more than others? How might such a situation come about and what would be the likely consequences for society? These are questions that you will be invited to consider as part of your study of sociology. You will also examine how power is exercised in various institutional contexts: in the family, the education system, the media, religious organisations and through the agencies of globalisation. The links between power and inequality will be explored at different points and you will be introduced to the concept of ideology, which is a form of power that can influence the way people think and view the world. Another dimension to the study of power and control is the phenomenon of social **resistance**, where individuals and groups challenge or resist the existing social order or dominant way of life. There are many examples of individuals and groups who engage in non-conformist behaviour. Why does this happen and what do such groups aim to achieve? These, too, are questions that your study of sociology will help to answer.

### Activity

*Social control: a police officer using her powers to prevent someone breaking the law.*

Make a list of people and/or organisations that have the capacity to direct or influence the behaviour of other people. Examples might include head teachers, police officers, law courts, employers. For each example, consider how the person or organisation is able to exercise control over the behaviour of others. Also, consider why people accept being controlled in this way and what might happen if they resist.

## Social change and development

Understanding how societies have changed and developed helps sociologists to make sense of the way people live today. Social change refers to changes in both behaviour and in the institutional arrangements that govern society. Sociologists have been particularly interested in understanding the transition from **traditional society** to modern industrial society (also sometimes referred to as '**modernity**'). A traditional society is one where behaviour is governed by customs that remain little changed from one generation to another. The economy is based around agriculture, with people working the land in small groups with strong family and kinship ties. Literacy is low and there are few opportunities for people to change their social position. Religion often plays a key part in shaping the norms and values of the society. By contrast, modern industrial society is shaped by technological innovation, science and entrepreneurship. Ties to family and community are weaker and behaviour is more individualistic. There are more opportunities for people to change their social position by, for example, setting up businesses or gaining higher educational qualifications. The use of advanced machinery and factory production based on mass labour brings about a shift in population from agricultural areas to towns and cities. Religion loses some of its social influence and people are more likely to explore new ways of life, turning away from the customs and beliefs that earlier generations had followed unquestioningly.

Most societies today combine elements of the traditional with the modern focus on individual freedom, innovation and change. How these two ways of life can exist together is one of the subjects that you will study in sociology. There will also be a chance to consider the role of religion today. Questions that will be addressed include: has religion lost its social significance and, if so, what belief systems have replaced it? Belief in the power of science helped bring about modernity (where traditional ways of thinking were replaced by a focus on technological innovation and economic advancement). However, some sociologists think that people have become more questioning about the role of science in recent years. They see this as one of several changes that have transformed modern society since the late 20th century. These changes are thought to be so fundamental that, they argue, we have moved to a new stage of society, known as postmodernity or post-industrial society. Sociologists who put forward this view are known as postmodernists. Exploring the relationship between modernity and postmodernity is central to understanding the social world today, and it forms a key part of the syllabus for AS & A Level Sociology.

## Socialisation, culture and identity

We mentioned earlier that social control describes the situation where our thoughts and behaviour are regulated by the norms, rules and laws of society. The processes though which people learn about these rules and laws is known as **socialisation**. Sociologists argue that socialisation begins in childhood within the family and later in the education system. Parents, guardians and teachers play an important role in helping children to understand how they are expected to behave in different social situations. Other institutions also contribute to the socialisation process and these include religion, the media and the legal system. Through socialisation, people acquire knowledge of their culture. Culture refers to the way of life, especially the customs and beliefs, of a particular group or society. A wide range of cultural groups can be found in most societies. These groups reflect differences between people based on factors such as social class, ethnicity, gender, religion, occupation, status, personal interests and lifestyle choices. '**Social identity**' is the term that sociologists use to describe a person's sense of who they are based on their group membership. It is possible for a person to have multiple social identities depending on the range of groups they associate with or to which they belong. For example, a 20-year-old female who is studying at university and who is a citizen of Australia and a member of her local church may have the following social identities: young person, student, Australian national, Christian. Her sense of who she is and her way of life is likely to be influenced by the culture of each of the groups (or categories) to which she belongs.

The different ways in which socialisation, culture and identity are linked will form an important part of your study of sociology. You will discover how interaction between people plays an important role in the socialisation process and how the particular social identities of male and female are formed. The question of why some people act against the rules and laws of society will be examined and studies will reveal what happens when the socialisation process proves inadequate. Different influences on social identity will be investigated and there will be a chance to debate how far people are free to choose their identities today. The extent to which established national and local cultures are being replaced by a single global culture is another dimension that will be explored. There will also be an opportunity to study how culture and identity are affected by new technology, including social media and the internet.

## Activity

*Social identity describes a person's sense of who they are based on their group membership.*

Think about your social identity. What social groups are important in your life? In what social activities do you participate? Make a visual representation of your social identity. This could be a collage of pictures or drawings depicting the social activities and groups that influence your identity. Or it could be a diagram (a pictogram, for example) showing the main influences that shape your way of life and sense of identity.

## Structure and human agency

A central debate in sociology concerns the relationship between the individual and society: should we think of society as a structural force that constrains and regulates the way people think and behave, or is society better understood as the product of the individual actions of people interacting with each other? Sociologists are divided on this question. Some support what is known as the structural perspective. They emphasise the importance of institutions in creating social order and regulating human behaviour. Structural theorists believe that the main institutions of society form a structure that shapes social action and makes it predictable. Other sociologists, known as interactionists, think that structural theorists exaggerate the extent to which the social world is fixed and ordered. Interactionists view society as more changeable and they suggest that individuals, as they interact with each other, are able to influence the way that social rules are interpreted and applied. In this view, each person has a degree of freedom in how they think about and react to the social world rather than being dominated by a structure of institutions and regulated relations between people. The power people have to think for themselves and act in ways that shape their experiences and way of life is referred to by sociologists as '**human agency**'.

As you study sociology, the importance of these two major perspectives – structural and interactionist – will become very apparent. Which perspective a sociologist favours plays a major part in shaping their explanations and theories about the social world. Structural theorists generally adopt a macro approach which emphasises the analysis of large-scale social processes and trends within the overall **social structure** and population. Interactionists are associated more with micro-level sociology, which looks at small-scale interactions between individuals, such as conversation or group dynamics, that reveal truths about the everyday lives and experiences of people. To what extent the macro and micro approaches are complementary is a question worth bearing in mind as you are introduced to more details about the two approaches. Research studies undertaken by sociologists are a useful source for thinking about the relationship between the individual and society, and as your knowledge of such studies develops you will be better positioned to form judgements about the rival claims of the structural and interactionist perspectives.

## Activity

1. Why might early sociologists have been unsure whether industrialisation would be a positive development?
2. Give four examples of social inequality.
3. How might a person achieve a higher social position?
4. What reasons might a person have for resisting the processes of social control?
5. Why are ties of family and kinship so important in traditional society?

## Key terms

**Culture** The way of life of a particular group or society.

**Social change** The transition from one form of social arrangement, or type of society, to another.

**Development** Improvement in the social and economic conditions of life of a society or people.

**Globalisation** The process through which the world is becoming increasingly interconnected as a result of increased trade and cultural exchange.

**Opportunity** The number of desirable options available to an individual or group in a particular society.

**Inequality** The uneven distribution of resources so that some people have more benefits and opportunities than others in a society.

**Power** The ability to direct or influence the behaviour of others.

**Social control** The ways in which our behaviour, thoughts and appearance are regulated by the norms, rules and laws of society.

**Resistance** Individual or group opposition to social control.

**Traditional society** A type of society based on an agricultural economy where behaviour is regulated by largely unchanging customs and beliefs.

**Modernity** A period in history or a type of society that is characterised by the use of advanced technology, belief in science, innovation and economic progress.

**Socialisation** The processes through which people learn about the norms, rules and laws of society.

**Social identity** A person's sense of who they are based on their group membership.

**Social structure** The system of social institutions and patterned relations between large social groups.

**Human agency** The power people have to think for themselves and act in ways that shape their experiences and way of life.

## Summary

1. European sociologists in the 19th century sought to understand the impact of industrialisation on society.
2. A leading French sociologist of the time, Émile Durkheim, advocated a scientific approach to social analysis.
3. Sociologists have developed a set of concepts and theories to help make sense of our complex social world.
4. Five Key Concepts have been identified as the basis for the Cambridge International AS & A Level Sociology syllabus: inequality and opportunity; power, control and resistance; social change and development; socialisation, culture and identity; structure and human agency.
5. Sociologists seek to understand why inequality exists and how it affects different groups in society.
6. Inequality is linked to power and social control. Some people are able to acquire more privileges and wealth than others through the exercise of power. Their power may be enhanced through the use of social control to regulate the way people think and behave in society.
7. Studying social change is important for understanding the way people live in society today. Sociologists are interested in understanding the differences between traditional society and modern industrial society. Some also draw a distinction between modernity and postmodernity (also sometimes referred to as post-industrial society).
8. Culture is the way of life of a people or society. People acquire an understanding of their culture through a process known as socialisation. Social identity refers to a person's sense of who they are based on group membership.
9. Structural theorists believe that the institutions of society create a structure that regulates the way people think and behave. Interactionists have a different view. They believe that the individual has more freedom to influence the norms and rules of society and the processes of social control are constantly changing and fluctuating.

# Unit 1.1.2 Structural perspectives

The structural perspective and interactionist perspective are so crucial to the study of sociology that it is worth studying the two perspectives in more detail as part of this introductory chapter. It is particularly important to understand that there are different versions of both the structural perspective and the interactionist perspective. The structural perspective includes Marxist, functionalist and feminist theories; the interactionist perspective has versions that include symbolic interactionism, labelling theory, the dramaturgical approach, and social exchange theory. A summary of these different versions of the structural and interactionist perspectives is provided below. The summary concludes with an introduction to postmodernist theory, which is an approach to understanding society that combines elements of both the structural and interactionist perspectives.

## The functionalist theory of society, culture and identity

Functionalism is a good example of a structuralist approach to understanding the relationship between society and the individual. The founder of functionalism, Émile Durkheim (1858–1917) believed that society and culture were more important than the individual. This belief was based on a simple observation: that society exists before the individual is born into it and continues relatively undisturbed after the death of the individual. In other words, 'society' is a thing that exists 'out there' despite the birth and death of individuals.

Durkheim (1893) noted that modern industrial societies are characterised by social order rather than chaos, and people's behaviour is generally patterned and predictable. Durkheim argued that this was because society's members were united by a **value consensus**, meaning that they shared the same cultural values, goals and norms. Functionalists see culture as the cement that bonds individuals together in the form of society and allows people to interact successfully with each other.

Durkheim argued that society is a social system composed of social institutions such as the family, education, work, religion, media and so on. According to functionalists, the social system has a number of crucial functions. First, it socialises individuals into the value consensus responsible for the social order that underpins most societies. For example, in most societies, people exchange money in the form of paper and coins in shops for goods. Functionalists argue that this is because members of society agree to invest these notes and coins with value. Second, the social system promotes **social integration** – socialisation results in a **collective consciousness** that binds individuals together so they feel that they belong to a greater social group known as society. Third, the social forces of collective consciousness and social integration promote **social solidarity** – people feel socially connected and consequently experience a common identity.

### Activity

*The role of consensus in regulating traffic and preventing road accidents.*

Using the functionalist argument about consensus, explain the following.

a. Why we are able to exchange bits of paper and metal coins for goods in shops.

b. Why traffic rules generally are effective in terms of reducing the number of road deaths despite the fact there are millions of cars on the roads at any given time.

c. Why we are generally happy to allow people in uniforms the power to stop, question and arrest us.

When you think about these questions, consider the functional value of currency, traffic laws and policing.

Functionalists often use a **biological analogy** to describe how society works. They liken the social system to the human body. All the organs of the body work together to bring about good health just as all the social institutions of society work together as a social system to bring about social order.

Durkheim also saw culture as playing a major role in the formation of the social roles that constitute people's identity. He observed that 'when I perform my duties as a brother, a husband or a citizen and carry out the commitments I have entered into, I fulfil obligations which are defined in law and custom and which are external to myself and my actions' (quoted in Giddens 2009).

### Evaluation of functionalist views

However, functionalism has been criticised by Dennis Wrong (1961) as **over-deterministic**. He criticises functionalism for painting a picture of members of society as over-socialised individuals. He rejects the idea that all social behaviour is moulded by the social system. In particular, he refutes the functionalist view that social actors passively accept their experience of socialisation and uncritically internalise all that they are taught by becoming docile citizens and workers. In contrast, Wrong argues that human beings should be seen as social without being entirely socialised. Moreover, the existence of social problems such as crime and deviance supports Wrong's observation that functionalist theory is possibly over-idealised, because their existence suggests that the socialisation process has not been totally effective in bringing about conformity.

Other structuralist thinkers such as Marxists and feminists are critical of functionalists because they believe that functionalists exaggerate the degree to which societies are characterised by consensus, stability, conformity and order. In particular, functionalists are criticised because they tend to neglect and ignore the conflict that exists within the same society between particular groups, such as the rich and the poor or men and women.

However, on the positive side, Durkheim is probably correct to suggest that there is a core culture that is widely shared by a majority of people in a society. The fact that you are sitting reading this text now in pursuit of an A Level education and the achievement of a qualification in sociology supports this observation.

## Key terms

**Value consensus** Common or shared agreement.

**Social integration** Fitting into society.

**Collective consciousness** A shared set of cultural beliefs, values, norms and morality which function to unite society.

**Social solidarity** A feeling of community or social belonging which results in feeling a bond with others.

**Biological analogy** The human body resembles society in that, as an effective totality, it is the sum of all its parts working together to ensure good health.

**Over-deterministic** Believing that everything that happens could not happen in any other way.

## Summary

1. Functionalism is a structural theory which argues that the social actions of members of society are shaped by social forces over which the individual has little or no control, such as value consensus, integration and social solidarity.
2. The function of the social institutions that make up the social system of society is to socialise members of society into a collective consciousness so that we share much the same set of beliefs, values and norms or common culture.
3. The same institutions also function to promote social integration and social solidarity.

### The Marxist theory of society, culture and identity

Another important structuralist perspective is the Marxist perspective. This takes a **conflict** approach to society and rejects the functionalist idea that modern societies are characterised by consensus. Marxism is essentially a critique of **capitalism**. Most societies in the world are capitalist societies in which trade, manufacturing industry and services are privately owned and controlled by a wealthy minority (rather than the state). Economic elites compete to produce and market consumer goods and services in order to maximise profit and wealth, often at the expense of ordinary waged workers. Marxists believe that the way that modern capitalist societies are organised has led to a potential conflict of interest between socio-economic groups, who are often set apart from one another by deep inequalities in income, wealth, access to education, living standards and life chances.

Karl Marx (1818–83) saw the pursuit of private profit as the most important goal of capitalist societies. Marx's forensic analysis of capitalism divided this social system into two interrelated parts: the **infrastructure** and the **superstructure**.

**Infrastructure** Marx claimed that the most important part of the capitalist social system is the infrastructure or economic system. He claimed that the infrastructure was dominated by a wealthy and powerful minority – a **bourgeoisie** or ruling capitalist class – who own and control the **means of production**. This refers to the sum of those resources required to manufacture goods, for example, *capital* (large sums of money for investment), *land* on which to build *factories*, distribution centres, shops and so on, *technology* (such as machines, computers, robots and so on) and the *raw materials* (for example, coal, iron ore and so on), which need to be extracted, processed and transformed into manufactured goods for consumption.

However, an essential ingredient in the manufacture of goods is the **labour power** provided by the **proletariat**. Marx referred to the relationship between the bourgeoisie and proletariat as '**the social relations of production**'. However, Marx argued that this relationship is unequal because the supply of workers' labour often outstrips capitalism's demand for them, meaning that the bourgeoisie have the power to set wages at an exploitatively low level. Owners also have the power to control the organisation of the workplace, especially the speed of the assembly line in factories and consequently the quantity of goods produced by individual workers.

Marx argued that profit and wealth inequality are produced by the ability of the bourgeoisie to exploit the **surplus value** generated by the labour power of the proletariat. Marx defined surplus value as the difference between what labour is actually worth in terms of the selling price of the product that the worker's labour produces and the wage that the worker is paid. This surplus value constitutes profit and is the main cause of **social class inequality** in wealth today in all capitalist societies worldwide.

## Activity

I am a worker who works 40 hours a week for my employer, who manufactures motorbikes. I am such a skilled worker that I can assemble a finished bike in 40 hours. The costs of the raw materials and parts that make up the bike and the costs of the power required to assemble it come to a total of $3000. I receive a wage of $500 for my skill and the hours I have worked. The motorbike that my labour power has produced is a bestseller and consequently is in high demand. It sells for $12,000. What is the total surplus value that my labour power has generated and which my employer will receive?

The global evidence generally supports Marx's argument that capitalism is an exploitative economic system that generates excessive profits which contribute to massive inequalities in income and wealth. For example, in 2018, Oxfam estimated that 82 per cent of the wealth generated by capitalist economies across the globe went to the richest 1 per cent of the global population, while the 3.7 billion people who make up the poorest half of the world saw no increase in their wealth between 2017 and 2018. Oxfam's report *Reward Work, Not Wealth* reveals how the global economy enables a wealthy elite to accumulate vast fortunes, while hundreds of millions of people are struggling to survive on poverty pay. The report generally agrees with the Marxist claim that socio-economic inequality and the wealth of the bourgeoisie are the product of the systematic exploitation and **appropriation** of the surplus value produced by the labour power of the global proletariat.

Marxists argue that people who share similar economic experiences constitute a socio-economic hierarchy or stratification system in which an extremely wealthy and powerful few sit at the top, while the bulk of society, who are employed as low-paid manual workers, occupy the bottom layers of this capitalist system, which resembles a pyramid in shape. Marx claimed that the behaviour of social classes is determined by their social class position and consequently that there is little an individual can do to resist these economic pressures.

**Superstructure** However, the existence of stratified capitalist societies in which there are these deep divisions of inequality begs the question as to why the proletariat continue to tolerate exploitation, inequality and poverty. Marx suggested that it was the role or function of the second part of the capitalist social system – the superstructure, made up of social institutions such as the family, education, the mass media and religion – to transmit **bourgeois ideology**. This is best defined as ideas that originate with the wealthy and powerful capitalist class, which the majority of members of society are 'encouraged' to accept as 'normal' or 'natural'. For example, the idea that hard work and ability regardless of social background will always be rewarded with material success is widely believed despite sociological evidence to the contrary. This idea is crucial to the success of the capitalist system because it motivates most ordinary people to get up in the morning and go to work. Marxists argue that ruling-class ideology is particularly transmitted through the family (for example, parents encourage their children to take their place within the capitalist system as workers and consumers) and the education system which seeks to convince students that unequal educational outcomes are 'fair' because schools and societies operate on the basis of 'equality of opportunity' (despite a reality in which the children of the bourgeoisie are often in receipt of a more privileged and successful education).

Marx concluded that the role of the superstructure was to assist with the reproduction of the inequalities in wealth and income brought about by the organisation of the infrastructure. He argued that it does so by legitimating or justifying ideas and attitudes which 'rationally' explained such inequalities in terms of a 'deserving' and hardworking elite of rich people and an 'undeserving' mass of poor people.

Marx claimed that the existence of this superstructure has produced a working class which exists in a state of '**false class consciousness**' – this group is deliberately told lies by the ruling class and, consequently, is kept in a state of ignorance about the true causes of its economic position. The people in this class are persuaded by the ideology pumped out by the superstructure that their failure is somehow the product of their own inabilities and weaknesses. This ideology acts as a smokescreen and hides the true reason why many workers struggle to provide for their families, which according to Marx is the systematic and unjust exploitation of the labour power of workers and the appropriation of its surplus value by the bourgeoisie.

The relationship between the infrastructure (or base) and the superstructure is summarised in Figure 1.1.1. Note that, from a Marxist perspective, all inequality is rooted in the infrastructure or economy because this is where the exploitative relationship between employer and employee is first established. The diagram clearly shows that the superstructure is dependent on the infrastructure – it cannot stand alone. Everything that goes on within the social institutions that constitute the superstructure (the family, education, religion, politics, mass media and justice-legal system) is determined and shaped by the inequalities in wealth, privilege and power generated by the economic base or infrastructure.

**Figure 1.1.1 Marxism: the relationship between the infrastructure and the superstructure.**

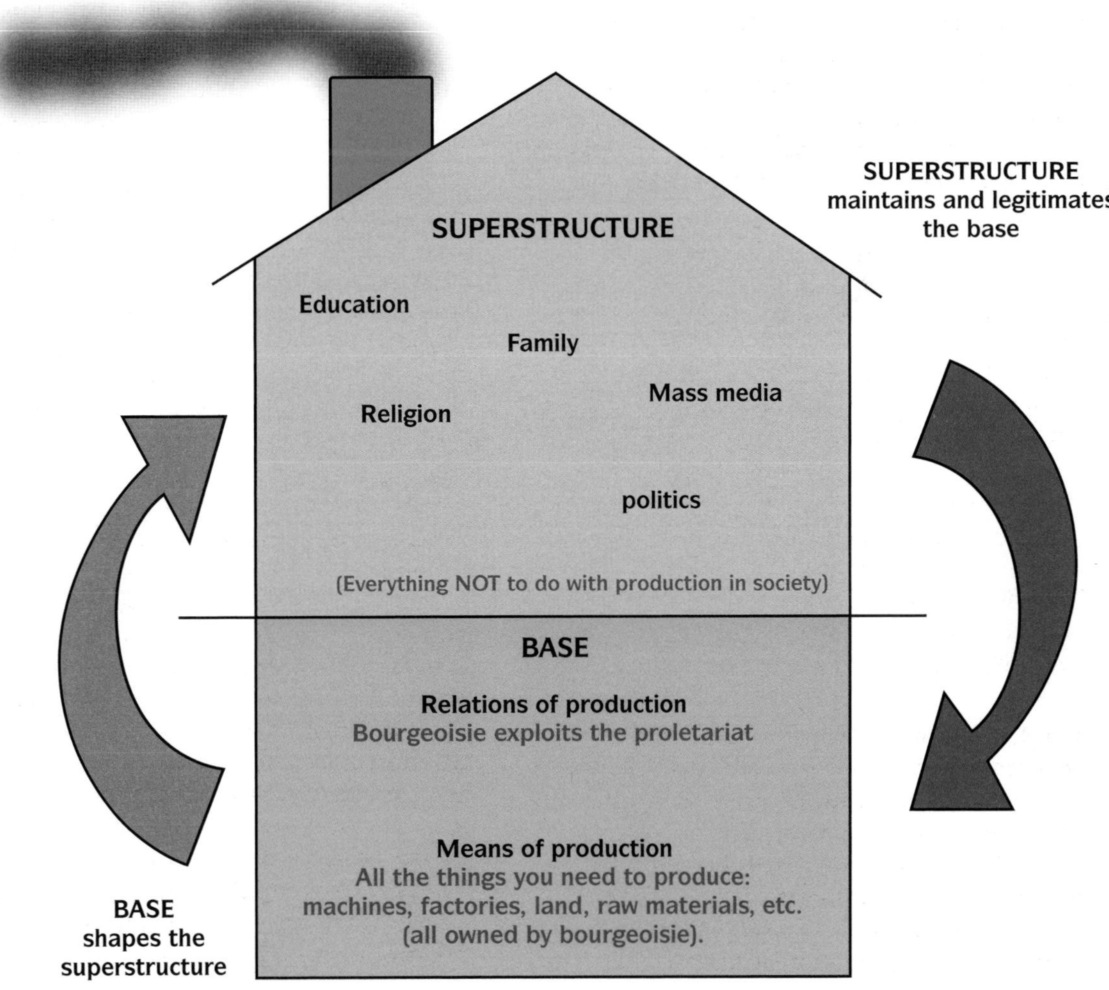

## Criticisms of Marxism

Like functionalism, Marxism has also been criticised by Wrong as being over-deterministic because it produces what he calls 'over-socialised' individuals whose identity and behaviour is wholly determined by their social class position, which in turn is the product of the social relations of production formed in the infrastructure. Critics of Marxism argue that the theory rarely acknowledges that people may be free to make their own choices or that working-class people may experience the same social-class situation in very different ways and consequently choose to react differently compared with their peers.

Secondly, Marxism portrays working-class people as '**cultural zombies**' brainwashed by ideology who inhabit a permanent state of 'false class consciousness'. This picture of compliant and docile workers fails to consider that such workers might actually be aware of class inequality (sociological surveys conducted in Europe indicate that they are), but that they feel that the benefits of capitalism (such as the high standard of living it provides) compensate for it. There is also evidence that some sections of the working class have actively resisted capitalist exploitation. Industrial action in the form of strikes, riots and voting for political parties that oppose the present organisation of capitalism suggest that many working-class people can and do see through ruling-class ideology.

The neo-Marxist Antonio Gramsci (2005) argued that what goes on in the superstructure is not always shaped by the infrastructure. He argues that some institutions that make up the superstructure can act independently of the economy and social class, and therefore equip the working class with the ideas that they need to overthrow the capitalist elite. Gramsci believed that both religion and the media have the power to socialise the working class into revolutionary ideas independently of the infrastructure and to mobilise them to take revolutionary action against the capitalist system.

### Key terms

**Conflict** Disagreement or clash of interest.

**Capitalism** An economic and political system in which a country's trade and industry are controlled by private owners for profit.

**Infrastructure** The economic system.

**Superstructure** All of the cultural and social institutions that function to transmit capitalist ideology, especially the idea that the existence of wealth and poverty are justified.

**Bourgeoisie** The socio-economic group that owns the means of production and is responsible for the organisation of capitalism.

**Means of production** The resources required to manufacture a product; for example, capital for investment, raw materials, machinery and so on.

**Labour power** The effort, skill and hours which a worker puts into the manufacture of a product.

**Proletariat** The labouring or working class.

**Social relations of production** The relationship between employers and workers.

**Surplus value** The excess of value produced by the labour of workers over the wages they are paid.

**Social class inequality** Inequalities in income and wealth, political power, life chances, levels of education, health and so on between the richest and poorest groups in capitalist society.

**Appropriation** Dishonest and unethical seizure of value or profit by the capitalist class of something produced by the labouring class.

**Bourgeois ideology** A set of ideas that originates with the capitalist class which attempts to convince members of society that inequality is a natural or normal outcome and that those who succeed or fail in the capitalist system deserve to do so.

**False class consciousness** Being unaware that socio-economic position is caused by the organisation of the capitalist system.

**Cultural zombies** Workers who have been convinced by bourgeois ideology that they are responsible for their own fate and that they should uncritically accept their social position.

### Summary

1. Marxism is a structural theory which argues that the social actions of those who belong to particular social classes are shaped by economic and social forces over which the individual has little or no control. These powerful influences originate in the infrastructure of capitalist societies.
2. The economic infrastructure is deliberately organised by the capitalist class, with the intention of exploiting the surplus value earned by the labour power of the working class.
3. Surplus value is pocketed by the capitalist class and is the main cause of social class inequalities in wealth, income and power.

4. The social institutions that make up the superstructure function to reproduce, justify and legitimate class inequality by transmitting ruling-class ideology. This ideology aims to persuade poorer and powerless sections of society that wealth is earned, inequality is 'natural' and that the poor are deserving of their fate.

### Status inequality: the theory of Max Weber

Another critic of Marx was Max Weber (1864–1920), who claimed that Marx had over-emphasised the power of economic factors, particularly the social class relationships formed in the economic infrastructure, as the main source of social inequality and as the principal influence on identity and social behaviour.

Weber suggested that the main source of inequalities in all societies was differences in **status** and power. He criticised Marx because Marx failed to recognise that social class was merely one type of status inequality and that other types of status inequality based on gender, ethnicity, religion, nationality and coercion (for example, the power to commit or threaten violence) – which have little to do with economic features such as wealth, profit or surplus value – are important sources of conflict in society.

Weber observed that status also derives from **authority**, which again has little to do with either economic status or class. Some people, for example, parents, teachers, social workers, police officers and judges, acquire authority from the state or society which equips them with the right to give orders, make decisions and to enforce obedience and conformity. A few unique individuals may acquire status because they possess a **charismatic personality** that inspires both devotion and obedience in others. For example, political and religious leaders often fall into this category. The important criticism that Weber is making of Marx is that none of these types of status originates in the way capitalism is organised.

Weber's analysis is important because he notes that it is not always the capitalist class that is responsible for inequality, exploitation, suffering and conflict. In many societies around the world, and in many walks of life, social groups that possess power and status repress other groups that they interpret as 'inferior'. For example, men dominate women, majority ethnic groups and religions persecute ethnic and religious minorities, and nationalist groups intimidate migrants.

## Key terms

**Status** Social standing or the prestige attached to particular social roles.

**Authority** The power or right to give orders, make decisions and enforce obedience. It normally derives from a legal source.

**Charismatic personality** Somebody with a compelling personality who has the ability to influence the behaviour of others.

## Summary

1. Weber identifies several sources of status inequality in addition to economic inequality.
2. He argues that inequality can be caused by status differences that originate in gender differences, power and authority, tribalism, ethnicity, religion and nationalism.

### The feminist theory of society, culture and identity

Feminism is another structuralist theory of society. It attempts to explain **gender inequality** by focusing on differences and conflict between men and women. It argues that most societies are patriarchal. This means that male domination, female subordination and therefore gender inequality characterise the social structure of the society.

According to feminists, **patriarchy** is the dominant form of status inequality in most societies around the world. They claim that patriarchy pre-dates the capitalist system and social class differences. They argue that patriarchy currently shapes what goes on in every social institution that makes up the social system. In social institutions such as the family, the education system, the mass media, the political system and the economic system, women are systematically disadvantaged and oppressed. They are deliberately kept under-represented in positions of power. Furthermore, male violence against women is a norm in patriarchal societies.

However, mainstream feminism (which as you will see in Chapter 4, Unit 4.3.1, comprises three distinct approaches: liberal, radical and socialist/Marxist) was criticised in the 1990s for being ethnocentric. Bri Morales (2017) claims that when the experience of non-Western women is considered by Western feminism, the solutions offered are West-orientated and aim to bring non-Western women to the same level of 'freedom' that has been allegedly achieved by Western feminism. However, Morales claims that this approach completely disregards the global diversity of culture. She argues that Western feminists need to have a better understanding of how individual cultures shape the everyday oppression of women in developing societies. Morales argues that, even within the USA, White middle-class feminists rarely engage with movements such as '**Black Lives Matter**' or protests against official government policy on immigration because they regard these issues as irrelevant to their brand of feminism. White feminists do not see alleged police brutality towards the Black community or immigration controls as problems because White women are rarely directly affected by such issues. However, Morales insists that such issues are part and parcel of the experience of subordination and oppression faced by millions of non-White women in the USA and therefore should be the focus of feminist analysis and protest.

In response to these concerns about the **ethnocentrism** of feminism, intersectional feminism appeared in the 1990s. The term '**intersectionality**' was coined by Kimberlé Crenshaw (1989) in an attempt to demonstrate that women experience patriarchal oppression in varying ways and in varying degrees of intensity. Crenshaw observes that women's experience of patriarchal oppression is not universal; that is, not all women experience patriarchy in the same way. Crenshaw and others, such as Aileen Moreton-Robinson (2000) and Reni Eddo-Lodge (2018), argue that cultural patterns of oppression are bound together and influenced by the intersectional systems of society such as race, gender, class, ability, sexuality and ethnicity. In other words, certain groups of women have to cope with multi-layered forms of patriarchy. There is no one-size-fits-all type of patriarchal experience or feminism. Similarly, a Black woman is subjected to patriarchal influences like all other women but that experience may be more negative because her experience of patriarchy interacts with other forms of inequality and oppression, such as racism and possibly the poverty caused by her social class position. Consequently, her experience of patriarchy is unique to her individual identity and experience.

The relative affluence of middle-class women may mean that, to some extent, the impact of patriarchy does not qualitatively undermine their lifestyle or life chances to the extent of that experienced by a Black single mother in precarious employment working for subsistence wages. Likewise, some religions encourage women to make the most of educational and employment opportunities, while others restrict women to the home and closely control what they can and cannot do outside the home. Intersectional feminism has also drawn attention to intra-feminist disputes. For example, in 2018, high-profile feminists such as Germaine Greer have questioned the right of those with transgender identities, and especially those who have transitioned from male to female, to call themselves women.

## Key terms

**Gender inequality** Refers to inequalities in wealth, pay, political power, access to certain types of jobs, and in the distribution of domestic tasks such as childcare and housework.

**Patriarchy** Male domination of society and the social institutions that comprise it.

**Black Lives Matter** An international activist movement, originating in the African-American community, that campaigns against violence and systemic racism towards Black people.

**Ethnocentrism** A tendency to see the experience of others in terms of one's own culture. It often involves making unconscious negative judgements, because people assume that their cultural experience is 'normal' and all other experiences are 'abnormal'.

**Intersectionality** The acknowledgement that middle-class White women are not as exploited or as unequal as women from working-class and ethnic minority backgrounds, who may be held back by poverty, racism and religion.

## Summary

1. Feminism is a structural theory which argues that the social actions of both males and females are shaped by the patriarchal structure of society over which the individual has little or no control.
2. Gender inequality is, therefore, found in most spheres of social life.
3. However, intersectional feminists point out that the experience of women is not universally the same.

4. The experience of patriarchy depends on how other types of status inequality – social class, ethnicity and sexuality – intersect with patriarchy. Consequently, the gender inequality experienced by Western White women may differ from that of Black and Asian women living in both Western and non-Western societies. Heterosexual women may experience patriarchy in different ways compared with lesbian or transgender females.

# Unit 1.1.3 Interactionist perspectives

There are four variations on social action theory or interactionism: symbolic interactionism, labelling theory, the dramaturgical approach and social exchange theory.

## Symbolic interactionism

**Symbolic interactionism** – the full name for interactionism – derives from the writings of George Herbert Mead (1863–1931) and then Herbert Blumer (1900–87) at the University of Chicago. Mead (1934) provided the foundation for the perspective, while Blumer (1962) helped apply the ideas to sociological issues. The theory of symbolic interactionism has three core ideas: the symbol, the self, the interaction.

a. *The symbol* – The world around us consists of millions of unique objects and people. Life would be impossible if we treated every separate thing as unique. Instead, we group things together into categories, which we then classify. Usually, we then give each group a name (which is a **symbol**). Examples of symbols include 'trees', 'students', 'parents'. You will immediately see that the symbol may evoke some feelings in us; they are not necessarily neutral terms. So, the world is composed of many symbols, all of which have some meaning for us and suggest a possible response or possible course of action. But the course of action that we feel is appropriate may not be shared by everybody.

b. *The self* – In order for people to respond to and act upon the meanings that symbols have for them, they have to know their selves; that is, who they are within this world of symbols and meaning. Crucially, this involves us being able to see ourselves through the eyes of others. Blumer suggests that we develop this notion of the self during childhood socialisation and, in particular, in role-playing. When we engage in a game with others, we learn various social roles and also learn how these interact with the roles of others. This brings us to the third element of interactionism, the importance of the interaction itself.

c. *The interaction* – For sociology, the most important element of symbolic interactionism is actually the point at which the symbol and the self come together with others in an interaction. Children learn (again through role-playing) to take the viewpoint of other people into account whenever they set out on any course of action. Only by having an idea of what the other person is thinking about the situation is it possible to interact with them. This is an extremely complex business – it involves reading the meaning of the situation correctly from the viewpoint of the other (What sort of person are they? How do they see me? What do they expect me to do?) and then responding in terms of how you see your own personality (Who am I? How do I want to behave? How do I want to be seen?). There is great scope for confusion and misunderstanding, so it is important that everyone involved in an interaction interprets the rules and symbols in the same way.

Interaction, therefore, involves people interpreting what is going on around them and applying symbolic meaning to particular social situations and to the actions of others. People interpret what is going on around them by looking for shared signs and symbols. For example, our actions are often dependent on our successful interpretation of signs and symbols signalled by others via facial expression, body language, gesture, tone of voice and so on, which indicate approval or disapproval of our actions. In reaction to others, we may modify our behaviour accordingly.

Symbolic interactionism also argues that individuals and groups are constantly and actively engaged in re-negotiating **social meanings** and interpretations. People's roles and social identities as parents, children, teachers, students, workers and so on are often open to individual interpretation and negotiation. For example, society collectively agrees that the role of a teacher is to teach students the knowledge and skills to ensure that they successfully pass exams. However, social action theory acknowledges that each teacher will negotiate this role differently depending on the quality of their interaction with students. For example, teachers may judge that young students may only respond positively to a highly disciplined or controlled approach, whereas a more relaxed approach might be used with A Level students.

## Activity

Some sociologists use **semiology** – the study of signs and symbols – when they study human behaviour. However, it can be difficult to successfully interpret the true meaning of symbolic behaviour. Consider, for example, how the following symbolic forms of behaviour expressed by a student might have alternative and conflicted meanings from both a student and teacher point of view:

- smiling/laughing/grinning
- a look of rapt attention
- eyes closed
- slumped in chair.

Think, too, about the sort of symbolic behaviour you might expect to see in the following situations:

- at a funeral
- in a shop
- at a birthday party
- in a church, temple or mosque.

## Labelling theory

This type of interactionist theory argues that powerful social actors have the power to change our behaviour by applying symbolic labels which shape our sense of self so that we may end up identifying with whatever label or stereotypical symbol is pinned on us. For example, a teacher's initial judgement of a student as a potential failure (a label which may be based on a range of both subjective and objective criteria) may be consciously or unconsciously transmitted to the student by the teacher's interaction with the student in the classroom. The student, who may still be in the early stages of constructing their sense of self at school, may symbolically identify the teacher's facial expression, tone of voice and vocal criticism of their behaviour with the view that the teacher does not think highly of their ability. They may respond by indulging in behaviour that disrupts lessons and confirms the teacher's initial label or prediction and consequently underachieve. From a **labelling theory** perspective, the interaction between the powerful teacher and the less powerful student has constructed or shaped the 'failure'. This effect is known as a **self-fulfilling prophecy**. It can, of course, work in the opposite direction. Some students may be positively motivated towards success by both positive labels and interaction with their teachers.

## Activity

*Interaction with teachers can have a powerful positive or negative effect on our self- image and work ethic according to interactionist sociologists.*

Imagine that you are a new student in a school and you are about to be taught by a teacher who taught your older sibling. When you introduce yourself to the teacher, they remark that they were not impressed with your older sibling. You receive your first assignment, which you hand in on time after putting a lot of effort into it. However, when the teacher hands out the grades, they make a remark in front of your class accusing you of copying the work of others 'like your brother or sister used to do'. You protest your innocence but the teacher does not seem convinced. You submit other pieces of work but the accusations of copying and cheating continue. What do you think will be the long-term effect of this teacher stereotyping on your interpretation of the teacher's lessons and your future work ethic?

## Activity

*A first-time mother or father has no experience of the social identity associated with parenting. However society provides them with a set of expectations that they know they should live up to, especially when interacting with other parents.*

Consider what behaviour constitutes a 'good' mother or father and a 'bad' mother or father. Which gender, in your opinion, is most likely to be judged as a 'bad' parent?

Interactionism suggests that the people who make up a particular society share a universal stock or library of meanings and that this is the source of social order in society. For example, we all share similar interpretations of the symbols of authority, such as wearing a cap/helmet and uniform, and we generally react in the same way when we are stopped by the police, showing respect and deference.

## The dramaturgical approach

Erving Goffman (1990) took a '**dramaturgical**' **approach** to social action. He referred to members of society as '**social actors**'. He claimed that people in a variety of daily social contexts act out or perform identity. Goffman suggested that every social situation in which we find ourselves is a scene in the larger drama of social life or society. To paraphrase Shakespeare, 'all the social world is a stage'. As actors, Goffman observed that our role is to manage other people's impressions of ourselves. We do this by putting on a '**front**' or by projecting a particular image of ourselves. For example, teachers might be shy, introverted and fairly quiet personalities in the company of their peers, friends and family, but the 'front' that they project in the classroom in order to control their students may be full of confidence, authority and even arrogance. Such teachers are, therefore, 'playing a role' in order to satisfy social or cultural expectations about how successful teachers should behave.

This **impression management** can be quite stressful and exhausting, because people need to be constantly aware when the need arises to 'act' and when they can drop the front and act more like their 'real' selves. Goffman, therefore, argued that our negotiation of social interaction and reality is dependent on our ability to successfully switch 'fronts' depending on what social situation or 'scene' we are participating in.

## Activity

*Teachers juggle several fronts during the course of their school day.*

Make a list of all the fronts that you have performed since you got up this morning. How many performances have you put on so far today?

## Social exchange theory

**Social exchange theory** is built on the assumption that all human relationships can be understood in terms of an exchange in roughly equivalent values. These values are rarely monetary ones. Examples include:

- subtle exchanges of affection (for example, a child might receive parental love depending on whether he or she conforms to parental wishes)
- social status (for example, if a professional behaves in a respectable fashion, their clients may reward that person with social status)
- **social capital** (in return for a favour, an influential friend might be made)
- **cultural capital** (for example, a teacher might reward the industry of a student in the classroom with knowledge essential to gaining a qualification).

George Homans (1961) observed that social exchange theory involves people rationally weighing up each interaction to decide whether it will come at a cost or whether there is some reward to be gained from it.

Social exchange theory, therefore, defines social action as the pursuit of rewards and the avoidance of punishment and other types of cost. The basic unit of analysis of this theory is the micro – the relationship between social actors. It is particularly interested in how the power possessed by one or both individuals shapes the social exchange.

However, social exchange theory is also interested in the macro. It observes that individual interaction can become complex and formal, especially when individuals congregate together in social associations or institutions. Individuals choose to form such groups because they expect some form of reward from membership. Those members who fail to conform to the expectations of the group may face a cost in terms of punishment such as exclusion. Peter Blau (1986) saw power as the key dynamic of the social exchange that occurs between individuals as well as that between individuals and societies or social structures. For example, we can observe social exchanges taking place between teachers (who have power in the form of authority invested in them) and students. Note that the latter have less opportunity than the former to reward the other.

## Activity

Think about the interaction between yourself and your teachers and carry out these three exercises. First, list both the rewards you hope to obtain from your teachers and the types of behaviour you probably need to adopt in order to achieve those rewards. Second, discuss with your class and your teacher whether it is true that the relationship between teacher and student is so one-sided that your behaviour is unlikely to reward the teacher. Third, list the costs to both students and teachers of negative social exchanges in the classroom.

We can also observe social exchanges between individuals and social structures. Teachers, for example, may find that how they teach and what they teach (that is, the nature of the social exchange between teacher and student) may itself be a product of a social exchange between the teacher and society as represented by social institutions such as the government, the exam board and the type of school they teach in. In other words, if the teacher achieves good exam results by conforming to the expectations of these structures and institutions, they may expect, in exchange, social approval, prestige and promotion.

Linda Molm (1997) links social exchange to social control. She investigated the role of coercion in social exchange. She defined **coercion** as the power to control negative events by withholding rewards and by inflicting punishments on others during the course of an interaction. She found that coercion is actually used less often by those in power because it may be viewed as unjustified in terms of the losses it imposes on the less powerful group in the exchange. Moreover, the powerful may fear retaliation by the less powerful group, who may feel that the coercion was too costly in terms of its effect on them and consequently feel a strong sense of grievance and hostility. Bo Anderson and David Willer (1981) claim that the ability to exclude others is actually more effective than coercion and consequently the most powerful outcome of social exchange.

## Evaluating interactionist perspectives

On the positive side, first, interactionist perspectives recognise that people or social actors are complex beings who exercise a degree of free will and consequently possess a diverse stock of social meanings and interpretations, which they use to flexibly negotiate their way through their interactions with others and social reality. Second, interactionist theories acknowledge that social actors play an active rather than passive role in the social construction of society. Third, labelling theory recognises the importance of micro-level interactions in shaping people's identities and what goes on within social institutions. They also acknowledge that 'power' is a crucial element in the social construction of society.

However, interactionist theories have been criticised by functionalists, Marxists and feminists for, first, failing to pay sufficient attention to the influence of structural social forces such as value consensus, social class inequalities, patriarchy and institutional racism on individual action. Second, although interactionist theory emphasises the role of power in the social construction of society, it is often vague about the source of the power that allows some groups to impose their social interpretation of reality on others. Finally, interactionist theory is keen to stress how voluntarist human action is and how over-deterministic structuralist theories are. However, interactionist theory is not totally innocent when it comes to determinism. It can be argued that the process of labelling is deterministic. If, as interactionists tend to argue, it leads to a self-fulfilling prophecy, this implies that it is very difficult for an individual to escape the consequences of being labelled by powerful institutions such as teachers/schools, the police or the media. For example, it is almost impossible for a powerless student to voluntarily opt out of an educational context such as being constrained by a physical detention, which has come about as a result of a mistaken label or biased stereotype imposed by an incompetent teacher.

## Key terms

**Symbolic interaction** A social action theory that claims that identity is developed through interaction with others. A key feature of such interaction is the process of interpreting the symbolic behaviour of others, for example, their facial expression and body language.

**Symbol** A thing that represents or stands for something else, especially a material object representing something abstract. For example, language in the form of writing is symbolic of spoken sounds. The word 'cat' is symbolic of a general group of domesticated pet, whereas the word 'Siamese' is symbolic of a particular breed of cat.

**Semiology** Sometimes called 'semiotics', this is the sociological study of signs and symbols. Sociologists have used it to study the content of media, for example, some feminists argue that the frequent use by journalists of the word 'girls' instead of 'women' symbolises patriarchal subordination.

**Social meanings** When we interpret the actions of others, we apply meaning to that action and respond accordingly.

**Labelling theory** The idea that people come to identify and behave in ways that reflect how more powerful others label or stereotype them.

**Self-fulfilling prophecy** This involves the application of a false definition or label to a person which makes a prediction about future behaviour. This labelling results in a new behaviour which confirms the initial label or prophecy.

**Dramaturgical approach** The idea that people's day-to-day lives can be understood as resembling performers in action on a theatre stage.

**Social actors** Term used by social action theories to describe people or individuals who freely enter into interaction with others.

**Front** The way we present ourselves in any given social situation to create specific impressions in the mind of others.

**Impression management** The conscious or subconscious process in which people attempt to influence the perceptions of other people about a person, object or event.

**Social exchange theory** A sociological theory which explains social order and stability as a consequence of negotiated exchanges between social actors. Interaction involves transactions between individuals that result in mutual value being exchanged. For example, if a group of people agree to abide by the law, the whole community benefits.

**Social capital** The collective value of all social networks (the value of knowing influential people), and the obligations that arise from these networks to do things for each other (for example, to return a favour).

**Cultural capital** The social, intellectual and cultural assets of a person that contribute to their educational success or social mobility, for example, knowing how to 'dress for success'.

**Coercion** The action or practice of persuading someone to do something by using force or threats.

## Summary

1. Social action theories reject the idea that the structure of societies releases irresistible social forces that shape social behaviour.
2. Social action theory sees social actors taking charge of their own destinies rather than being the puppets of society.
3. Society is actively constructed by social actors choosing to come together to interact and using their stock of interpretations or social meanings to make sense of and negotiate their way through any given social situation.
4. Agency or free will is, therefore, more important than social structure.
5. The social world is a social stage on which social actors perform and play roles.
6. Our self-awareness and social identities are the product of symbolic interaction with others.
7. When people interact with one another, they are engaged in social exchanges which involve potential costs and rewards.

# Unit 1.1.4 The postmodernist theory of culture, society and identity

Postmodernism is a theory that became very popular in the late 20th century. It claims that modern Western societies have evolved into a new postmodern form. It contains elements of both structuralist and interactionist theories. For example, it argues that in modern societies, people's actions were constrained by the scarcity of choices made available to them by culture and the economy. This scarcity often derived from the way in which such societies were structured. In postmodern societies, a greater range of choices is available to the individual, which empowers them to act in ways permitted by society.

## Postmodernist perspectives

Postmodern societies radically differ from modern societies in four crucial respects:

1. The economic systems of modern societies are focused on industrial manufacturing. Consequently, work is the main source of identity. In contrast, postmodern economies are **post-industrial** and the vast majority of workers are non-manual and engaged in the production of services (in government, the financial sector, leisure and tourism) rather than manufacturing.

   Postmodernists such as Dominic Strinati (2004) argue that the main economic activity found in postmodern societies is the **consumption** of goods (which are mainly imported) and personal services. A. Fuat Firati and Alladi Venkatesh (1995) argue that **consumerism** has had a liberating effect on individuals because the market provides a greater range of consumer choices from which individuals can pick in order to construct their identity. For example, the wealthy may wish to show off their status by using or wearing expensive luxury brands. This is known as **conspicuous consumption.**

2. Modern industrialised states were self-contained units or **nation-states** which were largely independent of the influence of the other societies that made up the world. In contrast, globalisation has had a major impact on the postmodern world in that most societies are now global societies, because advances in digital technology have transformed local economic and political systems. What were once free-standing and disconnected societies are increasingly inter-dependent and linked by global forces beyond their control. For example, in 2008, a financial crisis which originated in the collapse of the sub-prime mortgage market in the USA had a global ripple effect on the economies of other societies across the world.

3. In modern societies, explanations for the way society and culture worked were dominated by grand theories known as '**meta-narratives**' that originated in science, religion, philosophy, political ideologies, journalism, historical belief systems and even sociology. In contrast, Jean-François Lyotard (1984) argued that postmodern societies reject such meta-narratives. For example, experts and the mainstream media who justify their theories on the basis of facts or absolute truth are routinely ridiculed, and scientific theories such as climate change and evolution are frequently denied. Postmodernists claim that public faith in religion and mainstream politicians, especially in Western societies, has declined. They argue that, in postmodern societies, the pursuit of absolute truth favoured by traditional meta-narratives has been abandoned in favour of **relativism** – the idea that all points of view, whether backed up by facts or evidence or not, have value. This has led to some commentators, such as James Bull (2017), describing postmodern societies as **post-truth** societies.

4. In modern societies, identity was something that was largely inherited (for example, being born into religions, social classes or ethnic groups) and something that was largely imposed from without. Traditional values such as duty and obligation to a wider social group – the extended family, religion, community – shaped people's identity. In contrast, in postmodern societies, Lisa Zanetti and Adrian Carr (1999) argue that concepts such as citizenship, tradition, duty and community have been swept away by a postmodern focus on **individualism** – a value system which has been particularly encouraged by global social media and marketplace that stress self-interest, free will, freedom of choice and **narcissism**. In this postmodern world, citizens are encouraged to express their individuality through consumption and by selecting components of their identity from a marketplace of alternative ideas and symbols which originate in globalisation, social media, **New Age** or **self-religions**, and **new social movements**, especially those found online.

## Evaluating postmodernism

Many sociologists reject the postmodernist claim that a new type of society emerged in the late 20th century that was radically different from the 'modern' one that had preceded it. Rather, these critics argue that modern societies have experienced some relatively important changes rather than wholescale transformation. For example, Ulrich Beck (2004) argued that modern industrial-capitalist societies had not undergone transformation but instead the way manufacturing is organised has brought about a period of '**high modernity**' in which citizens are exposed to high levels of '**manufactured risk**' because consumer demand for new products and the failure to dispose of obsolete products are resulting in ecological crises and environmental destruction. Beck argued that citizens were often blinded to this risk because **individualisation** characterises highly modern **risk societies**. Consequently, people act selfishly and rarely consider what the outcomes of their consumerist actions might be for the rest of society.

Zygmunt Bauman (2000) also rejected the term 'postmodern' because he claimed that it has become corrupted by too much diverse usage and disagreement about what it actually entails. He claimed that modern societies are undergoing a process he called '**liquid modernity**'. This means that modern societies are in a state of constant change and uncertainty in spite of all attempts to impose order and stability.

Giddens (1998) too rejects the notion that modern societies have evolved into postmodern ones. He argues that modern societies are experiencing social changes but that none of these are important enough to transform them into an entity that is dramatically different to those societies that dominated the 20th century. Giddens argues that contemporary societies are **late-modern societies**. However, the social change that these societies have experienced is merely an extension of social forces and processes which have been around for some time. Giddens highlights two extensions. First, interaction and communication between individuals in early-modern societies used to be constrained by time, space and geography. However, these things have now become instantaneous because of the technological revolution in digital forms of communication, especially the internet, smartphones and email. Second, Giddens argues that the traditional ways of thinking and practices that dominated early-modern societies have been replaced by thinking and social action based on **reflexivity**. This means that citizens are now more individualistic and consequently make choices about their actions and about who they want to be. Giddens argues that people living in late-modern societies understand and treat their self-identity as a reflexive project. Instead of taking for granted or passively inheriting who they are, people frequently and actively shape or construct their identity.

Finally, Marxists, too, are critical of postmodernism, because they argue that the logic of capitalism which underpinned modern societies continues undisturbed today. Marxists claim that capitalism has expanded to become global in nature and capitalists have modified their outlook to embrace the idea that those who own capital no longer have any need for nationality. Other Marxists, such as John Bellamy Foster (2014) and Robert McChesney (2012), note that in **late capitalism**, there has been an economic tendency to **monopoly** and **oligopoly** as exhibited by the dominance of Google, Facebook, Amazon and Apple. David Graeber (2018) observes that capitalism has evolved to produce more profitable ways of exploiting labour to the extent that many of the jobs found in late capitalist societies serve no meaningful purpose beyond perpetuating the capitalist system. Jurgen Habermas (1984) argues that modernity should be seen as an incomplete project that requires revolutionary change in the form of more democracy, freedom and rational socialist policy.

### Activity

Read the following eight theoretical statements carefully and categorise them as either functionalist, Marxist, feminist or as social action theory. There are two statements for each theory.

1. Marriage is based on the domination of women by men.
2. In general, societies such as ours operate reasonably well because most people generally agree on most things.
3. 'Deviance' is a label given by people with the power to define what is normal and what is not normal.
4. Laws are created by the capitalist class to protect their own interests.
5. Religion and the mass media have always been used by the powerful as a way of persuading those without power, such as the poor, to accept without question the ways things are.
6. The role of social institutions is to encourage a sense of belonging to society.

7. People construct society by choosing to socially interact with one another.
8. Housework is slave labour – unpaid and done largely for the benefit of men.

## Key Terms

**Post-industrial** A stage in a society's development when the service sector of the economy generates more wealth than the industrial or manufacturing sector of the economy.

**Consumption** Consumers spending money on commodities/goods (shopping).

**Consumerism** The preoccupation of society with the acquisition of consumer goods.

**Conspicuous consumption** Expenditure on, and consumption of, luxuries on a lavish scale in an attempt to enhance one's prestige.

**Nation-states** A sovereign state of which most of the citizens or subjects are united by factors which define a nation, such as language, possession of a territory with borders and/or common descent.

**Meta-narratives** Grand theories which aim to explain society and human behaviour.

**Relativism** The view that there is no such thing as absolute truth and that all opinions and experiences have validity.

**Post-truth** A situation in which expert opinion and facts are less influential in shaping public attitudes than emotion, faith and personal belief.

**Individualism** Being free from external pressures such as tradition and duty and being able to pursue one's own interests (sometimes at the expense of others).

**Narcissism** Extreme selfishness, with a grandiose view of one's own talents and a craving for admiration.

**New Age religion** A type of religion which aims to help people find spiritual fulfilment through practices such as meditation, healing and self-discovery.

**Self-religions** New Age religions which claim to improve self.

**New social movements** Political movements, which are often radical, global in reach and disproportionately supported by young people and coordinated online.

**High modernity** The later stages of modern societies identified by Beck, associated with manufactured risks to the ecology of the planet and high levels of individualisation.

**Manufactured risks** The risks produced by consumer demand for more consumer goods and the inability of capitalism to manufacture goods without risking the environment (for example, through pollution).

**Individualisation** A social feature of late or postmodernity which encourages members of society to put the interests of themselves before the interests of the wider social group. It encourages selfishness rather than selflessness.

**Risk society** Beck's idea that technology used by capitalist societies has many negative consequences for humankind in terms of pollution, new diseases and environmental destruction.

**Liquid modernity** A term used by Bauman to describe the later stages of modernity, which he sees as characterised by uncertainty.

**Late modernity** A term used by Giddens to describe the later stages of modern society, which he claims is characterised by globalisation and reflexivity.

**Reflexivity** The state of being able to examine one's own feelings, reactions and motives for acting and being able to adjust one's behaviour or identity accordingly.

**Late capitalism** A term used by Marxists to describe the later stages of modern capitalist society, especially capitalism's ability to exploit new global markets and to create new forms of labour in order to generate profit.

**Monopoly** The exclusive possession or control of the supply of, or trade in, a commodity or service.

**Oligopoly** A state of limited competition, in which a market is shared by a very small number of producers or sellers.

## Summary

1. Postmodernists argue that societies have entered a new era as the modern features of society go into decline and are subsequently replaced by a completely new set of postmodern characteristics.
2. Postmodernists claim that modern societies have specific features: they have economies dominated by industrial manufacturing; they are politically autonomous societies and are not influenced by global processes; the citizens of such societies obtain their world views from meta-narratives supplied by tradition, religion, science and so on; identity is mainly derived from structural influences over which they have little control, for example, work, social class and patriarchy.
3. Critics of postmodernism claim that modern societies are merely going through some important changes rather than undergoing a total transformation. They use terms such as 'high modernity', 'late modernity', 'liquid modernity' and 'late capitalism' to describe these changes.

# 2 SOCIALISATION AND IDENTITY

## Chapter contents


| | | |
|---|---|---|
| **Section A** | **Socialisation and the creation of social identity** | **25** |
| **Exam-style practice questions** | | **73** |


Sociologists observe that there is a strong relationship between culture, **socialisation** and identity. At birth, you joined a social world or **society** with a distinct way of life or culture that had probably been in existence for hundreds of years. This chapter will focus on helping you to identify the key features of the culture that you experience daily. The chapter will also focus on the process of 'socialisation' – how you and other members of your society 'learn' or acquire those aspects of culture which shape your identity. There are two aspects to identity:

The first is personal or self-**identity** – this refers to how you view yourself in your daily interactions with others. For example, you may regard yourself as 'shy' or 'introverted' or as 'outgoing' and 'confident'. This type of identity undergoes extensive change over the years as other people react to your personality and you respond by changing aspects of it. For example, your personality is likely to be very different today compared to how it was at the age of 11.

The second is social identity – this refers to how society expects you to think and behave as members of a particular social group. For example, we often hold an opinion as to whether we are 'good' students, parents, children or employees according to a set of cultural expectations about those roles.

This chapter will examine how agencies of socialisation influence social action and the effects of structure and agency on the process of social learning. It will explore social control, conformity and resistance. Finally, it will examine social identity and change.

# SECTION A
# SOCIALISATION AND THE CREATION OF SOCIAL IDENTITY

## Contents


| | | |
|---|---|---|
| Part 1 | **The process of learning and socialisation** | 26 |
| Part 2 | **Social control, conformity and resistance** | 42 |
| Part 3 | **Social identity and change** | 53 |


In our approach to the study of socialisation and identity, it is important to distinguish between two crucial sociological concepts: *structure* and *agency*. Structuralist sociologists believe that individual human actions and identities are the product of impersonal social forces which are beyond the control or understanding of the individuals that make up a society. In contrast, social action sociologists claim that agency is more important than structure in determining an individual's identity and explaining people's actions. Agency refers to individuals' ability to exercise free will and to make choices about how they should behave and present themselves to others.

Another important concept is *inequality and opportunity*. Many societies are hierarchical and consequently stratified. Inequality is a fact of life in most societies. Some individuals and groups have greater access to opportunity and consequently enjoy better lifestyles and life chances than others who through no fault of their own may be located or stratified at lower levels of society. For example, if the society in which you live is a racist one, and you are a member of an oppressed minority, it is likely that you are going to be assigned a low status and that your opportunity to improve will be limited. The future life chances of your children are likely to be similarly restricted. Very importantly, people are generally unconscious of this process. They may genuinely believe that they are 'masters of their own universe'.

A third key concept is *social change and development*. Societies do not, on the whole, remain static. Social change is fairly common. Sometimes this change is sudden, radical and revolutionary. Often, it is gradual and slow. Whatever form social change takes, it is usually significant in that it alters both the social organisation – the structure – of society and its social institutions. It also disrupts, hopefully for the better, people's choices about how they should behave. A good example of how social change may positively impact both society and the individual is the way that many societies have improved the rights of women. This may be translated into individual action as men increasingly regard women as their equals and consequently choose to behave in less sexist ways towards the women they interact with daily.

The fourth key concept is *power, control and resistance*. There are many different theories about who holds power and how power is used to shape human behaviour.

This chapter is divided into three parts. Part 1 examines how agencies of *socialisation* work in practice, and explores the effect of structure and agency on learning culture and the construction of *culture and identity*. Sociologists put forward the idea that individuals learn how they are expected to behave via agents of socialisation. The norms and values learned through these agencies may vary across time and between cultures.

Part 2 explores and evaluates theories relating to social control, conformity and resistance from the perspective of *structure* and *agency* as well as examining key concepts such as *power, control and resistance*.

Part 3 examines social identity and change. Understanding how societies have developed helps sociologists make sense of the way people live today. Particularly important is the change from traditional society to modern industrial society. The terms 'pre-modernity', 'modernity' and 'postmodernity' are often used to understand this transition. Sociologists are particularly interested in how social change may be driven by contemporary phenomena such as the economic and cultural globalisation that has resulted from digital interconnectivity and capitalism's relentless pursuit of profit.

# PART 1 THE PROCESS OF LEARNING AND SOCIALISATION

Contents

| | | |
|---|---|---|
| Unit 2.1.1 | Culture | 26 |
| Unit 2.1.2 | The importance of socialisation | 35 |
| Unit 2.1.3 | The nature versus nurture debate | 40 |

The process of learning to behave in ways that are culturally acceptable to society is known as socialisation. In this part, we consider how the concept of 'socialisation' is linked to 'culture', and explore these social processes using global examples. Abdullahi An-Na'im (1992) observes that the impact of culture and socialisation on human behaviour is often underestimated because it is so powerful and embedded in our identity. Unit 2.1.1, therefore, examines the key features of the culture that you experience daily and how this concept differs from 'society'. Unit 2.1.2 explores the comparative importance of different agencies of socialisation. For example, is primary socialisation more important than secondary socialisation? Have parenting skills declined? Unit 2.1.3 investigates the nurture versus nature debate. For example, how important are biology, genetics, hormones and heredity in terms of human development? Are they more or less important than the immediate social environment in which we are nurtured as children?

## Unit 2.1.1 Culture

Christopher Jencks (1993) defines culture as 'the whole way of life of a society'. From this point of view, culture refers to the sum of knowledge, beliefs, language, values, norms, customs, traditions, mores, cuisine and the arts and music shared by a particular society. At birth, you joined a social world with a distinct culture that has been in existence for thousands of years.

It is important at this stage to clearly differentiate between culture and society. As Anthony Giddens (1997) argues, the concept of 'culture' cannot exist without the concept of 'society' because they are inter-dependent ideas. Giddens suggests that, without culture, there would be no such thing as self-consciousness or 'identity', which sociologists argue separate human beings from other animals.

A society constitutes a group of people who live alongside one another in a more or less ordered community. Sociologists argue that society is made up of all the formal and informal social institutions that people create by interacting with one other. These institutions include marriage and the family, the peer group, education, government (sometimes referred to as the state), religion, the workplace, traditional forms of media such as newspapers and television, and new forms of media such as the internet and social platforms such as Facebook.

Sociologists argue that culture is mainly responsible for shaping how societies work in practice. Culture sets out the key values that individuals who belong to the social institutions who make up society need to possess. For example, members of families are strongly encouraged to value marriage and the nurturing of children, while legal institutions such as the law and the police are expected to value and deal with all members of society equally. Culture is also responsible for putting values into practice by providing norms or guidelines for behaviour which regulate how people should act in specific social contexts.

### Beliefs

**Beliefs** are strong convictions or principles that individuals or social groups generally hold to be true, usually without evidence that such beliefs are actually true. If we compare societies past and present, we can see that certain cultural beliefs dominate in particular societies. These beliefs may originate in religion, political ideology and historical tradition. For example, in the past, some cultures believed in the 'divine right of kings': that some people, because they have royal blood, have been divinely chosen by God to rule over society. In Japan, for example, the emperor retained divine status until 1945, meaning that his people thought he was literally a 'God'. This belief has largely been replaced in modern times and in many cultures by a belief in 'republicanism' – the view that a head of state should be appointed by members of society through democratic elections in which people have the right to vote.

However, some societies such as Saudi Arabia, Bahrain, Oman and Brunei continue to be ruled by monarchies, which exercise considerable power within their own country. There is evidence to suggest that strong cultural beliefs in traditional hierarchies and deference to authority exist in these societies. These beliefs are underpinned by a strong commitment to religious beliefs, texts and structures which promote the idea that monarchs are not only kings and queens but are also the primary 'custodians of the faith'.

In the USA, Americans are encouraged to subscribe to the belief of the American Dream. James Truslow Adams (1931) defined this as the belief that 'life should be better and richer and fuller for everyone, with opportunity for each according to ability or achievement regardless of social class or circumstances of birth'. This belief system has been very important in terms of integrating very diverse migrant groups into a single collective and unified sense of American identity.

Other important cultural beliefs that underpin Western European societies include rationalism – the principle of basing opinions and actions on reason underpinned by scientific evidence rather than on superstition, religious belief or emotion. Eva Bellin (2004) argues that the people of many Middle Eastern, North African and Asian societies have a strong belief in patrimonialism and authoritarianism – a form of governance in which all power flows directly from a sole autocratic leader or oligarchic elite. She claims that this is one reason why in some societies in this region, Western-style democracy has not been successful.

### Activity

Can you identify four core beliefs that dominate your society relating to each of the following:

- politics
- religion
- family
- education.

## Language

However, 'beliefs' are only one of several components of 'culture' worth investigating. Culture is underpinned by communication. Language, therefore, is an important part of culture. As James Carroll (2009) observes, 'language is to humans, what water is to fish'. We swim in language. We think in language. We live in language. There can be no society without language; it is the social glue that binds members of society together.

Language functions to bind people to their culture by promoting a sense of belonging to a specific social grouping or society, for example, in India, the adoption of Hindi as the language of the government which binds India's disparate cultures to a greater sense of India as a society distinct from others in the region such as Pakistan.

## Symbolic cultural artefacts

Other important components of culture include **artefacts** which have shared symbolic cultural meaning for members of a society. Cultural artefacts include material objects, such as flags, dress and monuments, and cultural products, such as music, sport and cuisine (some types of food are often linked with particular countries or regions – for example, sushi with Japan, burgers with the USA, pizza with Italy and dhal with India).

Sport is a good example of a cultural artefact and often national sports events such as the football (or soccer) World Cup and Olympic Games become contexts in which symbolic 'cultural wars' are fought. For example, the Trinidadian Marxist author C.L.R. James (1963) argued that there is a strong relationship between the game of cricket, colonialism and imperialism. He observed that it was puzzling that those nations subjugated and exploited by the British Empire should retain such an affection for the sport, although he also suggested that Australians, Pakistanis, Sri Lankans, Indians and African-Caribbeans derive great cultural satisfaction when their cricket teams defeat their former imperialist master, England.

## High and mass culture

Within some cultures, sociologists often make a distinction between '**high**' culture and '**mass**' or '**popular**' culture.

## High culture

High culture refers to the fact that the educated elite or upper class of a particular society view particular cultural products, such as art, theatre, opera, ballet or classical music, as having great aesthetic value because they are the product of unique exceptional skills and talents. For example, in the English-speaking Western world, the plays of Shakespeare are generally regarded as high culture because they supposedly have no equal in terms of dramatising the human condition. However, other cultures may subscribe to a version of high culture that is distinctly different to that of the English-speaking world. For example, Japanese culture values Kabuki, a stylised form of theatre in which actors wear elaborate costumes and make-up. It is considered high culture because for almost 300 years it was a favourite of the powerful imperial court and its associated aristocracy.

### Activity

*In the English-speaking world, the plays of Shakespeare have been given great aesthetic value in terms of use of language and insight into human motivation. However, they were originally written for mass audiences as well as the elite.*

In your opinion, what are the similarities and differences between the plays of Shakespeare, such as *Romeo and Juliet*, and television soap operas or series, such as *The Simpsons*?

### Activity

*Japanese Kabuki theatre.*

How does Kabuki theatre differ from your cultural experience of drama?

## Mass or popular culture

In contrast, mass or popular culture refers to those cultural products which are normally mass produced by corporations for mass audiences and profit, such as television programmes, films and pop music and social media platforms such as Facebook. It is argued that these cultural products lack the aesthetic value associated with the products of high culture. Popular culture is often criticised as superficial, immoral or sensationalist and as a corrupting and harmful influence on children.

## Folk culture

In many societies, a '**folk culture**' often exists alongside high culture and popular culture. Mike Haralambos and Martin Holborn (2013) define folk culture as 'the culture of ordinary people, particularly those living in pre-industrial societies. Dominic Strinati (1995) observes that folk culture is often self-created and directly reflects the everyday lives and experiences of ordinary people. Examples include national costume and folk art, traditional folk songs, dances and folk tales passed down from generation to generation. Strinati observes that folk culture is often viewed as less worthwhile than high culture but its distinctiveness is accepted and regarded as worthy of some respect because it focuses on true stories about real lives and experiences.

The existence of these hierarchies of culture suggests that the experience of socialisation might differ across social groups. For example, high culture is often a key part of the curriculum taught in private fee-paying schools to privileged children, that is, the children of the ruling elite. Such students may be offered high culture subjects such as classics, Latin and art history. Acquisition of such high culture is often regarded as a natural part of the socialisation and education of society's future leadership because it is seen to equip them with governance skills.

In contrast, high culture may not appeal to some sections of a society's population because they see it as having little relevance to their lives. They may be more receptive to popular forms of culture such as television soap operas, which they see as being more relevant to their everyday experience. Folk culture, too, may be regarded as having more value, particularly to those members of society who possess a strong sense of national identity. In many societies, socialisation into folk culture involves the passing down of national or religious myths to the younger generation, thus strengthening their national or ethnic sense of identity. Sometimes, as in India, both popular and folk cultures may be combined. Bollywood films, for example, take many of their storylines from Hindu mythology.

## Values

**Values** are widely accepted beliefs that something is worthwhile and desirable. They often stem from beliefs but, unlike beliefs, they are not based on information from the past, nor are they based on context. Rather, values are related to our needs. Whatever we need—whatever is important to us—is what we value. A collection of values is known as a '**value system**'.

Value systems do not have to be supported by everyone in a society, but to influence or shape behaviour they need to be accepted by the majority of those who make up that society. Some values are universal, which means that they can be found in most societies around the world. For example, most societies value human life, compassion for others, marriage, children, taking responsibility for the elderly and family life.

However, other values are **relative** or specific to particular historical periods and societies. As life conditions change, and as societies evolve and advance, value systems are likely to change.

If we examine the culture of the USA today, we can see the dominance of values which are unique to that society. For example, first, American culture values allegiance and loyalty to the American way of life. Surveys show that schools in 50 per cent of US states practise patriotic assemblies in which the national flag is paraded and in which whole classes pledge allegiance to their country. Second, many Americans value the right to bear arms. Research by the Pew Research Center in 2014 found that more Americans (52 per cent) think it is important to 'protect the right of Americans to own guns' than to 'control gun ownership'. This value has been included in the Second Amendment of the American Constitution.

Francis Loh Kok Wah (2004) observes that many cultures value freedom, justice and solidarity because these values stem from a belief in a superior moral force such as a God. Kok Wah argues that loyalty to these values often 'transcends' loyalty to particular ethnic groups, governments or nations. A good example of this is the Muslim value of 'Ummah Islamiyyah' – the view that an important duty of Muslims is to contribute to the whole Islamic community, that is, to assist all Muslims in need wherever they are in the world.

Jefferson Plantilla (1996) argues that Asian value systems differ considerably from European and American value systems. He observes that Western value systems are often focused on the rights of the individual, whereas he argues that traditional cultures in Asia often do not recognise the rights of the individual. Instead the group to which the individual belongs – the family, clan, tribe or society – is regarded as the basic unit of society and their values or rights are more important.

Plantilla points out that in many South-east Asian cultures such as China, Malaysia and Singapore, 'authoritarianism' (that is, strict obedience to others at the expense of personal freedom) is valued because the dominant philosophical belief system of these societies is influenced by the teaching of Confucius. Confucius argued that rulers should be paternalistic (that is, they should act in a fatherly fashion and make decisions that are beneficial for all family members) and that in return the ruled should respect hierarchy and accept inequality without question. Plantilla, therefore, argues that South-eastern Asian culture consequently tends to value strong totalitarian leadership rather than democratically elected governments.

Plantilla claims that a specific set of South-east Asian values dominate cultural life in China, Malaysia and Singapore. These include:

- respecting the need for hierarchy
- submitting to strong leadership
- placing the needs of society, community and family above oneself
- doing one's duty to extended kin, especially to parents and grandparents and those who share the same religious beliefs
- avoiding bringing shame on the family and community by failing to meet obligations and duties.

A study conducted by Eva Krockow et al. (2018) compared the role of 'trust' in the national value systems of Japan, the UK and the USA. Their research found that Japanese values are shaped by the competing religious belief systems of Shintoism and Buddhism and prioritise the group over the individual. Consequently, Japanese society is comprised of close-knit communities with strong interpersonal bonds. The study concluded that Japanese people strongly trusted those who belonged to their community and displayed a strong sense of formal duty towards members of communities in which they lived. They also found that Japanese people value the notion of status inequality, hierarchy and difference, and therefore knowing one's place in society.

In contrast, Krockow et al. found that the value systems of Western societies such as the UK and USA are largely characterised by Christian values. C.S. Lewis (1952) claimed that Christianity thinks of human individuals not as mere members of a group, but as organs in a body – different from one another and each contributing what no other can. Consequently, both British and American societies tend to stress the values of self-help, self-interest, freedom and personal choice at the expense of the community. Krockow et al. conclude that, as a result, British and American people were more self-reliant and less trusting of others compared with the Japanese.

## Norms

**Norms** are rules of behaviour that relate to specific social situations, and they govern all aspects of everyday human actions. In a sense, norms are values put to practical use.

For example, people in Western societies tend to value privacy because of the individualistic nature of their societies. For example, Europeans and Americans prefer to keep their personal matters and what goes on within their personal relationships and in their bathrooms private. As a result, all sorts of norms of behaviour exist in order to preserve privacy. For example, when people visit someone else's home they knock and wait to be invited in. They ask permission to use toilet facilities. It is regarded as deviant to read other people's mail or personal diaries, to ask intrusive questions about their intimate lives or their toiletry habits. However, in contrast, Daniel Miller (2011) argues that it is a cultural norm in Trinidad and Tobago to pry into all aspects of the lives of your family, friends and neighbours.

Norms also shape how people interact with one another. Henry Hitchings (2013) argues that most societies have unique cultural norms which shape how members of those societies should behave when meeting, greeting and addressing others. Such norms exist because cultures value cooperation, respect for others, authority, hierarchy and the avoidance of conflict. For example, young people in the USA often use the word 'Sir' when addressing authority figures, such as their father or police officers. Members of Western cultures greet one another with a handshake, which is symbolic of the cultural value of cooperation. Some cultures have unique norms with regard to greeting and showing respect for others.

### Activity

*The act of bowing to others in Japan is a mark of respect and deference which is employed when greeting others. Generally, an inferior bows longer, more deeply and more frequently than a superior. A superior addressing an inferior will generally only nod slightly, and some may not bow at all.*

Research how norms differ across different societies such as Japan, Russia, France and Saudi Arabia with regard to greeting the following four groups of people:

- people with more power than you
- people of the opposite sex who you like
- relatives
- strangers.

Note that sometimes you will need to take into consideration your own gender and the gender of the group that is being greeted.

Cultural norms also determine aspects of our behaviour when socialising with others. Marzieh Gordan et al. (2013) observe that the basic cultural norms of communication especially with regard to the use of body language differ considerably between Arabs and Americans. These cultural differences often lead to gross misinterpretations of the intentions of the other cultural group. For example, they illustrate this cultural divide by observing that in the USA minor hand-gesturing and subtle facial expression are norms during everyday conversation. However, in contrast, Arab modes of communication tend to be considerably more physically animated and this body language is often accompanied by pronounced facial expressions. Gordan et al. observe that Americans often misinterpret such body language and facial expressions as aggression or anger. The potential for cultural misunderstanding is therefore enormous. Similarly, in most cultures making eye contact during conversation is the norm and desirable, but in some Native American tribal cultures eye contact is interpreted as over-familiar and as a sign of hostility.

Patience Akumu (2018) observes that kneeling in deference to men and older people is a common cultural expectation and norm for females from many African ethnic groups; anything less and a female risks being considered poorly brought up, elitist and disrespectful. However, Winnie Byanyima (2018) argues that 'curtsying, kneeling, foot binding, genital cutting are all cultural practices (or norms) that subordinate women'. Some are more harmful than others. She argues that all have 'no place in an equal world'.

## Activity

In a class discussion, debate the relative merits of the arguments for and against kneeling or curtsying in deference to men or the elderly.

In Muslim societies, the dominance of collectivistic values means that norms often reflect the view that society or community is more important than the individual and that individuals should not bring 'shame' (or sharat) to their family or community. For example, in some Muslim societies, 'purdah' or 'parda' is an important cultural norm. This involves the seclusion of women from public observation by means of clothing that conceals their hair and body (for example, by wearing a hijab, niqab or burka) and using high-walled enclosures, screens and curtains within the home. The norms associated with children's behaviour in some Muslim societies also reflect the importance attached to the value of social respectability or moral character. Children are expected to defer to the wishes of their parents; this continues even when they are adults, for example, with respect to marriage.

Cultural norms govern what is acceptable to eat, at what time, where and how we organise eating. For example, cannibalism is a cultural taboo in most societies because most cultures generally value human life. However, anthropologists have observed that the Korowai tribe that lives in Western Papua New Guinea consume the bodies of members of their tribe because they value the power of magic. They believe that witches are responsible for death and it is therefore their duty to consume the bodies of dead tribe members in order to take revenge on the witch that caused their death.

## Activity

*Deep-fried insects are a popular snack in Thailand.*

Compare the food norms of the society in which you live with the food norms of other societies.

- In Vietnam, millions of dogs are eaten every year, whale meat is popular in Japan, horsemeat is commonly eaten in France and deep-fried insects and worms are popular snacks in Thailand. How might people in the culture in which you live respond to these sources of food?
- In the USA, the first meal of the day is breakfast. The most common foodstuffs eaten at this time of day in the USA are cereal, pancakes, toast, fried or scrambled eggs, and coffee. In India, a typical breakfast includes a flatbread or roti, thin crepes made of lentils, spiced dips, chutney, potatoes and fresh seasonal fruits. How do breakfast norms differ in the society in which you live?
- How we eat is also shaped by cultural norms. For example, cultural norms determine whether we eat with crockery and cutlery, chopsticks or with fingers. Many cultures also have rules about table manners; for example, some cultures make a blessing before eating or forbid talking while eating. What cultural norms dictate how eating food should be organised in the society in which you live?

Norms, therefore, govern most aspects of life. However, they also shape how cultures approach and deal with death.

## Contemporary issues: Norms about death

*A funeral in the UK.*

*Mexican Day of the Dead celebrations.*

Caitlin Doughty (2018) carried out an ethnographic review of several societies around the world to investigate their attitudes and practices towards death, and especially how these compared to how death is dealt with in Western societies.

Doughty worked as a funeral director in the USA and observed that Americans and Europeans generally regard death as a taboo subject. Funerals are private family gatherings, marked by sadness, dignity and testimonies praising the character of the deceased. She also observes that American funerals tend to be quasi-religious regardless of the beliefs of the deceased. Kin are still generally expected by Western culture to express grief by wearing black, although increasingly people are turning to alternative **secular** arrangements which personalise funerals so that they are a genuine reflection and celebration of the life of the deceased.

However, Doughty found that other societies subscribed to completely different norms about death and funerals. For example, she found that an Indonesian tribe – the Toraja – believed that, although a person might have died, the corpse was still 'living'. Consequently, the body of a deceased relative was mummified and kept in the home for several months before being buried. Every few years, the grave was opened up and the mummified corpse was taken on a 'walking tour' to meet relatives and neighbours, who often conversed with the corpse and took photographs of themselves posing with the mummified body.

In Tibet, Doughty documented the norm of 'sky burial', which involves a skilled monk known as a 'burial master' cutting the body of a deceased person into small pieces which are left on the mountain-side for vultures to eat. The bones of the deceased are then crushed and ground into powder and scattered to the wind. This treatment reflects the Buddhist belief that the dead should be returned to nature.

In Ghana, there is a tradition of honouring the dead with coffins that celebrate the interests of the person when they were alive. People have been known to be buried in coffins in the shape of aeroplanes, giant beer bottles, cars and lizards.

Doughty found that when a baby or child dies in Mexico, families hold a party to honour the child to impress its spirit and to gain its favour, because the dead are regarded as possessing great spiritual power. On 1 November, Mexicans celebrate the Day of the Dead. Families gather at altars set up in their homes. Children dress up as skeletons and are given special treats such as sugar skulls. Relatives decorate the graves of their loved ones with candles and incense and whole families sit in vigil by the grave for hours.

There are signs that Western attitudes to death are slowly changing and this is influencing funeral norms. For example, deceased people often leave instructions that their funerals should celebrate their individuality. Mourners are often asked to wear bright colourful clothing and the music that is played during the service is often upbeat and cheerful.

Source: Caitlin Doughty *From Here to Eternity* (2018)

## Questions

1. Explain why Doughty's research can be described as ethnographic.
2. Why do you think Western attitudes towards death and funerals are so solemn?
3. What were your emotional reactions when you read about the Tibetan 'sky burial' and the Torajan and Mexican attitudes towards death?
4. What values and norms underpin the cultural approach towards death of the society in which you live? For example, how are funerals organised and conducted?
5. Research how the religions of Islam, Judaism and Hinduism approach death and funerals.

### Roles

**Roles** are a set of norms or patterns of behaviour that are culturally expected of a person or social group that occupies a particular status or social position in a society. For example, doctors are expected by both society and their patients to act in a professional manner and to maintain confidentiality. Roles are also attached to gender in that society often expects males and females to behave in very distinct masculine and feminine ways, which are learned through **gender role socialisation**.

### Customs

**Customs** refer to traditional and widely accepted norms of behaving that have been passed down through the generations. They are often associated with specific social situations, events and anniversaries, which are often accompanied by rituals and ceremonies. For example, it is the custom of Muslim people to fast and devote time to prayer, purification and charitable acts during the holy month of Ramadan. It is also the custom to mark the end of the fasting month with a feast and the exchange of gifts known as 'Eid-ul-Fitr'.

Millions of Hindus, Sikhs and Jains across the world practise the custom known as 'Diwali' or the 'Festival of Lights'. This is a celebration of new beginnings and the triumph of good over evil and light over darkness.

### Social mores and laws

Some social values are regarded as so important that the breaking of them can result in moral outrage, scandal and disgrace. These values mainly govern moral and sexual behaviour and are known as '**social mores**'.

### Deviance

The opposite of a 'norm' is '**deviance**' – behaviour which is culturally interpreted as different to the extent of being unusual or abnormal. Such behaviour is often condemned because it breaks the everyday rules which regulate people's behaviour.

Norbert Elias (1978) argued that actions that are related to the body are more likely to be viewed as deviant because in many traditional cultures the human body is often viewed as sacred and potentially shameful. He notes that as societies evolve and grow more modern and 'civilised', the body and its functions become more privatised. This means that the failure to control or cover up our bodies in public is more likely to be interpreted as deviant. For example, in many Western societies spitting in public is regarded as highly deviant. However, in some Asian cultures, public spitting is still an acceptable social norm. In 2015, the Chinese government officially advised Chinese tourists visiting Europe that spitting and breaking wind in public were considered offensive and deviant by Europeans and that they should avoid such behaviour in order not to bring disgrace to China's global reputation. In Japan, it is considered deviant and rude to blow one's nose in front of another person. In 2018, 29 women were arrested by the Gasht-e Ershad or 'morality' guidance police in Iran for removing their headscarves in public in protest at the compulsory law that states that women should dress modestly in public places.

**Deviance as law-breaking** Some values are deemed as so important that they are expressed in **law.** For example, most societies value human life. Consequently, they have laws which criminalise those deviant acts which may result in the death or injury of people, such as murder, manslaughter, criminal negligence and parental neglect or abuse of children. Failure to abide by such laws is regarded as highly deviant and usually results in criminal prosecution and punishment, if found guilty.

## Key terms

**Socialisation** The process of social learning that occurs in the period from birth to death in which individuals acquire and absorb the cultural values and norms of the society in which they live.

**Society** A community of people who share a common territory and culture and consequently interact with one another daily.

**Identity** The qualities, beliefs, personality, looks and/or expressions that constitute both how you see yourself and how other people may see or judge you.

**Beliefs** Ideas that members of society hold to be true.

**Artefacts** Material objects such as flags or monuments and buildings or cultural products such as sport, music and national dishes which have symbolic meaning for members of particular societies.

**High culture** Cultural products, such as art and literature, that are regarded as rare, unique and the product of exceptional talent.

**Mass or popular culture** Cultural artefacts such as pop music or Hollywood blockbusters that are mass produced for mass consumption.

**Folk culture** A type of culture which stems from the experiences, customs, traditions and beliefs of rural communities such as the peasantry or tribes that make up part of a wider culture, and which is passed down by word-of-mouth.

**Values** General guidelines about how members of society should behave. Values generally shape norms of behaviour. For example, many societies value marriage.

**Value system** A collection of values, norms, traditions and customs agreed upon and shared by a social group or society.

**Relativity of culture** The idea that what constitutes culture differs across time periods, societies and even between social groups living in the same society.

**Norms** The rules that govern what behaviour is normal in any given social situation.

**Secular** Not subject to religious routines or rules.

**Role** The behaviour that is expected from those who occupy a particular status.

**Gender role socialisation** The process of learning behaviour that is culturally expected from males and females.

**Custom** A regular pattern of behaviour that is accepted as a routine norm in a particular society; for example, shaking hands when greeting someone.

**Social mores** Values, often influenced by religion, which set out the moral principles and rules of societies; for example, that sexual relationships should only be conducted in the moral context of marriage.

**Deviance** Behaviour that is regarded as either offensive or odd to a social group or society and is therefore regarded as requiring some form of formal or informal regulation.

**Law** A rule or system of rules which a society agrees to follow and which regulate the behaviour of all. The role of the police and the courts is to enforce those rules by arresting those who break them and to impose punishments if found guilty of doing so.

## Summary

1. Culture is a crucial component of a society because it provides a template that most members of a society share and follow, in terms of what they should believe, what they should value and how they should behave in any given social context.
2. Cultures are relative. They are unique to specific societies and historical periods.
3. Social groups living within the same society may share cultural values and norms, but regard particular aspects of culture – high, folk and popular – as more worthy of their attention.
4. Without culture, individuals would not be able to live as members of a society.
5. Those who fail to conform to dominant values and fail to follow the norms of particular societies run the risk of being seen as deviant and may consequently face some form of punishment.

# Unit 2.1.2 The importance of socialisation

## Introduction

At birth, we are faced with a social world that already exists. Joining this world involves rapidly learning 'how things are done' in it. The process of learning culture is known as socialisation. It involves absorbing the cultural values, norms, language, mores and customs of a society in order to live successfully alongside others, to communicate effectively and to avoid unnecessary conflict. We also learn what is socially acceptable and what sort of behaviour is viewed as deviant and likely to be punished.

This learning experience is a lifelong process. Although most of this cultural learning goes on in childhood and adolescence, adult humans continue to internalise cultural norms as they interact with their peer and friendship groups and other family members. Adults continue to gather knowledge, cultural experience and skills from religious teachings, television, newspapers, the internet and from the workplace.

## Primary socialisation and the family

The main agent of **primary socialisation** is the family. The first few years of socialisation in the family are crucial to a person's development because it often exerts a profound effect upon all later social learning. Leon Kuczynski (2012) observes that primary socialisation is a process through which parents aim to introduce cultural continuity and competence into their children. Primary socialisation involves parents teaching their children how to interact and behave in particular social contexts, how to think and reason, how to communicate appropriately in a range of social situations, how to skilfully regulate the expression of their emotions, and how to successfully manage relationships with familiars, strangers and those in authority. Roy Baumeister (1986) argues that the process of primary socialisation results in young children believing that their family will love and care for them as long as they conform to behavioural norms approved by their parents. Parental love and approval (and the fear of losing these) provide a very powerful motivation to adopt ways of behaving encouraged by their parents.

Jean Piaget, a developmental psychologist, is useful to reference at this stage because he identified four stages of childhood socialisation or development which occur on the path to adulthood.

1. The 'sensorimotor' stage lasts between birth and the age of two. The child learns about itself and its environment through reflex (for example, hunger or pain may cause it to cry), motor (for example, crawling, walking and so on) and sensory actions (for example, through touch, taste and sound). In this stage, the child learns that it is separate from its environment and that external stimuli such as parents and toys continue to exist even when they are outside the child's sensory field.
2. The 'preoperational' stage begins when the child starts to talk and lasts until about the age of seven. In this stage, children begin to use symbols to represent objects, and begin to absorb and categorise information. For example, children's language use becomes more mature, and memory and imagination develop. Learning cultural norms through play becomes an important component of socialisation.
3. The 'concrete operational' phase lasts until early adolescence and is the stage in which socialisation starts to achieve real progress in terms of conformity to parental instructions and social norms. This is because in this stage of development children begin to think abstractly and to apply reason when making decisions based on observable evidence. They have internalised social norms and, in so doing, have developed a **conscience** – a sense of judgement about what constitutes 'right' and 'wrong'.
4. The final phase is the 'formal operational' stage. This begins at puberty and takes the adolescent through to adulthood. In this stage, the teenager is capable of hypothetical and deductive reasoning, and able to make rational judgements and construct complex and logical arguments.

Primary socialisation is likely to be at its most effective during Piaget's second and third stages. However, in stage four, parents may encounter some resistance to primary socialisation because adolescents may develop sophisticated moral arguments to counter their parents' authority and therefore rebel, with the support of their peers, against the socialisation process. This is explored further in Chapter 4.

George Herbert Mead (1934) argued that children develop a sense of self-identity through their interaction with other people, especially their significant others (any person who has a strong influence on an individual's self-concept), such as their parents, grandparents and older siblings. Charles Cooley (1998) developed Mead's ideas further. His concept of the 'looking glass self' states that a person's self grows out of a person's social interactions with others. The view we have of ourselves does not come from who we really are, but rather from how we *believe* others see us.

Albert Bandura's (1963) social learning theory suggests that observation and **imitation** play a major role in the socialisation process. He claims that children can learn behaviour by watching others, especially **role models** that they love and look up to. Moreover, the primary socialisation process may also involve children in empathetic role-play (imagining themselves as someone else), which allows them to practise interaction with others and to appreciate that certain types of behaviour in particular contexts may not be acceptable. Play also encourages children to solve problems, understand stimuli, learn about sharing and intimacy, to deal with conflict, to learn discipline and self-control and to discover the limits of both their physical and emotional power.

Gabriel Tarde (1903) also emphasised the role of imitation in the process of socialisation. Imitation in Piaget's first stage is probably limited to mimicking, but in his second and third stages it probably evolves into role-play. For example, a female child may play the role of mother by imitating the actions of her own mother. Feminists such as Ann Oakley (1972) argue that mothers and fathers as role models provide their children with gendered guidelines; that is, examples and illustrations of how to behave as males and females that children can then copy. (For a more detailed version of Oakley's ideas on **gender role** socialisation, see Chapter 4, Units 4.3.1 and 4.3.2).

All of the processes involved in primary socialisation contribute to children becoming aware of themselves as 'social beings'. They recognise that they have particular identities, that they occupy particular social roles – such as son, daughter, brother, sister – inside the family unit and outside it, too, as students, friends, neighbours and so on. The gradual process of taking on these roles and identities results in children's realisation that they are capable of social action that has consequences for others.

In the 21st century, most modern societies recognise that childhood is an important phase in the formation of civil society (that is, communities of like-minded individuals with common interests which demand from all members that they demonstrate a 'civilised character'). The experience of childhood socialisation ensures that most children subscribe to a moral code that does not harm others and ensures that they are fair, tolerant, courteous and compassionate in their dealings with other members of society.

## Feral children

As the primary socialisation process develops, children therefore acquire uniquely human skills. A useful way to understand the importance of the primary socialisation process in the cultivation of the civilised child is to examine examples of **feral** or 'wild' **children**. These are children who, for whatever reason, have either been kept isolated from regular human contact or have been abandoned into the wild and supposedly been partly raised by animals.

Case studies of children 'raised' by animals show that they often lack the human characteristics that we take for granted. Douglas Candland (1996) observes that feral children are often ignorant of language and seem to have internalised by imitation the behaviour of the animals they have spent time with. For example, such children may grunt, growl or bark. They cannot walk upright but instead crouch and move using both their arms and legs like an animal. They lap water from a bowl and eat raw rather than cooked meat. They have no 'toilet manners' and will often urinate and defecate in public without embarrassment. Many are unable to smile or laugh, and their emotional response to threatening or unfamiliar situations is frequently aggressive and violent.

### Activity

*Feral children often lack human characteristics.*

Identify six characteristics that you believe make you human but which feral children are likely to lack.

### Primary socialisation by others

It is important to understand that primary socialisation may be delivered by agents other than parents. For example, in many modern societies, both parents are in full-time work, which means that some responsibility for the socialisation of children may be in the hands of professional childminders, nannies and nurseries. There is evidence, too, that grandparents are now playing a significant role in the rearing of their grandchildren.

## Secondary socialisation

**Secondary socialisation** refers to situations in which children learn ideas, attitudes, values, norms and skills both inside and outside the home from sources other than their parents or other kin. As children get older, they come into everyday contact with several agents of socialisation that have a significant influence on their actions and their perception of social reality. The most important type of secondary socialisation is probably the education system, in which children spend most of their childhood and adolescence.

### Formal education and secondary socialisation

The education system contains two social devices that play an integral role in the socialisation of children. A visible academic curriculum equips children with the appropriate knowledge and skills required to achieve the qualifications used by employers to sort people into jobs that suit their abilities. However, sociologists have also highlighted the existence of a '**hidden curriculum**'. These are lessons that are learned that are mainly unintentional side-effects of the way schools, classrooms and lessons are organised. Many schools operate with a set of unwritten norms; for example, many expect their students to respect and defer to authority in the school and classroom, to respect other students' opinions, to attend school and lessons regularly and punctually, to pay attention and concentrate during lessons, to aspire to success and refrain from deviant and non-academic behaviour. Marxist and feminist sociologists argue that working-class, ethnic minority and female students are likely to experience the hidden curriculum in ways that are intended to undermine their academic achievements (see Chapter 5, Units 5.1.2 and 5.3.2). Interactionist sociologists such as Howard Becker (1995) argue, too, that teachers unconsciously promote an 'ideal pupil' stereotype in the classroom which has a hidden curriculum effect, in that those students closest to that ideal benefit from greater and more positive teacher attention, while those furthest from it may find that their behaviour meets with teacher disapproval and punishment (see Chapter 5, Unit 5.5.3).

Karl Thompson (2017) observes that the hidden curriculum today is most likely to be reflected in a school's 'ethos' – the character or atmosphere of the school that is articulated in the school prospectus or website. He lists the following values and norms that may be central to the role of the school, college or university as an agency of secondary socialisation:

- whether there is an emphasis on academic success, and/or artistic or sporting achievement
- whether there is an emphasis on equal opportunities for all students (does the school focus on helping disadvantaged students, for example?)
- whether there is an emphasis on respect for diversity (does the school promote multiculturalism and discourage racism and sexism?)
- whether the school encourages students to participate in community life
- the extent to which there is an entrepreneurial culture and strong ties with local businesses at the school
- whether parents are encouraged to get actively involved in the life of the school
- the type of learning a school encourages – whether formal, traditional 'chalk and talk' or independent learning, for example.

### Activity

Get hold of a copy of any brochures, prospectuses or the website for your school. Analyse the content, especially the head teacher's contribution, the photographs used and what is said about the ethos of the school. In your opinion, what 'hidden' values and norms are being encouraged?

Critics of the concept of the hidden curriculum argue that most, if not all, of the norms of behaviour allegedly encouraged by the hidden curriculum are, in fact, written down and formally encoded in school rules. Thompson questions whether these aspects of school organisation actually constitute an invisible and effective form of secondary socialisation. For example, Paul Willis (1977) and Paul Corrigan (1979) conducted ethnographic research into how working-class students experienced and interpreted school and came to the conclusion that the boys in their studies could resist the influence of the hidden curriculum and consequently were relatively unaffected by it.

### Activity

*The hidden emphasis of school sport is probably on teamwork, self-discipline, competition, fair play and achievement.*

List the 'hidden' values you think are being promoted by the wearing of school uniform and by lessons such as history or religious education. Do you think school events such as assemblies, sports days or prize/speech days promote unconscious ways of thinking and behaving? If so, make a list of the values and norms you think are being promoted.

## Peer groups and friendship networks as agents of secondary socialisation

The **peer group** refers to people of similar status who come into regular contact with each other, either socially or through work. Peer groups therefore include friendship networks, school subcultures and occupational subcultures (that is, workmates).

Peer groups have a particularly strong influence over adolescent behaviour and attitudes. Teenagers may feel a tension between parental controls and their desire for more responsibility and independence, and so come into conflict with their parents. A common site for this conflict may be the teenager's choice of friendships, especially with members of the opposite sex. Adolescents may also feel a great deal of peer pressure to fit in with their friends, and this may lead to radical changes in their identity during their teenage years in terms of image and behaviour. Some teenagers may feel peer pressure, for example, via bullying, to engage in 'deviant' or risky behaviour in order to be accepted by their peers. James Cote (2000) suggests that, in young adulthood, peer group or friendship networks eventually become more important than relationships with parents as a source of knowledge about how to live one's life.

## The workplace as an agent of secondary socialisation

The workplace is another important source of peer-group relationships. James Suzman (2018) observes that work is the social glue that holds societies together. It determines what, where and with whom we spend most of our time; shapes our sense of dignity, self-worth and identity; moulds our political beliefs and defines our status or social standing. The experience of paid work and the workplace teaches young people specific occupational skills and work discipline, as well as the informal norms that underpin working processes, the so-called 'tricks of a trade'. For example, skilled workers involved in craft work may believe their work has dignity and consequently experience greater levels of job satisfaction than workers who carry out repetitive unskilled work on assembly lines. The behaviour and attitudes of workers may be shaped by the nature of their work and the size of the workplace and workforce. Dangerous working conditions in which workers depend on others for their safety may produce collectivist values and a strong sense of group and political solidarity which divides society into conflicting social classes – 'them' (employers, managers and the wealthy) versus 'us' (the workers).

### Activity

Suzman identifies at least four effects of being a worker. Identify these effects and illustrate each one with a specific practical example of how workplace socialisation might affect a person's identity.

## Religion as an agent of secondary socialisation

Until the late 20th century, religion played a key role in socialisation in Western European societies, as both church attendance and belief in God were high. However, in the 21st century, social surveys suggest that Europeans are increasingly non-religious. Danièle Hervieu-Léger (2000) claims that Western societies have experienced a religious decline or secularisation, which she describes as a form of '**cultural amnesia**'. She notes that for centuries children used to be taught religion and morality by the extended family and at school. Religion was handed down generation by generation. However, in many European societies today, religious socialisation in families and schools has largely ceased. Instead, parents often encourage their children to decide for themselves whether they want to believe in God.

However, in contrast, there is little sign of this secular socialisation outside of Europe. For example, surveys conducted over the past 50 years indicate a consistently high level of belief in God in the USA. Dominic Sandbrook (2012) argues that the socialisation of children into an American identity in the 'Bible Belt' involves children being encouraged to believe in a literal interpretation of the Bible, to reject scientific explanations of the world's creation such as evolution theory and to adhere to strict moral codes based on the word of God. (The 'Bible Belt' is an informal region of the USA in the southern and midwestern states in which a socially conservative and evangelical form of Protestant Christianity plays a strong role in both politics and society.)

An examination of religion in a global context suggests that religious beliefs systems such as Islam, Hinduism and Buddhism continue to exert great influence over the socialisation of children and young adults. Adrian Wooldridge and John Micklethwait (2010) argue that, in non-Western societies, religion is probably the most influential source of socialisation.

These world religions generally teach children and young people humanitarianism, altruism, compassion for others and 'to do unto others what you would have them to do to you'. Norms include the avoidance of immoral, shameful and evil actions, to do good, to respect one's parents and elders, to be generous and charitable to others and to help the needy. However, critics of religion argue that it teaches a range of values and norms that can also create conflict and division, such as intolerance of other religious beliefs, segregation and the oppression and exploitation of women and girls.

### Activity

Conduct a social survey among your year group. Compile a list of, say, 10 moral statements (for example, 'It is important to be honest', 'It is important to respect your elders' and so on). Ask your sample of students whether they strongly believe that they and their peers abide by these codes. Ask them to identify the source of these codes. Did they come from their parents, school, peer group or from their experience of religious teachings?

## The media as agencies of secondary socialisation

Some sociologists – for example, Neil Postman (1985) – claim that in Western societies the media replaced the family in the 20th century as the main source of socialisation, especially for children and young people. It is argued that the media in all its varied forms has a significant influence on the type of social values and norms acquired by both children and adults. For example, numerous feminist studies of media products, such as newspapers, magazines, films and television, claim that the media socialise females into a restricted and ultimately damaging form of feminine identity. For example, Jeremy Tunstall (1983) argues that the media present young females with questionable role models to emulate, in that women are over-represented as 'busy housewives, as contented mothers and as eager consumers'. Similarly, Naomi Wolf (1990) argues that the dominant media message aimed at women is that their bodies are a project in constant need of improvement.

Jean Twenge (2014) argues that there is increasing evidence that the socialisation experience provided by social media platforms often results in high levels of mental ill-health, especially anxiety, narcissism, depression and self-harm in young people. This has been shown in most societies around the world in which children and adolescents have easy access to such technology.

## Activity

Carry out a social survey to find out the extent of use of smartphones and social media sites in your class or year group. Find out what percentage of your peers use a smartphone or visit social media sites. Observe your friends' use of their smartphones inside and outside of school. How often do they look at their phones over a period of, say, 30 minutes? Ask them how many texts they send and receive during the course of the school day. Finally, ask them what they like about smartphones and social media sites and what they see as the drawbacks of smartphones and social media sites. What do your results suggest to you about the role that social media play in the socialisation of young people? Do your results support Twenge's conclusions?

## Activity

Construct two tables. The first should list the values, norms and skills that are taught to children in the family. The other table should list the values, norms and skills that are taught by secondary agencies of socialisation such as the educational system, religion, the media, the peer group and the workplace.

## Key terms

**Primary socialisation** The process of learning that occurs in the family when parents teach children the language, attitudes, values, norms and ethics of the culture in which they live so that they grow up to be citizens and workers who conform to what society expects of them.

**Conscience** Refers to the moral sense of right and wrong introduced to children from a very young age during the socialisation process which aims to deter deviant behaviour by setting off feelings of guilt if the child thinks about doing wrong.

**Imitation** Children copying the actions of significant role models in their lives, especially their parents.

**Role models** Significant others who are respected by those with less status (such as children) and whose behaviour sets an example to be imitated.

**Gender roles** The social expectations that underpin what is expected of a boy/man and a girl/woman in any given society.

**Feral children** Children who have been deprived of interaction with other humans because they have been abandoned into the wild (and, in some cases, allegedly raised by animals) or kept in isolation.

**Secondary socialisation** The process of social learning that is in addition to that which occurs in the family. Agents of secondary socialisation include formal education systems, religion, the workplace and the media.

**Hidden curriculum** The unwritten, unofficial and often unintended lessons, values and attitudes that encourage conformity that students allegedly learn in classrooms and schools.

**Peer group** A group of people of approximately the same age, status and interests.

**Cultural amnesia** The collective loss of memory.

## Summary

1. People's role and place in society depends upon them learning and internalising the key elements of culture during the primary socialisation experienced during childhood.
2. However, socialisation is a lifelong process because of the existence of secondary sources or agents of socialisation.
3. Some secondary agents of socialisation – for example, TV, the internet and social media – may be undermining the effectiveness of the family and primary socialisation.
4. The most powerful agency of secondary socialisation in Western societies is the mass media.
5. Religion is probably the most influential agency of secondary socialisation in non-Western cultures.

# Unit 2.1.3 The nature versus nurture debate

In contrast to the sociological point of view that culture is the product of social learning or nurture, sociobiologists generally believe that culture is the product of biology or nature, especially heredity and genetics. In this unit, we will consider the argument between these two points of view, often known as the **nature versus nurture** debate. The focus of this debate is often on gender and whether males and females are acting in ways which are hard-wired by biology into the brain at birth or whether they are acting according to social expectations.

## The nature or biological argument

Sociobiologists such as Desmond Morris (1968) argue that biology shapes culture, because sharing culture is based on the inbuilt or genetic need to continue the life of the social group over time. Similarly, Lionel Tiger and Robin Fox (1971) argue that gender roles are biologically determined and consequently any attempt to interfere with what they see as the 'fixed' nature of masculine and feminine behaviour is bound to end in failure. Other neuroscientists and psychologists, such as Simon Baron-Cohen (2012), argue that the female brain is genetically hard-wired for empathy while the male brain is hard-wired for understanding and building systems.

On the other hand, sociologists argue that if human behaviour is influenced by biology at all, it is only at a reflex or physical level. For example, we may biologically feel the physical sensation of hunger but culture determines what and how we eat. Indeed, sociologists argue that many aspects of social life that are taken to be natural are in fact produced by society; that is, they are **social constructs**.

Sociologists argue that most aspects of social behaviour are the product of the social environment which nurtures members of society via the experience of socialisation. Cordelia Fine (2011) argues that neuroscience is a patriarchal ideology used to justify gender inequality, such as the pay gap and the exclusion of females from particular occupational sectors. She argues that the scientific evidence does not support the view that boys and girls are 'hard-wired' to have different skills. Through a quote in her book, Fine criticises these neurological approaches to gender roles because they coat 'old-fashioned stereotypes with a veneer of scientific credibility' without convincing evidence.

However, Fine argues that gender roles cannot be separated from culture, which enjoys a – as Fine quotes – 'deep reach' into our minds. She argues that all cultures contain stereotypical beliefs about gender which have a cultural 'ripple effect' on the mind. Such beliefs can 'change self-perception, alter interests, debilitate or enhance ability, and trigger unintentional discrimination'.

### Activity

'Nature is more important than nurture in the formation of gender roles.'

Explain this statement and, using sociological material, outline one argument against it.

### Key terms

**Nature versus nurture debate** The debate as to whether human behaviour is the product of innate biological influences such as instinct or genetics or whether it is the product of environmental influences such as social upbringing or the quality of socialisation.

**Social construct/construction** A belief, characteristic or set of behaviours and assumptions that is produced or manufactured by the actions of those who constitute society or powerful social groups.

### Summary

1. Sociologists reject the idea that nature in the form of biology or genetics is responsible for social behaviour.
2. In contrast, sociologists highlight the influence of nurture – they believe that the social environment in which socialisation occurs is more important.

# END-OF-PART QUESTIONS

| | | |
|---|---|---|
| 0 1 | Describe two types of secondary socialisation | [4 marks] |
| 0 2 | Explain two reasons why families are very effective at socialisation. | [8 marks] |
| 0 3 | Explain one strength and one weakness of schools in the socialisation process. | [6 marks] |

# PART 2 SOCIAL CONTROL, CONFORMITY AND RESISTANCE

## Contents


| | | |
|---|---|---|
| Unit 2.2.1 | The role of structure and agency in shaping the relationship between the individual and society | 42 |
| Unit 2.2.2 | Mechanisms of social control, social order and conformity | 44 |
| Unit 2.2.3 | The influence of social pressure, sanctions, individualism and social exchange on social order and expectations | 50 |
| Unit 2.2.4 | Explanations of deviance and non-conformity | 52 |


The first part of the chapter focuses on outlining sociological theories that aim to explain the relationship between the individual, socialisation and society. Some of these sociological theories claim that the only way of understanding the relationship between identity, socialisation and culture is to examine how societies are organised or structured. These *structuralist* theories focus on how identity and the social actions of individuals may be shaped by social forces which emanate independently from the social organisation of societies. Such theories claim that the influence of structure is so pervasive that social actors unconsciously establish predictable patterns of behaviour. Human behaviour is therefore seen by structuralists to be ultimately caused and shaped by social forces which are beyond the control of individuals and consequently difficult to oppose and resist.

In contrast, another group of sociological theories reject the notion that structure determines individual action or shapes identity. These interactionist or *social action* theories stress the concept of 'agency' or free will, and claim that people can act independently of social structure and are responsible for their own actions.

In addition to sociological theory, this part will examine the concept of social control and the social agencies that societies employ to ensure conformity, consensus and social order. Social processes such as social pressure, individualism and social exchange will be explained and evaluated in terms of their influence on social expectations and social stability. Finally, structural and social action theories of crime, deviance and non-conformity will be briefly outlined and evaluated.

## Unit 2.2.1 The role of structure and agency in shaping the relationship between the individual and society

Structuralist theories, which include functionalism, Marxism and feminism, suggest that the **social structure** of society mainly determines or shapes the behaviour of individuals. In contrast, social action theories argue that people are not the pawns of structural forces over which they can exercise little control. Rather, social action theories stress the active role of individuals and social groups in the social construction of society. They point out that people have **agency** and free will and consequently make choices to behave in particular ways.

### Structuralist theories of society, culture and identity

**Structuralist theories** of society claim that society and the social forces that radiate from its social structure determine the behaviour of individuals. This approach to understanding human behaviour is '**macro**' because it focuses on the effects of large-scale processes such as economic forces and the influence of social institutions such as the educational system or the economy on human behaviour rather than the motivations of the individual social actors who make up society. It is, therefore, a 'top-down' theory in that it sees society as exerting influence over the actions of individuals. This approach is also '**positivist**' because it claims to be scientific; that is, underpinned by a rational evidence-based way of thinking.

Julian Salisbury (2018) points out that structuralist theories are divided into two broad types: **consensus** and **conflict theories**. Consensus theories such as functionalism believe that societies and social structures are organised around common agreement or consensus, while conflict theories such as Marxism and feminism believe that societies are characterised by difference and inequality, and consequently underpinned by potential conflict.

## Interactionist theories of society, culture and identity

Salisbury (2018) observes that social action theory starts with the premise that society is not an entity 'out there', and 'if it exists at all it only does so inside people's heads'. This alternative way of looking at society is a 'micro' or **humanistic** approach which is underpinned by a focus on how social reality is 'interpreted' by individuals during everyday interaction with others. Social action theory is a 'bottom-up' theory in that it sees individuals as more important than societies or social systems, in contrast with structuralist theories that are 'top-down' in their insistence that society is more important than individuals.

In contrast to structural theories of society, social action theories argue that people's behaviour and life chances are not determined by the structural features of particular societies or their social background. Rather, social action theory can be described as a **voluntarist** approach because it stresses the role of **free will** and choice in shaping personal identity, culture and wider society. It sees people as in charge of their own destiny rather than being propelled along by social forces beyond their control.

Social action theory argues that society is the net sum of people interacting with each other at home, at work, at college, in the street and so on. Consequently, social action theory argues that society, culture and identity are social constructions – for example, society and culture are the product of people voluntarily choosing to associate with one another and to share in common agreement particular values, norms, customs and so on. Identity or **self** too is gradually socially constructed, as we adapt our outlook, personality and social behaviour in reaction to how others respond to us in particular social contexts.

Social action approaches argue that the concept of society as a social construct means that societies should not be seen as rigid and unchangeable. Rather they argue that 'social constructs' can gradually change over time. For example, many societies across the world have changed their internal structures as values, norms and social meanings with regard to the rights and roles of women have shifted.

### Summary

1. Structural theories of society see the social behaviour of both individuals and social groups as the product of social forces over which people have no control. These forces originate in the social structure of society; that is, from the way they are organised.
2. In contrast, social action theories reject structural theories as too deterministic, because they fail to appreciate that people have agency and free will and therefore have the ability to choose how they should behave.

### Key terms

**Social structure** The social organisation of society.

**Social construction** An interactionist concept that refers to behaviour that is thought to be natural but is actually the product of cultural expectations and processes.

**Agency** Free will or the ability to choose particular courses of action.

**Structuralist theories** Theories such as functionalism, Marxism and feminism which claim people's actions are the product of the ways their societies are organised or structured.

**Macro approaches** A top-down approach which is mainly interested in how society or aspects of it influence individual actions.

**Positivist** A scientific approach which aims to document the impact of social forces on human behaviour by collecting large-scale data using sociological methods which are regarded as highly reliable and objective.

**Consensus theory** A type of structuralist approach which sees society as characterised by agreement and order; for example, functionalism.

**Conflict theories** Theories such as Marxism and feminism which see societies as characterised by conflict between social classes or between men and women.

**Humanist approach** A micro or 'bottom-up' approach which is interested in how social reality is 'interpreted' by individuals during their everyday interaction with others.

**Voluntarism** The idea that human action is voluntary rather than imposed externally by social forces beyond the individual's control. Voluntarists as represented by social action theories believe that social behaviour is the result of people having free will and the ability to choose how to act.

**Free will** The power to make decisions or choices that are not shaped by social forces beyond the control of the individual.

**Self** This is composed of two parts; the 'I' is how people see themselves, while the 'me' is how we present ourselves when interacting with others.

# Unit 2.2.2 Mechanisms of social control, social order and conformity

We have seen that socialisation specifically refers to the process by which people learn the skills, knowledge, values, motives and roles (that is, culture) of the groups to which they belong or the communities in which they live. Socialisation is generally quite effective but there is always the possibility that members of society may be tempted to deviate from agreed standards, norms and rules. Consequently, most societies feel the need to use '**social controls**', to regulate and reinforce 'ideal' behaviour to make sure that citizens conform to the rules or laws agreed upon by a society and to publicly punish those who fail to abide by cultural values and norms. Members of society agree to consent to these social controls because they realise that they benefit from them in the long term.

Sociologists tend to distinguish between two broad agencies of social control: formal and informal.

## Formal agencies of social control

**Formal agencies of social control** tend to deal in repressive or coercive types of control which are expressed in formal written laws. They often involve negative or 'hard' sanctions that may result in physical punishment, removal from society or some other restriction on individual liberty. Examples of formal agencies of social control that function to ensure conformity include the military (although this agency tends only to be used as an emergency measure), the security or intelligence services, and the criminal justice system, which includes agencies such as the police and the judiciary, responsible for enforcing laws and civil order. If a person is found guilty of breaking the law, a range of **negative sanctions** is available to the courts.

### Activity

Identify three negative sanctions available to the courts in the country in which you live.

Some of the more extreme sanctions available to formal agencies of control across the world may also include capital punishment, extra-judicial (not legally authorised) execution by police officers or death squads, torture, imprisonment without trial, solitary confinement and the denial of basic civil liberties.

However, evidence suggests that the regular use of extreme negative sanctions such as violence and physical coercion by formal agents of social control often leads to hostility, dissent, defiance, protest and social instability. This oppositional resistance to the real and symbolic violence used by some agents of social control may mean that social order is constantly under threat because citizens see themselves as outsiders and feel forced to engage in deviant action such as rioting (which they may interpret as 'uprisings'), public protests and demonstrations and, in extreme cases, terrorism (which they may interpret as 'freedom fighting').

### Control by consent

These potential problems with formal social controls have led to many governments seeking to **control by consent**. This involves those in power 'persuading' society that the law is 'blind', that it seeks to protect all social groups equally and that all formal agencies of social control operate in a just way according to that law. For example, members of society are persuaded to follow the traffic laws laid down by the state because they protect life, and citizens are persuaded to follow the law and consent to policing because the state is willing to pursue justice on their behalf if they are ever victims of crime.

However, control by consent is criticised by Marxists as an **ideological** device which functions to convince members of society that social controls are both fair and necessary. Marxists claim that social controls are actually aimed at controlling the poor and the proletariat, who are seen by the wealthy and powerful as a potentially dangerous class.

### Activity

'Control by consent is generally more successful than control by coercion.' Explain this statement and, using sociological material, outline one argument in favour of it.

### Education as both formal and informal social control

Education is an important agency of social control. On the one hand, educational systems qualify as formal agencies of social control, because in many societies education is compulsory by law and parents who fail to send their children to school may be criminalised. Moreover, many schools operate a set of formal rules, and failure to abide by these may result in a range of official and negative sanctions ranging from letters home to parents, detentions, corporal punishment (this is banned in many countries but is still an option in countries such as China, Japan, Korea and Singapore), suspension and exclusion. However, schools and particularly individual teachers can also be seen as informal agencies of social control because teachers usually have a great deal of discretion in terms of how they manage their classrooms and interact with students. They may, for example, use informal modes of praise and reward such as constructive criticism of students' work and friendly chat with students to make sure that classroom behaviour is mainly focused on academic work.

### The workplace as both formal and informal social control

The workplace is an important agency of social control because it is in the factory, office and so on that people learn specialised skills 'on the job' that are essential to the smooth running of the economy. It is important that those skills are effectively learned, especially if workers are engaged in dangerous work such as coal-mining, where a mistake made by one individual could have severe consequences for the whole workforce. Consequently, employers will employ a number of positive sanctions to reward those who demonstrate skill but also the appropriate attitude towards work such as industry, dedication and commitment to following orders. Employers may reward those who show skill and willing commitment with pay rises and promotion to supervisory and management positions. Employers may encourage groups of workers with promises of future reward if they continue to work hard. However, employers can also use hard negative sanctions which are often underpinned by the state in the form of the law. If an employee is interpreted as lazy, incompetent or is frequently late to work or absent, employers have the power to give them both informal and formal warnings before eventually dismissing them. Threats by whole groups of workers to take industrial action may be countered by the employer with mass redundancy or by the threat to move production to other parts of the world in which workers are more easily controlled.

## Informal agencies of social control

**Informal agencies of social control** are mainly made up of primary groups such as families, communities and tribes in which relationships are close, direct and intimate. Social control is often maintained by informal mechanisms such as customs, traditions, mores and religion.

### The family as an agency of informal social control

David Morgan (1996) suggests that a great deal of family interaction between parents and children is concerned with social control and encouraging **conformity**. For example, parents often use **positive sanctions** to reinforce and reward socially approved behaviour, and negative sanctions to discipline and punish 'naughty' or deviant behaviour. Positive sanctions might include praise, sweets and the promise of extra television-viewing or new toys, while negative sanctions may include the threat to 'withdraw' love, sending children to sit on a 'naughty step' or to their room. Parents may punish adolescents by banning them from going out at night or by temporarily confiscating their smartphone, tablet or laptop. Some cultures may even encourage the physical punishment of children via smacking or beating. A 2013 study by Sylvia Y.C.L. Kwok, Wenyu Chai and Xuesong found that about 72 per cent of Chinese children said that their parents had beaten them. Kwok, Chai and He conclude that the evidence suggests that at the time of their study, Chinese parents used physical and emotional punishment to solve parent–child problems and conflict, which sometimes leads to child abuse. Chinese law, specifically the Law on the Prevention of Juvenile Delinquency, authorised 'strict discipline' of children by parents and guardians. However, over 40 countries around the world have now made parental smacking, beating and spanking of children illegal.

## Activities

1. What does the law say about smacking children in the society in which you live?
2. Compose a brief questionnaire asking adults whether they believe that smacking children is justified. Ask them to identify in what circumstances it might be used.
3. Can you think of any other harms that might be caused by smacking in addition to those listed by the research?
4. How might you criticise the reliability and validity of this research?

## Contemporary issues: Smacking

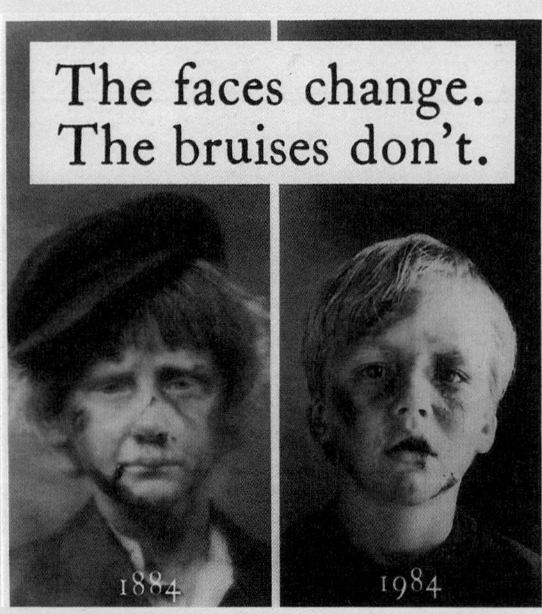


*Campaign poster for the UK's National Society for the Prevention of Cruelty to Children. © National Society for the Prevention of Cruelty to Children (NSPCC) Archive created 1983/1984.*

Research by UNICEF shows that around the world 80 per cent of children are subjected to some routine form of hitting, smacking or beating as a form of discipline by their parents. In many societies, this use of physical punishment is not illegal.

However, longitudinal research suggests that children who are smacked by their parents are more likely to have mental health issues as well as anti-social behaviour problems once they grow up.

Cognitive difficulties and increased aggression are the other side-effects recorded in a meta-analysis of 50 years of research conducted by Joan Durrant and Ron Emson (2012) on more than 160 000 children. The study assesses the long-lasting impact into adulthood that smacking has on children's mental health, life skills and development.

The researchers use the term 'spanking' to denote smacking; that is, 'hitting a child on their buttocks or extremities using an open hand'. Their review concludes that smacking has numerous negative effects. For example, some teenagers may engage in anti-social disruptive behaviour in the classroom. There is also evidence that adults who have been physically punished as children grow up into adults who demonstrate mental health problems (such as high levels of anxiety and depression) who find it difficult to form trusting relationships with others. There is evidence, too, that such adults demonstrate low self-esteem compared with their peers who had not been smacked.

The researchers concluded that smacking or spanking is a widespread practice, but there is no evidence to suggest that it was effective in correcting or improving children's behaviour. Rather, the research concludes that smacking does more harm than good.

Source: Durrant, J. and Ensom, R., *Physical punishment of children: lessons from 20 years of research*, available online at https://www.ncbi.nlm.nih.gov/pmc/articles/PMC3447048/.

Parental or family sanctions are frequently aimed at encouraging the development of a conscience or 'inner policeman' in children. This conscience is supposed to equip children, adolescents and adults with a moral compass which aims to guide their future actions and to deter them from potential deviant behaviour by invoking strong feelings of guilt.

## The peer group/friendship network as an agency of informal social control

There is evidence that peer groups, friendship networks or **subcultures** are also successful informal agents of social control. (A subculture is a group that exists within a wider society which has a very distinct and separate identity, for example, in terms of the way they dress or behave – that stands out from mainstream culture.) These groups, networks and subcultures may put considerable peer pressure on teenagers to conform to subcultural values and norms which may differ from those of adult society, and consequently encourage deviant and even criminal behaviour. Some adolescents may identify with **spectacular youth subcultures** (highly visible groups of young people whose behaviour is often interpreted by the media as 'threatening' the moral order of society), for example, mods, punks, soulboys, skinheads, metallers, goths or hippies – that they see portrayed in the global media. They may aim to copy the distinctive and often symbolically 'shocking' dress and hairstyles of these global subcultures in order to challenge and oppose adult society's attempt to turn them into conventional citizens.

### Activity

*The influence of peers might mean membership of a spectacular youth subculture such as these punks in Myanmar.*

Look closely at the photograph.

1. What features that you can see unite this pair of young people as a subculture or community?
2. What visible features of this subculture might create anxiety among older conventional members of Myanmar society?

This **symbolisation** makes the group stand out from 'normal' society as 'different' and therefore deviant. However, the majority of youth rarely come into contact with spectacular youth subcultures. Rather, their lives are much more likely to revolve around their peer group in the mundane contexts of school, the street and social media. Peer groups may use positive sanctions such as the endowment of respect or status (although this is often awarded for deviant activities), as well as negative sanctions such as gossip, ridicule, sarcasm, criticism, shame, bullying, discrimination and exclusion, to socially control the attitudes and behaviour of those in their orbit. Consequently, the peer group sometimes has more of an influence on the behaviour of adolescents than their parents do, although sociological studies generally demonstrate that the majority of adolescents usually end up conforming to the same set of cultural values and norms as their parents.

### Activity

Think about how your peer group operates in your local community or the school or college you attend. Make a list of the ways in which the peer groups and friendship networks that operate around you reward and punish young people. Research how peer group use of social media is now being used by peer groups as a means of social control.

## The media as agencies of informal social control

A principal agency of social control in many cultures is the media. Tabloid newspapers, magazines, television and films often reinforce what count as the boundaries between 'normal' and 'deviant' behaviour. Journalists are responsible for representing the actions of particular social groups and their relationship to specific social problems as part of the news reported in newspapers and on TV news programmes. Critics of the media point out that these representations are often ideological in that they stereotype particular social groups as engaged in either 'right' or 'wrong' behaviour. For example, females may be '**demonised**' or negatively labelled because their behaviour is interpreted by journalists as not sufficiently 'feminine'. Some women may be '**fat-shamed**' by the media because journalists subscribe to patriarchal stereotypes which interpret slimness as best representing femininity. Similarly, both men and women may be 'persuaded' by the media that their social destinies should be on very different trajectories. The media may reinforce the idea that the certain arenas of work, such as science, business, medicine and engineering, are best suited to male abilities and traits. A great deal of media content may represent females as either nurturers and domestic workers, so reinforcing the notion that women's skills are better suited to the home and the raising of children.

On a more positive note, Deirdre McKay (2016) found that Filipinos living and working in Europe used social network sites to stay true to the social duties and obligations encouraged by Filipino culture in their home villages and towns, despite being thousands of miles away.

## Contemporary issues: An archipelago of Care: Filipino Migrants and Global Networks

Deirdre McKay (2016) focuses on the experience of Filipino caregivers in London, some of whom are living and working illegally in their host country. She considers what migrant workers must do to navigate their way in a global marketplace. She draws on interviews and participant observations, her own long-term fieldwork in communities in the Philippines, and digital ethnography, to present an intricate consideration of how these caregivers create stability in potentially precarious living situations. McKay found that they used social network sites to insulate themselves from the individualism that they saw as dominating Western culture. Social networking with relatives and friends in the Philippines meant they could digitally return to the comfort of the types of cultural relationships that they had left behind, which were characterised by obligations to the extended family and ancestors, involvement in the local community and religious traditions. McKay argues that these workers gain resilience from the bonding networks they construct for themselves through social media, faith groups and community centres. These networks generate an elaborate 'archipelago of care' through which migrants create their sense of self.

### Questions

1. What methods did McKay use to research Filipinos living in London?
2. How does the culture of the Filipinos living in London differ from Western culture?
3. In what ways do social media function for the benefit of the culture and families of Filipino migrants?

### Religion as an agency of social control

Another informal agency of socialisation is religion, although in some societies religion is intertwined with both the law and state and consequently acts as a formal agency of social control. Those who believe in God, who regularly attend church, temple or mosque and conform to religious norms, may find that that their behaviour is controlled by the fear of what might happen to them in an 'afterlife' if they fail to have faith or to abide by religious mores. Religion awards the faithful with promises of spiritual rebirth, heavenly reward, nirvana and redemption, while it threatens the sinful and wicked with hellfire and eternal suffering. In those countries in which religion shapes most social institutions, especially the law and politics, non-believers and people who question religion may be threatened with prison or death.

## Activity

Construct a table with five columns labelled 'peer group', 'schools', 'media', 'family' and 'religion', and list in those columns the ways in which these agencies of control regulate behaviour and ensure conformity.

## Key terms

**Social controls** Regulations and rules which aim to reinforce 'ideal' behaviour and to ensure conformity. Failure to abide by social controls may result in public punishment.

**Formal social control** Sanctions enforced by official agencies such as government in reaction to the breaking of written formal rules.

**Negative sanctions** Punishments aimed at deterring deviance.

**Control by consent** Persuading a social group that they should obey rules because they will benefit from them in the long term.

**Ideological** Based on untrue information, propagated by a powerful group, aimed at justifying and legitimating some type of inequality.

**Informal social controls** The negative reaction of friends, relatives and peers to deviance that encourages conformity to the informal rules employed by such groups.

**Conformity** Abiding by or complying with social norms, rules and laws.

**Positive sanctions** Rewards which encourage conformity.

**Subculture** A distinct group that exists within a wider society. A subculture has a very distinct and separate identity, for example, in terms of the way they dress or behave – that stands out from mainstream culture.

**Spectacular youth subculture** Highly visible groups of young people who commit themselves to a certain 'shocking' look in terms of hairstyle, dress codes and so on, and whose behaviour is often interpreted by the older generation and the media as 'threatening' the moral order or stability of society.

**Symbolisation** A process found in some news reporting of social groups in which journalists identify key features of particular groups, especially young people, so that they can be avoided by others or be easily identified and targeted by the police.

**Demonisation** The social practice of treating some groups as if they were 'social problems' or a threat to those who belong to mainstream law-abiding society.

**Fat-shaming** The action or practice of humiliating someone judged to be fat or overweight by making mocking or critical comments about their size.

## Summary

1. The process of socialisation is generally effective but sometimes needs to be reinforced by formal and informal means of social control.
2. Formal agencies of social control are normally organised by the state, for example, the police, courts and prisons.
3. State agencies of social control can use coercion or force, as well as hard sanctions, to ensure conformity. However, coercion can often lead to resentment and further non-conformity. The state prefers to use 'consensual' control, which is achieved by persuading citizens that rules benefit them.
4. There also exist informal agencies of social control, such as the family, peer group, media and religion, that tend to use 'softer' controls to ensure that people fit into social groups or society.
5. Some agencies of social control, for example, educational institutions and workplaces – use a combination of hard and soft strategies of social control.

# Unit 2.2.3 The influence of social pressure, sanctions, individualism and social exchange on social order and expectations

Our examination of social control and the agencies that regulate our behaviour clearly show that both socialisation and social control function to exert **social pressure** to ensure conformity and social order. Such pressure is intended to deter any temptation to behave in a socially unacceptable way. Furthermore, **sanctions** are also available to agencies of control to reward and reinforce the conformity of those citizens who accept that complying with the rules brings about a social exchange that benefits both themselves and their community.

For example, in exchange for conformity, the criminal justice system is authorised by society to protect the lives, rights and property of its citizens. Consequently, the police forces of most societies engage in **consensual policing**; that is, most citizens accept the need for policing and voluntarily cooperate with the police when needed. Another example of this social exchange is that in return for adherence to the law, if a citizen is unlawfully killed or robbed, a team of strangers employed by the state (police detectives, forensic experts and so on) will work towards finding and punishing those responsible. As we saw earlier, social control agencies can also use negative sanctions or punishments. Again, in return for their acceptance of cultural values and norms, citizens accept that punitive action may need to be taken by the state against those who act outside the law, including themselves. In other words, as argued earlier by social exchange theory, members of society engage in **cost-benefit analysis** – they weigh up the benefits of conformity in obeying the law against the costs of rejecting it (for example, their lives, and those of their family may be put at high risk if a state of **anarchy** – a lack of laws and rules – was allowed to dominate society). Law is not just imposed on people from on high. Rather, members of society choose to submit to laws and regulations in return or exchange for benefits that appeal to their self-interest (for example, the protection of their families and private property, and some retribution or recompense if crime is committed against them).

**Social exchange** is an important social glue holding varied groups of citizens together. As we saw earlier, there are everyday norms or rules relating to civility, such as politeness, etiquette, morality, deference to those in authority, duty and obligation and so on, to which most citizens subscribe in exchange for social capital, social affiliation, community and reducing the possibility of conflict. As Edward Shils and Steven Grosby (1997) observed, 'civility is a belief which affirms the possibility of the common good'.

The concept of social capital refers to social bonds or relationships that have productive benefits. It refers especially to the reciprocal benefits that members of a society or community might share. The concept has especially been applied to the increasing popularity of social media platforms such as Facebook in recent years. First, it is argued that accumulating connections or online relationships is empowering and enriching because it produces resources and opportunities which have collective value for all concerned. Membership of an online community may provide opportunities for people with similar interests to find and interact with one another. This type of capital is known as '**bonding social capital**' and produces shared information flows that may throw up opportunities for jobs or mutual aid. For example, belonging to a Facebook community of A Level Sociology students may bring about benefits in terms of shared information about how to do well in the subject.

Second, membership of an online community may lead to relationships being established with others who seem to be very different to one another in terms of their social characteristics and interests. This is known as '**bridging social capital**'. For example, feminists may wish to bond with other feminists, but social networking sites such as Twitter may lead to feminists realising that seemingly different political causes such as fighting racism or economic inequality have a great deal in common with their cause. This may lead to social and political alliances or networks which increase the potential for social change.

However, social exchange (and its reciprocal benefits) works well in societies with collectivist value systems in which the individual is encouraged to put the needs of the society first. This can be illustrated using the work of Durkheim. He argued that some societies were characterised by '**mechanical solidarity**'. This concept suggests that agencies of socialisation and social control, particularly the family, community and religion, are so effective that the values, norms and laws of these societies are rarely questioned or challenged. These societies are, therefore, characterised by moral certainty. Individuals are expected to submit to the collectivistic interests of the wider society. The individual is expected to carry out civic duties and meet social obligations. In contrast, individualistic behaviour is defined as deviance. Punishments for such behaviour are harsh and may include exile or death. Consequently, the fear of losing one's place in such a tightly integrated society is sufficient for people to avoid deviant and criminal behaviour.

Durkheim suggested that these types of society were the norm in medieval times. However, contemporary examples of mechanical solidarity can be found in pre-industrial cultures as well as societies such as China or North Korea, where individuals are expected to put the interests of the state or the Communist Party before their own. Similarly, cultures such as Iran and Saudi Arabia may also be good examples of mechanical solidarity in action, as citizens are expected to submit their individuality to the greater good of the Islamic community.

In contrast, Durkheim sees the social structure of modern industrial societies as characterised by '**organic solidarity**'. Industrialisation in these societies has generated massive urbanisation. The impersonality of urban life (that is, living alongside thousands of strangers) generates a diversity of novel ideas which challenge traditional ways of thinking, especially ideas that promote self-interest or individualism, which have undermined the effectiveness of the family, community and religion as agents of both socialisation and social control. Consequently, community and neighbourhood ties are often weak. Values and norms in regard to morality in such societies are constantly shifting. Such societies and cultures are therefore plagued by '**anomie**' or moral uncertainty, which means that people act primarily in their own interests rather than in the interests of society as a whole. Such societies are therefore likely to be unstable because people are more likely to manage social interaction and exchanges in ways that personally benefit them rather than both parties. Such one-sided exchanges are more likely to break down into disorder.

## Key terms

**Social pressure** Influence exerted on an individual or group by a more or equally powerful person or group. The influence might take the form of rational argument, persuasion or coercion (threats, violence and so on). For example, a peer group may exert social pressure on an adolescent to behave in an anti-social manner.

**Sanctions** A negative sanction is a threatened penalty for disobeying a law or rule. A positive sanction may take the form of approval or a reward.

**Consensual policing** The power of the police to fulfil their functions and duties is dependent on public approval of their existence, actions and behaviour and on their ability to secure and maintain public respect.

**Cost-benefit analysis** A process that involves members of society rationally weighing up the benefit of, say, obeying the law against the costs of not doing so or of rejecting the need for law altogether.

**Anarchy** A state of disorder due to absence or non-recognition of authority or agencies of social control.

**Social exchange** Interaction and negotiation between individuals that involves maximum benefit and minimum cost for mutual or reciprocal benefit.

**Bonding social capital** The sharing of information or resources that may create opportunities for jobs or mutual help.

**Bridging social capital** Social and political alliances or networks that increase the potential for social change.

**Mechanical solidarity** The sense of togetherness in a society that arises when people perform similar work and share similar experiences, customs, values and beliefs. Such societies view society as more important than the individual.

**Organic solidarity** A type of system in which community ties are loose because people are exposed to a greater range of ideas, which encourages individualism and less moral certainty.

**Anomie** According to Durkheim – a state of normlessness or moral uncertainty in which the social rules of behaviour are not clearly drawn, therefore making people more prone to deviance.

## Summary

1. Members of society are generally happy to cooperate with the processes of socialisation and social control because cultural conformity brings about social benefits in the form of social exchange for those who comply.
2. Those who comply with the law benefit from it because the law aims to protect us all equally.
3. We are happy to behave civilly towards others because this behaviour ensures that others are civil in return, thus maximising social bonds and minimising the potential for conflict.
4. Another consequence of this social exchange is the acquisition of bonding social capital (information and resources that mutually benefit those with similar interests) and bridging social capital (the capacity to form alliances with others of like mind).

# Unit 2.2.4 Explanations of deviance and non-conformity

Deviance is any behaviour that violates cultural or social norms. Another term for deviance is 'non-conformity'. Non-conformists are generally seen as a threat to social order because they challenge convention. This challenge may be symbolised by rebellion, protest and dissent against the prevailing norms. Non-conformist behaviour may range from the 'odd' and the 'eccentric' to the extremes of dropping out of society altogether, committing crime or committing acts of terrorism. Deviant behaviour that breaks the law is known as crime. A number of academic disciplines – biology, psychology and sociology – have attempted to explain criminal and deviant behaviour. For example, in the 19th century, Cesare Lombroso (1835–1909) claimed that criminals were 'born' with certain visible physical features that differentiated them from law-abiding citizens. Later variations on this idea in the 20th century claimed that criminals have inherited certain genetic defects. However, these biological explanations for crime and deviance are generally unsupported by evidence.

Psychologists have also attempted to explain the origin of criminality. Their explanations tend to focus on 'weak' character and personality traits (such as poor self-control) which they see as shaped by childhood experience, poor parenting, inadequate socialisation or lack of intelligence.

In contrast, most sociologists tend to view crime as the product of society. Some sociologists take a 'structural' or 'macro' approach and claim that the social and economic organisation of societies creates inequalities and tensions which give rise to criminal behaviour. Other sociologists take a 'micro' approach to explaining crime and deviance by locating its cause in the interaction between relatively powerless groups and agents of social control, such as the police. These sociologists are interested in how some social groups are more likely to be labelled as 'criminal' and how criminality may be a legitimate and even rational response to the circumstances in which powerless groups, such as young people, find themselves.

## Summary

1. Biologists claim that criminals have distinctive physical or genetic characteristics which differentiate them from members of mainstream society although there is little evidence to support these ideas.
2. Psychologists claim that criminality is the product of weak character or personality traits brought about during childhood.
3. Sociologists, in contrast, claim that both macro and micro social factors are responsible for the extent and character of crime and deviance. Some sociologists argue that macro factors originate in the structure of society while others suggest micro factors originate in everyday social interaction.

# END-OF-PART QUESTIONS

**0 1** Describe two agencies of formal social control. **[4 marks]**

**0 2** Using sociological material, give one argument against the view that crime and deviance is a product of social structure. **[6 marks]**

# PART 3 SOCIAL IDENTITY AND CHANGE

## Contents


| | | |
|---|---|---|
| Unit 2.3.1 | **The construction of social identity** | **53** |
| Unit 2.3.2 | **Globalisation, identity and social change** | **71** |


This part of the chapter aims to examine the relationship between social identity and social change. Structuralist sociologists argue that the identity of many individuals originates in their membership of particular social groups. In this sense, identity is not voluntarily chosen. Rather, it is imposed on people from without. Good examples of these types of identity include those related to social class, gender, ethnicity, religion and age.

In contrast, social action theory argues that the identity we adopt is socially constructed via the voluntary choices that we make. The process of social change is also contributing to this process because, as structural forces such as social class, patriarchy, consensus and culture decline in influence, so people seek out other sources of identity, particularly those associated with global change. This part will therefore examine how and why these external social influences on identity have undergone change and how identities have consequently shifted and/or become hybrid in nature.

# Unit 2.3.1 The construction of social identity

Sarah McLaughlin (2017) observes that 'the concept of identity is important to sociologists because it is only by establishing our own identities and learning about the identities of individuals and groups, that we come to know what makes us similar or different, to other people. This helps us to form social connections and establish group solidarity and identification with others. It also creates disconnections and divisions'.

## Self-identity and social identity

McLaughlin argues that identity is made up of two components. The first is how we see ourselves. This is part of our identity is referred to as the 'self'. Mead argued that the self can be broken down into the 'I' and 'me'. The 'me' is the way you project yourself to the world – your outgoing personality that other people see and interact with. The 'I' is your private self, which is only revealed to your closest relatives and friends. It may be at odds with the 'me' in the sense that someone with a confident and extrovert, outgoing personality might express to their close friends that this masks a lack of confidence and insecurity about their ability to deal with others.

The second aspect of identity is how others see us. This is called 'social identity' and is the net sum of all the socialisation experiences a person has been through. In that sense, it is shaped by the family, peer group, education, religion and workplace. During the socialisation process (which never really ends), we internalise all the social expectations associated with the social roles that we occupy. As part of our primary and secondary socialisation, we learn how children, parents, siblings, friends, students, workers and good citizens are supposed to behave and adjust our social identity accordingly. When we reach adulthood, we have normally acquired a social identity that fits social expectations about what constitutes a beloved family member, a trustworthy friend, a respectable citizen and a reliable worker. We also learn what to expect in terms of appropriate behaviour from people with more status than ourselves, such as our parents, teachers, doctors, police officers and so on. Furthermore, our social identity reflects our commitment to conformity and our desire to avoid being defined as deviant.

### Activity

Make a list of words that sum up how you view your self-identity. For example, do you believe that you are honest, reliable, shy, confident, an introvert or an extrovert? Also make a list of the various social identities that you possess, for example student, son, daughter, brother, sister, friend, best friend and so on. What cultural expectations are attached to each of these identities?

## Approaches to identity

Structuralist sociologists argue that aspects of our identity are imposed on us by social forces such as social class, gender, sexuality, ethnicity, religion and nationality. Structuralist sociologists such as functionalists see the identity of individuals as the product of social structures including the family, religion, schooling and work. They see identity as essential to the functioning of society because it helps to create a sense of common community, consensus and solidarity across disparate groups.

Social action theories, on the other hand, argue that identity is the product of choice. For example, we may choose to identify with certain sports teams, types of music, fashion and leisure activity. Goffman, for example, claims that individuals perform and actively construct their own identities.

Sociologists such as Giddens take a **structuration** approach to identity in that they argue that structure and agency often interact and intersect to bring about identity. Bauman argues that consumers in the 21st century have greater freedom of choice in what they can purchase but affluent consumers have greater freedom than poorer consumers. In this sense, structure in the form of the economy still constrains free will. However, Giddens argues that individuals are not passive receivers of identity. He argues that they are actually 'reflexive', which means that they often reflect on how others view them and alter their identities accordingly. Both Bauman and Giddens saw identity as relatively changeable and co-dependent on both social factors such as family expectations, education, laws and culture and how we interpret and respond to such social influences.

## Contemporary issues: Facebook and self-identity

Derek Egan (2013) investigated the relationship between Facebook use and self-identity among a small section of the Irish population. He was particularly interested in the impact of online social networks on reflexivity, users' sense of self, and the ways in which they presented their self to a wider online audience.

Egan used Facebook as his main **sampling frame** because it is by far the most popular online social networking platform. He employed an online survey questionnaire consisting of 23 questions in hopes of reaching as many Facebook users as possible. Sixteen of the questions took the form of statements, while two questions asked respondents to rank the importance of Facebook to their social life as a whole, and the importance of trust within online social networks. Respondents were also asked to divulge their age, gender, number of Facebook friends, and the frequency of their Facebook use. In addition, he carried out in-depth interviews with a small focus group composed of four individuals who had taken part in the online survey.

The online survey yielded 40 respondents, and was relatively gender balanced, with a split of 55 per cent female to 45 per cent male. The results unearthed a certain degree of uncertainty among Facebook users regarding their relationship with the site. There was a noticeable reluctance to divulge too much information about oneself online. However, respondents also demonstrated some ambiguity regarding how they viewed their relationship with Facebook. For example, when they were asked to respond to the statement 'I feel that Facebook is useful in allowing me to display aspects of my personality', 55 per cent responded in the affirmative, while a further 50 per cent reported that they would miss their Facebook profile if they were denied access to it for a prolonged length of time. Finally, although users appeared to regard Facebook as a separate sphere distinct from their offline sense of self, they also espoused a degree of reflexivity about how one should conduct oneself when online – for example, many said it was tempting to exaggerate one-self's sense of identity online.

Source: *Facebook and its Effect on the Shaping of Social Self in Late Modernity* by Derek Egan (2013), available at https://www.maynoothuniversity.ie/sites/default/files/assets/document/Derek%20Egan.pdf

## Questions

1. What research methods did Egan use?
2. What sampling frame did he use and why?
3. Identify and explain three criticisms of Egan's methodology.
4. How might Egan's findings be used to support Goffman's conclusions about how people construct and project their self-identity?

### Subcultures and identity

The identity of most members of society is likely to shaped both by the dominant culture of the society in which they live but also by their membership of **subcultures**. These are groups which exist within a larger culture but which have their own separate and distinct values and cultural practices. Subcultural values normally exist in harmony with the wider cultural value system of societies, and their values often overlap with mainstream culture. We can see the existence of subcultures based on social class, ethnicity, religion, nationality, gender, age and globalisation.

## Social identity and social class

Socio-economic status or **social class** derives from a number of economic sources. For a tiny minority of people in capitalist societies worldwide, it may derive from inheritance or the acquisition of wealth through profit, especially if an individual owns or controls companies that dominate particular financial, manufacturing and consumer markets. For example, the Mittal and the Ruia family own and control the largest steelmaking companies in India. Lakshmi Mittal was ranked by *Forbes* magazine in 2018 as the third richest man in the world.

However, socio-economic status for the vast majority of the world's citizens derives from their occupation and particularly the income they earn, which shapes both their lifestyle and future life chances. For example, lack of income may result in a lifestyle in which poverty and low life expectancy may be the norm. Income also determines standard of living and consumption practices, for example, the ability to buy a car or other consumer goods that the rest of the society takes for granted.

In capitalist societies, socio-economic status is synonymous with social class, a pyramid-shaped set of hierarchical social categories based on occupation that indicate an individual's or household's relative position in capitalist societies (see Figure 2.3.1).

Before we can begin to examine the relationship between identity and social class, three important observations need to be made.

1. **Social stratification** is a global phenomenon. This has been reliably documented in 2018 by the Credit Suisse Global Wealth Report (CSGWR), which concluded that 82 per cent of wealth globally generated in 2017 went to the richest 1 per cent of the global population, while the bottom 50 per cent of income earners shared only 1 per cent of the world's total wealth. Furthermore, the CSGWR also observed that 42 people now own the same wealth as the poorest half of humanity.
2. Class stratification is mainly found in capitalist societies. The vast majority of societies worldwide are capitalist in terms of their social organisation and experience similar levels of economic inequality. However, we have to acknowledge that the nature of capitalism may differ and, consequently, so too may people's potential to be aware of their socio-economic status and identity. For example, some societies, particularly in the West, have well-established capitalist systems which have been in place for over 300 years. It is therefore likely that class identity is relatively well-developed in such societies. In societies such as China, capitalist enterprise is jointly managed by private entrepreneurs and the state, and consequently it may be more difficult for wealth to be monopolised by particular individuals or families.

   Religion may also shape the nature of capitalism in some countries. For example, Buddhism is the dominant belief system in Bhutan, Tibet and Thailand. Western capitalist ideologies that promote money and power as ends in themselves may not be compatible with Buddhist teachings such as '**satipatthana**', which encourages Buddhists to divest themselves of the need to measure happiness through the acquisition of material things and to practise altruism – to work for the common good and to assist those worse

**Figure 2.3.1 Class pyramid.**

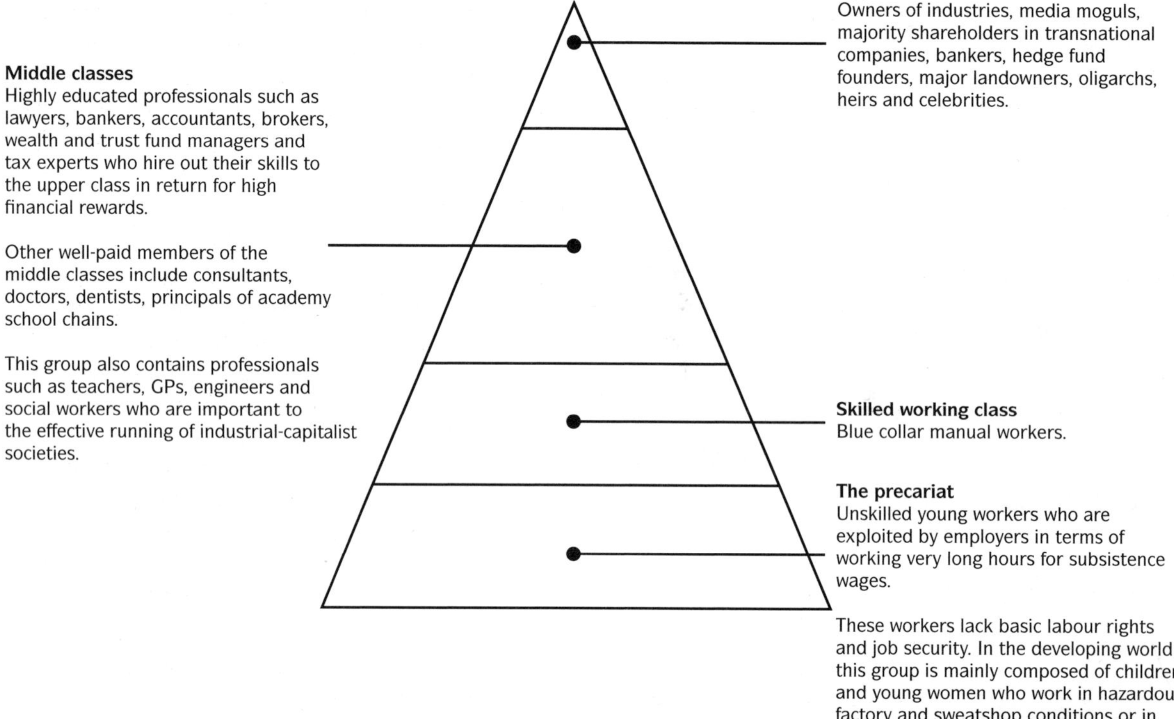


off than themselves. Some Buddhists, therefore, believe that socio-economic status undermines the spiritual ethos of Buddhist teaching.

3. Socio-economic status in Hindu India is the result of the **caste system**. This system has traditionally functioned to place all Hindus at birth into five hierarchical categories or '**jatis**', based on levels of religious purity. Membership of such jatis is fixed for life and determines job, and consequently income, wealth and socio-economic status. In addition to the five jatis, there exists a sixth socio-economic category or non-caste of people known as '**Dalits**', or untouchables, that do the 'dirty' unskilled jobs in Indian society and are generally shunned by the five castes. Hindus believe that if people accept their place in this hierarchy, do not complain or challenge the caste system, and humbly fulfil their duties, they will reincarnate after death into a higher caste in their next life. Donald and Jean Johnson (2018) argue that the caste system is important to Indian culture and identity because Indians primarily identify themselves as members of the caste community to which they belong or as Dalits. For example, it is rare that an Indian marries outside their caste group.

Sociologists have generally identified four very distinct and separate socio-economic groups or social classes in capitalist societies:

- a bourgeoisie or capitalist class
- a **middle class** composed of those who manage capitalism on behalf of the bourgeoisie
- a **working or labouring class** that carries out the skilled and semi-skilled work that is responsible for either extracting the raw material essential to the manufacture of goods in factories or whose labour power is directly responsible for the manufacture of the goods marketed and sold by the bourgeoisie
- An **unskilled class** (often referred to as the '**underclass**') which is employed in low-paid insecure work and which often experiences both unemployment and poverty.

## Identity and the bourgeoisie or capitalist class

This socio-economic group is largely made up of the economic elite that owns the means of production and which benefits directly in terms of wealth acquisition from the profits made in the capitalist system. This group may have different labels attached to it in other societies. For example, in the USA the terms '**super-rich**' or '**uber-wealthy**' are often used to describe this group. In Europe, the term '**upper class**' is sometimes used. It is important to understand that not all members of this class may be actively involved in the capitalist system. Some may have inherited wealth or extensive landholdings that generate wealth via rents. Some may belong to royal or aristocratic houses. Some may have gained entry to this group via marriage or because they have talents in sport, film or music, which are highly regarded (and therefore highly rewarded) by society. Some members of this group may be part of a kleptocracy – their wealth may have been accumulated by stealing the assets of society or by exploiting its natural resources or via corruption.

In terms of social identity, it can be argued that the capitalist class's identity shares the following common features.

- They monopolise global wealth and live a lavish lifestyle beyond the reach of most individuals. For example, a major influence on their social ability may be the ability to engage in 'conspicuous consumption' spending their wealth on high-end luxury goods (yachts, high-performance cars, jewellery, antiques and art) as well as designer brands and labels.
- Members of this class wield great political power and influence because a **symbiotic** relationship often forms between the super-rich and the political class. For example, politicians can guarantee low tax rates, while political elites benefit from the sponsorship of the wealthy in the form of generous donations to their political parties and, more controversially, corruption in the form of bribes.
- Members of this class wield disproportionate **ideological power**. As Marx (1845) observed, 'the ideas of the ruling class are in every epoch the ruling ideas, i.e. the class which is the ruling material force of society, is at the same time its ruling intellectual force'. In other words, this social class has the power to shape public opinion and debate by setting the agenda of the media and political debate about issues such as wealth and poverty.
- Members of this class are likely to share the view that the products of high culture have greater value than the products of folk and popular culture.
- Members of this class often share the experience of a privileged high-cost private education. For example, male children belonging to this class in Asian and African countries may be sent abroad to board at exclusive fee-paying schools in the UK or at military academies in the USA. The children of the uber-wealthy are disproportionately more likely than the children of other social classes to enter the most prestigious and costly universities, either in their home countries or abroad (for example, Oxford or Cambridge in England, the Sorbonne in France, or Yale and Harvard in the USA).
- Members of this social class are more likely to possess the cultural and social capital that opens the door to top jobs in their societies. The concept of social capital was first used by Jane Jacobs (1961) to refer to social contacts established between privileged elites, contact that can prove very useful when making business deals in the global economy. For example, if a Western billionaire wants to invest in a developing country, the fact that an important government minister went to the same prestigious school or university can prove very helpful in overcoming any official obstacles that might exist.
- This social class often practises '**social closure**', in that parents strongly encourage their children to marry only those from a similar socio-economic background to ensure that wealth and property stays in the hands of this minority stratum.

## Identity and the middle class

### Activity

*Doctors are members of the professional middle class. They are usually highly educated, earn high incomes and consequently enjoy high status.*

Consider your society and rank professional and managerial jobs in terms of status. Compare your selection with other students and discuss the differences and similarities in your ranking.

The second most economically powerful status group which exists in most capitalist societies is known as the middle classes. This is a fairly diverse group made up of professionals such as surgeons, doctors, lawyers, accountants, architects and so on, as well as the company executives, directors and senior managers of private corporations. Sociologists argue that in most capitalist societies worldwide, a distinctive middle-class identity can be perceived that shares the following traits or characteristics.

- This status group enjoys high salaries and job security because they are responsible on behalf of the bourgeoisie for the day-to-day management and smooth running of the capitalist system. They possess expert knowledge that is not available to other socio-economic groups. This furnishes them with the authority to hire, direct and control workers of lesser status.
- Members of the middle class share a cultural outlook and lifestyle that values economic security based on home ownership, self-discipline, thrift, saving, ambition and a sense of ethical responsibility. Members of this stratum tend to believe in '**deferred gratification**' – the idea that it is worth making sacrifices in the short term in order to receive rewards in the long term.
- Members of this social class are more likely to subscribe to an individualistic work ethic, as they compete with others for jobs, promotion, pay and so on.
- Members of this group share a similar experience of education and training. For example, professionals tend to be university-educated and consequently this socio-economic group generally subscribes to a positive view of higher education and encourages their children from an early age to aspire to educational achievement, especially at degree level.
- Higher education furnishes this particular social class with 'cultural capital', which they pass onto their children in the home. Sociologists argue that this group sees the educational advantage of giving their children higher-cultural experiences such as visits to theatres, museums and art galleries. Sociological studies of parental attitudes towards education in India, Nigeria and China suggest that parents who are professionals and managers are focused on equipping their children with the appropriate cultural capital for educational success in the form of positive attitudes towards study, respect for teachers and so on.

## Identity and the working class

### Activity

*Some members of the working class are skilled crafts people, while others are either semi-skilled and unskilled.*

Consider a number of working-class jobs (for example, electrician, road-sweeper, bus driver, assembly-line worker, plumber, window cleaner, shop assistant, car mechanic, care assistant, coal-miner). In your opinion, which level of skill is the person doing each job likely to possess?

A third type of social identity that exists in capitalist societies worldwide is that associated with the proletariat or working class. This group of global workers probably share the following aspects of working-class identity.

- Most members of this group are manual or blue-collar workers because they are engaged in physical manual labour, although many of them may possess a scarce technical skill for which they are paid an above-average wage. However, in contrast, groups such as the middle classes often claim higher status because they are engaged in supposedly 'superior' mental or intellectual labour.
- Members of this group share a **collectivist** identity because they work in dangerous jobs and are dependent on their fellow workers for mutual health and safety or because they spend their days working alongside hundreds or thousands of other workers in factories, sweatshops, foundries, shipyards, mines and so on.
- Working-class identity is often underpinned by **class consciousness**. Workers are often aware of exploitation, inequality, injustice and class division and conflict because of their everyday experience of working life, and contact with supervisors, managers and so on.
- Class consciousness means that they often express solidarity with workers in other industries.

- Working-class consciousness and identity may also be expressed via affiliation to **socialist** associations and organisations such as trade unions, which aspire to goals such as equality of opportunity, fair pay and workers' rights.
- Working-class identity may be expressed via a strong attachment to a localised community or neighbourhood in which they live and work, symbolised by leisure pursuits such as following a local football team, meeting in local pubs and belonging to working men's clubs.
- Sociological studies of the working class suggest that many members of the working class live in extended families that mutually support each other by lending money, helping each other to find jobs and so on.

## Class identity and social change

Jan Pakulski and Malcolm Waters (1996) argue that working-class identity is under threat, especially in Western societies, because the global expansion of capitalism has led to the decline of the industries closely associated with working-class identity as companies close their factories in the USA and Europe and open cheaper and more profitable operations in the less industrialised world. It is argued that this massive change has had three major effects on the class consciousness of manual workers in the West.

- In times of high unemployment, workers have become more individualistic as they compete with their peers for scarce skilled jobs. There are signs that the collectivistic identity of manual workers may be in decline.
- Despite the fact that capitalism has largely abandoned the working class, there are few signs that this has raised their class consciousness in terms of their opposition to capitalism. Rather, the evidence suggests that this class may be particularly susceptible to the influence of a **populist** 'divide and rule' ideology that suggests that they should blame 'outsiders', particularly immigrants and ethnic minorities, for their social and economic situation. In the USA, this disenchanted working class may have voted for Trump's promise to 'Make America Great Again'. There is evidence that across Europe such workers are voting for nationalistic, **xenophobic** and racist politicians and political parties.
- Many skilled workers have been forced to take on unskilled and insecure low-paid jobs in order that their families survive.

Consequently, a fourth socio-economic identity has recently emerged in many modern capitalist societies that Guy Standing (2016) has termed the '**precariat**'. These are workers who in the past would have been highly skilled manual workers but, because such skills are no longer in demand, have been forced to take on whatever casual work is available. This work tends to be unskilled and insecure and, accordingly, the precariat is particularly prone to long periods of unemployment. Such workers work long hours with few legal rights for very little economic reward.

In modern capitalist societies, Standing argues that young people who are reasonably well educated are disproportionately likely to be members of this precariat. This group has little choice but to eke out a living in what is known as the **gig economy**, working for fast-food chains and as delivery couriers or Uber drivers. Standing points out that young people are often denied the career choices that were available to previous generations because the specialised jobs that the economy required people to do in the late 20th century have largely disappeared. Standing argues that the precariat in Western economies is often supplemented by migrants and minorities.

In less industrialised societies, the precariat tends to be young women and children. For example, children are often illegally employed in factories and sweatshops in developing societies such as Bangladesh producing consumer goods, including textiles and sportswear for Western consumer markets, for very long hours for very low rates of pay. Another example of this type of unskilled worker is the 'untouchables' or Dalits of India. What all these workers have in common is that they have little or no status because the work they do is unskilled. Employers exploit the fact that there are more of these workers than there are jobs available by paying such workers the bare minimum, denying them the rights enjoyed by other socio-economic groups and by refusing to guarantee them job security.

The identity of those who belong to the precariat is likely to be shaped by the nature of the jobs available to them.

- Such workers are probably very **present-day-orientated** and focused on survival. They are likely to lack positive aspirations as to their future because they have little or no job security or promotion prospects.
- Such workers are more likely to subscribe to a **fatalistic** outlook – the belief that they cannot

change the way events will happen and that bad events cannot be avoided. Feelings of marginalisation are probably habitual, because they feel powerless to change their situation.

- The identity of such workers is probably underpinned by constant anxiety about whether they can earn enough to pay their rents and debts and whether they can feed their families. Living on the margins of poverty is the norm.
- The precariat lacks the occupational identity that is central to the self and group identities of the skilled working class and the professional/managerial middle class.
- Research by Kate Pickett and Richard Wilkinson (2018) suggests that the everyday experience of insecurity and inequality experienced by members of this global precariat can lead to a social identity characterised by low levels of psychological and social well-being and high levels of stress and anxiety, which in turn may result in high levels of criminality and suicide because they feel cheated, devalued, useless, helpless, unhappy and bitter.
- Standing claims that the precariat is potentially a dangerous class because the social identity of the precariat is likely be shaped by feelings of anger, hostility, envy, resentment, insecurity, hopelessness, depression, unhappiness and social anxiety which may spill over into social resistance in the form of crime, anti-social behaviour and riots.

### Activity

'Social class identity is in decline in the 21st century.' Explain this view and, using sociological material, give one argument against this view.

## Social identity and gender

Gender also has a significant independent effect on both our self-identity and social identity because the social structure of most societies worldwide is organised along patriarchal lines. This means that males are culturally regarded as having greater value than females. This can be illustrated in a number of ways.

1. Men rather than women are likely to constitute the wealthy minority of societies.
2. Men usually monopolise positions of political, religious, military and cultural power.
3. Women are less likely to experience the same educational, job and social mobility opportunities as men; for example, they may be excluded from particular jobs or management roles because these are thought to be 'better suited' to men.
4. Women tend to be paid less than men even when they have similar jobs and responsibilities.
5. Inheritance of wealth, property and titles is often patrilineal, that is, inheritance follows the male rather than female line.
6. Women are often confined to the domestic sphere as mothers and wives and are expected to defer to the authority of their husbands. In many societies, girls are expected to defer to the wishes of parents with regard to arranged marriage.
7. There is evidence that many cultures do not take sexual violence against girls and women seriously.
8. In some societies, religious rules, laws and police may attempt to apply social controls to the activities of women. For example, in Iran it is compulsory for women to keep their heads covered in public, while in Saudi Arabia women have only very recently been allowed to drive cars.
9. In some societies, it is regarded as legitimate for male members of the family to use violence and even kill a female relative if that girl or woman is deemed by males to have brought 'shame' on the family by marrying someone from a different religion or by refusing to marry the man the family has chosen for them.

Sociologists such as R.W. Connell (1987) argue that many cultures believe that the behaviour of both men and women should conform to **hegemonic** or dominant sets of ideas about what constitutes masculine and feminine identity and behaviour. Boys and girls learn what is culturally expected of them – the norms of behaviour associated with each gender – through gender role socialisation. In other words, boys learn how to be masculine and girls learn how to be feminine. Any failure to conform to these gender role expectations is likely to be interpreted as deviant.

### Feminine identity

It is argued mainly by feminist sociologists that throughout the 20th century gender role socialisation was generally successful in terms of teaching female children to take on a feminine identity that reflected **hegemonic** (male-dominated) **definitions of femininity**. For example, girls and women were often encouraged to defer to the power and authority of males, especially their fathers and husbands, and to regard themselves as having a subordinate identity compared with boys. Additionally, it was rarely questioned that the acquisition of a feminine identity meant prioritising becoming full-time mothers and housewives.

## Feminine identity and social change

However, there are signs in the 21st century that the hegemonic and patriarchal version of femininity is being challenged as societies modernise and economies and workforces become feminised. For example, Sue Sharpe (1990) and Helen Wilkinson (1994) observe that women experience greater educational and employment opportunities in modern capitalist societies worldwide and there is evidence that women's economic power has increased, although it is probably still only a fraction of that possessed by men. Natasha Walter (1999), Kat Banyard (2011), Catherine Redfern and Kristin Aune (2013) suggest that the gradual acquisition of greater opportunity and economic power has had two major effects on the attitudes of girls and women. First, girls today are more likely than their mothers and grandmothers to aspire to educational success and professional careers. Second, young women have acquired a range of rights in many societies, which means that they have more cultural power at their disposal than previous generations of women. For example, they can now choose to initiate divorce in order to escape unhappy or abusive marriages. Women in many societies have acquired **reproductive rights,** which has given them access to contraception. They no longer defer to their husbands with regard to when they should have children or how many they should have. A consequence of this is that many women in modern industrial societies are abandoning hegemonic or patriarchal definitions of feminine identity and instead seeing themselves as equal in status, rather than subordinate, to men.

There are also signs that women globally are actively resisting the sexism and **misogyny** that characterise their everyday experience of social life. It can be argued that internet campaigns such as that coordinated by www.everydaysexism.com and social media movements such #MeToo and #TimesUp indicate the emergence of a more assertive feminist identity which is successfully challenging the patriarchal exploitation of women in society in general.

## Masculine identity

James Messerschmidt (2018) argues that the hegemonic masculine value system that is visible in modern industrial societies often stresses difference from women, and in particular a set of masculine goals that need to be achieved in order to become a 'real man'. Messerschmidt argues that **hegemonic masculinity** emphasises the need to demonstrate power, authority and control over women via promiscuity and violence. Messerschmidt argues that this version of masculinity expects boys and men to acquire the respect of other males by demonstrating indifference to emotion and by avoiding any hint of vulnerability. Males are encouraged to use violent confrontation and to aggressively pursue their ambition to 'prove' (usually to other men) their masculinity. Furthermore, socialisation into this hegemonic form of masculinity also involves contempt for both homosexuality and physical weakness. The socialisation of boys into these hegemonic characteristics means that they may be brought up by their fathers unable and unwilling to see females as their equals.

## Masculine identity and social change

Some sociologists believe that the hegemonic way of bringing up boys is leading to two major social problems. First, '**toxic masculinity**' refers to the ways in which patriarchy may be harmful to males. Jaclyn Friedman (2017) argues that hegemonic masculinity encourages males to subscribe to a type of 'hostile sexism' which dehumanises women by calling them degrading names and by justifying sexual violence. It also encourages misogyny (woman-hating) and the view that women's needs are subservient to those of men.

Second, some sociologists argue that hegemonic masculinity has been made redundant by global economic recession and the resulting decline of industries that mainly employed men. It is argued by Máirtín Mac an Ghaill (2004) that men are experiencing a '**crisis of masculinity**' in many societies. Research by Malgorzata Matlak (2014) suggests that many men feel that their masculinity is undermined when they fail to find a job and cannot perform what they see as their most important gender role – providing for their families. Consequently, they may suffer from depression and suicidal thoughts. However, their experience of gender role socialisation convinces them that seeking help or counselling is a sign of weakness and therefore unmanly. Mac an Ghaill argues that some working-class boys may deliberately underachieve at school and may be turning to risky behaviour such as crime and territorial street gangs in order to compensate for what they see as their uncertain futures as men.

## Activity

*Charities including CALM aim to prevent male suicide by encouraging men to seek help.*

Draw two columns. Label the first 'Toxic masculinity' and the second 'Crisis of masculinity'. List the types of deviant behaviour that might arise if boys and men are exposed to these experiences.

## Contemporary issues: Jordan Stephens on toxic masculinity

*In an article in the UK* Guardian *newspaper (23/10/17), Jordan Stephens (one half of hip-hop duo Rizzle Kicks) discusses the effects of toxic masculinity.*

'[...] Any man who has read a woman's account of harassment or assault and thought "that doesn't apply to me": what you're experiencing in that moment is the exact privilege, power and entitlement that women are finding space to battle against. We have subconsciously benefited since we were born from patriarchal privilege – in many ways it's invisible to us. I've been outspoken in my support for women's rights, but I'm not afraid to admit that I've fallen foul of the patriarchy's malicious hardwiring. But in confronting it, rather than continuing to abuse my power, I've found more inner peace, understanding, love and truth then I ever could have done had I continued as I was [...]

I was raised predominantly by a strong mother, and I'd like to think that I journey into the world with good intent. I want to love, spread joy, help people and inspire. But I've still found myself in pockets of self-destruction [...]

If you're one of these guys who takes pride in jumping from girl to girl or brags about breaking hearts, you have no idea what it feels like to truly love and trust yourself [...]

I believe that the false power gifted to men in our patriarchal society does not allow them the space to understand, cry, and work through the pain of their past. As far as I can see, this toxic notion of masculinity is being championed by men who are so terrified of confronting any trauma experienced as children that they choose to project that torture onto the lives of others rather than themselves [...]

Accepting the patriarchy from a place of false benefit will prevent you from ever truly loving yourself or understanding others. It's OK to feel sad. It's OK to cry. It's OK to have loved your mum and dad growing up. It's OK to have missed them or wanted more affection. It's OK to take a moment when you're reminded of these truths. When you allow your brain to access these emotions, it knows exactly what to do. So nurture yourself. Talk honestly to the people around you, and welcome the notion of understanding them more than you have ever done before.'

Source: Adapted from 'Toxic masculinity is everywhere. It's up to us men to fix this.' Adapted from *Guardian*, 23/10/17

### Questions

1. What is the cause of toxic masculinity according to Jordan Stephens?
2. What are the symptoms of toxic masculinity?
3. What are the effects of toxic masculinity for men and women?

In response to the debate about toxic masculinity, some sociologists claim to have seen the emergence of what Connell calls '**subordinate** forms of **masculinity**'. They are subordinate because hegemonic sexist and misogynist forms of masculinity are still dominant in many areas of social life.

Sociologists have noted the emergence of a feminised version of masculinity promoted by male role models such as Frank Ocean, David Beckham and Barack Obama, which encourages men to seek healthier versions of masculinity, for example, to be open about their feelings, to admit unashamedly to emotional vulnerability, to empathise with others (especially women), to take equal responsibility for the care and upbringing of their children and to interpret life crises like unemployment or poverty as 'bearable rejection' rather than 'unbearable failure'. This version of masculine identity may eventually replace the rigid masculinity associated with the toxic hegemonic version. Sarah Schoppe-Sullivan et al. (2017) suggest that males in modern societies in 2018 are more likely than their fathers or grandfathers to attend the birth of their children and to be actively and emotionally involved in parenthood. The 21st century has also seen the emergence of the **metrosexual** male in some Western countries – an urban heterosexual male given to enhancing his personal appearance by fastidious grooming, beauty treatments and fashionable clothes.

## Activity

*Barack Obama and his daughters.*

Make a list of celebrities which suggests that both masculine and feminine identities are no longer shaped by patriarchal influences about how a man or woman should look and behave. Clearly state how each celebrity represents a new type of femininity.

There is a strong overlap between gender identity and sexual identity. For example, the hegemonic definition of masculine identity sees females as sexual objects who are fair game for sexual exploitation by heterosexual males. In many societies around the world, traditionally both masculine and feminine identities are assumed to be heterosexual because this sexual identity has close links to reproduction.

Connell and others point out that our choices with regard to gender identity have become more numerous in postmodern societies as cultures have become more open to the idea that homosexuality is socially acceptable. For example, in the 1980s and 1990s many societies decriminalised homosexual behaviour and prohibited discrimination against lesbian and gay people in employment, housing and services. Many Western societies have recently endorsed same-sex marriage. However, homosexuality is still a criminal offence in 72 countries worldwide, and in some countries it is punishable by death. And, despite the fact that gay culture is more socially acceptable in most Western cultures, there is evidence that **homophobic** attitudes and practices still persist.

The last 20 years have also seen a great deal of debate in Western societies about what constitutes a man or a woman. For example, in recent years a significant minority of both males and females have reported a mismatch between the sex they were assigned by biology and their personal sense of gender identity. Some people who are biologically male report that they feel female, and vice versa. This has led to the emergence of a third type of gender identity in both the USA and Europe known as **transgender identity**. Often those who experience this mismatch between their objective biological characteristics and their sense of subjective self will seek surgery in order to align their physical biology with their sense of masculine or feminine self. Some will transition from a man to a woman or from a woman to a man. The increasing acceptability of **transsexual** identity in Western societies has led to a debate about the meaning of gender and whether gender identity is fixed into just two distinct and opposite (often called **binary**) gender categories: masculinity and femininity. This debate has led to the conclusion among some sociologists that gender identity is actually a very changeable concept. There is evidence from other cultures which supports this supposition.

The Indian government officially recognises a group known as 'Hjiras' or two-spirited people as being neither completely male nor female. Individuals categorised in this way may be transgender, transsexual, cross-dressers or eunuchs (men who have been castrated). Germany, Australia, Nepal and Pakistan officially recognise that there now exist more than two gender categories and offer a third gender option on official forms.

## Activity

*Members of the Hjira community in India.*

Using the internet, research the stories of 'two-spirited' people found in Native American tribes.

Another global example of the flexibility of gender roles are the 'sworn virgins' of Albania.

## Activity

*'Sworn virgins' of Albania. A 'sworn virgin' vows to practise celibacy for the rest of her life. She is then allowed to dress in male clothing, use a male name, take on male work such as policing and act as the head of a household. The men of the village treat such women as equals.*

In what ways do the sworn virgins of Albania resemble men? In what ways do they differ from the Western hegemonic version of femininity?

There is also evidence that an increasing number of people subscribe to an '**intersex**' **identity.** This refers to the increasing recognition that some individuals may be born with biological characteristics such as genitalia and chromosomes that do not fit the typical definition of male and female. It is estimated that at least 1 in 5000 babies in the USA are born each year with intersex conditions – ambiguous genitals because of genetic glitches or hormone problems – which mean that doctors are unable to classify these children as either male or female.

An increasing number of people in the USA and Europe are claiming to possess '**non-binary**' gender identities. This is a catch-all category for gender identities which are not exclusively masculine or feminine. People who possess non-binary self-identities see themselves as neither male nor female. Non-binary people often prefer to forego the use of gendered pronouns such as 'he' or 'she' and favour more neutral pronouns such as 'they' or 'their'. In 2014 Facebook responded to the growing range of non-binary identities by giving its users in the USA a choice of 56 gender options to use when registering.

## Social identity and ethnicity

An ethnic identity can best be defined as a sense of cultural awareness and identity within groups that share a common language, history, religion or national ancestry and heritage. The notion of national ancestry and heritage can be expanded to include regional roots. For example, Indian society contains a diverse range of ethnic identities based on regional origins, including Punjabis, Gujaratis, Goans, Tamils and so on. These ethnic groups have distinctive identities organised around unique traditions and customs. For example, ethnic groups may differ in terms of dress, diet and how they organise marriage and family life.

Some aspects of ethnic identity may be based on visible racial characteristics such as skin colour. In the 1960s and 1970s, Black Americans and African Caribbeans living in European societies such as the UK and Germany were encouraged by their political leaders to emotionally invest and believe in 'Black Power'. In the USA, radical Black leaders who felt that that the Reverend Martin Luther King's civil rights movement was too conservative in its dealings with the White racist establishment set up the 'Black Panther' movement, which advocated violent confrontation between Blacks and Whites. Politicised young Blacks were encouraged to subscribe to slogans such as 'Black is Beautiful', to grow their hair Afro-style and to wear African-style dress in order

## Contemporary issues: The case of Caster Semenya

'Caster Semenya is a woman who is too much a man, according to new wrongheaded rules in track and field.

The South African runner moved up to gold in the women's 800 meters after the 2012 London Games because the Russian winner was caught doping. Semenya finished first in the 800 at the 2016 Rio Games – but can't score a three-peat at the 2020 Tokyo Games unless she's the one who's doping.

[...]

The IAAF, governing body for track and field, released new rules recently that are scheduled to go into effect in November. The rules say women who have high levels of naturally occurring testosterone may not compete in women's middle distance races unless they take medication to reduce those levels.

The IAAF says the new rule – really a new version of an old rule – is about fairness for the vast majority of female athletes. That sounds like a noble motive, but how do you balance athletes' rights with human rights?

Testosterone helps build muscle, endurance and speed. It is one of the reasons that men and women compete separately in most sports. But science simply can't say with precision how much advantage female athletes with high levels of testosterone have. And yet the IAAF would have these athletes take medication to alter what their bodies produce naturally.

The governing body says its new regulations are not "intended as any kind of judgment on, or questioning of, the sex or the gender identity of any athlete," though it would seem that is precisely what it does, no matter what's intended.

[...]

[Semenya] burst onto the world scene in 2009 and, almost immediately, unseemly speculation about her powerful physique burbled up. An Australian newspaper said she had internal testes and three times the testosterone level of most women. At one point, IAAF general secretary Pierre Weiss infamously said, "She is a woman, but maybe not 100%."

Some women are born with differences of sex development, also known as intersex, which means they "do not fit typical binary notions of male or female bodies," according to a definition by the human rights arm of the United Nations.

[...]

Men have varying levels of naturally occurring testosterone, but no one checks to see if that gives some men an advantage over others. So why would authorities assert an advantage for women? [...]

Elite athletes are typically born with natural advantages. Many basketball players are tall; some gymnasts are small. Michael Phelps, history's greatest Olympian, is blessed with a perfect swimmer's body. But genetics are not destiny; elite athletes must work inexpressibly hard to make the most of their God-given gifts. Why shouldn't it be the same for athletes such as Semenya?

[...]

Semenya is her own best spokesperson on all of this.

"God made me the way I am," she wrote on Twitter, "and I accept myself."

So why won't the rest of us?'

Source: 'Is this woman too much a man?' by Erik Brady, *USA Today*, 8/5/18

### Questions

1. Is intersex a biological or social condition?
2. What is a binary notion of male and female?
3. In your opinion, should Caster Semenya be allowed to compete in female athletics? Give reasons for your answer.

to reinforce their Black identity and its inherent opposition to the Jim Crow segregation laws and the racism practised by state governments and police forces in the Deep South of the USA.

Some ethnic identity groups may use their ethnicity to actively construct notions of cultural differences or boundaries between themselves and other ethnic groups – that is, to reinforce the notion of 'them' and 'us'. Majority ethnic groups may use ideologies of superiority and inferiority to suppress the identities of less powerful ethnic minority groups. Particularly horrifying examples of this include:

- the Holocaust – the Nazi attempt to wipe out Jewish identity in Europe during World War II
- the **ethnic cleansing** carried out by Serbs and Croatians in the 1990s of those Bosnians with a Muslim identity
- the mass slaughter of between 500 000 and 1 000 000 people with a Tutsi identity in Rwanda in 1994 by militias that identified with the Hutu ethnic group.

A common consequence of these cultural clashes is racism in the form of prejudice and discrimination.

A notorious example of this in action was the **apartheid** system that dominated South Africa between 1948 and 1993. This involved the White ruling elite constructing an institutionalised system of racial segregation that discriminated against those with a Black or Asian identity.

## Ethnic identity and social change

**Global migration** has dramatically increased in the past 50 years. There are a number of reasons for this; for example, many migrants to Europe are refugees aiming to escape from persecution or conflict in Syria, Iraq and Afghanistan. Many of those hoping to travel to the USA or Europe are economic migrants who are migrating in the hope of economic self-improvement, because these parts of the world are made up of relatively stable economies in which there are opportunities for both education and work.

In recent years, ethnic majority groups have expressed their fears and anxieties about **cultural diversity**, **multiculturalism** and global migration by voting for far-right nationalistic parties that legitimate racism and attacks on refugees and immigrants. In the USA, President Trump has banned people from particular Muslim countries from entering the USA and has promised the American people he will build a wall on the border between Mexico and the USA.

It is important to understand that ethnicity intersects with other important aspects of identity such as nationality, age, gender, social class and age. For example, most people with a Muslim identity living in Europe are third or fourth generation – this means that they were born in the countries in which they live. Most are aged under 30 years old and are bilingual. Many are in low-paid semi-skilled or unskilled jobs or are unemployed. Research into young Muslims in the 1990s carried out by Jessica Jacobson (2015) found that some young Muslims living in European societies are adopting a strong Islamist identity in response to what they see and interpret as a deliberate Western or Christian attack on Islam and the Muslim ummah in areas such as Afghanistan and Iraq. They also express unhappiness at Western support for the Israeli occupation of Palestinian territories. Finally, research suggests that they interpret their experience of everyday life in Western societies as tainted with **Islamophobia**; that is, they feel that the media, politicians and the general public are generally anti-Islamic.

### Activity

Class discussion: evaluate the view that ethnic identity is a source of power and pride rather than a source of conflict.

There are some positive signs that a new hybrid ethnic identity is beginning to emerge in some societies. For example, in the UK, 2.3 million people in Britain are either married to or living with someone of a different ethnicity. In 2018, the wedding of Meghan Markle to Prince Harry resulted in the first **bi-racial** member of the British monarchy. In many European societies, children of mixed-race or **dual heritage** identity are now very common. However, Tony Sandset (2012) argues that, although official **discourses** in Europe refer to the emergence of a **post-racial identity** or colour-blind era, colour and the racism that it attracts still matters in the lives of people who might be described as possessing a dual-heritage identity. Moreover, Sandset argues that, despite the increasing numbers of mixed-race children, some ethnic minority and religious identity groups have constructed cultural obstacles preventing intermarriage and what they see as the potential dilution of their ethnic identity.

# Age and identity

Robert Roberts et al. (1999) observe that age is an important aspect of identity which is experienced by all regardless of socio-economic status, gender and ethnicity.

Harriett Bradley (1996) identifies five major generational stages of age identity that exist in most modern industrial societies. These stages are also relative to particular societies. The movement from one stage to another may be symbolised and celebrated by cultural markers such as rites of passage. For example, the Bar-Mitzvah is a Jewish coming of age ritual for boys that indicates that they are ready to take part in adult religious activities.

## 1. Childhood

In modern industrial societies, childhood is generally regarded as a special, innocent and vulnerable time in which children's identity should be developed through their interaction with their parents. In addition to the parental contribution to a child's identity, Karen Wells (2014) notes that many modern states also intervene in family life to manage childhood identity. This management is almost entirely organised around saving children from internal threats (for example, neglectful or abusive parents) and external threats (germs and viruses, media representations of violence and adult exploitation). In this sense, the state aims to take responsibility for the emotional, physical, intellectual and spiritual development of the child so that they grow up to be a normal law-abiding citizen.

Many states have attempted to shape the identity of children by forbidding particular types of behaviour which are defined by adults as 'deviant'. Many societies have, for example, introduced a legal age at which children can officially be regarded as having a criminal identity. In the UK, 10 is the lowest age at which a child can be held to be responsible for a criminal offence, compared with 16 in Azerbaijan and 12 in China. However, in some US states it can be as low as six.

An important influence on a child's identity is the fact that they spend many of their formative years in school and college. Many modern states have made education compulsory. However, Wells observes that, in many less industrialised societies, many children – especially girls – are denied basic education and consequently grow up lacking numeracy and literacy skills.

Wells also points out that childhood identity in some less industrialised societies may be radically different to that encouraged in richer societies. Very young children may find themselves working for very long hours for little reward in extremely hazardous conditions. In some societies, for example, Uganda, Liberia and Sierra Leone, children have been recruited as child soldiers and been actively involved in the killing of other children and adults.

### Activity

Using the contents page of this book, read and note the childhood section of Chapter 4 on the family so you can discuss the way that childhood has changed in the past century and how the experience of childhood differs across other societies.

## 2. Adolescence

Adolescence or youth is the period between puberty and the achievement of full adult status – that is, the teenage years. Entrance to adulthood in Western societies is usually celebrated on the 18th or 21st birthday, because this is the age at which the state confers legal adulthood via the right to vote, marry, sit on a jury and so on. There is evidence that before the 1950s this life stage was not recognised as the distinctive social stage as it is today. For example, adolescents and their parents in the 1940s frequently shared similar leisure interests.

In modern industrial societies, youth subcultures appeared in the 1950s based on a growing consumer market in teenage products such as clothes, cosmetics, magazines, hairstyles and music, which the older generation found threatening. These youth subcultures were often defined as a problem of morality by the older generation and consequently, according to studies by Jock Young (1971) and Stanley Cohen (1973), were policed quite harshly by agents of social control.

However, global studies of teenagers have found that what young people value is not significantly different to the values held by their parents. Most young people are generally conformist – they respect and get on well with their parents and place a high value on traditional goals such as getting a job, getting married and setting up a home.

In contrast to more industrial societies, many pre-industrial societies do not recognise youth or adolescence as a distinctive life stage. As soon as a child reaches puberty, the community or tribe expects them to go through ceremonies or rituals called **rites of passage**, after which they take on the status of adults. Girls are initiated in domestic skills by older women to prepare them for marriage, while boys are trained by older men to prepare them for their adult role as hunters or farmers. For example, in Papua New Guinea, the Sepik tribe believe that boys should progress through a rite of passage that involves a painful and bloody skin-cutting ritual which leaves distinctive scars on the face and body which symbolise manhood.

## Activity

*Ceremonial henna tattoo of the rite of passage of a young Nepali girl.*

Research examples of rites of passage used across the world to initiate adolescents into adulthood.

## 3. Young adulthood

Young adulthood generally refers to the period between leaving the parental home and middle age. Gill Valentine (2003) suggests that private and public **cultural** '**markers**' exist in modern cultures which signify the beginning of adult identity. For example, private markers might include choosing and buying one's own clothes or going out clubbing for the first time, whereas public markers may include moving out of the parental home, getting a job, getting engaged or getting married. Young adulthood often involves independence from parents and taking responsibility for the first time, for example, paying rent, being faithful to one person and so on.

## 4. Middle age

Bradley claims that those who achieve middle age in capitalist societies generally have higher status than the young and elderly, because the middle-aged make up the majority of those who constitute the most successful socio-economic groups. Social indicators of middle age include children leaving home for university and more money being available for leisure pursuits. There may also be emotional or psychological indicators, such as the so-called 'midlife crisis'.

## 5. Old age

In many pre-industrial and tribal cultures, the elderly are accorded great respect and status by the young and their experience and wisdom is seen as an important resource. The same is true of communities in which religion is a prime shaper of morality and family life. For example, failure to look after aged parents is viewed as shameful in Hindu, Sikh, Muslim and Confucian cultures.

In contrast, in societies which are heavily influenced by Western culture and consumerism, attitudes towards the elderly are often indifferent and sometimes even hostile. Survey evidence collected by Ulrich Orth and Kali Trzesniewski (2010) suggested that consequently many elderly people in modern Western societies subscribe to a negative self-identity characterised by low self-esteem, because such societies value youth and those in work but fail to appreciate the experience and knowledge accumulated by the elderly. Christin-Melanie Vauclair et al. (2017) found that this negative self-identity is compounded by the elderly's experience of **ageism** – prejudice and discrimination – which stereotypes the elderly as vulnerable, dependent, inferior and as a financial and social burden on the rest of society. Consequently, the elderly are likely to feel marginalised, isolated and lonely. Moreover, the elderly are subjected to **infantilisation** – they are assumed to be helpless and dependent on others. They are rarely treated as independent adults capable of actively making choices and decisions of their own free will.

In evaluation, postmodernists argue that old age is intersected by other influences such as social class and ethnicity. Life expectancy, particularly for affluent Whites in Western societies, is increasing. Consequently, age identities are becoming flexible and becoming less significant as markers of self-identity. Mike Featherstone and Mike Hepworth (1991) argue that global media images of ageing are becoming less derogatory and condescending towards the elderly. In part, this is due to the fact that many global celebrities have become elderly, but their wealth and status have meant that they can project a relatively youthful and dignified image of old age to the world. For example, elderly celebrities such as Sir Mick Jagger do not conform to the dominant stereotype of that age group as vulnerable, dependent and in constant need of care.

## Activity

*Mick Jagger.*

Discuss with the rest of your classmates your perceptions of the elderly. Would you conclude that your generation is ageist?

## Key terms

**Structuration** A theory of society invented by Giddens which argues that human behaviour is caused by a combination of structure and agency.

**Sampling frame** A list of people who might take part in a sociological study.

**Subculture** A culture within a broader mainstream culture, with its own separate values, practices and beliefs.

**Social class** A socio-economic status and identity which is hierarchically organised on the basis of occupation, wealth, income and life chances.

**Social stratification** A system of social ranking, usually based on wealth, income, race, education and power.

**Satipatthana** A Buddhist concept that stresses mindfulness or awareness of others.

**Caste system** A religious and ascribed system of stratification mainly found in India and Indian communities abroad that categorises people into five status groups, which determine their occupation and the Hindu concept of religious purity.

**Jati** The caste system.

**Dalit** The non-caste of 'untouchables' who occupy the lowest social rung of the Indian caste system and who do the dirtiest jobs.

**Middle class** Those occupations that require a professional qualification or who manage capitalism on behalf of the capitalist class. This group tends to be highly rewarded in terms of income and status.

**Unskilled class/underclass** The lowest social stratum or status group found in a society consisting of the unskilled, low-paid and possibly unemployed and welfare-dependent poor.

**Super-rich/uber-wealthy** An expression used to describe the richest 1 per cent of billionaires and multi-millionaires.

**Upper class** The social group that has the highest status in society. This status is often inherited. It is often called the 'ruling class'.

**Symbiotic** Inter-dependent.

**Ideological power** Dominating culture or ideas.

**Social closure** Exclusionary practices employed by wealthy high-status groups to protect their monopoly and ownership of both wealth and property, so preventing other groups from becoming members of their class.

**Deferred gratification** The ability to forego or postpone gratification or pleasure now by making the decision to gain greater rewards later – say, by saving for the future or studying for a degree.

**Collectivism** The practice or principle of giving a group priority over each individual with in it.

**Class consciousness** A Marxist concept that relates to awareness of one's place in a system of social class, especially as it relates to the class struggle.

**Socialism** A left-wing political ideology or set of beliefs that states all people are equal and should enjoy equal opportunities with regard to access to education, qualifications, jobs and wealth creation.

**Populism** A system of ideas that claims to support the will of the people.

**Xenophobic** Fear or hatred of foreigners such as refugees or migrants.

**Precariat** People whose employment and income are insecure, especially when considered as a class.

**Gig economy** A labour market characterised by the prevalence of short-term contracts or freelance work as opposed to permanent jobs.

**Present-day orientation** A view likely to be held by members of the precariat, whose members may believe that people should live for today and that there is little hope for the future because of their experience of job insecurity.

**Fatalism** The belief that all events are predetermined and inevitable, and that we are powerless and incapable of bringing about social change.

**Hegemonic** Culturally dominant.

**Hegemonic femininity** A version of feminine identity which stresses that females are subordinate and their 'natural' roles should be confined to the spheres of motherhood and the home.

**Reproductive rights** The right of women to control their own bodies.

**Misogyny** Hatred of women.

**Hegemonic masculinity** A version of masculine identity which defines a 'real man' in terms of toughness, emotional hardness and the power to provide for his family.

**Toxic masculinity** A consequence of hegemonic masculinity in that males may suffer from depression or suicidal thoughts because they believe they cannot publicly display emotion or vulnerability. It may also be expressed through violence and misogyny.

**Crisis of masculinity** The struggle of men who have been socialised into the hegemonic version of masculinity to cope with the disappearance of traditional male roles.

**Subordinate masculinity** A type of masculine identity that is only subscribed to by a minority of men, for example, gay masculinity, men who look after their children full-time while their partner works, metrosexual men and so on.

**Metrosexual** A heterosexual urban man who enjoys shopping, fashion and similar interests traditionally associated with women or homosexual men.

**Homophobia** Hatred of homosexuals.

**Transgender identity** An umbrella term for people whose gender identity, gender expression or behaviour does not conform to that typically associated with the sex to which they were assigned at birth.

**Transsexual** A person who emotionally and psychologically feels that they belong to the opposite sex.

**Binary** The idea that there are only two sexes.

**Intersex identity** A general term used for a variety of conditions in which a person is born with a reproductive or sexual anatomy that does not seem to fit the typical definitions of female or male.

**Non-binary identity** A term used to describe somebody whose gender identity is not exclusively male or female.

**Ethnic cleansing** The mass expulsion or killing of members of one ethnic or religious group in an area by those of another.

**Apartheid** A system of state-approved institutionalised segregation that existed in South Africa between 1948 and 1991.

**Global migration** A situation in which people go to live in foreign countries, especially in order to find work.

**Cultural diversity** The existence of a variety of cultural or ethnic groups within a society.

**Multiculturalism** The practice of giving equal attention to the cultural needs, interests and traditions of all ethnic identity groups that exist in an ethnically diverse society.

**Islamophobia** Dislike of or prejudice against Islam or Muslims, especially as a political force.

**Bi-racial** Someone who is the product of parents who belong to different ethnic groups.

**Dual heritage** Another term for bi-racial.

**Discourse** A dominant debate.

**Post-racial identity** The idea that race and ethnicity are no longer important as a source of identity.

**Rite of passage** A ceremony or event marking an important stage in someone's life.

**Cultural markers** An event which symbolises a significant change in self or social identity or one's place in a culture, for example, going from being single to being married.

**Ageism** A form of prejudice and discrimination that devalues a group because of their age.

**Infantilisation** Treating or condescending to someone as if they were a young child.

## Summary

1. Most societies around the world are capitalist societies and consequently characterised by social class inequalities in wealth and income as well as exploitative work practices.

1. Four distinct social class identities can be observed as existing in capitalist societies; the bourgeoise or upper class, the middle classes, the working classes and the precariat.
2. Capitalist societies are characterised by conflict between social classes.
3. Standing argues that the precariat is a dangerous class because it feels a strong sense of grievance and hostility, especially towards the bourgeoisie, because it feels that the wealthy are denying them job security and a living wage.
4. The 20th century saw major changes in gender identity. During most of this century, feminine identity and aspirations were shaped by male or hegemonic definitions about how females should behave. For example, it was believed that females were subordinate to men and that they should only aspire to be mothers and housewives. However, economic changes in the late 20th century saw women acquiring more economic and cultural power which meant they aspired to higher education and careers. Surveys consistently showed that females no longer saw themselves as inferior or subordinate to males.
5. Male identity was focused on acquiring particular masculine characteristics such as physical and emotional toughness and avoiding vulnerability.
6. However, in many Western societies, women's identities began to change as they acquired more economic power and became more aspirational with regard to education and careers. In many societies across the world, many young women are questioning the idea that females should be subordinate to males. In many Western societies, it is being increasingly recognised that traditional expressions of masculinity are toxic and may be responsible for a 'crisis of masculinity;' which has emerged among boys and young men.
7. There is an increasing realisation among sociologists worldwide that gender identity has become more complex because sexual identities are becoming less binary and more diverse. In multicultural societies, ethnic and religious identities live alongside each other in relative harmony.
8. However, ethnic identity can lead to powerful ethnic groups imposing their identity in negative ways on minority groups via racism, segregation and ethnic cleansing.
9. As societies evolve and intermarriage increases, hybridised mixed-race identities are increasing in number.
10. All members of society have or will experience a range of identities based on age relative to their culture.

# Unit 2.3.2 Globalisation, identity and social change

This unit aims to briefly explore the relationship between globalisation and social change, and in particular the effect of this relationship on both self-identity and social identity today. Many of the issues, especially those relating to the debate about how globalisation should be defined and the sociological debates about the nature, extent, causes and significance of globalisation, are discussed in greater depth in Chapter 8. We also briefly explore how social class, gender, ethnicity and age identities may be increasingly shaped by globalisation, and particularly the increased choices that supporters of globalisation claim it has brought about. Finally, we conclude by briefly investigating whether globalisation has brought about the social construction of new forms of identity which are a hybrid or fusion of local and global influences.

## Defining globalisation

Globalisation can be defined as an ongoing process which involves the increasing interconnectedness and inter-dependency of the world's nations and their people into a single global economic, political and cultural system. As Allan Cochrane and Kathy Pain (2000) note, 'the lives of ordinary people everywhere in the world seem increasingly to be shaped by events, decisions and actions that take place far away from where they live and work'.

## The impact of globalisation on identity

Many sociologists argue that globalisation has had a significant effect on local identities which have traditionally been shaped by socio-economic status, gender, ethnicity, religion and age. For example, Giddens (1999) observes that globalisation is often interpreted by some Islamic cultures as a deliberate Western attempt to undermine traditional relationships between Islamic parents and children and to encourage liberal social norms which supposedly weaken Islamic identity among the young. Western norms such as equal rights for women, free speech and the promotion of democracy are regarded as threatening traditional authoritarian power bases such as rule by elites based on divine right, and particularly the male dominance common in these societies.

Furthermore, globalisation has exposed many traditional societies to the influence of Western consumerism and materialism, whose '**decadence**' or spiritual emptiness is seen by those who subscribe to a fundamentalist Muslim identity as a threat to their faith and identity, and especially the commitment of the next generation to religious rules regarding religious lifestyle and identity. The focus on materialism, fashion, pop culture and so on in Western culture is seen to be corrupt, in that it distracts young people in traditional societies away from religion. In response, in 2014, Iran sentenced six teenagers to a year in prison and 91 lashes for dancing in public to the global pop hit 'Happy' by Pharrell Williams.

Bauman (1992) also saw globalisation as having a profound effect upon local identities, because he claimed that it has undermined the collectivist identity of many traditional societies. Globalisation has increased the number of choices available to citizens and consequently promoted the identity of the individual at the expense of society. However, globalisation has made us more aware of **global risks** to our identity, thus promoting fear and uncertainty. This has resulted in the questioning of the old certainties which have governed our lives for hundreds of years. In this situation, while some embrace the new freedoms, others are attracted to **fundamentalist** forms of identity because these promise absolute truth and certainty.

## Hybrid identities

It is important, too, that we understand that local identities interact with the global, especially via social media, mass tourism and cultural commodities such as film, television, sport, fast food and pop music. The fusing of global products with local culture to produce unique hybrids is known as '**glocalisation**'. Luke Martell (2010) claims that glocalisation has two elements to it. First, Western media and cultural producers often adapt their products so that they appeal to local markets and audiences. For example, MTV adapts its programming according to the cultural likes and dislikes of particular countries such as Japan, India, Mexico, Spain and France and mixes Western music with that produced locally. Moreover, global brands such as McDonald's, Starbucks and KFC often adapt their menus to reflect local tastes and to avoid offending local cultural traditions.

Second, local cultures select and appropriate elements of Westernised global culture that please them, which they modify and adapt to local culture and needs. In other words, they localise the global to produce a **hybridised** popular culture and **identity**. A good example of this is the Indian film industry, known as 'Bollywood', which combines contemporary Western ideas about entertainment with traditional Hindu myth, history and culture.

Miller (2011) argues that the Trinidadian use of Facebook is a good example of glocalisation. He argues that Trinidadians use Facebook in ways that reflect their cultural priorities. He observes that locals refer to Facebook as 'Fasbook' or 'Macobook'. These labels deliberately mirror the cultural inclinations of Trinidadian society, especially the characteristic 'to be fas' that refers to the uniquely Trinidadian way of trying to get to know another person rather too quickly and 'maco', which Miller claims is a unique Trinidadian cultural trait meaning 'wanting to meddle in other people's business'. So, activity on Facebook in Trinidad is mainly geared to getting to know somebody of the opposite sex but, once users become friends with one another, they use Facebook to gossip about one other and to constantly pry into other people's lives. Fasbook, then, is a good example of cultural hybridity, because it has appropriated the Western idea of a social network to project one's identity but it has been adapted by Trinidadians for use as a source of gossip and as a means of interfering in the private lives of others.

However, another effect of globalisation is **cultural appropriation**. This is a sociological concept which views the adoption or use of elements of one culture by members of a different culture as a largely negative phenomenon because it is a form of cultural theft. When the cultural element is used in the West, it is sometimes used in a disrespectful way and/or its cultural source is rarely acknowledged. A number of cultural artefacts which originated in other cultures have been appropriated by Westerners in order to construct their self-identity, including tattoos (from Polynesian culture), manbuns (from Japan), body or facial piercing (from India) and dreadlocks (from Rastafarianism).

### Activity

1. 'Globalisation has generally had a positive effect on the world.' Explain this view and, using sociological material, outline one argument in support of the view and one argument against it.
2. Explain using examples what is meant by cultural appropriation.

## Key terms

**Decadence** Spiritual emptiness.

**Global risks** Globalisation has increased people's risk of being victims of global warming, terrorism, crime and so on.

**Fundamentalism** A very conservative version of religion which believes that God's word and religious texts are infallible and need to be interpreted literally.

**Glocalisation** A trend which sees global actors flexibly altering their global brands so that they suit the needs of and respect local cultures. Local cultures may take aspects of a global product and adapt it so that it appeals to local consumers.

**Hybridised identity** A form of identity that is constructed by combining aspects of two or more cultures.

**Cultural appropriation** This involves members of a dominant culture taking cultural artefacts from a marginalised group without permission, and usually with little respect for or knowledge about that culture.

## Summary

1. Globalisation refers to the increasing interconnectedness of the world.
2. Developments in digital communication mean that people who were previously separated by geographical distance and national boundaries, as well as time zones, can now be linked instantaneously.
3. Globalisation may be viewed by some cultures as a threat. There is some evidence that globalisation may have questioned old moral certainties and consequently it may have encouraged the rise of religious fundamentalism in some parts of the world.
4. Globalisation has resulted in the cultural appropriation by Westerners of some cultural features of the less industrialised world.
5. Globalisation has led to two types of glocalisation, which have produced hybrid cultural forms as Western global brands have adapted their products to meet the needs of local markets.
6. Some local cultures have adapted Western cultural products such as Hollywood and Facebook so that they meet their own cultural needs.

# END-OF-PART QUESTIONS

| 0 | 1 | Describe the two components that make up identity. **[4 marks]**

| 0 | 2 | Explain one positive and one negative effect that globalisation might have on local cultures and identity. **[6 marks]**

| 0 | 3 | Explain two reasons why traditional notions of femininity are undergoing change in modern societies. **[8 marks]**

# EXAM-STYLE PRACTICE QUESTIONS

| 0 | 1 | Describe two factors that might influence a person's social identity. **[4 marks]**

| 0 | 2 | **a.** Explain two reasons why people usually conform to social expectations. **[8 marks]**

**b.** Explain one strength and one limitation of the view that individual behaviour is shaped by the social structure. **[6 marks]**

| 0 | 3 | 'The role of socialisation in shaping human behaviour has been exaggerated.'

**a.** Explain this view. **[10 marks]**

**b.** Using sociological material, give one argument against this view. **[6 marks]**

| 0 | 4 | Evaluate the view that social control serves the interests of the ruling class. **[26 marks]**

| 0 | 5 | Evaluate the view that people are free to choose their social identities today. **[26 marks]**

# 3 RESEARCH METHODS

## Chapter contents


**Section A Research methods, approaches and issues** **75**

**Exam-style practice questions** **141**


We are bombarded with information online, on the television and radio, in newspapers and magazines, in academic books and journals – facts and figures telling us what is happening, keeping us informed, and claiming to reflect reality. However, do any of these facts and figures come close to the truth?

What do we really know? How do we find out what is true? We could observe something happening and then find evidence that supports our observation and confirms what we see. But we tend not to look for evidence that might contradict what we think we see. We could rely on common sense. But today's common sense may well be tomorrow's nonsense. We could listen to experts. But they often disagree among themselves. So how do we decide what to believe?

This chapter looks at the methods of research that sociologists use to gather information and find out what may or may not be true. Although these methods are not perfect, they do show us how information is produced and we can recognise their strengths and limitations. This helps us to form judgements about the quality of the information that each method produces. These methods range from observations of people's behaviour to interviews and questionnaires. They include interpreting and analysing information from photographs, websites, television broadcasts and autobiographies.

The chapter assesses the strengths and limitations of each method. It also examines the different theoretical approaches to sociological research and the debates about whether sociology can and should be based on the natural sciences. It then looks at the different factors – practical, ethical and theoretical – that influence sociological research and some of the possible sources of bias in research findings.

# SECTION A
# RESEARCH METHODS, APPROACHES AND ISSUES

## Contents


| | | |
|---|---|---|
| Part 1 | Types of data, methods and research design | 76 |
| Part 2 | Approaches to sociological research | 112 |
| Part 3 | Research issues | 132 |


The key concept of *structure and human agency*, which you were introduced to in Chapter 1, is particularly important in this section. The idea of structure is concerned with the influence of society on the individual. Structural approaches emphasise the way that society and its social structures – such as families, class and education systems – influence, shape and constrain our behaviour. For example, through the socialisation process, education systems have scope to influence students' beliefs, values and behaviour. Such approaches tend to see people as playing a passive role within the socialisation process, as being socialised into, rather than challenging, their society's norms and values. How do structural approaches investigate the social structures that they see as influencing our behaviour? Are some methods more appropriate than others for researching structure?

The idea of agency concerns the freedom that individuals have to act in ways that can shape and change society. For example, people might try to influence decision-making in society and bring about change by actively participating in feminist or environmental groups. The emphasis here is on people's power to make choices and to act on these choices. How do sociologists research the significance of agency and self-determination? In other words, how do they investigate the choices and decisions that individuals make in their daily lives? Are qualitative research methods such as unstructured interviews more suitable than quantitative methods for capturing creative human agency, meaningful action and the choices we make? Or is it possible and desirable for sociologists to combine quantitative and qualitative methods in one study to capture aspects of both structure and agency?

This chapter comprises just one section, which is divided into three parts. Part 1 examines different types of data and research methods that sociologists use, and explores their strengths and limitations. It also looks at the stages involved in planning and designing a piece of research.

Part 2 explores different approaches to research, including debates about whether sociology can be seen as a science and the role of values in research. It also looks at the debate between positivist and interpretivist approaches to research.

Part 3 focuses on issues arising from research, including sources of bias in sociologists' findings and the question of how we assess the value of different research methods.

# PART 1 TYPES OF DATA, METHODS AND RESEARCH DESIGN

## Contents


| | | |
|---|---|---|
| **Unit 3.1.1** | **Different types of data used in sociological research** | **76** |
| **Unit 3.1.2** | **Quantitative research methods** | **80** |
| **Unit 3.1.3** | **Qualitative research methods** | **88** |
| **Unit 3.1.4** | **Secondary sources of data** | **97** |
| **Unit 3.1.5** | **The stages of designing research** | **105** |


This part begins by looking at different types of information produced by and used in sociological research studies. What kind of information might sociologists want and what are the best methods for collecting it? What are the strengths and limitations of the different **research methods** that sociologists use? How useful is pre-existing information such as official statistics or autobiographies?

How do sociologists go about designing their research? Put yourself in the position of a researcher. What topic would you choose to investigate? How would you choose to research it? Is the way you plan to conduct your research **ethical** – is it morally the right way to treat your **research participants**? These are some of the questions that this part answers.

## Unit 3.1.1 Different types of data used in sociological research

When carrying out research, sociologists collect **data** in an organised way in order to address their research aims and questions. They may generate new data during the course of their research and/or draw on pre-existing sources of information. The term 'data' refers to the information produced and used in a research project. Data provide sociologists with evidence to explain the social world. This unit looks at the different types of data that sociologists use in their research. It distinguishes between primary and secondary data, and between quantitative and qualitative data.

### Primary and secondary data

There are two main types or sources of data – **primary data** and **secondary data**. Often, researchers use both sources within a single project.

Primary data were not present before the research began. They are generated by the researcher during the research process and include information produced by questionnaires, interviews and observations. By collecting primary data rather than relying on pre-existing sources, researchers are more likely to find out exactly what they want to know about a particular issue. However, it is usually more expensive and time consuming to generate primary data compared to using secondary sources.

Secondary data existed before the research began. They include data from official statistics such as crime and unemployment rates, personal documents such as diaries and letters, media sources such as newspapers and television programmes, and digital content such as emails and blogs. Many sociological studies draw on secondary sources in one form or another.

Using secondary data can save time and money because the information has already been collected. Many public documents are readily available and easily accessible. For example, sociologists researching education can usually view prospectuses and newsletters from school websites at no cost. Government departments in many countries often publish vast quantities of official statistics each year. Sociologists do not have the resources to compile these statistics themselves. In some cases, secondary data may be the only source of information on a particular topic, such as birth rates in different parts of the world. However, a sociologist who uses secondary sources has no control over the collection or the quality of the data. Some secondary data, such as students' school reports or emails, may be difficult to access. In other instances, the required information may not actually exist. (See Unit 3.1.4 for a discussion of other limitations of secondary data.)

## Quantitative and qualitative data

There are two other categories of data – **quantitative data** and **qualitative data**. Researchers often use both forms within one piece of research.

Quantitative data are information in the form of numbers or percentages. Examples include **official statistics** on births and marriages, or statistical data from questionnaires. Quantitative data are particularly useful for measuring the strength of possible relationships between various factors, for example, between age and internet use, or gender and employment. With quantitative data, sociologists can compare social groups and measure trends (for example, educational attainment by ethnicity) over time.

'Qualitative data' refers to all types of data that are not in the form of numbers, including:

- descriptive data from observations, for example, a description of behaviour in a workplace or classroom, or at a football or soccer match
- quotations from interviews, for example participants' views on marriage
- written sources, for example diaries, novels and autobiographies
- pictures, for example photographs, paintings and posters
- films and recorded music.

Qualitative data are naturally occurring rather than being structured by researchers. As a result, they often give a richer and more in-depth picture of people's lives than the numbers provided by quantitative data. While crime statistics, for instance, might provide figures on the number of thefts recorded by the police, qualitative data might help us to understand what it means to be a victim of theft. Based on qualitative data, sociologists can not only explore how people make sense of their experiences but also explain the meaning behind the statistics. In practice, many sociologists combine quantitative and qualitative data in their research.

### Activity

*Collecting qualitative data by observing fans' behaviour at a soccer or football match.*

**Table 3.1.1 Quantitative data from a soccer or football match**

| | Goals | Possession | Pass success | Shots at goal | Yellow cards | Penalties |
|---|---|---|---|---|---|---|
| **Winner** | 3 | 56% | 82% | 16 | 1 | 1 |
| **Loser** | 1 | 44% | 74% | 11 | 3 | 0 |

1. Give one example of a:

   a. quantitative, primary source of data

   b. qualitative, secondary source of data.
2. Using the material above, outline the difference between quantitative and qualitative data.
3. How might a combination of both types of data provide a fuller picture than just one type?

## Validity and reliability of data

When conducting research, sociologists are concerned about the **validity** and **reliability** of the data they produce or use. Ideally, they want to draw on data that are both valid and reliable.

### Validity

Data are valid if they present a true and accurate description or measurement. For example, official statistics on crime are valid if they provide an accurate measurement of the extent of crime. Statistics on crimes recorded by the police are used to measure the extent of crime in many countries. However, this is not a valid measure for two main reasons. First, many crimes are not reported to the police and therefore cannot be recorded by them. Second, research by Her Majesty's Inspectorate of Constabulary (2014) in the UK indicated that around 800 000 crimes reported to the police each year (19 per cent of all reported crime) were not recorded. Clearly, police-recorded crime statistics do not provide valid data on the extent of crime.

### Reliability

Data are reliable when different researchers using the same methods obtain the same results. For example, if a number of researchers use the same procedures to measure attendance rates at the same school and they all get the same results, then the data would be reliable. However, this does not necessarily mean that the data are valid. For instance, the researchers may have used class registers to measure attendance and the registers may not have been filled in accurately. As a result, the registers would not measure what they were designed to measure and the data drawn from them would be invalid. (See also Unit 3.3.2.)

### Activity

*The children were asked to place wooden blocks into appropriate holes.*

Yakima Native American children were given an intelligence test that consisted of placing variously shaped wooden blocks into appropriately shaped holes. The children had no problem with the test, but they were all given low scores because they failed to finish it in the required time. Unlike Western culture, Yakima culture did not place a high priority on speed (Klineberg, 1971).

1. Explain why the test results are reliable.
2. Explain why the test results are not valid.

## Different theoretical approaches

A number of sociologists have suggested that there are two main research traditions or approaches in sociology – **positivism** and **interpretivism**. They are based on different views of human behaviour and sometimes lead to the use of different research methods. These approaches are explored in Unit 3.2.2, but here is a brief introduction to them.

### Positivism

Positivist sociology favours quantitative data. It attempts to measure behaviour by presenting it in the form of numbers. This makes it possible to use statistical tests to measure the strength of relationships between two or more factors. A **correlation** – a statistical link – may indicate a causal relationship, that one factor causes another. However, correlation does not necessarily indicate causation; it does not mean that one thing necessarily causes another.

Some research methods are more likely than others to generate quantitative data. It is fairly easy to translate the answers to a questionnaire and responses to certain types of interview into numbers. As a result, positivists are likely to prefer these research methods. In terms of secondary data, they tend to prefer information in a numerical form – for example, official statistics such as unemployment and crime statistics.

Positivists aim to make **generalisations** about human behaviour. A generalisation is a statement made about a whole group based on findings from a relatively small number of members of that group. To do this, they need to study a **representative sample** (a subgroup that reflects the characteristics of the **population** or wider group from which it is drawn). So, if the study is based on middle-class, African-American women aged 20–30 the sample should have these characteristics. If the sample is representative, then data from the sample are more likely to reflect the group in society as a whole.

## Interpretivism

Some sociologists argue that understanding human behaviour involves seeing the world through the eyes of those being studied. People give meaning to their own behaviour and to the behaviour of others. They define situations in certain ways and act accordingly. To understand their behaviour, it is essential to discover the meanings and definitions that guide their actions. This approach is sometimes referred to as interpretivism – the sociologist's task is to discover and interpret the meanings and definitions of the situation.

Interpretivists tend to favour particular research methods. Many see participant observation as one of the best ways to discover meanings. It provides researchers with the opportunity to observe people in their normal, everyday situations, to see life as it is lived. Interpretivists also favour in-depth, unstructured interviews, which allow research participants to express their own view of the world and define situations in their own way. Interpretivists see these methods as more likely to provide qualitative data, which they believe is richer and more meaningful than quantitative data. In terms of secondary data, they prefer personal documents such as diaries and autobiographies in which people express their meanings and feelings in their own way.

## Key terms

**Research methods** Techniques for collecting data such as interviews or questionnaires.

**Ethical** Relating to moral principles that state what is right and wrong.

**Research participants** The people who researchers study.

**Data** Information that a researcher draws on and/ or generates during a study.

**Primary data** New information produced by the researcher during the research process.

**Secondary data** Pre-existing information used by the researcher.

**Quantitative data** Information in the form of statistics.

**Qualitative data** All data (such as quotations from interview participants) that is not in numerical form.

**Official statistics** Numerical data produced by government departments and agencies.

**Validity** Data are valid if they represent a true or accurate measurement.

**Reliability** Data are reliable when different researchers using the same methods obtain the same results.

**Positivism** An approach based partly on the methods used in the natural sciences. It favours quantitative data.

**Interpretivism** An approach that explores people's lived experiences and the meanings they attach to their actions. It favours qualitative data.

**Correlation** A statistical link between two or more variables or factors.

**Generalisation** A statement based on a relatively small group which is then applied to a larger group.

**Representative sample** A subgroup that is typical of its population.

**Population** The group under study from which a sample is selected.

## Summary

1. Sociologists draw on different types of data in their research – primary and secondary data, and quantitative and qualitative data.
2. When undertaking research, researchers are concerned about the reliability and validity of their data.
3. In some cases, data may be reliable but lack validity.
4. Some sociologists argue that there are two main research traditions or approaches in sociology – positivism and interpretivism. Each of these favours particular research methods and types of data.

# Unit 3.1.2 Quantitative research methods

Quantitative research methods produce statistical data. This unit looks at some of the research methods that provide sociologists with primary sources of quantitative data. It begins by focusing on questionnaires and structured interviews, which are the main ways of gathering data in **social surveys**. However, what are the similarities and differences between these two methods? The unit then examines experiments, which are usually designed to test **hypotheses**. Do all experiments necessarily take place in laboratories? What are the main strengths of these different quantitative methods? What are their limitations?

## Questionnaires

A social survey involves systematically collecting the same type of data from a relatively large number of people. Survey research is often carried out by using **self-completion questionnaires** delivered to respondents by post, email, the internet or by hand. A questionnaire comprises a list of questions to which participants provide the answers. The questions are usually designed to measure, for instance, how many people voted for a particular political party in the last election according to gender and ethnicity. They produce data that can be easily quantified – put into numerical form.

### Types of question

There are two main types of question – **closed questions** and **open-ended** (or **open**) **questions**.

In closed questions, the range of responses is fixed by the researcher. The respondent (the person from whom information is sought) has to select their answer from two or more given alternatives. Table 3.1.2 provides an example of a very simple closed question which offers two possible answers. This type of question can usually be answered quickly and the answers are easily quantified.

**Table 3.1.2**

| Do you have any brothers or sisters? (Please tick as appropriate.) | |
|---|---|
| Yes | |
| No | |

Table 3.1.3 gives an example of a closed question in which the respondent has to select the answer that best fits their experiences from seven alternatives. It is taken from the Global School-based Student Health Survey (GSHS), a self-completion questionnaire carried out in many countries, including Mauritius, Tunisia and Morocco. The results relate to the survey carried out in Mauritius in 2011.

**Table 3.1.3**

| Question: During the past 30 days, on how many days were you bullied? | | | |
|---|---|---|---|
| **Results for Mauritius, 2011** | | | |
| | | **Frequency** | **%** |
| 1 | 0 days | 1364 | 65.2 |
| 2 | 1 or 2 days | 418 | 20.0 |
| 3 | 3 to 5 days | 156 | 7.5 |
| 4 | 6 to 9 days | 47 | 2.2 |
| 5 | 10 to 19 days | 29 | 1.4 |
| 6 | 20 to 29 days | 10 | 0.5 |
| 7 | All 30 days | 60 | 2.9 |
| | Missing | 84 | |

Source: http://www.who.int/ncds/surveillance/gshs/MUBH2011_public_use_codebook.pdf?ua=1

The answers to this question are easy to quantify. The third column shows the actual number of respondents who chose each alternative. The fourth column shows the percentage of respondents who chose each alternative.

## Activity

1. Devise your own example of a closed question with pre-set answers.
2. Identify one disadvantage of closed questions.

Closed questions are the simplest way to produce numerical data. The data are suitable for statistical analysis. They make it possible to discover whether there is a correlation between two or more variables or factors, for example, between age, gender and the incidence of bullying.

Open questions ask respondents to answer questions in their own words. Several lines are left blank on the questionnaire for the respondent to write their answer. Open questions give the respondent more freedom to respond in their own way.

Most researchers see closed questions as suitable for simple, factual information such as age, gender and income level. Open questions are usually seen as more appropriate for data on meanings and beliefs, where respondents are required to express how they feel.

## Constructing questionnaires

Questionnaires are based on the idea that all respondents answer exactly the same set of questions. This means that any differences in their answers should indicate real differences between them. The questions must mean the same thing to all respondents so that their answers can be directly compared. The researcher must ensure that the questions are clear and unambiguous, that participants are able to understand the words and phrases used and that the instructions for completing the questionnaire are straightforward. This not only provides good quality data; it is also an **ethical issue**. If participants cannot understand the questions, they might feel stupid, defensive or offended and this may affect their answers. For this reason, a **pilot study** (a small-scale trial run) is recommended to sort out any problems with the questionnaire before the main survey (*The Research Ethics Guidebook*, 2017).

## Operationalisation and coding

Questionnaires are designed to measure things. In order to do this, those 'things' (concepts or variables) must be **operationalised** – put into a form that can be measured and quantified. For example, concepts

## Activity

*Examples of questions to avoid when devising a questionnaire.*

1. What is wrong with each of these questions?
2. Select one of these questions and rewrite it in a more appropriate way.

such as poverty, inequality, power and identity must be defined in such a way that they can be measured in a questionnaire. The concept of poverty, for instance, could be operationalised in terms of low incomes and measured at below 60 per cent of the average income in a particular country.

However, when concepts, beliefs and attitudes are operationalised, they may not measure what they are supposed to measure. It is often difficult to assess whether operational definitions provide valid measurements.

The answers to questions are **coded** or classified into various categories. Answers to closed questions are pre-coded. For example, possible answers to the questionnaire in Table 3.1.3 are pre-coded into seven categories. The researcher simply has to count the number of people who chose each category. Quantifying the data is easy.

Open questions are coded after the answer has been given. It is sometimes difficult to code and quantify a written answer. Consider the following.

| | |
|---|---|
| ***Question*** | Have you experienced bullying in the workplace during the past 30 days? Give reasons for your answer. |
| ***Answer*** | It depends what you mean by bullying. Do you mean teasing? Or something physical? My workmates often tease each other and occasionally they can go a bit too far and people get upset. This happened to me last week. But I wouldn't necessarily call it bullying. |

This answer is difficult to code. Researchers usually have a list of categories in terms of which written answers are coded. Sometimes, however, written answers do not fit neatly into any of the categories provided.

## Response rates

The **response rate** is the percentage of the **sample** (a subgroup of research participants drawn from the larger group being studied) that actually participates in the research. For example, if half the sample completes a questionnaire, then the response rate is 50 per cent. Response rates vary widely. For instance, Shere Hite's *The Hite Report on the Family* (1994), based on questionnaires in magazines, had a mere 3 per cent response rate. A low response rate may result in an unrepresentative sample. Those who do not respond may differ in important respects from those who do – for example, in terms of their age, gender, ethnicity or social class. If this is the case, the findings may be biased.

There are many reasons for non-response to self-completion questionnaires, including lack of time or interest. It is also easy to throw away the questionnaire with few consequences.

## Activity

*Language difficulties may result in incomplete questionnaires, group efforts to complete them and low response rates.*

Explain why a low response rate may be problematic in sociological research.

## Strengths of questionnaires

- Questionnaires can be a cost-effective way of collecting large amounts of data from many people over a relatively short period of time.
- The same questionnaire can be given to all research participants and their answers can be directly compared.
- It is relatively easy to quantify the results of questionnaires, particularly if closed questions are used. The data can be analysed quickly and efficiently with the use of computers.

- From a positivist perspective, a questionnaire survey based on a representative sample provides data for generalisations. Questionnaire surveys are seen as a reliable method because they are fairly easy to replicate (to repeat using the same questions and a similar sample). **Replication** allows the researcher to check the reliability of the findings. If the findings are reliable, then it is possible to generalise from them.

### Limitations of questionnaires

- If a questionnaire has a low response rate, the findings may be biased. Those who respond may not be typical of the sample and this will affect how far sociologists can generalise from the results.
- Self-completion questionnaires are inappropriate for some research participants, such as those with limited literacy skills or language difficulties.
- Some researchers argue that the data produced by questionnaires lack validity for several reasons, including the following:
  - Respondents may interpret the questions differently from each other.
  - The questions might not be relevant to research participants' lives.
  - What people say in response to questionnaires may not reflect their behaviour in everyday life.
- Interpretivists question the validity of responses to questionnaires. They argue that, when operationalising concepts, researchers simply impose their own interpretations on the meanings they intend to discover. Translating operationalised concepts into questions is problematic because the questions reflect the researchers' concerns and priorities rather than those of the participants. Coding the questions and answers further distorts social reality. Pre-coded questions give participants little opportunity to express themselves or to say exactly what they mean. Coding answers to open-ended questions also involves imposing the researchers' interpretations on the participants' answers. From an interpretivist view, this whole process takes the researcher further and further away from the meanings that direct participants' actions.

## Structured interviews

Some social surveys are based on **structured interviews,** which are questionnaires or lists of questions that the interviewer reads to the participant. The same questions are read in the same order to all participants. They are usually simple and straightforward. For example, 'How old are you?' 'What is your occupation?' 'Did you vote in the last election?' Most questions are designed to produce answers that do not require explanation.

### Activity

*In a structured interview, the interviewer reads the questions from a standardised interview schedule.*

Evaluate the view that structured interviews have limited use in sociological research because they restrict participants' responses.

### Non-response

In the case of structured interviews, reasons for non-response include the following:

1. Failure to make contact because, for example, people have moved, are on holiday, in prison, working away from home or simply not at home when the researcher tries to make contact.
2. Contact is made, but the interview cannot be conducted because, for instance, the person is ill or experiencing a personal tragedy.
3. The person refuses to participate due to lack of time or interest. They may also dislike or be suspicious of the researcher.

### Strengths of structured interviews

- Structured interviews are usually faster and cheaper to conduct than less structured interviews (see Unit 3.1.3).
- Compared to other types of interview, virtually all the interviewer has to do is read out the

questions and record the answers. Because of this, there is less chance of **interviewer bias** – of the participant's answers being influenced by the interviewer, by their age, gender, ethnicity and manner, for example.

- When closed questions are used, the responses are relatively easy to quantify.
- Structured interviews are more likely to produce data that can be directly compared. Participants are asked standardised questions so their answers are not affected by possible differences in the wording of questions. As a result, researchers can identify patterns and correlations in the data.
- Positivists favour structured interviews because they generate responses that can be coded and compared. Structured interviews can also be replicated to check for reliability and allow generalisations.

### Limitations of structured interviews

- Researchers set the questions based on their priorities and concerns. In this respect, they have imposed on the participant what they see as important. With closed questions, the researcher also determines the possible answers in advance. Participants have little control over the interview and no opportunity to qualify their answers or to introduce issues that reflect their concerns.
- **Interview bias** is a potential problem with all interviews, including structured interviews. For example, participants may give answers that they see as socially acceptable or that they think will be viewed positively rather than reveal their true thoughts, particularly on controversial topics. This is known as the **social desirability effect**.
- Interviewer bias arising from the interviewer's social characteristics, such as their age, gender, ethnicity or class, is another potential problem. Interview and interviewer bias can reduce the validity of the findings.
- From an interpretivist perspective, standardised interviews cannot provide rich data or meaningful insights into people's lives.

### Activity

Evaluate the usefulness of self-completion questionnaires to investigate people's experiences of bullying.

## Experiments

There are two types of experiment in which people are asked to participate – **laboratory experiments** and **field experiments**. Laboratory experiments are usually conducted in closed rooms, cut off from outside factors such as noise or passers-by. Field experiments usually take place in everyday surroundings, such as streets or workplaces.

### Laboratory experiments

A laboratory experiment is a setting and a situation that is designed to test a hypothesis – an assumption or proposition about the relationship between two or more **variables**. Variables are things that can vary, such as social class, gender and ethnicity or temperature, sound and light. In a laboratory experiment, they can be held constant (kept the same) or manipulated (changed). Experiments are usually designed to see whether one variable – the independent variable – has a causal effect on another variable – the dependent variable. The variables and results of laboratory experiments are usually quantified.

The main aspects of the experimental method can be illustrated by the example of an experiment designed to test the hypothesis that noise has an effect on memory. The hypothesis is stated in such a way that it can be tested – the louder the noise, the more it will reduce the ability to remember. Every variable in the laboratory except the level of noise – the independent variable – is held constant throughout the experiment. For example, the temperature and lighting remain the same. The participant is given a list of 20 random numbers, asked to memorise them within one minute and then to recall them. The experiment is repeated five times with the noise starting from nothing – silence – then steadily rising in measured units. If the participant recalls fewer and fewer numbers, then this may provide support for the hypothesis being tested.

If the experiment's results show a correlation between the independent variable (the level of noise) and the dependent variable (the amount of recall), this might indicate that one causes the other. Correlation does not, of course, necessarily mean causation. However, the ability to control variables in the closed system of a laboratory helps the researcher to judge whether the correlation is causative or coincidental, as does the use of quantitative measurements.

### Activity

If two things are correlated, they may increase together, decrease together, or one may increase as the other decreases. This might be due to one causing the other, to a third factor which causes both, or due to chance.

Select one of the above possibilities for the following correlations and give reasons for your choice.

1. In Copenhagen, Denmark, for 12 years following World War II, the number of storks nesting in the city and the number of human babies born went up and down together.
2. There appears to be a link between yellow grass and the sale of cold drinks. The yellower the grass, the more cold drinks are sold.

### Research example: Researching teacher expectations and social class

Dale Harvey and Gerald Slatin (1975) carried out research to assess how far teachers' expectations of students' performance were related to their perceptions of the children's social class. The experiment involved a sample of 96 teachers from four elementary schools (which are similar to primary or first schools) serving 'lower-class' and 'middle-upper-class' neighbourhoods in a US city. They asked this sample to judge the potential (for example to succeed or fail academically) and the socio-economic background of a set of 18 anonymous photographs of Black and White school children aged 8–12 years.

Harvey and Slatin found that perceived socio-economic class was more strongly associated with success among the White children and with failure among the Black children. However, the experiment did not show that the middle-class bias in teachers' perceptions affected students' academic performance in real-world classrooms or that this bias would be communicated to children. It is also difficult to generalise from a small sample of teachers.

#### Questions

1. Why do you think the researchers used photographs rather than real children in their experiment?
2. Evaluate the view that teachers' responses to photographs are a valid measure of the judgements they make in the classroom.

## Field experiments

Field experiments take place in normal, everyday settings such as classrooms, factories or street corners.

### Research example: Researching social class and interaction between strangers

Mary Sissons (1970) devised a field experiment to test the effect of social class on interaction between strangers. A male actor stood outside Paddington Station in London, England, and asked people for directions. The actor, place and request were kept the same but the actor's dress varied from that of a businessperson to a labourer.

The experiment indicated that people were more helpful to the 'businessperson'. It could therefore be argued that people were responding to what they perceived to be the actor's social class. However, there are other possibilities. For example, the actor may have behaved more confidently in his role as a businessperson and people might have responded to his level of confidence rather than to his class.

Field experiments are always going to be inexact and 'messy'. It is impossible to identify and control all the variables that might affect the results. For example, it is difficult, if not impossible, to control the social class of the people who were asked for directions in Sissons' experiment. Most of them may have been middle class. If so, they may have been more helpful to the 'businessperson' because he seemed 'more like them'.

#### Questions

Explain why it is difficult to control all variables in a field experiment, and why this is likely to be problematic for social researchers.

## Strengths of experiments

Laboratory experiments have been very successful in the natural sciences such as physics and chemistry.

- Laboratory experiments allow researchers to control variables.
- They can provide quantitative data.
- Laboratory experiments can be replicated and the results can be directly compared in order to check reliability.
- Field experiments provide a more realistic setting than laboratories.

## Limitations of experiments

- Whether in the laboratory or in more everyday social contexts, people are often aware that they are participating in an experiment. This in itself is likely to affect their behaviour. Any unintended impact of an experiment on participants is referred to as an **experimental effect**.
- People act in terms of how they perceive others. They will tend to respond differently if the experimenter is young or old, male or female, Black or White and so on. People also tend to act in terms of how they think others expect them to act. This might explain the results in the experiment involving the actor dressed as a businessperson and a labourer (see the research example 'Researching social class and interaction between strangers'). He might have been conveying two different expectations and this may have affected the responses to his request for directions. For example, he may have expected more help in his role as businessperson and unintentionally conveyed this to the participants. The unintended effect of the experimenter on those being studied is known as **experimenter bias**.
- Experiments sometimes involve deception and can therefore be seen as unethical. If participants are not informed of the true purpose of the experiment, they are not given the information necessary for **informed consent**. If they were, the experiment might not work. Participants might change their behaviour if they knew what the experiment was about.

## Research example: The Hawthorne effect

One example of the experimental effect is known as the **Hawthorne effect**, because it was first observed during a study at the Hawthorne Works of the Western Electricity Company in Chicago, USA, in the late 1920s. The researchers conducted an experiment to discover whether there was a relationship between the workers' productivity and variables such as lighting and heating levels and the frequency of rest periods. The researchers were puzzled because the results appeared to make little or no sense. For example, productivity increased whether the temperature in the workplace was turned up or down. The only factor that appeared to explain the increase in productivity was the workers' awareness that they were part of an experiment – which explains the term 'Hawthorne effect'.

*The Hawthorne Works – productivity increased whether the lighting was turned up or down.*

1. Explain what is meant by the term 'Hawthorne effect'.
2. Suggest reasons for the Hawthorne effect.
3. Identify one difference between experimenting with people and with variables such as heat or light.

For example, if the participants in Harvey and Slatin's experiment (see the research example 'Researching teacher expectations and social class') knew what was being measured, then they would probably have changed their responses. In some circumstances, it is considered acceptable not to provide participants with the full information. This might be the case if, for instance, there is no alternative method, and participants are debriefed after the experiment and given the opportunity to withdraw their consent.

- Most sociologists have serious doubts about the use of laboratory experiments with human beings. This is partly because people act in terms of their definitions of situations. They are likely to define laboratories as artificial situations and act accordingly. As a result, their behaviour in a laboratory may not reflect their behaviour in the 'real' world. Although field experiments may provide more realistic contexts, it is not possible to control all the important variables.

## Key terms

**Social survey** Systematic collection of the same type of data from a fairly large number of people.

**Hypothesis** A testable statement about the relationship between two or more variables.

**Self-completion questionnaire** A questionnaire that the respondent fills in.

**Closed questions** Questions in which the range of responses is fixed by the researcher.

**Open-ended/open questions** Questions which allow the respondent to answer in their own words.

**Ethical issue** A concern with morals and how to conduct morally acceptable research.

**Pilot study** A small-scale study to check the suitability of the methods to be used in the main study.

**Operationalise** Translate abstract concepts into a form that can be measured.

**Coded** Answers are classified into various categories.

**Response rate** The percentage of the sample that participates in the research.

**Sample** A subgroup of research participants from the larger group to be studied.

**Replication** Repeating an experiment or research study under the same conditions.

**Structured interview** A questionnaire which the interviewer read outs and fills in.

**Interviewer bias** The effect of the interviewer on a research participant's answers.

**Interview bias** The effect of the interview situation itself on a participant's responses.

**Social desirability effect** Bias resulting from a research participant's desire to reflect in their responses what is generally seen as the right way to behave.

**Laboratory experiment** An experiment conducted in a specially designed setting.

**Field experiment** An experiment conducted in everyday social settings.

**Variables** Factors that affect behaviour. Variables can vary, for example, temperature can increase or decrease.

**Experimental effect** Any unintended impact of the experiment on participants.

**Experimenter bias** The unintended effect of the experimenter on a participant.

**Informed consent** The participant only agrees to participate in the research once the sociologist has explained fully what the research is about and why it is being undertaken.

**Hawthorne effect** Changes in participants' behaviour resulting from an awareness that they are taking part in an experiment.

## Summary

1. Questionnaires are the main method for collecting data in social surveys.
2. In theory, questionnaires provide directly comparable data.
3. Closed questions are pre-coded and produce data that are easy to quantify. Answers to open questions can be difficult to code and quantify.
4. It is difficult to assess whether operational definitions provide valid measurements.
5. Positivists favour social surveys based on questionnaires that produce quantitative data. However, the response rate may be low. Interpretivists argue that numerical data produced by questionnaires often lack validity.
6. Positivists prefer the quantitative data produced by structured interviews, but interpretivists prefer less standardised approaches to interviewing.

7. There are two main types of experiment – laboratory experiments and field experiments.
8. Experiments are designed to test hypotheses. They are usually intended to measure the strength of relationships between two or more variables.
9. Ideally, laboratory experiments allow the researcher to control all important variables. However, critics argue that laboratories are artificial situations and therefore, that findings from laboratory experiments may not apply to everyday social situations. Field experiments help to avoid artificiality, but do not provide the same control of variables.
10. Both laboratory and field experiments are criticised for experimental effect and experimenter bias. As a result, their findings may be low in validity.

# Unit 3.1.3 Qualitative research methods

Qualitative research methods produce data in verbal or visual form. This unit looks at different research methods that generate primary sources of qualitative data. It explores semi-structured, unstructured and group interviews. What are the differences between semi-structured and unstructured interviews? How do group interviews work?

The unit also looks at different forms of observation including participant and non-participant observation. Why might sociologists use one of these rather than the other? How do participant observers gain entry into groups of people? Should they tell those they are observing what they are really doing? What are the strengths and limitations of each of these qualitative methods?

## Semi-structured interviews

Each **semi-structured interview** in a particular study is usually based around the same set of questions. In this respect, semi-structured interviews share some of the advantages of structured interviews. However, a semi-structured interview enables the interviewer to 'probe' – to jog participants' memories and ask them to develop, clarify or give examples of particular points. This adds depth and detail to the answers.

This gain, however, is accompanied by a loss of standardisation and comparability. Although the basic questions are pre-set, the probes are not so each interview is different. Consequently, the data are not directly comparable because, to some extent, participants are responding to different questions.

## Unstructured interviews

An **unstructured interview** is more like a guided conversation. Rather than using an interview schedule, the researcher usually draws on a list of topics or prompts that they want to cover during the course of the interview. Unstructured interviews are more informal, open-ended, flexible and free-flowing than semi-structured and structured interviews. The setting tends to be less formal and the atmosphere more relaxed – for example, armchairs and a cup of coffee.

### The interview process

Interviewers are often trained to conduct effective interviews and to avoid pitfalls. The standard advice is to be **non-directive**, to avoid leading participants and to allow them to express themselves in their own way. The idea is to minimise interviewer bias. It is important to establish **rapport** – a friendly and understanding relationship – while at the same time appearing professional. Probing – digging a little deeper with further questions – is used in order to get participants to clarify or develop their answers. However, this must be utilised carefully, as it can result in leading questions – questions that direct participants to a certain answer (Fielding, 1993). Advice about how to conduct interviews usually focuses on asking questions. However, Rosalind Edwards and Janet Holland (2013) point out that listening to participants is the key to probing and following up their answers.

### Strengths of unstructured interviews

An unstructured interview offers more opportunities for participants to take control and direct the interview into areas that they see as interesting and significant. In this way, they have more chance to express their own viewpoints. This can lead to new and important insights for the researcher.

Many researchers see unstructured interviews as particularly suitable for discovering meanings. They give participants the opportunity to express how they feel about a range of issues. Meanings are complex. A skilled interviewer can help participants to spell out this complexity. For example, what does family life mean to the participant? The pre-set questions in a structured interview are unlikely to capture the shades of meaning associated with issues such as family life. However, if participants open up and say what they really mean in an unstructured interview, they are more likely to provide data that are valid, rich and colourful.

Members of some groups, such as a religious group or gang members, may be less likely to provide information for researchers. They might be suspicious of outsiders, hostile towards them, afraid of them or simply uncomfortable in their presence. An unstructured interview can reduce these feelings, as it provides an opportunity for rapport and trust to develop between interviewer and participant.

Unstructured interviews are seen as particularly suitable for sensitive topics such as people's experiences of racism or bullying. Participants may be more likely to discuss sensitive and painful experiences if they feel that the interviewer is sympathetic and understanding. Unstructured interviews provide the opportunity for developing this kind of relationship. Joan Smith et al.'s (1998) study about the family background of homeless young people produced in-depth information using unstructured interviews.

Interpretivists prefer unstructured interviews, in particular in-depth interviews that are designed to discover meanings. They give participants the freedom to express themselves in their own way. The qualitative data produced are seen as more likely to be valid than the information generated by structured interviews.

## Limitations of unstructured interviews

Unstructured interviews involve interaction between an interviewer and a participant, and this can lead to interviewer bias. To some extent, this bias is unavoidable. Interviewers are people with social characteristics – they have a nationality, ethnicity, gender, social class and so on. They also have particular personalities – they may be shy or outgoing, caring or uncaring, aggressive or unaggressive. These social and psychological characteristics will be perceived in certain ways by participants and will have some impact on their responses.

Several studies have examined the effect of the social characteristics of interviewers. J. Allen Williams Jr (1971) claims that the greater the status difference between interviewer and participant, the less likely participants are to express their true feelings. He found that African Americans in the 1960s were more likely to say they approved of civil rights

## Activity

*In a study of business organisations, Martin Parker (2000) found that participants saw him in different ways.*

1. How did each participant see Parker, and how might this affect their answers?
2. How might Parker's age, gender and dress affect the participants' responses?

demonstrations if the interviewer was Black rather than White.

In general, people like to present themselves in a favourable light. Participants might emphasise socially desirable aspects of their behaviour and attitudes in the presence of interviewers. This can reduce the validity of interview data, particularly in unstructured interviews that develop into friendly conversations.

## Activity

*What does it mean to be a parent for the first time? Some methods are more appropriate than others for discovering people's subjective experiences and the meaning of their actions.*

1. Explain one reason why unstructured interviews are more appropriate than structured interviews for investigating women's subjective experiences of motherhood.
2. Write brief notes to summarise the strengths and limitations of unstructured interviews.

Unstructured interviews can develop in all sorts of directions. As a result, data from one interview to the next can vary considerably and it is difficult to make comparisons between them. From a positivist perspective, they are difficult to replicate, and lack reliability and generalisability.

## Group interviews

In a **group interview**, the researcher interviews and collects data from a number of people at the same time. A group interview usually covers several areas, themes or topics. A **focus group** is a group interview that focuses on one particular topic.

| Group interviews | Focus groups |
|---|---|
| *are interview situations in which the interviewer asks questions and the participants respond | *explore how partic-ipants interact within the group and how they respond to each other's views |
| *usually cover a wide range of themes or topics | *focus on one particular theme or topic in depth |
| *may be used to save time and money. | *are used to gain extra insights into group interaction rather than to save time and money. |

### Strengths of group interviews

- The researcher can access wide-ranging views and experiences and obtain a rich source of information on relevant topics.
- By interviewing several people together, the researcher can save time and money.
- Individuals may feel more comfortable describing their experiences in a group setting because they are supported by others.
- Participants may be recruited to take part in follow-up individual interviews.
- Group interviews may generate new ideas for the researcher to explore.

### Limitations of group interviews

- The researcher must manage the group interview carefully, particularly when the topics are potentially sensitive.
- In a group setting, the participants may influence each other. Some may dominate and others may be less open than in an individual interview.
- If participants talk over each other, it is difficult to transcribe (write down) the contents of group interviews.
- Confidentiality and privacy can be problematic when using group interviews. The researcher can request, but cannot guarantee, that participants' identities and what they say remain within the group.

## Focus groups

Focus groups are sometimes called group interviews but they are usually more like discussions. Group members are asked to talk among themselves. They are guided by a **moderator** who asks them to focus on particular topics. Focus groups usually have between 4 and 10 members.

## Activity

*Five focus groups each made up of four boys or men of similar ages were asked to discuss body image, diet and exercise. According to the researchers, the participants were more likely to disclose sensitive, personal feelings in a small group of people like themselves than in a one-to-one interview situation (Grogan and Richards, 2002).*

1. Would you prefer to participate in a focus group or in a one-to one interview? Or would you rather not participate in either? What factors would influence your decision?
2. Assess the view that the similarities of the focus group members help them to disclose sensitive and personal feelings.

### Strengths of focus groups

- Often focus group members have certain things in common – for example, similarities of age, gender, experience or expertise. These similarities can encourage discussion and interest, and minimise the intervention of the moderator (Morgan, 2006).
- A focus group involves interaction between participants. Compared to a one-to-one interview, this can produce different kinds of data. Participants in a focus group discuss and debate, agree and disagree. This encourages them to really think about their views. Focus groups can also show how people make sense of things collectively and develop a shared viewpoint.
- Focus groups have been successfully used to study sensitive topics such as homelessness. They can provide social support and empowerment for vulnerable participants with shared experiences (Edwards and Holland, 2013).

### Limitations of focus groups

- Researchers have less control than in standardised interviews. (This, however, can also be seen as a strength.)
- Despite trying to minimise their intervention, the moderator sometimes has to get involved to ensure that things run smoothly – for example, to prevent one member of the group dominating the discussion.
- It is not clear how far agreement on particular views reflects group pressure rather than the actual beliefs of all participants.
- It can be difficult to assess how far social desirability influences the views expressed in a group context.
- The discussion may move onto unanticipated topics that some participants would not have agreed to discuss in public. Although participants should be told that they can withdraw at any time, some may feel under pressure to remain.

## Activity

1. Explain one difference between focus groups and group interviews.
2. Explain one reason why a researcher might choose to use focus groups rather than group interviews as a research method.

# Observation

One of the aims of sociological research is to discover how people behave in their normal, everyday settings – at work, in their leisure time or with their friends and family. One way to do this is by interviewing them, but another way is to observe group members in their everyday settings. This might involve joining the group and getting involved in some of its activities in order to gather data. This is referred to as **participant observation**. The researcher can also observe people

## Activity

*In focus groups, the moderator's role is to encourage rather than control discussion so there is less of a power imbalance than with individual interviews. However, the moderator must be able to manage a group.*

In each case above, explain how the moderator might respond to the participant (for example, verbally or using non-verbal communication such as eye contact).

without directly joining them. This is known as **non-participant observation**.

### Participant observation

Participant observation has been used in a variety of settings. It was used by John Howard Griffin (1960), a White journalist who dyed his skin black in order to discover what it was like to live as a Black man in the southern states of the USA in the late 1950s. It was also used by the sociologist Erving Goffman (1968) when he adopted the role of assistant to the athletics director in order to study the experience of patients in a psychiatric hospital in Washington, DC.

Participant observation gives researchers the opportunity to observe people in their normal settings as opposed to the more artificial contexts of laboratories or interviews. It allows researchers to see what people do as opposed to what they say they do.

**Gaining entry** Participant observation cannot work unless the researcher gains entry into the group and acceptance from its members. Achieving this can be difficult. Many groups do not want to be studied, especially those whose activities are seen as criminal or anti-social by the wider society.

In some instances, researchers have to participate directly in order to gain entry. Dick Hobbs (1988) wanted to research the relationship between criminals and detectives in the East End of London, England. He was coaching a local soccer team when he discovered that Simon, a detective, was the father of one of the players. He developed a friendship with Simon, who provided him with introductions and vouched for him (said he was OK). Hobbs also spent time in a local bar that was frequented by several detectives. These contacts enabled him to gain entry into the world of the detectives – he joined in their conversations and observed their activities.

**Covert and overt research** The above method of gaining entry involves the researcher hiding their identity and purpose. This is known as covert or hidden research. **Covert observation** has certain advantages. If the group sees the observer as 'one of them', they will be more likely to behave normally and reveal information they may not give to an outsider. However, many sociologists regard covert research as unethical – morally wrong. For example, it does not give those being observed the opportunity to consent (or otherwise) to participating in the research.

**Overt observation** (open research) has its own problems of entry and acceptance as Sudhir Venkatesh (2009) found during his first day with the Black Kings, an African-American gang in Chicago, in the USA. Some gang members saw him as a possible threat or a harmless source of amusement. One gang member saw him as a spy from a rival Mexican gang. The gang leader, J.T., gave Venkatesh his support, which provided entry and eventual acceptance into the world of the Black Kings.

One of the advantages of overt participant observation is that it can lead to the development of key informants, who go out of their way to assist in the research. A **key informant** is a member of the group being studied who has a special relationship with the researcher, provides important information and often acts as a sponsor, telling the rest of the group that the researcher can be trusted. J.T., the leader of the Black Kings, was a key informant for Sudhir Venkatesh. In Venkatesh's words, 'I felt a strange kind of intimacy with J.T., unlike the bond I'd felt even with good friends'.

## Activity

Suggest reasons why the gang members initially rejected Venkatesh.

Participant observation involves looking and listening while trying not to influence people's behaviour. As the aim is to observe people in their normal setting, the researcher must not disturb that setting. Blending into the background is usually recommended, though this is not always possible. For example, a participant observer in a classroom can stand out in an obvious way. This may result in an artificial and untypical lesson which can reduce the validity of the observations. But it is surprising how soon the researcher becomes 'invisible' and taken for granted. In his study of a British secondary school, Geoffrey Walford (1993) found that it took four weeks of observation before any students misbehaved. However, the situation changed rapidly after this time and Walford was soon watching 'mock wrestling' and chairs flying around the classroom!

## Research example: Researching the service sector in China

*A five-star hotel in Beijing was a setting for Eileen M. Otis's study of the service sector in China.*

Eileen M. Otis (2016), a Mandarin-speaking American sociologist, used observations and semi-structured interviews in a luxury, five-star hotel in Beijing, China, operated by an American firm. The majority of the guests were male and Western. She gained access to the hotel by working there as an unpaid English teacher. She observed training courses, meetings and training exercises and also shadowed workers.

Otis explored the mode of femininity that the hotel's managers sought to introduce among the young, working-class, female staff who worked there as hostesses, waitresses, butlers and cleaners. The female workers were trained 'to perform an American variant of middle-class femininity' which involved, for example, displaying elegance, poise and sociability.

### Question

Drawing on this information, explain one advantage and one disadvantage of using overt participant observation in the workplace.

## Strengths of participant observation

- Participant observation gives researchers the opportunity to observe people in their normal, everyday situations and in a variety of contexts. It can provide insights and knowledge which may not be available from other research methods. William Whyte (1955) undertook a lengthy study of an Italian-American gang in Boston based on participant observation. He discovered things that he had previously known nothing about. In his words, 'As I sat and listened, I learned the answers to questions that I would not even have had the sense to ask if I had been getting my information solely on an interviewing basis.'
- Participant observation generates rich and in-depth qualitative data. Spending possibly years observing a fairly small group of people means that the researcher can get to know them well. This provides a real opportunity to discover the meanings that direct their behaviour, and how they construct their view of the world and make sense of their experiences. By using participant observation, a researcher can capture the 'insider's view' and see the world from the viewpoint of those being observed. By contrast, quantitative research methods such as questionnaires provide one-off, snapshot accounts rather than a full picture.
- Supporters of participant observation see it as the best method for obtaining valid data – for providing a true picture of the topic being investigated.
- Interpretivists are concerned with the meanings and definitions that direct action. Often, these meanings and definitions are taken for granted – people are unaware of them. Observing their behaviour provides an opportunity for the researcher to interpret these taken-for-granted meanings. Consequently, interpretivists tend to favour participant observation as a method for collecting data.

## Limitations of participant observation

- It can sometimes be difficult to gain entry to, and acceptance by, the group being studied because, for example, the members distrust the researcher's motives or fear their criminal or anti-social activities will be exposed.
- Participant observation can be a long and expensive process that requires dedication, stamina and courage. Researchers are often cut off from the normal supports of family and friends, sometimes living a double life in an unfamiliar setting. Participant observation can also be dangerous if, for example, the researcher is studying gangs involved in violent and criminal activities. However, given the quality of information that participant observation can produce, some might see these risks as acceptable.
- The presence of an observer in an overt observation study may change the behaviour of the group being studied. This is known as the **observer effect**. The relationship between a researcher and a key informant may have drawbacks. In his study of an Italian-American gang (1955), Whyte had a special relationship with Doc, the gang leader. In Whyte's words, 'Doc became, in a very real sense, a collaborator in the research.' However, this close relationship may cause problems if it changes the informant's behaviour. In Doc's words, 'Now, when I do something, I have to think what Bill Whyte would want to know about it and how I can explain it. Before, I used to do things by instinct.' It might also change the researcher's behaviour, as the picture in the Activity box indicates.
- The personal involvement that participant observation demands can reduce **objectivity** and prevent an impartial view. This can affect the validity of research observations. An observer can identify so strongly with a group that the behaviour of its members is seen in a positive light. In rare cases, this identification is carried to its extreme when observers join the group and never return to their former lives.
- From a positivist viewpoint, participant observation has its uses. For example, it provides information that can be used to construct relevant questions for questionnaires. This will improve the quality of the questions and of the quantitative data they produce. However, positivists do not see a participant observation study as particularly useful as an end in itself. The numbers observed are too small to provide a representative sample from which to generalise. Participant observation is difficult to replicate and lacks reliability, in that different researchers are unlikely to produce the

## Activity

*Doc on the left, Whyte on the right.*

What problems for Whyte's research are indicated in the picture?

same results. There are various reasons for this. Participant observation is unsystematic, as there are no fixed procedures to follow, things happen and the observer tags along. Data are rarely quantified. Participant observation also relies heavily on the personal qualities of the individual researcher. To some degree, these qualities will affect how well they get on with those they observe, what they see and note down, and how they interpret particular events or incidents.

## Activity

Explain one strength of covert participant observation.

### Non-participant observation

The researcher need not participate in order to observe people's behaviour. A non-participant observer is a bit like a birdwatcher in a hide, observing behaviour without joining in. For example, a researcher may observe children's behaviour in a school playground from an upstairs staffroom or stand back and observe the audience at a music festival.

**Types of non-participant observation** There are two main types of non-participant observation – structured and unstructured observation. **Structured observation**, sometimes known as **systematic observation**, is a quantitative research method. It uses a pre-set **observation schedule**, which tells the observer exactly what to look for and how to record it. Completing an observation schedule is a bit like ticking pre-set boxes on a questionnaire.

**Unstructured observation** is a qualitative research method. As its name suggests, it does not use an observation schedule to record specified aspects of behaviour systematically. Instead, it simply describes the behaviour being investigated (such as gendered behaviour in a classroom) as seen by the researcher.

### Ethics and non-participant observation

Non-participant observation is often covert – people are not aware that they are being observed. As a result, informed consent is not sought at the outset. However, there are many cases where obtaining consent is impractical – for instance, observing a crowd at a baseball match. Examples such as this do not necessarily break **ethical guidelines** if the research takes place in a public setting and is unlikely to put participants at risk.

### Strengths of unstructured non-participant observation

- Because people are often unaware that they are being observed, the researcher is unlikely to affect their behaviour.
- Interpretivists favour the qualitative data provided by unstructured non-participant observation. There is no observation schedule to impose rules on the descriptions of the behaviour observed.

### Limitations of unstructured non-participant observation

- Non-participant observers are less likely than participant observers to get to know the people they observe or to see them in various contexts. This reduces the chances of discovering the meanings that direct their behaviour. Consequently, non-participant observers are more likely to impose their meanings and interpretations on the behaviour of those they observe.

- Positivists prefer structured non-participant observation based on an observation schedule because the results can be quantified. The strict instructions of the observation schedule make this method easier to replicate. If different observers produce similar results, then the data can be seen as reliable. By contrast, unstructured non-participant observation is difficult to replicate and different observers are unlikely to produce consistent results.

## Key terms

**Semi-structured interview** Similar to a structured interview, but the interviewer probes with additional questions.

**Unstructured interview** An interview with few, if any, pre-set questions, though researchers usually have certain topics they wish to cover.

**Non-directive interviewing** An interviewing technique that seeks to avoid leading participants to answer in particular ways.

**Rapport** A friendly, trusting and understanding relationship.

**Group interview** A type of interview covering a range of themes or topics; the researcher questions and collects data from several people at once.

**Focus group** A group discussion about one particular theme or topic guided by a moderator; it explores how participants interact and respond to each other's views.

**Moderator** An interviewer who guides focus group discussions.

**Participant observation** A qualitative method in which the researcher gathers data by joining a group and taking part in its activities.

**Non-participant observation** An observation-based study in which the researcher does not join those they are studying.

**Covert observation** Observation-based research in which the observer's true identity and the purpose of their study are hidden from participants.

**Overt observation** Open research in which the observer's true identity and the purpose of their research are revealed to participants.

**Key informant** A member of the group being studied who provides important information and often sponsors the researcher.

**Observer effect** This occurs in an observation-based study when the observer's known presence changes the behaviour of the people being studied.

**Objectivity** A value-free, impartial, unbiased view.

**Structured/systematic observation** An observation-based study which usually employs an observation schedule to generate quantitative data.

**Observation schedule** Instructions which tell the observer what to look for and how to record it.

**Unstructured observation** An observation-based study that produces a detailed description of behaviour as seen by the researcher.

**Ethical guidelines** Guidance provided by social science organisations and universities on how to conduct morally acceptable research, covering issues such as informed consent and confidentiality.

## Summary

1. Various types of interview generate qualitative data, including semi-structured, unstructured and group interviews, and focus groups. Each has its strengths and limitations.
2. To some extent, all qualitative interviews are influenced by interviewer bias and social desirability effects.
3. Interpretivists prefer qualitative data produced by unstructured and group interviews, while positivists prefer quantitative data produced by structured interviews.
4. The standard advice to interviewers is to avoid direction and develop rapport. Interviewers are advised that listening is a 'crucial skill'.
5. Participant observation involves the researcher joining those they wish to study. It can be overt (open) or covert (hidden). Covert participant observation is usually regarded as unethical.
6. Participant observation is based mainly on looking, listening and, where possible, standing back to avoid influencing participants' behaviour.

7. Positivists tend not to favour participant observation, as it produces little, if any, quantitative data, the samples are too small for generalisation and the method is not seen as reliable. Interpretivists favour participant observation, seeing it as an excellent method for discovering meanings, and for providing rich and valid data.
8. There are two main types of non-participant observation – structured and non-structured observation – which generate different kinds of data.
9. Structured observation is based on an observation schedule and produces quantitative data. Non-structured observation provides a detailed description of the behaviour observed.

# Unit 3.1.4 Secondary sources of data

So far, this chapter has examined methods that produce primary data – information that was created during the research process. This unit explores secondary data – information that already existed before the research began. It looks at two types or forms of secondary data: quantitative and qualitative secondary data. Official statistics are an example of quantitative secondary data. But do they really measure what they are intended to measure? Personal documents, digital content and media sources are examples of qualitative secondary data. How do sociologists use these different sources of data? What are their strengths and limitations?

## Official statistics

Official statistics are numerical data produced by national and local governments. They cover a wide range of issues, including births, deaths, marriages and divorces, the distribution of income and wealth, crime and sentencing, and unemployment. Sources of official statistics include government departments and agencies, and surveys such as censuses of the population.

### Crime statistics

Crime statistics are a widely used form of official statistics. In many countries, they are published annually, reported by the media and commented on by the government of the day.

In the USA and the UK, for example, there are two sets of official statistics that measure the extent of crime – one that counts crimes recorded by the police and one that counts crime victimisation. In the USA, for instance, the Uniform Crime Reports are based on law enforcement agencies' monthly crime reports to the Federal Bureau of Investigation (FBI). The National Crime Victimization Survey is based on a survey of households and individuals. It covers reported and unreported crime from the victims' perspectives.

**Police recorded crime** Police recorded crime (PRC) consists of crimes actually recorded by the police. Most PRC is based on reports by the public. Although statistics on PRC may appear to be a straightforward measure of the extent of crime in any one year, they have limitations. Critics argue that they do not provide an accurate or complete picture of the total amount of crime committed. For example, they exclude crimes that have

- not been discovered or witnessed
- been witnessed but not reported to the police because, for example, the victim sees the crime as too trivial (for instance, petty vandalism)
- been reported to the police but not recorded by them because they are under pressure to meet performance targets.

## Activity

*A crime or an accident?*

One reason why victims might not report a crime to the police is that they suffered no financial loss as a result of the crime. What other reasons can you think of to explain why some victims do not report crimes to the police?

In theory, PRC statistics allow researchers to identify **trends** in crime over time. However, changes in the classification of offences mean that trends cannot necessarily be identified (Office for National Statistics, 20.10.2016). Police priorities are a particular problem for the accurate identification of trends in crime. For example, if the police prioritise weapons offences, then time, money and personnel may be directed at apprehending criminals who commit these offences. Partly due to this, PRC statistics on weapons offences may increase over time even though the actual number of these offences remains stable.

Victim surveys **Victim surveys** are another source of official statistics on crime. They might take the form of a structured interview and ask participants whether they have been victims of particular crimes over the past year. They are used to measure trends in the crimes they cover.

Victim surveys include unreported crime, so they give information on offences that are not included in PRC statistics. However, a victim survey does not cover the full range of crimes recorded by the police. For example, it excludes murder (or homicide), given that the victim is dead, so-called victimless crimes such as possession of drugs, and crimes such as theft from a shop where the victim is a business rather than a person or household. Until recently, victim surveys have not included cyber-crime.

## Strengths of official statistics

- In more industrialised societies today, official statistics are often readily available and cost little or nothing to use. Sometimes official statistics are the only major source of information on a particular topic.
- Care is taken to select representative samples, and sample sizes are often large. Such big surveys are usually outside sociologists' research budgets.
- Many government surveys are well planned and organised, with detailed questionnaires or interview schedules. As such, they meet the rigorous standards of sociological research.
- Surveys are often conducted regularly, for example on a three-monthly, annual or ten-yearly basis. This can allow for comparisons over time and the identification of trends.
- Some official statistics, such as those on births, deaths, marriages and divorce in contemporary Western societies, are seen as both valid and reliable. Definitions of these events are clear and there is no disagreement about what is being measured. There are also standardised procedures for reporting and recording these events. As a result, the statistics are likely to be valid in that they will provide a true and accurate picture of what they are intended to measure. The statistics are also likely to be reliable in that the use of the same procedures for measurement will produce similar statistics.
- Positivists recognise the problems of validity and reliability with some official statistics. Nonetheless, they favour the quantitative data available from this source. They argue that statistics based on large, representative samples can provide reliable data from which to draw generalisations.

## Limitations of official statistics

- Official statistics from previous periods in the history of Western nations and from less industrialised societies today may be less reliable than those currently collected in the West. This is due to, for example, the underfunding of government research and the relatively low levels of literacy and numeracy in the target population.
- Some official statistics (such as PRC) are seen as less likely to be valid and reliable than others.
- Victim surveys do not provide an accurate measure of the extent of crime in a particular country. For example, they do not include victimless crimes.
- The definitions on which official statistics are based – for example, the definition of unemployment – can change. As a result, it may not be possible to measure trends over time.
- Official statistics measure what governments decide is important. To some extent, this is a political decision.
- Interpretivists tend to focus on how statistics are constructed and to question their validity. Some go further and argue that statistics are simply meanings. For example, J. Maxwell Atkinson (1978) states that suicide is a social construction, a meaning used by coroners to officially classify certain deaths as suicide (see Unit 3.2.2). There is no reality beyond that meaning. The job of a sociologist is simply to discover the meanings used to construct suicide statistics and other statistics.

### Activity

Evaluate the usefulness of official statistics as sources of data.

# Personal documents

**Personal documents** are a type of qualitative data. As secondary sources, they have not been generated by sociologists using sociological research methods or at the request of a researcher for research purposes. Instead, they are produced by people during their everyday lives – as part of their family life, paid employment, education or leisure activities. Such data are ready-made forms of evidence.

Written personal documents include letters, diaries, notes and autobiographies, while visual personal documents include family photographs. Personal documents can be an expression of people's hopes, feelings, worries and concerns – just the kind of data that many sociologists look for.

## Assessing documents

John Scott (1990) offers four 'quality control criteria' for assessing documents including personal documents and other qualitative secondary sources. These are authenticity, credibility, representativeness and meaning.

**Authenticity** Is the document original or a copy? If it is a copy, is it an exact copy? Has it been tampered with in any way, such as the photograph below of Lenin (one of the founders of the Soviet Union)? Is the document a forgery?

**Credibility** Is the author of the document 'sincere' and honest in revealing their true feelings or do they distort the evidence in order to mislead the audience? There are plenty of examples of distortion, deceit and lies in documents.

**Representativeness** To what extent is the document representative? For example, is an old family photograph that was kept in an archive typical of those taken at the time? Did people throw away photographs that they disliked? Were the authors of **historical documents** typically middle-class men rather than women or working-class people? The question of representativeness is particularly important in the case of historical documents, as many have been lost or destroyed. Those that remain may not be typical.

**Meaning** What does a document mean? Researchers must be able to understand words and phrases when analysing written material such as notes and letters. Ideally, they should know the meanings intended by the writer and what is understood by various members of the audience.

## Ethics and documentary research

Data protection legislation may prevent certain documents from being used without permission from the individuals concerned and from possible copyright holders. The use of some documents, including visual

### Activity

*(Left) Lenin addressing troops in Moscow. On the right of the podium are Trotsky and Kamenev.*

*(Right) When Stalin came to power, he 'removed' Trotsky (he was murdered) and Kamenev (he was executed). They were then also 'removed' from the photograph.*

Why is it important to know whether an original document has been altered?

## Research example: Researching immigrants to the USA and their families in Poland

The importance of personal documents is illustrated by a classic sociological work entitled *The Polish Peasant in Europe and America* by William I. Thomas and Florian Znaniecki (1919, originally published in five volumes from 1918 to 1920). It is partly based on 764 letters exchanged between immigrants to the USA and their families in Poland. The letters give a valuable insight into village life in Poland and the experience of migration to the USA. The letters also represent the writers' world view, their picture of their lives, and their reflections on their relationships with families and friends (Stanley, 2010). Personal documents such as these provide data that are not available from primary data generated by standard sociological research methods.

### Question

Drawing on this information:

**a.** Describe one type of personal document.

**b.** Identify one strength and one limitation of this type of personal document as a source of data.

data, raises issues of 'confidentiality, anonymity and consent' (Ali, 2011). For example, can individuals be recognised and identified in family photographs? If so, should the people concerned or their relatives (if the people have died) be informed and their permission requested? These are some of the questions about ethics which need to be considered when conducting documentary research.

### Strengths of personal documents

- Personal documents provide a unique and valuable source of information on people's hopes and fears, wishes and desires, their world views and reflections on their situation. Such data may not be available from primary sources.
- As personal documents were not created specifically for research purposes, they are seen as non-reactive. For example, they are not subject to interview bias or the observer effect.
- In some respects, personal documents are just the kind of data that interpretivists seek. They can provide qualitative data with a richness and depth not always found in data produced by sociological research. Most have not been influenced by sociologists. Documents might present a false picture (either intentionally or unintentionally), they may distort, they may be based on ignorance and misunderstanding. However, they are still valid in that they are actual products of human behaviour.

### Limitations of personal documents

- Like many documents, personal documents are often written for a particular audience. They may say more about the writer than the events they describe.
- The writer may not be representative of the group they belong to.
- Rather than providing an objective account, personal documents tend to be one-sided, prejudiced, and based on particular viewpoints and value judgements. However, not all sociologists would necessarily see this as a disadvantage, as it does provide people's perspectives.
- Analysis of personal documents is often based on the researcher's interpretation of the contents. This may result in the imposition of the researcher's meanings and priorities.
- Positivists tend not to use personal documents as their main source of data. It is often difficult to quantify documents. It is also difficult to obtain representative samples of documentary material and to make generalisations from the data. This is particularly true of historical documents, as the authors were not representative of the wider population. In many eras, literate people were in a minority and were usually the better off, and documents were more likely to be written by men than women.

## Digital content

**Digital content** relies on the internet for distribution. It includes virtual or online documents such as websites, email, postings to online forums and blogs, videos and social media such as Facebook and Twitter.

The four criteria (authenticity, credibility, representativeness and meaning) for assessing personal documents can also be applied to digital content. For example, why was a particular website built? Does it exist to promote a cause or sell something?

## Contemporary issues: Fake news

*US presidential candidates Hillary Clinton and Donald Trump debating before the election in 2016.*

The Macedonian town of Veles in Eastern Europe has launched over 140 United States political news websites. Almost all support Donald Trump, mostly with fake news stories. Here are a couple of false news stories for Trump supporters about Hillary Clinton, his opponent for the presidency.

**A 'quote' from Hillary Clinton** Hillary Clinton is falsely quoted on one website as saying, in 2013, 'I would like to see people like Donald Trump running for office. They're honest and can't be bought and sold.' In its first week on Facebook, this post had 480 000 shares, reactions and comments.

Source: Buzzfeed News online.

**'Your Prayers Have Been Answered'** Under this headline, the article claimed that Hillary Clinton would be indicted and tried in 2017 for crimes related to her supposed misuse of her personal email. This fake news produced 140 000 shares, reactions and comments on Facebook.

### Questions

1. Why is it important to study fake news?
2. Should fake news be censored? Think about freedom of expression in your answer.
3. How might fake news have influenced the US presidential election in 2016?

### Strengths of digital content

- An enormous amount and variety of digital content is available to researchers. Information can usually be accessed at no cost.
- Digital content provides researchers with a rich source of qualitative data that can be used as an object of study.
- Researchers can apply both quantitative and qualitative forms of analysis to digital content.
- As the content was not created for research purposes, it is not influenced by an interviewer or observer.

### Limitations of digital content

- Not everyone has access to the internet to post blogs, and the people who post on forums may differ significantly from those who do not post. As a result, the authors of digital content may not be typical of the wider population. In general, for example, younger people are more likely to post blogs than people in their 80s.
- There is no quality control of material on most websites and, as a result, they cannot be seen as a source of reliable and valid information.
- The researcher cannot probe to find out more about the poster or their postings.
- The number of research questions that can be explored via postings is limited compared to the use of unstructured interviews, for example.

## Traditional media sources

Traditional media sources include radio and television broadcasts, music, films, novels, newspapers and magazines. They contain both visual and written text and are usually referred to as the 'mass media' as opposed to the 'new media' of digital content. Although some parts of the mass media may provide sociologists with useful data, their main importance is as objects of study. Mass media reports can be used to analyse the ideologies of those who produce them. Some sociologists have been highly critical of parts of the mass media for producing distorted images of society that might mislead the public or adversely affect the socialisation of children.

### Strengths of media sources

- The media provide a useful source of information on a variety of issues and events.

### Activity

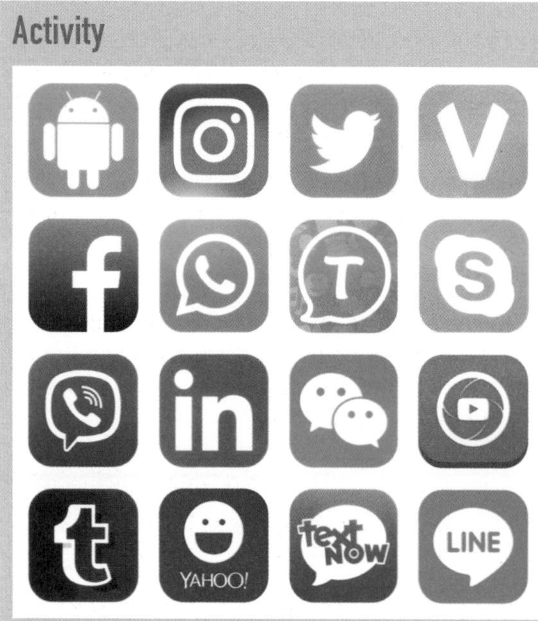


*Digital content and social media are important secondary sources of qualitative data.*

1. Why do you think it is important to study digital sources?
2. Roughly what proportion of people in your society have access to the internet on a daily basis?
3. Explain the view that digital content does not provide a representative source of information.

- Television programmes and newspaper articles were not produced by, or for, a researcher for research purposes. As a result, there is no reactive effect to limit the validity of the data.

### Limitations of media sources

- Many parts of the mass media are notoriously inaccurate and are unlikely to provide objective accounts of social life.

## Methods used to analyse qualitative secondary data

Various types of content analysis are used to analyse qualitative secondary data such as media images on television or in newspapers. Ray Pawson (1995) identifies four main approaches to content analysis: formal content analysis, thematic analysis, textual analysis and audience analysis.

**Formal content analysis** is a quantitative research method that attempts to classify and quantify the contents of a source in a systematic way. At its simplest, it counts how often words, phrases and images appear. An example is provided by the Global Media Monitoring Project (GMMP). Every five years, the project presents a content analysis of women in the news media. In 2015, it had contributors from 114 countries. The 2015 report showed persistent under-representation of women in global news media (Global Media Monitoring Project, 2015). In Mauritius, for instance, no women were presented in print, radio and television stories for politics-related news on the day of the monitoring.

### Activity

*The GMMP monitors the presentation of women in the media in countries such as Mauritius, Pakistan, the USA and Cyprus.*

1. What type of data does formal content analysis provide?
2. Why is it important to monitor the presentation of women and men in the media?

**Thematic analysis** looks for the guiding themes of the professionals (such as newspaper journalists) who produce mass media reports. It focuses on the motives, intentions and underlying ideologies of the authors. For example, a news broadcast or newspaper article about a war or an international conflict may reflect the interests of particular groups in society. Rather than reporting events neutrally, war correspondents may take sides by describing one side as terrorists, guerrillas or subversives.

**Textual analysis** involves a close examination of the 'text' to see how the words and phrases used encourage a particular reading of it. The Glasgow

University Media Group's (1976) study of televised reporting of strikes in Britain provides an example. Strikers tended to be reported using verbs such as 'claim' or 'demand', while management were reported using verbs such as 'offer' and 'propose'. As a result, managers appeared to be reasonable and ready to negotiate, whereas the strikers appeared to be demanding and uncompromising. Textual analysis often involves the use of **semiology** or the analysis of signs (see 'Semiotic analysis' in this section).

With **audience analysis,** the focus of research is on the audience as well as on the content of the media. For example, what do different audiences make of a particular television programme? Researchers might focus, for example, on how TV news broadcasts about an international conflict affect the audience's knowledge and understanding of the conflict. The emphasis is on what audiences make of particular television programmes.

Researchers who adopt this approach see audiences as actively negotiating the meaning of messages rather than passively consuming them. The outcomes of these negotiations range from acceptance of the messages, to indifference, to opposition (Pawson, 1995).

## Activity

1. Have you noticed any instances of media professionals in your country taking sides when reporting on issues such as wars or conflicts between groups or states? Do they take sides when covering international sporting events such as the World Cup or the Olympics? Or do they report in neutral terms? In your view, should they remain neutral? Explain your reasoning.
2. Give one argument against the view that photographs can be taken at face value as a source of secondary data.

### Strengths of content analysis

- Formal content analysis provides a way of dealing systematically with a variety of personal documents and visual images. It generates quantitative data from qualitative secondary sources and allows researchers to systematically compare products such as different advertisements on television.
- With formal content analysis, the researcher works with a set of predetermined categories so the analysis can be replicated to check the reliability of the findings.
- Positivists are likely to favour formal content analysis when suitable documentary data are available, for quantification by counting words and images, for obtaining representative samples and for making generalisations.
- Forms of content analysis that focus on newspaper articles or television programmes do not involve research participants who may be influenced by the researcher.
- Audience research allows researchers to discover the meanings that people give to media sources such as televised news and the understandings they draw from them.

### Limitations of content analysis

- All types of content analysis can be time consuming and laborious.
- Formal content analysis says little about what a particular text or image means to an audience. It also involves subjective judgements, which may create quantitative but invalid data.
- While thematic analysis may uncover motives, it has its problems. The sociologist's interpretation of underlying themes is subjective and audiences may not interpret the articles in the same way as the researcher.
- As with thematic analysis, textual analysis relies on the researcher's interpretation, which may not correspond to the audience's view.
- Audience research involves 'asking the audience', but the research methods employed to do this, such as interviews or focus groups, have their limitations.

## Semiotic analysis

Semiology is the study of signs and symbols, what they stand for and how they work together to create meanings. **Semiotic analysis** is often used as a method to analyse the hidden meanings underlying visual images such as those in photographs, films and advertising. It aims to reveal how signs are designed to affect the people who consume them. One key area that semiology explores is advertising in magazines, websites and on television.

The methods used to analyse documents tend not to meet positivist requirements. Methods such as semiology, and thematic and textual analysis rely heavily on the researcher's interpretations. This makes them difficult to replicate (to check for reliability).

## Research example: Researching magazine covers

*The magazine cover analysed by Barthes.*

Roland Barthes (1986, cited in Ali, 2011) provides an example of semiotic analysis. Barthes analysed the cover of a 1966 edition of *Paris Match*, a French-language news magazine. Barthes noted that the image represented a young black man wearing a military uniform saluting something that is out of sight. The image was accompanied by text in French.

Barthes claimed that the connotations, or the meanings, of the magazine cover were as follows. Although there was no flag in the image, a flag was implied by the way the young man was raising his eyes and looking into the middle distance. The image was published within the context of fighting by Algerians for independence from France. However, this image implies continuing loyalty to France among ethnically diverse groups who see themselves, above all else, as French.

### Questions

1. What background information would you need to know in order to carry out your own semiotic analysis of this image?
2. Give two criticisms of semiology from a positivist approach.

### Key terms

**Trend** The general direction in which statistics on something (such as the divorce rate) change or move over time.

**Victim surveys** Surveys that ask respondents whether they have been victims of particular crimes during a specified period and, if so, whether they reported them to the police.

**Personal documents** Letters, diaries, notes and photographs.

**Historical documents** Documents from the past.

**Digital content** Information such as social media that is distributed via the internet.

**Formal content analysis** Counting how often particular words, phrases and images occur.

**Thematic analysis** Interpreting the meanings, motives and ideologies that underlie documents.

**Textual analysis** Examining how the words and phrases chosen encourage a particular reading of a document.

**Semiology** The analysis of signs.

**Audience analysis** Examining how audiences respond to and interpret documentary material.

**Semiotic analysis** The study of signs and symbols and how they combine to create meaning.

### Summary

1. Secondary sources of quantitative data include official statistics. Secondary sources of qualitative data include personal documents, digital content and traditional media sources. Each has its strengths and limitations.
2. Researchers need to know how official statistics are constructed in order to assess their validity.
3. Police recorded crime is regarded as an inadequate measure of the extent of crime and trends in crime.
4. Some researchers argue that official statistics can be politically biased in order to present governments in a favourable light.

5. Despite their shortcomings, official statistics can provide valuable data for sociological research.
6. Personal documents provide data on people's feelings and concerns, and hundreds of years of history and visual images in the form of photographs.
7. Various types of content analysis can be used to analyse documents. They include formal content analysis, thematic analysis, textual analysis and audience analysis.
8. Visual images such as photographs and advertisements in magazines can be analysed and interpreted in a variety of ways, including formal content analysis and semiotic analysis.
9. Qualitative secondary data can be assessed in terms of:
   - authenticity – are they genuine?
   - credibility – are they true?
   - representativeness – are they typical?
   - meaning – are they comprehensible?

# Unit 3.1.5 The stages of designing research

So far, this chapter has looked at the different research methods and sources of data available to sociologists. But how do sociologists go about designing their research? Where do they get their research questions? How do they select samples of research participants? This unit examines the various stages involved in planning and designing a piece of sociological research from deciding on a research strategy to interpreting the results.

## Deciding on a research strategy

A research strategy is 'a general orientation to the conduct of social research' (Bryman, 2016). Alan Bryman (2016) distinguishes between quantitative and qualitative research strategies. Quantitative research emphasises quantification or measurement during the process of collecting and analysing data. By contrast, qualitative research puts more emphasis on words than on numbers. (See also Unit 3.2.2 for a discussion of positivism and interpretivism.) A researcher must decide which of these strategies they will use.

## Formulating research questions and hypotheses

Sociologists ask questions about the social world and, during the research process, they may address these questions in the form of aims or hypotheses. Research aims set out what the researcher is planning to investigate and provide a clear focus to the study. A hypothesis is a supposition, hunch or informed guess to be tested. It is usually written as a statement that can either be supported by the evidence or refuted.

Researchers develop their research questions, aims and hypotheses from several sources, including:

- a critical review of the existing literature (including relevant books and journal articles) on a particular area – by carrying out a literature review, researchers may spot a gap, focus their own study on new ground and ensure that their research will contribute original knowledge to the field
- a previous study they carried out in which, for example, something struck them as unexpected, puzzling or interesting
- new developments in technology such as the internet and social media
- their personal lives, experiences or interests
- a pressing social problem such as poverty or racism.

## Samples, sampling frames and sampling techniques

Nearly all social surveys are based on a sample of the population under investigation. The population might be female prisoners, male manual workers, 16- to 19-year-old students and so on. Samples are necessary because researchers rarely have sufficient time or funding to study the full population.

Most researchers aim to select a sample that is representative of its population. Thus, if a researcher is studying the attitudes of Malaysian women, the sample should *not* consist of 1000 single women or 1000 university-educated women, as such groups are hardly representative of Malaysian women. With a representative sample, generalisations are more likely to be true – findings from the sample are more likely to apply to their overall population.

## Sample design and composition

In many cases, it is fairly easy to define a **sampling unit** – that is, a member of the population to be studied. Dentists, males between 30 and 40 years of age, females who own their own businesses or people with degrees can be defined without too many problems. However, other groups are less easy to define – how would you define a semi-skilled manual worker or a person living in poverty?

### Activity

*A sample is a subgroup drawn from the population.*

1. What is a representative sample?
2. Explain one reason why a researcher might want a representative sample.

## Sampling frames

Once the research population has been defined, the sample is selected from a **sampling frame** – a list of members of the population to be studied. In some cases, an appropriate sampling frame is readily available. In countries such as Mauritius and the UK, for example, the register of electors (a list of people registered to vote) is likely to be used for a study of voting behaviour. In other cases, researchers may have to rely on listings such as telephone directories, which may not be entirely suitable for their purposes.

All listings have drawbacks. Not everyone is included, they are often out of date and certain groups are likely to be under-represented. For instance, younger people may be less likely to appear on electoral registers in many countries, as they are less likely to register to vote.

## Sampling techniques

A **sampling technique** is a procedure used to obtain a sample. Tim May (2001) divides sampling into two categories: random (or probability) sampling and non-probability sampling. With **random sampling**, each member of the sampling frame has a known chance of being selected. Non-probability sampling is used where a sampling frame is unavailable.

Random sampling **Simple random sampling** gives every member of the sampling frame an equal chance of being included in the sample. Every name is given a number and then a list of random numbers is used to select a sample. This avoids bias in selection. It prevents the researcher from selecting a sample that provides a result that fits their theory or supports their hypothesis.

Random samples are not necessarily representative. For example, if the sample is intended to represent parents, it might include mostly fathers. This can happen when the sample is randomly drawn, even though fathers might make up only half of the population.

Stratified random sampling **Stratified random sampling** offers a possible solution to the problem of representativeness. The sampling frame is divided into groups or strata which reflect the wider population – for example, age, gender, ethnic and class groups. For instance, if the sampling frame is based on women in Malaysia, the researcher might divide the women into age, ethnic and class groups and then draw a random sample from each of these groups. This would be more likely to provide a representative sample of Malaysian women. In practice, researchers include strata that are important to their research.

Non-random sampling **Quota sampling** is a type of stratified sampling in which the selection of people within each stratum is not random. For example, a market researcher stands on a street corner looking for people to fill her quota. She has to find 20 women aged between 30 and 45 years to answer a questionnaire on magazine readership. She fills her quota with the first 20 women passing by who fit the required age group and agree to answer her questions. The sample is not randomly selected from a sampling frame. The researcher simply fills their quota from the first available people.

### Activity

Give one reason why quota sampling is unlikely to produce a sample that is representative of its population.

Quota sampling is often used for opinion polls and market research. It has its advantages – it is simpler, quicker and cheaper than stratified random sampling. However, it is less likely to produce a

## Activity

*Deciding whether or not to take part in the survey.*

1. With reference to the picture, why might volunteer samples be unrepresentative?
2. Why might some people be more likely to participate in a web survey than a structured interview when the subject concerns illegal behaviour and/or sensitive issues?

representative sample. For example, where and when a quota is filled can make significant differences to the sample. Stopping people on the street during weekday working hours would exclude many people in paid employment. The fact that researchers can choose who they interview can bias the sample still further. If faced, for example, with two young men, many researchers would probably choose the one who is more smartly dressed and 'pleasant' looking.

In quota sampling, people in the same stratum do not have an equal chance of being selected.

**Snowball sampling** is used when researchers have difficulty obtaining people for their samples. First, lists for a sampling frame might be unavailable. Second, the research population might be so small that normal sampling methods would not supply the numbers needed. Third, members of the research population (such as burglars, former prisoners or people who avoid paying tax) might not wish to be identified. One possibility is to use a network of like-minded or like-situated individuals. This is the basis of snowball sampling.

With snowballing, the researcher finds one member of the population and gradually gains their confidence until they are willing to identify others. In this way, a network of members of the population is built up and forms the basis for the sample. Additionally, if the researcher establishes a good relationship with the first member of the sample, then that person can vouch for the researcher with their friends and acquaintances.

Snowballing has the advantage of creating a sampling frame when other methods have failed. However, it is unlikely to provide a representative sample because it is not random and relies on personal contacts.

**Volunteer samples** are made up of people who volunteer to participate in the research.

For example, posters, radio or television broadcasts, magazine articles, social media and emails announce the research and request volunteers for the sample.

One advantage of volunteer samples is that those who take part are likely to be interested in the topic and keen to participate. However, volunteer samples are unlikely to be representative because they are self-selected. Those who volunteer may have a particular reason for doing so – they may have a grievance or a strong view to express (Seale, 2012).

### Activity

1. Explain one reason why sociologists may be unable to obtain a representative sample.
2. Explain one strength and one limitation of snowball sampling.

## Pilot studies

Before starting their main research, some sociologists conduct a pilot study. This is a small-scale feasibility study to check the suitability of the methods to be used in the main research. It can save time and money in the long run. Pilot studies often use a small sample of the main group to be studied. Members of this sample will not, however, take part in the final research. The uses of a pilot study include the following:

1. If interviews or questionnaires are to be used, the questions can be tested to ensure that they are understood by, and make sense to, the research participants.
2. With self-completion questionnaires, the researcher is not present to explain any difficulties or clear up any confusion. A preliminary test might reveal that the questionnaire's instructions or the wording of a question need clarifying.
3. Piloting an in-depth interview may prove useful when constructing a questionnaire for the main research. It may identify participants' concerns and priorities, which could be incorporated into the questionnaire.

## Operationalisation

Sociological research is designed to measure or explore things. In order to do this, those 'things' must be operationalised – put into a form that can be measured. However, when designing questionnaires or interview schedules, it is difficult to operationalise or define abstract concepts such as social class or poverty in order to measure them.

When investigating the influence of social class on educational achievements, for example, the researcher must operationalise the concept of social class. Students' social class is often measured in terms of their parents' occupation. However, this data may be missing. In Africa, students' socio-economic status is often measured by the type of school they attend (Morley and Lussier, 2009).

Alice Sullivan (2007) investigated students' knowledge of the dominant culture (focusing on the arts, science and politics) in four schools in England. In her questionnaire survey, she operationalised the concept of 'cultural knowledge'. She did this by testing students' knowledge of 25 famous cultural figures, including Karl Marx, Mahatma Gandhi and Bill Clinton. The data from the survey allowed her to compare the levels of cultural knowledge of students aged around 16 years old from graduate and non-graduate homes. (See Unit 5.5.2 for details of Sullivan's findings.)

However, it is often difficult to assess whether operational definitions provide valid measurements of what they are supposed to be measuring.

## Conducting the research

The next stage in the research process involves carrying out the research in an organised manner to collect the raw data. In practice, a researcher may use one or more quantitative or qualitative methods, or a combination of these. They may use primary or secondary sources of data, or both of these. (See mixed methods in Unit 3.2.2.) The raw data provide the researcher with evidence to help explain the social world and contribute to our knowledge about society.

## Interpreting the results

Research produces vast quantities of raw data, for example, in the form of completed questionnaires or interview transcripts. The researcher then has the task of interpreting the data, that is, analysing and making sense of the information and presenting the main findings.

## Assessing the quality of the research

Sociologists present conference papers and submit articles about their research to academic journals. Research outputs such as journal articles are evaluated by other experienced sociologists before being accepted for publication. This is known as peer review and operates as a form of quality control.

In order to evaluate a piece of research, sociologists focus on several key features including validity and reliability (see Unit 3.1.1). They also focus on objectivity, representativeness and generalisability.

### Objectivity

Most sociologists try to be objective when conducting their research. This means that they try to prevent their values, political views, religious beliefs and prejudices from influencing their research.

### Representativeness and generalisation

When planning research, sociologists must decide whether they want to generalise. Generalising involves making a statement about the sample and applying that statement to members of its population. For example, making a statement about the attitudes of all men aged 20 to 30 in Pakistan based on the attitudes of some men aged 20 to 30 in Pakistan. If a sociologist aims to generalise, then they must try to select a representative sample, one that is typical of the whole group.

## Research ethics

One important criterion for assessing a piece of research concerns how far it is ethical. Ethics are moral principles – beliefs about what is right and wrong. In terms of research, ethics are the moral principles that guide research. Sociological associations in many countries have a set of ethical guidelines for conducting research. Sociologists may have to submit their research proposals to a **research ethics committee** (REC) at their university. RECs ensure that research conducted by staff complies with ethical guidelines. They help to safeguard research participants, advise on the ethical implications of a study and grant approval (or otherwise) to the research.

### Ethical considerations when conducting research

Here are some of the ethical guidelines that sociologists usually follow when designing and conducting research.

**Informed consent** Many researchers argue that prospective participants should be given the opportunity to agree, or refuse, to participate in research. The decision should be 'informed' – information must be made available on which to base this decision. Researchers should therefore provide information about the aims of the research, what the conduct of the research involves and the purposes to which the findings will be put.

**Deception** Ethical guidelines often state that research participants should not be deceived. Deception can take various forms. Information might be withheld from participants or they might be given false information. They might be unaware they are participating in a research study. They might be misled about the purpose and conduct of the study.

Some researchers argue that deception is justified if there is no other way of gathering data. Others argue that, in certain instances, ethical guidelines should not apply. For example, in a study of child abuse, deception might be judged as acceptable if it helps to bring abusers to justice.

**Privacy** Researchers generally agree that participants' privacy should be respected, but most research intrudes into people's lives. One view is that if participants consent to take part in research, then they accept this. However, they may be unaware of the extent of the intrusion. With hindsight, they may see it as an invasion of privacy.

Certain research methods which are generally considered ethical may involve an invasion of privacy. For example, an in-depth, unstructured interview often develops into a friendly chat and, in this relaxed atmosphere, participants may reveal personal and private matters which they later regret.

**Anonymity and confidentiality** It is generally agreed that research participants' identities should be kept secret and information about them should be confidential. The International Sociological Association's (2001) *Code of Ethics* states that the 'anonymity and privacy of research subjects and informants should be respected rigorously ... The sources of personal information obtained by researchers should be kept confidential, unless the informants have asked or agreed to be cited.' One argument is that there may be a case for naming names when people in powerful positions misuse their power (Homan, 1991).

**Protection from harm** There is general agreement that research participants should be protected from physical and psychological harm. This includes any harmful effects of participating in the research and any harmful consequences of the research. For example, publication of research findings may harm those who participated. Particular care should be taken to protect members of vulnerable groups, for example, victims of domestic violence.

### Activity

1. Researching children raises particular ethical concerns that may not apply when researching adults. Why might it be more difficult to get informed consent from children than from adults?

2. Assess the view that it would be unethical to use social media postings for research purposes without permission.

## Research example: Research ethics in action

The American Psychological Association justifies the use of deception if no other procedures are available. However, it cannot be used if it may cause 'physical pain or severe emotional destress'. Informed consent must follow after the data collection. Participants can then withdraw the use of their data (Behnke, 2009).

*Milgram's experiment on obedience is now widely seen as unethical.*

Experiments are often used in psychology. The American psychologist Stanley Milgram (1963) conducted an experiment to investigate how far people would obey commands which they felt were wrong and would harm others. The research participants were told that the experiment was a 'scientific study' of the effect of punishment – electric shocks – on learning. Unknown to the participants, the shocks were not real.

The man on the left of the picture is a participant, but the two other men are actors. The man on the right is pretending to be in extreme pain. Milgram describes the response of one of the participants. 'At one point he pushed his fist into his forehead and muttered: "Oh God, let's stop it". And yet he continued to respond to every word of the experimenter, and obeyed to the end.' The participants were only free to withdraw from the experiment after several commands to continue.

Milgram defends his experiment by arguing that the importance of his findings justifies his methods. For example, his findings raise questions about what governments, with their authority and status, could order people to do. Milgram admits that, in some cases, there was psychological harm, but claims that this was only short-term. He hired a psychiatrist to interview the participants one year after the experiment. There appeared to be no long-term harm.

Milgram's experiment was based on deception throughout the conduct of the research. He justifies this by saying, 'I had to deceive them for the experiment to work.' Over 80 per cent of the participants saw the deception as necessary and therefore acceptable.

### Questions

1. Make brief notes on the role of ethics in sociological research.
2. Evaluate the view that Milgram was justified in conducting this experiment.

## Key terms

**Sampling unit** A member of the research population such as a household or a student.

**Sampling frame** A list of members of the research population.

**Sampling technique** A procedure (such as snowball or stratified random sampling) used to obtain a sample.

**Random sampling** A sampling technique in which every member of the sampling frame has a known chance of being selected.

**Simple random sampling** A technique in which all members of the sampling frame have an equal chance of being selected.

**Stratified random sampling** A technique in which the population is divided into strata and the sample is randomly drawn from each stratum. It attempts to reflect particular characteristics, such as age and gender, of the population.

**Quota sampling** A type of stratified sampling in which selection from the strata is not random.

**Snowball sampling** A technique in which members of the sample select each other.

**Volunteer sample** A sample in which members of the sample are self-selected.

**Research ethics committees** Bodies in universities that scrutinise research proposals.

## Summary

1. Designing research involves several stages from deciding on a research strategy to interpreting the results.
2. There are two categories of sampling: random (or probability) sampling and non-probability sampling.
3. Examples of random sampling include simple random and stratified random sampling. Examples of non-random sampling include quota, snowball and volunteer sampling.
4. To make generalisations, sociologists try to ensure that their sample is representative of its population.
5. Whatever type of sample is used, there is no guarantee that it will be representative.
6. Pilot studies can save time and money in the long run.
7. Operationalising or measuring concepts such as social class and poverty can be difficult.
8. Research studies are subject to peer review. The quality of research can also be assessed in terms of its validity, reliability, objectivity, representativeness and generalisability.
9. Research ethics cover issues such as informed consent, deception, privacy, confidentiality and protection from harm.
10. There are occasions when ethical guidelines may not be followed – for example, when research participants are harming others.

# END-OF-PART QUESTIONS

| 0 | 1 | Describe two secondary sources of qualitative data. **[4 marks]**

| 0 | 2 | Explain one strength and one limitation of unstructured interviews as a research method. **[6 marks]**

| 0 | 3 | 'Overt participant observation lacks validity.'

Using sociological material, give one argument against this view. **[6 marks]**

# PART 2 APPROACHES TO SOCIOLOGICAL RESEARCH

## Contents


| | | |
|---|---|---|
| **Unit 3.2.1** | **Different approaches to sociological research** | **112** |
| **Unit 3.2.2** | **Positivism, interpretivism and mixed methods** | **117** |
| **Unit 3.2.3** | **Sociology, the natural sciences and values** | **124** |


Some approaches to sociological research – such as case studies and surveys – provide a framework or a structure for a study and draw on different research methods. Part 2 begins by examining examples of such approaches. It then explores positivist and interpretivist approaches, two important research traditions in sociology. What does positivism involve? How does it view the pursuit of objectivity and reliability? What emphasis does interpretivism place on meaning and validity? How do positivism and interpretivism influence sociologists' choice of data and research methods? **Mixed-methods approaches** have become increasingly popular in sociology, but why is this the case? What are the uses of mixed methods? Finally, this part examines debates about sociology, the natural sciences and value freedom. Can sociology be based on the natural sciences? Should it strive for value freedom?

## Unit 3.2.1 Different approaches to sociological research

Some approaches provide frameworks or structures for sociological research. Examples include case studies, social surveys, ethnographies and longitudinal studies. They are not research methods as such, but they do draw on one or more methods. A case study of an individual's life, for instance, might use unstructured interviews as a means of gathering data, while an ethnographic study of a group might combine participant observation with unstructured interviews. This unit explores these approaches to sociological research that draw on different methods.

### Case studies

A **case study** is a detailed study of a particular instance of something – for example, a study of an individual or a community.

#### Strengths of case studies

- Focusing on a particular case can provide an insider's view, a richer and more detailed picture than research based on large samples. This may result in new insights and fresh ideas.
- Case studies can provide useful information for a larger research project. There is a better chance of a questionnaire or interview being relevant and meaningful if it is based, at least in part, on a case study.
- Case studies are an important warning against sweeping generalisations. The findings from a single case study can call into question those of a much larger study. Case studies can provide data that might lead to the modification or rejection of a theory.

#### Limitations of case studies

Case studies have sometimes been criticised as being limited and unrepresentative. As they are one-off instances, they cannot be used as a basis for generalisation. However, as noted above, this can sometimes be a strength – it can question the results of a larger study.

### Ethnographies

**Ethnography** involves the study of the way of life of a group of people in, for example, a community, a gang or a boarding school. It explores the group's lifestyle, culture and the structure of their society. Often researchers attempt to 'walk a mile in their

## Research example: Researching an individual

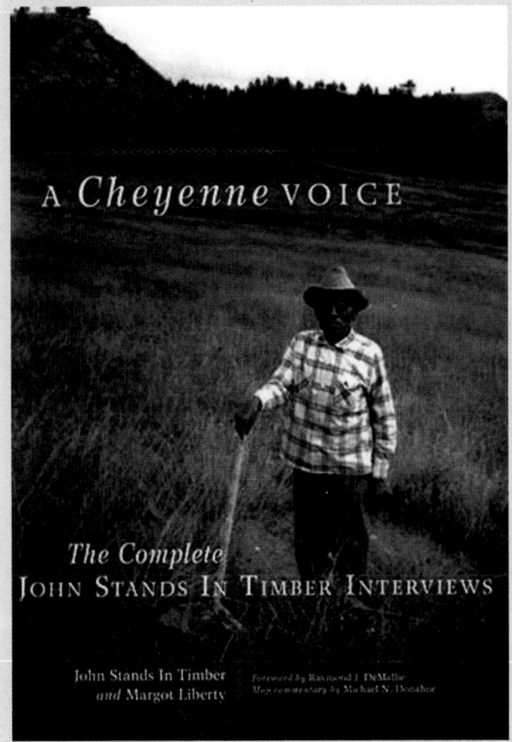


*Case studies based on life histories such as that of John Stands In Timber can provide a unique insider's view.*

A **life history** is a case study of an individual, usually based on a series of in-depth interviews. The American anthropologist Margot Liberty produced a life history of John Stands In Timber, one of the last Cheyenne Native Americans to have lived their traditional way of life. According to Liberty, 'John's narrative provides white readers with a rare insight into the history and culture of his people...[He] has given us a history of the Cheyennes as they themselves recall and interpret it...His kind of inside view will never be achieved again' (Stands In Timber and Liberty, 1967).

### Questions

1. Why do you think life histories are often based on a series of in-depth interviews?
2. Explain one advantage and one disadvantage of life histories as an approach to research.

shoes' – to see the world from their perspective, discover their meanings and appreciate their experiences. Ethnographers immerse themselves (either overtly or covertly) in the daily lives of the group being studied, often for a long time. They usually gather their data by using several qualitative methods, such as participant observation and in-depth interviews. A number of classic ethnographies are based on participant observation including Whyte's (1955) account of an Italian-American gang in Boston in the USA (see Unit 3.1.3).

## Research example: Researching a community

Paul Heelas, Linda Woodhead et al. (2005) undertook a detailed study of spirituality and religion in Kendal, a town in the Lake District in England. Kendal was small enough to investigate systematically, but large enough to have a range of spiritual and Christian activities. The research methods they used included a church attendance count, a questionnaire, participant observation, semi-structured and unstructured interviews.

Heelas et al. found a decline in traditional Christianity. They also discovered a rise in spirituality expressed, for example, in yoga and Tai Chi (see Unit 7.5.2).

### Questions

1. Can you think of any communities in your society that could form the basis of an important or valuable case study? Explain your reasoning.
2. Evaluate the view that case studies are of limited value because they do not provide a basis for generalisations.

## Research examples: Ethnography in practice

### Researching clothing factories in Sri Lanka

*Ethnography allows researchers to gather rich and detailed data.*

Kanchana N. Ruwanpura (2015) carried out an ethnographic study of two clothing factories in a semi-rural location in Sri Lanka based on participant observation and in-depth interviews. The period of extended fieldwork lasted around seven months. During this time, Ruwanpura visited the factories daily to get to know the workers. She also stayed in a local home and got to know the workers outside the workplace. After this period, she made return field trips, maintained contact and gathered data through monthly telephone conversations with groups of the workers. This allowed her to gather rich and detailed data about specific incidents linked to unionisation at one factory as events played out. By using an ethnographic approach, she was able to explore the interactions between management and workers during a struggle over the formation of a union in this factory.

### Researching deviant students' subculture in China

Lin Liu and Ailei Xie (2017) used an ethnographic approach to investigate the subculture of a group of deviant students in a school located in a city in the south of China. Lin Liu (a postgraduate student researcher at the time) carried out the fieldwork. She used participant observation and unobtrusive observation as the main methods to collect the data. While at the school, she also helped the teachers with tasks such as grading the students' work and provided tutoring to students who were experiencing difficulties in maths and Chinese. This helped her to build rapport with the research participants.

The first phase of data collection lasted one month and during this time Lin Liu undertook classroom-based unobtrusive observation. This allowed her to gather information on the atmosphere within the class and the school, on the daily interactions between students and their teachers and peers, and on relationships between students and their teachers.

After the first month, Lin Liu also began to focus on a group of five students (one girl and four boys) from one class who were seen as 'notorious troublemakers' within the school. She used participant observation and unstructured interviews to gather data about this group's activities beyond the school. She spent time with them in places such as cafes, interviewed them individually and arranged group discussions with them. She also interviewed relevant teachers at the school in order to develop a deeper understanding of issues such as school policies and teachers' perspectives on handling deviant students. (See Unit 5.5.3 for an account of their findings.)

### Questions

1. How do you think the students in your school or college might react to the presence of a researcher carrying out an ethnographic study in their classroom? How might their reactions affect the quality of the data collected?
2. Drawing on these two studies, explain one strength and one limitation of ethnography.

### Strengths of ethnography

Many of the strengths (and limitations) of participant observation apply to ethnography. For example, an ethnographer using overt participant observation can openly question participants about their behaviour and take field notes while observing or questioning them. Ethnographic studies also enable the researcher to gather rich, detailed data and gain extra insights by participating in activities.

### Limitations of ethnography

The limitations linked to overt participant observation include difficulties in accessing the group and in maintaining trust, and the Hawthorne effect. Limitations linked to covert participant observation include the impracticality of taking field notes, the risk of being exposed as a researcher, and ethical dilemmas concerning informed consent and deception. Other problems with ethnography include the risk of over-involvement and loss of objectivity.

## Longitudinal studies

Many sociological studies are like a snapshot and show what is happening at a particular point in time. However, situations and people change. A **longitudinal study** is concerned with change. It studies the same group of people over an extended period of time. In this respect, it can be seen as similar to an ethnographic study. However, in ethnography based on participant observation, the researcher participates in group members' daily lives on an ongoing basis and gathers data throughout the course of the fieldwork. By contrast, in a longitudinal study, the researcher revisits the same sample at particular points in time to gather data.

Quantitative longitudinal studies are usually based on self-completion questionnaires or structured interviews. The sample is questioned at the outset, and the same people are surveyed again at least once more to build a picture of how their lives are changing over time.

Bryman (2016) identifies two types of longitudinal design which differ in terms of their sample:

1. A cohort study, in which either a whole cohort of people or a random sample of them is selected. Everyone in the cohort shares a particular experience or characteristic, such as being born in the same week.
2. A panel study, in which a sample is selected from the full population. The sample might comprise, for example, people, schools or households.

### Research example: The General Household Survey Panel

The panel survey component of the General Household Survey (GHS) in Nigeria is a national longitudinal survey that runs every two to three years. The first wave was conducted in 2010/11, the second wave in 2012/13 and the third wave in 2015/16. The GHS Panel follows the same households over time and questions household members on topics such as their living standards, education, health and welfare. The data inform policy makers.

A total of 5000 households were selected in the first wave and, of these, 4916 were interviewed. By the third wave, 4581 households were interviewed. The National Bureau of Statistics in Nigeria produces the survey and the World Bank is involved in its implementation. The survey is funded by the Federal Government of Nigeria and the Bill and Melinda Gates Foundation.

#### Questions

1. Would you be willing to participate in a longitudinal study? Explain your reasoning.
2. Suggest two possible reasons for the decrease in the number of households participating in the GHS over time.

Although longitudinal studies are usually associated with quantitative research methods, qualitative longitudinal studies are becoming increasingly popular among sociologists. The Timescapes Initiative, for example, was a major qualitative study that ran from 2007 to 2012. It involved seven different research projects in five UK universities which explored how people's personal and family relationships developed and changed over time. Research methods included in-depth interviews, observation, video diaries and photography.

### Ethics and longitudinal studies

Longitudinal studies raise particular ethical concerns. For example, participants may have experienced divorce, bereavement, longstanding illness and, as they grow older, they may be unable to give informed consent. Researchers need to be prepared to deal with the grief, stress or embarrassment that talking about such issues may cause.

### Strengths of longitudinal studies

- Longitudinal studies provide a picture of social trends and developments over time. By studying the same individuals, researchers can be sure that any changes in behaviour and attitudes are not simply due to changes in the make-up of the sample.
- They focus on continuity (what stays the same) as well as social change.
- Longitudinal studies avoid asking people to recall events from much earlier in their lives, when memory might fail them. In this respect, the data are more likely to be valid.

### Limitations of longitudinal studies

- The main problem with longitudinal studies is **sample attrition**, the reduction in size of the original sample. This may be due to death, emigration, refusal to participate or the researcher's inability to locate participants. The researchers make considerable efforts to maintain contact. Despite this, samples inevitably grow smaller and probably less representative of the population if more people from particular social groups (such as homeless or older people) withdraw. This makes it more difficult to generalise.
- Few organisations can afford to fund an investigation that may last for 20 years or more. Even a longitudinal study over a shorter time period can be very expensive.
- Involvement in a longitudinal study may affect participants' behaviour, in that they might think about an issue more and act differently as a result of their involvement in the research.

### Activity

Explain one similarity and one difference between an ethnographic study and a longitudinal study.

## Social surveys

A social survey involves the systematic collection of the same type of data from a fairly large number of people at one point in time. Questionnaires and structured interviews are the main methods used to collect data in survey research.

### Research example: The Nepal Demographic and Health Survey

The Nepal Demographic and Health Survey (NDHS) is a national survey that provides data on basic demographic and health indicators in Nepal. The 2016 survey was based on six questionnaires – including one for households, one for women and one for men – which were delivered via structured interviews. The household questionnaire, for example, collected information on each household's dwelling unit, its residents and visitors. The response rates were relatively high. For instance, a total of 13 089 women aged 15–49 were eligible to be interviewed. Of these, 12 862 were interviewed – a response rate of 98.3 per cent.

The NDHS provides information on a wide range of issues, including education and literacy, exposure to the mass media, internet usage and employment. Trends can be identified by comparing data from 2016 to data from previous surveys. For example, 83 per cent of women were employed in 2006, but this fell to 68 per cent in 2016.

Demographic and Health Surveys (DHS) are carried out in over 90 developing countries, including Pakistan, Guyana, Brazil, Nigeria and Kenya. They provide comparative, cross-national data on population and health issues. The surveys are funded by the United States Agency for International Development (USAID), a US government agency.

#### Questions

1. In your view, how important is it to gather cross-national data on population and health issues in developing countries in this way. Explain your answer.
2. Should participants be paid for taking part in research such as the DHSs? How far would it be ethical to pay people who participate? Should prospective participants be told who funds the DHSs? Explain your reasoning.
3. Make brief notes on the strengths and limitations of case studies, ethnographies, longitudinal studies and social surveys.

## Key terms

**Mixed-methods approaches** Using more than one method in a research project, often combining both qualitative and quantitative techniques.

**Case study** A study of a particular instance of something.

**Ethnography** The study of the way of life of a group of people in order to understand their world from their perspective.

**Life history** A case study of an individual's life.

**Longitudinal study** A study of the same group of people over time.

**Sample attrition** The reduction in the size of the original sample over time.

## Summary

1. A case study is an in-depth study of an individual (known as a life history) or a community.
2. Case studies can produce new insights and generate data that question existing generalisations and theories.
3. An ethnography involves the study of a group in its everyday setting and is usually based on participant observation and unstructured interviews.
4. Many of the strengths and limitations of participant observation also apply to ethnographies.
5. Longitudinal studies are usually based on quantitative methods, but qualitative longitudinal studies are increasingly popular.
6. Longitudinal studies provide data for studying social change, developments and continuities over a fairly long period of time.
7. The data from longitudinal studies are more likely to be valid compared to relying on people's long-term memory. However, they are costly and sample attrition is problematic.
8. A social survey is usually based on presenting all participants with standardised questions in the form of a structured interview or a self-completion questionnaire.

# Unit 3.2.2 Positivism, interpretivism and mixed methods

In broad terms, it is possible to identify two main approaches or research traditions in sociology: positivism and interpretivism (see Unit 3.1.1). Positivism argues that sociologists should study the social world in the same way that scientists such as physicists and chemists study the natural world. It stresses the importance of objectivity, value freedom, reliability and generalisability in sociological research. By contrast, interpretivism emphasises meaning, subjectivity and validity. This unit looks at the positivist ideas of Comte and Durkheim. It then explores the ideas of Atkinson, Douglas and Weber, whose approaches are influenced by interpretivism. Finally, it examines mixed-methods approaches to sociological research.

## Positivism and quantitative methods

The founders of sociology in the 19th century saw sociology as a scientific discipline. By following the rules and logic of the scientific method, sociology could discover the laws underlying the development of human society. In this respect, it was a science just like the natural sciences of physics and chemistry, which seek to discover the laws underlying the behaviour of matter.

### Auguste Comte and positivism

Auguste Comte (1798–1857) is credited with inventing the term 'sociology'. He argued that sociology should be based on the methods of the natural sciences. According to Comte, this would produce a 'science of society' that would reveal the 'invariable laws' that governed the evolution of human society. Comte's approach is known as positivism.

Comte insisted that only directly observable 'facts' were acceptable in a positive science of society. This ruled out anything that could not be directly observed, such as meanings. Positivism assumes that behaviour in the natural and social world is based on similar principles. The behaviour of matter is a reaction to external factors such as temperature and pressure. In much the same way, human behaviour is a reaction to external forces beyond the individual, such as economic and political systems.

Behaviour in both the natural and social worlds is determined by external stimuli. As a result, natural science **methodology** is appropriate for the study of human behaviour.

Scientists explain the behaviour of matter in terms of cause and effect relationships. In order to discover these relationships, behaviour must be objectively quantified. It must be measured in the form of numbers and these measurements must be objective – unbiased and **value free**. They should not be affected by the researcher's values, morality or politics.

Statistical analysis of quantitative data can be used to discover possible correlations – links or connections – between social facts. Correlations may indicate relationships between social facts. Theories can then be developed to explain these relationships. In this way, the 'positive science of sociology' may uncover the 'invariable laws' governing human behaviour.

## Activity

*Comte argued that sociology should be based on the methods of the natural sciences.*

1. Did Comte place more emphasis on structure or human agency? Explain your answer.
2. How far do you agree that your behaviour is a reaction to external forces beyond your control such as the economic and political system in your society?

## Émile Durkheim – the rules of sociological method

The French sociologist Émile Durkheim (1858–1917) is one of the founders of sociology. He saw sociology as a science and his approach illustrates many aspects of positivism.

**Social facts** In *The Rules of Sociological Method*, first published in 1895, Durkheim outlined the logic and methods to be followed in order for sociology to become a science of society. The starting point, 'the first and most fundamental rule is: Consider social facts as things'. **Social facts** are the institutions, norms and values of society. As 'things', social facts can be treated in the same way as the material objects of the natural world. They can be studied with the same degree of objectivity that scientists apply when studying the natural world. Social facts can be objectively measured, quantified and subjected to statistical analysis. Correlations can be drawn between social facts, cause and effect relationships established and theories developed to explain those relationships. In this way, 'real laws are discoverable' in the social world as in the natural world.

## Activity

1. How similar are the subject matters of sociology and the natural sciences?
2. To what extent can they be studied in the same way?

Critics question whether social facts can be treated as things. In their view, human beings have consciousness and are, therefore, fundamentally different from the inanimate objects that make up the natural world. Consequently, critics question whether natural science methods are appropriate for the study of human behaviour.

Durkheim accepted that social facts form part of our consciousness – they have to in order for society to exist. Without shared norms and values, for example, society could not operate. However, although they are a part of us, social facts also exist outside of us. In Durkheim's words, 'collective ways of acting and thinking have a reality outside the individuals'. Members of society do not simply act in terms of their own particular psychology and personal beliefs. Instead, they are directed and constrained to act by social facts, by values and beliefs that are over and above the individual and part of the wider society. In this respect, social facts 'have a reality outside the individuals' and can therefore be studied objectively 'as external things'.

Thus, just as matter is constrained to act by natural forces, so human beings are constrained to act by social facts. Matter reacts to external stimuli, and people react to social facts in the wider society. Given this, social facts can be studied using the methodology of the natural sciences.

Durkheim adopted a structural perspective and put more emphasis on structure than on human agency. He saw social structure as being external to the individual and as limiting people's behaviour. For instance, the legal system and social customs existed before a particular individual was born and they constrain that individual's behaviour. However, critics argue that structural approaches downplay human agency and the existence of free will.

## Activity

Drawing on your own experiences, how far do you agree that social structures limit your behaviour in your daily life? Can you think of any ways in which you exercise agency during your everyday activities?

## Research example: Durkheim's study of suicide

Durkheim's *Suicide: A Study in Sociology* (1897) exemplified his rules of sociological method. Durkheim argued that the causes of suicide rates (the number of suicides per million of the population) are to be found in society, *not* in the psychology of individuals. Suicide rates are social facts. They are also a product of social facts, of 'real, living, active forces which, because of the way they determine the individual, prove their independence from him'.

Durkheim compared official statistics on suicide (a secondary source of quantitative data) from a number of European countries. He found that: 1) suicide rates within each country were fairly constant over a number of years, and 2) there were significant differences in the rates both between societies and between social groups within the same society. Durkheim found correlations between suicide rates and a wide range of social facts. For example, he found statistical relationships between suicide rates and religion, age and family situation. Some of these are illustrated in Table 3.2.1. In each of the pairs, the group in the left column had a higher suicide rate than the group in the right one.

**Table 3.2.1 Some of the variations that Durkheim identified in the suicide rates between different social groups**

| Higher suicide rate | Lower suicide rate |
|---|---|
| Protestants | Catholics |
| City dwellers | Rural dwellers |
| Older adults | Younger adults |
| Unmarried | Married |
| Married without children | Married with children |

Having established correlations between social facts, Durkheim looked at whether he could discover causal connections. He argued that variations in suicide rates were caused by variations in levels of social integration – that is, the extent to which individuals are part of a wider social group. In the case of the examples given in Table 3.2.1, the groups on the left have lower levels of social integration than those on the right. For example, older adults are less socially integrated than younger adults, because their children have grown up and left home, many of their friends and relatives have died, and if they have retired from work they may have lost contact with their workmates. Using examples such as this, Durkheim claimed that 'suicide varies inversely with the degree of integration of the social groups of which the individual forms a part'. So, the higher an individual's social integration, the less likely they are to take their own life.

Durkheim's final task was to explain why suicide rates vary with levels of social integration. Part of his explanation runs as follows. As members of society, people are social beings – they have been socialised to play a part in society. The greater their social isolation, the less they can participate in society. Their lives lack meaning and purpose unless they are shared with others. In a situation of social isolation, 'the individual yields to the slightest shock of circumstance because the state of society has made him a ready prey to suicide'.

Durkheim did not claim to explain all aspects of suicide. For example, he did not explain why only a small minority of socially isolated individuals commit suicide. He saw this as the job of the psychologist because it concerns individual behaviour rather than social facts.

Durkheim believed that his research on suicide proved that scientific methodology was appropriate for the study of society because it had shown that 'real laws are discoverable'. However, few sociologists would agree with this view today.

## Questions

1. Drawing on Durkheim's ideas, explain why married people without children might have higher suicide rates than married people with children.
2. 'In his study of suicide, Durkheim focused on structure while largely overlooking human agency.'

   Give one argument to support this view.

## Activity

1. 'Social surveys closely fit into the positivist perspective.'

   Give one argument to support this view.
2. 'Quantitative methods enable researchers to study the social facts that constrain human behaviour.'

   Explain this view.

# Interpretivism and qualitative methods

Interpretivists reject the view that the methods and assumptions of the natural sciences are applicable to the study of human beings. They argue that matter lacks agency and simply reacts to external stimuli such as temperature and pressure. Human beings have agency – that is, free will and self-determination – and their actions can shape and change society. For example, individuals make choices and decisions about their education, religion and family life. They act in terms of meanings, which they use to direct their behaviour.

Interpretivists tend to prefer qualitative methods. The aim of qualitative research is to see the world through the eyes of the research participants, to discover their subjective experiences, the meanings of their actions and their definitions of the situation. This means avoiding the imposition of the researcher's categories, classifications and frameworks. David Silverman (2013, 2015) argues that 'Qualitative research gives deeper understanding. It provides naturally occurring data rather than data structured by the researcher.' Obtaining 'naturally occurring data' often means studying research participants in their normal, everyday settings through, for example, participant observation.

### Suicide and the construction of meaning

Interpretivist approaches to the study of suicide can be contrasted with Durkheim's approach. This illustrates some of the differences between positivist/quantitative and interpretivist/qualitative approaches.

## Research example: Atkinson's study of suicide

In *Discovering Suicide*, Atkinson (1978) asks, 'How do deaths get categorised as suicides?' Atkinson rejects the view that the suicide rate is a 'social fact', arguing that there is no such thing as a 'real' or objective suicide rate.

Atkinson sees suicide as a meaning. His research attempts to discover the meanings that coroners in England and Wales use to classify deaths as suicide. Coroners are officials who examine the reasons for someone's death, particularly a sudden or violent death. Atkinson held discussions with coroners, attended inquests (official inquiries into the cause of death), observed a coroner's officer at work and analysed a coroner's records. He argues that coroners have a 'commonsense theory of suicide', which they use to classify and explain deaths as suicide. In terms of his theory, the following evidence is seen as relevant for reaching a verdict:

1. Whether suicide threats were made or suicide notes were left.

2. The type of death – hanging, gassing and drug overdose are seen as typical suicide deaths.
3. The location of death – death by gunshot at home is more likely to be seen as suicide than in the countryside, where it may be interpreted as a hunting accident.
4. The biography of the deceased – a recent divorce, the death of a close friend or relative, a history of depression, problems at work, financial difficulties and lack of friends are seen as typical reasons for suicide.

The closer the deceased fits this common-sense theory of suicide, the more likely their death will be defined as suicide. In Atkinson's words, coroners 'are engaged in analysing features of the deaths and of the biographies of the deceased according to a variety of taken-for-granted assumptions about what constitutes a "typical suicide", "a typical suicide biography", and so on'.

According to Atkinson, suicides are not objective 'social facts' with causes that can be explained. Trying to discover the 'causes' of suicide will simply result in uncovering the meanings used to classify a death as suicide. Thus, it comes as no surprise that the 'typical suicide biography' – the friendless, divorced loner – is very similar to Durkheim's socially isolated individual. For Atkinson, suicides, like any other aspect of social reality, are simply constructions of meaning.

### Question

Explain two differences between Durkheim's and Atkinson's approach to the study of suicide.

**The social meanings of suicide** Compared to Atkinson, Jack Douglas (1967) takes a less extreme interpretivist view of suicide. He argues that suicide is not simply a meaning; it has a reality. He claims that it is possible for researchers to discover whether a death actually was suicide.

In *The Social Meanings of Suicide*, Douglas (1967) argues that suicide is an act that is defined and given meaning by the victim, their family, friends and acquaintances, and the coroner. The job of the sociologist is to discover these meanings and to judge whether or not they indicate actual suicides. To do this, Douglas suggests three steps.

**Step 1** Examine the meanings that victims give to their possible suicide. This involves:

- an analysis of suicide notes, if available
- an examination of diaries, if kept
- interviews with families and friends
- building up a biography of the victim.

**Step 2** Look for the meanings that appear common to a number of possible suicides. These might include:

- a 'cry for help' suicide when all else has failed
- a self-punishment suicide for one's misdeeds
- an escape suicide when life becomes unbearable.

**Step 3** Link these patterns of meaning with the wider beliefs of the culture. For example:

- In Western culture, suicide is often seen as an act of desperation when all else fails.
- In some nomadic hunter-gatherer bands, such as the traditional Inuit, older people who can no longer physically keep up with the band leave the encampment to die.

Douglas argues that suicide statistics (on which Durkheim based his research) are the result of negotiated meanings and social interactions. For example, although family and friends might believe that the deceased has committed suicide, they might nevertheless do their best to conceal the 'suicide'. This, in turn, may lead the coroner to deliver a verdict of accidental death or death by natural causes. Douglas argues that only by discovering meanings by following the above steps can the researcher have a chance of judging whether or not a death is suicide.

### Activity

1. Explain one difference between Atkinson's and Douglas' approach to the study of suicide.
2. 'Qualitative methods allow sociologists to explore how people exercise agency in their lives.'

   Explain this view.

## Max Weber, social action and verstehen

Max Weber (1864–1920) saw sociology as based on 'the interpretive understanding of social action'. By social action, he meant action that is subjectively meaningful to the actor and takes account of other people. His social action approach involves interpreting the meanings and motives that direct individual action. For example, what meaning does an actor give to the action of chopping wood? Weber calls his approach **verstehen**, which roughly translates as 'empathetic understanding'. It involves researchers putting themselves in the place of those they are researching and attempting to see the world through their eyes.

Weber accepted that social structures existed. However, he saw these structures as created by the actions of individuals. In this sense, he emphasised human agency.

## Activity

*Weber's social action approach involved understanding the meanings and motives that direct individual action.*

1. What are the possible meanings and motives for the action of the person in the photograph?
2. a) Which research method would you use in order to understand this individual's meanings and motives?

   b) Why would you use this method?

# Criticisms of the positivism vs interpretivism dichotomy

So far, this unit has divided sociological approaches or research traditions into two distinct parts – positivist/quantitative and interpretivist/qualitative. To some extent, this division reflects real differences in the assumptions and theories underlying these two approaches and the research methods favoured by each. However, this split has been criticised by some sociologists. According to Pawson (1989), rather than just two approaches, there is a whole range of approaches with different assumptions and emphases.

A second criticism focuses on an examination of actual research. This indicates that sociologists often use a mixture of qualitative and quantitative methods and combine the different kinds of data that each produces. For instance, they might use participant observation and questionnaires within a single research project.

## Mixed-methods approaches

A mixed-methods approach uses more than one method in a particular study. Ethnographic studies, for example, usually combine qualitative methods such as participant observation and unstructured interviews. Alternatively, a mixed-methods approach might combine both quantitative and qualitative methods such as questionnaires and group interviews within the same study. This is sometimes referred to as **methodological pluralism**.

For example, Johnson Oluwole Ayodele (2015) combined qualitative and quantitative approaches to study reporting of crime among female market traders in Oyo town, Nigeria. He used questionnaires with female traders and five focus group discussions with female traders, their customers and police officers. Ayodele found that many crimes committed against the female traders were not reported to the police. One possible reason for this under-reporting is that the women did not regard the police as able or willing to apprehend the perpetrators of the crimes. The majority of those who reported the crimes to the police were dissatisfied with the way the police handled their complaints.

## Uses of mixed methods

- In practice, many sociologists do not think in terms of positivism versus interpretivism. Because of this, they see no problem in combining methods that some might see as more appropriate for one or the other approach.
- Mixing methods can generate different types of data within a study. Qualitative data might provide rich data and meanings, while quantitative data might provide reliable and generalisable findings.
- By mixing methods, the researcher can draw on the strengths of several different methods to obtain a more detailed picture and reduce the limitations of one method.

- Using one method can help to develop another method. For example, information from in-depth interviews can be used when designing a questionnaire to make it more relevant to participants.
- Mixed methods is used in the process of **triangulation** (see below).

**Triangulation** Triangulation is a way of cross-checking the validity of research findings. This can be done in several ways. First, it can be done by using more than one method. If the two methods produce conflicting rather than consistent results, this raises questions about validity. Have one or both methods generated incorrect data?

Second, triangulation can combine different types of data – for example, primary and secondary data and/or qualitative and quantitative data. If one form of data contradicts the other, this suggests that further research is needed to get a true picture. If the findings from the quantitative and qualitative methods are consistent, then they are likely to be more reliable and valid than the findings from just one method.

Third, if two researchers' findings differ, then one of them may have made an incorrect observation. Again, this raises the question of validity and suggests the need for additional research.

Triangulation is useful for cross-checking one source of data or evidence, or one set of research findings against another. It offers a means of improving validity. However, different findings do not necessarily mean that one is correct and another incorrect. They may simply reflect different perspectives, with neither being right nor wrong.

## Activity

1. Identify one way in which sociologists might use mixed methods in a study to capture aspects of both structure and agency.
2. Make brief notes to summarise positivist and interpretivist approaches to sociological research.

## Key terms

**Methodology** A theory about how research should proceed.

**Value free** Objective, impartial and unbiased.

**Social facts** The institutions, norms and values of society.

**Verstehen** As used by Weber, an approach for interpreting the meanings and motives that direct individual action. It involves understanding research participants' situations as they themselves understand them.

**Methodological pluralism** The use of a plurality or range of research methods, including both quantitative and qualitative methods.

**Triangulation** A way of cross-checking the validity of research findings by, for example, using mixed methods.

## Summary

1. Positivism argues that sociology should be based on the methods of the natural sciences with an emphasis on objectivity, value freedom, reliability and generalisations.
2. Comte assumed that behaviour in the natural and social worlds is determined by external stimuli. As a result, natural science methods are appropriate for the study of human behaviour.
3. Durkheim saw social facts (society's institutions, norms and values) as external to individuals. They become part of human consciousness, and direct and constrain behaviour. He emphasised structure rather than human agency.
4. Durkheim argued that social facts can be considered as things and studied in the same way as the subject matter of the natural sciences.
5. Interpretivism focuses on discovering the meanings that direct action. Interpretivists emphasise meaning, subjectivity and validity.
6. Ethnography and methods such as participant observation and in-depth, unstructured interviews are favoured for discovering meanings and generating rich, deep and more valid data.
7. Weber advocated verstehen, which involves developing an empathetic understanding of the meanings that direct individuals' actions. He emphasised human agency and saw structures as created by individuals' actions.
8. In practice, sociologists often mix methods or use methodological pluralism in a single project.
9. Triangulation provides a way of checking the validity of research findings.

# Unit 3.2.3 Sociology, the natural sciences and values

Natural sciences such as physics and chemistry often enjoy high status as superior forms of knowledge. Sociology is sometimes referred to as a social science. Can it be seen as a scientific discipline? For many years, sociologists have been debating whether sociology is a science, could be a science or should be a science. Answers to these questions depend on a number of factors, including how science is defined and how human beings and society are viewed. This unit explores the question of whether sociology can and should be based on the natural sciences. It also examines debates about the role of values in sociological research. Is value freedom possible? If so, is it necessary or desirable?

## Positivism and natural science methodology

As discussed in Unit 3.2.2, the early positivists saw sociology as a 'positive science of society'. They argued that natural science methodology was appropriate for the study of human behaviour. Its use would reveal the 'invariable laws' that governed society. Data consist of observable facts which could be directly measured and quantified. The research process would be objective – free from the researcher's values.

Positivism aims to discover the cause and effect relationships that are seen as underlying human behaviour. Statistical techniques are applied to numerical data in order to identify and measure possible cause and effect relationships. A hypothesis or prediction is developed. A hypothesis translates the theory into a form that can be tested. Observation and measurement are then used either to accept or reject the hypothesis. This, in turn, can result in a confirmation, modification or rejection of the theory.

This process is known as a **deductive approach**. It is sometimes described as a 'top-down' approach, as it starts at the top from a theory and moves downwards, as shown in Figure 3.2.1.

Today, few quantitative researchers would call themselves positivists. This is partly because the term 'positivist' is sometimes used in a

**Figure 3.2.1 A deductive approach.**

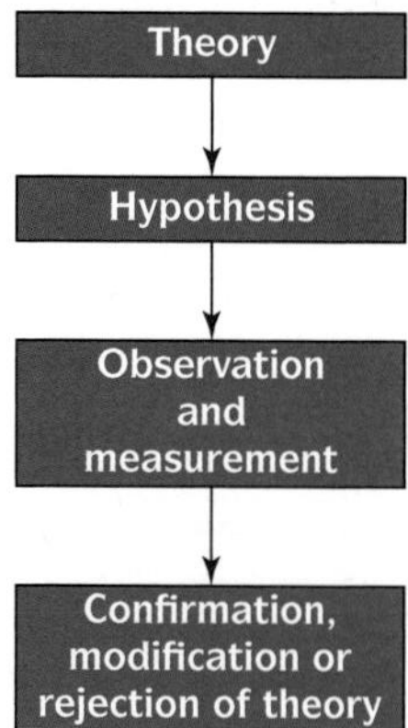


negative way. It is also partly because quantitative sociologists do not look for 'laws' underlying human behaviour, as few (if any) now believe that such laws exist. Nor do they necessarily start their research with a hypothesis. They do, however, attempt to generalise from quantitative data based on representative samples.

## Karl Popper and falsification

Like positivists, the philosopher of science Karl Popper (1902–94) adopted a deductive approach but in a rather different way. He started with a theory and used data to test that theory. However, instead of looking to confirm theories, Popper argued that scientists should look for evidence to disprove or falsify theories. This means that theories must be constructed in such a way that **falsification** is possible, that theories can be shown to be untrue.

Theories that survive falsification tests, however, are not necessarily true. They have simply not been falsified. The following example illustrates this point. 'All swans are white' is a scientific statement because it can be falsified. But, however many times it is confirmed by observation, it cannot be accepted as true because the very next swan might be black, red, blue or yellow. In this respect, there are no absolute truths in science. Scientific knowledge is provisional rather than certain or true for all time.

Popper saw no reason why the methodology of the natural sciences cannot be applied to the social sciences. Theories of human behaviour which are open to the possibility of falsification can be developed. However, not all sociological theories are open to falsification. Theories that cannot be falsified are non-scientific.

## Activity

*In Popper's view, we only need one observation of a black swan to falsify the idea that all swans are white.*

To what extent do you agree with Popper's view that all scientific knowledge is provisional?

## Grounded theory and induction

**Grounded theory**, as its name suggests, starts from 'concrete data' 'on the ground'. It then builds upwards to theory. This is known as an **inductive approach**. As shown in Figure 3.2.2, it moves in a 'bottom-up' rather than a 'top-down' direction. Starting with data, an inductive approach moves on to an analysis of the data looking for connections, patterns and relationships. From this, it develops a theory to explain these relationships.

**Figure 3.2.2 An inductive approach**

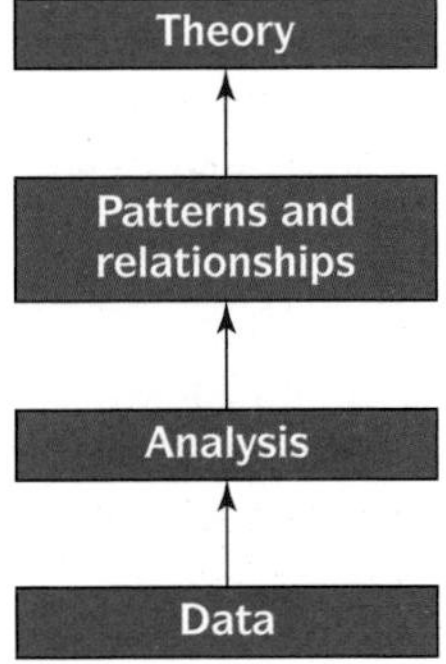


Inductive grounded theory does not start with a hypothesis to test. It tends to begin with a largely blank sheet without preconceptions. Durkheim (1895) argued that sociological research should be based on an inductive approach. He stated that researchers should start with a recognition of their 'complete ignorance' and that 'all preconceptions have to be eradicated'.

## Activity

Identify two differences between an inductive and a deductive approach.

Today, participant observation and in-depth qualitative interviews are the main methods used in grounded theory. Participant observers often begin their research by looking and listening with no fixed ideas about what they might find and no hypotheses to test. Their observations lead to the discovery of patterns and relationships from which theories are developed. This was the starting point for Venkatesh's (2009) participant observation study of the Black Kings, an African-American gang in Chicago (see Unit 3.1.3). In his words, '[I had] no experience whatsoever in an urban ghetto...[I was] an outsider looking at life from the inside.'

In practice, many researchers combine inductive and deductive approaches. For example, Durkheim began his research on suicide with an inductive approach. He examined and compared official statistics on suicide from 11 European countries (see Unit 3.2.2). He found patterns in the statistics, from which he moved towards theories which may have explained them. Then he tested these theories by using a deductive approach (Swedberg, 2011).

## Thomas Kuhn – normal science

For Durkheim, science consists of accumulating evidence and developing theories from that evidence. For Popper, science consists of creating testable theories and attempting to falsify them. For Thomas Kuhn, **normal science** – the vast majority of work which is called science – differs from both these views. Kuhn (1962) argued that the way science has developed bears little relationship to conventional views of the scientific method.

### Paradigms

According to Kuhn, most of the time scientists are busily preoccupied with 'normal science'. Normal science operates within a **paradigm**. A paradigm is a framework of concepts and theories which states how the natural world operates. It identifies appropriate methods for studying that world and specifies what questions to ask and how to answer them. A paradigm is shared by members of the scientific community. It shapes the way they see the world that they study.

Normal science operates within the confines of a paradigm – developing and refining it but not challenging it. For example, until the 16th century Western astronomy was based on the theory of terracentricity – the idea that planets and the sun move around the earth. It is perfectly possible to confirm this idea with observations and measurements. It is also possible to ignore or explain away contradictory evidence that might challenge it. Scientists are so committed to the existing paradigm that they operate within it rather than attempting to falsify it.

### Scientific revolutions

Kuhn rejects the conventional view that sees science as a progressive accumulation of knowledge based on the testing and proving or disproving of hypotheses. Change does occur, but only when one paradigm is replaced by another. Kuhn calls this process a **scientific revolution**. It is sudden and revolutionary, because a whole way of thinking about the world is swept away within a relatively short period of time. An example is the replacement of Newton's paradigm in physics with Einstein's. Once a new paradigm is established, normal science resumes and any real change has to wait until the next scientific revolution or breakthrough.

Scientific revolutions occur when evidence accumulates that cannot be explained in terms of the existing paradigm. This evidence builds to the point where it cannot be ignored or dismissed as the result of incorrect observation and measurement.

### Sociology and paradigms

In terms of Kuhn's view of science, it has been argued that sociology is in a pre-paradigmatic and therefore pre-scientific situation. There is a range of competing sociological perspectives but scant indication that this variety will develop into a single paradigm that would be acceptable to the sociological community.

However, Kuhn's view of paradigms and scientific revolutions has been criticised as a distortion of the history of science. For example, Imre Lakatos (1970) rejects the view that normal science is dominated by a single paradigm. Instead, he sees the development of science as a history of constantly competing paradigms. In terms of Lakatos' view, this does not disqualify sociology from being a science. In fact, sociology's history of competing perspectives largely accords with his view of the history of science.

## The realist approach to science

The **realist view** of science, while accepting that there are basic differences between the social and natural worlds, maintains that a social science is possible. It argues that events in both the social and natural worlds are produced by underlying structures and mechanisms. According to Roy Bhaskar, the essential task of realism is to uncover and explain these structures and mechanisms (Bhaskar, 1978).

### Open and closed systems

Andrew Sayer (1992) distinguishes between open and closed systems as arenas of study. The laboratory is the prime example of a **closed system**. Sciences such as physics and chemistry have the advantage of being able to create closed systems in which conditions can be fixed and variables controlled. This allows them to reveal 'more clearly the operation of mechanisms' (Sayer, 1992).

However, a large body of scientific research takes place within **open systems** where it is not possible to control variables. Meteorology is an example of a natural science where closed systems are rare. As a result, it is unable to predict the weather with any degree of accuracy, as weather forecasts indicate. However, it is able to offer an explanation of the weather after the event in terms of underlying mechanisms.

One of the most famous non-predictive explanations is the theory of evolution. This specifies mechanisms such as natural selection and mutation which are seen to underlie the evolutionary process. However, because evolution takes place within an open system, it is not possible to predict its future.

Human behaviour takes place in open systems. As a result, it is not possible to predict its course with any degree of accuracy. There is no way of controlling all the variables that affect human action. However, from a realist viewpoint, this does not rule out a social science. It is still possible to explain human behaviour in terms of underlying structures and mechanisms, just as meteorologists, geologists and evolutionary biologists explain behaviour in the natural world.

### Realism, sociology and science

From a realist viewpoint, events in both the natural and social worlds are produced by structures and mechanisms. Given this, social science is based on the same principles as natural science. Both are concerned with the identification and explanation of structures and mechanisms. In this respect, the social scientist's job is the same as the natural scientist's. So just as an evolutionary biologist identifies mechanisms such as natural selection to account for biological change, so a sociologist identifies mechanisms such as the class struggle to account for social change.

## Interpretivism and natural science methodology

Interpretivism starts from the view that the subject matter of the natural and social sciences is fundamentally different. The natural scientist investigates the behaviour of matter. Matter is inanimate and does not have agency, so it reacts in predictable ways to external stimuli. Human beings act and interact rather than react. They have agency and their actions and interactions are directed by meaning. Any understanding of human action must, therefore, involve an understanding of these meanings. For many researchers, this necessitates employing methods that are very different from those used in the natural sciences.

The sociologist's job is to discover meanings. This involves observation and interpretation. Qualitative methods, in particular participant observation and in-depth interviews, are seen as the main ways of discovering meanings. The research process is viewed as an art rather than a science.

Interpretivists accept that objectivity is not possible. The discovery of meanings cannot be value free. It is inevitably affected by the researcher, who becomes personally involved and immersed in their research.

There are many views of science and scientific methods. As a result, there are many views about the relationship between sociology and science, and about the appropriateness of applying the assumptions and methods of the natural sciences to the study of human behaviour.

### Activity

*Some feminists see Western science as dominated by privileged White men.*

1. Which research method would you use to investigate whether Western science is dominated by White men from privileged backgrounds?
2. Evaluate the usefulness of your chosen method to investigate this particular topic.

## The role of values in sociological research

The founders of sociology saw the subject as an objective science of society. Objectivity involves value freedom, impartiality and lack of bias. It means that the research process and findings are not influenced by the researcher's values, their moral, political or religious beliefs, their gender, ethnicity, social class, nationality, sexual orientation, their world view or by their personality. **Subjectivity** is the opposite of objectivity. It refers to a personal viewpoint, based on a particular individual's values and beliefs.

Until the mid-1950s, many sociologists believed that an objective, value-free sociology was possible and desirable. Since then, growing numbers have questioned this view. The American sociologist Alvin W. Gouldner (1975) stated that 'a value-free sociology is a myth'; that it is 'absurd' to claim that it is possible. He believes that his political views led him to condemn the system of social inequality which generates poverty and powerlessness. Gouldner argues that this belief will inevitably influence his choice of research project, the research process, his findings and his conclusions.

The American sociologist Howard S. Becker (1970) shares this view. He states that it is impossible to conduct research and produce findings that are 'uncontaminated by personal and political sympathies'. He argues that 'There is no position from which sociological research can be done that is not biased in one way or another.' Becker sees society as divided into the powerful and the powerless. He believes that 'we cannot avoid taking sides' and he sides with powerless 'underdogs'.

## Activity

*'We cannot avoid taking sides.'*

1. How does this picture reflect Becker's views?
2. Do you have any values that could influence the way you conduct research? Do you think people are necessarily aware of the values they hold? Explain your reasoning.

Does the view that a value-free sociology is impossible mean that sociologists should no longer be concerned about objectivity? Many sociologists see the pursuit of objectivity as essential. Becker puts it this way: 'Our problem is to make sure that, whatever point of view we take, our research meets the standards of good scientific work, that our unavoidable sympathies do not render our results invalid.'

What does this mean in practice? According to Becker, it means 'we must not misuse the tools and techniques of our discipline'. It means that sociologists should avoid asking leading questions and advertising their sympathies to research participants or encouraging them to give a particular response. Sociologists should not reject findings which go against their sympathies. Becker argues that sociologists should be as objective as possible, guard against their 'personal and political commitments' and do their best to 'avoid the distortion' they might bring to the findings.

Today, most sociologists recognise that complete objectivity is impossible. But this does not mean giving up on objectivity. Clifford Geertz (1973) makes the following case for the pursuit of objectivity: 'I have never been impressed by the argument that, as complete objectivity is impossible… one might as well let one's sentiments run loose… [That] is like saying that as a perfectly aseptic [germ-free] environment is impossible, one might as well conduct surgery in a sewer.'

## Activity

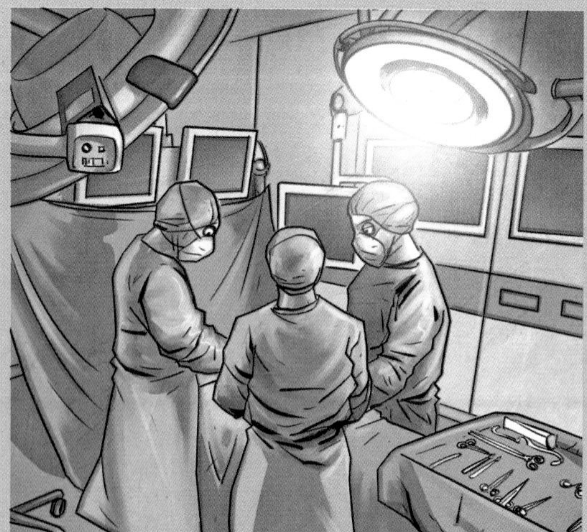

*Geertz argued that complete objectivity may be impossible but sociologists cannot let their beliefs and views run loose.*

1. How do these pictures reflect the arguments of Becker and Geertz?
2. To what extent do you agree with their arguments?

## A postmodernist view of objectivity and research

Most sociologists aim to be objective, to present the social world of those they are studying as it really is, to give us the 'facts'. Many sociologists accept that complete objectivity is an unattainable ideal. However, they do their best to get there and believe that their research reports are a lot better than the views of other people.

From a postmodernist view, objectivity is a myth. Research findings are constructions that are designed to persuade, to give the impression of rational, analytical thinking and to convince the reader that the researcher's view is 'the truth'. Often, the persuasion works. Sociologists are a bit like conjurers. They deceive, they play tricks, they create illusions. For example, they skilfully present an illusion of objectivity where none exists.

This view is an extreme version of **relativism**, the idea that all knowledge is relative to time, place, culture and the individual. According to this view, there is no such thing as objective knowledge, because everything is seen through the lens of our values and experience, the time we live in and our culture. Sociological research is not, and cannot be, objective.

Postmodernism rejects the idea that it is possible to produce valid knowledge. Instead, many postmodernists argue that all knowledge (including that produced within sociology and the natural sciences) is relative and uncertain rather than absolute. There are many versions of reality, none of which is superior to any of the others. A sociologist's account of religion or education, for example, is no better than anyone else's.

Postmodernists see knowledge as a product rather than as absolute truth. They use the idea of narratives (or stories) rather than truths. Different people have different backgrounds and, as a result, they will have different narratives. Rather than search for the truth, postmodernism compares these narratives.

Postmodernists argue that **meta-narratives** or grand theories (such as functionalism, feminism or Marxism or world religions including Islam, Judaism and Christianity) that claim to have discovered the truth are misleading. They reject all meta-narratives that claim to provide definitive, authoritative or complete guides to the truth. Jean-François Lyotard (1984) argued that people no longer have faith in meta-narratives or big, all-embracing theories about how the world works. They are increasingly sceptical about the claim that any set of beliefs, including scientific and religious beliefs, can provide a way of understanding and resolving the problems faced by humanity.

## Feminist politics and methodology

Some feminists argue that the 'women's struggle' against patriarchal oppression is inseparable from **feminist methodology**. The term 'malestream' sociology refers to the male bias built into the assumptions of mainstream sociological approaches such as functionalism. Many feminists argue that malestream sociology is so saturated with assumptions of male dominance that a feminist alternative is required. Maria Mies (1993) provides an example of this approach. She argues that the idea of so-called value-free research has to be replaced by conscious partiality. In practice, this means that feminist researchers cannot be neutral; they must positively identify with the women they study.

Mies argues that valid knowledge can only emerge from the struggles waged by the oppressed against their oppressors. The journey to truth involves just the opposite of value freedom. It requires a wholehearted commitment to women's liberation. In her view, feminist research must become an active part in the women's struggle to bring about change.

Feminists have been at the forefront of recent developments in methodology. For example, feminist researchers have emphasised the significance of **reflexivity** – that is, reflecting on and critically examining the process of research. (See Unit 3.3.2 for a discussion of reflexivity.) They have generated important debates about the ethical implications of research and power relationships within the research process. Many feminists challenge the notion of objectivity and argue that sociology is not, should not and cannot be value free. They emphasise the importance of capturing women's experiences and of expressing these experiences directly. They argue that emotion has an important part to play in the research process. As a result, they have opened up, questioned and presented alternatives to established research methodology.

## Research example: Researching subject choice and gender identity from a feminist perspective

In *Gender and the Politics of the Curriculum*, Sheila Riddell (1992) examines the relationship between subject choice and gender identity among 14-year-old students who were selecting their exam-level options. She focuses on the role of the family, the school and students' construction of masculinity and femininity. What part did these factors play in producing gender divisions in subject choice?

Riddell carried out case studies of two schools in England: Millbridge Upper School, where she had previously worked as a teacher; and Greenhill Upper School. Her research focused on the question of why working-class girls continue to make option choices that are likely to mean that they will experience disadvantages in the labour market in the future.

Riddell used a mixed-methods approach. She observed students interacting daily with their peers and teachers in the classroom. She also carried out detailed, in-depth, semi-structured interviews with students, parents and teachers in the two schools. This enabled her to cross-check her own observations with the students' accounts of events. She reflects that her status as a former teacher or non-teacher impacted on her interaction with students and teachers. As a former teacher at Millbridge, she was accepted by teachers but not by students. At Greenhill, her role as a non-teacher resulted in her being more accepted by students than teachers.

The qualitative data enabled Riddell to explore the participants' lived experiences and their subjective meanings. However, she also wanted to explore the connections between key variables and to compare different groups. Consequently, she administered questionnaires to parents and students. She also drew on school-based documentary sources. By mixing methods, she was able to use the qualitative and quantitative data in a complementary way to provide a more rounded and complete picture of the social world that she was investigating.

Riddell found that the option choice system (for example, the information and advice that the schools provided) generated clear differences based on gender and social class. Students tended to make traditional choices (with girls, for instance, likely to choose arts subjects and unlikely to choose physics) and these decisions were influenced by their gender identities. Once the students had made their subject choices, this further reinforced their gender identities. For their part, few teachers saw gender segregation in the curriculum as a problem.

Working-class female students were not passively subordinate in their attitudes and behaviour. They were hostile to gender discrimination and supported the idea of equality within paid work. However, many still chose subjects that would result in them taking low-paid jobs rather than becoming financially independent.

Riddell's choice of research methods was influenced by her political position as a feminist and by debates on feminist methodology. In broad terms, she tried to stick to the principle of reflexivity, making her theoretical and political position and its impact on the data collection process explicit. Drawing on the ideas of Mies (1983), Riddell states that feminist research insists on respect for research participants within a more democratic research relationship. Consequently, she provided the two schools with feedback on her findings and discussed the data with interested students and teachers, incorporating their ideas into the analysis and achieving a degree of accountability to the research participants.

### Questions

Drawing on this information, explain:

1. one strength of using a mixed-methods approach to investigate subject choice and gender identity
2. two features of a feminist methodology
3. one advantage and one disadvantage of a feminist approach to sociological research.

## Key terms

**Deductive approach** Starting with a theory and using evidence to test that theory.

**Falsification** Looking for evidence to disprove a theory.

**Grounded theory** Starting from 'concrete data' and building upwards to theory.

**Inductive approach** Starting with evidence and developing a theory from that evidence.

**Normal science** Science which operates within an established paradigm.

**Paradigm** A framework of concepts and theories which states how the natural world operates.

**Scientific revolution** The overthrow of an established paradigm by a new paradigm.

**Realist view** An approach which assumes that events in both the natural and social worlds are produced by underlying structures and mechanisms.

**Closed system** A system in which all the variables can be controlled.

**Open system** A system in which it is impossible to control all the variables.

**Subjectivity** A personal view based on an individual's values and beliefs.

**Relativism** The idea that all knowledge is relative to time, place, culture and the individual.

**Meta-narratives** Grand stories which claim to explain things.

**Feminist methodology** A methodology designed to reflect feminist ideals and values.

**Reflexivity** In the context of research, reflecting on yourself, looking back at your research, and examining how your values and background might have influenced your findings.

## Summary

1. The early positivists saw sociology as a 'positive science of society'.
2. According to Popper, natural science methodology could be applied to explain human behaviour. However, he argued that not all sociological theories are 'scientific', because they cannot be falsified.
3. According to Kuhn, 'normal science' operates within a paradigm. A scientific revolution occurs when the existing paradigm is overthrown by a new paradigm.
4. Sociology has a range of competing perspectives rather than a single paradigm. In terms of Kuhn's view of science, it is in a pre-paradigmatic and, therefore, pre-scientific situation.
5. From a realist viewpoint, events in both the social and natural worlds are produced by underlying structures and mechanisms. In view of this, there is no reason why sociology cannot be a science.
6. Human society is an open system. So is the world that sciences, such as meteorology and geology, study. In this respect, there is no reason why sociology cannot be a science.
7. In view of the differences between the natural and social worlds, between inanimate objects and human beings, interpretivists argue that natural science methodology is inappropriate for the study of society.
8. Most, if not all, sociologists now recognise that complete objectivity and value freedom are impossible, but many see objectivity as an important aim for sociological research. However, postmodernism sees objectivity as a myth.
9. Some feminists argue that feminist politics and methodology are inseparable and that true knowledge can only emerge from the struggle between the oppressed and their oppressors.

# END-OF-PART QUESTIONS

| 0 | 1 | Describe two features of the interpretivist approach to sociological research. **[4 marks]**

| 0 | 2 | Explain one strength and one limitation of the positivist approach to sociological research. **[6 marks]**

| 0 | 3 | 'Sociology should be based on the methods and procedures of the natural sciences.' Using sociological material, give one argument against this view. **[6 marks]**

# PART 3 RESEARCH ISSUES

## Contents

Unit 3.3.1 Practical, ethical and theoretical influences on sociological research 132
Unit 3.3.2 Sources of bias and assessing the value of different methods 136

This chapter has examined some of the theoretical and ethical influences on sociological research. This part focuses on these and other issues that sociologists have to consider when planning and conducting their research. How might feminist or Marxist perspectives influence sociologists' choice of topic? How might ethical issues affect the way you conduct your research? How do practical issues such as your budget affect your choice of method? This part also explores the issue of bias in research findings. What are the possible sources of bias? How might your findings be biased by your actions and the choices you make? Finally, it provides a summary of the criteria that sociologists use when assessing the value of different research methods. Why are validity, reliability and representativeness important criteria?

# Unit 3.3.1 Practical, ethical and theoretical influences on sociological research

This unit looks at some of the practical, ethical and theoretical factors that influence sociological research. How do these different factors affect a sociologist's choice of topic? What impact do they have on the choice of research methods? How do they inform the conduct of the research? The unit addresses these and other questions.

## Practical influences on sociological research

The practical influences on research include accessibility, money, time, and the nature of the topic and research questions.

### Access to and availability of data

It does not make sense to choose a research topic if there is little chance of generating data about it. Ease of access to people and research sites varies. Getting access to public places is relatively easy. People can usually be observed without too much trouble in streets, shopping malls, clubs, museums, art galleries and music festivals.

However, permission is needed from **gatekeepers** to research in sites such as schools, hospitals and prisons (or jails). It can be difficult to gain access to, and conduct research with, groups such as criminal gangs or young children in schools. Similarly, gatekeepers are unlikely to allow access to a country's secret service organisations for research purposes.

#### Activity

Why do you think some people might not want to participate in sociological research on families?

### Interests of the researcher

Researchers sometimes choose a research topic because it reflects their hobbies and interests. For example, they might like a particular type of music such as rap and examine whether it reflects the concerns of young African Americans.

#### Activity

1. Think about your interests or hobbies. Make a note of three possible research questions arising from your interests.
2. Which research method would you use to investigate your research questions?
3. Explain why you would use this particular research method in your investigation.

### Funding

Choosing a research topic is influenced by cost and funding issues. Most research undertaken by sociologists requires funding. Research grants may be available from various sources, including charitable foundations, government and business organisations.

Each funding body has its own priorities. For example, industrial organisations tend to fund projects dealing with their particular concerns, such as solutions to workplace stress. Choice of topic is sometimes shaped by the priorities of the funding body. When making competitive applications for funding, sociologists must take funding bodies' priorities into account if they are to be successful.

Financial considerations also influence choice of methods. Research is expensive and the costs of travel, stationery and transcribing interviews, for example, must be covered. Some methods are more expensive than others, so sociologists must choose methods that match their budget. For example, if they were doing research into equality in the workplace, their budget might not cover lengthy unstructured interviews but it might be enough for group interviews or a self-completion questionnaire. Funding also affects the number of interviews that can be conducted.

### Time

Some methods are more time consuming and labour intensive than others. For example, participant observation sometimes takes more than a year. A researcher's time is limited and, given this, they might decide to conduct interviews rather than a lengthy participant observation study.

### The topic and research questions

The topic and research questions influence the choice of methods. For example, a researcher studying the experience of becoming a parent for the first time is more likely to use qualitative methods such as unstructured interviews rather than standardised questionnaires to capture participants' subjective experiences and meanings.

### The people being studied

Some methods are less suitable than others for studying certain groups. For example, self-completion questionnaires are unsuitable for people with literacy problems or for young children. Asking teenage gang members to participate in interviews or complete questionnaires is unlikely to produce the required information. However, joining in their activities, gaining their trust and observing their behaviour can generate valuable data.

### Characteristics of the researcher

Researchers have a number of characteristics such as age, gender, ethnicity and class which must be considered when selecting methods. An older participant observer, for example, may find it more difficult to be accepted by members of a teenage gang than a younger researcher.

## Ethical influences on sociological research

Today, professional bodies and funding bodies have ethical guidelines that cover the right and wrong ways to conduct research. For example, people should be made aware that they are participating in research, be able to decide whether to take part, and be protected from physical and psychological harm. These guidelines apply to all stages of the research process, including choice of topic and methods, and the conduct of the research. They also relate to any publications arising from the research. In practice, ethical issues may arise during the course of the fieldwork and the sociologist must be prepared to deal with them. (See Unit 3.1.5 for a full discussion of research ethics.)

## Theoretical influences on sociological research

A sociologist's theoretical position can influence their choice of research topic. Every theoretical position sees certain aspects of society as particularly important. For example, Marxism sees the class system as the foundation of capitalist society. As a result, Marxists tend to focus on topics such as class inequality, class conflict and class identity.

## Then and now: Becky Francis, *Boys, Girls and Achievement* (2000)

In *Boys, Girls and Achievement*, Becky Francis (2000) explored the ways in which students aged 14 to 16 years construct gender in the classroom. She used a combination of research methods including classroom observation and semi-structured interviews with individual students in three schools in London, England. She used classroom observation so that she could see gendered interaction and student behaviour first-hand. She followed this up with interviews to ask the participants about their views on, and interpretations of, this interaction. (See Unit 5.7.4 for a summary of Becky Francis's findings.) In the following account, she reflects on her study and raises some key questions about research ethics.

'It is interesting to reflect back on my study today. Since that time I have continued with mixed-methods research, because gathering data in different ways and from different perspectives sheds so much more light on an issue than just a single methodological approach. Most recently, I have been involved with very large-scale longitudinal studies, including both qualitative and quantitative research. But each time I embark on an educational research project that doesn't involve classroom observation, I find that it misses the richness and directness that direct observation provides.

There are of course issues of power and ethics involved with observation that it is important to consider – and to try to address. In this, I think Sociological researchers are more sensitive than other scientists (including social scientists). For example, in different branches of Psychology it is quite common not to reveal all the circumstances of the experiment in which subjects are asked to participate. This is often seen as legitimate in the interests of the pursuit of science. I think it is right that we balance such interests with attempts to ensure that the subjects of our research are not disempowered.

Working with young people in schools adds an additional ethical dimension – school relies on young people obeying adults, and of course they have no choice about attending school either! I have found that piloting research approaches and interview questions with young people can help to ensure sensitivity, enabling a change of question or even method if this seems more appropriate. (For example, at times I have changed from focus group to individual interviews if topics seem too personal; or from individual interviews to focus groups on topics where young people appear to appreciate "strength in numbers").

But it's the revelations within qualitative work with children that still trouble me. We researchers tell young people that their interviews are confidential. Yet sometimes children reveal awful things that need addressing: being smacked by a teacher, for example; or that they are being bullied. Each time something like this happens, it requires a judgement from the researcher. And how would you feel as an interviewer if your respondent says something racist or homophobic – do you just continue to listen, because your role is to accurately capture the respondent's views, rather than exercise a judgement or hierarchal power relationship? Or, does not intervening to challenge those views legitimate and perhaps even perpetuate them? These are dilemmas for all researchers, but especially for feminist researchers concerned to avoid disempowering respondents, while also contesting inequality.'

### Questions

1. Why does Becky Francis continue to use a mixed-methods approach?
2. How does she try to ensure sensitivity when researching young people in schools?
3. How do ethical considerations influence the way Becky Francis conducts research?
4. What concern does Becky Francis identify for feminist researchers?

Feminist sociologists tend to focus on gender issues – in particular, gender inequality. Some feminists prefer a qualitative approach to research because, for example, unstructured interviews can reduce the power relationships between researcher and participants. (See also the discussion of feminist methodology in Unit 3.2.3.)

## Activity

*Feminist researchers often want to avoid disempowering research participants and this has implications for their choice of methods and the conduct of their research.*

Give one argument for and one argument against the view that unstructured interviews reduce power imbalances between researchers and participants.

Theoretical issues also concern questions about the validity, reliability and generalisability of the data gathered during research. For example, studies of gangs are usually based on participant observation. This allows the researcher to build a strong rapport with participants and gather rich and detailed data. However, if gang members do not trust the participant observer or question their motives, for instance, this may reduce the data's validity.

### Positivism and interpretivism

According to some sociologists, positivist and interpretivist approaches are a key influence on the choice of data and the selection of methods (see Unit 3.2.2). Increasingly, however, sociologists mix quantitative and qualitative methods within one project. The choice of methods in mixed-methods approaches is likely to be determined by the research questions and practical factors rather than by issues related to positivism or interpretivism.

## Activity

1. Explain one factor that may influence the choice of methods in mixed-methods research.
2. 'Positivism and interpretivism favour completely different research methods.' Evaluate this view.
3. Assess the view that ethical considerations are the most important influence on sociological research.

## Activity

Here are three topics for research:

- the relationship between gender and choice of TV programmes
- the relationship between ethnicity and tastes in music
- the relationship between social class and diet.

1. Select one of these topics for research and say why you chose it.
2. Which factors will you need to consider when choosing a method for your research?
3. Which issues will you need to consider when conducting your research?

## Key term

**Gatekeeper** The person or group in a particular setting such as a school with responsibility for allowing (or otherwise) a researcher to undertake research in that site.

## Summary

1. Practical, ethical and theoretical factors influence sociological research.
2. Practical considerations – such as whether the data are available, whether the research sites

and participants are accessible, whether the funding is sufficient, and whether the topic fits the funding body's priorities – affect choice of research topic.

3. Practical issues – including whether funding and time are sufficient, and whether the method suits the people being studied – affect choice of methods.
4. Ethical considerations relate to the choice of topic and methods, and the conduct of research.
5. Choice of topic is linked to theoretical position when, for example, feminists focus on research linked to gender inequality.
6. Theoretical considerations include questions about the validity and reliability of different methods and types of data.
7. One view is that positivist and interpretivist approaches are linked to the choice of data and methods. In practice, however, researchers are likely to mix quantitative and qualitative methods in one study.

## Unit 3.3.2 Sources of bias and assessing the value of different methods

There are many potential sources of **bias** (errors or distortions in the data) in sociological research arising from the way that evidence is collected or interpreted. If bias is introduced into the research process, then this would raise questions about the validity and reliability of the findings and distort the conclusions. Many of the potential sources of bias have been touched upon in this chapter already. Findings may be biased by researchers' actions and values, and by their choices in funding, designing and conducting research. Bias can occur, for example, as a result of the way that a sample is selected. A sociologist's values, for instance, may lead them to side with a particular group and influence how they collect and analyse the data, and interpret the findings. This unit examines some of the sources of bias in research findings. It then looks at the criteria that sociologists use to assess the value of different research methods, including validity and reliability.

### Bias linked to research design and conduct

The choices that a sociologist makes in designing and conducting their research may lead to bias in the findings.

- Sociologists must choose one or more research methods, each of which is potentially subject to bias. For example, interviews are subject to interview bias and experiments are subject to the Hawthorne effect.
- If a sociologist chooses a non-random sampling technique, sampling bias may occur. With non-random sampling, some members of the population have less chance than others of being selected. In practice, researchers use their own judgement when selecting non-random samples. They may be more likely to select some members of the population (for example, people like themselves) than others. In these cases, the sample will not be representative of the wider population, making generalisations difficult.
- Sampling bias is linked to non-response when people in the sample cannot be contacted or refuse to participate. Systematic bias in a study's findings may occur if, for instance, schools without strong equal opportunities policies decline to participate in a study on equality in education. It may also occur if particular groups, such as working-class men, refuse to participate in research.
- Sampling bias is also linked to the use of an inadequate sampling frame, for example, one that is incomplete or out of date.
- When gathering primary data, the researcher's presence could impact on the participants and the findings. This can be seen, for instance, with interviewer bias, experimenter bias and the observer effect.
- Bias can arise from the social desirability effect, which may invalidate the findings. With survey research, the way the survey is administered makes a difference. For example, self-completion questionnaires reduce the chances of socially desirable answers and eliminate interviewer bias.

- If the researcher asks leading questions in unstructured interviews, this may impact on participants' answers.
- Coding errors may be introduced when the researcher processes responses to questionnaire surveys.

### Activity

To what extent do questionnaires eliminate the social desirability effect?

## Researchers' values

Researchers are likely to study something they consider to be important. What they see as important is influenced by their values – their beliefs about right and wrong, good and bad. For example, a sociologist's belief in gender equality may influence how they view participants' responses during interviews. A sociologist's values may lead them to take sides (for example, siding with the underdog) and influence how they analyse interview data.

Many researchers argue that values affect the whole research process from the choice of topic to the collection and interpretation of data to the final conclusions. Karl Marx (1880–83) saw capitalism as an evil and exploitative system. Today, David Harvey (2010) shares Marx's vision and values. They direct his research and the questions he asks. Harvey's values are clear from his words, 'We need revolutionary politics to replace capitalism with a just and fair society.'

## Funding

Research in higher education is funded by several sources, including public bodies such as governments, and private bodies such as charities, industrial and commercial organisations.

If a public funding body identifies a skills shortage in quantitative methods, it might try to address this deficit by funding more studies based on quantitative methods. This might, in turn, have an impact on what researchers investigate, the types of data they collect and their research findings.

Public funding bodies often have research priorities such as housing or digital media. If a researcher applies for funding from one of these bodies, they will tailor their proposal to these priorities. Applying for funding is usually a highly competitive process. Research funds may be allocated according to criteria such as the impact of the work on people, its benefits to society and its success in bringing about change. This might pressurise sociologists to research topics and produce findings in which the impact is visible in the short term.

### Activity

1. Why is it important to know who funded a particular piece of research?
2. How might sociologists cross-check the validity of their research findings?

### Activity

*Marx's view of capitalist society.*

1. How does this picture illustrate Marx's political views, sympathies and values?
2. Some contemporary sociologists share Marx's views. How might this influence their research findings?

## Research examples: Reflexivity in action

In the 1920s, Robert Redfield (1930) studied the village of Tepoztlán in Mexico. He found a warm, generous and close-knit community. Oscar Lewis (1951) studied the same village 17 years later. He saw a community divided by envy, distrust and conflict. Redfield and Lewis reflected on themselves and their research to try and explain why their pictures of Tepoztlán were so different (Critchfield, 1978).

They agreed that the 17 years between their research projects could not account for the different pictures. According to Redfield, the main reasons were 'personal differences between the investigators' – 'differences in interests and values' which resulted in 'different questions asked' and different conclusions drawn. Redfield clearly liked the people of Tepoztlán. He found them friendly, generous and welcoming: 'I found doors were open to me.' Lewis did not appear to like them. He wrote that the kindness, generosity and joy described by Redfield 'appeared much less often than anger, hate, irritability, jealousy, fear and envy'.

The studies of Tepoztlán indicate the importance of reflexivity. Looking at themselves and looking back at their research, Redfield and Lewis recognised what a difference the personal characteristics of the researcher can make to the results of research.

Meghan Hollis (2014) used participant observation to study female and ethnic minority police officers in the USA. As part of her research, she observed a fight on a Saturday night outside a club in a New England city. The police officer she was with accidentally pepper sprayed her. Despite her discomfort, Hollis spent a further four hours on patrol with the officer. She had proved herself in a male-dominated occupation. As a result, she gained the trust, respect and cooperation of the police.

Looking back on her research, she notes that 'the officers were increasingly likely to talk to me and accept me as part of the group after this incident'. Reflexivity allowed her to assess the quality of the data she collected. Gaining acceptance from the police officers probably indicated to Hollis that her data were more likely to be valid.

*Meghan Hollis outside the club.*

### Questions

1. Explain one way in which a researcher's personal characteristics might influence their findings.
2. Why was it important for Meghan Hollis to 'prove herself'?
3. How might reflexivity help researchers to assess the validity of their data?

## Reflexivity

Sociologists are increasingly looking at themselves, at their values, beliefs, concerns, theoretical assumptions and their position in society, to see how these factors might influence their research. This process is known as reflexivity. It means reflecting on yourself, how you as a person might have affected the findings you produced and the conclusions you reached. Sociologists can assess their research by being reflexive and also provide lessons for others to apply to their own research.

## Assessing the value of different research methods

This chapter has examined different types of research method used by sociologists as well as different approaches to sociological research. But how do sociologists assess the value of the methods available to them? The short answer is that they use the concepts of validity, reliability, objectivity, representativeness and ethics. These concepts have been discussed already in this chapter and Table 3.3.1 provides a summary of them.

**Table 3.3.1 Criteria used to assess the value of a particular research method**

| | |
|---|---|
| **Validity** | *Validity concerns whether the method used to gather data actually measures what it is intended to measure. Does it generate data that give a true and accurate description of what they are supposed to describe?<br><br>*If participants open up in an unstructured interview and say what they really mean, for example, they are likely to provide rich and valid data. However, validity may be reduced by the social desirability effect. |
| **Reliability** | *Reliability concerns whether the method produces the same or consistent results the second time round. Official statistics on birth and death rates are more likely than others to be both reliable and valid. With questionnaires, different researchers can ask the same questions and are likely to get the same results from the same participants. However, reliable results may lack validity.<br><br>*With qualitative methods such as unstructured interviews and participant observation, it is difficult to check reliability, because the study cannot be replicated easily. |
| **Objectivity** | *Objectivity concerns whether the method produces impartial and unbiased data and whether the researcher's values intrude.<br><br>*Participant observation, for example, demands a high level of personal involvement. If this reduces objectivity and prevents an impartial view, it is likely to affect the validity of research observations. |
| **Representativeness** | *Representativeness concerns whether the sample is typical of the population that it is drawn from. It is possible to generalise from a representative sample. Questionnaires based on stratified random samples can form a basis for generalising.<br><br>*With participant observation, the numbers observed are too small to provide a representative sample. |
| **Ethics** | *Ethics concern whether the researcher conducted the research and used the methods in ways that comply with ethical guidelines on informed consent, confidentiality, privacy, deception and harm.<br><br>*A researcher would be seen as unethical if, for example, they used a particular method in a way that caused distress or involved deception. |

## Activity

Take each of these five criteria in turn and apply it to **one** of the studies discussed in this chapter.

## Key term

**Bias** Error or distortion in the data arising from the way evidence is collected or interpreted.

## Summary

1. Findings may be biased by the choices a sociologist makes in funding, designing and conducting the research.
2. Findings from all research methods may be subject to bias. Distortion may arise, for example, because of interview bias or the Hawthorne effect.
3. Sampling bias is linked to non-random sampling.
4. The social desirability effect can impact on research findings.
5. Findings may be distorted by the sociologist's values if they affect the research process.
6. Funding providers' priorities may influence sociologists' decisions to research particular topics, the methods they use and the types of data they collect.
7. Reflexivity is increasingly seen as an important part of the research process. It provides researchers with an opportunity to assess possible sources of bias within their findings.
8. Sociologists use the concepts of validity, reliability, objectivity, representativeness and ethics to assess the value of the different research methods.

# END-OF-PART QUESTIONS

0 1 Describe two sources of bias in research findings. **[4 marks]**

0 2 Explain one strength and one limitation of using reliability to assess the value of questionnaires. **[6 marks]**

0 3 'Theoretical considerations are the most important influence on sociological research.'
Using sociological material, give one argument against this view. **[6 marks]**

# EXAM-STYLE PRACTICE QUESTIONS

0 1 Describe two types of sampling method. **[4 marks]**

0 2 **a.** Explain two reasons why laboratory experiments are rarely used in sociological research. **[8 marks]**

**b.** Explain one strength and one limitation of questionnaires. **[6 marks]**

0 3 'Qualitative research data lack validity.'

**a.** Explain this view. **[10 marks]**

**b.** Using sociological material, give one argument against this view. **[6 marks]**

0 4 Evaluate the use of structured interviews in sociological research. **[26 marks]**

0 5 Evaluate the view that sociological research should be value free. **[26 marks]**

# 4 THE FAMILY

## Chapter contents


| | | |
|---|---|---|
| Section A | Theories of the family and social change | 143 |
| Section B | Family roles and changing relationships | 177 |
| Exam-style practice questions | | 225 |


The problem with studying the family is that we all think we are experts – not surprisingly, given that most of us are born into families and socialised into family roles and responsibilities. For many of us, the family is the cornerstone of our social world, a place to which we can retreat and where we can take refuge from the stresses of the outside world. It is the place in which we are loved for who we are, rather than for what we are. Moreover, studying the family is important because it is often a primary source of love, nurturance, support, affection, commitment, responsibility, obligation, duty and sense of belonging, yet at the same time it can also be a site of significant conflict, tension and violence. Family life can be both positive and negative. It often provokes strong and contradictory feelings in most of us. This chapter, therefore, deals with sociological theories of the family that have contributed in some way to our understanding of family life in the 21st century. What all these theories tell us is that, although we all operate with a common-sense definition and understanding of what we mean by the 'family', once we examine sociological theories of families and family life, it soon becomes obvious that the way family life is organised is not so straightforward. There is both a huge cultural and global variation in how families are organised and how family life is lived. It is important to understand that there is no such thing as a 'right' or 'wrong' way to organise family life and that family groupings may differ according to cultural location.

# SECTION A
# THEORIES OF THE FAMILY AND SOCIAL CHANGE

## Contents


**Part 1 Perspectives on the role of the family 144**

**Part 2 Diversity and social change 157**


Three of the key concepts that you were introduced to in the introductory chapter are particularly relevant to your study of the family.

- First, *power, control and resistance*. The family has enormous power to shape children's understanding of the wider world, and to mould children and adolescents into the type of citizens and workers that are going to benefit society. It is, therefore, important to examine how the family shapes social action via the processes of socialisation and social control. Moreover, as we shall see during the course of this chapter, some sociologists genuinely believe that what is taught to children by parents is the product of consensus and ultimately beneficial to society in terms of bringing about order and stability. However, other sociologists are critical of what happens during family life. They argue that the cultural values passed down from parents to children are potentially damaging to society, because these values 'enslave' our minds and consequently we are unable to fully see or understand how society works in practice.
- Second, *social change and development*. The family, as we shall see, was an integral feature of the movement from traditional to modern industrial societies. But what role does it play in *social change* and *development* today? We will particularly examine the relationship between the family and globalisation. Some sociologists, particularly postmodernists, argue that the concept of 'family' should be abandoned because it has become too prescriptive. Instead, these sociologists argue that we should focus on the everyday components of people's personal lives that contribute to their overall family experience.
- Third, *socialisation, culture and identity*. As we saw in Chapter 2, the family is central to the reproduction, generation by generation, of both society and culture. The interaction between parents and children is organised around the socialisation of children into the central values and norms of society so that they grow up to be law-abiding citizens and willing workers. Our identity, too, as individuals and as members of a social group is formed within the family unit.

Section A is divided into two parts.

In Part 1, we seek to gain an overview of how different sociological perspectives view the relationship between family, society and the individual. Some are extremely positive about the contribution that the family has made towards society and social change, while other perspectives have been critical and even go as far as suggesting that the relationship between the family, society and the individual is unhealthy.

In Part 2, we look at how social change has produced diversity in family forms and family life. We consequently examine how changes in the nature of adult relationships, especially with regard to marriage, have impacted on family life, relationships and structure.

# PART 1 PERSPECTIVES ON THE ROLE OF THE FAMILY

## Contents


| | | |
|---|---|---|
| Unit 4.1.1 | Definitions | 144 |
| Unit 4.1.2 | Functionalist accounts of the family | 146 |
| Unit 4.1.3 | Marxism, the family and capitalism | 153 |


Functionalist theories of the family see the family as making a very positive contribution to society. For example, George Peter Murdock (1949) went as far as to argue that it is such an important institution that it is universal – meaning that it can be found in virtually every society in the world. Talcott Parsons (1902–79) argued that the multi-functional extended family was exceptionally well-suited for meeting the needs of agricultural pre-industrial societies but evolved and adapted to the needs of industrial society by becoming a smaller, more streamlined unit, shedding some of its functions and adopting more specialist functions better suited to modern demands. Not all functionalist sociologists agree with this 'loss of functions' argument, though. Finally, Marxist explanations of family life tend to question the functionalist view that family life is beneficial both for its members and for society. Marxists tend to argue that the family benefits a select few – especially those who benefit from capitalism, and men – rather than the many.

## Unit 4.1.1 Definitions

It is important that you have a clear understanding of some of the common concepts used in different theoretical perspectives on the family. For example, **kinship** refers to people who are biologically related by descent or who have attained the status of relatives via marriage, cohabitation, adoption or fostering. Kin normally enjoy legal rights such as those relating to the inheritance of property. Moreover, they may feel obliged to offer each other material and emotional support.

The most common family type experienced by the majority of people in modern industrial societies, especially among urban populations, is the '**nuclear family**'. Traditionally, this has been defined as a two-generational social group – two parents and one or more children – who share a common residence. Evidence suggests that the most common type of family found in pre-industrial societies or the rural districts of societies which are rapidly undergoing urbanisation such as China is the '**extended family**'. There are three types of extended family:

1. The vertical extended family, in which three generations of kin – grandparents, parents and their children – live under the same roof.
2. The horizontal extended family, in which brothers and their wives and children live under the same roof. These are mainly found in Sikh communities.
3. The attenuated extended family, in which extended kin live in close proximity to each other, and contact between them – which is shaped by a strong sense of duty and obligation – is frequent and based on offering each other mutual support.

### Activity

*An extended family.*

Construct a family tree that includes all your relatives or kin. Set it out so different-coloured arrows symbolise the strength of the relationship and/or the frequency with which you interact with them. For example, a dark-blue line might indicate kin you see every day because you live with them. A green line might indicate relatives you see fairly frequently. A red line might indicate kin you only ever see at special events such as funerals, weddings or religious ceremonies. Show the tree to your parents, and ask them to identify kin not included in your tree. Some people regard close friends – symbolic 'uncles' and 'aunts' – and pets as members of their families. If you do, feel free to add them.

Finally, the concept of '**household**' is central to an understanding of family. All families that share a common residence are households. However, there are also household set-ups that are not families. For example, a single person who lives alone, a couple of friends who share a rented apartment, students who share a house and elderly people who live in a retirement home are all examples of non-family households. In the USA in the 1960s and 1970s, some members of a youth counter-culture known as 'hippies' as well as members of religious sects such as the Moonies, set up types of households known as **communes**. Communes are self-sustaining collectives based on sharing property and responsibilities – for example, for raising children. In Israel, communes (known collectively as **kibbutzim** and based on socialist values such as economic cooperation and equality) are popular. In 2016, it was estimated that 150 000 people lived in 274 kibbutzim.

## Activity

Colin Turnbull was an anthropologist who specialised in studying primitive communities or tribes. Between 1964 and 1967, he lived among the Ik – a tribe of hunter-gatherers who spent most of the year moving around Northern Uganda in search of food. The Ik had a harsh life and were constantly on the verge of starvation. Turnbull noted that this struggle for survival had led to them rejecting basic human values such as love, kindness, sentiment or honesty. Instead, the Ik were motivated almost entirely by individual self-interest.

The Ik regarded anyone who could not take care of themselves as a useless burden and a hazard to the survival of the others. This included children, the sick and disabled and the elderly, who were often abandoned by parents and other relatives to die. Children were thrown out of the village at the age of 3 and formed themselves into gangs which raided crops, fought each other and generally competed for survival.

## Questions

1. What positive features of your experience of family life simply do not exist in Ik culture?
2. Identify three similarities between modern family life and Ik family life.
3. Why is it a sociological mistake to judge Ik culture negatively?

## Key terms

**Kinship** Relationship between people who are related to each other by blood, marriage or adoption.

**Nuclear family** A unit that comprises mother, father and children, natural or adopted.

**Extended family** A unit consisting of the nuclear family plus other kin who may live under the same roof or in close proximity so that contact is regular and frequent.

**Household** This includes all those who live under the same roof or occupy the same dwelling. These people need not be necessarily related.

**Commune** A type of cooperative household made up of mainly unrelated people who agree to share work, possessions and religious or social objectives.

**Kibbutz** A type of commune or household found in Israel (plural 'kibbutzim').

## Summary

1. Sociologists agree that there are two types of family: the nuclear unit, which is common in modern industrial societies, and the extended family, which is more common in pre-industrial societies.
2. Some people choose to live in households or non-family units with friends, fellow students, or in communes or kibbutzim with people who share their collectivist ideals.

# Unit 4.1.2 Functionalist accounts of the family

Functionalism is a structuralist or systems theory in that it believes that society and the way it is organised (that is, its social structure/system) is more important than the individuals who comprise it. Functionalism examines the social institutions (such as the economy, education, media, law, family, religion) that make up society. It sees these social institutions as moulding and shaping the individuals who belong to them. Functionalists often assume that if a social institution such as the family exists, then it must have a function or purpose – it must do something useful. As a result, the family is usually seen to perform functions which benefit both its members and society as a whole. In this unit, we will examine the functionalist idea that the nuclear family is so important to the maintenance of social order and stability that it is a universal institution; that is, it is found in every known human society. We will also examine the functionalist argument that the family, whether it is extended or nuclear, functions for the benefit of both society and the individuals who comprise it.

*The traditional nuclear family.*

## The universality of the family argument

The functionalist sociologist, Murdock (1949) claimed that the nuclear family is universal (that is, it is the most common type of family found in any society) and that it performs four basic functions:

- *Reproductive* – it provides new members of society, without which society would cease to exist.
- *Sexual regulation* – the idea that sex should be confined to marriage contributes to social order and stability because such **fidelity** sets the moral rules for sexual behaviour in general.
- *Economic* – parents take responsibility for the economic welfare of their children.
- *Educational* – parents socialise the next generation into **consensual** social values.

However, Murdock's view that the nuclear family is universal has been criticised because, although families do tend to exist in most societies, his argument fails to take account of the increasing diversity of modern family structures and relationships. For example, in many societies today, reproduction and sex are no longer exclusive to family and marriage. In some societies, households rather than families (for example, communes and kibbutzim) have successfully raised children. Finally, Murdock's idea of a family is an ideological construct in that it is conservative. He seems to suggest that marriage and heterosexuality are central to the concept of family and consequently excludes alternative set-ups involving single, gay or surrogate parents, as not 'proper' families.

## Talcott Parsons

Parsons (1965), an American sociologist, was the most important contributor to the functionalist theory of the family. His theory of the family examined how the social and economic change associated with industrialisation and modernisation shaped family structures and relationships.
He argued that most pre-industrial societies are composed of relatively small farming or hunter-gatherer communities. Land and other economic resources were commonly owned or rented by extended families. For example, it was not uncommon to live with and work alongside extended kin on the land, either tending herds of animals or raising crops. Parsons claimed that there was a functional 'fit' between extended families and the social or cultural requirements of pre-industrial societies in that such families performed a range of functions which was beneficial to both society and the kin that made up such families. In this sense, the pre-industrial family was a **multi-functional** unit. The extended family, therefore, functioned:

- To meet the basic needs of extended kin through the production of food, clothing and shelter. They would trade or barter with other family groups for those things they could not produce or make themselves. In times of poor harvest or famine, the extended family rallied around to provide a subsistence living.

- To educate children in whatever skills the family specialised in. These skills were not highly specialised and were probably limited to hunting, gathering, growing particular crops, soldiering and providing the community with basic services such as baking, brewing, metalwork, shoeing horses and so on. Most of these skills were shared and passed down through generations from parents to children. However, this socialisation rarely extended to literacy or numeracy. Specialised occupational roles which required these skills were often restricted to children from high-status families.
- To take responsibility for the health of its members in the absence of a system of universal healthcare. However, the high infant mortality rates and low life expectancy of the pre-industrial period suggest that this was probably a constant struggle.
- To take responsibility for the welfare of disabled and elderly members of the family. For example, the relatively few family members who did make it into old age would be cared for by extended kin, in exchange for services such as looking after very young children.
- Extended kin, in the absence of a criminal justice system, often pursued vendettas to seek revenge for perceived slights. If a family member was unlawfully killed, blood feuds between extended families could last for three or four generations. For example, the War of the Roses in England in the 15th century was a conflict between two extended families, as represented by the royal Houses of Lancaster and York.

## The decline of the extended family and the growth of the nuclear family

Parsons argued that extended families were very effective for the needs of pre-industrial society, but he claims that they were too unwieldy and impractical to continue in societies that experienced industrialisation and the **urbanisation** that inevitably followed the industrial revolution. Parsons claimed that the extended kinship network was generally unsuitable in meeting the needs of an economy based on manufacturing industry.

Consequently, Parsons argued that the extended family evolved into the smaller and more streamlined **isolated nuclear family** in order to function in a way that effectively met the needs of an industrial-capitalist society. He argued then that the industrial revolution brought about five fundamental social changes to the family.

1. The new industrial economy demanded a more **geographically mobile** workforce. The responsibilities and duties that underpinned extended families (for example, members of such families felt a strong sense of obligation to remain near to their extended kin and to defer to their elders) did not suit these modern economic demands. Members of extended families were consequently reluctant to move to the urban areas in which factories and textile mills were being built. Nuclear families, on the other hand, because they were smaller, were more geographically mobile than extended families. Parsons, therefore, argued that as industrialisation spread nuclear families broke away from their extended kin to move to the growing urban centres to take advantage of the jobs and wages offered by the new factories and textile mills. In the UK, in which the world's first industrial revolution occurred, this resulted in a mass migration from rural areas to cities. Most of this urbanisation occurred between 1700 and 1830, when the proportion of the UK population living in cities and towns increased from 15 per cent to 34 per cent.

   We can see similar trends in countries which have experienced rapid industrialisation during the past 20 years. For example, in 1982 China was still a mainly rural society and only one in five Chinese people lived in cities. However, the massive and rapid industrialisation and urbanisation that has taken place in China over the past 20 years now means that just over 50 per cent of China's population now live in cities. It is predicted that 75 per cent of the Chinese population will be living in cities by 2030.

2. Another social change brought about by industrialisation was the opportunity to improve oneself materially. This is known as social mobility. In pre-industrial societies and in extended families, social mobility and status was/is ascribed. For example, the head of the household to whom all other members of the family were expected to defer was usually the oldest male. However, Parsons claimed that **ascription** was not suitable as a means of allocating roles in an industrial society. This is because such societies needed to ensure

that the most skilled and talented occupied the most important occupational roles if they were to be economically successful.

Parsons claimed that industrial societies needed to be meritocratic in order make sure that the most skilled and talented are allocated to jobs in which they will be most effective.

3. Parsons believed that members of nuclear families were more independent as individuals and less prone to the sorts of social pressures from extended kin and community that might have made them less adventurous in their social ambitions and choice of jobs or location. Parsons argued that the **ascribed roles** that were part and parcel of the extended family were likely to come into conflict with the roles required by a competitive industrial-capitalist economic system in which jobs and status were allocated on the basis of ability and qualification rather than being passed down and/or inherited. For example, the social stability of a family and community may be undermined if junior members of an extended family wield more economic power than the traditional head of the household.

4. A key difference between rural extended families and urban nuclear families was that the latter had experienced a separation between home and workplace, as they had become wage-earners in the factory system. They were no longer in a position to grow or rear their own food, build their own homes or make their own clothing. Consequently, as industrialisation extended its influence over society, specialised agencies gradually took over many of the functions of the pre-industrial extended family. Parsons referred to this process as '**structural differentiation**' and argued that it was often accompanied by a social process that he called 'functional specialisation'. This meant that more effective specialist institutions evolved to produce the goods and services previously provided by extended families. Members of urban nuclear families, therefore, became dependent on outside agencies – businesses – which evolved to meet many of their needs. For example, processed canned and frozen food was mass produced in factories and sold in stores that eventually developed into supermarket chains. Other products which had traditionally been produced by extended families, such as clothing, furniture and even homes, were produced by businesses which specialised in these commodities. In this sense, Parsons saw the nuclear family as largely losing its most important economic function – that of production.

5. Industrialisation also encouraged the development of the modern bureaucratic state as society and the economy grew more formal and complex. For example, the development of a monetary system resulted in people entering contractual relationships in which they were expected to engage in official legal exchanges such as money for goods. Bureaucratic government increasingly took on the responsibility of regulating such relationships. The state also increasingly took over the functions of education, health, welfare and justice, which prior to industrialisation had largely been the responsibility of the extended family.

   Parsons suggested that this process of structural differentiation meant that the multi-functional family effectively disappeared and was replaced by the isolated nuclear family, which focused on performing two **basic and irreducible functions**: (a) the primary socialisation of children and (b) the **stabilisation of adult personalities**.

**Primary socialisation of children** Parsons believed that the family should bear the main responsibility for the socialisation of children into the core cultural values of industrial-capitalist societies, such as:

- achievement
- competition
- equality of opportunity
- respect for private property.

For a more detailed account of the functions of the family as an agent of primary socialisation and its effectiveness in helping bring about value consensus, conformity, social solidarity – the main foundation stones of social order – you should refer to Unit 2.2.2.

Parsons viewed the nuclear family as a 'personality factory' whose manufactured products were young workers and citizens committed to the rules, patterns of behaviour and belief systems that make positive involvement in economic life and good citizenship possible. In this sense, Parsons saw the family as a crucial bridge connecting the individual child/adult to wider society.

## Activity

What evidence would you use to challenge Parsons' idea that primary socialisation is successful in producing young citizens committed to the rules?

## Home and family

Commuting · Deadlines · Competition
Pace of life · Budgets · Money
Productivity · Stress · Overtime
Hard work · Promotion · Hiring and firing
Job insecurity

*The 'warm bath' theory.*

**Stabilisation of adult personality** Parsons argued that the second major specialised function of the family is to relieve the stresses of modern-day living for its adult members. He observes that modern-day workplaces are very hectic, competitive and stressful places.

Members of a nuclear family no longer have extended kin easily available for advice and guidance to help them cope with modern-day living. However, Parsons saw this as an opportunity for spouses and children in the nuclear family to positively reinforce their relationships.

Parsons claimed that the nuclear family could act as a 'warm bath' – he suggested that immersion in family life could relieve the pressures of work and contemporary society just as a warm bath soothes and relaxes the body. John Pullinger (2014) claims that Parsons viewed the nuclear family as a 'retreat', especially for the male breadwinner, 'from the competitive demands and formality of the workplace, so as to provide replenishment within a haven of emotional security. Moreover, it caters for the therapeutic needs of adults to act out childish residues – affective, childlike behaviour which would not be acceptable in the outside adult world but which nevertheless need release.

### Activity

*A father relaxes with his child after work.*

How might playing with children help to stabilise the adult personalities of parents?

This emotional support and security, and the opportunity to engage in play with children, acts as a safety valve that prevents stress from overwhelming adult family members. As a result, it both stabilises the adult personality by de-stressing the individual and strengthens social bonds within the family as well as stability in wider society.

### Activity

| Feature | Pre-industrial society | Modern industrial society |
|---|---|---|
| Family type | | |
| Family functions | | |
| Ascribed or achieved roles? | | |
| Relations with extended kin? | | |

### Question

Drawing on what you have read so far, fill in the table.

**Instrumental and expressive roles** Parsons particularly saw marriage as essential to the health, happiness and stability of adults in modern societies. Parsons therefore viewed the family as a positive and beneficial place for all its members – as 'home sweet home', as a 'haven in a heartless world' and a place in which people could be their natural selves.

Parsons argued that this new nuclear unit provided the husband and wife with very clear and distinct social roles. Parsons claimed that the male should be the '**instrumental leader**' – responsible for the economic welfare and living standards of the family group and the protection of other family members. He is the wage-earner and consequently the head of the household.

Parsons claimed that the female is best suited to being the '**expressive leader**' – this means that the mother and wife should be primarily responsible for the socialisation of children and particularly the emotional care and support of family members. Parsons argued that this sexual division of labour is 'natural', because it is based on biological differences. However, Parsons did see the relationship between husbands and wives as complementary, with each equally contributing to the maintenance of the family but in a qualitatively different way.

In conclusion, then, Parsons argued that extended families, with their emphasis on tradition, hindered progress and modernity. In contrast, he argued that the nuclear family unit was superior because it was more adaptable to the needs of modern industrial societies. Parsons believed that only the modern nuclear family could produce dutiful citizens and the achievement-orientated and geographically mobile workforce required to make modern industrial economies successful.

### Activity

If possible, interview your grandparents and/or great-grandparents about their experience of family life.

- Ask them how they met, what cultural expectations in their day governed their contact with one another before marriage and how their wedding was organised.
- Ask them what was expected by society about the role of men and women in marriage with regard to parenting, housework, decision-making, women taking on paid work and so on.
- Ask about their contact with (and the influence of) extended kin, especially parents, on how they managed their marriage and family life.
- Ask them what they think has changed for the better and what has changed for the worse.
- Think about how their recollections might support or challenge the sociological studies mentioned in this chapter.
- Finally, compare your own experience of family life to theirs.

## Evaluating the functionalist theory of the family

Functionalism was the first theory to point out that in almost all societies throughout the world we can see the two-generation nuclear family with adults of both sexes and dependent children. Furthermore, many state policy initiatives aimed at regulating family life, especially those in modern industrial societies, have their origin in functionalist theories of the family. However, the functionalist theory of the family has been criticised for several reasons:

1. Ronald Fletcher (1988) argued that Parsons was wrong to suggest that the nuclear family had undergone a '**loss of functions**'. Fletcher argued that the nuclear family continues to perform three unique and crucial functions that no other social institution can carry out in most of the societies in which it is found. These include: satisfying the long-term sexual and emotional needs of parents; raising children in a stable environment; and the provision of a home to which all family members return after work, school and so on. Moreover, Fletcher argued that the nuclear family continues to perform the functions that Parsons believes it lost to the state. He observed that most parents continue to take primary responsibility for providing their children with educational supports and daily healthcare. Moreover, even after children have left home to marry or have moved away to work, parents continue to provide welfare for their children and extended kin. Deborah Chambers (2012) agrees and observes that many nuclear families continue to 'opt in' to provide care or financial support to extended kin.

   Fletcher argued that Western governments never intended to replace the family and that the role of social policy is actually to supplement the functions of the family, for example, by providing social, economic and educational supports such as postnatal care, free healthcare from the cradle to the grave and compulsory education.

Fletcher accepted that the nuclear family has largely lost its economic function of production, although many family-based companies continue to be successful. However, Fletcher argued that the family functions as a major unit of economic **consumption**, because the modern nuclear family spends a great proportion of its income on family or home-orientated consumer goods, such as the family car, garden paraphernalia, the latest electrical appliances for the kitchen and leisure use, and toys. The consumption function of the family, therefore, motivates its members as workers to earn as much as possible, as well as motivating capitalist entrepreneurs and businesses to produce and market what families want. In other words, the nuclear family is essential to a successful economy.

2. Parsons failed to consider the impact of global migration on family life in the USA and other industrial nations. This migration has resulted in a diversity of family types existing alongside each other. The nuclear family is, therefore, no longer as dominant as it once was.
3. Parsons neglected agency and free will. Interactionist sociologists argue that Parsons paints a picture of children as 'empty vessels' being pumped full of culture by their parents. They claim that this is an over-deterministic and passive view of children which fails to acknowledge that in reality socialisation is a two-way interaction in which children have the power to modify their parents' behaviour – for example, by taking part in family decision-making with regard to consumer spending, television viewing, use of social media sites and so on.
4. Historians suggest that Parsons was far too simplistic in his interpretation of the impact of industrialisation on the family. They point out that the evidence suggests that industrialisation follows different historical patterns in different industrial societies. For example, until the 1980s, the Japanese experience of industrialisation stressed the importance of a job for life with the same company. Employees were encouraged to view the company and their workmates as part of a larger extended family and consequently duty and obligation were encouraged as important cultural values. As a result, Japanese extended kinship networks continue to exert a profound influence on their members and the isolated nuclear family failed to gain a significant foothold in Japanese culture.
5. Some sociologists and social historians claim that Parsons confused cause and effect. For example, Parsons hypothesised that industrialisation resulted in the decline of the extended family and its replacement with the nuclear family. However, this is not supported by the limited historical data that we have. Social historians now hypothesise that industrialisation was able to take off so quickly and effectively in some societies because nuclear families already existed in large numbers, so people could move quickly to those parts of the country where their skills were in demand.
6. Similarly, studies of urban areas undergoing industrialisation suggest that the need for the extended family was actually strengthened by migration to towns and cities. For example, extended kinship networks probably functioned as a mutual economic support system for migrants. It is very likely that migrants sought out extended kin when they arrived in an urban area and that such kin pooled their wages in order to share the high cost of rents and to help out kin who were sick, disabled and elderly. Moreover, in European countries such as the UK, social surveys indicate that the extended family continued to exist well into the late 20th century.
7. Parsons presented a very positive picture of relationships within the nuclear family, but evidence suggests that living in such a unit can sometimes be very dysfunctional or harmful to its members. As David Cheal (2002) notes, functional relationships can easily slip into damaging relationships, and love can often turn into hate in moments of intense emotion. He notes that 'we have to face the paradox that families are contexts of love and nurturance, but they are also contexts of violence and murder' (Cheal 2002). Feminists are critical of functionalists for ignoring the 'dark side of family life'. They point out that, in many societies, most recorded murders of women and children, assaults and abuse of children, sexual or otherwise, take place within the family unit. For example, the United Nations Commission on the Status of Women (UNCSW) estimated that of all women who were the victims of homicide globally in 2012, almost half were killed by intimate partners or family members, compared to less than 6 per cent of men killed in the same year.

The UNCSW also observed that 43 per cent of women in the 28 European Union member states have experienced some form of psychological violence by an intimate partner in their lifetime.

8. Finally, Parsons' theory of family has been criticised as '**ethnocentric**'. This means that Parsons assumed that his American experience of the nuclear family life was a universal experience. However, he failed to consider the fact that wealth or poverty may determine whether women stay at home to look after children or not. Religious and ethnic subcultural differences may mean that Parsons' version of the family is no longer relevant in societies that are multicultural.
9. Feminists are particularly critical of functionalism, which they describe as a patriarchal ideology that justifies sexism, misogyny and gender inequality in its insistence that family roles are somehow biological in origin, and that males and females are somehow more 'naturally' suited to being instrumental leaders and expressive leaders respectively. Feminists such as Cordelia Fine (2017) point out that there is absolutely no scientific evidence for such assertions. Moreover, such ideas seep into popular consciousness and undermine the aspirations of females, consequently limiting the number of positive female role models that are available to girls and young women. As Sally Ride, the first female commander of the Space Shuttle commented, 'you can't be what you can't see'.

## Activity

Evaluate the view that Parsons' ideas about the relationship between men and women in families are patriarchal.

## Activity

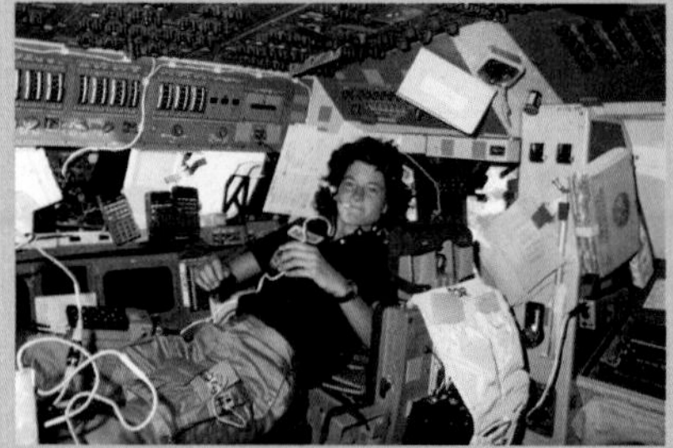

*Sally Ride in the flight deck of Space Shuttle* Challenger *STS-7 in June 1983.*

Why are female role models so important to the aspirations of girls and young women?

## Key terms

**Fidelity** Faithfulness, usually in a relationship.

**Consensual** All involved agree willingly.

**Multi-functional** Performing lots of functions, such as the pre-industrial family.

**Urbanisation** The process of people who had previously lived in the countryside moving to the towns and cities, usually to find work in factories, mills and so on.

**Isolated nuclear family** A family that is self-contained and which has little contact with extended kin.

**Geographical mobility** Refers to people and families physically moving across the country, usually in search of work or education.

**Ascription/ascribed role** A role assigned at birth over which an individual has little choice or say. For example, members of a royal family inherit a role. In patriarchal societies, females involuntarily occupy a subordinate role.

**Structural differentiation** The emergence of specialised agencies which gradually took over many of the functions of the pre-industrial extended family.

**Basic and irreducible functions** The two crucial functions performed by the nuclear family in modern capitalist societies: the primary socialisation of children, and the stabilisation of adult personalities.

**Stabilisation of adult personality** An irreducible function of the nuclear family according to Parsons, in which the male worker's immersion in his family supposedly relieves him of the pressures of work and contemporary society, just as a warm bath soothes and relaxes the body.

**Instrumental leader** The role of economic provider or breadwinner for the nuclear family. Parsons claimed that this is usually the role of the male.

**Expressive leader** The role of nurturer of children, primarily responsible for the primary socialisation of children, and emotional caretaker. According to Parsons, females have a 'natural' empathy for this role.

**Loss of functions** The functionalist idea that the multi-functional extended family of the pre-industrial era lost many of its functions after the industrial revolution.

**Consumption** Refers to the spending of money on goods and services. A successful economy needs to competitively market its goods and services in ways that attract consumers to spend their cash on them.

**Ethnocentric** Judging other cultures according to preconceptions originating in the standards and customs of one's own culture.

## Summary

1. The functionalist sociologist Talcott Parsons believed that there was a strong relationship between structural social change and changes in family life.
2. Parsons claimed that multi-functional extended families were the norm in pre-industrial societies because they functionally fitted the needs of that type of society.
3. Industrialisation was the catalyst of family change.
4. Parsons claimed that the nuclear family evolved out of the extended family, and became the universal norm in more industrialised societies because it met the functional needs of industrial society for a geographically and socially mobile workforce.
5. Parsons claimed that the nuclear family was functionally beneficial for both modern industrial societies and for the individuals that comprised it.
6. However, Parsons has been criticised for being ethnocentric and over-deterministic and for neglecting or ignoring the 'dark side of family life'.

# Unit 4.1.3 Marxism, the family and capitalism

Marxism and functionalism are both examples of structural theories (see Unit 2.2.1 on structuralism). They are mainly interested in how the family contributes to the overall running of society rather than how people experience family life on a daily basis. Like functionalists, then, Marxists are keen to find out what the overall purpose or function of the family is for society.

Marxists reject the functionalist view that society is based on value consensus and therefore operates for the benefit of all. Instead they argue that capitalist society is organised around conflict between social classes and exploitation rather than social order (as functionalists believe). This unit will examine the two main Marxist approaches to the family that originate with Engels and Zaretsky.

## Friedrich Engels: the family, the bourgeoise and private property

Engels speculated that the history of humanity could be divided into two main eras:

1. *The era of primitive communism* – Engels claimed that during the early stages of human evolution there was no private property and the family as we know it today did not exist. Human beings lived in 'promiscuous hordes' or tribes. There were very few rules limiting sexual relationships, and marriage as we know it today also did not exist. Children were brought up by the whole tribe rather than parents.
2. *The era of capitalism* – Engels claimed that the nuclear family based on monogamy (marriage between one man and one woman) only developed with the emergence of capitalism, which led to the accumulation of private property and wealth. Engels claimed that the monogamous nuclear family was adopted by capitalists because it provided the most efficient way of ensuring that wealth and private property was inherited by a person's direct descendants. If there is only one husband and one wife in a family, questions about the paternity of children or about which wife's children should inherit were unlikely to arise. Engels claimed that monogamous marriage, in particular, was useful to the capitalist class because it conferred legitimacy on children and, therefore, members of the bourgeoisie were able to ensure that their fortunes were inherited by their direct descendants.

### Evaluating Engels

- There is strong evidence that suggests that monogamous nuclear families have grown in popularity as capitalism has evolved although there is also evidence that nuclear families existed in large numbers pre-capitalism.
- Feminists point out that there is no historical evidence of an era of primitive communism. This is pure speculation on Engels' part.
- However, anthropologists (people who study primitive tribal societies) such as Kathleen Gough (1973) have supported Engels' idea that primitive human societies were characterised by promiscuous sexual relations because our nearest relatives – chimpanzees – live in promiscuous groups.

## Eli Zaretsky: The family as an ideological agency

Eli Zaretsky (1976), like most other Marxists, claims that the modern nuclear family is an ideological agency which operates as part of the superstructure of capitalist society to reproduce and legitimate the inequality and exploitation found in the economic infrastructure. Consequently, nuclear family life mainly benefits capitalism and the capitalist class at the expense of other members of society. This can be illustrated in four key ways:

1. Zaretsky saw the family as a crucial agent of socialisation. However, Zaretsky believed that the family socialised children into capitalist **ideology** in order to turn them into passive and **falsely conscious** workers, citizens and consumers who uncritically accept the inequality that is generated by the organisation of capitalist societies. Zaretsky argues that a working-class child's experience of socialisation usually involves learning obedience, conformity, showing respect for those in authority and so on. Marxists, therefore, suggest that the family is partially responsible for the ideological control of the working class and especially the suppression of ideas which might challenge the current organisation of the capitalist system.
2. Zaretsky is very critical of Parsons' 'stabilisation of adult personality' argument. In contrast, he argues that the role of the family is more sinister because its real function is to help workers manage their resentment of the capitalist workplace, which generally oppresses and exploits them. Zaretsky notes that the nuclear family dampens such feelings because the worker who has a family is unlikely to engage in actions which threaten their income and therefore their family's standard of living. Research by Huw Beynon (1984) found that companies such as Ford would only employ married men with families in the 1980s, because they were more reluctant than single men to take strike action, feeling that their main responsibility was to their wives and children rather than their fellow workers.

   Similarly, Fran Ansley (1972) argued that capitalism has stripped male workers of dignity, power and control at work. Surveys of factory workers suggest that many are bored by the tedious nature of their work. Many are alienated – meaning that they cannot identify with or bring themselves to care about the product they are producing. They feel powerless and consequently feel that their masculinity is being challenged. However, Ansley argues that this male frustration and **alienation** is often absorbed by the family and particularly the female partner. She argues that the powerlessness that men experience in the workplace leads to problems such as **domestic violence** and **child abuse**, as men attempt to assert power, control and authority in the home. Wives, therefore, act as safety valves for capitalism because these men are not directing their anger at the real cause of their problems – the nature and organisation of capitalism.
3. Some Marxists have claimed that the extended family was deliberately discouraged by the capitalist class. This is because the mutual support system on which the extended family depends encourages socialist ideas such as collectivism, altruism, equality of opportunity, egalitarianism and selflessness rather than capitalist values, which encourage competitiveness, individualism, greed and selfishness.
4. Zaretsky argued that the nuclear family is an essential component of capitalism because it is the major unit for the consumption of manufactured goods and services and therefore it is essential to the success and profitability of the capitalist system. Moreover, the pursuit of consumerism may have the added bonus for the capitalist class of distracting workers from the unjust organisation of capitalism. For example, Marxists argue that parents are encouraged to teach their children that the main route to happiness and status lies in consumerism and the acquisition of material possessions. Consequently, the inequalities in wealth and income produced by capitalism often go unchallenged by a generation fixated on the acquisition of the latest designer labels and gadgets.

   Similarly, the neo-Marxist Herbert Marcuse (1964) noted that the profitability of capitalism depends on the family spending money on '**false needs**'. These are consumer goods which are mainly bought to be conspicuously consumed; that is, their ownership is noticed by others because they are 'trendy' or high-status items. However, the logic of capitalism dictates that these items quickly become obsolete as they are replaced by improved technology or more fashionable items. Capitalist ideology transmitted by advertising and the mass media, and aimed at the family, ensures that family income continues to be spent on such items. This ensures that the capitalist class continues to make vast profits.

## Activity

*Shopping for the latest technology.*

What sort of consumer items could be described as 'false needs'? Do you, and your family or your friends, own any of these?

## Evaluating Marxist theories of the family

In terms of strengths, Marxist sociologists have questioned the notion that the nuclear family is always good for society and have drawn sociological attention to the possibility that powerful interests may be shaping family life. For example, there is little doubt that the nuclear family is deliberately targeted by advertisers as a **unit of consumption** and that the family is essential to the health of the capitalist economy.

However, Marxists such as Zaretsky tend to be over-deterministic in their view of human behaviour and consequently they fail to take account of agency and free will. Interactionists point out that Marxists rarely consider that some working-class parents may actually resist ruling-class ideology by teaching their children values and norms which are the product of working-class culture, therefore empowering their children with knowledge of capitalist inequality and exploitation. Another possibility is that working-class parents may be well aware of the pitfalls of capitalism, such as inequalities in wealth, but feel that the standard of living provided by capitalism is so comfortable that they are willing to dismiss inequality as a lesser evil.

Marxism also fails to consider how individuals interpret their family set-up and its relationship to other social institutions. Consequently, interactionists argue that Marxism may be guilty of ignoring the very real emotional and social satisfaction that people get from being members of a family. The Marxist tendency to write off such satisfaction as the product of capitalist ideology is both too simplistic and patronising.

Feminists make two very important criticisms of Marxism. First, they point out that the great weakness of Marxist theory is its economic reductionism; that is, Marxists see women's experience in the family solely as a reflection of class experience and fail to consider that non-economic factors, particularly patriarchy, misogyny, ethnicity and religious beliefs, can also shape women's experience of the family. Second, feminists argue that this Marxist account of the family is very dated and does not take account of recent global economic and educational changes which have transformed women's experience of family life and their attitudes towards it. Women in many countries have acquired a greater number of reproductive and legal rights, which mean that they, rather than their husband, choose when to have children or how many children they wish to have. Improved legal rights mean that they can now escape unhappy marriages.

## Activity

Interview a sample of females from different generations in order to see how female attitudes towards education, employment, family, children and equality with males have changed in the society in which you live. Do your data support the feminist case?

## Key terms

**Ideology** A set of ideas which most people believe to be true but which in fact are myths or misrepresentations. They are usually encouraged by powerful groups because such ideas tend to justify and legitimate the power and wealth of those groups.

**Falsely conscious** A way of thinking that prevents a person from perceiving the true nature of their social or economic situation.

**Alienation** A concept which Marxists in particular suggest is now becoming a common characteristic of how workers feel about their jobs. Alienation refers to the lack of satisfaction, identification and control that workers experience on a daily basis and the fact that they work merely for a wage.

**Domestic violence** Violence, usually committed by the male spouse on his female partner and/or his children.

**Child abuse** Physical maltreatment or sexual molestation of a child.

**False needs** According to Marxism, the logic of capitalism as expressed through advertising is to sell as many commodities to consumers as possible. This often involves 'persuading' consumers to indulge in false wants or needs, that is, to buy commodities that are not essential and not built to last.

**Unit of consumption** The family is the main unit of consumption in capitalist society because agents of capitalism such as advertisers and the media promote consumer items in such a way that they are specifically aimed at encouraging family members to buy them.

## Summary

1. Marxists claim that the nuclear family evolved in order to meet the needs of capitalist society rather than all sections of industrial society.
2. Marxists argue that nuclear families exist to socialise their members into false class consciousness, so that they conform to their expected roles as obedient citizens and passive workers, and do not challenge the present organisation of capitalist society that only benefits the ruling classes.

# END-OF-PART QUESTIONS

**0 1** Describe any two functions of the nuclear family. **[4 marks]**

**0 2** Explain two ways in which the nuclear family is supportive of the capitalist system according to Marxists. **[6 marks]**

**0 3** Explain two reasons why the isolated nuclear family is functional for modern industrial societies according to functionalist theory. **[8 marks]**

# PART 2 DIVERSITY AND SOCIAL CHANGE

## Contents


| | | |
|---|---|---|
| **Unit 4.2.1** | **Changing patterns of marriage and cohabitation** | **157** |
| **Unit 4.2.2** | **Marital breakdown** | **163** |
| **Unit 4.2.3** | **Family diversity** | **165** |
| **Unit 4.2.4** | **New Right perspectives on family diversity** | **169** |
| **Unit 4.2.5** | **Postmodernist perspectives on family diversity** | **171** |


Part 2 focuses on the concept of social change and how family structure and internal organisation has been transformed by changing patterns in marriage. The idea that marriage is in decline and is being replaced by cohabitation (living together and having children without being married) is explored and examined. Moreover, some sociologists are anxious that the nuclear family is under threat from the fact that many societies have experienced fairly high increases in divorce over the past 30 years. These trends in divorce have resulted in family diversity, as variations on the nuclear family – the single-parent family, the reconstituted family and the blended family – have significantly increased in number. This part particularly explores the idea that families in modern societies are increasingly diverse and that the nuclear family is no longer dominant. Some sociologists, notably Robert Chester (1985), argue that most people at some stage in their lives spend time in a nuclear family. A similar argument that originates in New Right thinking suggests that state policies have severely damaged the nuclear family by encouraging cohabitation, divorce and the legalisation of gay marriage, as well as encouraging married women with children to go out to work.

Finally, this part examines postmodern ideas about family, which argue that the concept of the 'family' is too rigid to describe the current state of family dynamics in modern societies.

# Unit 4.2.1 Changing patterns of marriage and cohabitation

Sociological studies of the family worldwide suggest that marriage is a universal institution that is practised by most societies, although the form that marriage takes and the functions it performs may differ. This unit will consider various forms of marriage as well as global trends in marriage and cohabitation.

## Marriage

Marriage may exist in several forms depending upon culture. Until fairly recently, Western societies promoted **monogamy**; that is, lifelong heterosexual marriage. The functionalist sociologist Murdock surveyed 1231 societies from around the world and observed that 186 practised legalised monogamy. This means that these societies had laws which only permitted marriage between one man and one woman at any one time. Consequently, **bigamy** – the act of being married to more than one person at the same time is illegal and therefore a punishable crime.

However, the nature of monogamy is undergoing some significant change in Western societies. For example, **serial monogamy** is probably now the norm – because of divorce and cohabitation, people in Western societies are likely to experience more than one long-term monogamous relationship over the course of their lifetime. Moreover, a number of Western societies have now legalised **same-sex** or gay **marriage**.

### Other types of marriage

In some societies, particularly in the Middle East and Africa, people are more likely to practise **polygamy** – marriage to more than one partner at the same time. There are essentially two types of polygamy. First, **polygyny** is the most common type. This is when a religion or culture allows a man to take more than one wife. In 1998, the University of Wisconsin found that 453 societies practised occasional polygyny, while in another 588 societies it was a common practice. For example, in 2012, the then President of South Africa, Jacob Zuma, married his sixth wife in a traditional KwaZulu ceremony in the presence of his other three wives (he had previously divorced one wife and a second committed suicide).

*Jacob Zuma and his sixth wife, Gloria Bongekile Ngema.*

Ndela Ntshangase (2017), an expert in Zulu studies at the University of KwaZulu-Natal, observes that the British colonial powers which ruled South Africa in the late 19th century attempted to stamp out polygyny in the Zulu nation, and to replace it with the Christian tradition of monogamy, by charging extra taxes for each additional wife and allocating land on a basis which did not provide sufficient space for polygamous families. However, he notes that polygyny is still a fact of life in rural Zulu communities in South Africa today, because it is the outcome of the Zulu cultural expectation that every family member should work for the betterment of the family. Young males are strongly encouraged during family socialisation to demonstrate adult responsibility by becoming a husband. A common way of achieving both the status of adult and of improving a family's status and income is to add extra members in the form of co-wives.

Second, '**polyandry**' is the term used when cultures allow a woman to take more than one husband. It is less common than polygyny, but Katherine Starkweather and Raymond Hames (2012) identified nearly 80 cultural groups that practise it. For example, in some parts of Tibet, India and China women are often married to four or five husbands at the same time.

## Same-sex marriage

Same-sex marriage refers to the marriage of a same-sex couple, whether they are gay men or lesbians. In 2018, same-sex marriage was recognised in law by 27 societies worldwide. A further three countries recognise such marriages if they are entered into in another country. However, there are 72 societies that have criminalised homosexuality and in which same-sex marriage and families are illegal. In some of these societies, homosexuality is punishable by death.

### Activity

Copy the table shown and complete it by adding two strengths and two weaknesses for each type of marriage. Consider strengths and weaknesses for both the individuals concerned and for society as a whole.

| Identify | strengths | weaknesses |
|---|---|---|
| **Monogamy** | 1.<br>2. | 1.<br>2. |
| **Polygyny** | 1.<br>2. | 1.<br>2. |
| **Polyandry** | 1.<br>2. | 1.<br>2. |

### Arranged marriages

Some societies practise **arranged marriage**, especially Middle Eastern and Asian societies in which the religions of Islam, Hinduism, Sikhism and Orthodox Judaism are the main source of cultural values and beliefs. It is important to note that such marriages do not involve parents forcing a child to marry against his or her will. Instead, an arranged marriage usually involves children and parents in mutual discussion about a proposed marital match. Children and parents may even jointly consult online sites that list potential wives and husbands, who, for example, share the same religious beliefs, caste and socio-economic status. No decision can usually be agreed unless both families, as well as the potential bride and groom, consent.

## Global trends in marriage

If we examine societies worldwide, we can make a number of general observations about trends in marriage.

- There is some evidence that in many societies worldwide the **marriage rate** (the number of marriages per 1000 people per year) has gone into significant decline. For example, in the UK in 1972, 480000 couples got married, compared with only 239020 couples in 2015. Mark Regnerus (2017) observes that, in 2000, 55 per cent of Americans aged between 25 and 34 were married but that in 2015 this figure had dropped to 40 per cent. According to the Ministry of Civil Affairs, China, which had seen an annual increase in marriage since 2000, is now experiencing a steep decline. For example, in 2016 new marriages fell by 6.7 per cent to 11.4 million, marking the third consecutive year of decline since 2013. Moreover, fewer Japanese couples got married in 2017 than at any time since 1945.
- The age at which both men and women are getting married is rising in many countries worldwide. For example, in the UK, the average age for a first marriage is 37.5 years for men and 35.1 years for women. In 1988, it was 30.9 years and 28.3 years respectively.

  Evidence from China also suggests that the average age at which people first get married is creeping up and that this is creating some cultural anxiety because in Chinese culture an individual was traditionally looked down upon if they were not married by the age of 25 years. Since 2007, single women over the age of 27 in China have been commonly known as '**leftover women**', or 'sheng nu' in Chinese. In contrast, the average age at which people get married in societies dominated by religions such as Islam is much younger. For example, three-quarters of Pakistani and Bangladeshi women are married by the age of 25.
- Women worldwide tend to marry at a younger age than men. This pattern reflects the fact that men generally tend to marry women younger than themselves.
- People worldwide tend to marry people who come from similar groups to themselves, whether this is religion, caste or socio-economic group.
- People from poorer backgrounds are less likely to get married than those from more affluent backgrounds. Sarah Corse et al. (2013) found in the USA that the decline of full-time factory jobs and the rise in precarious and casual low-paid employment mean that working-class men and women are now less likely to get (and stay) married and have children within marriage. The research also found that the unemployed and those living on low wages or in poverty were less likely to marry because of the high cost of traditional weddings.

  Recession and austerity have been the norm in Western societies for some time now and may account for the 7.5 per cent decline in marriage rates for the poorest sections of those societies since 2001. Consequently, marriage is increasingly becoming a middle-class institution.
- Global migration means that there is a greater likelihood of inter-ethnic marriage in modern Western societies.
- Most marriages worldwide are based on choice and consent, but there is evidence that **forced marriage** is acceptable in some societies, and that many of these involve children. A forced marriage is defined as 'a marriage conducted without the valid consent of both parties where duress (emotional pressure in addition to physical abuse) is a factor'. According to a 2017 UNICEF report, Niger has the highest rate of forced child marriage in the world – 76 per cent of girls aged under 18 years were forced to marry between 2010–2016. The charity WorldVision in 2015 observed that, in at least 12 less industrialised countries in Africa, as well as in Bangladesh (in which 65 per cent of girls experience forced marriage), one in three girls are married before reaching the age of 18. According to the Indian Ministry of Home Affairs,

nearly 34 000 women and nearly 17 000 girls were forced into marriage in 2016 in India. It is important to understand that, because of global migration, forced marriage is also found in modern Western societies. For example, statistics from the UK in 2013 suggest that there are 8000 forced marriages a year in Britain. However, it can be very difficult to assess the real degree of this problem, as victims are reluctant to come forward because they are often unwilling to report their parents to the authorities. They may also not wish to bring shame upon themselves or their families by not fulfilling what they see as a family duty. They may also be fearful of the consequences.

## Explanations for global trends in marriage

Much of this cultural shift in attitudes towards marriage is rooted in the social change that many females across many societies experienced in the latter part of the 20th century. For example, education for girls improved considerably across the world, although not at the same pace in all societies. Education in many societies meant that many women worldwide were able to take advantage of the economic opportunities that opened up because of globalisation (many Western transnational companies transferred their service call centres and manufacturing hubs to developing countries or contracted out manufacturing – for example, in textiles, sportswear and electronics – to local manufacturers, particularly in China).

These economic trends improved women's economic power and significantly increased the global number of **dual-career/income families** in which a woman's earnings were just as important to a couple's living standards as the earnings of her husband. In China, the evidence suggests that these economic changes have resulted in an increase in **DINK** – dual income, no kids – **families**. Surveys conducted in China suggest that 7 per cent of married people identified themselves as living in this type of family. Beijing, for example, now has 10 000 DINK families. When combined with those in Shanghai and Guangzhou, the figures rise to about 600 000, according to Youth League Committee of Beijing statistics. Moreover, many governments responded to this economic change by introducing social policies which strengthened women's position in their societies and consequently their determination and ability to make successful marriages and to reject unsuccessful ones.

### Activity

*Enjoying the DINK lifestyle.*

Why might this type of family be on the rise?

Helen Wilkinson (1994) argues that young women worldwide now weigh up the costs of marriage and having children against the benefits of a career and economic independence. The result of this is that many women, particularly middle-class graduates, are postponing or delaying both marriage and family life until their careers are established. For example, Chinese sociologists have suggested that a significant number of Chinese women working in high-income jobs are voluntarily choosing to marry at a later age in order to ensure that they find a partner who is willing to enter into a companionate marriage.

From the feminist perspective, then, the global decline in marriage rates is not a negative trend. It indicates that couples in general, and especially women, are less carefree about marriage. People now see marriage as a serious proposition and as as a result are more careful in their choice of partner and more willing to make the personal sacrifices necessary to make the marriage work. As a result, the institution of marriage has become stronger rather than weaker.

There are other pieces of evidence that also suggest that marriage is far from dead. First, surveys indicate that most people, whether single, divorced or cohabiting, still see marriage as a desirable life-goal. For example, European surveys have found that, although members of society are now more liberal about pre-marital sex, the most common view was that marriage should precede parenthood. Marriage is still considered by both married and unmarried people to be the 'gold standard' – there is nothing beyond marriage and the wedding ceremony, which publicly expresses overall and complete commitment to another person.

Second, around 40 per cent of all marriages in the USA and Europe are **remarriages** (in which one or both partners have been divorced or widowed). More men than women remarry. This is probably because taking responsibility for children reduces women's opportunities in the re-partnering market. Whatever the reasons for remarriage, the fact that it occurs so often indicates that marriage is still popular as a social institution, despite some people's previous negative experience of it.

Finally, there is a danger that concerns about the decline of marriage have been exaggerated. Despite the decrease in the overall number of people marrying over the last 40 years, marriage is still the main type of partnership for men and women in most societies worldwide. In addition, New Right perspectives on marriage and family life can be criticised for using statistics selectively. For example, the New Right often highlight the number of single people who remain unmarried. However, the emphasis on single people ignores the fact that the majority of them will eventually marry or remarry at some stage.

### Activity

Design a questionnaire aimed at both males and females and different generational groups, asking whether people in the society in which you live value marriage and/or can see themselves getting married in the future. Design your questions around some of the issues just discussed.

## Cohabitation

**Cohabitation** is an arrangement where two people who are not married but are romantically and emotionally involved with one another voluntarily choose to live together intimately as a couple. Research by Zoya Gubernskaya (2008) suggests that worldwide cohabitation is becoming a popular domestic set-up or family option. She looked at cohabitation practices in 28 nations and found considerable cross-country variation in both the prevalence and level of support for cohabitation. Sweden has the highest cohabitation rate (24 per cent), followed by Finland, Norway, Brazil and Denmark, while the lowest cohabitation rates are found in Israel (3 per cent), Mexico (2.43 per cent) and Poland (2.36 per cent). Cohabitation tends to be less popular in Roman Catholic societies such as Poland and those found in Central and South America, although Brazil has recently experienced an increase in the number of couples living together outside of marriage.

In societies with large Islamic populations and which are subject to sharia law, cohabitation is generally regarded as deviant, and in some societies, such as Indonesia, it is defined as a crime punishable by a two-year prison sentence. Islamic societies generally disapprove of cohabitation outside of marriage. There is also some evidence that discussion of cohabitation is taboo and that the families of those who do cohabit feel that the couple are bringing shame on their wider extended family. Cohabitation is virtually non-existent in highly Islamic countries such as Pakistan. In India, cohabitation attracts great disapproval in rural districts but has grown in popularity in urban areas.

Máire Nī Bhrolchain and Éva Beaujouan (2011) carried out an extensive study of cohabitation in Britain which concluded that cohabitation actually strengthens marriage rather than bringing about its decline. They found that the vast majority of marriages in the UK – 80 per cent in 2008–10 – are actually preceded by a spell of cohabitation. Only 30 per cent of marriages were preceded by cohabitation in 1980–84. Indeed, they note that 'marriage without first living together' is now as unusual as pre-marital cohabitation was in the 1970s.

Nī Bhrolchain and Beaujouan's research found that, at the 10th anniversary of moving in together, half of cohabiting couples in their study had married each other, whereas just under four in ten had separated and just over one in ten were still living together unmarried. They conclude from this evidence that cohabitation should be viewed as an increasingly popular option taken up by couples who want their future marriages to succeed. Moreover, they also point out that surveys and official statistics indicate that marriage rather than cohabitation is still the main cultural goal for most people in most societies. For example, 84 per cent of women are married by their 40th birthday in both the USA and Europe. Some sociologists argue that this indicates that marriage is stronger in 2018 than it has been for a generation.

Beaujouan and Nī Bhrolchain also suggest that cohabitation may be responsible for the decline in marital breakdown that can be seen across a range of modern societies. They argue that the experience of cohabitation 'screens out' weaker relationships which without cohabitation might have immediately progressed to marriage. In other words, marriages are more likely to last today because couples have undergone a severe test of compatibility during the cohabitation process. Those couples who successfully survive the cohabitation test and marry have already worked out and resolved the potential problems that might sabotage their marriage.

Finally, there are also a number of other practical reasons for the rise in cohabitation; for example, people may be separated from a previous partner and awaiting a divorce. Once the official separation period is over, they may intend to marry a new partner. In the meantime, they may cohabit with that new partner. The couple may also cohabit to save money that they intend to invest in a wedding. For example, the average cost of an American wedding was $35,329 in 2016.

## Key terms

**Monogamy** The state of only being married to one person at any one time.

**Bigamy** The state of being married to two people at the same time. It is a criminal offence in Western societies.

**Serial monogamy** The practice of engaging in a succession of monogamous cohabiting relationships or marriages.

**Same-sex marriage** Also known as gay marriage – the marriage of same-sex couples recognised by law as having the same status and rights as marriage of opposite-sex couples.

**Polygamy** A cultural norm which allows spouses to have more than one husband or wife.

**Polygyny** A type of polygamy in which a man can marry more than one woman or can be married to a set of co-wives.

**Polyandry** A type of polygamy in which a woman can marry more than one husband. It is quite rare compared with polygyny.

**Arranged marriage** A type of marriage organised or arranged by the parents of the couple and/or matchmakers.

**Marriage rate** The number of marriages per 1000 people per year.

**Leftover women** A term used in China to describe women who are still not married by the age of 27. They are seen to be 'left on the shelf'.

**Forced marriage** A marriage in which one or more of the parties is married without his or her consent or against his or her will.

**Dual-career/income families** Families in which both adult partners pursue a career and in which each contribute income that is important to the family's standard of living.

**DINK families** 'Dual income, no kids'. A term which refers to a couple who both earn an income and do not (yet) have children.

**Remarriage** The act of marrying again after experiencing a divorce.

**Cohabitation** The state of living together and having an intimate relationship without being married.

## Summary

1. Marriage is a universal practice. It can be found in some shape or form in virtually every society worldwide.
2. Across the world, there are three main types of marriage systems: monogamy, polygyny and polyandry.
3. Marriage rates are in decline in industrial societies.
4. However, most people in most societies still see marriage as an ideal goal to achieve. They also note that people are delaying marriage rather than opting out of it altogether. Most people eventually marry.
5. Studies of cohabitation suggest that it is not always an alternative to marriage and that experience of cohabitation before marriage may actually strengthen marriage.
6. Same-sex marriages are increasingly being recognised and permitted worldwide.

# Unit 4.2.2 Marital breakdown

Marital breakdown can take three different forms: divorce, separation and empty-shell marriages. This unit will discuss these different forms, trends in divorce and possible explanations for the increase in divorce.

## Types of marital breakdown

- **Divorce** refers to the legal ending of a marriage. Every nation in the world allows its residents to divorce under some conditions, except the Vatican City, an ecclesiastical sovereign city-state which has no procedure for divorce.

  Many societies have no-fault divorce in which couples agree that the marriage has **'irretrievably' broken down**. In Britain, for example, if the couple have lived apart for two years and agree that the marriage cannot be salvaged, divorce is usually granted by the courts. However, if one partner disagrees, the court may insist on a five-year separation before granting the divorce.

  The vast majority of countries introduced divorce into law between 1960 and 2005. However, some countries, for example, only grant divorce if one partner is 'guilty' of a 'marital offence' such as cruelty, desertion, adultery, impotency and so on.
- **Separation** is where a couple agrees to live apart after the breakdown of a marriage. Some people, especially those with strong religious beliefs, often prefer this option rather than undergoing the 'shame' of divorce proceedings, although in many countries their partner can still obtain a divorce after a certain period of time has passed even if the other party objects.
- **Empty-shell marriages** are those in which husband and wife stay together in name only. There may no longer be any love or intimacy between them. Today, such marriages are likely to end in separation or divorce, although this type of relationship may persist for the sake of children or for religious or economic reasons. The couple may wish to avoid bringing shame down on themselves and their extended family.

## Trends in divorce

Four distinct major trends in divorce can be observed since 1970 worldwide:

a. The global divorce rate has increased by over 250 per cent since 1960. The United Nations estimates that the Maldives has the highest divorce rate in the world: 11 divorces for every 1000 people. The average Maldivian woman, by the age of 30, has been divorced three times. The lowest divorce rates are found in less industrialised societies in which religions such as Islam and Hinduism still exert a powerful influence and marriages are generally arranged by parents and matchmakers.

   Another way of looking at divorce is to examine the percentage of marriages that end in divorce. For example, 87 per cent of marriages in Luxembourg break down, compared with 46 per cent in the USA, 42 per cent in the UK and 38 per cent in Australia. In contrast, only 15 per cent of marriages break down in Kenya, 17 per cent in Egypt and 1 per cent in India.

b. Divorce statistics from both the USA and Europe suggest that the younger a couple are when they get married, the more likely it is that the marriage will end in divorce. For example, divorce is highest in the 25–29 age group – these people are more likely to have married in their late teens or early twenties.

c. In both the USA and Europe, about 30 per cent of marriages end in divorce by the couple's 20th wedding anniversary. About 60 per cent are ended by the death of one of the spouses.

d. In the USA, divorce is more likely to be the outcome if one or both partners have been married before, compared with marriages in which both partners are marrying for the first time.

## Explanations for the increase in divorce

Explanations for the increase in divorce obviously differ by country and to some extent religion.

### Changes in the law

There is no doubt that the introduction of divorce laws, especially the no-fault and 'irretrievable breakdown' options, have made divorce both easier and cheaper to obtain in most countries around the world. However, sociologists argue that there are other important influences to consider in addition to divorce laws, including changes in social attitudes, a more secular society, the declining influence of the extended family and the late-modernist theory of divorce.

### Changes in social attitudes

Sociologists note that legal changes often reflect other changes in society, especially changes in social attitudes. In particular, sociologists argue that social expectations about marriage have dramatically changed over the past 50 years. This can be illustrated in a number of ways.

- Functionalist sociologists argue that high divorce rates are evidence that marriage is more valued today and that people are demanding higher standards of marital behaviour from their partners compared with the past. Couples are no longer prepared to put up with unhappy, 'empty-shell' marriages or to take their relationships for granted. People want more from their marriage than just companionship – they are increasingly demanding emotional and sexual compatibility and equality in decision-making and domestic tasks. Functionalists argue that some people are willing to go through a number of partners to achieve these goals.
- Feminists note that women's expectations of marriage have radically changed compared with previous generations from the 1970s on. In 2012, the majority of divorce petitions in the USA and Europe were initiated by wives. Barbara Thornes and Jean Collard (1979) argue that this trend supports the view that women expect far more from marriage than men and, in particular, that they value friendship in marriage and emotional gratification more than men do. Women may be using divorce to escape marriages when their husbands fail to live up to their high expectations.
- Before the 1970s, if women were unhappily married and/or trapped in empty-shell marriages, they found it difficult to escape the marriage because they were likely to be highly dependent on their husband's wages. The entry of women into the labour force in large numbers resulted in women becoming independent wage-earners and improved the range of choices available to women when it came to the ending of a marriage.
- Nicky Hart (1976) notes that increasing divorce rates may also be a reaction to the frustration and injustice that many working wives experience if they feel that the distribution of housework and childcare tasks between themselves and their husbands is unequal and unfair.
- Similarly, increased divorce may be the outcome of tensions produced by women taking over the traditional male role of breadwinner in some households, especially if the male is long-term unemployed. Some men may regard this as a threat to their masculinity and traditional head of household status and then react with violence. However, modern women are no longer tolerant of male violence and are more likely than previous generations of women to react by petitioning for divorce on the grounds of unreasonable behaviour or by legally separating from the husband.

## Secularisation

Western Christian societies in particular saw some profound attitudinal change as church attendance and religious belief went into decline (**secularisation**). Divorce was no longer associated with stigma and shame. Increasingly, divorce began to be seen as a 'lesser moral evil' or source of shame than unhappiness. In contrast, divorce rates are very low in societies in which religious belief and practice are still strong.

## The declining influence of the extended family

In modern urban societies in which geographical mobility has become the norm, the social controls exerted by extended kin and close-knit communities have declined. These extended kin and communities traditionally put pressure on couples to stay together in order to avoid the 'shameful' labels associated with divorce. In societies dominated by privatised nuclear families, the view that divorce can lead to greater happiness for the individual became more acceptable. It was even more so if divorce involved escaping from an abusive relationship or if an unhappy marriage was causing emotional damage to children. However, it is important to recognise that such attitudes are not necessarily a sign of a casual attitude towards divorce. Most people experience divorce as an emotional and traumatic event, equivalent to bereavement. They are normally also very aware of the severe impact it may have on children.

## Individualism

The late-modernist sociologist Ulrich Beck (1995) argued that increasing divorce rates are the product of a rapidly changing world in which the traditional rules, rituals and traditions of love, romance and relationships no longer apply. He argued that more industrialised societies are characterised by two important social influences: **individualisation**, and **conflict**.

- *Individualisation* – People are under less pressure to conform to traditional collective goals set by members of the extended family, religion or culture. They now have the freedom to pursue individual goals. This makes them more egoistic and narcissistic (self-centred and obsessed with self-identity).
- *Conflict* – However, Beck observes that there are now more potential points of conflict between spouses because there is a natural clash of interest between the selflessness required by marriage and the selfishness encouraged by individualisation. He argues that partners may enter a marriage wanting different things. For example, one partner may be focused on their career while the other may want children. In a highly individualistic society, Beck argues that this potential conflict, which he terms the '**chaos of love**', means that all too often marriage becomes a battleground in which self-interest triumphs over self-sacrifice.

## Key terms

**Divorce** The legal dissolution of a marriage by a court or other competent body.

**Irretrievable breakdown** When both spouses agree that the marriage is over and that there is no hope that it will be ever revived.

**Separation** Informal separation occurs when spouses live apart, but do not pursue formal separation or divorce.

**Empty-shell marriage** A loveless marriage in which husband and wife stay together for financial or religious reasons or for the sake of the children, but essentially lead separate lives in the same house.

**Secularisation** A general decline in religious belief in God and religious practices such as regularly going to church.

**Individualisation** A concept associated with Beck that refers to a dominant ideology that stresses freedom from obligation or community pressure and gives people the freedom to look out for themselves first and foremost.

**Conflict** A clash of interests that can cause inequality.

**Chaos of love** Beck believes that marriage is potentially a battleground, because the institution of marriage demands compromise and selflessness but people often look out for their own interests first.

## Summary

1. Divorce has increased worldwide.
2. There are a number of explanations for rising divorce rates; states have generally moved in the direction of making divorce both cheaper and less complex so that it is universally available; social attitudes towards divorce have grown more liberal and consequently divorce is no longer regarded as shameful; society has become less religious and people have become more individualised.
3. Feminists argue that high divorce rates may be evidence that marriage is actually highly valued and that women in particular are no longer willing to tolerate the unhappy empty-shell marriages experienced by previous generations.

# Unit 4.2.3 Family diversity

The availability of divorce in more industrialised societies has had a significant influence on family and household diversity in those types of society.

## Types of family diversity

Three very distinctive forms of family diversity are probably the direct consequence of the availability of divorce: the single-parent family (also known as the lone-parent family and one-parent family), the reconstituted family and the blended family. Divorce has probably increased the number of single-person households in more industrialised societies too.

### Single-parent families

If we use the case-study of the UK, in 1961 only 2 per cent of all UK households were made up of **single parent families**. However, by 2012, it was estimated that there were approximately 2 million such families with dependent children in Britain, making up about a quarter of all families in the UK. Similar trends can be found elsewhere. According to the US Census Board, there were 12 million single-parent families in the USA in 2017.

However, according to United Nations data on families and households collected in 2017, the lowest numbers of single-parent families headed by females are found in less industrialised societies located in Africa and Asia.

Over 80 per cent of single-parent families worldwide are headed by women. About 50 per cent of these mothers had their children within marriage but are now separated, divorced or widowed. It is culturally expected in many societies that women should take on the main caring responsibilities for any children when relationships break down. Family courts are therefore more likely to award custody of children to mothers, unless fathers can prove that the mother is incapable of performing the role of primary carer.

## Reconstituted families

**Reconstituted families** are one of the fastest growing types of family in Europe and the US. A reconstituted family is a family unit where one or both parents have children from a previous relationship, but they have combined to form a new family. They are sometimes referred to a step-families, because one or both of the adults is a step-parent rather than a natural parent. The main causes of this family form are divorce and remarriage. For example, in 2009, 19.1 per cent of marriages in the UK involved the remarriage of one partner, while 15.8 per cent involved the remarriage of both partners. In France, 940 000 children live with a natural parent and a step-parent. In the US, over 50 per cent of families are remarried or recoupled; 80 per cent of remarried people bring children to the relationship. Consequently, about 30 million children under the age of 13 in the US have a step-parent. In contrast, reconstituted families are fairly rare in less industrialised societies because of cultural disapproval of divorce. If such families exist, it is often because a widow has come under family or community pressure to remarry, because such cultures believe that men should be responsible for the welfare of women and children.

Erica De'Ath and Dee Slater's (1992) study of step-parenting identified a number of challenges facing reconstituted families:

- Children may find themselves pulled in two directions, especially if the relationship between their natural parents continues to be strained. They may feel they are being disloyal to their natural parent if they are seen to like or get on with the step-parent. Wednesday Martin (2013) notes that the step-mother with good intentions may become a target for the children's resentment about the amount of change in their lives and their natural mother's unhappiness. In the children's minds, she is transformed into the 'wicked' step-mother who is the cause of all their problems.
- Strained relations between step-parents and children may, therefore, be the norm in these families, especially if the step-child is unwilling to accept the newcomer as a 'mother' or 'father' or is unwilling to accept disciplinary action from the step-parent. Martin argues that such conflict is normal in the first few years of step-family life.

## Blended families

A **blended family** is a variation on the reconstituted family. In this type of family, couples who have remarried have chosen to have more children with their new partner. These 'new' children become the half-brothers and sisters of the step-children. For example, in 2001, it was estimated that 57 per cent of married couples in step-families in the UK have their own children, while in France about 530 000 children live in blended families with a parent and a step-parent and half-brothers or half-sisters.

## Single-person households

One of the most dramatic post-war changes in modern urban societies has been the increase in **single-person households**. In 2013, 7.7 million people (13 per cent of the UK population) lived alone. This is nearly four times higher than it was 40 years ago. However, this reflects a common trend across Europe where the average proportion of single households is 14 per cent of all households. A report by China National Radio estimated that in 2013 there were 58 million single-person households in China, accounting for 14 per cent of all Chinese households.

Wherever such households appear in the world, the majority of them are made up of males aged between 20 and 50 years of age. There are a number of reasons for this. First, in societies such as China, males outnumber females in urban areas because of the traditional preference for sons and China's one-child policy. Daisy Guo (2017) also reports that highly educated and high-earning young women prefer to remain single rather than to marry a husband who is likely to occupy a lower social status. In European countries and the USA, males are more likely than females never to marry and to take longer to remarry if divorced. In contrast, such single households are less likely to exist in less industrialised societies, because such men would be incorporated into extended kinship networks.

## Contemporary issues: Single-person households in Mongolia: Lily Kuo (2018)

A society which has seen a rapid increase in single-person households is Mongolia. However, most of the single-person households in this culture are composed of successful women. Kuo (2018) observes that Mongolian families have been investing in their daughters by sending them to school and university in the capital, Ulaanbaatar. She notes that some parents believe their daughters will take better care of them in their old age. Others think women need to learn other skills such as herding, but livestock is work reserved for men. In Mongolia, boys are kept at home to tend the animals. Kuo argues that this trend has given rise to a 'reverse gender gap'. Women are more educated than men. They are less likely to be unemployed. They also live longer – by a decade, on average. However, by outpacing men, Mongolian women in the city struggle to find husbands the way their parents did. The marriage rate has consequently fallen steeply because there is a shortage of men in the capital city. For example, Ulaanbaatar has about 60 000 more women than men. Kuo argues that Mongolian women face the dual cultural pressures of establishing a career and getting married before the age of 29. However, many women in their 30s remain single and unmarried and many Mongolian women now rely on social media such as Facebook, Instagram and Tinder in order to meet the right sort of educated and cultured man who can match their expectations in terms of education, intelligence and professional status, and so escape from the undesirable state of singlehood.

### Questions

1. Identify two reasons why Mongolian females are better educated than Mongolian males.
2. What are the main features of the 'reverse gender gap' in Mongolian society?
3. Explain why female singlehood is regarded as an 'undesirable state' in Mongolian society.

## Dimensions of family diversity

- **Organisational diversity** – this simply refers to variations in internal structural organisation. For example, some of these families involve marriage while others are a product of cohabitation. Rhona and Robert Rapoport (1982) observed that whether family structure is underpinned by marriage or cohabitation, the nuclear family structure is still the most common type of family set-up in more industrialised societies. However, they also pointed out that the **vertical extended family** (three generations of the same family living under the same roof or in very close proximity so that there is daily contact) is the norm in most less industrialised societies, especially those found in Africa and Asia. There is even a case for arguing that nuclear families, wherever they are located, are members of '**dispersed extended families**', which means that, although their extended kin are geographically scattered, nuclear family members still retain contact via digital technology such as Skype, email and social media platforms. There is evidence too that extended kin still physically come together for special occasions and that they feel a strong sense of duty or obligation to help and support one another in times of family crisis – for example, when children are born or when elderly relatives suffer debilitating illnesses such as dementia.

- **Domestic diversity** – The Rapoports argued that there are often variations in the way men and women divide and manage childcare and housework. The domestic division of labour in some nuclear families may be equally distributed. However, in some nuclear units, and particularly in traditional extended families, the domestic tasks are likely to be segregated in that some domestic tasks are allocated to men or women on the basis of patriarchal beliefs about the roles of men and women. In some **dual-income or dual-career nuclear families**, women may find themselves with a 'dual burden' – they work all day for pay yet are still responsible for most of the childcare and housework. In a very small minority of households, roles may have been swapped. Women may be the main breadwinners while men may be househusbands.
- **Cultural diversity** – global migration has led to multiculturalism becoming a major feature of many more industrialised societies. This has had a significant effect on family structures and relationships. For example, migrants bring their own cultural and religious beliefs and values about how they should organise family life to their host countries. This can sometimes cause cultural conflict.
- The evidence suggests that an important aspect of assimilation is intermarriage between indigenous ethnic groups and migrant groups. In many European societies, **dual-heritage children** – the offspring of **inter-ethnic marriages** – are the fastest growing group of children in those societies. Some sociologists have suggested that young people from mixed-race backgrounds face their own unique problems in the form of prejudice and discrimination from the communities from which their parents originate.
- **Class diversity** – this refers to social class variations in the quality of family relationships and lifestyles. For example, the family life experienced by the affluent may be very different to that experienced by middle-class or working-class families. In some countries, the children of the rich may spend most of their childhood in a fee-paying boarding school. The children of the educated middle classes may receive more economic help from their parents while studying at university. The children of the poor, especially in less industrialised societies, may not be able to afford to send their children to school, and, if they can, may only choose to send their male children.

### The beanpole family

Julia Brannen (2003) claims that a new type of family has appeared in industrialised societies, which she terms the '**beanpole family**'. This is a four-generational family which includes great-grandparents and great-grandchildren. Brannen argues that these families are less likely to experience horizontal intra-generational ties – for example, millennials are likely to have fewer aunts, uncles and cousins compared with previous generations. Brannen argues that we are now more likely to experience closer ties with both grandparents and great-grandparents.

## The debate about the extent of family diversity and the dominance of the nuclear family

Chester (1985) claims that arguments about family diversity are exaggerated, and that the basic features of family life modelled on the nuclear family (which he calls the **neo-conventional family**) have remained largely unchanged for the majority of the population since the 1950s. Chester argues that it is important not to dismiss the nuclear family as irrelevant. He argues that most adults still marry and have children. Most children are reared by their natural married parents. Most people live in a household shared by a married couple. Most marriages continue until parted by death. It may be true that about 40 per cent of all marriages will end in divorce, but 60 per cent are successful.

Chester concludes that nuclear families are still very common, although he acknowledges that they have undergone some changes over the generations – for example, mothers are more likely to go out to work rather than staying at home full-time. He therefore argues that nuclear families are the most conventional family type because most people will pass through one at some stage in their life.

### Key terms

**Single-parent families** Families with children under age 18 headed by a parent who is widowed or divorced and who has not remarried, or by a parent who has never married.

**Reconstituted family** Also called a step-family – a family unit where one or both parents have children from a previous relationship but have combined to form a new family.

**Blended family** A variation on the reconstituted family that includes, in addition to step-children, the natural children of the remarried couple.

**Single-person households** A person living alone.

**Organisational diversity** Differences in the size or organisation of families. Extended families are obviously larger than nuclear families, which in turn are larger than one-parent families.

**Vertical extended family** Families composed of three generations that may live under the same roof or in very close proximity who are in frequent daily contact.

**Dispersed extended family** Extended kin (grandparents, aunts, uncles and cousins) who normally live in geographically scattered nuclear families but who feel a sense of duty and obligation to provide mutual support and assistance to each other in times of need or to get together on symbolic occasions such as Christmas.

**Domestic diversity** Differences of internal arrangements of families. For example, in some families the mother has a career and goes out to work. In others, the mother stays at home full-time, and in a rare number of families the father stays at home as a full-time carer.

**Dual income/dual career nuclear families** A family in which both adults have a career and in which the wage of each partner makes a significant contribution to the lifestyle of the family.

**Cultural diversity** Refers to how families might differ in organisation across different societies and across ethnic and religious groups within the same society.

**Dual-heritage children** The children of inter-ethnic marriages.

**Inter-ethnic marriage** Marriages that take place between people who are from different racial or ethnic groups.

**Class diversity** Refers to how social class, especially wealth and poverty, may shape family living arrangements and the opportunities for a quality childhood.

**Beanpole family** A four-generational type of family that has few extended kin such as aunts, uncles and cousins.

**Neo-conventional family** Chester's term for the modern form of nuclear family. According to Chester, most of us will live as a child or adult in this type of family at some point in our lives.

## Summary

1. Divorce has certainly increased family and household diversity because it has resulted in an increase in single-parent, reconstituted and blended families as well as single-person households.
2. Other diverse family and household forms include the vertical extended family, the beanpole family, the dual-career family, the bi-nuclear family and gay families.
3. Not all sociologists believe in family diversity. Chester believes it to be exaggerated and convincingly argues that most people in more industrialised societies will find themselves living in a nuclear family at some stage of their lives.

# Unit 4.2.4 New Right perspectives on family diversity

New Right perspectives on the family are very similar to functionalist theories in that they agree that the nuclear family is the best possible type of family to bring children up in. However, they also believe that the nuclear family is under attack and in decline because of state policies.

## The state and social policy as influences on the family

Patricia Morgan (2007) argues that government social policy across the world, particularly in more industrialised societies in which religion has declined in influence, has done little to protect marriage and nuclear family life. In her view, government social policy should promote marriage (through, for example, lower rates of taxation for married couples). She argues that government social policy should aim to penalise those who cohabit rather than marry and to make divorce more difficult to obtain.

Morgan argues that state social policies have actually weakened both marriage and family life by introducing laws and social policies which have encouraged females to enter education and the workforce on equal terms with males, therefore encouraging them to abandon their aspirations to marry and to have children, and to forego their 'natural' roles' as caregivers and nurturers. It has even been suggested that the rise in juvenile crime rates and anti-social behaviour seen in some Western societies may be a result of the supposedly inadequate socialisation that occurs if females are not fully focused on raising children because they go out to work.

New Right sociologists are also critical of liberal social policies such as the reform of divorce laws, which have supposedly made it cheaper and easier for couples to divorce; the failure to use taxation to encourage marriage and discourage cohabitation; and the legalisation of gay marriage.

It is alleged by Charles Murray (1994) that state policies aimed at economically helping poorer couples have created a **dependency culture** which has encouraged the emergence of a criminal **underclass** composed of **welfare-dependent** 'problem' families. Robert Rector (2014) claims that social policies which offer financial benefits to the poor have seriously damaged the institution of marriage. He argues that such social policies have encouraged single parenthood at the expense of married parenthood, because the payment of welfare benefits reduces the financial need for marriage. He notes that less educated mothers in European countries such as the UK are symbolically married to the state and to the taxpayer rather than to the fathers of their children. This is because, if such mothers get married, the rules which underpin eligibility for benefits reduce the amount of money they can claim from the state. He therefore argues that welfare has become a substitute for a husband. He notes that welfare benefits create a destructive feedback loop: they promote the decline of marriage, which generates a need for more welfare.

Murray claims that there is a large group of single mothers who have never married or cohabited, who are long-term unemployed and less educated *and* attracted to lone motherhood by the '**perverse incentive**' of being able to claim state welfare benefits in the USA and those European societies that offer welfare assistance. Murray sees the single-parent family as an inherently second-rate imperfect or 'broken' family that is doing a poor job in terms of raising children.

In criticism of the New Right view of lone mothers and single-parent families, Reuben Ford and Jane Millar (1998) suggest that the New Right analyses strongly imply that the poverty that single mothers experience is the effect of 'choosing' this lifestyle. However, Ford and Millar argue that the New Right have misinterpreted this relationship. Their survey of single mothers in the UK suggests that poverty is a major cause rather than effect of single parenthood. Single women from poor socio-economic backgrounds living in deprived areas with higher than average rates of unemployment are more likely than others to become single mothers. Motherhood is regarded as a desired and valued goal by these women because it is a realistic alternative to their poor economic prospects. Surveys of such women suggest that children are a great source of love and pride, and most lone parents put family life at the top of the list of things they see as important.

## Key terms

**Dependency culture** According to New Right sociologists, a way of life characterised by dependency on state benefits.

**Underclass** The lowest social stratum in a country or community, consisting of the poor and unemployed. The New Right claim that members of the underclass are most likely to be welfare-dependent and criminal.

**Welfare-dependent** The New Right claim that some individuals are no longer capable of taking responsibility for themselves because they have grown too dependent on state benefits. They are no longer motivated to seek work.

**Perverse incentive** An incentive that results in unintended negative consequences; for example, females may find it advantageous to get pregnant and bring up a child alone rather than get married, because state benefits are generous.

## Summary

1. New Right sociologists claim that the nuclear family has been undermined by government policies which have encouraged cohabitation and divorce at the expense of marriage.
2. They also argue that state policies have encouraged married women to go out to work, therefore undermining their roles as wives and mothers.

# Unit 4.2.5 Postmodernist perspectives on family diversity

Postmodernist sociologists argue that sociological studies of the family should focus on the 'life-courses' of individuals rather than family structures or units. In other words, sociologists should examine the way that lives evolve and change as people experience personal events or rites of passage such as marriage, the birth of a child or the death of a partner. Other postmodernist sociologists argue that we should focus on '**personal life**' instead of the 'family'.

## Life-course analysis

Tamara Hareven (2000) noted that the **life-course** is made up of several stages:

a. Birth
b. Early childhood (being a baby)
c. Infancy (being a toddler)
d. Childhood (beginning with compulsory schooling)
e. Adolescence (being a teenager)
f. Young adulthood (18–29)
g. Adulthood (30–50)
h. Middle age (51–64)
i. Old age (officially begins with retirement)
j. Death

Hareven notes that a life-course might affect the structure and dynamics of family life in a number of ways. For example, a child might experience a settled nuclear family from early childhood to adolescence but experience a single-parent family thereafter because their parents separate and divorce. This in turn might lead to a dual-parenting arrangement or the child may no longer have any contact with the father. As adolescence develops, they may experience the reconstituted or step-family (in which relationships might be tense).

As people progress through the life-course stages into young adulthood, they may leave home for, say, university, leaving an '**empty nest**' **family** behind. They may share houses or apartments with friends, who become more important than kin for a while. They may decide to cohabitate with someone from the opposite sex. They may decide to come out as gay, trans or intersex and enter relationships that reflect their sexual identity. Such relationships are likely to impact, both positively and negatively, on their relations with parents, siblings and extended kin. In middle and old age, family life and interaction experiences continue to evolve. For example, when the children leave home, parents have to cope with the concept of the empty nest household or the family may evolve into a '**boomerang**' **family** as the children return home after a period at university because they cannot find secure well-paid employment or afford to buy or rent a home of their own. Some older people may choose to divorce at this stage. Many of them will derive emotional satisfaction from being grandparents and helping their adult children with childcare. However, many of these decisions and choices may be shaped by events such as death, sickness, disability, migration and influences such as wealth, poverty, ethnicity and globalisation. Some people will decide to

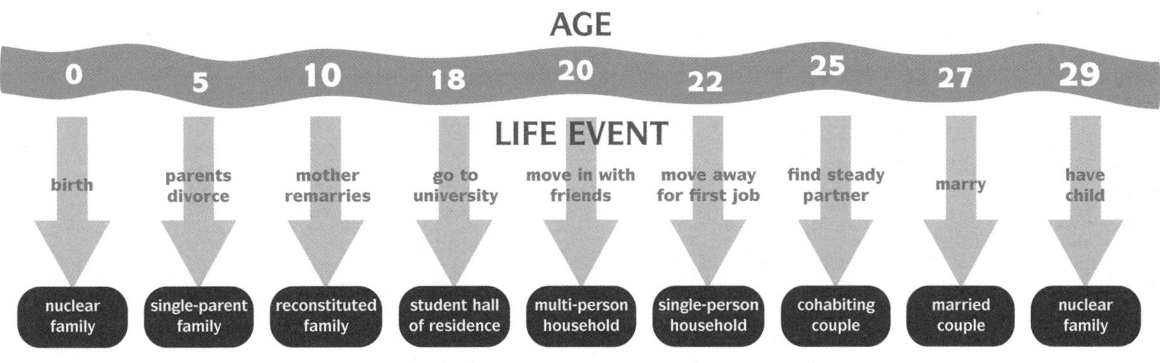


*How an individual can live in eight types of household before the age of 30.*

continue as a single-person household after the death of their partner. Others may elect to live with their children or go into a residential home or sheltered accommodation.

Life-course analysis, therefore, focuses on the diversity and flexibility of family practices that occur during these stages. Postmodernists argue that family life is not about living in a static and unchanging ideal type of family structure. Families and households are not concrete things that people should strive to attain, as argued by functionalist and New Right sociologists. Rather, family life is in a continual state of fluctuation and change. There is, therefore, no such thing as the perfect family because interactions between family members, and the family dynamics that result, are unique to that group of people. If every experience of family is different, there can be no universal criteria by which 'families' can be judged as right or wrong. Postmodernists, therefore, argue that sociologists need to focus on what family members regard as important (as opposed to what sociologists think are important) in order to find out how family dynamics give meaning to people's lives.

Ray Pahl and Liz Spencer (2001) also argue that the concept of 'family' is no longer useful to describe personal relationships in the 21st century. They argue that people no longer feel they have to maintain relationships with other kin out of duty or obligation. Instead, people are now more likely to subscribe to '**personal communities**', which are made up of a combination of those relatives, **fictive kin** (close friends of spouses who are unrelated by birth or marriage but who have such a close emotional relationship with them that they are regarded as 'honorary' aunts and uncles of the spouses' children and considered part of the family).

## The sociology of personal life

Another postmodernist, Carol Smart (2007), recommends using the term 'personal life' instead of 'family' because the latter concept is too often associated with value judgements about 'ideal' or 'normal' family types. Smart argues that the concept of 'personal life' is more neutral and flexible, because it goes beyond marriage and biological kin to include newer types of relationships such as post-divorce relationships, same-sex relationships, fictive kin and friendships. For example, she notes that the wide range of choices open to both men and women may result in the following diverse forms of family and person life.

1. Women's control of their own fertility has seen an increasing number of women voluntarily choosing to reject child-bearing altogether. Some studies note that one in three female graduates in European societies have opted not to have children. More and more women are choosing to be child-free in more industrialised societies.

   Catherine Hakim (2010) argues that **voluntary childlessness** is a relatively new lifestyle choice that could only have been brought about by the contraception revolution. However, deciding not to have children can still attract social disapproval, especially from parents who wish to be grandparents. There may also be social pressure from relatives, friends and colleagues because, as Hakim notes, a woman's fertility status is still considered public property. Many regard **childlessness** as a type of feminine defect because the role of motherhood is still regarded as central to female identity. Hakim argues that the positive term '**child-free**' should replace the rather negative phrase 'childless'.

   Rosemary Gillespie (2003) identifies two motivational factors for choosing to be child-free.

- There may be a 'pull' factor in that some women will be attracted by the increased freedom and better relationships with partners that it affords. A number of studies indicate that couples are happier without children. Ed Wallander (2001) notes that married couples without children have more disposable income than households with children.
- There may be a 'push' away from motherhood. Kristin Park (2005) found that women who were motivated by this factor tended to see parenting as conflicting with their careers or leisure interests. These women claimed to be uninterested in children and often rejected the notion of a maternal instinct.

2. Another fairly new 'family' type that can be spotted by highlighting the personal life of children is the **co-parenting** model in which a divorced couple may agree to share the custody of a child or children. For example, many children may spend the week living with their mother but spend every weekend and half the holidays living at the home of their father and his partner. Both mother and father and their respective partners share legal

co-parenting responsibility for their children. Some family experts see co-parenting as a characteristic of **bi-nuclear families** – two separate post-divorce or separation households are really one family system, as far as children are concerned.

3. Gay and lesbian couples are increasingly choosing to start families via adoption, **surrogacy** or **in vitro fertilisation.**
4. A very small minority of couples in long-term relationships agree to bring up their children while living in separate households. These are known as **living apart together (LAT)** households. LAT households may be popular among young couples because, as Simon Duncan (2014) notes, they allow individuals to combine the freedom of living alone with the intimacy of being part of a couple. However, research by John Haskey and Jane Lewis (2006) suggests that younger LAT households are likely to evolve into cohabitation, marriage and eventually nuclear families. Irene Levin (2004) observes that some people entering a relationship in old age may prefer to maintain a relationship with a partner who lives elsewhere.
5. The existence of a 'boomerang' and a '**failure to launch' generation** has been highlighted by recent studies of family practices and personal life. Many young adults may return (like a boomerang) after initially leaving home for university or work, or they may never leave in the first place (fail to launch). Both these situations may be caused by a range of structural constraints beyond the control of family members (for example, the precarious nature of a minimum wage, zero-hours economy; the nature of the housing market; the lack of political will to help young people become independent of their parents and so on). Living with parents provides various types of support but may inhibit children's ability to be independent and responsible. It may also negatively impact on parents' ability to enjoy their later years free of the burden of childcare. Roles and expectations of both parents and children need to be refined and revised if this aspect of personal life is to be successful.
6. Some families are dependent upon new reproductive technologies – for example, the first **'test-tube' baby**, Louise Brown, was born 40 years ago through in vitro fertilisation. Other children are the product of surrogate motherhood where one woman carries a foetus produced by the egg of another woman. This raises questions about who the parents of the child are, because the birth parents and the genetic parents are different. It adds to the complexity of possible family types and has even led to a grandmother giving birth to her own grandchild. Such technologies have also extended the period when a woman can give birth. For example, the actress Brigitte Nielsen gave birth to her fifth child in 2018 when aged 54. Maria del Carmen Bousada de Lara, a Spanish mother, gave birth to twins at the age of 66 years.

The radical feminists Shelley Budgeon (2011) and Sasha Roseneil (2013) suggest that the traditional nuclear family does not appeal to some women because it is based on the **hetero-norm** – the idea that women should marry men forms the heart of the family. They argue that intimate and emotional relationships are often part and parcel of female friendship and that for many women friendships with other females are just as important as relationships with lovers, work colleagues and other family members. They also argue that there has been a '**decentring of conjugal relationships**', which means that some women do not subscribe to the hetero-norm and are not interested in solely building their lives and identities around a relationship with a man, marriage or a nuclear family. For these women, the most important relationship in their lives may be with someone such as a best female friend or male gay friend who she regards as much a member of her 'family' as any of her blood relatives. Roseneil argues that such friendships are no longer tied together by heterosexuality. It is now normal for heterosexuals, especially women, to have strong emotional relationships with gay people. However, Yvette Taylor (2011) points out that Roseneil and Budgeon's evidence is limited to a small number of case studies and may not be generalisable to the population at large.

1. Beck and Elisabeth Beck-Gernsheim (2001) argued that the spread of the ideology of individualisation in the 21st century has seen the emergence of what they call '**families of choice**', in which individuals may choose to include people as family members who are not traditionally related. For example, a cohabiting couple may interpret each other as 'husband' and 'wife' despite the fact that they are not formally married, or close friends of parents may be adopted as honorary aunts and uncles. Studies

of how children interpret the concept of families suggest that some even see pets such as dogs and cats as family members.

2. Eric Klinenberg (2014) argues that people in more industrial societies such as the UK and USA are influenced by the '**cult of the individual**' in which people put their own needs before those that are expected of them by society. Klinenberg argues that this philosophy may be responsible for the large increase in single-person households. For example, while a woman is expected to settle down with a man and start a family, the cult of the individual means she puts her needs before, say, her parents' desire to be grandparents and this may mean she lives alone while establishing a career and independent lifestyle for herself. Klinenberg notes that the digital revolution, especially the availability of smartphones and the popularity of social media, make such single-household lifestyles more attractive.

## Then and now: Carol Smart, *Personal Life* (2007)

*Personal Life* was published in 2007. It was the culmination of many years of research, both **empirical** and theoretical, and so it is important to recognise that its intricate roots go much further back than the date of publication. When I was a sociology student I could never relate to courses on 'The Family' (as they were then called) because the idealised image of families we were presented with bore no resemblance at all to my own family or the families of my friends. Yet, paradoxically, as a teacher I was always keen to put on courses for students on families and relationships. This was because by then I had become fascinated by how close relationships work and because I wanted to explore and expose the complexities and challenges of these important relationships. These interests set in train a number of empirical projects which gave me the opportunity, over several decades, to talk to hundreds of people about their relationships. So *Personal Life* is not a single study, but rather distilled insights from many of my projects.

Given this history to the book, I was somewhat taken aback to discover that some sociologists felt that I had abandoned my interest in family life and that I was trying to devalue the study of families – simply because I was trying to stretch the study of important relationships beyond the conventional limits of families by using the term 'personal life'. It remains a mystery to me how anyone could come to the conclusion that *Personal Life* is not substantially about family life. It is true that it is more than just this, of course. Yet I prefer to think of it as being about 'family life *plus*', although we should always remember that families do not provide the primary source of relationships for all people or for all time.

It was because I felt it was more important to study what people do, and how they relate to one another, that I moved decisively away from the study of the structures of the family and the kind of sociology I had been taught as an undergraduate. Instead I moved towards studying what David Morgan (1996, 2011) has called family practices. This **epistemological** shift away from structures towards practices opened up a completely new way of understanding relationships as well as providing much more engaging methods of researching families, kinships and friendships. These included such things as basing discussions of relationships on photographs to evoke memories and stories; using vignettes or hypothetical situations as ways of eliciting sensitive ideas; and using written accounts of family histories. It even led me to the study of family secrets as a way of getting 'behind' the public front of family life.

Since the book was published, families and relationships have inevitably continued to change. Same-sex marriage is now well established in England, Wales and Scotland (although not in Northern Ireland). Assisted reproduction (in the form of egg, sperm and embryo donation) and surrogacy are changing the shape of many families as children born from such methods may not be genetically related to one or both of their parents. This in turn means they are not genetically related to their grandparents. We need to understand how these new relationships work, and from my perspective, and from the perspective of *Personal Life,* this is a much more important question than simply bemoaning the fact that families in 2017 don't look like the families formed in 1917 or 1957.

In the second chapter of the book I stated that family 'relationships are very sticky' and I went on to say 'it is hard to shake free from them at an emotional level and their existence can continue to influence our practices and not just our thoughts' (2007: 45). I still stand by that statement but wish to underline that this does not mean that such relationships are ideal, unremittingly positive or even supportive. I wanted this 'warts and all' perspective on family/kin/friend relationships to be more clearly understood without throwing the baby out with the bathwater – to use an overworked cliché. I hope that this at least is what future students will take from the book.

D. Morgan (1996) *Family Connections*, Cambridge: Polity
D. Morgan (2011) *Rethinking Family Practices*, Basingstoke: Palgrave Macmillan

## Key terms

**Personal life** Smart believes that, rather than study families, sociologists should study how individuals negotiate their way through their personal lives. By doing this, we can see that a vast range of people beyond immediate kin play important roles in our lives.

**Life-course** The stages that all human beings go through during their life, covering birth to death.

**Empty nest families** Households in which only the parents remain once their grown-up children have left home.

**Boomerang family** Families in which children leave home, but because of circumstances beyond their control they are forced to return to live with their parents as young adults.

**Personal communities** A network of close friends and kin (even pets) that a person might regard as closest to them.

**Fictive kin** Normally, close friends of the family, particularly parents, who have been given the honorary title of 'uncle' or 'aunt'.

**Voluntary childlessness** Consciously and voluntarily choosing not to have children. It should be distinguished from the state of not being able to have children for medical or biological reasons.

**Child-free** The decision usually taken in conjunction with a partner not to have children.

**Childlessness** The state of not having children. This may be voluntary or involuntary.

**Co-parenting** When a separated, divorced or unmarried couple share the duties of parenting, for example, a child may spend part of a week living with one parent and the rest of the week living with the other.

**Bi-nuclear family** Children of divorced or separated couples often belong to two nuclear families because their natural parents have remarried or are cohabiting with a new partner.

**Surrogacy** The process in which a woman agrees to bear a child on behalf of another woman, either from her own egg fertilised by the other woman's partner, or from the implantation in her uterus of a fertilised egg from the other woman.

**In vitro fertilisation** A medical procedure whereby an egg is fertilised by sperm in a test tube or elsewhere outside the body.

**Living apart together (LAT)** A modern household set-up in which a couple who are romantically involved make the decision to maintain separate households rather than move in together.

**Failure to launch generation** Children who for a variety of reasons have not been able to leave home and therefore still live with their parents despite being adults.

**Test-tube babies** Children who are the product of reproductive technology such as in vitro fertilisation or artificial insemination because their parents cannot conceive naturally for medical reasons.

**Hetero-norm** The idea that relationships should be heterosexual.

**Decentring of conjugal relationships** A radical feminist idea that rejects the idea that the most important relationship a woman has is with a man. Radical feminists believe that women can have the same quality family relationships with other women and/or gay men.

**Families of choice** An idea which suggests that members of our family are who we choose them to be – for example, we might regard close friends as symbolic family members, as well as cats and dogs.

**Cult of the individual** An idea very similar to Beck's concept of individualisation. It refers to the increasing trend to put ourselves before others and a desire not to live or mix with others, thus the trend towards living in single-person households.

**Empirical** Based on experience or observation.

**Epistemological** Relating to how knowledge of a given subject is obtained.

## Summary

1. Postmodernists argue that the concept of the family is too rigid and judgemental. They argue that sociologists need to study concepts such as 'life-course', 'personal life' and 'families of choice' in order to truly understand the social changes that 21st-century families are experiencing.
2. Postmodernists consequently are strong believers in family diversity and have identified a range of new ways of managing family dynamics and personal life.

# END-OF-PART QUESTIONS

| | | |
|---|---|---|
| 0 1 | Describe two types of marriage that exist worldwide. | **[4 marks]** |
| 0 2 | Explain two limitations of the New Right view of marriage and cohabitation. | **[6 marks]** |
| 0 3 | Explain two ways in which divorce has contributed towards family diversity. | **[8 marks]** |

# SECTION B
# FAMILY ROLES AND CHANGING RELATIONSHIPS

## Contents


**Part 3** **Gender equality and experiences of family life** **178**

**Part 4** **Age and family life** **203**


Section B focuses on different feminist perspectives on the family, and especially the key concept of *power, control and resistance*. Most feminist theories of the family see it as a patriarchal institution and attempt to explain how and why the family may be responsible for the general subordination and lack of power widely experienced by females in a range of societies. Our examination of these theoretical arguments is followed by an exploration of evidence relating to the internal organisation of families, particularly its domestic division of labour, and whether family life may be damaging for family members who lack power. The key concept of *inequality and opportunity* is particularly relevant here in the analysis of who takes the major responsibility for housework, childcare, decision-making and emotion work. The key concept of *social change and development* is important here, too, as we consider whether the family's domestic organisation has 'progressed' from segregated families in which males dominate and exercise power because of their superior earnings to more egalitarian families based on shared responsibilities. This section will also focus on age and family life. In particular, the idea that childhood and the role of grandparents have undergone *social change and development* will be examined. As we shall see, the concepts of *inequality and opportunity,* particularly with regard to social class, gender and ethnicity, are also important in understanding both the experience and quality of childhood today.

Part 3 will focus on how females experience family life. We will particularly examine the view that marriage is now more likely to be characterised by equality today and that family life is generally a positive experience for women and children. Part 4 will examine the relationship between age and family life, and especially changes in the role and social position of children in families, the changing role of grandparents, and how the social meaning of concepts such as motherhood and fatherhood have changed over time.

# PART 3 GENDER EQUALITY AND EXPERIENCES OF FAMILY LIFE

## Contents


| | | |
|---|---|---|
| Unit 4.3.1 | Feminist theories of the family | 178 |
| Unit 4.3.2 | Conjugal roles and debates about gender equality in the family | 194 |
| Unit 4.3.3 | The dark side of family relationships | 200 |


This part of the chapter generally focuses on the experience of women within the family and the development of a specific theory – feminism – which has evolved to explain the existence of a gender-specific form of oppression, exploitation, inequality and male supremacy known as 'patriarchy'. Patriarchy refers to any social system in which males hold primary power and predominate in leadership roles, moral authority, social privilege and control of property. At its simplest, Charlotte Higgins (2018) observes that 'male supremacy' operates at the expense of women in much the same way that 'White supremacy' operates at the expense of Black people.

This part, therefore, critically reviews a range of feminist theories in some depth before going on to examine the evidence collected from sociological research relating to the organisation of the domestic division of labour and especially those tasks relating to childcare, housework and the management of emotion. We particularly examine the view that power and decision-making in marriage in most societies in 2018 is **egalitarian**. Finally, using sociological research and official statistics, we need to examine whether family life is positive or negative for family members, because some radical feminists believe that the family as an institution is a patriarchy ruled by fear, intimidation and coercion.

## Unit 4.3.1 Feminist theories of the family

Feminists aim to describe the extent of gender inequality that exists across the world. This unit briefly outlines the history of feminism before discussing a number of feminist perspectives on the family, including liberal feminism, radical feminism, Marxist-feminism and intersectional feminism.

### Sociological history of feminism

If we examine the sociological history of feminism, we can see four eras or waves which have made a significant contribution to the position of women today both in society and in the family.

#### First-wave feminism

The **first wave of feminism** began with the 1792 publication of Mary Wollstonecraft's book *A Vindication of the Rights of Women*, which argued that females should have the same right to education as males because this would make them more effective partners in marriage as well as more successful mothers. Wollstonecraft also highlighted blatant inequalities in marriage that allowed unscrupulous husbands to exploit the inherited wealth of their wives. Over the 19th century, Wollstonecraft's followers won a notable set of victories for married women's rights. Legislation was eventually passed in both the USA and in many European nations protecting women's property rights (previously a husband could claim ownership of his wife's property once married) and allowing women to initiate divorce proceedings (previously only husbands could instigate divorce). This first wave of feminism culminated in some groups of women being given the vote in the USA and several European countries after a sustained (and sometimes violent) campaign by a group of feminists known as the women's **suffrage** movement.

## Activity

*A suffragette protester is arrested, London, 1913.*

Describe the contribution that first-wave feminism made to the position of women today.

## Second-wave feminism

The **second wave** of feminism began in the 1960s and continued into the 1970s with the publication of feminist classics such as Betty Friedan's *The Feminine Mystique* (1963), Germaine Greer's *The Female Eunuch* (1970) and Kate Millett's *Sexual Politics* (1970). Three distinct schools of feminist thought and action emerged in this period.

Some feminists who can be termed '**liberal feminists**' believed that sociological analysis of gender inequality in fields such as education, employment, pay, social mobility and family life would demonstrate the pervasive influence of patriarchy and put pressure on governments to pass **civil rights** legislation and social policy that would put females on an equal footing with males. This was reasonably successful in that it led to governments introducing equal opportunities legislation that banned discriminatory practices against females by employers and encouraged more married women into the workplace. The law was also changed to make divorce more accessible to married women. In the 1980s, many liberal feminists claimed that the influence of patriarchy was weakening because studies carried out by feminist sociologists such as Sue Sharpe (1976) clearly demonstrated that young women no longer shared the same aspirations and priorities as their mothers and grandmothers with regard to marriage and family life. All of these trends were viewed by liberal feminists as evidence that patriarchy was in retreat and that equality might be achieved in the not-too-distant future.

However, another feminist school of thought – **radical feminism** – did not share this optimism. This group of feminists argued that men and women would always be locked in a state of conflict with one another because the continued existence of patriarchy ensured men's power over women. Radical feminists argued that patriarchy is a system of male domination in which males use ideological, economic and physical power to control and subordinate females. Moreover, they argued that all men were naturally inclined to exploit and oppress women and that violence against women, especially rape and domestic abuse, was the main means by which men controlled women. These feminists believed that women needed to **liberate** themselves from men and to set up women-only communities. The more extreme wings of this movement advocated refusing to have children and encouraged feminists to avoid marriage and to shun family life.

A third type of feminism – **socialist** or **Marxist feminism** – parted ways with both the liberals and radical wings by insisting that patriarchy is an ideology invented and employed by capitalism in its relentless search for profit rather than an apparatus that exists solely for the benefit of men.

## Third-wave feminism

The **third wave** of feminism can be dated to the late 1980s and 1990s, and was essentially made up of critics of the second wave. There were two types of critics: **intersectional feminists** and **post-feminists**. Intersectional feminists, many of whom were Black feminists, pointed out that liberal and radical feminists were guilty of '**theoretical imperialism**' and **ethnocentrism** because they assume that their Western, White and often middle-class experience of patriarchal oppression is the norm for all women wherever they are located in the world. From an intersectional feminist perspective, this assumption is an over-simplification of the subtle realities of the patriarchal oppression experienced by different groups of women across the world. For example, Western feminists claimed that the family is the main site of patriarchal oppression, but Black feminists in the USA suggest that in societies characterised by White supremacy, apartheid and institutional racism, the family is often a site of refuge and liberation from the trauma and stress of living in a society that is hostile to the presence of minority groups.

The third wave also saw the emergence of a group of female academics who described themselves as 'post-feminists'. These academics who included Camille Paglia (1990) and Naomi Wolf (1990) argued that women in the 1980s had acquired a great deal of economic power and that 'young women had never had it so good'. Stacy Gillis and Rebecca Munford (2004) argue that these post-feminists claimed that the 1990s generation of young women reviled and rejected conventional feminism and consequently few young women self-identified as feminists. Post-feminists rejected the idea that women were the victims of men and advocated an alternative **power-feminism** that applauded the economic success of the 1990s generation of young women. These women (who were sometimes called '**ladettes**') were encouraged by post-feminists to adopt traits normally associated with masculinity – for example, to focus on their careers, to be sexually active and to drink heavily without fear of judgement. Post-feminists, therefore, extolled the virtues of the '**girl power**' symbolised by the global success of the Spice Girls and Madonna and the global popularity of the American TV series *Sex and the City*. However, Gillis and Munford conclude that post-feminism was viewed with scepticism by many, and turned out to be merely a short-lived fashion rather than a genuine indication that women had reached the next stage in the feminist struggle.

## Fourth-wave feminism

The **fourth wave of feminism** is articulated very clearly by Higgins (2018), who observes that this type of feminism is made up of those who have lost their trust in forward progress or those who were born too recently – the millennial generation – to have experienced it. Higgins describes this wave of feminism as a **digital** form of **feminism** and claims that it is more concerned with action than theory. She observes that this digital feminism has 're-discovered' patriarchy because of recent scandals in the worlds of celebrity, film and politics that produced the #MeToo movement. Marina Watanabe (2014) observes that this fourth-wave feminism sees patriarchy as perpetuating sexism, **misogyny** and violence on a daily basis against women. However, fourth-wave feminism also sees patriarchy as oppressive and limiting for males too. It argues that both society and families are responsible for inculcating men with **a toxic** form of **masculinity**, which has negative consequences for males as they grow up to become adults, and particularly husbands and fathers.

### Activity

*Take Back the Workplace and #MeToo survivors march, November 2017.*

Why does Higgins describe the fourth wave of feminism as digital feminism?

Digital feminism has also been influenced by intersectionality and consequently it encourages the view that the experience of patriarchy is qualitatively different for a range of social groups, including the **LGBT** (lesbian, gay, bisexual and transgender) **community**. Digital or **millennial feminists** are particularly critical of the radical feminist refusal to accept the idea that transsexuals who have transitioned from male to female should be considered to be women. They have accused radical feminists such as Greer, who argue that trans women are not 'real' women, of being **transphobic**. They are also critical of the idea that masculine and feminine identity can be reduced to a simple **gender binary**.

In this sense, digital feminism has been very influenced by the work of Judith Butler (2006), who argues that academics need to view both sex and gender as constituting separate continua. The biological sex continuum is bookended at one end by biological males as represented by their possession of male sex organs, and at the other end by female biology as represented by the possession of female sex organs, ovaries and a womb. However, between these two extremes is found a range of biological conditions that does not conform to the biological norms of male and female. For example, some people may be born with intersex biological features, some females may be born without ovaries or a womb, and some people's bodies may produce too much testosterone or oestrogen.

With regard to gender, Butler argues that this is largely socially constructed by individuals and societies. For example, societies have dominant ideas about how boys should behave (known as masculinity) and how girls should behave (known as femininity). Butler claims that sex is biologically determined but that gender is performed. Most members of society conform to dominant or hegemonic definitions of gender and perform according to cultural expectations. However, some do not – for example, transvestites transgress social norms regarding both masculinity and femininity. Some individuals experience gender dysphoria, meaning that, although they occupy biological bodies which are deemed male or female, their internal sense of gender does not fit how they have been biologically categorised. Many of these individuals may choose to transition to the biological gender they feel inside by electing to undergo physical change via surgery and drugs. People who identify as gay, lesbian or bisexual may be content with their biology but be sexually attracted to those of their own sex, and consequently perform in stereotypical gendered ways that the rest of society recognises as 'gay' rather than masculine or feminine.

## Feminism and sociology

Feminists have generally been critical of sociology for a number of reasons. Very few sociologists before the development of feminist sociological research in the 1970s seemed interested in patriarchy, probably because most of them were men, and as Higgins argues, 'the persistence of male domination was so much part of the oxygen of life that it was not even regarded as a concept'. Moreover, she argues that male supremacy was seen as 'natural' by some sociologists, especially functionalist sociologists such as Parsons. The idea that patriarchy was a 'natural' feature of society was self-fulfilling because those who wrote sociological theory were, very largely, men. Consequently, many contemporary feminist researchers into the family dismiss much of the sociology of the family as the product of '**malestream**' thinking. In other words, it has a masculine bias.

Pamela Abbott, Claire Wallace and Melissa Tyler (2005) argue that such malestream sociology has generally neglected women's issues and particularly issues of oppression and inequality relating to marriage and the organisation of family life. Consequently, until feminist research such as Hannah Gavron's *The Captive Wife: Conflict of Housebound Mothers* (1966), Ann Oakley's *The Sociology of Housework* (1974) and Hart's *When Marriage Ends* (1976), there was little sociological interest expressed by male sociologists in women or family issues such as childbirth, domestic labour, women's physical and mental health, women's leisure, domestic violence and the difficulty of combining motherhood with paid work or a career.

### Key terms

**Egalitarian** The principle that all people are equal and deserve equal rights and opportunities.

**First wave of feminism** Ideas that appeared in the 18th and the 19th century that challenged male domination of the family and eventually led to women being allowed to vote.

**Suffrage** The right to vote.

**Second wave of feminism** Liberal, radical and Marxist feminist ideas that appeared in the 1960s and 1970s, often collectively known as the 'women's liberation movement'.

**Liberal feminism** A collection of feminist sociologists who highlighted gender inequality in areas such as education and put pressure on governments to challenge it by introducing equal rights and opportunities legislation and social policies.

**Civil rights** The rights of citizens to political and social freedom and equality.

**Radical feminism** A group of feminists who attempted to explain gender inequality by constructing structural theories that saw patriarchy as a complex inter-dependent social system. The theory was often seen as men-hating because it is hyper-critical of what it saw as male exploitation and oppression of women.

**Liberate** To free somebody from oppression or exploitation.

**Socialist/Marxist feminism** A type of feminism that argued that gender inequality was linked to class inequality. Both were seen to be the product of capitalism – for example, capitalist employers profit from women's unpaid domestic labour.

**Third wave of feminism** Refers to two unrelated forms of feminism that appeared about the same time (1980s/1990s) – intersectional feminism and post-feminism.

**Intersectional feminism** A critique of liberal and radical feminism which implied that the experience of patriarchy was the same for all women. Black and Asian feminists, and Marxist feminists pointed out that gender often interacts or intersects with social class, race and patriarchy to produce unique experiences of patriarchy.

**Post-feminism** A 1990s trend that suggested that females no longer had any need for second-wave feminism because they now had girl power. Many critics saw it as a media construction and as reflecting a male backlash against radical feminism.

**Theoretical imperialism** The insistence that one particular type of experience should take precedence over all other experiences. Radical feminism was accused of this by intersectional feminists for implying that all women experienced patriarchal control in the same way.

**Ethnocentrism** Judging one's own cultural experience to be 'better' than that of other cultures.

**Power-feminism** Another term for post-feminism.

**Ladettes** A term used by the media in the 1990s to describe young women who used their leisure time to act in the same way as men.

**Girl power** A media-invented term which claimed that females wielded cultural power in the 1990s because they imitated role models such as Madonna.

**Fourth wave of feminism** Type of feminism, particularly the digital feminism practised by millennials.

**Digital feminism** Feminists, who mainly belong to the millennial generation, who challenge sexism and misogyny using online digital sites such as Twitter and Facebook and by setting up internet websites such as Everydaysexism.com.

**Misogyny** Dislike of, contempt for, or ingrained prejudice against women.

**Toxic masculinity** A type of masculinity which exhibits negative traits such as violence, sexual aggression and an inability or reluctance to express emotions because of a belief that it is weak to do so.

**LGBT community** A loose grouping of lesbian, gay, bisexual, and transgender organisations, and subcultures, united by a common culture and social movements. These communities generally celebrate pride, diversity, individuality and sexuality.

**Millennial feminists** Feminists who were born in the late 1980s and who in the early 21st century were in their 20s and early 30s. This generation, especially if it has experienced higher education, is thought to be highly politicised. Surveys suggest that they see females as equal to males and consequently they are less likely to tolerate inequality, sexism and misogyny and more likely than previous generations to challenge patriarchal processes.

**Transphobia** Refers to a range of negative attitudes, feelings, actions or hate crimes toward transgender or transsexual people.

**Gender binary** The classification of sex and gender into two distinct, opposite and disconnected forms of masculine and feminine.

**Malestream** A concept developed by feminist theorists to describe the situation when male sociologists carry out research which either ignores or neglects women's experience and/or focuses on a masculine perspective and then assumes that the findings can be applied to women as well.

## Liberal feminism

Liberal feminism, which emerged as part of the second wave of feminism, is not a unified perspective but the outcome of several pieces of research by a group of feminists who came to exercise a great influence over the campaign to establish equal rights for females in the fields of education, employment, family and reproduction. Liberal feminists tend to see patriarchy originating in the practice of gender role socialisation, which mainly occurs in the family during childhood. Research by Oakley (1972) revealed two crucial components of gender role socialisation, which she termed:

- '**manipulation**' – parents discourage particular types of behaviour which society believes is inappropriate for a child of a particular gender
- '**canalisation**' – parents channel children's interests into toys and activities approved by society in terms of the gender of the child.

The result of this manipulation and canalisation is that children are subtly and not so subtly pressured into conforming to cultural expectations about how they ought to behave as boys or girls. Oakley argues that, through a series of codes (relating, for example, to colours, dress, appearance, toys, play activities, etiquette, speech, imitation and social control), socially expected gender behaviour and conceptions of power are internalised by children in preparation for adult roles.

## Activity

*A boy playing with a doll.*

Consider your own childhood and list examples of how your parents introduced these gender-orientated codes into your lives. For example, what colour clothing did your parents dress you in as a baby? Consider your present wardrobe if you are a male – how many of your clothes are predominantly pink? How are clothing, appearance in terms of hairstyles, ornaments and cosmetics gender-typed? What sorts of advice were you given in terms of gender etiquette – for example, how you should sit, behave and so on? What sorts of images adorned the cover of birthday cards given to you? What types of toys were you encouraged to play with? What sorts of household tasks were seen to be your responsibility? If you are a female, is your behaviour, especially outside the home, more strictly controlled than your brothers or male peers?

These stereotypes and biases are confirmed as males and females progress into adulthood by agents of secondary socialisation. For example, by schools which may steer males and females towards or away from particular subjects; the focus on women's appearance and bodies in the media rather than their abilities or achievements; and patriarchal ideologies that claim that there are 'natural' or genetic differences between males and females that cannot be changed or challenged (such as the idea that females are naturally more suited to childcare and domestic work, which is widely accepted but not supported by scientific evidence).

However, liberal feminists argue that, in addition to individuals practising sexism or misogyny, many social institutions suffer from **institutional sexism**, that is, conscious and unconscious patriarchal attitudes and ways of doing things that are embedded in their everyday routine practices. We can illustrate this with regard to a major family problem, domestic violence – that is, violent or aggressive behaviour within the home, typically involving the violent abuse of a spouse or partner. The evidence worldwide suggests that such violence is fairly common and is mainly male on female.

A husband may commit violence because his socialisation as a child involved witnessing such behaviour by his father and the passive acceptance of this abuse by his mother. Talking to childhood friends may confirm his father's behaviour as 'normal' in the context of his peer group or neighbourhood. His experience of a culture in which males are regarded as powerful and females as subordinate may reinforce a view that men have the 'right' to physically discipline women.

## Activity

*A UK Home Office poster placed in men's washrooms in 2014 to coincide with the World Cup (football) tournament.*

1. Why do you think the UK Home Office produced a poster reminding men that domestic abuse was not just about violence?
2. Suggest reasons why it was released to coincide with the World Cup.

On an institutional level, the society in which the abuser lives may have a legal system that historically was designed by men and consequently legally defines domestic violence as a minor offence compared with street violence. The police, who are likely to be disproportionately male, may carry a legacy of sexism and/or be reluctant to interfere in what they see as a 'private' family affair. Consequently, few abusive husbands are arrested. The judicial system may not prioritise domestic violence, either, because most magistrates and judges are male. Light sentences that do not deter future offenders may be handed out if the case progresses to court (which it often does not). Cultural and religious attitudes may unconsciously support the social control of wives by husbands or, if this progresses to violence, not speak out loudly or clearly enough against it. Mass media reports may imply that aggressive behaviour by husbands was 'provoked' in some way by the wife's 'unacceptable' behaviour. Finally, victims of domestic violence may be encouraged by a range of institutions, including their own extended family, not to speak out for fear of bringing shame to the family. They may be encouraged to accept the situation for the 'greater' good of their children. They may be dissuaded from breaking up the family and filing for divorce. In conclusion, then, failure by these institutions to deal with the problem effectively usually leads to the cycle of violence starting up again.

## Then and now: Rebecca Dobash and Russell Dobash, *Violence Against Wives* (1979)

Sociology has traditionally focused on social problems yet not all problems are widely recognised as such nor is it always possible to gain public and state recognition and support.

*Then* – At the outset of efforts to deal with intimate partner violence, in the US and UK some commentators rejected demands to deal with violence in the home dubbing it a family affair in which society and the state should not intervene. Women's Aid, the early battered women's movement, thought otherwise and we agreed. It was the early reports of this violence from Women's Aid that led us to embark on research on what is now widely recognised as serious social problem. In the late 1970s and 80s, there was a paucity of research on violence against women. The project we conducted involved the examination of over 34 000 police files revealing that 25 per cent of all assaults involved violence against a woman by an intimate male partner. This coupled with the results of intensive interviews of women who had been the victims of such an assault led us to conclude that violence against women in the home was a widespread problem resulting in serious physical injuries and emotional harm. Evidence from this study led to the publication of *Violence Against Wives*, in which we used the quantitative data to assess prevalence and main patterns and qualitative interviews to demonstrate the experiences of victimised women at the hands of their partners. This evidence reinforced the claims of the battered women's movement in the UK and USA.

That was then – what about *Now*? While it is difficult to assess the impact of research on any social problem, it is clear that in conjunction with the pressure of the women's movement, research has played an important role in bringing about change. National surveys conducted in many countries reveal that on average 35 per cent of women who have ever been in an intimate relationship have experienced domestic violence. The WHO describes the violence as a 'global pandemic' having 'devastating consequences'. Our latest research (*When Men Murder Women,* 2015) confirms these conclusions. Based on 866 casefiles and interviews of 180 men who have committed a murder, we found that when a woman is killed the murderer is most likely to be an intimate partner or ex-partner. The murders occurred in the context of the man's sense of entitlement, possessiveness, and women's attempts to escape. Internationally based research conducted by the UN, WHO, UNESCO and the Council of Europe reveals important developments, including: creation of 'restraining orders' for abusers; legislation making the violence a crime; increased arrest and prosecution; national and international legislation aimed at curbing the abuse of women; and identifying the abuse as an infringement of women's rights. Protection has developed and expanded. The shelter movement is now national and international and multitudes of women have benefited from the battered women's movement. A one-day survey in 2015 of thousands of shelters in 46 countries found that over 53 000 women and 35 000 children were being given safe housing and support. In the 1970s there were only three shelters in the UK, two in Scotland and one in England. The feminist-inspired shelter movement has been an extraordinary development – demonstrating the importance and strength of feminism.

Liberal feminists have tended to seek gradual or piecemeal reform of attitudes. For example, they are very much in favour of the gender-neutral socialisation of children so that boys are not infected with a toxic version of masculinity which normalises domestic violence. Moreover, liberal feminists have successfully campaigned to challenge overt forms of patriarchy and to pressure governments to improve the civil rights of women in order to reduce gender inequalities so that women have access to many of the same opportunities as men. They have been particularly successful with regard to improving the experience of women in marriage and families, as the following examples illustrate;

a. In the 1960s and 1970s, many Western economies went through profound change because of globalisation. This led to the decline of manufacturing industry and massive male unemployment. However, it also resulted in economies shifting to the provision of service industries – for example, the numbers of jobs in government, retail, finance, hotel, personal services and fast food expanded. Consequently, the opportunity for married women with children to go out to work, to earn a wage and to have a professional career which was equivalent to her husband's in terms of status and income dramatically improved. European and American governments responded to this profound economic change by outlawing employer discrimination against female workers and by bringing in legal requirements for women to be fairly paid compared with men.

b. Governments, often under pressure from feminist research findings, reformed their education systems so that females could receive the same quality schooling as males. In many European countries, female attainment outstripped that of males in terms of qualifications and entry to university, which meant that young women now had the qualifications and ability to take advantage of the new economic opportunities coming their way.

   There is some evidence that as a result of these educational experiences young women today have undergone a '**genderquake**' experience, which means that compared with earlier generations of females they are less likely to want to get married or to want children. They are also more willing to escape unhappy relationships and marriages and are less likely to tolerate domestic violence.

c. Many governments now acknowledge that not all marriages can be successful and have put cheap and accessible legal means into place so that married people can sue for divorce.

d. By setting up health services, women in many societies now have access to contraception. This has restored '**reproductive rights**' to women which were previously in the hands of men. For example, traditionally in many societies it was usually husbands who decided on behalf of their wives if they were going to start a family, when a woman was first going to have a child and how many children she would eventually have. In some societies, women were often at high risk of maternal death because of this. Women's control of contraception restores control over their bodies.

Liberal feminism has proved very successful over the years. Women now have greater control over their destiny especially with regard to their experience of family life. Many can choose to go out to work rather staying at home full-time to bring up and look after children. Many now choose to be child-free because they are more interested in their vocation and lifestyle. Many are choosing to have their children later in their lives because they enjoy going to work and earning an independent income. Many are choosing to divorce rather than tolerating or exposing themselves or their children to marital stress or abuse.

Liberal feminists are, therefore, optimistic about the future and can see a day when gender equality is likely to be achieved in many sectors and when the influence of patriarchy is much reduced.

### Evaluation of liberal feminism

- Although they see patriarchal influence as in decline, liberal feminists acknowledge that there is still a long way to go before full equality is achieved between men and women, especially in the family and home. Liberal feminism can also be given credit for bringing about massive attitudinal change among women. The continuing relevance of feminism today, especially digital feminism, is very much a product of the success of liberal feminism.
- However, popular culture in the form of advertising and mass media representations of women are still infected with patriarchal stereotypes. Female politicians are often judged in terms of their bodies and what they wear in ways in which male politicians are not. There is clearly still a need to eradicate toxic forms of masculinity, which are symptomatic of patriarchy.
- In addition to the continuing existence of toxic and brutal forms of masculinity, there are signs that women themselves are still being encouraged by popular culture to be unhappy with their bodies, as can be seen in increasing rates of eating disorders, self-harm, fat-shaming and bullying, particularly on social media sites, and the demand for cosmetic surgery. There are also concerns that girls are becoming sexualised at an earlier age and consequently are more susceptible to grooming. Furthermore, online pornography increasingly shapes male expectations of women as sexual partners.
- Intersectional feminists argue that most of the liberal reforms have assisted White middle-class women living in the developed Western world rather than all women. There is still a long way to go to achieve gender equality in pre-industrial societies in which tradition and religion interact to keep women both subordinate and powerless. In some of these societies, females are denied the most basic human rights. For example, female babies may be killed at birth, girls might be denied education and young females may be forced to work in brutal and dangerous working conditions.
- Marxist feminists are critical of liberal feminists for failing to acknowledge that some men are oppressed more than some women in capitalist societies.
- Radical feminists such as Greer are critical of liberal feminists because they argue that women will never be truly liberated until women do not have to ape or imitate men and are free from men's control over the way they dress or behave. Radical feminists argue that societies require revolutionary change to convert them into **matriarchal** or **matrifocal** societies.

### Key terms

**Manipulation** A component of gender role socialisation in which parents encourage behaviour which is culturally acceptable for boys or girls but discourage behaviour that might be interpreted as not fitting cultural norms.

**Canalisation** A component of gender role socialisation where parents lead or channel their children's interests and activities to gender-appropriate areas. For example, toys are often classified as suitable for either boys or girls.

**Institutional sexism** Ideas and practices that may be consciously or unconsciously embedded in the regulations and actions of an organisation such as a school or police force.

**Genderquake** A radical change in attitudes compared with previous generations, so radical that it symbolises a seismic (earthquake-type) upheaval.

**Reproductive rights** The right of females to control their own bodies; for example, the right of women to decide whether they want to have children or be child-free, when to have children and how many children to have.

**Matriarchal** A society or community dominated by women – the opposite to patriarchal.

**Matrifocal** A society or culture based on the mother as the head of the family or household.

## Radical feminism

In contrast to liberal feminism, which has been mainly concerned with challenging prejudice and discrimination against females when expressed by individuals or social institutions, radical feminism is both a structuralist and a conflict theory of society.

Radical feminism is a structuralist theory because, like functionalism and Marxism, it believes that societies are social systems composed of collections of inter-dependent social institutions such as the family, the criminal justice system, education, the media, the state and so on. Like other structuralist theories, radical feminism believes that the way societies are organised or structured exercises an effect on the actions of individuals. The social structure of an institution such as the family determines the actions of individuals, both men and women, who make up those institutions.

Radical feminists argue that most societies and social systems are patriarchal. Millett (1970), for example, stated that patriarchy is everywhere and consequently it is society's most fundamental source of power.

Patriarchy is, therefore, a structural feature of society which is present in all aspects of social life and, for this reason, it is very difficult to challenge or change. Moreover, patriarchal influence means that the oppression of women is multi-layered. As Higgins observes, it operates through inequalities at the level of the law and the state, but also through the home and the workplace. It reproduces itself endlessly through these norms and structures that are themselves 'patriarchal in nature'. Radical feminists are critical of liberal feminist attempts to challenge patriarchy because they claim that their successes are too limited in scope. Radical feminists believe in more revolutionary forms of social change in order to defeat patriarchy and bring about gender equality.

Radical feminism is also a conflict theory; it argues that males and females are in fundamental conflict with one another because in patriarchal societies males exercise power over women and deliberately exploit and oppress them. Most importantly, in patriarchal societies women are expected to passively defer to male authority.

In fact, radical feminists such as Millett (1970) and Shulamith Firestone (1970) argue that men and women constitute separate and often conflicting 'sex classes' or status groups. Millett believed that women often occupy a subordinate status compared with men because it is impossible for women to acquire the power to compete equally with men. She argues that gender differences are more influential than either socio-economic or ethnic differences. For example, as evidence for this she points out that even higher-class women are subordinate to men.

Radical feminists believe that the interaction between the sexes, especially in marriage and the family, is responsible for the most important and longstanding form of inequality and conflict that exists in human societies. This clash of gender interest has resulted in battle lines being drawn between males – patriarchs – and their female victims.

Radical feminists reject the functionalist idea that the family is a cooperative unit founded on common interests and mutual support between husband and wife. Instead, they view the family as a patriarchal institution ruled by fear, intimidation and coercion. Radical feminists, therefore, focus on how the nuclear family functions to mainly benefit heterosexual men. They claim that patriarchy shapes the dynamics of family life because, in most families, the father possesses economic power and authority and boys are trained for public life. Girls, on the other hand, are prepared for their future roles as wives and mothers and, especially, taught that the idea that the gendered division of labour is 'natural' and unchangeable.

Furthermore, radical feminist thinkers have drawn attention to a range of ways in which the patriarchal nuclear family has oppressed or exploited women. For example, Firestone claimed that 'love [...] is the pivot of women's oppression today', while Christine Delphy and Diana Leonard (1992) claimed that husbands consciously and unconsciously exploit their wives despite genuinely loving them. They also argue that a woman's role within a marriage is to 'flatter' her husband and to provide emotional support for him. In contrast, men rarely perform this function for women.

Greer (2000) argues that even in marriage today women remain subservient to their husbands. She believes that single women are generally happier than married women and this is reflected in the high number of divorces instigated by women. Greer claims that wives are much more likely to suffer physical and sexual abuse than husbands, and that daughters are often victims of sexual abuse by male relatives within the family.

## The origin of patriarchy

Firestone (1970) argued that patriarchy is based upon a sexual class system that she speculates is based on biology. She claims that women were at a biological disadvantage when power was distributed in pre-industrial societies because of pregnancy and childbirth, which made them relatively weak and vulnerable. They were also tied down by the requirements of breastfeeding and hindered by menstruation. Similarly, Laura Purdy (1997) believes that the source of men's exploitation is the fact that women have babies, which restricts their ability to challenge men for power and status. Firestone and Purdy believed that men have taken advantage of these biological facts to make women dependent on them, particularly in families. This biologically derived dependency enabled men to monopolise and consolidate power and leadership positions across a range of social institutions.

Millett, while not fully sharing Firestone's arguments about the role of biology, does acknowledge that biology plays some role in establishing patriarchal power, because men can use their size and body strength to threaten physical and sexual violence against those women who fail to conform to patriarchal expectations by challenging male power.

## Radical feminism – the role of ideology

However, radical feminists also argue that men have used their biological advantage to dominate cultural institutions that can be used to spread patriarchal ideology, which aims to persuade both men and women that it is natural that men rather than women wield power and authority. This ideology has become embedded over the centuries in historical tradition, myth and religious texts. It is also often underpinned by scientific claims, for example, that males and females are biologically programmed to perform different tasks or that male and female brains are hard-wired in different ways. However, this ideology is rarely underpinned by hard scientific data. For example, there is no scientific evidence that women are better suited to raising children compared with men. Rather, these ideas have been socially constructed by men in order to justify their false claim to power over women and to ensure that women cannot compete with them for scarce resources such as jobs. In the family, this ideology is embedded in the primary socialisation process, which teaches female children that they are weak, vulnerable and not as important as their male siblings.

Furthermore, in contemporary societies, radical feminists argue that this ideology functions to dilute female aspiration and to convince women that their natural inclination is towards passivity, docility and being decorative rather than adopting 'unladylike' traits such as assertiveness and ambition. Friedan (1963) argued that mass media and advertising help to persuade women to accept that domesticity is their destiny. Millett claimed that patriarchal ideology tells women how to look, dress and behave if they are to avoid negative judgement and cultural chastisement. Millett claims that patriarchal ideology is a most ingenious form of 'interior colonisation' because it has convinced the majority of women that it is not possible to put an end to male control or **cultural hegemony.** Consequently, she believed patriarchy to be sturdier and more rigorous and enduring than any other form of segregation and inequality. When this ideology fails (which is rare), radical feminists argue that men resort to physical coercion to ensure women's conformity to patriarchal controls.

### Activity

*The archetypal 1950s housewife, UK.*

How are men and women represented in advertisements in your society?

This has motivated some radical feminists to examine why the nuclear family is often the site of violence against women and children. Catherine Redfern and Kristine Aune (2013) conclude that violence against females inside families takes many different forms, including female genital mutilation, acid throwing, the forced marriage of children, marital rape, honour killings, domestic violence and psychological bullying. Radical feminists working in these fields point out that such violence is often fuelled by a self-fulfilling patriarchal ideology which sees women as second-class citizens. Andrea Dworkin (1974) actually claimed that all men benefit from rape because women become dependent on them in order to be protected from other men.

Many radical feminists see patriarchy as a universal feature of all societies which needs to undergo fundamental or revolutionary social change. However, the exact proposed solutions to male dominance vary. Purdy (1997), for example, advocates that mothers should go on a '**baby strike**' and refuse to reproduce. However, many radical feminists are pessimistic about the possibility that patriarchal gender relations can be transformed, while current nuclear family set-ups that ultimately benefit men continue to exist. Separatists believe that women should set up alternative ways of living that exclude men. Firestone, for example, argued that women should use new reproductive technologies, such as in vitro fertilisation (IVF), to exclude men from families, because she believes that women's dependence on men derives from their childbearing and child-rearing functions. Greer (2000) also argues in favour of all-female matriarchal communes, households or families. Some argue for the abolition of the nuclear family and traditional forms of gender-role socialisation altogether, because these are seen as the primary source of patriarchal ideology.

## Evaluating radical feminism

Radical feminism has offered an important challenge to traditional sociological views and has highlighted some very important features of women's oppression. For example, radical feminists were the first to emphasise the role of violence in maintaining male power and this has led to an important recognition of the significance of problems such as domestic violence and rape. They have also been able to emphasise and give insight into the enduring and apparently intractable problem of male dominance.

However, six key criticisms can be made of radical feminism and how it views the family;

- It has dated fairly significantly, because it fails to account for recent economic and social changes, such as the educational success of young females, women's use of divorce, and many women's rejection of domestic labour as their exclusive responsibility. Liberal feminists argue that radical feminists tend to underestimate the extent to which women have become less oppressed and more liberated in families (especially in Western societies) and the range of non-patriarchal options that they can now choose from in terms of how they want to organise their futures.
- Jennifer Somerville (2000) and Hakim (2000) both argue that radical feminism probably exaggerates the exploitation of women in the family. They argue that most women value their relationships with men and that the bulk of male–female relationships are based on mutual love and respect rather than exploitation, domination and subordination.
- Radical feminists ignore those accounts of family life in which females experience motherhood as fulfilling and rewarding, or they dismiss this experience as less rewarding than having a career. Hakim argues that this is condescending. Many women choose to be mothers and gain great satisfaction from this role. She argues that, as an option, it should be judged no differently from any other.
- Like other structural theories, radical feminism is guilty of over-emphasising the nuclear family and neglecting the rich diversity of other family types in modern society. For example, who exactly is guilty of exploitation in the female-headed single-parent family?
- The radical feminist concept of patriarchy may be over-simplistic, because it does not accommodate the idea that some men do not enthusiastically uphold or want to benefit from patriarchy. Furthermore, it fails to acknowledge that women's actions contribute to the maintenance of patriarchy (although radical feminists often dismiss these women as 'cultural dopes' or victims of patriarchal ideology).
- Intersectional feminists who are part of the third wave of feminism argue that radical feminists exaggerate the degree to which all women are similar and share similar interests. Consequently, they ignore or neglect other important social divisions (such as ethnicity). Sara Delamont (2001) suggests that there are many divisions between women on grounds of income and social class, ethnicity and religion which radical feminists neglect. For example, the influence of factors such as religion or racism may mean that Black or Asian women may experience more male exploitation than White women.

Black feminists have accused radical feminism of ethnocentrism. They claim that White radical feminists have tended to portray Black women as the helpless victims of both racism and sexism. Black feminists argue that White feminists cannot claim to speak for the experience of all women and Black women can provide a unique and essential contribution to feminism in general. For example, the pioneering American Black feminist bell hooks (1981) argued that the legacy of slavery had given Black women a unique insight into the nature of oppression, which White feminists do not have.

Similarly, Safia Mirza (1997) argues that a distinctive Black British feminism is essential in order to challenge distorted assumptions that Black women are passive victims of racism, patriarchy and class inequality. She argues that this is simply not true, because such women have fought to overcome sexism and racism in education and elsewhere. Black feminism has also been important in developing postcolonial feminism, which is particularly concerned with challenging gender inequalities that result in part from colonialism in the developing countries of Africa, Asia and Latin America. For example, they have analysed how the legacy of colonialism has affected women caught up in the AIDS/HIV epidemic in Africa.

## Socialist or Marxist feminism

Rosemarie Tong (2017) observes that 'although it is possible to distinguish between Marxist and socialist feminist thought, it is quite difficult to do so'. She argues that the main difference is one of emphasis rather than substance. For example, she observes that Marxist feminists are particularly indebted to and influenced by the work of one of the co-authors of *The Communist Manifesto*, Engels, and especially his critique of marriage and the nuclear family. Marxist feminists also tend to see patriarchy as a product of capitalism and social class inequality rather than seeing it as a free-standing social system.

Socialist feminists, like radical feminists, recognise the fundamental oppression of women and the importance of patriarchy in bringing about women's subordination. However, socialist feminists do not insist that gender is the only source of women's oppression. They also recognise that social class and ethnicity are important, and that any analysis of patriarchal oppression needs to examine the role of social class and ethnicity in bringing about women's subordination.

Socialist feminism opposes the separatism demanded by radical feminists and argues instead that women need to work with socialist men to bring about gender equality. They also differ from liberal feminists who believe that progress towards equality can be achieved within the constraints of the way societies are currently organised. Socialist feminists, like Marxist feminists, believe that society needs to be radically restructured so that it is truly meritocratic. This means that rewards in the form of status, power, jobs, income, qualifications and social mobility should be neutrally based on merit (levels of ability, talent, skill, hard work measured by objective examination), regardless of gender.

Both socialist and Marxist feminist theories of the family are influenced by the work of Engels, who argued that patriarchy was a crucial factor in the emergence of capitalism in the 18th century (see Unit 4.1.3). He claimed that patriarchy emerged alongside the development of the nuclear family and particularly monogamous marriage. Engels suggests that these processes resulted in the 'world-historical defeat of the female sex', because thereafter men commanded both the family and home, while the woman's role in the family was reduced to the servicing of male needs. However, Engels' ideas are not based on any convincing historical evidence. They are mere speculation.

Marxist feminists such as Margaret Benston (1972) and Martha Gimenez and Jane Collins (1990), like all feminists, saw patriarchal oppression by men as central to women's experience, but they did not see this oppression as the main source of social inequality. Like Marxism in general, they saw social class relationships as the major cause of inequality. From a Marxist feminist perspective, all labour – paid and domestic – is exploited by the capitalist class for profit. Gender oppression is, therefore, part and parcel of the general oppression of all workers, waged or unwaged. Moreover, Marxist feminists see patriarchy as a deliberate ideology designed and constructed by the capitalist class to justify the exploitation of women's domestic labour, which ultimately functions to benefit the ruling class.

Most Marxist feminist analysis of the family has focused on the contribution of female domestic labour – housework and childcare – to capitalist economies. They point out that domestic labour is unpaid but observe that it has great value for capitalist economies. For example, Benston (1972) suggested that the nuclear family, and especially women's nurturing role within it, is important to capitalism because it produces and rears the future workforce at little cost to the capitalist state. She also argued that domestic labour ensures that the male workforce is fit, happy and healthy to go to work and consequently to be productive. In other words, the housework role (which involves feeding the male worker, shopping to meet his needs, bringing up his children and making sure he has a clean and relaxing environment to return home to every day) contributes to the effectiveness of male labour and the value of the work he produces for his employer. Moreover, if his emotional and physical needs are met by his wife, he is less likely to interpret his work or his workplace as alienating or lacking in satisfaction.

There is no question that Marxist feminists are correct in their view that domestic labour makes a tremendous contribution to the economy and that employers benefit from the unpaid labour of women in the home. For example, in the UK, in 2014, the government estimated that laundry and ironing in the home was worth an estimated £97.2 billion in 2012, while unpaid childcare was estimated to be worth £343 billion in 2010 – three times higher than the contribution to the British economy made by the financial sector.

### Activity

Convert the figures into the local currency of the society in which you live. What other 'free' labour, mainly carried out by your mother, might also be assigned a monetary value? Think about healthcare, cooking (how much do restaurants or canteens charge for this?) or transporting you to various places. If you had to pay your mother for these services, what might a fair weekly wage be?

Marxist feminists argue that women's work is being exploited by the capitalist class because the wage received by the male worker only includes payment for his labour – it does not include payment for the domestic labour of his female partner, which makes an essential contribution both to his value as a worker and the capitalist economy.

Another important Marxist feminist is Ansley (1972), who suggests that capitalism has stripped male workers of dignity, power and control at work. Surveys of factory workers suggest that many are bored and dissatisfied by the tedious nature of their work. Many are alienated, meaning that they cannot identify with or bring themselves to care about the product they are making. They feel powerless and consequently feel that their masculinity is being challenged. However, Ansley argues that this male frustration, dissatisfaction and alienation is often absorbed by the family, and particularly by their female partner, in the form of domestic violence. Wives, therefore, act as safety valves for capitalism because these men are not directing their anger at the real cause of their problems – the nature of capitalism and the alienation that results from its organisation of production.

## Evaluating Marxist and socialist feminism

On the positive side, Marxist feminists have shown how gender roles within the family may be

## Contemporary issues: Wages for housework

Both socialist and Marxist feminists have campaigned for wages to be paid for housework. In 2014, Selma James founded the International Wages for Housework (WFH) campaign to re-ignite the global domestic labour debate.

The WFH campaign has only been partly successful, in that Venezuela has been the only country that has agreed to pay women for childcare and housework. In 2007, President Hugo Chavez announced that 200 000 poor women who were head of households would receive 80 per cent of the legal minimum wage (amounting to approximately $180 per month).

However, Zoe Fairbairns (1988) is critical of the WFH campaign. She claims that demanding money for unpaid domestic work was a 'sad indictment' of feminism, because it demonstrated that it had lost the battle to force men to do their fair share of childcare and housework. Similarly, Lisa Tuttle (1986) claims that 'paying women for child-, house-, and husband-care simply reinforces the very traditions and prejudices that keep women in the home', whereas Daniela Del Boca (2014) objects to WFH because it acts as a disincentive for women to get jobs and have careers. In her view, it also dilutes the powerful message that working mothers with careers send out to their daughters, which is that a female career is fundamental if women are to escape economic dependency on men. Fiona Cameron (2018) points out that WFH is discriminatory, because women who already have paid work are unlikely to receive additional payments for the extra work that they currently do for free in the home.

### Questions

1. Why do Socialist and Marxist feminists believe that women should receive a wage for their domestic labour?
2. Identify four criticisms of the Wages for Housework campaign.

created and perpetuated by the requirements of capitalist society rather than being 'natural', as functionalists argue.

However, like Marxists, they see the family as performing predetermined functions for the good of capitalist society rather than for society as a whole. They therefore insist that the nuclear family only benefits the capitalist class and men. However, this can be criticised because it ignores the day-to-day experiences and interpretations of women who choose to live in such families because they enjoy and benefit from the experience of being a mother, wife, partner and so on.

Radical feminists are critical of Marxist feminists because they argue that patriarchy pre-dates capitalism. Moreover, there is no guarantee that a radical change in the economic organisation of society will eradicate patriarchy or gender inequality. There is no evidence that women's everyday conditions have changed (with the exception of Venezuela) relative to those in capitalist countries in countries which claim to be communist or socialist. Female opportunities in terms of careers and paid work might improve, but domestic conditions probably undergo little change, as Wayne Ellwood (1982) observed when he noted that in communist Russia women went into space but they still had to do the washing and ironing when they got home.

Moreover, the Marxist feminist model of the family is still largely based upon the rather dated model of the nuclear family of working husband and economically dependent full-time housewife. Many families no longer fit into this category, because modern families are extremely diverse in their organisation and structure. Many nuclear families are dual-career and consequently women may now have the economic and cultural power to resist any attempt to allocate them to exclusively domestic and maternal roles.

**Triple systems feminist theory** Sylvia Walby's (1990) **triple systems theory** is an attempt to deal with some of the common weaknesses of feminist theory. In particular, she addresses the intersectional feminists' argument that the impact of patriarchy on female experience is made complicated by the influence of both social class and ethnicity. Walby makes it very clear that any theory of patriarchy must not restrict itself to gender, because a working-class woman's experience of patriarchy may be more negative than a middle-class woman's experience. In other words, social class in the form of poverty, living in a deprived neighbourhood and lack of educational qualifications may all worsen the experience of patriarchy, while being fairly affluent and well-educated may mean that a middle-class woman is better equipped to deal with patriarchal pressures. Similarly, women from ethnic minority groups may find that their negative experience of patriarchy is reinforced by powerful traditions and religious belief systems which very clearly state that females should be ascribed second-class citizenship. This compares with White women living in secular European societies in which traditional obligations have been largely replaced with individualistic value systems and indifference towards religious beliefs.

Walby has analysed how systems perpetuate and reinforce patriarchy. She identifies two types of patriarchy. She argues that '**private patriarchy**' is found in personal relationships and the home/family, while '**public patriarchy**' is found in those social institutions that form a part of public life such as the education system, religion, the economy, the law, the state, and cultural institutions such as the media and the arts. Both private and public forms of patriarchy interact with other socio-economic and cultural factors to create a unified system of patriarchy that shapes the subordination of women across a range of social situations. For example:

- In the public sphere of the economy, women have a legal right to equal pay and opportunity in the workplace but this has not resulted in the eradication of the gender pay gap. However, talented and well-qualified females are prevented from obtaining top jobs by a **glass ceiling** – an invisible but real, unacknowledged barrier to female advancement in management and the professions which prevents them from achieving economic equality with men. There is evidence too from a range of more industrialised societies that White women are more likely to be in employment, to earn higher rates of pay and to break through this glass ceiling compared with similarly qualified and experienced women from ethnic minority backgrounds.
- Sometimes private and public forms of patriarchy combine to exclude women from occupational success. Walby highlights the existence of powerful ideologies employed to foment guilt in women and so prevent them from competing on an equal playing field for jobs. For example, 'a woman's place is in the home' or 'all women have a maternal instinct' or working mothers risk causing their children 'psychological damage' are all-powerful cultural ideas which seep into the private world of

relationships and family and may shape decisions taken by couples which ultimately disadvantage women rather than men.

These ideologies might lead women to delay going back to work after giving birth or to have more children. Some cultures, especially in pre-industrial societies, may not give women a choice between motherhood and career because cultural tradition demands they become homemakers.

In conclusion, then, Walby clearly demonstrates that patriarchal power emanates from a complex web or system of interlinked private and public institutions underpinned by gender, social class and ethnicity. However, Beatrix Campbell (2014) argues that sociologists need to add a fourth factor – globalisation – to this list. She argues that patriarchal oppression is unlikely to be the same experience across different societies. It is likely to have a greater impact in societies in which fundamentalist religions dominate, in which female infanticide, female circumcision, child marriages and the **dowry system** are common. In many less industrialised societies, girls are deliberately excluded from education, which is seen to be an exclusively male privilege. In Pakistan, Malala Yousafzai was shot by the Taliban in 2012 for campaigning in favour of girls' education. She was 15 years old. Moreover, in those societies which have experienced industrialisation because of the outsourcing by Western capitalism of products such as textiles, sportswear and electrical items, young women are seen as an easily exploitable group in terms of working long hours in dangerous conditions for very low rates of pay. Often these women have no rights and are dismissed if they suffer accidents, fall pregnant or protest against their working conditions.

## Conclusion

In conclusion, Higgins notes that feminists have drawn attention to both the longevity and the peculiar elusiveness of patriarchy and gendered power. Feminism, in all its varied forms, has clearly shown us that patriarchy is not located in any one place or social institution, and that individual examples of gender inequality actually interact and reinforce each other to create a complex and largely invisible system of oppression. They have also made us very aware that the eradication of patriarchy is a task of enormous complexity that is not likely to be achieved any time soon.

### Key terms

**Cultural hegemony** Domination or rule maintained through ideological or cultural means.

**Baby strike** A call by radical feminists for women to refuse to have babies, claiming that motherhood is the biggest obstacle to women's progress and that it reinforces patriarchy.

**Triple systems theory** A feminist theory of patriarchy associated with Walby which argues that there are three crucial influences on a woman's experience of inequality and oppression – gender, social class and ethnicity.

**Private patriarchy** A type of male domination found exclusively in the home, family and in personal relationships.

**Public patriarchy** Institutionalised forms of sexual prejudice and discrimination found across a range of social institutions, including government, education and the law.

**Glass ceiling** The unseen, yet unbreachable, barrier that keeps women from rising to the upper rungs of the corporate ladder, regardless of their qualifications or achievements.

**Dowry system** Refers to the cash and property that the bride's family gives to the bridegroom, his parents, or his relatives as a condition of the marriage.

### Summary

1. Feminists aim to describe the extent of gender inequality that exists across the world. Most aim to explain male domination and female subordination with reference to the concept of patriarchy.
2. Liberal feminists have challenged gender inequality in a range of social areas of modern life and put pressure on governments to introduce measures that either empower females or outlaw gendered discrimination. They are optimistic that social change will eventually lead to the disappearance of patriarchy, although they acknowledge that there is still some distance to travel.

3. Radical feminism argues that patriarchy should be considered as a complex social system which has embedded its ideology into the foundation of every social institution and consequently determines how structures are organised and the social actions of both men and women. Radical feminists argue that men and women have little in common with one another and that males use their power in all areas of society to exploit, oppress and dominate women.
4. From a radical feminist perspective, love and romance are merely patriarchal devices that men use to manipulate women.
5. Marxist feminists believe that social class inequality is the main source of power, and that patriarchy is consequently a product of capitalism. Marxist feminists argue that women's family labour contributes to the profits made by the capitalist class, because women ensure that men are fit and healthy to work and that children will grow up to be the future workforce.
6. Intersectional feminists believe that gender needs to be considered as exerting a similar influence as social class and ethnicity over the experience of women. Some women have more means at their disposal to resist patriarchy because they possess wealth, status and education, while others may find that their experience of patriarchy is more oppressive because they live in poverty or in a racially segregated society or are subject to strict religious controls. Walby's triple systems theory is a good example of intersectional feminism.

# Unit 4.3.2 Conjugal roles and debates about gender equality in the family

This unit aims to examine the empirical or first-hand evidence regarding the role each spouse takes on within the home with regard to domestic labour – that is, to work out who is responsible for the lion's share of housework and whether specific tasks such as childcare are regarded primarily as a male or female responsibility. There have been literally hundreds of pieces of sociological research conducted by sociologists looking at how domestic labour is divided up between males and females in order to provide evidence for the points raised by the feminist perspectives in Unit 4.3.1.

## The distribution of domestic labour in the home

Most sociological studies of **domestic labour** in the home have been carried out in Western societies. For example, one classic study was carried out by Michael Young and Peter Willmott (1957) in a working-class district of London in the 1950s. They observed that marital or **conjugal roles** in working-class families in this period were clearly segregated. Men were primarily wage-earners and were responsible for very few domestic tasks around the home. It was rare for a father to attend the birth of his child or to be involved with the day-to-day care of his children. Men regarded themselves as the head of the household – they exercised this social power on the basis of their superior earning power and consequently were responsible for family discipline and decision-making. Furthermore, they spent their leisure time with other men rather than their spouses. In contrast, few females worked outside the home and consequently they were often economically dependent on their husband, who would allocate their 'housekeeping' money. Women were usually exclusively responsible for all aspects of housework and childcare. They generally exercised little power over decision-making and sometimes were the victims of their spouse's physical power in the form of domestic violence. The **domestic division of labour** and power relations in the home therefore were generally unequal.

### Activity

*Conjugal roles in the 1950s, UK.*

Describe the conjugal roles found by Young and Willmott in 1950s London.

However, on the basis of further research that they conducted in the 1970s, Young and Willmott (1973) claimed that men and women's attitudes towards the distribution of labour in the home had undergone radical change in the modern UK so that in both middle-class and working-class households conjugal roles were more likely to be jointly shared. They argued that this trend towards joint conjugal roles meant that marriage in the 1970s was likely to be egalitarian. They claimed that this domestic change had been brought about by three important social changes:

- Greater educational and job opportunities led to larger numbers of working-class people experiencing geographical mobility. Moving away from the areas in which they were born and raised meant they were often isolated from extended kin and free from traditional influences about how they were supposed to organise domestic tasks that had favoured segregated conjugal roles.
- Women started going out to work in greater numbers than ever before and began making a significant economic contribution to the standard of living of their family. Families could afford to buy goods (for example, televisions) and time- and labour-saving devices (for example, vacuum cleaners), which made the home a more attractive place to be in for both males and females.
- Women acquired more power in a variety of ways. They acquired power over their own fertility because of contraception. They acquired economic power because going out to work meant they were no longer exclusively dependent on housekeeping money from their husband's wages. These powers therefore meant women could put pressure on men to do more around the home.

Young and Willmott concluded that these changes had resulted in a new family form – the **symmetrical family** (a type of nuclear unit) – in which women experience equality with men. Young and Willmott argued that in this type of family both spouses were involved in paid work and therefore made a joint contribution to the family income and bills, and that housework and childcare tasks were more equitably distributed. Decision-making was shared and spouses enjoyed spending leisure time together.

## Activity

*A symmetrical family.*

Explain how the symmetrical family differs from the domestic division of labour described by Young and Willmott in their 1957 study.

## The feminist response to Young and Willmott

The liberal feminist sociologist Oakley (1974) responded to Young and Willmott's ideas that marriage was increasingly becoming egalitarian with her own academic study of domestic work. As Chambers (2012) notes, until Oakley's study appeared, housework had not been considered worthy of study by male sociologists because it was regarded as an everyday private activity.

The idea that equality was a central characteristic of marriage in the 1970s was strongly opposed by Oakley, who rejected the notion of a symmetrical family. She argued that patriarchy was still very much a major characteristic of modern nuclear families and that women still occupied a subordinate and dependent role within the family and in wider society.

Oakley interviewed 40 housewives living in suburban London and found some quantitative evidence of husbands helping in the home but found little evidence of symmetry or equality. Only 15 per cent of husbands had a high level of participation in housework, but even this group saw housework as 'her work' rather than something to be jointly shared.

Oakley's research was carried out over 40 years ago, but recent research suggests that her view that domestic labour was organised in a deeply unequal way and consequently her rejection of symmetry may still hold true. Contemporary feminist sociologists suggest that there is little hard evidence in the 21st century for equality in marriage in Western societies with regards to domestic labour, despite the fact that many women are now engaged in paid work and working long hours outside the home.

For example, research by Lyn Craig (2007) found that women do between one-third and one-half more housework than men. She argues that this inequality begins when a couple move in together and before they have children. She calls this aspect of domestic inequality the '**partnership penalty**'. Her research found that when couples marry, the wife's unpaid domestic labour rises in volume, while the husband does less housework compared with when he was single. Moreover, when the couple do have children, the female also experiences an additional '**motherhood penalty**'. The decision to have children results in the mother being financially worse off across her lifetime compared with men in general and child-free women.

A survey of 1000 men and women in Britain in 2014 carried out by the BBC found that modern marriage was often characterised by outbreaks of '**chore wars**' rather than equality and symmetry. It found evidence of consistent conflict emerging between partners over domestic chores. Two-thirds of those aged between 18 and 34 years admitted that they regularly argued with their partners over housework. Women were particularly frustrated with their partners over how little they did around the home or about the male standard of cleanliness, which many felt did not achieve their own standards.

The quantitative evidence collected from American, Australian and European surveys that measure how much time men and women allocate to childcare and housework (known as **time-budget studies**) clearly supports the feminist argument that women today are experiencing a '**second shift**' or '**dual burden**' with regard to housework. This means that married women are mainly responsible for the bulk of domestic tasks despite holding down full-time jobs. This second shift usually starts before they go to work (for example, preparing breakfast and packed lunches for children) and resumes when they return (for example, laundry, cleaning and cooking). Women therefore work two shifts, because in reality they have two jobs – one paid and one unpaid – and they experience the double burden of trying to be effective at both. Some feminists are critical of time-budget surveys because both men and women are often unaware of the invisible 'work' that women do around the home. They argue that women unconsciously view housework as a 'norm' to be done unthinkingly and men are simply ignorant of the full extent of women's contribution to the home.

However, the reliability of time-budget studies has been criticised because those sociologists conducting them have to trust that participants are accurately estimating their contribution in terms of minutes and hours. There may be a tendency for some research subjects to either exaggerate or understate their involvement in housework or childcare. Time-budget studies may therefore lack objectivity.

Sociological studies have also noted that the distinction between work and leisure or free time is less clear-cut for married women. For example, Annabel Venning and Guy Walters (2018) found that wives usually interpret leisure time as time free from both paid work and family commitments, but felt they were on call with regard to domestic duties and especially childcare 24 hours a day, whereas husbands saw all time outside paid work as their leisure time. Consequently, time-budget studies consistently show that in the UK men experience 43 hours of 'he-time' per week, while the number of leisure hours experienced by women per week who have families has actually fallen in recent years.

**Leisure hours taken per week**

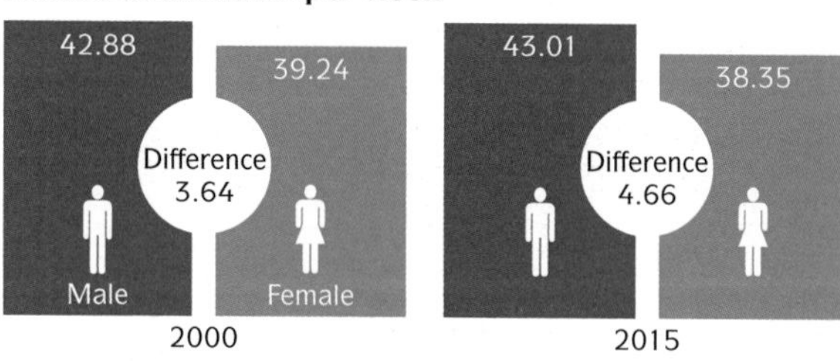


**Women's leisure time at different ages**
**Hours per week**

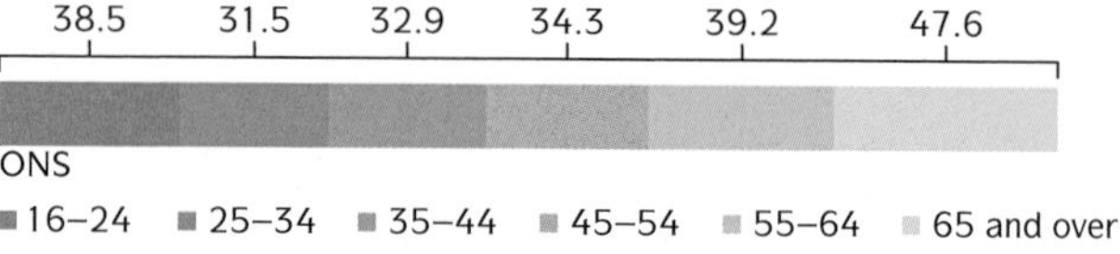


Venning argues that the moment working women leave their desks, they plunge into another workplace of childcare, food shopping, multiple loads of laundry, filling in school forms and booking doctors' appointments. She observes that 'each individual task doesn't take long but add them together and it's a wonder we women have time to brush our teeth, let alone luxuriate in a long bath. Even our thinking time is taken up tackling what has been dubbed the "mental load" – all the planning of what needs to be done.'

However, although the gender revolution in terms of domestic labour is unlikely to happen for some time, there may be good news in favour of equality occurring at some future date. First, men today are doing a great deal more around the home compared with their fathers and grandfathers. Second, there is also evidence that, as women's earning power increases relative to men's, so men take more responsibility for domestic labour. In 2018, women's earnings still remain unequal, at about three-quarters of those of men across most European societies. However, Rosemary Crompton's (2006) analysis concluded that if female earnings were to improve, then so too will the division of labour in the home. Third, research does indicate that men are more likely to be involved in childcare rather than housework. There is a wealth of evidence which supports this. For example, Judith Treas and Giulia Dotti Sani (2016) found that fathers across most Western countries are spending more time with their children than parents did in the mid-1960s. Time spent with children is highest among better-educated parents. Their research, which covered the period 1965–2012, asked 122 271 parents (68 532 mothers, 53 739 fathers) in Canada, the UK, the US, Denmark, Norway, France, Germany, the Netherlands, Italy, Spain and Slovenia to keep a diary of all their daily activities. Researchers then analysed differences by randomly selecting one day from each diary and tabulating the amount of time recorded for both interactive and routine childcare activities. The research concluded that fathers' time with children had nearly quadrupled. In 1965, dads spent a daily average of just 16 minutes with their kids, while today's fathers spend about 59 minutes a day caring for them.

However, sociologists need to be cautious in their interpretation of this data, because they do not say a great deal about the quality of the relationship between the father and the child. For example, Craig (2007) found that often men only engage in childcare when the mother is nearby and that most of the time fathers spent with their children was spent playing with them or talking to them. Craig noted that women's time with children was mainly spent practically servicing them – that is, feeding, clothing or cleaning them. Women often found it difficult to find the time for the sorts of quality interaction with children enjoyed by men because they were more likely to be looking after children while undertaking other tasks such as preparing meals.

### Activity

Design and carry out a time-budget survey to find out how much time your parents spend on specific household tasks (make a list; for example, cooking, vacuuming, making beds, cleaning the toilet, washing clothes, ironing and so on). Ask them who is or was responsible for particular childcare tasks (for example, cooking for children, preparing their school lunch, getting them up and dressed in the morning, dropping them off at school or picking them up from school, making them dinner, arranging with other parents for their friends to come for a sleepover, organising birthday parties, supervising bathtime, reading to them, helping them with homework and putting them to bed). Which partner is or was responsible for planning, for example, anticipating when children will need new shoes or clothes (because they are growing)?

## Decision-making in families

An important aspect of equality and symmetry for Young and Willmott was the spouses' sharing of family decision-making, which in traditional patriarchal families with segregated roles had always been dominated by men. Some sociologists have, therefore, focused on decision-making in couples and argue that true equality in terms of the domestic division of labour can only occur if decision-making or power is shared equally between a couple.

Stephen Edgell's (1980) study of professional couples found that decision-making in nuclear families could be allocated to three broad categories:

- Very important decisions – these generally were economic or financial decisions involving finance, a change of job or moving house. Edgell found that these decisions were either taken by the husband alone or taken jointly but with the husband having the final say. Edgell concluded that the husband's power mainly derived from his superior earning power.
- Important decisions – these decisions focused on the quality of family life or children's lives, such as those about children's schooling (for example, whether to choose private or state schools) or where to go on holiday. These were normally taken jointly but seldom by the wife alone, probably because such decisions were likely to involve a substantial economic investment.

- Less important decisions – these decisions focused on the everyday minutiae of family life, such as shopping for food, domestic items and children's clothing and were usually made exclusively by the wife.

Irene Hardill et al. (1997) repeated Edgell's research over a decade later and found few signs of change. They discovered that middle-class wives generally deferred to their husbands in major decisions involving where to live, the size of the mortgage, buying cars and so on. They concluded that the men in their sample were able to demand that the interests of their wives and families should be subordinated to the man's career because he was the major breadwinner. However, Gillian Leighton's (1992) research did discover that the power to influence and make family decisions changed when males became unemployed. In her study of professional couples, working wives often took over responsibility for bills and initiated cutbacks in spending.

### Activity

Using Edgell's categories, investigate whether these decisions in your home are jointly undertaken or whether they are taken exclusively by your mother or father. For example, do you live where you do because of your father's job or your mother's job?

## Emotion work

A number of feminist sociologists have argued that it is important to go beyond merely counting what men and women do within marriage, and to examine how women feel about it. Susan Brownmiller (1975) argues that housework is often experienced as a thankless and alienating task because other members of the family rarely witness it first-hand. Moreover, other members of the family often undo what housework achieves during the course of the day. Housework has been compared with hacking a way through a jungle, only to turn around to see that the path just cut has grown over again. Michèle Barrett and Mary McIntosh (1980) described the housewife role as like 'being banged up in a solitary (prison) cell while the guards attend to other, more important business'.

This sort of qualitative exploration of women's feelings about marriage and domestic labour has led some sociologists to an examination of the 'emotional work' that goes on within the family unit. Jean Duncombe and Dennis Marsden (1995) argued that any measurement of equality within households must take account of '**emotion work**'. This involves thinking about the emotional well-being and happiness of other members of the household and acting in ways which will be of emotional benefit to others. This might include:

- sustaining the relationship between fathers and children
- complimenting family members for their achievements
- trying to ensure that family members are happy or enjoying life
- smoothing over arguments between family members
- buying presents and cards for birthdays so that the family keeps in touch with close relatives and extended kin
- hugging family members and reassuring them of love
- planning and organising social events that others will enjoy.

### Activity

*Emotion work.*

Who does most of the 'emotion work' in your family?

Duncombe and Marsden argued that women take the major responsibility for the emotional well-being of their partners and children in addition to paid work and responsibility for housework and childcare. In this sense, women actually work a '**triple shift**'. Jacqui Gabb (2008) argues that the activities that women routinely do, such as feeding the family, not only serve a pragmatic purpose, but they also perform a symbolic function, with mothers literally constructing a sense of family community and sense of belonging. The message of women's work in the family is essentially emotional. It is a practical way of confirming love and care and reinforces family bonds.

However, feminists point out that most family members generally benefit from women's emotion work, but women rarely do. Arlie Hochschild (2003) argues that mothers are rarely thanked for this work because what they do is **gender bound** – it is seen by other family members as part of their gendered duty. For example, if the father provides childcare, it is often interpreted by him as a gift to the mother, but not so if the mother provides it because it is seen as her job.

Duncombe and Marsden carried out in-depth interviews with 40 couples and found that women felt that their male partners were lacking in terms of '**emotional participation**'; that is, men found it difficult to express their feelings, to tell their partners how they felt about them, to relate emotionally to their children and to show gratitude for the work women did in the home. Duncombe and Marsden argued that this increases the burden on women because women feel they should attempt to compensate and please all parties in the family. Consequently, women spend a great deal of time soothing the emotions of partners and children but other family members do not pay similar attention to their wives' or mothers' emotional needs.

This triple shift and the inequality in the exchange of emotion associated with it often leads to the neglect of women's well-being, which can have negative consequences for women's happiness and their mental and physical health. A number of studies of marriage confirm this inequality in the exchange of emotion.

For example, Jesse Bernard's classic study of marriage (1982) found that the men in her study were more satisfied with their marriage than their wives, many of whom expressed emotional loneliness. Moreover, these men had no idea that their wives were so unhappy.

Karyn Loscocco and Susan Walzer (2013) reviewed sociological and psychological studies of contemporary marriage and found the following:

- Women often express their unhappiness in marriage more than men do.
- Women are more likely than men to see problems in their marriage.
- Women are more likely to initiate divorce proceedings and are more than three times as likely as their former husbands to have strongly wanted the divorce. Michael Bittman and Jocelyn Pixley (1997) suggest that inequality in the distribution of childcare, housework tasks and emotion work is the major cause of divorce in UK society.
- Once-married men are more likely to say that they want to marry again compared with once-married women.

Loscocco and Walzer also note that women find it exhausting to be the one who maintains the emotional temperature of a relationship and who keeps the ties to family and community going. This creates resentment, which can lead to marital tension and divorce.

## Lesbian couples and gender scripts

Gillian Dunne (1997) argues that the traditional division of domestic labour continues today because of what she calls deeply ingrained '**gender scripts**'. These are the traditional or conventional social expectations or norms that set out the different gender roles that heterosexual men and women in relationships are expected to play. Such expectations are normally contained within familial and patriarchal ideology.

In her study of 37 cohabiting lesbian couples with dependent children, Dunne found that such gender scripts do not operate to the same extent. Many of the characteristics of the traditional domestic division of labour do not exist in the lesbian family or household. For example, Dunne found evidence of symmetry and egalitarianism in her sample of lesbian households – both partners gave equal importance to each other's careers and viewed childcare positively. However, she did find that where one partner did much more paid work than the other, the time that each partner spent on domestic work was likely to be unequal.

Dunne's conclusions were challenged by Chris Carrington (1999), who carried out an **ethnographic** study of gay and lesbian couples. He found tension in these relationships because of inequalities in the distribution of household tasks which were similar to those experienced by heterosexual couples. Carrington remained unconvinced that the domestic arrangements of lesbian and gay couples were somehow an example of equality that heterosexuals should aspire to imitate.

## Key terms

**Domestic labour** Unpaid labour – housework, childcare and so on – carried out within the home, often by women.

**Conjugal roles** The roles played by a male and female partner in marriage or in a cohabiting relationship.

**Domestic division of labour** The way that men and women divide up housework and childcare between themselves.

**Symmetrical family** A type of nuclear family identified by Young and Willmott in which husband and wife supposedly share domestic labour, decision-making and leisure time.

**Partnership penalty** An idea associated with Craig. She claims that the decision of a couple to live together or marry benefits the male but penalises the female, in that she ends up responsible for the bulk of domestic labour.

**Motherhood penalty** Craig claims that motherhood often means that women have more responsibility for domestic labour and less time for leisure.

**Chore wars** The conflict that results between a couple about who should be responsible for domestic labour.

**Time-budget study** A type of social survey which asks respondents to estimate the amount of time they spend on a particular task.

**Second shift** The idea that married women have two jobs and consequently no leisure time. They spend their day in paid work but still do most of the unpaid labour in the home.

**Dual burden** Another term for the second shift.

**Emotion work** The idea that women are responsible for the emotional health and well-being of family members.

**Triple shift** The idea that women have three pressures on their time – paid work, unpaid domestic labour and emotion work.

**Gender bound** The idea that men and women are culturally obligated to perform certain tasks – for example, that men provide for their families and women are emotional caretakers.

**Emotional participation** Sharing one's feelings, experiences and emotions, particularly within an intimate relationship or family context.

**Gender scripts** The idea that male and female behaviour is performed according to cultural expectations about masculinity and femininity.

**Ethnographic** Sociological research which studies social groups in their own environment going about their everyday business.

## Summary

1. Functionalist sociologists such as Young and Willmott argue that modern nuclear families are symmetrical families in which marriage is egalitarian and housework and childcare tasks are fairly distributed between spouses, and leisure and decision-making are shared.
2. However, sociological studies generally do not support the view that marriage has become egalitarian.
3. Studies of domestic labour suggest that women still take most of the responsibility for childcare and housework, although men have increased their participation worldwide in child-rearing. However, many women work second shifts – they go to work full-time yet still do the lion's share of domestic labour.
4. Moreover, men still largely control decision-making in families.
5. Women are also mainly responsible for emotional labour in families and, in this sense, they work a triple shift.
6. Overall, sociological studies suggest that women are more likely to be unhappy in marriage than men.

# Unit 4.3.3 The dark side of family relationships

Unit 4.1.2 outlined the functionalist theory of the family, which tends to present a very idealised picture of family life. Parsons, for example, saw the nuclear family as a system of positive loving relationships which meet the basic human need for love and intimacy. Marriage is seen as particularly important as a source of companionship, emotional gratification and psychological support. Other writers in the functionalist tradition such as Willmott and Young suggest that the nuclear unit is egalitarian in the distribution of domestic tasks and decision-making. Overall, then, the nuclear unit is seen as good for society and positive for the individuals who comprise it. Such thinking is echoed by New Right thinkers, who portray nuclear family life as the ideal to which we should all strive.

However, this positive picture of nuclear family life has come under sustained attack in the last 30 years. We have already looked at feminist and Marxist critiques of family life (see Units 4.1.2 and 4.1.3) which suggest that the ways in which modern families are organised suit men and the ruling class at the expense of women and the working class respectively. This unit focuses on what is called the 'dark side' of family relationships, notably the idea that living in families can sometimes be very dysfunctional or harmful to women and children.

## Domestic violence and abuse

Cheal (2002) observes that family relationships can easily slip into damaging relationships, and love can often turn into hate in moments of intense emotion. He notes that 'we have to face the paradox that families are contexts of love and nurturance, but they are also contexts of violence and murder'. Similarly, Anthony Giddens (1992) argues that it is the nature of family life that makes violence in families a common occurrence. He argues that family life is characterised by 'emotional intensity and personal intimacy' – this means that it is normally charged with strong emotions, often mixing 'love' and 'hate'. In these circumstances, even minor arguments can escalate into acts of violence. The growing isolation of the nuclear family from extended kinship networks may be increasing this intensity.

A review of global family-related violence suggests that families may be toxic and dangerous environments, particularly for women and children. Global statistics demonstrate that murder by other family members, domestic violence (which is mainly perpetrated by husbands on their wives) and child abuse (which can take several forms ranging from neglect to various types of abuse – emotional, physical and sexual) are shockingly common. In the UK, there are three domestic murders of women every two weeks, accounting for 40 per cent of all female murder victims. European Union statistics show that 18 women are victims of homicide each day in Europe on average, and 12 of these are murdered by intimate partners or other family members. The United Nations Office on Drugs and Crime (UNODC) reported that 437 000 women were the victims of murder worldwide in 2012 within the family. An ongoing study by WHO and the London School of Hygiene and Tropical Medicine shows that more than 35 per cent of the murder of females globally (known as **femicide**) is committed by an intimate partner. In contrast, the same study estimates that only about 5 per cent of all murders of men are committed by their spouse or other family member. These statistics are probably conservative, given the high amount of missing data, especially in less industrialised countries.

Three-quarters of all global violence is domestic (and these are only the reported cases) according to WHO. On average, about 200 children are murdered each year by family members in the UK. WHO reports that nearly 60 000 children are murdered each year worldwide.

A Thomson Reuters Foundation Survey in 2018 surveyed 548 experts on women's issues and ranked India as the most dangerous country in the world for women, because it is still heavily engaged in customary practices such as forced child marriages, child trafficking and slavery, stoning and female infanticide. The USA was ranked joint third when respondents were asked where women were most at risk of sexual violence, harassment and being coerced into sex.

### 'Honour'-related murders

**'Honour'-related murders** involve a girl or woman being killed by a male or female family member for an actual or assumed sexual or behavioural transgression, including adultery, sexual intercourse or pregnancy outside marriage – or even for being raped. Often, the perpetrators see this femicide as a way to protect family reputation, to follow tradition or to adhere to a particular interpretation of a religious teaching. Murders in the name of 'honour' may also be used to cover up cases of incest, and there are reports of people using the 'honour defence' as a way to receive community and legal acceptance of a non-'honour' murder. WHO estimates that there are 5000 murders in the name of 'honour' each year worldwide, although this is believed to be an underestimate. These killings occur mainly in parts of the Middle East and South Asia, but also among some migrant communities in countries including Australia, Europe and North America.

## Toxic masculinity

Another negative consequence of family life is that boys are often socialised into a form of hegemonic masculinity that is often toxic in terms of its negative effect on relationships between men and women. This toxic masculinity often underpins patriarchy and legitimates the abuse of male power in many areas of social life. Some sociologists claim that masculine norms and boundaries have become so distorted in family socialisation that some men believe that sexist and abusive behaviour against women is socially acceptable.

Jordan Stephens (2017) argues that gender role socialisation – that is, the way boys are brought up in modern families – partly accounts for this (see Contemporary issues box in Unit 2.3.1). He claims that males are brought up to believe that they are 'hard-wired' to behave in a patriarchal way – to brag about breaking hearts, to speak to girls and women inappropriately and to see the investment of love and trust in others as weakness and vulnerability. He argues that many males have experienced a traumatised childhood in which they were not allowed by older men, often their fathers, to express weakness in any shape or form. Instead, they are told to 'man up' and to exert their male power over others via physical violence and emotional manipulation. Consequently, he observes that as boys become adults, they fail to learn from these childhood experiences and to understand why they desire power over others.

Stephens argues that men need to recognise that the way they have been brought up is a problem, that they are suffering a **crisis of masculinity** that denies them the capacity to acknowledge and understand their childhood pain. It is this which prevents them from ever truly loving themselves, which prevents them from trusting others and treating women as equals. He argues that males need to learn that it is OK to feel sad or to cry and to have loved their mother and father while growing up. He claims that it is only when young males acknowledge and realise that they have been wounded by their childhood socialisation that masculinity will undergo detox.

## The radical psychiatrist view

Finally, some psycho-sociologists known as **radical psychiatrists** argue that family relationships have the potential to cause mental illness in some individuals. For example, Edmund Leach (1967), argued that the nuclear family with 'its privacy and tawdry secrets is the source of all our discontents'. Leach argues that because the nuclear family is isolated and privatised, family members tend to make great emotional demands of each other. For example, parents expect a great deal from their children. However, more often than not, children fail to live up to their parents' expectations in the field of education and parents may be disappointed, even disillusioned with their children. Spouses too make unrealistic demands of each other. Leach argues that the result is that 'parents fight and children rebel'.

The radical psychiatrist R.D. Laing (1971) suggested that some family members may become mentally ill because of the nature of family relationships. He suggested that schizophrenia, for example, is partly caused by experiences within the family. Laing argues that family relationships are potentially destructive, because the intensity of nuclear family life means that we worry about how much we are loved by other family members, particularly our parents. For example, we might suspect that a particular brother or sister is the favourite of our parents. Laing argued that we react to this anxiety by forming alliances within the family in order to maximise our chances of receiving love. For example, we might side with one parent against another in an argument.

Laing argued that as a result of these processes family members become like gangsters, offering each other mutual protection and love to be used against other family members. We consequently become mutually suspicious of each other's motives, and this becomes the basis of mental breakdown and family arguments and feuds which can last for years.

### Key terms

**Femicide** The murder of females.

**'Honour'-related murders** The murder of a girl or woman by a family member for an actual or assumed sexual or behavioural transgression, including adultery, sexual intercourse or pregnancy outside marriage, or even for being raped.

**Crisis of masculinity** The idea that men are more likely to suffer from anxiety and depression because their traditional roles as breadwinner and head of household are fast disappearing.

**Radical psychiatry** A school of psychiatric thought that believes psychiatric problems are caused by alienation brought about by the intensity of family relationships.

### Summary

1. Families may not be as functional and beneficial as functionalists suggest.
2. A lot of evidence from around the world shows that people, especially women and children, are more likely to be murdered, assaulted and abused by other family members.
3. Traditional families may be producing toxic forms of masculinity and possibly even mental illness in some societies.

# END-OF-PART QUESTIONS

| 0 | 1 | Describe two negative consequences of family life. **[4 marks]**

| 0 | 2 | Explain two limitations of the view that marriage is egalitarian. **[6 marks]**

| 0 | 3 | Explain two ways in which women emotionally maintain family relationships. **[8 marks]**

# PART 4 AGE AND FAMILY LIFE

## Contents


| | | |
|---|---|---|
| **Unit 4.4.1** | **The social construction of childhood** | **203** |
| **Unit 4.4.2** | **Theoretical approaches to childhood** | **209** |
| **Unit 4.4.3** | **The impact of changing life expectancy upon the family** | **218** |
| **Unit 4.4.4** | **Changes in the concepts of motherhood and fatherhood** | **222** |


Some sociologists argue that childhood as we experience it today did not exist 200 years ago. These sociologists argue that childhood is actually a very recent social invention, specifically a 20th-century phenomenon. Moreover, they argue that the way children are treated today constitutes progress, because childhood in the past was a short and often a dangerous and brutal experience, whereas in modern societies it has been categorised as a special period in which children are treated as a valued resource to be protected from the threats and risks of the adult world.

However, some sociologists point out that the experience of childhood is not that dissimilar from adult experience in that children, too, are subjected to inequalities that stem from social class, gender and ethnicity. In addition, they experience unique forms of oppression and inequality that stem entirely from the view that adults know what is best for children. This has led sociologists who identify with social action perspectives to examine how children act as active agents in the construction of their own childhood. Similarly, postmodernists have attempted to ascertain the influence of factors such as family diversity, choice, consumption and globalisation on childhood experience, and how these might have changed the role and social position of children in the family.

After examining childhood in the first two units of Part 4, we consider the role of grandparents and the enhanced role they may now play in the experience of childhood. Finally, we consider changes in concepts of motherhood and fatherhood.

## Unit 4.4.1 The social construction of childhood

Common sense tends to assume that childhood is merely a developmental or biological stage that we all go through on the way to adulthood. However, sociologists argue that experiences of childhood appear to vary between different societies and different historical periods. They have, therefore, come to the conclusion that childhood is a social construction – something created by society, rather than simply a natural stage of physical and mental development. Sociologists argue that what people mean by childhood and the position that children occupy in society is not fixed but differs between different times, places and cultures.

### Childhood in pre-industrial society

The social historian Philippe Ariès (1962) suggested that what children experience today as childhood is a recent 'invention' or **social construction**. As John Clarke (2009) notes, 'this view holds that sometime between 1600 and the twentieth century the idea of childhood was "invented" and what we now think of as childhood would not have made sense to our ancestors'.

Ariès claimed that, in pre-industrial society, the type of childhood that exists in modern societies today simply did not exist. He argued that as soon as children were no longer physically dependent on their parents – that is, around the age of 7 years – they were treated no differently to adults. Childhood did not extend beyond this age. He argues that children in medieval societies were treated as 'miniature adults' who took part in the same work and play activities as grown-ups. They certainly did not enjoy the special and unique treatment in terms of protection, responsibilities and rights that many more industrialised societies believe children are entitled today.

Ariès claimed that the main reason for treating children in much the same way as adults was that the concept of age in medieval societies and its interpretation was very different from how it is viewed today. In many pre-industrial societies, people did not generally know their date of birth or their exact age. The registration of births that is a legal obligation today simply did not exist.

Ariès argues that this uncertainty about age meant that people in medieval societies did not see individuals in terms of their chronological age, but rather in terms of their physical appearance, abilities and habits. Consequently, if a 7-year-old had a distinct personality, if he or she could perform physical tasks and could converse with older people, then he or she was regarded as little different to their adult peers. It was, therefore, perfectly normal for such mini-adults to be working alongside their older peers in agricultural work or for royal or aristocratic 7-year-olds to be fully participating in formal ceremonies or to find themselves engaged to be married. One area which illustrates the lack of distinction between the world of children and adults in pre-industrial society is crime and punishment. For example, between the 16th and 18th centuries in Britain, dozens of children aged between 7 and 17 years of age were hanged for crimes such as arson and housebreaking.

## Activity

Try to find out at what age a child is held responsible for criminal actions in the country in which you live. How does that age of criminal responsibility compare with other societies? Debate the question 'How young is "old enough" to be prosecuted as an adult criminal?'

Ariès based his ideas about the medieval experience of childhood on an analysis of representations of children in medieval paintings. He claimed that there was no qualitative difference in the way children and adults were portrayed in the art of the medieval period because children were seen as simply 'reduced' versions of adults. Paintings showed infants wearing baby clothes which were generally the same for boys and girls, but artists portrayed those children aged over 7 years as wearing smaller versions of adult clothing styles and as having the same but miniaturised physiques as their adult peers. They were often portrayed with serious adult-like expressions on their faces. There were rarely any of the stylised features that are often associated with paintings of children today, such as vulnerability, innocence, dependency, chubbiness, large eyes, small hands or smiling faces. Children were very rarely painted playing.

## Activity

*Antoon Claeissens* – A Family Saying Grace Before the Meal *(1585)*.

What evidence does the painting provide to suggest that children were seen as 'little adults' and therefore part of adult society?

Ariès argues that the medieval concept of childhood first began to evolve into the modern version of childhood towards the end of 17th century. He notes that paintings of children during this period start to specifically show them as children rather than mini-adults. He suggests that the main reason for this was a steady decrease in the infant mortality rate, which meant that it became more likely that children would survive childhood. Consequently, parents began treating them with more interest and affection.

Ariès argues that a distinct culture of childhood started to emerge from the 17th century onwards in both America and Europe and took on the following features:

- Certain styles of clothes were seen as exclusive to children.
- Games and toys were invented and manufactured specifically for children – Ariès claimed that those 'childish' games that had existed in the medieval period were played by both adults and children.

Ariès argued that the biggest influence on the emergence of modern childhood was that there was a profound social change in the 17th century, especially among the merchant class or bourgeoisie in terms of their everyday lifestyles. Up to the 17th century, Ariès claimed, everyday social life and interaction with others was based on '**sociability**' – it was normal for citizens to spend most of their time in the community with their friends and neighbours – but during the course of the century, everyday life based on privacy became more dominant as a lifestyle. This meant that members of society chose to spend most of their time at home with their extended kin. Ariès argued that this coincided with more attention being paid to children. Clarke suggests that a middle-class model or **ideology of the family** became popular in this era, based on the idea of the self-contained family led by a strong father organised around the 'proper' upbringing of children. Ariès claimed that child-rearing gradually became the central purpose of family life in industrial societies, although this was not fully achieved until the second half of the 19th century.

### Critique of Ariès

Linda Pollock (1983) criticises Ariès' for using a limited and highly selective set of sources and evidence, such as paintings. She argues that such sources were generally unrepresentative of medieval society. Paintings in the medieval period were mainly commissioned by wealthy elites whose approach to children and childhood may not have been typical of wider society, especially the peasant class. Moreover, a piece of art may only reflect the artist's subjective experience or point of view or his or her desire to follow an artistic trend. Pollock argues that sociologists need to examine qualitative data that focuses on actual child–parent relationships rather than images. These can be found in diaries, autobiographies and other first-hand accounts from these historical periods.

### Activity

Using your knowledge of research methods, identify three reasons why Pollock is critical of Ariès' use of secondary sources such as medieval paintings. She recommends diaries, autobiographies and other first-hand accounts instead. Identify three potential weaknesses of using these secondary sources to investigate the experience of childhood in medieval society.

Adrian Wilson (1980) argues that Ariès makes the mistake of being ethnocentric. This means that he views the past from the perspective and judgement of the present. Consequently, Ariès argues that medieval society had a limited awareness of childhood because they lacked modern society's 'awareness' of what children are like and how they should be treated. Ariès, therefore, is seen to be guilty of applying modern standards to past societies. However, it may be quite simply that these societies had different standards of childhood – they may have loved their children in ways in which people in modern societies might not understand.

Despite these criticisms, Ariès' work has been very influential. Most historians agree that modern society has experienced a massive change in sentiment about children. It is generally accepted that childhood was experienced and imagined quite differently in the medieval period. The way that parents treat children today would be unrecognisable to those from previous centuries. Ariès clearly showed that childhood is not just a natural category which is experienced in the same way at all times and in all societies – rather, it is an ever-shifting social concept or invention.

## Childhood and industrialisation

However, it is very important to understand that the changes in childhood that Ariès documented took some time to filter down to ordinary families from the bourgeois experience. Ariès acknowledged that industrialisation did not lead to a radical change in the way working-class children were treated. An examination of European societies in the industrial 18th and 19th centuries suggests that the concept of childhood as it is known today was still evolving. Many children's lives were actually characterised by poverty, hard labour and exploitation.

During the early industrial period, working-class children in European societies such as Britain were frequently found working in factories, mines and mills. This had an adverse effect on their health, as children were often killed or injured at work and were exposed to toxic substances which shortened their lives. However, despite these risks, children's labour was often regarded as an economic necessity by parents in order to stave off poverty and the threat of the **workhouse**. Children were also viewed as economic assets by their parents because their wage, in the absence of a **welfare state**, could help support parents when they were too old or sick to work themselves.

## Activity

*Child labour in the early industrial period.*

Describe the differences in childhood for bourgeois children and working-class children during the early industrial period.

Social attitudes towards children started to radically change in the middle of the 19th century. In Britain, for example, government legislation known as factory acts were passed that excluded children from working in mines and in certain types of mill and factory work. This legislation also reduced the number of hours they could do paid work. Many 19th-century campaigners in Britain were concerned about the number of children who had become pickpockets, beggars and even prostitutes, and consequently legislation was passed by the British parliament to get them off the streets and away from predatory adults. In the late 19th century, organisations such as Dr Barnardo's were formed in societies such as Britain and the USA in order to protect vulnerable and especially abandoned children from adult exploitation and cruelty. These organisations petitioned their respective governments to legislate in favour of children and childhood.

European countries such as Germany and the UK, and the USA introduced compulsory mass education for children aged 5–12 between 1870 and 1920. However, some working-class parents resisted state attempts to compulsorily educate their children, because their family wage and standard of living were very dependent on sending their children out to work. Nevertheless, as Clarke notes, by the end of the 19th century, 'while the lives of most children were still dominated by poverty, ignorance and illness, the idea of **child-centredness** as a key focus for policy development had firmly taken root' in both the USA and most European societies.

Most sociologists now accept the validity of Ariès' argument that the separation of the status and identity of childhood from other life-stages is a modern social construction. Colin Heywood (2001), for example, argues that what people expect of children today is very different compared with medieval times. Dr Tony Chapman (2004) argues that 'it was not until the nineteenth century that childhood became socially constructed as a significant life transition that required, in middle-class families at least, particular forms of nurturing, supervision, discipline and even distinctive clothing, play and dedicated space in homes. Instead of children bringing economic advantage to households through gainful employment, they now represented a very significant cost to parents and for longer periods of time'. Chambers (2012), too, argues that the idea of a 'protected or sheltered childhood' became very popular in the late 19th century, and this was reflected in social policy which sought to regulate child labour and to establish compulsory schooling.

## A child-centred 20th century

The 20th century, therefore, saw the emergence of child-centred societies in both the USA and Europe in which childhood is seen as a very distinct and separate life-stage category from adulthood. Chambers argues that in the 20th century childhood came to be seen as sacred and set apart from other life-stages. This idea continues today in that children are often perceived by more industrial societies as 'special people with unique needs who need separate forms of treatment, as well as protection from the dangers and 'corrupting influences' of the adult world'. Today, children are cherished for their sentimental value – they now occupy a central place in the emotional life of the home in the sense that having and rearing children is seen as symbolic of commitment and family stability.

Hugh Cunningham (2006) notes that child-centred society has three major features:

**a.** Childhood (which legally extends to the age of 18 years in most societies) is regarded as the opposite of adulthood – children are viewed as innocent, vulnerable and dependent beings in need of adult protection from a range of potential 'threats' such as bad parenting, neglect, exploitation and so on.

b. The social worlds of adults and children are physically and symbolically separated. For example, children occupy social spaces such as the home and schools in which they are expected to engage in play and learning respectively. They are excluded from adult spaces such as the workplace, bars and so on.

c. Childhood is associated with certain rights – for example, the right to 'happiness', to be 'safe', to be healthy, to play and to enjoy childhood.

## Children and the state

In both the USA and Europe, the 20th-century state contributed to the social construction of childhood as a sacred and special period in the life cycle by passing legislation aimed at the protection of children and childhood. Karen Wells (2009) notes that this government of childhood is almost entirely organised around saving children from internal threats (for example, neglectful or abusive parents) and external threats (germs and viruses, ignorance, media representations of violence, exploitation by employers and so on). In this sense, the state aims to take responsibility for the emotional, physical, intellectual and spiritual development of the child so that he or she grows up to be a normal law-abiding citizen. As Chambers notes, this is the state taking on the role of the 'good parent'.

Social policy aimed at safeguarding children has taken a variety of forms:

- State health services often oversee children's health in a variety of ways – via antenatal, maternity and post-natal care, health visits to the homes of new mothers, the mass vaccination of children, through family GPs and through the availability of consultants who specialise in children's illnesses (paediatricians) and specialist children's hospitals and wards.
- The state shapes and supervises the secondary socialisation of children through compulsory state education which is available for much of childhood.
- A major role of social services and social workers is to police those families in which children are thought to be at risk of neglect or abuse.
- The law has been used by the state to exclude children from activities which may harm them. For example, children may not be allowed to buy alcohol or smoke, they may not be allowed to see certain types of films at the cinema and they may not be allowed to marry without their parents' permission until they are 18 years old (although, as we shall see later in this section, many countries do not set an age minimum for marriage; therefore, a large number of child marriages take place worldwide in the 21st century). A good example of how the law has helped shape the social construction of childhood is the age of sexual consent. In the 19th century, English common law set it about 10–12 years, but in the light of child prostitution scandals it was officially raised to 13 years in 1875 and then 16 years in 1885. The majority of countries around the world have an age of consent between 16 and 18. However, the age of consent is 21 years in Bahrain and 20 years in South Korea. In contrast, in Nigeria the legal age of consent is only 11 years, whereas in Japan it is 13 years. Additionally, several Middle Eastern and African countries have no legal age of consent, but ban all sexual relations outside of marriage. This has raised concerns by many international organisations, especially in some countries where girls are married at as young as 9 or 10 years old.

### Activity

*Learning to drive.*

Research the ages at which young people are permitted in your society to participate in particular activities – for example, taking on paid work, driving a vehicle, going to the cinema, serving on a jury, voting and so on. At what age can a person marry without parental permission in the society in which you live?

- Preventing child abuse is seen as a priority by the majority of more industrialised societies. Therefore, laws and punishments have been put into place to deter physical and sexual abuse and neglect (the most common type of mistreatment of children) and female genital mutilation (FGM). However, FGM is practised legally in 29 countries in Africa and the Middle East, according to a 2013 United Nations International Emergency Children's Fund (UNICEF) report. Many Western societies have taken legal steps to criminalise FGM in order to deter migrant communities from the practice.

- Many modern states take some economic responsibility for children by paying benefits to parents. In the 1970s, Singapore introduced a 'Stop at Two' children policy, while an estimated 200 million births were prevented by China's 'one-child' policy between 1979 and 2011. These policies that financially rewarded parents for limiting the number of children they had and penalised some parents for having too many children were put into action because of concerns about over-population. In Western societies, governments have attempted to lift families out of poverty in order to improve children's future educational and job opportunities.
- Some modern states protect children's welfare in the event of parental separation and divorce, emphasising that decisions taken by parents and the courts should be in the best interests of the child. Therefore, the courts, when making decisions about custody, have to take on board what children themselves say about their experiences and what they want with regard to parenting.

State family policy and the law are, therefore, central in today's modern societies in defining and shaping parental responsibility towards children. The state sets out the duties of parents and gives them rights over children's bodies and children's time. However, some critics argue that the state does not always protect children. Some governments seem to be very reluctant to legislate with regard to parental violence – for example, smacking children, which is banned in 30 countries including Scotland but remains legal in England and Wales, the USA, Canada and Australia.

UNICEF measures children's well-being by using five dimensions of children's lives – wealth, health and safety, education, behaviour and risks, and housing and environment. For example, more industrialised societies in which children generally enjoy a good standard of living and housing and good health, as well as high levels of literacy and numeracy, are ranked highly. However, UNICEF also asks children about their subjective well-being. Those societies in which few children express anxiety, depression or problems such as self-harm or eating disorders are classed highly on the basis of well-being.

## Activity

Using the internet, find out how UNICEF ranks the experience of childhood in the society in which you live.

## Conclusion

Sociologists generally accept that childhood is a social construction, but they also point out that this concept of social construction is not straightforward in the 21st century because there are significant variations on children's experience of childhood due to influences such as gender role socialisation, social class, culture, ethnicity, religion, region and globalisation. Heywood (2018), for example, stresses that although progress has been made in the protection of children, inequalities between classes, regions and ethnic groups continue to exist. Therefore, an important aspect of the social construction argument is the understanding that childhood is not a fixed, universal experience. Rather it is a relative experience – it can be experienced positively and negatively, and most importantly not all cultures construct it as a sacred and special experience. In some parts of the world, childhood is a dangerous and risky period of a person's life which often involves early death and suffering.

## Key terms

**Social construction** A term used by social action theories to indicate that some social processes are the product or invention of society, dominant social groups or cultural norms.

**Sociability** The quality of liking to meet and spend time with other people.

**Ideology of the family** A set of dominant ideas and beliefs which have the effect of instructing members of society about how families and the roles within them should be organised.

**Workhouse** A British public or charitable institution in which the poor, especially children, the elderly and the sick and disabled, received somewhere to live in return for work. Most poor people feared being sent to the workhouse because it was a humiliating and shameful experience.

**Welfare state** A system whereby the state undertakes to protect the health and well-being of its citizens, especially those in financial or social need, by means of grants, pensions and other benefits.

**Child-centredness** The notion that the child should be the focus of attention. Child-centred families see raising children as the most important component of family life.

## Summary

1. Sociologists argue that childhood is more than just a biological or psychological stage of human development. The experience of childhood is socially constructed, which means that it is the product of particular historical periods and cultures. Even within the same society, childhood is often not a universal or common experience, because it is often shaped by the status inequalities embedded in the structural organisation of a society. For example, the experience or quality of a working-class, male or ethnic minority childhood may differ in comparison with that of children who come from ruling or middle-class backgrounds, who are female and members of majority groups, respectively.
2. Ariès argued that the contemporary experience of childhood is a distinct improvement (or progress) compared with the medieval experience of children, which was often short and brutal.
3. The 20th century saw the emergence of child-centred families in which children were treated as a precious but vulnerable commodity to be protected at all costs from the risks and threats associated with adult society.
4. The state in many societies has taken on the duty of protecting children from both internal and external threats.

# Unit 4.4.2 Theoretical approaches to childhood

In addition to the social constructionist argument outlined in Unit 4.4.1, there are six other sociological approaches to childhood: the conventional or march of progress approach, the New Right approach, the social conflict approach, the feminist approach, the social action or interactionist approach and the postmodernist approach. Most agree with the view that childhood is socially constructed, but there are differences with regard to how each approach views the role and social position of children in the family today.

## The conventional or 'march of progress' approach

Many functionalists and New Right thinkers tend to subscribe to what has been termed a 'conventional' approach to childhood. They highlight the role of parenting and suggest that primary socialisation is the key to a successful and happy childhood. Successful parenting and, therefore, happy childhoods involve parents socialising their children into positive social values such as working hard, showing respect to others and always demonstrating good manners. Good parents from this perspective should exercise sensible control and discipline over their children's behaviour and seek to ensure that negative outside influences do not undermine their children's upbringing and that children are kept safe from threats to their innocence. This approach is sometimes referred to as the '**march of progress**' approach because it assumes that childhood has progressed from a state in which children were at great risk and threat from neglectful parents, adult predators and an indifferent state to a society in which parents and the state are united in their goal of turning the period of childhood into a positive, safe, happy and healthy phase of social development.

The conventional approach to childhood has always assumed that successful child-rearing requires two parents of the opposite sex, and that there is a 'right' way to bring up a child. Consequently, they tend to see the experience of childhood as being potentially undermined by what they term 'deviant family' units such as single-parent families or gay families. Some argue that 'working mothers' are denying their children qualitative family interaction because they are too busy working and this may be the cause of what the conventional approach sees as the decline of civilised childhood in which children always respected their elders.

## The New Right approach

As we saw earlier in this chapter (see Unit 4.2.4) New Right sociologists see family life as under attack, especially from the state and government policies.

Melanie Phillips (1997) is typical of this New Right approach to childhood. She argues that parenting has been undermined by state policies, which she claims have given too many rights and powers to children. However, she argues that parents are often penalised for resorting to what she argues are necessary sanctions, such as smacking.

Phillips believes that the media and the peer group have become more influential than parents. She sees the media in the form of magazines aimed at young girls, pop music videos and television as a particular problem, because they encourage young girls to envisage themselves as sexual beings at a much younger age. According to Phillips, these trends mean that the period of childhood has been shortened – it is no longer a sacred and innocent period lasting up to 13 or 14 years. Phillips complains that adulthood and particularly the **sexualisation of childhood** encroaches upon the experience of children a great deal earlier compared with the past. She argues that many children do not have the emotional maturity to cope with the rights and choices that they have today. The result, she believes, is an increase in social problems such as suicide, eating disorders, self-harm, teenage pregnancy, depression and drug/alcohol abuse.

### Activity

List arguments for and against the views advanced by Phillips.

Neil Postman (1994) too saw childhood as under threat because television and the internet have resulted in '**social blurring**'. This means that there is no longer any distinction or boundaries between the world of adults and the world of children. Traditionally, in order to protect children, these two worlds have been kept separate. However, Postman complained that traditional children's games are now disappearing and that children are now playing the same computer games as adults. Consequently, he concluded that children are less child-like today. They speak, dress and behave in more adult ways, while many adults are going through **infantilisation** – they are increasingly starting to dress more like their children and youth. Over time, nearly all the traditional features that mark the transition to adulthood – getting a job, religious confirmation, leaving home, getting married – no longer apply in any clear way. The fact that children are spending longer living at home and are economically dependent on their parents for longer periods compared with the past has compounded this problem.

However, Postman's analysis has been heavily criticised. His arguments do not appear to be based on any solid evidence, while recent studies indicate that adults are actually taking more and more control of their children's lives. For example, David Brooks (2001) diagnoses parents today as obsessed with safety, and ever more concerned with defining boundaries for their kids and widening their control and safety net around them.

Postman's concerns are supported by research from Australia conducted by Trina Hinkley et al. (2014) which found that young children who spend hours each day in front of the television or playing computer games are more likely to suffer from a range of emotional problems and to be overweight. They found that the more TV children watched, the more likely they were to suffer from difficult family relationships, one of the primary causes of unhappiness.

## The social conflict approach to childhood

Conflict sociologists such as Marxists dispute the idea that children's lives have improved for two reasons:

1. Inequalities based on social class and ethnicity still exist between children in terms of the qualitative experience of childhood and their future life opportunities. Within more industrialised societies such as the USA and Britain, there are clear differences in childhood experience that are the result of socio-economic, gender and ethnic inequalities.
2. There are also major inequalities of power between children and adults. This is known as '**age patriarchy**'.

### Social class as a factor affecting the experiences of children in the family

Marxist sociologists have drawn attention to the fact that childhood is not a universally positive or similar experience, because of inequalities in family life, especially inequalities in family income, housing, life chances and standard of living caused by the organisation of the capitalist system. They point out that childhood experience is qualitatively more advantageous for those children born into affluent and professional households compared with children who are born to economically disadvantaged groups – for example, to low-paid workers or those in poverty.

Experiences of childhood in more industrialised societies may vary, therefore, according to the social class of families. Children from wealthy families may spend most of their formative years in private prestigious boarding schools from which they progress to high-status universities. Similarly, the children of professionals may be encouraged by their parents from an early age to aim for university in order to embark upon a professional career. They are likely to receive considerable economic and cultural support from their parents in pursuit of these goals.

## Activity

Think about the parental support offered by the three groups of parents highlighted in this table. Copy the box and list in it the economic, educational, social, cultural, emotional and psychological support which these three groups of parents can offer their children.

| Children from wealthy families | Children whose parents are professionals | Children from poverty-stricken backgrounds |
|---|---|---|
| | | |

Research on middle-class parenting by Annette Lareau (2011) found that social class influences patterns of family life and childhood. She found that the experience of middle-class childhood was socially constructed by parents who were engaged in a '**concerted cultivation**' of children. This involved such parents enrolling children at a young age in a range of specific cultural, artistic and sporting activities and courses. In addition, these children would be encouraged to join libraries and parents would take them on visits to museums, art galleries and sites of historical interest. This cultivation of children dominated middle-class family life and was both costly and labour-intensive, especially for mothers. A study of middle-class childhood by Carol Vincent and Stephen Ball (2007) found that middle-class parents raise '**renaissance children**' who are provided with a range of expensive enrichment activities organised around sport and creative pursuits such as music, art and drama. Vincent and Ball argue that middle-class parents see their children as a 'project for development' and consequently invest considerable time and money in their childhood. Vincent and Ball conclude that the renaissance child is equipped with the skills to make better choices than working-class children.

In contrast, Lareau found that working-class parents emphasised the 'natural growth' of their children – they did not develop their children's special talents. Instead, they believed that as long as they provided their children with love, food and safety, their children would grow up to be healthy well-rounded individuals.

Working-class childhood may be made more difficult by the experience of poverty. For example, research by Barbara Jefferis et al. (2002) found that children who experienced poverty had significantly fallen behind children from middle-class backgrounds in terms of maths, reading and other ability tests by the age of 7. Poverty also increases the chance of illness during childhood. Children from low-income families often miss out on childhood activities and events that most children take for granted, such as going on school trips, inviting friends around for dinner or spending holidays away from home, because their parents cannot afford them.

## Ethnicity as a factor affecting the experiences of children in the family

Other forms of status inequality in addition to that of social class are ethnicity and religion. In multicultural countries, the experience of childhood may differ because of inequalities and differences that exist according to ethnicity and religion. For example, it is highly likely that in India the childhood of the highest caste – the Brahmins – is likely to be qualitatively different to that of children who belong to the non-caste of 'intouchables' or Dalit.

Paul. A. Singh Ghuman (2003) found that religion had a significant impact on the childhood experience of Asians in Britain. For example, many Muslim children spend some of their week at a mosque or madrasah learning the Qur'an. Alison Shaw (2000), who carried out an ethnographic study of British-Pakistani Muslims in Oxford, England, found that third-generation Muslim children were happy to follow Islamic values and family traditions. However, she also found that female children were treated in more traditional ways than their brothers and that their daily activities, and in particular their contact with the opposite sex, was strictly monitored.

Ghuman argues that generational conflict between Asian parents and children living in Western societies was likely to emerge as children came into contact with Western institutions and peers. This potential conflict was likely to be provoked by children, especially female children, over issues such as Westernised dress, the dating of boys, arranged marriages and the aspirations of girls with regard to higher education and future working careers. Ghuman cites increasing evidence that Muslim girls living in Western societies had expectations that went beyond the traditional pathways and cultural beliefs that stress motherhood and domesticity. However, Charlotte Butler's (1995) study of Muslim girls in Britain found that they respected both the teachings of Islam and the wishes of their parents, and that they preferred to resolve any potential conflict through compromise.

## Age patriarchy

Conflict sociologists argue that many of the things that march of progress writers see positively as care and protection are in fact new forms of oppression and control by adults. This adult or parental control, which is known as age patriarchy, takes a number of forms.

- *Controls over children's space* – children's movements are often subjected to control and surveillance by parents, teachers and police officers. Parental fears about road safety and 'stranger danger' mean that children spend far more time in the home compared with other generations of children, under adult supervision. For example, Mayer Hillman et al. (1990) found that in the UK in 1971, 80 per cent of 7- to 8-year-olds were allowed to go to school without adult supervision compared with only 9 per cent in 1990. Cunningham (2006) notes that the 'home habitat' of 8-year-olds (the area in which they are able to travel alone) has shrunk to one-ninth of the size it was 25 years ago.

### Activity

*Adult supervision.*

Do children walk to school by themselves in your society?

- *Controls over behaviour* – parents judge what behaviour is appropriate or inappropriate for children. If they consider their child's behaviour to be inappropriate, the child may be punished by being sent to 'sit on the naughty step' or by being banished to their room. If they are teenagers, they may be grounded (not allowed to go out and see their friends) or have their mobile phone, tablet or laptop confiscated for a period. In some countries, they may legitimately be physically smacked or beaten.
- *Controls over children's time* – adults in more industrialised societies control children's daily routines, including the times when they get up, eat, go to school, come home, go out, play, watch television and sleep. Adults also control the speed at which children 'grow up'. It is they who decide whether a child is too old or too young for this or that activity, responsibility or behaviour.
- *Control over children's bodies* – adults exercise enormous control over children's bodies, including how they sit, walk and run, what they wear (sunhat, make-up, glasses and so on), their hairstyles and whether or not they can have their ears pierced. It is taken for granted that children's bodies may be touched (in certain ways by certain adults); they are washed, fed and dressed, have their heads patted and hands held, are picked up, cuddled and kissed. At the same time, adults restrict the ways in which children may touch their own bodies. For example, a child may be told not to pick their nose, suck their thumb or play with their genitals.

## Global experiences of childhood

Conflict sociologists also point out that in many non-industrialised societies, the experience of childhood is extremely different compared with that found in more industrialised societies.

- Children in such countries are constantly at risk of early death because of poverty and lack of basic healthcare. For example, UNICEF notes that measles kills over 500 000 children a year in Africa and malaria kills over 1 million children a year, most under the age of 5.
- Moreover, children in these countries are less likely to have access to education. According to UNESCO, 67.4 million children do not attend school in the less industrialised world, while an estimated 122 million children aged 18 and under cannot read or write. Two-thirds of these are thought to be girls, who face more challenges than boys in receiving an education because of cultural and

religious discrimination and social **stigma**. Often, girls' education is seen as secondary to childcare, looking after the sick and elderly and other household responsibilities.

- Children in less industrialised societies may find themselves occupying roles as workers much like European children did in the 18th and 19th centuries. According to the International Labour Organisation (ILO), about one in five of the world's 1.5 billion children are involved in paid work. Many of them (126 million) are engaged in hazardous work – that is, work that has adverse effects on safety, physical or mental health or moral development. Many of them are working excessive hours, often more than 30 hours per week, for exploitative rates of pay. Many of them are employed in sweatshops producing goods for Western markets.
- War also shapes childhood because wars not only kill a disproportionate number of children but they also increase the likelihood of children becoming orphans, refugees, hostages, slaves and soldiers. In 1995, UNICEF reported that in the previous decade approximately 2 million children had been killed in wars around the world – this figure exceeded the number of soldiers killed in the same period. In 2013, it was reported that over 11 000 Syrian children had been killed in the civil war. Nearly one in four of civilian casualties between 2014 and 2018 in Syria were children. In Afghanistan, almost 35 000 children have been the victims of land mines since 1979. Female children have been forcibly taken and sold into slavery during civil conflicts in countries such as Nigeria.
- Thousands of children, some as young as 10 years old, are serving as child soldiers around the world. They are used as fighters, cooks, suicide bombers and human shields. Girls are often used for sexual purposes. P.W. Singer (2006) observes that African states have been at the epicentre of the child soldier phenomenon, although children have also fought in wars in Palestine, Iran, Iraq, Afghanistan and Sri Lanka. In Northern Uganda, as many as 14 000 children were abducted between 1995 and 2006 to serve as soldiers in the Lord's Resistance Army which operated across Uganda, Sudan and the Congo, while during the civil war in Sierra Leone in the 1990s many children were drugged and brainwashed by rebel militias and forced to kill and maim civilians and government soldiers.
- Most children are cared for within the family unit. However, in many countries, a large number of children live on the streets because they have been abandoned by their parents. UNICEF estimates that 100 million children are growing up on urban streets around the world. For example, there are estimated to be 11 million street children in India and 400 000 street children in Bangladesh (of which nearly 10 per cent have been forced into prostitution in order to survive). Charities estimate that there are 1.9 million children in Mexico sleeping rough on the streets. About 240 000 of these have been abandoned by their parents.
- Controls over children's access to resources – children only have limited opportunities to earn money and so they remain economically dependent on adults. Pocket money may be dependent on 'good behaviour' and there may be restrictions on what it can be spent on.

## The feminist approach to childhood

Feminist sociologists argue that the experience of childhood in both traditional and modern societies may differ according to gender.

### Gender as a factor affecting the experiences of children in the family

Evidence from feminist studies such as Sharpe (1976), Oakley (1985) and Fine (2011) shows that boys and girls in more industrialised societies such as the USA and Britain are socialised into a set of behaviours based on cultural expectations about masculinity and femininity. Consequently, girls have a qualitatively different experience of childhood compared with boys in terms of toys given to them, the nature of their play activities, the chores they do around the home and their interaction with their parents and relatives compared with boys. This gendered socialisation according to feminist analysis is mainly aimed at them learning the feminine skills and attitudes needed to perform the adult role of homemaker and mother.

McRobbie (2000) also suggests that girls' experience of childhood may differ from boys because parents see them as in need of greater protection from the outside world. Consequently they are subjected to stricter social controls from their parents, compared with boys, when they reach adolescence, and consequently spend more time in the family home than their brothers.

In contrast, boys' experience of childhood involves what Chapman (2004) calls 'toning down their emotionality and familial intimacy' so that they effectively require the masculine skills and attitudes required for their adult roles as wage worker and breadwinner. As we saw in Unit 4.3.3, some sociologists are concerned about the exposure of boys to toxic forms of masculinity during this socialisation process. Moreover, boys are rarely seen as in need of protection from external threats and consequently spend a lot of their childhood outside the home socialising with their peers. Evidence from Susan McHale et al.'s study (2003) suggests that where families have limited budgets, they are more likely to invest in activities which enhance the development of their sons rather than their daughters.

However, William Corsaro (2011) is critical of gender role socialisation arguments. He argues that there is little research on parent–child interaction in the home and there is no real and convincing evidence and analysis of how toys are used or symbolically valued. He argues that much of the sociological research on gendered play that does exist assumes rather than proves that playing with 'female' toys such as dolls leads to a gendered experience of childhood or outcomes such as mother or breadwinner. He argues that no sociological research has established such a link for certain.

## Child abuse

Feminists have particularly drawn attention to the fact that female children are often at risk of sexual violence and abuse. It is a fact that, despite the emphasis on the protection of children in child-centred societies, some children's experiences of childhood may be extremely damaging. Different types of child abuse have been rediscovered in recent years in Western societies, such as neglect and physical, sexual and emotional abuse. In Britain, for example, 30 000 children are on child protection registers because they are at risk of abuse from family members. It is a fact, then, that not all children experience their childhood as happy, positive, secure and safe – for many children and teenagers, childhood is an exploitative, abusive and sometimes very dangerous experience. Moreover, the negative emotional and social effects of divorce on children have also been documented in several surveys.

Marije Stoltenborgh et al.'s (2011) global survey of child sexual abuse estimated that for every 1000 children in the world, 118 had been the victim of sexual violence. Most of these victims were female. Rates of abuse were found to be particularly high in parts of Africa and Asia (despite the suspicion that many girls were under-reporting their experiences; in contrast, Western girls were more confident in talking about their experience of abuse because the cultural environments in which they were located were more supportive). The study concluded that child sexual abuse was a major problem in India, where government statistics released in 2017 indicate that a child is sexually abused every 15 minutes. In 2016, over 100 000 cases were officially recorded. These statistics are likely to be an underestimate, because Indian culture is a highly collectivistic one in which the needs of the group are considered to be more important than the needs of the individual. Consequently, there exists the possibility that children's experience of abuse may be ignored, to protect the family from the shame of being associated with a reported case of abuse. The study also found that child sexual abuse in many African societies was not regarded as 'abuse' by parents and locals, because this sexual activity was regarded as a 'normal' part of initiation rites of passage which symbolised the transition into adulthood in early and mid-adolescence. These rites sometimes encouraged sexual contact with older persons, often in the form of child marriage. Stoltenborgh et al.'s study also observes that in some African societies FGM is practised routinely for the benefit of the adult men that young girls are forced to marry. In some African societies, such as Zimbabwe and Zambia, young girls were considered less likely to have HIV and therefore were preferred as sexual partners. Suzanne Leclerc-Madlala (2002) found evidence in 1990s South Africa of a popular myth which stated falsely that having sex with a virgin girl or infant child would cure a man of HIV/AIDS or other sexually transmitted disease. Catherine Mbagaya (2010) argues that the socialisation of African children to unquestioningly obey older people puts them at risk of sexual abuse by people to whom they are expected to pay their respects. She also argues that the rapid social changes in Africa, along with increases in urbanisation and individualism, have led to greater isolation of families. In situations where children are left with biologically unrelated caregivers when parents go to work, the risk of sexually abusive experiences increases.

## The social action or interactionist approach to childhood

The conventional 'march of progress' approach has been criticised by social action sociologists, who have focused on researching how children see and interpret the world around them, and how children's decisions and social actions can help to bring about social change in the role and social position of children in the family.

Social action approaches to childhood suggest that functionalist and New Right arguments wrongly assume that children are simply empty vessels waiting to be passively filled with values, parental wisdom and appropriate behaviours. Family life is presented as a one-way process in which parenting and socialisation aim to transform children into good citizens. However, social action theory argues that socialisation is actually a two-way process in which children are actively engaged in the social construction of both parenthood and childhood. In other words, parents learn as much from their children as children do from adults. There are three big themes in the interactionist or social action approach to childhood and family life:

1. Social action theory, also known as interactionism (see Chapter 1), criticises the conventional view of childhood for ignoring the idea that children develop their own unique interpretation of family life, which they actively employ when they socially interact with their parents, siblings and other family members. In other words, children are social actors who actively contribute to the social construction of their childhood. They can choose to influence the nature and quality of family life as much as their parents do. For example, research by Virginia Morrow (1998) found that children can be constructive and reflective contributors to family life. Most of the children in Morrow's study had a pragmatic view of their family role – they did not want to make decisions for themselves but they did want a say in what happened to them.

   Chambers therefore argues that sociologists need to examine how children themselves see and interpret their childhood. They should no longer be treated as the passive recipients of parental care and socialisation. She notes that they 'need to be acknowledged as moral and social practitioners of family life in their own right', while Allison James and Alan Prout (1997) argue that children must be seen as social actors who can express how they feel about their family life and childhood and make choices about the direction their childhood should take. They note that one of the reasons families and childhood have become more egalitarian in recent years is because research shows that children are actively engaged in shaping family relationships.

2. Social action theory believes that children should have the right to make an active contribution to both their childhood and family life in general. For example, Gill Valentine (1999) argues that children and adults often fight over the 'right to independence'. She notes that children can influence the process of acquiring this right by behaving in particular ways. It is the job of parents to make judgements about how much freedom to grant and whether children can master the skills required to survive independently in the outside world. Children may learn how to manipulate their parents' judgement or they may convince one parent that they are competent and responsible in order to secure the right to more independence and freedom.

3. Social action theory points out that age is highly contested in most households – both the child and parent insist that the child is old enough to do one thing but too young to do something else. There are also gendered assumptions about what children can do – girls may be regarded as more mature than boys but also in need of more adult protection.

Childhood, therefore, is not a static and universal experience, because children contest it every step of the way. They generally want more rights as they get older. However, social action theory acknowledges that this can lead to tension and conflict. This can be illustrated in three ways:

a. Children often want the right to more independence but this potentially conflicts with the state's desire to construct a legal framework in which children can be protected. Chambers argues that legislation passed by governments in many countries to protect children often does not transmit a consistent image of the rational independent self-directed child. It assumes that children should never be given the power or freedom to decide how they should behave in particular situations. In other words, the notion that children can be totally free to make their own decisions may be illusory.

b. There is also tension between the idea of children being active agents of their own behaviour and the need for parents to protect children from external threats such as bullying. Julie Evans and Joan Chandler (2006) found that peer pressure was an important aspect of children's rationale for putting pressure on their parents to buy them consumer goods. The children in their study were conscious of what clothing and designer labels were approved by their peers and which were not. Moreover, they were very aware of the possibility of the teasing, name-calling and bullying that might result if they did not conform or fit in because they lacked these items. They therefore actively put pressure on their parents to devote a percentage of their household expenditure to the purchase of consumer goods in order to avoid such treatment. However, Chambers argues that the negative side of this is that 'consumption now saturates children's relationships' with their parents and each other. Richard Layard and Judy Dunn's (2009) study found that 90 per cent of parents believed that today's children were more materialistic than previous generations.

c. Chambers identifies a tension between parents and children caused by children's use of new media. She notes that since 2000 there has been a revolution in the range of new media gadgets, especially smartphones, being used in the family home and that this has prompted a re-negotiation of relations between children and parents.

## Postmodernist approaches to childhood

There are a number of themes that postmodernists have highlighted as having a significant effect on the experience of childhood.

1. Postmodern theory suggests that the status of children may be changing because of the emergence of new kinds of intimate relationships and new versions of the family. Giddens (1991) argues that there has been a transformation in the nature of family life that has led to the emergence of more democratic relationships in families. Children are now gaining the right to determine and regulate their association with parents. Chambers argues that in families where children are involved in decision-making 'parents now have to be answerable to them and to offer them respect in order to be respected'.

   Chapman notes that the experiences of children and home are clearly also very varied because of new versions of the family that exist today. He argues that the experiences of children in gay and lesbian households, of children who have experienced their parents' divorce, co-parenting and bi-nuclear families, children who live in single-parent families and reconstituted or step-families, children who have to care for adults and so on, cannot directly be compared with children who live in conventional two-parent nuclear families. Indeed, he points out that even if children did all live in the same type of household, their experiences of childhood would still be shaped by a variety of factors such as their parents' occupation, social class, education, ethnicity, religion and so on.

2. Postmodernists suggest that childhood is undergoing a process of individualisation. Children are becoming autonomous of their parents and increasingly exercising influence over the family's economic consumption. Postmodernists argue that there has been a corresponding decline in the traditional relationship between parents and children, especially a decline in deference and obedience. This individualisation may mean that in the future the growing autonomy of children may mean that families may experience difficulties in fitting children into society and that more social problems involving children are likely to appear in the future.

   This idea can be illustrated by examining how children have increasingly been influenced by **consumerism** and consumption. It is estimated that, in the UK, children aged between 7 and 11 are worth about £20 million a year as consumers. Advertisers have, therefore, targeted children in order to encourage '**pester power**' – the power of children to train or manipulate their parents to spend money on consumer goods that will shape and increase the status of their children in the eyes of their peers. Two related sociological concerns have arisen from this trend:

   a. Commentators often hark back to a so-called 'golden age' of their own childhoods as being much less stressful and complex. They suggest that the shift into a more consumer-orientated society has resulted in children cynically manipulating their parents with regard to consumer goods. Allison Pugh (2002), for example, suggests that parental spending on children is '**consumption as compensation**' – parents who are 'cash-rich but time poor' alleviate their guilt about not spending time with their children by buying them whatever consumer goods they desire.

**b.** There is evidence that some parents are using their children as symbols of **conspicuous consumption**. For example, it is suggested that some parents deliberately spend large amounts of money on children's parties or presents in order to symbolically mark themselves out as having more wealth and status than others.

## Activity

Make a list of consumer goods that you own. Why are these important to you? Did you pay for these yourself or were they bought for you by your parents? Have you ever engaged in pester power? How do you think your parents justify spending money buying consumer goods for you? Do you compare what your parents buy you with what the parents of your close friends buy them and feel relatively deprived in comparison?

However, there is evidence that these concerns about childhood and consumerism may be exaggerated. Many parents seem to be using consumption as a strategy to keep their children safe. Evans and Chandler found that many parents justified their consumption of children's products on the basis that the world had become a much riskier place for children and that spending money on consumer goods meant that children spent more time in the home. Parents justified their spending on items such as DVDs and computer games as 'safer leisure options'. Most parents and children, then, saw buying consumer goods for their children as indicative of 'good parenting'. There were also signs that both parents and children interpreted the giving of material possessions as a means of communicating and measuring love respectively.

3. Postmodernists are interested in the appearance of new forms of media, particularly how the use of digital forms of media by children such as smartphones, tablets and laptops are shaping both childhood and the nature of modern family life. Sonia Livingstone (2009) notes the rise of a youth-centred media and 'screen rich bedroom culture'. Most parents believe that a very important part of a good childhood is that children should have the right to their own personal space – that is, their own bedroom in the family household. Adolescents now spend significant amounts of leisure time in the privacy of their own bedrooms using new media such as gaming consoles and laptops in a solitary way. Livingstone notes that children communicate more with the virtual outside world than with adult members of their own family. Parents often have to text or Facebook their children to gain their attention at mealtimes.

Some sociologists fear that children's new-found freedom to actively engage with new media has resulted in a fragmentation of family life and childhood. It is argued that children have disengaged from family life. Veerle Van Rompaey and Keith Roe (2001) argue that children's active use of new media has led to a new type of family interaction, which they call 'living together but separately'. However, there may be tension and conflict between children and parents as parents feel obliged to restrict access to phones, computers, the internet and computer games because of fears that violence or sexual content seen by children may harm them or because they fear that their children may be sexually groomed online or experience cyberbullying. Moreover, conflict between parents and children often arises when parents are perceived as invading their children's personal territory in order to investigate their activities. Parents want to know what their children are doing because they want to protect them. However, children are not keen on their parents knowing what they are doing, because they want their autonomy.

## Activity

Consider your own family situation and interaction with other family members. Do you eat, watch TV or socialise together as a family, or would you agree that you have 'disengaged' from family life in that you spend more time in your bedroom using digital media?

## Key terms

**March of progress** The idea that features of contemporary life are an improvement on how they were previously organised.

**Sexualisation of children** The idea that children are growing up too quickly because the media are introducing them to adult themes such as sex far too early in their development.

**Social blurring** The idea that the distinction between children and adults is beginning to disappear as children aspire to behave like adults and as adults treat children as their equals.

**Infantilisation** To reduce something to a childish state or condition.

**Age patriarchy** A system of inequalities caused primarily by age differences and especially the idea that adults, particularly the heads of households, know what is best for children.

**Concerted cultivation** A type of middle-class socialisation of children which aims to develop or encourage cultured behaviour and knowledge, such as knowledge of art, history, literature and so on, which may be advantageous in educational contexts.

**Renaissance children** Middle-class children possessing lots of cultural capital that is, knowledge valued by schools and universities.

**Stigma** A negative label or a mark of disgrace associated with a particular circumstance, quality or person.

**Consumerism** The act of shopping for consumer items or commodities.

**Pester power** The ability of children to pressurise their parents into buying them products, especially items advertised in the media.

**Consumption as compensation** The idea that parents buy their children consumer items to compensate for not spending quality time with them.

**Conspicuous consumption** Expenditure on, or consumption of, luxuries on a lavish scale in an attempt to enhance one's prestige.

## Summary

1. There are six theoretical approaches to childhood. The conventional approach is highly influenced by functionalism and generally has a very positive view of the relationship between the nuclear family and childhood. From this perspective, the function of childhood is to inculcate children with the values and skills required to be successful citizens and workers.
2. In contrast, New Right sociologists generally argue that primary socialisation in childhood is no longer effective because of toxic influences such as the media, and that consequently childhood is in danger of disappearing.
3. Conflict sociologists note that childhood experience in more industrialised societies is often shaped by power inequalities. They also highlight the fact that the experience of childhood differs enormously across the world.
4. Similarly, feminist sociologists highlight how patriarchal inequalities mean that the experience of childhood differs for male and female children.
5. Social action theorists claim that children actively contribute to the social construction of their own childhood and have more power over parents than previous theories have acknowledged.
6. Postmodernists argue that we need to examine how contemporary processes such as individualisation, family diversity, digital media saturation, consumption patterns and globalisation are impacting on childhood.

# Unit 4.4.3 The impact of changing life expectancy upon the family

In many more industrialised societies, life expectancy has increased dramatically over the last 50 years for a variety of reasons. This trend has led some sociologists to reflect on the impact that this social change may be having on family structure and dynamics. In particular, some sociologists are now paying attention to the role of grandparents and the positive contribution that some now make to the experience of childhood. This section, therefore, examines why death rates have fallen and life expectancy has increased, and discusses the implications for family life. Moreover, a range of sociological research on the role that grandparents play in families today, especially with regard to their grandchildren, is considered.

## Explanations for the decline in death rates and rise in life expectancy

In many more industrialised societies death rates dramatically fell during the course of the 20th century, because rising wages increased living standards, particularly the quality of diet and housing, and lifted people out of poverty (which many sociologists agreed was a major cause of death). Moreover, many governments took on the responsibility of looking after their citizens from the cradle to the grave by creating public health programmes, investing in public health – clean water supplies and sanitation systems which safely removed sewage (which was a major cause of water-borne diseases) and public hygiene programmes which made clear the link between germs, disease and lack of cleanliness. Governments also invested heavily in healthcare, especially maternal healthcare, which significantly cut the maternal and infant death rates, as did the mass vaccination of children to protect them against measles (a major killer in 19th-century Western societies). Advances in medical technology, drugs and surgery now mean that people are more likely than ever to survive cancer, heart disease and other life-threatening diseases. Consequently, life expectancy in many societies has increased.

The dramatic decline of death rates and a parallel fall in women's fertility (they are having fewer children) have led to an ageing population in many more industrialised societies. For example, in Japan, 26 per cent of the population is over 65 years old and in Italy, 22 per cent of the population is over 65 years old. In the USA, about 15 per cent of the population is aged over 65, and this population is expected to nearly double from its present 48 million to 88 million by 2050. One in three babies born in Great Britain in 2013 is expected to celebrate its 100th birthday. In contrast, only 1 per cent of those born in 1908 lived to be 100 years old. However, Chambers (2012) notes that it is important to understand that:

a. The elderly population of most Western societies is not a uniform group – there are differences in the experience of ageing because of a variety of factors including social class, gender, sexual orientation, location, migration and the degree of family support.

b. The elderly are often stereotyped as part of a culture of decline – for example, as 'unproductive, infirm and dependent, whilst the reverse is often the case'. Chambers argues that many elderly people remain independent until death. They are active players in family life and they often remain in paid work post-retirement age. For example, in many Western societies, around 50 per cent of the elderly population report that they enjoy good health. Furthermore, about one in five people aged between 65 and 74 is still economically active in Western societies such as the USA and UK.

## The impact of changing life expectancy upon the family

Changing life expectancy is impacting on the family and consequently childhood in significant ways:

1. It has led to a significant increase in the number of elderly one-person households as a proportion of all households. Most of these households are female, because women tend to outlive men. They may be housebound and consequently very dependent on family members, social services and neighbours for support. In traditional pre-industrial societies, such single-person households are less likely to exist because the collectivistic value systems of such families mean that it is seen as a duty for adult children to invite their parents to live with their family.

2. The number of extended families, especially in more industrial societies, may increase as adult children may feel obliged to invite their parents to live with them. Old age can be socially isolating and lonely and, furthermore, living alone can be potentially dangerous for the elderly because of limited mobility or declining mental functions. In contrast, in traditional pre-industrial societies, extended families are the norm, because in many of these societies it is regarded as shameful for family members not to look after their elderly kin. In more industrial societies, there is evidence that working-class families, in particular, still see great virtue in maintaining ties with elderly kin.

   Feminist sociologists have noted that daughters tend to take on a disproportionate responsibility for the care of elderly parents compared with sons. Judith Healey and Stella Yarrow (1997) studied parents living with children in old age and found that most of their sample had moved into their daughter's household. Women are also more likely to be '**sandwich carers**', which means that they combine care of the elderly and the care of grandchildren. Feminists point out that this increases both the domestic and emotional burden on women, who already take on most of the responsibility for caring in families in terms of childcare and housework. Women's disproportionate responsibility for caring for elderly relatives may lead to economic inequality between the sexes. Women are more likely than men to give up work in order to care for elderly relatives. Caring responsibilities may mean that some women are excluded from the full-time labour market. This potentially means that some women carers may have to be economically dependent on men. They may also be more likely to suffer anxiety and emotional problems because of the stress of caring for a physically or mentally deteriorating parent.

3. Beanpole families – Brannen (2003) claims that increasing life expectancy has produced this new type of family, which contains four generations of direct kin.

## The role and social position of grandparents in the family

The fact that many elderly people are active players in family life has led many sociologists to embark on the study of the impact of grandparenting on childhood and family life. Chambers notes that there is a growing recognition that families benefit from the presence of grandparents and that the interaction between grandparents and grandchildren is of a higher quality compared with the past. This is because grandparents today live longer. They are more healthy and active compared with previous generations. Consequently, they make a significant contribution to the parenting and socialisation process. In this sense, elderly people are a resource rather than a burden. A study carried out by a British insurance company in 2012 estimated that 5.8 million, or 47 per cent, of grandparents aged over 50 regularly look after their grandchildren for an average of 10 hours a week. This amounts to saving nearly £11 billion in childcare costs over a year. As well as donating free childcare, nearly half these grandparents were also spending around £142 a month towards the children's upbringing and an average of £293 towards holiday costs per grandchild.

Dalia Ben-Galim and Amna Silim (2013) found that grandmothers are putting in a greater number of informal childcare hours than grandfathers, and play a crucial role in helping families with childcare. June Statham (2011) found that in families in which the mother is in work or education, 71 per cent receive some level of childcare from grandparents, and 35 per cent relied on grandparents as the main providers of childcare.

There is evidence that caring for grandchildren is associated with a higher quality of life. Jill Rutter and Ben Evans (2011) found that an overwhelming majority of grandparents reported that caring for grandchildren had had a positive impact on their lives. Ninety-three per cent of grandparents and older carers aged between 55 and 64 years old found it a rewarding experience. In particular, it was found that grandparents enjoyed taking care of their grandchildren because they were able to form strong ties with the children they cared for, and because they enjoyed the ability to experience new things.

### Activity

*The positive impact of caring for grandchildren.*

What positive effects might grandparents caring for grandchildren have on grandparents, parents and children?

Nicola Ross et al. (2005) explored the relationship between grandparents and teenage grandchildren, looking at the ways teenage grandchildren and their grandparents related to one other. The research looked at the care and support they offered each other and how the relationship between them changes over time.

Ross et al. found that grandparents spoke positively about becoming and being a grandparent. When grandchildren were younger, time was spent together on outings and playing together, or with the grandparents teaching skills and providing childcare. As grandchildren grew older, the relationships were more likely to revolve around talking, giving advice and support. Grandparents often referred to providing financial support to assist their grandchildren, ranging from pocket money to school fees. Both generations in Ross et al.'s study described how grandparents usually played a key role in 'listening' to grandchildren. Many young people said they could share problems and concerns with their grandparents and referred to the way grandparents would sometimes act as go-betweens in the family, particularly when there were disagreements between themselves and their parents. The research also found that grandparents also provided a bridge to the past by acting as sources of family history, heritage and traditions: storytellers who kept grandchildren aware of their own family experiences and their culture. They were also active in keeping wider sets of relatives connected. It was also apparent that the direction of care and support altered during the teenage years, with some grandchildren taking greater responsibility for their grandparents. Grandchildren sometimes acted as a source of support for a grandparent with health issues, or as emotional and practical support for the other grandparent of the pair.

## Cross-cultural comparisons of children's perceptions of grandparents

There are over 500 Native American nations, and each has its own traditions and attitudes toward ageing and elderly care. However, in many tribal communities, elders are respected for their wisdom and life experiences. Within Native American families, it is common for young people to ask their elders for advice and guidance. Tribal elders are expected to pass down their experience to younger members of their extended family.

Both Korean and Chinese culture are influenced by the Confucian principle of '**filial piety**', which means that one must respect one's parents. Younger members of the family are brought up to have a duty of care for ageing members of their families. Even outside the family unit, young Chinese and Koreans are socialised to respect and show deference to older individuals as well as authority figures. For example, it is customary in Korea to have a big celebration to mark an individual's 60th and 70th birthdays. The *hwan-gap*, or 60th birthday, is a rite of passage when children celebrate their parents' move into old age. It is celebrated in part as an acknowledgement that many of their ancestors would not have survived to this age. A similar large family celebration is held for the 70th birthday, known as *kohCui* (which means 'old and rare').

In China, Westernisation and the one-child policy have lessened the power of filial piety but adult children are still generally expected to care for their parents in their old age. Placing parents in retirement homes often results in children being labelled as 'uncaring', 'dishonourable' or as 'bad' sons or daughters.

Many Indian grandparents live with their adult children and their grandchildren in joint extended family units, with the elders acting as the head of the household. The elders are supported by the younger members of the family and they in turn play a key role in raising their grandchildren. Advice is always sought from these elders on a range of issues, from the investment of family money to the nitty-gritties of traditional wedding rituals and intra-family conflicts. This is not just passive advice, because the word of elders is often final in settling disputes. Moreover, the elderly act as positive role models for the young in that they are often the most religious and charitable members of the family. If family members disrespect their elderly, this can result in younger family members being negatively stigmatised by the community in which they live.

However, attitudes about being a grandparent are not universally positive. Linda Burton and Vern Bengtson (1985) interviewed African-American grandmothers and found that those women who became grandmothers early (for example, in their early to mid-30s) were discontented and feeling obligations that they felt they were not ready for. They were also affected by the stereotypes associated with grandparenting and age. For example, 'I am just too young to be a grandmother' was a typical quote. Those grandparents who experienced a late transition to grandparenting (for example, in their 70s) often expressed regret and disappointment that they were not physically active enough to make the most of the grandparental role, whereas grandparents aged 50–65 were more likely to find the role rewarding, and feel very close to their grandchild, than younger or older grandparents. John Jessel et al. (2011) researched migrant families of Bangladeshi origin living in the UK and found examples of **synergistic** learning interactions between grandparents and grandchildren – the grandmother would help the grandchild learn about their Bengali language and heritage, while the grandchild would help their grandmother learn how to use computers.

In parent-maintained households with co-resident grandparents, there is much greater opportunity for helping with childcare. Although this is more the norm in some less industrialised societies,

Jane Pearson et al. (1990) studied a predominantly African-American community in Chicago, and found that 10 per cent of households with 6- to 8-year-old children had co-resident grandmothers. The grandmothers had substantial child-rearing roles in these families and exercised control over the punishment of children. Daphna Oyserman et al. (1993) examined families where teen mothers of children under two were assisted by grandparents. She found that involved grandfathers had a positive influence on children as male role models who demonstrated skills rarely associated with masculinity such as nurturance and cooperation.

Some children are exclusively brought up by grandparents because of the death of their parents or because a parent is in prison or some other institution. Studies of families headed by grandparents found that these often experience problems associated with poverty. Studies clearly show that grandchildren reared in these low-income grandparent-headed households experience poorer academic performance than children raised in two-parent-headed households.

## Key terms

**Sandwich carers** Refers to those looking after young children at the same time as caring for older parents. It can also be used much more broadly to describe a variety of multiple caring responsibilities for people in different generations.

**Filial piety** A Confucian belief that children should have a great respect for their elders, especially parents and grandparents.

**Synergistic** The interaction or cooperation of two individuals, such as grandparents and grandchildren, which produces a combined effect greater than the sum of their separate effects.

## Summary

1. Many more industrialised societies are experiencing an ageing population because of a dramatic decline in death rates and a corresponding rise in life expectancy.
2. The ageing of the population has significantly impacted on family life. It has particularly led to an enhanced role for grandparents. However, sociologists acknowledge cultural differences in treatment of the elderly and grandparents.

# Unit 4.4.4 Changes in the concepts of motherhood and fatherhood

It is impossible, of course, to examine childhood without examining motherhood and fatherhood. An examination of the social attitudes that dominate particular societies suggest that there exist ideologies of both motherhood and fatherhood. Ideologies are dominant sets of ideas that make clear cultural expectations about how fathers and mothers should ideally behave. For example, most societies expect parents to care for their children. Consequently, most societies have laws which punish parents who do not live up to society's cultural expectations about how parents should treat their children. However, an examination of parenting suggests that in patriarchal societies the cultural expectations regarding motherhood are generally harsher in terms of their judgements than the cultural expectations about fatherhood. However, there are signs that social attitudes about fatherhood held by males may be undergoing positive change.

## Parenting: motherhood

Luca Arfini (2016) points out that in the pre-industrial period of many societies the role of parenting was not clearly differentiated between mothers and fathers because the whole family was involved in both agricultural and domestic labour. However, industrialisation led to a major change in the organisation of parenting for two reasons. First, home and work became separate domains, but it was men who left the home in order to earn the family wage. Second, the state eventually banned child labour, and restricted women's labour opportunities too, because children needed a family member to look after them. Consequently, an ideology of motherhood and domesticity evolved as societies grew more modern, during the 19th and 20th centuries.

Arfini argues that the 20th century in particular saw the emergence of the traditional idea of motherhood, which defined being a 'good mother' as someone who stayed at home full-time and who was happy to be economically dependent on the male breadwinner and to be fulfilled by her 'natural predisposition' to be a combined domestic goddess, nurturer of children and emotional caretaker and caregiver. According to functionalist sociologists such as Parsons, mothers performed an 'expressive' role within families, taking charge of their children's education and taking exclusive responsibility for household affairs. Fathers were 'instrumental leaders' – economic providers and heads of households responsible for imposing strict discipline (on both his wife and children) and ensuring the living standards of the nuclear family unit. He was not expected to play any significant role in domestic or childcare activity.

Arfini argues that the mother's parenting style in early 20th-century families in the USA and Europe was culturally expected to be nurturing and indulgent, while those cultures expected a good deal less from the parenting style of fathers, which could be best summed up as authoritarian and neglectful. However, ideas about parenting styles began to shift in more industrialised societies during the 1950s and 1960s, when more and more mothers began to enter the workforce, accomplishing a double role as a mother at home and as an earner at work. In combining these two aspects, the mother's role shifted from 'expressive' to 'intensive'. About the same time, fathers became more involved in their children's lives and there was no longer a distinctive separation between the two roles of father and mother. In the 1970s, feminists started to critique both motherhood and fatherhood, and to claim that both these roles were socially constructed by patriarchal ideology and institutions.

Chambers argues that in both modern and less industrialised societies today there exists an ideology of motherhood which is organised around the idea of 'putting (children's) needs first'. She says 'the mother is perceived as the core of the family', as the emotional stabiliser that keeps the whole family together. Data from surveys conducted around the world generally support Chambers' observations. For example, data from attitude surveys conducted in a range of European societies suggest that a dominant cultural expectation is that women should prioritise their caring role over having a job. In addition, most surveys suggest that there is a deep-seated belief in society in general that the role of mother is just as fulfilling as the role of worker. These surveys indicate that a majority still believe that children are negatively affected if their mothers work. Women, therefore, are expected to take on jobs that are compatible with family commitments. Moreover, the popularity of such beliefs means that large numbers of mothers feel guilty about working full-time. Some actually give up work altogether because they believe that their absence somehow damages their children. Madeleine Leonard (2000) argues that women who continue to see housework and childcare as an essential part of being a 'good wife and mother' are more likely to be satisfied with an unequal domestic division of labour than women who reject such roles. However, there are signs that attitudes towards motherhood may be undergoing some significant change in more industrial societies, as the following examples illustrate:

- Wilkinson (1994) argues that surveys of young women indicate a radical shift in attitudes towards motherhood among young women compared with the attitudes held by their mothers and grandmothers. She argues that this attitudinal shift is so great that it can be termed a 'genderquake'. Wilkinson notes that previous generations ranked motherhood at the very top of, or very high on, their list of priorities. However, recent surveys suggest that this priority is no longer so high on young women's 'to-do' lists as careers and consumption of leisure have become more important. This change is reflected in two other trends:
- There is evidence that educated women, and especially those in professional and managerial jobs, are postponing motherhood until their late 30s and early 40s and electing to have fewer children. Moreover, some women are electing to raise their children alone. They are rejecting the notion that they or their children need a male in their lives.
- A significant number of women are choosing voluntary childlessness. They are rejecting motherhood in order to be child-free. Giddens (1992) claims that this trend stems from the ideology of individualisation that has supposedly swept through modern societies and which has allegedly led to a decline in romantic love and marriage.
- The renewed popularity of activist or digital feminism has led some females to see motherhood as an oppressive ideology and practice which restricts independence and their ability to compete equally with men in the workplace.

## Parenting: fatherhood

Tina Miller (2010) argues that the responsibilities and practices associated with fatherhood are not so clear-cut or as morally regulated as those of motherhood. However, there is an ideology of fatherhood which is mainly associated with concepts such as 'breadwinner', family provider, head of the household, unemotional disciplinarian and how absent fathers are disapproved of.

Research by Hanan Hauari and Katie Hollingworth (2009) found that Pakistani, African-Caribbean and Black African families continue to define and judge fathers in terms of how well they economically provide for their families. Sarah Salway et al. (2009) studied four ethnic-religious Asian groups – Bangladeshi Muslims, Pakistani Muslims, Gujarati Hindus and Punjabi Sikhs. The study found that the community had great respect for those fathers who took economic responsibility for their family. Men who did not or could not support their children were labelled as 'shameful'.

Jo Warin et al. (1999), in their study of 95 families in Rochdale, UK, also found that fathers, mothers and teenage children overwhelmingly subscribed to the view that the male should be the breadwinner, despite changes in employment and family life. The majority of the sample believed that mothers should dominate childcare because they were the experts in parenting.

However, there are signs that men have become more willing to involve themselves in childcare in modern societies. In the early 1990s, many sociologists concluded that the role of fathers was changing. For example, men in the 1990s were more likely to attend the birth of their babies than men in the 1960s, and they were more likely to play a greater role in childcare than their own fathers. Louie Burghes (1997) found that fathers were taking an increasingly active role in the emotional development of their children. Beck (1992) argued that, in the 21st century, fathers can no longer rely on jobs to provide a sense of identity and fulfilment. Increasingly, they look to their children to give their lives purpose and meaning. Research by Anne Gray (2006) supports this view. Her research showed that fathers emphasised the need to spend quality time with their children. They wanted more time to get to know their children, to take them out, to help them with homework and to talk to them. Fathers viewed time spent with children in outings, sport, play and conversation as an expression of fatherhood rather than as a form of domestic work.

However, it is important not to exaggerate men's role in childcare. Looking after children is still overwhelmingly the responsibility of mothers, rather than jointly shared with fathers. Recent research has focused on the pressures of work in the 21st century. A survey of British males conducted by La Valle et al. in 2002 found that 30 per cent of fathers (and 6 per cent of mothers) worked more than 48 hours a week on a regular basis. Gray found that many fathers would like to spend more time with their children but are prevented by long work hours from bonding effectively with their children.

Barbara Risman's (1986) research on single fathers as homemakers rejects the view that women have a natural predisposition to be mothers and that the raising of children should be their responsibility. She found that single fathers were just as effective and competent as mothers in terms of their parenting skills. She concludes that we need to re-examine the general belief that only mothers have the 'natural' skills to raise children and that children belong with their mothers after divorce. We need to stop thinking that nurturing is only a female skill. We must adapt to the fact that a father can also fulfil the traditional role of the mother.

### Summary

1. An examination of culture clearly demonstrates the existence of dominant ideologies which dictate how mothers and fathers are supposed to behave.
2. However, there is evidence that these ideologies, especially with regard to fatherhood, are now undergoing some change, although traditional ideas, particularly about motherhood, have only slightly shifted over the past 50 years.

# END-OF-PART QUESTIONS

| | | |
|---|---|---|
| 01 | Describe two ways in which governments contribute to the social construction of childhood. | **[4 marks]** |
| 02 | Explain two contributions grandparents make to family life. | **[6 marks]** |
| 03 | Explain two ideas about childhood associated with interactionist theories. | **[8 marks]** |

# EXAM-STYLE PRACTICE QUESTIONS

| | | |
|---|---|---|
| 0 1 | Describe two types of family structure. | **[4 marks]** |
| 0 2 | **a.** Explain two ways in which government policies may influence family life. | **[8 marks]** |
| | **b.** Explain one strength and one limitation of the Marxist view that the family is an agency of social control. | **[6 marks]** |
| 0 3 | 'Family diversity is the norm in most societies today.' | |
| | **a.** Explain this view. | **[10 marks]** |
| | **b.** Using sociological material, give one argument against this view. | **[6 marks]** |
| 0 4 | Evaluate the view that the family is a patriarchal institution. | **[26 marks]** |
| 0 5 | Evaluate the view that family life is harmful for many people. | **[26 marks]** |

# 5 EDUCATION

## Chapter contents


| | | |
|---|---|---|
| **Section A** | **Education and society** | **227** |
| **Section B** | **Education and inequality** | **270** |
| **Exam-style practice questions** | | **323** |


In many parts of the world today, education is a privilege rather than a right. In low-income countries, although access to formal schooling has increased, it is still limited. By contrast, in societies with compulsory mass education, many people are likely to have spent 11 or more years at school before progressing to further and higher education.

Some sociologists would see these experiences as worthwhile. Students learn to read, write and perhaps later to study academic subjects at A Level and beyond, and to prepare for life in the wider society. Others examine education within the context of social formations such as capitalism or patriarchy and, consequently, view it in a more negative light. They see education as benefiting some social groups – for instance, the rich and powerful – rather than all members of society. Such approaches see education as preparing students to accept life in an unequal society. They also argue that students are largely unaware of what education is doing to them and to the rest of society. This chapter looks at the positive and negative views of education and assesses the evidence for and against the different theories about the role of education in society.

Education is often seen as a key route to social mobility, enabling hard-working and talented individuals to achieve their potential and move up the class structure into high-status jobs. This chapter examines important debates about how far education operates on merit to provide equal opportunity to all regardless of their social background, class, gender or ethnicity.

Some sociologists explore what actually gets taught in educational settings. What factors influence the content of the curriculum? Does a hidden or covert curriculum operate alongside the official curriculum in schools and colleges? If so, how does it influence students?

A main focus of this chapter is inequalities in educational attainment linked to social class, ethnicity and gender. Why do those at the top of the class system tend to get the best exam results and go to the highest-ranking universities? Why do different ethnic groups have different levels of educational attainment? Why are girls now outperforming boys at every level of the education system in some societies? How far does intelligence influence educational attainment? To what extent do material and cultural factors linked to students' home backgrounds influence their attainment? Alternatively, are school-based factors such as student subcultures and teacher expectations more significant? Answers to these and other important questions are suggested throughout this chapter.

# SECTION A
# EDUCATION AND SOCIETY

## Contents


| | | |
|---|---|---|
| **Part 1** | **Theories about the role of education** | **228** |
| **Part 2** | **Education and social mobility** | **247** |
| **Part 3** | **Influences on the curriculum** | **259** |


Section A focuses on the role of education in society. Three of the key concepts that you were introduced to in Chapter 1 are particularly important here. First, *power, control and resistance*. Potentially, education systems have enormous power to control people and shape their behaviour and ideas. Do education systems have an ideological role in keeping people in their place? Do they play a part in reproducing the power and privileges of dominant classes over time? Sociologists are interested in the control of the curriculum. Are powerful groups able to influence the content of the school curriculum? Resistance is an important concept within the sociology of education. How do some students exercise power in classrooms and resist their teachers' efforts to exercise authority over them?

Second, *inequality and opportunity*. The sociology of education explores structural inequalities in society such as differences in the distribution of resources including income and wealth. Are these class-based inequalities in the wider society reflected within education systems? Do they create barriers to educational attainment for some groups of students? Is equality of opportunity a reality within education systems? Do all students have equal opportunities to achieve their potential and to succeed, regardless of their backgrounds, gender or ethnicity? Does education provide a route of upward social mobility to students from less privileged backgrounds and to females? Or do social inequalities inhibit equality of educational opportunity and mobility?

Third, *structure and human agency*. Perspectives such as functionalism and Marxism adopt structural approaches that focus on the role of education in maintaining the social structure in its present form. How do schools contribute to maintaining the social structure? Do education systems shape individuals and constrain their behaviour through processes such as socialisation? Or do students exercise agency and choice within schools and classrooms by, for example, resisting their teachers' authority? Do schools produce conformists, rebels or both? The concepts of structure and agency are also important in the debates about the factors affecting educational attainment. Structural accounts focus more on material factors – for example, parental income – to explain differences in attainment between social groups such as working-class and middle-class students. Interactionist accounts focus more on classroom interaction, teacher–student relationships and individual agency when exploring topics such as differential educational attainment or student subcultures.

This section is divided into three parts. Part 1 looks at different theories about the role of education in society, including functionalist, Marxist and New Right approaches.

Part 2 explores the relationship between education and social mobility. It examines the idea of equal opportunity, different accounts of meritocracy (in which achievements are based on individual merit) and whether education systems are meritocratic.

Part 3 focuses on the curriculum. It examines some of the factors that influence the content of the curriculum, including power, economic factors and gender. It also looks at the hidden curriculum – the things that students learn in school (such as conformity and obedience) that are not part of the formal curriculum of history, geography and so on.

# PART 1 THEORIES ABOUT THE ROLE OF EDUCATION

## Contents


| | | |
|---|---|---|
| **Unit 5.1.1** | **Functionalist views on education** | **228** |
| **Unit 5.1.2** | **Marxist views on education** | **232** |
| **Unit 5.1.3** | **Education and cultural reproduction** | **239** |
| **Unit 5.1.4** | **Social democratic and New Right views on education** | **241** |


Part 1 looks at different theories about the role of education in society. It begins by examining functionalist and Marxist accounts of the role and function of education. Does education perform vital functions and contribute to the well-being of society as a whole? Or does it mainly serve the interests of the rich and powerful and maintain the capitalist economic system? Next, Bourdieu's ideas on the role of education in transmitting or reproducing the culture of dominant classes is explored. How does this cultural reproduction take place?

This part also looks at two perspectives on the relationship between education and the economy that have influenced the development of education in many societies – social democratic and New Right views. The New Right approach (or neoliberalism), with its emphasis on competition, the market and economic growth, is steadily becoming the driving force in global education. But should there be more to education than servicing the economy?

## Unit 5.1.1 Functionalist views on education

Functionalists see society as a system made up of interrelated parts, such as the education system, the family and the economy. These parts work together to maintain society as a whole. A sociologist's job is to examine the function of each part – that is, how it contributes to the maintenance of the social system. Functionalists argue that certain things are essential for the maintenance of society. These include a shared culture, in particular shared norms (accepted ways of behaving) and values (beliefs about what is right and desirable). Functionalists focus on how the parts of society contribute to the production of shared norms and values.

Two related questions have guided functionalist research into education:

- What are the functions of education for society as a whole?
- What are the functional relationships between education and other parts of the social system?

As with functionalist analysis in general, the functionalist view of education tends to focus on the positive contributions that education makes to the maintenance of the social system. This unit examines and evaluates some of the main functionalist theories of education.

### Émile Durkheim – education and social solidarity

The French sociologist Émile Durkheim (1858–1917) saw the major function of education as the transmission, the passing on, of society's norms and values. Durkheim (1961), furthermore, argued that a vital task for all societies is to join a mass of individuals together into a united whole – in other words, to create **social solidarity**. This involves a commitment to society, a sense of belonging, and a feeling that the social unit is more important than the individual.

Education, and in particular the teaching of history, provides the link between the individual and society. If the history of their society is brought alive to children, they will come to see that they are part of something larger than themselves; they will develop a sense of commitment to the social group.

### Activity

*Schoolchildren take the Pledge of Allegiance to the American flag. The USA is home to people from a range of cultural backgrounds. Education has helped to provide a common language, shared values and a national identity.*

How might this picture illustrate Durkheim's view that schools develop social solidarity?

### Education and social rules

Durkheim saw the school as society in miniature, a model of the social system. In school, the child must interact with other members of the school community in terms of a fixed set of rules. This experience prepares them for interacting with members of society as a whole in terms of society's rules.

### Activity

In your view, to what extent do children learn to respect society's rules by first learning to respect school rules?

### Education and the division of labour

Durkheim argued that education teaches the skills needed for future occupations. Industrial society has a **specialised division of labour** – people have specialised jobs which require specific skills and knowledge. For example, the skills and knowledge required by plumbers, electricians, teachers and doctors are very different. According to Durkheim, the specialised division of labour in industrial societies relies increasingly on the education system to provide the skills and knowledge required by the workforce.

### Evaluation of Durkheim

Durkheim laid the foundation for functionalist theories of education. However, his work has been criticised:

1. Durkheim assumed that a society has a shared culture that can be passed on by the education system. Some commentators now see countries such as Australia, Canada, Mexico and Singapore as multicultural – as having a variety of cultures. As a result, there is no single culture for schools to pass on. However, it can be argued that in a multicultural society *some* shared norms and values are essential to hold society together – for example, a common language and a shared belief in tolerance and freedom of speech.
2. Marxists argue that the education system serves the interests of the ruling class rather than those of society as a whole (see Unit 5.1.2). Radical feminists see education as serving the interests of patriarchy or male dominance in society.
3. Some researchers argue that schools emphasise individual competition through the exam system, rather than encouraging cooperation and social solidarity (Hargreaves, 1982).

## Talcott Parsons – education and universalistic values

The American sociologist Talcott Parsons (1951) outlined what has become the main functionalist view of education. Parsons argued that, after **primary socialisation** within the family, the school takes over as the main socialising agency. It acts as a bridge between the family and society as a whole, preparing children for their adult roles. This is known as **secondary socialisation**.

Within the family, the child is treated and judged largely in terms of **particularistic standards**. Parents treat the child as their particular child rather than judging them in terms of standards that can be applied to every individual. However, in the wider society the individual is treated and judged in terms of **universalistic standards**, which are applied to all members, regardless of their kinship ties.

Within the family, the child's status is **ascribed**; it is fixed at birth. For example, a child is a daughter and, in some cases, a sister. However, in advanced industrial society, status in adult life (such as occupational status) is largely **achieved.** Thus, the child must move from the particularistic standards and ascribed status of the family to the universalistic standards and achieved status of adult society.

The school prepares young people for this transition. It establishes universalistic standards in terms of which all students achieve their status. Their conduct is assessed against the criteria of the school rules; their achievement is measured by performance in examinations. The same standards are applied to all students regardless of ascribed characteristics such as gender or ethnicity. Schools operate on **meritocratic** principles: status is achieved on the basis of merit – that is, ability and motivation.

Like Durkheim, Parsons argued that the school represents society in miniature. Modern industrial society is increasingly based on achievement, on universalistic standards, and on meritocratic principles that apply to all its members. By reflecting the operation of society as a whole, the school prepares young people for their adult roles.

### Activity

*Taking exams.*

How does this picture illustrate:

1. Individual achievement?
2. Judgement by universalistic standards?

## Education and value consensus

As part of the process of secondary socialisation, schools socialise young people into the basic values of society. Parsons, like many functionalists, maintained that **value consensus** – an agreement about the main values – is essential for society to operate effectively. According to Parsons, schools in American society introduce two major values:

1. the value of achievement – by encouraging students to strive for high levels of academic attainment, and by rewarding those who succeed
2. the value of **equality of opportunity** – by placing individuals in the same situation in the classroom and allowing them to compete on equal terms in examinations.

These values have important functions in society as a whole. Advanced industrial society requires a highly motivated, achievement-orientated workforce. This necessitates differential rewards for differential achievements, a principle that has been established in schools. Both the winners (the high achievers) and the losers (the low achievers) will see the system as just and fair, because their status or position is achieved in a situation where all have an equal chance. Again, the principles of the school mirror those of the wider society.

## Education and selection

Finally, Parsons saw the education system as an important mechanism for the selection of individuals for their future role in society. Thus schools, by testing and evaluating students, match their talents, skills and capacities to the jobs for which they are best suited. The school is therefore seen as the major mechanism for **role allocation**.

## Evaluation of Parsons

Like Durkheim, Parsons fails to adequately consider the possibility that the values transmitted by the education system may benefit a ruling minority rather than society as a whole. His view that schools operate on meritocratic principles is open to question – a point that will be examined in detail in later units.

Support for Parsons comes from the view that the increasing cultural diversity and difference in today's societies require the transmission of at least some shared norms and values. In this respect, schools have an important role to play (Green, 1997).

# Kingsley Davis and Wilbert E. Moore – education and role allocation

Like Parsons, Davis and Moore (1967, first published 1945) saw education as a means of role allocation. However, they linked the education system more directly to the system of **social stratification** – in Western societies, the class system. Davis and Moore viewed social stratification as a mechanism for ensuring that the most talented and able members of society are allocated to positions that are functionally most important for society. High rewards, which act as incentives, are attached to these positions. This means that, in theory, everybody will compete for them and the most talented will win through.

The education system is an important part of this process. It sifts, sorts and grades individuals in terms of their talents and abilities. It rewards the most talented with high qualifications, which in turn provide entry to society's functionally most important occupations.

### Evaluation of Davis and Moore

Critics of Davis and Moore's theory argue that:

1. There is considerable doubt about the claim that the education system grades people in terms of ability. In particular, it has been argued that intelligence has little effect upon educational attainment. (See Part 4).
2. There is widespread evidence to suggest that social stratification largely prevents the education system from efficiently grading individuals in terms of ability.

These points will be considered throughout the rest of the chapter.

## Activity

*Many functionalists argue that the education system rewards highly talented people with the credentials to enter functionally important occupations. But do members of some groups face more barriers than others in accessing key jobs in society?*

Explain one strength and one limitation of the functionalist view of education.

## Key terms

**Social solidarity** This involves a commitment to society, a sense of belonging, and a feeling that the social unit is more important than the individual.

**Specialised division of labour** A labour force with a large number of specialised occupations.

**Primary socialisation** The earliest and probably the most important part of the socialisation process, usually within families.

**Secondary socialisation** The socialisation that takes place during later life, for example, within schools and workplaces.

**Particularistic standards** Standards that apply to particular people, for example, to particular children in families.

**Universalistic standards** Standards that apply to everybody – for example, to all college students or to all employees in the workplace.

**Ascribed status** Status or positions in society that are fixed at birth and unchanging over time, including hereditary titles linked to family background (for example, King or Princess) or the status of a daughter or son within a family.

**Achieved status** Status or positions in society that are earned on the basis of individual talents or merit.

**Meritocratic** Description of a system in which a person's position is based on merit – for example, talent and hard work – rather than on their social origins, ethnicity or gender.

**Value consensus** Agreement about the main values of society.

**Equality of opportunity** A system in which every person has an equal chance of success.

**Role allocation** A system of allocating people to roles which best suit their aptitudes and capabilities.

**Social stratification** The way that society is structured or divided into hierarchical layers or strata, with the most privileged at the top and the least privileged at the bottom. Examples include caste and social class.

## Summary

1. Émile Durkheim argued that education:
   - transmits society's norms and values
   - produces social solidarity
   - prepares young people to act in terms of society's rules
   - teaches the skills and knowledge needed for occupational roles.
2. Talcott Parsons stated that schools socialise young people for adult roles by:
   - judging them in terms of universalistic rather than particularistic standards
   - transmitting society's values and creating value consensus
   - developing an achievement-oriented workforce
   - allocating young people to positions in adult society for which they are best suited.
3. Davis and Moore argue that education works with the stratification system to grade and select young people so that the most able are allocated to the most important jobs in society.
4. Functionalist theories have been criticised for assuming that education always makes positive contributions to society as a whole and that it benefits all members of society.


# Unit 5.1.2 Marxist views on education

This unit examines Marxist theories of the role of education in society. There are several varieties of Marxist theory and they largely share the following ideas. In capitalist society, there are two main social classes – the ruling class (the bourgeoisie) and the subject class (the proletariat). The powerful ruling class own the means of production (the factories and the raw materials) and the capital (money) to invest in the production of goods and services. The relatively powerless subject class produce the goods and services and sell their labour in return for wages. However, the value of their wages is considerably less than the profits taken by the ruling capitalists. In this respect, the subject class are exploited.

The economic base of society (the infrastructure) largely shapes the rest of society (the superstructure), including, for example, education, families, religion and the legal system. The economic relationships between the two classes, the relations of production, are reflected in the superstructure, which represents the interests of the ruling class. Beliefs and values form a **ruling-class ideology** which produces a **false class consciousness** – a distorted and false picture of society that blinds the subject class to their exploitation and justifies and legitimates (makes right and legal) the position of the ruling class.

## Samuel Bowles and Herbert Gintis – Schooling in Capitalist America

The Marxist economists Bowles and Gintis (1976) see the role of education in capitalist society as reproducing labour power over time. The education system does this by 'the forms of consciousness, interpersonal behaviour and personality it fosters and reinforces in students'. This is achieved through a **hidden curriculum**, a curriculum apart from the actual subjects taught, a curriculum that students and teachers are largely unaware of.

Bowles and Gintis' theory is known as a **correspondence theory**. They see 'a close correspondence between the social relationships in the workplace and the social relationships of the education system'. This correspondence or fit produces the hard-working, obedient and motivated workforce required by capitalism. It does this in the following ways.

### Submission to authority

Schools are organised on a hierarchical principle of authority and control. Teachers give orders, students obey. Students have little control over the subjects they study or how they study them. This prepares them for relationships within the workplace where they will be required to accept the authority of supervisors and managers. Bowles and Gintis argue that social relationships in schools mirror 'the hierarchical division of labour in the workplace'.

### External rewards

Students have little control over their work and, as a result, they get little direct (intrinsic) satisfaction from it. They are motivated by external (extrinsic) rewards – the possibility of examination success and the promise of employment that it offers. Responding to external rewards is mirrored in the world of work. Workers are motivated by wages rather than by the work itself. Lack of personal involvement and fulfilment in school reflects **alienation** from work in later life – a feeling of being cut off from and unable to find satisfaction from work.

### Activity

*The external rewards of education – celebrating examination success.*

How does this picture illustrate Bowles and Gintis' view of 'external rewards' and education?

## Legitimating inequality

For capitalism to operate efficiently, the inequalities it produces must be seen as legitimate and just. Bowles and Gintis suggest that the education system provides a large part of the justification for and acceptance of the inequalities of capitalist society.

Education legitimates inequality by creating the belief that schools provide the opportunity for fair and open competition whereby talents and abilities are developed, graded and certificated. The education system is thus seen as a meritocracy. Those with the highest qualifications have earned them on merit. The same belief is then applied to the economic system. It is assumed that those with the highest qualifications receive the highest rewards in the world of work. In this way, the education system justifies inequalities in the economic system.

Bowles and Gintis reject the view that rewards in the educational and economic system are based on merit. They argue that educational and occupational attainment are related to family background rather than to talent. Thus, the children of the wealthy and powerful tend to obtain high qualifications and highly rewarded jobs irrespective of their ability. However, the education system disguises this with its myth of meritocracy. In this way, education provides 'the legitimation of pre-existing economic disparities'.

## Evaluation of Bowles and Gintis

According to David L. Swartz (2003), *Schooling in Capitalist America* is undoubtedly one of the classics in the sociology of education 'having had a major impact on education theory and research'. As a result, it has received both widespread support and criticism.

The main criticism is that the argument is too deterministic – it sees education as determined by the economy. As such, it ignores the possible effects of other aspects of society. It also gives too much emphasis to capitalism. For example, Karabel and Halsey (1977) maintain that education in communist Cuba places 'heavy reliance on grades and exams as sources of student motivation' and teaching is based on a 'generally authoritarian and teacher-centred method of instruction'. Critics have also argued that Bowles and Gintis saw the social structure as shaping individuals but they largely ignored resistance in schools and in the wider society to the type of education they describe. This oversight may be due to the fact that their theory was not based on extensive research in school settings. Numerous studies show that many students have little respect for school rules or for teachers' authority (see, for example, Unit 5.5.3). As Henry Giroux (1984) argues, schools can be seen as **sites of ideological struggle** – with clashes based on conflicting views occurring within and between various groups such as teachers, school managers, parents, students, school inspectors and politicians.

### Activity

*Bowles and Gintis saw schooling as producing a hard-working, obedient and motivated workforce to meet the needs of capitalism.*

Evaluate the view that Bowles and Gintis exaggerate the power of the education system to form personalities and attitudes.

## Louis Althusser – the reproduction of labour power

Louis Althusser (1972), a French philosopher, argues that in order for the capitalist ruling class to survive and prosper, the 'reproduction of labour power is essential'. In this respect, Althusser's account is similar to that of Bowles and Gintis. Generations of workers must be reproduced over time to create the profits on which capitalism depends. Althusser argues that the reproduction of labour power involves two processes: first, the reproduction of the skills necessary for an efficient labour force; second, the reproduction of ruling-class ideology and the socialisation of workers in terms of this ideology. These processes combine to reproduce a technically efficient, submissive and obedient workforce. The role of education in capitalist society is the reproduction of such a workforce.

### Ideological control and education

Althusser argues that no class can hold power for any length of time simply by using force. Ideological control provides a far more efficient means of maintaining ruling-class power. If members of the subject class accept their position as normal, natural and inevitable, and fail to realise the true nature of their situation, then they will be unlikely to challenge ruling-class dominance. The maintenance of class rule largely depends on the reproduction of ruling-class ideology.

The subject class is kept in its place by a number of **Ideological State Apparatuses**, which include education, religion, the mass media and the law. Ideological State Apparatuses transmit ruling-class ideology, which creates a false class consciousness – a false and distorted picture that makes society seem reasonable. False class consciousness disguises the exploitation of the subject class and justifies the position of the ruling class. In pre-capitalist society, Althusser sees the church as the main Ideological State Apparatus. In capitalist society, it has largely been replaced by the education system.

Althusser identifies another means of keeping the subject class in its place, which he refers to as the **Repressive State Apparatuses**. This includes the army, the police and the prison system, which are ultimately based on force. However, he sees this as much more obvious and far less effective than the Ideological State Apparatuses.

### Evaluation of Althusser

As Althusser himself admits, he has presented only a very general framework for an analysis of education in capitalist society. He provides little evidence to support his views. Althusser has been criticised for picturing members of society as 'cultural dopes', passively accepting their position in society and failing to question the dominant ideology. There is no indication of any opposition or resistance to the ruling class and 'no sense of the politics of ideological struggle' (Elliott, 2009).

### Activity

1. Identify one similarity and one difference between Ideological and Repressive State Apparatuses.
2. 'Althusser fails to explore human agency and resistance.' Evaluate this view.

## Paul Willis – *Learning to Labour*

In an important ethnographic study Paul Willis (1977) developed a distinctive, neo-Marxist (new Marxist) approach to education. Willis studied a boys' school in England in the 1970s. He did not just rely on an analysis of the relationship between education and the economy. He also tried to understand the experience of schooling from the students' perspectives and how they saw the present and the future. He soon found that schools were not as successful as Bowles and Gintis supposed in producing docile and conformist workers.

### The counter-school culture

The school that Willis studied was situated in a working-class area in a mainly industrial town. The main focus of his study was a group of 12 working-class boys, whom he observed over their last 18 months at school and their first few months at work. The 12 students formed a friendship group with a distinctive attitude to school. The 'lads', as they called themselves, had their own **counter-school culture**, which opposed the values that the school promoted.

This counter-school culture had the following features. The lads felt superior both to teachers and conformist students, whom they referred to as 'ear 'oles' (ear holes). The lads attached little or no value to academic work and had no interest in gaining qualifications. While avoiding work, the lads kept themselves entertained with 'irreverent marauding misbehaviour'. 'Having a laff' (a laugh) was a high priority.

According to Willis, the lads were eager to leave school at the earliest possible moment, and they looked forward to their first full-time jobs. While the ear 'oles were concerned about the types of job they would eventually get, the lads were content to find any job, as long as it was a male, manual job. Such jobs were considered 'real work', in contrast to the office jobs which the ear 'oles were heading for.

The education system appears to be failing to produce the kind of workers that some would see as ideal for capitalism. The lads neither accepted authority nor were they obedient and docile. Despite this, Willis argues that the lads were well prepared for the work that they would do. It was their very rejection of school that made them suitable for male, unskilled or semi-skilled manual work.

## Working-class masculinity

The lads saw themselves and their future work as tough, hard and manly. Manual work was masculine, mental work was 'sissy' (or effeminate). The lads' construction of masculinity was both offensive and defensive. It gave power to their resistance, superiority over those the school defined as successful, and self-respect where teachers saw them as failures.

### Activity: The lads' view of life

Extract from a poem written by one of the lads in an English lesson:

*On a night we go out on the street*

*Troubling other people,*

*I suppose we're anti-social, But we enjoy it.*

*The older generation*

*They don't like our hair,*

*Or the clothes we wear*

*They seem to love running us down,*

*I don't know what I would do if I didn't have the gang.*

In what ways does this poem reflect the lads' view of life?

## Shop-floor culture and counter-school culture

When Willis followed the lads into their first jobs in factories, he found strong similarities between **shop-floor culture** (the shop floor is the factory floor) and the counter-school culture. There was the same lack of respect for authority, the same emphasis on masculinity, and the same belief in the worth of manual labour. Having a 'laff' was equally important in both cultures, and on the shop floor (as in the school) the maximum possible freedom was sought.

According to Willis, both the counter-school culture and the shop-floor culture were ways of coping with tedium and oppression. Life was made more tolerable by having a 'laff' and winning a little space from the supervisor, the manager or the teacher. In both settings, though, the challenges to authority never went too far. The lads and workers hoped to gain a little freedom, but they did not challenge the institution head-on.

Willis concluded that the lads are neither persuaded to act as they did by the school nor forced to seek manual labour. Instead, they actively created their own subculture, which led them to look for manual jobs. They learned about the culture of the shop floor from male relatives and other men in their community. They saw the school and its values as irrelevant to their chosen work.

## Evaluation of Willis

According to Madeleine Arnot (2004), Willis' study 'has greater, not less, relevance in the current school climate'. First, schools are increasingly exam-driven, competitive and pressured. Second, the de-industrialisation of Western society and the disappearance of the majority of manual jobs have led to growing uncertainty about occupational futures. These factors might make working-class masculinity and resistance to schools even more relevant today.

Willis provided a framework for studying and understanding the relationship between class, gender, schooling and the economy. As Liz Gordon (1984), states, Willis 'has provided the model on which most subsequent cultural studies investigation within education has been based'. Nonetheless, Willis' work has been criticised.

- Critics suggest that Willis' sample is inadequate as a basis for generalising about working-class education. Willis focused on only 12 boys, who were typical of neither the students at the school he studied nor working-class students in the wider population.

- They accuse Willis of largely ignoring the existence of a variety of subcultures within the school. They point out that many students came somewhere in between the extremes of being totally conformist and being totally committed to the counter-school culture.
- Feminists are critical of such studies of education based on all-male samples, particularly when the results are generalised to apply to all students, not just to boys. Since the 1970s, however, feminism has had a marked impact on the sociology of education (see Part 7).
- Critics question the relevance of Willis' study in today's increasingly de-industrialised society where manual jobs are rapidly disappearing.

However, Michael Ward's (2015) study of young men in South Wales shows that, in several respects, working-class culture has remained the same despite the disappearance of many traditional working-class jobs (see Unit 5.7.3).

## Then and now: Paul Willis – *Learning to Labour* (1977)

My Research Question has always been as much to do with the 'How' of it as with the 'Why' of it. Therefore, the subtitle of my book: *How Working-Class Kids Get Working-Class Jobs.* When I did the research in the 1970s, there were many ideas about why working-class students so often 'failed' in education, ideas which were usually very insulting of them. But there were very few ideas concerning the 'how'. I wanted to fill this gap with a detailed account of their 'lived culture', the meanings they gave to the context in which they lived, how they came to accept a future of manual labour, how it seemed natural to them.

To do this I chose ethnography as my research method – studying behaviour in the situation in which it occurs and discovering the meanings used to make sense of the present and future. This type of research requires a specific focus – in this case a focus on class and gender in order to understand the experience of 'the lads'.

I believe that this approach is essential for an in-depth understanding of the 'meanings world', the 'social grammar' and the 'structure of feeling' of a social group. For this reason, I think that my approach continues to be highly, perhaps even more, relevant to understand today's working class and what is going on both in and out of school. It is very pleasing to me to have opened up a new approach which can be applied to the study of any social group.

I have been criticised for having an 'old fashioned view' of class, a view that has been outdated by economic change and de-industrialisation. There often seems to be an assumption that that class has largely disappeared and is no longer relevant. This greatly overstates things. The working class is undoubtedly being re-formed and fractured in complex ways but certainly not abolished. Some working-class students proceed to still available industrial, construction and maintenance jobs, following more or less traditional patterns. Some find intermittent and insecure work. Some are 'parked' for long periods of time in colleges or on government schemes. Others move to non-manual and 'mental work' while retaining many aspects of working-class culture. These experiences demand ethnographic attention with a focus on the 'how'. My main hope for the continuing contribution of my book is to remind scholars and researchers that the 'how' question should always be included and to show respect for the 'lived culture' of those under study. Find that creative 'cultural production' which always lives no matter how deeply buried in the belly of the beast of social reproduction! Despite everything, that is always a source of optimism and hope.

### Questions

1. Explain one similarity and one difference between the ideas of Bowles and Gintis and those of Willis.
2. Why do you think Willis focused on both class and gender?
3. With reference to Willis' study, explain what the following terms mean:
   - social reproduction
   - resistance
   - human agency.
4. Assess the contribution of Willis' study to the sociology of education.
5. Drawing on this information and your own knowledge of research methods, evaluate the use of an ethnographic approach in sociological research on counter-school cultures.

## Glenn Rikowski – education, capitalism and globalisation

Glenn Rikowski (2002, 2005) argues that the development of education systems can be understood within a Marxist framework. Marx claimed that, as capitalism developed, social services such as education and health would become increasingly capitalised. This means that they would be **privatised** – privately rather than state owned. In this way, education becomes like any other **commodity** – a product to be bought and sold in the market with the aim of making a profit. Rikowski (2005) argues that 'educational services operating within markets' are 'being transformed into commodities'.

Marx claimed that a constant expansion of the market is necessary for the development of capitalism. As a result, there is a built-in tendency for capitalists to create a world market. This can be seen today from the rapid expansion of multinational companies. Rikowski (2002) argues that today's '**globalisation** is essentially capitalist globalisation'. He sees education as part of this process. Education is becoming a global commodity. The driving force behind global educational institutions is the generation of profit. However, although there are considerable pressures within the system to move capitalism in this direction, the process is not inevitable.

### Globalisation and education

A world market in educational services would be extremely profitable. According to Rikowski (2002), the World Trade Organization and the World Bank support global educational businesses as a way to increase productivity and economic growth, especially for developing nations. This is welcomed by many governments who see education as the key to success in an increasingly competitive global economy.

The UK company Nord Anglia Education is a forerunner in the trend that Rikowski anticipates. According to its website, Nord Anglia operates '42 International schools located in 15 countries across China, Europe, the Middle East, North America and Southeast Asia' with 32 000 students aged 2 to 18. It has a 'global campus' and offers a 'global education' (Nord Anglia Education, 2016). Universities are increasingly operating in a similar way to business institutions. For example, departments of education in UK universities generate large amounts of income by acting as consultants for developing school systems in countries such as Chile, Poland and Romania. Universities are also establishing campuses in various countries. For instance, Middlesex University in England has international **branch campuses** in Mauritius, Dubai and Malta, and there are American universities in places such as Beirut, Dubai and Paris. Rikowski sees a global trend in which 'education services will be progressively commercialised, privatised and capitalised'.

## Activity



*The Middlesex University branch campus in Dubai was opened in 2005. By 2016, it had over 2500 students of more than 90 different nationalities.*

1. How do this picture and the caption indicate the increasing globalisation of education?
2. What are your views on the use of British or American curricula (plural of 'curriculum') in international schools in countries across the world? Why do you think some international schools teach students through the medium of English rather than the local languages? How far does this reflect globalisation?

### Opposition to global capitalism

Rikowski is optimistic about the possibility of opposing the influence of global capitalism in education. He argues that teachers and lecturers may prevent the smooth flow of labour production – the production of students suited for the workforce required by capitalism. Many educators are concerned with social equality, justice and human rights, principles that are opposed to education as a commodity. According to Rikowski, teachers and lecturers are in a uniquely strong position to challenge global capitalism with teaching based on these principles.

### Evaluation of Rikowski

Over the last 30 years, Marxist sociology has become unfashionable. Rikowski has given a new lease of life to

Marxist perspectives on education. As he admits, he is looking at the beginnings of a possible trend.

Rikowski's critics accept that schools in many countries are increasingly run on business lines, that they are exposed to market forces, and that there is a growing market for the export of educational services. However, this is a long way from saying that education is becoming a global commodity, controlled by global capitalism for the primary purpose of generating ever-increasing profit. Critics argue that governments control education and will do so for the foreseeable future. Schools for profit are unlikely to appear as part of present or future educational policy in places such as the UK (Hatcher, 2005). Despite these criticisms, recent evidence provides some support for Rikowski's concerns about the possible future of education (see Unit 5.1.4).

## Activity

1. Explain one similarity and one difference between the functionalist and Marxist views of education.
2. Explain two limitations of the Marxist view of education.

## Key terms

**Ruling-class ideology** A system of ideas that justify the position of the ruling class (the bourgeoisie in capitalist societies).

**False class consciousness** A false picture of society that disguises the exploitation of the subject class (the proletariat in capitalist societies).

**Hidden curriculum** The messages schools transmit which are not part of the standard taught curriculum and which are largely hidden from teachers and students.

**Correspondence theory** A theory that states that there is a similarity between two things.

**Alienation** A feeling of being cut off from and unable to find satisfaction from work.

**Sites of ideological struggle** Places where there are conflicts based on different beliefs and values.

**Ideological State Apparatuses** Institutions, including the education system, that transmit ruling-class ideology.

**Repressive State Apparatuses** Institutions, such as the army and the police, that keep the subject class in its place.

**Counter-school culture** A school-based subculture whose members reject the norms and values of the school and replace them with anti-school norms and values.

**Shop-floor culture** The culture of low-skill workers which has similarities to the counter-school culture.

**Privatise** Move from state to private ownership.

**Commodity** Something that can be bought and sold.

**Globalisation** The process by which societies, cultures and economies become increasingly interconnected.

**Branch campus** A campus which is a branch of the main university.

## Summary

1. According to Bowles and Gintis, education in capitalist society reproduces labour power. It does this by:
   - rewarding discipline
   - legitimating inequality and disguising exploitation by promoting the myth of a meritocracy.
2. Critics argue that Bowles and Gintis:
   - give a deterministic view in seeing education as shaped by the economy
   - ignore resistance to and conflict within the education system.
3. According to Althusser, education, as part of the Ideological State Apparatuses, transmits ruling-class ideology and is linked to ideological control.
4. Critics argue that Althusser:
   - provides only a general framework with little evidence to support his views
   - treats people as 'cultural dopes' who passively accept ruling-class ideology.

5. According to Willis, the lads developed their own counter-school culture. This involved:
   - having a 'laff'
   - misbehaving and rejecting authority
   - doing as little work as possible
   - getting involved in the male, adult world outside school.
6. The similarity between counter-school culture and shop-floor culture prepared the lads to accept and cope with low-skill, manual work.
7. Critics argue that:
   - Willis' sample is too small to generalise from
   - he ignored other student subcultures and girls' experiences
   - his study is no longer relevant because of economic change.

   Despite these criticisms, Willis' work has been very influential and provided a model for later research.
8. According to Rikowski:
   - the globalisation of educational services is increasing
   - many governments welcome educational businesses; they see education as the key to success in an increasingly competitive global economy.
9. Critics argue that Rikowski may have overstated the case for education becoming a global commodity.

# Unit 5.1.3 Education and cultural reproduction

This unit looks at the views of Pierre Bourdieu (1930–2002) on the role of education in society. Pierre Bourdieu is regarded by many as one of the most important sociologists of the late 20th century. He saw the main role of education as cultural reproduction. However, this does not involve the transmission of the culture of society as a whole, as Durkheim argued. Instead, it involves the reproduction of the culture of the 'dominant classes'. How does this cultural reproduction take place? What role does the education system play in this process? How is it linked to inequality?

## Different forms of capital

Bourdieu (1986) describes the main resources that determine people's position in society as **capital**. He identifies four interrelated forms of capital – economic, social, symbolic and cultural capital.

**Economic capital** refers to financial resources such as income and wealth. People can use their economic capital to further their children's educational success by investing in private education, buying a house close to a 'good' school and employing personal tutors.

**Social capital** refers to networks of family, friends and acquaintances. Social contacts can be seen as a resource. They may provide advice on the best schools and universities, the top jobs and appropriate training.

**Symbolic capital** refers to honour, prestige and reputation. In some societies, for example, symbolic capital is high among the nobility. Families with high symbolic capital can raise their children's expectations and boost their confidence.

**Cultural capital** refers to manners, tastes, interests and language. It includes so-called 'high culture' such as classical music, ballet, opera and visual art. Cultural capital is the culture of the 'dominant classes'. According to Bourdieu, cultural capital is a resource, because the more of it an individual has, the more likely they are to succeed in the education system and enjoy the rewards that this can bring. It can be reproduced or transmitted between the generations through the process of socialisation in families.

### Activity

*Cultural capital, the culture of the dominant classes, includes opera.*

To what extent is Bourdieu's concept of cultural capital based on a Western conception of culture?

In general, the greater the amount of capital an individual or group possesses, the higher their position in the class system. Each form of capital can contribute to success in the education system, with cultural capital being the most important. Bourdieu relates success or failure in education to the distribution of cultural capital between social classes.

## Conversion of capital

The various forms of capital can reinforce and increase each other. Their interaction can, in Bourdieu's terms, lead to **conversion**. For example, the rich tend to mix with the rich, which may increase their social capital. Similarly, the ability to pay for private education may also increase their social capital. Valuable social contacts may result from friendships made at private schools.

## Cultural capital and education

Bourdieu (1986) identified three forms of cultural capital: objectified, institutionalised and embodied. Objectified cultural capital includes material cultural goods such as books, dictionaries and computers, and institutionalised cultural capital includes academic qualifications and titles. In its embodied form, wealth is converted into a **habitus**, an integral part of the person, including ways of speaking and acting. Although habitus is learned or acquired through socialisation and upbringing in families, it appears to be innate.

Bourdieu (1974, 1986) claimed that the possession of cultural capital is the key to high educational attainment. Cultural capital is concentrated in the 'dominant classes'. He also claimed that educational success depends mainly on the culture learned during a child's early years. Children of the 'dominant classes' have a head start when they begin school and this advantage continues throughout their educational career.

Schools and families are both central to Bourdieu's analysis of the cultural reproduction of inequality in society. He focused on how social inequalities were reproduced or transmitted 'through the interactions between the pedagogical practices of schooling and the cultural practices of students and their families' (Gewirtz and Cribb, 2009).

## Social reproduction

Bourdieu argued that cultural capital and the educational qualifications it produces are essential to **social reproduction** – to perpetuating social inequality from generation to generation and maintaining the power and privileges of the 'dominant classes'. In addition, educational success legitimates social reproduction – makes it appear just, right and deserved. The so-called talent and ability which are seen to produce educational success are basically 'the investment of cultural capital'.

This process is hidden within families and, as such, it is safeguarded. This helps to maintain social reproduction. The 'invisibility' of cultural capital largely prevents any criticism and challenge to the advantages it brings.

## Evaluation of Bourdieu

Bourdieu's views have been extremely influential and have stimulated a large body of research. He provided a framework for the study of education which has been used by a number of prominent sociologists (see, for example, Unit 5.5.2).

Bourdieu's views brought both praise and criticism. His critics claim that he presented an overly rigid picture of a society which constrains behaviour and structures action. There appears little room for creativity, resistance or human agency. People were presented as creatures of the social system (Elliott, 2009).

Marxists argue that Bourdieu neglected the economy and placed too much emphasis on cultural capital and not enough on economic oppression.

Critics also argue that Bourdieu's description of cultural capital lacked precision and detail. Additionally, he failed to spell out how cultural capital is converted into educational qualifications (Sullivan, 2001). These criticisms are examined in the section on social class and educational attainment (see Part 5).

### Activity

1. Make brief notes to summarise Bourdieu's account of the relationship between cultural capital and education.
2. Assess the view that the influence of cultural capital on educational attainment reproduces social inequality.

### Key terms

**Cultural reproduction** The transmission of cultural norms, values and experiences between the generations.

**Capital** In Marxist terms, wealth derived from ownership of the means of production. Bourdieu broadened this to include the main social, cultural and symbolic resources as well as economic resources that determine people's position in society.

**Economic capital** Financial resources in the form of income and wealth.

**Social capital** A social network that can be used as a resource.

**Symbolic capital** Honour, prestige and reputation.

**Cultural capital** The manners, tastes, interests and language of the 'dominant classes' which can be translated into wealth, income, power and prestige.

**Conversion** The process by which one form of capital reinforces another.

**Habitus** The dispositions, expectations, attitudes and values held by particular groups.

**Social reproduction** The reproduction of social inequality from one generation to the next.

## Summary

1. According to Bourdieu:
   - the 'dominant classes' have the highest amount of capital
   - the more cultural capital an individual has, the greater their chance of educational success
   - cultural capital gives the children of the 'dominant classes' a head start when they begin school.
2. Critics state that Bourdieu's description of cultural capital lacked precision and detail.
3. Some Marxists argue that Bourdieu ignored the power of the economy to shape the education system.
4. Other critics argue that Bourdieu underplayed resistance and agency among working-class students in schools.

# Unit 5.1.4 Social democratic and New Right views on education

The social democratic perspective is a political ideology that has had a major influence on the development of Western democracies. It has also influenced thinking within the sociology of education. This unit begins by examining social democratic perspectives on education. How do social democratic approaches view equality of opportunity? How do they link education to economic growth?

The New Right, also known as neoliberalism, is a political and economic ideology rather than a sociological theory. It has become a global perspective, guiding the economic policies of governments across the world. The unit explores New Right views on education and, in particular, on how standards can be raised in schools.

## Social democratic views on the relationship between education and the economy

From a social democratic perspective, the state should represent the interests of the population as a whole. This requires a democratic system in which adult members of society elect those who govern them. Democracy is seen as the best way to ensure equal rights such as equality under the law and to ensure equality of opportunity so that every member of society has an equal chance of becoming successful.

In some respects, social democratic views are similar to those of functionalism. Both see education as a means of providing equality of opportunity and as essential for economic growth. However, many social democrats argue that inequalities in society can (1) prevent equality of educational opportunity, and (2) reduce the effectiveness of education in promoting economic growth. Social democratic views have had an important influence on the sociology of education, particularly during the 1960s. They continue to influence government educational policy, for example, in some European countries.

### Equal opportunity and meritocracy

Social democrats such as the British sociologist A.H. Halsey argue that the inequalities produced by a free market economy prevent equality of opportunity. In class-based societies, those who succeed in the education system tend to be the sons and daughters of the middle and upper classes, and those who fail are disproportionately from working-class backgrounds. The class system appears to stand in the way of equal opportunity. Social democrats believe in a meritocracy – a society in which a person's status is achieved on the basis of merit, on their talent and motivation. For a meritocracy to operate effectively, equality of opportunity is essential. Educational reforms are directed at providing equality of educational opportunity.

### Economic growth

According to social democrats such as Halsey et al. (1961), education has a major role to play in economic growth in advanced industrial societies, where the demand for professional and managerial workers is relatively high.

Equality of educational opportunity would make society more meritocratic. It would provide everyone with the opportunity to develop their potential and so maximise their contribution to the economy. In doing so, they would make greater contributions to economic growth, which would bring prosperity to all.

### Evaluation of social democratic theory

**Equality of opportunity** According to social democratic theory, there are two ways of moving towards equality of opportunity – either by changing the education system in order to provide all students with an equal chance to succeed, or by changing the class system and reducing the inequalities that divide society. Despite attempts by various governments in states such as Britain to address these issues, there has been little change in class differences in educational attainment from the 1940s to the present day.

Social democratic theory has been criticised for placing too much importance on changing the education system as a means of reducing inequality of educational opportunity. For example, over the past 60 years, educational reforms within British education do not appear to have significantly reduced class differences in attainment. It appears that 'education cannot compensate for society' (Bernstein, 1971). In other words, education cannot make up for inequalities in the wider society.

Many social democrats now argue that only a reduction in inequality in society as a whole can reduce inequality in educational opportunity. However, the evidence does not hold out much hope for such a reduction. For instance, inequality has grown steadily in most member states of the Organisation for Economic Cooperation and Development (OECD) including Israel, New Zealand and the USA over the past 30 years, according to a report by the OECD (Cingano, 2014).

From a feminist perspective, schools do not provide equality of opportunity, nor are they based on meritocratic principles. Gender inequalities in schools and wider societies favour boys rather than girls. Kate Millett (1970), a radical feminist, saw education as linked to patriarchy. She argued that educational inequalities reinforce economic ones. For example, females tend to study humanities subjects, which often have a lower status than the sciences. As a result, women do not compete on equal terms with men to access the best job opportunities in the labour market (see Part 7).

### Activity

*Feminists question how far societies provide equality of opportunity to women.*

1. Explain why equality of opportunity is essential for a meritocracy to work effectively.
2. In your view, do girls and boys tend to have different attitudes towards science and humanities subjects? How might such differences limit girls' later opportunities to acquire economic power through paid employment?

**Economic growth** Does education promote economic growth, as social democratic theory claims? Critics make the following points.

- First, the school curriculum often fails to meet employers' requirements. It is not designed to provide the skills needed for economic growth.
- Second, more education does not necessarily lead to increased growth in the economy. Alison Wolf (2002) analysed educational expenditure and economic growth in a number of countries. She found that, 'among the most successful economies, there is in fact no clear link between growth and spending on education'. In Switzerland, for example, expenditure on education is relatively low, but in terms of per capita income Switzerland is one of the richest countries in the world. Among less

developed countries, Egypt massively expanded its education spending between 1980 and 1995 but failed to improve its economic position relative to other countries.

- Third, according to the OECD, the level of economic growth depends on the extent of inequality. Countries with the lowest level of inequality have the highest growth rates. The OECD report argues that an increase in the income of the poor would reduce inequality and boost growth. The way to do this is 'to promote equality of opportunity in access to, and quality of, education' and 'promoting employment for disadvantaged groups' (Cingano, 2014).

Governments see more education for more people as vital for economic growth in an increasingly competitive global economy. As competition intensifies, growth is seen to be increasingly dependent on the development of scientific knowledge, technological innovation, and a more highly skilled workforce. Education is seen as crucial for these developments (Lauder et al., 2006).

## New Right views of the relationship between education and the economy

The New Right or neoliberalism informs the economic policies of governments across the world. This approach focuses on competition in national and global markets. It sees competition as the key to efficiency and economic growth. In this view, competition only works in a free market, a market free from government regulations and restrictions.

According to the New Right, competition offers choice to consumers, and choice is only available when companies compete with each other to provide goods and services. There is no choice when the state has a monopoly. The New Right argues that state-owned monopolies such as the provision of education and healthcare should be privatised – sold to private investors. Competition between private companies in a free market will bring choice, efficiency, economic growth and improvements in the quality of goods and services.

There is increasing evidence that neoliberalism is shaping government educational policy in many nations across the globe, including India, New Zealand, the USA and the UK. Also, as we have already seen, there has been a growth in global education companies, some of which view education as a commodity and are mainly concerned with profit.

### Education and the market

From a New Right perspective, education is central to economic growth. Raising standards in education will raise living standards and promote growth.

Marketisation According to neoliberalism, **marketisation** is the key to raising standards in education. Schools, colleges and universities must compete for customers in a free and open market. Parents and students should have the freedom to select the educational institutions of their choice. This will improve standards as parents will choose to send their children to the most successful schools and students will apply to the top universities. Educational institutions will, therefore, have an incentive to raise their standards in order to attract students. In a market system, public money from the state will follow the choices made by parents and children. This will give successful institutions the funds to expand and failing institutions an incentive to improve or face closure.

For an educational market to work efficiently, the New Right argue that information on school standards must be widely available. Without this, parents, students and politicians cannot make informed decisions. In order to provide information on which to base choice, testing regimes must be put in place. Students must be regularly assessed and the results published. Schools can then be directly compared and ranked in 'league tables'. Measuring school performance is essential for informed choice and for raising standards. In order to compete in the market, educational institutions must behave like businesses. Not only students, but also teachers and educational institutions, should be continually assessed. Teachers are assessed in terms of their students' test results. The guiding concept is **performativity** – a focus on performance and its measurement. In Stephen J. Ball's words, this leads to 'audits, inspections, appraisals, self-reviews, quality assurance, research assessment and output indicators'. It directs teaching and research towards areas 'which are likely to have a positive impact on measurable performance' (Ball, 2012).

### The school choice process in India

Private sector provision of low-fee schools in India has grown over the last 20 years. In order to increase parental choice, some private schools are required to set aside one-quarter of their places for students aged 6–14 from disadvantaged backgrounds who attend for free. Eleanor Gurney (2017) argues that one potential consequence of this is greater social segregation.

## Contemporary issues: School choice in the USA

*A rally in Texas in the USA in support of the right to choose schools.*

In a number of US states, the School Choice Program provides students with the opportunity to attend a school other than their neighbourhood school. However, Jeanne H. Ballantine and Joan Z. Spade (2015) argue that the question of school choice in the USA is controversial and, in the 1970s, it became a political issue. Those in favour of school choice argue that it gave working-class families an opportunity to send their children to better schools. Critics argue that only parents with the necessary cultural capital would be able to work through the system in order to secure places for their children in the best schools. In practice, many White parents prioritise the school's racial composition when making choices. The effect of this is to reinforce 'the resegregation of schools' along racial lines.

### Questions

1. Why do you think the people in the photograph are demonstrating for the right to choose schools?
2. What potential problems are associated with policies to extend school choice?

Gurney explored the factors affecting parents' school choices among low-income families in Delhi. She found that parental identity played an important role in choices. For some mothers, making decisions about their children's schooling enabled them to assert power within the domestic setting. The parents' own educational experiences shaped their values concerning schooling and their identity within the market for education. Many of the parents identified themselves as 'uneducated' and this influenced their decision-making. For example, this identification was a driving force in some parents' focus on their children's schooling and their willingness to make financial sacrifices in order to invest in their children's education.

Some parents saw private schooling as connected to social status. Gurney argues that, unless efforts are made to address the effects of children from relatively privileged families leaving the state sector, then pro-market approaches may entrench rather than challenge the 'reproduction of social inequalities through education'.

## Neoliberalism, globalisation and education

Neoliberal perspectives have become global. Education is seen as the key to success in an increasingly competitive global market. It provides the skills needed to compete and the scientific knowledge and new technology to stay in the race.

With this emphasis on education and the economy, schools and colleges have increasingly focused on **vocationalism** – training and preparation for occupations. According to Brown and Lauder (2006), 'Schools, colleges, universities, think-tanks, design centres and research laboratories are now on the front line in the search for competitive advantage.'

In *Global Education Inc.*, Ball (2012) looks at the growth of 'global education policy' based on neoliberal ideology. He argues that global organisations such as the World Bank and the World Trade Organization, international businesses and think-tanks are increasingly involved in 'producing and disseminating global educational policies'.

Ball points to the development of **multinational education businesses** (MNEBs) that sell educational policies and practices based on neoliberal principles. For example, UK-based MNEBs work with other nation-states to provide consultancy, training, management services, professional development and a range of assessment materials.

## Contemporary issues: Global educational league tables

A number of organisations produce international comparisons of educational attainment. One of the most important is the PISA (Programme for International Student Assessment) survey provided by the Organisation for Economic Cooperation and Development based in Paris. It ranks over 70 countries every three years using tests for maths, science and reading given to samples of students aged around 15 years old. Results published in 2016 show that Asian countries tend to dominate the rankings – for example, with 7 in the top 10 for maths (BBC News online, 09.12.2016). Singapore came top in the rankings for science, maths and reading in the 2015 tests.

Global educational league tables are taken very seriously. In some countries, for example, low rankings can result in changes in educational policy. But how seriously should they be taken? Not very seriously, according to Harry Torrance (2006), who has assessed the main providers. Each uses different tests, different samples and different age groups so their results cannot be directly compared. In addition, Torrance states, 'The core of the studies – the basic test results and rankings – are almost meaningless since they could be used to argue virtually any case that one wanted to present.'

### Questions

1. Why do you think the PISA survey ranks students on maths and science rather than on other subjects?
2. To what extent can global educational league tables be seen as reflecting New Right thinking?
3. How useful are the results of international league tables to policy makers?

## Activity

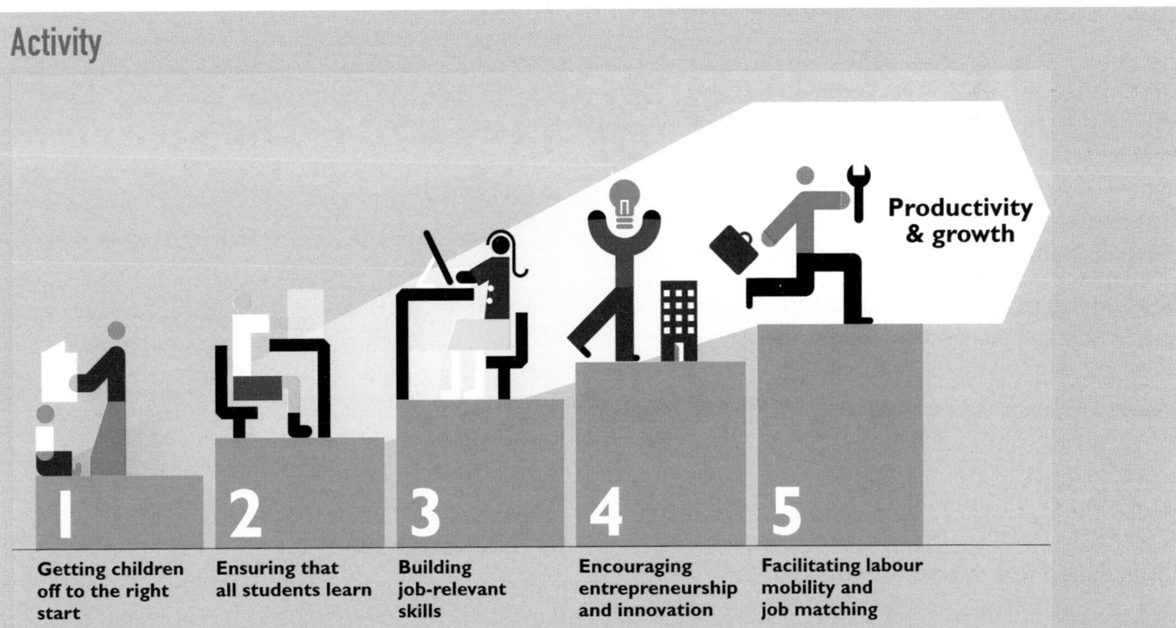


*The World Bank's STEP framework for productivity and economic growth. The World Bank encourages countries to see education as a means of developing the skills needed for economic growth.*

How does the World Bank's STEP framework illustrate their view that education is vital and should be directed to economic growth?

## Evaluation of New Right perspectives on education

**Educational markets are unfair** Do parents have an equal choice in the educational market? Some parents have more knowledge and understanding of the education system and more money. They are in a better position to manipulate educational markets to get the most out of them. For example, middle-class parents will be more likely to get their children into state schools with the best reputations or to afford private schools' fees. In some areas, for some parents, choice is not available – there is no alternative to the local schools.

**Raising standards** Will competition and choice raise standards? A detailed study of evidence from the USA indicates the following. Based on findings of 25 separate studies, the data suggest that competition and choice do produce small improvements in student achievement (Levin and Belfield, 2006). However, these 'modest' improvements are well below the levels expected by supporters of market approaches.

Will this modest improvement be spread evenly across the student population, or will some gain more than others? Evidence from the USA suggests that market approaches will lead to greater social inequalities – in particular, the children of higher-income parents will gain most, leading to a wider **attainment gap** between rich and poor (Levin and Belfield, 2006).

Neoliberal ideas have been widely applied in New Zealand. In some low-achieving schools, student numbers did decline as expected with competition and freedom of choice. However, this was mainly because middle-class students moved to schools with higher reputations, leaving their working-class counterparts behind in inferior schools (Lauder et al., 1999).

**Selection by schools** In an open market, consumer choice may sometimes result in provider choice. This may lead to schools (the providers) choosing students, rather than parents (the consumers) choosing schools. For example, the most successful schools may not have enough places for all the students who wish to attend. This means that schools must select (Ranson, 1996).

Given their desire to remain at the top of the league table, there is pressure on these schools to select students who they see as the most able. In practice, such students are usually from middle-class backgrounds. This process is sometimes known as **creaming.**

**Education as a means to an end** Some critics believe that the marketisation of education leads to a narrow view of education as a means to an end. Stewart Ranson (1996) argues that markets are based on the assumption that each individual will pursue an 'instrumental rationality' in which their sole concern will be to maximise their own self-interest. Ranson believes that when individuals act in this way, it is because the market encourages them to do so. It undermines values that stress the importance of selflessness and cooperation with others.

Frank Coffield and Bill Williamson (2011) claim that schools have been turned into 'exam factories'. Exam results have become a measure of success for students, teachers and schools. Teachers 'teach to the test' and students are 'mark hungry and obsessed by exams'.

Hugh Lauder et al. (2006) do not agree with the view that 'education is a servant of the economy'. What about creativity, critical thinking, questioning and self-awareness? There is little room for such concerns in New Right education policy.

### Activity

1. Assess the view that schools have become exam factories.
2. Explain two limitations of the New Right approach to education.

### Key terms

**Marketisation** The process in which organisations compete in the market.

**Performativity** How well an individual or organisation performs.

**Vocationalism** Education and training designed to prepare young people for employment and to teach work skills to meet the needs of industry.

**Multinational education businesses** Private education companies which have branches in two or more countries.

**Attainment gap** A difference in achievements between groups which is based, for example, on class, gender or ethnicity.

**Creaming** Selecting students who appear most likely to succeed for entry to educational institutions.

## Summary

1. Social democratic perspectives support equal opportunity in education and in the wider society. They argue that social class inequalities prevent equality of educational opportunity.
2. Some social democratic perspectives argue that changes in the education system can reduce inequality of opportunity in schools. Others argue that only a reduction in social class inequality in the wider society can reduce inequality of opportunity in education.
3. Social democratic perspectives state that education promotes economic growth. Critics argue that:
   - the school curriculum is not designed to provide the skills needed for growth
   - there is not a clear link between spending on education and economic growth
   - while education plays a part, reductions in inequality in society lead to growth.
4. Neoliberalism or New Right approaches see competition in the market as the way to improve standards in education. This involves consumer choice, measuring school performance and privatisation.
5. Neoliberal perspectives are now global:
   - Education is seen as essential for providing the skills needed in an increasingly competitive global market.
   - Multinational educational businesses are rapidly growing to meet this demand.
6. Critics of neoliberalism argue that:
   - educational markets are unfair
   - competition only leads to 'modest' improvements
   - some schools select students by 'creaming'
   - there is more to education than servicing the economy.

# END-OF-PART QUESTIONS

| 0 | 1 | | Describe two functions of education. | **[4 marks]** |
| 0 | 2 | | Explain two limitations of the New Right view of education. | **[6 marks]** |
| 0 | 3 | | 'Education promotes economic growth in modern industrial societies.' Using sociological material, give one argument against this view. | **[6 marks]** |

# PART 2 EDUCATION AND SOCIAL MOBILITY

## Contents

**Unit 5.2.1** **Equal opportunity, meritocracy and education** **248**

**Unit 5.2.2** **The links between education and social mobility** **252**

Some sociological approaches see education as operating on meritocratic principles and as providing equal opportunity. In a meritocracy, class, gender and ethnicity do not form barriers to opportunity or achievement. But how far are education systems meritocratic today? Is meritocracy a reality? Or is it an ideology that hides the reality of marked inequalities in opportunity?

In a meritocratic society, education is associated with social mobility. Talented people have the chance to achieve qualifications and credentials that enable them to move up into higher social classes. This part looks at evidence and arguments about the links between education and social mobility. To what extent does education determine people's chances of upward and downward social mobility? Does education provide a route of upward social mobility for talented people, regardless of their social class, gender or ethnicity? Or does it provide more opportunities to those from privileged backgrounds? This part addresses these and other questions.

# Unit 5.2.1 Equal opportunity, meritocracy and education

In a meritocracy, an individual's achievements are based on their own talents and abilities rather than on factors such as their social origins, gender or ethnicity. A meritocratic society provides equality of opportunity so that everyone has an equal chance to achieve (see Unit 5.1.4). Rewards (such as high incomes and status) are distributed and occupations are allocated on the basis of ability and effort as measured by educational achievements and examination results. Although inequality exists, it is based on innate differences in talents or intelligence rather than on social differences in opportunity. But do societies necessarily provide equality of educational opportunity for all children to achieve their potential? Or do education systems favour groups such as those at the top of the class system in unequal societies? This unit explores the idea of meritocracy and different views on the extent to which education systems are meritocratic today.

## Functionalist accounts of meritocracy

According to Parsons, schools promote the key shared values of achievement and equal opportunity (see Unit 5.1.1). Education gives students the central value of individual achievement through, for instance, competitive assessments and examinations. These examinations are based on meritocratic standards that are applied to all students in the same way. The education system is also seen as meritocratic in allocating individuals to their future jobs and status in society on the basis of individual merit and ability rather than gender, ethnicity or class. Even those who do not achieve high grades in examinations or high-status jobs nonetheless accept that the education system operates in a fair way.

In Parsons' view, as societies modernised, social selection would be based on achievement rather than on ascription. An individual's educational attainments would determine their future occupational success. Parsons argued that, if there is fair access to opportunity, it is fair to give different rewards to people for different levels of achievement. According to Parsons, equality of opportunity does not imply equality of outcome.

### Activity

*In Parsons' view, if access to opportunity is fair, then it is fair to reward people on the basis of their achievements.*

How does Parsons justify inequality of outcome?

Davis and Moore (1945) saw the education system as sorting and grading students in terms of their abilities and talents. The system rewards the most talented with academic credentials which provide them with entry to the most functionally important occupations in society (see Unit 5.1.1). In Davis and Moore's view, meritocracy operates as a mechanism for allocating individuals to suitable occupations. Although social inequalities persist in a meritocracy, people accept them as fair.

### Criticisms of functionalist accounts

- Critics question whether education systems are based on equality of opportunity. For example, not all students have access to fee-paying schools. Some students gain advantages based on their parents' financial capital.
- Others question whether schools are meritocratic. The underachievement of working-class students and those from some minority ethnic groups results from social factors such as their lack of access to different forms of capital rather than from lack of ability or talent.
- Many sociologists see meritocracy as a myth rather than as a reality (see below).

## New Right accounts of meritocracy

Peter Saunders (1995, 1996) argues that a meritocracy allocates positions such as occupations on the basis of effort in addition to ability. He differentiates between equality of opportunity and equality of outcome (in which everyone ends up the same). In his view, a meritocracy is based on equality of opportunity (for example, having the right to a free state education) but it generates unequal outcomes (for example, in terms of the overall examination results of females and males). In his view, social inequality is not necessarily unfair. In other words, it is possible for a meritocratic society to be unequal but fair.

According to Saunders, many sociologists focus on class divisions, social advantage and disadvantage rather than on intelligence or innate ability. These sociologists examine the social causes for the differences in educational attainment and levels of social mobility between groups. In doing so, they overlook the possibility that genetic factors might play a part in explaining these differences. Saunders argues that intelligence and effort are the main factors that influence an individual's social class position in British society (see Part 4).

## Social democratic accounts of meritocracy

Social democratic views on equal opportunity and meritocracy were examined in Unit 5.1.4. To summarise, social democrats support the ideal of meritocracy but argue that, in practice, social inequalities can prevent equality of educational opportunity.

### Activity

1. Give one similarity and one difference between functionalist and social democratic accounts of meritocracy.
2. Explain two limitations of the functionalist view of meritocracy.

## Marxist accounts of meritocracy

Marxists see notions of equality of opportunity as ideological in that they help to disguise the realities of class exploitation and domination under capitalism. They reject the idea that schools provide equality of opportunity. Instead, they argue that schools provide capitalist enterprises with the workforce they need.

Bowles and Gintis view meritocracy as a myth (see Unit 5.1.2). It is an ideology via which the education system disguises the social and economic inequalities that are built into capitalist society. Poverty, for example, is seen as acceptable because it results from innate individual failings.

Bowles (1976) rejects the idea that schools in the USA evolved as 'part of a pursuit of equality'. Instead, he argues that they developed 'to meet the needs of capitalist employers for a disciplined and skilled labour force'. Bowles describes class inequality in the school system in the USA as persistent and pervasive.

In Bowles' view, educational inequality is rooted in the class structure of capitalist societies. At the same time, education legitimises and reproduces the class structure. Schooling appears to be open to all. Thus, an individual's position in capitalist society is portrayed as resulting from their talents and efforts rather than their birth. Bowles rejects the idea that schools in the USA are moving towards equality of opportunity. He argues that 'The close relationship between educational attainments and later occupational success thus provides a meritocratic appearance to mask the mechanisms that reproduce the class system from generation to generation.'

Schooling operates on the principle of rewarding excellence. However, the upper class are able to define excellence in such a way that their 'children tend to excel', for example, in relation to examination results. Sticking to the principle of rewarding excellence leads to unequal outcomes – for instance, in terms of unequal access to university – while at the same time 'maintaining the appearance of fair treatment'.

## Life chances

In a meritocracy, there is equality in **life chances**. The term 'life chances' refers to an individual's chances (opportunities) of obtaining those things defined as desirable and avoiding those things defined as undesirable in their society. In Western societies, for example, life chances relate to educational attainment, life expectancy, health, housing, wealth, income, job security and promotion prospects.

Life chances are distributed unequally between different individuals or groups. Those in higher social classes, for example, have access to more of the things considered desirable (such as a good education and high-status credentials) than those in other social classes.

Sociologists, politicians and policy makers see education as an important influence on life chances. In many countries around the world, policy initiatives focus on improving the life chances of people from less privileged backgrounds.

## Activity

*The Doon School is a fee-charging boys' boarding school in Northern India that provides some bursaries or means-tested awards to cover the costs of school fees.*

1. Why might young people's life chances be influenced by the type of school they attend?
2. Is it possible to have equality of opportunity when education is provided by the private sector alongside the state or government sector?

## The consequences of educational underachievement

Educational underachievement among particular social groups such as working-class boys from low-income families or some minority ethnic groups has consequences for the individuals and groups concerned, and for society. The arguments put forward include the following points:

- Educational underachievement has a negative impact on economic growth if human resources are not put to their most appropriate use.
- It results in wastage of talent if some groups' talents are not being used to the full. This may, in turn, affect economic efficiency and reduce international competitiveness.
- The motivation and productivity of people who underachieve may be affected. In this case, it may impact on economic growth.
- If members of some social groups underachieve, it means that inequality will be maintained over time.
- Educational underachievement may suggest a lack of equal opportunity in society.

Some sociologists question the usefulness of the concept of underachievement (Gorard and Smith, 2004; Smith, 2003a, 2003b). They point out that there is little agreement on how to define or measure it. For example, underachievement has been defined in terms of low or poor achievement in formal tests or examinations, low achievement relative to that of other social groups and lower achievement than would be expected.

## Contemporary issues: School 'dropout' in developing countries

*A school in Bangladesh, one of the 30 countries included in Huisman and Smits' study of the factors behind the decision to withdraw from school in less industrialised nations.*

Janine Huisman and Jeroen Smits (2015) see education as an important means of reducing poverty, achieving economic growth, improving people's earning potential and building a competitive economy. They note that millions of children in less industrialised countries withdraw from school at a relatively young age – in some countries, a quarter of children who enrol in school leave before completion. This is problematic because, for example, the children do not achieve their full potential and the countries waste scarce resources.

Huisman and Smits undertook research to investigate the factors behind the decision to withdraw from school in developing nations. They drew on secondary sources of statistical data on 30 countries, including India, Bangladesh, Senegal and Malawi. This gave them information on more than 134 600 children aged 12–15 years in over 360 districts of the 30 developing countries. They examined variables linked to household characteristics such as parental occupation and education, and household wealth. They also examined contextual characteristics such as the availability of schools and teachers, and labour market opportunities at the district level.

In almost all of the countries, children tended to begin school when they were older than the legal age to start primary education. Rates of participation in education were highest among 9- to 12-year-olds. At age 15, the rates were significantly lower than those at age 12. This indicated high dropout rates in most of the countries studied.

Children from households with more socio-economic resources were much more likely to remain in school. The researchers found that 'higher educated parents, a wealthier household, and a father with a higher-level job are strongly positively associated with children staying in school'. Of these factors, household wealth and parental education – particularly the mother's education – were the most important. For example, the odds of remaining in school rose for daughters by 77 per cent and for sons by 40 per cent if their mothers had a minimum of some primary education.

The availability of teachers as measured by a relatively high teacher–student ratio had a significant positive effect on students' likelihood of remaining in school. There was also a higher likelihood of remaining in school in contexts where education increased the chances of finding higher-paid occupations.

Huisman and Smits identified a significantly increased risk of withdrawal from the education system among most students immediately after they finished their primary schooling. The researchers saw this as representing 'a critical choice moment'. However, children – particularly boys – in households with grandparents were less likely to withdraw at this point. Therefore, family capital is important for educational attainment in less industrialised countries.

## Questions

1. What factors affect the educational life chances of children in less industrialised countries?
2. How does gender impact on the chances of remaining in school?
3. Why is it important to gather data on school 'dropout' in these nations?
4. Evaluate the view that research based on quantitative data is limited because it fails to capture human agency.

## Key term

**Life chances** An individual's chances of achieving positive or negative outcomes – relating, for example, to education, health and housing – as they progress through life.

## Summary

1. Parsons argues that the education system is seen as meritocratic in allocating individuals to jobs on the basis of ability.
2. Saunders argues that a meritocracy is based on equality of opportunity rather than outcome. Social inequality is not necessarily unfair.
3. Bowles and Gintis see meritocracy as an ideology. Through the myth of meritocracy, the education system disguises the social and economic inequalities that are built into capitalist society.
4. Life chances are distributed unequally between different social groups. Members of higher social classes have access to more of the things considered desirable in a society, such as high-status credentials, than members of other social classes.

# Unit 5.2.2 The links between education and social mobility

The issue of social mobility is high on the political agenda in many countries. Sociologists are interested in studying social mobility as a way of examining the extent to which a society is meritocratic and how far it offers opportunity for talent and effort to be rewarded. Social mobility is an important factor in an individual's life chances.

Education is widely seen as a key route to social mobility – to movement between social classes – in industrialised and developing countries. Sociologists explore the role of education in promoting social mobility. In many societies, educational attainment is a key factor in determining people's mobility chances, their jobs and their social class. However, what role does an individual's educational attainment play in determining their chances of social mobility? Does education promote mobility for working-class and female students? Or does it restrict mobility levels? Do people with higher-level educational qualifications achieve higher social class positions? This unit explores these and other important questions.

## Defining social mobility

The term 'social mobility' refers to movement between different strata or layers in society. In industrialised societies, it refers to movement between social classes. Social mobility can be upward – for example, moving from the working to the middle class – or downward. Societies that provide little opportunity for social mobility are described as closed and those with a relatively high rate of social mobility are called open. In closed systems, an individual's position is largely ascribed. Often, it is fixed at birth and there is little that people can do to change their status. In open systems, status is achieved and the individual has some chance of changing their position. The traditional caste system in India provides an example of a closed stratification system. Individuals automatically belonged to their parents' caste and, except in rare instances, spent their life in that status. In class-based systems, social mobility is possible. Some people will be upwardly mobile and improve their position on the basis of merit through talent, ability, ambition and hard work. In such cases, characteristics such as class of origin, gender and ethnicity have little influence on an individual's social status.

### Types of social mobility

Sociologists have identified two main types of social mobility: intragenerational and intergenerational mobility. (*'Intra'* refers to 'within' and *'Inter'* refers to 'between'.)

1. **Intragenerational mobility** refers to social mobility *within* a single generation. It is measured by comparing the occupational status of an individual at two or more points in time. Thus, if a person begins their working life as an unskilled manual worker and 10 years later is employed as an accountant, they are upwardly socially mobile in terms of intragenerational mobility.
2. **Intergenerational mobility** refers to social mobility *between* generations. It is measured by comparing the occupational status of sons or daughters with that of their fathers (or, less frequently, with that of their mothers). Thus, if the daughter of an unskilled manual worker becomes an accountant, she is socially mobile in term of intergenerational mobility. Contemporary studies of social mobility are more likely to take gender and ethnicity into account than those carried out in the 20th century.

Sociologists distinguish between absolute and relative intergenerational mobility. **Absolute mobility** refers to the total amount of social mobility in a society. **Relative mobility** refers to the comparative chances of people from different class backgrounds reaching particular positions in the social structure.

## Measuring social mobility

Sociologists often use occupation to measure mobility between different classes. The Oxford Mobility Study (OMS), widely seen as a classic study of social mobility, was conducted in 1972 and published in 1980 (Goldthorpe, 1980). It provides an example of quantitative research using a survey of 10 000 men in England and Wales. The OMS is based on a seven-class scheme devised by John Goldthorpe. It produced data on the impact of the 1944 Education Act on educational achievement and social mobility. The 1944 Act introduced a test for 11-year-olds, the results of which determined the type of secondary school they would attend.

The study found high rates of absolute mobility. There was more upward than downward mobility, because the proportion of non-manual jobs in the occupational structure had increased while the proportion of manual jobs had decreased. It also found that the chances of those from working-class backgrounds reaching a higher social class had improved during the course of the 20th century.

On the surface, these findings seem to support the claim that British society was becoming more open and meritocratic. However, the study found that relative mobility chances varied greatly between the classes, and the relative chances had changed little during the 20th century. Thus, 45.7 per cent of sons with class 1 fathers (the highest social class, containing professionals and high-grade managers) ended up in class 1. However, just 7.1 per cent of sons with class 7 fathers (the lowest social class, containing unskilled and semi-skilled manual workers) ended up in class 1.

The chances of members of all social classes attaining class 1 and 2 jobs increased over the period studied. However, this absolute mobility largely resulted from changes in the occupational structure. The growth of professional occupations, for example, created more room at the top. Mobility was more due to this and less the result of increased equality of opportunity or reductions in inequalities in life chances. The relative chances of those from different classes taking advantage of the increasing room at the top of the class system changed little. In other words, there was no significant increase in the openness of the British **stratification system**.

## Problems with the Oxford Mobility Study

1. The OMS suggests that there was a relatively high rate of mobility into the top of the British class system and that class 1 as a whole appeared fairly open. However, critics argue that the OMS ignores the existence of small elites or, in Marxist terms, a ruling class. The OMS's class 1 is a relatively large grouping, containing 10–15 per cent of the male working population. Studies that concentrate on small elite groups within class 1 reveal a much lower degree of openness.
2. The OMS ignores women. It views the family as the unit of stratification in industrial societies. The class position of a family was based on the occupation of the main earner, usually a man. Feminist sociologists criticise such approaches as having a male bias and as telling us little about the social mobility experiences of women.

## Activity: Social class and life chances

*Each row shows a person at different stages of their life. The top row shows a man born into and remaining in the upper middle class. The bottom row shows a man born into and remaining in the lower working class. The pictures illustrate the life chances of the two men – their chances of obtaining desirable outcomes and experiences and of avoiding undesirable outcomes and experiences.*

Data from research in Britain based on a longitudinal approach show that the class people are born into increasingly shapes their life chances. How do the pictures illustrate this?

### Activity

Phillip Brown (2013) argues that 'high levels of "absolute" social mobility do not confirm the hypothesis of merit-selection because they do not depend on narrowing inequalities in education or the labour market'.

Explain why high rates of absolute mobility in a particular society do not necessarily mean that it provides equality of opportunity.

## Comparative studies of education and social mobility

Technical difficulties in carrying out studies of social mobility have made it difficult to compare international rates of mobility. For example, the occupational classification schemes employed to distinguish classes have varied from society to society and comparable sets of data have not always been available.

In recent years, however, international comparisons of social mobility rates have become possible. One reason for this is that a number of countries have adopted similar occupational classification schemes.

An international comparison of mobility rates in European countries was published in 2004 by Richard Breen (discussed in Scott, 2005). This study examined how far class origins influenced educational success and how far occupations were determined by educational qualifications. In the most meritocratic countries, class should have little effect on educational success, while occupational status should be strongly influenced by qualifications. Sweden was found to be the most meritocratic of the countries, and Britain was the least meritocratic in terms of how changeable or open the class structure was, taking both upward and downward social mobility into account.

Jo Blanden, Paul Gregg and Stephen Machin (2005) conducted research on intergenerational mobility in eight major industrial counties (six European countries, the USA and Canada). However, they used income rather than occupation as a measure of mobility. This allowed them to make simple comparisons between countries and cohorts (groups of people born at different times). They found that Britain and the USA had the lowest rates of intergenerational mobility, while Norway, Denmark and Canada had relatively high rates. They also found that the extent of intergenerational income mobility had declined significantly in Britain over time: the cohort born in 1970 were less mobile than the cohort born in 1958. By contrast, a marked fall in mobility was not found in the USA. They explain the decline in mobility in Britain partly in terms of the 'increasing relationship between family income and educational attainment between these cohorts'.

Based on his review of the literature on comparative studies of mobility in Western societies, John Scott (2005) argues that an individual's chances of upward or downward social mobility depend on their class background significantly more than on their educational attainments. In his words, 'Education does not seem to matter very much when it comes to determining occupational success and improvements in income... the chances of a person rising or falling in the social hierarchy depends on their class background far more than it does on their individual educational achievement.' People born in the higher classes have much more chance of experiencing upward social mobility and avoiding downward social mobility.

### Activity

Different studies of social mobility use different definitions and methods. Why might this make it difficult to compare rates of mobility between countries?

The Organisation for Economic Co-operation and Development (Going for Growth, 2010) compared earnings between fathers and sons in several developed nations. In France, Italy, the UK and the USA, a young person from a less well-off family had relatively low chances of earning higher wages or getting a higher level of education than their parents. By contrast, countries such as Denmark, Austria and Canada had relatively high levels of earnings mobility across the generations.

One view is that levels of mobility are associated with public expenditure on education. For example, lower levels of mobility tend to be found in countries with lower levels of spending on education per person as a percentage of their gross domestic product.

When making international comparisons of mobility, researchers may be limited by lack of relevant data. For instance, when measuring income mobility, researchers must have access to parental income and also children's income 20 or more years later. By contrast, data on parents' and children's social class or occupation are relatively easy to collect. However, it is important that the international measures of social class are comparable, to ensure that class has the same meaning across countries. It is also difficult to ensure cross-national comparability in terms of qualification levels.

## Functionalist accounts of social mobility

From a functionalist perspective, education systems in industrial societies have a key role in training the future workforce so that it can meet the growing demand for professional, managerial and technical workers. Recruitment to important occupations is increasingly based on merit. In this context, the role of education becomes that of determining class position. Functionalist accounts argue that the relationship between educational attainment, social class and occupational destinations will grow stronger over time in response to the demands of industrial societies' economic organisation and technology. In order to maintain technological and economic dynamism, employers must recruit staff on the basis of the relevant knowledge and skills that educational qualifications certify. The increasing demand for qualified staff will necessitate the expansion of education systems along with reforms in order to increase equality of educational opportunity. This will ensure that human resources are used as effectively as possible. In the functionalist account, ascribed status will be replaced over time by achieved status via education. As a result, societies will become increasingly socially mobile and meritocratic. The association between class origins and educational attainment will weaken over time and intergenerational social mobility will increase.

### Criticisms of the functionalist approach

- Critics argue that functionalism focuses on the needs and demands of society as a whole rather than on how individual social actors make sense of these needs.
- Goldthorpe (2013) points out that there has not been a tendency in most advanced industrial societies for the association between educational attainment and class destinations to strengthen. Nor is there definite evidence of a general weakening trend in the association between social origins and class destinations.
- Brown (2013) argues that many studies highlight continuing inequalities in social origins, education and destinations linked to class, ethnicity and gender. In his view, it is necessary to address class inequalities in opportunity and life chances in order to increase intergenerational social mobility rates.

### Activity

*Unpaid internships are becoming more widespread in many countries.*

Why might the growth in unpaid internships benefit some young people more than others?

Brown suggests that within a mass system of higher education characteristic of many countries today, credentials become less valuable to employers as a way of screening job applicants. There is also more emphasis now on competency-based recruitment, which combines 'the "hard currencies" (credentials, sporting achievements, work experience, etc.), along with the "soft currencies" of personality, character and social confidence'. This benefits students from privileged backgrounds who, for example, take for granted learning opportunities in the form of unpaid internships, **extra-curricular activities** (activities outside school) and foreign travel. Brown argues that job candidates are now excluded because they lack the personal qualities that make up employability rather than because they lack the relevant credentials. As a result, the relationship between educational attainment and class destination will become weaker rather than stronger.

## Neoliberal approaches to social mobility

New Right or neoliberal approaches focus on giving people from disadvantaged backgrounds the chance to compete in the market with people from more privileged backgrounds.

### Activity

*New Right approaches believe in giving everyone the chance to compete in the market for positions. Open competition provides some people with the opportunity to become socially mobile.*

Criticise this view from:

1. a Marxist approach
2. a feminist approach.

### Criticisms of neoliberal approaches

Brown (2013) argues that this approach focuses on absolute rather than relative mobility. It sees the way to increase absolute social mobility in terms of raising the aspirations of people from disadvantaged backgrounds and increasing the opportunities available to them. However, it fails to address the issue of relative social mobility. In Brown's view, the neoliberal approach ignores the sociological evidence that absolute social mobility can occur without any reduction in inequalities in life chances.

Brown argues that many families – both working-class and middle-class – experience 'social congestion' rather than intergenerational social mobility. In his view, the economy does not have the capacity to deliver enough professional occupations to meet demand. This has led to crowding in the labour market. In industrialised countries with mass higher education, a large middle class and wide inequalities in income, the labour market's failure to supply enough professional occupations is particularly marked. Job applicants have to compete with each other. They try to use the education system to 'stand out from the crowd'. The tactics they use to get ahead often add to the congestion, because so many applicants adopt the same tactics. Universities and employers respond by raising their entry requirements or adding requirements such as work experience as well as higher education qualifications.

### Activity

*No jobs at the top!*

1. What problem for social mobility is depicted in the picture?
2. Assess the view that social mobility can be increased by raising the aspirations of people from disadvantaged backgrounds.

## Feminist approaches to social mobility

Feminists are critical of the male bias involved in the practice of categorising women in social mobility studies according to the class of their male partners (Acker, 1973). Many prefer an approach in which individuals are allocated to a class according to their own job.

Quantitative studies of social mobility have tended to focus on social class rather than on gender (Abrantes and Abrantes, 2014). However, evidence suggests that women's chances of upward social mobility are more constrained than those of men. One reason for this relates to gendered subject choices at school and beyond. Qualifications in Science, Technology, Engineering and Maths (STEM) subjects are highly valued in labour markets and can lead to well-paid careers. Female students are less likely than males to study STEM subjects at school and at university. Feminists argue that subject choice may impact negatively on females' future career options, earnings from paid work and their social mobility chances (see Part 7). Careers information and guidance provided by educational institutions or by families might not challenge gender stereotypes surrounding subject choice. This, in turn, might limit females' chances of social mobility.

## Contemporary issues: Gendered social mobility across Europe

*Some fields of study, such as Business and Law, may provide a route of upward social mobility for more male than female graduates across Europe.*

Pedro Abrantes and Manuel Abrantes (2014) drew on statistical data from the European Social Survey. This large-scale survey provided information covering 22 countries, including Sweden, Germany, Spain and Poland. Based on their comparison of these countries, Abrantes and Abrantes argue that the relationship between gender, education and intergenerational social mobility is not uniform across Europe. They found marked variation between countries, social classes and fields of study such as the Business and Law field or the Health, Education and Care field.

Male graduates in Business and Law, for example, 'are 2.2 times more likely to access class A or B [the dominant or affluent classes] than the total population average. The chances of women in the same situation remain *below* the average'. Thus, fields such as Business and Law offer routes of upward social mobility for significantly more male than female students. One possibility is that some females may avoid some fields of study and areas of employment because they are aware that they are more likely to experience discrimination in them.

### Questions

1. Identify one research method that you would use to investigate females' choice of field of study and employment area, and explain why you would use this particular method.
2. In your view, to what extent are people in your culture likely to experience gender discrimination in fields of study or areas of employment?

Many sectors of labour markets (such as architecture, engineering, nursing and childcare) are segregated on gender lines. Male-dominated sectors (such as information technology) are often more highly paid than female-dominated ones (such as teaching), even when they require the same level of educational qualifications for entry. As a result, women may have less chance of experiencing income generational mobility than men. Furthermore, gender discrimination in the labour market (for example, in relation to recruitment and promotion) can have a negative impact on women's social mobility chances.

### Key terms

**Intragenerational mobility** An individual's movement up or down between the strata or layers of society over the course of their life.

**Intergenerational mobility** Movement up or down between the strata or layers of society as measured between the generations of a family.

**Absolute mobility** The total amount of social mobility in a society.

**Relative mobility** The comparative chances of people from different class backgrounds reaching particular positions in the social structure.

**Stratification system** The way a society is structured or divided into hierarchical strata or layers, with the most privileged group at the top and the least favoured at the bottom.

**Extra-curricular activities** Activities undertaken outside lessons at school such as clubs and debating societies, or hobbies undertaken outside school such as yoga or dance.

## Summary

1. Social mobility refers to movement – either upward or downward – between different strata or layers in society.
2. Sociologists differentiate between intragenerational and intergenerational social mobility, and between absolute and relative mobility.
3. Occupation is generally used to measure mobility between social classes.
4. The Oxford Mobility Study (OMS) found high rates of absolute mobility linked to changes in the occupational structure rather than to increased equality of opportunity. Critics argue that the OMS ignored women and the existence of small elites.
5. In the most meritocratic countries, class should have little effect on educational success and occupational status should be strongly influenced by qualifications. Breen (mentioned in Scott, 2005) found that Sweden was the most meritocratic of the European countries studied, while Britain was the least meritocratic.
6. Researchers may be limited by lack of data when making international comparisons of social mobility.
7. Functionalist accounts argue that, in response to the economic demands of industrial societies, social mobility and meritocracy will increase and the link between class origins and educational attainment will weaken over time.
8. Brown argues that the relationship between educational attainment and class destination will weaken rather than strengthen. Job candidates with the relevant credentials are now excluded because they lack personal qualities that make up employability.
9. New Right or neoliberal approaches to social mobility focus on giving people from disadvantaged backgrounds the chance to compete in the market with those from more privileged backgrounds.
10. Critics argue that neoliberal approaches focus on absolute mobility, which can occur without reductions in inequalities in life chances. Brown argues that many families – both working-class and middle-class – experience social congestion rather than intergenerational mobility.

# END-OF-PART QUESTIONS

**0 1** Describe two consequences of educational underachievement for society. **[4 marks]**

**0 2** Explain two limitations of the view that education systems provide equality of opportunity today. **[6 marks]**

**0 3** 'Education provides a key route of social mobility in modern industrial societies.' Using sociological material, give one argument against this view. **[6 marks]**

# PART 3 INFLUENCES ON THE CURRICULUM

## Contents


| | | |
|---|---|---|
| **Unit 5.3.1** | **Knowledge and the curriculum** | **259** |
| **Unit 5.3.2** | **Education and the hidden curriculum** | **266** |


Education is often seen as involving the transmission of knowledge from teachers to students. But what is knowledge based on? Is there such a thing as valid knowledge? It is easy to see the school curriculum as something that simply exists rather than as something that has been constructed or put together. However, what factors shape what actually gets taught in schools? Why are some subjects included in the curriculum and others excluded? Why do some subjects have higher status than others? How far is this linked to the distribution of power in society? Unit 5.3.1 addresses questions about the nature of knowledge and the curriculum.

What do students learn in schools, apart from subject knowledge and skills? Unit 5.3.2 looks at particular aspects of the curriculum in more detail. It also examines different views of the hidden curriculum – the ideas, norms and values that are transmitted as part of everyday school life.

# Unit 5.3.1 Knowledge and the curriculum

Large amounts of knowledge are transmitted in schools daily. But what do we mean by knowledge? Sociologists see knowledge as problematic rather than as taken for granted. They question how societies make or construct knowledge. Who has control over the production of knowledge? How is knowledge transmitted? This unit questions the nature and construction of knowledge.

## The social construction of knowledge

Many sociologists and philosophers reject the view that knowledge is something that simply exists 'out there', awaiting discovery. Instead, they emphasise the social basis of knowledge and the role of people in constructing or producing it. Some argue that all knowledge, including scientific and educational knowledge, is socially constructed. In other words, knowledge and 'truth' are created by members of society in particular social situations or group settings. For example, one view is that scientific knowledge is produced by communities of like-minded scientists who interact and work together in their laboratories rather than being discovered through the use of logical procedures and objective criteria (see Unit 7.1.2).

Constructionism sees knowledge as produced within the context of power relationships based on social class, gender and ethnicity. In this view, truth is relative rather than absolute. It is relative to the setting or context within which it is produced – for example, to a particular culture at a particular point in time. This implies that there is no such thing as objective knowledge and that all knowledge must be equally valuable.

Michael F.D. Young (1971b, 1973) focused on educational knowledge and who controls it. In his earlier work, he adopted a social constructivist approach to knowledge. He argued that all knowledge is socially constructed. Knowledge is a product of human practices rather than something that simply exists in reality. This led Young to question 'what counts as educational knowledge' (1971a) rather than taking school knowledge for granted or treating it as a 'given'. Consequently, he viewed the curriculum as an area of sociological investigation rather than as something that exists independently of people.

Young saw the content of the curriculum and the different subjects taught in schools as socially constructed. In his view, some groups (such as university subject specialists, politicians, examination boards and heads of departments in schools) are able to impose their constructions on other groups.

## Postmodernism and knowledge

Modernist thinking is based on the idea that it is possible to generate valid knowledge about the social and natural worlds. Postmodernists, however, are sceptical about such claims. They reject grand theories or meta-narratives and the idea that objective truth exists. To them, knowledge is relative rather than absolute. For example, truth claims are relative to the context within which they were produced. From a postmodernist perspective, knowledge is also partial in the sense that it is both limited and biased. The extension of this view is that it is impossible to discover valid knowledge.

## Activity

*Harvard University in Massachusetts, USA, dates back to 1636 and is regarded as one of the most prestigious universities in the world. Many of its staff engage in research to develop human knowledge.*

Why might the idea of extending human knowledge through research be seen as based on modernist thinking?

According to Jean–François Lyotard (1984), in the postmodern era certainty has been replaced with uncertainty. There are now a multitude of answers, none of which can be shown to be definitively true or untrue. In his view, knowledge is relative to time and place and to particular cultures. Truth and falsehood, and right and wrong, are defined in different ways by different cultures.

Lyotard welcomed the downfall of meta-narratives. From his perspective, grand stories presented a single version of the truth and of right and wrong. He believed that this led to intolerance and prevented many voices from being heard. Lyotard argued that postmodern society provides an opportunity to hear the voices of a wide variety of groups who were largely silenced in modern society – for example, the voices of minority ethnic groups.

## Postmodernism and educational knowledge

According to Robin Usher and Richard Edwards (1994), the task of education under modernity was to bring out people's potential to think for themselves and to make rational decisions. Within modernity, education is the key to developing individuals and, in doing so, making social progress possible.

Usher and Edwards follow writers such as Lyotard in arguing that modernity is characterised by a belief in meta-narratives of human progress. It is education that expresses and disseminates the big stories about progress and helps to give people their belief in progress itself and their faith in science and reason as ways of achieving it.

Postmodernists, however, oppose any belief that there is a firm foundation to knowledge. They are critical of any attempt to impose one version of the truth on people. They also oppose the belief that rationality can solve all human problems. Consequently, postmodernists would question grand claims such as the following:

- Human potential can be achieved through education.
- Education can produce shared values and social solidarity.
- Education can produce equality of opportunity and a just society.

To Usher and Edwards, postmodernism denies that there is any single best curriculum that should be followed in schools. If there is no one set of truths that can be accepted, then there is no basis for saying that one thing should be taught in all schools and other things should be excluded. Instead, Usher and Edwards argue that education should teach many different things and accept that there can be different truths rather than attempt to impose one set of ideas on all education.

## Activity

*Science is usually seen as a high-status subject and is often a compulsory part of the curriculum for girls and boys.*

1. How might postmodernism view the knowledge that is transmitted in science lessons?
2. On what basis does postmodernism question the idea that education can produce equality of opportunity?

### Criticisms of postmodernism

- Critics object to the claim that all truth is relative on logical grounds. Rob Moore (2004) points out that, for *all* truth to be relative, 'there must be one truth that is *not* relative: namely, the truth that all truth is relative. Therefore, it is *not* true that *all* truth is relative.' Moore believes that objective knowledge is possible.
- Michael W. Apple (1997) argues that postmodernists tend to ignore the wider political and economic forces such as capitalism and economic power that shape the education system.

## Factors affecting the content of the curriculum

During the 1970s, sociologists such as Young, Basil Bernstein and Nell Keddie began to explore knowledge within education. They focused on the content of education and the transmission of knowledge via curricula. They questioned the content of curricula and how curricula content, subjects and skills are selected. Various factors have been identified as influencing the content of the curriculum including the status of different subjects, power, culture, economic demands and gender.

### High- and low-status subjects

Young (1971b) argued that knowledge, including educational knowledge, is socially organised. One key dimension of this organisation is the 'stratification of knowledge'. There is a hierarchy of knowledge and some forms of knowledge are more highly valued than others. Within education, the curriculum is stratified into high- and low-status subjects. Traditional academic subjects such as chemistry, mathematics and history have more status than practical or vocational subjects. According to Young, areas of the curriculum or individual subjects have high status if they are:

- formally assessed (for example, via examinations rather than coursework)
- taught to the 'most able' students
- taught in same-ability sets or groups rather than in mixed-ability groups.

Young (1971b) argued that educational knowledge is stratified or ranked on four dimensions:

- how abstract it is
- whether it involves written communication rather than oral work
- whether it emphasises individual rather than group assessment
- whether it is directly related or relevant to everyday life or activities outside school.

Academic curricula have high-status knowledge which tends to be abstract rather than concrete, stresses written work and individual work, and is not strongly related to non-school activities. By contrast, non-academic knowledge is organised in terms of oral presentation, group work and assessment, and concrete knowledge. It is related to non-school knowledge and is more practical or work related than high-status, academic knowledge. Young saw these dimensions as socially defined. This means that an academic curriculum and formal examinations are social inventions. They are linked to cultural choices which reflect the beliefs and values of dominant groups such as universities.

Kate Reynolds (1991) sees the distinction between 'academic' subjects such as maths and the sciences and 'non-academic' subjects such as art and woodwork as based on a division between mental labour and manual labour. In Reynolds' view, this serves to legitimate class divisions in society.

### Knowledge and power

Young (1971b, 1973) and his associates related knowledge to the overall distribution of power in society. They argued that people in positions of power will try to define:

1. what is seen as valued knowledge
2. how far any knowledge is accessible to different social groups
3. the accepted relationships between different areas of knowledge, and between those who have access to these areas and 'make them available' (Young, 1971b).

Groups in powerful positions will tend to define their own knowledge as superior, to institutionalise it in educational settings, and to measure educational attainments in terms of it. This is not because 'some occupations "need" recruits with knowledge defined and assessed in this way' (Young, 1971b). Rather, it is to maintain the established order and to ensure that power and privilege remain within the same social groups.

## Criticisms of Young

Young and his associates claimed that all knowledge is socially constructed and, consequently, of equal value. This suggests that there is no objective way of evaluating knowledge, of assessing whether one form of knowledge is superior to others. If any knowledge is seen as superior, it is simply because those with power have defined it as such and imposed their definition on others. It therefore follows that all knowledge is equally valid and valuable.

This view is known as cultural relativism or a relativist position on knowledge and the curriculum. Taken to its extreme, it poses serious problems. For example, it becomes impossible to assess whether a particular view is right or wrong. Thus, from the standpoint of cultural relativism, Young's views are no more valid than any others. However, despite the criticisms of the views of Young and his associates, the content of the curriculum is now a central issue among groups such as politicians, policy makers and teachers in many countries.

## Culture and the curriculum

Stuart Foster and Jason Nicholls (2008) investigated the influence of culture on the content of textbooks. They examined eight popular history textbooks, two from each of four countries, in order to analyse how the US's role in World War II was described. The textbooks were drawn from: the US; England, a close ally of the US during the war; Japan, a wartime enemy of the US and England; and Sweden, a neutral country.

The researchers compared, for example, how the different textbooks covered the outbreak of World War II. The US textbooks mentioned the outbreak of war in Europe in 1939. However, the war only received extended treatment when the US entered the war in 1941 after the Japanese navy attacked the US naval base at Pearl Harbor in Hawaii. The English and Swedish books focused on the war from a European perspective and gave little attention to the war in the Pacific. By contrast, the Japanese textbooks focused on the war in the Pacific rather than in Europe or North Africa. They examined events in the Pacific between 1930 and 1941 and, in this way, gave much more context to events leading to the bombing of Pearl Harbor.

Foster and Nicholls argue that the textbooks tended to examine World War II from a nation's own cultural, historic and geo-political perspective. For example, the US textbooks portrayed America's entry into the war as being decisive to the outcome. However, Swedish textbooks concentrated on the war in Europe and North Africa and, consequently, portrayed the US as playing a supporting rather than leading role.

Foster and Nicholls argue that historical information and interpretation of world events that are conveyed to school students in different countries vary considerably. Their research illustrates how the four countries treat historical events differently and the influence of culture and geopolitical perspectives on the production of knowledge.

### Activity

*Cultural factors may influence the information presented in textbooks.*

1. To what extent does Foster and Nicholls' study support the idea that knowledge is socially constructed?
2. How might the knowledge learned in school socialise the members of a society?
3. In your view, how far would it be possible to remove the influence of culture in the production of knowledge?

## Economic demands and the curriculum

Governments across the globe see education as linked to economic growth (see Unit 5.1.4). Curriculum reforms are often a response to economic demands, including global recessions or changes in the global market for labour (McDougall and Trotman, 2009). Vocational courses attempt to make education fit the requirements of industry and to prepare students for future employability.

Functionalism (see Unit 5.1.1) focuses on the economic requirements for a skilled and literate workforce in industrial societies. Neoliberal approaches see education as playing a key role in providing a country with a competitive edge in the knowledge economy (see Unit 5.1.4). The New Right emphasises efficiency and value for money rather than principles such as equality of opportunity (Ball, 1990). Alan Skelton (1997) points out that the competitive, marketplace ideology of the New Right sees education mainly in terms of its economic function. Wilfred Carr and Anthony Hartnett (1996) describe this economic role in terms of 'training an efficient workforce, creating a culture of entrepreneurship and enterprise, and fostering a positive view of industry and wealth creation'.

**The knowledge economy and education** In a knowledge economy, production and services are based on knowledge-intensive activities or intellectual skills that contribute to rapid advances in science and technology. It includes science-based industries, newer industries based on biotechnology and information technology, and jobs such as computer programming.

Knowledge is seen as a way of promoting economic growth and enabling countries to compete in a global economy. There is more reliance on the intellectual capacities of workers than on factors such as natural resources (for example, land) or machinery and manual labour. Car manufacturing, for instance, now involves computer technology. One view is that a knowledge economy increases the demand for highly educated and skilled workers. To remain competitive globally, nations need to stay ahead in terms of technology.

Ideas about the knowledge-based economy influence education policy around the world (Robertson, 2008). Investment in education is justified in terms of strengthening the economy in order to compete in international knowledge-based markets. Expansion in higher education provision is seen as a way to increase the pool of skills available to employers. It is also seen as increasing the employability of young people by equipping them with the necessary knowledge and skills for work in the global knowledge economy.

**The OECD (1996)** The Organisation for Economic Cooperation and Development (OECD) (1996) argues that 'Knowledge is now recognised as the driver of productivity and economic growth, leading to a new focus on the role of information, technology and learning in economic performance.' In knowledge-based economies, 'productivity and growth are largely determined by the rate of technical progress and the accumulation of knowledge'.

## Contemporary issues: Promoting gender equality in education in Africa

The Forum for African Women Educationalists (FAWE) is a charitable organisation that was set up in 1992. The organisation operates through 34 National Chapters across African countries including Nigeria, Kenya, Namibia and Mozambique. FAWE campaigns for and promotes gender equality in education. One of its programmes focuses on girls' involvement in Science, Technology, Engineering and Mathematics subjects.

*Delegates at a FAWE conference.*

'Many girls in sub-Saharan Africa do not participate significantly or perform well in Mathematics, Science and Technology subjects. This situation becomes more pronounced as the level of education increases and a combination of factors perpetuate the imbalance. These factors include cultural practices and attitudes and biased teaching and learning materials.

FAWE developed its Science, Technology, Engineering and Mathematics (STEM) model to increase and sustain access, interest, participation and performance of girls in STEM subjects at all levels.

The model trains teachers to adopt and use STEM curricula, teaching and learning materials and classroom practices that are gender-responsive. It involves not only teachers but education planners, curriculum developers, publishers and women leaders, and sensitises parents and stakeholders on the importance of girls' participation in STEM.

The Science, Mathematics and Technology model was initiated in 2005 and has been introduced in Burkina Faso, Cameroon, Kenya, Malawi, Mali, Mozambique, Rwanda, Swaziland, Tanzania, Uganda, Zambia, Zanzibar and Zimbabwe.

Over 15 000 students have benefited from FAWE's STEM programme since 2005.

**Features of FAWE's STEM model**

The STEM model features extensive use of activities and resources including:

- Science camps and clubs
- Study tours
- Profiles on women achievers in science-based fields
- Exposure to role models
- Awards to female achievers in STEM subjects.

**Impact of FAWE's STEM model**

- Higher rates of girls' participation in SMT [Science, Mathematics and Technology] subjects
- Improved test scores for girls
- Improved teachers' attitudes towards girls' abilities and participation in SMT
- Improved instructional materials for SMT subjects
- Girls' positive attitudinal change to SMT
- Greater confidence for girls in tackling academic challenges.
- Enhancement of girls' chances for career progression.'

Source: http://fawe.org/home/our-programmes/interventions/science-mathematics-and-technology/

## Questions

1. How does this source explain girls' levels of participation and performance in Science, Mathematics and Technology subjects in sub-Saharan Africa?
2. In your view, why is it important for girls to study these subjects?
3. How might girls' participation and performance in these subjects improve if they are exposed to role models?
4. Are you aware of gender differences in participation and performance in SMT subjects in schools in the region in which you live? If so, are there any programmes to address this?

Workers are required not only to have relevant skills but also to update their skills regularly. Education and training are key elements of the knowledge-based economy. In the OECD's view, government policies need to provide broad-based formal education and to incentivise companies and individuals to participate in lifelong learning and continuous training.

## Criticisms of the knowledge economy

André Spicer (2016) describes the knowledge economy as 'largely a myth'. He argues that Western economies such as the USA and the UK do not have enough degree-level knowledge-intensive jobs to meet the demand for them from graduates. In his view, increasing the number of people with degrees or expanding the higher education sector will not create a more competitive economy in these countries. Other commentators point out that the expansion of higher education in many countries has created credential inflation because the demand for professional and managerial jobs is greater than the supply.

## The influence of gender on curriculum content

From a feminist perspective, Reynolds (1991) argues that gender is highly significant in terms of the construction of knowledge. For example, females are under-represented in images in textbooks (see Unit 5.3.2 for an account of the gendered curriculum). Consequently, feminist sociologists argue that educational knowledge is defined 'from a white "male" perspective whereby the achievements, struggles and even existence of women is omitted from the picture'.

The Australian sociologist Dale Spender (1982) argued that education is largely controlled by men, who use their power to define men's knowledge and experiences as important, and women's knowledge and experiences as insignificant. She examined the content of the school curriculum from a feminist perspective. In her view, many subjects were riddled with sexism. Science textbooks, for instance, focused mainly on men's achievements and ignored the contributions of female scientists. In this way, women were rendered invisible to science students. As a result, science failed to provide girls with positive role models or to engage them in science subjects. In Spender's view, the curriculum was dominated by male interests and neglected issues that were of concern to women. For example, history textbooks focused on military and political events. Furthermore, schools taught men's knowledge and understandings of the world.

Anthony Giddens and Philip Sutton (2017) argue that the **formal curriculum** in schools in industrialised societies was differentiated along the lines of gender in the past. In the 1960s, for example, subjects such as domestic science and typing were seen as suitable for girls, while subjects such as maths and woodwork were considered more appropriate for boys. Today, however, the curriculum in secondary schools in nations such as Britain does not explicitly distinguish between girls' and boys' subjects in this way.

## The curriculum and cultural capital

Bourdieu (1971, 1974) argued that the education system is systematically biased in favour of dominant social classes who have high amounts of economic and cultural capital. As such, it devalues the knowledge and skills of the working class. Dominant groups have the power to impose their own meanings as legitimate. They are able to define their own culture as 'worthy of being sought and possessed', and to establish it as the basis for knowledge in the education system. However, there is no objective way of showing that the dominant culture is any better or worse than other subcultures in society. The high value placed on dominant culture simply stems from the ability of the powerful to impose their definitions of reality on others.

Bourdieu linked the school curriculum to cultural capital. Dominant classes who possess cultural and economic capital have greater access to the highest levels of the education system and to higher-level qualifications. By contrast, the working class is excluded from these.

The curriculum in schools restricts the life chances of working-class students. Bourdieu saw the curriculum as biased rather than as neutral because it makes demands on all students but, in reality, not all students are able to meet these demands. Children whose families have provided them with the necessary cultural and social skills and attitudes that lead to academic success are rewarded with qualifications. Although their success is seen as being based on their natural or innate ability, Bourdieu argued that it is, in fact, based on the cultural capital that their families have equipped them with from an early age. Children whose families have not provided them with the necessary skills to succeed are excluded from the education system.

In addition, Bourdieu argued that the way that knowledge is transmitted assumes that all students have a certain cultural capital that conforms to that which the school demands. This is because the curriculum largely involves knowledge being transmitted for its own sake rather than for practical purposes.

Schools appear to award qualifications in an impartial way on the basis of merit. However, these qualifications are awarded 'for socially conditioned aptitudes' which schools treat as though they were unequal abilities or unequal natural 'gifts'. As a result, schools help to perpetuate inequalities over time and legitimise the transmission of cultural capital.

Bourdieu saw schools as a conservative force that perpetuates the myth of schools as a liberating force for gifted and hard-working people in society. Society lets the most privileged classes 'monopolise educational institutions'.

### Activity

*A graduation ceremony at Yale University in Connecticut in the USA. Yale is one of eight Ivy League universities, which are regarded as prestigious centres of academic excellence by some people and as elitist by others. Former USA Presidents George H.W. Bush, George W. Bush and Bill Clinton studied at Yale, as did presidential candidate Hillary Clinton.*

1. Drawing on Bourdieu's ideas, explain why some social groups have greater access than others to universities that are seen as prestigious.
2. Drawing on functionalist ideas, explain why some individuals have access to universities that are seen as prestigious.

## Summary

1. Young argued that all knowledge, including the curriculum, is socially constructed.
2. Postmodernism sees knowledge as relative and partial. However, critics argue that objective knowledge is possible.
3. Factors affecting curriculum content include status, power, culture, economic demands and gender.
4. Bourdieu argued that dominant groups in society have the power to establish their own culture as the basis of knowledge within education.
5. He linked the curriculum to cultural capital and saw it as biased in favour of students whose families have equipped them with cultural capital.

# Unit 5.3.2 Education and the hidden curriculum

This unit examines the concept of the hidden curriculum – the attitudes and ideas transmitted by schools that are not part of the official school curriculum. Different approaches see the hidden curriculum as transmitting ruling-class ideology, patriarchal ideology, neoliberal ideology or society's core values. How are these ideas transmitted? Are teachers and students aware of the hidden curriculum? The covert messages conveyed by the hidden curriculum are seen as both gendered and **ethnocentric** (judging one culture or ethnic group as superior to others). This unit explores some of the arguments behind these views.

## The hidden curriculum

The **formal curriculum** of schooling consists of the stated knowledge and skills that students are expected to acquire during lessons in sociology, maths, geography and so on. The hidden curriculum refers to the messages that schools transmit to students covertly, without directly teaching them or spelling them out. It consists of ideas, beliefs, norms and values which are often taken for granted and transmitted as part of the normal routines and procedures of school life. It includes the unwritten and often unstated rules and regulations that guide and direct everyday school behaviour (Ballantine and Spade, 2001). For example, through sports education, schools might transmit messages about the importance of teamwork or individual competition. Some schools might encourage students to compete with each other to achieve the highest exam grades. Schools often transmit messages about gender through practices such as lining up girls and boys separately or by not making provision for girls to play sports such as football. Different approaches interpret the content of the hidden curriculum differently. However, some critics question whether the hidden curriculum is actually hidden at all today, given the amount of research on it.

## A functionalist view of the hidden curriculum

As outlined earlier, functionalists see the transmission of society's core values and norms as one of the main functions of the education system, which helps to promote social order and stability. These norms and values are transmitted through the socialisation process in schools. This can be seen as part of the hidden curriculum. It is hidden in the sense that teachers and students are often unaware of the process. Parsons (1951, 1961) provided an example using the value of individual achievement, one of the major values in Western industrial society. In schools, young people are required to achieve as individuals. They take exams on their own, not as members of a team. Their individual achievements are carefully graded and assessed. Outstanding achievement is rewarded with praise, high status, good grades and valuable qualifications. In this way, young people are encouraged to value individual achievement. This prepares them to achieve as individuals in the wider society.

### Activity

*A student receives a trophy during a prize-giving ceremony in a Malaysian school.*

1. How might functionalists view prize-giving ceremonies in schools?
2. Does your school have similar ceremonies? If so, on what basis does it award prizes (for example, for academic achievement or effort)? In your view, should schools have such ceremonies? Explain your reasoning.

Critics argue that functionalist accounts:

- over-simplify the relationship between schools and the wider society, pointing out that society is not necessarily based on consensus
- present students as passively accepting the messages of the hidden curriculum rather than resisting or challenging them. In other words, functionalist accounts present students as lacking agency. By contrast, interactionist approaches view students as actively creating meanings in classrooms. They argue that the functionalist approach to the hidden curriculum puts too much emphasis on how schools contribute to maintaining the social structure.

From a Marxist perspective, functionalist accounts do not explore the potential role of the hidden curriculum in maintaining and reproducing social class. From a feminist perspective, they do not examine the gendered nature of the hidden curriculum.

## A Marxist view of the hidden curriculum

Marxists argue that the main job of schools is social reproduction – producing the next generation of workers who have been schooled to accept their roles in capitalist society. (See Unit 5.1.2.) For Bowles and Gintis (1976), this is done primarily through the hidden curriculum. This consists of the things that students learn through the experience of attending school, rather than as a result of the stated objectives of institutions. Bowles and Gintis claim that schools in the USA socialise children to become subservient, well-disciplined workers who will submit to control from above and take orders rather than question them. Schools do this by rewarding conformity, obedience, hard work and punctuality, and by penalising creativity, originality and independence. The hidden curriculum encourages an acceptance of hierarchy which prepares students for hierarchical relationships in the workplace. It also socialises students to be motivated by external rewards such as exam results and wages.

Schools are also seen as transmitting ruling-class ideology – a false picture of society that justifies social inequality and the capitalist system (see Unit 5.1.2).

Critics argue that Bowles and Gintis:

- did not carry out detailed research into school life. Instead, they tended to assume that the hidden curriculum was actually influencing students.
- ignore the influence of the formal curriculum. Even if the hidden curriculum could be shown to encourage docility, the presence of Bowles and Gintis themselves within the formal curriculum (for example, in sociology syllabuses and textbooks) would undermine their claims about education.
- see teachers and students as passively receiving the messages of the hidden curriculum rather than as active agents who have the capacity to resist these messages.

## A radical view of the hidden curriculum

Giroux (2011) is a radical thinker who argues that there is a hidden curriculum in American, and increasingly global, education based on neoliberal ideology (see Unit 5.1.4). In Giroux's view, 'Neoliberal ideology emphasises winning at all costs, even if it means a ruthless competitiveness, an almost rabid individualism and... a market driven rationality!' As noted earlier, government education policy in many countries is at least partly based on neoliberal views. Schools compete in an educational market place and aim to be top of the educational league tables. The job of schools is mainly to promote economic growth in an increasingly competitive global market.

How is this translated into the classroom? According to Giroux, 'Students are educated primarily to acquire market-oriented skills in order to compete favourably in the global economy'. They are taught to compete as individuals in an examination-based system, to climb the educational ladder and prepare themselves to succeed in a competitive labour market.

What should replace this hidden curriculum? In Giroux's view:

- 'knowledge and power should always be subject to debate, held accountable, and critically engaged'
- students should be taught to think critically
- students should be taught to be citizens of the world. This means that they should have 'duties and responsibilities to others' in a global society.

This is not possible as long as schools are based on neoliberal thinking which 'strips education of its public values, critical content, and civil responsibilities'.

## Illich's account of the hidden curriculum

Ivan Illich (1971) regards schools as repressive institutions which indoctrinate students, smother creativity and imagination, induce conformity and stultify students into accepting the interests of the powerful. He sees the hidden curriculum operating in the following ways:

1. Students have little or no control over what they learn or how they learn it. They are simply instructed by an authoritarian teaching regime and, to be successful, must conform to its rules. Illich argues that real learning is not the result of instruction, but of direct and free involvement by the individual in every part of the learning process.
2. The power of the school to enforce conformity to its rules and to coerce its inmates into accepting instruction stems from its authority to grant credentials that are believed to bring rewards in the labour market. Those who conform are selected to go on to higher levels of the education system. Conformity and obedience bring their own rewards.
3. Students emerge from the education system with a variety of qualifications which they and others believe have provided them with the training, skills and competence for particular occupations. Illich argues that 'The pupil is "schooled" to confuse teaching with learning, grade advancement with education, a diploma with competence.'

## The ethnocentric curriculum

Ivan Reid (1996) argues that the processes of selection and presentation of knowledge generate a curriculum that is more culturally acceptable to some groups than others. In his view, much school knowledge can be seen as ethnocentric. The term 'ethnocentric' refers to the belief that your own ethnic group or culture is superior to others. **Ethnocentrism** focuses on and prioritises a particular ethnic or cultural group to the exclusion of others.

Ethnocentricity has been identified within particular subjects and textbooks. María Inés Tāboas-Pais and Ana Rey-Cao (2015) examined the representation of 'race' in 36 physical education textbooks used in secondary schools in Spain. They undertook a content analysis of 2583 photographic images drawn from the textbooks and found marked differences in how frequently different groups were represented. For example, White people appeared in 87.3 per cent of the photographs, people from different groups appeared together in 7.4 per cent and people of Latin American origin appeared in just 0.2 per cent of the images.

Tāboas-Pais and Rey-Cao argue that the images reproduce racial stereotypes associated with physical education and sport by showing different groups participating in different types of physical activity. For example, the images showed White people participating in a wide variety of activities, including sports, fitness and artistic activities such as dance. By contrast, Black people were more frequently depicted in competitive, elite sport than in other physical activities.

The researchers also examined 87 school students' perceptions of 15 images from the textbooks. They found that the images of minority groups generated more racial prejudice among the students than the images of the White, Western group.

The school curriculum in Britain has been described as ethnocentric because White British culture and ethnicity are presented as superior and dominate the curriculum while minority ethnic cultures are largely excluded from subjects such as history, literature, art and music. A study based on interviews with 84 African-Caribbean students provided evidence to support this view (Tikly et al., 2006). It found that 'A significant number of African-Caribbean pupils noted their invisibility in the curriculum and were exasperated by the White European focus'. When Black history was included, 'many pupils reported their frustration with the tendency to focus on slavery'.

Tikly et al. argue that Black Caribbean students have a need for 'curriculum inclusion' so they do not feel marginalised and excluded. They suggest that this can be done by including Black Caribbean history, culture and experience across the curriculum.

## Feminist views of the gendered curriculum

Many feminist sociologists see aspects of both the formal and hidden curricula as gendered rather than gender-neutral. For example, women are often absent from history textbooks, both in terms of their individual achievements and contributions to society and in terms of issues that are particularly relevant to their gender. Additionally, in classrooms, many girls still tend to be less boisterous and demanding than boys. The gendered curriculum in schools reinforces gendered socialisation processes in families and society. From a radical feminist perspective, schools transmit **patriarchal ideology** – the idea that male dominance in society is reasonable and acceptable.

Subject choices, particularly at A Level and university, are still influenced by gender (see Unit 5.7.1). Male students tend to choose subjects such as physics, chemistry, engineering and business studies, which are more likely to lead to highly paid jobs. Gender divisions are also present in vocational courses such as childcare, hairdressing and beauty therapy, which are largely taught and taken by females and which usually lead to lower paid jobs.

In *A Feminist Manifesto for Education*, Miriam David (2016) argues that schools must ensure that 'women and girls are afforded dignity and respect in all aspects of their lives'. Schools must address issues of abuse, harassment and violence against girls. Failure to recognise and prioritise sexual harassment at school or college can be seen as part of a hidden curriculum that ignores female suffering and abuse.

## Activity

*Although girls' educational attainments have improved, they are less likely than boys to choose subjects such as physics and chemistry.*

1. Describe two ways in which the curriculum can be seen as gendered.
2. Make notes to summarise different sociological accounts of the curriculum.

## Key terms

**Ethnocentric** Evaluating one's own culture or ethnic group as superior to others.

**Formal curriculum** The stated knowledge and skills which students are expected to acquire.

**Ethnocentrism** The belief that one's own culture or ethnic group is superior to others.

**Patriarchal ideology** The idea that male dominance in society is reasonable and acceptable.

## Summary

1. Views of the hidden curriculum include:
   - functionalist – the transmission of societies' core values and norms
   - Marxist – the transmission of ruling-class ideology
   - radical – the transmission of neoliberal ideology
   - feminist – the transmission of patriarchal ideology.
2. The curriculum is seen as ethnocentric in evaluating one culture as superior to others.
3. The curriculum is seen as gendered in rendering females invisible.

# END-OF-PART QUESTIONS

| | | |
|---|---|---|
| 0 1 | Describe two characteristics of the knowledge economy. | [4 marks] |
| 0 2 | Explain one strength and one limitation of the Marxist view of the hidden curriculum. | [6 marks] |
| 0 3 | 'Power is the most important influence on the content of the school curriculum.' Using sociological material, give one argument against this view. | [6 marks] |

# SECTION B
# EDUCATION AND INEQUALITY

## Contents


| | | |
|---|---|---|
| Part 4 | Intelligence and educational attainment | 271 |
| Part 5 | Social class and educational attainment | 277 |
| Part 6 | Ethnicity and educational attainment | 301 |
| Part 7 | Gender and educational attainment | 307 |


Section B focuses on education and inequality. Two of the key concepts that you were introduced to in Chapter 1 are particularly important here.

First, *inequality and opportunity*. Stephen Ball (2003) sees social inequality as at the heart of the sociology of education. In many countries, marked inequalities in educational attainment based on social class, gender and ethnicity are evident. Some explanations link these to inequalities in the wider society. How do class-based material factors impact on educational attainment? What impact do racism and sexism have? How influential are school-based factors such as labelling and student subcultures on achievement?

Second, *socialisation, culture and identity*. Cultural explanations for the differences in educational attainment focus on areas such as parental attitudes, values and speech codes. How important is the possession of cultural capital to educational success? How does membership of school-based subcultures affect students' identities and achievements? How do class, gender and ethnicity combine to shape students' identities? Schools are an important agency of socialisation. What part does gender socialisation play in explaining the differential achievements of female and male students?

Section B is divided into four parts. Part 4 explores debates about the relationship between intelligence and educational attainment. It examines some of the difficulties in defining and measuring intelligence, and the problems associated with IQ tests. It asks whether there is evidence to suggest that some groups are more intelligent than others and, therefore, perform better within education systems.

Part 5 examines the relationship between social class and attainment. It looks at factors outside schools such as material and cultural influences. It also explores in-school factors such as teacher expectations, labelling processes and subcultural membership.

Part 6 examines the relationship between ethnicity and attainment. It looks at various explanations for the underachievement of some minority ethnic groups such as racism in schools and teachers' perceptions of ethnicity. It also examines cultural and subcultural explanations.

Finally, Part 7 looks at the relationship between gender and attainment. It examines factors inside schools and in the wider society that help to explain the relationship between gender and attainment. It explores the role of gender socialisation processes in explaining differences in attainment. It also looks at recent social and economic changes that may have impacted on female and male achievements.

# PART 4 INTELLIGENCE AND EDUCATIONAL ATTAINMENT

## Contents

**Unit 5.4.1** **Defining and measuring intelligence** 271

**Unit 5.4.2** **Intelligence and educational attainment** 275

Perhaps one of the most obvious explanations for differences in educational achievement is individual differences in intelligence. The work of some educational psychologists, such as Cyril Burt (1883–1971), appeared to show that intelligence was largely inherited and could be measured by the use of a test. However, Burt's work has since been discredited. Nonetheless, such approaches have justified the use of selective education systems which place students in particular types of school based on the results of tests. But what is intelligence? Why is it difficult to define? Is intelligence based on innate differences between people? How do we measure it? How valid are IQ tests? Questions such as these are addressed in Unit 5.4.1.

Many studies show a correlation between measured intelligence and achievement in education. Working-class students, for example, continue to score less well in intelligence tests than middle-class children. This might lead to the conclusion that intelligence explains class differences in achievement. But is this necessarily the case? Unit 5.4.2 focuses on the relationship between intelligence and educational attainment.

## Unit 5.4.1 Defining and measuring intelligence

What is intelligence? There are difficulties associated with defining intelligence, not least because it includes different qualities. For example, someone who solves abstract mathematical puzzles with ease may struggle to understand literary fiction (Giddens and Sutton, 2017). How do we explain differences in the level or amount of intelligence between individuals? Is intelligence an innate quality or is it largely based on environmental factors? Can it be measured accurately through intelligence tests? Or are intelligence tests influenced by social factors? This unit focuses on some of the key issues surrounding the definition and measurement of intelligence.

### Difficulties in defining intelligence

The American psychologist Arthur Jensen (1973) defined intelligence as 'abstract reasoning ability'. He argued that intelligence is a selection of just one portion of the total spectrum of human mental abilities'. It is the ability to discover the rules, patterns and logical principles underlying objects and events, and the ability to apply these discoveries in order to solve problems. However, the psychologist N.J. Mackintosh (2011) argues that 'there is no agreed definition of the nature of intelligence'. Similarly, Robert Plomin et al. (2013) point out that the term 'intelligence' has numerous different meanings within psychology.

### Gardner's theory of multiple intelligences

Some critics challenge the idea that intelligence can be easily defined and measured on a single scale. Howard Gardner (1999), a psychologist, argues that the standard, traditional Western view of intelligence is that there is 'a single, underlying general intelligence' (referred to by psychologists as *g* or general intelligence) that is fixed and heritable (transmissible from parents to children) and which can be measured by a test. However, the East Asian view is based on a different set of beliefs, which stress that how smart a person is reflects how hard they work.

Gardner rejects the idea that there is just one intelligence. His theory of multiple intelligences highlights eight (and possibly more) different forms of intelligence. They include linguistic intelligence linked, for example, to being good with language and poetry; and logic and mathematical intelligences linked, for example, to science or interpreting graphs. These two intelligences are both assessed via IQ tests and are focused on and valued in schools. Other forms of intelligence include:

- musical intelligence – for example, being able to compose music
- spatial intelligence involved, for example, in navigating
- bodily kinesthetic intelligence or being able to use parts of the body or the whole body to make products or solve problems. Dancers, athletes, actors and surgeons, for example, display this particular intelligence.
- interpersonal intelligence involved, for instance, in understanding other people's emotions
- intrapersonal intelligence, involved in understanding one's own emotions, skills or motivations.

In Gardner's view, these capacities are relatively independent of each other. Each individual has a 'unique blend of intelligences'.

## Activity

*According to Gardner, top athletes possess a particular form of intelligence.*

1. What sort of intelligence is involved in being an outstanding athlete?
2. In Gardner's view, why is it possible to have high levels of intelligence in some areas but not in others?

Mackintosh (2011), however, argues that many of Gardner's intelligences are, in fact, talents or skills. Therefore, Gardner's account does not allow us to distinguish between intelligence, talents and skills.

### Intelligence, ideology and power

Paul Henderson (1976) sees the concept of intelligence as ideological in that it serves to legitimise the allocation of high-status positions in society. The middle class have the power to establish definitions of intelligence. These definitions largely refer to abilities that the middle class already have. According to Henderson, intelligence is a 'label' that is applied to the 'behavioural characteristics' of members of a dominant class in society. In his words, 'The middle class are able to *select* and *define* those behavioural characteristics which are to be considered "intelligent".' These characteristics are ones that the middle class are most likely to possess, given their position in the social class structure. Rather than arguing that intelligent people achieve privileged positions, Henderson argues that it is 'due to their privileged positions that people are intelligent'.

## Activity

Give one argument against the view that intelligence can be easily defined.

## Measuring intelligence

Intelligence is measured by intelligence tests which give an individual's intelligence quotient (**IQ**) and enable comparison between people's levels of intelligence. Such tests are designed to measure verbal ability, spatial ability and abstract reasoning ability. They would exclude questions such as 'Which is the highest mountain in the world?' that test knowledge and memory rather than the ability to reason. Thus, a simple IQ test may ask for the next number in the following sequence: 2, 4, 6, 8. This question requires individuals to discover the pattern underlying the sequence of numbers and to apply their discovery to solve the problem. The average score on IQ tests is 100. People with an IQ of 150 and above are often seen as being exceptionally intelligent, while those with IQs below 100 are seen as having below average intelligence.

IQ tests were developed for use within education to measure differences in intelligence between individual students. Despite their widespread use, a large body of evidence suggests that IQ tests are not a valid measure of intelligence, particularly when they are used to compare the intelligence of members of different social groups.

### The validity of IQ tests

The British sociologist Saunders (1996) accepts that there are difficulties associated with measuring intelligence accurately via IQ tests. However, he sees IQ as a reasonably valid and reliable indicator of intelligence. He argues that IQ 'can be used to measure approximate differences in average levels of intelligence between different social groups, particularly when they live under similar cultural conditions'. In his view, ability in one area (such as in verbal reasoning) tends to correlate with ability in other areas (such as spatial or mathematical ability). While this does not necessarily support the idea of one common factor, *g* or general intelligence, it does suggest that there are differences in the average levels of intelligence between different social groups.

Researchers such as Otto Klineberg (1971) and Philip Vernon (1969) question the validity of IQ tests as measures of intelligence. Critics argue that IQ tests are culturally biased. This makes it easier for some groups to get higher scores on them than others. One view is that they are biased in favour of the middle class, as they are largely constructed by and standardised upon members of this group. If it is accepted that social classes and other social groups have distinctive subcultures and that this affects their performance in IQ tests, then comparisons between groups in terms of measured intelligence are invalid.

This argument can be illustrated by the testing of non-Western populations with Western IQ tests. The Canadian psychologist Klineberg (1971) gave a test to Yakima Native American children living in Washington State, USA (see the Activity in Chapter 3, Unit 3.1.1). The test consisted of placing variously shaped wooden blocks into the appropriate holes in a wooden frame 'as quickly as possible'. The children had no problem with the test but produced low scores because they failed to finish within the required time. Klineberg argues that this does not indicate low intelligence but simply reflects the children's cultural background. Unlike Western culture, the Yakima do not place a high priority on speed.

Such examples suggest that Western IQ tests are inappropriate for non-Western people as they do not measure pure ability. The same argument has been applied to the use of IQ tests within Western societies which contain different subcultural groups, including social class subcultures. Thus, the British psychologist Vernon (1969) stated: 'There is no such thing as a culture-fair test.' In this view, IQ tests are biased towards some groups, such as White, middle-class people. This suggests that conclusions based on comparisons of the average measured IQ of different social groups must be regarded at best with caution.

## Activity

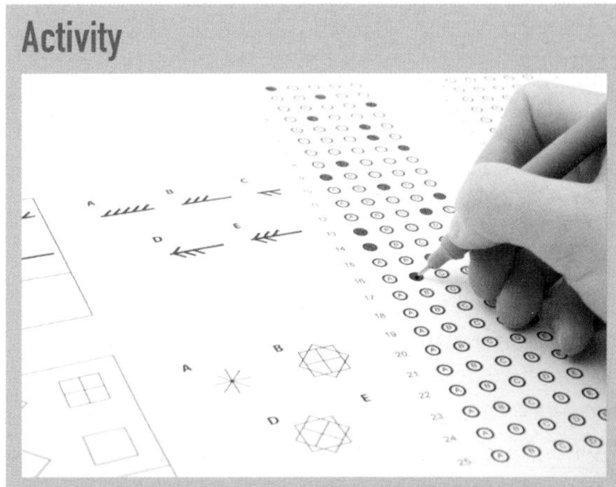

*IQ tests are used to measure intelligence. However, their validity is questioned.*

Assess the view that IQ tests provide a valid measure of intelligence.

## Genes, the environment and intelligence

One view is that intelligence is due to both genetic and environmental factors. It stems partly from the genes that individuals inherit from their birth parents, and partly from the environment in which they grow up and live. Environmental influences include everything from diet to social class, from quality of housing to family size. They include factors such as household income, parental education and occupation, parent–child relationships and the quality of schooling. For example, malnutrition during the early years may impact negatively on children's cognitive development. In this view, genetic and environmental factors interact to influence intelligence. For instance, intelligent parents are more likely to provide an appropriate environment (such as a nutritious diet, books and involvement in extra-curricular activities) for developing their children's intelligence.

Some social scientists, such as Jensen (1973) and Richard Herrnstein and Charles Murray (1994) in America, and Hans Eysenck (1971) in Britain, argue that intelligence is largely inherited. Differences in people's IQ scores are largely explained in terms of genetic differences between them. These researchers variously estimate that between 60 and 80 per cent of intelligence is genetically based.

Saunders (1996) argues that intelligence is determined by both genetics and the environment, which interact is complex ways. In his view, this means that sociologists cannot justifiably ignore biological factors and differences in intelligence when researching topics such as social mobility. It is very difficult to ascertain the precise influence of genetics and the environment or of nature and nurture. However, drawing on Eysenck's account of research on identical twins, Saunders argues that, although intelligence is not entirely genetic, it has a substantial genetic component, possibly 50 per cent or more. For example, research suggests that identical twins who were brought up separately have much more similar scores on IQ tests than non-identical twins who were brought up together.

Critics, however, argue that the view that genes largely determine intelligence is an ideology. It benefits rich and powerful social groups by justifying inequalities as natural and inevitable.

## Genes, intelligence and the cognitive elite

Herrnstein and Murray (1994) argue that more intelligent people tend to have greater success in their careers than less intelligent people. In their view, between 60 and 70 per cent of the variation in human intelligence is genetically transmitted between the generations. The remaining variation in human intelligence is linked to environmental factors.

Herrnstein and Murray argue that intelligence has become increasingly necessary for the performance of the top jobs in industrial societies. They also argue that the best universities in the USA now admit students on the basis of their performance in standardised tests rather than on the basis of inherited wealth. In other words, admission is based on meritocratic principles. Due to these changes, society (and, in particular, well-paid, prestigious and powerful positions) is increasingly dominated by a 'cognitive elite' whose members are better trained and more intelligent than other people. Members of the cognitive elite tend to intermarry and have intelligent children. In this way, the elite is perpetuated over time. This implies that the existence of an elite in society is both natural and inevitable. It also suggests that inequality between social groups, such as different ethnic groups or classes, has a genetic basis.

The ideas of Herrnstein and Murray have provoked much controversy. Critics argue that:

1. Herrnstein and Murray overestimate the extent to which intelligence is determined by genetic factors. Other estimates suggest that no more than 40 per cent of intelligence is inherited.
2. There are various forms of intelligence, including emotional intelligence.
3. An individual's innate abilities cannot be separated easily from the effects of their environment or socialisation.
4. Herrnstein and Murray do not take account of the effects of inherited wealth, high incomes, cultural and social resources, and the process of socialisation in bolstering intelligence test results.
5. The existence of an elite is neither natural nor inevitable.

## The environment and intelligence

Some commentators argue that it is not possible to estimate the degree to which intelligence is determined by genetic and environmental factors. However, research has indicated that a wide range of environmental factors can affect performance in IQ tests. Klineberg argues that successfully solving the problems in IQ tests depends, for example, on the test taker's education and previous experience, their motivation, emotional state and physical health. For instance, if people feel anxious about taking an IQ test, this may affect their performance. Other critics argue that IQ scores can be raised with tuition and practice. Social factors such as early socialisation can also influence performance.

## Approaches to the heredity and environment debate

Henderson (1976) identifies three main approaches to the heredity and/or environment debate:

1. Intelligence is mainly acquired through heredity – it is inherited.
2. Intelligence is mainly acquired through the process of learning.
3. It is impossible to assess the relative contribution of inheritance and learning because intelligence is acquired from an interaction between these factors.

Henderson is critical of all three approaches because they fail to question the 'social basis of the concept of intelligence and the functions performed by this concept in a class society'.

## Activity

*Herrnstein and Murray argue that intelligence is increasingly necessary for the performance of top jobs in industrial societies.*

1. Some sociologists see 'intelligence' as a socially constructed concept rather than as objective and value free. What do you think they mean by this?
2. Evaluate the view that the existence of an elite group in society is both natural and inevitable.

## Key term

**IQ** Intelligence quotient – a score based on a test designed to measure a person's intelligence.

## Summary

1. There are difficulties in defining intelligence. Some psychologists argue that the term has various meanings.
2. Gardner argues that there are at least eight different forms of intelligence.
3. Henderson sees the concept of intelligence as ideological, in that it serves to legitimise the allocation of high-status social positions.
4. Intelligence is measured by IQ tests. However, critics question their validity, arguing that they are culturally biased.
5. There are debates about the influence of genes and environment on intelligence.
6. Herrnstein and Murray argue that the US is increasingly dominated by a cognitive elite composed of highly trained, intelligent people. However, their views have provoked fierce criticism.

# Unit 5.4.2 Intelligence and educational attainment

This unit examines the relationship between intelligence and educational achievement. How far does intelligence influence educational attainment? Do differences in intelligence account for individual differences in attainment? Do they account for group differences? Do middle-class students, for example, perform better than working-class students because, on average, they are more intelligent?

## The influence of intelligence on attainment

Social scientists, such as Jensen (1972, 1973), Herrnstein and Murray (1994) and Eysenck (1971) argue that class differences in intelligence largely account for class differences in educational attainment. Eysenck (1971) claims: 'What children take out of schools is proportional to what they bring into schools in terms of IQ.' Jensen (1972) is more cautious when he suggests that 'genetic factors may play a part in this picture'. However, he does argue that there is better evidence for the influence of genes on educational attainment than for the influence of environmental factors. Saunders (1996) suggests that middle-class students perform better within education than working-class students because, on average, they are more intelligent. Controversially, Herrnstein and Murray (1994) argue that intelligence is linked to 'race'. However, their research has been widely challenged.

Such approaches tend to see intelligence as fixed and innate. Consequently, it is not possible to develop or improve people's intelligence over time. However, Klineberg (1935, discussed in Boronski and Hassan, 2015) found that the IQ scores of Black students rose after they moved from the south of the USA to better-resourced schools in northern states.

Nicholas Mackintosh (2011), a psychologist, argues that IQ scores correlate with a number of different indices of educational achievement, such as how long students remain in education, results in public examinations and qualifications, and whether students complete high school and obtain degrees. He points out that children who achieve high scores on IQ tests tend to perform better than students with lower scores. Furthermore, evidence suggests that IQ predicts 'both educational and occupational success, but the predictions are far from perfect'.

Mackintosh is sceptical of some sociological claims that IQ scores are not causally linked to educational attainment and that the correlation between IQ scores and educational attainment results from family and class background. He argues that research studies show that the correlation between children's IQ scores and their subsequent educational attainment is bigger than the correlation between family background and attainment. In his view, some sociologists overestimate the significance of family background. However, Mackintosh does not suggest that intelligence is the only determinant of educational attainment and points out that other factors may be more important. These include students' determination, study skills, self-discipline and their willingness to defer gratification (to make sacrifices in the present for future reward).

Stephen Murdoch (2007), however, argues that the tests 'do not test intelligence and have negligible ability to predict academic achievement'. (Murdoch, 2007, discussed in Mackintosh, 2011) Furthermore, Bowles and Gintis (1976) argue that IQ accounts for only a small part of educational achievement. They examined a sample of individuals who had average IQs. Within this sample, they found a wide range of variation in educational attainment. This led them to conclude that there is little relationship between IQ and academic qualifications. They found a direct relationship between educational attainment and family background. In their view, the causal factor is not IQ, but the class position of the individual's parents. In general, the higher a person's class of origin, the longer they remain in the education system and the higher their qualifications.

But why do students with high qualifications tend to have higher than average intelligence? Bowles and Gintis argue that this relationship is largely 'a by-product' of continued education. The longer an individual stays in the education system, the more their IQ develops. Thus, IQ is a consequence of length of stay rather than the cause of it. From this evidence, Bowles and Gintis concluded that, at least in terms of IQ, the education system does not function as a meritocracy.

Reid (1996) is another critic of arguments that explain different educational attainment in terms of intelligence or IQ. He argues that it is 'absurd to expect individual variables to explain group differences'. Therefore, IQ cannot be used to explain the differential educational achievement of different social groups. He rejects the idea that social groups such as different classes, ethnic groups or genders have different genes that would explain their educational achievements. Nor do these social groups 'represent a gene pool, to the extent that they have differing overall levels of inherited intelligence'. In Reid's view, the marked changes in educational performance based on gender and the improvements in girls' achievements (see Unit 5.7.2) indicate that educational attainment is influenced by social and cultural factors.

## Activity

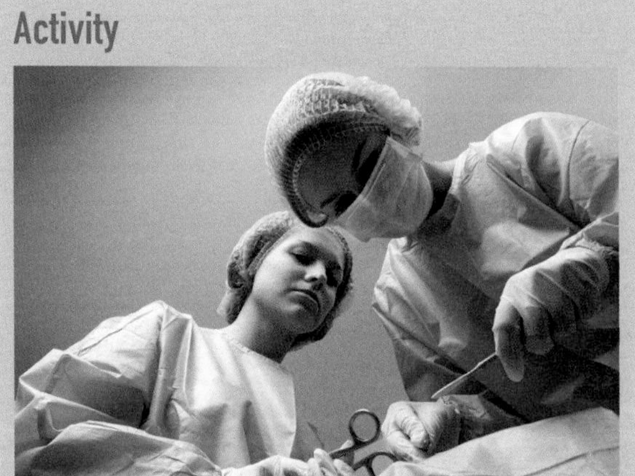

*In many countries, improvements in females' educational achievements mean that more women are entering professional occupations such as medicine and law.*

Assess the view that differences in intelligence account for group differences in educational attainment.

The final parts of this chapter explore a range of social, cultural and economic factors that influences the educational attainment of different social groups based on social class, ethnicity and gender.

## Summary

1. Some social scientists argue that intelligence largely determines educational achievement.
2. Mackintosh links IQ to educational and occupational success. Other relevant factors include being conscientious and deferring gratification.
3. Bowles and Gintis found little relationship between IQ and academic qualifications. They link attainment to family background and social class.
4. Reid argues that individual variables such as IQ cannot be used to explain group differences in attainment.

# END-OF-PART QUESTIONS

| 0 | 1 | Describe two difficulties in defining intelligence. **[4 marks]**

| 0 | 2 | Explain two limitations of the view that intelligence is largely determined by genetics. **[6 marks]**

| 0 | 3 | 'Intelligence is the most important influence on educational attainment.' Using sociological material, give one argument against this view. **[6 marks]**

# PART 5 SOCIAL CLASS AND EDUCATIONAL ATTAINMENT

## Contents

**Unit 5.5.1** **Material factors and educational attainment** **278**

**Unit 5.5.2** **Cultural factors and educational attainment** **280**

**Unit 5.5.3** **In-school factors, social class and educational attainment** **292**

**Differential educational attainment** refers to the fact that different social groups – for example, different class, ethnic and gender groups – have different levels of educational achievement. This part looks at evidence and explanations for social class differences in educational attainment. Social class, the main form of stratification in Western societies, refers to groups that are divided in terms of income, wealth, power and status. The essence of class is economic inequalities.

Although the focus here is on social class, it is important to bear in mind that each student is a member of a social class and an ethnic group; they are also either male or female (Joan Garrod, 2004). This means that class is just one of several variables linked to educational attainment. Furthermore, class, gender and ethnicity are not separate categories that each work in isolation. Instead, they intersect with each other. For example, Reid (1996) argues that many differences within education that appear to be related to ethnicity can be explained in terms of social class. However, it may not be easy to disentangle the various factors involved.

Research shows that the higher a person's social class, the higher their educational attainment is likely to be. The children of parents in higher social classes are more likely to attain high grades in formal examinations; they are more likely to stay on and be successful in post-compulsory education and to progress to university. These class differences were a feature of education in many countries throughout the 20th century and persist today.

This part begins by examining the relationship between material factors and educational attainment. It then focuses on cultural explanations for class differences in attainment, including parental attitudes, values and speech codes, and various compensatory education programmes that seek to help less privileged children to compete on equal terms with other students. More recent explanations based on Bourdieu's idea of cultural capital are also explored.

The part then investigates factors within schools. It looks at how students' class position affects their treatment in the classroom and how this might impact on their educational attainment.

This part raises important questions. To what extent does class affect educational attainment? What can be done to provide equality of educational opportunity? Can it be done by schools and teachers? Or is the answer to reduce inequality in the wider society?

# Unit 5.5.1 Material factors and educational attainment

Some explanations for the relationship between social class and educational attainment focus on factors outside the school such as material and cultural influences. This unit examines the relationship between social class, material factors and educational achievement. Class is about material differences in income and wealth, and the things that money can buy. Many sociologists argue that material circumstances play an important part in determining levels of educational attainment. In particular, they see **material deprivation** – a lack of material resources – as a major factor accounting for the relatively low attainment of those in the lower levels of the class system.

## Cognitive development

Parental income can make an important difference to educational attainment. Research by Jane Waldfogel and Elizabeth Washbrook (2010) looked at the relationship between parental income and children's cognitive development. They drew on rich and detailed data about the cognitive ability of 5-year-old children taken from the UK Millennium Cohort Study, a longitudinal study of 12 644 children from birth onwards.

Cognitive ability (mental processes such as reasoning) was based on the results of three tests taken by the 5-year-olds. The test results allowed the researchers to identify the children's cognitive developmental age. The researchers divided the children into five groups based on parental income. They compared the test results of the lowest income group (the bottom 20 per cent) with the results of the middle-income group (the middle 20 per cent). There was a significant test score gap between the lowest and the middle groups. The largest gap, that of 11.1 months, was on the Naming Vocabulary Test, a verbal ability test in which children were shown pictures of objects and asked to name them. This test indicated that the cognitive development of children in poverty when they started school was nearly a year behind that of middle-income children. This gap was reduced to nine months for children who spoke only English at home. But the gap remains important, because it is likely to be reflected in the attainment gap throughout the children's educational career.

The researchers then attempted to identity factors which might help to explain the income-related cognitive development gap. In terms of material factors, lack of a home computer and a car were the most apparent. Lack of an annual holiday was a distinguishing factor. In terms of health, lower birth weight and poorer health generally appeared to make a 'modest contribution' to lowering cognitive development. Factors which seemed to make a positive contribution to cognitive development were parents reading to children and family trips to places of interest.

## Private tuition and extra-curricular activities

Private tutors provide students, at a cost, with direct help with their schoolwork. A study commissioned by the Sutton Trust in 2017 drew on data from the Programme for International Student Assessment (PISA) which showed that one in six students in Year 11 (aged 15–16) in England had private tutors in maths and science. This proportion was similar to that in China but higher than that in countries such as South Korea and Australia. In England and Wales, students aged 11–16 years from the highest-income families were much more likely to have received private or home tuition than those from the lowest-income families (John Jerrim, Sutton Trust, 2017).

Research indicates that involvement in extra-curricular activities can have a positive effect on educational attainment. However, parents in higher-income groups are more likely than those in lower-income groups to pay for their children to attend extra-curricular activities such as classes in sport, dance, drama and music.

## Activity

*Some students may benefit from private tuition or involvement in extra-curricular activities such as piano lessons.*

1. How might involvement in extra-curricular activities have a positive impact on educational attainment?
2. Are students in your school encouraged to participate in extra-curricular activities? If so, why are they encouraged to do so? As far as you know, do many students in your school have private tutors?

## Schools in disadvantaged areas

Organisations such as Ofsted, the official schools' assessment body in England, report that, in general, the higher the level of deprivation in an area, the lower the quality of schools. Ruth Lupton (2004) studied schools in deprived low-income areas in England. Teachers had serious student welfare issues to worry about. Compared to better-off areas, students tended to be 'anxious, traumatised, unhappy, jealous, angry or vulnerable'. They were more likely to disrupt lessons and truant from school (to be absent without permission). Teachers had difficulty maintaining high expectations, as they were often disappointed. They were careful to select inexpensive school trips because parents often lacked the money to pay for them.

Claudia Rangel and Christy Lleras (2010) examined the effects of school quality and family background on the academic achievements of students in their final year of high school in 2003 in Cartagena, Colombia. They found that family socio-economic background had a significant effect on student achievement as measured by their mathematics and reading test scores. For example, students from more privileged backgrounds had significantly higher achievements in mathematics than less privileged students.

This variation in achievement was partly explained by school-level factors such as the quality and the composition of the school. Measures of school quality included the number of well-trained teachers and the availability of educational resources such as libraries, science equipment, and language and computer laboratories. School composition refers to factors such as the proportion of students from less privileged families and whether the school was in the private or the public (state) sector. The significantly higher mathematics achievements among students from more privileged socio-economic backgrounds was partly linked to their greater likelihood of attending private schools and schools with lower levels of poverty among the intake.

## Barriers to learning

In a study of the effects of poverty on schooling, Theresa Smith and Michael Noble (1995) list some of the 'barriers to learning' that can result from low income. These include:

- There may be insufficient funds to pay for school uniforms, school trips, transport to and from school, classroom materials and, in some cases, school textbooks. This can lead to children being isolated, bullied and stigmatised. As a result, they may fall behind in their schoolwork.
- Children from low-income families are more likely to suffer from ill-health, which can affect their attendance and performance at school.
- Low income reduces the likelihood of a desk, educational toys, books and space to do homework, and a comfortable well-heated home.
- The marketisation of schools is likely to increase the division between successful, well-resourced schools in affluent areas and under-subscribed, poorly resourced schools in poor areas. This will 'reduce rather than increase opportunities for children from poor families, by concentrating socially disadvantaged children in a limited number of increasingly unpopular schools' (Smith and Noble, 1995).

## Activity

*Research suggests that factors such as having internet access and a quiet study space at home can influence students' educational achievements.*

Write brief notes to summarise the relationship between educational attainment and material deprivation.

## Key terms

**Differential educational attainment** The different attainment levels of different groups of children, for example, class, gender and ethnic groups.

**Material deprivation** A lack of material resources.

## Summary

1. Evidence suggests that parental income is linked to cognitive development. This can be explained in terms of material factors.
2. Children from affluent families may benefit from private tuition and involvement in extra-curricular activities.
3. One view is that disadvantaged areas may have lower-quality schools.
4. Some researchers argue that material factors, particularly poverty, can be 'barriers to learning'.

# Unit 5.5.2 Cultural factors and educational attainment

So far, explanations for class differences in educational achievement have focused on material factors. This unit examines the view that cultural factors account for class differences in educational attainment. In this approach, the relatively low attainment of working-class students is due mainly to working-class subculture. This leads to government policies which aim to compensate for the supposedly negative effects of working-class subcultures on educational attainment.

This approach is sometimes known as **cultural deprivation theory**. It suggests that the subculture of low-income groups is deprived of factors that are necessary for high educational attainment. The so-called culturally deprived child is pictured as lacking the language and reasoning skills needed for intellectual tasks, and as deficient in important attitudes and values required for educational success. Cultural deprivation theory has been strongly criticised and this unit examines some of these criticisms.

The unit also explores how Bourdieu's ideas of cultural, social and economic capital have been used to explain class differences in achievement. In doing so, it raises a complex question. Will equality of opportunity ever be possible when those at the top have an armoury of cultural, social and economic capital to keep themselves up there?

## Class subcultures and educational attainment

It has been argued that a social class's **subculture** – its distinctive norms and values – affects performance in the education system. Norms are guides to appropriate behaviour in particular situations. Values are beliefs that something is important and worthwhile. While sharing the culture of mainstream society, members of a class-based subculture also have some of their own norms and values.

The view that social class subcultures affect educational attainment was first spelled out in detail by the American sociologist Herbert H. Hyman (1967). He argued that the value system of the lower classes creates 'a self-imposed barrier to an improved position'.

Using a wide range of data from opinion polls and surveys conducted by sociologists, Hyman outlined what he saw as differences between working-class and middle-class value systems:

1. Members of the working class place a lower value on education.
2. They also place a lower value on achieving high occupational status.

3. Compared to their middle-class counterparts, members of the working class believe that there is less opportunity for personal advancement.

These values did not characterise all members of the working class – a sizeable minority did not share them. In general, however, Hyman concluded that motivation to achieve, whether in school or outside it, is generally lower for members of the working class.

### Attitudes and orientations

The British sociologist Barry Sugarman (1970) argued that middle- and working-class subcultures contain different attitudes and orientations, which may account for class differences in educational attainment. In particular, he claims that working-class subculture emphasises fatalism, immediate gratification, present-time orientation and collectivism.

1. **Fatalism** involves an acceptance of the situation rather than efforts to improve it. As such, it will not encourage high achievement in the classroom.
2. **Immediate gratification** and **present-time orientation** emphasise the enjoyment of pleasures in the moment rather than sacrifice for future reward. This will tend to discourage sustained effort, with its promise of examination success. It will also tend to encourage early school-leaving for the more immediate rewards of wages, adult status and freedom from the disciplines of school.
3. **Collectivism** involves loyalty to the group rather than the emphasis on individual achievement that the school system demands.

Sugarman, therefore, concluded that the subculture of students from working-class backgrounds places them at a disadvantage in the education system.

### Criticisms of the concept of class subcultures

1. So-called working-class subculture may simply be a response in terms of mainstream culture to the circumstances of working-class life. Thus, members of the working class may be realistic rather than fatalistic. They might defer gratification if they had the resources to do so. They might be future-oriented if the opportunities for successful future planning were available.

   From this point of view, members of the working class share the same norms and values as any other members of society. Their behaviour is not directed by a distinctive subculture. It is simply their situation that prevents them from expressing society's norms and values in the same way as members of the middle class.
2. The content of working-class subculture is sometimes derived from interviews and questionnaires. Hyman's and Sugarman's data were largely obtained from these sources. However, what people say in response to interviews or questionnaires may not provide an accurate indication of how they behave in other situations.
3. In a criticism of American studies, R.H. Turner (discussed in Colquhoun, 1976) notes that social-class differences reported from interview and questionnaire data are often slight. Sociologists are inclined to ignore the similarities between classes and emphasise the differences. Sometimes this is because the differences tend to support their views – in this case, that class subcultures help to explain class differences in educational attainment.

## J.W.B. Douglas – *The Home and the School*

J.W.B. Douglas and his associates (Douglas, 1964; Douglas et al. 1970) conducted an influential longitudinal study (that is, a study of the same group over time). They followed the educational careers of 5362 British children born in the first week of March 1946, through primary and secondary school, up to the age of 16 in 1962.

Douglas divided the students into groups in terms of their ability, which was measured by a range of tests including IQ tests. He also divided the students into four social-class groupings and found significant variations in educational attainment between students of similar ability but from different social classes. He found that length of stay in the education system was related to social class. Within the 'high ability' group, 50 per cent of the students from the lower working class left secondary school in their fifth year (aged 15–16), compared with 33 per cent from the upper working class, 22 per cent from the lower middle class and 10 per cent from the upper middle class.

### Parental interest in education

Douglas related educational attainment to a variety of factors, including the student's health, the size of their family and the quality of the school. The single most important factor appeared to be the degree of parents' interest in their children's education. In general, middle-class parents expressed a greater interest, as indicated by more frequent visits to the school to discuss their children's progress. They were more likely to want their children to stay on at school beyond the minimum leaving age and to encourage them to do so. Douglas found that parental interest and encouragement became increasingly important as a spur to high attainment as the children grew older.

Douglas also attached importance to the child's early years, as, in many cases, performance during the first years of schooling is reflected throughout secondary school. He suggested that, during primary socialisation, middle-class children receive greater attention and stimulus from their parents. Middle-class parents were likely to encourage their children to do their best in a wide variety of activities. This formed a basis for high achievement in the education system.

### Activity

*Douglas argued that middle-class children receive more parental attention and stimulus during primary socialisation.*

1. How does Douglas explain class differences in education?
2. Explain one strength and one weakness of using a longitudinal approach to investigate class differences in educational attainment.

## Evaluation of explanations based on class subcultures

The studies discussed above appear to strongly support the view that class subcultures influence educational attainment, particularly through differences in parental encouragement. However, these studies should be viewed with some caution.

A number of arguments suggest that working-class parents are not necessarily less interested in their children's education just because they go to their children's schools less frequently than their middle-class counterparts. Tessa Blackstone and Jo Mortimore (1994) make the following points:

1. Working-class parents may have less time to visit school because of the demands of their jobs. Manual jobs typically involve longer and less regular hours than non-manual jobs.
2. Working-class parents may be very interested in their children's education but they are put off going to the school because of the way teachers interact with them. Blackstone and Mortimore (1994) argue that it is possible that 'working-class parents feel ill at ease or the subject of criticism when they visit school. Teachers represent authority and parents who have had unhappy experiences at school or with authority figures may be reluctant to meet them.'
3. The data used by Douglas may not actually measure parental interest in education. It may measure teachers' perceptions of their interest. It is possible that teachers perceive middle-class parents as more interested than working-class parents because of the way they interact with teachers when they attend school.

### Activity

*One way of measuring parental support is by means of teachers' assessments of parental interest in their children's education. But is this necessarily a valid or reliable measure?*

Explain one strength and one limitation of using teachers' assessments of parental interest in their children's education to measure parental support.

## Basil Bernstein – speech patterns

The English sociologist Bernstein suggested that class differences in speech patterns are related to educational attainment. As speech is an important medium of communication and learning, attainment levels in schools may be related to differences in speech patterns. Bernstein (1961,1970,1972) identified two forms of speech pattern, which he termed the **restricted code** and the **elaborated code**. In general, members of the working class are limited to the use of restricted codes, whereas members of the middle class use both codes.

Restricted codes are a kind of shorthand speech. Those conversing in terms of this code have so much in common that there is no need to make meanings explicit in speech. Restricted codes are characterised by 'short, grammatically simple, often unfinished sentences'. Meaning and intention are conveyed more by gesture, voice intonation and the context in which the communication takes place.

Restricted codes tend to operate in terms of **particularistic meanings** and are tied to specific contexts. Because so much is taken for granted and relatively little is made explicit, restricted codes are largely limited to dealing with objects, events and relationships that are familiar to those communicating. Thus, the meanings conveyed by the code are limited to a particular social group: they are bound to a particular social context and are not readily available to outsiders.

By contrast, an elaborated code explicitly verbalises many of the meanings that are taken for granted in a restricted code. It fills in the detail, spells out the relationships and provides the explanations omitted by restricted codes. As such, its meanings tend to be **universalistic**: they are not tied to a particular context. The listener need not be plugged in to the experience and understanding of the speaker, because the meanings are spelled out verbally.

## Speech patterns and educational attainment

Bernstein used class differences in speech codes to account in part for differences in educational attainment:

1. Education in schools is conducted in terms of an elaborated code and involves 'the transmission and development of universalistic orders of meaning'. This places working-class children at a disadvantage because they tend to be limited to the restricted code.
2. The restricted code, by its very nature, reduces the chances of working-class students successfully acquiring some of the skills demanded by the education system.

### Activity: Transformation to an elaborated code

*The pictures illustrate part of a series of interviews used to assess the language skills of African-American boys. They were asked to describe a toy plane. In the first interview, the boy gives short answers followed by long silences. In the second interview, where he is joined by his best friend and given a packet of crisps (potato chips), the boy gives a detailed description of the plane (Labov, 1973).*

1. Suggest reasons for the boy's different responses in the two interviews.
2. How might this be used to question Bernstein's findings?

Bernstein did not dismiss working-class speech patterns as inadequate or substandard. He described them as having 'warmth and vitality' and 'simplicity and directness'. However, particularly in his earlier writings, he did imply that, in certain respects, they are inferior to an elaborated code. He suggested that an elaborated code is superior for analysing relationships, logically developing an argument, making generalisations and for handling higher-level concepts. Because such skills form an important part of formal education, limitation to a restricted code may provide a partial explanation for the relatively low attainment of working-class students.

### Evaluation of Bernstein

- Bernstein lumps together all manual workers into the working class and all non-manual workers into the middle class. This ignores the various levels within these classes.
- He provides little evidence of the existence and use of the restricted and elaborated codes.
- Much of his evidence is drawn from interviews with children. The context of an interview and the appearance, gender, age and ethnicity of the interviewer can affect the results.
- Although Bernstein does not actually state that working-class speech patterns are substandard, he appears to imply this. Critics argue that he has created the myth that middle-class speech patterns are superior (Rosen, 1974).

## Evaluation of cultural deprivation theory

Cultural deprivation theory portrays working-class subculture as substandard, inadequate and deficient. It was developed mainly by White American middle-class psychologists in the 1960s, partly in an attempt to explain the low educational attainment of African-American students. The theory has been criticised for placing the blame for educational failure on the children and their families, their neighbourhoods and the subculture of their social groups.

Nell Keddie (1973) calls this theory 'the myth of cultural deprivation'. She argues that this myth largely accounts for educational failure. The myth informs and directs interaction in schools, 'teachers' ways of assessing and typifying students and the ways in which teachers and students give meanings to educational situations'. As a result, children from low-income, working-class and minority ethnic backgrounds are seen 'as less "educable" than other children'. Keddie argues that 'The perception of working-class subcultures as deficient seems to arise from the ignorance of those who belong to what they perceive as the dominant cultural tradition.'

## Compensatory education and positive discrimination

From the viewpoint of cultural deprivation theory, equality of educational opportunity could only become a reality by compensating for the deprivations and deficiencies of low-income groups. Only then would low-income students have an equal chance to seize the opportunities provided for all members of society.

From this kind of reasoning developed the idea of **positive discrimination** in favour of culturally deprived children. They must be given a helping hand to compete on equal terms with other children. This took the form of **compensatory education** – additional educational provision for the culturally deprived. According to many educational psychologists, most of the damage was done during primary socialisation, when a substandard culture was internalised in an environment largely devoid of 'richness' and stimulation. Therefore, compensatory education should concentrate on the pre-school years.

This thinking lay behind many of the programmes instituted by the Office of Economic Opportunity during President Johnson's 'War on Poverty' in the USA (from the 1960s to the early 1970s). Billions of dollars were poured into **Project Head Start**, a massive programme of pre-school education, beginning in Harlem in New York City and extending to low-income areas across the US. This and similar programmes aimed to provide planned enrichment – a stimulating educational environment in which to introduce achievement motivation and lay the foundation for effective learning in the school system.

The results were very disappointing. In a large-scale evaluation of Project Head Start, the Westinghouse Corporation concluded that it produced no long-term beneficial results. Despite such gloomy conclusions, there is still support for compensatory education. Some argue that it has failed because the programmes developed have been inappropriate, or because the scale of the operation has been insufficient.

### Educational Priority Areas, Education Action Zones and Excellence in Cities

Nations such as Britain, Portugal and France have compensatory education programmes. In Britain, compensatory education began in the late 1960s with the government allocating extra resources for school building in low-income areas and supplements to the salaries of teachers working in those areas.

Four areas were designated as **Educational Priority Areas** (EPAs). Programmes of compensatory education were introduced in these EPAs. They were based mainly on pre-school education and additional measures in primary schools to raise literacy standards. Although it is difficult to evaluate the results, reports from the EPAs were generally disappointing.

Halsey, who directed the EPA projects, argued that positive discrimination in England has yet to be given a fair trial. It has operated on a shoestring compared to American programmes – for example, in 1973 only 0.2 per cent of the total education budget was spent on compensatory education. Writing in 1977, Halsey stated: 'Positive discrimination is about resources. The principle stands and is most urgently in need of application.'

More recent examples of compensatory education include Education Action Zones (EAZs) and Excellence in Cities (EiC). These programmes directed resources to low-income, inner-city areas in an attempt to raise educational attainment. Available evidence indicates that, at best, they produced only small improvements.

In Portugal, one aim of the national compensatory education programme is to reduce the gap in academic performance between schools in deprived areas and those in more privileged areas. Tiago Neves, Hélder Ferraz and Gil Nata (2017) carried out a longitudinal analysis of quantitative data to assess how far the Portuguese compensatory education programme has narrowed this gap. They measured the performance of schools in national examinations that enable students to access higher education. Neves et al. found that the programme has not been effective in improving the academic results of schools in deprived areas compared to those of other schools.

### Evaluation of compensatory education

Critics see cultural deprivation theory as a smokescreen that disguises the real factors preventing equality of educational opportunity. By placing the blame for failure on the children and their backgrounds, it diverts attention from the deficiencies of the education system. William Labov (1973) argued that Project Head Start was 'designed to repair the child rather than the school; to the extent it is based upon this inverted logic, it is bound to fail'.

Sharon Gewirtz (2001) sees EAZs as being firmly based upon the idea of cultural deprivation. She argues that they involve a 'massive programme of resourcing and re-education which has as its ultimate aim the eradication of cultural difference by transforming working-class parents into middle-class parents'.

Geoff Whitty (2002) criticises EAZs for being based on a cultural deprivation model in which the working class are seen as lacking the necessary culture to succeed in education. In his view, rather than the working class having to change to fit in with education, it is education that should change and place a higher value on working-class culture. Whitty argues that EAZs are likely to have only limited success in raising achievement because they involve quite a modest redistribution of resources to poor areas. They are, therefore, unlikely to do much to compensate for the inequalities in the wider society, which lead to low attainment in deprived areas in the first place.

Any positive effects of EAZs and the EiC programme that replaced them may become more evident in the long term, but so far there is little evidence that they have made a major impact on educational disadvantage.

### Activity

*US President Johnson with some of the children involved in Project Head Start.*

Explain one advantage and one disadvantage of compensatory education programmes.

## Conclusion

So far, this part has focused on factors outside schools in the wider society rather than on what happens in classrooms. It has examined material differences between social classes and class-based subcultures. Some sociologists argue that a combination of these factors explains class differences in educational attainment. Bourdieu's ideas of cultural, social and economic capitals bring together both cultural and material factors, and factors external and internal to schools.

## Bourdieu, capitals and differential attainment

As outlined earlier, the French sociologist Bourdieu saw the main role of education in society as social reproduction, in particular, the reproduction of inequalities of wealth, power and privilege between social classes. Bourdieu (1971, 1974) argues that the education system is based on the culture of the dominant classes, who have the power to impose their definitions of reality on others. (See Unit 5.3.1.) This is very different from cultural deprivation theory, which suggests that the subculture of those in the lower levels of the class system is substandard and deficient compared to the subcultures of those above them.

### Cultural capital

Bourdieu refers to possession of the dominant culture as cultural capital because, via the education system, it can be translated into wealth, power and status. Cultural capital is not evenly distributed throughout the class system, and this largely accounts for class differences in educational attainment. Students with upper-class and, to a lesser extent, middle-class backgrounds have a built-in advantage because they have been socialised into the dominant culture.

Bourdieu claims, 'the success of all school education depends fundamentally on the education previously accomplished in the earliest years of life'. Education in school merely builds on this basis – it does not start from scratch but assumes prior skills and prior knowledge. Children from the dominant classes have internalised these skills and knowledge during their pre-school years. Their success is based on 'the cultural capital previously invested by the family' (Bourdieu, 1986). They possess the key to unlock the messages transmitted in the classroom. In Bourdieu's words, they 'possess the code of the message'.

The educational attainment of social groups is therefore directly related to the amount of cultural capital they possess. Thus, upper and middle-class students have higher success rates than working-class students because they have more of the dominant culture and therefore more cultural capital.

Bourdieu is somewhat vague when he attempts to pinpoint the skills and knowledge required for educational success. He places particular emphasis on style, on form rather than content, and suggests that the way students present their work and themselves counts for more than the actual scholastic content of their work. He argues that, in awarding grades, teachers are strongly influenced by 'the intangible nuances of manners and style'. The closer students' style is to that of the dominant classes, the more likely they are to succeed.

The emphasis on style discriminates against working-class students in two ways:

1. Because their style departs from that of the dominant culture, their work is devalued and penalised.
2. They are unable to grasp the range of meanings that are embedded in the 'grammar, accent, tone, delivery' of the teachers. Because teachers use 'bourgeois parlance' as opposed to 'common parlance', working-class students have an in-built barrier to learning in schools.

## Habitus, class and education

Bourdieu used the concept of habitus to develop his ideas (see Unit 5.1.3). Habitus refers to the values, attitudes, dispositions and expectations held by particular groups. It defines everyday ways of doing things – in Bourdieu's words, 'ways of walking or blowing your nose, ways of eating or talking'. It constructs ways of seeing the world and states what is reasonable, appropriate, and to be expected. As a result, habitus generates 'thoughts, perceptions, expressions and actions'. Habitus is learned from an early age within the family. It is a major part of primary socialisation and varies from class to class.

Bourdieu argues that the habitus of the dominant classes provides them with an advantage in the education system. As a result of their habitus, parents and children are likely to have a positive attitude towards education. This means that they will be inclined to do what is required to succeed in education – from parents investing money in fee-paying schools, private tutors and extra-curricular activities, to children seeing education as important and working hard to pass exams and gain admission to a top university.

This dominant class habitus will be recognised by teachers as a readiness for school knowledge. Teachers will take the view that they and the students are working towards the same goal. As a result, teachers will tend to favour the children of the dominant classes.

### Activity

*During question and answer sessions or group work activities in classrooms, teachers assess and compare their students' vocabulary, language skills and knowledge.*

How might a teacher recognise a student's dominant class habitus and 'readiness for school knowledge'?

By comparison, the habitus of the working class tends to have a more negative attitude towards education. It has lower expectations of success and sometimes rejects the values of school. It may encourage resistance to the school and a 'negative withdrawal which upsets teachers'. This may lead to low attainment among some working-class students.

## Taste, class and education

Using survey data as evidence, Bourdieu (1984) claims that people's tastes – for example, in art, films, music and food – are related to their upbringing, their class and their educational attainment.

The tastes of the dominant classes, which Bourdieu refers to as 'legitimate taste', tend to have the highest prestige. They include so-called 'high culture' – classical music, opera, ballet, theatre, fine art and 'good' literature.

Legitimate taste on its own does not guarantee educational success or a well-paid job. However, it helps some students to get into the most prestigious schools and universities. It also shapes teachers' perceptions of their students. Unconsciously, teachers recognise different tastes and the types of behaviour typical of different classes. They value and reward legitimate taste more than middlebrow taste, and, in turn, middlebrow taste is valued more than popular taste. Such tastes may not even be part of the formal curriculum, but they play an important role in giving those from higher-class backgrounds more chance of success.

## The social function of elimination

Bourdieu claims that a major role of the education system is the social function of **elimination** (Bourdieu, 1974; Bourdieu and Passeron, 1977). This involves the elimination of members of the working class from higher levels of education. It is accomplished in two ways:

1. examination failure
2. self-elimination.

Due to their lack of cultural capital, working-class students are more likely to fail examinations, which prevents them from entering higher education. However, their decision to vacate the system of their own accord accounts for a higher proportion of elimination. Bourdieu regards this decision as 'reasonable' and 'realistic'. Working-class students realise that they are in a disadvantageous position and know what is in store for them. Their attitudes towards education are shaped by 'objective conditions', and these attitudes will continue 'as long as real chances of success are slim'.

## Conclusions

Bourdieu concluded that the major role of education in society is the contribution it makes to social reproduction. Social inequality is reproduced in the education system and as a result it is legitimated. The privileged position of the dominant classes is justified by educational success; the underprivileged position of the lower classes is legitimated by educational failure.

The education system is particularly effective in maintaining the power of the dominant classes, because it presents itself as a neutral body based on meritocratic principles providing equal opportunity for all. Unlike economic capital, 'the transmission of cultural capital is heavily disguised or even invisible'. As such, it 'escapes observation and control'. Bourdieu (1986) concludes that, in practice, education is essentially concerned with 'the reproduction of the established order'.

## Alice Sullivan – a test of Bourdieu's theory

Alice Sullivan (2001, 2002) conducted a questionnaire survey of 465 16-year-old students in four English schools in order to test Bourdieu's theory of class differences in educational attainment. (See Unit 3.1.5.) She used parental occupations to determine the children's social class. Where there were two parents, she chose the one with the higher-status job. She used educational qualifications to measure parents' cultural capital.

A number of measures of students' cultural capital were used. For example, students were asked about the books they read, the television programmes they watched, the music they listened to, whether they played a musical instrument, and their attendance at art galleries, theatres and concerts.

The research then examined which of these factors, if any, are linked with educational performance in GCSEs (formal examinations taken by 16-year-olds). Students who read widely and watched more intellectual and 'highbrow' television programmes such as arts, science and current affairs documentaries, and more sophisticated drama, developed wider vocabularies and greater knowledge. These students were more likely to achieve higher GCSE grades. Watching television programmes such as soap operas (popular drama serials) and game shows did not improve GCSE performance. Attendance at cultural events and involvement in music had no significant effect, suggesting that these should not be considered important aspects of cultural capital.

Sullivan found that students' cultural capital was strongly correlated with parental cultural capital (that is, their parents' educational qualifications), which in turn was closely linked to their social class. Graduate parents in higher professions had children with the most cultural capital and who were most successful in exams.

On the surface, this research provides strong support for Bourdieu. However, Sullivan found significant differences in GCSE attainment between middle-class and working-class children even after the effects of cultural capital had been taken into account.

This led her to conclude that Bourdieu's theory could only account for part of the class differences in attainment. Sullivan (2001) argues that 'Other mechanisms, such as class differentials in material resources and educational aspirations, must account for the remaining differentials in educational attainment.' Her conclusion suggests that cultural capital, *and* parental interest in education, *and* parents' economic situation, all contribute to class inequality in educational attainment.

## Activity

*A family from the dominant social classes.*

1. Which forms of capital are depicted in this picture?
2. Briefly suggest how these capitals might help the children's education.

### Evaluation of Bourdieu

The evaluation on Bourdieu's views on the role of education in society outlined in Unit 5.1.3 also applies to this section.

1. Bourdieu has been criticised, particularly by Marxists, for downplaying certain material factors – in particular, economic exploitation and oppression.
2. Critics argue that Bourdieu places too much emphasis on the structure of society in shaping people's behaviour rather than looking at how individuals can change and transform society. For example, they argue that habitus is presented as determining behaviour rather than as providing opportunities for individuals to direct their own actions. As Sullivan (2002) puts it, 'Bourdieu's theory has no place not only for individual agency, but even for individual consciousness.'
3. Concepts such as cultural capital and habitus have been criticised as vague, lacking in precision and detail, and as difficult to operationalise (to put into a form that can be measured).
4. Sullivan's test of Bourdieu's theory suggests that cultural capital explains only a part of educational attainment.
5. Despite the above criticisms, Bourdieu's work has been extremely influential. It has informed many studies in many countries. Concepts such as cultural, social and economic capital and habitus have inspired and directed many important research projects.

## Activity

Briefly evaluate the view that Bourdieu's theory does not account for individual agency.

## Class, capitals and choosing schools

Studies of class differences in choosing schools in England conducted by Ball, Bowe and Gewirtz (1994) show the importance of cultural, social and economic capital. As a result of their greater capitals, middle-class parents were in a better position than working-class parents to assess available schools for their children. They also had a wider choice of schools. They had more knowledge, contacts, time and money to help them make decisions.

Middle-class parents were more likely to have the economic capital to widen their choice of schools – money to pay for coaching for entrance exams into selective or private schools, fees for private schools, the expense of moving house to be close to a successful school and the costs of transportation to more distant schools.

With their greater cultural capital, middle-class parents were better able to judge the quality of schools, analyse league tables and gather information from teachers on open days.

Added to the above is the greater likelihood of middle-class parents having more social capital – a wider and more informative network of relatives, friends and acquaintances who can provide advice and information on school choice. Ball (2003) states that 'Middle-class parents have enough capitals in the right currency to ensure a high probability of success for their children.'

### Activity

*A parent getting information on the school's examination results as part of the process of deciding which school their child will attend to study A Levels.*

What does the picture suggest about the parent's cultural capital?

### Activity

The following quotations about school choice are from two middle-class mothers (Ball, 2003):

> *You talk to other people who've got children there who come from Riversway [School], how they are coping. You spend a lot of time talking outside the school gates to people you know in the same situation, that's how you discover things really.* (Mrs Grafton)

> *We spoke to teachers in the schools, spoke to other parents, and spoke to my friends ... about where their children went and what they thought about it.* (Mrs Gosling)

1. Drawing on this and other sociological evidence, explain how some middle-class parents use their capitals in relation to their children's education.
2. Evaluate the use of semi-structured interviews with parents to investigate class differences in school choice.

## Class, capitals and higher education

Diane Reay, David and Ball (2005) investigated the influence of social class on university choices. Their sample was based on students from six schools and colleges in and around London, England. They gave a questionnaire to 502 students, ran focus groups and conducted 120 in-depth interviews.

### Habitus

Reay et al. found Bourdieu's concept of habitus (see Unit 5.1.3) particularly useful. They argue that the habitus acquired in the family has an important influence on higher education choices. For example, many of the privileged middle-class students came from families where university attendance was taken for granted, and where elite universities were seen as appropriate for 'people like them'. These views were usually confirmed by the habitus of the fee-paying schools they attended. Progression to elite universities was seen as normal and natural for their kind of students.

Privately educated, middle-class students often had detailed knowledge of premier-division universities, which they had acquired from both family and school. In addition, they had a 'confidence, certainty and sense of entitlement', which led many to choose the top universities. By comparison, many working-class students lacked this knowledge and confidence. They tended to see elite universities such as Oxford and Cambridge as 'not for the likes of them'. They had insufficient cultural capital to avoid 'feelings of risk, fear, shame and guilt', which resulted from their perception of a greater likelihood of academic and social failure should they attend an elite university. For many, this led to a 'process of self-exclusion'. By not applying, they barred themselves from the top universities.

## Activity

*Grandfather, father and son.*

How does this picture illustrate the working of habitus?

## Evaluation of the concepts of capitals and habitus

The concepts of cultural, social and economic capital and the idea of habitus have directed a range of research projects on social class and educational attainment. They have been extremely useful in throwing new light on the importance of:

- socialisation within families
- choosing schools and universities
- social class attainment and the wider society.

The concepts of capitals and habitus have shown the connection between money, social contacts, ways of thinking, and attitudes and expectations. As a result of the ideas of capitals and habitus, researchers have asked new questions and provided new answers.

These ideas have brought together cultural and material factors, and factors both internal and external to schools and the education system.

## Activity

Make brief notes on the relationship between cultural factors and educational attainment.

## Key terms

**Cultural deprivation theory** The idea that certain groups are deprived of, or deficient in, things seen as necessary for high educational attainment.

**Subculture** The distinctive norms and values of a particular social group.

**Fatalism** Accepting a situation rather than making efforts to improve it.

**Immediate gratification** Focusing on the pleasures of the moment rather than putting them off for future reward.

**Present-time orientation** A focus on the present rather than the future.

**Collectivism** Emphasis on the group rather than the individual.

**Restricted code** A kind of shorthand speech in which meanings are not spelled out.

**Elaborated code** Speech in which meanings are made explicit and spelled out.

**Particularistic meanings** Meanings that are tied to a particular social context and not readily available to outsiders.

**Universalistic meanings** Meanings that are not tied to a particular context or situation.

**Positive discrimination** Treating a particular group more favourably than others.

**Compensatory education** Making up for, or compensating for, the supposed deficiencies of so-called culturally deprived groups.

**Project Head Start** A programme of pre-school compensatory education in the USA.

**Educational Priority Areas** Programmes of compensatory education in parts of England.

**Elimination** The elimination of members of the working class from higher levels of education.

## Summary

1. Some researchers see differences in class subcultures as the main reason for social class differences in educational attainment.
2. Class differences in parental interest in children's education have been seen as a reason for class differences in attainment.
3. Bernstein argued that class differences in speech patterns contribute to class differences in attainment.
4. Cultural deprivation theory states that the reason for the relatively low attainment of working-class children is due to a lack of the skills, attitudes and values required for high educational attainment. It has been criticised for blaming the child and their background rather than the school for educational failure.
5. Compensatory education aims to compensate for the supposed deficiencies of children from low-income families and give them a head start in school.
6. According to Bourdieu, educational success is mainly based on cultural capital. In general, the higher a person's position in the class system, the more cultural capital they possess.
7. Dominant class habitus includes attitudes and expectations which provide a significant advantage in the education system.
8. Students from the lower levels of the class system tend to eliminate themselves from higher levels of the education system.
9. Sullivan's test of Bourdieu's theory suggests that cultural capital explains only a part of educational attainment.
10. The greater capitals of the middle and upper classes give them advantages in choosing schools.
11. The habitus of the dominant classes leads them to select the highest-ranking universities.
12. The concepts of capitals and habitus have directed important research projects.

# Unit 5.5.3 In-school factors, social class and educational attainment

The previous units focus mainly on factors outside schools to explain the relationship between social class and educational attainment. They look at the wider society and argue that an individual's position in the social structure has an important effect on their educational attainment. Structural explanations, in this case explanations based on the class structure, see behaviour as shaped by external factors over which the individual has little control. Behaviour is seen as largely determined by the directives of class subcultures, by material factors and by cultural, social and economic capitals.

This unit has a different focus. It looks at small-scale interaction situations in the classroom. It examines teachers' perceptions of students' social class and how this might affect their placement in ability groups – for example, the tendency for working-class students to be placed in lower sets (where students are placed in ability groups for specific subjects such as English or maths) and streams (where students are placed in a particular ability group and taught in this group for all subjects). This, in turn, might affect how students see themselves and their attainment. This unit asks whether interaction in the classroom reinforces factors in the wider society which result in class differences in educational attainment.

## Teachers' perceptions of social class

Teachers' perceptions of students' social class are an important in-school factor that can influence students' educational attainment.

### Class and the ideal pupil

An early study of teachers' perceptions of social class was conducted by the American sociologist Howard Becker. He interviewed 60 teachers from Chicago high schools and found that they tended to share an image of the 'ideal pupil', who was intelligent, motivated to learn and well dressed.

Teachers perceived middle-class pupils as closest to this ideal, and pupils from the lower working class as furthest from it. Those in the lowest class grouping were seen as less able, lacking motivation and difficult to control. As a result, teachers felt the best they could do was 'just try to get some basic things over to them' (Becker, 1970).

Teachers were unaware that their assessments were influenced by pupils' social class background. Nor did they realise that perceptions of class also influenced the level of work they felt appropriate for pupils.

### Class and 'ability'

David Gillborn and Deborah Youdell (2001) conducted research in two secondary schools in London, United Kingdom, from 1995 to 1997. They discovered that teachers had a 'common sense understanding of ability'. Using this as a measure, the teachers had allocated pupils to different sets.

Working-class pupils were more likely to be seen as disruptive, as lacking in motivation and lacking in parental support. As a result, they 'face a particular problem in convincing teachers that they have "ability"'. Consequently, they were more likely to be placed in lower-level sets.

As a result of making a link between so-called 'ability' and social class, teachers systematically discriminated against working-class pupils.

### Cultural capital and habitus

According to Bourdieu (1984), teachers recognise the high levels of cultural capital possessed by students from the 'dominant classes'. As a result, they see them as having the skills, attitudes and ambitions to succeed. Teachers also recognise the habitus of these students and believe that it encourages a positive view of education.

### Class and teacher–pupil relationships

Generally, teachers prefer to teach pupils who they see as able and highly motivated. They place these students in higher sets and respond more favourably towards them. As a result, such teacher–pupil relationships tend to be positive.

Conversely, teachers' views of students who have been defined as less able and placed in lower sets tend to be less favourable. These students may respond with resentment and hostility. This can result in discipline problems and negative relationships between teachers and pupils.

This can be seen from teachers' views of the 'Macho Lads' in Maírtín Mac an Ghaill's (2004) study of a secondary school in the United Kingdom. The Macho Lads were working-class boys in the lowest sets. The teachers saw them as low-ability, non-academic troublemakers. Their main priority was policing the Macho Lads, who, in turn, saw the teachers as controlling and hostile.

### Activity

**Teaching top and bottom sets**

*Teacher A:* You don't find any behaviour problems with the top set – they've got the intelligence.

*Teacher B:* When you get your next year's timetable and you see that it is a top or bottom set then you get certain images. If you get a top set you tend to think that their behaviour will be better. You tend to think with a bottom set you will get more discipline problems. I look forward to teaching my top-set third year but dread my bottom-set third year. With the bottom group I go in with a stony face but I know that with the top set if I say fun's over they will stop. But if I give a bottom set rope they'll take advantage of you.

Source: Abraham, 1995.

*Teaching a top set.*

What effects might the teachers' views have on the students' behaviour and attainment?

## Interactionist perspectives

Structural explanations argue that an individual's position in the social structure has an important effect on their educational attainment. By contrast, interactionist perspectives on social class and educational attainment focus on the classroom rather than on the wider society. **Interactionism** directs attention to small-scale interaction situations and the meanings that develop and guide action within those situations. Studies of teacher–pupil relationships within classrooms, and student subcultures provide good examples of how the interactionist approach has been applied within a substantive area of sociology.

Interactionists argue that a person's **self-concept**, their view of themselves, develops from interaction with others. Interaction in the classroom, with teachers and students, helps to shape a person's self-concept. Their self-concept can have a significant effect on their educational attainment.

The way students are classified as 'high attainers' and 'likely to succeed', and 'low attainers' and 'unlikely to succeed', is often influenced by their social class. Middle-class students tend to be classified as 'high attainers' and working-class students as 'low attainers'. This can affect teachers' expectations of students' achievements.

In this respect, students have been labelled. A **label** defines how others see a person and how they behave towards them. It can also influence how a person sees themselves and how they behave in response to the label.

## Labelling and social class

In a study of an American kindergarten, Ray C. Rist (1970) found that as early as the eighth day of school the children were permanently seated at three separate tables. Table 1 was reserved for 'fast learners', tables 2 and 3 for the 'less able'. According to Rist, it was not ability that determined where each child sat, but the degree to which they conformed to the teacher's own middle-class standards. For example, the teacher appeared to take account of whether the children had neat and clean appearances, and whether they were known to come from an educated family with one or both parents in middle-class occupations. In other words, the kindergarten teacher was evaluating and labelling students on the basis of her perception of their social class, not on their abilities.

The labelling of students can have important effects on their progress in education. Aaron V. Cicourel and John I. Kitsuse (1963) conducted a study of the decisions of counsellors in an American high school. The counsellors played a significant part in the students' educational careers because they largely decided which students should be placed on courses designed for preparation for college entry. The counsellors claimed to use grades and the results of IQ tests as the basis for classifying students in terms of achievement. However, Cicourel and Kitsuse found significant differences between these measures and the ways in which students were actually classified.

They argue that the students' social class was an important influence on the way they were evaluated. Even when students from different social backgrounds had similar academic records, counsellors were more likely to perceive those from middle-class and upper-middle-class origins as natural 'college prospects' and to place them on higher-level courses.

## The self-fulfilling prophecy theory

Labelling theory argues that, once a label is attached to a person, there is a tendency for them to see themselves in terms of the label and act accordingly. There is also a tendency for others to see them in terms of the label and act towards them on this basis. This may result in a **self-fulfilling prophecy**.

The self-fulfilling prophecy theory argues that predictions made by teachers about the future success or failure of students will tend to come true. The teacher defines the student in a particular way, such as 'clever' or 'not so clever'. Based on this definition, the teacher makes predictions or prophecies about the behaviour of the student – for example, that they will get high or low grades.

The teacher's interaction with students will be influenced by their definition of the students. They may, for example, expect higher-quality work from, and give greater encouragement to, those they have defined as 'bright' students. The students' self-concepts will tend to be shaped by the teacher's definition. Their actions will, in part, be a reflection of what the teacher expects from them. In this way, the prophecy is fulfilled – the predictions made by the teacher have come to pass. Thus, the student's attainment level is to some degree a result of interaction between the student and the teacher.

There have been a number of attempts to test the validity of the self-fulfilling prophecy theory. The most famous one was based on a field experiment conducted by Robert Rosenthal and Lenore Jacobson (1968) in an elementary school in California in the USA. They selected a random sample of 20 per cent of the student population and informed the teachers that these children could be expected to show rapid intellectual growth. They tested all students' IQ at the beginning of the experiment. After one year, the children were re-tested and, in general, the random sample showed greater gains in IQ. In addition, report cards indicated that teachers believed that this group had made greater advances in reading skills.

Although Rosenthal and Jacobson did not observe interaction in the classroom, they claimed that 'teachers' expectations can significantly affect their students' performance'. They suggested that teachers had communicated their belief that the chosen 20 per cent had greater potential and that the children responded by improving their performance. Rosenthal and Jacobson speculated that the teachers' manner, facial expressions, posture, degree of friendliness and encouragement conveyed this impression, which, in turn, produced a self-fulfilling prophecy.

## Activity

*The researchers gave teachers a list of the names of pupils who were likely to show greater intellectual growth within the next year, but these pupils were, in fact, randomly selected. Teachers might respond to this false information by giving the named pupils more challenging tasks or special attention.*

1. With reference to this photograph and other information, explain how labelling can lead to a self-fulfilling prophecy.
2. Evaluate Rosenthal and Jacobson's field experiment from an ethical viewpoint.

### Evaluation of labelling and the self-fulfilling prophecy

Despite seeming reasonable, the self-fulfilling prophecy theory has been criticised. One area of criticism concerns the evidence. Rosenthal and Jacobson have been strongly attacked for the methods they used in their study. In particular, it has been suggested that the IQ tests they used were of dubious quality and were improperly administered.

In almost all research based on labelling and the self-fulfilling prophecy, the actual process that is supposed to have led to changes in self-concept and behaviour has not been directly observed. For example, Rosenthal and Jacobson only speculated on how the changes in the children's performance came about. They were not in the classroom to observe how changes in the teachers' attitudes might have led to changes in the students' behaviour (Rist, 2016).

There is evidence that students sometimes reject negative labels. In a study of a group of Black girls in a comprehensive school in London, United Kingdom, Margaret Fuller (1984) found that the girls resented the negative stereotypes associated with being both female and Black. They felt that many people expected them to fail, but, far from living up to these expectations, they tried to prove them wrong. The girls devoted themselves to schoolwork in order to try to ensure their success. Heidi Safia Mirza (1992) also challenges the labelling theory of underachievement among Black female students in two schools in London, United Kingdom. Although there was evidence of racism from some teachers, Mirza argues that this did not undermine the Black girls' self-esteem. They had positive self-esteem, were concerned with academic success and were prepared to work hard.

This suggests that labels can have a variety of effects. They may produce a self-fulfilling prophecy. However, they may be rejected and result in the opposite behaviour to that implied by the label.

## Ability grouping

In many schools, students are placed in **ability groups** – groups of pupils who are seen as having similar abilities. There are several types of ability grouping, including the following:

- **Streaming:** Students are placed in a class on the basis of their overall ability. They remain in that class for most or all subjects. For example, a student is placed in class 3 and taught at that level for all subjects.

- **Banding:** This is a less rigid form of streaming. Each band contains two or more classes, which may be regrouped for different subjects.
- **Setting:** Students are placed in subject groups on the basis of their attainment in those subjects. For example, they may be in set 1 for English and set 3 for maths.
- **Mixed-ability groups:** Students are randomly or intentionally mixed in terms of their perceived ability (Ireson and Hallam, 2001). For example, in Finland, students are taught in mixed-ability classes. Students who fall behind receive additional support from a teacher to help them to catch up. In Shanghai (China), Singapore and Hong Kong, students are not streamed or set by ability during mathematics lessons. Instead, they are all taught together and teachers provide support on a daily basis to individual students who need additional tuition.

## Ability grouping, social class and attainment

Research by Jo Boaler (2005) suggests that the selection of students for ability groups is affected by their social class and that ability grouping influences students' attainment. She studied students aged 13 to 16 in mathematics classes in two schools in Britain. The two groups were similar in terms of social class and previous attainment. In School A, students were taught in mixed-ability classes until a few months before their GCSEs. In School B, students were placed in one of eight sets for maths at the age of 13. Middle-class students tended to be placed in higher sets, and working-class students in lower sets.

In School A, there were no significant social class differences in exam results and the results were significantly higher than those of School B. However, in School B, most of the higher grades were attained by middle-class students, and most of the lower grades by working-class students. Boaler concludes that ability grouping in sets 'reproduces social class inequalities' rather than promoting high achievement for all.

## Streaming in primary schools

Streaming by ability in primary schools appears to increase the gap between higher- and lower-attaining pupils. It also widens social class differences because those from low-income families tend to be placed in lower streams, and those from better-off homes are put in higher streams. Evidence for this comes from a study of 2544 Year 2 pupils (aged 6 and 7) born in the UK in 2000–2001, who took part in the longitudinal Millennium Cohort Study (Centre for Longitudinal Studies, 2014).

## Contemporary issues: Setting – a global survey

*Students in the top sets gain from setting.*

Adam Gamoran (2010) conducted a survey of research on setting in a range of countries, from the UK and the USA to Germany, Belgium, South Africa, Japan and Australia. The results of this large body of research all point in the same direction:

1. Those in high sets gain, while those in low sets lose.
2. In terms of the overall exam results of the school, 'the gains of the high achievers are offset by the losses of the low achievers'.
3. Over the course of schooling, the attainment gap between students assigned to high and low sets grows steadily wider.
4. As middle-class students tend to be placed in high sets and working-class students in low sets, setting tends to reinforce social inequality in the wider society.

**Possible solutions** How might the negative effects of setting be reduced or removed? Based on his survey, Gamoran suggests two possibilities:

- First, academic standards in the lower sets should be raised and combined with specific rewards for high performance, such as entry to further education and access to jobs.
- Second, mixed-ability classes should have specially designed supplementary instruction available for students who are having difficulty.

Both approaches have been tried with varying degrees of success.

### Question

Explain how setting might reinforce social inequality.

One in six children in English primary schools were placed in streams. Compared to children in mixed-ability teaching groups, pupils in the top streams did better in reading and maths, while those in the bottom streams did 'significantly worse'. The study found that working-class pupils were 'disproportionately placed in lower streams' and that streaming, particularly when it begins at a very early age, is likely to increase the attainment gap between top and bottom streams, and between social classes.

How does streaming do this? 'Grouping children by ability changes teachers' expectations. This impacts on what is taught to different groups, how it is taught and the unspoken messages given to pupils' (Hallam and Parsons, 2014).

## Pupil subcultures

Student or **pupil subcultures** are the distinctive norms and values developed by young people in schools and colleges. Most sociological research focuses on counter-school cultures, also known as **anti-school cultures.** These are subcultures which reject the norms and values of the school. They are usually found among students in lower sets who tend to be working-class. However, class, ethnicity and gender are all influential in the formation of student subcultures and intersect with each other. (See Units 5.6.3 and 5.7.3.) Membership of counter-school cultures shapes students' identities, how they see the education system, their progress and their examination results. It also affects the way that teachers see students and the sets they place them in.

Many studies of counter-school cultures focus on working-class boys. For example, Willis' study examined the counter-school culture of 12 White working-class 'lads' (see Unit 5.1.2). The 'lads' saw no value in academic work and had no interest in gaining qualifications. They misbehaved, disrupted lessons and focused their attention on 'having a laff'.

In his study of an English secondary school, Mac an Ghaill (2004) identified a group he called the 'Macho Lads' – working-class boys in the lowest sets (see Units 5.5.3 and 5.7.3).

Defined as troublemakers and as underachievers with little or no chance of academic success, the Macho Lads reacted by developing an anti-school culture. They saw schoolwork as meaningless and disrespected students who conformed to school rules. Their main concerns were 'acting tough', 'looking after your mates' and 'having a laugh'. They refused to accept the teachers' authority. In the words of one boy, 'schools are for keeping you down and bossing you around'. Stuck in the bottom sets, they saw the teachers as 'just looking down on us'.

As with the 'lads' in Willis' research, the anti-school culture developed by the working-class Macho Lads gave them little chance of gaining qualifications. (See Units 5.6.3 and 5.7.3 for further coverage of student subcultures.)

### The subculture of deviant students in China

Lin Liu and Ailei Xie (2017) undertook an ethnographic study of a subculture of at-risk, deviant students in a secondary school in a city in China. High expectations for educational achievement are placed on young people in the Chinese school system and, in general, parents see education as important regardless of their social background.

The study focused on five students (four boys and one girl) who attended a school in a relatively affluent city on China's southern coast. They were labelled first by the head teacher and later by others as the '4 + 1' group (based on their gender).

The school was under pressure to perform well and to achieve a high position in the ranking system used there. It emphasised academic attainment and examination results rather than other achievements. Students were expected to undertake a lot of homework to improve their academic performance.

Teachers and some students experienced conflict over issues such as homework. The '4 + 1' students were labelled as deviant, mainly because they were seen as low achievers. Such students tended to be from a 'low social class'.

Lin Liu and Ailei Xie argue that eventually the students came to accept and internalise this label and it became part of their identity. They worked against the school regime's standards of behaviour, which were based on regulations deemed necessary for academic achievement. Teachers favoured well-behaved students who made an effort to achieve. They were more tolerant of poor behaviour among high-achieving students than among underperforming students.

In Lin Liu and Ailei Xie's view, the label became a self-fulfilling prophecy. The '4 + 1' students, who were 'lower class', had little chance of escaping the self-fulfilling prophecy, because they lacked familial or community resources to 'overcome their previous deviant behaviour'. By contrast, middle-class students had opportunities to attend cram school (where they train, for example, to pass university entrance examinations) or to hire private tutors.

The 4 + 1 students were marginalised by the school and, in response, formed part of a 'muddling through' subculture. This term means applying 'easy strategies to survive' or cope with the education system. It involved resisting teachers' authority in relation, for example, to the strict regulations regarding dress and hairstyles. Their subcultural resistance to authority, however, was 'displayed at an acceptable level'. For instance, they saw their resistance and confrontations as having failed if they resulted in oppressive responses from teachers or parents.

The group members did not reject school entirely and saw credentials as important to their employment prospects. However, they did not 'fully embrace school either'. Their attitude to school was pragmatic, in that they wanted to leave school with the relevant diploma rather than dropping out, but, at the same time, they wanted to soften the process of schooling. Their 'muddling through' subculture bonded them together and helped them to endure their schooling by negotiating 'control of the schooling process' from teachers and, at the same time, graduating with a diploma.

Lin Liu and Ailei Xie argue that, although it is assumed that schools will help disadvantaged students to improve their performance, the education system can contribute to students' engagement in deviance.

## Activity

*The 'muddling through' subculture involved resisting teachers' authority regarding, for example, regulations on hairstyles and dress.*

Drawing on Lin Liu and Ailei Xie's study and other evidence, evaluate the view that schools can contribute to students' engagement in deviance.

## The educational triage

Gillborn and Youdell (2000) looked at some of the effects on teaching of league tables and the marketisation of schools. Their detailed research over a two-year period was based on interviews and observations in two secondary schools in London, United Kingdom. They found that teachers divided students into three groups in terms of their predicted performance at GCSE. The first group consisted of students who were expected to attain A* to C grades (the highest grades) with little difficulty. These students tended to be middle class. The second group were seen as 'borderline cases' – students on the border of grades C and D. The third group were seen as 'hopeless cases' – students with little or no hope of reaching a grade C or above. They tended to be working-class. Gillborn and Youdell call this three-part grouping the **educational triage**.

Gillborn and Youdell found that teachers' main focus was the second group – the 'borderline cases'. This group received additional teaching provided by the most experienced teachers, aimed at boosting their GCSE grades.

The main measure for judging secondary school performance was the proportion of students obtaining five or more GCSEs with grades A* to C. The aim of the educational triage was to maximise this proportion in order to improve the school's league table position. The most effective way of doing this was seen in terms of directing additional resources of time, effort and money at the borderline cases.

This focus on borderline cases discriminated against the first and third triage. It was particularly harmful to the third triage – those in the lower sets, who arguably needed the most help. In the schools studied by Gillborn and Youdell, these were mainly working-class and Black Caribbean heritage students.

### Conclusion

This unit has shown that what happens inside schools often reinforces class inequalities. The inequalities of social class outside school produce social class differences in educational attainment. Rather than reducing these differences, what happens in the classroom may well increase them and widen the achievement gap between different groups.

## The relationship between social class, ethnicity and gender

This part has focused on social class. When looking at educational inequalities, however, it is apparent that different factors intersect, overlap and combine to affect people's experiences and identities. For example, sociologists are aware of the influence of class, ethnicity and gender on the formation of student subcultures.

### Intersectionality

The theory of **intersectionality** examines how different factors intersect, overlap or interact to form people's identities and their experiences. For example, it looks at how the interaction of class, ethnicity and gender shapes their lives and educational experiences, and interconnects to form their identities. The experience of being a girl or a boy will interact with being from a particular ethnic group and social class to shape the experience of schooling.

Louise Morley and Kattie Lussier (2009) examined intersections between factors such as gender and socio-economic status in their study of participation and achievement patterns across four universities in Tanzania and Ghana. By exploring how gender intersects with socio-economic status, Morley and Lussier show that gains in relation to gender such as the increase in the participation of women within higher education in Tanzania and Ghana can hide socio-economic privilege and inequality. For example, although the LLB Law programme at one of the Tanzanian universities had a relatively high rate of female participation in 2007/08, poor females were under-represented.

The idea of intersectionality is important, because it suggests that social factors such as class, ethnicity and gender are not separate categories that act independently or in isolation. When investigating the underachievement of some working-class students, for example, it is also important to examine factors linked to their ethnicity and gender. The final parts of the chapter focus on ethnicity and gender.

### Activity

Make brief notes on the relationship between school-based factors, social class and educational attainment.

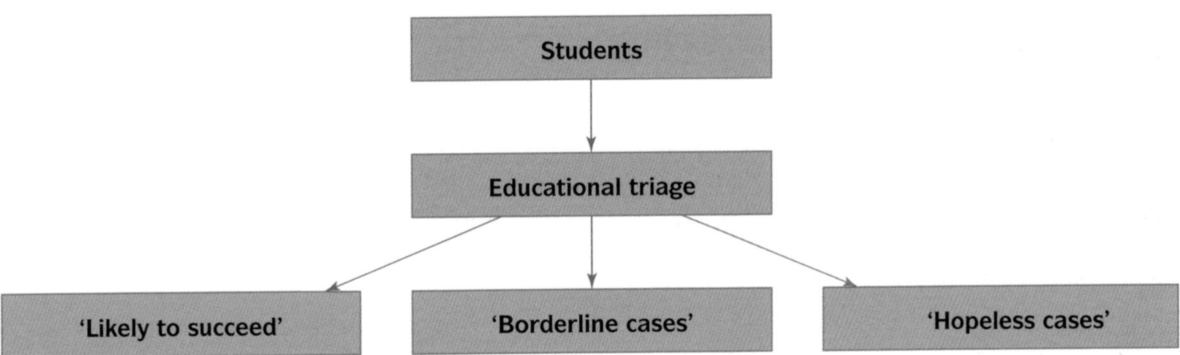


*The educational triage (Adapted from Gillborn and Youdell, 2000).*

## Key terms

**Interactionism** A sociological theory which examines interaction between members of small social groups.

**Self-concept** An individual's picture or view of themselves.

**Label** A definition of a person placed on them by others.

**Self-fulfilling prophecy** A tendency for the way people are labelled to shape their actions.

**Ability groups** Groups in which students are placed on the basis of their perceived ability.

**Streaming** Placing students in a particular group for all subjects. The whole class becomes an ability group.

**Banding** Placing students in a band containing two or more classes, which may be regrouped for different subjects.

**Setting** Placing students in an ability group for particular subjects.

**Mixed-ability groups** Groups in which students are randomly placed or intentionally mixed in terms of their perceived ability.

**Pupil subculture** The distinctive norms and values of a particular group of students.

**Anti-school culture** Student subculture which rejects the norms and values of the school.

**Educational triage** The division of students into three groups in terms of their expected GCSE grades.

**Intersectionality** The idea that factors such as class, gender and ethnicity interact and combine to shape people's identities and experiences.

## Summary

1. The interactionist perspective explores how:
   - students' self-concepts might be shaped in the classroom
   - students are sometimes labelled
   - labelling might lead to a self-fulfilling prophecy.
2. Students might reject negative labels.
3. In many schools, students are placed in ability groups based on their perceived ability.
4. There is a tendency for middle-class students to be placed in higher-ability groups and working-class students in lower groups, even when their grades are similar.
5. Placement in ability groups is likely to widen the attainment gap between the higher and lower groups and, as a result, to reproduce social class differences in educational attainment.
6. Counter-school/anti-school cultures are usually found in lower sets consisting of mainly working-class students. These cultures reduce their chances of gaining qualifications.
7. By focusing time and effort on borderline cases, the educational triage discriminates against the first, largely middle-class, group and particularly against the third, mainly working-class, group.
8. Sociologists increasingly recognise that factors such as gender, ethnicity and social class do not work in isolation. They intersect and combine to shape people's identities and experiences of schooling.

# END-OF-PART QUESTIONS

**0 1** Describe two examples of how cultural deprivation may affect educational attainment. **[4 marks]**

**0 2** Explain one strength and one limitation of the interactionist approach to education. **[6 marks]**

**0 3** 'Cultural capital is the most important factor in determining educational attainment.' Using sociological material, give one argument against this view. **[6 marks]**

# PART 6 ETHNICITY AND EDUCATIONAL ATTAINMENT

## Contents


| | | |
|---|---|---|
| **Unit 5.6.1** | **Racism in schools** | **301** |
| **Unit 5.6.2** | **Cultural explanations** | **304** |
| **Unit 5.6.3** | **Ethnicity, subcultures and attainment** | **305** |


In culturally diverse countries, differences in the educational attainment of different ethnic groups can be identified. On average in England, for example, students of Chinese and Indian heritage have the highest attainment at GCSE while White British students and those of Pakistani and Black Caribbean heritage tend to achieve below the national average. Chinese heritage students also have the highest percentage in terms of university admissions, while White British students have the lowest. As is the case with attainment based on social class, material deprivation and income appear to affect the educational attainment of ethnic groups. For example, in many cases students from low-income households perform less well than students from higher-income households. However, the performance of different ethnic groups does not appear to be affected by low income in a uniform way. For example, British Bangladeshi students achieve better GCSE results than White British students even though their average household income is significantly lower.

Clearly, factors other than material deprivation may affect the relationship between ethnicity and educational attainment. This part examines some of these other factors, including school-based influences such as racism in classrooms and home-based factors such as parental expectations. It moves on to explore the workings of cultural capital in relation to ethnicity and achievement. Finally, it looks at how ethnic group subcultures might impact on educational attainment. Many sociologists make the important point that ethnicity is only one variable when it comes to understanding educational attainment. Social class and gender are also relevant factors.

## Unit 5.6.1 Racism in schools

This unit examines explanations for the relationship between ethnicity and educational attainment that focus on racism in schools. Unit 5.3.2 examined ethnocentrism in the curriculum and this can be seen as one key aspect of racism within educational settings. In what other ways does racism operate in schools and classrooms? Do teachers view students from different ethnic groups in different ways? Do they view girls and boys from the same ethnic group differently? This unit explores these and other important questions.

### David Gillborn and Deborah Youdell – Racism in the classroom

Gillborn and Youdell (2000, 2001) argue that, with the increasing concern with league tables and marketisation, 'some students are sacrificed to the more important goal of raising attainment in the league table statistics'. The students 'sacrificed' tended to be working-class and Black Caribbean heritage (see Unit 5.5.3). These students were seen as 'less able' and placed in lower sets. Students in higher sets had the most experienced teachers and were given more teacher time, support and effort. Students in lower sets were 'systematically neglected'.

Gillborn and Youdell found that 'widespread inequalities of opportunity are endured by Black children'. Teachers had an expectation that 'Black students will generally present disciplinary problems, and they therefore tended to feel that "control and punishment" had to be given higher priority than "academic concerns"'.

Most Black students felt they were disadvantaged by their treatment in schools. By and large, they expected to be blamed for disciplinary problems. They also expected teachers to underestimate their future achievements. In these circumstances, it was hardly surprising that they ended up doing, on average, less well than the White students attending the same schools.

Gillborn and Youdell see teachers' perceptions of and behaviour towards Black Caribbean students as racist. However, most teachers are unaware of this. In fact, 'many teachers are passionately committed to challenging the very inequalities that they participate in reinforcing'. Their racism takes the form of **institutional racism** – part of the taken-for-granted operation and assumptions of institutions such as schools.

## Teachers' perceptions of ethnicity

Some teachers tend to view different ethnic groups in different ways. This can affect their expectations of each group and the way they teach them. This, in turn, can affect the behaviour and attainment of different ethnic groups.

### Black Caribbean boys

**Racism** From their research in schools, Gillborn and Youdell (2001) found that teachers tended to see Black Caribbean boys, whatever their social class, as less able and more disruptive than White boys. They were more likely to place Black boys in lower sets and give priority to 'control and punishment'. Gillborn and Youdell saw the teachers' behaviour as racist.

**Types of teacher** Tony Sewell (1997), a Black Caribbean researcher, studied a boys' 11–16 school in Britain and found that Black Caribbean boys were singled out for punishment. For example, they made up 32 per cent of the student population but comprised 85 per cent of those excluded from school.

Relationships with teachers were often strained and difficult. According to Sewell, teachers were sometimes frightened by the physical size and aggression of some of the more assertive students. There was a tendency to lump all Black Caribbean boys together. Those who conformed to the school's values and those who rebelled against them were often judged and treated in terms of the same negative stereotypes.

Sewell divided the teachers into three groups in terms of their relationships with Black Caribbean students:

1. **Supportive teachers** did their best to support and guide students and usually established good relationships (about 10 per cent of staff).
2. **Irritated teachers** could be supportive but felt firmer discipline was needed. They blamed the boys' street culture for many of the school's problems (about 60 per cent of staff).
3. **Antagonistic teachers** were either openly racist or objected to Black Caribbean street culture – for example, hairstyles and 'bopping' (a stylised walk). Their relationships with Black Caribbean students were strained and sometimes hostile (around 30 per cent of staff).

### Black Caribbean girls

A study by Mirza (1992) of two secondary schools in London, England focused on 62 young Black students, aged 15–19 (see Unit 5.5.3). Mirza identifies five types of teacher in terms of their relationships with and attitudes towards Black students.

1. **Overt racists** were a small minority who the girls avoided where possible.
2. **The Christians** tried to be 'colour blind', claiming to see no difference between ethnic groups and the White majority, and refusing to see racism as a problem. They sometimes expected too little from the girls and gave them glowing reports for average achievement.
3. **The crusaders** were anti-racists who tried to make their lessons relevant to Black students. Because they knew little about their students, lessons tended to be confusing and irrelevant.
4. **Liberal chauvinists** like the crusaders, were well-meaning, but tended to underestimate their students' ability.
5. **Black teachers** made up a small group who showed no favouritism and were liked and respected. The girls found their help and advice extremely valuable.

In general, the girls in Mirza's research were ambitious, hard-working and determined to succeed. They rejected the negative views of their blackness, the low expectations of their potential, and the patronising and unhelpful 'help'. They tended to keep their distance and maintain a cool relationship with their teachers.

### South Asian students

**Primary students** Paul Connolly's (1998) study of a British multi-ethnic, inner-city primary school focused on the relationship between South Asian 5- and 6-year-olds and their teachers. The children were seen as obedient, hard-working and conformist. Teachers expected them to produce high-quality work.

Girls were seen as models of good behaviour. When the boys did misbehave, this was seen as 'silly' rather than as a challenge to the teachers' authority. As a result, they were not punished as much as Black Caribbean boys. Boys were often praised for good work, while girls tended to be left alone – teachers felt they did not need the same help and encouragement.

**Gang Girls** In her research on schools in England, Farzana Shain (2010) termed one group of Asian heritage girls the 'Gang Girls' (see Unit 5.7.3). Teachers saw these Gang Girls as troublemakers. They objected to assertive girls in gangs partly because this challenged their stereotypical perception of Asian 'passive femininity'. This negative view of the girls and their placement in bottom sets convinced teachers that they were low achievers. As a result, the girls gradually stopped taking part in learning. As one girl put it, 'I'm not interested. I don't want to do anything. I just like coming to school to meet my friends.'

## Discrimination linked to setting in schools

Critics of setting in a British context argue that the students allocated to lower sets or streams tend to be from working-class and/or minority ethnic backgrounds. This can prevent them from obtaining the knowledge required for high grades in examinations. By contrast, a disproportionate number of White, middle-class students are placed in the upper sets. Ability groups discriminate in favour of the White middle class and against students from working-class and minority ethnic backgrounds.

In practice, perceptions of behaviour have been used as a basis for allocating students to ability groups. For example, there is evidence that Black Caribbean heritage students have been placed in examination sets below their measured ability because their behaviour was seen as unsuitable for higher sets (see Unit 5.5.3, Gillborn and Youdell).

Many schools across the USA, for example, have a system of tracking or grouping based on students' perceived ability. Critics argue that, in practice, tracking means that students are stratified in terms of their ethnicity and socio-economic status. Critics also point out that, in cases where schools have switched from tracking to mixed-ability teaching and learning, the achievement gap between minority and White students has narrowed. According to William Mathis (2013), opposition to the elimination of tracking in the USA is linked to the desire to preserve privilege.

### Activity

1. Describe two examples of how gender and ethnicity might intersect to inform the experiences of students in schools.
2. Describe one way in which ethnicity and social class might interact to shape students' school-based experiences.

### Key term

**Institutional racism** Racial prejudice and discrimination that form part of the taken-for-granted assumptions and operations of institutions.

### Summary

1. Differences in educational attainment between ethnic groups have been identified in culturally diverse societies.
2. Income and material deprivation appear to affect the educational attainment of ethnic groups. But, to some extent, they affect different groups' performance in different ways.
3. Ethnic group differences in attainment are affected by social class and gender.
4. According to Gillborn and Youdell, the relatively low attainment of Black Caribbean heritage students in England is due to institutional racism.
5. Some teachers have tended to see Black Caribbean heritage boys in Britain as less able and more disruptive than White boys. This view is seen as racist.
6. Black Caribbean heritage girls reject the low expectations that some teachers have of their potential. Many are ambitious and hard-working.
7. Shain found that teachers see Gang Girls as troublemakers who challenge their stereotypes of passive Asian femininity.
8. Ability groups may discriminate in favour of White middle-class students and against those from working-class and minority ethnic backgrounds.

# Unit 5.6.2 Cultural explanations

The previous unit examined racism in schools and its implications for educational attainment. This unit has a different focus. It examines some of the factors outside the school that might help us to understand the educational attainments of different ethnic groups. It explores cultural explanations by looking at parental factors and the workings of cultural capital. What impact do parents' expectations have? How might access to cultural capital make a difference to the attainment of different ethnic groups?

## Parental factors

Steve Strand (2015) used a longitudinal study of 15 000 students in England to analyse the differences in attainment between various ethnic groups. He found that the attainment gap associated with social class was twice as large as the biggest ethnic gap and six times as large as the gender gap. However, he found that class, ethnicity and gender were not sufficient to explain differences in attainment. Other factors included parental attitudes and behaviour, which were 'significantly associated with attainment'. Parents' expectations that students would continue their education after age 16 were particularly important, as were providing a computer for their children and a private tutor. In general, ethnic minority parents were more likely than White British parents to have positive attitudes and behaviour towards education.

## Cultural capital

Bourdieu's idea of cultural capital may help to explain the educational attainment of some minority ethnic students. For example, people of Chinese and Indian heritage in Britain have the largest proportion of middle-class members and the highest attainment. Their high attainment may result from having the largest amount of cultural capital. But what about people of Bangladeshi and Pakistani heritage who are doing much better than their class position would suggest? In view of their relatively high proportion of low-income members, these groups should not, in theory, have the cultural capital to produce their level of attainment. Tariq Modood (2004) argues that many members of minority ethnic groups may have more cultural capital than would be expected from their current class position. This may be because their jobs after migrating to the UK were lower in pay and prestige than their previous jobs. This might be due to the time taken to find suitable jobs after arrival in the UK or to discrimination in the labour market.

A number of things may result from this, including:

1. a reservoir of cultural capital that derives from earlier occupations
2. a powerful desire on the part of migrants to improve their own position and their children's prospects
3. a high value placed on education as a means for doing this
4. this value being passed on to their children.

### Activity

*Sociologists are interested in how families use their cultural, social and financial resources to support their children's education.*

1. Which resources is the mother in the photograph drawing on to support her daughter's education? Explain your answer.
2. Evaluate the view that group interviews provide a valid account of parental support for their children's education.

## Themina Basit – British Asians and educational capital

Basit (2013) studied a group of 36 British Asian students of Indian and Pakistani heritage – Hindus, Sikhs and Muslims aged 15–16 years – and their parents and grandparents. The grandparents were working-class and some parents were also working-class while others were middle-class. The research was based on individual interviews and focus groups.

Whatever their ethnicity, religion, age or social class, 'It was strikingly clear that education was seen as capital that would transform the lives of the younger generation.' Parents and grandparents impressed on young people the importance of a good education and how it would lead to a well-paid job and a high standard of living. According to Basit, 'Migrants and their children always have aspirations of upward social mobility. This is a key attribute of peoples who leave their country of origin in search of a better life for themselves and their future generations.'

Students, both girls and boys, accepted the advice of their elders, as the following quotations indicate:

- 'I think it's good that they're encouraging me.'
- 'My parents are always telling me education is good.'
- 'My parents are working hard for us to do our best in the future and go to university.'

## Summary

1. Ethnic differences in educational attainment are influenced by parental expectations and attitudes.
2. They are also affected by the amount of cultural capital within the family.
3. Basit's research showed that British Asian families impressed the value of education on young people.
4. As migrants, they had high hopes for upward social mobility and a better life.

# Unit 5.6.3 Ethnicity, subcultures and attainment

This unit focuses on the relationship between ethnicity, subcultures and educational attainment. To some extent, an ethnic group has its own subculture – a set of distinctive norms and values. How do these subcultures influence their members' educational attainment? And do members of a subculture have other identities that might also influence their achievement? How easy is it to disentangle the influence of ethnicity, class and gender on attainment?

## British Chinese students' subculture

British Chinese students have the highest grades at GCSE, the highest grades of those entitled to free school meals and the highest percentage of students going to university. Louise Archer and Becky Francis (2007) conducted semi-structured interviews with 80 14- to 16-year-old British Chinese students, 30 Chinese parents and 30 teachers from schools in London, England that had Chinese students. Parents from all social classes placed a very high value on education, as did their children. Working-class parents with little formal education were 'passionately committed to providing their children with the opportunities they had lacked'. Both middle- and working-class parents saw university as 'a must'. All 80 students interviewed said they wanted to go to university.

Parents invested considerable time, energy and money in their children. They monitored their children's progress and often hired home tutors and arranged supplementary schooling. Education was a 'family project'. A family's standing in the community was partly related to the educational performance of their children. The children appreciated their parents' high expectations, encouragement and support. These findings applied to both middle- and working-class families. To some extent, the high value placed on education is due to Chinese subculture. In this respect, the high attainment of Chinese students may be partly the result of their subculture.

## Tony Sewell – Black masculinities and schooling

Sewell (2008) questions some accounts which suggest that Black underachievement is based on institutional racism in schools. In his view, 'The idea that teachers are directly or indirectly holding back Black students is questionable. More likely, it is to do with the inability or unwillingness of these students to break away from an anti-education peer group that loves the street rather than the classroom.' However, Sewell's (1997) conclusions discussed below are based on his earlier findings from an ethnographic study of Black Caribbean boys in an 11–16 boys' school in Britain (see Unit 5.6.1). He emphasises the complex interplay between factors such as teacher racism, student subcultures and negative peer group pressure within the school.

### Black masculinities in school

Sewell (1997) identified four main groups of Black students in the school he studied which reflect different versions of black masculinity:

**Conformists,** the largest group, made up 41 per cent of the sample. They saw education as the route to success and conformed to the norms and values of the school.

**Innovators** (35 per cent) also saw education as important but rejected the process of schooling and the demands they saw it as making on their identity and behaviour. Although anti-school, they attempted to keep out of trouble.

**Retreatists** (6 per cent) were loners and kept themselves to themselves. Many had special educational needs.

**Rebels** (18 per cent) rejected both the norms and values of the school and the importance of education. Many saw educational qualifications as worthless, as racism would disqualify them from high-status, well-paid jobs. The rebels reacted aggressively to what they saw as racism in school. They were confrontational and challenging, adopting a macho masculinity and demanding respect.

### Evaluation

Critics argue that Sewell blames Black Caribbean males for their underachievement. They suggest that, in the process, Sewell has diverted attention from what they regard as the real cause of Black underachievement – a racist society, a racist education system and economic deprivation.

Supporters of Sewell reject this criticism. They argue that he is attempting to describe and explain rather than to allocate blame. In addition, his research rejects the stereotype of the young aggressive Black male personified by the Rebels by showing that they formed only a relatively small minority (18 per cent) of the Black Caribbean boys in the school he studied.

### Activity

1. Which of the four groups does this boy appear to fit into?
2. Explain one way in which Sewell's explanation takes account of both ethnicity and gender.
3. Evaluate the view that racism in schools is the most significant influence on minority ethnic students' educational attainment.

### Summary

1. Ethnic differences in educational attainment are affected by ethnic group subcultures.
2. Archer and Francis argue that the high attainment of many British Chinese students may be partly due to the high value placed on education in their subculture.
3. According to Sewell, the relatively low attainment of some Black Caribbean heritage males is mainly due to subcultural influences and their perceptions and performance of their masculinity.
4. Critics argue that Sewell overlooked the real causes of underachievement, including racism in society and within education, and economic deprivation.

# END-OF-PART QUESTIONS

| 0 | 1 | Describe two examples of how racism in schools may affect educational achievement. **[4 marks]**

| 0 | 2 | Explain two limitations of focusing on material factors to explain the educational attainment of students from different ethnic groups. **[6 marks]**

| 0 | 3 | 'Education provides equality of opportunity to all students, regardless of their ethnicity.' Using sociological material, give one argument against this view. **[6 marks]**

# PART 7 GENDER AND EDUCATIONAL ATTAINMENT

## Contents


| | | |
|---|---|---|
| Unit 5.7.1 | Gender socialisation and educational attainment | 307 |
| Unit 5.7.2 | Social changes and gendered achievement | 310 |
| Unit 5.7.3 | Gender and subcultures | 315 |
| Unit 5.7.4 | Teacher expectations and gendered classroom behaviour | 320 |


Across cultures and continents, from the USA to Japan, from Mexico to New Zealand, from Portugal to South Korea, girls and young women outperform their male counterparts at every level of the education system. This dramatic change has happened during the last 30 years.

In the 1970s the focus of research was on girls' 'underachievement'. Since the 1990s, 'underachieving boys' have been the focus of research on gender in education. It is important to place the 'gender effect' in perspective. Class and ethnicity have more effect on educational achievement than gender. But, as the following units show, the effect of gender on educational attainment is still significant.

This part begins by looking at the impact of gender socialisation on attainment. How does this process, both inside and outside school, affect girls' and boys' achievements? It moves on to examine some of the social and economic changes that help to explain the rapid improvement in girls' educational attainment from the 1990s onwards. What impact has feminism had on this? How important are labour market changes? Next, it explores the relationship between gender and subcultures. How significant are these? It then focuses on school-based factors and asks how far they explain the links between gender and education. Are teachers' gendered expectations significant? Do girls and boys behave differently in the classroom? If so, does this affect their educational attainment?

## Unit 5.7.1 Gender socialisation and educational attainment

In the 1970s and 1980s, the main focus of gender research in education in many countries was girls' 'underachievement'. In England and Wales, for example, this was particularly marked at A Level and degree level. This unit looks at explanations for this gender difference that focused on gender socialisation. In one respect, these explanations have become redundant, given that girls now outperform boys at every level of the education system. However, some of the explanations may still be relevant – they may point to factors which, even today, are preventing girls from reaching their full potential.

### Early gender socialisation

As Fiona Norman and her colleagues (1988) point out, before children start school, gender socialisation has already begun. From the types of play that girls and boys are encouraged to engage in and the types of toys they are given, different sets of aptitudes and attitudes may be developed. Tina Rampino (2015) links the toys that boys are encouraged to play with to the development of spatial skills which make them better at mathematics than girls.

The educational aspirations of girls may be influenced through playing with dolls and other toys that reinforce the stereotype of women as 'carers'. Boys tend to be encouraged to be more active than girls, and this may be reflected in their attitudes in classrooms. Furthermore, boys are more likely to be given toys that can help develop scientific and mathematical concepts. The media, through magazines, books, computer games, television and advertising, can further reinforce gender stereotypes.

One possible consequence of early gender stereotyping is that girls may at that time have attached less value to education than boys. Research conducted by Sue Sharpe (1976) into a group of mainly working-class girls in schools in London, England, during the early 1970s found that the girls had a set of priorities that were unlikely to encourage them to attach great importance to education. She found that their concerns were 'love, marriage, husbands, children, jobs, and careers, more or less in that order'. Sharpe argued that, if girls tended to see their future largely in terms of marriage rather than work, then they might have little incentive to try to achieve high educational standards.

In the 1990s, Sharpe repeated her research and found that girls' priorities had changed. Now jobs or careers were their chief concern for the future (Sharpe, 1994). This change may help to explain why the educational attainment of girls at school is now higher than that of boys.

## Contemporary issues: Gendered toys

Let Toys Be Toys is an UK-based organisation that campaigns to stop manufacturers and retailers from promoting some toys and books as only suitable for girls and others for boys. Their 2012 survey showed that 50 per cent of shops used signs for 'Boys' toys' and 'Girls' toys'. Their 2016 survey showed that these signs had 'pretty much disappeared'. However, their research gave a different picture for toy manufacturers, whose packaging, ads and catalogues were still based on stereotypes (Let Toys Be Toys, 2016).

Similar findings come from research by the Institution for Engineering and Technology. They found that, on toy retailers' websites, 31 per cent of toys with a science, technology, engineering and maths focus were listed for boys and only 11 per cent for girls.

### Questions

1. Assess the view that parents are responsible for gendered toys.
2. What effect might gendered toys have on gender subject choices at school and university?

## Gender socialisation in school

Many sociologists have claimed that there is bias against girls in the education system. Research by Glenys Lobban (1974) found evidence of gender bias in some educational reading schemes used in Britain. (See also Unit 5.3.2 on the gendered curriculum.) From a study of 179 stories in six reading schemes, Lobban found that only 35 stories had female heroes, while 71 had male heroes. Girls and women were almost exclusively portrayed in traditional domestic roles and it was nearly always men and boys who took the lead in non-domestic tasks. In at least three of the schemes, females took the lead in only three activities in which both genders were involved: hopping, shopping with parents, and skipping. Males took the lead in seven joint activities: exploring, climbing trees, building things, looking after pets, sailing boats, flying kites and washing cars.

Lobban's research was conducted in the 1970s, but more recent research has also found evidence of gender stereotyping in some of the educational materials used in many countries. For example, in his study of a Japanese English language textbook, Ian Clark (2016) found that, while females and males were represented in equal numbers, bias in the representation of gender roles was evident. Kazi MM Islam and M. Niaz Asadullah (2018) undertook a comparative study of gender stereotypes in secondary school textbooks from Malaysia, Indonesia, Pakistan and Bangladesh based on content analysis. They found some indications of stereotypes in all of the textbooks. For example, females were much more likely to be represented in domestic roles than males. However, the extent of stereotyping varied across the four countries. The textbooks from Pakistan and Bangladesh showed a less equal representation of females than the textbooks from the other two countries.

Research carried out in Australia, the USA and the UK also reveals differential gender representations in school textbooks. For example, Jackie F.K. Lee and Peter Collins (2010) found that only

42.5 per cent of the characters in a sample of 10 English language textbooks used in Australia were female. Furthermore, women and men were often represented in traditional gender stereotyped ways in terms of their occupations and domestic roles.

### Activity

*The cover of a children's book in the Ladybird Reading Scheme published in Britain in the 1960s.*

1. To what extent does the cover of this book reflect traditional gender stereotypes?
2. Identify one advantage and one disadvantage of using content analysis to investigate gender bias in textbooks.

## Gender, subject choice and socialisation

Despite significant changes in girls' educational attainment, there are still marked gender differences in subject choice, particularly at A Level (and the equivalent) and university level in many countries. Such differences may disadvantage women in the labour market in terms of job status and pay. The subjects they tend to choose may lead to lower-status and lower-paid occupations than those chosen by men.

Maria Charles et al. (2014) note that the representation of females in STEM fields varies over time and by place. For example, mathematics and technical degree programmes are less male dominated in many 'poorer' societies than in affluent societies which are often seen as more equal in gender terms. Furthermore, drawing on their analysis of cross-national data from 50 countries, Charles et al. argue that boys were more likely than girls to aspire to mathematically related jobs in all countries except Botswana, Malaysia and Indonesia. However, the gender gap in aspirations varied widely in size. For instance, the gap was only 1 percentage point in South Africa and Ghana, but 23 percentage points in the Netherlands.

A variety of reasons have been suggested for gender differences in subject choice, one of which is socialisation. In this view, gender differences in socialisation may reinforce stereotypes, affect gender identity and, in turn, subject choice. For example, boys tend to be given, and to play with, toys related to construction, which may influence their choice of engineering in later life. Another explanation focuses on teachers' gendered expectations (see Unit 5.7.4).

## Contemporary issues: The gender gap in education

*In 2015, Latvia had the highest share of female graduates among OECD countries.*

The Organisation for Economic Cooperation and Development (OECD) regularly collects wide-ranging data from its member countries, including data on education. OECD data show a reversal in the gender gap in education. Less than a century ago, girls were excluded from, or experienced discrimination within, education. In 2013, however, the majority (55 per cent) of students who graduated from a programme of general secondary education in OECD countries were female.

This trend also extends to higher education within OECD countries. Of the 6 million students who graduated with a bachelor's degree from an institution of higher education in 2013, a majority (58 per cent) were female. The gender gap is marked when the field of study is taken into account. For example, approximately 64 per cent of degrees in social sciences, humanities and education were awarded to women. By contrast, less than one-third (31 per cent) of bachelor's degrees in engineering and sciences were awarded to females.

The OECD argues that these gender differences in the proportion of bachelor's degrees awarded across fields of study reflect the different career expectations among 15-year-old female and male students, as recorded by the Programme for International Student Assessment (PISA), and the gendered career choices that people make later in life. These gender differences also account for a significant proportion of the gender pay gap (the gap in earnings from paid employment).

Source: http://www.oecd.org/gender/data/gender-gap-in-education.htm

## Questions

1. How might gender socialisation explain subject choice at university?
2. How might gender socialisation limit young people's life chances?

### Criticisms of socialisation theory

Critics argue that socialisation theories place too much emphasis on the way the social structure moulds people. These theories tend to see children as passively receiving messages about gender through the socialisation process. However, they do not explore human agency and the way that people resist the gendered expectations and roles passed on through families and the education system.

## Summary

1. Some explanations for girls' underachievement in the 1970s and 1980s focused on early gender socialisation at home – for example, girls' and boys' toys.
2. Another possible explanation is socialisation at school – for example, gender stereotypes in reading schemes and textbooks.
3. There are still important differences in subject choice. One explanation for this gender gap focuses on differences in primary socialisation processes and secondary socialisation within schools.
4. Critics of socialisation theory argue that it underestimates individual agency and resistance.

# Unit 5.7.2 Social changes and gendered achievement

Over the past 30 years, the improvement in the educational attainment of girls and young women in many countries has been dramatic and unprecedented. Yet relatively little has been written to explain it. Instead, the focus has been on the so-called 'underachievement' of boys. According to feminist sociologists Francis and Christine Skelton (2005), 'this reveals the marginalisation of girls, how their school performance is seen as peripheral to that of boys, how they do not count'. This unit looks at some of the explanations for the changes in gendered educational achievement that focus on wider social changes. It is important to bear in mind, however, that some groups of girls underachieve today. For instance, there are high-achieving, middle-class boys who tend to perform better in examinations than working-class girls. This example highlights the significance of taking both gender and social class into account.

## Changing expectations and attitudes

As noted earlier, Sharpe's (1976) study of working-class schoolgirls in the early 1970s showed that their main priorities for the future were 'love, marriage, husbands and children'. When she repeated this study in the 1990s, she found significant changes. Now, the girls' main concerns were 'job, career and being able to support themselves' (Sharpe, 1994). They were more confident, assertive and ambitious. They saw education as the main route to a good job and financial independence.

In the 1970s, over 80 per cent of girls wanted to get married; by the 1990s, this had dropped to 45 per cent. The girls were increasingly wary of marriage. With the rapidly rising divorce rate in Britain throughout the 1980s and 1990s, they had seen adult relationships breaking up around them. They had also seen women who were financially independent rather than depending on financial support from a man. Paid employment and financial independence were now major concerns.

Although many of the girls in the 1990s expected to work in 'women's jobs' such as primary school teaching, nursing, beautician work and clerical work, they were more likely than girls in the 1970s to consider 'men's jobs' such as car mechanics and firefighters, and to look forward to professional careers in medicine or law. Given their hopes and concerns, educational success was more important to the 1990s girls than their 1970s counterparts.

The changing expectations and attitudes of girls were reflected both by their parents and by their schools. A number of studies, particularly those of girls from middle-class families, indicate that parents increasingly expect exam success, and in some cases make their daughters feel that they could 'never be good enough' (Francis and Skelton, 2005).

### Activity

To what extent have girls' expectations and attitudes towards education, paid employment and financial independence in your society changed over the last 20 years? Are girls coming under increasing pressure from teachers and family members to succeed in examinations and progress to university? Are they under more pressure to succeed than boys? Explain your reasoning.

## The women's movement and feminism

In societies across the globe, many of the rights that feminists and the women's movement fought for in the 1960s and 1970s have now been translated into law. The ideals on which those rights are based have been increasingly taken for granted. Although today's young women may not see themselves as feminists, they often expect equal opportunity in education and in the labour market. According to Eirene Mitsos and Ken Browne (1998), the women's movement has provided both incentives and direction for young women in education. In their view, the 'women's movement and feminism have achieved considerable success in improving the rights and raising the expectations and self-esteem of women'.

## Changes in the labour market

Over the last 50 years, many countries have experienced significant changes in the labour market, such as a decline in heavy industry (for example, mining and shipbuilding), a growth in service sector work (such as care work, call centre and office work) or an increase in the employment of 'flexible' part-time workers and workers on fixed-term contracts. Such changes have expanded employment opportunities for women.

This growth in employment opportunities, along with the rise in young women's occupational ambitions, has increased their incentives to gain educational qualifications. Studies of both primary and secondary school students show that many girls are now looking forward to jobs that require degree-level qualifications (Francis and Skelton, 2005).

### Contemporary issues: Barriers to girls' education in North-West Pakistan

*A teacher and her female students in North-West Pakistan.*

Although the position of women in many countries has changed significantly over the last few decades and barriers to girls' education have been removed, such changes have not necessarily occurred in all societies. Aamir Jamal (2016) undertook research on the perceptions of men from the Pashtun region in North-West Pakistan on the education of girls aged 7–15 years. Jamal's research identified several key barriers to girls' education in this region including household poverty and the costs of education. In his words, 'In a situation where it is hard for parents to feed and clothe their children, education becomes a low priority, especially for girls as they are expected to marry early and thus will not contribute income to the household.'

In some areas, schools were not accessible because of their location. The lack of female teachers meant that some parents would not allow their daughters to attend school. The curriculum was seen as irrelevant to the needs and priorities of the community in which the girls lived and sometimes this led people to resist the education of girls.

Gender discrimination in the Pashtunwali (the tribal codes that set out the cultural and social traditions that define the Pashtun population's identity) was highlighted by some of the research participants. However, many pointed out that some geographical areas, such as urban areas, were more accepting of social changes and less inclined to support gender discrimination.

Another issue was that particular interpretations of Islam – via practices such as the veiling of women, early marriage and defining women's responsibilities in terms of the home – could restrict girls' access to education.

### Questions

1. List the barriers to girls' education that this study identified.
2. Jamal is from the area in which this research was carried out. How might his 'insider' status have impacted on his research?

## Individualisation and the risk society

Ulrich Beck (1992) argued that the West is moving from modernity into a new phase of modernity, which he calls the **second modernity**. His views have been used to help explain the dramatic change in women's educational achievements.

According to Beck, today's society is characterised by risk and uncertainty and by a process of **individualisation**. For example, with the rising divorce rate in many countries, marriage is increasingly associated with risk and uncertainty. Employment is becoming more unstable. There are fewer 'jobs for life'; people are changing jobs more often, retraining, improving and/or learning new skills. As a result, the job market and career paths become less predictable.

A process of individualisation accompanies risk and uncertainty. People are increasingly thrown back on themselves as individuals. They are more and more responsible for their own fate, their own security and their own future. People are becoming more self-sufficient and self-reliant. Beck sees women as at the forefront of the individualised self – they are 'setting the pace for change'. He argues that this is due to changes in women's family life, education, occupations and the laws on gender equality.

In this increasingly insecure, individualised society, individuals must equip themselves for self-reliance and self-sufficiency. Financial independence is seen as one of the main ways of doing this, and education is regarded as one of the main routes to well-paid jobs that can provide financial independence.

However, education is not simply a means to financial security. Sociologists who picture a second modernity generally agree that there is an increasing emphasis on the construction of self and the creation of identity. Studies of girls in primary and secondary schools illustrate this emphasis. According to Francis and Skelton (2005), 'The majority appear to see their chosen career as reflecting their identity, as a vehicle for future fulfilment, rather than as simply a stopgap before marriage.'

### Activity

*For women, living in the second modernity might involve being financially independent, buying their own place to live, getting promoted at work, developing new work-related skills and completing a postgraduate degree.*

1. In what ways does this photograph and caption indicate individualisation and self-reliance?
2. How does individualisation impact on females?

## The educational achievements of boys

In the 1970s and 1980s, concern about the 'gender effect' focused on girls' 'underachievement'. By the 1990s, this concern was reversed. Now boys were 'underachieving'. But was this necessarily the case?

In general, the educational attainment of boys and young men has steadily improved over the past 50 years. This does not indicate underachievement. However, certain boys are underachieving – a higher proportion of working-class boys are doing badly compared with other social groups. But the same can be said for working-class girls. In the UK, for example, White working-class boys from low-income families who receive free school meals are the lowest-performing group in terms of ethnicity, class and gender.

What has changed is the overall rate of improvement for boys and girls. Girls' educational performance over the last 30 years has improved at a faster rate than boys', resulting in a significant widening of the gender gap. This applies to boys and girls from all social classes. Whether this should be seen as 'boys' underachievement' is a matter of opinion. Some commentators suggest that this concern had reached the level of a '**moral panic**' among the press and politicians in nations such as Britain (Francis and Skelton, 2005) and the US.

There have been many attempts to explain boys' failure to keep pace with girls. They are based on the assumption that boys are underachieving and that something should be done to raise their educational attainment. Some of these will now be examined.

## Constructions of masculinity

The school is a major setting for the construction of masculinity. Recent research argues that the form of masculinity constructed in the classroom contributes to the underachievement of male students. Earlier research had made a similar argument with reference to the anti-school subculture developed by some working-class boys, particularly those placed in lower-ability groups. However, studies now indicate that 'laddish' behaviours have spread to most boys – both working-class and middle-class – and to some extent to girls (Jackson, 2006).

Carolyn Jackson (2006) examined 'laddish behaviour' among 13- to 14-year-old boys and girls. Her research was based on interviews with 203 students in eight English schools and questionnaire data from 800 students in six schools.

Laddish behaviour is based on the idea that it is 'uncool' to work and that appearing 'cool' is necessary to be popular. This aspect of laddishness was accepted by the vast majority of boys and girls, whatever their social class background.

Boys' laddish behaviour was constructed within a framework of **hegemonic masculinity** – the dominant and pervasive view of masculinity. It was based on heterosexuality, toughness and competitiveness. It was expressed in acting 'hard', being one of the lads, disrupting lessons, having a laugh and being demanding and assertive. Academic work was defined as effeminate and uncool.

Students are faced with a dilemma. They want to do well academically, yet they also want to appear cool and to be popular. But if they are seen to work hard, they are a 'geek', a 'nerd' or a 'swot' – terms of derision. The solution is to appear to reject schoolwork, do the requisite amount of messing around, but work secretly, usually at home. This favours middle-class boys who have home-based resources to do their homework quickly and efficiently – the space, privacy, a desk and a computer. They are better able to balance being popular and academically successful.

### Activity

*By working secretly at home, some boys might be successful academically without being seen as a 'nerd', a 'geek' or a 'swot'.*

1. Why might middle-class boys be better placed than working-class boys to do well academically and, at the same time, to be popular?
2. To what extent does 'laddish' behaviour occur at your school or in other local schools? Is being seen to work hard ever ridiculed?

If laddish behaviour is holding boys back, then its development should parallel the widening of the gender gap in attainment. Some researchers argue that this is the case. The following are some suggested explanations for the development of laddish behaviours. They point to changes in the wider society which have occurred at the same time as the widening gender gap in educational attainment.

**Pressure to succeed and fear of failure** A number of sociologists have seen competitive individualism and

## Activity

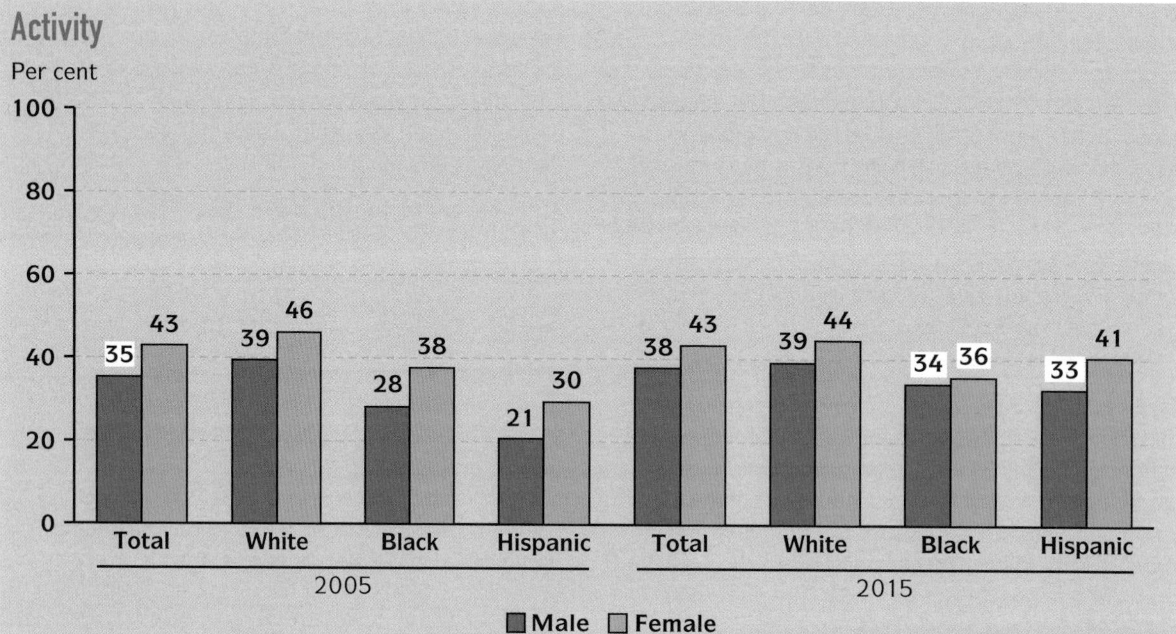


*Total college enrolment rates of 18- to 24-year-olds in degree-granting institutions in the USA, by ethnicity and gender: 2005 and 2015.*

Source: *Digest of Education Statistics, 52nd edition*, https://nces.ed.gov/pubs2017/2017094.pdf

1. What percentage of Hispanic females aged 18 to 24 years were enrolled in degree-granting institutions in the USA in 2005?
2. What percentage of Black males aged 18 to 24 years were enrolled in degree-granting institutions in the USA in 2015?
3. Did the total college enrolment rate for males increase or decrease between 2005 and 2015?
4. Among which groups did the total college enrolment rate remain the same between 2005 and 2015?
5. Among which groups did the total college enrolment rate increase by more than 10 percentage points between 2005 and 2015?

individual responsibility as major themes in today's society. This promotes fears of academic failure and directs responsibility for failure to the individual. Laddish behaviour can be seen as a response to this. The argument that it is uncool to work can be used as an excuse for poor academic performance.

The marketisation of schools has placed further pressure on students. Schools compete in the educational market, striving to raise standards and climb league tables. The importance of examination success is increasingly emphasised and students are under growing pressure to achieve high grades. Laddish behaviour can be seen as a defensive strategy to reduce the fear of poor academic performance or to excuse the reality of failure (Jackson, 2006).

**The crisis of masculinity** Some sociologists argue that boys and men are experiencing a **crisis of masculinity** in contemporary societies. This has been linked, in part, to changes in the labour market and the rapid decline in unskilled and semi-skilled manual jobs over the last 25 years. These 'macho' manual jobs reflected traditional male working-class identities. Their disappearance has left these identities uncertain and under threat. The new jobs in the service sector require what were traditionally seen as feminine skills and sensitivities.

Working-class boys may have responded to these threats to their traditional identities by turning to laddish behaviour in school to restore their sense of masculinity (Jackson, 2006). If working-class boys believe that males no longer have a clear-cut role in society, this could impact on their self-esteem and motivation at school.

**Educational aspirations and attitudes** Research by Rampino and Mark Taylor (2013, 2015) based on self-completion questionnaires given to 13- to15-year-olds in Britain produced the following findings. Girls were more likely than boys to see education in a positive light, to want to continue in school after age 16 and go on to university. These gender differences remained, whatever their parents' income and education.

Boys' educational aspirations and attitudes tended to become less positive from the ages of 12 and 13, whereas those of girls stayed the same or improved as they grew older. Unlike boys, girls were more aware of economic downturns when it was harder to get a job. They were more likely to see education as important for employment.

**Conclusion** Boys' 'underachievement' has become a major concern. Large amounts of time and money were spent on a range of government initiatives aimed at raising boys' educational attainment. Some critics, however, argue that the whole question of equality of educational opportunity has been reduced to gender and focused on boys. This has diverted attention from class, ethnicity and girls (Francis and Skelton, 2005). According to Ball (2013), 'To a great extent the problem of boys' underachievement is a working-class one, and one for those from some minority ethnic groups, but this is often lost sight of in both the media and policy initiatives.'

## Key terms

**Second modernity** A new phase of modernity characterised by risk, uncertainty and individualisation.

**Individualisation** An emphasis on the individual, on self-construction, self-reliance and self-sufficiency.

**Moral panic** A widespread panic that something is morally wrong.

**Hegemonic masculinity** The dominant and pervasive view of masculinity.

**Crisis of masculinity** The idea that males see their traditional masculine identity as under threat today.

## Summary

1. The following reasons have been given for the recent changes in the relationship between gender and educational attainment:
   - Changing expectations and attitudes. Girls' main concerns have become more focused on jobs and financial independence rather than on marriage and motherhood.
   - The women's movement and feminism have raised women's expectations and self-esteem.
   - Changes in the labour market have created more job opportunities for women, but also, according to some accounts, a crisis of masculinity, particularly among working-class males.
2. Changes in society linked to individualisation, risk and uncertainty have led to an emphasis on self-reliance and self-sufficiency among females.
3. The concern about boys' supposed 'underachievement' became a moral panic.
4. The spread of 'laddish behaviour' as an expression of masculinity, has been seen as a major reason for boys' 'underachievement'.
5. The following reasons have been suggested for the spread of laddish behaviour:
   - as a defensive strategy resulting from pressure to succeed and fear of failure
   - changes in the labour market threatening traditional male, working-class identities.
6. Boys are less likely than girls to see education in a positive light.

# Unit 5.7.3 Gender and subcultures

Examples of subcultures based on gender, class and/or ethnicity have already been discussed in this chapter (see, for example, Willis, Unit 5.1.2). This unit looks at studies that focus on gender and other aspects of identity. It begins with a summary of a contemporary study of working-class masculinities and education. It then examines a study of British Muslim boys of Pakistani and Bangladeshi heritage. It examines their gender and religious identities, the value they place on education as a means of getting a well-paid job, and their positive view of their family as a source of love and security. The unit finally looks at examples of studies of female subcultures, including the educational identities of middle-class Rebel Girls and Asian heritage Gang Girls.

## From labouring to learning

Ward (2015) examines a group of young working-class men in a de-industrialised community in South Wales (see Unit 5.1.2). This study provides evidence to suggest that de-industrialisation and the decline of traditional manual jobs has led working-class boys to place a higher value on education and to progress to further and sometimes higher education.

Like most young people in the UK today, they continued their education after 16 in order to gain qualifications and because there were few other options open to them. Manual jobs in the local area had all but gone – in particular, the coal mines had closed down. This challenged the traditional working-class culture of masculinity – the emphasis on physical labour, toughness and having a laugh. Unlike the lads in Willis' research, they had no available manual jobs in which to express this form of masculinity.

Ward identified two main groups in his study – the Boiz (who were in some respects similar to Willis' 'lads') and the Geeks.

**The Boiz** At school and in further education, the Boiz continued to enact the more traditional form of working-class masculinity. They tended to take 'male' subjects such as physical education, motor vehicle studies and A Levels in maths, science, electronics and business studies. In class they were boisterous, disruptive, joking and having a laugh. Despite this behaviour, four members of the Boiz (one-third of the group) went on to university.

In their leisure, the Boiz followed traditional activities of young, working-class men – for example, sports such as rugby and football, and fast cars. They looked down on the Geeks, as they called them. They saw the Geeks as effeminate and socially inadequate, and bullied and teased them.

**The Geeks** Compared to the Boiz, the Geeks were studious, quiet and well-behaved. They followed school rules and wore school uniform. They were determined to achieve, got high grades and nearly all went to university. They took a mixture of A Levels – maths, science, English, history and media studies.

Outside school, the Geeks read books and comics, wrote poetry and played computer games. At times, they followed traditional working-class leisure pursuits. However, they looked forward to escaping from their working-class community and taking up middle-class occupations.

**Continuity and change** The two groups adapted to de-industrialisation in different ways. The Boiz continued with traditional working-class masculinity in terms of their identities and behaviour, apart from recognising the need to continue to further education and, for a third of them, to go to university.

The Geeks made greater changes. Their masculinity was now based on educational success and a desire for a new way of life outside the working-class community in which they were raised.

### Activity

Ward spent two and a half years following the educational and social lives of 32 young men. His research was based on participant observation, semi-structured and unstructured interviews, and conversations with individuals and groups.

1. Evaluate the usefulness of participant observation to investigate the educational and social lives of young men.
2. Identify one similarity in the research approach adopted by Ward and Willis.
3. Explain one difference between the findings of Ward and Willis.

### Evaluation of Ward's study

This study moves away from the so-called 'crisis of masculinity'. It suggests that, at least to some extent, traditional working-class masculinity can co-exist with educational success. In this respect, the 'lads' and 'ear 'oles' of Willis' 1970s study have adapted fairly well to become the 'Boiz' and the 'Geeks' of the 2010s.

### Activity: Data from Máirtín Mac an Ghaill's research into the Macho Lads

*Darren:* It's the teachers that make the rules. It's them that decide that it's either them or us. So you are often put into a situation with teachers where you have to defend yourself. Sometimes it's direct in the classroom. But it's mainly the head cases that would hit a teacher. Most of the time it's all the little things.

*Gilroy:* Acting tough by truanting, coming late to lessons, not doing homework, acting cool by not answering teachers, pretending you didn't hear them; that gets them mad. Lots of different things.

*Noel:* Teachers are always suspicious of us. Just like the cops, trying to set you up.

Source: adapted from Mac an Ghaill, 2004.

1. How does the boys' behaviour indicate an anti-school subculture?
2. Suggest intersected factors which might explain the boys' behaviour.

## Louise Archer – Muslim boys and education

In *Race, Masculinity and Schooling: Muslim Boys and Education* (2003), Archer examined how British Muslim boys saw themselves, their schooling and their future. Her sample consisted of 31 Muslim boys aged 14–15 and her data came from discussion groups led by three interviewers/discussion leaders – two British women of Pakistani heritage and Archer herself, a White British middle-class woman. The boys were mainly of Pakistani and Bangladeshi heritage. Archer's main aim was to see how the boys 'constructed and negotiated their masculine identities'.

### Muslim and Black identities

In the discussion groups, all the boys identified themselves first and foremost as Muslim. They were proud of belonging to a local and global Muslim brotherhood. They saw this as a strong masculine identity as opposed to the traditional stereotype of a 'weak', 'passive' Asian masculinity.

Although most of the boys were born in England, they did not feel they belonged in England, nor in the countries of origin of their parents or grandparents – mainly Pakistan and Bangladesh. Although they saw themselves as Muslim, many were not particularly religious in terms of their behaviour – for example, most did not attend the mosque on Friday.

When constructing their identities, the boys drew partly on Black Caribbean and African-American styles of masculinity. They sometimes referred to themselves as 'Black' in comparison to the 'White' majority. However, the boys' Black identity was ambiguous – Black 'gangsta' forms of masculinity were drawn on, rather than forming the basis for their identities.

### Gendered identities

The boys' gender identity as male was constructed in relation to girls. They were aware of boys' supposed 'underachievement' and girls' superior exam performance and they complained that teachers unfairly favoured girls. They responded to this with laddish remarks, seeing 'messing around' and 'having a laugh' as typical of a desirable macho masculinity. This response probably reflected their class position as well as their gender – most of the boys came from working-class families.

The boys saw part of their gender identity as deriving from their Asian Muslim subculture. Men are the breadwinners – they have freedom and autonomy, power and control. Women are primarily concerned with domestic matters as housewives and mothers – as such, they are subservient. It is a man's duty to make sure that women's behaviour is appropriate – for example, that their appearance and clothing are respectable. The boys admitted that in certain respects gender roles were unfair but believed that this was part of their religious/cultural tradition and therefore they should abide by it.

However, the boys recognised that the gender relations outlined above were not reflected in their everyday experiences. Muslim girls often refused to do as they were expected – from the boys' point of view, they were often 'out of control'.

### Education and the breadwinner identity

The boys saw themselves as future breadwinners and viewed education as a means towards successfully performing this role. They held a strong belief in the value of education for 'getting ahead' and obtaining a well-paid job. Most of the boys expressed an interest in continuing their education beyond GCSE and were encouraged by their parents to do so.

Despite this view of education, some of the boys felt that the value of qualifications was reduced by racism. They believed that this made it more difficult for them to translate qualifications into appropriate occupations. Because of this, some saw falling back on family businesses (for example, restaurants). which did not require qualifications, as an alternative route.

The boys described their family lives in 'overwhelmingly positive terms' – home was a source of warmth, love and security. They saw adult Muslim masculinity as involving a breadwinner providing for his family, caring for his parents in their old age, and supporting relatives locally and 'back home' in Bangladesh or Pakistan. Successfully performing this role was a 'source of pride and a symbol of masculinity', and education was seen as a means to this end.

### Evaluation

This is an important study because it illustrates that identities are changeable and complex – they derive from different sources, they change according to the social context and they are always in the process of construction and reconstruction. For example, the boys 'shifted across and between' Muslim, Black, Asian, Bangladeshi/Pakistani, English and British identities, selecting one or more depending on the situation, context or topic of conversation. Additionally, the boys' gender, ethnicity, religion, class and experiences of family life influenced their identity. Their attitudes towards and experience of education must be seen in terms of this complex and changing social context.

Archer's insistence on the importance of social context may indicate a weakness in her research method. The data came from small discussion groups led by two British Pakistani women and one middle-class White British woman. Each boy had an audience, consisting of other boys in the group and one of these women. Each boy's projection of particular identities will reflect his perception of the audience. Archer recognises this. However, it may place limitations on her data – for example, what would the boys say in the presence of their father, mother, sister, brother, male friends, female friends and so on? Wider sources of data drawn from different contexts would provide a fuller picture.

## Female school subcultures

Although many of the earlier studies of student subcultures focused on boys and saw girls as peripheral, more recent studies have explored subcultural formation among females.

### Activity

*A White-British woman leading a discussion with 14- to15-year-old Pakistani and Bangladeshi heritage boys.*

1. How might the gender and ethnicity of the researcher influence the responses of the students?
2. With reference to this study, explain what is meant by the term 'intersectionality'.

### Rebel girls

Alexandra Allan (2010) conducted a two-year study of 25 middle-class, 11- to12-year-old girls in a single-sex, high-achieving school in the UK. Some of the girls were seen by teachers as 'underachievers'. They were seen by many of the other girls as 'rebels', 'bad girls' and 'misbehavers'. The rebels played practical jokes and were known for their humour and their view that it was uncool to work.

The rebels saw themselves as different. Although they were middle-class, they regarded themselves as 'common', as 'lacking the right know-how to compete'. They defined most of the other girls as 'posh' – wealthy, overly confident, haughty and 'stuck up'. In the words of one rebel, 'They have been to private schools which means they are taught better because you pay for the privilege. You can tell they are different because they are just so confident.'

The rebels downplayed the importance of academic achievement and were not impressed with those who achieved – 'they are not really that clever, their parents had used their money to make them clever'. This view can be seen as a defence mechanism, as 'self-worth protection by those defined as underachievers'.

However, despite all this, the rebels achieved well on a national scale, but not in a high-achieving school.

Yet they saw themselves as 'common', as below most of the girls in social class terms and as lacking in cultural and economic capital.

### British Asian girls

Shain (2010) studied 44 Asian girls, aged 13–16, mostly from Pakistani backgrounds. The girls attended eight schools in economically deprived areas of England. Shain identifies four main groups:

1. **The Gang Girls** opposed the culture of their school, which they saw as White and racist. This led to an emphasis on Asian subculture and a withdrawal from the other students (see Unit 5.6.1).
2. **The Survivors** conformed to the values of their school in order to achieve academic success despite their experience of racism and sexism.
3. **The Rebels**, so-called by the teachers, were critical of what they saw as unequal gender relations in their home community and of the subculture of the Gang Girls.
4. **The Faith Girls** gave priority to religion but were well integrated with other ethnic groups and followed a survival strategy in order to achieve academic success.

**The Gang Girls** Shain (2010) explores the subculture of the Gang Girls. She argues that setting by ability is 'a critical factor in friendship patterns which were central to the girls' academic and social experiences throughout schooling'. The Gang Girls were defined by the teachers as 'underachievers' and placed in lower sets.

Like most Asian girls, they experienced racist abuse. They fought back, insulting those who insulted them. They responded to racist abuse and relegation to lower sets by forming an all-Asian female subculture. They wore traditional dress, which they 'fiercely defended' as a 'visible marker of Asian identities'. They rejected what they saw as the White, racist culture of the school and excluded from their group Asian students who appeared to mix in friendship with White students.

Teachers saw the Gang Girls as troublemakers. Confined to lower sets and regarded as failures, the Gang Girls 'gradually withdrew from learning'.

## Conclusion

This and previous units have looked at some of the many examples of students' gendered subcultures. The idea of intersectionality is a useful approach to understanding how students' subcultures and identities are formed by several interconnected factors. These factors include gender, ethnicity and class, the pressure to succeed and the fear of failure, ability grouping and the changing labour market.

## Activity

1. Make brief notes on the relationship between student subcultures and educational attainment.
2. Evaluate the usefulness of the concept of intersectionality to an understanding of student subcultures.
3. Reid (1996) argues that 'education is both the cause of inequality and the reflection of inequality'. Explain this view.

## Summary

1. The boys in Archer's study saw themselves first and foremost as Muslims.
2. In terms of their gender identity, they felt males should have power over women. They saw themselves as future breadwinners taking pride in caring for their family and parents.
3. They had a strong belief in the value of education and hoped to continue beyond their GCSEs. However, some felt that racism might reduce their chances in the job market.
4. The data came from discussion groups led by two British Pakistani women and one middle-class White British woman. Their gender and ethnicity might influence the results.
5. With the absence of manual jobs, the Boiz had little alternative but to continue their education after 16. Ward argues that the traditional working-class culture of masculinity does not necessarily prevent educational achievement.
6. The middle-class rebel girls were seen as underachievers and downplayed the importance of education to protect their self-worth.
7. The Asian Gang Girls rejected the culture of their school, which they saw as White and racist.
8. Many factors intersect to make up students' identities and school subcultures, including gender, ethnicity, class, ability groups and the changing labour market.

# Unit 5.7.4 Teacher expectations and gendered classroom behaviour

Previous units have examined the processes of labelling and the self-fulfilling prophecy in classrooms. We have also seen that teachers' expectations of behaviour and attainment might differ depending on students' gender, ethnicity and class. This unit looks at teachers' gendered expectations in more detail.

## Teachers' gendered expectations

Teachers' perceptions of students are often based on gender. For example, what is acceptable behaviour for one gender may not be regarded as acceptable for another. Diane Reay (2001), in her study of 7-year-olds in an English primary school, noted that teachers in the staffroom sometimes referred to girls who misbehaved as 'scheming little madams'. Their behaviour was seen as inappropriate for girls. However, boys who behaved in a similar way were simply seen as 'mucking about'. Girls who misbehaved were sometimes seen as having a problem, but, in the case of boys, misbehaviour was usually dismissed as 'high spirits'.

**Perceptions of ability** A number of studies have indicated that teachers tend to see boys as naturally talented but lazy. By contrast, girls' achievements are seen as a result of hard work rather than ability as such. This may help to explain why boys often overestimate their ability while girls underestimate theirs (Francis and Skelton, 2005).

**Attending to boys** Spender (1982) recorded lessons given by herself and other teachers. Boys received over 60 per cent of teachers' time – 62 per cent in her case, even though she tried to divide her time equally between boys and girls. Compared with boys, girls were 'invisible'. They tended to blend into the background, a strategy encouraged by the fact that boys often poked fun at girls' contributions to lessons. In addition, teachers usually allowed boys to get away with insulting comments to girls.

Michelle Stanworth's (1983) study of A Level students and teachers in a college of further education reflects this focus on boys (see next page). Stanworth found that teachers gave more time and attention to boys, were more likely to know boys' names, and expressed more concern and interest in them.

### Teacher expectations and subject choice

Research from the 1980s indicated that teachers and careers officers tended to steer girls and boys towards gender-stereotypical subject choices. However, later research suggested that these directives were less apparent (Francis and Skelton, 2005).

## Behaviour in the classroom

The active and dominant males in reading schemes (see Unit 5.7.1) may be reflected in the behaviour of boys and girls in the classroom. From their own classroom observations and their analysis of other studies, Barbara G. Licht and Carol S. Dweck (1987) argue that girls lacked confidence in their ability to carry out intellectual tasks successfully. Despite the superior performance of young girls compared to boys in primary schools, it was the girls who generally expected to encounter most difficulty when learning new things.

According to Licht and Dweck, boys are able to shrug off failures by attributing them to a lack of effort on their part, or unfair assessment by teachers. Girls, on the other hand, constantly underestimate their ability, fail to attach significance to their successes, and lose confidence when they fail.

### Francis – gender in the classroom

In *Boys, Girls and Achievement*, Francis (2000) reviews studies on gender in the classroom and describes her own research in this area (see Unit 3.3.1). She says:

> ***Almost two decades on, research shows that girls' educational achievement has improved despite the continuing male dominance of the classroom, curriculum content (for example, history's focus on the lives of men) and greater demands on teacher time.*** **Francis, 2000**

Francis conducted her own research in three English secondary schools in 1998–99. The schools had different levels of overall achievement and were located in different areas, but all had a majority of working-class students. She observed four different classes of 14- to 16-year-olds in each school, visiting each class three times. In addition to classroom observations of English and maths lessons, she interviewed a sample of students.

Like earlier researchers, Francis found evidence that classrooms were gendered and that boys tended to dominate. She found that 'boys tend to monopolise space in the classroom and playground, and girls tend to draw less attention to themselves than do boys'. In 8 of the 12 classes, boys were considerably noisier than girls. A number of the teachers, though not all, treated male and female students differently.

There were a number of incidents where boys were disciplined more harshly or more frequently than girls. Francis notes that sometimes this might have reflected the greater noisiness of boys. Girls who were not paying attention tended to talk quietly rather than disrupt the classroom with more obvious, noisy behaviour.

Francis found evidence that girls were still getting less attention than boys and that schools remained largely male-dominated. However, in some classes there was little evidence that boys and girls were treated significantly differently. Furthermore, Francis did find that some things had changed. For example, students no longer took for granted the belief that girls were less academically able than boys.

## Activity

*Francis found that boys received more attention than girls in some English and maths classes.*

1. On what evidence did Francis base her view that classrooms were gendered spaces?
2. Why do you think these students no longer took for granted the belief that girls were less academically able than boys?
3. In your experience, to what extent do students, teachers or parents believe that one gender is more academically able than another?

### Michelle Stanworth – gender differences in further education

Stanworth (1983) examined A Level classes in a British further education college (which enrolled students aged 16 plus). She interviewed teachers and students from seven different classes in the humanities department. Her findings suggested that a number of the attitudes displayed by teachers would impede the educational progress of girls.

Teachers found it much more difficult to remember the girls in their classes. Without exception, all the students whom teachers said it was difficult to name and recall were girls. Quiet boys were remembered, but quiet girls seemed to blend into the background and made little impression on their teachers.

Stanworth found that teachers held stereotypical views of what their female students would be doing in the future. Only one girl was seen as having the potential to enter a professional occupation. Interestingly, she was the most assertive of the girls in the classroom but her academic performance was not particularly good. One teacher described the most academically successful girl as likely to become a 'personal assistant for someone rather important'. Even for this girl, marriage was suggested as one of the most significant aspects of her future life. Male teachers mentioned nothing other than marriage as the future for two-thirds of the female students.

When asked which students were given the most attention by teachers, the students themselves named boys two and a half times as often as girls, although girls outnumbered boys by nearly two to one in the classes studied. The students reported that boys were four times more likely to join in classroom discussions, twice as likely to seek help from the teacher, and twice as likely to be asked questions.

Furthermore, girls were consistently likely to underestimate their ability, while boys overestimated theirs. Students were asked to rank themselves in terms of ability in each class. In 19 of the 24 cases in which teachers and students disagreed about the ranking, all of the girls placed themselves lower than the teachers' estimates, and all but one boy placed themselves higher.

Stanworth claimed that classroom interaction disadvantaged girls. Teachers had an important role in this, but students themselves also 'played an active part in the regeneration of a gender hierarchy, in which boys are the indisputably dominant partners'.

Stanworth's work was based on interviews and not direct classroom observation. It therefore gives some indication of what teachers and students perceive to be happening in classrooms, but does not actually establish, for example, that teachers give more attention to boys (Randall, 1987). However, later research supports the claim that boys tend to dominate classrooms.

## Activity

Once you have revised Section B of this chapter, make notes on:

1. the relationship between school-based factors and educational attainment
2. the relationship between factors outside school and educational attainment.

## Summary

1. Teachers' perceptions of students were often based on gender.
2. Some teachers tended to see aspects of girls' behaviour as misbehaviour, while similar behaviour from boys was seen as 'high spirits'.
3. Research suggests that teachers may have different perceptions of girls' and boys' abilities.
4. Teachers often gave girls less time in lessons than boys.
5. Francis found evidence that classrooms were gendered and that boys tended to dominate.
6. Stanworth argued that classroom interaction disadvantaged girls.
7. Later research supports the claim that boys tend to dominate classrooms.

# END-OF-PART QUESTIONS

**0 1** Describe two examples of how gender socialisation may affect educational achievement. **[4 marks]**

**0 2** Explain two limitations of focusing on in-school factors to explain the educational attainment of girls and boys. **[6 marks]**

**0 3** 'Education provides equality of opportunity to girls and boys.' Using sociological material, give one argument against this view. **[6 marks]**

# EXAM-STYLE PRACTICE QUESTIONS

**0 1** Describe two examples of student subcultures. **[4 marks]**

**0 2** Explain two ways in which education may contribute to social solidarity. **[8 marks]**

**0 3** 'Educational systems in modern industrial societies are meritocratic.'

Using sociological material, give two arguments against this view. **[12 marks]**

**0 4** Evaluate the view that intelligence is the most important factor determining how well a child performs at school. **[26 marks]**

# 6 THE MEDIA

## Chapter contents


| | | |
|---|---|---|
| **Section A** | **Ownership and control of the media** | **325** |
| **Section B** | **Media representation and effects** | **365** |
| **Exam-style practice questions** | | **391** |


Our knowledge of the world beyond our immediate circle of relatives, friends and acquaintances is dependent on the mass media. The term 'mass media' refers to means of communicating messages (media) to large, geographically dispersed audiences (mass). For the sake of brevity, the word 'mass' is often omitted and people talk simply about 'the media'.

The media is made up of two main categories. The 'traditional media' consists of print media such as newspapers, magazines, comics and, indeed, the book you are currently reading, and audio-visual media such as radio, television and film. The second category, which has only emerged in recent decades and is therefore termed the 'new media', consists of digital media which rely on the internet for the distribution of messages via desktop computers and mobile devices such as laptops, tablets and mobile phones.

An increasingly important subset of the new media consists of what is known as 'social media': digital platforms which bring people together for the exchange of a wide variety of information. These include Facebook, YouTube, Twitter, Snapchat, Instagram, WhatsApp and so on. According to *statista,* in the third quarter of 2017 Facebook, for example, had over 2 billion active monthly users, more than a quarter of the world's population!

Sociologists are interested in a wide range of issues connected to the media and how they work, both globally and in particular societies. In broad terms these can be divided into two sets. The first, addressed in Section A of this chapter, has to do with the crucial issue of power and therefore asks questions about the ownership and control of the media. Where does control of the media lie in different types of society? Where the media are owned by private corporations, do they have control or do they have to defer to audiences? Is the growth of digital technology giving more power to ordinary citizens compared to governments and corporations? And what effect is the growth of the new media having on social relationships and social identity?

The second set of issues, addressed in Section B, has to do with how the media represent the world to their audiences and what effects these representations have on people's attitudes and behaviour. Can viewing violence on screen cause violence in real life, for example? Do the media simply reflect the world around them, acting like a mirror to society, or do they act more like a hall of mirrors in a funfair providing a distorted picture of reality? Do audiences simply accept the messages they read, see and hear or are they able to stand back a bit, and maybe even challenge them?

# SECTION A
# OWNERSHIP AND CONTROL OF THE MEDIA

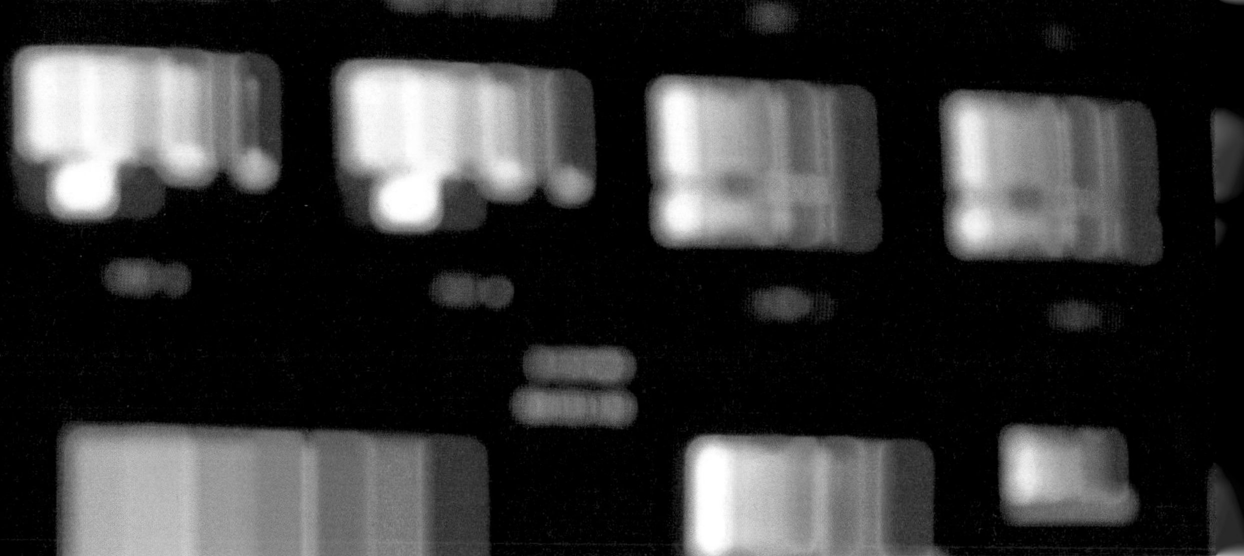

## Contents


| | | |
|---|---|---|
| **Part 1** | **The media in global perspective** | **326** |
| **Part 2** | **Theories of the media and influences on media content** | **336** |
| **Part 3** | **The impact of the new media** | **350** |


Two of the sets of key concepts that you were introduced to in the introductory chapter are particularly relevant in this section.

First, *power, control and resistance.* Potentially, the media would appear to have enormous *power* to shape our understanding of the wider world because we are otherwise not in a position to know what is happening beyond our immediate surroundings. This raises the question of who *controls* the media and therefore the information we are able to access. Are we able to gain an accurate and detailed knowledge of the world through the media or is the picture we gain partial, biased, maybe even deliberately slanted to benefit those who are in control? In addition, if the state or commercial media organisations use the media to serve their own vested interests, what tools do ordinary people have to *resist* such manipulation?

Second, *social change and development.* The mass media were an integral feature of the movement from traditional to modern industrial societies. The invention of the printing press, for example, revolutionised the ability to communicate the same message to large numbers of people. But what role do the mass media play in *social change* and *development* today? Could globalisation have occurred without the growth of the internet and the World Wide Web? Are the traditional media in decline as people increasingly look for information online? And are the new media, as some sociologists argue, bringing about a further stage of development leading to a 'postmodern' society?

Section A is divided into three parts. In Part 1, we seek to gain an overview of the different ways in which the media operate in different societies and look particularly at the relationship between the media and the state. We also examine current trends affecting the organisation of the media both nationally and globally.

In Part 2, we look at the operation of the media in those societies where the media have at least some independence from the state and at the competing theories that sociologists have developed to explain the relationship between ownership, control and media content. We also examine the postmodernist view of the media.

Finally, in Part 3, we focus on the new media and the various sociological debates that the growth of the new media has prompted. In particular, we explore the debate between those who see the new media as positive developments and those who emphasise their downside.

# PART 1 THE MEDIA IN GLOBAL PERSPECTIVE

## Contents


| | | |
|---|---|---|
| Unit 6.1.1 | The media: a global overview | 326 |
| Unit 6.1.2 | The media, the state and state censorship | 329 |
| Unit 6.1.3 | Global trends in media organisation and access | 332 |


Some of you will live in countries where you have relatively easy access to a wide variety of media outlets and different points of view – for example, to newspapers that display different political allegiances. Others will live in societies where there is much less diversity of viewpoints and where the state exercises considerable control over both the traditional media and access to new media. In Part 1, we try to identify broad patterns in the degree of media freedom in different countries and look particularly at the role of the state in relation to the media. This relationship, however, is not fixed: it can and does change – for example, in response to political changes in countries and to changes in media technology. We will, therefore, also seek to identify those trends currently affecting the organisation and control of the media globally.

## Unit 6.1.1 The media: a global overview

Across the globe there are enormous differences in the degree to which the media are able to function independently of the government. Freedom from government control is important, for example, if journalists are to be able to fulfil the function of 'talking truth to power': identifying corruption, incompetence, hypocrisy, oppression and so on in the government's dealings with its citizens.

### Activity

*A memorial to the murdered Maltese journalist Daphne Caruana Galizia, who had reported on corruption in local politics and was killed by a car bomb in October 2017.*

How free are journalists to report critically on political or religious authorities in the country where you live?

There are two main sources of information about the relative degree of media freedom existing in different countries globally and which cover most of the world's countries. These two sources are the World Press Freedom Index produced by Reporters Without Borders (a French organisation, *Reporters Sans Frontières,* or RSF) and the Freedom of the Press Report produced by Freedom House, based in the USA. Both are **non-governmental organisations** (NGOs), but as Freedom House receives some of its funding from the US government it could be argued that it is not as free of possible political pressure as RSF. Therefore we will use the latter's latest report (2017) to provide an overview.

### Activity

Why might it matter that Freedom House receives some of its funding from the US government?

## The World Press Freedom Index

The World Press Freedom Index covers 180 countries (over 90 per cent of the total) and is compiled from the responses of journalists, media lawyers, researchers and other media specialists in these countries to a questionnaire devised by RSF. This qualitative data is combined with quantitative data on abuses and acts of violence against journalists during the period in question.

The questionnaire measures six indicators of media freedom:

- *Pluralism*: the degree to which a variety of opinions are represented in the media.
- *Media independence:* the degree to which the media are able to function independently of sources of political, governmental, business and religious power and influence.
- *Environment and self-censorship*: the nature of the environment in which news and information providers operate (for example, freedom from harassment or intimidation).
- *Legislative framework*: the impact of the legal framework governing news and information activities.
- *Transparency*: how open the institutions and procedures that affect the production of news and information are.
- *Infrastructure*: the quality of the infrastructure that supports the production of news and information (for example, the availability of internet access and distribution facilities for print media).

Countries are awarded a score between 0 and 100 on the basis of these criteria (the higher the score, the lower the level of journalistic freedom). In 2017, the country judged to offer journalists the greatest degree of freedom, with a score of 7.60, was Norway; the least, with a score of 84.98, was North Korea. Table 6.1.1 provides a summary of the report's findings.

## Explaining the findings

Broadly speaking, the degree of media freedom relates to the nature of the political system operating in different countries. There are a number of ways in which political systems can be classified, but one widely used classification distinguishes between **democratic** and **authoritarian** regimes.

In democracies – 'democracy' translates literally as 'rule by the people' – there is generally a range of political parties which competes with each other to form the government, regular elections which are fair and free, universal suffrage (that is, virtually all adults have the right to vote in elections), civil rights/liberties (such as freedom of expression and freedom of assembly) which are generally respected, and the legislature (the body which makes the law) and the **judiciary** with some degree of independence from the government.

In authoritarian regimes, all these features are either lacking or severely compromised. There may be superficial elements of democracy – for example, elections may be held, but all candidates belong to one political party or there are undue pressures placed on voters to support the official candidate. Also, infringements and abuses of civil liberties are commonplace, government criticism is suppressed and the judiciary is not independent of the government.

The Economist Intelligence Unit (linked to *The Economist* magazine) produces an annual estimation of how democratic countries are – the 'Democracy Index'. It covers most of the countries of the world and uses 60 indicators to allocate each country

**Table 6.1.1 Summary of World Press Freedom Index findings, 2017**

| Freedom score range | Classification | Number of countries | Examples |
|---|---|---|---|
| 0–15 | Good | 16 | Norway, Sweden, Finland, Denmark, New Zealand, Jamaica, Iceland, Germany |
| 16–25 | Fairly good | 33 | UK, USA, Cyprus, Australia, Spain, South Africa |
| 26–35 | Problematic | 59 | Nepal, Mauritius, Guyana, Kenya, Italy, Japan, Israel, Brazil, Greece |
| 36–55 | Bad | 51 | Pakistan, UAE, Nigeria, Malaysia, Indonesia, Brunei, Singapore, Mexico, Russia, India |
| 56–100 | Very bad | 21 | China, North Korea, Saudi Arabia, Cuba, Eritrea |

Source: RSF World Press Freedom Index 2017.

to one of four categories: full democracies, **flawed democracies**, **hybrid regimes** and authoritarian regimes (see Unit 8.3.1). In 2016, it looked at 167 countries and categorised 19 as full democracies, 57 as flawed democracies, 40 as hybrid regimes and 51 – covering roughly one-third of the world's population – as authoritarian regimes.

All the countries rated 'good' in terms of media freedom by RSF in 2017 were rated as 'democratic' by the 2016 Democracy Index (13 as 'full democracies', 3 as 'flawed democracies') and all the countries covered by the Democracy Index rated as 'very bad' in terms of media freedom by RSF were classified as 'authoritarian'. This is because full democracies tend to have a diverse and independent media and support freedom of expression, while in authoritarian regimes the media are often state-owned or controlled by groups closely associated with the government and there is widespread media censorship. Interestingly, the country rated most highly for media freedom (Norway) also came top in the Democracy Index and the lowest-rated country for media freedom (North Korea) also came last in the Democracy Index.

## Activity

Summaries of both the Democracy Index and the World Press Freedom Index are freely available on the World Wide Web (assuming access is not restricted by the state). Look up the country you live in. Are you surprised by its ranking or is it what you expected? Do you agree or disagree? Why?

Explain why democracies tend to be associated with greater media freedom than authoritarian regimes.

To summarise, we can say that democracies tend to allow greater media freedom and authoritarian regimes less. However, outside the two extremes of full democracy/'good' media freedom and authoritarian regime/'very bad' media freedom, the situation is variable and it is important to avoid over-simplification. For example, both Japan and Mauritius are classified as 'full democracies' by the Democracy Index, but RSF classifies their level of media freedom as 'problematic'. While it describes Mauritius as a model African country for democracy and human rights, RSF claims that abuses against journalists occur. These include 'threats by the authorities against the daily newspaper *L'Express*, the 2011 jail sentence of the editor of the weekly *Samedi Plus,* and the Mauritius Broadcasting Corporation's warnings to journalists who spoke during public debates'. Similarly, in Japan, RSF claims that since the re-election of Shinzo Abe as Prime Minister in 2012, media freedom has been declining, with both local and foreign journalists experiencing harassment by government officials.

In Unit 6.1.2, we will look more closely at the variable relationship between the state and the media in different countries and particularly at the role of state censorship.

## Key terms

**Non-governmental organisation** A non-profit organisation that operates independently of any government.

**Democratic regime** A political system in which power is ultimately held by the people.

**Authoritarian regime** A political system that concentrates political power in an authority not responsible to the people.

**Judiciary** The branch of the state which interprets and applies the law.

**Flawed democracies** Nations where elections are fair and free, and basic civil liberties are honoured, but which may have significant democratic failings in other respects.

**Hybrid regime** A political system which combines elements of democracy with authoritarianism.

## Summary

1. There are two main sources of information about media freedom globally: the World Press Freedom Index produced by Reporters Without Borders (RSF) and the Freedom of the Press Report produced by Freedom House.
2. The 2017 RSF report covered 180 countries and categorised 16 as 'good', 33 as 'fairly good', 59 as 'problematic', 51 as 'bad' and 21 as 'very bad'.
3. Broadly speaking, the degree of media freedom relates to the nature of the political system operating in different countries, with democratic systems offering greater media freedom and authoritarian systems less.
4. However, while this pattern holds true at the extremes, countries with similar political systems can differ in terms of the level of media freedom.

# Unit 6.1.2 The media, the state and state censorship

In the last unit, we looked at the global picture in terms of media freedom and saw that this varies with the nature of the political regime in different countries. In this unit, we will take a closer look at the role of the state in relation to the media and the role played by state censorship.

## Authoritarian regimes

In authoritarian regimes, the state usually seeks to control both the traditional and new media in order to control public opinion. In extreme cases, such as North Korea, Eritrea and Turkmenistan, there are no independent traditional media sources and the government seeks to prohibit access to new media. For example, in North Korea the Korean Central News Agency is the sole source of official news for the print and broadcast media and the people are fed a daily diet of stories extolling the virtues of its leader Kim Jong-un. According to the Open Net Initiative, online access within North Korea is exceedingly rare and limited to sites that comprise the domestic intranet, whose content is chosen (and user activity monitored) by the authorities.

However, according to Robert Orttung and Christopher Walker (2014), most authoritarian regimes today do not seek total domination of all means of mass communication. This is both because of a desire to avoid condemnation in the court of international opinion and because of aspirations to economic modernisation. The latter would be handicapped by wholesale media repression and the restrictions on information flow that this would entail. Instead, according to Orttung and Walker, they want 'effective media control – enough for them to convey their strength and puff up claims to legitimacy while undermining potential alternatives'.

### Activity

Many authoritarian regimes *claim* to be democratic (the official name of North Korea is the Democratic People's Republic of Korea, for example) and have media freedom enshrined in their constitution. Assuming that the country you live in has a written constitution, carry out research to discover whether it enshrines media freedom.

Orttung and Walker identify four distinct audiences that authoritarian-controlled media seek to influence:

1. Regime elites: authoritarian governments need to reassure elite groups that they are in control and warn potential opponents among the elite that any defections will be punished (for example, through smear campaigns) because any splits could lead to regime collapse.
2. The general population: state-dominated media are used to make mass audiences both fear and respect the regime at the same time as encouraging political apathy and passivity. State-controlled television is typically the main tool for achieving this goal.
3. The political opposition and independent civil society organisations (where these exist): state-run media are used to try to discredit in the public's mind any opposition to the regime, painting opponents as corrupt, self-interested or as agents of malign foreign powers.
4. Regular internet users: as the number of people online grows, authoritarian governments have realised that they need to at least control politically sensitive online content as well as that of the press and broadcasting.

## Censorship

Writing in the introduction to *Attacks on the Press: The New Face of Censorship,* produced by the international NGO, the Committee to Protect Journalists, Joel Simon (2017) claims that strategies used by authoritarian and hybrid states to control and manage information fall into three broad categories:

- *Repression 2.0*: new forms of direct censorship and the intimidation and/or imprisonment of critical journalists. These are similar to the direct control of the media exercised by the Communist Party in the former Soviet Union before Mikhail Gorbachev came to power ('Repression 1.0').
- *Masked political control*: systematic efforts to hide repressive actions taken against the media by dressing them up 'in the cloak of democratic norms'. For example, justifying an internet crackdown by claiming that it is necessary to suppress hate speech, incitements to violence or to tackle terrorism. In Turkey, for example, according to RSF, since the failed coup of July 2016 the authorities have used the 'fight against terrorism' as a pretext for eliminating dozens of media outlets and imprisoning dozens of journalists.

- *Technology capture*: using digital technologies to stop internal dissent by monitoring and surveilling critical voices, blocking websites and using **state-sponsored trolling**. According to the 2016 *Freedom on the Net* report produced by Freedom House, two-thirds of the world's internet users live in countries which blocked or restricted access to social media sites and communication services during that year.

To this list might be added a fourth category, namely self-censorship, where journalists avoid criticising the regime through fear of harassment or because of financial considerations. According to the NGO, the World Association of Newspapers and News Publishers (WAN-IFRA), in Malawi and Cambodia, for example, governments use the threat of withdrawing state advertising from independent media outlets as a tool to pressurise them to avoid criticising the government (MacDowall and van der Zee, 01/12/2017).

The *Freedom on the Net* report referred to above identified China as the country with the most restrictions on internet freedom (North Korea was excluded from the report). China has a comprehensive internet censorship system known colloquially as 'The Great Firewall of China' that seeks to control both internet traffic originating outside of China and internal traffic.

Until recently, **tech-savvy** Chinese internet users had been able to bypass the government's efforts to block foreign websites by using what are known as Virtual Private Network services (or VPNs) (Baker, 2017). However, since 2018 new laws require that all VPN operators are licensed by the government. Moreover, the state-run telecom companies China Mobile, China Unicom and China Telecom have been required to ensure that their 1.3 billion subscribers cannot access blocked content with VPNs.

## Democratic regimes

State control, including state censorship, of the media is generally seen as incompatible with democracy, at least in times of peace. Sebastian Stier (2015) examined data relating to the situation in 149 countries over the period 1993 to 2010, and found that democracies lead to 'significantly higher levels' of media freedom than **autocracies,** other things being equal.

This is not to say that the state plays no part in the operation of the media in democracies. The state may well pass laws which limit the freedom of the press in ways which are seen as in the public interest – for example, hate-speech legislation. It is also likely to pass laws limiting the ability of any one company to monopolise a particular media sector in order to ensure at least some **media plurality**. For example, in January 2018 the UK Competition and Markets Authority (CMA) concluded that it was not in the public interest for 21st Century Fox to take over Sky broadcasting: 'The CMA has provisionally found that if the deal went ahead, as currently proposed, it is likely to operate against the public interest. It would lead to the Murdoch Family Trust (MFT), which controls Fox and News Corporation (News Corp), increasing its control over Sky, so that it would have too much control over news providers in the UK across all media platforms (TV, Radio, Online and Newspapers), and therefore too much influence over public opinion and the political agenda' (https://www.gov.uk/government/news, 23/01/2018).

However, media freedom cannot be taken for granted in democracies. As indicated in the introduction to Part 1, changes in government and in the political climate can lead to attacks on media freedom even in democratic societies. In its accompanying analysis of the 2017 World Press Freedom Index, RSF states that 'violations of the freedom to inform are less and less the prerogative of authoritarian regimes and dictatorships'. Among numerous examples, it draws attention to recent developments in Europe and the USA where the rise of **right-wing populism** has seen the election of **neo-conservative governments** who are intolerant of media criticism.

In the USA, the election of Donald Trump has seen repeated attacks on journalists, with Trump accusing them of being 'among the most dishonest human beings on earth' and of deliberately spreading 'fake news'. In Poland, the election of the Law and Order Party in 2015 was followed by legislation bringing public radio and television under its control and the replacement of the existing directors with government appointees. It also acted to restrict the distribution of newspapers that were critical of the government and ordered all state agencies to cancel their subscriptions and not place any advertisements in the targeted newspapers. Similarly, in Hungary, since the Fidesz party came to power in 2010, the government under Viktor Orbán has sought to tighten its control over the media through legislation and through the purchase of independent media outlets by wealthy supporters of the government.

## Contemporary issues: State control of the media in Russia

### PREDATOR OF PRESS FREEDOM

**Vladimir PUTIN**
President of the Russian Federation
Aged 64

**Predator since 2000**

**Vladimir Putin has alternated between the positions of prime minister and president since 2000. He was FSB (former KGB) director in 1998 and 1999.**

**Attack technique:** nationalistic authoritarianism

Catapulted into the presidency in 2000 after a decade of dilution of authority, Putin has always had an overriding obsession with control. The media quickly felt the effects of his concern to impose topdown authority, called the "power vertical," during his first two terms as president, when all the national TV channels were gradually brought under the Kremlin's control from the start of the 2000s. The authoritarianism became even more pronounced after Putin's return to the presidency in May 2012 and string of draconian laws criminalizing protests and limiting free speech. And the previously free Internet was reined in. Websites were blocked without reference to the courts, bloggers were tightly regulated and social network users found they could be jailed over a single post. While the leading TV channels inundate viewers with propaganda, the climate has become very oppressive for those who question the new patriotic and neo-conservative discourse or simply try to defend quality journalism. Leading independent media have been picked off one by one. The editors of *Lenta.ru* and *RBK* were ousted. *Dozhd TV* was dropped from satellite and cable TV services. The main Russian media defence NGOs were all declared to be "foreign agents."

**Kill tally:** There is less freedom of expression in Russia now than at any time since the fall of the Soviet Union.

4 journalists are currently in prison: Zhalaudi Geriyev (Kavkazsky Uzel) since 16 April 2016; Alexander Sokolov (RBK) since 27 July 2015; Sergei Reznik since 26 November 2013; and Alexander Tolmachev (Upolnomochen Zayavit and Pro Rostov) since 20 December 2011.

**Enforcers:**

- The Duma (parliament's lower chamber), which is always keen to pass draconian legislation
- Oligarchs and businessman, who buy independent media outlets and then bring them into line
- The security services

**Favourite targets:** independent investigative media, especially those that investigate high-level corruption.

**Official discourse:** brazen hypocrisy

*"The media's active and responsible attitude and a truly independent and courageous journalism are more than ever desired and indispensible for Russia."* (Address to the Union of journalists, April 2013)

**Country score:** Russia is ranked 148th out of 180 countries in RSF's 2016 World Press Freedom Index.

The role of the state in relation to media control in authoritarian regimes can be illustrated by the situation in Russia. The panel shown here, published by RSF, describes President Putin as a 'predator of press freedom' and details some of the ways in which he has sought to exercise control over the media landscape in Russia since coming to power in 2000.

Source: 'Predator of Press Freedom: Vladimir Putin: https://rsf.org/en/predator/vladimir-putin-0, Reporters Sans Frontières/Reporters Without Borders

### Questions

1. Identify the main ways in which Putin has acted to gain control of the media in Russia, according to the RSF report.
2. What does RSF say has happened to independent media outlets under Putin?
3. Explain RSF's reference to 'brazen hypocrisy' (that is, saying one thing and doing another) in relation to Putin's address to the Union of Journalists in April 2013.
4. Using the RSF report above, produce a summary in your own words of the state of the media in Russia in 2016.

## Activity

Explain, using examples, why it is misguided to imagine that media freedom is guaranteed in democratic societies.

However, these developments have been met with resistance from sections of civil society in these countries. Kenneth Roth, the director of the NGO Human Rights Watch, speaking at the launch of its 2018 annual report, stated that 'The lesson of the last year is that resistance matters. The only way to limit the rise of autocrats is to stand up to them. The only way to preserve the values populists attack is to defend them' (*Guardian*, 19/01/2018).

## Key terms

**State-sponsored trolling** Where governments employ people to manipulate online discussions in ways which promote the interests of those governments, both home and abroad.

**Tech-savvy** Someone who is knowledgeable about, and skilled in, the use of modern technology, especially computers.

**Autocracy** A political regime in which power is concentrated in the hands of one individual – common in authoritarian regimes.

**Media plurality** The situation where there is a range of agencies owning and providing media content.

**Right-wing populism** A political strategy that involves support for traditional morality, a strong state and laissez-faire capitalism combined with anti-immigrant and nationalistic rhetoric, and which *claims* to speak up for the ordinary person against the elite (therefore, 'populist').

**Neo-conservative governments** Governments that embrace right-wing ideas as set out above.

## Summary

1. In authoritarian regimes, the state typically seeks to control both the traditional and new media, although only in extreme cases do they seek total control.
2. In seeking to exercise control, according to Orttung and Walker, they have four distinct audiences in mind: members of the elite, the general population, opposition groups and internet users.
3. Simon identifies three types of state censorship: Repression 2.0, masked political control and technology capture. Also important in authoritarian and hybrid regimes is self-censorship by journalists and programme makers.
4. State control, including state censorship, of the media is seen as incompatible with democracy.
5. However, media freedom is never guaranteed and RSF argues that recent years have seen attacks by the state on media freedom in a number of formally democratic countries.

# Unit 6.1.3 Global trends in media organisation and access

Units 6.1.1 and 6.1.2 have sought to provide an overview of the global media landscape in terms of the degree of media freedom in different countries and the role played by the state. In Unit 6.1.3, we seek to complete the picture by looking at the underlying trends in the global organisation of, and access to, the media over recent years.

## The global context

The global organisation of the media today reflects a number of developments in recent decades that have impacted on the economic organisation of countries around the world and the relationships between these countries. Four developments stand out: the globalisation of capitalism, the spread of neoliberal ideas, deregulation and digitalisation:

1. **Capitalist globalisation** Globalisation involves all parts of the world becoming increasingly interconnected, so that national boundaries – in some respects, at least – become less important. According to William I. Robinson (2004), globalisation represents the latest stage in the historical transformation of **capitalism**. For most of the 20th century, capitalism was organised on a nation-state basis, but in the 1970s the system was faced with a crisis of stagnant growth and rising prices ('stagflation') and falling profits. Over the next two decades, Robinson argues, capitalism was reorganised on a global scale with the growth of multinational or **transnational corporations (TNCs)**. Moreover, with the

so-called **'collapse of communism'** at the end of the 1980s, regions and areas that had previously operated outside capitalism's scope (China, the former USSR, Angola, Mozambique and others) were incorporated into a global capitalist system.

2. **Neoliberalism** These developments were guided by a political philosophy called 'neoliberalism'. Neoliberals believe that prosperity and freedom are best promoted by allowing businesses to pursue profits with as little state regulation as possible. Consequently, according to Robinson, global organisations such as the IMF, World Trade Organisation and World Bank became promoters of neoliberalism and hundreds of multilateral, bilateral and global free trade agreements were concluded, enabling the growth of TNCs.
3. **Deregulation** Deregulation is the process of removing or reducing state regulations that limit the activities of businesses. Neoliberals see this as desirable. Critics see it as removing potentially important safeguards for consumers. What Robert McChesney (2001) describes as the centrepiece of these neoliberal policies was the 'call for commercial media and communication markets to be deregulated'. This allowed foreign companies – particularly, but not only, American ones – to buy into national media markets, and as a result media and telecommunications companies were able to expand on an enormous scale, both domestically and internationally.
4. **Digitalisation** The replacement of analogue electronic and mechanical devices with digital technology – the 'digital revolution' – began in the 1980s and underpins the growth of the new media. At the centre of this development is the global spread of the internet. By 2017, nearly half the world's population (3.5 billion out of a global population of 7.5 billion) were connecting to the internet through PCs, laptops, tablets, smartphones or other devices (Statista, 2018). However, the proportion of the population able to access the internet varies significantly between the industrialised and less industrialised world, as the figure in the second activity shows (see below).

## Activity

Discuss the extent to which these four processes have impacted on the media in the country you live in.

## Activity

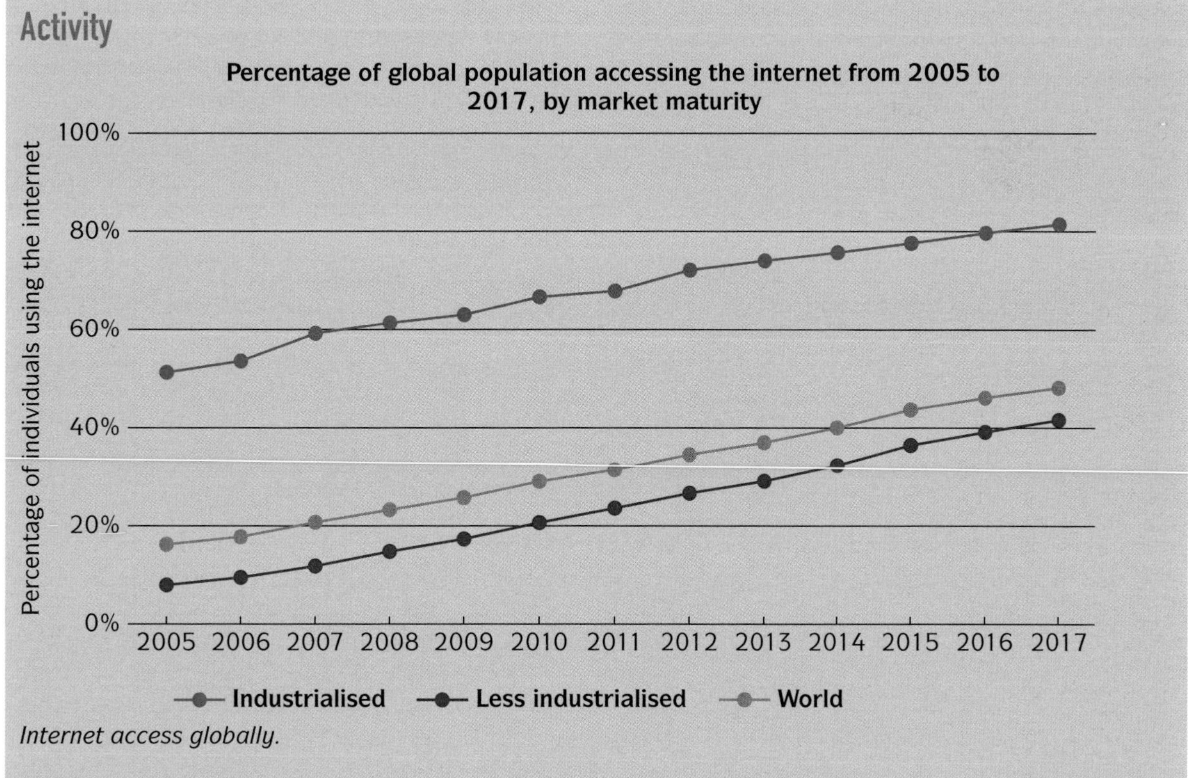


*Internet access globally.*

What percentage of the population was accessing the internet in 2017 in the more industrialised world, and what percentage was doing so in the less industrialised world?

## Trends in global media organisation

Outside of the world's authoritarian regimes, the general trend that is evident over the last decade according to Mike Jensen (2016) is that more and more of both the traditional and new media, along with the infrastructure needed to deliver messages, is owned and operated by TNCs operating on a global scale.

This has come about through two distinct processes known in economics as horizontal and vertical integration:

Horizontal integration is also known as **cross-media ownership** and refers to the fact that the bigger media companies often own a diverse range of types of media. For example, the Murdoch family, which owns News Corp and 21st Century Fox, in addition to newspapers in Britain, Australia and the USA, owns book and magazine publishers, film companies and TV companies.

Vertical integration involves the combination in one company of two or more stages in the production and distribution process normally operated by separate firms. It enables companies to exert greater economic control over their operating environment. For example, Time Warner owns the Warner Bros. film studios, but also owns an international chain of cinemas in which it shows films produced by Warner Bros. Similarly, since 2013, Netflix, which provides an online video streaming service in 190 countries has also produced its own original films and TV programmes.

Vertical and horizontal integration has led to the creation of enormous media TNCs or **media conglomerates** that increasingly dominate the global picture. A conglomerate is a corporation that is made up of a number of different, seemingly unrelated businesses. The companies operate independently of each other, but are overseen by a holding company. For example, YouTube is actually a subsidiary of Google, but Google itself is owned by Alphabet, a holding company set up in 2015 by Google's founders, Larry Page and Sergey Brin.

Table 6.1.2 lists the 10 largest media companies globally by revenue in 2016.

### Activity

How many of the top 10 companies are American? Evaluate the extent to which this implies that globalisation of the media can be equated with Americanisation.

## Trends in global media access

Surveying global trends in media access in 2018, UNESCO states that access increased between 2012 and 2016, although the extent of this increase varied significantly across regions. This development has been accompanied by significant changes in how audiences

**Table 6.1.2 The 10 largest media corporations in the world**

| Rank | Corporation | Revenue 2016 |
|---|---|---|
| 1 | Alphabet Inc. (Mountain View/US) | €82.0 billion |
| 2 | Comcast (Philadelphia/US) | €72.6 billion |
| 3 | The Walt Disney Company (Burbank/US) | €50.3 billion |
| 4 | AT&T Entertainment Group (DirecTV)(El Segundo/US) | €32.9 billion |
| 5 | News Corp. Ltd./21st Century Fox (New York/US) | €32.1 billion |
| 6 | Time Warner Inc. (New York/US) | €26.5 billion |
| 7 | Charter Comm. Inc. (St. Louis/US) | €26.2 billion |
| 8 | Sony Entertainment (Tokyo/JP) | €25.9 billion |
| 9 | Facebook, Inc. (Palo Alto/US) | €25.0 billion |
| 10 | Altice Group (Amsterdam/NL) | €23.5 billion |

Source: Institut für Medien- und Kommunikationspolitik/Institute of Media and Communications Policy.

combine old and new media for accessing news and entertainment. The internet has registered the highest growth in users, although television continues to be the most popular medium. At the same time, consumption of newspapers and radio has declined overall, though this trend is not evident in all countries.

### Internet and mobile

While the numbers accessing the internet have continued to grow, the rate of growth has been slowing down recently, with a 5 per cent annual growth rate in 2017 compared to 10 per cent in 2012. At the same time, mobile internet connectivity has played an important part in expanding access, particularly in Asia and the Pacific and in Africa. The number of unique mobile phone subscriptions increased from 3.89 billion in 2012 to 4.83 billion in 2016, two-thirds of the world's population.

### Broadcast media

In Western Europe and North America, the primacy of television as a source of information is being challenged by the internet, particularly among younger generations. In other regions, such as Africa, television is replacing radio as the main source of information.

The switch from analogue to digital television has been uneven across the globe. The switch is significant in that it potentially opens up a wider range of channels to viewers, as satellite broadcasting had done previously. According to the International Telecommunications Union, in 2017, 28 per cent of 198 countries had completed the process, it was ongoing in 35 per cent, was yet to start in 7 per cent and the situation in the remaining 30 per cent was not known.

### The press

Print newspapers have been the most severely affected by the growth of the internet. Newspaper circulation globally declined by nearly 8 per cent between 2012 and 2017 according to the World Association of Newspapers and News Publishers (WAN-IFRA), although it rose significantly in some Asian and Pacific countries such as China, India and Indonesia. Many newspapers have started producing online versions in an attempt to counteract this trend – some allowing free access, others requiring payment.

## Key terms

**Capitalism** A system for organising the production, distribution and exchange of goods and services based on private ownership and the profit motive.

**Transnational corporations (TNCs)** Companies that operate across national boundaries.

**Collapse of communism** A series of events between 1989 and 1991 that led to the fall of communist regimes in Eastern Europe and the Soviet Union and led other communist regimes (such as China and Cuba) to introduce elements of capitalism into their previously socialist organisation of the economy.

**Cross-media ownership** The ownership of different kinds of media organisations by a single company.

**Media conglomerates** Media corporations that are made up of a number of different, seemingly unrelated businesses.

## Summary

1. The global media landscape today reflects the historical influence of four main factors: capitalist globalisation, neoliberalism, deregulation and digitalisation.
2. Outside of authoritarian regimes, the 21st century has seen increasing media industry consolidation with the creation of media conglomerates through processes of vertical and horizontal integration.
3. Consequently, media production is increasingly dominated by TNCs, particularly American ones.
4. Access to different types of media globally continues to grow, with access to the internet growing fastest. However, television remains the most popular medium, while consumption of radio and print media has declined overall.

# END-OF-PART QUESTIONS

| | | |
|---|---|---|
| 0 1 | Describe four differences between democratic and authoritarian regimes. | **[4 marks]** |
| 0 2 | Explain why authoritarian regimes generally seek to limit media freedom. | **[6 marks]** |
| 0 3 | Evaluate the role of media censorship by the state in authoritarian regimes. | **[8 marks]** |

# PART 2 THEORIES OF THE MEDIA AND INFLUENCES ON MEDIA CONTENT

## Contents


**Unit 6.2.1 Who controls the media? Competing theories 336**

**Unit 6.2.2 Understanding news production and its effects 341**

**Unit 6.2.3 The postmodernist contribution to understanding the media 347**


There is little debate among sociologists over where control of the media lies in authoritarian regimes. As we saw in Part 1, control lies firmly with the state, which uses the media to paint a positive picture of the regime and its leaders and seeks to exclude or, at least, marginalise any voices of dissent. For this reason, it also seeks to limit its citizens' access to new media.

The situation in democratic societies is less clear-cut. Given that the media are mainly in the hands of commercial organisations, it might seem obvious that it is the owners of these companies who are in control. However, notions such as those of '**editorial independence**' and 'creative freedom' suggest instead that control lies with those who actually produce media content: journalists, programme makers, editors and so on. On the other hand, maybe neither of these sets of actors has much control, because if they fail to provide audiences with what they want they will go out of business/lose their jobs. So maybe it is the audience who exercise ultimate control.

Unit 6.2.1 examines the competing theories produced by sociologists aiming to understand the relationship between owners, media professionals and audiences in the production of media content. Unit 6.2.2 focuses on one aspect of media content which is seen as playing a crucial role in the political life of democratic societies; namely, the news. This will provide an opportunity to evaluate the theories examined in Unit 6.2.1. Finally, in Unit 6.2.3 we will examine the views of postmodernists.

## Unit 6.2.1 Who controls the media? Competing theories

The sociological debate over where control of the media lies in democratic societies is mainly between pluralists and Marxists, although Marxists are divided among themselves over exactly where control lies.

### Pluralist theories

**Pluralist theories** of the media derive from pluralist theories of power in democratic societies; for example, Robert Dahl's study of the USA *Who Governs?* (1961). These argue that political power is spread out among a wide range of competing interest groups representing different sections of society – businesses, trades unions, religious organisations, pressure groups, voluntary organisations and so on – none of which are powerful enough to dominate the political decision-making process.

For pluralists, a similar picture applies to the media landscape in democratic societies. Not only are there a variety of mediums – television, radio, print, film, the internet and so on – but, within each sector of the media, companies compete with each other for audiences. Indeed, for pluralists, readers, viewers and listeners are the real power-holders because ultimately it is they who choose which media **messages** to consume: which TV programmes to watch, which magazines to buy, which social media to sign up to and so on. If they did not like the products that media owners were making available to them, or if they suspected the media product was biased one way rather than another, the potential audience would respond by not consuming the product and the media company would go out of business. As John Whale (1977) puts it in relation to the press, 'It is readers who determine the character of newspapers.' Power, then, according to pluralists, lies with the consumer or audience rather than with owners or media professionals. The media have no choice but to give the public what it wants!

Moreover, pluralists argue that the rationale for the increasing concentration of media ownership described in Unit 6.1.3 is essentially economic rather than political or ideological. They argue that media products are costly to produce. Concentration of ownership is aimed at maximising audience size in order to reduce costs and to attract advertising revenue. The globalisation of the media and the conglomerates that have resulted from this are also merely attempts at finding new audiences in order to increase profits, rather than covert efforts to spread, say, American ways of life across the globe.

Indeed, pluralists argue that it is practically impossible for owners to interfere in media content because their businesses are economically far too complex. Whale, for example, argues that 'media owners have global problems of trade and investment to occupy their minds' and so – allegedly – do not have the time to think about the day-to-day detailed running of their media businesses or the everyday content of their newspapers or television programmes.

In addition, many democratic societies have public service broadcasters (PSBs) that are formally independent of the state and required by their charters to display 'due impartiality' in the reporting of matters of public policy or political or industrial controversy. For example, the World Service of the British Broadcasting Corporation (BBC) – the first public service broadcaster – is widely respected around the world for its objectivity and has provided the blueprint for many subsequent PSBs. Pluralists see PSBs as an additional source of media diversity and a counterweight to any potential bias in the commercial sector.

## Activity

*The headquarters of the Telewizja Polska (TVP) public broadcasting corporation, Warsaw, Poland.*

Does the country you live in have a PSB? If so, research how it is funded (the BBC is mainly funded by an annual licence fee paid by every household with a TV receiver), how independent it is of the government and what its audience share is. Do your findings support or undermine a pluralist view of the media?

Finally, the growth of the new media is seen as opening up an even greater range of choice of content with every conceivable taste and shade of opinion catered for on the World Wide Web.

### Evaluation

A number of issues can be raised in relation to the pluralist theory:

- Just how diverse are the media in terms of the range of views presented? Critics argue that the media operate within a 'consensus band' which largely excludes radical views. Moreover, there may be a range of viewpoints, but these viewpoints may be skewed in a particular direction. For example, the press in the UK is predominantly right-wing.
- There is plenty of evidence that owners of the press are not neutral when it comes to the editorial line taken by their newspapers.
- Do the public get what they want, or come to want what they are given?

- PSBs are rarely completely immune from government pressures. In the UK, for example, it is the government which determines the cost of the TV licence and it can use this as a lever to pressurise the BBC.
- Does the concentration of media ownership really not matter? Tim Berners-Lee, the inventor of the Web, writing in 2018 argues that 'What was once a rich selection of blogs and websites has been compressed under the powerful weight of a few dominant platforms. This concentration of power creates a new set of gatekeepers, allowing a handful of platforms to control which ideas and opinions are seen and shared (*Guardian*, 12/03/2018).

## Marxist theories

Karl Marx (1818–1883) lived at a time when the only mass medium was the printing press. Consequently, he wrote little or nothing about the media. However, since the 1960s sociologists influenced by Marx's ideas have written extensively on the media.

For Marxists, the key feature of modern societies is not the level of technology or the fact that they are based on markets, but the fact that they are capitalist. Marxists see capitalist societies as organised around an inevitable conflict of interest between those who own the means of production and those who provide the labour. These 'social relations of production' (or class relations) are seen as central to understanding how capitalist societies work. Moreover, because these class relations are unequal and – in the view of Marxists – because wealth translates into power, Marxists are sceptical about claims made by such societies of being truly democratic.

In analysing Marxist views of the media, a distinction can be drawn between conventional or 'instrumental' views, which emphasise the power of the wealthy, and neo-Marxist views, which emphasise the institutional constraints within which the media operate under capitalism – for example, the need to attract advertising and to make a profit.

### Conventional Marxist views

Conventional Marxist views, exemplified by Ralph Miliband's *The State in Capitalist Society* (1973), argue that the media are directly controlled by a dominant class who use it as an instrument to control the working class. The key role of the media is to transmit a set of ideas which justifies the inequalities inherent in capitalist societies – '**ruling-class ideology**'– and which persuade people that the system is basically fair and operates in the interests of all rather than the dominant class. For conventional Marxists, ruling-class ideology represents a distorted picture of reality. Consequently, working-class people experience '**false consciousness**' – they come to believe that capitalism is a fair system that benefits all people equally. They therefore fail to see the reality of their situation – that they are being exploited by a system that, in the view of Marxists, only benefits a powerful minority. This is why the notion of 'mass manipulation' is sometimes used to refer to the conventional Marxist view of the media in democratic societies.

One of the ways in which ideologies work is by presenting a partial view of reality as if it were the whole story. An example is provided by the notion of the 'freedom of the press'. For pluralists, this is a cornerstone of democratic societies, referring to the idea that the press should be free from government control so that it can help to hold governments to account. Conventional Marxists, however, would argue that the press in capitalist societies is not really 'free'. Rather, newspapers provide a mouthpiece for extremely wealthy individuals – '**press barons**' – to promote their interests to an unsuspecting public on a daily basis!

#### Activity

How do you think pluralists might respond to this Marxist put-down of the notion of freedom of the press?

Miliband rejects the pluralist view that the media represent a diversity of viewpoints. In relation to the press, for example, he argues that 'most newspapers in the capitalist world have one crucial characteristic in common, namely their strong, often their passionate hostility to anything further to the Left than the milder forms of **social democracy**, and quite commonly to these milder forms as well' (Miliband, 1973). Miliband accepted that there is some diversity of opinion within the media, but argued that the range of ideas and opinions is very limited and that radical views are demonised.

**Neo-Marxist views and the propaganda model** Neo-Marxists contest a number of the claims of conventional Marxists. For example, they challenge the idea that the owners of capital constitute a 'ruling class' in contemporary democracies and that the state is simply an instrument of this class. Rather, they argue that the state has some independence from the capitalist class or, in their words, is 'relatively autonomous'. Additionally, they argue that the class structure is more complicated than a simple division into 'bourgeoisie' (owners) and 'proletariat' (workers).They also recognise that there are important non-class interests in capitalist societies – linked, for example, to gender, ethnicity, sexuality and disability – which may all have grievances that they wish the state to address.

Neo-Marxists share the view of conventional Marxists that the media play an important ideological role in justifying capitalist arrangements, but they do not see this mainly as the result of a kind of conspiracy by members of the capitalist class to intentionally brainwash the proletariat. For a start, they argue that the capitalist class is not a unified grouping. The interests of industrial capitalists (low interest rates, say) may not be the same as those of finance capitalists (high interest rates). Moreover, what may be in the short-term interests of *capitalists* (low wages, say) may not be in the long-term interests of the *capitalist system* (as, if workers cannot afford to buy the goods and services produced, capitalists cannot make profits).

Consequently, for neo-Marxists the culture of the dominant class is reproduced through the media, not so much by design, but as a kind of by-product of the structural location of the media and the logic of capitalist production. This is part of what is known as **cultural hegemony**: the domination of one set of ideas over others.

This hegemonic model is associated with the work of the Italian Marxist Antonio Gramsci, as well as with members of the Frankfurt School for Social Research, such as Theodor Adorno and Max Horkheimer. Such thinkers see ideology as a natural, almost accidental, outcome of the pursuit of economic interest. Neo-Marxists believe that most media professionals – such as journalists, editors, television producers, advertising executives – genuinely shape media content in professional ways in order to maximise their audiences. However, unconsciously they produce a 'culture industry' which reflects their class position and which ideologically benefits the wealthy.

## Activity

*Antonio Gramsci 1891–1937.*

Carry out research to find out more about Gramsci's concept of cultural hegemony.

Writing in 2005, David Harvey, for example, argues that the media have played a part in promoting neoliberal ideas globally: 'Neoliberalism has, in short, become hegemonic as a mode of discourse. It has pervasive effects on ways of thought to the point where it has become incorporated into the common-sense way many of us interpret, live in and understand the world' (2005). Almost all states, from those emerging from the collapse of the USSR, old-style social democracies like New Zealand and Sweden, post-apartheid South Africa to China, the UK and the USA, have embraced neoliberal tenets such as deregulation, privatisation and the withdrawal of the state from many areas of social provision.

Closely related to neo-Marxist perspectives is the 'propaganda model' of media control put forward by Edward S. Herman and Noam Chomsky in their book *Manufacturing Consent – The Political Economy of the Mass Media* (1988). Like neo-Marxists, they reject conspiracy views of the media, but nevertheless argue that the media (in the USA) systematically promote elite interests.

They identify five news 'filters' through which 'money and power are able to filter out the news fit to print, marginalise dissent, and allow the government and dominant private interests to get their messages across to the public':

1. the size, concentrated ownership, owner wealth and profit orientation of the dominant mass media firms
2. advertising as the primary income source of the mass media
3. the reliance of the media on information provided by government, business and 'experts' funded and approved by these sources
4. 'flak' as a means of disciplining the media and keeping them in line (through complaints, lawsuits, government sanctions and so on)
5. (at the time they were writing) anti-communism as a kind of national religion. (Today, the 'war on terror' and 'free market' beliefs serve a similar function.)

## Evaluation

A number of issues can also be raised in relation to Marxist and propaganda theories:

- The instrumental Marxist notion of a unified capitalist elite controlling media content is problematic in a number of ways. First, as neo-Marxists argue, there are divisions within the capitalist class. Second, notions of editorial independence and journalistic integrity are not entirely without substance. Third, the fact that Marxist critiques of the media can be easily accessed (for example, through the internet) raises problems for a theory which claims that capitalists control content.
- The idea that the media produce 'false consciousness' is also problematic. First, the concept of *false* consciousness rests on the validity of a Marxist analysis of society. Second, it assumes that the public simply accepts whatever the media tell it. As we shall see later, sociologists have questioned the idea that audiences passively soak up media messages.
- While it is true that extreme wealth as such is rarely criticised in the media, corruption, incompetence and unethical behaviour on the part of the wealthy is likely to be exposed. For example, in recent years, the Panama Papers and the Paradise Papers have exposed the offshore financial affairs of hundreds of politicians, multinationals, celebrities and high-net-worth individuals. The documents were leaked to the German newspaper *Süddeutsche Zeitung,* which called in the International Consortium of Investigative Journalists (ICIJ) to oversee the investigation involving nearly 100 media groups globally.
- The internet has drastically reduced the start-up costs of new media outlets. In recent years, this has enabled radical voices, both on the left and on the right politically, that fall outside the mainstream consensus to establish a platform and communicate with audiences – the so-called 'alternative media'. Their typical audiences are relatively small, but they have certainly expanded media diversity.

## Activity

Draw up a table summarising the key strengths and weaknesses of the pluralist, instrumental Marxist and neo-Marxist theories of media control in democratic societies.

## Key terms

**Editorial independence** The idea that editors should be able to make decisions without interference from the owners of media outlets.

**Pluralist theories** Theories which argue that power and influence in democratic societies is spread out across a variety of competing interest groups.

**Messages** In the context of studies of the media, 'messages' is a generic term for anything the media transmits. It could be a newspaper story, a movie, a television programme, a tweet, an email or any of a wide variety of other types of message.

**Ruling-class ideology** The set of ideas and beliefs which justify the dominant position of the capitalist class.

**False consciousness** A view of the world which is mistaken.

**Press barons** Wealthy owners of newspapers who are considered to have too much influence.

**Social democracy** A left-wing political philosophy which supports government intervention in capitalist societies in order to protect the general welfare of citizens.

**Cultural hegemony** Rule or domination achieved by persuading people that values, beliefs and ideas that serve the interests of a dominant class are 'common-sense'.

## Summary

1. While it is clear that the state controls the media in authoritarian regimes, sociologists disagree about where control lies in democracies.
2. Pluralists argue that ultimately it is the audience who exercise control in democracies and that a diversity of viewpoints are covered by the media. Critics argue that this diversity is largely contained within a relatively narrow band of mainstream views which provide limited criticism of the status quo.
3. Instrumental Marxists argue that control lies with the capitalist class, who use the media to generate false consciousness.
4. Neo-Marxists reject the idea of a capitalist conspiracy to mislead the public via the media, but nevertheless argue that the media unwittingly promote the interests of the dominant class via a process of cultural hegemony.
5. The propaganda model argues that elite interests are promoted through the news media.
6. Critics of Marxist and propaganda models argue that the media in democratic societies do provide a platform for views that are critical of the status quo and that the internet has extended the range of viewpoints that can be relatively easily accessed by the public.

# Unit 6.2.2 Understanding news production and its effects

What pictures form in your imagination when you see the words 'news' and 'journalist'? A typical sequence of pictures might involve the occurrence of some unexpected event, a journalist being dispatched to find out the facts about what has happened, the same journalist writing up a report of what they have discovered and the publication of this report in a newspaper or its broadcast on the radio or TV.

The problem with such a common-sense view of the news and of the role of journalists in reporting it, is not that it is untrue, but that it massively over-simplifies what is involved in the production of the news. Moreover, it suggests that the news is purely factual. In this unit, we will explore the many hidden processes that go into the production of the news and why it is more accurate to talk about the news as a manufactured product combining facts and values rather than to talk about it as a simple matter of reportage.

We will also use the topic of the news to evaluate the debate between pluralists and Marxists we explored in the previous unit. Does journalism provide citizens with the information they need to participate actively in democratic societies and make informed political decisions, or does it systematically mislead them about what is going on in a way that benefits dominant groups, including governments, corporations and the wealthy?

## The social manufacture of the news

The first thing to note about the news is that it involves a highly partial account of reality. Millions of events occur within societies and across the globe every day, but only a tiny fraction of these are ever reported. 'News' is the end result of a process of selection by editors and journalists who therefore act as **gatekeepers**, controlling the flow of information. This selection is guided by **news values,** general guidelines or criteria that determine the worth of a news story and how much prominence it is given by newspapers or broadcast media. Specifically, news values refer to what journalists, editors and broadcasters consider as 'newsworthy' – that is, something which is seen as socially significant and interesting enough to appeal to an audience.

Johan Galtung and Marie Ruge (1970) supply one of the best-known lists of news values. Although their research was conducted in 1965 and was focused just on the coverage of international events, it is still widely seen as of general and continuing relevance. Galtung and Ruge identified the following set of news values used by journalists:

- Extraordinariness – events that are unexpected, rare, unpredictable or surprising. (As Charles A. Dana famously put it: 'If a dog bites a man, that's not news. But if a man bites a dog, that's news!').
- Threshold – perceived as socially significant.
- Unambiguity – events that can be reported in black-and-white terms.
- Reference to elite persons – involve the rich, high-status or well-known people.
- Reference to elite nations – involve countries that are seen as globally prominent.

- Personalisation – can be reduced to the actions of the individuals involved.
- Frequency – events are newsworthy, long-term social processes are not.
- Negativity – bad things are seen as more newsworthy than good things.

## Activity

*British newspaper front pages following the announcement of the royal engagement of Prince Harry and Meghan Markle.*

How might the focus on events and personalities make it difficult for the news to offer a more sociologically informed understanding of social processes and structures that shape the events it reports?

The second thing to note about the news is that the facts do not speak for themselves. In order to be meaningful, facts have to be interpreted. The news media do not simply tell us about what is happening, but offer us particular ways of understanding what they have selected – what Stuart Hall (1973) called **'interpretative frameworks'** or **'frames'.** Framing refers to the way an issue is presented to the public or the 'angle' it is given by the news media. It involves calling attention to certain aspects of an issue while ignoring or obscuring other elements.

In principle, a clear distinction can be drawn between facts and comment or opinion. A former editor of the *Guardian* newspaper in the UK, C.P. Scott, famously stated that 'comment is free, but facts are sacred'. Moreover, newspapers typically distinguish comment and opinion pieces (including their editorial column) from news stories. However, in practice this distinction is difficult, if not impossible, to maintain.

The crucial point to recognise is that the same facts can be interpreted in different ways. Subtle changes in language, for example, can transform how an event or issue is perceived. This is because words that have the same denotation (dictionary definition) can have very different connotations (associations). Governments can 'intervene' in the economy (neutral) or can 'interfere' (negative); a leader can be 'strong-willed' (positive) or 'inflexible' (negative); policies can be 'bold' (positive) or 'reckless' (negative) and so on.

Another example of framing is provided by **media sensationalism**: the use of emotive and colourful language to grab the viewer's or reader's attention. For example, rapists are never presented as ordinary men in tabloid journalism, but instead are labelled 'fiends', 'beasts', 'monsters', 'maniacs' or 'rippers'. (See also Unit 6.5.1.)

The consequence of these two processes – of selection and framing – is that the news media play an important role in what is called **agenda-setting:** shaping the public's view of what the important issues facing society are *and* how they should be understood.

## Activity

Apply the concept of agenda-setting to the issues which currently dominate the news coverage of what is happening in your society. Which issues are at the top of the agenda and how have they been framed?

# Sociological research on the news

Hall and colleagues argued that, because journalists are supposed to avoid offering their own interpretations of events, they have to turn to others to contextualise the events they report. Those in positions of power tend to be the **primary definers** of what is happening. For example, in their work on 'mugging' (street robberies) in the UK in the 1970s, it was government ministers, senior police officers and judges whose definitions were drawn on to explain what was happening, rather than ethnic minority spokespeople, let alone the young Black men who were the principal perpetrators. These definitions helped to create, in the view of Hall et al., a '**moral panic**' around mugging at that time.

Other research in the 1970s by the Glasgow University Media Group (GUMG, now known as the Glasgow Media Group) looked at television news reporting of industrial conflict. The UK was experiencing an economic crisis at that time of 'stagflation': stagnant economic growth combined with price inflation. There were competing explanations of these events: the Conservative government blamed over-powerful trades unions and strikes; left-wing critics blamed incompetent management and a lack of investment in new technology.

In *Bad News* (1976) and *More Bad News* (1980), the GUMG argued that television news failed to adequately reflect this divergence of opinion and was skewed towards the government's position, not because of any kind of conspiracy, but because the social background of TV journalists led them to view the world from a politically conservative perspective. There was an illusion of balance, but in practice the coverage portrayed the workers and trades unions as the culprits for the country's economic problems. For example:

- The Prime Minister, Harold Wilson (Labour), made a speech about the car industry in which he appealed to unions *and* management to cut down on what he called 'manifestly avoidable stoppages'. Subsequent news bulletins reported the PM as calling just on workers to cut down on avoidable stoppages.

## Contemporary issues: Framing welfare and welfare recipients

*In a comment piece in the UK* Guardian *newspaper, Mary O'Hara criticises the way in which welfare and social security recipients have been demonised by right-wing governments and politicians in the UK and USA.*

'Since the emergence almost a decade ago of the poisonous rhetoric of "**skivers and strivers**" that has helped to prop up the fiasco that has been Tory [*Conservative Party*] **austerity**, a culture of dismissing poor people has become well and truly entrenched. The despicable idea that being poor is somehow the by-product of personal flaws rather than bad policy, and that strong welfare systems should be rejected, is pervasive.

In the US – which barely has a welfare safety net and which is the ultimate poster boy for British advocates of rolling back the state – the campaign to demolish what little support there is for poor people has reached a new crescendo. And, as with austerity in the UK, cruel and counterproductive policies are wrapped in language carefully crafted to demean and "**other**" those in need of assistance.

Since the start of the year, the Trump administration has launched an all-out policy assault on America's poor. The opening salvo came when Medicaid, the national social insurance programme providing essential health benefits for about 74 million Americans – was subject to a brazen, calculated attack.

It isn't enough that Republicans have been trying to demolish the 50-year-old programme (despite it being effective as well as popular nationwide) for decades. With a new set of guidance issued by the administration last month, unless legal challenges are successful, individual states will be able to take healthcare provided by Medicaid away from people unable to find a job who fail to meet certain "work requirements". Early estimates suggest that as many as 6.3 million people could lose access to healthcare.

And how are they trying to sell their proposed cuts to vital programmes that help the poor? You've guessed it. It's all about framing. The speaker of the House of Representatives, Paul Ryan, has been cheerleader-in-chief, wheeling out phrases such as "helping people" and positioning cuts to Medicaid as a boon for "workforce development". Others justify the proposals by saying it's all about promoting individual fulfilment.'

Source: adapted from: Mary O' Hara Let's Tell the Truth About Poverty – And Stop This Assault on Welfare, *Guardian*, 20/02/18.

### Questions

1. The policy of 'rolling back the state' (that is, reducing the role of governments, particularly in relation to welfare provision) is part of neoliberalism. How does demonising welfare recipients help to promote this policy?
2. Explain in your own words 'language carefully crafted to demean and "other" those in need of assistance'.
3. How might those who oppose these policies rephrase 'helping people' and 'workforce development'?
4. What are the implications for the debate between pluralists and Marxists of the appearance in a mainstream newspaper of this highly critical attack on neoliberal policies?

- Coverage of strikes focused on the disruption they caused to the public rather than on the workers' grounds for striking.
- Union **shop stewards** were interviewed on **picket lines** while management were brought into the television studios for lengthy discussions with the newscaster.

Overall, the GUMG argue that 'The news is underpinned by a key ideological assumption. It is that production in our society is normal and satisfactory unless there are problems with the workforce' (GUMG, 1982). All of the other problems that may impede production in a system based on private capital – inefficient management, failure to invest, profits being used to distribute high dividends to shareholders rather than for wages or research and development and so on – remain unexamined.

A later study by GUMG entitled *Bad News from Israel* (2004), of the reporting of the Israel /Palestine conflict on the two leading terrestrial TV channels in the UK (BBC and ITV), again argued that it was the perspective of the more powerful side – Israel – that framed the coverage. Greg Philo and Mike Berry argue that there are two very different perspectives on this conflict. They say that Israeli authorities and much of the Israeli population see the conflict in terms of their security and the survival of their state in the face of threats from terrorists and hostile neighbours. In contrast, Philo and Berry believe the Palestinians see themselves as resisting a brutal military occupation by people who have taken their land, water and homes and who are denying them their own state.

Philo and Berry found the following.

- News reports failed to provide a historical context to the events they reported, leaving viewers

## Then and now: Glasgow University Media Group, *Bad News* (1976)

'When we published *Bad News in* 1976, our criticisms of television news in the UK were greeted with some astonishment. It was unusual to criticise the BBC, which was seen as an august, rather stately institution offering an objective window on the world. But we were social scientists and we knew there were many accounts of controversial issues such as strikes, the economy and conflict. We compared the news with other sources such as government figures on the number of strikes and found no relation between the level of news coverage and the other measures of what was actually happening. We examined who got on and showed how the most powerful figures in our society were able to shape news agendas and the way in which our society is explained. This included who was blamed for its problems and what was seen as necessary, possible or desirable within it.

Not all journalists are the same and there are some critical journalists but overall our conclusion was that the news offered a perspective which accorded with the views of the powerful and excluded the powerless.

What has changed? The most obvious difference now is the growth of new media and the use of these as alternative sources of news. This presents its own problems as the internet carries many false stories, but it has been important as a way of organising alternative political movements and avoiding traditional media. Of course, this also means that it can be used by unscrupulous political groups to spread propaganda and ideologies of discrimination and racism. The media are in this sense always a battleground of ideas. Some politicians routinely attack it, accusing it of 'fake news'. This is a good way of insulating their followers from the inconvenient truths that the best journalists sometimes uncover. But some of it is fake and social science helps a great deal in telling the difference.

The question remains, does all this matter in the sense that the media have powerful effects on public belief? Some would point to the 2016 Brexit vote in the United Kingdom, to the years of negative propaganda about the European Union which preceded it and to the publicity at the time suggesting, for example, that leaving would release £350 million a week to be spent on health services. This seemed convincing for some voters though critics suggested that the likely effect of leaving would be a contraction of economic growth and less money for public services. Still the vote was carried with very little understanding of its potential consequences.

All of this underlines the importance of studying media – of learning to spot false and distorted accounts, to inform yourself and get as close as possible to the truth.'

(Professor Greg Philo, Glasgow University, Scotland, August 2018.)

'extraordinarily confused'. For example, they found that many viewers thought it was the Palestinians occupying the occupied territories.

- The reports framed the issue as one of terrorism, with the Palestinians presented as terrorists who had initiated the conflict, to which the Israelis 'responded'. Thus, the Israelis were described as responding to what had happened to them about six times as often as the Palestinians.
- Israelis were quoted and spoke in interviews about twice as often as Palestinians, as were US politicians (who tended to support Israel) compared to British politicians.
- There were significant differences in the language used for the casualties on both sides. Words such as 'mass murder', 'atrocity' and 'brutal murder' were used to describe the death of Israelis, but not Palestinians.

More recently still, Mark Curtis (2017) has argued that news media coverage of British foreign policy is systematically skewed towards elite interests. He attacks what he sees as the key ideological concept underpinning this coverage: the idea of Britain's *basic benevolence* in its dealings with other countries, arguing instead that foreign policy is shaped essentially by the elite's perception of what is in Britain's economic and strategic interests.

Drawing on the history of Britain's dealings with Kenya, Malaya (now Malaysia), British Guiana (now Guyana), Egypt, Iraq and others, he argues that media reporting distorts Britain's role in the world by:

- not reporting some policies at all (that is, gatekeeping)
- framing discussion within narrow parameters
- ignoring relevant history
- reiterating and failing to counter elite explanations.

Curtis concludes by quoting approvingly the view of the GUMG: 'The news is not a neutral and natural phenomenon; it is rather the manufactured production of ideology.'

## Conclusion

Pluralists are correct in arguing that in democratic societies a variety of points of view are represented in the news media – for example, that there is likely to be a range of newspapers and magazines which reports what is happening from the perspective of different political positions. They are also correct in arguing that the World Wide Web has provided a platform for views which fall way outside the consensus – even though their audience reach is likely to be limited.

However, there are severe limitations to the pluralist view.

First, in relation to the press, newspapers reflecting right-wing views tend to predominate and newspaper readers may not realise that their favoured newssheet is providing them with a biased view. A YouGov (market research organisation) poll of readers of national newspapers in the UK in 2017 found between 39 per cent and 49 per cent of respondents said that they 'didn't know' whether the newspaper they read was 'left', 'right' or 'centre'.

### Activity

Identify the main national newspapers (in terms of circulation) in the country you live in. In discussion with your classmates, try to reach a consensus on the political slant displayed by each of them.

Second, while it is true that media organisations have to be responsive to the concerns of their audiences, they can do this without doing or saying anything that threatens the status quo. As Philo (2012) argues in relation to UK media responses to the policy of austerity which followed the 2008 global financial crisis: 'the role of the mainstream media is largely to act as a forum for grumbles and discontent, but not to explore serious alternatives'.

Third, broadcast news, unlike the press, presents itself as impartial and objective. Indeed, PSBs are generally legally required to show 'due impartiality' in the reporting of current affairs, which they seek to achieve by providing a 'balanced' coverage. However, research indicates that in practice broadcast news unwittingly tends to be skewed towards the frames preferred by the powerful: governments, large corporations and political elites.

Most researchers reject the view that this is a result of some kind of conspiracy. Instead, they point to various factors – such as the social backgrounds of journalists, the operating practices of news organisations, the need to not upset advertisers and so on – as producing a view of the world that tends to reflect how powerful groups and organisations see it.

## Contemporary issues: Fake news

'Fake news' is lies and propaganda told for a commercial or political purpose which employs digital technology, especially social media, to go viral.

The term appeared after the 2016 US Presidential Election, when it became apparent that fake news stories posted on social media, such as Facebook and Twitter, had been prevalent during the campaign.

Some, such as stories posted by young people in Macedonia claiming that the Pope had endorsed Trump, were motivated purely by commercial considerations. The youths realised that outlandish stories captured so much interest that they could make money through automated advertising that rewarded high traffic to their sites. Others, such as stories undermining Hillary Clinton's campaign that suggested she had approved weapons sales to Islamic jihadists when Secretary of State, were politically motivated.

In November 2017, the US Senate Select Committee on Intelligence provided a list of 2753 Russian-linked Twitter accounts (now suspended) which had posted fake news stories supporting Trump during the election campaign.

Since Trump's election, he has made frequent use of the term 'fake news'. However, it could be argued that his (mis)use of the term is designed to undermine and misrepresent legitimate criticisms of his presidency. As the news media editor of BuzzFeed has written, Trump has 'redefined the term to mean, effectively, news reports he didn't like' (BuzzFeed News, 31/12/2017).

While the term 'fake news' is of recent origin, what it refers to is far from new. 'Disinformation' has played a prominent part in political conflict throughout history. However, the sheer scope and immediacy of digital media has led to worries that fake news could undermine democracy by misleading voters or encouraging a cynical attitude in which all sources are treated as equally untrustworthy. As a result, a number of governments around the world are either considering or have enacted legislation to try to tackle this problem. For example, in 2017 the UK government's Digital, Culture, Media and Sport Committee began an inquiry into fake news and the German government passed the Network Enforcement Act, which requires social networks that have more than 2 million German users to take down fake content within 24 hours of it being reported.

### Questions

1. Explain the origins of the term 'fake news'.
2. Why might Donald Trump's use of the term 'fake news' be seen as disingenuous (devious)?
3. Why is fake news an issue for democracies?
4. Research the conclusions that the UK's select committee inquiry reached about fake news.

### Key terms

**Gatekeepers** Individuals or organisations that control the flow of information reaching the general public.

**News values** Journalists' ideas about what is and is not newsworthy.

**Interpretative frameworks/frames** Ways in which the news media interpret the events that they report.

**Media sensationalism** The use of exaggeration or distortion to represent people or events in ways which will provoke a strong emotional reaction in the audience.

**Agenda-setting** The role of news media in shaping the public's opinion of what the important issues are facing society and how they should be understood.

**Primary definers** Individuals or organisations to whom journalists turn first to comment on the events they report.

**Moral panic** Widespread public concern about a particular group or activity that is seen as a threat to society.

**'Skivers and strivers'** Terms used by Conservative politicians in the UK to divide the working class by suggesting that some were lazy ('skivers') while others were hard-working ('strivers').

**Austerity** The policy, adopted by right-wing governments in a number of countries following the 2008 financial crisis, of cutting welfare expenditure and public services.

**'Other'** 'Othering' involves persuading people that certain individuals or groups are unlike themselves and undeserving of their respect or concern.

**Shop stewards** Trades union members elected as representatives of a 'shop' (or department) in dealings with the management.

**Picket line** A boundary established by workers on strike, especially at the entrance to their place of work, which other workers are asked not to cross.

## Summary

1. News can be seen as socially manufactured rather than merely reported.
2. Journalists act as gatekeepers in terms of the flow of information through society, selecting events to report on the basis of their news values – ideas about what makes an event newsworthy.
3. The news also provides particular ways of understanding the events it reports by framing them in one way rather than another – for example, through the language chosen. Powerful groups tend to be the ones whose frames provide the primary definition of events.
4. The news plays an important role in setting the agenda for public opinion.
5. Sociological research suggests that the mainstream media report events in ways that, while acknowledging some degree of diversity of opinion, rarely challenge the basic arrangements or basic assumptions of a society.
6. Pluralists are justified in arguing that the news media cover a variety of viewpoints in democratic societies and that the internet has extended the range of viewpoints that audiences can access.
7. Newspapers are usually partisan, but audiences may be unaware of the degree to which the press provides a partial and one-sided account of what is happening. Broadcast news may or may not be partisan, but even when it is legally required to be impartial it may nevertheless limit the range of views presented to those that fall within a consensus band of opinion.
8. Fake news has become a matter of concern for democracies, as it can misinform voters or promote a cynical view which treats all news media as equally untrustworthy.

# Unit 6.2.3 The postmodernist contribution to understanding the media

The term 'postmodernism' refers to two distinct things. One is an artistic, architectural and cultural movement which is characterised by a mixing of artistic styles and genres. Postmodernism in this sense emphasises **irony**, **pastiche** and playfulness and challenges the traditional distinction between high culture and popular culture. The art of Andy Warhol and films such as *The Matrix* and *Reservoir Dogs* could be seen as examples. The other is a philosophical movement which has produced some influential claims about how society is changing and also challenges much of mainstream sociological theorising. It is with the latter that we are concerned in this unit.

## Postmodernism as a sociological perspective

Postmodernism as a sociological perspective is associated particularly with a number of influential 20th-century French philosophers and social theorists such as Jean-François Lyotard, Jacques Derrida, Jean Baudrillard and Michel Foucault (although, confusingly, both Derrida and Foucault rejected the label of 'postmodernists').

All of these writers were interested in the role of language not merely in describing the world, but in shaping our understanding of it. For this reason, they were also sceptical about the possibility of discovering objective truths about the world because it is only through language that we can describe the world, but language is not neutral and the meaning of words can change. Additionally, they claimed that people no longer believed in the inevitability of progress, the power of science to solve all problems, the perfectibility of humanity or the possibility of running societies in a rational way. In Lyotard's view, people had rejected what he called 'grand narratives': all-embracing philosophical systems such as Marxism, religion, science and so on that claim to explain human experience and history.

For example, Foucault rejected the Marxist notions of ruling-class ideology and false consciousness because these assumed that Marxism provided the 'truth' about how history and society developed. In Foucault's view, all knowledge was bound up with power and the two together produced 'discourses': ways of talking and writing about the world, but also – at the same time – ways of understanding the world, which reflected the interests of those who produced them. The search for objective truth was therefore a mistaken quest, in his view, but one could nevertheless usefully analyse discourses in order to expose the interests they promoted. For example, one could analyse the medical discourse around insanity and reveal how psychiatry had been used as a mechanism of social control.

For postmodernists, society in the latter part of the 20th century was moving into a new era, a postmodern era in which the main focus of people's lives was not labour but consumption, in which traditional social structures like social class subcultures had fragmented and been replaced by consumption-based 'lifestyle choices' and in which the media had come to play an increasingly central role. However, before moving on to look at how postmodernists view the role of the media, it is worth pointing out the extent to which their theories took for granted that what was happening in Western Europe and North America at that time was true more generally. For example, for most people in developing countries, hard physical labour rather than consumption continued to define their lives and many had no access to traditional media, let alone the new media which postmodernists saw as crucial features of this new era. Similarly, while Western Europe and North America were, arguably, becoming increasingly secular, religious beliefs were still a central feature of the lives of people elsewhere, with the growth of religious fundamentalism and the Sunni/Shia split in Islam crucial features of the Middle East, for example.

### Activity

To what extent do you think the ideas of postmodernism are applicable to your society?

## Postmodernist views of the media

For postmodernists, the media play a central role in people's lives. For example, Baudrillard argues that we live in a media-saturated society in which we are surrounded by media images and spend an increasing part of our days consuming media messages. Moreover, in this new world the traditional distinction between 'representation' (media images) and 'reality' (the world outside of the media) has broken down. Instead, we live in a world of '**hyperreality**', a world in which people can no longer distinguish between what is real and what is fake – between media **simulations** and the real thing – because media images have come to constitute such an important part of this lived reality. In fact, Baudrillard goes further, arguing that the media provide us with **simulacra:** images of things that do not exist in reality. For him, modern society is based on the production and exchange of free-floating signs (words, images and so on) that have no connection with anything real.

### Activity

Does the fact that people confuse fake news with truth support or undermine the concept of hyperreality?

For Baudrillard, entertainment, information and communication technologies provide experiences that are so intense and involving that everyday life cannot compete. Disneyland (now, Disneyland Park) in California, for example, represents the epitome of hyperreality for Baudrillard. People go to see simulations of worlds – Frontierland, Main Street, USA, New Orleans Square – which either never really existed in the first place or which represent idealised and sanitised versions of historical reality. 'Reality' television shows – such as *Big Brother,* the *Real Housewives* franchise and *Keeping up with the Kardashians* – which are supposedly unscripted live broadcasts or recordings of real-life situations, and often feature an otherwise unknown cast of individuals who are not professional actors, provide another example of the blurring of fiction and reality. Are the people we are watching acting or just being themselves? Does this distinction even make sense?

Sherry Turkle (1995) echoes Baudrillard when she talks about television as part of the postmodern 'culture of simulation', where we allegedly learn to identify with the simulated world of television more readily than we do with the real world around us. According to Turkle, such simulation laid the groundwork for the next development in the relationship between reality and simulation: the development of virtual reality. 'Virtual reality' (or 'VR') is a term used to describe three-dimensional, computer-generated environments that simulate our experience of the real world. An early example was provided by Second Life, where users can create their own characters, using **avatars.** Increasingly popular today, however, are virtual reality games using VR headsets such as Oculus Rift, HTC Vive, PlayStation VR, Gear VR or Daydream.

## Activity

*A gamer wearing a VR headset.*

How far do you think virtual reality games blur the boundary between real life and simulations of real life?

# Evaluation

Postmodernism does seem to have captured something about a world in which media images have become all-pervasive and where people spend a vast amount of time looking at television, mobile, tablet and computer screens. Moreover, **anecdotal evidence**, such as the stories that actors who have played villains in soap operas tell about being accosted in the street by angry members of the public attacking them for their 'evil behaviour', suggests that some people do indeed have trouble distinguishing between representation and reality. However, postmodernism has been the subject of extensive criticism.

## Activity

Why are sociologists cautious about using anecdotal evidence?

First, its claim that the pursuit of objective truth is misguided is **epistemologically** flawed. This claim rests on the assertion that all knowledge is relative, yet the claim itself is stating that this particular assertion is not relative, but true. Presumably, postmodernists want us to take the claims they make about society seriously, that they are saying something that is true, yet at the same time they are denying the possibility of objective truth!

Second, the claims that postmodernists make about the power of the media today are not generally backed up by extensive empirical research. For example, the claim that people are unable to distinguish between media representations and reality because the two have become fused in people's minds is a strong claim about media effects that is open to empirical investigation. But postmodernists do not seem to be interested in carrying out such investigations.

Greg Philo and David Miller (2001) argue that it is perfectly possible to compare media images with reality and to highlight inaccuracies and misrepresentations: 'a media image is a measurable part of reality in its own right and the processes by which it is manufactured can be analysed and exposed'.

Moreover, research that has been carried out on, for example, reality TV programmes, suggests that audiences have few illusions about what they are viewing. Annette Hill (2002) studied audience responses to *Big Brother* in the UK. When asked about the programme, regular viewers felt that there were elements of reality (in that it was not scripted and featured non-actors), but they were well aware that they were watching something that had been contrived by the producers to make entertaining television.

Finally, left-wing critics attack postmodernists for adopting what *appear*s to be a radical posture, but which actually functions to undermine the examination of structures of power and inequality in society. Instead, it encourages an ironic detachment from any issue which seems to take the idea of objective truth seriously.

## Activity

In your own words, describe three criticisms of postmodernist views of the media.

## Key terms

**Irony** Saying the opposite of what you mean. For example saying, 'Well, that's brilliant!' when what you mean is that it's dreadful.

**Pastiche** A composition in literature, music or painting made up of bits of other works or imitations of another's style.

**Hyperreality** The reality created by a media-saturated society where it is no longer possible to separate representations of reality from reality.

**Simulations** Copies of reality.

**Simulacra** (singular 'simulacrum') Signs (words, images and so on) which no longer bear any connection to the real world.

**Avatars** In computing, an avatar is the graphical representation of the user or the user's alter ego or character in a virtual reality setting.

**Anecdotal evidence** Evidence collected in a casual or informal manner and relying heavily, or entirely, on personal testimony.

**Epistemology** The branch of philosophy concerned with studying the grounds of knowledge – that is, the basis on which someone can claim to know that something is true.

## Summary

1. Postmodernism refers to both an artistic and aesthetic movement that developed in the second half of the 20th century and to a theory of how society was changing at that time.
2. Postmodernism is particularly associated with a number of French philosophers and social theorists: Derrida, Lyotard, Baudrillard and Foucault.
3. Postmodernists argue that societies have become increasingly fragmented and diverse, that people no longer accept grand narratives that claim to explain how the world is and how it could be different, and they reject the search for objective truths about the world.
4. Postmodernists also argue that people today live in a media-saturated society of hyperreality where it is no longer possible to distinguish between representation and reality. So-called 'reality TV' programmes illustrate this blurring of fact and fantasy.
5. Postmodernist theories have been subjected to extensive criticism. Critics reject the relativism they embrace on the basis that this is epistemologically flawed. Also, the large claims they make about the role of the media in contemporary society are not supported by empirical evidence and the research that has been done does not provide strong support for these claims. Left-wing critics accuse postmodernists of adopting a radical pose which undermines efforts to address the real problems of wealth and power inequalities that characterise late capitalism.

# END-OF-PART QUESTIONS

| | | |
|---|---|---|
| 01 | Describe two ways in which pluralist and Marxist views of the media differ. | **[4 marks]** |
| 02 | Explain the role of selection and framing in the production of the news. | **[6 marks]** |
| 03 | Evaluate the postmodernist view of the media. | **[8 marks]** |

# PART 3 THE IMPACT OF THE NEW MEDIA

## Contents

**Unit 6.3.1** **Understanding new media: sociological issues** **351**

**Unit 6.3.2** **The new media as challenges to existing power structures** **356**

**Unit 6.3.3** **The impact of the new media on social identities and interpersonal relationships** **359**

The media landscape has been transformed over the last three decades by the growth of new digital technologies and their rapid global spread.

In Part 3 we examine some of the many issues that this has raised for sociologists, from their impact on global politics, at one end of the scale, to their impact on social identity and interpersonal relationships at the other.

In Unit 6.3.1 we will seek to clarify the nature of the new media, explore the role it has played in globalisation and outline the debate between those who see these developments as mainly beneficial and those who see them as mainly detrimental.

In Units 6.3.2 and 6.3.3, we seek to examine at least some of the many areas of disagreement between digital optimists and digital pessimists.

Like all new technology, the new media have provoked wildly optimistic claims about how they will transform society for the better, on the one hand, and equally exaggerated predictions of disastrous consequences for social life, on the other. Where does the truth lie?

# Unit 6.3.1 Understanding new media: sociological issues

As we have seen, the term 'new media' consists of digital media which rely on the internet for the distribution of messages via desktop computers and mobile devices such as laptops, tablets and mobile phones. It entails a wide range of new means of communication including email, wikis, blogs, vlogs, mobile phone applications such as Twitter and Instagram, virtual reality sites, social media sites and so on. But what do these all have in common?

## The characteristics of new media

The new media – whether they have evolved from traditional media delivery systems or are new in their own right – share a number of characteristics that differentiate them from the media delivery systems that dominated only 30 years ago:

- *Digitalisation*: the growth of digital technology in the 1990s resulted in changes in the way information is stored and transmitted. In particular, it led to the translation of all information, regardless of format (for example, images, texts, sounds), into a universal computer language. The new media all share this common digital format.
- *Convergence*: digitalisation resulted in the realisation that different ways of presenting a variety of types of information – text, photographs, video, film, voices and music – could all be combined into a single delivery system. This is known as '**technological convergence**'. What were once separate and unconnected technologies are now part of a converging media landscape that blurs the lines about how we use these technologies. For example, people use smartphones not only to call others, but to send texts, access the internet, take photographs, stream music, play video games and watch videos.
- *Compression*: digital technologies enable the compression of signals. This has led to a proliferation of radio and television channels, because it means that many signals can be sent through the same cable, telephone line and so on. This has resulted in the development of new markets organised around the concept of '**narrowcasting**' – the transmission of particular types of media content to niche audiences. For example, TV channels are dedicated to programmes about homes, sewing, wildlife, fishing, sports, business, cooking, sailing and many more.
- *Interactivity*: communication via traditional media is essentially one-way – from the producer of a message to the audience. The new media enable a much greater degree of interactivity between the originators of media messages and their recipients. This development is captured in the term 'Web 2.0', which refers to various applications of the **Internet and World Wide Web**, including blogs, wikis, video sharing services, and social media websites such as Facebook and MySpace, which focus on interactive sharing and participatory collaboration rather than simple content delivery.

## Activity

*A 'smart' or 'hybrid' TV set with integrated internet and interactive 'Web 2.0' features.*

How do such devices illustrate technological convergence?

## The new media, globalisation and digital divides

Globalisation involves all parts of the world becoming increasingly interconnected, so that national boundaries – in some respects, at least – become less important. It is associated with increasing global flows of information, ideas, goods and people.

The new media have undoubtedly played a part in the process of globalisation through their ability to compress both space and time: people who are geographically distant are able to communicate with each other more or less instantaneously even when they are on the other side of the globe. It is also possible for people to become part of virtual communities of like-minded individuals – say, scholars researching global warming – who may be based in many different countries. Also, information, including audio-visual material, can be transmitted via the internet across national boundaries by groups and organisations for educational, cultural, commercial or political purposes.

However, it is important to recognise the existence of a number of 'digital divides' – inequalities in access to the new media – globally, regionally and within nations.

By the end of 2017, roughly half (48 per cent) of the world's population regularly connected to the internet according to the International Telecommunications Union (UNESCO, 2017/2018). However, this means that there are large numbers for whom the new media are out of reach. Only about 35 per cent of people in developing countries have access to the internet and in the Least Developed Countries (LDCs) the figure drops to 10 per cent.

Equally significant as the level of economic development is the nature of the political regime that people live under. As we saw in Unit 6.1.2, access to online media for people living in authoritarian regimes is often limited by governments and – on top of this – censorship further limits the content that people can access.

Within countries, other digital divides are apparent, along the lines of age, class and gender particularly. Unsurprisingly, those who have grown up with digital technology – younger generations – are more confident about using it than older generations and generally spend more time online. Marc Prensky (2001) refers to those who have grown up in the digital age as '**digital natives**', whom he contrasts with older people (or 'digital immigrants'), likening digital literacy to the contrast between those who are socialised into a culture from birth and those who have to adjust to it as recent immigrants. Also, access to new media depends on the ownership of appropriate hardware – computers, tablets and mobile phones, for example – the cost of which may prohibit access for those who are poorer.

### Activity

If you are in a position to do so, compare your use of digital technology with that of your parent(s) and your grandparent(s). Is a generational divide apparent?

Finally, there is some evidence that digital technology has been gendered as more 'masculine'; that because it involves technology it will somehow be more congenial to males than females. The *Final Report of the European Commission* on 'Women in the Digital Age' (2018) found that male graduates in Information and Communications Technology (ICT)-related fields outnumber women by roughly three to one in the European Union. The report suggests that gender inequality in the digital sphere is 'essentially a result of the persistence of strong unconscious biases about what is appropriate and what capacities each gender has, as well as about the technologies themselves'.

### Activity

How far do you think such unconscious gender biases in relation to digital technology still exist in your own generation? Also, do you think they apply equally to using digital technology as a consumer or just to working with it?

Other statistics support this picture. Global figures on age and class divides are not available, but in the UK, for example, in terms of age, according to the Office of National Statistics (ONS), nearly 90 per cent of the population aged 16 and over had used the internet in the last three months in 2017. However, the proportion declines with age from 99 per cent for those in the 16–34 age group, down to 41 per cent of those aged 75 and over. Similarly, figures from 2012 provided by ONS indicate that internet use declines with income, with 100 per cent of those with a weekly income of over £2000 having ever accessed the internet, compared with 93 per cent of those earning less than £200.

In terms of gender, according to the International Telecommunications Union, the global internet-user gender gap was 12 per cent in 2016. In other words, 12 per cent fewer women accessed the internet than men. The gap was largest in the world's LDCs, at 31 per cent. The regional gender gap is largest in Africa (23 per cent) and smallest in the Americas (2 per cent).

# Digital optimism versus digital pessimism

As far back as the 1960s, an influential media theorist called Marshall McLuhan predicted that new communication technologies would unite the world into a 'global village'. The growth and rapid spread of digital technologies in recent decades – ongoing digital divides notwithstanding – has provoked an extensive literature concerned to understand this development and evaluate its likely impact on society.

This writing can be divided into two broad camps. On the one hand, digital optimists (also known as cyber- or techno-optimists) are hopeful that the new technology will lead, for example, to greater global understanding, interconnectedness and fellow feeling as people in different countries become more aware of the many things that unite them, rather than those which divide them. On the other hand, digital pessimists (also known as cyber- or techno-pessimists) are doubtful whether new technologies alone will transform international relations in the face of enormous global military, economic and political inequalities and are sceptical of the ability of this new technology to promote democracy.

## Activity

*Like primitives, we now live in a global village of our own making, a simultaneous happening... The global village is a world in which you don't necessarily have harmony; you have extreme concern with every else's business and much involvement in everybody else's life.'*

*A photograph of, and quotation from, McLuhan.*

Going by the quote above, do you think McLuhan would be classified today as a digital optimist or digital pessimist?

## Digital optimists

A clearly optimistic view of the digital revolution is provided by Nicholas Negroponte. In *Being Digital* (1998), he talks about the 'triumph of the digital age', which in his view displays four powerful qualities – decentralisation, globalisation, harmonisation and empowerment. Digital technology will empower the ordinary citizen and reduce the extent to which power is centralised in the state in the future. People will be able to cooperate with each other on a global scale, even though they are geographically distant. Such cooperation will lead to greater harmony and strengthen international social bonds.

A more recent example of digital optimism is provided by the work of Henry Jenkins. In *Convergence Culture: Where Old and New Media Collide* (2006), he suggests that interactivity and convergence have produced a '**participatory culture**'. In other words, media producers and consumers no longer occupy separate roles – they are now participants who interact with each other according to a new set of rules that are constantly evolving. This has produced more control at the user end compared with the past. For example, Jenkins notes that the print fanzine magazines of the 1980s have now migrated to the online digital world of bloggers, because these websites have greater accessibility and the speed of feedback is almost instant.

Jenkins also suggests that interactivity has produced a '**collective intelligence**', because consuming new media tends to be a collective process. He notes: 'none of us can know everything; each of us knows something; and we can put the pieces together if we pool our resources and combine our skills'. He claims that such collective intelligence can be seen as an alternative source of media power to that of media owners.

The internet provides the main means through which people can interact with each other in a participatory culture and build collective intelligence. They can engage in online discussions or play online live games with each other through mediums such as Xbox LIVE. They may simply be interested in networking with others through sites such as Twitter and Facebook. Some of this interactivity will be creative – for example, people may wish to convey their thoughts, feelings and opinions through the setting up of their own websites or blogs. They may produce their own films and music and post these on sites such as YouTube. User-generated content and information sites such as Wikipedia and IMDb are a popular source of knowledge.

## Digital pessimists

The work of Andrew Keen can be seen as a direct riposte to that of Jenkins. In *The Cult of the Amateur* (2008), he agrees that the internet has enabled a multitude of new voices to be heard, but disagrees that this represents progress and is extremely sceptical about Jenkins' notion of 'collective intelligence'. He makes four main claims:

1. Social networking sites such as Facebook and YouTube are creating a culture of 'digital narcissism' – an excessive desire for personal attention. Keen argues that these websites have become 'shrines for self-broadcasting' – they exist so 'that we can advertise ourselves: everything from our favourite books and movies, to photos from our summer vacations, to "testimonials" praising our more winsome moments or recapping our latest drunken exploits'.

   He notes that 50 per cent of bloggers blog for the sole purpose of reporting and sharing experiences from their personal lives. Consequently, Keen argues that 'the internet has become a mirror to ourselves. Rather than using it to seek news, information or culture, we use it to actually BE the news, the information, the culture.'

### Activity

How far do you think the now widespread habit of taking selfies on smartphones and posting them online supports Keen's claims about increasing narcissism?

2. Open-source sites such as Wikipedia are undermining the authority of experts and teachers and encouraging plagiarism. Keen claims that on Wikipedia, 'everyone with an agenda can re-write an entry to their liking. No one is being paid to check their credentials or evaluate their material.' Consequently, internet sites such as these are vulnerable to untrustworthy material. Moreover, the internet is undermining 'the very concept of ownership, creating a generation of plagiarists and copyright thieves with little respect for intellectual property'. Keen argues that students are using this stolen property to cheat their way through school and university – 'the digital revolution is creating a generation of cut-and-paste burglars who view all content on the internet as common property'.
3. Anonymous blogs, as well as sites such as Twitter, and their amateur content are undermining informed expertise and professional journalism. Keen argues that the majority of blogs and tweets do not deliver anything worthwhile, because essentially blogging and tweeting are merely about expressing shrill superficial opinion rather than considered analysis and judgement. Blogs and tweets spread rumours as facts and actually undermine truth as 'one person's truth becomes as "true" as anyone else's'. Moreover, he argues that blogging undermines democracy, because the only conversations bloggers want to hear are those with people like themselves – they use the Web to confirm their own partisan views and to link to others with the same ideas.
4. The rise in digital literacy has led to a decline in cultural literacy. Keen claims that the more skilled young people become in using the tools of the digital revolution, the more ignorant they become about the objective world around them. He argues that the informational abundance of the Web is creating a famine of intelligence and that this has produced what Mark Bauerlein (2009) terms 'the dumbest generation'. Keen claims that the internet is 'eroding our ability to concentrate and contemplate intellectually, the mental requisites that allow us to read and digest books'. The digital revolution is therefore transforming internet users into skimmers – with low attention spans and poor cognitive skills.

Keen's negative view of Wikipedia is shared by some academics, but many others value it as a remarkable example of what can be produced by ordinary people when they cooperate with each other, and who argue that its open-source nature means that, because everyone has an equal stake in ensuring the reliability of the information provided, falsehoods are likely to be spotted and corrected. On the other hand, his claim that blogs and tweets spread rumours as facts can be seen as **prescient**, anticipating the current concern over the ability of social media to spread 'fake news' (see Unit 6.2.2). So, too, can his concern over the rise of plagiarism, which has led colleges and universities to employ software that can check for plagiarism in students' assignments.

A similarly negative view of the digital revolution is taken by McChesney in his book *Digital Disconnect: How Capitalism is Turning the Internet Against Democracy* (2013). He writes: 'For all of the digital revolution's accomplishments, it has failed to deliver on much of the promise that was once seen as inherent in the technology.'

McChesney's main concern is with the third of Keen's four claims: the impact of the internet on journalism, especially print journalism. For

McChesney, journalism is a public good which plays a vital role in democracies, but as internet companies have grown they have sucked advertising money away from the press. The four most visited sites in 2012 in the USA were Google, Microsoft, Yahoo and Facebook and these companies had attracted two-thirds of the revenue from advertising on the internet in the USA by 2012. Moreover, people increasingly obtain their news online rather than buying newspapers, but the writers providing this news content are often either amateurs or poorly paid freelancers who focus on gossip and celebrity culture rather than '**hard news**'.

## Activity

See whether you can find out the proportion of advertising expenditure spent on online advertising in the country you live in.

The result has been that many smaller newspapers in Western Europe and the USA have closed and those that remain are financially vulnerable. Consequently, in McChesney's view, the internet has undermined journalism's watchdog role, undermined professional journalistic standards and resulted in the trivialisation of content.

### Conclusion

Clearly, there is a lack of consensus about how the new media are impacting society. There is not the space to evaluate all the points of disagreement between digital optimists and pessimists, so instead in the next two units we will focus on the issues which have perhaps received the greatest attention: the impact on politics and the impact on interpersonal relationships and social identity.

## Key terms

**Technological convergence** In the context of ICT, refers to the combination of two or more technologies in a single device.

**Narrowcasting** Transmitting media messages to a specific segment of the audience (in contrast to *broad*casting).

**The internet and World Wide Web** These terms are often used as if they refer to the same thing. Strictly speaking, they do not. The internet is a massive network of computer networks (a networking infrastructure) begun in the 1960s that connects millions of computers and other digital devices together globally. The Web (or World Wide Web), on the other hand, is the system of webpages and sites that is accessed via the internet. It was developed in the late 1980s by Tim Berners-Lee.

**Digital natives** People who have grown up since birth with digital technology.

**Participatory culture** A participatory culture is a culture with relatively low barriers to artistic expression and civic engagement, strong support for creating and sharing one's creations, and some type of informal mentorship whereby what is known by the most experienced is passed along to novices.

**Collective intelligence** The notion that people working together collaboratively can produce an outcome that is superior to that produced by people working alone.

**Prescient** Knowing or correctly suggesting what will happen in the future.

**Hard news** News stories that focus on politics, economics, war and crime; in contrast to 'soft news', which focuses on human interest stories.

## Summary

1. The new media share four characteristics which differentiate them from traditional media: digitalisation, technological convergence, compression and interactivity.
2. The new media have played an integral role in the process of globalisation, although there are a number of significant digital divides related to the level of a country's economic development and political structure and to class, age and gender.
3. The digital revolution has generated fierce debate between digital optimists and digital pessimists about its (likely) effects on society.
4. Digital optimists such as Negroponte and Jenkins think that the digital revolution will bring people together across national and ethnic boundaries, promote democracy and harness the collective intelligence of the masses.
5. Digital pessimists such as Keen and McChesney argue that this has not happened. Instead, the digital revolution has encouraged narcissism, undermined the authority of experts and teachers by providing the ignorant and bigoted with the same opportunity to promote their views as those with genuine expertise, and reduced people's ability and willingness to concentrate. In addition, by increasingly monopolising advertising revenue it has undermined traditional journalism, which has weakened democracy.

# Unit 6.3.2 The new media as challenges to existing power structures

For digital optimists, the digital revolution was seen as empowering ordinary citizens through providing easy access to information, interpretations and viewpoints which were unlikely to be found in the conventional mainstream media that traditionally set the agenda for debate in the wider society. Additionally, digitalisation facilitated communication and data-sharing and the internet offered people the ability to network with thousands of other like-minded individuals. Some media sociologists, therefore, have suggested that the internet can revitalise democracy because it gives a voice to those who would otherwise go unheard, both in democratic and authoritarian societies. It can turn ordinary citizens into '**citizen journalists**' who can join together and take action that may lead to social change – '**digital activism**'.

## Digital activism: the optimist view

In their book *Digitally Enabled Social Change: Activism in the Internet Age,* Jennifer Earl and Katrina Kimport (2011) argue that digital technology has had two main effects on activism: one quantitative ('scale change') the other qualitative ('model change').

In terms of scale change, activists carry out the same activities as in the analogue era, but more quickly, on a larger scale and at lower cost. They provide the example of online petitions (or e-petitions). E-petitions collect signatures in the same way as paper petitions, but at larger scale because they can be signed by anyone at any time, and at lower cost because they can be started and distributed for free.

### Activity

Are you aware of any e-petitions that have been circulated in your country? Have you ever signed one?

In terms of model change, Earl and Kimport contrast traditional activism, organised by formal organisations such as trade unions and NGOs, with what happened in the Arab Spring (anti-government movements which spread across the Middle East and North Africa between late 2010 and mid-2012) and the Occupy movement (demonstrations against 'corporate greed', social inequality and the political domination of the richest 'one per cent', which began in New York in Wall Street in 2011 and subsequently spread to over 900 cities). The new media allow participants to organise themselves without formalised, central leaders. Leaders emerge as a result of individuals choosing to follow certain people – for example, on Twitter.

### Activity

*The Arab Spring: protesters gather in Tahrir Square, Cairo, Egypt, in January 2011.*

Research the role that social media played in the Arab Spring protests. For further discussion on this topic, see Unit 8.3.2.

Digital optimists argue that digital activists have used the internet to challenge power elites in a number of ways:

- It has been used to monitor the illegal or immoral activities of big businesses.
- It has been used to harness mass support for causes such as Make Poverty History.
- It has also been used to coordinate protests and activism ranging from the promotion of animal rights to disrupting G8 meetings about climate change and debt in developing nations.
- Hacktivist networks such as Anonymous have defaced corporate and government websites and engaged in virtual sabotage such as web-sit-ins and email bombing (sending so much information to a site that it crashes) and information theft, especially computer code theft.

Owen Spencer-Thomas (2008) uses the example of Burma (also known as Myanmar) to illustrate the growing influence of citizen journalists. He notes that the mass anti-government demonstrations in Burma in 1988 failed to receive much media attention because the military regime banned overseas journalists from the country. By contrast, the mass demonstrations in 2007 received far more attention because civilians themselves had the technology, in the form of modern mobile phones and camcorders, to send instant messages and pictures out of the country to waiting international media such as Reuters, the BBC and CNN. In other words, the digital revolution enabled citizen journalism.

## Twitter

Dhiraj Murthy (2013) has empirically investigated the impact of Twitter, which had 140 million users worldwide at that time, and rejects the cultural pessimist view that Twitter represents the dumbing down of society, the victory of short attention spans, the death of meaningful communication, or the rise of what Keen calls 'me-cultures'. Instead, Murthy claims that Twitter has proved extremely useful as a news-gathering medium in terms of communicating information about events such as the Tohuku earthquake in Japan in 2011, and social movements such as the Occupy protests and the Arab Spring.

Murthy argues that Twitter was particularly effective in the Egyptian protests that toppled President Mubarak, in two ways. First, Twitter helped enable a mass movement of people out onto the streets protesting about high unemployment, persistent poverty and police brutality. Indeed, Murthy notes that both the internet and Twitter were regarded by the Egyptian authorities as so threatening in their dissemination of activist information that they were shut down for a week by the government in January 2011. Second, Murthy argues that Twitter helped to bring international attention to what was going on by acting as a valuable news source for international journalists.

Murthy concludes that, 'even if tweets did not bring feet to Egyptian streets, they helped to facilitate a diverse global network of individuals who participated in a wide-ranging set of mobilisation efforts from the re-tweeters in Starbucks to those sending letters to their Congress people/Ministers or participating in activist movements both online and offline' (Murthy, 2013).

He argues that although Twitter may not topple governments, as a young communications medium it has the potential to shape many aspects of people's social, political and economic lives.

A recent example of digital activism is the #MeToo campaign seeking to raise awareness of the widespread nature of the sexual abuse and harassment of girls and women by men. (See the Contemporary issues box below.)

## Contemporary issues: The #MeToo Campaign

*Seoul, South Korea, 8 March 2018. South Korean Workers Confederation Union Members support the #MeToo campaign.*

*The following is drawn from an American blog.*

'The #MeToo campaign continues to rock our world. It has spread across the globe and crossed racial, economic, and other boundaries. The digital campaign gained traction on October 15, 2017, when – in response to allegations of sexual harassment against Hollywood film producer Harvey Weinstein – actress Alyssa Milano posted a tweet urging women who had been sexually assaulted or harassed to post a status on social media with the words "Me Too," to "give people a sense of the magnitude of the problem." When she awoke the next morning, she found that over 30 000 people had used #MeToo.

Besides hitting Hollywood, media, politics, national security, and other sectors, the movement has rapidly spread across the world – a mirror of the numerous women's marches across the globe this past January. By early November, #MeToo had been tweeted 2.3 million times from eighty-five countries.

However, the #MeToo campaign has been somewhat less visible in the Arab world. According to reporting from CNN, "Experts believe that the burden of harassment and abuse there is as rife as in any other region but that the voices heard are few and far between." Lina Abirafeh, director of the Institute for Women's Studies in the Arab World in Lebanon suggests that "There are so many reasons behind this silence... I've heard trickles... [but] people are scared," in part due to norms that attach stigma and shame to speaking out.'

Source: Adapted from *#MeToo Goes Global and Crosses Multiple Boundaries,* blog post by Catherine Powell, 14/12/2017.

### Questions

1. Why can #MeToo be seen as an example of digital activism?
2. Do you agree that it can be seen as a 'global' movement, given that there are over 200 countries in the world?
3. Why might girls and women in some countries be reluctant to join the campaign even if they are aware of it?

## Limitations of the digital optimist view

The evidence and arguments outlined above provide strong support for the claim that the digital revolution has empowered ordinary citizens and facilitated, if not promoted, political action against authoritarian governments and against powerful interests within democracies.

However, this is only one side of the story. As already stated, the Occupy protests in Wall Street spread to over 900 cities worldwide, yet Wall Street is still standing and the interests of finance capitalism appear not to have suffered any major setbacks. The Arab Spring led to protests and demonstrations across many countries in the Middle East and Northern Africa. Yet, as of 2018, only the uprising in Tunisia has resulted in a transition to constitutional democracy. In other countries authoritarianism still prevails (as in Egypt) or civil wars continue (as in Syria). As Thomas Carothers (2015) argues: 'The number of democracies today is basically no greater than it was at the start of the century' and many existing democracies today 'are experiencing serious institutional debilities and weak public confidence'.

How can this be explained? A number of factors are relevant.

First, protests and demonstrations can usually be withstood by established authorities unless they succeed in engaging enormous numbers. Rakesh Rajani (quoted in Carothers), reflecting six years later on the limited successes of Twaweza, a digital social change initiative in East Africa which he launched in 2009, commented that 'Technology does not *drive* anything. It creates new possibilities for collecting and analysing data, mashing ideas and reaching people, but people still need to be moved to engage and find practical pathways to act. Where the fear of being beaten or the habits of self-censorship inhibit agency, technology, however versatile, is a feeble match.'

Second, as we saw in Unit 6.2.1, authoritarian governments increasingly seek to limit the liberating potential of the new communication technologies by means of censorship, masked political control and technology capture: using the same technologies that have enabled the global information explosion to stifle internal dissent by monitoring and surveilling critical voices. For example, in Turkey, the 2014 Internet Law requires internet service providers (ISPs) to store the data they collect on Web users' activities for two years and to make it available to the authorities upon request. (It should be noted that similar laws have also been passed in democracies – for example, the UK's Investigatory Powers Act of 2016 – despite opposition from civil rights groups. However, the political context matters: according to Amnesty International in Turkey, since the failed coup of July 2016, over 281 journalists have been imprisoned (winter 2017, issue 195)

In other words, it is not only pro-democracy activists who can use digital technology; it is equally available to those who oppose democracy or wish to undermine democratic processes in established democracies. For example, IS (also known as ISIS or Daesh) has made sophisticated use of digital technology to seek to radicalise young Muslims and recruit them to their cause of jihad (holy war). According to the anti-radicalisation think-tank Quilliam, in 2015 IS produced daily an average of three videos, more than fifteen photographic reports and nine radio news bulletins in multiple languages, all available online. In addition, IS makes extensive use of social media, including YouTube, Twitter, Instagram and Tumblr (Davies, 2016).

Finally, as Senem Düzgit (quoted in Carothers) argues, it is important not to lose sight of the fact that, outside the wealthy, established democracies, large numbers of people still lack access to digital technologies. In Turkey, for example, approximately half of households still lack internet access. They are, therefore, reliant on government-controlled traditional media.

## Activity

Give three arguments against the digital optimist view of the impact of the new media on democracy.

### Conclusion

As Mary Joyce (2013) argues, the reality of digital activism is more complicated than either cyber-optimists or digital pessimists suggest: 'Digital technology does not have uniquely positive or negative effects on activism. Much depends on context, on the political system in which activists are operating, and on the complexity of the problem they seek to remedy.'

However, as Martin Tisné (quoted in Carothers) argues, the focus on the impact of digital activism at the national level may be missing significant developments at the local level which are extending democracy. He cites the examples of FixMyStreet (a website and app that helps people in the United Kingdom inform their local authority of problems needing their attention, such as potholes, broken streetlamps and so on), BudgIT (a Nigerian digital activist platform holding local and regional officials to account on spending issues) and Mejora Tu Escuela (a Mexican initiative which allows parents to track the performance of local schools).

## Key terms

**Citizen journalists** Members of the general public who collect and disseminate news over the internet.

**Digital activism** The use of new information and communication technologies in social and political campaigning.

## Summary

1. Digital optimists have argued that digital technologies have reinvigorated democracy by promoting citizen journalism and digital activism.
2. Digital technologies have facilitated activism by allowing it to be conducted more quickly, more cheaply and on a larger scale, and by democratising activism itself.
3. The Arab Spring protests and the Occupy movement were both facilitated by digital media.
4. However, digital pessimists point out that only one of the many countries involved in the Arab Spring is now a democracy and that the Occupy movement does not appear to have had any long-term impact on finance capital.
5. They also point out that authoritarian governments have either censored digital technology or used it themselves to undermine democracy in various ways and that digital divides continue to limit the radical potential of new technologies.

# Unit 6.3.3 The impact of the new media on social identities and interpersonal relationships

The growth of **hyper-connectivity** – the ability to be digitally connected to others pretty much constantly across a wide range of platforms – has led to intense speculation about how this might impact on people's social lives. In this unit, we will explore what the resulting literature has suggested will be the impact on people's social identities and their interpersonal relationships.

## Social identity

Social identity has to do with group membership and has both an objective and subjective component. Objectively, people may see us as belonging to a particular group because of some characteristic we share with others – say, gender or ethnicity – irrespective of how important this aspect of identity is to ourselves. Subjectively, social identity has to do with how we see ourselves in terms of group membership, which group or groups we see ourselves as belonging to.

As groups differ in their social status, people may be looked up to or looked down upon by others in terms of their objective social identity. Similarly, subjectively they may experience different levels of self-esteem in terms of their self-identification or they may even refuse to identify with a social identity that they actually belong to. For example, someone with a physical impairment may not identify themselves as disabled or someone who is attracted to the same sex may not see themselves as gay if they believe that such identities are stigmatising.

Interpersonal relationships are the relationships we have with others, both face to face and online – family, friends, acquaintances, colleagues, strangers and so on.

## Case study: changing identities in the UK

In 2013, a government-commissioned report looking at 'a rapidly changing, globalised, technology-rich, and densely networked UK' was published called *Future Identities: Changing Identities in the UK: The Next 10 Years*.

The report observed that most people in the UK were now connected to the internet and 60 per cent of internet users were members of one or more social networking sites. As a result, it argued, the UK is now a virtual environment as well as a real place and UK citizens are increasingly globally connected. Moreover, as people increasingly post information about themselves online on social media, so the distinction between people's private and public identities is becoming blurred. The report also argued that, while the internet has not produced a new kind of identity, it has been instrumental in raising awareness that identities are more multiple, culturally contingent and contextual than had previously been understood. In simpler terms, each of us has numerous (potential) social identities; the social identities we have available to us depend on the culture of the society we live in, and which identities matter to us at any particular time depends on social context.

A similar picture could be painted for other industrialised societies and less industrialised societies are likely to follow a similar trajectory. Are these developments to be welcomed or feared?

## The digital optimist view

For digital optimists, the digital revolution has opened up the chance to try out and take on an infinite range of different identities, in line with the postmodernist theme of greater variability and flexibility in social identities. For example, Thusha Rajendran (2018) refers to the opportunities provided by virtual worlds such as Second Life and video games such as World of Warcraft where people 'can take on different identities and imagine a completely new existence for themselves'.

Rajendran refers approvingly to the liberating effect of the internet for those who feel 'trapped in the wrong body' – that is, people who identify as transgender – or who feel constrained by binary notions of sex – that is, the division into male and female – and who embrace gender fluidity (that is, gender that varies over time). Similarly, for people who are attracted to the same sex, particularly those living in societies where homosexuality is illegal or heavily stigmatised, the internet has provided reassurance that in many societies it is not homosexuality, but **homophobia**, that is outlawed.

Rajendran concludes: 'We no longer have to feel ourselves straitjacketed by fixed ideas of national, cultural or sexual identity. In 2018 technology can help take us beyond who society tells us we are, where we can explore whole new worlds and different ways of life, and decide exactly who we want to be.'

Digital optimists also argue that the digital revolution has massively expanded people's range of potential contacts and field of relationships. Fulvio Castellacci (quoted in Holsten, 2018) argues that 'social networking sites like Facebook and Instagram can have positive effects on our social life. It can make it easier for us to keep track of existing acquaintances, and... can help us develop relationships with people who are far away geographically.' For example, it is now much easier for members of migrant communities to stay in touch with their families and friends back home, and online dating, using apps like Tinder, Happn and Melt, has expanded the range of potential partners people can meet. Also, engagement with others through social media can break down feelings of social isolation for those who are housebound or struggle with face-to-face interaction because of shyness.

### Activity

Evaluate the digital optimist view of social identity. How far do you think it is true that digital media allow us to choose our social identity?

## The digital pessimist view

For digital pessimists, the digital revolution has opened up new opportunities for people to misrepresent their identities online with detrimental consequences. For example, the anonymity afforded by the internet has allowed paedophiles

## Contemporary issues: Keeping the family together through new media

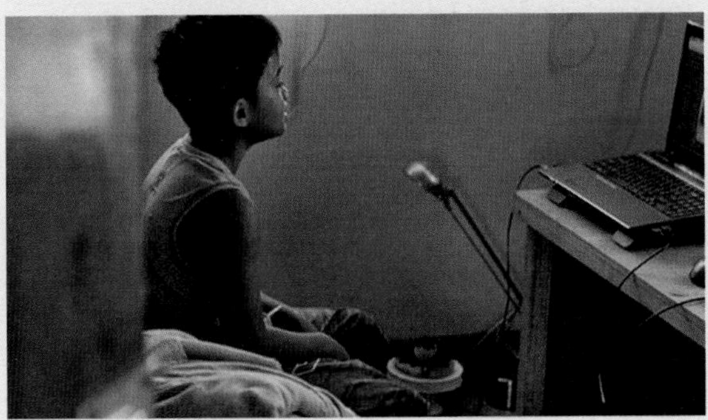

*Migrant parents are using social media to keep in touch with their children. Image by Geric Cruz. Philippines, 2016.*

'Imagine a life in which you have to live away from your children, maybe for several years.

Ask yourself how you could keep the ties close between you, watch them growing up, and continue to be a daily part of their lives.

In their book *Migration and New Media – Transnational Families and Polymedia*, Mirca Madianou and Daniel Miller reveal how new media have come to be at the heart of such family relationships.

Their research looks at the long-term separation between migrant mothers and their children from the Philippines where migration is critical to the economy.

Madianou has talked to both migrant mothers and their left-behind children who keep in touch through new media such as Skype, social networking sites, mobile phones and email and her study builds up an understanding of how relationships are maintained through new media and how they are changing.

Before the advent of the mobile phone migrant families could only communicate through occasional letters and very infrequent (and expensive) phone calls.

Mothers often felt they had become remote from their families, and in some cases might return home to the Philippines to find that their children had not been cared for as they expected.

Digital media change all that. A migrant mother can now call and text her left-behind children several times a day, peruse social networking sites and leave the webcam on for 12 hours achieving a sense of co-presence. Skype, in particular, with the use of webcams, has revolutionised communications between mothers and children, especially small children who might have been no more than babies when their mothers left.

Mirca Madianou commented: "Digital media do not necessarily solve relationship problems. Our interviews with left-behind children revealed that the constant communication made possible through digital media often amplifies family conflicts and is resented by older children who experience it as a form of monitoring."

However, what we found is that new media are beginning to transform the whole experience of migration as the promise of constant communication affects decisions relating to migration and settlement in the UK."

Source: abridged from *Migration and New Media: Transnational Families and Polymedia by* M. Madianou and D. Miller, Routledge, 2011.

### Questions

1. How have digital technologies made it easier for migrant Filipino mothers to keep in touch with their children?
2. What limitations of digital technology does the article mention?
3. How far do you think such online communication can compensate for the physical separation of mothers and their children?

to masquerade as children and engage in **online grooming.** Less seriously, but still undesirably, people's idealised portrayals of their life on social platforms such as Facebook are seen as likely to generate feelings of inadequacy or envy among those who view them as truthful representations of people's lives.

In terms of relationships, digital pessimists are concerned that people may devote so much time to online platforms that they neglect their offline relationships. The addictive nature of online communication – the need to check the number of 'likes' (or other responses) one's latest post on Facebook or YouTube has attracted, say – may lead to people marginalising their immediate relationships. Moreover, many online relationships are seen as superficial. For example, pessimists deride the competitive urge to boast that one has a large number of 'friends' on Facebook or 'followers' on Twitter. Are such friends and followers genuine substitutes for real friends?

Pessimists are also concerned about the way the internet appears to exacerbate the worst features of human nature; for example, the **misogynistic** abuse of women in the public eye who challenge traditional conceptions of femininity, and cyberbullying of children by their peers.

### Evaluation

In evaluating the debate between digital optimists and pessimists as it relates to the impact of the new media on social identity and interpersonal relationships, it is important to recognise the relative youthfulness of the technology involved. The World Wide Web has only been around for about three decades and social media for only about two decades. As such, people's relationship with such media is still evolving and much of what has been written about it from both sides of the debate is speculative.

Nevertheless, quite a lot of research has been carried out already and some preliminary conclusions are advanced below.

## Social identity

Clearly, it is true that people can experiment with alternative online 'virtual' identities and can engage in what Erving Goffman called 'the presentation of self' – or **impression management** – in creative ways online. Whether this is beneficial is a matter of debate. However, Rajendran's suggestion that this means we can 'decide exactly who we want to be' overlooks the fact that social identities are not simply chosen, but are, to an important degree, imposed on us by others. The fact that someone who belongs to an ethnic minority group can be whoever they want online, for example, may not prevent them from being targeted by racist abuse in their everyday life.

What is less in question is the fact that people with access to the internet can now acquire a vast amount of information online about debates relating to identity. Clearly, as in the case of people for whom same-sex attraction is viewed negatively in the country where they live, this could be seen as beneficial. However, there is also information available which could be seen as potentially unhelpful for, say, young people struggling with identity issues. For example, young women and men concerned about their body image could access 'pro-ana' or 'pro-mia' sites which celebrate and encourage anorexic/bulimic practices.

Similarly, young people struggling with issues of sexuality and/or gender identity could access sites supporting gender-transitioning procedures. It is unlikely that gender reassignment would be the best way forward for any but a tiny fraction of such youngsters, yet increasing numbers of children and young people are being referred to **gender dysphoria** clinics in the West. This is not to suggest, however, that there is not an important global battle being fought by activists seeking to secure the human rights of people who choose to transition.

It is also true that identities can be manipulated online. For example, IS has sought to radicalise Muslim youngsters in Britain by implying that you cannot be both Muslim and British. Shamender Talwar (quoted in *Guardian*, 06/09/2015) says that IS 'deliberately targets youngsters and home[s] in on the whole question of identity. They ask them "Are you Muslim or are you British?" By doing this they sow doubt in their minds and it becomes easier to split their loyalties.'

## Social media use and interpersonal relationships

Research carried out by Sonia Livingstone, Alicia Blum-Ross, Jennifer Pavlick and Kjartan Ólafsson (2018) at the London School of Economics as part of their *Parenting for a Digital Future* report challenges the digital pessimist view that digital media are separating family members and diverting them from traditional, shared activities. Their report is based on a large-scale social survey of 2032 UK parents of children aged 0–17 in late 2017. They argue that 'digital media brings families together' and that watching television and movies and playing video games together are now deeply integrated into family life. Moreover, they also argue that 'Parents are working hard to enable children's online opportunities, and address risks.'

Among the 'risks' the parents had in mind were compulsive social media use and cyberbullying, both of which have also been researched.

Digital pessimists are concerned about the possibility of social media 'addiction'. Globally, mental disorders are formally recognised when they are listed in one or other (or both) of the World Health Organisation's (WHO) *International Classification of Disorders* or the American Psychiatric Association's *Diagnostic and Statistical Manual*. Neither recognises 'social media addiction', although in January 2018 the WHO announced that it would include video-gaming addiction as a disorder.

However, research carried out in Hungary (Bányai et al., 2017) suggests that there is a small but not insignificant risk of problematic social media use among youngsters. Their research, carried out in 2015, was based on a large-scale social survey of nearly 6000 adolescents in Hungary. They made use of a specially developed research instrument – the Bergen Social Media Addiction Scale (BSMAS) – to examine respondents' social media usage and found that 4.5 per cent of the adolescents belonged to an 'at-risk' group, and reported low self-esteem, a high level of depressive symptoms, and elevated social media use. Adolescents in this group were more likely to be female and to spend more than 30 hours per week on the internet or using social media.

According to Alex Hern (2018), the risk of social media addiction is not an unfortunate, unintended by-product of social media use, but something which the designers of platforms such as Facebook and Twitter ignored in their efforts to ensure that users spent as much time on their platforms as possible. Hern quotes Sean Parker, the founding president of Facebook, who said at a conference in Philadelphia in 2017: 'The thought process that went into building these applications, Facebook being the first of them... was all about: "How do we consume as much of your time and conscious attention as possible?" That means that we need to sort of give you a little dopamine hit every once in a while, because someone liked or commented on a photo or a post or whatever. And that's going to get you to contribute more content and that's going to get you... more likes and comments," he said. "It's a social-validation feedback loop... exactly the kind of thing that a hacker like myself would come up with, because you're exploiting a vulnerability in human psychology. The inventors, creators – me, Mark [Zuckerberg], Kevin Systrom on Instagram, all of these people – understood this consciously. And we did it anyway' (*Guardian*, 24/01/2018).

## Activity

How much time on average do you spend on social media each week? How does this compare with your classmates?

Bullying is generally seen as an abuse of power in situations where there is a power imbalance and involves repeated acts of aggression carried out by one or more persons against a victim. Cyberbullying involves bullying that makes use of new media and communication devices such as mobile phones and the internet.

Ruthaychonnee Sittichai and Peter K. Smith (2015) suggest that, while the form cyberbullying takes can be conditioned by cultural and schooling factors, it occurs in all societies where there is a relatively high level of digital penetration. Moreover, digital technology is seen as exacerbating the problem of bullying because perpetrators can block or hide their identity. Additionally, cyberbullying can have particularly profound effects, as the content used to harass the victim can be spread or shared widely and can remain accessible indefinitely.

## Activity

*Graffiti Artists came together as part of an anti-cyberbullying campaign in Brighton, UK.*

Is cyberbullying a significant problem for young people in the society where you live? Why do you think this is?

## Conclusion

It is difficult to avoid the conclusion that the advent of digital media has been associated with a great deal of hype about its potential to transform identities and relationships, both for good and bad. Digital media do indeed offer opportunities for people to form new social identities, but offline identities both constrain people's freedom to do so and continue to exert a powerful influence on their lives. Similarly, digital media do indeed offer opportunities to establish new contacts with others or new ways of communicating with existing contacts, but people can use the technology to spread hate as well as fellow feeling and there are real dangers for some of becoming 'hooked' on social media. At this point in time, it is an open question whether the digital optimist or digital pessimist view will turn out to be nearer the mark.

## Key terms

**Hyper-connectivity** The state of being constantly connected to others through a variety of digital platforms such as mobile phones, tablets and computers.

**Homophobia** The irrational fear or hatred of people who are sexually attracted to the same sex.

**Online grooming** Using digital technology to build an emotional connection with a child to gain their trust for the purposes of sexual abuse, sexual exploitation or trafficking.

**Misogynistic** Reflecting hatred of, contempt for, or ingrained prejudice against girls and women.

**Impression management** Efforts to control how other people see us.

**Gender dysphoria** A condition where a person experiences discomfort or distress because there is a mismatch between their biological sex and gender identity.

## Summary

1. Digital optimists argue that the new technology has opened up opportunities for people to choose and express their social identities and to form new relationships or maintain existing ones at a distance.
2. Digital pessimists argue that social identities are imposed as well as chosen and that digital technologies have created new problems in terms of relationships such as online grooming, compulsive social media usage and cyberbullying.
3. Both sides in the debate have been guilty of exaggeration. There are both benefits and problems associated with the growth of digital technology in terms of its impact on identities and relationships.

# END-OF-PART QUESTIONS

| 0 | 1 | Describe four key features of the new media. | **[4 marks]** |
|---|---|---|---|
| 0 | 2 | Explain three ways in which the new media can be seen as promoting democracy. | **[6 marks]** |
| 0 | 3 | Evaluate the digital optimist view that the new media have had a positive effect on interpersonal relationships. | **[8 marks]** |

# SECTION B
# MEDIA REPRESENTATION AND EFFECTS

## Contents


**Part 4** **Media representations** 366

**Part 5** **Media effects** 381


Three of the sets of key concepts you were introduced to in the introductory chapter are particularly relevant here.

First, *power, control and resistance,* which was covered in the introduction to Section A.

Second, *socialisation, culture and identity.* Sociologists have long recognised the media as important agents of secondary *socialisation* alongside education, peer groups and the workplace. But do the media simply reflect the *culture* of the society which produces them or play a part in changing that culture? And are the new media, by enabling people to interact easily with members of other, distant societies, contributing to a kind of 'global culture'? Also, how do the media shape our perception of the *identity* of people who belong to different social groups from us? For example, do people living in Europe and North America gain a rounded picture of Muslim ethnic minorities living in their country or one that mistakenly equates Muslims with Islamic fundamentalists?

Third, *structure and human agency.* Sociologists are faced with a paradox when considering society. On the one hand, social behaviour is clearly shaped by the culture and institutional *structure* of the society to which people belong. The lives of people who lived in South Africa under the system of apartheid were very different from those, say, living in Japan today. Yet, on the other hand, society is a human product. It was the actions of people – their exercise of *agency* – that produced these societies. In considering the media, therefore, sociologists have to grapple with the issues of both how the media shape society and of how people can nevertheless exercise agency both as the producers and the consumers of media messages.

Section B is divided into two parts. In Part 4 we examine how the media represent the members of a number of important social categories: gender groups, racial and ethnic groups, social classes and age groups. To what extent do the media reflect the diversity and complexity of such groups or, intentionally or unintentionally, stereotype them?

Finally, in Part 5 we examine the various models that sociologists have produced to try to understand both the nature and extent of media effects on society and on the attitudes and behaviour of its audience. We conclude by examining these effects in terms of the relationship between the media, crime and deviance.

# PART 4 MEDIA REPRESENTATIONS

## Contents


| | | |
|---|---|---|
| Unit 6.4.1 | Media representations of gender | 366 |
| Unit 6.4.2 | Media representations of race and ethnicity | 371 |
| Unit 6.4.3 | Media representations of class and age | 376 |


In Part 4, we return to the question posed in the chapter introduction. Do the media simply reflect the world around them, acting like a mirror to society, or do they act more like a hall of mirrors in a funfair, providing a distorted picture of reality?

Sociological interest in the topic of media representation has tended to focus on media representation of social groups: gender groups, racial and ethnic groups, age groups and social classes. We will examine each in turn in the units of Part 4.

For functionalists, the main focus has been on the role of the media as important agents of secondary socialisation. For example what messages do the media transmit about the appropriate behaviour for boys and girls, men and women, or for different age groups. For conflict theorists, such as Marxists and feminists, the focus is on ideology: do media representations simply reinforce **sexism, racism, ageism and classism** or can the media play a role in challenging such ideologies?

## Unit 6.4.1 Media representations of gender

Sociologists typically distinguish between 'sex' and 'gender'. Sex, in the sense of being male or female, is seen as biologically determined. Gender, in the sense of society's expectations of how males and females should behave – embedded in notions of masculinity and femininity – is seen as socially constructed. Ideas about what is appropriate behaviour for males and females vary both historically and cross-culturally, although the degree of this variation and whether biology plays any role at all in shaping male and female behaviour are fiercely disputed topics among both social scientists and natural scientists.

One of the ways in which the media can influence audiences is through the transmission of gender **stereotypes.** The Council of Europe explains these as follows: 'Gender stereotypes are generalised views or preconceived ideas, according to which individuals are categorised into particular gender groups, typically defined as "women" and "men", and are arbitrarily assigned characteristics and roles determined and limited by their sex. Stereotypes are both descriptive, in that members of a certain group are perceived to have the same attributes regardless of individual differences, and prescriptive as they set the parameters for what societies deem to be acceptable behaviour.'

### The global context

Gender roles and gender relations are a core feature of every society and are the key concern of feminist sociologists. Feminism, loosely defined, refers to a body of ideas and a social movement dedicated to achieving gender equality. It dates back a long way and encompasses a wide variety of tendencies and strategies. Its history is conventionally divided into three phases or 'waves'. The first wave, which began at the end of the 18th century, was narrowly focused on gaining the vote for women. The second wave, associated with the women's liberation movement, ran from the 1960s to the 1980s and embraced a wide range of demands, including equal pay and the outlawing of sexual discrimination. The third wave runs from the 1990s to the present day and has been associated with what Sylvia Walby (2011) has called the 'mainstreaming' of gender issues.

Thanks to the success of feminist activism, efforts to achieve gender equality are now globally recognised. Research carried out for the World Bank in 2010/2011, published as *On Norms and Agency* (2012), found that in industrialised as well as less industrialised societies there is widespread recognition of issues of gender. The research covered 20 countries in all world regions and involved over 4000 men and women who lived in both remote villages and in urban areas being interviewed in focus groups about the effects of gender differences and inequalities on their lives. The researchers reported that 'Participants acknowledged that women are actively seeking equal power and freedom, but must constantly negotiate and resist traditional expectations about what they are to do and who they are to be. When women achieve the freedom to work for pay or get more education, they must still accommodate their gains to these expectations, especially on household responsibilities.'

### Activity

How prominent are efforts to promote gender equality in the society where you live?

## The global situation

In 1995, 189 Member States of the United Nations reaffirmed their commitment to gender equality in what became known as the 'Beijing Declaration': 'Ensure the full implementation of the human rights of women and of the girl child as an inalienable, integral and indivisible part of universal human rights...'. The Declaration identified women and media as one of 12 critical areas of the Beijing Platform for Action and called on media everywhere to make 'a far greater contribution to women's advancement'.

20 years later, reviewing progress, UN Women noted that:

> *There has been some progress since the Beijing Conference. The percentage of stories reported by women has edged up in most issue areas and women are amongst the most active social media users. But even a cursory look at media content shows how far there is to go.*
>
> *Women in all types of media tend to be thin and sexualised. They talk less than men. They have fewer opinions. And they are far less likely, in the entertainment industry, to play roles as leaders or professionals, or even as women who work for a living.*

Except from web article 'Women and the Media', beijing20.unwomen.org, UN Women 2015.

One of the areas where there is reliable quantitative data relates to women in the news. Every five years, since 1995, the Global Media Monitoring Project has analysed one day's coverage of women in news reports in national newspapers and television, radio and internet news broadcasts and tweets. In 1995, 71 countries were covered; in 2015, 114 (more than half the countries in the world) were covered.

The 2015 report found:

- Worldwide, only 24 per cent of the people heard, read about or seen in newspaper, television and radio news are women, the same as in 2010.
- That percentage only rises to 26 per cent on digital news-delivery platforms and in social media 'tweets'.
- The gender gap in coverage is widest in news about politics and government.
- In the past 10 years, the only category where coverage has risen significantly is in the portrayal of women as survivors of domestic violence.
- A global gender disparity also exists between female and male news reporters – a **'glass ceiling'** for women in the newsroom.

This evidence, even though it is only concerned with one small area of media coverage – news reporting – supports feminist complaints that women are both under-represented in the media and misrepresented. What does research carried out in particular countries show?

### Activity

Roughly what proportion of TV newscasters are women in the country where you live? Why does this matter in terms of the audience's perception of gender roles?

## Research in the UK

Bob Connell (1995) argues that cultural expectations about gender roles in the UK in the 20th century were dominated by hegemonic definitions of masculinity, femininity and sexuality. These cultural ideas stressed two broad traditional ideas with regard to gender:

1. Paid work was central to men's identity and role. Men were expected to be breadwinners (primary earners) and heads of households, responsible for the economic security of their dependants. Masculinity was perceived to be individualistic, competitive, ambitious and aggressive. Men were not expected to openly demonstrate emotion.
2. Women were categorised primarily as homemakers, mothers and carers. They were confined to a life defined by the family, the home and personal relationships. They were expected to be less rational and more emotional and neurotic than men.

Connell argues that these ideas about gender constituted a patriarchal ideology, which assumed that masculinity was dominant and femininity was subordinate because males exercised economic, social and physical power over females. This ideology was transmitted from one generation to the next through the process of gender role socialisation that mainly occurred in the family.

However, the mass media, a secondary agent of socialisation, were also seen as playing a key role in teaching and reinforcing these cultural expectations about how each gender was supposed to operate in the social world.

A study carried out in the 1980s of women's magazines supports Connell's claims. Marjorie Ferguson (1983) conducted a content analysis of women's magazines from between 1949 and 1974, and 1979 and 1980. She argued that the magazines from the earlier period were organised around 'a cult of femininity', which promoted a traditional ideal where excellence was achieved through caring for others, the family, marriage and appearance. Writing about those from 1979/80, she argued that, although they were gradually moving away from these stereotypes, they still tended to focus narrowly on 'him, home and looking good (for him)'.

Naomi Wolf (1990) suggests that the images of women used by the media, especially the print media and advertising, present a particular 'beauty ideal' through which they transmit the strong ideological message that women should treat their bodies as a project in constant need of improvement. Guy Cumberbatch (2004) found that being 'attractive' fitted the description for nearly two-thirds of females featured in television advertising but only one-quarter of males. He concluded that women generally occupy a passive 'decorative' role in television advertising. Other research (for example, see the *Just the Women* report described in 'Research in the 21st century in the UK') suggests that the same applies to print advertising.

## Activity

*An advertisement from the 1960s in the UK.*

How does this illustrate the use of images of women to sell products?

## Activity

Assuming that you have access to commercial television channels, spend an evening monitoring the advertisements. Do your findings match those of Cumberbatch?

## Research in the 21st century in the UK

Gender roles in the UK have changed significantly over the last 50 years. Indeed, Helen Wilkinson (1994) describes the changes as a 'genderquake', likening them to the profound impact of an earthquake in geology. In particular, there has been an enormous increase in the employment of women, particularly married women, so that by 2017 the male employment rate for those of employment age was about 80 per cent, while that for women was not much lower, at about 70 per cent. There has also been some decline in **gender segregation** in the labour market, with some movement of women into jobs traditionally seen as 'men's jobs' (for example, law and construction) and of men into jobs traditionally seen as 'women's jobs' (for example, nursing and social care). This can be explained as a product of the passing and enforcement of equality legislation since the 1970s, advances of women in education, the progressive loss of importance of physical attributes for productivity, change in family roles and, last but not least, the challenging of traditional gender norms by feminism.

How far have these changes been reflected in changes in media representations?

Jane Martinson et al. (2012), in a report entitled *Seen but Not Heard*, based on a random sample of the front pages of 18 national daily and Sunday newspapers, found that 78 per cent of all front-page bylines were male and that 84 per cent of all those mentioned by name or quoted in lead stories were men. There were very few stories about women's professional abilities or expertise, and most press coverage continues to rely on men as experts in the fields of business, politics and economics.

A joint report by four women's organisations published in November 2012 – *Just the Women* – focused on the representation of women, and violence against women in particular, in British newspapers. The report's findings, which were based on a fortnight's analysis of 11 national newspapers in September 2012, found that over 1300 news reports involved sexism. The *Just the Women* report came to six conclusions about the press reporting of women and women's lives:

1. Press reporting often lacks context and this often leads to inaccurate, incomplete, misrepresentative and misleading impressions of women and women's lives.
2. Photographs and coverage often focus on women's appearance and the degree to which women's behaviour conforms to a stereotyped code of acceptable femininity, which has the potential to reduce women's aspirations.
3. Press reporting, especially in the tabloid press, excessively objectifies women and reduces them to sexual commodities in a way that would not be broadcast on television or allowed into the workplace because of equality legislation.
4. Selective and de-contextualised reporting perpetuates stereotypes and myths about victims of sexual violence and the perpetrators of such violence, which negatively impacts on women's confidence in the criminal justice system.
5. The reporting of rape and violence, and the advertising of pornography in newspapers, often glamorise and eroticise violence against women and girls.
6. 'Women's issues' are often covered in a very narrow and stereotyped way, and women who have achieved some level of political and societal power are often infantilised, denigrated and humiliated.

## Magazines for young women

Research by Cyndi Tebbel (2000) suggests that magazines for teenage girls concentrate heavily on beauty and slimming. Tebbel reports that women's magazines have 10.5 times more advertisements and articles promoting weight loss than men's magazines do, and over three-quarters of the covers of women's magazines include at least one message about how to change a woman's bodily appearance – by diet, exercise or cosmetic surgery. The *Just the Women* report supports this observation and notes that newspapers are often critical of celebrities who put on weight, and they actively encourage girls to compete with each other to achieve an ideal of 'thinness'. The report concludes that this impacts negatively on the self-esteem of young women.

However, David Gauntlett (2008) argues that magazines aimed at young women in particular have changed dramatically. He argues that such magazines:

> ***are emphatic in their determination that women must do their own thing, be themselves, and/or be as outrageously sassy and sexy as possible. Many recent movies have featured self-confident, tough, intelligent female lead characters... Female pop stars sing about financial and emotional independence, inner strength, and how they don't need a man.***

This set of media messages from a range of sources suggests that women can be tough and independent while 'maintaining perfect make-up and wearing impossible shoes'. Gauntlett claims that surveys of young women and their lifestyles suggest that these media messages are having a positive and significant impact on the way young women construct their identities today.

### Representations of masculinity

Gauntlett also carried out research on men's magazines. He suggests that, rather than reinforce traditional conceptions of masculinity, they have an almost obsessive relationship with the socially constructed nature of manhood. He argues that such media are positive because they stress that 'the performance of masculinity can and should be practised and perfected'. His study of the content of one men's magazine in particular, *FHM*, concludes that the masculine values it transmits are 'fundamentally caring, generous and good-humoured'. Gauntlett argues that these magazines are often centred on 'helping men to be considerate lovers, useful around the home, healthy, fashionable, and funny – in particular, being able to laugh at themselves'.

However, Jim McNamara (2006) is sceptical that media representations of masculinity positively celebrate being a man. He analysed a wide variety of media – newspapers, magazines and television – over a six-month period, and argued that:

> *Men are predominantly portrayed in mass media as villains, aggressors, perverts and philanderers. More than 75 per cent of all mass media representations of men and male identity categorized into profiles portrayed men in one of these four ways. In total, more than 80 per cent of media profiles of men were negative, compared with 18.4 per cent which showed positive profiles or themes... There is little equivocation in relation to men in the media; they are predominantly evil. Men are mostly reported in mass media news, current affairs, talk shows and lifestyle media in relation to violence and aggression.*
> (McNamara, 2006)

### Comment

One of the striking features of research into contemporary representations of gender in the UK media is the extent to which researchers disagree with each other about how far sexist representations continue to be transmitted. This is likely to reflect differences in the value positions of different researchers, diversity within the media and ongoing ideological conflict around what constitutes sexism.

#### Activity

Social researchers are expected to strive for objectivity. How does research into media representations of gender in the UK illustrate the difficulty of achieving this?

What is clear is that there have been significant changes over recent decades. For example, it is no longer seen as 'inappropriate' for women to be newsreaders on TV or radio or to present programmes focusing on politics, economics or business. Also, blatant sexist comments made by broadcasters are likely to be punished – for example, two football pundits on Sky Sports were sacked in 2011 for making derogatory remarks about a female football official. On the other hand, representations of women in the tabloid press and in popular magazines continue to focus on their appearance, and women in the public eye who upset traditionalists are often subjected to a stream of vile, misogynistic abuse online.

#### Activity

*A woman, Gabby Logan, was a pitch-side reporter at the 2010 FIFA World Cup.*

How does this challenge traditional representations of gender?

## The continuing influence of patriarchy

In many countries around the world, patriarchal ideologies continue to have a powerful influence on media representations. For example, Ahmed Rameez Ul Huda and Roshan Ali (2015) argue that, despite the fact that women are increasingly playing an active role in the media in Pakistan, they continue to be objectified. For example, in advertisements female models are often 'sensually dressed up for the sake of alluring customers', even when they have nothing to do with the product.

Digests of short stories are popular in Pakistan. Ul Huda and Ali maintain that in these collections young women are portrayed as preoccupied with getting married, and married women as preoccupied with household chores and childcare, fashion and their appearance. Also, for both, their main duty in life is portrayed as serving their 'patti daive' (Hindi word for 'husband' that means 'divine/god-like husband'). This service is considered to be a labour of love.

Equally popular are drama serials and morning shows on TV, particularly among housewives. Ul Huda and Ali argue that these are mainly concerned with pre-marital and post-marital situations and with conditions of life for both housewives and working women. The women in these dramas are 'almost always' subjected to some form of violence or other hardships regarding their domestic or external affairs. The morning shows highlight fashion and cooking and interviews with glamorous celebrities.

Finally, they argue that, while women are increasingly accessing social media such as Facebook, Twitter and Tumblr, they are often subjected to '**Eve teasing**' online by men – that is, the use of sexual innuendo or the making of indecent suggestions.

## Activity

How far do you think the mainstream media in your society reinforce traditional conceptions of masculinity and femininity?

## Key terms

**Sexism, racism, ageism and classism** Belief systems which suggest that certain groups – men, white people, middle-aged people and upper classes – are inherently superior to others.

**Stereotypes** Shared preconceptions, often of a negative kind, about the characteristics of a social group which assume that all members of the group are alike.

**Glass ceiling** An invisible barrier making it difficult for women to achieve top positions in society.

**Gender segregation** Organisational structures which separate boys and girls/men and women.

**Eve teasing** A euphemism used in South Asia to refer to sexual harassment of women and girls.

## Summary

1. The media are an important agent of secondary socialisation.
2. Sociologists are interested in the role the media play in generating and reinforcing gender stereotypes.
3. Research suggests that feminism has had a global impact and in 1995 the UN called on the media to 'make a far greater contribution to women's advancement'.
4. Commenting on the progress made by 2015, UN Women argued that there was still a lot of progress needed.
5. Research on gender representation in UK media suggests that there have been significant changes over recent decades, but researchers disagree about the extent to which the media are still sexist.
6. The influence of patriarchal ideas on media representations of men and women is still evident in many societies, such as Pakistan.

# Unit 6.4.2 Media representations of race and ethnicity

While media representations of gender have probably received the most attention from sociologists, representations of race and ethnicity have also attracted a considerable amount of research.

## The meaning of 'race' and ethnicity

Both race and ethnicity are **social constructs**. Normally, to refer to something as a social construct is *not* to imply that it is 'imaginary' or 'doesn't really exist'; just that the thing being talked about could be understood or perceived differently at a different time or in a different society. However, in respect of race, it turns out that races do not exist, objectively speaking.

In the 19th century, European scholars developed a theory that human beings could be divided into three broad racial categories: Negroid, Caucasoid and Mongoloid, with the Caucasoid race being the most evolved. This provided a convenient but pseudo-scientific rationale for both slavery and colonialism. However, most scientists and sociologists now accept that in the 20th century, the science of genetics has clearly shown that all human beings have evolved from a single set of African ancestors and that race as a scientific concept is 'well past its sell-by date', as Steven and Hilary Rose (2005) have put it. However, this scientific consensus has not prevented the continued use of the word 'race' in popular discourse to refer to people with different **phenotypical** characteristics, such as skin colour. As such, races should be understood as *social* categories of people who are mistakenly regarded as biologically distinct because they share certain visible physical characteristics.

Today, the term 'ethnicity' has largely replaced 'race' in academic writing. Ethnic groups are groups of people defined by 'race', religion and/or national origin who share a common cultural heritage, so the focus is more on culture than biology. Yet, ethnicity is still a social construct in that the categorisations can and do vary over time and cross-culturally. For example, in the 1950s people who came to Britain from the Caribbean were referred to as 'Coloured'. Today, the same people and their descendants are referred to as 'Black'.

In everyday life, the topics of race and ethnicity are associated with numerous misunderstandings. For example, people confuse ethnicity with ethnic minority status. Everybody has an ethnic identity, but when a group of people with a different cultural heritage live in a society where they are in a numerical minority, they constitute a minority ethnic group. Similarly, people often confuse 'ethnic minority' with 'immigrant'. Immigrants are people born in another country from the one where they are now living. Someone who belongs to an ethnic minority group may well have been born in the country where they live. Indeed, in some countries, surviving members of the indigenous population – for example, Maoris in New Zealand, Native Americans in the USA and Canada – may constitute a minority ethnic group.

## Activity

Explain why the idea that human beings can be divided into biologically distinct 'races' is problematic.

## Media representations of race and ethnicity

The racial theories developed in the 19th century have had a profound global impact because they were spread across the world as an integral feature of the European – particularly, French, Spanish, Portuguese and British – empires that had developed from the 17th century, colonising countries in Eastern and Southern Asia, Africa and South America. Those empires may now have disappeared, but the ideas of racial superiority which accompanied them have proved much harder to eradicate. A telling example is the thriving market for skin-lightening creams in countries that were once colonies of these European countries, a market estimated to be worth $19.8 billion globally in 2018 (*Latin Post*, 26/04/18).

## Activity

*An advert for a skin-whitening product in Bangkok, Thailand.*

Are skin-lightening creams sold in the country where you live? How are they promoted in advertisements?

In the 19th and early 20th centuries, representations of Black people as ape-like or as 'savages' were commonplace in Western media, although they were not the only group to be depicted in this way. Irish people were similarly represented in British media in the 19th century when Ireland was part of the British Empire. In both cases, whole populations were '**racialised**' as a way of justifying their exploitation as colonial subjects.

## Activity

MR. G-O'RILLA, THE YOUNG IRELAND PARTY, EXULTING OVER THE INSULT TO THE BRITISH FLAG. SHOULDN'T HE BE EXTINGUISHED AT ONCE!

*A cartoon from the English magazine* Punch *in the 1840s depicting a member of the 'Young Ireland' Irish nationalist movement.*

Explain how 19th-century racial theories informed this depiction of an Irishman.

Such grotesque misrepresentations of ethnic groups are now rare outside the pages of White Supremacist blogs, but the colonialist attitudes which contributed to such misrepresentations did not entirely disappear. In a remarkable special edition of the *National Geographic* magazine – based in the USA – published in April 2018, the editor, Susan Goldberg, wrote:

> *For decades, our coverage was racist. To rise above our past, we must acknowledge it. Until the 1970s* National Geographic *all but ignored people of colour who lived in the United States – rarely acknowledging them beyond labourers or domestic workers... while picturing 'natives' elsewhere as exotics, famously and frequently unclothed, happy hunters, noble savages – every type of cliché.*

Another example of colonialist attitudes is reflected in the news reporting of indigenous populations. Typically, indigenous peoples have been exploited and marginalised by the colonists and a wide range of social and economic problems have subsequently developed among indigenous communities, such as alcoholism and substance abuse, mental health problems, unemployment and involvement in crime. However, news reporting implies that it is the indigenous people who are the problem rather than being the victims of the problems caused for them by colonialism.

For example, according to Michael Meadows (2004), many representations of Indigenous Australians (Aborigines) 'focus...on conflict (violence, criminality) and difference. Indigenous people have been represented... as the exotic other,...a dying race, welfare dependent, the drunk, the activist, the threat to existing order, the invisible.' Moreover, according to David Hollinsworth (2005), their behaviour is often represented as irrational and out of control.

A final example of the racialisation of minorities is provided by contemporary Indian society. Lucy Fedrick (2012) argues that the Dalits in India have been racialised as a way of justifying continuing discrimination against them, particularly in rural areas. The Dalits constitute about 160 million of India's total population of around 1.3 billion and were previously classified as 'untouchables' under the Indian caste system, which saw them as religiously 'impure'. 'Untouchability' was outlawed in 1950 shortly after India gained its independence from Britain and there have been efforts made by governments since then to help the so-called 'scheduled castes' by means of **affirmative action**. However, Fedrick argues that 'realistically the caste system is still resisting its extinction and in particular is thriving in smaller villages throughout India causing discrimination to thousands of people'.

## Contemporary issues: The representation of Dalits in Bollywood films

An expert in Indian cinema at Birmingham City University has said that Bollywood is creating the wrong perception of an entire community in its portrayal of Dalits.

As he begins the first study of its kind in 40 years, Vishal Chauhan, from Ajmer in Rajasthan, is highlighting the representation of marginalised people in Indian cinema, and says that their stereotyped depictions on screen are fuelling further **social stratification**.

Dalit, meaning 'thrashing' or 'pressing' in Sanskrit and 'broken' or 'oppressed' in Hindi, is a term for the members of lower castes in India. In popular Indian cinema, Dalits are traditionally portrayed as ill-dressed, under-confident and ugly. Furthermore, characters from lower castes are rarely played by Dalit actors, instead, they are performed by upper-caste actors donning **blackface.** According to Chauhan:

> *Dalits represent around 22 per cent of India's population, yet they do not receive equal screen time compared with other societal groups. For example, a recent analysis of lead characters of more than 250 films released in 2013 and 2014 by* The Hindu *newspaper revealed that only six lead characters belonged to a lower caste.*
>
> *Where filmmakers have attempted to honestly portray Dalits, their films tend to be labelled as an art house picture and receive a limited release. In big budget films, Dalits will more than likely be played by higher caste actors, and lower caste peoples are barely reflected in positions behind the camera either. Most worrying, however, is the stereotypical portrayal of Dalit peoples – when they do appear – as intellectually inferior and only able to survive on the good will of upper caste peoples. The Indian film industry has helped create an untrue perception of an entire community.*

Source: 'Bollywood Needs to Rethink Dalit Representation, Media Scholar Says', *University News*, 08/08/2017, Birmingham City University.

### Questions

1. How are Dalits stereotyped in Bollywood films, according to Chauhan?
2. What evidence is there in the passage of the racialisation of Dalits?
3. Why is it significant that there are few Dalits working behind the cameras?

## Media representations of ethnic minorities in the UK

People who belong to Black, Asian and (other) minority ethnic (BAME) groups in the UK were, for a long time, seriously under-represented in the mainstream UK media, except as sportsmen and sportswomen and as entertainers. An example of what George Gerbner and Larry Gross (1976) called 'symbolic annihilation'. Today, this is no longer the case. Black and Asian faces on TV, for example, as newsreaders, presenters and as actors, and in TV and magazine adverts, are now commonplace.

Nevertheless, research suggests that BAME groups continue to be represented in stereotyped and negative ways across a range of media content. In particular, newspapers and television news have a tendency to present minority ethnic groups as a problem, or to associate Black people with physical rather than intellectual activities, and to neglect and even ignore racism and the inequalities that result from it.

Peter Akinti (2003) suggests that television often reflects an inaccurate and superficial view of Black life, focusing almost exclusively on stereotypical issues such as gun crime. Toyin Agbetu (2006) suggests that 'a Black person constructed in the media has three attributes: they are involved in criminality, involved in sports or involved in entertainment'. He suggests that anything that lies outside those classifications is not of interest to the media.

Agbetu notes that the media frequently focus on Black people as the perpetrators of crime rather than as victims. The word 'Black' is often used as a prefix if an offender is a member of a minority ethnic group – for example, 'a Black youth'. The word 'White' is rarely used in the same way. Furthermore, African Caribbean people are portrayed as 'only interested in carnival and dancing and, of course, they all come from Jamaica, and they're all yardies'. Agbetu argues that 'Black people are troublesome but exciting for the media'. In other words, they are newsworthy because they almost always constitute 'bad news'.

In a perceptive study of 'race' and violent crime reporting in the national and regional press, Kjartan Sveinsson (2008) argues that 'culture' has replaced 'race' as a way of representing the relationship between ethnicity and crime, but serves the same function, as it conceives of culture as an innate quality: as a way of life determined by birth. Thus, gang, gun and knife crime are conceptualised as products of a **pathological**, inner-city Black culture which leads young Black men to engage in criminal behaviour.

As Sveinsson argues:

> *The claim that 'culture' is the source of violent crime necessarily attaches violence to certain 'communities' defined by their ethnic 'identity'. This implies that most members of those groups are violent. The effect is that entire 'communities' are criminalised on the basis of their (alleged) cultures.*

In other words, the complex relationship between ethnic minority status, relative deprivation, residential segregation, discrimination, unemployment and involvement in certain types of crime is reduced to a supposed **criminogenic** Black culture. Moreover, as Sveinsson points out, concepts of 'culture' and 'community' are seldom drawn upon when talking about White Britons or crimes carried out by members of the (White) ethnic majority.

### Activity

Explain how the idea of a criminogenic Black culture involves the use of stereotypes.

## Media representations of Muslims in the UK

Around 4.5 per cent of the UK population are Muslims, mainly from Pakistan and Bangladesh. Kerry Moore et al. (2008) carried out a content analysis of five alternate years of British newspaper reporting between 2000 and 2008, focused on the key phrases 'British Muslim' and 'Islam'. They deliberately avoided looking at coverage in 2001 and 2005 in the aftermath of the 9/11 and 7/7 terrorist attacks (in New York and London, respectively) because they wanted to focus on routine everyday coverage of British Muslims. This approach generated 23 000 stories in all.

Moore et al. found that the four most newsworthy and therefore common stories about British Muslims in 2000 involved terrorism (28 per cent), religious and cultural issues (20 per cent), community relations (13 per cent) and attacks on Muslims (10 per cent). However, between 2000 and 2008, stories on terrorism or the war on terror accounted for 36 per cent of all stories.

Generally, Moore et al. conclude that news stories about Muslims in the UK contain four ideological messages about Islam. First, that Islam is dangerous, backward and irrational compared with Western thought and actions. Second, that multiculturalism, with its stress on diversity and tolerance, is allowing extremist Islam too much freedom to disseminate its anti-Western views in Muslim communities. Third, that there is a fundamental clash of civilisations between the democratic and free West and an oppressive Islam which restricts or suppresses the rights of women, homosexuals and others. Fourth, that Islam is a threat to the British way of life.

## Ethnicity, migration and media in the UK

Philo and Liza Beattie (1999) argue that moral panics often arise because of negative media representations of issues such as immigration and asylum seekers. They note that this coverage creates fear and concern among the general UK population because journalists construct immigrants and asylum seekers as problems and threats. The Information Centre about Asylums and Refugees (ICAR) (2005) found that the British media often repetitively used certain terms and types of emotive language in their reporting – for example, asylum seekers were often described as a 'flood' or 'wave' and as 'bogus' or 'fraudulent'. Philo and Beattie found that media coverage broadly hinted that immigrants wished to take advantage of the UK's benefit and health systems.

### Activity

To what extent are immigrants in the country where you live **scapegoated** for social and economic problems?

Both the ICAR and Philo and Beattie note that media coverage often excludes essential information such as the contribution that immigration has made to the economy or the fact that asylum seekers are often escaping political persecution, torture and poverty in their home countries. Philo and Beattie conclude that news about immigration tends to be **xenophobic** in tone and seems to be about reinforcing a narrow and nostalgic version of British identity. The ICAR argues that there is often a link between media coverage and community tensions. It conducted research in London and discovered that unbalanced and inaccurate media images of asylum seekers made a significant contribution to their harassment by local residents.

### Conclusion

Our discussion of the representation of race and ethnicity has indicated the power of the media to reinforce negative stereotypes of racial and ethnic minorities. The media in some countries have made real efforts to address this issue and promote greater diversity, but further progress is likely to depend on the extent to which members of such minorities gain positions in the media production process.

## Key terms

**Social construct** A feature of a society which appears to be a natural or given phenomenon, but which is actually a product of social processes.

**Phenotypical** Relating to visible biological characteristics.

**Racialised** Identified as belonging to a racial group.

**Affirmative action** Action designed to compensate for past discrimination through the use of quotas, for example.

**Social stratification** The ordering of society into layers with different amounts of wealth, status and power.

**Blackface** The use of make-up to darken the skin.

**Pathological** Causing social sickness.

**Criminogenic** Generating or causing crime.

**Scapegoated** Blamed for problems not of their making.

**Xenophobia** Hatred or fear of foreigners.

## Summary

1. Both race and ethnicity are social constructs.
2. Racial theories developed in Europe in the 19th century have had a global impact despite the fact that they have been shown to be scientifically invalid.
3. The media played an important role in the historical transmission of these theories.
4. Dalits in India have been racialised as a way of justifying continuing discrimination against them. Bollywood films do little to challenge this misrepresentation.
5. While Black and Asian faces are now commonplace on TV in the UK, media coverage tends to associate Black people with crime and Muslims with terrorism.
6. Immigration is often presented via the media as a threat to the 'British way of life' and the media rarely draw attention to the economic contribution made by immigrants.

# Unit 6.4.3 Media representations of class and age

Sociological research on media representation of social class and of age groups has been less extensive than that on gender and ethnicity, though that is not to say that it is any less important.

## Media representations of class

Social class is the system of social stratification associated with industrial capitalism. Social classes are social categories or groups of people who share a similar economic position in terms of occupation, income and ownership of wealth.

All systems of stratification require legitimation; that is, some means of justifying the inequalities they represent. Class systems are typically legitimated on the basis that they are open or **meritocratic.** That is, people can move up the class hierarchy if they are prepared to work hard enough and make the necessary sacrifices. Indeed, this is the basis of the **American Dream**. The logical consequence of the notion of meritocracy is that whatever position you occupy in the class structure is one you deserve: if you are at or near the top, it is because you are talented, hard-working and deserving of success; if you are at or near the bottom, it is because you are talentless, lazy and undeserving. Class systems may also be legitimated by 'classism', the belief that people from certain social or economic classes are superior to others. Some sociologists argue that the media play an important role in processes of legitimation by the ways in which they represent different social classes.

Media representations of social classes rarely focus on the social tensions or class conflict that some critical sociologists see as underpinning society. In fact, as we saw in Unit 6.2.1, neo-Marxist sociologists suggest that the function of the media is to ensure the cultural hegemony of the dominant capitalist class and that inequality and exploitation are not defined as social problems, so that they do not become the focus of social debate and demands for social change.

### Media representations of class in the UK

Neo-Marxists argue that media representations of social class tend to celebrate hierarchy and wealth. Those who benefit from these processes – the monarchy, the upper class and the very wealthy – generally receive a positive press as celebrities who are somehow deserving of their position. The UK mass media hardly ever portray the upper classes in a critical light, nor do they often draw any serious attention to inequalities in wealth and pay or the over-representation of those who have been to public school in positions of power.

Sociological observations of media representations of the upper classes suggest that popular films and television costume dramas tend to portray members of this class either in an eccentric or in a nostalgic way. In films such as *The King's Speech*, and television costume dramas such as *Downton Abbey*, a rosy, idealised picture is painted of a ruling elite characterised by honour, culture and good breeding.

## Activity

*Promotional picture for* Downton Abbey, *season 4.*

Downton Abbey ran for six series between 2010 and 2015 on ITV, with an average audience of around 10 million. How might such programmes help to legitimise wealth inequalities?

Robert Reiner (2010) argues that the media tend to represent the UK as a meritocratic society, in which intelligence, talent and hard work are rewarded. Marxists point out that this is an ideological myth, because the evidence suggests wealth is more important than ability in opening up access to top universities such as Oxford and Cambridge and top jobs. Moreover, Jock Young (2007) suggests that British culture is a monetary culture characterised by a 'chaos of rewards', whereby top businessmen are rewarded for failure and celebrities are over-rewarded for their 'talents'. In contrast, ordinary people in functionally important jobs struggle to get by. However, the media very rarely focus on these issues. Rather, they celebrate celebrity culture and its excesses, and encourage their audiences to engage in a popular culture underpinned by materialism and **conspicuous consumption**.

David Newman (2006) argues that the media focus very positively on the concerns of the wealthy and the privileged. He notes that the media over-focus on consumer items such as luxury cars, costly holiday spots and fashion accessories that only the wealthy can afford. In the UK, the upper classes have magazines exclusively dedicated to their interests and pursuits, such as *Country Life, Horse and Hound* and *Tatler*. Newman also notes the enormous amount of print and broadcast media dedicated to daily business news and stock market quotations, despite the fact that few people in the UK own stocks and shares. He notes that 'international news and trade agreements are reported in terms of their impact on the business world and wealthy investors, not on ordinary working people'.

### Representations of the working class

It can be argued that some mass media representations of the working class are also part of capitalist ideology. Newman (2006) notes that there are very few situation comedies, television dramas or films that focus on the everyday lives of the working class, despite the fact that this group constitutes a significant section of society.

He argues that when working-class people are featured, the media depiction is often either unflattering or pitying. Blue-collar heads of households on prime-time television have typically been portrayed as well-intentioned but dumb buffoons or as immature macho exhibitionists. Newman argues that when news organisations focus on the working class, it is generally to label them as a problem – for example, as welfare cheats, drug addicts or criminals. Working-class groups – for example, youth subcultures such as mods or skinheads – are often subjected to moral panics, while reporting of issues such as poverty, unemployment or single-parent families often suggests that personal inadequacy is the main cause of these social problems, rather than government policies or poor business practices. Studies of representations of industrial relations reporting by the Glasgow University Media Group (GUMG) (1976) suggest that the media portray 'unreasonable' workers as making trouble for 'reasonable' employers (see Unit 6.2.2).

Owen Jones (2011), too, claims that media coverage of the working class, and particularly the poor, symbolises an assault on working-class values, institutions and communities. He observes that from the 1980s onwards, it became fashionable to disparage working-class life. Jones notes that journalists are keen to suggest that those who constitute an – alleged – unqualified, unskilled and unemployed **underclass** are feckless, foul-mouthed, promiscuous and probably racist. He argues that many journalists suffer from a 'liberal bigotry' in that they assume that all working-class White people hate immigrants and **multiculturalism.**

Jones claims that there is also an assumption among journalists that the old, 'decent' working class, which had a great deal of self-respect, has died out, leaving behind a detritus of '**chavs**', 'gym-slip slum mums', 'alcopop-slurping feral street urchins' and '**bling**-dripping' thugs who lack any moral compass. He concludes that the genuine hopes and fears of ordinary working-class people and the everyday experiences of their surroundings, communities and working lives do not exist as far as journalists and TV programme makers are concerned. He notes that, 'coupled with the ludicrous mainstream view that Britain is now a classless society, the "chav" phenomenon obscures what it means to be working-class today'.

## Activity

*A group of youths hanging around the streets of London, Britain, that may be labelled as 'chavs'.*

How are poor members of the society you live in represented in the media?

John McKendrick et al. (2008) studied a week's output of mainstream media in 2007, and concluded that coverage of poverty is marginal in the UK media, in that the causes and consequences of poverty were very rarely explored across the news, documentaries or drama. Furthermore, reporting of poverty-related issues, where it existed, was negative, inaccurate and partial – it often strongly implied that poverty was the result of individual irresponsibility, that those in poverty were too content to live off benefits, and that a culture of poverty was the main cause of anti-social behaviour. It was rare to find news stories exploring more structural reasons for poverty, such as government economic and social policies, global recession, inequalities in the distribution of wealth and income and so on.

# Media representations of age

Most sociological research on media representations of age groups have focused on young people and old people. This is because it is these age groups which have most commonly been found to have been negatively stereotyped by the media, at least in the West. In other words, youths and old people have suffered from the effects of ageism, the belief that certain age groups are inherently inferior to others.

### Media representations of youth in the UK

There are generally two very broad ways in which young people have been targeted and portrayed by the media in the UK. On the one hand, there is a whole media industry aimed at socially constructing youth in terms of lifestyle and identity. Magazines are produced specifically for young people. Record companies, internet music download sites, mobile phone companies and radio stations all specifically target and attempt to shape and/or respond to the musical tastes of young people. Networking sites on the internet, such as Facebook, Twitter and Instagram, allow youth to project their identities around the world.

However, youth are often portrayed by news media as a social problem, as immoral or anti-authority, and consequently constructed as **folk devils** as part of a moral panic (see Unit 6.5.2). The majority of moral panics since the 1950s have been manufactured around concerns about young people's behaviour, such as their membership of specific 'deviant' subcultures (for example, teddy boys, hoodies), or because their behaviour (for example, drug taking or binge drinking) has attracted the disapproval of those in authority.

Research by Mike Wayne (2007) confirms this overwhelmingly negative portrayal of youth in the UK. His analysis looked at 2130 news items across all the main television channels during May 2006 and found 286 stories that focused specifically on young people. Of these, 28 per cent focused on celebrities, but 82 per cent focused on young people as either the perpetrators or the victims of violent crime. In other words, young people were mainly represented as a violent threat to society. Given that – in terms of recorded crime – offending peaks in the late teens and early twenties, the association of youth with crime is unsurprising. However, most young people do not offend, so the resulting stereotyped view of youth is misleading.

Wayne also found that it was very rare (only 1 per cent) for news items to feature a young person's perspective or opinion. He notes that the media only deliver a one-dimensional picture of youth, one that encourages fear and condemnation rather than understanding. Moreover, he argues that it distracts from the real problems young people face in the modern world – such as homelessness, not being able to get onto the housing ladder, unemployment, mental health problems and so on – that might be caused by society's or the government's failure to take the problems of youth seriously.

Research conducted by the UK National Children's Bureau in 2008 confirms this picture. The research was based on stories about young people which appeared in a sample of national and regional newspapers and BBC/ITV news over a two-week period in 2008. The research found that:

- The media produce more negative stories than positive ones about youth.
- The media focus particularly on youths belonging to minority groups.
- Bad news sells.
- Journalists are under pressure to cover negative stories.

## Activity

How far are such negative representations of youth in the media mirrored in the country where you live?

### Media representations of old people

Age Concern UK (2000) argues that the elderly are under-represented across a variety of mass media. For example, in 2000, 21 per cent of the population were aged 65 plus, yet only 7 per cent of representations on television were of that age group. Colin Milner, Kay Van Norman and Jenifer Milner (2012), in a comprehensive review of the global mass media's portrayal of old age, conclude that media portrayals of ageing:

> ***not only reflect the widespread ageism in society, but largely reinforce negative stereotypes. In addition, when ageing is depicted in a manner that appears positive, the aim is often to push anti-ageing messages and frame defying ageing as the only example of successful ageing.*** **(Milner et al., 2012)**

The cosmetics industry certainly reinforces this view with endless advertisements for products which claim to remove, disguise or even reverse the visible signs of ageing such as wrinkles and grey hair.

Milner et al. argue that the media categorise the elderly into two very contrasting groups. At one end of the scale are 'super seniors', who are portrayed, especially by advertisers, as healthy, wealthy and as defying the ageing process. At the opposite end is 'bad' old age, characterised by illness, decline and a strain on the economy as well as social and health services. Such media portrayals reflect the intersection of age with class: representations of wealthy old people tend to be positive; representations of poor old people, negative.

Feminists argue that representations of old age are also modified by gender. For example, older men are highly visible on film and TV, but older women less so. While TV presenters in the UK are broadly reflective of the general population in age terms, a large majority (82 per cent) of those over 50 are men. Overall, women over 50 make up just 5 per cent of on-screen presenters of all ages and both sexes, and 7 per cent of the workforce both on and off screen (Commission on Older Women, 2013).

## Activity

*Co-presenters attend the* Strictly Come Dancing *series 11 launch show at Elstree Studios, England, 2013.*

How does the image above of Bruce Forsyth (then 85) and Tess Daly (then 44) illustrate TV's differential treatment of men and women by age?

## Cross-cultural variations and recent developments

It is important to recognise that, as Izian Idris and Lynn Sudbury-Riley (2016) point out, the findings described above cannot necessarily be applied to the East because of cultural differences. Respect for older adults is 'profoundly rooted in the norms of Asian collectivist culture', while Western culture is more individualistic. In their study of both print and television advertising in Malaysia, they found that 'while older women are still slightly underrepresented, there appears to be progress made in that greater numbers of older adults are now included in mainstream advertising. Moreover, these seniors are depicted as relatively happy, active, and physically strong and are utilized in ads for a range of different products.' However, it is possible that Malaysia is not typical of East Asian countries in general. Research carried out around the same time (Michael Prieler, Alex Ivanov and Shigeru Hagiwara, 2017), which analysed 432 television advertisements from Hong Kong, Japan and South Korea, found that 'older people are highly underrepresented'.

In the West, recent research suggests that media producers may be gradually reinventing how they deal with the elderly, especially as they realise that this group may have disposable income – that is, extra money ('grey pounds') – to spend on consumer goods. Monica Lee et al. (2007) note that representation of the elderly in advertisements is still fairly low (15 per cent ), but the majority of these advertisements (91 per cent) portray the elderly as 'golden agers', who are active, alert, healthy, successful and content. Nevertheless, Lee et al. suggest that this stereotype may be unrealistic, in that it does not reflect the wide range of experiences that people have as they age, including loss of status, poverty, loneliness and loss of their partner.

### Key terms

**Meritocratic** Relating to a society or organisation in which success or failure is based on merit, defined as effort plus ability.

**American Dream** The belief that anyone who works hard enough and has the necessary talent can reach the top of the ladder in the USA.

**Conspicuous consumption** The purchase and display of expensive items in order to demonstrate one's wealth.

**Underclass** A social category or group existing beneath the class structure of a society.

**Multiculturalism** A social policy in which the co-existence of different ethnic groups is accepted without pressure for ethnic minorities to assimilate into the majority culture.

**Chavs** An insulting word for people, particularly young people, whose way of dressing, speaking and behaving is thought to show their lack of education and their low social class.

**Bling** Cheap and showy jewellery.

**Folk devils** People belonging to a deviant subculture who are seen as a threat to society.

### Summary

1. Systems of stratification need to be legitimated. The media help to legitimise class systems by suggesting that they are meritocratic or by transmitting classist views.
2. Media representations of upper classes are generally positive, while those of lower classes are generally negative – for example, representing poor people as 'chavs' or 'skivers'.
3. The media have been accused of reinforcing ageism through their portrayal of young people and the elderly.
4. Media treatment of age is modified by considerations of class and gender.
5. The growth in numbers of relatively affluent old people has led to some changes in media representations of this group, particularly in advertisements.

# END-OF-PART QUESTIONS

**0 1** Describe how the media can promote stereotypical views of the members of social groups. **[4 marks]**

**0 2** Give three examples of ways in which the attitudes associated with European colonialism have impacted on media treatment of ethnic groups. **[6 marks]**

**0 3** Evaluate the view that the media are ageist. **[8 marks]**

# PART 5 MEDIA EFFECTS

## Contents

**Unit 6.5.1 Models of media effects 381**

**Unit 6.5.2 The media, deviancy and crime 385**

So far we have largely taken for granted that the media have important effects on society, both for good and ill. For example, we have seen how authoritarian regimes try to control the messages their citizens receive through the media and how these citizens have used the new media to seek to resist their oppression. We have also looked at the role of the media in democratic societies and the debate between those who see it as promoting democracy and those who see it more as a vehicle for promoting the interests of elites. In addition, we have looked at the wider debate between those who see the new media as bringing about a more connected, open and democratic world and those who are more pessimistic about its impact.

However, social scientists disagree with each other about just how powerful the media are and about exactly how they affect both attitudes and behaviour (to the extent that it does). Consequently, in this, the final part of the chapter, we turn our attention to these issues.

Unit 6.5.1 examines the main competing sociological models of media effects and Unit 6.5.2 analyses how they have been applied to understand the relationship between the media, deviancy and crime.

## Unit 6.5.1 Models of media effects

In sociology, models are simplified attempts to represent real-life social processes. Over the years, a number of competing models of media effects have been developed offering alternative views of the processes involved.

### The hypodermic syringe model

One of the earliest models was the hypodermic syringe model that was developed after World War I to explain how propaganda messages had affected the morale of enemy soldiers. The model suggested that propaganda worked like a drug injected directly into a vein using a hypodermic syringe, having a direct and powerful effect.

In 1938, when Orson Welles and the Mercury Theatre broadcast a dramatisation of H.G. Wells' *War of the Worlds* on the radio in the USA in the format of a news bulletin and the *New York Daily News* reported that thousands of people were gripped by mass hysteria, fearful that the earth was being invaded by Martians, it seemed like the theory had been validated.

However, subsequent commentators have queried the *New York Daily News'* claims. They point out that the *New York Daily News'* report was based largely on anecdotal evidence that was never fully investigated and that local hospitals had no records of hysterical or shocked patients being admitted following the broadcast. They also point out that newspapers were concerned at the time that the relatively new medium of radio could deprive them of some of their advertising revenue and were, therefore, keen to paint it as irresponsible. In addition, if hundreds or even tens of thousands really had been gripped by mass hysteria, it seems likely that this would have been an ongoing story to be explored at length, yet the newspaper coverage was dropped after a day or two.

## Activity

DAILY NEWS FINAL

FAKE RADIO 'WAR' STIRS TERROR THROUGH U.S.

"War" Victim

"I Didn't Know"

*Front page of the* New York Daily News *following the broadcast of* War of the Worlds.

Explain why the headline above should be treated with caution?

Later researchers have argued that the hypodermic syringe model over-simplifies media effects in a number of ways. First, it wrongly assumes that audiences are passive and that audience members are all affected in the same way. It also pictures the audience as an '**atomised mass'** whose response to media messages is unaffected by their social relations with others. This latter view is challenged by the next model we will look at.

### The two-step flow model

Elihu Katz and Paul Lazarsfeld (1955) suggested that personal relationships and conversations with significant others, such as family members, friends, teachers and work colleagues, result in people modifying or rejecting media messages. They argued that 'opinion leaders' – that is, people of influence whom others in a social network look up to and listen to – usually dominate social networks. These people usually have strong ideas about a range of matters. Moreover, these opinion leaders expose themselves to different types of media – newspapers, television news, documentaries, soap operas and so on – and form an opinion on their content. These interpretations are then passed on to other members of their social circle.

Katz and Lazarsfeld thus suggested that media messages have to go through two steps or stages:

1. The opinion leader is exposed to the media content.
2. Those who respect the opinion leader internalise their interpretation of that content.

Consequently, the media do not directly influence media audiences. Rather, they choose to adopt a particular opinion, attitude or way of behaving after negotiation and discussion with an opinion leader. The audience, therefore, is not passive, but active.

Clearly, the two-step flow model is itself rather simplistic, because audience members may or may not discuss what they see, read or hear with others and, even if they do discuss some messages, many messages will go undiscussed. Nevertheless, the general idea that audiences are not passive and that effects are dependent on audiences' social relations with others is now widely accepted.

### The uses and gratifications model

The next model to be developed not only accepted that audiences are active consumers of the media, but turned the basic research question on its head. Instead of asking what the media did to audiences, it asked how audiences use the media.

Jay Blumler and Denis McQuail (1968) suggest that people use the media in order to satisfy particular needs that they have. They argue that these needs may be biological, psychological or social. Moreover, these needs are relative – the way that the audience use the media to gratify their needs will depend upon influences such as social position, age, gender, ethnicity and so on. For example, Julian Wood (1996) illustrated how teenagers may use horror films to gratify their need for excitement.

Blumler and McQuail identifed four basic needs which people use television to satisfy:

1. *Diversion.* As James Watson (2008) notes, 'we may use the media to escape from routines, to get out from under problems, to ease worries or tensions'. People may immerse themselves in particular types of media to make up for lack of satisfaction at work or in their daily lives. For example, women may compensate for the lack of romance in their marriages by reading Mills & Boon romantic novels. Some people even live alternative lives and identities as avatars on websites such as Second Life.
2. *Personal relationships.* Watson notes that we often know more about characters in soap operas than we do about our own neighbours. The media may, therefore, provide the means to compensate for the decline of community in our lives. For example, socially isolated elderly people may see soap opera characters as companions they can identify with and worry about in the absence of interaction with family members. Users may also see cyber-communities on the Web as alternative families.
3. *Personal identity.* People may use the media to 'make over' or to modify their identity. For example, a teenager who suspects he is gay may use the experience of a gay character in a teenage soap opera such as *Hollyoaks* or *Skins* to help him make decisions about how he might deal with his own sexuality. Social networking sites such as Facebook allow people to use the media to present their preferred identity to the wider world.
4. *Surveillance.* People use the media to obtain information and news about the social world in order to help them make up their minds on particular issues. In recent years, the gratification of this need is increasingly taking on an interactive quality with the growing popularity of online blogging and websites to which people can add their own knowledge – for example, Wikipedia.

Later researchers have used this approach to establish that people may use the media to satisfy a wide range of needs. For example, James Lull (1995) found that members of families use television to satisfy their sometimes somewhat contradictory needs for communication with each other, affiliation, social learning and demonstration of competence, as well as for avoidance and dominance (for example, taking control of the remote control).

Recognition of the fact that audiences seek to satisfy particular needs as consumers of media is a useful reminder that audiences are not passive, but tells us nothing about possible effects. The next model to be developed sought to understand better how the idea of an active audience might modify the impact of media messages.

## The reception analysis model

The reception analysis model identifies a number of ways in which audiences are active in terms of their reception of media messages. In particular, they draw attention to processes of:

- *Selective exposure:* audience members select which media messages they will expose themselves to – for example, which newspapers they will buy or which TV programmes they will watch.
- *Selective interpretation:* audience members do not necessarily simply absorb unquestioningly the messages they receive, but may challenge them.
- *Selective recall:* audience members may forget information that does not fit in with their pre-existing world view.

The issue of selective interpretation has received particular attention from researchers. The key assumption these researchers have made is that media messages are **polysemic** – that is, carry many potential meanings. To put it another way, media messages are open to different interpretations.

The reception analysis model suggests that the way people interpret media content differs according to their class, age, gender, ethnic group and other sources of social identity. Research by David Morley (1980) examined how the content of a well-known 1970s BBC evening news programme, *Nationwide*, was interpreted by 29 groups made up of people from a range of social, cultural and educational backgrounds. Members of these groups took part in in-depth group discussions following the viewing of one of two extracts (one about strike action taken by a group of workers, the other about the budget plans of the government) in order to see how they had decoded the preferred interpretation of events offered by the programme makers.

Morley concluded that people chose to make one of three 'readings' or interpretations of media content:

1. *Preferred (or dominant) reading:* the viewer shares the programme's 'code' (its meaning system of values, attitudes, beliefs and assumptions). This was the reading associated with, for example, a group of bank managers, print management trainees, apprentices and school students.
2. *Negotiated reading:* the viewer partly shares the programme's code and broadly accepts the preferred reading, but modifies it in a way that reflects their social position and interests. This was the reading associated with, for example, teacher training college students, university arts students and photography higher education students.
3. *Oppositional reading:* the viewer does not share the programme's code and rejects the preferred reading, bringing to bear an alternative frame of interpretation. This was the reading associated with a group of **shop stewards**.

Moreover, Morley argued that social class alone did not determine how a group interpreted the programme. People within the same social class could belong to distinct subcultures within that class and consequently read the programme extracts differently. For example, the apprentice group and shop stewards group were both working-class, but – as indicated above – read the extracts differently.

Overall, then, the reception analysis model argues that audience members actively interpret media messages according to their pre-existing attitudes, values, beliefs and social position. Chris Livesey (2014) has suggested that models such as this which focus on how media messages are filtered by audience groups can be referred to collectively as 'normative models', reflecting the emphasis given to the importance of understanding how the norms and values of audience members may influence the way media messages are interpreted and applied.

## The cultural effects model

It is but a short step from the reception analysis model to the conclusion that the media have little real effect on audiences, because the latter interpret what they see, hear or read according to their pre-existing views, attitudes and opinions. However, such a step has been challenged by a range of media sociologists who insist that the fact that audiences are active does not preclude the possibility that the media can have significant effects on both attitudes and behaviour.

In relation to the reception analysis model, they pose the question as to where these pre-existing ideas come from and query whether it is plausible to suggest that the media have played no part in their formation. They also ask what happens when audience members have no direct experience or other knowledge of an issue. For example, Philo (2001) notes that when he and his colleagues began their examination of media coverage of the Gulf War of 1991, it was clear that public knowledge about the background to this conflict was low, meaning that media outlets were in a stronger position to 'instruct' their audiences.

Left-wing sociologists in particular are critical of models which suggest that the media are ineffectual. Jenny Kitzinger of the Glasgow University Media Group argues that:

> *Many of the terms widely used in media/cultural studies obscure vital processes in the operation of media power. Concepts such as 'polysemy', 'resistance' and 'the active audience' are often used to by-pass or even negate enquiry into the effects of cinema, press or televisual representations. Our work shows that the complex processes of reception and consumption* mediate, *but do not necessarily* undermine, *media power. Acknowledging that audiences can be 'active' does not mean that the media are ineffectual. Recognising the role of interpretation does not invalidate the concept of influence.* (Kitzinger, 1999)

The neo-Marxist cultural effects model argues that, over the long term, constant exposure to the media results in the internalisation of an ideology which portrays capitalism as both natural and inevitable and, in recent decades, portrays neoliberal policies as in the interests of all. For example, they argue that in the UK and the USA media coverage of benefit fraud in recent years has resulted in the demonisation of welfare claimants and the undermining of public support for the **welfare state**.

Ben Baumberg, Kate Bell and Declan Gaffney (2012) examined a database of national daily newspapers in Britain from 1995 to 2011 and located about 6600 articles concerned with benefit and working-age claimants. They found an 'extraordinarily disproportionate' focus on benefit fraud, with 29 per cent of news stories referencing fraud over this time period, despite the fact that the Department for Work and Pensions' own estimate of fraud across all benefits is just 0.7 per cent. Moreover, the reporting of benefit fraud often makes use of sensationalism in order to provoke a strong negative emotional reaction in the reader.

The authors also conducted focus groups and commissioned a MORI survey of public opinion to examine public attitudes towards benefit claimants. The survey asked respondents to estimate the proportion of claims that were fraudulent. Their estimate was one in four, a proportion pretty much in line with the proportion of news reports about benefits that focused on fraud. The hypothesis that the newspapers were largely responsible for these estimates is further strengthened by their finding that there was a strong relationship between the amount of news coverage of fraud in particular newspapers and the estimates provided by the readers of those titles.

## Activity

*The cover of Baumberg, Bell and Gaffney's study.*

Describe the evidence presented by this research of newspaper coverage influencing their readers' view of benefit fraud.

### Conclusion

Clearly, the issue of media effects is one which divides sociologists and other social scientists. Perhaps this is unsurprising given the difficulty of isolating the effects of the media from other possible influences and given the complexity of the possible effects: short-term or long-term; direct or indirect; intended and unintended and on individuals, groups and society as a whole.

One way of evaluating these competing models is to examine an area of social life which has been extensively researched: the relationship between the media, crime and deviance. It is to this topic we turn in the final unit.

## Key terms

**Atomised mass** A view of the media audience as made up of a very large number of people who lack relationships with others.

**Polysemic** Having many possible meanings.

**Shop stewards** Trades union members elected as representatives of a 'shop' (or department) in dealings with the management.

**Welfare state** All those services provided by the state intended to maintain the well-being of its citizens.

## Summary

1. There are a number of competing models of media effects within sociology.
2. The main ones are: the hypodermic syringe model; the two-step flow model; the uses and gratifications model; the reception analysis model; and the cultural effects model.
3. There is a lack of consensus among sociologists over both the nature and extent of media effects. Nevertheless, recognition of the fact that audiences are not passive does not preclude the possibility that the media have measurable effects, both in the short and long term.

# Unit 6.5.2 The media, deviancy and crime

In sociology, 'deviance' refers to behaviour that breaks social norms, while 'crime' refers to behaviour that breaks criminal laws. The two overlap, but are not the same. To the extent that social norms vary from one society and one time to another, so too does what counts as deviant behaviour. Similarly, to the extent that the criminal law varies from one society to another and over time, so too will what counts as criminality. There is, of course, wide-ranging global agreement over some types of criminality: murder, grievous bodily harm, burglary and robbery, for example. Yet, there are also areas of the law where societies differ. Homosexuality, for example, is still criminalised in 72 countries (*Guardian*, 27/07/17).

As Geoffrey Pearson (1983) argued, the public are both fearful of and fascinated by crime and in virtually all societies the media have sought to satisfy the public's apparently near-insatiable appetite for stories about crime and deviance, more or less since its inception in the form of 18th-century news sheets.

In this unit, we will examine some of the alleged effects of the media's coverage of crime and deviance as a way of evaluating the models of media effects covered in the previous unit.

## Media violence and real-life violence

One area that has been the focus of extensive research over a long period of time is the possible relationship between the portrayal of violence in the media and violent behaviour in the real world, particularly by children and adolescents.

Early studies of the relationship between the media and violence focused on conducting experiments in laboratories. For example, Albert Bandura et al. (1963) looked for a direct cause-and-effect relationship between media content and violence. They showed three groups of children real, film and cartoon examples of a self-righting doll ('bobo doll') being attacked with mallets, while a fourth group saw no violent activity. After being introduced to a room full of exciting toys, the children in each group were made to feel frustrated by being told that the toys were not for them. They were then led to another room containing a bobo doll, where they were observed through a one-way mirror. The three groups who had been shown the violent activity – whether real, film or cartoon – all behaved more aggressively than the fourth group. On the basis of this experiment, Bandura and colleagues concluded that violent media content could lead to imitation or **copycat violence**.

In a similar vein, Gregory McCabe and Kimberly Martin (2005) argue that imitation was a likely outcome of media violence, because often it is the hero who uses violence to deal with a problem, violence which not only goes unpunished but also brings rewards to its perpetrator. Consequently, it is argued that such media violence has a **disinhibition effect** – it convinces children that in some social situations the 'normal' rules that govern conflict and difference can be suspended – that is, discussion and negotiation can be replaced with violence.

A third alleged consequence of media violence is **desensitisation**. Elizabeth Newson (1994) noted that children and teenagers are subjected to thousands of killings and acts of violence as they grow up, through viewing television and films. She suggested that such prolonged exposure to media violence may have a 'drip-drip' effect on young people over the course of their childhood and result in their becoming desensitised to violence – they become socialised into accepting violent behaviour as normal, especially as a problem-solving device. Newson concluded that, because of this, the latest generation of young people subscribe to weaker moral codes and are more likely to behave in anti-social ways than previous generations.

### Evaluation

There can be no disputing the claim that real-life violence can and does mimic media violence. Numerous examples are available. For example, in 1995, two 18-year-olds, Sarah Edmondson and her then-boyfriend, Benjamin Darras, went on a violent crime spree in the southern USA following repeated viewings of the film *Natural Born Killers*. Darras shot and killed a businessman in Mississippi and Edmondson shot and wounded a store clerk in Louisiana. Similarly, in 2014, 16-year-old Steven Miles stabbed his girlfriend to death in his bedroom in Surrey, England, and then dismembered her body, mimicking the actions of *Dexter*, a vigilante serial killer in a cult US TV series.

### Activity

Poster for *Natural Born Killers*.

Can you think of any reasons for questioning the idea that this film 'caused' the crimes committed by Sarah Edmondson and Benjamin Darras?

However, the claim that these screen depictions of homicidal violence *caused* real-life killings needs to be treated with caution. First, correlation does not necessarily prove causation. That is to say, just because two variables are associated, it does not follow that one is causing the other. The direction of cause and effect could be the other way round – homicidally inclined people may be attracted to watching screen violence – or a third factor, mental instability, say, or childhood abuse may lead to *both* a taste for screen violence *and* murderous tendencies. Second, recognising that the violent acts mimicked those viewed on screen still leaves unexplained why these specific people acted in this murderous way when the vast majority of viewers of *Dexter* and *Natural Born Killers* did not subsequently kill others. Finally, the question has to be asked: would these or similarly fatal actions have been carried out at some point by those convicted *whether or not they had viewed these instances of screen violence?* Clearly, we can never know for sure, but – at the very least – it has to count as a distinct possibility.

Overall, the evidence for a direct causal relationship between screen violence and violence in real life is quite weak. For example, studies that have looked at how children are affected when television first arrives in a society have found little change. The latest study was in St Helena, a British colony in the South Atlantic Ocean, which received television for the first time in 1995. Before-and-after studies showed no change in children's social behaviour (Tony Charlton et al., 2000). Similarly, Richard Rhodes (2000) found that violent crime rates in Europe and Japan either stayed the same or declined in the years following the introduction of television. Nevertheless, it may well be the case that certain children who have grown up in a violent environment are more vulnerable to being negatively influenced by screen violence.

Cumberbatch (2004) looked at over 3500 research studies into the effects of screen violence, encompassing film, TV, video and, more recently, computer and video games. He states that, 'If one conclusion is possible, it is that the jury is still out. It's never been in. Media violence has been subjected to a lynch mob mentality with almost any evidence used to prove guilt.' In other words, there is still no conclusive evidence either way that violence shown in the media influences or changes people's behaviour.

## Moral panics and deviancy amplification

Two further alleged effects of the media's representation of crime and deviance which have received considerable attention from sociologists are moral panics, which have to do with how the media can affect public opinion, and **deviancy amplification**, which is concerned with how the media can affect behaviour.

The term 'moral panic' was popularised by Stan Cohen (1972) in his classic work *Folk Devils and Moral Panics: The Creation of the Mods and Rockers*. The term refers to widespread feelings of anxiety and concern held by the general public which develop when – in Cohen's words – 'a condition, episode, person or group of persons emerges to become defined as a threat to societal values and interests'.

According to Erich Goode and Nachman Ben-Yehuda (1994), there are five distinguishing features of moral panics:

- *concern* – the belief that the behaviour of the group or activity deemed deviant is likely to have a negative effect on society
- *hostility* – hostility toward the group in question develops, and they come to be seen as 'folk devils'
- *consensus* – there must be widespread agreement that the group in question poses a real threat to society
- *disproportionality* – the level of anxiety and concern is disproportionate to the actual threat posed by the accused group
- *volatility* – moral panics are highly volatile (unstable) and tend to disappear as quickly as they appeared due to a waning in public interest or news media turning their attention elsewhere.

Moral panics are closely linked to the concept of deviancy amplification. The concept was coined by Leslie Wilkins (1967) and draws upon the **labelling theory** notion that the social reaction to deviant behaviour can unintentionally – and ironically – actually make it worse. It could, for example, attract more people to engage in this form of deviancy or encourage those already involved to become more deviant.

Deviancy amplification needs to be distinguished from what Young (1971) called a **fantasy crime wave**, which occurs when there is no *real* increase in the deviant behaviour, but where there *appears* to be an increase, either because the police devote more effort to detection, thereby uncovering more instances, or because the public become more willing to report instances as victims or witnesses, thereby inflating the crime statistics.

Moral panics go through a number of stages, with the media implicated at every stage:

- The news media (especially, the tabloid press) report on a particular activity/incident or social group, using sensationalist and exaggerated language and headlines.
- **Moral entrepreneurs** – for example, politicians, religious leaders and so on – react to media reports and make statements condemning the group or activity; they insist that the police, courts and government take action.
- The media over-simplifies the reasons why the group or activity has appeared (for example, young people out of control, a lack of respect for authority, a decline in morality and so on), and follow-up articles demonise the group as a social problem or 'folk devils' – that is, the media give them particular characteristics, focusing particularly on their dress and behaviour, which helps the general public and police to identify them more easily.
- The authorities stamp down hard on the group or activity – this may take the form of the police stopping, searching and arresting those associated with the activity, the courts severely punishing those convicted of the activity, or the government bringing in new laws to control the activity or group.
- The reporting of incidents associated with the group or activity to the police by the general public rises as the group or activity becomes more visible in the public consciousness.
- The media report the arrests and convictions that result from the moral panic, thereby fulfilling the initial media prophecy or prediction that the group or activity would be a social problem.
- The group may react to the moral panic, over-policing and so on by becoming more deviant in protest, or the activity may go underground, where it becomes more difficult to police and control.

### The mods and rockers

The focus of Cohen's path-breaking study was two working-class youth subcultures that emerged in Britain in the 1960s: the 'mods' and 'rockers'. Cohen argued that the media themselves played a part in crystallising the distinctive identities of these two subcultures by exaggerating their differences from each other (in terms of dress, musical preferences, preferred mode of transport and so on) and, at the same time, generated a moral panic around their activities.

## Activity

*Picture of rockers (left) and mods and their preferred modes of transport.*

Cohen focused on the media's reaction to youth 'disturbances' beginning on Easter Monday 1964. He demonstrated how the media blew what were essentially small-scale scuffles and vandalism out of all proportion by carrying stories on their front pages and using sensationalist headlines such as 'Day of Terror by Scooter Gangs' and 'Wild Ones "Beat Up" Margate'.

He argued that the media tapped into what it saw as a social consensus – it assumed that decent law-abiding members of society shared their concerns about a general decline in the morality of the young, symbolised by the growing influence of youth culture. Subsequently, groups labelled 'mods' and 'rockers' by the media were presented and analysed in a distorted and stereotyped fashion as a threat to law and order. A **deviancy amplification spiral** was set in train, with the news media eager to 'expose' new examples of delinquency, increasing numbers of working-class youths identifying with one or other group, further run-ins between the youth groups and calls by moral entrepreneurs to 'do something' about this growing menace to social order and civility.

The decades since the 1960s have seen a succession of further moral panics in Britain around such issues as 'mugging', 'bogus asylum seekers', 'raves', 'predatory paedophiles', 'dangerous dogs', 'road rage', 'girl gangs', 'hoodies', 'scary clowns' and so on.

Can you identify any (similar) moral panics in the society where you live in the last two decades?

## Contemporary issues: The moral panic over 'boat people' in Australia

*'Boat people' travelling to Australia.*

In 1976, five refugees sailed into Darwin Harbour in a small junk that they had piloted from Vietnam. The government of the day publicly declared it would 'offer sanctuary' to those seeking asylum, promising that the government's 'full resources' would be made available to them.

Today, asylum seekers who arrive in Australia by boat are mandatorily detained before being removed from the country for 'offshore processing' and resettlement in another country. Moreover, asylum seekers who arrive in Australian waters now are officially referred to in government statements as 'illegals'. Using sensationalist language, ministers have publicly alleged asylum seekers 'could be murderers, could be terrorists' and report 'whole villages' are coming to Australia in uncontrollable 'floods' (Doherty, 2015).

This change in both discourse and policy, according to Greg Martin (2015), is the product of a moral panic that has developed over 'boat people', which has taken hold because it resonates with deep-rooted anxieties about Australia's national identity and way of life related to fears of Asian 'invasion' and anxieties related to multiculturalism.

In addition, Martin argues, moral panics over asylum seekers are now a more or less permanent feature of Australian society following US President George Bush's declaration of a 'war on terror' shortly after the 9/11 terrorist attack on the Twin Towers of the World Trade Center in New York. The result of Bush's speech has been the construction of the 'Muslim/terrorist/refugee' as a transnational folk devil, Martin suggests.

Sources: Adapted from B. Doherty (2015), *Call Me Illegal: The Semantic Struggle over Seeking Asylum in Australia* and G. Martin (2015), *Stop the Boats! Moral Panic in Australia over Asylum Seekers.*

### Questions

1. Contrast the language used to refer to asylum seekers in the 1970s with today's language.
2. Explain the final sentence in your own words.
3. 'Moral panics can have real consequences.' How does the moral panic over boat people in Australia illustrate this claim?

## Moral panics and deviancy amplification: a critique

A number of issues have been raised about moral panics and deviancy amplification:

- The key feature of a moral panic is the disproportion between the level of public concern and the real threat that the deviant behaviour poses to society. However, estimation of whether the level of concern is disproportionate hinges on a value judgement and so is not a simple matter of fact.
- Analyses of deviancy amplification usually leave the original causes of the initial deviant behaviour unexplored and unexplained.

- The appearance of interactive new media, according to Angela McRobbie and Sarah Thornton (1995), has radically changed the relationship between the media and its audience and has consequently undermined the overall impact of moral panics. Audiences are allegedly now more sophisticated in terms of how they interpret media content. Competition between different types of media – newspapers, television, 24-hour rolling satellite news channels, Facebook, Twitter, blogs and other internet gossip websites – means that audiences are exposed to a wider set of interpretations about potential social problems and are consequently more likely to be sceptical of their moral panic status.
- These points notwithstanding, both concepts continue to provide powerful ways of understanding two significant features of the relationship between crime/deviance and the media.

## The new media and crime

The new media have offered criminals the opportunity to commit old crimes in new ways (such as terrorist offences), but also opportunities to commit a wide range of entirely new types of crime (such as computer hacking).

Such offences are known as cyber-crimes. The term refers to any type of criminal activity conducted through, or using, an ICT device. The UK government's National Cyber Security Strategy (2016) distinguishes between:

- *cyber-dependent crimes* – crimes that can be committed only through the use of ICT devices, where the devices are both the tool for committing the crime, and the target of the crime; and
- *cyber-enabled crimes* – traditional crimes which can be increased in scale or reach by the use of computers, computer networks or other forms of ICT.

Cyber-dependent crimes fall into two main categories: illegal intrusions into computer networks such as hacking (where criminals gain entry to computers or computer networks in order to gather personal data or information that they can then exploit in some way) or the disruption or downgrading of computer functionality and network space, such as malware and Denial of Service (DOS) attacks.

Cyber-enabled crimes take many forms:

- economic-related cyber-crimes including fraud and intellectual property crime, such as piracy, counterfeiting and forgery
- malicious and offensive communications, such as cyberbullying and trolling
- offences that specifically target individuals, such as cyberstalking and harassment
- child sexual offences, such as online grooming
- extreme pornography and obscene publications.

### Activity

Explain in your own words the distinction between cyber-dependent and cyber-enabled crimes.

## Conclusion

Our review of research on the relationship between the media and crime/deviance clearly indicates that the media can and do have real effects on individuals, groups and society as a whole. Equally clearly, it reveals that sometimes – despite extensive and detailed research – the issue of effects remains uncertain.

Critics of sociology see this as a weakness. They are wrong. Even if the truth of the matter remains frustratingly out of reach, research deepens our understanding of the social world and it is far better to live with uncertainty than to pretend that there are simple answers to complex social issues.

### Key terms

**Copycat violence** Violence which mimics an earlier violent episode.

**Disinhibition effect** An effect which reduces the power of in-built barriers to acting in a deviant or criminal way.

**Desensitisation** An effect which dampens the emotional impact of something which would otherwise be distressing, such as viewing violent behaviour.

**Deviancy amplification** A social process in which actions intended to reduce deviance have the opposite effect.

**Labelling theory** A theory of deviance drawing upon symbolic interactionism and pluralism.

**Fantasy crime wave** An imaginary increase in crime.

**Deviancy amplification spiral** A vicious circle in which attempts to control deviance feed back on themselves, producing increased deviance.

**Moral entrepreneurs** People who make moral judgements and seek to bring about social change in line with these judgements.

## Summary

1. The claim that media violence leads to real-life violence is not well supported by the evidence, but the issue remains unresolved.
2. Two well-attested media effects in relation to crime are moral panics and deviancy amplification.
3. Moral panics are characterised by concern, hostility, consensus, disproportionality and volatility.
4. Deviancy amplification needs to be distinguished from a fantasy crime wave.
5. The media play a crucial contributory role in the process of deviancy amplification.
6. The key feature of moral panics is that the level of public concern is disproportionate to the real threat. Whether the level of public concern is disproportionate in a particular case involves making a value judgement, so is not a simple matter of fact.
7. The new media, associated with digital technologies, have produced new ways of committing traditional crimes as well as entirely new types of offences.
8. It is possible to distinguish between cyber-dependent crimes (where ICT devices are both the means for committing offences and the target of such offences) and cyber-enabled crimes (where the use of ICT facilitates the commission of offences that can also be carried out without the use of ICT).

# END-OF-PART QUESTIONS

0 1 Give the names of four different models of media effects. **[4 marks]**

0 2 Evaluate the claim that media violence causes real-life violence. **[6 marks]**

0 3 Explain how the media can generate moral panics. **[8 marks]**

# EXAM-STYLE PRACTICE QUESTIONS

0 1 'Pluralist theory is mistaken in claiming that the media reflect a wide range of different interests in society.' Evaluate this view. **[35 marks]**

0 2 'The uses and gratification model of media effects has more strengths than limitations.' Evaluate this view. **[35 marks]**

# 7 RELIGION

## Chapter contents

| | | |
|---|---|---|
| **Section A** | **Religion and social order** | **393** |
| **Section B** | **The influence of religion** | **439** |
| **Exam-style practice questions** | | **461** |

Globally, millions of people identify themselves as Muslim, Jewish, Hindu or Christian, while less conventional beliefs include Scientology and Paganism. Sociologists are not concerned with evaluating these different religious beliefs. Instead, they focus on the significance of religion in society. This chapter explores religion in its social context. It begins by examining different ways of defining religion. It asks why science often enjoys higher status than other sources of knowledge and belief, such as religion. Sociologists are interested in the relationship between religion and social class, gender, ethnicity and age. Are young people, for example, less likely to participate in religion than older people?

The chapter then focuses on sociological accounts – both positive and negative – of the role of religion in society. How far do religious beliefs bind people together? To what extent does religion promote social order? Is religion linked to oppression? Can religion be a source of social change?

The chapter explores feminist perspectives on religion. How far can religions be seen as patriarchal and as promoting gender inequality? What evidence is there to suggest that religious practices can benefit women?

The chapter also asks whether religion is declining and becoming less significant in the modern world. Or are different things happening to religions in different societies across the globe?

The chapter concludes by looking at different accounts of the relationship between religion and postmodernity. How significant are new religious movements and New Age ideas for understanding religion today? How do sociologists explain the growth of fundamentalist religions? This chapter suggests answers to these and other important questions.

# SECTION A
# RELIGION AND SOCIAL ORDER

## Contents


| | | |
|---|---|---|
| **Part 1** | **Religion and society** | **394** |
| **Part 2** | **Religion and social order** | **414** |
| **Part 3** | **Gender, feminism and religion** | **421** |
| **Part 4** | **Religion as a source of social change** | **429** |


Section A focuses on the relationship between religion and social order. Four of the key concepts that you were introduced to in Chapter 1 are particularly important here. The first of these is *power, control and resistance*. Many sociologists see religion as a significant agency of social control. Potentially, religions have enormous power to shape their followers' ways of thinking and behaving, and to encourage them to accept the status quo. However, religious movements can sometimes spearhead (lead or be at the forefront of) resistance to governments. Both functionalist and Marxist approaches see religion as a powerful force in society. Functionalism sees it as contributing to social order and social solidarity, and thereby benefiting society. By contrast, Marxist accounts see religion as oppressive and as serving the interests of capitalism.

The second concept is *socialisation, culture and identity*. Religion seems to be more relevant to some social groups than others. For example, globally, women tend to be more religious than men and this may be due to gender socialisation processes. Religion is bound up with people's culture and their identities. The vitality of religion among some minority ethnic groups may be due to the group protecting its cultural heritage and sense of identity.

The third concept is *social change and development*. Sociological debates about the relationship between religion and social change are longstanding. Max Weber (1864–1920) argued that religious ideas played an important part in the development of capitalism. More recently, religion has contributed to far-reaching political, economic and social changes across the world.

The fourth concept is *structure and human agency*. Functionalism and Marxism focus on the role of religion in maintaining the social structure in its present form. Critics argue that these structural theories fail to recognise that religion involves individual choice, decision-making and active human agency.

Section A is divided into four parts. Part 1 examines different ways of defining religion and some of the difficulties involved in measuring religious belief. It looks at both religion and science as examples of belief systems and discusses whether they are compatible. It also explores the relevance of religion for different social groups such as women and young people.

Part 2 focuses on the relationship between religion and social order. It explores functionalist and Marxist accounts of the role of religion in society and examines their strengths and weaknesses.

Part 3 explores feminist perspectives on religion and the relationship between religion, gender and patriarchy.

Part 4 examines debates about the role of religion in promoting or inhibiting change in society. It explores Max Weber's account of the role of Calvinist Protestantism (a form of Christianity) in the rise of capitalism. It also discusses the influence of religious movements on political debates and struggles around the world.

# PART 1 RELIGION AND SOCIETY

## Contents


| | | |
|---|---|---|
| Unit 7.1.1 | Defining and measuring religion | 394 |
| Unit 7.1.2 | Religion and other belief systems | 401 |
| Unit 7.1.3 | Religion and different social groups | 406 |


How do sociologists define religion? How do they measure it? Part 1 examines different ways of defining religion and some of the difficulties involved in measuring religious belief. It looks at both religion and science as examples of belief systems and discusses whether they are compatible. It also explores the relevance of religion for different social groups such as women and young people.

## Unit 7.1.1 Defining and measuring religion

In order to study **religion**, sociologists must define it. Any definition has to take account of the rich diversity of religions that exists on a global scale. However, sociologists disagree on the question of what religion means. What are the sources of this disagreement? Is there necessarily a clear-cut boundary between religious and non-religious phenomena? This unit looks at some of the issues involved in defining religion. It then examines some of the difficulties in measuring religious **beliefs**. It also explores different types of religious organisation, such as churches and sects.

## Different ways of defining religion

Initially, defining religion might seem to be a straightforward task. **Belief systems** such as Judaism, Islam and Christianity are clear examples of world religions. Each has its own set of beliefs and values, its own practices, **rituals** and symbols. However, it is difficult to devise a definition that is broad enough to encompass a wide variety of beliefs without also including phenomena that are not usually considered to be religious, such as astrology or fortune telling.

The different sociological definitions of religion can be divided into three types: substantive definitions, functional definitions and social constructionist approaches.

### Substantive definitions of religion

**Substantive definitions** focus on the substance or content of religion and are concerned with what religion is. A substantive definition, for example, might define religion in terms of a belief in the supernatural, in divine forces, powers or spiritual beings such as a god or gods that are above the laws of nature. Malcolm Hamilton (2001) argues, however, that such definitions are problematic because some belief systems that are commonly regarded as religions, such as forms of Buddhism, do not necessarily include a belief in supernatural beings. This highlights the potential problem of defining and using the concept of religion from a Western perspective.

### Functional definitions of religion

**Functional definitions** view religion in terms of the functions or roles it performs for individuals or society. They focus on what religion does rather than what it is (Hamilton, 2001). J. Milton Yinger, for example, adopted a functional definition of religion as 'a system of beliefs and practices by means of which a group of people struggles with the ultimate problems of human life' (1970, quoted in Hamilton, 2001). However, Hamilton notes several problems with such a definition. First, it is too broad. For instance, by this definition, a political belief system such as communism could be seen as a religion because of the function it performs, even though it explicitly rejects religious beliefs. Second, phrases such as 'the ultimate problems of human life' are open to interpretation. Hamilton points out that for many people the ultimate problems of life might be 'simply how to enjoy it as much as possible, how to avoid pain and ensure pleasure'. Many other aspects of social life, apart from religion, address such issues – for example, medicine and leisure.

**Inclusive and exclusive definitions** Alan Aldridge (2007) distinguishes between more inclusive and more exclusive definitions of religion. With **inclusive definitions**, it is relatively easy for a belief system to qualify as a religion if, for example, it promotes unity or reinforces social cohesion. Religion is defined broadly and could include devotion to a soccer team or loyalty to a rock band or rap artist. Inclusive or broad definitions would also include political belief systems such as nationalism, fascism and communism.

One potential problem with using broad definitions is that they would result in religion being found everywhere. With narrower or **exclusive definitions**, the criteria are more restrictive. The focus is on the content of religion – for example, a belief in a supernatural power such as a god or gods. Generally, functional definitions tend to be more inclusive and substantive ones tend to be more exclusive.

## Activity

*Inclusive, functional definitions would classify devotion to a soccer team as a religion.*

1. How far does soccer or football support involve the following characteristics?
   a. Rituals
   b. Sacred symbols
   c. Faith
   d. A sense of group identity and being bound together
2. To what extent would you see loyal devotion to a football team as a religion?

### Social constructionist approaches to the study of religion

**Social constructionist approaches** are sometimes referred to as 'definitions in use' (Giddens and Sutton, 2013). James Beckford (2003), for example, focuses on the uses that individuals, groups and agencies such as the mass media, schools and the state make of religion in everyday life. Research in this area explores what people say and mean when they talk about religion and participate in practices that they consider to be religious. This approach places more emphasis on whatever passes for religion in society and the meanings that people give to it rather than on questions about what religion is or what it does.

## Difficulties in measuring religious belief

Sociologists are interested in examining the extent of religious belief in different societies and changes in **religiosity** (the quality of being religious) over time. However, there are difficulties in measuring levels of religious belief.

- Sociologists do not agree on a single definition of religion. The definition they adopt (for example, an inclusive rather than an exclusive one) will influence what they class as religious belief, how they measure it and how many people they count as holding such beliefs.
- Beliefs differ between religions (for instance, between Buddhism and Christianity), which can make direct comparisons difficult.
- The lack of reliable evidence about the extent of religious belief in earlier periods makes historical comparison difficult when researching changes in religiosity over time.
- Reliable data may not be available to allow international comparisons of the nature and extent of religious belief.
- Particular measures of religiosity are open to criticism. For example, can church attendance figures be seen as a reliable indicator of religiosity? Some people may attend a place of worship to meet up with friends or because it is the norm in their community to do so rather than because they hold religious beliefs. Others may see themselves as religious and practise in private, without engaging in socially recognised religious practices and rituals such as attending a place of worship.
- There may be a difference between 'belonging' to a religion and 'believing' in its teachings. For example, many people profess a religious identity (when completing a census form, for instance), but this would not necessarily provide a reliable guide to how many people in a society hold religious beliefs.
- Surveys of social attitudes are often used to measure the extent of religious belief but there are problems in relying on evidence from such surveys. For example, some people might be reluctant to admit that they have religious beliefs in contemporary secular societies. Others might be reluctant to deny religious belief in societies where religion remains a major social force. Another problem is that we do not know whether all respondents understand terms such as 'belief', 'religiosity' and 'faith' in the same way. Such terms may mean different things to different

research participants. For instance, some respondents may associate religious belief with participation in established religious practices, while others think of it in a broader context as belief in transcendental forces or some general sense of spirituality. Moreover, it is hard to probe such a deeply personalised subject as religious belief (in attitude surveys, for instance) without the potential problem of misinterpretation on the researcher's part.

## Activity

Questionnaire-based surveys are used in quantitative research on religious beliefs, including studies of trends over time. Questionnaires are designed to measure concepts or variables (see Unit 3.1.2). To do this, concepts must be operationalised – put into forms that can be measured. One way of operationalising religious belief is shown by the British Social Attitudes survey. Respondents had to select the answer which best fitted their beliefs from six alternatives. Answers to this question are easily quantified. The first column of figures shows the percentage of respondents who chose each alternative and the second column gives the actual number of respondents.

**Table 7.1.1 Belief in God**

| Year of research | 2008 | |
|---|---|---|
| I don't believe in God. | 18% | 356 |
| I don't know if God exists and there is no way to find out. | 19% | 368 |
| I don't believe in a personal God but I do believe in some kind of higher power. | 14% | 282 |
| I believe in God some of the time but not at others. | 13% | 255 |
| I have doubts but I feel that I do believe in God. | 18% | 357 |
| I know God really exists and I have no doubts about it. | 17% | 332 |
| Not answered | 1% | 24 |
| Total | | 1974 |

Source: National Centre for Social Research (2016) – British Social Attitudes Survey 33.

1. To what extent does this survey measure religious beliefs from a Western perspective?
2. Assess the view that, although these data can be seen as reliable, they lack validity.

Quantitative data from attitude surveys are suitable for statistical analysis. They make it possible to discover whether there is a correlation – a statistical link – between two or more variables, for example between belief in a god and social class.

A survey provides a broad snapshot but different surveys can produce different pictures of religious belief in the same society, depending, for example, on how the questions are worded. Surveys about religious belief tell us little about other aspects of religion such as the importance of religion in people's everyday lives.

## Activity

'Qualitative methods such as unstructured interviews are useful for exploring the nature of religious belief but they are less useful for measuring belief.'

Evaluate this statement.

# Types of religious organisation

Most people who hold religious beliefs express them through particular religious organisations. Sociologists such as Roy Wallis have attempted to classify the diverse range of organisations into different types.

## Roy Wallis on types of religious organisation

Wallis (1976) classified religious organisations in terms of whether they are:

- *respectable* because they support the norms and values of the wider society or *deviant* because their beliefs do not conform to those of most members of society
- *uniquely legitimate* in claiming a monopoly of the religious truth or *pluralistically legitimate* in accepting that other organisations could also have legitimate religious beliefs.

Wallis' typology (a classification of different types of something) is illustrated in Table 7.1.2.

**Table 7.1.2 Wallis' typology of religious organisations**

| | Respectable | Deviant |
|---|---|---|
| **Uniquely legitimate** | church | sect |
| **Pluralistically legitimate** | denomination | cult |

Source: R. Wallis, *The Road to Total Freedom: A Sociological Analysis of Scientology*, Heinemann, London, 1976, p.13.

## The church

The term '**church**' is associated with Christian worship and refers to a large religious organisation that represents the main religion of a society. Churches are formal organisations with a hierarchy of professional, paid officials. Examples include the Roman Catholic Church and the Church of England.

In principle, a church might try to be universal – to embrace all members of society – and to be, in Wallis' words, 'uniquely legitimate' (the only 'true' religion). In practice, however, there might be substantial minorities who do not belong to it.

Churches are traditionally likely to be ideologically conservative and to support the status quo. This type of organisation accepts and affirms life in this world: members can play a full part in social life and are not expected to withdraw from society.

Steve Bruce (1996) argues that the definition of a church discussed above is mainly useful in describing pre-modern Christian societies where, for example, Catholic or Orthodox churches tried to be the only religion. Religious pluralism in societies undermines the dominance of the church, because it does not have a monopoly on religious belief.

## Denominations

Wallis (1976) defined **denominations** as respectable religious organisations that are 'pluralistically legitimate' – they accept other religious organisations and belief systems. Denominations have often broken away from a church and exist alongside the original church and other groups that have broken away. Examples include Methodist and United Reformed churches.

Like churches, denominations have a hierarchy of paid officials and freely admit new members. Unlike a church, a denomination does not have a universal appeal in society. For example, the United Reformed Church had an average of 33 100 attendances each week in the UK in 2015 (Faith Survey, 2015).

A considerable number of denominations usually exist within a particular society. The USA, for example, has no established church, but a large range of denominations. Denominations do not claim a monopoly on religious truth. They are prepared to tolerate and cooperate with other religious organisations.

## Sects

Wallis (1976) saw **sects** as deviant religions that are in tension with the wider society, partly because they claim a monopoly of the religious truth. Other characteristics of sects that sociologists have identified include the following:

1. Sects are smaller than other religious organisations.
2. Sect members are mainly drawn from lower social classes and are likely to be in conflict with the outside world. They reject the wider values of society in favour of their own religious beliefs.
3. Members may be expected to withdraw from life outside the sect, perhaps giving up connections with friends and family, and living in a commune. They are expected to be deeply committed to the sect's beliefs and may be excluded if they fail to demonstrate their commitment. Members must sacrifice 'worldly pleasures' in order to devote themselves to their religious life. Thus, sects exercise a relatively strong control over individuals' lives.
4. Sects do not have a hierarchy of paid officials. If central authority exists within a sect, it usually rests with a charismatic leader, whose personality and perceived special qualities attract the followers.

Wallis' definition of sects is broadly supported by most other sociologists. However, examples of sects that do not possess the above characteristics can be found.

## Cults

There is no single definition of **cults** that all sociologists accept. Many different religious organisations and spiritual beliefs have been described as 'cults', including Scientology, Transcendental Meditation (TM) and the Heaven's Gate organisation.

Wallis (1976) saw cults as being deviant but pluralistically legitimate (see Table 7.1.2). However, although this definition could cover a wide range of religious organisations, it does not cover all organisations that are seen as cults.

Cults often have customers rather than members and these customers may have relatively little ongoing involvement with the organisation once they have learned the cult's basic beliefs.

## Activity

*Yogic flying.*

Transcendental Meditation (TM) is a technique that is taught on courses during which individuals learn to concentrate on a personal mantra (a word or sound). TM was founded by the Indian Guru the Maharishi Mahesh Yogi. It is claimed that when successfully practised, meditation can lead to stress reduction, self-development and spiritual awareness. If meditation became widespread, the Maharishi believed that it could combat crime and reduce unhappiness. The most advanced practitioners, who undertake specialist training called the Sidhi-Program, claim to be able to levitate while sitting cross-legged. This is known as yogic flying.

In what ways does TM differ from church religions, denominations and sects?

## Activity

**Wallis' typology of new religious movements**

If you have access to online sources of data, research into any *one* organisation in each of the four categories in the figure. Briefly describe their main characteristics and identify some of the main differences between the four movements you have chosen.

# Wallis' account of new religious movements

Wallis was among the first sociologists to develop a typology for the increasing range of **new religious movements** evident since the 1960s (Wallis, 1984). His typology relates specifically to Britain in the 1970s and 1980s but it has been applied to other contexts. A version of Wallis' account is illustrated in the image in the Activity box 'Wallis' typology of new religious movements'.

Wallis divides new religious movements into three main groups according to whether the movement and its members *reject, accommodate* or *affirm* the world outside the movement. He notes the existence of some groups (those in the middle circle) that do not fit neatly into any single category.

## World-rejecting new religious movements

The **world-rejecting new religious movements** have many of the characteristics of a sect. They are usually unambiguously religious organisations but they are highly critical of the outside world and may seek social change. They often have a communal lifestyle with members living in relative isolation and the organisation having a strong influence over its members. Many are seen as morally puritanical, for example the Unification Church (often referred to as Moonies, due to their founder's name, Sun Myung Moon) is particularly strict about restricting sex to monogamous marriage. World-rejecting new religious movements vary enormously in size: the Moonies have an international following with hundreds of thousands of followers, while other groups are small and locally based.

Despite the differences between world-rejecting groups, none of them is content with the world as it is, and they are hostile to competing religions.

## World-accommodating new religious movements

The **world-accommodating new religious movements** are usually offshoots of an existing major church or denomination. For example, neo-Pentecostalist groups are variants of Protestant or Roman Catholic religions, while Subud is a world-accommodating Muslim group.

Typically, these groups neither accept nor reject the world as it is; they simply live within it. They are primarily concerned with religious rather than worldly questions and often want to restore the spiritual purity that they believe has been lost in more conventional churches and denominations.

### World-affirming new religious movements

The **world-affirming new religious movements** may not appear to resemble a conventional religion in that they often lack a church, rituals and a theology. However, they claim to be able to provide access to spiritual or supernatural powers and, in this sense, can be regarded as religions.

World-affirming groups accept the world as it is, and they are not particularly critical of other religions. They offer followers the potential to be successful by unlocking their spiritual powers. Salvation is seen in terms of a personal achievement and as a solution to personal problems such as unhappiness or suffering. Individuals usually overcome such problems by adopting a technique such as meditation or 'primal screams' that heightens their awareness or abilities.

World-affirming movements seek as wide a membership as possible. Rather than attempting to convert people, they try to sell them a service. Followers carry on their normal lives except when undergoing training. There is little social control over the members or customers. Examples of world-affirming new religious movements include Transcendental Meditation (TM) and Erhard Seminars Training (known as est).

### The 'middle ground'

Wallis appreciated that no religious group would conform exactly to the categories he outlined. Some, such as the Healthy, Happy, Holy Organization (3HO), combine elements of different types of movement. The 3HO is like world-affirming movements in that it is an offshoot of an established religion, in this case Sikhism. Like world-affirming movements, it employs techniques including yoga that it is claimed will bring personal benefits, such as happiness and good health. Like world-rejecting movements, the organisation has a clear concept of God, and members live in communes or ashrams but hold conventional jobs outside the movement. Occupying the middle ground, 3HO allows its followers to combine elements of an alternative lifestyle with conventional marriage and employment.

## Rodney Stark and William Sims Bainbridge

According to Stark and Bainbridge (1985), there is no clear-cut, definitive way of distinguishing different types of religious organisation. For example, not all churches try to convert all members of society and not all sects are exclusive. Stark and Bainbridge, therefore, argue that typologies of religious organisations should be abandoned. They claim that religious groups can be compared in terms of a single criterion: the degree of conflict that exists between them and the wider society.

### Sects and cults

Stark and Bainbridge argue that there are different kinds of religious movement in a high degree of tension with their social environment:

1. Sects are formed as an offshoot of an existing religion as a result of division or schism within that religion.
2. Cults are new religions, or at least they are new in a particular society. Some result from *cultural importation*, where a religion from other societies is introduced into a society. Examples of imported cults include Eastern religions introduced into the USA. Other cults are entirely new and result from *cultural innovation*; they are unconnected to existing religions.

Stark and Bainbridge suggest that cults exhibit different degrees of organisation and can be divided into three:

1. **Audience cults** are the least organised and involve little face-to-face interaction. Contacts are often maintained through the mass media and conferences. Many members of the audience for such cults may not know each other. Examples include astrology and belief in UFOs.
2. **Client cults** are more organised and usually offer services to their followers. Scientology, for example, offers its clients the opportunity to clear 'engrams' (repressed memories of painful experiences) from the brain with the help of a device called an e-meter.
3. **Cult movements** involve followers much more. They try to satisfy all the religious needs of their members and, unlike client and audience cults, membership of other faiths is not permitted. Some require little more than occasional attendance at meetings and

acceptance of the cult's beliefs, but others shape the whole of a person's life. The Unification Church is an example of a cult movement.

## The New Age

The **New Age** is associated with alternative forms of spirituality that became popular in the 1970s and 1980s. The New Age incorporates some world-affirming new religious movements and cults (particularly client cults and audience cults), but it is also present in the wider culture of Western societies in shops, meetings, music, television programmes, public lectures and so on. This lack of a tie to particular organisations makes the New Age distinctive from most other religious and some spiritual belief systems.

Examples of New Age beliefs include: an interest in clairvoyance; belief in 'spirit guides'; various types of meditation and psychotherapy; belief in astrology; and an interest in self-healing and natural or traditional remedies for ill-health (for example, yoga, aromatherapy and reflexology).

Paul Heelas (1996) argues that the central feature of the New Age is a belief in **self-spirituality**. People with such beliefs have turned away from traditional religious organisations in their search for the spiritual and have begun to look inside themselves instead. According to Heelas, the New Age values personal experience above 'truths' provided by scientists or conventional religious leaders.

### Key terms

**Religion** Often defined narrowly as a belief system related to supernatural beings or divine forces. However, there are several ways of defining religion including substantive, functional and social constructionist approaches.

**Beliefs** Ideas or convictions that individuals or groups hold to be true even when they are not based on evidence.

**Belief system** A set of ideas held by individuals or groups that help them to interpret and make sense of the world.

**Rituals** Religious practices or ceremonies comprising a set of actions that are carried out in an established order.

**Substantive definitions (of religion)** Definitions that focus on the substance or content of religion – what religion is rather than what it does.

**Functional definitions (of religion)** Definitions that focus on the functions or roles of religion – what religion does rather than what it is.

**Inclusive definitions (of religion)** Broad definitions that include traditional religions and other belief systems such as nationalism, communism and humanism.

**Exclusive definitions (of religion)** Narrow definitions that include traditional religions but exclude other belief systems.

**Social constructionist approach (to defining religion)** Rather than trying to provide a single definition, this approach focuses on how religion is used in daily life.

**Religiosity** The quality of being religious, linked to beliefs and values.

**Church** The dominant religious organisation in a society, which is associated with Christian worship and usually claims a monopoly of the religious truth.

**Denomination** A religious organisation that has broken away from the main religious organisation in a society and accepts the legitimacy of other religious organisations.

**Sect** A relatively small religious organisation which is in conflict with other belief systems in a society.

**Cult** To Wallis, a cult is a relatively small organisation with beliefs that are considered deviant by most people but which coexists with other belief systems in society.

**New religious movements** Religious/spiritual organisations and movements such as Seventh-Day Adventists, the Unification Church and Pentecostalism that are of relatively modern origin and are in some form of opposition to (or differentiation from) longer-established, more powerful religious organisations such as the Roman Catholic Church.

**World-rejecting new religious movements** Religious movements that developed from the 1960s onwards and are hostile to the social world outside the movement.

**World-accommodating new religious movements** Religious movements of relatively recent origin that hold strong religious beliefs but reject mainstream religious doctrine. Nevertheless, they allow members to have conventional lives outside their religious practice.

**World-affirming new religious movements** Religious movements that developed from the 1960s onwards; they are positive about mainstream society, and their religious practices tend to encourage or facilitate social and economic success.

**Audience cults** Cults that do not require much commitment from followers and involve little face-to-face interaction.

**Client cults** Cults that offer services (courses or rituals) to their followers but require little commitment.

**Cult movements** Cults that involve followers/believers fully and act as full religious organisations.

**New Age** A term for a wide range of broadly spiritual beliefs and practices that emphasise the discovery of spirituality within the self. People seek spiritual experiences, inner peace or growth through, for example, meditation, crystal healing and/or aromatherapy.

**Self-spirituality** The practice of searching for spirituality inside oneself.

## Summary

1. Sociologists disagree on how to define religion and there are several different definitions of the concept.
2. Substantive definitions focus on what religion is and its content, such as belief in supernatural forces or supreme beings.
3. Functional definitions focus on what religion does and the purposes, functions or roles that it performs.
4. Inclusive definitions define religion in broad terms. Exclusive definitions are narrower in focus.
5. Rather than searching for a correct or agreed definition of religion, social constructionist approaches focus on the uses that individuals, groups and agencies make of religion in everyday life.
6. There are difficulties in measuring the extent of religious belief in different societies.
7. Wallis defined churches as respectable organisations that claim to be uniquely legitimate, denominations as respectable organisations that claim to be pluralistically legitimate, sects as deviant organisations that claim to be uniquely legitimate, and cults as deviant organisations that claim to be pluralistically legitimate.
8. Wallis distinguished between different types of new religious movement (world-rejecting, world-accommodating and world-affirming) that emerged since the 1960s.
9. Stark and Bainbridge question other typologies of religious organisation and claim that a single criterion, tension with the wider society, can be used to distinguish different types of organisation.
10. However, Stark and Bainbridge do distinguish three types of cult:
    i. audience cults that involve little face-to-face interaction
    ii. client cults that offer services to their members, and
    iii. cult movements that dominate their followers' lives.
11. The New Age refers to a range of spiritual beliefs focusing mainly on the development of the self that became popular in the 1970s.

# Unit 7.1.2 Religion and other belief systems

Religion and science are both examples of belief systems that make claims about the world. In many societies, science is often seen as superior to other belief systems. Science earns its high status because of the methods it uses to generate knowledge that is generally considered to be objective and based on evidence. This knowledge is often utilised for the benefit of humankind. For example, medical research has led to the eradication of smallpox and the control of leprosy. But does science really deserve its high status? Is scientific knowledge genuinely superior to other sources of knowledge and beliefs in society? This unit looks at contrasting views of science and questions some of the **knowledge claims** of science. It explores the relationship between scientific and religious belief systems. It also examines religion and science as examples of ideologies.

## Science and the Enlightenment

The **Enlightenment** refers to a range of scientific, social and philosophical beliefs that developed in Western Europe in the 17th and 18th centuries. Enlightenment thinking rejected belief in the supernatural and in superstition as ways of understanding the world. It argued that knowledge could only come from rational ways of thought. Enlightenment thinking is seen as the foundation of modernity, a phase in human history during which trust was placed in scientific views of the world. For example, it was believed that humankind could use scientific knowledge to bring about progress, improve people's lives, fight disease and tackle natural disasters.

## Open and closed belief systems

Science and religion are both sources of knowledge and beliefs but they differ in important respects. Some approaches distinguish between **open belief systems** and **closed belief systems**. (Bear in mind that these are not the same as Andrew Sayer's open and closed systems discussed in Unit 3.2.3.) Robin Horton (1993), for example, argues that science is an open system of ideas, as its knowledge claims are based on evidence. Science operates in an open environment and is characterised by questioning, testing and revising ideas. As a result, science is constantly developing. By contrast, he suggests that closed systems of ideas such as religion are not open to criticism or to alternative views. Consequently, religion is conservative and does not modify its ideas over time.

Horton argues, however, that religion and magic are in some respects similar to science. Each tries to understand how the world operates in order to control it for human purposes. Critics disagree, arguing that religion and magic are fundamentally different from science. For example, scientific propositions are testable, whereas religious beliefs are based on faith. The **truth claims** of religion (the beliefs and ideas that followers of a religion hold to be true) cannot be tested by rational procedures (Wilson, 1966). Unlike non-scientific belief systems, science enables people to explain, predict and control the world. It can also confirm its explanations in terms of its practical results – for example, by eradicating diseases or predicting when a volcano will erupt. Religion, however, is unable to confirm its explanations in this way.

### Karl Popper

Popper (1959) argued that science is an open belief system. Scientists put forward statements and test them systematically by observation and experiment. Scientific theories are open to testing by peers. However, Popper argued that it is impossible to verify a theory (see Unit 3.2.3). In his view, all scientific knowledge is provisional, 'for the time being' (Popper, 1974), rather than certain or true for all time.

According to Popper, scientific knowledge is distinctive because it is not absolute or sacred truth and can be questioned and tested. By contrast, with non-scientific thought, such as religion or magic, explanations are not tested. Popper argued that subjective experiences or strong feelings of conviction 'cannot be decided by science' (Popper, 2002). Someone may be completely convinced of the truth of something but this conviction cannot be seen as an objective scientific statement if it cannot be tested. For example, statements such as 'God exists' are not scientific because they cannot be tested or falsified. Scientific statements must be open to testing, falsification, criticism and revision.

### Activity

Drawing on Popper's ideas, explain one difference between scientific knowledge and religious thought.

## Critical views of science as an open system

Sociologists and philosophers now question how far science is an open system. This suggests that scientific knowledge may not be as trustworthy as is usually assumed.

### Thomas Kuhn and paradigm shifts

Kuhn (1962) challenged the view that scientific discovery is based on rational and critical enquiry (see Unit 3.2.3). He saw science as a closed system of ideas and argued that progress in science is neither linear nor gradual. Science is committed to a particular paradigm, a set of beliefs shared by a group of scientists. Kuhn did not agree that scientists are completely objective or that they accept or reject a paradigm on the basis of evidence alone. For example, they may ignore any evidence that contradicts the paradigm and resist new ideas. Change in scientific knowledge comes about via the replacement of one scientific paradigm by another during a scientific revolution. For instance, the shift from Newtonian mechanics to Einsteinian relativity can be seen as an example of a paradigm shift, a move from classical to modern physics involving a radical change in the way that many scientists viewed the physical world.

### Laboratory-based studies of science

Over the last 50 years, traditional views about science have been challenged. One area of scrutiny is the practice of science: the way that scientific knowledge is manufactured or constructed inside laboratories.

Michael Lynch (1983) conducted research in a psycho-biological laboratory and his findings suggest that scientists may be less objective than they claim. The scientists studied brain functioning by examining thin slices of rats' brains under microscopes. Photographs and slides of the brain slices were examined to see how useful they were in developing theories of brain functioning.

Sometimes, unexplained features were found in the photographs. There was much discussion in the laboratory about whether these features were **artefacts** rather than real features of rats' brains. They were frequently viewed as errors in the production of the photographs or slides. For example, some were believed to result from scratching of the specimen when it was being sliced. In reaching their conclusion, the scientists were influenced by their existing theories, and the types of feature they were looking for and expected to find. If the visible marks on the slide or photograph did not fit the scientists' theories of how rats' brains functioned, they were much more likely to be dismissed as errors. The scientists' interpretations of the data were guided by their theories.

Far from following Popper's methodology and striving to falsify their theories, the scientists tried to use the evidence to confirm them. Many scientists may be reluctant to dismiss perhaps years of research because a single piece of evidence does not support the theory that they have developed.

Steve Woolgar (1988) is sceptical about the knowledge claims of science. He is interested in what goes on in science on a daily basis and what scientists do in laboratories. He argues that science is not, in fact, distinct from other forms of social activity or knowledge production. There is nothing inherently special about 'the scientific method' and, in practice, scientists do not necessarily stick to it. In Woolgar's view, science activities are constructive (in that scientific 'facts' are constructed in laboratories) rather than descriptive.

### Activity

*Some sociologists undertake laboratory-based studies to explore how scientists construct scientific knowledge.*

1. Explain two strengths and two limitations of using an ethnographic approach to study the work carried out by scientists in laboratories.
2. Give two arguments for the view that science is an open belief system.

## Postmodernism and science

Most postmodernists challenge the objectivity and truth of all belief systems. In their view, truth is not something that exists 'out there' waiting to be discovered through the use of objective scientific methods. Instead, truth is created or constructed by people.

Postmodernists argue that people no longer place their trust unquestioningly in science or scientists. People increasingly question the power of science to solve global problems such as famine or natural disasters and to produce a better world. In fact, science and technology can have negative side effects. For example, cars and aeroplanes contribute to air pollution and global warming. Rather than providing truth, the truth claims of science have been challenged by sceptical philosophers and historians of science.

Jean-François Lyotard (1984) argued that science and religions rest on **'meta-narratives'** – grand theories, 'big stories' or myths – that give meaning to other narratives or stories. For example, science provides a meta-narrative or a big story about evolution by natural selection. Meta-narratives give a sense of purpose to scientific endeavour and a sense of direction to social life. They suggest that humans can progress, through science, towards defeating ignorance and oppression, and that science can help humans to conquer nature.

Lyotard associated postmodernism with the decline of scientific, religious, political and other meta-narratives.

An 'incredulity towards meta-narratives' develops in postmodern societies. People no longer put their faith in these big, all-embracing theories about how the world works. They become sceptical that any set of beliefs can provide a means of understanding and resolving the problems of humanity. They no longer believe that reason can conquer superstition.

Lyotard's critics point out, however, that religions and other meta-narratives are still powerful forces in some countries. They also argue that, although Lyotard dismissed the possibility of objective knowledge, he nonetheless claimed to have accurately described key changes in society such as an increased scepticism about science. However, if objective knowledge is not possible, then there is no reason to believe that Lyotard's claim about science is any more 'true' than claims made by sociologists who disagree with him.

## The relationship between science and religion

Some commentators see science and religion as compatible belief systems that can coexist without tension. Others see them as competing with each other in terms of how they explain the world. In this view, they are incompatible because their ideas clash.

### Science and religion as compatible

Science and religion can be seen as compatible for several reasons including the following.

- Stephen Jay Gould (1999, cited in Bainbridge, 2009) was a scientist who supported evolutionary theories of biology. Nevertheless, he argued that there is no conflict between science and religion, because they are concerned with different aspects of human life and needs. Gould claimed that one type of human need is the need to understand the facts about how nature works. Science has the authority and power to teach about this. However, humans also have a drive to give meaning to their own lives and to find a basis for their moral views. Religion can fulfil this need without directly conflicting with science.
- Bruce (2011) argues that science and religion can coexist quite easily. Not many people have a great deal of knowledge about scientific methods and discoveries. In his view, science is unlikely to disprove religious faith if that faith is backed up and supported by a strong religious community.

### Science and religion as incompatible

An alternative view is that science and religion are fundamentally incompatible. Richard Dawkins (2006) argues that belief in 'supernatural gods' is simply a delusion completely at odds with scientific beliefs. Dawkins rejects Gould's idea that religion can provide answers to questions which science cannot. Although he accepts that science may not have answers to questions about the meaning of life, he sees no reason why religion should be seen as offering any expertise in such areas.

Dawkins argues that religion is based on faith. In his view, faith is an inadequate and positively harmful basis for believing in something. It involves believing without question despite the lack of evidence to support it. This can lead, for example, to violent acts being carried out on religious grounds (see Part 4).

### Activity

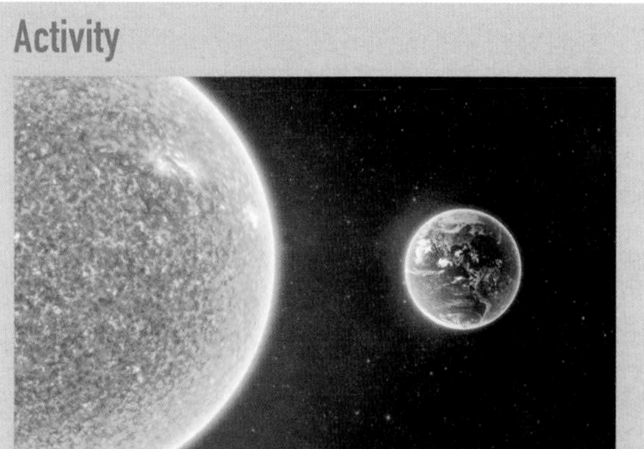

*People used to believe that the sun went around the earth. In the 17th century, the Roman Catholic Church convicted Galileo, an Italian astronomer, of heresy for his hypothesis that the earth revolves around the sun.*

1. Drawing on Galileo's experience, explain one way in which religion can be seen as a closed belief system.
2. Evaluate the view that science and religion are compatible belief systems.

## Ideology

An **ideology** refers to a set of shared ideas, beliefs or values that provide a way of interpreting the world. This can result in a partial, false or distorted view of reality. In practice, an ideology often legitimises or justifies the position and actions of powerful groups in society, such as the ruling class or men. Religion can be seen as an ideology.

### Marxist accounts of religion as an ideology

Marxists focus on the ideology of the ruling class. In this sense, ideology is a viewpoint that distorts reality and justifies the position of a particular social group. Marxists see ruling-class ideology as a set of beliefs and values that express the interests of the bourgeoisie in capitalist society. Ruling-class ideology legitimises existing power relationships in society.

Karl Marx saw religion as an ideology in that religious beliefs uphold the interests of the ruling class and justify inequalities of wealth and power (see Unit 7.2.2). This can be seen in Christian teachings such as 'blessed are the meek' (those who are gentle and unwilling to disagree with others) and 'the meek shall inherit the earth'. Religious beliefs also make the social order appear natural, acceptable and inevitable. Marxists link religion to false class consciousness in that religious ideas keep the subject class from recognising its own interests and disguise the true extent of its exploitation.

By justifying the status quo, religion distorts reality. False class consciousness blinds members of the subject class to their true situation and their real interests. In this way, religion diverts people's attention from the real source of their oppression and helps to maintain the power of the ruling class.

## Activity

*Religious beliefs and practices can be seen as a way of justifying social inequality. In this sense, religion has an ideological role.*

To what extent do you agree with the view that religions can have an ideological role?

## Key terms

**Knowledge claims** Information or statements (for example, claims about what the world is like) that a particular individual, group or belief system such as science holds to be true but which are nonetheless open to debate.

**Enlightenment** The period from the 17th century in Europe that emphasised reason, was sceptical about belief systems such as religion and put its faith in natural science and progress.

**Open belief system** A set of ideas that makes knowledge claims based on the testing of evidence. Consequently, its beliefs develop over time. Science is seen as an open belief system that tests evidence through observation and experimentation.

**Closed belief system** A set of ideas that is not open to testing or criticism, so its beliefs tend not to change. Religion and magic are seen as examples of closed belief systems. Religion, for instance, is based on faith rather than on the testing of evidence.

**Truth claims** Statements or ideas that particular individuals, groups or belief systems (such as religions) hold to be true, and which are not open to debate.

**Artefacts** Things produced by the research process (for example, resulting from a technical error) that do not exist in the phenomenon being studied.

**Meta-narratives** Large-scale singular explanations of society.

**Ideology** A set of dominant ideas in society that distort reality and serve the interests of a particular group, such as men or the ruling class.

## Summary

1. Science is seen as an open system of ideas, because its knowledge claims are based on testing and revision. Religion is seen as a closed system, as its beliefs are based on faith and it is not open to testing.
2. Popper saw science as an open belief system that is based on falsification. Religious beliefs are not scientific statements, because they cannot be tested.
3. Kuhn saw scientists as conservative rather than as completely objective. Progress in science comes about during a scientific revolution when one paradigm replaces another.

4. Sociological research inside science laboratories highlights the processes involved in the manufacture of scientific knowledge.
5. Postmodernism suggests that science is a meta-narrative rather than the truth. Lyotard argues that people have lost faith in science and scientists.
6. Science and religion are seen as compatible because they are concerned with completely different aspects of human life. They are seen as incompatible because belief in gods conflicts with scientific beliefs.
7. The term 'ideology' refers to a set of shared beliefs and values that provide a way of interpreting the world which results in a partial – and usually distorted – view of reality.
8. Marxists see religion as ideological and link it to false class consciousness. Religious ideas keep the proletariat from recognising its true interests in capitalist society and help to maintain ruling-class power.

# Unit 7.1.3 Religion and different social groups

Religious organisations and movements tend to attract more members or believers from some groups than others. The main social divisions linked to religious belief and participation are social class, gender, ethnicity and age. This unit examines the relationship between social groups and religiosity, asking questions such as how does social class influence religious belief? Why do women appear to participate more than men in most religions and spiritual groups? How closely is ethnicity associated with differences in religious affiliation? And do people get more religious as they age?

## Social class and religiosity

Evidence suggests that different types of religion tend to appeal to different social classes. However, the evidence is not clear-cut and there is no straightforward relationship.

### Marxist theories of social class and religion

According to Marxists, religious participation and social class are closely related. Marx (1844) described religion in capitalist societies as the 'opium of the people'. He saw it as acting like a drug by giving its followers a false sense of well-being and distorting reality. Marx argued that religion started in the subject classes as a way of coping with oppression, but it was later adopted by the ruling classes as a way of justifying their advantaged position in society. Marx, therefore, argued that all classes believed in religion, although for different reasons. As the subject class (the proletariat in capitalist societies) developed greater class consciousness, they could potentially lose some of their religious beliefs. This leaves open the possibility that higher classes (particularly the ruling class, or the bourgeoisie under capitalism) might become more religious than subject classes.

### Max Weber, class and religious beliefs

Sociologists highlight the links between social class and different types of religious organisation. This idea originated in the work of Weber (cited in Christiano, Swatos and Kivisto, 2008) who believed that different classes tended to develop different types of religious belief and that this was linked to different religious organisations.

Weber distinguished between different theodicies (religious explanations) for suffering on earth.

- Some religions have a **theodicy of misfortune**, which claims that wealth and worldly success are indicators of evil. This type of belief tends to be associated with religious organisations that are popular with lower social classes.
- By contrast, a **theodicy of good fortune** suggests that worldly success indicates virtue. This is associated more with higher classes.

Weber, however, did not suggest that religious beliefs were simply dictated by class position. Instead, particular classes and status groups played an active role in creating and recreating beliefs. They were influenced by their class position and class interests, but these did not directly determine their beliefs.

**Activity**

Briefly explain how Weber recognised that religion involves human agency.

### Social class and social mobility

Drawing on USA-based research, Stephen Hunt (2004) notes that generally sociologists argue that upwardly mobile groups and individuals tend to belong to religious organisations with more liberal beliefs – for example, about sexuality. However, conservative or **fundamentalist beliefs** are likely to be supported by those who feel that their stake in society might be threatened by upwardly mobile social groups. Lower social classes who feel excluded tend to support sects that offer some religious compensation for their low status and reject mainstream norms and values.

Hunt argues that New Age beliefs (for example, different types of meditation) are supported by those 'who have sufficient time and means to pay for a narcissistic journey of self-discovery'. They are particularly supported by middle-class people in 'expressive' professions (such as artists and writers) who have university-level education. Hunt also claims that, in the USA, occult practices and superstitious beliefs are more popular with lower classes, who have limited education and live in rural areas.

## Activity

*A woman giving psychic readings in Washington, DC, USA, and an outdoor Tai Chi class in Milan, Italy.*

Suggest reasons why the above practices might appeal to different social classes.

## Social class and religious organisations

Evidence suggests a link between different types of religious organisation and their members' social class.

- Churches aspire to include members from all social classes. Because of its size, members of a church are drawn from all classes in society, but the upper classes are particularly likely to join because churches are often closely connected to the established political order. For example, the Roman Catholic Church in the Middle Ages had important political, educational and social functions.
- Denominations tend to be slightly anti-establishment, as they have broken away from the religious mainstream. However, Wallis (1984) noted that they are respectable organisations and therefore appeal most to the upper working class and the lower middle class. They are not usually closely identified with the upper classes.
- Sects have traditionally recruited the most disadvantaged people in society. They require members to give up their previous life, so those with much to lose are unlikely to join. They tend to appeal to the deprived because membership offers a way of coping with disadvantage by finding meaning and a sense of self-worth within the sect. Wallis (1984) argued that in the 1960s and 1970s, sects also began to appeal to the 'relatively deprived' middle class of affluent students who were seeking compensation for their lack of a spiritual life.
- World-affirming new religious movements (Wallis, 1984) such as TM are positive about mainstream society. Their religious practices tend to facilitate social and economic success. Client cults (Stark and Bainbridge, 1985) such as Scientology offer services to their followers but require little commitment. Both world-affirming new religious movements and client cults appeal to the successful and affluent who want to become even more successful.
- Cult movements such as the Unification Church involve their followers or believers fully and are similar to sects in opposing mainstream society. Consequently, they tend to attract the disadvantaged or relatively deprived.
- According to Heelas (1996), **New Age movements** tend to appeal to the middle class (particularly

women). Like Hunt (2004), Bruce (2002) believes that they attract those in expressive professions such as the media, teaching and counselling who believe in self-improvement.

### Evaluation

In the USA, detailed data are available on social class, religious belief and participation. However, there is a shortage of such data in many other countries. It is therefore difficult to assess the accuracy of claims about class and different religious organisations. Consequently, most of the claims discussed here should be treated as hypotheses rather than as well-supported theories. Furthermore, class intersects with other social divisions, particularly gender, ethnicity and age, in shaping religious belief and participation.

## Gender and religiosity

Statistical evidence suggests that women tend to be slightly more religious than men on a global scale. The Pew Research Center (2016) estimated that globally, 83.4 per cent of women identified with a faith group compared with 79.9 per cent of men. In 61 of 192 countries, women were at least two percentage points more likely than men to express a religious affiliation, but there were none in which the reverse was true.

### Alan S. Miller and John P. Hoffman – Risk and religion

Miller and Hoffman (1995) note two main types of sociological explanation for women's greater religiosity.

1. **Differential socialisation**
   According to the differential socialisation view, 'females are taught to be more submissive, passive and obedient and nurturing than are males and these attributes are associated with higher levels of religiosity' (Miller and Hoffman, 1995). These characteristics are more often found in traditional religious beliefs. For example, religions such as Christianity emphasise obedience to God and characteristics such as being loving, which are associated with female gender roles. Male roles place less emphasis on these characteristics. This theory is supported by USA-based evidence discussed by Miller and Hoffmann which indicates that men who are submissive, passive, obedient and nurturing tend to be more religious than other men.

2. The **structural locations** of women and men (their location in the social structure)
   According to this view, women are less involved in the labour force than men and more involved in raising children. Not only do women have more time for church-related activities but their lower-level involvement in paid work also gives them a greater need for the sense of personal identity which religion can provide. Some US research suggests that religion is seen as a household activity. Socialising children by taking them to church can be regarded as an extension of female childcare roles.

### Activity

*A woman and child at a church.*

1. Do you agree that women in your society are more religious than men? Explain your answer.
2. To what extent do women and men have different structural locations in your society? Do women lack a sense of occupational identity? Do they have more time than men for activities related to religion?

These two explanations are not mutually exclusive. Indeed, the socialisation of females and males tends to lead to them occupying different social locations, which in turn reinforces gender differences. However, Miller and Hoffman argue that these explanations cannot fully explain the gender differences in religiosity. They quote research which suggests that, even when socialisation and structural location are taken into account, women are still more religious than men. They argue, therefore, that a third factor, **attitude to risk**, is also important. There is nothing to lose by being religious. However, not being religious can be seen as risk-taking behaviour because it risks condemnation to hell after death. Using survey-based research from the USA, Miller and Hoffman show that men tend to be less averse to risk than women. Furthermore, both men and women who are more risk averse have higher levels of religiosity. They conclude that women's greater concern about risk is an important additional factor, alongside socialisation and structural location, in explaining women's greater religiosity.

**Evaluation** The argument put forward by Miller and Hoffman that women have more time for church-related activities is highly debatable given that a great deal of research suggests that women spend more time on housework and childcare than men. Furthermore, rates of female participation in the labour market are high in nations such as the USA and the UK, making it questionable whether women lack a sense of occupational identity.

## Steve Bruce – religion and secularisation

Bruce (1996) suggests that religion tends to have an affinity with aspects of femininity that make women 'less confrontational, less aggressive, less goal oriented, less domineering, more cooperative and more caring'. This affinity applies to traditional religion and is particularly strong with New Age spiritual beliefs. Many women are attracted to the 'healing, channelling and spirituality' side of New Age beliefs because these are more in keeping with female gender roles. The minority of men involved in the New Age tend to be more interested in the paranormal than in the more feminine aspects of the movement.

Bruce argues that women are more attracted to traditional religions than men because 'the churches have always been interested in the control of sexuality and in the instruction of the next generation, both matters which are concentrated on the domestic hearth and in which women have a major role to play'. According to Bruce, there is a division in the modern world between the **public sphere** (of paid work, politics and so on) and the **private sphere** (the domestic world of the family and personal life). Bruce believes that as a result of **secularisation** (the decline in the significance of religion in society – see Unit 7.5.1), religion has become less important in the public sphere and increasingly confined to the private sphere. Since women are more involved with the private sphere than men, and religion has become a largely private matter, women have tended to become more religious than men. As religion has declined generally, men with their predominantly public-sphere social roles have lost their religiosity more quickly than women.

To Bruce, within an overall pattern of decline, religion has declined less among women than men. However, the type of religion that has retained an appeal for some women varies by social class. Working-class women tend to retain a belief in forms of religion and spirituality in which they are more passive. They believe in a powerful God, or in 'obscure forces beyond their control', such as fortune telling and superstition. By contrast, middle-class women have more experience of controlling and improving their own lives. Consequently, they tend to follow religions that allow more individual autonomy, and forms of spirituality which facilitate personal development. They are attracted to New Age beliefs that promote self-growth and development.

## Linda Woodhead – female religiosity and secularisation

Woodhead (2005) believes that processes of secularisation and the decline in Christianity have influenced Western societies, but they can only be understood with reference to gender. From the 19th century, **modernisation** led to a process of **rationalisation** in which people calculated the best and most rational means to achieve given objectives rather than relying on faith or tradition to guide their actions. This had a 'corrosive effect' on religion, as it left little room for the non-rational faith required by religion. However, this process largely affected men. The housewife role became increasingly important for middle-class women and this isolated them to some extent from rationalisation. Women were not 'absorbed into rationalized values' and so were less likely than men to become disillusioned with the church's teachings.

Church attendance among men declined and women became the majority of those involved in churches. Churches became 'increasingly feminized or domesticized'. They placed more emphasis on 'love, care and relationships' and less on God as an all-powerful and punitive ruler. However, they continued to reinforce male power through paternalistic images of God as a 'loving father'. As churches became feminised, they lost prestige and became even less appealing to most men.

### Religion and different spheres of life

By the 1970s in Western societies, many married women were returning to the labour force and were increasingly exposed to the rationalised culture of paid work. This led to a rapid decline in churchgoing among women. Woodhead believes that the changes in women's lives largely account for the decline of Christian churches and denominations in Western

## Activity

*Comforting hands from heaven and dramatic lightning.*

1. Explain why these two images can be seen as representing feminine and masculine views of a Christian God.
2. If churches emphasise the message given in the first image, how could that account for gender differences in church attendance?
3. To what extent do these images present a Western, Christian bias?

countries since the 1970s. However, women are still more interested than men in religion and spirituality, for a number of reasons.

1. Women are still less involved in the public world of work than men. More women than men work part-time and women are still much more likely to have the main responsibility for childcare.
2. Woodhead argues that there are three rather than two spheres in contemporary societies. These are:
   - **primary institutions** such as those associated with work and politics
   - **secondary institutions** associated with caring for others, including the family and religion
   - an **individual sphere** in which people are concerned with their own autonomous and individual selves.

   Religion remains relevant to those women whose lives are based in secondary institutions. Given this, women are still more likely than men to be involved in churches and denominations.
3. New Age beliefs also tend to be dominated by women. Woodhead argues that this helps to resolve a contradiction between 'traditional' female roles in the home and more 'masculine' roles in the workplace. In paid work, your sense of self largely derives from your position or job, whereas in family roles your sense of self is more concerned with relationships with others (as wife, parent and so on). New Age beliefs allow this tension to be bypassed because they create a new 'type of selfhood in which identity is not dictated by social position and experience, but discovered from within'. The contradiction between roles in primary and secondary institutions is resolved by seeking your identity in the individual sphere.

## Religion and ethnicity

Most evidence suggests that members of minority ethnic groups in Western countries such as Britain are more likely than majority ethnic groups to see themselves as religious; religions that are mainly followed by minority ethnic groups are more likely to be practised by believers; and their religion is more likely (in most respects) to influence their lives. However, there are exceptions to these tendencies.

### John Bird – explanations for high levels of religiosity

Bird (1999) identifies five important reasons for the higher levels of religiosity among minority ethnic groups in Britain:

1. Many ethnic groups 'originate in societies with high levels of religiosity'. For example, Bangladesh and Pakistan have high levels of religious observance and belief. First-generation immigrants tend to bring these high levels of religiosity to the UK.

2. For minority ethnic groups, religion can 'act as a basis for community solidarity'. Solidarity based on religious affiliation can perform important social functions for new migrants, giving them 'a point of contact in a new country, a source of marriage partners, social welfare and so on'.
3. Bird argues that 'Maintaining a religious commitment is also a way to maintain other aspects of cultural identity such as language, art, patterns of marriage, cooking and so on.' Religion and minority ethnic cultures can be mutually reinforcing.
4. The importance of religion can be maintained through socialisation and 'there is often strong family pressure to maintain religious commitment'.
5. Some minority ethnic groups might also have strong religious beliefs because it helps them cope with oppression. Disadvantaged minority ethnic groups tend to be working-class, and their religious beliefs can be seen as a response to their position in the social structure. Bird suggests that Pentecostalism might perform a dual function for British African Caribbeans. First, it can be 'a way to adjust to a society in which (they) face discrimination and social injustice'. Pentecostalism can act as the 'opium of the people' (see Unit 7.2.2). Second, it can also help people to combat disadvantage by improving their social and economic position. For example, Ken Pryce (1979) pointed out that Pentecostalism encouraged hard work and thrift, which could result in Pentecostalists gaining greater economic security.

## Steve Bruce – cultural defence and cultural transition

Bruce argues that minority ethnic groups are more likely to engage in religious activity than the ethnic majority, mainly due to social reasons. The vitality of religion is largely a response to the social situation of minority ethnic groups rather than an expression of deep religious commitment. Bruce sees the strength of minority ethnic religions as caused by either:

1. **cultural defence**, where an ethnic group is protecting its sense of identity and maintaining ethnic pride through religion; or
2. **cultural transition**, where an ethnic group uses religion to cope with the upheaval of migration.

These two processes can work together as immigrant minority ethnic groups try to both adapt and defend their religious/cultural heritage. For example, Meredith McGuire (2002) describes how Vietnamese-American Buddhists simultaneously attempt to continue socialising their children into their culture and also to gain acceptance in US society. She describes how, in 'Houston, Texas, the Vietnamese community has created their Temple with many features reminiscent of Vietnam'. However, the Temple is also used as a community centre, assisting people to integrate into US society – for example, by facilitating networking to help people find jobs. In such centres, minority ethnic groups can 'negotiate a Buddhist religious identity and work to have it accepted as legitimate in their new community'.

### Activity

*A Buddhist Temple in Houston, Texas.*

Explain how centres such as Vietnamese Buddhist Temples in US cities can be seen as linked to cultural defence and cultural transition.

## Decline or revival in ethnic minority religions?

Bruce argues that, over time, minority ethnic groups in many Western societies become more integrated and are increasingly influenced by the wider secular society. As a consequence, their religious beliefs will decline.

George Chryssides (1994) argues that, in Britain, the religions of immigrant groups and their descendants have had three main paths open to them:

- **Apostasy**, when a particular set of religious beliefs is abandoned in a hostile environment. For example, a Sikh might convert to Christianity.
- **Accommodation**, when religious practices are adapted to take account of the changed situation. For example, a Sikh might remove his turban because he believes it could improve his chances at a job interview.
- **Renewed vigour**, when the religion is reasserted more strongly as a response to actual or perceived hostility towards it. For example, parents might insist on strong religious orthodoxy from their children.

Chryssides acknowledges that minority ethnic religions have faced difficulties in Britain. They have had to establish places of prayer and deal with situations in which religious observation might be difficult. However, he argues that the general pattern has been characterised by accommodation and renewed vigour rather than apostasy. Buildings have been bought and converted into mosques and temples, and religious beliefs and practices have been retained or adapted rather than abandoned. For example, many Muslim women have found ways to dress modestly while incorporating Western elements into their clothing.

## Age, generation and religiosity

Evidence suggests that, in most countries, the young tend to be less religious than the old. For example, the World Values Survey (discussed in Burkimsher, 2008) found that younger people (classified as those under 30 years) were less likely to say they attended places of worship than older people (those aged 50 or over) in the majority of countries surveyed.

### Reasons for age differences in religiosity

David Voas and Alasdair Crockett (2005) identified three possible explanations for age differences in religiosity. The differences could be due to age, a period effect or the progressive decline of religion.

1. **Age**. Many commentators have suggested that people tend to get more religious as they get older and see themselves as coming closer to death. Religious belief might also be affected by life events such as having children. Parents might return to active involvement in religion because they think it is important for their children's socialisation.
2. A **period effect**. Those born in a particular period (a **cohort**) might be particularly likely or unlikely to be religious because of specific events or social changes during the era in which they grew up. For example, Peter Brierley (2006) notes the rapid decline in churchgoing among the young in the 1990s and argues that 'Those in "Generation Y", defined by some as those born in the 1980s, have been found to have little spiritual interest, being rather focused on "happiness".'
3. The progressive decline of religion could mean that each generation is less religious than the previous one. Supporters of this view generally favour the secularisation thesis (see Unit 7.5.1).

### Evidence

Voas and Crockett examined data from the British Social Attitudes survey to consider which of these theories was most plausible. The data allowed them to see whether a cohort was more or less religious than other cohorts and whether their attitude to religion changed as they aged.

Voas and Crockett found little evidence that people became markedly more religious with age, or that specific cohorts were becoming less religious. Instead, they concluded that in Britain 'change has occurred because each generation has entered adulthood less religious than its predecessors'. This was partly because each generation was less likely to socialise their children into religious beliefs than the previous generation.

Voas and Crockett's conclusions may not apply to all types of religious and spiritual beliefs. For example, Heelas et al. (2005) claim that New Age spiritual beliefs are growing rapidly despite few young people being involved, because people do not usually start to engage with such spiritualities until middle age.

Marion Burkimsher (2008) identified similar patterns across many, but not all, countries. She examined statistical evidence from the European Values Surveys of 2002, 2004 and 2006 and the World Values Surveys of 1995 and 2004. She found that evidence from 'stable developed countries' (including Western Europe) suggested that recent generations were less religious than earlier generations. Although there was generally a trough in religiosity among people in their early 20s, and a slight increase in their late 20s, attendance did not generally increase after the age of 30. There was, therefore, little evidence of increased religiosity as people aged.

However, in some ex-communist countries in Eastern Europe and in much of Africa, there is evidence of increased religiosity among the young. In the USA, youth attendance fell between 1980 and 1995 but rose again between 1995 and 2000. Furthermore, Puerto Rico, Mexico and Brazil have all had rising rates of attendance among the young.

## Key terms

**Theodicy of misfortune** A religious explanation for suffering which claims that wealth and worldly success are indicators of evil.

**Theodicy of good fortune** A religious explanation for suffering which claims that wealth and worldly success are indicators of virtue.

**Fundamentalist beliefs** A set of religious beliefs that advocates returning to the 'fundamental' original teachings of a particular religion.

**New Age movements** Diverse and loosely organised groups that became popular in the 1970s and 1980s, within which people seek spiritual experiences focusing primarily on the development of the self. They are sometimes viewed as a subset of new religious movements. Examples include est, Heaven's Gate and Dianic Wicca.

**Differential socialisation** The contrasting ways in which females and males are brought up within and outside the family.

**Structural location** The position of different social groups within the social structure – for example, the greater involvement of men in full-time paid employment than women.

**Attitude to risk** The extent to which individuals are willing to expose themselves to social practices, beliefs and situations that carry a possibility of danger.

**Public sphere** The social world outside the family and personal life.

**Private sphere** The social world inside families involving personal relationships.

**Secularisation** A process involving a decline in the social significance of religion.

**Modernisation** The process of moving from traditional society to a modern developed society.

**Rationalisation** A process in which people calculate the most efficient means to achieve given objectives rather than relying on faith or tradition to guide their actions.

**Primary institutions** Institutions associated with work and politics.

**Secondary institutions** Institutions associated with caring for others, such as the family and religion.

**Individual sphere** The sphere of social life concerned with individual identity.

**Cultural defence** An ethnic group using religion to reinforce and maintain ethnic identity and pride.

**Cultural transition** An ethnic group using religion to cope with social change and migration.

**Apostasy** Abandoning a set of religious beliefs in a hostile environment.

**Accommodation** Adapting religious beliefs in response to a changed environment.

**Renewed vigour** An increase in the intensity of religious feelings in response to perceived hostility.

**Age** The length of time a person has lived.

**Period effect** The effects of being born in a particular era on social beliefs and practices.

**Cohort** A group of people born in a particular time period.

## Summary

1. Marxists believe that religion originates among subject classes to help them cope with oppression, but it is also adopted by the ruling classes to justify their position.
2. Weber argued that different theodicies appealed to different social groups. A theodicy of misfortune attracts lower classes and a theodicy of good fortune attracts higher classes.
3. Hunt argues that socially mobile groups tend to join liberal religious organisations and social groups who feel under threat tend to join more conservative organisations.
4. Churches aspire to attract members from all classes but tend to be predominantly middle- and higher-class institutions because they generally support the establishment.
5. Denominations tend to appeal to the upper working class and lower middle class, while sects generally attract the disadvantaged or the relatively deprived.
6. World-affirming new religious movements appeal to the affluent. The New Age mainly attracts middle-class professionals, particularly women in expressive professions.
7. Statistical evidence suggests that women tend to be more religious than men in all types of religious organisation in most countries.
8. Miller and Hoffman explain gender differences in terms of gender socialisation, the structural locations of men and women, and men's greater willingness to take risks.
9. Bruce argues that secularisation has led to religion being largely confined to the private sphere, in which women are more involved than men.
10. Woodhead believes that secularisation has impacted on men more than women, which has resulted in churches becoming feminised and appealing to women more than men. New Age beliefs appeal to women because they help women to develop a new sense of selfhood which bypasses the contradiction between their family and work roles.
11. The religion of minority ethnic groups in countries such as Britain is closely connected with the ethnicity and countries of origin of first-generation immigrants. Most minority

ethnic groups in Britain tend to be more religious than their White counterparts.

12. Bird explains higher levels of religiosity among minority ethnic groups in terms of ethnic origins, community solidarity, cultural identity, socialisation and oppression.
13. Bruce argues that religion acts as a form of cultural defence or a way of coping with transition to a new society. In his view, minority ethnic religions in the UK will decline over time. However, Chryssides suggests that they can develop in three ways: apostasy, renewed vigour or accommodation.
14. Statistical evidence suggests that, in most countries, young people are less religious than older people. Voas and Crockett suggested that the statistical patterns could be due to people getting more religious as they age, a period (or cohort) effect or secularisation.
15. Data from the British Social Attitudes survey suggest that, in Britain, secularisation is the main cause of age differences in religiosity. However, Heelas claims that New Age beliefs are growing rapidly, despite relatively few young people being involved.
16. Burkimsher found that secularisation is affecting most industrialised countries, but in Eastern Europe and Africa there is evidence of young people becoming more religious.

# END-OF-PART QUESTIONS

| | | |
|---|---|---|
| 0 1 | Describe two types of definition of religion. | **[4 marks]** |
| 0 2 | Explain two limitations of the view that science is an open belief system. | **[6 marks]** |
| 0 3 | 'Science and religion are incompatible belief systems.'<br>Using sociological material, give one argument against this view. | **[6 marks]** |

# PART 2 RELIGION AND SOCIAL ORDER

## Contents

**Unit 7.2.1 Functionalist accounts of religion 414**

**Unit 7.2.2 Marxist accounts of religion 418**

Religions, one of the most important belief systems in contemporary societies, are a key area of sociological interest. Sociologists focus on the significance of religion in society. What is religion really about beneath the surface? How does it shape relationships between people? Does religion perform a positive or negative role in society? This part examines how functionalist and Marxist perspectives address questions about the role and function of religion in society and its relationship to social order.

## Unit 7.2.1 Functionalist accounts of religion

In the functionalist view, society has functional prerequisites or basic needs such as value consensus (broad agreement on society's values) which must be met if it is to survive over time. Functionalism examines social institutions such as religion in terms of their functions. It focuses on the positive role of religion in society and its contribution to meeting society's needs. This unit examines some of the main functionalist theories of religion.

### Émile Durkheim's account of religion, the sacred and the profane

Durkheim (1912) argued that all religious beliefs divide the world into two completely separate parts: **the sacred** (things that are set apart and forbidden)

**and the profane** (ordinary, everyday things). However, the 'sacred' are not simply things such as gods or spirits. According to Durkheim, anything could potentially be sacred, including a tree or a rock. What sacred things have in common is the reverential attitudes (feelings of great respect and awe) that they inspire among believers.

Durkheim argued that sacred objects such as trees do not have any intrinsic qualities that make them sacred. Consequently, they must be symbols. In order to understand the role of religion in society, he believed that it is necessary to examine the relationship between sacred symbols and what they represent.

Durkheim examined reports of **totemism**, the religion of Australian Aboriginal groups. Aboriginal society is divided into clans. Each clan has its own unique totem, usually a plant or an animal such as a kangaroo. The totem is a sacred symbol and ritual observances separate it from profane or ordinary things. A representation of the totem – the totemic emblem or image – is placed or painted on objects or people. The totemic emblem is also surrounded by rituals and is considered more sacred than the totemic object itself. The totem provides clan members with their shared name. This means that clan members themselves possess sacred qualities because of their sacred name.

Durkheim argued that the totem is the symbol of both God and society. From this, he argued that God and society are, in fact, the same thing. He suggested that, in worshipping god, people are actually worshipping society. Society is more important and powerful than the individual. Durkheim argued that 'Primitive man comes to view society as something sacred because he is utterly dependent on it.' People invent a sacred symbol such as a totem because it is easier for someone to 'visualize and direct his feelings of awe toward a symbol than towards so complex a thing as a clan'.

## Religion and the collective conscience

Durkheim viewed religion as performing valuable functions for society. He argued that social life would be impossible without the shared values and moral beliefs that form the collective conscience. Without them, he argued, there would be no social order or social control. In short, there would be no society. Religion performs a key function by reinforcing the collective conscience. The worship of society strengthens the values and moral beliefs that form the basis of social life. In this way, religion acts like a cement that binds members of society together and promotes social solidarity.

### Activity

*Among many Roman Catholics around the world, statues of angels are seen as sacred.*

Sarah Dunlop and Peter Ward (2014) asked young Polish Catholics living in England to take photographs of what is sacred to them. Their photographs included images of churches, statues and people.

If you were asked to take photographs of what is sacred to you, what would you include?

Durkheim emphasised the importance of collective worship. The social group comes together in religious rituals full of drama and reverence. Together, its members express their faith in their common values and beliefs. In this highly charged atmosphere, the integration of society is strengthened.

### Activity

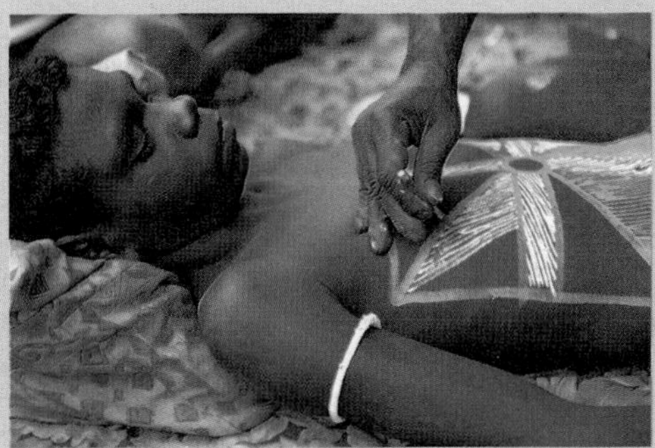

*An Aboriginal teenager being painted with his totem for a ceremony to mark his initiation as an adult member of the community.*

1. Why do you think Aboriginal teenagers are painted with a totem as part of their initiation ceremony?
2. What functions might this ceremony perform for the group?

### Evaluation of Durkheim

1. Critics argue that Durkheim studied only a small number of Aboriginal groups, which were not typical. It might be misleading to generalise about Aboriginal beliefs and religion as a whole from this sample.
2. Andrew Dawson (2011) suggests that some of the fieldwork data that Durkheim relied on were of doubtful validity. Other critics argue that totemism is not a religion.
3. Durkheim's views on religion are more relevant to small, non-literate societies whose members share a common belief and value system. They are less relevant to modern societies with diverse subcultures, social and ethnic groups, and a wide range of religious beliefs, rituals and institutions.

Despite these criticisms, many sociologists recognise Durkheim's contribution to an understanding of religion. William E. Paden (2009) argues that Durkheim's observations about the importance of religion for social solidarity remain valid in many circumstances today. The symbolic importance of the Western (or Wailing) Wall in Jerusalem for Jews is an example of the continuing symbolic importance of sacred objects.

### Activity

*Jewish women praying in the women's section of the Western (or Wailing) Wall in Jerusalem, a sacred site for prayer and pilgrimage.*

1. How might the example of the Western Wall be used to support Durkheim's account of religion?
2. Why might some feminists use this example to support the view that religion is patriarchal?

## Talcott Parsons' account of religion

Parsons (1937, 1964, 1965) argued that religious beliefs provide guidelines for human action and standards against which people's conduct can be evaluated. In a Christian society, for instance, the Ten Commandments show that many of the norms of the social system can be integrated (or brought together) by religious beliefs. For example, the commandment 'Thou shalt not kill' integrates diverse norms such as how to drive a car, settle an argument and deal with the suffering of the aged. The norms that direct these areas of behaviour prohibit manslaughter, murder and euthanasia, but they are all based on the same religious commandment.

In this way, religion provides general guidelines for conduct, which are expressed in a variety of norms. By establishing general principles and moral beliefs, religion helps to provide the value consensus that is necessary for social order and stability.

### Religion and social order

Parsons saw religion as addressing particular problems that occur in all societies and disrupt social life. These problems fall into two categories. The first relates to 'the fact that individuals are "hit" by events which they cannot foresee and prepare for, or control, or both'. One such event is death, particularly premature death. Parsons saw religion as a mechanism for adjustment to such events and as a means of restoring the normal pattern of life.

The second problem area is that of 'uncertainty'. This refers to endeavours in which a great deal of effort and skill has been invested, but where unknown or uncontrollable factors can threaten a successful outcome. One example is humanity's inability to predict or control the effect of weather upon agriculture. Parsons argued that religion provides a means of coming to terms with such situations through rituals which act as 'a tonic to self-confidence'. In this way, religion maintains social stability by relieving the tension and frustration that could disrupt social order.

### Religion and problems of meaning

Parsons argued that religious beliefs give meaning to life; they answer questions about humanity and the world we live in. One of the major functions of religion is to 'make sense' of all experiences, no matter how meaningless they appear. One example is the question of why some people experience suffering. Religion provides answers to this: suffering tests a person's faith; it is a punishment for sins; and those who endure suffering with strength will be rewarded in heaven. In this way, suffering becomes meaningful.

Parsons (1965) saw a major function of religion as providing meaning to events that people do not expect or feel ought not to happen. This allows them to adjust to these events. On a more general level, this adjustment promotes order and stability in society.

### Evaluation of the functionalist perspective

1. Critics argue that the functionalist perspective over-emphasises the role of religion in maintaining social order and stability. It underplays dysfunctional or negative aspects of religion and neglects the many instances where religion can be seen as a divisive and disruptive force. Functionalism gives little consideration to hostility between different religious groups within the same society, such as Shia and Sunni Muslims in Iraq, Hindus and Muslims in India or Catholics and Protestants in Northern Ireland. In such cases, religious divisions can be seen as a direct threat to social order.

2. The functionalist approach focuses on religion as a conservative force in society and does not explore religion as a radical force that is linked to social change. (See Part 4 of this chapter.)

3. Functionalism tends to see religion as a product of socialisation and to assume that people will be socialised into the religious culture of their society. However, other approaches adopt a more individualistic stance. For example, **rational choice theory** sees religion as meeting the needs of individuals rather than those of social groups or society as a whole. This theory argues that there are rational choices behind belief in religion – people believe in religion because there is something in it for them. Unlike functionalism, rational choice theory focuses on individual choice and decision-making, and sees religion as involving active agency.

4. From a feminist perspective, functionalism fails to examine the role of religion in maintaining patriarchy and female oppression. From a Marxist perspective, it fails to examine religion's role in maintaining capitalism.

## Key terms

**The sacred and the profane** Durkheim's distinction between things that are set apart and inspire reverential attitudes among followers (the sacred) and ordinary, everyday things (the profane).

**Totemism** A form of religion practised by the Australian Aboriginal peoples in which a sacred totem (usually a plant or animal) symbolises the clan.

**Rational choice theory** An approach that assumes most people are naturally religious, that religious belief is based on rational choices and that religion meets individuals' needs.

## Summary

1. Functionalism focuses on the positive role of religion and its contribution to meeting society's needs.
2. Durkheim argued that, in worshipping god, people are actually worshipping society. Religion is functionally important in reinforcing the collective conscience and promoting social order and social solidarity.
3. Critics question the validity of the data that Durkheim used, the relevance of his views to modern, diverse societies and his account of religion as the worship of society.
4. Parsons linked religion to value consensus, order and stability in society. Religious beliefs give meaning to life and make sense of all experiences, regardless of how meaningless they appear.
5. Critics argue that functionalists pay insufficient attention to dysfunctional aspects of religion and its role in generating conflict, division and change.
6. Unlike functionalism, rational choice theory sees religion as involving individual choice, decision-making and active agency.

# Unit 7.2.2 Marxist accounts of religion

While functionalism focuses on the positive role of religion in society, Marxism is critical of religion in all class-based societies. Marxists identify two main classes in capitalist society: the ruling class and the subject class. The ruling class – the bourgeoisie – own the forces or means of production, while the subject class – the proletariat – only own their labour power and are forced to sell their labour to the bourgeoisie in order to survive. The relationship between these two classes is based on exploitation, as the proletariat's wage is much less than the profits that the bourgeoisie makes.

Marxists see capitalist society as made up of the economic base which largely shapes the superstructure. They see beliefs (including religious beliefs) and values in society as forming a ruling-class ideology. This produces false class consciousness (a distorted picture of society that disguises class-based exploitation) and the subject class are not aware that they are being exploited. At the same time, false class consciousness legitimates the ruling class's position in capitalist society. This unit examines Marxist perspectives on the relationship between religion, capitalism, exploitation and oppression.

## Karl Marx's views on religion

Marx argued that 'Man makes religion, religion does not make man.' He challenged the Christian belief that God created man in his own image by arguing that man created God in his own image. In Marx's view, people create imaginary beings or forces which stand above them and control their behaviour. People project their own human powers and capabilities onto God, who is seen as all-powerful. As a result, they become detached from themselves. Marx saw religion as a form of alienation in capitalist society in that it disguises the fact that people can take control of their own destiny. In this way, religion prevents them from realising their own potential such as their power to control their own lives on earth.

Marx saw religion in capitalist society as an ideology in that religious beliefs support the bourgeoisie's interests and justify inequalities of wealth and power. Religion is linked to false class consciousness because religious ideas distort reality, disguise the extent of exploitation in capitalist society and prevent the proletariat from recognising its own interests.

In order to achieve true happiness and fulfilment, religion and the social conditions that produce it must be abolished. In Marx's future classless communist society, religion would not be necessary because the social conditions that produce it, such as alienation and exploitation, would no longer exist.

### Religion as 'the opium of the people'

Marx described religion as 'the opium of the people' (Marx, in Bottomore and Rubel, 1963). He argued that religion acts as a drug to dull the pain produced by oppression (see Unit 7.1.3). It helps to make life more bearable for the proletariat and therefore dilutes demands for change. As such, religion merely numbs or stuns its followers rather than bringing them true happiness and fulfilment.

From a Marxist perspective, religion can dull the pain of oppression in the following ways:

1. It promises a paradise of eternal bliss in life after death. Engels argued that Christianity appeals to oppressed classes because it promises 'salvation from bondage and misery' in the afterlife. The Christian vision of heaven can make life on earth more bearable by giving people something to look forward to.

2. Some religions see the suffering produced by oppression as a just punishment for sins. Suffering is also seen as a trial set by God, promising rewards for those who endure poverty with dignity and humility. Religion makes poverty more bearable by offering a reward for suffering and promising compensation in the afterlife for injustice.

3. Religion can offer the hope of supernatural intervention to solve problems on earth. Members of religious groups such as the Jehovah's Witnesses wait for the day when supernatural powers will descend from on high and create heaven on earth. Anticipation of this future can make the present more acceptable.

4. Religion often justifies the social order and an individual's position within it. God can be seen as creating and supporting the social structure. This can make particular social arrangements appear as God-given and therefore inevitable. It can also help the proletariat to come to terms with their situation and make life more bearable for them.

## Religion and social control

From a Marxist viewpoint, religion does not simply cushion the effects of oppression; it is also an instrument of that oppression. It acts as a **mechanism of social control**, maintaining the existing system of exploitation and reinforcing class relationships. Marx argued that Christianity preaches 'submissiveness and humbleness' to the proletariat. In doing so, it keeps them in their place. Furthermore, by making unsatisfactory lives bearable, religion tends to discourage people from attempting to change their situation. By offering an illusion of hope in a hopeless situation, it prevents thoughts of overthrowing the system. In this way, it acts as a conservative force in society (see Unit 7.4.1).

Marx did not believe that religion would last forever. Religion was rooted in societies that alienated, exploited and oppressed their members. When such societies were replaced, religion would no longer be necessary. Ultimately, the proletariat would remove the need for religion by replacing capitalist society with communism.

In Marx's vision of the ideal communist society, exploitation and alienation are things of the past. The means of production are communally owned, which results in the disappearance of social classes. Members of society are fulfilled as human beings; they control their own destinies and work together for the common good. Religion does not exist in this communist utopia because the social conditions that produce it have disappeared.

## Activity

*In Marxist terms, religion acts as a means of social control and keeps people in their place.*

1. From a Marxist perspective, how might religious beliefs and practices act as an opiate or a painkilling drug?
2. Explain one similarity between Marxist and functionalist theories of religion.
3. What key differences are there between Marxist and functionalist perspectives on religion?

## Evidence to support Marxism

There is considerable evidence to support the Marxist view of the role of religion in society.

The caste system of traditional India, for example, was justified by Hindu religious beliefs. In medieval Europe, kings and queens ruled by divine right. The Egyptian pharaohs went one step further by combining both god and king in the same person. Slave-owners in the southern states of America often approved of the conversion of slaves to Christianity, believing it to be a controlling and gentling influence. It has been argued that, in the early days of the industrial revolution in England, employers used religion as a means of controlling the masses and encouraging them to remain sober and to work hard.

Pentecostalism (a form of Christianity that has grown significantly among poor people in Latin America, Africa and parts of Asia) emphasises sobriety (not drinking alcohol) and hard work. Pentecostal churches have conservative teachings on issues such as abortion, sexuality and the role of women in society and within the church. Consequently, Pentecostals are seen as likely to support the status quo and to work hard in order to try to improve their social position (see also Unit 7.4.1).

Bruce (1988) points out that, in the USA, conservative Protestants – the '**New Christian Right**' – consistently support right-wing political candidates in the Republican Party, and attack more liberal candidates in the Democratic Party (see Unit 7.4.2). Although Bruce emphasises that the New Christian Right have had limited influence on American politics, they have tended to defend the interests of the rich and powerful at the expense of other groups.

## Evaluation of Marxism

1. McGuire (2002) argues that the relationship between religion and social and political action is more complex and unpredictable than Marx claimed. Although religion can act as an opiate, it can also be linked to social and political change.
2. Marxism does not explain the existence of religion where it does not appear to contribute to the oppression of a particular class. Critics argue that Marxism fails to explain why religion might continue to exist when, in theory at least, oppression has come to an end. Under communism in the USSR after the 1917 revolution, the state actively discouraged religion and many places of worship were closed. The communist state placed limits on religious activity and banned the religious instruction of children. Nevertheless, religion did not die out under communism, as Marx predicted. Religious activity increased again once communism had ended. This suggests that Marx was wrong to believe that religion would disappear under communism. It also suggests that there may be other reasons for the existence of religion apart from those put forward by Marx, or that communism failed to end oppression.
3. Functionalist approaches accept that religion may act as a means of social control. However, they see this as functional for society.
4. Some feminists link religion to patriarchy rather than to capitalism. They see religion as legitimising male power rather than ruling-class power.
5. Rational choice theory adopts a more individualistic stance than Marxist (and functionalist) approaches and sees religion as a matter of individual choice and agency.

### Activity

*Rational choice theory views religion in similar terms to a market.*

1. How far do you agree that when people make choices about religion, they act like consumers choosing between different products in the marketplace?
2. In your view, to what extent is religion a matter of individual choice?

### Key terms

**Mechanism of social control** A means by which individuals are persuaded to conform to the rules in society.

**New Christian Right** A term originating in the USA to describe Christian groups with links to the right-wing Republican Party. They have conservative views on social issues and want religious culture to be central in public life.

## Summary

1. Marx argued that people create religion. They project their own powers or capabilities onto superhuman beings and become detached or alienated from themselves.
2. In Marx's view, religion is an ideology in that religious beliefs support the ruling class's interests and justify inequalities.
3. Marx saw religion as an opiate – a painkilling drug – which makes life more bearable for the proletariat under capitalism. In doing so, religion dilutes demands for radical change in society.
4. Marx linked religion in class-based societies to alienation and oppression. However, by replacing capitalism with communism, the proletariat would remove the need for religion.
5. Examples such as the caste system of traditional India and the divine right of kings support the Marxist view of the role of religion in society.
6. Critics point out that, although religion can inhibit change, it can also encourage social, economic or political change. They also argue that Marx was wrong to believe that religion would disappear under communism.
7. Functionalism sees the social control aspect of religion as functional for society.
8. Feminists see religion as justifying male rather than ruling-class power and as legitimising patriarchy rather than capitalism.

# END-OF-PART QUESTIONS

| 0 | 1 | Describe two functions of religion. **[4 marks]**

| 0 | 2 | Explain two limitations of the Marxist account of religion. **[6 marks]**

| 0 | 3 | 'Through its contribution to meeting society's needs, religion performs a positive role.' Using sociological material, give one argument against this view. **[6 marks]**

# PART 3 GENDER, FEMINISM AND RELIGION

## Contents

**Unit 7.3.1 Feminist perspectives on religion 422**

**Unit 7.3.2 Patriarchy and gender inequality in religion 426**

There are several different feminist approaches within the sociology of religion, including radical feminism and liberal feminism. These different approaches agree that power and authority are not distributed equally between women and men within most religious organisations and traditions. Male domination can be seen in many religious teachings about women and men, in the leadership structures of religious institutions and in the practices of religions. Therefore, the feminist views of religion relate well to the key concept of power and control. Feminist approaches use the term 'patriarchy' to refer to a system of male domination in society and they argue that patriarchy is supported by a set of religious beliefs. But are all religions necessarily patriarchal? Can religion empower women rather than oppress them? Can religion be a form of resistance? This part looks at the different feminist views on the role of religion in society and its links to patriarchy.

# Unit 7.3.1 Feminist perspectives on religion

Feminist theories of religion, like Marxist theories, often argue that religion can be an instrument of domination and oppression. However, they tend to see religion as a product of **patriarchy** rather than of capitalism. Many feminists see religion as part of a wider ideology or set of ideas which serve the interests of men rather than those of a capitalist class.

Religion is seen as a patriarchal institution that perpetuates gender inequality over time. Feminist sociologists draw on evidence from a variety of religious beliefs and practices to support this view. They highlight four main ways in which religion can be seen as patriarchal.

1. **Religious organisations.** Most religious organisations are hierarchical in their structures and male-dominated in their leadership. Women continue to be excluded from key roles or positions of power in many religions. The Church of England finally allowed the ordination of female priests in 1992 and female bishops in 2014. Roman Catholic women, however, cannot become priests. This exclusion is despite the fact that women often participate more in organised religion (when they are allowed to) than men (see Unit 7.1.3). Orthodox Jewish women cannot become rabbis and, in Hinduism, only men can become Brahmanic priests. Sikhism is perhaps the most egalitarian of the major religions, as all offices are equally open to men and women. However, even in Sikhism, only a small minority of women have significant positions within the religion.
2. **Laws and customs.** In most religions, women have fewer rights than men. The Roman Catholic Church, for instance, has strict rules on abortion and contraception. Women often have fewer rights than men regarding divorce and are subject to more rules about what is seen as appropriate dress when praying. In countries where the cultural norms are influenced by religion, men and women may be treated unequally by, for example, receiving different punishments for adultery.
3. **Sacred texts.** Sacred texts tend to give women subordinate roles. In most religions, the gods are male and women are portrayed in minor roles. All the apostles in the New Testament, for example, are men. One explanation for this is that the sacred texts were usually written by men. The position of women in many societies across the globe has improved over the last 50 years. Faced with such changes to women's social status, some groups want women's traditional roles (for example, as wives and mothers) to be re-established. Such groups often appeal to sacred texts in order to justify their views on gender.
4. **Places of worship.** Some places of worship segregate men and women. Women's second-class status is often related to their female identities. Jean Holm (1994) points out that 'Menstruation and childbirth are almost universally regarded as polluting. In many traditions women are forbidden to enter sacred places or touch sacred objects during the menstrual period.' For example, Hindu women are prohibited from approaching family shrines when pregnant or menstruating. Muslim women are not allowed to touch the Qur'an, go into a mosque or pray during menstruation.

## Activity

*Many feminists see the majority of religious organisations as male-dominated in their leadership.*

1. How far do you agree with the view that religions are patriarchal?
2. Can you think of any arguments to counter this view?

Fang-Long Shih (2010) identifies two main feminist perspectives on religion: the **radical feminist** perspective and the **liberal feminist** perspective. However, other feminist-inspired viewpoints have also developed which challenge the view that religion is necessarily patriarchal.

# Radical feminist perspectives on religion

Radical feminist perspectives argue that gender inequality is the central type of inequality in society. Furthermore, a radical transformation of society is necessary to remove gender inequality. Unlike liberal feminists, they believe that small-scale reform will not be enough to bring about change.

## Simone de Beauvoir's account of female oppression within religion

De Beauvoir (1953) argued that religion acts for women in similar ways to those suggested by Marx for oppressed classes. Oppressors (men) can use religion to control the oppressed group (women). Religion also serves as a way of compensating women for their second-class status. De Beauvoir notes that men have generally exercised control over religious beliefs in different faiths and use divine authority to support their dominance over women. The fear of God serves to keep women in a subordinate position.

Religion gives women, like Marx's proletariat, the idea that they will be compensated for their sufferings on earth by equality in heaven. In this way, the subjugation of women through religion helps to maintain a status quo in which women and men are unequal. Furthermore, in terms of their role within religion, women are seen as vital because they do much of the work for religious organisations and introduce children to religious beliefs.

## Goddess religion and feminist spirituality

Some feminists argue that the subordination of women has not always been a characteristic of the majority of religions. Karen Armstrong (1993), for example, argues that in early history women were at the centre of 'the spiritual quest'. In the Middle East, Asia and Europe, archaeologists have uncovered numerous symbols of the Great Mother Goddess. She is pictured as a naked pregnant woman and seems to represent the mysteries of fertility and life. There were very few early effigies of gods as men. As societies developed religious beliefs in which there were held to be many different gods and goddesses, the Mother Goddess still played a crucial role. However, the final death knell for goddesses came with the acceptance of monotheism – belief in a single male god (such as Yahweh, the god of the prophet Abraham) rather than in many gods.

## Mary Daly and Goddess religion

Some feminist approaches, such as that of de Beauvoir, assume that religion is inevitably patriarchal and must be abolished. Others accept that religion is patriarchal but do not believe that religion itself needs to be abolished. Instead, they argue that patriarchal religions need to be replaced with feminist religion. In particular, they need to be replaced with **Goddess religion**.

Daly (1973) was one of the earliest advocates of this approach. She was strongly influenced by de Beauvoir and agreed that religion was oppressive to women. She argued that existing religions are based on an 'inadequate God', and that women are oppressed in several ways:

1. Religions such as Christianity have often proclaimed that the subordination of women is God's will.
2. God is portrayed as a man and as Father. 'One-sex symbolism' of this sort alienates women and places them in an inferior position to men.
3. Religion tells believers that redemption comes through prayer, not through actively trying to change the situation and abolish exploitation. For this reason, it tends to support the continuation of patriarchy.

Daly argued for a new feminist spirituality. This sense of spirituality can come from within women themselves and can lead to the revolutionary overthrow of dominant, male gods. Together, women can 'struggle towards self-transcendence' so that religious and spiritual insight comes from within and not from the teachings of male preachers imposing a male god on women.

In this way, some religions may oppose rather than support male domination. Woodhead (2007) describes the Goddess feminist movement as seeking 'to honour the "divine feminine" in their own lives and in society'. It is committed to the empowerment of women.

Radical feminist approaches which emphasise the importance of Goddess religion have demonstrated that, while a belief in God can help to maintain patriarchy, non-patriarchal religions are possible. However, critics argue that Daly's work is rather generalised and, in places, lacks detailed evidence to support her claims. Nevertheless, Shih (2010) believes that this type of research has been significant in developing the sociology of religion in general, by helping to open up female and feminist perspectives. For example, Woodhead (2007) has discussed how involvement in New Age activities such as Reiki in Kendal, Britain, can be a way for women to gain self-esteem, which may be low as a result of patriarchal ideology. For example, women may have found that their sense of self-worth has been undermined by male partners and that involvement in New Age activities is a way to overcome these feelings.

### Activity

*The Glastonbury Goddess Temple in Somerset, England.*

1. How might replacing existing religions with Goddess religions help overcome patriarchal ideology?
2. Why might New Age movements be less patriarchal than other forms of religion?

### Patriarchy, Islam and the limited role of religion

Both de Beauvoir and advocates of Goddess religion write from the perspective of Western, Christian women. Furthermore, they assume that religion itself is a main cause of patriarchy. However, Nawal El Saadawi (1980), an Egyptian feminist writer, discusses female oppression in the Arab world and elsewhere. She examines the importance of religion in creating and perpetuating oppression but does not see religion itself as the main underlying cause of oppression. Instead, she sees it as just one aspect of a wider patriarchal system which needs to be overthrown.

El Saadawi denies that the oppression of women is directly caused by religion in general, or by Islam in particular. She notes that oppressive practices such as female circumcision have often been attributed to the influence of Islam. However, female circumcision has been practised in a considerable number of countries, not all of them Islamic. In her view, genuine religious beliefs tend to be opposed to any such practices and aim at 'truth, equality, justice, love and a healthy wholesome life for all people, whether men or women'.

Furthermore, she believes that other religions, including Christianity, are often more oppressive than Islam. To El Saadawi, female oppression is not essentially due to religion but to patriarchy. Men have often distorted religion to serve their own interests, to help justify or legitimate the oppression of women. El Saadawi is not hostile to religion itself, but only to the domination of religion by patriarchal ideology.

### Evaluation of radical feminism

1. Critics argue that much radical feminism tends to generalise about religion and to see all religions as equally patriarchal. However, some liberal feminists have identified certain religions, such as Quakerism, that are not clearly or strongly patriarchal.
2. Radical feminists also tend to ignore evidence that progress has been made and that aspects of patriarchal ideology within religion have been successfully challenged.
3. Radical feminists such as de Beauvoir and Daly have not backed up their views with detailed research. In other cases, the validity or representativeness of the research may be open to question.
4. Radical feminists are not particularly sensitive to the ways in which women may find space within, or use, apparently patriarchal religions to further their own interests.

## Liberal feminist perspectives on religion

Radical feminists tend to believe that patriarchy is so built into existing religions that only their destruction or replacement with an alternative can lead to the furthering of feminism. However, liberal feminists, while also regarding existing religions as patriarchal, focus more on reforming religions in order to remove patriarchal elements from them. In their view, religion and feminism are compatible. They start off by identifying the aspects of religion which, in their view, need reforming.

### Inequalities in major religions

Holm (1994) argues that, while the classical teachings of many religions have stressed equality between men and women, in practice they have usually been far from equal. In Japanese folk religions, for example, women are responsible for organising public rituals but only men can take part in the public performances. In Chinese popular religion, women are associated with Yin and men with Yang. However, Yang spirits are more important and powerful. In Buddhism, both men and women can have a religious role, as monks and nuns, respectively. However, all monks are seen as senior to all nuns. Orthodox Judaism only allows males to take a full part in ceremonies. In Islam, in some regions, women are not allowed to enter mosques for worship, and men have made all the legal rulings. In Christianity, it is still impossible for women to take the highest positions in church hierarchy.

### The limits to patriarchy and progress towards greater equality

Many liberal feminists suggest that the patriarchal oppression of women within religion is not universal. Essays in a book edited by Holm (1994) identified three main reasons for this:

1. Some religions are generally patriarchal but aspects of them can still provide significant opportunities for women. For example, Leila Badawi (1994) noted aspects of Islam that are positive for women. Unlike Christian women, Muslim women keep their own family name when they get married.
2. There are a few religions which do not have a strong tradition of patriarchy and have always been relatively egalitarian. According to Alexandra Wright (1994), some Christian religions, particularly Quakerism, have never been oppressive to women. For example, Quakers believe in totally democratic organisational structures and value men and women's contribution to the day-to-day running of the religion in equal measure.
3. Patriarchal aspects of some religions are changing, partly as a result of liberal feminists' actions and campaigns for gender equality within religions. For example, some have campaigned for women to hold senior posts within the Church of England hierarchy on equal terms to men. Partly due to such campaigns, women have been consecrated as bishops within the Church of England since 2015. Others are currently campaigning for the Roman Catholic Church to ordain women as priests.

### Activity

In Berlin, Germany, a new mosque, Ibn Rushd-Goethe, has been built which seeks to challenge patriarchal interpretations of Islam. It does this by allowing men and women to pray together as well as allowing women imams. The founder and imam, Seyran Ates, a self-proclaimed Muslim feminist, argues that the way to overcome problems such as radicalisation (where individuals are encouraged to take on extreme and sometimes violent actions in the name of religion) and hostility towards Islam is to introduce more a progressive, feminist brand of faith. The mosque is part of a small but growing number of similar mosques around the world that have received both hostile criticism and also some hopeful support.

1. Outline two ways in which the Ibn Rushd-Goethe mosque challenges radical feminist views of religion.
2. Explain why this new mosque may appeal to women more than traditional mosques.

### Evaluation of liberal feminism

1. Although there is evidence of some progress as a result of liberal feminism, the extent of this progress is open to question. Radical feminists tend to believe that patriarchy is so embedded within existing religions that reform will never be enough to significantly improve the position of women within religion and within society in general.
2. Some feminists, while not rejecting liberal feminism altogether, believe that it has had only a limited impact. Shih (2010) refers to research which suggests that, even with increasing numbers of women ordained within the Church of England, relatively little has changed and sexist attitudes within the Church remain strong.
3. Statistical evidence suggests that there is still a long way to go before women achieve equality within the Church of England. For example, in

2012, women made up 12 per cent of senior staff (including cathedral clergy, archdeacons and bishops); in 2015, this figure stood at 19 per cent (Church of England, 2016).

## Key terms

**Patriarchy** A pattern/structure of male dominance and control.

**Radical feminists** Those who believe that society is dominated by men and the only way to improve the position of women is via radical changes in society.

**Liberal feminists** Those who believe that gender equality is possible within existing social structures, with changes in attitudes, laws and social policies.

**Goddess religion** Religion that honours the 'divine feminine', the female side of the divine.

## Summary

1. Feminist theories see religion as a patriarchal institution in terms of its hierarchical organisations, its laws and customs, its sacred texts and its places of worship.
2. Radical feminists such as de Beauvoir argue that religion is inevitably patriarchal and must be abolished.
3. While accepting that religion oppresses women, some feminists argue that patriarchal religions need to be replaced with non-patriarchal religions such as a new feminist spirituality or a Goddess religion.
4. El Saadawi sees religion as playing a role in women's oppression but rejects the idea that it is the main cause of oppression. Instead, she sees religion as one aspect of a wider patriarchal system.
5. Critics of radical feminism point out that not all religions are equally patriarchal and that aspects of patriarchal ideology within religions have been successfully challenged. Furthermore, women may use apparently patriarchal religions to further their own interests.
6. Liberal feminist perspectives focus on removing patriarchal aspects from religion and argue that progress has been made towards greater equality. Critics question the extent of this progress and reform.

# Unit 7.3.2 Patriarchy and gender inequality in religion

## Patriarchy and women in conservative religions

Conservative religions, which tend to support traditional values, are often seen as the most oppressive types of religion for women. **Fundamentalism** and **evangelicalism**, which advocate traditional morality and the importance of the domestic role and modesty for women, seem to be particularly patriarchal. In Catholicism there are strict rules governing men and women's sexuality – for example, prohibiting sex outside marriage or abortion. Furthermore, there are strict rules concerning women's sexuality even within approved relationships, such as marriage among orthodox Jews. These examples also suggest that religion might affect women in different ways and therefore generalisations about religion are inappropriate.

However, some feminist sociologists question whether they necessarily always succeed in oppressing women. A number of researchers have found evidence that women find space within such religions to develop their own ideas or use aspects of these religions to further their own interests. For example, Sophie Gilliat-Ray (2010) points out that some British-born Muslim girls and young women wear the hijab (a scarf covering their head and hair) as a means of negotiating approval from their parents to go into higher education or paid employment. This may help to explain why many conservative religions are embraced by a significant number of women.

### Islam and the veil

Many feminists view the issue of veiling and modest dress among Islamic women as controversial. Rachel Rinaldo (2010) notes that, as veiling regained popularity in the 1970s and 1980s, 'the reaction from feminists was overwhelmingly negative', seeing the practice as a 'reassertion of patriarchy'. After the Islamic revolution in Iran in 1979, for example, veiling was made compulsory, and some saw this as a direct attack on women's rights. However, these assumptions have been challenged by a number of other feminist writers.

Helen Watson (1994) argues that the veiling of Islamic women can be interpreted as beneficial to them. She examines three Muslim women's responses to veiling and finds that Islamic women in a globalised world can use veils in a positive way. As Western culture tries to influence Islamic countries, and more Muslims live in the Western world, the veil can take on new meanings for women. For example, Nadia, a second-generation British-Asian woman studying medicine at university, actively chose to start wearing a veil when she was 16. She was proud of her religion and wanted others to know that she was Muslim. She felt that 'It is liberating to have the freedom of movement and to be able to communicate with people without being on show. It's what you say that's important, not what you look like.' She found that, far from making her invisible, wearing a veil made her stand out, yet it also helped her to avoid unwanted comments and attention from men.

Watson concludes that veiling is often a reaction against an increasingly pervasive Western culture. It can be seen as the assertion of independence, separate identity and a rejection of Western **cultural imperialism**. Rather than seeing the veil as a sign of male oppression, it is 'part of the search for an indigenous Islamic form of protest' against patriarchy in society.

Watson's conclusions, however, should be treated with some caution. Her observations are based on a sample of three women. She appears to have made no attempt to find Muslim women who felt men or patriarchal society forced them into wearing the veil against their will.

The next section explores the extent to which new forms of religion follow similar patterns of reflecting patriarchal ideology, or alternatively if they provide alternative ideas and practices.

## Activity

In many parts of Europe, it is now illegal to wear any form of face covering in public places, but critics argue that this infringes people's freedom of expression and religion.

1. Why might some feminists support a ban on wearing a veil in public?
2. Why might other feminists oppose such a ban?
3. To what extent do you agree that the state should impose rules on what people wear in public?

## Do more recent forms of religiosity reflect patriarchal ideology?

Given the huge array of new forms of religions emerging in recent years, it can be difficult to make generalisations about the extent to which they perpetuate ideas which oppress women. However, this section explores some examples which both challenge and support the claim that religions continue to uphold patriarchal ideology.

### New religious movements

New religious movements (relatively modern forms of religion which are different from, or challenge, traditional religions in some way) are not easy to compare, as they vary considerably in relation to gender. Susan Palmer (2008) suggests that the majority, however, tend to reinforce conservative, simplistic ideas about the role of women as carers or mothers that uphold patriarchy. A minority of new religious movements offer opportunities for greater experimentation with gender roles. For example, the Raëlians encouraged experimentation with gender roles, encouraging transvestitism, as well as practising the removal of gendered identity and behaviour. Other new religious movements sought to challenge patriarchal assumptions, although these practices are not always long-term. For example, between 1981 and 1985 the Rajneesh movement granted women leadership positions, only shortly afterwards to be replaced by male leaders. Therefore, the overwhelming view is that new religious movements are unlikely to challenge patriarchy or, indeed, offer women any form of liberation.

### Pentecostalism

Some feminists express concerns about Pentecostalism's deep conservatism with respect to women's roles. However, Elizabeth Brusco (1996) carried out research into Pentecostalism in Colombia in the 1980s and found that Pentecostalism can be a source of change or emancipation for women. Brusco claims that Pentecostalism has the capacity to reform gender roles in ways that enhance female status. Brusco claims that Pentecostalism promotes female interests in simple, practical ways, such as involving them more in organisational roles and valuing their contribution in the family. Pentecostalism also has the potential to challenge machismo or male dominance that is so central to Latin American culture. This is possible through the expectations and teachings about the need for men to be respectful to their wives and other female relatives. However, this finding is only limited to Colombia, so the pattern may not be reflected elsewhere.

### New Age movements

New Age movements (see Unit 7.1.3) appear to attract women more than men. For example, the Kendal Project in the UK (see Unit 7.5.2) notes that women are more likely to be part of a growing number of people who are not affiliated to traditional religious organisations, but who instead attend New Age movements that practise techniques such as yoga. Michael York (2004) claims that much of the outlook of New Age movements, their spirituality and organisation lends itself to a more female-centred belief system. Cynthia Eller (1993) claims that New Age movements in the USA offer women the opportunity to be part of a feminist spirituality movement, as opposed to traditional patriarchal forms of religion.

### Key terms

**Fundamentalism** A form of religion whose adherents want to return to what they see as the core doctrines of the faith as set out in sacred texts such as the Bible or the Qur'an. Christian fundamentalists, for example, adopt a literal interpretation of biblical accounts of miracles and the Creation.

**Evangelicalism** A movement within Protestant Christianity that is seen as conservative in its support of traditional values.

**Cultural imperialism** The practice of imposing a culture, viewpoint or civilisation on people in another, less powerful country.

### Summary

1. Fundamentalism and evangelical Christianity are seen as particularly patriarchal. However, some feminist sociologists argue that women can find space within such religions to develop their own ideas.
2. Many feminists have reacted negatively to the popularity of veiling among Muslim women. However, Watson argues that wearing a veil in a globalised world can be beneficial to Muslim women.

# END-OF-PART QUESTIONS

0 1 Describe two ways in which religion can be seen as oppressive for women. **[4 marks]**

0 2 Explain two limitations of the liberal feminist view of religion. **[6 marks]**

0 3 'New forms of religion continue to maintain patriarchal ideology.'
Using sociological material, give one argument against this view. **[6 marks]**

# PART 4 RELIGION AS A SOURCE OF SOCIAL CHANGE

## Contents


| | | |
|---|---|---|
| **Unit 7.4.1** | **The relationship between religion and social change** | **429** |
| **Unit 7.4.2** | **Religious movements, political debates and struggles** | **435** |


Sociologists are interested in the relationship between religion and social change. To what extent is religion a source of stability in society? Can it promote social change and, if so, what sort of change does it bring about? In addressing these questions, this part draws on functionalist, Marxist and feminist approaches. It also explores the ideas of Weber on the links between religion and the rise of capitalism. Finally, it examines the influence of religious movements on political debates and struggles around the world. What role have religious leaders and beliefs played in political debates, struggles and conflict?

## Unit 7.4.1 The relationship between religion and social change

There are a number of possible relationships between religion, social change and social stability. In general, functionalist and many Marxist and feminist sociologists argue that religion may be a **conservative force**, a factor that inhibits social change. By contrast, neo-Marxists such as Otto Maduro (1982) argue that religion may also be a radical force that promotes change. This unit looks at different sociological accounts of the role of religion as a source of social change, including debates about the relationship between religion and the origins of capitalism.

### Religion as a conservative force

Religion can be seen as a 'conservative force' in two senses, depending on how 'conservative' is defined. The phrase 'conservative force' is usually used to refer to religion as preventing change and maintaining the status quo. Functionalists, Marxists and feminists generally agree that religion acts as a conservative force in society. However, they disagree in terms of how they interpret this. From a functionalist perspective, religion contributes to social order and stability (see Unit 7.2.1). In doing so, religion facilitates the continued existence of society in its present form and inhibits change. This is interpreted by functionalists in positive terms.

Marx had similar views to functionalism in that he saw religion as maintaining the status quo (see Unit 7.2.2). However, he argued that religion operates in the interests of the ruling class rather than those of society as a whole. By promising its faithful followers rewards in the next life, religion discourages people from demanding radical social changes in this life and acts as an agency of social control.

Many feminists see religion as a patriarchal institution that perpetuates rather than challenges gender inequality. From a feminist perspective, religion can be seen as ideological in that it socialises people into accepting patriarchy and gender inequality as natural and inevitable.

'Conservative' may also refer to traditional beliefs and customs. Usually, if religion helps to maintain the status quo, it will also maintain traditional customs and beliefs. For example, the stance of successive popes has restricted the use of abortion among Roman Catholic women. The Roman Catholic Church also has traditional views on issues such as marriage, divorce, sexuality, contraception and gender.

In some circumstances, however, religion can support social change while at the same time promoting traditional values. This often occurs when there is a revival in fundamentalist religious beliefs within, for example, Christianity or Islam. Such beliefs involve a return to what a group claims are the 'fundamentals' or basic, original beliefs of a religion. Christian fundamentalism in the USA, for example, involves an emphasis on the literal truth of scripture, a literal interpretation of the biblical account of the Creation and a rejection of the scientific theory of evolution. It advocates traditional roles for women in society, and control over female sexuality and reproduction expressed, for instance, in its attitudes to abortion. Bryan Turner (2005) argues that Christian fundamentalism has become an important force in the revival of right-wing politics in the USA.

Fundamentalism involves the reassertion of traditional religious and moral values to counter social changes that have taken place and to oppose the people who support these changes (see Unit 7.6.2). If fundamentalists are successful, they succeed in defending traditional values. At the same time, however, they change society by reversing innovations that took place earlier.

Islamic State (IS) can be interpreted as acting as both a force for change and a conservative force. On the one hand, it is a movement that wants to bring about change (the establishment of a state that is governed by Islamic law). On the other hand, IS is seen as an organisation that supports traditional, conservative values. This illustrates the importance of distinguishing between the two meanings of the word 'conservative'.

## Activity

*A preacher challenges students on an American university campus to abandon evolutionary theory and replace it with Christian beliefs.*

1. In what way might religion be seen as a conservative force in society?
2. Briefly explain one similarity between feminist and Marxist views on the relationship between religion and social change.
3. Briefly explain one difference between functionalist and Marxist views on the relationship between religion and social change.

## Religion as a change-promoting force

Marx is generally regarded as a materialist. He argued that the material world shaped people's beliefs, including their religious and political beliefs. In his view, the economic system largely determined the type of religion that was dominant in a particular society and the beliefs that people held.

Unlike Marx, Weber rejected the view that religion is always shaped by economic factors. In his view, under certain conditions, religious beliefs can have a major influence on economic behaviour and promote social change.

### Weber's theory of the role of religion in the rise of capitalism

Weber (1958, first published 1904/05) examined the relationship between the rise of Calvinism, a Protestant form of Christianity, and the development of Western industrial capitalism. He tried to demonstrate that:

- Calvinism emerged before the development of Western capitalism
- capitalism first developed in areas where Calvinism was influential.

**The Protestant ethic** Calvinist Protestantism originated in the beliefs of John Calvin (1509–64) and his followers in the 17th century. Calvin led the Protestant Reformation in Switzerland and France. The term 'Reformation' refers to attempts to reform the Roman Catholic Church and to the development of Protestantism in Western Europe.

Calvin believed in the doctrine of **predestination**: that God had predetermined the world and that a distinct group of people, the **elect**, were destined to go to heaven. The elect had been chosen by God even before they were born. Unlike members of other religions, such as Roman Catholics, Calvinists believed that those who were not among the elect could not earn themselves a place in heaven, no matter how well they behaved on earth. They could not change God's decision.

Weber pointed out that Calvinists had a psychological problem: they did not know whether they were among the elect. Consequently, they suffered from uncertainty about their status. However, they reasoned that only the elect would be able to live a good life on earth. If their behaviour was exemplary, they could feel confident that they were among those chosen by God to go to heaven after death. Their behaviour was not an attempt to earn a place in heaven; instead, it was an attempt to convince themselves that they had been chosen to go there.

The **Protestant ethic** developed first in 17th-century Western Europe among Protestants, including Calvinists. This ethic was **ascetic**, encouraging abstinence from life's pleasures, an austere lifestyle and self-discipline.

Calvinists saw their occupation or career as a **calling**, as something to which they had been called by God. The Protestant ethic produced individuals who worked hard and single-mindedly in their calling. Acquiring wealth provided ascetic Protestants with a clue to their fate. They saw financial success as a sign of God's favour – as a sign that they were one of the elect, saved rather than damned. The money they made, however, could not be spent on luxuries or frivolous entertainment. It had to be spent on the glory of God. In effect, this meant being even more successful in one's calling and, in practice, reinvesting profits in the business. Therefore, the interpretation that the Calvinists put on the original doctrine of predestination contributed to them becoming the first capitalists.

## Activity

*This cartoon from 1653 shows a Puritan (a follower of Puritanism, a strict form of Protestantism that was influenced by Calvinism) driving Father Christmas out of town. Christmas fun and games were banned in mid-17th-century England.*

How might this cartoon illustrate Weber's view of the Protestant ethic?

**The spirit of capitalism** Weber argued that modern capitalist enterprises are organised on rational lines and business transactions are conducted in a systematic manner. Underlying the practice of capitalism is the **spirit of capitalism** – a set of ethics, values and ideas such as to waste time loses money. The spirit of capitalism involved seeing the accumulation of capital as an end in itself rather than as a means to an end. It involved dedication to acquiring money through economic activity and avoiding the use of wealth for personal enjoyment.

Weber claimed that the origins of the spirit of capitalism were to be found in the work ethic of ascetic Protestantism. He saw ascetic Protestantism as a vital influence in the creation and development of the spirit and practice of capitalism. In his view, the methodical and single-minded pursuit of a calling encouraged rational capitalism. Making money became both a religious and a business ethic.

Finally, Weber noted that the importance of wealth creation and the restrictions on spending it encouraged saving and reinvestment. The ascetic Protestant way of life led to the accumulation of capital, investment and reinvestment. It produced the early businesses that expanded to create capitalism.

**Religion in non-Protestant societies** Weber compared religions and economic developments in different parts of the world in order to understand the relationship between religion and changes in society (Weber, 1963, first published 1922). Although other parts of the world beyond Western Europe possessed many of the necessary preconditions to develop capitalism, they were not among the first areas to develop it. For example, India and China had technological knowledge, labour and individuals engaged in making money. What they lacked, according to Weber, was a religion that encouraged the development of capitalism.

**Materialism and Weber's theory** In Weber's view, he had shown that some religious beliefs could promote economic change. He claimed to have found a weakness in Marx's materialism, which implied that the economic system always shaped ideas. Weber put much more emphasis than Marx on the influence of ideas in bringing about economic change. However, Weber also recognised the importance of the economy, material factors and technology in making capitalism possible. Material factors were as important as ideas in the development of capitalism. Neither could be ignored in any explanation.

## Activity

*A portrait of John Calvin. Weber examined the impact of Protestant religions such as Calvinism on the development of Western capitalism.*

Write a summary of Weber's ideas on the relationship between the Protestant ethic and the development of capitalism.

### Evaluation of Weber

1. Werner Sombart (1907) argued that Weber was mistaken about Calvinists' beliefs. According to Sombart, Calvinism opposed greed and the pursuit of money for its own sake. However, Weber pointed out that it was not the Calvinist beliefs in themselves that were important. The doctrine of predestination was not intended to produce the rational pursuit of profit. However, this was one of its unintended consequences, in that it led to the Protestant work ethic.
2. Critics point to parts of the world where Calvinism was strong but capitalism did not develop until much later. For example, Switzerland, Scotland, Hungary and parts of the Netherlands all contained large Calvinist populations but were not among the first capitalist countries. However, Gordon Marshall (1982) argues that Weber did not claim that Calvinism was the only factor necessary for the development of capitalism. Simply finding Calvinist countries that failed to become capitalist comparatively early cannot therefore disprove Weber's theory. In his own study of Scotland, Marshall found that the Scots had a capitalist mentality but were held back by a lack of skilled labour and capital for investment, and by government policies that did not stimulate the development of industry.
3. Karl Kautsky (1953), a Marxist, argued that early capitalism came before and largely determined Protestantism. He saw Calvinism as developing in cities where commerce and early forms of industrialisation were already established. Weber's defenders insist that a distinctive rational capitalist entrepreneur did not emerge until after Calvinism.
4. Others question whether it was Calvinists' religious beliefs that led to them becoming businesspeople. According to this view, Calvinists devoted themselves to business because they were excluded from holding public office and from joining certain professions by law. Like Jewish people in Eastern and Central Europe, they tried to become economically successful in order to overcome their political persecution. However, Weber's supporters argue that only Calvinists developed capitalist behaviour involving rational planning to accumulate capital. As a result, only they could develop capitalist businesses before capitalism was established.

Despite these criticisms, Weber successfully highlights the theoretical point that ideas – in this case, religious ideas – can lead to economic change.

## Contemporary issues: Pentecostalism

### Pentecostalism

Pentecostal movements are one of the faster-growing churches within world Christianity and have spread rapidly in Latin America and other less industrialised societies. One interpretation of Pentecostalism regards it as a new form of Weber's Protestant ethic (Martin, 2013). Pentecostals' lifestyle, based on hard work, saving money and self-discipline, is seen as encouraging upward social mobility and effective participation in a modern economy. Consequently, in this view, Pentecostalism is associated with economic and social change.

Pentecostalism is seen as a modernising movement in less industrialised societies in Latin America, Asia and Africa in terms of economic behaviour. Its beliefs are compatible with economic and industrial growth. It also seeks to transform family life and, in some cases, the role of women to bring about greater gender equality.

David Martin (2013) notes that Pentecostals believe in bettering themselves and self-help. They are prepared to change their circumstances themselves rather than expecting others to rectify their wrongs for them. He sees Pentecostal pastors as religious entrepreneurs who run enterprises, including transnational megachurches, that are religious versions of large-scale businesses. Becoming a pastor can provide a route of rapid upward social mobility for some.

Allan H. Anderson (2014) suggests that Pentecostalism can change its believers' values and motivate new economic behaviour. As a result, Pentecostalism has encouraged capitalism and development in, for example, parts of Africa. He agrees with Martin that Pentecostalism can create upward social mobility. It can also legitimise economic success.

### The Prosperity Gospel in Brazil

*The Temple of Solomon in São Paulo, Brazil, is the world headquarters of the neo-Pentecostal Universal Church of the Kingdom of God.*

Pentecostalism is the fastest-growing sector of Protestantism in Brazil, a predominantly Roman Catholic country in Latin America. Many neo-Pentecostal churches have introduced the Prosperity Gospel to Brazil. The Religious Literacy Project argues that one key belief of the Prosperity Gospel concerns the power of Jesus Christ and the gospel to heal not only people's emotional and physical illnesses, but also their financial ills. In effect, having faith, praying and donating money to a Pentecostal church can lead to financial rewards and riches. Wealth and prosperity are seen as signs of God's favour, while (by implication) poverty is linked to a lack of faith.

Neo-Pentecostalism's enthusiastic acceptance of the Prosperity Gospel associates devotion with upward social mobility. This has contributed to the widespread appeal of neo-Pentecostalism among the Brazilian urban poor as well as the middle class.

### Question

Drawing on the example of Pentecostalism and other relevant material, evaluate the view that religious ideas can encourage social and economic change.

## Examples of religions as vehicles for social change

G.K. Nelson (1986) argues that, 'far from encouraging people to accept their place, religion can spearhead resistance and revolution'. In cases when religion has been a force for change in society, the society that results may be strongly influenced by that religion. Numerous examples show that religion can act as a vehicle for social change.

- In the 1960s, a number of radical and revolutionary groups emerged within the Roman Catholic Church in Latin America. They preached **liberation theology**, arguing that it was the duty of church members to fight against unjust and oppressive right-wing dictatorships. Liberation theology is committed to the struggle for justice and to taking action on behalf of the poor and marginalised. In 1979, Catholic revolutionaries supported the left-wing Sandinistas (named after their leader, Sandino) when they seized control in Nicaragua and two priests became ministers in the first Sandinista government.

Maduro (1982), a neo-Marxist sociologist, accepts many aspects of Marx's analysis of religion but rejects the idea that religion is always a conservative force and claims that it can be revolutionary. He argues that religion is often 'one of the main (and sometimes the only) available channel to bring about a social revolution'. Maduro claims that, until recently, Catholicism in Latin America tended to support the bourgeoisie and the right-wing military dictatorships, which represented its interests. The Catholic Church has tended to deny the existence of social conflicts between oppressive and oppressed classes. It has recognised some injustices, such as poverty and illiteracy, but has suggested that their solution lies with those who already have power. It has also celebrated military victories but failed to support unions, strikes and opposition political parties.

On the other hand, Catholic priests have increasingly demonstrated their autonomy from the bourgeoisie by criticising them and acting against their interests. Maduro believes that members of the clergy can develop revolutionary potential where oppressed members of the population have no other outlets for their grievances. The oppressed can pressurise priests to take up their cause. Theological disagreements within a church can provide interpretations of a religion that are critical of the rich and powerful. All of these conditions were met in Latin America and led to the development of liberation theology.

- In the USA in the 1960s, Reverend Martin Luther King and the Southern Christian Leadership Council played a leading role in establishing civil rights and securing legislation to reduce racial discrimination.
- In South Africa, Archbishop Desmond Tutu was active in the struggle to bring apartheid (which was based on a government policy of racial segregation between 1948 and 1994) to an end.
- In Iran, Islamic fundamentalism played a part in the 1979 revolution, led by the Ayatollah Khomeini, a religious leader.

## Factors affecting whether religion promotes or inhibits change

McGuire (2002) identifies several significant factors in determining whether religion is a change-promoting or a change-inhibiting force.

1. **The beliefs of the particular religion.** Religions with strong moral codes are more likely to produce members who are critical of society and who seek to change it. If a religion stresses concern with this world, its members are more likely to engage in action that produces change than a religion that is more concerned with sacred and spiritual matters. Consequently, Protestantism can have more impact on social change than Buddhism.
2. **The culture of the society in which a religion exists.** In countries where religious beliefs are central to the culture (for example, in Latin America), anyone wishing to produce change tends to use religion to justify their actions. In Britain, however, religion plays a less central role in society's culture, so it tends to have a lesser role in legitimising social change.
3. **The social location of religion: the part that religion plays in the structure of society.** The greater the importance of religion, the greater its potential to participate in generating change. Where an established religious organisation plays a major role in political and economic life, it has considerable scope to impact on processes of change.
4. **The internal organisation of religious institutions.** Religions with a strong, centralised authority have more chance of affecting events. On the other hand, the central authority might try to restrain the actions of parts of its organisation. For example, at the Puebla Conference in Mexico in 1978, the Pope clashed with Latin American Roman Catholic bishops who advocated liberation theology and the need to bring about political change and support the poor.

### Activity

*Some religions, such as Buddhism, may have less impact on social change than others.*

Explain why the beliefs of some religions may be more likely than others to produce adherents who seek to change society.

### Key terms

**Conservative force** A factor such as religion or the mass media that inhibits social, economic or political change.

**Predestination** The belief that God has predetermined whether people will be saved or damned after they die.

**Elect** The people chosen by God to be saved and destined to go to heaven.

**Protestant ethic** Weber used this term to refer to the value that Calvinists placed on the importance of thrift, abstaining from pleasure and the duty to work hard in one's calling.

**Ascetic** An austere and self-disciplined lifestyle that does not involve indulging in any of life's pleasures.

**Calling** The vocation, position in society or particular way of life that some individuals believe they are called to by God.

**Spirit of capitalism** The essence of capitalism involving the single-minded pursuit of profit as an end in itself.

**Liberation theology** A movement of radical Roman Catholic priests in Latin America, dating to the 1960s, who promote political change, fight oppression and support the poor.

## Summary

1. Religion can be seen as a conservative force in terms of preventing social, political and economic change, and in terms of maintaining traditional customs and beliefs regarding, for example, abortion and divorce.
2. In the case of fundamentalism, religion can support social change and promote traditional values at the same time.
3. Functionalist, Marxist and feminist approaches see religion as a conservative force but disagree on how to interpret this.
4. Weber saw religion as a force for change and argued that the Calvinist way of life was a key factor in the development of capitalism.
5. While Marx argued that the economic base largely determines the superstructure, including religious beliefs, Weber argued that religious beliefs could have a major effect on economic behaviour and bring about social change.
6. Critics question Weber's interpretation of Calvinist beliefs and point out that capitalism preceded Calvinism.
7. Many examples – including liberation theology in Latin America – show that religion can generate change.
8. McGuire identifies several factors that affect whether religion promotes or inhibits change: the beliefs of a particular religion, the culture of the society within which the religion exists, the social location of religion and the internal organisation of religious institutions.

# Unit 7.4.2 Religious movements, political debates and struggles

Religious leaders and beliefs have influenced political debates, conflicts and struggles in many parts of the world including Bosnia, Northern Ireland, the Middle East and the Indian subcontinent. This unit explores the influence of religious movements on political debates and struggles. It does this by examining case studies including the evangelical movement in US politics and the ayatollahs in the Iranian revolution.

## The evangelical movement in US politics

In the USA, evangelicalism is made up of Conservative Christians who try to influence government and return to what they see as traditional Christian values in American life. It includes, for example, the Assemblies of God and the Southern Baptist Convention. Evangelicalism has grown dramatically in the USA since the 1970s. According to the Pew Research Center, 25 per cent of US adults identified with evangelical Protestantism in 2014.

Since the 1960s, Conservative evangelical Protestants have been concerned by many of the political and cultural changes taking place in the USA such as the women's liberation and civil rights movements, and the increase in divorce. Many oppose the teaching of the theory of evolution in schools. The evangelical movement promotes its cause partly through conventional democratic politics. Some commentators argue that evangelicalism helped to elect the Republican George W. Bush in the 2000 and 2004 presidential elections. According to a CBS News poll, Donald Trump, the Republican candidate, gained 80 per cent of the White evangelical vote in the presidential election in 2016. Anthony Giddens and Philip W. Sutton (2017) note that 'Evangelical organisations are highly effective in mobilising resources to help achieve their religious and political objectives.'

Bruce (2003) links the New Christian Right's (NCR) programme in national politics in the USA to evangelical Protestantism (see Units 7.2.2 and 7.5.2). In his view, the NCR wants to restore conservative religion to a central position in public life. The NCR seeks to influence politicians, has infiltrated the

Republican Party and is concerned with tackling issues such as abortion, homosexuality and divorce. According to Bruce (1988), the NCR support 'a more aggressive anti-communist foreign policy, more military spending, less central government interference, less welfare spending, and fewer restraints on free enterprise'. However, Bruce argues that the NCR has failed to achieve popular support. It has not made marked progress on issues that are specific to its conservative Protestant agenda, such as restricting divorce and abortion. This is partly because the NCR is not successful at building alliances with other groups in order to take political action on issues such as abortion. Furthermore, the NCR has powerful opponents among those who support tolerance and liberal ideas. More recently, however, activists in the USA who support the idea of a woman's right to choose whether to have an abortion argue that the Trump administration poses a threat to abortion rights.

## The Iranian revolution (1978–79)

Under the last shah or ruler of Iran, society underwent a process of change that was influenced by Western ideas, dress and music. One aspect of this change involved the liberalisation of traditional Islamic attitudes to women. However, many Iranian people resented the West's influence on the country and the existence of a rich elite whose wealth derived from the oil industry. Iran's ayatollahs (religious leaders) blamed poverty on Western influences and the decline of Islam. They saw the solution as involving a rejection of Western ideas and a return to a truly Islamic society based on the Qur'an.

In 1979, the Shah was deposed during a revolution that was partly inspired by Islamic fundamentalism. The liberalisation that took place under the Shah was reversed.

The Iranian revolution led to the introduction of an Islamic republic under the leadership of Ayatollah Khomeini. Western music and alcohol were banned, bars were burned and nightclubs were closed down. Women had to wear a veil and Islamic law was reinstated. The Islamic republic sought to 'Islamize the state – to organize government and society so that Islamic teachings would become dominant in all spheres' (Giddens and Sutton, 2017).

Fundamentalist religious beliefs contributed to revolutionary changes in Iranian society. By challenging the status quo, religion acted as a change-promoting force. However, by supporting traditional values, it acted as a conservative force.

### Activity

Drawing on your own examples, explain how religion can be linked to conflict or violent struggle.

## Contemporary issues: The Arab Spring

*Anti-government protesters gather in Tahrir Square, Cairo, Egypt, on 1 February 2011.*

The Arab Spring illustrates the role that religion can play in influencing political debates and struggles. This term describes a number of rebellions and protests that challenged undemocratic and corrupt regimes that held power in several Arab countries including Tunisia, Egypt, Libya and Syria. These protests involved Muslims and other groups who used social media networks to exchange views, demand reforms and generate political change.

The first uprising of the Arab Spring began in Tunisia in 2010 and resulted in the overthrow of the Tunisian president in 2011. In October

2011, open elections were held in Tunisia and a democratic government took power. The success of this uprising gave hope to other social movements, and demonstrations and protests led to the resignation of President Mubarak of Egypt in 2011. The Muslim Brotherhood played a part in these protests and formed a government in Egypt after winning an open and free election in 2012. The example of the Arab Spring suggests that religion can promote political change by helping to give a voice to dissent and demands for reform.

The democratic reforms introduced, however, may not necessarily be long-term ones. In Egypt, for instance, the army backed the overthrow of Egypt's elected president in 2013 and began a crackdown on critics, including the Muslim Brotherhood.

## Question

How far does the example of the Arab Spring illustrate the idea that religious movements can influence political debates and struggles?

## Bruce's account of the relationship between religion and conflict

According to Bruce (2000), there are three types of relationship between religion and conflict:

1. Religion is often used to justify 'what are essentially secular national or ethnic conflicts, even when the combatants are the same religion' (Bruce, 2000). The civil war in the former Yugoslavia in the 1990s illustrates this. Croats, Serbs and Bosnian Muslims fought one another and religion must have played some role since each group follows a different faith (Croats are Roman Catholic and Serbs are Orthodox). However, the war was largely based on ethnic divisions and concerned control of territories rather than the truth of different faiths.
2. Other conflicts are essentially to do with religion. Some participants in conflicts see themselves as engaged in a crusade (a Christian mission to spread their religion) or jihad (the Islamic equivalent). Bruce believes that Osama bin Laden had largely religious motives for his leadership of al-Qaeda, and that Iranian attempts to export its Islamic revolution have also been religiously motivated.
3. In most cases, however, religious and secular motives are 'inseparably intertwined'. There is often an overlap between religious groups, national boundaries and ethnic divisions, so a war might be fought for religion, country and ethnicity at the same time. In these circumstances, religion 'provides each side with a justification for seeing itself as superior (we obey God) and the enemy as inferior (they are the Infidel)' (Bruce, 2000).

## Activity

*Many people in the West see religion as inevitably linked to conflict, violent struggle and war. In practice, however, conflicts and wars are often based on interrelated rather than single factors.*

1. Explain two reasons why religion may be a source of struggle.
2. What other factors may have been involved in religious conflicts in recent history?

## Summary

1. The evangelical movement in the USA attempts to influence government policy and return to what adherents see as traditional Christian values.

2. Bruce links the New Christian Right's programme in national politics in the USA to evangelical Protestantism. In his view, the NCR has infiltrated the Republican Party and is concerned with tackling issues such as abortion, homosexuality and divorce.
3. According to Bruce, the NCR has not made marked progress on issues that are specific to its conservative Protestant agenda, such as restricting divorce and abortion (although access to abortion may be changing under the Trump administration). The NCR is not successful at building alliances with other groups and does not enjoy popular support.
4. The ayatollahs were influential in the Iranian revolution which led to the introduction of an Islamic republic under Ayatollah Khomeini's leadership.
5. Bruce argues that the role of religion in conflict varies. Religion can be used to justify conflict over secular concerns such as control of territories. Other conflicts are motivated by religion. Often, however, religious and secular motives are interconnected.

# END-OF-PART QUESTIONS

| | | |
|---|---|---|
| 0 1 | Describe two characteristics of the Protestant ethic. | **[4 marks]** |
| 0 2 | Explain two limitations of Weber's account of the role of religion in the rise of capitalism. | **[6 marks]** |
| 0 3 | 'Religion acts as a change-inhibiting force in society.' Using sociological material, give one argument against this view. | **[6 marks]** |

# SECTION B
# THE INFLUENCE OF RELIGION

## Contents


**Part 5 The secularisation debate 440**

**Part 6 Religion and postmodernity 454**


Three of the key concepts that you were introduced to in the introductory chapter are particularly relevant here.

First, the key concept of *social change and development* is central to the secularisation debate, the debate about the declining influence of religion in people's lives today in some parts of the world. There is a range of evidence for and against the secularisation thesis, for example, including attendance at religious services and religious affiliation. Rapid social changes in society have had a range of effects on the beliefs that people have, leading to some changes in religious beliefs and practices. Why are some groups responding to the process of **globalisation** by becoming more religious? Why are other groups responding to globalisation by becoming less religious?

Second, this section also relates to the key concept of *socialisation, culture and identity*, as we explore the different ways that religion continues to inform and shape people's lives, or not; for example, the extent to which religious beliefs continue to be powerful in shaping people's socialisation, culture and identity. Why is religion an important marker of identity for some cultural groups but not for others?

Third, the key concept of *inequality and opportunity* is also explored in this section through the emergence of new forms of religion as a response to growing inequalities in society, including fundamentalism. Why has fundamentalism grown significantly recently?

Why are some religions more attractive to those who experience a lack of opportunity?

Section B is divided into two parts. In Part 5, we explore the secularisation debate, using both arguments and evidence for and against, based on a range of different measures. This discussion highlights the fact that measuring religion can be difficult, as sociologists do not necessarily agree on a definition of religion and the fact that there is a lack of reliable evidence about religious belief in earlier periods.

Part 6 explores new forms of religion, including new religious movements and New Age movements and the reasons for their emergence. The influence of globalisation on religiosity is explored – in particular, the extent to which beliefs have shifted to become increasingly privatised and based on individual needs. One characteristic of religion in postmodern society has been the growth of a range of fundamentalist religions, and the causes and consequences of this change are examined.

# PART 5 THE SECULARISATION DEBATE

## Contents


| | | |
|---|---|---|
| Unit 7.5.1 | The secularisation thesis | 440 |
| Unit 7.5.2 | Evidence for and against secularisation | 444 |


The role of religion in society has long been debated, with some sociologists claiming that religion has become more significant in day-to-day life, while others see religion as taking a far less important role in complex societies. On the other hand, there are those who see religion as simply changing rather than declining in significance. Unit 7.5.1 explores the meaning of secularisation, as well as considering key arguments which claim that secularisation is occurring. Unit 7.5.2 explores empirical evidence from around the world, looking at patterns of religious participation, membership, affiliation (or belonging) and disengagement.

## Unit 7.5.1 The secularisation thesis

This unit begins by exploring what secularisation actually means, followed by some of the key arguments which claim that secularisation is occurring, including both classic and more contemporary perspectives. There are two significant factors to take into account when exploring the importance of religion in contemporary society. First, there are many more religions to choose from today; second, the process of globalisation has had a range of interesting effects on religious practices and beliefs.

### What is secularisation?

If we are to measure secularisation and discuss the extent to which it is happening, a definition is an important starting point. As seen earlier in the chapter, sociologists define religion in different ways and it is therefore no surprise that definitions for secularisation vary, as well.

#### Definition 1

Bryan Wilson (1966) provided a good 'classic' definition of secularisation, calling it 'the process whereby religious thinking, practices and institutions lose social significance'. This definition is useful because it makes clear that secularisation is a process. It is also a very broad definition that covers a range of different aspects of religion. However, it is hard to use this definition to measure or operationalise secularisation because Wilson is not clear about what he means by religious thinking, practice or institutions specifically. These three aspects of religion could be differently interpreted and therefore, when measured, may produce different results. Another problem with Wilson's definition is that he is not clear about when the process began, making it difficult to measure the extent to which secularisation has occurred.

#### Definition 2

In an attempt to produce a better definition, Bruce (2002) provides the following:

Secularisation is a social condition manifest in:

a. the declining importance of religion for the operation of non-religious roles and institutions such as those of the state and the economy

b. a decline in the social standing of religious roles and institutions

c. a decline in the extent to which people engage in religious practices, display beliefs of a religious kind, and conduct other aspects of their lives in a manner informed by such beliefs.

This definition is easier to operationalise, as it is more detailed; however, like Wilson, Bruce does not provide a timescale, nor does he explain exactly what 'beliefs of a religious kind' are. Part of the problem is that religion takes many different forms and is practised in an increasingly varied number of different ways in different contexts. As we saw in Unit 7.1.1, there are different definitions of religion and religiosity: more inclusive definitions of religion can include a range of activities and beliefs that may not be seen as religious by some. However, despite these difficulties, Wilson's and Bruce's definitions are a useful initial starting point.

### Definition 3

More recently, José Casanova (2003) identifies a significant division between two types of definitions of the term 'secularisation', reflecting two levels of approaching the issue; the macro (large scale) and the micro (small scale). One way of using the term sees secularisation as a macro process: the 'secularisation of societal structures or the diminution of the social significance of religion' (Casanova, 2003). In this definition, the main emphasis is on religious institutions and religious beliefs playing a decreasing role in influencing public life so that religion becomes an increasingly private matter. However, this definition is difficult to measure quantitatively with statistics, for example. The other way of measuring the term is at a micro level and refers to the 'decline of religious beliefs and practices among individuals' (Casanova, 2003). At this smaller scale, the emphasis is on how many people believe in God, how many people attend churches or other places of worship and how many may affiliate to a religion. Each of these measures is likely to produce a very different picture of the role of religion.

### Activity

1. Suggest one reason why it is difficult to define secularisation.
2. Explain why Bruce's definition might be considered easier to operationalise than Wilson's.
3. Suggest one reason why micro-level research on individuals produces a different picture of secularisation compared with macro-level evidence.

## What is the secularisation thesis?

The **secularisation thesis** is the hypothesis or theory which claims that secularisation is occurring. There is little agreement among sociologists about the rate at which this is happening or how best to operationalise (or measure) the process. There are also questions to be asked about *which* forms of religion are less important today and *which* have become more important. Secularisation theorists use a range of different sources of evidence to support their claims and we will look at this more closely in the next unit. The views of sociologists tend to reflect the ideas of the time in which they were written, so it is important to understand when these views emerged.

### Classical theories of secularisation

It is worth being aware that the majority of sociologists themselves take a secular view of the world; they claim that religion is a social construct and therefore changes over time and from place to place. Most of the founding key figures of early sociology predicted that, as societies developed, religion would either decline (as Durkheim suggested) or disappear altogether (as Marx predicted would happen as a result of communism). Remember that functionalism and Marxism relate to the key concept of structure, as they take the view that religion forms part of the structures of society that shape behaviour. Auguste Comte, an early sociologist, argued that the growth of science and scientific, rational thinking would replace religious thinking. Weber, an interpretivist, claimed that religion would decline due to the rise of modernity. Modernity and religion, according to Weber, cannot coexist.

**Has rationalisation led to a decline in religious belief?** Weber argued that religion would decline in importance because of the development of modernity. Modern societies are seen to be incompatible with religion having a central role in society. Weber thought that in modern societies people would act less in terms of emotion and tradition and more in terms of the rational pursuit of goals. Weber calls this process rationalisation, and he argued that this would gradually erode the influence of religion as people began to turn to science for their understanding of the world. People would no longer believe that prayer, for example, was a way to achieve their aims (Weber 1958, 1963, first published in 1904; Gerth and Mills 1954). Weber's approach and that of other classical secularisation theorists have been developed by a range of contemporary sociologists.

### Contemporary theories of secularisation

Bruce (2011) develops Weber's ideas further to establish his own theory of secularisation. Bruce claims, like Weber, that it was the particular characteristics of Protestant beliefs that, contributed to secularisation. However, Bruce argues it was also other changes that were happening in wider society that, along with Protestantism, created the conditions for secularisation. These changes are set out below, including **structural differentiation, social differentiation, societalisation** and **schisms.**

Structural differentiation in **modern Western societies** (the modern period was from around 1850 to around 1980, reaching its height in the 1950s) led to the separation of social institutions such as the church, the family and education as they became more specialised in their role. Churches, as part of this process, became less central to social life and the role of the church therefore more narrowly focused on providing a belief system for individuals. At the same time, social differentiation occurred. In feudal times (roughly from the 9th century through to the 15th century), in mainly agricultural societies, all social groups lived closely to each other and saw themselves as inhabiting the same social world, which was very unequal. As the process of urbanisation began between approximately 1750 and 1850, with the development of cities and towns, different social classes emerged and became more distinct and separate. At this time, there was greater social mobility and people were less likely to feel that they belonged to one social world.

These changes coincided with a shift towards the greater emphasis on the individual, a process known as **individualism.** This shift reflected the fact that people felt less need for collective experiences and institutions such as the church. As individualism occurred, the processes which were once linked to societalisation (for example going to church) were less relevant and necessary. Bruce sees the final reason for secularisation as the schisms or splits that occurred in established religions along with the increasing number of different social and cultural groups in society. Furthermore, an increase in new forms of religious beliefs may have made established religious beliefs weaker.

So, while Bruce accepts that scientific, rational thinking is a partial cause of secularisation, he claims that wider social changes meant that religion became a much less significant part of people's lives in contemporary society. Bruce feels that the most significant reason for the decline in religion is that there are many alternative views of the universe for people to choose from today rather than religion with its one particular account of the absolute truth.

There are other contemporary sociologists who support the view that secularisation is occurring, including Wilson (1994), who claims that religion has lost its significance at a societal, institutional and personal, individual level. For Wilson, secularisation is about the fact that religion no longer has authority to define morals and rules about the way people live their lives. Like Bruce, Wilson agrees that secularisation is linked to the decline in community in contemporary society and he expresses concern about the lack of moral guidance for young people now that the church no longer has this responsibility. However, the American sociologists Stark and Bainbridge (1987) argue that, while the secularisation process is occurring among traditional religions, at the same time there is a continual regrowth of new forms of religion or a religious revival, so the secularisation process will never be fully complete.

### Activity

Think about the society you live in.

1. What has happened to the role of traditional religion(s): has it/have they declined in importance or grown? How might you measure this?
2. Have alternatives to traditional religion grown in recent years and, if so, why?

## Evaluation of views on the secularisation thesis

One major problem with the secularisation thesis is that it assumes that at some point in the past religion *was* significant to most people, a view which some claim is false or not supported by sufficient empirical evidence. This view of the past as a 'golden age of religion' is difficult to measure, because in the past a range of reliable or valid records about beliefs and practices did not exist. Many people may have participated in churchgoing simply to conform to social expectations of the time, rather than because they believed in their religion. Before the 19th century, a significant number of people were illiterate and therefore many records do not reflect a representative sample of religious views and practices. We do know, however, that in the first ever Census in 1851 in England and Wales, only 40 per cent of the population attended church, which challenges the idea that there ever was a 'golden age of religion' in these countries.

Furthermore, secularisation theorists tend to come from Western cultures and their views may not be shared by sociologists and thinkers from around the world. Western sociologists are in danger of assuming that their ideas about secularisation can be applied to places where religion may be much more significant today. Furthermore it can be difficult to find a common definition for all forms of religion, making it difficult to compare levels of religiosity.

There is much debate about the role that religion will take and how far secularisation will go. Some claim that secularisation will occur as a result of globalisation and Westernisation. Others, including Bruce (2011), see secularisation as mainly occurring in Western societies. Bruce goes on to argue that once a society becomes secular it can no longer become religious again, as it is an irreversible process. However, others, such as Gilles Kepel (1994), disagree, citing evidence of the regrowth of some forms of traditional religions among some groups in the West and beyond. For example, there has been a significant growth in some traditional forms of religion such as Hinduism. This resurgence of religion may be due to a number of factors, including concerns over the loss of spirituality, the need for religion as a source of comfort or the fact that there is more immigration, and migrant populations tend to be more religious than non-migrants. There is a range of examples of new forms of religion which suggests we are now witnessing a revival of religious beliefs. This is known as **resacralisation**, the process of people reaffirming their beliefs in the sacred.

## Contemporary issues: Christian denominations in Cuba

*San Cristobal Catholic Cathedral in Havana, Cuba, where religion is flourishing.*

In Cuba, as socialist ideas fade, enforced atheism is also in decline, which has resulted in Christian denominations flourishing. National holidays such as Good Friday and Christmas have been reinstated and churchgoers no longer face discrimination. In particular, evangelical Christianity has been popular among migrants who arrive in Havana and find community through the church. There are some who say that, under socialism, young people in particular became more likely to be interested in buying material objects and having sex outside marriage. One evangelical pastor says, 'We are living in a society which has lost its values, Christ gives them back.'

### Questions

1. Suggest two reasons why religion has grown in Cuba in recent years.
2. Explain how this example might provide evidence of a resurgence in religion.

### Key terms

**Globalisation** Involves all parts of the world becoming increasingly interconnected, so that national boundaries – in some respects, at least – become less important.

**The secularisation thesis** The theory or hypothesis that religion is having less influence on people's lives.

**Structural differentiation** The process by which institutions become separated and specialised.

**Social differentiation** There are many different groups in society, such as age, gender and class.

**Societalisation** The process by which close-knit local communities lose power to larger towns and cities or bureaucratic states.

**Schisms** Splits in religious organisations to form separate groups.

**Modern Western society** The period approximately between 1850 and 1980s when many societies became industrialised and when structural differentiation occurred.

**Individualism** The process whereby individuals focused more on their own personal ideas and thoughts than on conforming to social expectations.

**Resacralisation** The process by which interest in and belief in the sacred is revived.

## Summary

1. There are a number of definitions of the concept of secularisation, which depend on how religion itself is defined.
2. Most classic early sociologists believed that the development of science and modern societies would lead to religion becoming less important.
3. Weber argued that rationalisation would erode the influence of religion. Bruce provides a contemporary theory of secularisation, which links it to the development of modernity and changes in the characteristics of social life that accompany it.
4. There are problems with the secularisation thesis, as it relies on the idea that there was in fact a time when people were a lot more religious, with little evidence to support the view that this is true. Also, secularisation theorists do not agree on the extent to which the process will occur.
5. There is also evidence suggesting that there is a religious revitalisation, which may in part be a response to the process of secularisation itself.
6. This debate comprises largely of the views of White, Western sociologists, who may fail to take into account the role of religion in a contemporary global context.

# Unit 7.5.2 Evidence for and against secularisation

As we have seen in the previous unit, most claims that secularisation is occurring come from European or American sociologists and reflect the views of those societies. This unit explores a wide range of empirical evidence from around the world. The data are complex and vary between and within geographical areas. For example, in the data from the World Values Survey (2000), 98 per cent of the public in Indonesia said that religion was very important in their lives, while in China only 3 per cent considered religion very important.

However, there are counterclaims that religious identities and religious beliefs have not declined as much as is widely assumed, that traditional religions are not in decline and that new forms of spiritual beliefs are also growing. Remember that these issues relate to the key concept of identity. This unit examines these competing arguments and evidence in relation to patterns of religious **participation**, **membership, affiliation** (or belonging) and **disengagement**, drawing on a range of examples from around the world.

## Measuring secularisation

### Activity

*The Holi Festival in Nepal. This is a Hindu religious festival that marks the arrival of spring. It is a celebration of fertility, colour and love, as well as the triumph of good over evil.*

1. Why do you think that religious festivals such as the Holi Festival (above) are still important today?
2. Give one example of a religious festival that is considered important in your society.
3. Suggest one reason why such festivals may be losing significance today.

### Different measures of secularisation

In a major piece of research, the International Panel on Social Progress (2017) investigates changing religious beliefs at a global level. The research, led by Grace Davie et al., shows how different ways of measuring religiosity reveal strikingly different results.

## Activity

New Zealand

| Affiliation | Worship Attendance | Salience of Religion | Belief in God | Practice of Prayer |
|---|---|---|---|---|
| 57% 35% | 19% | 36% | 57% | 35% |
| self-identification red: Christian yellow: non-religious | % who attend more than once a week, once a week, once a month | % very important, rather important | % yes | % several times a day, once a day, several times a week |

Jordan

| Affiliation | Worship Attendance | Salience of Religion | Belief in God | Practice of Prayer |
|---|---|---|---|---|
| 97% 3% | 57% | 100% | 100% | 91% |
| self-identification green: Muslim red: Christian | % who attend more than once a week, once a week, once a month | % very important, rather important | % yes | % several times a day, once a day, several times a week |

Circles represent all survey respondents; all religions

Data sources: Todd M. Johnson, Brian J. Grim, & Gina A. Zurlo, eds.World Religion Database. Leiden/Boston: Brill, accessed April 2017; World Values Survey Wave 6: 2010–2014.

*Measuring religion quantitatively produces some very different results depending on the measure used.*

1. In your opinion, do you think New Zealand or Jordan is more religious, and why?
2. Explain what the two case studies above reveal about the differences in religiosity between New Zealand and Jordan.
3. Explain which measures included above are most significant, and why?
4. Identify three problems with measuring religion quantitatively.
5. Can you think of other questions that you might want to ask? What do the measures above not tell us about the beliefs people hold?

## Religious participation

On a global level, numbers of those who regularly participate in religious services varies widely. It is worth noting that participation is not necessarily the same thing as believing, and many people choose to participate in religion for a range of reasons other than religious belief. For example, people may choose to participate for social reasons; therefore, the data may be neither reliable nor valid. Equally, participation in regular services is different to participating in major life events such as weddings, christenings and funerals. Nonetheless, it is worth exploring levels of participation for comparative reasons. Data from the World Values Survey, which includes 60 nations, reveals the following interesting patterns of attendance of religious organisations:

**Table 7.5.1 Percentages of the population who attend religious services regularly**

| Country | Percentage (%) |
|---|---|
| Nigeria | 89 |
| Ireland | 84* |
| Philippines | 68 |
| Northern Ireland | 58* |
| Puerto Rico | 52 |
| South Africa | 56 |
| Poland | 55 |
| Portugal | 47* |
| Slovakia | 47 |
| Mexico | 46 |
| Italy | 45* |
| Dominican Republic | 44 |
| Belgium | 44* |
| USA | 44 |
| Turkey | 43 |
| Peru | 43 |
| India | 42 |
| Canada | 38* |
| Brazil | 36 |
| The Netherlands | 35* |
| Venezuela | 31 |
| Uruguay | 31 |
| Austria | 30* |
| Chile | 25 |
| Argentina | 25 |
| Britain | 27* |
| Spain | 25 |
| Slovenia | 22 |
| Croatia | 22 |
| Hungary | 21* |
| France | 21* |
| Romania | 20* |

**Table 7.5.1 (Continued)**

| Country | Percentage (%) |
|---|---|
| South Korea | 14 |
| Switzerland | 16 |
| Australia | 16 |
| Lithuania | 16 |
| West Germany | 14 |
| Czech Republic | 14* |
| Bulgaria | 10* |
| Ukraine | 10 |
| Taiwan | 11 |
| Moldova | 10 |
| Georgia | 10 |
| China | 9 |
| Armenia | 8 |
| Azerbaijan | 6 |
| Serbia | 7 |
| Montenegro | 7 |
| Belarus | 6 |
| Latvia | 5 |
| Denmark | 5* |
| Norway | 5 |
| East Germany | 5 |
| Sweden | 4 |
| Iceland | 4* |
| Finland | 4 |
| Estonia | 4 |
| Japan | 3 |
| Russia | 2 |

Source: based on latest available data from the 1990–91 or the 1995–97 World Values surveys. Results with an asterisk are from the 1990–91 survey; all others are from the 1995–97 survey. https://news.umich.edu/study-identifies-worldwide-rates-of-religiosity-church-attendance/

## Activity

1. Explain why you think Russia has the lowest attendance rates according to Table 7.5.1.
2. Give two reasons for the patterns in Table 7.5.1.
3. Explain why these statistics might not be a reliable measure of religiosity.
4. Explain why these variations in religiosity may make it difficult to tell whether secularisation is occurring.

### Church attendance declining in the USA and in the UK

It is worth noting, again, that there is a lack of reliable data on religious attendance for many parts of the world. Similarly, there is a lack of data on religious participation in the past.

Some of the strongest evidence for the theory of secularisation as applied to the UK, and to a lesser degree the USA, is based on church attendance statistics. It is important to note that the USA is more ethnically diverse than the UK. Although both countries have a majority of Christian-based religions, there has been an increase in alternative religions, partly as a result of high levels of immigration in recent years. The earliest available survey statistics on church attendance in the UK originate from the 1851 Census of Religion. This found just under 40 per cent of the adult population attended church. In England and Wales, the numbers had dropped to 35 per cent by 1901 and 20 per cent by 1950. Between 1980 and 2015, attendance fell from 11.1 per cent to 5.4 per cent (BRIN, 2018). Other types of participation in organised religion have also declined. In the UK, in the 1920s and 1930s, over 90 per cent of babies were baptised, but by 2001 this was down to 45 per cent (Brierley, 2005) and by 2009 it had reduced to just over 20 per cent (Brierley, 2011).

As Figure 7.5.1 shows, according to the available statistics, there has been a fall in attendance in most churches in the UK between 1980 and 2015. However, there has been a rise in attendance at New churches (a range of new forms of recently formed Christian denominations), Orthodox churches and Pentecostal churches, though not high enough to offset the falls in other institutions.

**Figure 7.5.1 English church attendance by denomination.**

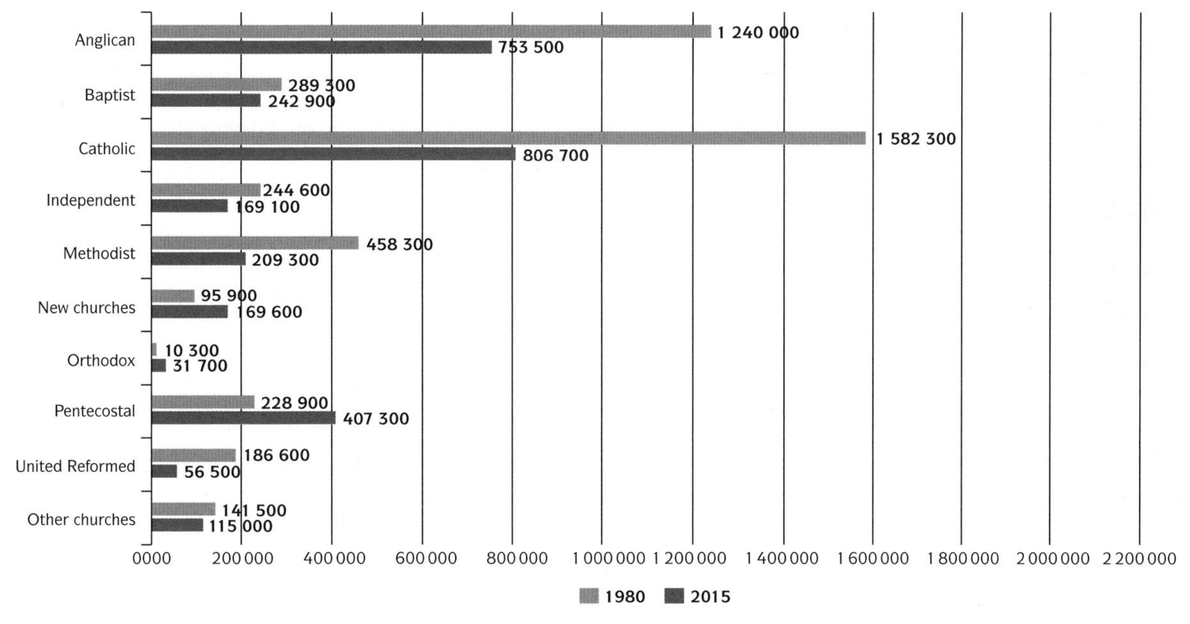


Source: English church attendance by denomination

## Activity

Does Figure 7.5.1 suggest that secularisation is taking place in England or instead that there has been a shift in the popularity of different denominations? Justify your answer.

In the USA, according to the Pew Research Center, the percentage of Americans who say they 'seldom' or 'never' attend religious services (aside from weddings and funerals) has risen slightly in the past 10 years. Twenty nine per cent of American adults in 2018 say they seldom or never attend worship services, up from 25 per cent in 2003. However, the proportion of people who say they attend services at least once a week has remained relatively steady: 37 per cent say they attend at least weekly today, compared with 39 in 2008. However, people *saying* they usually attend services is not necessarily a truthful or valid measure of religiosity, as people may exaggerate how often they actually do attend.

### Evidence that attendance is increasing

As seen in Figure 7.5.1, in the UK, there has been an increase in attendance at new denominations – for example, Pentecostal churches. However, this increase is not as significant as the number of those no longer attending the traditional churches. These growing denominations may well reflect increased immigration, as immigrants tend to be more religious than non-immigrants (see Unit 7.1.3). Elsewhere, there is evidence that attendance patterns are changing, for example in the USA. The pattern in the UK and the USA is that while there is a decline in traditional religions, there is a growth in new and non-Christian forms of religion.

## Membership of religious organisations

Religious membership numbers, although interesting, may be an unreliable source of information about religiosity because religious organisations have different requirements or criteria for religious membership, making it hard to compare religious organisations. Membership should not be confused with affiliation, which is discussed later in the section. The general pattern, however, is that the number of members of traditional churches in both the UK and the USA is declining.

## Evidence that religious membership in the UK is in decline

Table 7.5.2 shows the number of church members, and the number of denominations, in the UK in 2012 and 2017 (Brierley, 2017).

## Activity

**Table 7.5.2 UK church membership 2012–17**

| Religions | 2012 membership | 2017 membership | Percentage of change 2012–17 |
|---|---|---|---|
| Roman Catholic | 1 475 000 | 1 301 000 | –12% |
| Anglican | 1 424 000 | 1 167 000 | –18% |
| Presbyterian | 731 000 | 593 000 | –19% |
| Orthodox | 440 000 | 514 000 | 17% |
| Pentecostal | 359 000 | 400 000 | 11% |
| Methodist | 234 000 | 198 000 | –15% |
| Independent | 221 000 | 233 000 | 6% |
| Baptist | 191 000 | 180 000 | –6% |
| New churches | 186 000 | 210 000 | 13% |
| Smaller denominations | 177 000 | 193 000 | 9% |
| Fresh expressions | 41 000 | 96 000 | 135% |

Source: UK Church Statistics No.3, 2018 edited by Peter Brierley, http://brierleyconsultancy.com

1. Describe the main trends in church membership shown in Table 7.5.2.
2. Explain how far these trends support the secularisation theory.

### Evidence which suggests an increase in religious membership

While traditional Christianity is witnessing a decline in membership in the UK and other countries, other traditional religions, as well as non-traditional religions, are seeing an increase both in the UK and beyond.

**Demographic changes** This increase in religious membership is not necessarily due to increased interest in the religion. Some suggest that the patterns are a reflection of population changes in particular parts of the world. For example, membership of Islam is growing at a rapid rate globally. According to the Pew Research Center (2017), globally, babies born to Muslims will begin to outnumber Christian births by 2035. At the same time, people with no religion are predicted to sharply decrease in the number of children they have, based on current trends. By 2055 to 2060, it is predicted that just 9 per cent of all babies will be born to religiously unaffiliated women, while more than 70 per cent will be born to either Muslims (36 per cent) or Christians (35 per cent). This demographic evidence challenges the secularisation thesis, because it shows that it is population changes rather than beliefs which are at the heart of the changing patterns of religiosity globally.

Other religions that are growing as a result of an increasing birth rate include Hinduism, which is the fastest-growing religion in Pakistan and Saudi Arabia.

**A growth in membership of Christian denominations** In terms of new forms of religion, there has been a significant increase in denominations, particularly Christian denominations – for example, in places such as Nigeria, where rapid social change has led to people wishing to turn to a form of religion that they can relate to, that provides security and a sense of belonging in a time of uncertainty (see also Unit 7.2.1).

In sum, in 1900, there were fewer than 1 million Pentecostals/Charismatics in the world. In 2017, they increased to 669 million. By 2050, they will top 1 billion – the second Christian group to do so, behind Catholics.

## Contemporary issues: Christian denominations in Nigeria

*In Lagos, Nigeria, there has been a huge growth in Christian denominations.*

In Nigeria, there has been rapid social change and huge population growth. Christianity is on the rise, in various forms. For example, in Lagos, 'Redemption Camp' has been set up, with 5000 houses, roads, rubbish collection, police, supermarkets, banks, a funfair, a post office, even a 25 megawatt power plant. The church provides education and healthcare and a much reduced cost of living. In fact, the line between church and city is rapidly vanishing and it is the church, not the local authorities, that is organising the local community both practically and spiritually.

Source: https://www.theguardian.com/cities/2017/sep/11/eat-pray-live-lagos-nigeria-megachurches-redemption-camp

### Questions

1. Explain why new denominational forms of Christianity may appeal to people living in Nigeria.
2. Give one reason why this example challenges the secularisation thesis.

## Religious affiliation

Another way of measuring religiosity is to look at religious affiliation, that is, the number of people who identify themselves as belonging to a particular religion. While there may be a number of reasons why people claim affiliation, such as to conform to social norms, the measure is still interesting as it highlights those who may claim an affiliation but not attend religious services.

### A decline in religious affiliation

Generally, the decline in religious affiliation reflects the patterns in religious attendance, as seen in Table 7.5.2.

Table 7.5.3, based on affiliation in the UK, shows that, as well as a significant increase in the proportion of people saying they had no religion,

### Activity

**Table 7.5.3 Religious affiliation in the 2001 and 2011 UK Censuses (percentages)**

| | No religion | Christian | Muslim | Other | Not stated |
|---|---|---|---|---|---|
| 2001 | 14.8 | 71.7 | 3 | 2.8 | 7.7 |
| 2011 | 25.1 | 59.3 | 4.8 | 3.6 | 7.2 |

Source: ONS (2012) Religion in England and Wales, 2011.

1. Describe the trends in religious affiliation shown in Table 7.5.3.
2. Compare these trends with those in relation to participation and membership in Tables 7.5.1 and 7.5.2.

there has been a significant fall in the percentage of those claiming an affiliation with Christian religions and an increase in the percentage of those saying they were Muslim or affiliated with other religions.

It is also important to consider where the majority of people who are unaffiliated are located. According to the Pew Research Center (2017), as of 2015, three-quarters of unaffiliated people live in Asia and the Pacific. This may be due to the fact that China, which is home to a significant proportion of the global population, has been governed under communist ideology, which does not encourage or even allow religious beliefs.

### Evidence that there has been an increase in religious affiliation

Davie (2002) argues that, while there is evidence to suggest that affiliation to traditional Christianity is in decline in some parts of the world such as the UK, it is thriving in other areas, particularly in denominational forms. Also, there are parts of Europe where affiliation to Christianity continues to remain high, such as Poland and the Republic of Ireland.

## Religious disengagement

So far, we have explored measures of religiosity such as religious participation, membership and affiliation. However, some theorists argue that it is the changing role of religion in society which is also a key indicator of the significance of religion in society. From this point of view, individual beliefs are less important than the declining social significance of religion in shaping other aspects of society. Disengagement involves the withdrawal of the church from wider society as a result of its declining influence on other institutions, particularly politics and law; for example, there is less creation of laws based on religious ideas. This links to the key concept of socialisation: if religious disengagement is occurring, people are likely to receive a less religious upbringing and therefore less likely to develop a religious identity.

According to the Pew Research Center (2017), more than 20 per cent of countries have an official state religion, with the majority of these being Muslim states, and a further 20 per cent of countries identify a preferred or favoured religion. A small majority (53 per cent) of countries have no official or preferred religion, and 10 countries (5 per cent) are hostile to religion. Most of the 43 countries with state religions are in the Middle East and North Africa, with a cluster in northern Europe. Islam is the official religion in 27 countries in Asia and sub-Saharan Africa as well as North Africa and the Middle East. Thirteen countries – including nine in Europe – are officially Christian, two (Bhutan and Cambodia) have Buddhism as their state religion, and one (Israel) is officially a Jewish state. No country has Hinduism as its state religion. In some cases, the state religion is simply limited to playing a part in state ceremonies, but in other cases the role of religion is significant in shaping ideology and policies. In addition, countries with established religious affiliations tend to strictly regulate religious practice, including placing restrictions or bans on minority religious groups.

### Evidence that religious disengagement is occurring

Martin (1969) argues that in the UK today, compared with the Middle Ages (the 13th to 15th centuries), the power, wealth and prestige of the established church in Britain has declined dramatically. During the Middle Ages, the church carried authority and in many ways took the role that the state or the government takes today. Bruce (1995) agrees that the Church of England has lost power, as it has become more distant from the British state.

### Evidence that religious disengagement is not occurring

In the USA, religion appears to retain an important role in society, with little evidence of religious disengagement. Christians with strong religious beliefs are active in politics, particularly the so-called New Christian Right (Johnstone, 2007). The New Christian Right emerged in the 1970s and encouraged Americans to vote for politicians who supported their policies. They consist of the conservative and fundamentalist Christians who believe that what they see as a moral decline in American society should be opposed and that some aspects of the Bible should be taken literally. Casanova (1994) supports the view that disengagement is not happening everywhere. He believes that recent history shows that, while there has been some decline in religious beliefs and practices in parts of Europe, this has not been the case in other parts of the world. Furthermore, Casanova argues that religion is becoming stronger not weaker; 'public religions' are becoming more important in many countries as a global force.

Patterns of religious disengagement are complex. While there is some evidence to suggest that states express a desire to be secular, this is often accompanied by a public discourse which places religion at the heart of social and political debate.

## Activity

*Sitting down for prayers at school in Pakistan.*

1. In Pakistan and some other countries, education is often heavily influenced by religion. Can you think of examples of how religion has shaped your education?
2. How might this image challenge the idea that disengagement is occurring in Pakistan?

## Is the growth in new religious movements evidence of secularisation?

There are two key patterns over the past few decades: the decline in traditional dominant established religions and the growth of new religious movements. This could suggest that religion is becoming less important in people's lives, supporting the secularisation thesis, or alternatively it could be seen as evidence that in fact people continue to be religious simply through different forms of religion which they feel may be more relevant in contemporary society. Furthermore, the growth of new religious movements might be seen as a revival in religion. This perspective would appear to challenge the secularisation thesis.

## Contemporary issues: Between the religious and the secular – fuzzy fidelity

Over recent years, sociologists have begun to pay increasing attention to the large number of people who are neither atheists nor fully fledged followers of a religion. Although there is considerable evidence of quite rapid decline in religious participation and strong religious belief in the UK and some other parts of Europe, the number of self-proclaimed atheists has gone up much more slowly. Voas (2009) was the first to highlight this issue and he identified those with only vague connections to religion as having **fuzzy fidelity**. They come from a Christian background, but their faith is vague, generalised and weak. This group has come to be referred to as the 'fuzzies' and they might, for example, support a religion because it represents their national identity or because they like aspects of religious tradition (for example, carol services). Alternatively, they might have given up on Christianity altogether, but find New Age beliefs appealing.

A very different view is taken by Heelas (2015). Basing his arguments largely on Britain, he claims that there is little evidence to suggest that most people will end up as atheists with no spiritual beliefs at all. A survey in 2013, (Theos, 2013, cited in Heelas, 2015) found that just 13 per cent of Britons agreed that 'humans are purely material beings with no spiritual element'.

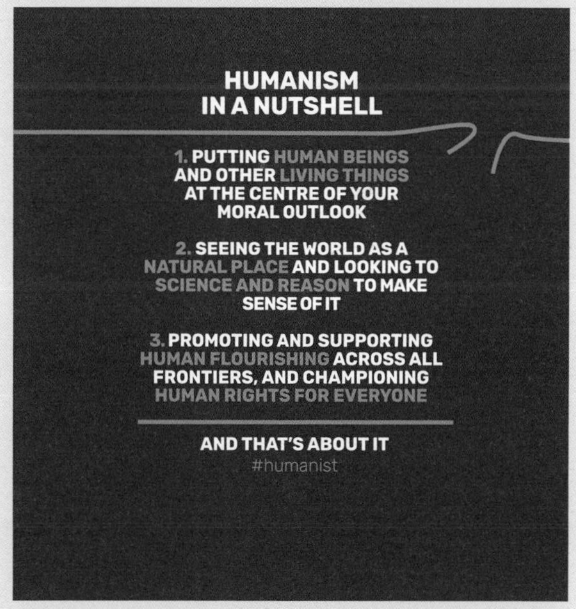


*A poster from Humanists UK, a campaigning and community-services-based charity which supports non-religious people to shape their own lives and have their voices heard.*

### Questions

With some reference to the image, discuss whether humanism is more likely to produce widespread atheism or increased spirituality.

## Does the emergence of New Age movements lead to secularisation?

It is debatable for some sociologists whether New Age movements can be seen as constituting a religion, while for others they can be seen as having a basis in spiritual and non-rational beliefs. As such, they represent a challenge to at least some theories of secularisation.

Bruce (2011) argues that the New Age has only a small number of followers who take it seriously and regard it as spiritual. Bruce believes that, by its very nature, the New Age has less effect on society than more conventional religious beliefs because the beliefs advocated by the New Age are **diffuse** (Bruce, 2002) meaning that people can believe whatever they choose and need not follow a single set of teachings. Bruce (1996) claims that the New Age is simply an extreme form of the individualism that is characteristic of modern societies.

### Arguments that New Age movements do not cause secularisation

It could be argued that Bruce underestimates the significance of the effects he identifies. If substantial numbers of people are willing to question scientific orthodoxy and place some trust in beliefs that require a degree of faith, this could be taken as evidence against the secularisation theory. Paul Heelas (1996) certainly regards the New Age as rather more significant than Bruce does. He quotes a 1993 Gallup opinion poll which found that in Britain 26 per cent of people believed in reincarnation, 40 per cent in some sort of spirit, 17 per cent in flying saucers and 21 per cent in horoscopes; while a 1989 Gallup poll found that no less than 72 per cent had 'an awareness of a sacred presence in nature'.

## The problems of measuring religiosity

There are a number of challenges to operationalising the concept of religion, as this discussion alone has shown. For example, individuals may belong without

### Contemporary issues: The Kendal project

Some indication of the vitality of the New Age is provided by a study conducted by Heelas, Woodhead and colleagues in the town of Kendal in Cumbria, in northern England (Kendal Project, 2001a, 2001b; Heelas et al., 2005). The study attempted to find every religious group, and groups with a spiritual dimension, in Kendal and within a five-mile radius.

The researchers identified 25 different churches, and on 26 November 2000 a total of 2207 people attended these churches. They also found 62 groups with a spiritual dimension, including yoga groups, healing groups, Tai Chi classes and Buddhist groups, all of which used a language of spiritual growth. They also found 90 people who practised alternative therapies, of whom 63 said their practice had a spiritual dimension. From their research, they were able to estimate that around 730 people were involved in spiritually inclined but non-Christian activities in a single week. This compared to 674 who worshipped in Anglican churches in a typical week.

These findings led Heelas et al. to suggest that both secularisation and **sacralisation** were occurring at the same time. These changes were seen as part of a **spiritual revolution** in which the nature of spirituality was changing.

Secularisation was defined as a decline in traditional theistic religions (based on a strong belief in God). The decline was evident in the falling numbers involved in the **congregational domain**, where members of congregations meet together to pray in places of worship.

On the other hand, sacralisation (an increased emphasis on the sacred) was taking place in the **holistic milieu**. The holistic milieu involves support for 'body–mind spirituality' and is evident in New Age beliefs and the beliefs of some religions. It exists in groups, therapy sessions, individual encounters and in shops selling products with spiritual connotations.

According to the Kendal Project, then, secularisation in the UK is only taking place in the narrow sense of a decline in traditional religion. From a broader perspective, beliefs are shifting away from traditional religion towards more individualist, spiritually inclined beliefs.

*The parish Church in Kendal, Cumbria.*

## Questions

1. Explain why a decline in attendance at this and other churches in Kendal does not necessarily show that secularisation is taking place.
2. How convincing do you find the arguments of Heelas et al. that sacralisation is occurring in Kendal with the growth of New Age spirituality?

believing and vice versa. Similarly, there may be issues with people claiming that they are religious when they are not, due to pressures to conform, for example. Alternatively, people may feel too embarrassed or shy to disclose their personal religious beliefs. There are also different levels of participation; for some, participation means attending key ceremonies such as weddings, while for others participation means regular attendance at religious services. Measuring the influence of religion from a range of different institutions is also subjective and can be interpreted in a number of different ways. There are multiple problems of comparing data across different geographical areas because interpretation of measures can vary significantly.

## Conclusions on the secularisation debate

Most of the long-term evidence on participation and membership in the UK and (to a lesser extent) the USA seems to support the secularisation theory, at least in terms of traditional religion. Although recent years have seen a growth in smaller, newer religious organisations, compared to the 19th century and early decades of the 20th there is little doubt that fewer people attend a place of worship or belong to a religious organisation. On the other hand, globally, non-Christian religions are growing and Islam is predicted to outgrow Christianity, so care needs be taken in making assertions about the secularisation process worldwide across all forms of religion. Affiliation patterns seem to reveal similarly complex patterns. Davie (2007) accepts that 'Secularisation is a multi-dimensional concept', meaning that there are a number of (sometimes conflicting) different parts of the process, and these frequently operate independently of each other.

Most theorists who either support or attack the theory of secularisation are now willing to admit that the theory cannot be unproblematically applied to all groups in all societies. It can, therefore, be argued that the national, regional, ethnic and social class differences in the role of religion make it necessary to relate theories to specific countries and social groups.

## Key terms

**Participation** The various ways in which people are involved with a religion – for example, attending services.

**Membership** The way some participants of religion have joined their church.

**Affiliation** A sense of belonging to a religious organisation.

**Disengagement** The withdrawal of churches from wider society because of their declining influence on other institutions, particularly politics and the legal system.

**Fuzzy fidelity** A vague belief that there may be some sort of religious or spiritual force without any adherence to specific religious belief.

**Diffuse** Spread across a wide area or among a range of people.

**Spiritual revolution** Radical change in the nature of spirituality, moving from the congregational domain to the holistic milieu.

**Congregational domain** The site of conventional religious organisations where congregations meet together to pray in a consecrated place of religious worship.

**Sacralisation** The process of becoming sacred.

**Holistic milieu** The varied settings in which New Age spirituality is promoted and practised, including groups and therapy sessions.

## Summary

1. Statistical evidence suggests that church attendance and other types of participation in organised traditional Christian religions (such as church weddings) has fallen considerably in Britain and the USA.
2. Some churches, such as Pentecostal churches, have seen an increase in attendance.
3. Islam is growing, but mainly due to demographic reasons such as a higher fertility rate and a younger population.
4. Membership of most types of religious organisation in the UK has fallen, although there have been increases in membership of some non-Christian religions and in some sects and denominations.
5. Global figures suggest that 80 per cent of the population affiliate themselves with a religion, although the numbers are declining in terms of traditional Christian churches.
6. Disengagement involves the declining influence of the church on other institutions. There is evidence that in the UK the church has less influence over politics and the law than in the past.
7. There are problems in interpreting all figures on religious participation, membership and affiliation.
8. There is some evidence of a move away from traditional religious belief towards spiritual beliefs, although the extent and significance of this change is disputed.
9. Religious pluralism can be seen as evidence for and against secularisation.
10. Bruce claims that the growth of New Age movements is evidence of secularisation, while Heelas disagrees and argues that they are a sign of a revival of religion.

# END-OF-PART QUESTIONS

**0 1** Describe two problems with measuring religiosity. **[4 marks]**

**0 2** Explain two ways in which the growth of New Age movements supports the idea that secularisation is occurring. **[6 marks]**

**0 3** 'The emergence of new religious movements means that there has been a religious revival.' Using sociological material, give one argument against this view. **[6 marks]**

# PART 6 RELIGION AND POSTMODERNITY

## Contents

**Unit 7.6.1** **New forms of religion: new religious movements and New Age movements** 455

**Unit 7.6.2** **Religion in postmodern global society: privatised belief and fundamentalism** 457

In this part, the role of religion in contemporary society is explored from a range of postmodern perspectives. Postmodernists explore the increasing flow of ideas about beliefs that are possible through greater interconnectedness globally. This has meant that not just religious ideas are spreading, but also rational scientific secular ideas. Unit 7.6.1 explores why the growth of new religious movements and New Age movements helps us understand the role of religion in people's lives around the globe today. Unit 7.6.2 looks at the main characteristics of religion in postmodern society, as well as exploring how the rise of fundamentalism can be explained from this perspective.

# Unit 7.6.1 New forms of religion: new religious movements and New Age movements

As discussed earlier in the chapter, new religious movements, New Age movements, sects and cults have grown at certain periods of history (see Unit 7.1.1). This unit explores why the growth of particular new religious movements and New Age movements help us understand the role of religion in people's lives around the globe today.

## Reasons for the growth of sects and cults

Religious sects and cults are not a new phenomenon; they have existed for centuries. Bruce (1995) traced the emergence of the first sects to the reformation of the Christian church in the 16th century in Europe. Despite this, most existing sects and cults originated in the 20th century, particularly in the 1960s and 1970s. The growth of sects and cults can be explained either in terms of why people choose to join them or by looking at changes in wider society. In reality, these two approaches are closely linked.

### Marginality

Weber (1963, first published in 1922) provided one of the earliest explanations for the growth of sects. He argued that they were likely to arise within **marginal groups** in society: members of groups outside the mainstream of social life, who often feel that they are not receiving the prestige and/or economic rewards they deserve. Marginalisation relates to the key concepts, as it represents the idea that some groups in society lack power and control, and see religion as a form of resistance. One solution to this problem is to join a sect based on what Weber called a '**theodicy of disprivilege**' (a theodicy is a religious explanation or justification; disprivilege is a lack of material success and social status). This enables people to explain their position in society and to find a way to improve it.

Wilson (1970) pointed out that a variety of situations could lead to the marginalisation of groups in society and provide fertile ground for the development of sects. These situations include defeat in war, natural disasters or economic collapse. In part, the growth of sects in the USA in the 1960s was accomplished through the recruitment of marginal and disadvantaged groups. The Nation of Islam, for example, aimed to recruit poor and marginalised African Americans, such as those serving a prison sentence. However, for the most part, in the 1960s and 1970s the membership of the world-rejecting new religious movements was drawn from among the ranks of young, White middle-class Americans and Europeans. Wallis (1984) argued that, despite this background, most were marginal because they were likely to be involved in alternative lifestyles such as those relating to hippy subcultures, drug use or surfing.

### Relative deprivation

The concept of '**relative deprivation**' refers to subjectively perceived deprivation – the feeling of having less than others. Certain members of the middle class, for example, may feel spiritually deprived rather than materially deprived in a world they see as too materialistic, lonely and impersonal. According to Wallis, this means that they therefore seek salvation in the sense of community offered by the sect; it becomes an opportunity.

Stark and Bainbridge (1985) also employed the concept of relative deprivation in explaining the origins of sects. They define sects as organisations that break away from an established church, and they believe it is the relatively deprived who are likely to break away. McGuire (2002) argues that the relative deprivation does not directly cause the growth of sects, but it can produce conditions which make growth more likely.

### Social change

Wilson (1970) argued that sects arise during rapid periods of social change when traditional norms are disrupted and social relationships come to lack consistent and coherent meaning. He gave the example of the rise of Methodism in the working-class communities during the early years of the industrial revolution in Britain. Methodism provided the support of a close-knit community organisation, well-defined and strongly sanctioned norms and values, and a promise of salvation. Similarly, Bruce (1995, 1996, 2011) attributes the development of a range of religious institutions, including cults and sects, to a general process of modernisation and secularisation.

## Reasons for the growth of new religious movements

The growth of new religious movements is a global phenomenon, evidenced through membership and affiliation, although patterns are variable. Wallis (1984) pointed to a number of social changes that he believed accounted for the growth of new religious movements in the 1960s, some of which particularly relate to young people. First, Wallis stated that the growth of higher education extended the transition between childhood and adulthood, giving young people the time to explore different ideas and lifestyles free from work and family responsibilities. Second, the young felt that new technology would lead to the end of economic scarcity, giving the economic freedom to try out new ways of living. Third, radical political movements in the 1960s encouraged the exploration of alternative lifestyles. These reasons coincide with the large-scale social change which led many individuals to turn to new religious movements for individual reasons, such as searching for identity, belonging and security.

## Reasons for the growth of New Age movements

John Drane (1999) argues that the appeal of New Age movements is connected to the failure of new religious movements to deliver personal satisfaction. Drane, along with postmodernist sociologists, claims that Western societies are turning against modern institutions and belief systems. They claim that people have lost faith in these due to the problems experienced in the modern era, such as the world wars and environmental destruction – for example, the depletion of the ozone layer. There is also considerable scepticism about science, such as the way that some drug companies have placed pursuit of profit over a desire to improve health and cure illnesses. Similarly, the church is treated with distrust due to its failure to keep in touch with people's need for spirituality and because it has been associated with corruption and abuse cases. This has led to people turning to New Age movements as an alternative, postmodern form of spirituality. However, many New Age movements are based on adapted versions of existing religions. For example, yoga is connected to Hinduism, Jainism and Buddhism, but can be practised today in a secular or spiritual way.

On the surface, New Age movements appear to contradict the view of sociologists such as Weber that the modern world is becoming increasingly rational. However, if Heelas and Bruce are correct, then the rationality of modernity also brought with it individualism, which led to the growth of non-rational beliefs.

### Activity

*Yoga is a relatively new practice in some parts of the world.*

Give two reasons why New Age movements particularly appeal to middle-class women in Western societies.

### Key terms

**Marginal groups** Members of groups outside the mainstream of social life, who often feel that they are not receiving the prestige and/or economic rewards they deserve.

**Theodicy of disprivilege** Weber's concept for a set of ideas which explain inequalities using religious beliefs. A theodicy is a religious explanation or justification; disprivilege is a lack of material success and social status.

**Relative deprivation** This refers to subjectively perceived deprivation – the feeling of having less than others.

### Summary

1. There are several reasons for the growth of sects, cults and new religious movements, including marginality, relative deprivation and social change.
2. Drane saw the New Age as a product of postmodernity and the rejection of modern belief systems.

# Unit 7.6.2 Religion in postmodern global society: privatised belief and fundamentalism

Postmodern thinkers claim that patterns in religiosity very much reflect the postmodern era in which we now live, with its emphasis on greater choice and individualism. Postmodern society is also characterised by a greater focus on consumerism and the commodification of religion, made possible partly through the increasing role of the internet, mass media and new forms of social media. This unit explores the main characteristics of religion in postmodern society, as well as exploring how the rise of fundamentalism can be explained from this perspective.

## Arguments for an increase in privatised religion – believing without belonging?

Some sociologists claim that religion today may be expressed in different ways. Religion for these thinkers has become increasingly privatised; people develop their own beliefs and relationship with God and see religious institutions as being less important. Davie (1994, 2007) coined the phrase 'believing without belonging' to describe this situation. If religion is increasingly seen as a choice open to an individual, rather than an obligation imposed by society, then people may increasingly hold religious beliefs in private without feeling the need to demonstrate them in public. Similarly, there are a wide range of new forms of **privatised religion** which are much harder to measure, as they take place in the private sphere of the home – for example, online.

### Lyotard – The rejection of meta-narratives

The postmodernist Lyotard (1979) argued that postmodernity involves growing 'incredulity towards meta-narratives' or a lack of faith in any big stories about society and human progress (see Unit 7.1.2). Both religion and scientific rational thought can be seen as types of meta-narratives that individuals are choosing to reject. From a postmodernist perspective, people no longer feel that they need to accept and adopt any single set of beliefs; rather, they wish to find their own individual truth. Technological advances have also lead to a plethora of new ways in which religious ideas can be accessed, meaning that individuals can participate in religion in different ways, such as viewing religious events online or through social media – for example, the emergence of televangelism, where people at home can participate in religious services remotely. These technologically based new forms of religious participation may be challenging to measure.

### Lyon – relocation of religion and re-enchantment of the world

These ideas have been developed by the postmodernist David Lyon (2000). According to Lyon, Western societies are becoming increasingly consumerist, which is, in turn, influencing religious ideas and practices. As consumers, people do not wish to be told which religion to believe in; they want to make up their own minds. According to Lyon, religion is not therefore declining, it is simply relocating to the sphere of consumption. Religion has moved out of the traditional institutions such as education and the law and instead become more commercial so that people can consume and celebrate religion in a number of ways. For example, in the USA, Christian values such as the importance of marriage are celebrated through Disney film characters in the theme parks known as Disneyland. Religion has become part of popular culture, through the media, social commentary or through the messages espoused by companies, and therefore Lyon does not believe that a decline in church attendance indicates that secularisation has occurred. Rather, there are alternative ways to participate in religion. He claims that over the past three to four decades there has been a **re-enchantment,** meaning that, although traditional religions may be in decline, alternative forms of religion and ways of practising religions have developed in the West and elsewhere.

## Activity

*Televangelism is becoming a popular way for people to participate in religion. It involves watching religious services on television or online.*

1. Evaluate the view that televangelism is evidence of a process of re-enchantment.
2. Explain how televangelism supports the idea of belief without belonging.

### Hervieu-Léger – spiritual shopping

Danièle Hervieu-Léger supports postmodern views of religion in Western societies; she also agrees with Davie in claiming that religion has become less public and more private. Hervieu-Léger argues that religion was traditionally part of a **chain of memory** (Hervieu-Léger, 2000) – something that is passed down from generation to generation which, as Durkheim argued, helps to integrate society. Rather than God being experienced in a direct and personal way, churches have acted as intermediaries and religion has been learned more than directly experienced. However, in many European countries, this chain of memory has, to some extent, been broken. Secularisation has weakened the hold of the traditional churches so that collective memories about religion are no longer passed down from parents to children with the force that they once were.

As a result of this, individuals have been left to choose (or to reject) their own religious path. This has resulted in individuals engaging in **spiritual individualism** (Hervieu-Léger, 2006) in which people shop around for the religion that suits them best, a process also called **spiritual shopping**. This suggests a shift towards people becoming consumers of religion in which they expect to gain something from their religious participation, usually self-improvement or fulfilment. They may try to experience a variety of religions and spiritual beliefs to see which they prefer.

Hervieu-Léger does not believe that the influence of Christian churches will disappear. Some individuals will choose them as a 'personal option'. Furthermore, many people will be nostalgic for church services and keen to maintain the fabric of beautiful church buildings. Churches, however, will become less and less important as a source of collective identity, individual beliefs and moral values.

### Evaluation of postmodernist views

As discussed earlier, patterns of religiosity are complex and there is evidence which suggests that some traditional religions such as Islam are in fact growing rather than new forms of religion beginning to overtake old forms. Furthermore, the postmodern thinkers explored above tend to reflect on Western religious practices, which are not necessarily representative of global patterns. They also ignore structural factors which affect the way that people engage with religion – for example, the fact that religion provides a source of comfort for structurally marginalised groups with fewer opportunities. Therefore, this approach may not offer a complete explanation of religion in contemporary global society.

## Religious fundamentalism as a characteristic of postmodern society

Despite the problems with postmodernist views, one reason why postmodernism may be useful for understanding the role of religion in society today is that it helps to explain the emerging forms of religion in contemporary society. While the secularisation thesis suggests a progressive decline in religion, previous sections have indicated that there are, in fact, many parts of the world where religion appears to be thriving or reviving. In a number of contexts, the term 'fundamentalism' has been used to describe the nature of religion today, particularly where it is undergoing an enthusiastic revival in strongly held beliefs.

In a major comparative study of *Strong Religion* (or fundamentalism), Gabriel Almond, R. Scott Appleby and Emmanuel Sivan (2003) identified fundamentalist movements among Jews in Israel; Muslims in Pakistan, Palestine, Egypt and the Russian regions of Dagestan and Chechnya; Sikhs and Hindus in India; Christians in the USA and Ireland; and Buddhists in Sri Lanka. Islamic fundamentalism has perhaps been subject to more attention than other forms, particularly after the Islamic fundamentalist group al-Qaeda's 9/11 attacks in the USA and the rise and fall of Islamic State in Syria and bordering countries. However, fundamentalism is by no means confined to Islam. Furthermore, most Islamic people (like most Christians, Hindus and the followers of other religions) are not fundamentalists.

### What is fundamentalism?

According to Bruce (2000), the term 'fundamentalism' was first used in the 1920s, when conservative evangelical Protestants published a series of pamphlets in which they called for a return to 'The Fundamentals of the Faith'. These Protestants were 'anti-modernist' in that they objected to the way in which, as they saw it, their religion was becoming diluted in the modern world. Almond et al. (2003) defined fundamentalism as 'a discernible pattern of religious militance by which self-styled "true believers" attempt to arrest the erosion of religious identity, fortify the borders of the religious community, and create viable alternatives to secular institutions and behaviours' (Almond et al., 2003).

### How can we explain the growth of fundamentalism?

Fundamentalism itself is not new; examples of such religious beliefs can be found throughout the history of religion. However, there has been a recent growth in the number of fundamentalist movements. There are a number of explanations for the growth of fundamentalist groups, which are in many ways a response to the forces of globalisation and rapid social change. Globalisation, the process whereby the world is becoming increasingly interconnected, has been happening over a long period of time. However, over the past 40 years globalisation has rapidly increased as a result of technological and communicative advances. The effects of recent globalisation have included the spread of **liberal Western values** (including tolerance to same-sex relationships, sex outside marriage, equality between the genders) and increased migration. These changes have been interpreted in different societies and social groups in a number of ways.

**Cultural defence** As discussed in earlier sections, Bruce (2002) regards one role of religion today as allowing people to protect and maintain their cultural or ethnic identity. They generally do this as they perceive their ideas, practices and beliefs to be under threat as a result of rapid social changes and the spread of liberal values. An assertion of traditional or fundamentalist values is a rejection of liberal values. Cultural defence can also be a response to discrimination – for example, Islamophobia. People may respond to such discrimination through the strengthening of their religious beliefs as a way of seeking comfort from a world that is otherwise hostile. Remember that this relates to the key concepts; for some, fundamentalism provides a form of resistance to social change.

**Cultural transition** Another feature of a global contemporary society is that there is far greater migration. As Bruce points out, religion plays an important social function in helping groups settle and create networks in new locations. This is especially true when moving into an area as a religious or ethnic minority. It may be the case that people who were less religious in their previous location become more religious in their new context, as a means of coping with all of the changes.

**Religious disengagement** As seen earlier (see Unit 7.5.2), where states become more separate from the influence of religious ideas, they may become more liberal in their ideology. In fact, religious disengagement within the state can actually lead to a resurgence in religion, including fundamentalist religion. This idea relates to the argument that, today, religion has not become more privatised; rather, it remains firmly part of public and political discourse. We have seen how in the USA Christian fundamentalist groups have had huge political presence, for example, culminating in the election of President Trump in 2016.

**Marginality** Individuals who find themselves at the edge of society – for example, those who experience discrimination, racism and material deprivation – may well be attracted to the security and strong sense of identity that fundamentalist groups provide. Also, individuals who feel left behind by the forces of globalisation and are affected adversely by rapid social change are also likely to feel more attracted to fundamentalist groups.

## Religious revival

Much of this section has explored how secularisation probably reached its height in the 1970s and, since then, how religious ideas have undergone a process of renewal or revitalisation. Fundamentalism is one such expression of this **religious revival**. Although we have seen the development of rational modernity, people still feel very much in need of religion as a compensator, and for some, this comes in the form of fundamentalism. Postmodernists claim that this means people are looking for alternative, new forms of religion which reflect the values and wishes of this era.

### Bruce – fundamentalism as a reaction to modernisation

Bruce (2000) sees fundamentalism as a reaction to modernisation (as discussed earlier in Unit 7.1.3). Modernisation, which according to Bruce has been occurring throughout the past century, involves societalisation (in which social life becomes increasingly fragmented) and differentiation (in which religious life is separated from other aspects of social life such as the economy). Modernisation also involves rationalisation, in which social life is planned to achieve certain goals, not based upon faith or prayer. A further feature of modernity is a tendency towards **egalitarianism**, in which all members of society share certain rights. For example, it involves increasingly egalitarian gender roles as women gain full citizenship rights. According to Bruce, all of these processes challenge the authority of religion, and in some circumstances groups with strongly held religious beliefs will try to defend their religion against the perceived threats.

In Western countries such as the USA, modernisation has provided a local and immediate challenge to some aspects of traditional religious belief. Elsewhere – for example, in Islamic countries such as Iran and Turkey – the process of modernisation has produced a range of responses.

In both sets of circumstances, Bruce believes that 'the main cause of fundamentalism is the belief of religious traditionalists that the world around them has changed so as to threaten their ability to reproduce themselves and their tradition' (2000). He sees fundamentalism as a 'rational response of traditionally religious peoples to social, political and economic changes that downgrade and constrain the role of religion in the public world' (Bruce, 2000).

### Almond et al. (2003) – fundamentalism as a response to secularisation and modernisation

Almond et al. (2003) discussed the findings of a major comparative study of fundamentalist religions throughout the world. Their findings correspond with postmodernist explanations and observations. A total of 75 case studies were carried out by researchers over a 20-year period, and interviews were conducted in the Middle East, North Africa and the United States.

They follow Bruce in seeing fundamentalism as a reaction to the social changes associated with modernisation and secularisation. Without secularisation, there would be no need for a fundamentalist movement. Furthermore, the development of communications has contributed to globalisation, and with it the influence of Western secular rationalism has spread to non-Western countries. However, it has also provided opportunities for fundamentalists to organise and spread their message. Thus, the New Christian Right in the USA have made extensive use of the media, including starting their own TV stations. The internet has been important in spreading Islamic fundamentalism worldwide. It also allows the 'demonstration effect' or copycat behaviours such as suicide bombings.

## Key terms

**Privatised religion** Religion of significance to the individual but which has relatively little connection to religious institutions and little or no importance in wider society.

**Re-enchantment** The process by which people re-engage with spirituality.

**Chain of memory** The way that memories (including religious beliefs) are passed down from one generation to the next.

**Spiritual individualism** Religion in which individuals follow their own spiritual path rather than following the teachings of a particular religious leader or religious institution.

**Spiritual shopping** The idea that people relate to religion as consumers, and that they select and consume various forms of religion, sometimes multiple forms at the same time.

**Liberal Western values** A set of ideas which focus on individualism and choice as well as rights.

**Religious revival** The idea that spiritual and religious ideas and practices are going through a period of growth as people re-engage with the same or new forms of belief systems.

**Egalitarianism** The tendency towards becoming more equal.

## Summary

1. Postmodern thinkers claim that patterns in religiosity very much reflect the postmodern era in which we now live, which includes greater individualism.
2. Davie believes that there is a general trend towards 'believing without belonging'.
3. The postmodernist Lyotard claimed that, as people reject major meta-narratives, they turn to new forms of religion or spirituality.
4. The postmodernist Lyon (2000) argues that Western societies are becoming increasingly consumerist, which is in turn influencing religious ideas and practices.

5. According to the postmodernist Hervieu-Léger, in many European countries the chain of memory (collective religious memories) has been weakened and spiritual individualism and spiritual shopping are replacing traditional forms of religion.

6. Bruce and Almond et al. argued that the growth of a range of fundamentalism is a response to modernisation, secularisation, globalisation and the spread of liberal values.

# END-OF-PART QUESTIONS

| 0 | 1 | Describe two reasons for the growth of sects and cults. **[4 marks]**

| 0 | 2 | Explain two limitations of the postmodernist accounts of religion. **[6 marks]**

| 0 | 3 | 'The growth of fundamentalist religions is a response to rapid social change.' Using sociological material, give one argument for this view. **[6 marks]**

# EXAM-STYLE PRACTICE QUESTIONS

| 0 | 1 | 'The arguments against the secularisation thesis are stronger than the arguments for.' Evaluate this view. **[35 marks]**

| 0 | 2 | 'The extent to which religious organisations are patriarchal has been exaggerated.' Evaluate this view. **[35 marks]**

# 8 GLOBALISATION

## Chapter contents

| | | |
|---|---|---|
| **Section A** | **Key debates, concepts and perspectives** | **463** |
| **Section B** | **Contemporary issues** | **518** |
| **Exam-style practice questions** | | **581** |

This chapter explores the concept of 'globalisation'. However, this concept is not easy to define. Anthony Giddens (1996), for example, claims that 'there are few terms that we use so frequently but which are in fact as poorly conceptualized as globalization'. Similarly, Wayne Ellwood (2015) describes globalisation as the 'least understood (concept) of the new millennium'. Consequently, a number of competing theories of globalisation exist, some of which view globalisation very positively, while others claim that it is extremely harmful to societies. What is evident is that sociologists do not agree on which dimensions of globalisation – if it is indeed occurring – are the most significant elements of its impact on the world.

Section A explores the debate about whether globalisation is a beneficial or harmful phenomenon. In particular, sociological perspectives are examined to work out whether they view globalisation as a positive or negative form of change. We also examine the possible impact of globalisation on the formation of individual and large-scale identity. For example, have cultures and therefore the identities of those who are part of those cultures been overwhelmed by a homogenised global culture? Or have they been able to resist globalisation? Finally, has Westernisation been mistaken for globalisation? We also explore the impact of globalisation on power and politics. For example, what has been the impact of globalisation on the nation-state? Why have social movements opposing globalisation emerged in recent years? How can the nation-state tackle problems such as environmental degradation brought about by globalisation?

Section B explores contemporary issues associated with globalisation. We explore how life chances relating to education, income and health are distributed around the world and sociological explanations for global inequalities. For example, is global capitalism responsible for these inequalities or are they self-inflicted?

We also consider the causes and consequences of global migration. For example, do migrants choose to leave their societies of origin or are they pushed out by social factors beyond their control? How are they received by the societies in which they arrive? Do migrants experience the same job opportunities and rights as members of indigenous populations? Are indigenous workers 'happy' to welcome migrant workers?

Finally, we explore the contemporary issue of global crime. A range of global crimes is examined, ranging from overtly criminal acts committed by international human trafficking gangs and drug cartels to corporate and green crimes committed by 'respectable' transnational corporations. In particular, we look at who benefits from the globalisation of crime and issues relating to the difficulties of policing and prosecuting such crimes.

# SECTION A
# KEY DEBATES, CONCEPTS AND PERSPECTIVES

## Contents


| | | |
|---|---|---|
| **Part 1** | **Perspectives on globalisation** | **464** |
| **Part 2** | **Globalisation and identity** | **477** |
| **Part 3** | **Globalisation, power and politics** | **494** |


Section A focuses on key debates, concepts and perspectives on the process and impact of globalisation. Three of the key concepts that you were introduced to in the introductory chapter are relevant here.

First, think about *power, control and resistance*. One of the reasons why digital technology, one of the cornerstones of globalisation, expanded so rapidly in influence across the world is because ownership and control of digital communication systems became increasingly concentrated in the hands of fewer transnational corporations. Some critics of this concentration of ownership argue that it amounts to an unhealthy control of news and information, and that consequently ordinary people may be unable to gain an accurate and detailed knowledge of the world. These criticisms have led to calls for the state to get more involved in the regulation of digital technology in order to prevent these corporations abusing their power. However, some Marxists argue that digital technology has produced a networked global society and has transformed the relationship between the electorate and the powerful. They argue that digital technology has the potential to revitalise democracy because it gives a 'voice' to traditionally powerless groups such as those in poverty, women, the LGBT community and the anti-globalisation movement. It gives oppressed people the ability to facilitate social change.

Second, keep *social change and development* in mind. Some sociologists claim that human history can be reduced to four major social changes or stages of development: the agricultural revolution, the industrial revolution, the computer revolution and the digital revolution. Globalisation is often portrayed as the final stage of history of both modern Western society and of those societies situated in the developing world. In the eyes of many politicians, economists and sociologists, globalisation is responsible for a permanent deindustrialisation of the West and the shifting of significant economic and cultural power permanently eastward.

Third, consider *socialisation, culture and identity*. We examine how globalisation may have impacted in both positive and negative ways on identity. Some sociologists claim that globalisation has the potential to produce a global consciousness in which difference and inequality in all their forms are eradicated so that human beings will view themselves primarily as citizens of a one-world society. Some sociologists dismiss this scenario as too utopian and argue that at best we should hope that the process of globalisation can raise social and political consciousness – for example, so that citizens across the world can unite to oppose breaches of human rights. Other sociologists argue that these aspirations are too ambitious and that globalisation may only impact on people's ability to construct their personal identity by providing them with increased consumer choices.

Section A is divided into three parts. Part 1 explores what sociologists mean by 'globalisation' and considers its economic, political and cultural dimensions. It examines three broad sociological perspectives on this phenomenon: 'globalists', who view globalisation in a very positive light; 'sceptics', who consider globalisation to be extremely harmful to societies, and 'transformationalists', who argue that globalisation may eventually have the positive effect of reducing national differences and global inequalities.

The second part of this section is focused on globalisation and identity, specifically on whether global forces have affected people's sense of self. For example, has globalisation produced a global identity or consciousness? Or has it reinforced people's sense of national or religious identity as they seek to resist global forces? How have individuals and cultures adapted to globalisation? How might global forces themselves be shaped by local cultures?

The third part of this section focuses on globalisation, power and politics. In particular, it explores two important concepts, liberal democracy and human rights, and the ability of nation-states to defend these important principles in the context of globalisation. Moreover, it examines how the nation-state tackles problems such as environmental degradation brought about by globalisation.

# PART 1 PERSPECTIVES ON GLOBALISATION

## Contents


| | | |
|---|---|---|
| Unit 8.1.1 | Key definitions and issues | 464 |
| Unit 8.1.2 | The significance of different dimensions of globalisation | 467 |
| Unit 8.1.3 | Theories of globalisation | 472 |


In Part 1, we explore key definitions and issues surrounding globalisation, which is a contested concept that sociologists rarely agree upon. In particular, it is important to understand that there are three main ways in which globalisation has impacted on the world at large and on individual cultures and nation-states. First, sociologists are interested in the consequences of economic globalisation for the economies of the world. Second, some sociologists claim that political globalisation has occurred and that consequently the nation-state may be in decline. Third, sociologists are also interested in socio-cultural globalisation and how this is impacting on local cultures and identities. Underpinning all three dimensions of globalisation is the debate as to whether it is a positive or negative process. Some sociologists – the globalists – are very positive about globalisation, while others (particularly Marxists and feminists), are more cautious and sometimes very sceptical about its effects. Postmodernists, on the other hand, believe that globalisation has the potential to 'transform' the world for the 'better'.

# Unit 8.1.1 Key definitions and issues

Globalisation is a complex process and one that is difficult to define. In this unit we consider the challenges of defining globalisation, the processes that make up globalisation and how globalisation has developed in different ways since the prehistoric period.

## Defining globalisation

Manfred Steger (2017) notes that the concept of **globalisation** has been used in both the popular press and academic literature to describe 'a process, a condition, a system, a force and an age'. He argues that, as these competing labels have very different meanings, their indiscriminate usage is often obscure and invites confusion. Consequently, he argues that globalisation as both a concept and a theory of social change is highly contested. Moreover, there is an unfortunate tendency to reduce the complex concept of globalisation to the simplistic metaphor of an 'unstoppable juggernaut' which is determined on spreading Western capitalism and cultural values and 'flattening or eradicating local, regional and national cultures and traditions'.

Steger suggests that sociologists need to adopt a more nuanced approach to understand globalisation. This approach sees globalisation as incorporating three very distinct concepts:

1. **'Globality'** signifies a social condition characterised by tight economic, political, cultural and environmental interconnectedness and flows underpinned by technological innovation that have rendered most national borders and boundaries irrelevant. However, Steger does argue that we should not assume that full globality is already upon us. He also warns that it is not known what form full globality will eventually take or what its effects will be, despite the sociological debate as to whether globalisation is a good or bad thing.
2. **'Global imagining'** refers to people's growing consciousness of 'thickening globality'. Steger claims that people across the world still have a sense of 'home' and generally still subscribe to a sense of local or regional or tribal or ethnic or religious identity. However, Steger argues that national identity is increasingly diluted as globality thickens.
3. **'Glocalisation'** – as globality evolves, it produces a dynamic global–local nexus which changes the character of both the national and local. Steger uses the world's most popular sports event, the men's football (soccer) World Cup, to illustrate these concepts. He points out that this four-yearly event is a great example of globality and globalisation in that it is organised by a global organisation – FIFA – which represents every country with an official football association

that has agreed to follow the same global rules and regulations. The globality of the event can be illustrated by the fact that the location of the tournament has rotated across continents since it began in 1930. Moreover, the World Cup is a global television event – every game is shown live to a global TV audience. The World Cup also has global sponsorship in that global **conglomerates** such as Coca-Cola and McDonald's pay billions of dollars to advertise their brands in stadiums during matches and in the commercial half-time TV breaks. However, Steger points out that the World Cup has localised dimensions too, in that countries compete with each other to host the tournament. The way it is organised into groups followed by knock-out rounds also encourages local pride as national teams with low positions in FIFA's rankings – for example, Tunisia (ranked 21st in 2017) – battle highly ranked football nations, for example, Belgium (ranked third in 2017), to a draw or inflict a shock defeat on them. Steger, therefore, concludes that the men's football World Cup is very much both a global and glocalised event.

## Activity

*Football fans in Moscow's Red Square during the 2018 men's World Cup. Steger sees the World Cup as an example of both globality and glocalisation.*

Draw two columns; label the one on the left 'Example of globality', and the one on the right 'Example of the glocal'.

Research the World Cup. Choose one of these events – the 2014 men's World Cup in Brazil, the 2018 men's World Cup in Russia or the 2015 women's World Cup in Canada. Focus on finding information on the following and categorise them as either exclusively global in character or as an example of glocalisation, a combination of the local and global.

- The qualifying group stage
- Ticket applications from fans of the countries that have qualified
- Spectators banging drums, blowing vuvuzelas, trumpets and so on, or doing Mexican waves
- The television audience that watched the World Cup Final live
- Brazilian/Russian/Canadian spending on building new stadiums and security
- Long-term effect on tourism to Brazil, Russia or Canada
- The manufacture and import of replica kits and World Cup footballs
- The artists chosen to perform at the opening ceremony
- Winner of the Golden Ball for the best player in the tournament
- The World Cup Final and the crowning of the champions.

Steger, therefore, sees globalisation as a set of social processes that transform our present local social conditions and life experiences into one of globality. At the **micro-level** of individual experience, this means that distance is no longer an obstacle to interaction between people separated by geography or time-zones. Individuals can now interact and communicate instantaneously with others who sit at computers thousands of miles away in different time zones. David Harvey (1990) refers to this global transformation as **space–time compression**.

Martin Albrow (1987) claims that this has resulted in the incorporation of the very different and varied people and cultures of the world into a single globalised culture and society, or 'global village'. At its simplest, globalisation means that the planet we live on now feels smaller – remote places are now more accessible than they were in the past.

On a **macro-level**, globalisation can be defined as a process characterised by a growing engagement and communication between societies wherever they are located in the world and regardless of what language they speak.

Robin Cohen and Paul Kennedy (2000) suggest that globalisation refers to the increasing interconnectedness and interdependency of the world's nations and their people, which has resulted in a single global economic, political and cultural system. As Allan Cochrane and Kathy Pain (2000) note, 'the lives of ordinary people everywhere in the world seem increasingly shaped by events, decisions and actions that take place far away from where they live and work'. Societies that were once distant, independent and very different to one another are today increasingly globally intertwined and inter-dependent, whether they want to be or not. Moreover, the macro and micro are also interwoven in that the everyday local lives of ordinary people are increasingly shaped by events, decisions and actions that take place thousands of miles from where they live.

## The causes of globalisation

Cohen and Kennedy argue that globalisation needs to be understood as 'a set of mutually reinforcing transformations' of the world. In order to understand these 'transformations' and the causes of globalisation, it is important to examine six interrelated dimensions of globalisation:

- the historical
- the technological
- the economic
- the cultural
- the political
- the moral.

### The historical dimension of globalisation

Steger argues that globalisation is not a modern phenomenon but has actually been going on in a piecemeal fashion for the past 2000 years. In particular, culture, language, religion, and even disease, have spread throughout the world as a result of the following:

- population growth which encouraged both trade and migration
- the development of technology, especially in the fields of weaponry, ship-design and navigation
- the control of such technology gave some countries, especially in Europe from the 1490s on, the military power to set up global empires and to transport people over long distances as part of a global slave trade.

### The contemporary period – from the 1980s to the present day

Steger argues that, although globalisation has always existed, it picked up 'quantum' speed from the 1980s onwards to the extent that it has resulted in a 'great convergence' in which 'different and widely spaced people and social connections are coming together more rapidly than ever before'. The reasons why globalisation has accelerated since the 1980s – particularly the development of digital technology – will be discussed in more detail in the rest of this chapter.

However, it is important to acknowledge that globalisation is not a single process. It is therefore vital to examine its different dimensions in order to understand that it is, in Steger's words, 'an intricate tapestry of overlapping shapes and colours'. Steger warns that we must resist the temptation to reduce globalisation to one single or overwhelmingly crucial feature.

## Key terms

**Globalisation** The trend of increasing interaction between societies and individuals on a worldwide scale due to advances in transportation and communication technology.

**Globality** A social condition characterised by tight economic, political, cultural and environmental interconnectedness and flows underpinned by technological innovation that have rendered most national borders and boundaries irrelevant.

**Global imagining** People's growing consciousness that they share a common global culture or that they share common interests with their neighbours in the global village.

**Glocalisation** A combination of the words 'globalisation' and 'localisation', used to describe a product or service that is developed and distributed globally, but is also adjusted to accommodate the user or consumer in a local market. The term is also used more generally as a hybrid fusing of the global and local, as in 'Bollywood'.

**Conglomerates** A corporation composed of a collection of companies which have been brought together by mergers and takeovers.

**Micro-level** Processes that occur at the level of individuals.

**Space–time compression** A term invented by David Harvey that refers to a set of processes that impact time and space, that is, they cause the relative distances between places as measured in terms of travel time or cost to shrink so that the world seems to be a much smaller place.

**Macro-level** Processes that happen at a societal or structural level.

### Summary

1. Globalisation is a complex process that is often over-simplified.
2. The most effective way to define globalisation is that it reflects the growing interdependency of world society and/or the increasing interconnectedness of societies which are usually separated by geographical distance, time zones and very different cultures.
3. Steger suggests that globalisation is made up of three processes: globality, the global imagination and glocalisation.
4. It is important to understand that globalisation is not a new process but that it has accelerated at an incredible speed in the last couple of decades.

# Unit 8.1.2 The significance of different dimensions of globalisation

In the previous unit we examined the historical dimension of globalisation. We now briefly examine the other five dimensions: the technological, economic, cultural, political (sometimes referred to as the 'ideological') and the moral. It is important to understand that, although these can be examined as separate entities, they actually overlap and are inter-dependent. For example, the technological dimension has had a considerable impact on the economic and cultural dimensions of globalisation.

### Activity

Go through Steger's five historical periods and list all the technological inventions and innovations that he highlights as contributing to increased globalisation.

## The technological dimension of globalisation

Although there have been numerous technological innovations that have contributed to increased globalisation, five related technological creations since the late 1980s have probably made the greatest contribution to globality, the global imagination and the formation of the local–global nexus known as glocalisation. These technologies more than any other have transformed our concept of time and space.

First, in 1989 Tim Berners-Lee created and developed the World Wide Web or internet – a global network of connected computers which transfers information around the world in seconds. The internet allows users to access websites – a collection of pages of multimedia content – located under a single domain name. Internet technology has rapidly developed in the last decade as related technological innovations have been harnessed to its use, including search engines, browsers, broadband, cloud storage and social media platforms.

Second, the development of digital technology means that all information, regardless of format (for example, images, text and sound), is now converted into binary code that can be transmitted instantaneously along the information superhighway of the internet. Digitalisation allows information to be delivered across a range of media platforms that were once separate and unconnected technologies. It is now possible to watch television and films, take photographs, consult maps and use GPS, download and listen to music, play games, send texts and emails, and upload photographs, videos and comments to social network and sharing sites on one device.

Third, the rapid evolution of microchip-based microprocessor computer technology means that digital computers are getting smaller and are therefore perfectly suited to practical domestic use. This has resulted in the sales of laptop or notebook computers exceeding those of desktop computers. For example, nearly three out of four computers sold worldwide in 2018 were laptops or tablets.

Four, a new breed of mobile phone – the smartphone – appeared in the early 21st century. This mass communications device is essentially a handheld personal computer supported by broadband and/or Wi-Fi which can connect to the internet and email. The Pew Research Center reported in 2017 that about three-quarters of US adults (77 per cent) say they own a smartphone, up from 35 per cent in 2011, making the smartphone one of the most quickly adopted consumer technologies in recent history. Smartphone ownership is more common among those who are younger or more affluent. For example, 92 per cent of 18- to 29-year-olds say they own a smartphone, compared with 42 per cent of those aged 65 and older. Interestingly, these devices are less likely to be used for talking or texting. American adults report that they mainly use smartphones to shop and to access the internet, especially social media platforms such as Facebook, WhatsApp, Instagram and Twitter. However, although smartphone ownership is climbing in less industrialised nations, a digital divide still remains. Over a third of people in less industrialised nations owned a smartphone according to a Pew survey carried out in 2015, but more industrialised economies have considerably higher rates of smartphone adoption and use. For example, the highest rates of smartphone use were found in South Korea, Sweden, Australia, the Netherlands, Spain and the USA.

Fifth, smartphone technology can now also be found in televisions. Smart televisions are the result of technological convergence between computers and flatscreen televisions. Internet access is integrated into the device, which can be used to access social media apps, terrestrial domestic as well as global satellite TV channels, and streaming services such as Netflix.

Steger argues that these technological innovations have contributed to globalisation in the following ways;

- They have created new social networks.
- They have multiplied existing connections that cut across traditional political, economic, cultural and geographical boundaries.
- They have expanded and stretched social relations, activities and connections, especially in the economic and cultural dimensions.
- They have intensified and accelerated social exchanges and activities, especially communication power, and in so doing have created what Manuel Castells (2009) calls 'a **global network society**'.

## Activity

*On public transport in Shanghai, China.*

Examine the statement by Steger shown here and answer the questions that follow it.

'If we asked ordinary citizens on the busy streets of global cities like New York, Shanghai, or Sydney about the essence of globalisation, their answers would probably involve some reference to growing forms of economic connectivity fuelled by digital technologies. People might point to their mobile devices such as Cloud-connected smart wireless phones like the popular iPhone and tablets linked to powerful internet search engines like Google Chrome that sort in a split second through gigantic data sets. Or they might mention accessible video-postings on YouTube; ubiquitous social networking sites like Instagram, Facebook and Twitter; the rapidly expanding blogosphere, satellite – and computer-connected HDTVs and Netflix movie streaming and interactive 3-D computer and video games.'

Using the list in this quote, design a questionnaire aimed at a reasonably manageable sample of people in your school or college – say 20–30 individuals. The first question should be an open question asking, 'What sorts of examples would you use to support the view that the society in which you live has become globalised?' They might, for example, cite global market brands or the fact that in the city or town in which they live there is a McDonald's or Starbucks. Follow this open question with closed questions based on whether they use the sorts of technologies mentioned by Steger in the extract. Then ask questions about what countries they have visited as tourists, and what global tastes they have in popular music, film and television. Ask them whether they like and enjoy food or drink that originates from outside their culture and society. Conclude by asking them whether they consider themselves global citizens of the world.

Discuss the results as a class. Were they expected or unexpected?

Consequently Steger concludes that globalisation is 'about growing worldwide interconnectivity'. He notes too that it involves 'both the macro-structures of a global community and the micro-structures of "global personhood"' or identity.

## The economic dimension of globalisation

There has been a rapid intensification of international trade and investment in the past 30 years and as a result distinct national or local economies have dissolved into a global **free-trade** and market economy. Countries have become economically inter-dependent because of the expansion of international trade, the development of 24-hour global financial trading markets and the global dominance of the so-called 'three sisters of trade'; the World Trade Organization (WTO), the World Bank and the International Monetary Fund (IMF). Moreover, global trade has led to the emergence of transnational corporations (TNCs), which have created an international division of labour by situating their manufacturing plants in different locations across the globe, by transferring money, technology and raw materials across national borders and by creating global markets and consumers for their products. TNCs dominate the fields of manufacturing, oil exploration, chemical and arms production, finance, popular culture and digital technology. Marxists claim that the overriding aim of such TNCs is to maximise profit by systematically exploiting global workers and consumers wherever they are situated in the world. Many TNCs are more economically powerful than individual countries, and consequently they wield disproportionate bargaining power over local economies, governments and labour forces. For example, of the 100 richest 'economies' in the world in 2018, 51 are TNCs and only 49 are actual countries.

Two examples of economic globalisation which are worth highlighting are:

- Tourism, which has been dramatically boosted by technological developments in air travel such as the creation of jumbo jets like the Airbus A380 and Boeing's Dreamliner. Air travel has also dropped in cost as budget airlines have flourished. In 2017, according to the World Tourism Organization, 1322 million people were recorded as arriving in a country from abroad because of tourism. This was worth nearly $1,000 billion in 2017, making tourism one of the world's largest industries. In 2017, the Middle East and Asia had the greatest growth of tourists. Europe still has the greatest number of tourists – nearly 671 million in 2017.
- Containerisation. Marc Levinson (2016) argues that the most significant influence on economic globalisation, but one that has been woefully under-appreciated, has been containerisation. He argues that container shipping has developed over the last 50 years into a huge industry that has transformed economic geography, slashed transportation costs and reshaped the global flow of trade in manufactured commodities. Levinson puts it more bluntly when he claims in the subtitle of his book that the shipping container made the world smaller and the world economy bigger. For example, containerisation is responsible for the transportation across the world of roughly 90 per cent of manufactured goods.

### Activity

Ask your teacher to pin up a map of the world on your classroom wall. Stick pins in those countries people in your class have visited, to ascertain the extent of your global footprint.

### Activity

*The container terminal in Rotterdam, the largest port in Europe, which serves a hinterland of 40 000 000 consumers.*

Can you think of ways in which containerisation might be useful for global criminals?

There is no doubt that the development of an increasingly unified global economy is having effects on domestic economies. Decisions made in one society about lifestyle preferences and leisure pursuits can cause problems such as unemployment, debt and the loss of livelihoods for workers and farmers thousands of miles away. Zygmunt Bauman (2007) observed that 'on a planet open to the free circulation of capital, and commodities, whatever happens in one place has a bearing on how people in all other places live, hope or expect to live… Nothing is truly, or can remain for long, indifferent to anything else – untouched and untouching'.

## The cultural dimension of globalisation

**Cultural globalisation** refers to the rapid movement of ideas, attitudes, meanings, values and cultural products across national borders. It refers specifically to the idea that there is now a global common culture transmitted and reinforced by the internet, popular entertainment media, transnational marketing of particular brands and international travel and tourism that goes beyond local cultural traditions and lifestyles. Sociologists cannot agree on whether cultural globalisation positively or negatively shapes the identities, perceptions, aspirations, tastes and everyday activities of young people, wherever in the world they may live.

It is argued that culture has become globalised as ownership and control of the world's media, internet providers and websites have become increasingly concentrated in the hands of fewer transnational corporations. Cultural products such as films, television, music, designer fashion, news, social networking sites, food, drink, brands and sport are primarily developed and manufactured for global consumption. This means that the populations of diverse societies now encounter and consume the same sorts of cultural products. Despite huge differences in distance, upbringing and social context, many of us now listen to the same popular music, read the same books and watch the same films, television programmes and sports.

### Activity

Make a list of sports that are global because countries worldwide annually host key events or competitions in that sport.

It is argued that global cultural icons such as pop stars Beyoncé, Jay-Z, Madonna, Kanye West and One Direction; global sport stars such as Cristiano Ronaldo, Lionel Messi, Kobe Bryant, Sachin Tendulkar, Rafael Nadal and Serena Williams; and Hollywood and Bollywood film stars are important global role models in that they export aspects of their home culture to their foreign fans, who read about their lifestyles as well as sometimes engaging in cultural appropriation – they may adopt aspects of other cultures such as tattoos, dress codes, jewellery and incorporate them into their own lifestyles, producing a popular hybridised culture that fans worldwide can tap into.

### Activity

*Stars such as Jay-Z and Beyoncé have a global following.*

Make a list of the most popular home-grown pop stars in the society or country in which you live. Examine your local pop charts. Are local stars outselling global stars? Can their music be described as hybridised?

Cultural globalisation has allegedly increased interconnectedness among different populations and cultures. For example, food is an important part of cultural experience. Most societies around the world have diets which are unique to them. However, the cultural globalisation of food and diet has been particularly promoted by American fast-food transnationals such as McDonald's, Burger King and KFC. It can be argued that the 35 000 McDonald's restaurants that operated in 118 countries in 2015 have had a global effect on local diets and eating habits. Moreover, many global cities such as London,

New York and Tokyo have restaurants that specialise in Chinese, Italian, Japanese, Indian and Thai cuisine.

### Activity

Either survey your classmates to find out whether they have global tastes in food and drink, *or*, if it is safe, walk around your city or town centre or local neighbourhood in order to list restaurants or takeaways that specialise in food that originates outside the society in which you live.

## The political or ideological dimension of globalisation

It is claimed that political globalisation is increasingly extending beyond local politics. Until the end of World War II, the governments of nation-states were traditionally responsible for maintaining the human rights, security and economic welfare of their citizens. However, many countries are joining and becoming actively involved in global political institutions such as the United Nations, NATO, the European Community and the G7. In turn, these global organisations shape and influence domestic political policies.

Politics is also intertwined with economic globalisation. For example, both the World Bank and IMF often lend money to individual countries on the condition that they adopt a neoliberal economic approach to free trade. This often involves these global political institutions insisting that, in return for aid, less industrialised countries should 'reform' their economies so that trade and banking is deregulated and public spending on, say, health or welfare is reduced and/or that state-owned agencies and services are privatised by being sold off to TNCs.

## The moral dimension of globalisation

Bauman argued that on a planet criss-crossed by 'information highways', everything that happens in any part of the world is eventually known. Bauman observed that the human misery associated with distant places and remote ways of life are vividly brought into our homes by a global news media.

He argued that in the global world, global inequality and the humiliation and injustice it brings are now very visible via digital technology. Moreover, he argued that the well-being of one place can ever be innocent of the misfortune of another. As Milan Kundera (2004) observes, 'there is nowhere one can escape to in a globalized society'.

Bauman argued that globalisation brings with it increased risk. Global risks have evolved in the sense that the world increasingly shares the same global problems such as disease, terrorism, crime, climate change and environmental degradation, which increasingly emanate from the same global sources.

### Activity

*Chernobyl nuclear power plant.*

Research the true story of the world's worst nuclear disaster, which occurred at Chernobyl on 26 April 1986 – at the time Chernobyl was in the USSR. What global effects did this disaster have?

Moreover, Bauman argued that global inequalities in wealth, income and life chances are likely to worsen the risks faced by the global population by increasing the fears, tensions and uncertainties of those trapped at the bottom of the global stratification system. He claimed that economic globalisation leads to unregulated markets that further widen inequality and the sense of hostility and grievance felt by those who go without across the world. This is a recipe for planetary lawlessness, which is then used by the powerful as another excuse for greater levels of surveillance, control and repression of powerless groups. Bauman also predicted the rise of fascist and racist movements, nationalism, populism, religious fanaticism and terrorism.

There is evidence that globalisation has produced a new set of shared moral problems and fears. For example, it has produced geo-political tensions between the USA and North Korea and, according to Samuel Huntington (2002), between the Christian and Muslim worlds. It has also led to the rise of right-wing nationalism in several European countries, especially Austria, Hungary, Poland and Italy, that have come to power because of popular fears about migrants and refugees. All of these countries have introduced tougher immigration policies and have seen significant rises in racist hate crimes.

Like Bauman, Michael Ignatieff (2017) believes that there is a need for a form of moral globalisation in an increasingly divided world, within which global citizens speak the same ethical language when confronting global ethical issues such as the behaviour of TNCs, corruption, public trust, tolerance, multicultural cities, reconciliation after war and conflict, and resilience in times of uncertainty and danger.

Examples of global morality can be found in the rise of global social protest movements, such as Amnesty International and Greenpeace, which aim to protect human rights and the environment respectively. In addition, an anti-capitalist global movement has developed symbolised by protests outside G7 conferences as well as the Occupy and Anonymous campaigns. These have used global communication systems to form alliances with activists in other countries to protest against the poverty, inequality, greed and corporate tax evasion they associate with global capitalism.

Globalisation has also led to the rise of social and political movements which are critical of capitalism, such as the radical Syriza government elected in Greece in 2015. Finally, there are signs that globalisation is being blamed by those suffering long-term unemployment and wage stagnation in both the USA and Europe.

### Summary

There are five important inter-dependent dimensions of globalisation: the technological, economic, cultural, political and moral.

# Unit 8.1.3 Theories of globalisation

Sociologists disagree about the effects of globalisation. Some sociologists argue that globalisation is a fact of life, and therefore irreversible. Optimistic **globalists** believe this to be a good thing, because they believe that this will eventually break down barriers between societies and promote greater tolerance and understanding. In contrast, critical sociologists believe that globalisation simply promotes economic and cultural forms of imperialism and therefore poverty, inequality and potential conflict between religions and cultures. Some perceive globalisation to be a threat to traditional ways of life which have been in place for centuries. They are, therefore, very pessimistic about globalisation, which they predict will inevitably lead to dystopia – that is, a world full of risks and conflict. This is in contrast to the utopia of human rights, universal access to education and communications, and multicultural understanding envisaged by those who see globalisation as a positive process.

### Activity

Explain why the civil war in Syria is often referred to as 'the world's war'. Think about how many nation-states are involved in the war either directly or indirectly. Think, too, about the geographical origins of the foreign fighters who volunteered to fight for Islamic State.

## Globalist theories of globalisation

Globalists are sociologists who believe that globalisation is a fact which is having real consequences for the way that people and organisations operate across the world. However, globalists are not united on the consequences of such a process. Some globalists – the **hyper-globalists** – see the process of globalisation as a positive phenomenon, while the pessimists or sceptics see globalisation as a type of **cultural imperialism** that is generally having a negative effect on the local cultures of less industrialised societies.

### Hyper-globalism

Hyper-globalists (sometimes called optimists or positive globalists) welcome globalisation because they believe that it will eventually produce tolerant and responsible world citizens. Amartya Sen (2002) suggests that globalisation represents hope for all humanity because it will produce a universal techno-scientific culture which will liberate people from poverty. Mario Vargas Llosa (2000) suggests that much war and conflict is caused by local cultural differences. Therefore, the quicker that local cultures merge into a single global culture the better.

Neoliberals such as Thomas Friedman (2000) argue that globalisation has occurred as a result of the global adoption of neoliberal economic policies. He identifies a neoliberal economic set of principles that he calls the 'golden straitjacket', which he argues all countries need to fit into if they are to achieve success in the global economy. These principles include the privatisation of state-owned enterprises and pensions, the maintenance of low inflation, a reduction in the size of government bureaucracy, the liberalisation of trade and investment and the reduction of corruption. He argues that this golden straitjacket is 'pretty much "one-size fits all"...it is not always pretty or gentle or comfortable. But it's here and it's the only model on the rack this historical season' (quoted on p. 21 of Ha-Joon Chang (2008)).

Friedman claims that the globalised world economy is the result of the fact that, since the 1980s, most countries have adopted similar economic policies focused on deregulation, privatisation and the opening up of free trade and investment. These countries were often shepherded onto the 'right' economic path by the 'good Samaritans' of Western governments, especially the USA and the 'three sisters of free trade'. Friedman argues that the world is now in a golden age of prosperity and predicts that this will eventually see the end of problems such as world poverty.

## Activity

*Sri Lankan soft drinks and coconut water compete with international brands.*

What examples of competing international and 'local' brands can you think of in your own society?

### Pessimistic or sceptical globalism

In contrast, pessimistic globalists, such as Jeremy Seabrook (2005), argue that globalisation is a negative phenomenon because it is essentially a form of Western (and especially American) imperialism, peddling a superficial and homogeneous form of popular culture and consumption.

Seabrook argues that, by definition, globalisation makes all other cultures local and, by implication, inferior. He suggests that globalisation implies a superior, civilised mode of living – it implicitly promises that it is the sole pathway to universal prosperity and security – consequently diminishing and marginalising local cultures. Seabrook suggests that globalisation sweeps aside the multiple meanings that human societies and cultures have derived from or imposed upon their environment. He argues that integration into a single global economy is a 'declaration of cultural war' upon other cultures and societies and that it often results in profound and painful social and religious disruption.

Many pessimistic globalists argue that Westernisation or Americanisation has been mistaken for globalisation. These sociologists are concerned about the concentration of the world's media in the hands of a few powerful American and Japanese TNCs. It is argued that these TNCs disseminate primarily Western, and especially American, forms of popular culture. There have been concerns that these cultural products reflect a cultural imperialism that results in the marginalisation of local culture. Peter Steven (2004) argues that, 'for the past century, US political and economic influence has been aided immensely by US film and music. Where the marines, missionaries and bureaucrats failed, Charlie Chaplin, Mickey Mouse and Mariah Carey have succeeded effortlessly in attracting the world to the American way.' Mass advertising of Western cultural icons such as McDonald's and Coca-Cola has resulted in their logos becoming powerful symbols to people, especially young people, in the less industrialised world, because they imply that they need to adopt Western consumer lifestyles in order to modernise.

It is argued that cultural globalisation may, therefore, eventually undermine and even destroy rich local cultures and identities. Ben Barber (2003) feared that the globalised world is turning into a 'McWorld', in which all cultures and consumption will be standardised. Other commentators have expressed similar anxieties about the 'coca-colonisation' or 'Disneyfication' of the developing world. In his critique of cultural globalisation, Seabrook suggests that 'it is not only the economies of countries that are reshaped, but also the minds and sensibility of the people. Their value systems are re-formed in the image of the global market.' This cultural change is interpreted by some sections of developing nations as a form of cultural imperialism – an attempt by the West to spread its supremacy – as a colonialism of the mind.

Seabrook argues that the principal response of most world leaders to globalisation has been one of fatalism. They imply that the world is simply powerless to resist globalisation, which is presented as inevitable and irreversible. Seabrook argues that most leaders of the industrialised world take this position because they are experiencing an 'impotence of convenience' – their confessed powerlessness disguises the fact that the forces of globalisation economically advantage their countries and their economic elites.

### Marxist theories of globalisation

Marxists do not believe that globalisation is a new phenomenon. Harvey (2011), for example, points out that capitalism has been an international phenomenon for hundreds of years. All we are experiencing at the moment is a continuation, or evolution, of the Western or American-dominated form of capitalist production and trade, as the logic of capitalism propels manufacturing and marketing to seek greater profits in the global arena. In his world-systems theory, Immanuel Wallerstein (2011) argues that globalisation has always been an important part of the way that capitalism organises itself. He argues that capitalism is responsible for creating a 'world order' or world system because capital from its very beginning has ignored national borders in its search for profit. In particular, Wallerstein observes that this world capitalist system is organised around an international division of labour consisting of three levels of exploitation. The 'core' or more industrialised countries control world trade and monopolise the production of manufactured goods. The 'semi-peripheral' zone includes what Jim O'Neill (2001) dubbed the **BRIC** countries – the fastest-growing market economies such as Brazil, Russia, India and China, which resemble the core countries in terms of their urban centres but also contain extremes of rural poverty. Countries in the semi-periphery are often connected to the core because the latter contract work out to them. For example, most Apple products are manufactured in China. The third tier of this capitalist global system is composed of countries that make up what Wallerstein calls the 'peripheral' sector – for example, much of Africa. These countries mainly supply minerals and cash crops to the core and semi-periphery, and are the emerging markets in which the core countries market manufactured goods such as cigarettes and mobile phones.

Wallerstein goes on to suggest that this global capitalist system is constantly evolving in its search for profit. The signs of this are:

- constant commodification (attaching a price to everything)
- de-skilling (the breaking down of complex skills into simple repetitive skills in order to pay people less)
- mechanisation, such as robot computerised technology.

Wallerstein argues that these processes, too, are becoming globalised and predicts that in the long term they will generate so many dispossessed, excluded, marginal and poor people who will unite in a global revolutionary movement that they will transform the global capitalist system into a more just socialist world economy.

### Evaluation of Marxist theories of globalisation

The main problem with Wallerstein's theory of global capitalism, as with Marxism generally, is that it is guilty of economic reductionism. It assumes that the economy is driving all other aspects of the system (politics, culture and so on). Albert Bergesen (1990) argues that political influences in the form of military conquest were more important than the logic of capitalism in bringing about globalisation.

However, despite these criticisms, Wallerstein's work was one of the first to acknowledge the 'globalisation' of the world (although he himself never uses the term). He draws attention to the international division of labour, which some see as the main source of global inequality. Lately, however, sociologists working from a globalisation perspective have noted that relationships within the world system are far from one-way. Economic interdependence can also mean that problems in the less industrialised world (such as financial crises caused by debt) can have a negative ripple effect on both the industrialised and less industrialised economies that make up the global capitalist system. For example, a financial crisis in South Korea in 1997 led to the car manufacturer Nissan-Hyundai making British workers redundant.

## Feminist theories of globalisation

Serena Parekh and Shelley Wilcox (2014) argue that economic globalisation must also be understood in terms of the effects it has had on women, who make up a disproportionate percentage of the global poor. Feminists tend to argue that these effects have been primarily negative for women. Feminists point out that globalisation has promised many things that are crucial to feminists: peace, prosperity, social justice, environmental protection, the elimination of racism and ethnocentrism and, of course, an increase in the status of women. However, economic and political globalisation have actually created the conditions for war and increased militarism, increased the gap between the rich and the poor and created a system that is hostile or antagonistic towards women.

Parekh and Wilcox argue that there are four key features shared by feminist approaches to globalisation.

First, early feminist analyses focused on issues that were widely believed to be of particular importance to women around the world, such as domestic violence, workplace discrimination and human rights violations against women. However, some feminists criticise this approach as too narrow because they argue that even apparently gender-neutral global issues often have a gendered dimension, including war, global governance, migration, southern debt and climate change.

Second, radical feminists have particularly focused on women's global subordination especially with regard to the gendered harms involved in sexual slavery, forced domestic labour, and the systematic withholding of education, food and healthcare from women and girls that follow from societies in which most live in poverty.

Third, intersectional feminists believe that attention needs to be paid to how patriarchal systems of oppression and injustice interact with other forms of oppression such as race, ethnicity, nationality, social class and sexuality to produce global disadvantage.

Fourth, feminist critiques of globalisation are committed to avoiding ethnocentrism, especially the idea that feminist ideas and the experiences of women worldwide are universal. They acknowledge that feminist ideas from Western cultures have been unfairly imposed on women from less industrialised countries. Feminism also recognises the role that women played as part of the colonial oppression of indigenous peoples. For example, Frances Kaye (2017) observes that 'in terms of working with the Indians, as missionaries, as matrons, as schoolteachers, White women got a lot of power out of the disempowering of native people. That's not something you can be happy about...if we don't recognise that then we're still justifying imperialism and colonialism.'

## Transformationalist and postmodernist theories of globalisation

Transformationalists agree with sceptics that the impact of globalisation has been exaggerated by globalists, but argue that it is foolish to reject the concept out of hand. This theoretical position argues that globalisation should be understood as a complex set of interconnecting relationships through which power, for the most part, is exercised indirectly. They suggest that the globalisation process can be reversed, especially where it is negative or, at the very least, that it can be controlled.

Transformationalists are particularly critical of the cultural-imperialist globalisation argument for three reasons:

1. These arguments make the mistake of suggesting that the flow of culture is one-way only – from the West to the less industrialised world. This focus fails to acknowledge how Western culture is enriched by inputs from other world cultures and religions.
2. It underestimates the strength of local culture. As Cohen and Kennedy (2012) observe: 'People in Lagos or Kuala Lumpur may drink Coke, wear Levi jeans and listen to North American pop artists, but that does not mean they are about to abandon their customs, family and religious obligations or national identities wholesale, even if they could afford to do so, which most cannot'.

   Roland Robertson (1992) argues that local cultures are not swallowed up by global or Western culture. Like Steger, Robertson emphasises the concept of 'glocalisation' and notes that the global and the local can work well together. He argues that local people tend to select only what pleases them from the global, which they modify and adapt to local culture and needs. Cohen and Kennedy also argue that the local 'captures' the global influence and turns it into a form compatible with local tastes. They refer to this process as '**indigenisation**'. A good example of this is the Indian film industry – 'Bollywood' combines contemporary Western ideas about entertainment with traditional Hindu myth, history and culture. There is evidence that this glocalisation or indigenisation eventually leads to hybridisation – for example, some world music fuses and mixes Western dance beats with traditional styles from North Africa and Asia.

## Activity

*The popularity of Bollywood films extends well beyond India.*

Take a close look at the popular culture of the society or culture to which you belong, and debate with your classmates whether young people in your society are adopting glocalised forms of leisure.

3. Transformationalists and postmodernists also see the global media as beneficial phenomena because they are primarily responsible for diffusing different cultural styles around the world and creating new global hybrid styles in fashion, food, music, consumption and lifestyle. It is argued that in the postmodern world such cultural diversity and pluralism will become the global norm. Postmodernists, therefore, see globalisation as a positive phenomenon because it has created a new class of global consumers, in both the industrialised and less industrialised world, with a greater range of choices from which they can construct a hybridised global identity.

## Key terms

**Globalists** Sociologists who believe that globalisation has had significant and real effects on the world, although they may disagree as to whether these effects are positive or negative.

**Hyper-globalists** Sociologists who are optimistic and positive about the effects of globalisation.

**Cultural imperialism** The process and practice of promoting one culture over another. Many sociologists see it as the consequence of the ubiquity of Western and especially American cultural products.

**BRIC** An acronym for the fast-growing economies of Brazil, Russia, India and China.

**Indigenisation** The action or process of bringing something under the control, dominance, or influence of the people native to an area.

## Summary

1. Some sociological theories welcome globalisation and believe that it will eventually promote tolerance, reduce inequality and promote the 'one world federation' approach we see portrayed in science fiction films such as *Star Trek*.
2. Other sociologists, however, claim that globalisation will never produce a global consciousness because it is not truly global. Rather, globalisation is really Westernisation or Americanisation disguised as globalisation. Consequently, it is argued that it functions like an 'evil empire' destroying local cultures and foisting its imperial value system in the form of Western popular and secular culture on traditional societies.
3. Marxists believe that globalisation is just another means by which the capitalist system has extended its reach in order to exploit the labour power and markets of less industrialised societies and thus increase global inequalities in wealth.
4. Feminist theory points out that globalisation has probably reinforced patriarchy and gender inequality rather than reduced these types of oppression.
5. Transformationalists and postmodernists argue that globalisation has increased the potential for the social interaction of people from very different cultures and has encouraged cultural exchanges that have produced glocalised and hybrid responses to globalisation.

# END-OF-PART QUESTIONS

| | | |
|---|---|---|
| 0 1 | Describe two ways in which technology has contributed to globalisation. | **[4 marks]** |
| 0 2 | Explain one positive and one negative effect of globalisation. | **[6 marks]** |
| 0 3 | Explain two reasons why transformationalists are positive about globalisation. | **[8 marks]** |

# PART 2 GLOBALISATION AND IDENTITY

## Contents


| | | |
|---|---|---|
| **Unit 8.2.1** | **The impact of globalisation on identity** | **478** |
| **Unit 8.2.2** | **Cultural convergence versus cultural divergence** | **484** |
| **Unit 8.2.3** | **The role of Western ideology in shaping identity and the concept of Westernisation** | **490** |


This part will explore the impact of globalisation, especially in the form of global social media on personal, social and cultural identity. In particular, it will examine how personal identity has been transformed by globalisation. It also considers three social reactions to globalisation: ethnic revitalisation, cultural defence and hybridisation.

An important question that needs to be asked is whether globalisation makes people around the world more alike or more different. Steger observes that pessimistic globalists suggest that globalisation is resulting in a convergence of cultures and that we are witnessing 'the rise of an increasingly homogenized popular culture': 'As evidence for their interpretation, these commentators point to Amazonian Indians wearing Nike sneakers; denizens of the Southern Sahara purchasing Yankees baseball caps; and Palestinian youths proudly displaying their Golden State Warriors basketball singlets in downtime Ramallah.' However, critics of this view argue that globalisation has actually produced cultural divergence or, in Steger's words, 'a cultural rainbow that reflects the diversity of the world's existing populations'. Bauman argued that some cultures and religions have seen globalisation as convergence and interpreted this as an attack on, or at least a threat to, their traditional way of life. These cultures have reacted in a 'defensive aggressive' way to this perceived danger by adopting **fundamentalist** beliefs and employing terror as a strategy of resistance to globalisation. A third way of approaching and interpreting the influence of globalisation is to analyse what Steger calls the 'global–local nexus' to see how globalisation has both responded, and adapted itself, to local needs and sensibilities. Such an analysis has seen the emergence of hybridised forms of local culture in which local services and consumers have borrowed aspects of globalisation and converted them to local use.

Finally, we need to examine the claim that what some theorists refer to as 'globalisation' is best understood as a form of Westernisation or Americanisation. For example, Marxists such as Wallerstein argue that globalisation is merely an extension of the Western capitalist quest for profit into new territories. Additionally, there is no doubt that many developing societies have seen globalisation as a smokescreen for the imperialist ambitions of Western governments. Certainly, Islamist movements such as al-Qaeda and ISIS seem to view globalisation as merely a means through which decadent Western values infect young Muslims. The Islamic Republic of Iran has actively sought to reduce the impact of Western values on Iranian young people by banning Western pop music and movies.

# Unit 8.2.1 The impact of globalisation on identity

Until the digital revolution of the 1990s, social networks generally involved people – friends, family or work colleagues – making the effort to physically meet face to face, to write letters or talk on the telephone. However, it can be argued that digital technology, particularly texting, email and the rapid and global spread of social media platforms such as Facebook and Twitter, have radically transformed the ways in which we communicate and interact with one another today.

## The growth of social media

The computer-digital age has produced **virtual communities** in which globally dispersed people with common interests are no longer constrained by geographical distance or time zones. The existence of the internet and its diversity of websites, newsgroups, discussion boards, social networking platforms and so on, as well as email and video applications such as Skype, has produced instant interaction and sharing at any time and from any place. It can, therefore, be argued that global social network platforms such as Facebook have replaced local institutions such as the family, the educational system, the workplace, religion and old media such as newspapers and television as the most important infrastructure through which people organise their lives, interact with others, construct and project their identity and exchange social capital in the 21st century.

Castells argues that digital networks and social platforms have dramatically changed the nature of social networking in the 21st century. In particular, Facebook has become the major agency for packaging, promoting and presenting the self for public consumption. In January 2017, 1.86 billion people – 96 per cent of all adults online worldwide – registered with Facebook. People, especially those who belong to the millennial generation, use Facebook, Twitter, Snapchat and Instagram, WeChat and Sina Weibo to engage in what Castells calls '**mass self-communication**'. This has transformed our traditionally subjective interpretation of personal identity or self into a social product which we project into cyberspace in return for mass admiration and social approval. According to Sherry Turkle (2016), internet-based social networks free people of the burdens of their physical identities and allow them to present 'better' and 'more attractive 'cyber-versions of themselves.

### Activity

Survey both your class and year group in order to find out the extent and frequency of use of social media platforms and **social media apps** among your age group.

## Globalisation, global social media and young people's identity

Howard Gardner and Katie Davis (2014) observe that young people are the most frequent users of social media. Jan Van Dijk (2012) claims that social network sites have replaced email and telephone as the preferred mode of interaction for teenagers. These observations are supported by research carried out in 2017 by the Education Policy Institute (EPI) which investigated internet use by 540 000 young people across 35 countries. This research found that more than one in three British 15-year-olds are 'extreme internet users' who spend at least six hours a day online, markedly higher than any other country in the study apart from Chile.

Gardner and Davis found that young people take a great deal of care in how they present themselves online for public consumption. They identify three trends in this online presentation and performance of self:

1. Many young people construct and perform a socially desirable and polished online self which generally exaggerates the more socially attractive aspects of a person's personality but downplays less 'cool' traits. This generally means that a young person's online identity may be more **outgoing** and extroverted than their everyday offline identity.
2. Some young people construct a range of fictitious identities because they are performing to different audiences who may have different expectations. For example, a person may construct a Facebook identity to attract maximum connectedness, a Twitter identity which is 'edgy' in its comments on current events, and a Reddit identity which is deliberately provocative and aggressive in the stance it takes on particular online debates.
3. Once the self has been constructed on a platform such as Facebook, there is evidence that

young people then engage in constant **identity performance** in that free time is mainly taken up checking phones in order to manage the online impressions others have of them by 'liking' what others upload as well as updating their own profile and status.

Gardner and Davis argue that there are several advantages for young people in social networking and constructing online relationships. For example, accumulating connections or online relationships may be empowering and enriching for some because it can produce **social capital** – they can make connections with others and share resources and experiences which are of mutual benefit to all concerned.

For example, membership of an online community may provide opportunities for people with similar interests to find and interact with one another. These opportunities may produce the possibility of benefiting from both '**bonding social capital**' and '**bridging social capital**' (see Unit 2.2.3).

Sociologists such as Daniel Miller (2011) suggest that social media platforms have a number of benefits. For example, texting and updating one's Facebook page and profile may function to micro-coordinate activity among friends and family who are physically scattered by geographical distance. Miller observes that Facebook extends and makes meaningful relationships which in the pre-social media age would have grown weaker or lapsed altogether as people got older or moved away.

Furthermore, social media platforms may act as a social lifeline, particularly for those who are isolated, shy or disabled. John Bargh and Kate McKenna (2004) found that social platforms can often help those with low self-esteem relate to others because social networking does not involve face-to-face interaction.

## The critique of digital social networking

However, critics of social networks suggest that the costs of this global online revolution may outweigh its benefits. They argue that digital forms of communication may be dysfunctional for the following reasons.

First, Marxists such as Christian Fuchs (2017) argue that powerful global corporations monopolise and control digital communication and social media and this fact undermines the concept of a participatory digital global culture. He argues that, as a result, connectedness is less important than connectivity. Van Dijk (2012) illustrates this when he observes that the algorithms developed by social networking sites like Facebook for commercial reasons increasingly determine what people like, want, know or find. The aim of these algorithms is not to connect people but to keep them online for as long as possible and to maximise the possibility that they will click on and connect to other commercial sites. Fuchs argues that social platforms like Facebook have resulted in the **commodification** of friendship and connectedness. He argues that social media activity is not as voluntary as users believe it to be. Algorithms shepherd people towards making 'choices' that benefit capitalist agencies such as advertisers. Social media content may, therefore, simply reflect the capitalist imperative to commodify and market all aspects of social life in order to make profit.

Second, there are concerns about how the data collected by sites such as Facebook might be used. Facebook in particular has been accused of violating the privacy of its users. In 2018, Facebook was criticised for permitting a company called Cambridge Analytica to 'harvest' personal data from global users of Facebook to sell onto political parties so that they could target political advertising at particular groups of individuals. This example supports the Marxist case that commodification is the major goal of social media platforms. It is also becoming apparent to politicians and law-makers across the world that global social media are very difficult to police.

Third, the quality of online relationships or 'friendships ' has been questioned by Turkle, who observes that people boast about how many people they have 'friended' on Facebook, but research on the nature of friendship in the USA concludes that Americans say they have few real friends. Miller observes that critics of Facebook suggest that 'friending' represents a 'kind of inflation' of superficial and weak relationships that actually diminishes the value of true friendship. He argues that the quality of Facebook relationships can feel non-genuine because they lack the intimacy, vulnerability and physical closeness that characterise real relationships. Gardner and Davis argue that such 'friends' may be connected but they may not always be connecting.

Fourth, Turkle suggests that the way people are mentally 'tethered' to their digital devices is unhealthy. She points out that, although digital forms of communication connect users to more people, it has also resulted in greater anxiety. She observes that devotion to checking one's mobile phone is almost religious. When mobile phones are misplaced, anxiety levels rise and people feel cut off from reality. Turkle argues that young people should be described as 'cyborgs' because they are always connected to one other, regardless of where they are, via their laptops, tablets and smartphones.

## Activity

*Young people using smartphones.*

Interview a selection of your classmates about how they see the differences in the quality of the friends they come into face-to-face contact with compared with their online friends. What are the differences and similarities that they see or interpret?

As an additional experimental activity, on the same day ask your classmates whether they would be prepared to leave their phones at home for a day. How many of them refuse? What is their excuse? How do those who agreed feel about it? Do they feel anxiety because they don't have access to their phone? How do they feel about Turkle's description of them as 'cyborgs'?

Danah Boyd (2014) argues that the constant tracking of social media performance is particularly unhealthy for teenagers, because it has weakened their ability to develop an autonomous sense of self in that they become too dependent on how other people react to them online. Research published in 2017 suggests the frequent use of global social media is making children and teenagers more anxious. It found that 40 per cent of its sample reported that 'they felt bad' if nobody 'likes' their selfies and 35 per cent said their confidence was directly linked to the number of followers they had. Jean Twenge (2017) also argues that fear of negative reaction to their identity performance is producing rising levels of moodiness, anxiety, sadness and isolation among teenagers.

Boyd's research suggests teenagers feel that their thoughts and feelings are not real until validated by others online. Gardner and Davis similarly argue that constant self-projection and self-tracking online reduces the time teenagers have for self-contemplation and real-life interaction with others. They observe that the maintenance of virtual identities means that teenagers today are more likely to suffer from **narcissism** compared with previous generations. There is also some evidence that digital interaction makes young people less **empathetic** and possibly 'meaner' online than in person. Online bullying, sexting, grooming, hate crimes and sexual harassment are now recognised as common problems of the digital age.

Fifth, digital technology may also be disruptive, because it potentially reduces interaction between family members. Turkle has argued that the **proto-communities** of social network sites are increasingly replacing real communities composed of family, extended kin and neighbours. As a result, the **'post-familial' family** in which family members spend more time interacting with their gadgets than with each other is becoming the norm.

However, not all sociologists are critical of global social media platforms. Marxist sociologist Castells claims that global media have helped heighten young people's sense of political identity by creating a **networked global society**. Castells argues that before the digital revolution of the internet, politics involved joining vertical organisations such as a political party or pressure group and/or reading the products of such organisations such as political manifestos. In addition, media organisations, which were also vertical organisations, attempted to influence voters as well. Consequently, political news or scandal travelled relatively slowly. Castells argues that new digital media have transformed the relationship that the electorate has with politicians and the way that politicians behave because political news and gossip that is instantaneously available can ruin political careers within minutes. Moreover, these networks are now able to highlight global political issues such as human rights abuses that in the past were largely invisible to people on the other side of the world. This means that states and governments may come under global pressure to clean up their records on human rights, too. For example, the leaders of Myanmar have come under considerable global pressure to halt their persecution of the Rohingya people in recent years.

Castells claims that the global reach of social media has transformed the attitudes of the millennial generation towards world politics because it has given them a political voice that they never had before. Traditionally, politics was dominated by older privately educated and wealthy elites. Global social media platforms have given ordinary young people the power and confidence to be heard on global issues such as human rights abuses, identity politics, global injustice and inequality. In both the USA and UK, the popularity of radical politicians such as Bernie Sanders and Jeremy Corbyn post-2016 is very much a product of this online networking by young people. The Black Lives Matter, MeToo, Make Poverty History, Occupy and **anti-globalisation movements (AGMs)** have all become major thorns in the side of mainstream establishment politicians because of the massive online support generated by young people for these causes. The success of other identity politics issues such as the legalisation of same-sex marriage and the increasing pressure on governments to recognise the rights of individuals who identify as transsexual, intersex and non-binary is partly the result of young people using global media to highlight these civil rights issues. Global social media, then, have proved extremely useful in giving a voice to groups which were previously muted or repressed by the powerful, such as the poor, ethnic minorities, the LGBT community, the disabled, and even oppressed people and tribes in remote parts of the world.

### The extent of social media's effect on identity

However, we have to consider that digital communication and social media may actually have a minimal effect on cultural identity and change for the following reasons;

1. Some critics argue that we have entered a 'post-truth' age and consequently young people may find it increasingly difficult to distinguish between facts and opinion, and between real news and 'fake' news.
2. Ellen Helpser (2017) points out that many people across the world do not have access to digital communications, and that the poor lack the resources to join in with this so-called digital revolution. Helpser refers to those who are excluded from digital communications as a **'digital underclass'**. Domestically, this group is made up of groups that are more likely to be unemployed, low-paid, and to have few educational qualifications. Globally, this digital underclass is mainly to be found in parts of sub-Saharan Africa.
3. Luke Martell (2010) points out that there is a growing tendency in the digital corporate world for power to be concentrated in fewer and fewer more powerful hands. He argues that digital technology gives a false impression of more power being given to a greater number of people. He suggests that digital technology may only be a quantitative rather than a qualitative improvement because political information could be obtained before the internet, although more awkwardly and slowly. Martell concludes that, technologically, the internet is revolutionary but that it does not necessarily follow that it will have a revolutionary impact on cultural or political life.
4. Some countries have taken control of digital media in order to regulate the ability of their citizens to access international websites. For example, China has blocked all references to the word 'democracy' on its most popular search engine and denies its citizens access to websites such as Wikipedia. All internet use is closely monitored by the authorities. This censorship and surveillance is referred to colloquially as the 'great firewall of China'.
5. Andrew Keen (2015) is also critical of the idea that the internet and digital technology have the power to politically change the world. He argues that the internet is too chaotically organised to be effective in bringing about change. Moreover, he argues that social networking sites do not contribute to the democratic process in any way because they are merely vehicles for shameless self-promotion. He further argues that the content of Twitter and blogs often go unchecked and, consequently, uninformed opinion, lies and trolling are the norm, rather than considered political analysis and expertise. Dhiraj Murthy (2018) argues, too, that the revolutionary power of Twitter to change the world is grossly exaggerated.

## Global social media and women's identity

Feminist theory has traditionally focused on how societies tend to be organised in patriarchal ways – that is, in favour of men.

Feminists were particularly critical of old media forms of communication such as newspapers and television, which they saw as patriarchal agencies mainly engaged in the **symbolic annihilation of women** – that is, they tended to show women in a narrow and limited range of social roles and suggest that their achievements are less important than their looks and bodies. Feminists are also critical of some online digital content, particularly the easy availability of pornography websites on the internet. Feminists also point out that control of the content of new digital forms of communication is in the hands of transnational corporations such as Apple, Microsoft and Facebook, which are mainly owned or controlled by men.

However, millennial feminists tend to more optimistic about the power of global social media to challenge global patriarchy, and its potential to change women's social position in society for the better. They argue that the anonymity granted by many forms of digital communication allows women to reach beyond their oppressed feminine identity and take on alternative identities that avoid the negative judgements and stereotypes often applied to female identity. Research by Simon Gottschalk (2010) into how users of 3-D virtual reality internet sites interact with other users and construct and present their virtual selves (known as 'avatars') found that users had a wide range of generic images to use to construct the look or image of their avatar, including buff male bodies, voluptuous female forms and asexual humanoid alternatives such as cyborgs. Gottschalk's research found that users did not feel limited by their real gender identities when choosing an avatar identity. For example, some women reported that they had deliberately chosen to adopt male bodies in order to experience a masculine identity, while other women preferred the cyborg identity because it was asexual or non-binary and therefore minimised the influence of patriarchy and sexual politics.

Moreover, Kira Cochrane (2013) has identified a millennial feminist movement powered by global digital technology that encourages women to build an empowering, popular and reactive feminist movement online. She observes that women are using digital forms of communication to protest about pornography, violence against women, the sexualisation of childhood and so on. She argues that digital technology has resulted in contemporary young women adopting an 'intersectional' form of feminism in which they are aware of how multiple oppressions – class inequality, poverty, race, age, sexuality, gender, ability, violence and so on – interact to bring about misogyny and patriarchal institutions.

Some feminists now argue that digital technology and particularly the internet is a feminine technology that has the potential to destabilise patriarchy because its use allows women to explore, subvert and create new identities and to resist sexist representations wherever they might occur. A good example of this online empowerment is Laura Bates' 'Everyday Sexism' project, which in 2018 had more than 315 000 followers on Twitter and Facebook. This is a consciousness-raising initiative encouraging women to send in everyday experiences of street harassment, workplace discrimination and body-shaming. Helen Lewis (2018) argues that the internet and social media have lowered the barrier to women speaking out against sexual exploitation. Individual women who experience sexual harassment are no longer isolated. They can now find each other by logging onto global media sites which show female victims that they are not alone and that there are many others who have similar stories to tell. Social networking via global media has the potential to create alliances among women that can challenge the patriarchal power structures that still exist in many societies.

Ariel Levy (2006) has been very critical of Instagram's role in the sexualisation of culture. She claims that social media encourage young women to 'celebrate' their bodies by presenting themselves in ways that seek male approval. However, Levy is criticised by Lynne Segal (2006) because she cannot decide whether to treat females who use Instagram as victims or as women who are 'essentially selfish, narcissistic and predatory'.

## Activity

*Laura Bates, author of 'The Everyday Sexism Project', in which women and girls are encouraged to upload their experiences of sexism to the project's website.*

If you have access to the internet, research feminist websites. Write 400 words describing two or three of these, identifying their target audience and their main goals. In your opinion, how might these sites 'empower' females in patriarchal and misogynistic societies?

However, despite these advances, women who use digital forms of communication are often subjected to online sexism, abuse and rape and death threats by 'critics' of feminism. The internet may help disseminate feminist ideas across the world but it also does the same for its polar opposite – woman-hating views.

## Key terms

**Fundamentalist** A strict, literal interpretation of scripture in a religion.

**Virtual communities** An online community that only meets in cyberspace.

**Mass self-communication** A type of communication in which a user selects the group of people symbolised by a website or online community that they want to communicate with and directs their message appropriately.

**Social media apps** Digital applications that are designed to allow people to share digital content quickly, efficiently and in real time.

**Outgoing** In terms of personality, someone who is sociable and easy to talk to.

**Identity performance** A type of impression management in which a person presents a particular version of themselves for public consumption – for example, on a social media site – in order to manage other people's opinion about them.

**Social capital** The collective value of all social networks (the value of knowing influential people), and the obligations that arise from these networks to do things for each other (for example, to return a favour).

**Bonding social capital** The sharing of information or resources that may create opportunities for jobs or mutual help.

**Bridging social capital** Social and political alliances or networks that increase the potential for social change.

**Commodification** Applying an economic value to a range of human activities.

**Narcissism** Self-obsession.

**Empathetic** Demonstrating the ability to understand and share the feelings of others.

**Proto-communities** An early form of community. Often used to describe online communities that have not been established or in place for very long.

**Post-familial family** A type of family that spends its leisure time online or playing with digital devices rather than actively spending it in each other's company. Parents today, for example, often Facebook their children to tell them to come downstairs for their meals.

**Networked global society** The idea that people sat at their computers are technologically linked to a global network of hundreds of thousands of others and consequently are potentially able to bring about economic, social and political change.

**Anti-globalisation movement (AGM)** A disparate collection of interest groups that feel that the problems of the group they represent have been brought about by global processes. The movement often uses global social media to coordinate and unify its protests against globalisation at events where world leaders meet.

**Digital underclass** People who are so disadvantaged that they cannot afford access to digital technology such as smartphones, laptops and broadband, ownership of which many people take for granted.

**Symbolic annihilation of women** A term invented by Tuchman that suggests that media representations of women rarely report their achievements or, if they do, tend to trivialise and devalue them. Women are often reduced in the media to being wives and girlfriends of men.

## Summary

1. The emergence of global social media has transformed the concepts of social interaction and identity. Young people, in particular, use global social media to engage in identity performance and to project their identity to all corners of the globe.
2. However, research suggests that the relationship between global media and identity has had some negative consequences in terms of addiction, anxiety and trolling.
3. Young people today are more likely to have developed a keen sense of political identity because of the existence of a networked global society, which means that the internet has given them the potential to possess a political voice that matters. Consequently, they are more likely to be actively engaged with identity politics or mass global political movements.

4. Marxists argue that global social media do not promote freedom of speech or democracy because it's ownership is concentrated in the hands of a small capitalist elite who aim to suppress criticism of capitalism.
5. Feminists have used global media to challenge patriarchy and misogyny and to construct a more empowered version of feminine identity.

# Unit 8.2.2 Cultural convergence versus cultural divergence

Some sociologists argue that globalisation has led to people across the world sharing the same cultural tastes. This argument is known as **cultural convergence** (also known as **homogenisation**). In contrast, other sociologists argue in favour of **cultural divergence** – they claim that some cultures react negatively to globalisation and resist it by proclaiming their separateness from other societies by becoming overtly nationalistic or turning back to traditional forms of culture, especially religious **fundamentalism**.

## Theories of cultural convergence and homogenisation

Martell argues that global processes are sweeping away significant territorial boundaries and bringing about the global homogenisation of cultural tastes. He also argues that national economies are declining in importance because of the free movement of capital, the activities of transnational corporations (TNCs) and the rise in influence of international organisations such as the UN, the WTO, the IMF and the EU. Moreover, the power and influence of nation-states is fast being eroded and devalued by the speed of digital technology, and especially the internet and social media as well as global migration and tourism.

Convergence theory argues that globalisation has resulted in a homogenised global culture in which national differences have become less clear as people consume culture from around the world rather than just their own national cultural products. There are three ways in which culture has become globally homogenised:

1. The use of English as the universal language of international business, finance, air travel and shipping. In contrast, other languages are in decline. For example, the number of spoken languages in the world has declined from an estimated 14500 in 1500 to 6400 in 2016, and it is predicted that least 50 per cent of languages spoken in the world in 2018 will have disappeared by the end of the 21st century. However, there are signs that the dominance of English is being challenged by Spanish in the USA and that, as China becomes more powerful, Cantonese and Mandarin may eventually challenge English, especially in Asia.
2. Leisure habits in many parts of the world are increasingly shaped by a global popular culture disseminated by global media that specialises in distributing the same music, television, film, computer/video games and video via social media platforms to a global audience.
3. It is suggested that tastes in food, drink, fashion and sport are also becoming homogenised as global brands in fast food and sportswear, as well as outlets for meeting friends, such as coffee houses, spread as the companies that dominate these markets expand across the world.

### Activity

Conduct a survey among your year group to examine whether aspects of their lives have become homogenised. Ask them questions such as:

- whether they own sportswear such as Manchester United, LA Laker or Barcelona tops
- whether they speak English when they are with their friends or whether they incorporate English phrases into conversation even when speaking in the local language
- whether they eat global fast foods such as burgers, pizza or chicken drumsticks, or drink Coke and Pepsi
- whether they discuss stuff they have seen on YouTube with their friends
- whether they buy products from Amazon or similar global companies.

## Theories of cultural divergence

However, the idea that the modern world is now characterised by homogeneity or sameness has been criticised by cultural divergence theory. David Held and Anthony McGrew (2007), for example, argue that if convergence was occurring it would be experienced evenly by all social groups across all societies. However, this is not the case for four reasons:

- Trade, investment and money flows are mainly concentrated in the 'triad' of Europe, Japan and North America.
- The UN, EU or WTO rarely act independently of or against the interests of the most powerful nations. All of these organisations have been accused by poorer nations of working in favour of the economic triad of Europe, North America and Japan.
- Globalisation has had some fairly unpleasant side-effects that have affected poorer societies more than wealthy ones, including the environmental destruction of local eco-systems, global warming – which according to some experts is resulting in rising sea levels and flooding – major crimes such as drug and people trafficking, corruption, terror attacks carried out in the name of religion, and even genocide and ethnic cleansing.
- Convergence theory has been criticised for making sweeping generalisations about 'global' processes. Critics note that these processes do not affect all areas of the world equally. There is considerable evidence that some nation-states – for example, the USA, Russia and China – continue to wield great global power and influence. There is also evidence that global inequality has widened. For example, African countries have tended to experience greater poverty as globalisation has progressed.

On the basis of these criticisms, some sociologists have concluded that so-called 'global processes' have resulted in cultural divergence rather than convergence. This can be illustrated in five ways:

## The resurgence of nationalism

According to supporters of globalisation, there should be less nationalism as the influence of nation-states recedes. However, there is a good case for stating that the past 10 years has seen a steep rise in nationalist movements – for example, in Italy, Hungary and Poland. Britain has voted to leave the EU. Masha Gessen (2017) claims that Russia's President Putin increasingly talks in increasingly nationalistic tones about Russia's 'destiny'. Sociologists have observed that nationalism is often accompanied by a rise in racism and **xenophobia** (fear of and hostility towards foreigners, especially migrants).

### Activity

Think of three other examples from around the world that suggest a resurgence in nationalism.

## A retreat to fundamentalism

The late 20th century and early 21st century in particular saw a rise in religious fundamentalism among Zionists in Israel, Hindus in India, Muslims in Saudi Arabia, Iran, Iraq and Afghanistan and Christian groups in the USA. Steger argues that the resurgence of fundamentalism that occurred in the 1990s and post-2000 is evidence of cultural divergence. He argues that globalisation resulted in a loss of traditional meaning in some cultures which were not quite ready for such modernity. Globalisation, therefore, created an uneasy tension and a less stable sense of identity, place and knowledge among some groups, who became very attracted by the certainties offered by fundamentalist religions.

Giddens (1999) argues that the growth of fundamentalism is a product of and a reaction to globalisation, which is seen by some religious scholars, especially in Islamic societies, as a threat to traditional beliefs and practices.

Global values and moral codes are interpreted by fundamentalist scholars as too liberal and as undermining traditional social norms relating to the family, gender roles and sexuality because they encourage equal rights for women and gay people, free speech and the promotion of democracy. Globalisation's promotion of these norms and values are regarded as threatening traditional authoritarian power bases, especially rule by elites based on divine right and male dominance of these societies.

Furthermore, globalisation has exposed many traditional societies to the influence of Western consumerism and materialism, whose 'decadence' or spiritual emptiness is seen by some fundamentalist members of less industrialised societies as a threat to their faith and identity, and especially the adherence of the next generation to religious rules of lifestyle. The focus on materialism, fashion and pop culture in Western culture is seen to be corrupt in that it distracts young people in traditional societies away from religion.

Giddens argues that fundamentalism is attractive to some because its rigid dogmatic beliefs promise certainty in an uncertain world. It is a retreat from the 'cosmopolitan' (and Western) modern world, with its demand for rational thinking and personal choice, into faith-based answers and submission to a higher spiritual authority. Giddens sees fundamentalism as the enemy of cosmopolitan thought and modernity.

### Activity

Research Hindu fundamentalism in India or Christian fundamentalism in the USA. How similar or different are the motives for these types of fundamentalism to the type of fundamentalism found in some Muslim countries?

## Ethnic revitalisation

James Banks (2017) argues that globalisation and the resurgence of nationalism have led to many nations questioning how they should deal with global migration. In the period following World War II, many nations were happy to accommodate immigration. For example, after 1945 thousands of European Jews emigrated to the USA and Israel, and in the 1950s and 1960s the shortage of male labour in Britain led employers to recruit hundreds of thousands of workers from Britain's ex-colonies in the Caribbean and on the Indian subcontinent. As both the German and French economies became successful in the 1960s, they recruited workers from Turkey and North Africa respectively.

### Activity

*The* Empire Windrush *packed with West Indian immigrants on arrival in the UK in 1948.*

What actions by the UK government in relation to the original Windrush generation have proved controversial in recent years?

Banks argues that it was assumed that migrant groups and their cultures would **assimilate** into the wider culture of the country in which they had settled, that migrants' values and norms would eventually become indistinguishable from those of the dominant group. However, Banks argues that in the 1960s marginalised racial, ethnic, and language groups argued that they should have the right to retain important aspects of their cultures and languages while participating fully in the national civic culture and community. This movement which became known as 'ethnic revitalisation' demanded that state institutions needed to be more sensitive to the cultural identities and experiences of minorities. Governments were encouraged to promote tolerance and to reduce prejudice and injustice by dismantling segregatory regulations in their education systems.

The result of these pressures was that **assimilation** was widely abandoned as a policy and the notion of **multiculturalism** became the norm in most modern societies. This is the view that all the different cultural or ethnic groups that make up a society have the right to retain and celebrate their own religious, historical and cultural traditions without fear or threat from the majority group. Multicultural societies promote the cultural needs and sensibilities of all social groups because these are regarded as equally important in terms of their civil and human rights.

The notion of 'ethnic revitalisation' has been of great influence. In Canada in the 1980s, it very nearly led to French Quebec declaring itself independent from mainly English-speaking Canada. It also brought down the apartheid regimes in Rhodesia (now Zimbabwe) in 1980 and South Africa in 1994.

However, there have also been doubts expressed about the effectiveness of multiculturalism in modern societies. These are explored in detail in Part 5 of this chapter.

## Cultural defence

Migration is a very stressful experience. Burhan Wazir (2018) argues that new arrivals tend to look in two directions; they gaze back at their homelands, religions, families and those they have left behind; and they also look anxiously at the customs, language, religions and laws of the country they have adopted. They have to cope with a range of negative reactions to their presence such as '**othering**' – the frequent reference to 'you people'. Afua Hirsch (2018) describes othering very succinctly as a migrant from Ghana to the UK when she says, 'I can't be British, can I, if British people keep asking me where I'm from?' Other negative reactions to the migrant's presence include **micro-aggressions**, subtle prejudice, institutional racism and open hostility, which may show itself through racial violence and attacks.

The concept of **cultural defence** has mainly been used by sociologists who are interested in how migrant groups cope with such stress and anxiety and to explain why they seem to be more religious than indigenous groups. For example, Asians, Africans and African-Caribbeans who have settled in the USA and Europe generally tend to be more religious in terms of both belief and practice than most White people. Steve Bruce (2002) claims that for many migrants religions act as a form of cultural defence (see Unit 7.6.2). In particular, religion offers migrants support and a sense of cultural identity in an uncertain and possibly hostile environment. It functions to defend and preserve culture and language and helps newcomers to cope with threats such as racism. James Beckford (2002) suggests that the evangelical Christianity offered by the Baptist and Pentecostal churches gave Black people a sense of community, purpose, hope and independence in countries such as Britain and the USA. Religion, therefore, offers more than just spiritual fulfilment to members of ethnic minorities. It has the power to reaffirm or revitalise ethnic identity.

Cultural defence can also promote ethnic revitalisation. In the 1960s, the civil rights movement led by a caucus of Black church organisations headed by the Reverend Martin Luther King, Jr was instrumental in persuading the US government to outlaw segregation in schools and other state institutions.

Amy Chua (2018) argues that sociologists should focus on the concept of 'tribes' rather than nation-states. Chua is not using the term 'tribe' in its conventional sense. She uses it to mean 'political interest group'. She argues that tribes are more likely than nation-states to culturally defend their interests and engage in ethnic revitalisation. She argues that most people do not simply seek to be free or to be rich as individuals. They actually want to thrive within their tribe while hurting other tribes. She argues that most societies contain rival competing tribes which can be economic, political, religious, ethnic or age-orientated in origin.

For example, in 2001, the USA identified the Taliban as an anti-democratic force that had to be eradicated and invaded Afghanistan with that goal in mind. However, Chua argues that the USA failed to understand that the Taliban was also a resistance movement, mainly made up of people from the Pashtun tribe. When the USA toppled the Taliban, it installed a new Afghan government mainly made up of the Tajik tribe (the main rival of the Pashtuns). The Afghan civil war continues to this day.

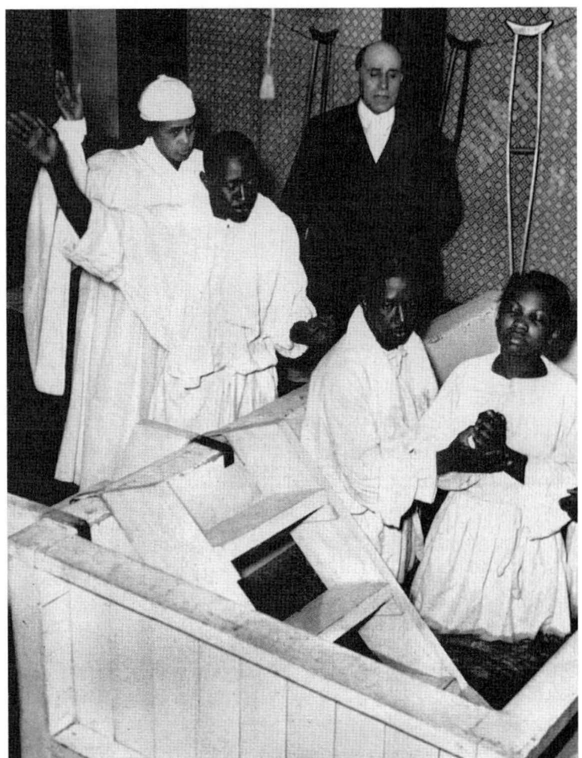

*Baptisms being performed at the Pentecostal Faith Church of All Nations in New York, 1934.*

Chua argues that even President Trump's victory in 2016 can be seen as a form of ethnic revitalisation. She argues that the White working-class tribe who were disaffected by economic recession and the USA's industrial decline mainly voted for Trump. Their vote was a rejection of the elite tribe – the political establishment – that dominated Washington. Chua argues that Trump epitomises and supercharges American tribalism. With him in power, all other American tribes – Blacks, women, Mexicans, the LGBT community and so on – feel more threatened than the straight White male tribe.

There is evidence that some groups are using global social media as forms of cultural defence and ethnic revitalisation. For example, migrant populations use social media to facilitate connections with their homeland. These connections help them to preserve and defend aspects of their culture, especially language, customs, traditions and religious rites (see the Contemporary issues box in Unit 6.3.2).

### Activity

Consider Chua's ideas about tribes. Think about the society in which you live. Are there tribes of the type that Chua describes? Do some of these dominate your society?

## Hybridisation: glocalisation or 'transformative change'

Held (2010) argues that globalisation has led to what he calls 'transformative change', which means that there are no longer any clear distinctions between the local/domestic and international in terms of economic, social and political processes. For example, aspects of local culture such as media, films, television, music, religion, food, fashion and sport are often now infused with inputs from global sources. This transformative process often produced a global–local nexus of exchange known as 'glocalisation' – a fusion or blending of global products with local products and services in ways that reflect the cultural priorities and eccentricities of a particular society.

Similarly, Steger observes that those who denounce the homogenising effects of Americanisation must not forget that hardly any society in the world today possesses an 'authentic or self-contained culture'. Rather, cultural hybridity is increasingly the norm. Steger argues that those sociologists who believe in cultural convergence or homogeneity need 'to listen to exciting Bollywood pop songs, admire the intricacies of the several variations of Hawaiian pidgin or enjoy the culinary delights of Cuban-Chinese cuisine'.

Roland Robertson (1995) argues that the hybridisation that stems from the cultural flow between the global and local can reinvigorate local cultures. The processes of hybridisation are clearly visible in fashion, music, dance, films, food, sports, language and social media.

Robertson argues that glocalisation often involves local people selecting from the global only that which pleases them, so that it becomes embedded in and accommodating to their local conditions and needs. They borrow, adapt and modify global products to match and blend with their domestic cultural requirements. The global is modified by its contact with the local fusion/creativity. The process of glocalisation should work both ways if global businesses wish to be successful. For example, McDonald's may have proliferated around the world but the ingredients of its products vary to fit in with local customs (from shrimp burgers in Japan to kosher burgers for Jewish customers in Israel and an emphasis on chicken burgers in Muslim countries). Global fast-food outlets, therefore, adapt to local eating customs that may vary from 'fast' to 'leisurely' in different contexts.

John Clammer (2014) identifies a form of glocalisation which he terms 'indigenisation'. He notes that Japanese culture is concerned with constructing distinctive styles of dress and other forms of consumption. Japanese people feel the need to express their identity by creating the right atmosphere at home. Moreover, Clammer argues that Japanese tradition has always fostered eclecticism – a delight in selecting new avenues of expression.

Consequently, Clammer argues that Japanese modern consumerism is a combination of ancient Japanese tradition – especially that relating to the giving and receiving of gifts (often in return for favours) – and global influences. For example, he observes that Japanese culture has had little difficulty incorporating the Christian festival of Christmas or American inventions such as Mother's Day and Halloween, all of which involve the exchange of gifts.

Similarly, the Indian film industry – Bollywood – exports 900 films a year to the rest of the world. These combine traditional Hindu and other mythological material relating to duty and kinship obligations with American themes such as those found in Hollywood musicals and romance.

Another form of glocalisation is **creolisation**, which generates altogether new and fused inventions. It is a form of creative blending. For example, in South Nigeria, the absorption of Christianity into local culture has led to a fusion of African music and language with traditional hymns and gospel and the traditional Christian rituals associated with worship. However, local worshippers have blended Christian worship with local cultural beliefs in magic and witchcraft (which originates in the pre-Christian religion of animism). Consequently, Nigerian churches and what goes on in them are very different to their Western counterparts.

Another good example of creolisation is the way that Trinidadians use Facebook ('Fasbook' or 'Macobook') to reflect their cultural priorities (see Unit 2.3.2).

Glocalisation often results in the hybridisation of food and drink. In the West, people often combine spices and sauces from around the world, such as soy sauce, chilli and curry spices, pesto or Italian sauces, and add them to traditional stews, soups, barbecue grills and pies.

## Activity

With the permission of your parents, go through the fridge and kitchen cupboards at home and list those products – spices, foods and drink – that are not produced by the country in which you live. How hybridised is your family's favourite food?

Cohen and Kennedy also point out that in societies in which there is conflict between rich and poor or between powerful groups and the powerless, hybridisation can often be a deviant or transgressive act that can empower an oppressed social group. Adopting a hybridised identity can be a form of political protest that challenges the authority of those in power.

In addition to glocalisation, Cohen and Kennedy point out there also exist what they call '**reverse cultural flows**'– for example, to the West from the East. Western culture has been enriched by cultural inputs from the popular culture of other societies. For example, many Western musicians have worked with African and Arab musicians to fuse genres of music into new forms. Some world music fuses and mixes Western dance beats with traditional styles from North Africa and Asia. Western cultural lifestyles and tastes have also been modified by aspects of Japanese culture in the form of alternative medicine and herbal therapy, meditative techniques and martial arts such as t'ai chi, judo, karate and kung fu. Hinduism was very influential in the 1960s and 1970s in terms of influencing many New Age religions. The influence of Chinese culture is apparent, with acupuncture being a staple of many Western healthcare systems.

## The postmodernist perspective on globalisation

Martell (2010) argues that postmodernists argue that what we think about is more important than globalisation itself. We interpret the world as globalising, whether it is or not. This may even have a self-fulfilling effect. Because we think the world is globalising, we act as if it is. Globalisation, then, has an ideational force on us. Furthermore, it starts to happen when we behave in a globalised way because of what we think as much as because of what is actually there. We need to analyse globalisation as a discourse and examine its signifiers (symbols of globalisation) and people's consciousness of the world.

From a postmodern point of view, one of the key developments in the history of globalisation was the popularisation of the idea of globalisation itself in the 1980s onwards, as much as any actual processes of globalisation. Martell, however, is sceptical that globalisation has actually occurred, because he argues that there is no evidence of a shared global consciousness – that is, that people around the world think and interpret the social world in similar ways. Some sociologists go as far as dismissing globalisation as an ideological construction of Western liberal intellectuals.

## Activity

Research the principles that the popular TV series *Star Trek* was organised around. The USS *Enterprise* and its ethnically diverse crew represented the United Federation of Planets. Debate within your class the possibility of the people of this planet adopting a one-world identity or being united by subscribing to the same global consciousness. What problems could be eradicated if such unity could be achieved?

## Key terms

**Cultural convergence** The process by which different cultures become very similar or the same.

**Homogenisation** The process of being or becoming the same.

**Cultural divergence** The process by which cultures become different from one another or even come into conflict with one another.

**Fundamentalism** A form of a religion, especially Islam or Protestant Christianity, that believes in and acts upon a literal interpretation of holy texts.

**Xenophobia** Fear or hatred of foreigners often expressed through open or subtle forms of hostility and aggression.

**Assimilation** The process in which an ethnic group subculture is absorbed into a wider culture. It involves ethnic groups either voluntarily or being forced to give up traditional aspects of their culture. The culture of the minority group comes to resemble that of the majority group.

**Multiculturalism** The presence of, or support and respect for, the presence of several distinct cultural or ethnic groups within a society.

**Othering** Viewing another person as different or inferior or alien compared with oneself. A form of stereotyping based on ignorance.

**Micro-aggression** Indirect, subtle or unintentional discrimination against members of a marginalised group – for example, giving disapproving looks.

**Cultural defence** In a racist or hostile society, ethnic minority groups may use aspects of their religion as a way of defending their culture if it is under threat.

**Creolisation** A hybrid mix of different cultures – for example, see Miller's work on how Trinidadian people use Facebook as 'Fasbook'.

**Reverse cultural flow** It is often assumed that the cultural flow of ideas and cultural products is from the West to other parts of the world. However, Western culture has also been heavily influenced by a cultural flow from the East in the form of religion, diet, exercise regimes and so on.

## Summary

1. Some critics of globalisation believe that it has brought about cultural sameness or homogenisation (also known as convergence) that destroys and devalues the richness and diversity of local cultures.
2. Other sociologists believe that globalisation has brought about cultural divergence and differences. The evidence suggests that there are six possible social reactions to globalisation, including a resurgence in nationalism, the rise of fundamentalist and ethnic revitalisation movements, cultural defence, and hybridisation or glocalisation.
3. There are a number of different types of hybridisation or glocalisation – that is, ways local people combine or fuse the global with the local.
4. Postmodernists believe that thinking about globalisation may be more important than globalisation itself. They argue that true globalisation can only occur when there exists a unified global consciousness possessed by all people in all societies. This consciousness does not exist yet.

# Unit 8.2.3 The role of Western ideology in shaping identity and the concept of Westernisation

This unit aims to examine the role of Western ideas in shaping identity around the world. Many sociologists believe that a close examination of the different dimensions of globalisation reveals that Western ideology and practices have exercised a disproportionate influence on these dimensions. For example, Marxist sociologists argue that economic globalisation is not a genuinely global phenomenon because most of its characteristics originate in Western capitalism, and particularly a Western set of economic ideas or ideology known as neoliberalism.

## Westernisation

Some sociologists suggest that the term 'internationalisation' more accurately describes economic globalisation and the world economy. These writers do not deny that globalisation is taking place. They are simply pointing out that global processes are mainly driven by Western, and especially American, influences and that therefore what we are talking about is **Westernisation**.

Marxists have provided sociology with the most compelling critique of capitalism. Most Marxists reject the idea that globalisation is something new. They tend to argue that the world economy is quite simply characterised by an advanced version or stage of capitalism in which capitalists search for new and expanding markets for their goods. In 1848, in *The Communist Manifesto*, Marx and Engels clearly stated that capitalism would exist across 'the entire surface of the globe. It must nestle everywhere, settle everywhere, establish connections everywhere.'

According to Paul Hirst and Grahame Thompson (2009), the modern world is dominated by a form of international capitalism dominated by Western governments, as well as multinationals and international organisations such as the WTO operating internationally rather than globally. The function of these agents of capitalism is to scour the world for raw materials, new markets and sources of labour, and thus to make even greater profits. Moreover, this international economic activity is underpinned by an economic ideology – neoliberalism – that originated in Western thought.

Neoliberal ideology states that individual freedom is best guaranteed by the 'free market' and that the role of the state is to promote private enterprise by removing any barriers such as tariffs, quotas and regulations which prevent or impede open markets and free trade. The influence of this ideology probably reached its peak in the 1980s. Martell argues that it carried in its wake another set of ideas which assumed that less industrialised nations needed to adopt Western forms of economic and political organisation such as capitalism, industrialism, rationalisation, urbanism, individualism and democracy if they wished to be seen as modern or global societies.

Hirst and Thompson argued that a world economy exists today made up of a collection of independent capitalist economies in which the richest nation-states (mainly located in North America, Europe and Japan) exercise a great deal of economic independent power and control. In contrast, globalisation suggests one global economy within which all countries, rich or poor, are interdependent and in which even rich countries are unable to escape the negative effects caused by this unified global economy running into problems.

George Ritzer (1993) argues that one negative consequence of the spread of capitalism across the world has been the global adoption of a mode of production and service that he calls 'McDonaldization', which originated with the fast-food franchise of the same name.

According to Ritzer, the four main dimensions of 'McDonaldization' are:

- Efficiency – quite simply, this refers to taking a task and breaking it down into smaller tasks. This process is repeated until all tasks have been broken down to the smallest possible level. All tasks are then rationalised to find the single most efficient method for completing each task. All workers perform this task in the same way. Individuality is not allowed.
- Calculability – all outcomes are assessed on quantifiable rather than subjective criteria. Quantity is valued more than quality.
- Predictability – the production process is organised to guarantee uniformity of product and standardised outcomes.
- Control – this is achieved by de-skilling the labour force or by replacing it with automation.

Ritzer is critical of 'McDonaldization' because it produces uniformity or homogeneity in production, labour and product, wherever it is situated in the world.

However, from a Marxist perspective, 'McDonaldization' is just another capitalist way of doing business. As manufacturing industry, especially in the West, went into decline in the 1980s, new opportunities for profit opened up in the service sector. As profits mounted, fast food was internationalised. Marxists suggest that the production of fast food was very much a component of the spread of Western tastes. This can clearly be seen when the arrival of the McDonald's 'Big Mac' in the communist states of Eastern Europe was seen as a powerful symbol of Western freedom and consumer lifestyle – the real taste of the USA.

Some sociologists claim that this internationalisation, because of its Western bias, is a form of cultural imperialism, and is destroying or eroding the richness and unique quality of local cultural production and destabilising local communities and dividing societies along socio-economic and generational lines. It was argued by Barber (2007) that this cultural imperialism is producing a type of consumerism that is increasingly soulless and unethical in its pursuit of profit. Benjamin Barber and Andrea Schulz (1995) coined the term **'McWorld'** to symbolise a global world in which

## Activity

*The opening of the first McDonald's restaurant in Moscow, 1990.*

Research how people in the former communist countries of Russia, East Germany, Poland, Hungary and Czechoslovakia reacted when McDonald's opened up their fast-food outlets in those countries.

they feared all cultures and consumption would be standardised and homogenised.

Those who argue that cultural imperialism is a problem have expressed concern about:

- Media concentration – most of the world's media and culture industry is owned and controlled by a few powerful media corporations (see Unit 6.2.1). These media conglomerates, which are mainly American (such as Disney, Microsoft, WarnerMedia, Apple, Facebook and AOL) have achieved near monopolistic control of newspapers, film archives, news programmes, advertising, satellites, internet search engines, social media platforms and the production of music, films and television shows. It is feared that this media concentration over cultural products may threaten democracy and freedom of expression.
- Marxist critical thinkers such as Robert McChesney (2008) highlight the similarity of digital content and social networking. American capitalism, as represented by corporations such as Facebook, Google and Twitter, for example, operates in hundreds of countries across the world. He claims that these companies are engaged in a form of cultural imperialism aimed at spreading the 'American way-of-life' and are, therefore, engaged in a 'colonialism of the mind' and resulting in millions of people behaving and thinking in the same way. McChesney argues that this 'cult of homogeneity' speaks to everyone in general and no one in particular and crowds out local cultural products. It has also reduced people's opportunity to speak out and challenge issues such as inequality.
- Fuchs (2013), too, argues that all forms of global communication and social media platforms are ideological in that they function on behalf of the global capitalist ruling class to reproduce and justify class inequality, especially that expressed via wealth and income inequalities (see Unit 6.2.1). Fuchs believes that the role of digital social media and the cultural products produced by modern capitalism is to bring about a state of 'false class consciousness' so that ordinary citizens and workers do not criticise or challenge the organisation of capitalist society, which allegedly favours the few at the expense of the many.
- The influence of American companies such as Coca-Cola, Nike, Pepsi and Microsoft as symbols of US power and materialism is illustrated by a story retold by Cohen and Kennedy about Fidel Castro and Che Guevara, the leaders of the Cuban revolution. Both were very conscious of the iconic power of American culture. Every day, Che would present Fidel with a bottle or can of Coke until one day Castro shook his head and said, 'It's no good, unless we crack the formula of Coca-Cola, the revolution is doomed.'

## Activity

What are the implications of Castro's conclusions about Coca-Cola?

- Other societies can rarely compete with this American domination of cultural production. This can be illustrated in three ways:

1. Music production and sales are dominated by American artists and studios. The only country that has made any significant inroads into the American dominance of the music industry is Britain. Held observes that many domestic record industries cannot compete with the **Americanisation** of music. France, for example, has maintained a relatively strong domestic music industry and market for its own particular brand of pop, although it is less popular outside French-speaking countries (however, French bands such as Daft Punk often use English lyrics to sell to a wider global market). He observes that 'Sweden has generated the disco equivalent of Volvo in the shape of Abba' but on the whole, world music (from the likes of Nigeria, Ghana, Cuba and South Korea (K-Pop and Gangnam) is expanding, but currently only takes up a tiny share of international music markets.

## Activity

'Globalisation is more likely to result in global convergence than global divergence'. Evaluate this view.

Films are made and released internationally by only 20 or so nations but the USA dominates the number of films shown in cinemas around the world. For example, over 80 per cent of domestic cinema receipts are generated by US-made films. There are few co-productions between US film-makers and film-makers in other countries. Some countries, notably France, have taken steps to protect their domestic film industry by introducing quotas on the number of English-speaking films shown in cinemas.

2. Tourism is often cited as evidence of the globalisation of culture, but neither the origins nor the final destinations of international tourists support this thesis. Tourist expenditure, for example, is not evenly distributed or divided across the globe. The vast majority of outward tourist movement is from the USA and Europe.

Jan Aarte Scholte (2005) takes issue with Hirst and Thompson and argues that, since the late 1980s, there are signs that 'superterritorialism' is becoming the dominant feature of the 21st-century world. He argues in favour of a form of globalisation that he claims goes far beyond the Marxist concept of internationalisation, because it 'involves more people, more often'. It also involves a greater volume of global transactions and is both more extensive and intensive. He claims that the world is now experiencing a more genuine form of globalisation characterised by two types of global connectivity not experienced before. This is something above, beyond and separate from geographical connectedness:

a) **Transworld simultaneity** – people in a diversity of distant and remote places are doing the same things as each other, such as consuming the same brand of coffee, watching the same global sports tournaments and worrying about and experiencing the same ecological problems or economic problems caused by events outside of the society in which they live.

b) **Transworld instantaneity** – people who are located in different parts of the world and time-zones, and who are culturally and linguistically different from one another, can now use social media such as Facebook and Twitter to interact with and communicate with one another at the same time. Moreover, they can instantaneously swap social capital and distribute political ideas that people in other societies can use to publicise or challenge the inequalities and human rights abuses that exist in their own society or worldwide.

However, Martell remains unconvinced. He argues that if globalisation had truly taken place, then a 'global consciousness' ought to be apparent and that most of the world's population would have an awareness of 'the globe as one place'. They would view themselves as citizens of the world. However, the evidence suggests that the nation-state mentality still dominates – for example, international surveys do not report that the majority of the world's people see themselves as part of a global community.

3. Finally, Scholte argues that globality is evident in social relations through global consciousness. In other words, people often do think globally. For example, some might regard the planet as a 'global village' or globally minded people might regard the planet as the main source of their food supplies as well as their entertainments, threats and friends. For example, Ghanaian traders and Filipino domestics may see the whole planet, rather than just the region they come from, as their potential workplace. Scholte also argues that transworld consciousness can also take the form of languages (such as English, Esperanto and Spanish) and is often symbolised by icons such as the Coca-Cola or Nike logo, as well as World Heritage Sites. Awareness of the planet as a single social place is, furthermore, evident in events such as global sports competitions – for example, the Olympic Games, World Cups in football, rugby and cricket), global exhibitions, global film festivals, global tours by music superstars, global conferences and global panics. In addition, global consciousness arises when people conceive of their social affiliations in transplanetary, supraterritorial terms – for instance, with transworld solidarities based on class, gender, generation, profession, race, religion, sexuality and, indeed, humanity. However, Scholte acknowledges that the world has not yet reached this stage. However, he is confident that one day it will. He illustrates this confidence by referring to humankind's obsession with aliens from outer space. He observes that when we discuss the possibility of aliens from other planets, the alien other is not conceived as just another nationality from another territory, but as another being from another planet, 'thereby defining humanity and the Earth as one'.

## Key terms

**Westernisation** The process whereby cultures adopt American or European ways of thinking or cultural practices.

**McWorld** A term used to indicate a particular standardisation of production techniques inspired by the McDonald's fast-food chain and seen to epitomise globalisation.

**Americanisation** The dominance of American cultural products such as Hollywood films or rap music.

**Transworld simultaneity** Scholte defines this as global connections that extend across the planet at the same time. For instance, people in lots of places doing the same thing, such as young people drinking Coca-Cola as a lifestyle choice.

**Transworld instantaneity** Scholte defines this as global connections that move anywhere across the planet in no time. For instance, digital technology can connect people at the same time wherever they are located in the world using devices.

## Summary

1. Marxists reject the idea of globalisation altogether. Rather, they believe that what is mistaken for globalisation is merely an expansion of capitalism into new markets. This has produced a negative by-product because capitalist values are often shaped by Western values and consequently accused of cultural imperialism.

# END-OF-PART QUESTIONS

0 1 Describe two examples of cultural convergence. **[4 marks]**

0 2 Explain one positive effect and one negative effect of the impact of globalisation on personal identity. **[6 marks]**

0 3 Explain two reasons why some societies and cultures attempt to resist globalisation. **[8 marks]**

# PART 3 GLOBALISATION, POWER AND POLITICS

## Contents

**Unit 8.3.1** **The spread of liberal democracy and human rights** **495**

**Unit 8.3.2** **Global social movements and attempts to oppose globalisation** **505**

**Unit 8.3.3** **Debates about the role of the nation-state in tackling global social and environmental problems** **511**

This part focuses on political globalisation, specifically the global spread of a particular type of political system known as liberal democracy or democratic capitalism. This system has a number of distinct social characteristics that differentiate it from other political systems, past and present. The main features of liberal democracy include the nation-state and the promotion and protection of human rights – basic rights and freedoms which, in principle, belong to every person in the world, from birth until death. Unit 8.3.1 explores the features of liberal democracies and contrasts them with other political systems – for example, authoritarian governments. The unit also considers which human rights are regarded as fundamental to liberal democracies and contrasts this with the human rights records of authoritarian states.

Unit 8.3.2 focuses on global social movements that have arisen since the 1980s to oppose the globalisation encouraged by liberal elites and democracies. However, some sociologists argue that such movements have also helped spread liberal democracy in their opposition to repressive totalitarian regimes that routinely ignore or abuse human rights. The effectiveness of these anti-globalisation, pro-democracy and human rights movements has been enhanced by the globalisation of digital technology, which has interconnected various protest groups based around the world at the click of a button.

Finally, Unit 8.3.3 examines whether the nation-state is capable of survival in the globalised world and whether it has the will or resources to tackle the social and environmental risks, threats and problems associated with globalisation.

# Unit 8.3.1 The spread of liberal democracy and human rights

This unit identifies and explores the social features that characterise **liberal democracies** and nation-states. It also contrasts liberal democracies with other political systems. For example, in recent years, there has been an increase in authoritarian governments in which autocratic leaders have taken power on a wave of populism motivated by resentment of liberal elites and globalisation. The unit concludes by examining the concept of human rights and evaluating the different definitions of which rights are regarded as fundamental to liberal democracies. In contrast, the record of authoritarian states with regard to human rights is considered, especially the view that, in many of these societies, human rights tend to be undervalued, ignored altogether and even abused.

## Defining liberal democracy and authoritarianism

Countries are territories inhabited by a distinct cultural or ethnic group. Throughout history, such groups have claimed sovereignty over that territory, which means that they have organised themselves into a government that has established borders between its territory and that of other groups, and claimed the right and power to govern what goes on within that territory. Until the 16th and 17th centuries, most territories were ruled by autocratic rulers such as kings, emperors and princes, and subjects had very little say in how governance was organised.

Anthony Pick (2011) argues that the first nation-states emerged in the 17th century. In nation-states, leaders are accountable to civil society. This means that the legitimacy of such leaders is derived from the people through the mechanism of democratic elections. Consequently, most nation-states today are based on liberal democracy although authoritarian regimes continue to exist.

### Liberal democracy

Held (2006) argues that a liberal or **representative democracy** means that decisions affecting a community such as a nation are taken by a group of representatives who have been chosen via an electoral process (voting) to govern within the framework of the rule of law.

He argues that liberal democracies are composed of a cluster of rules and institutions that distinguish them from other political systems, and which are necessary to their successful functioning. In 2006, the Economist Intelligence Unit (EIU) produced its first 'democracy index'. This aims to categorise countries into one of four regime types; **full democracies**, **partial or flawed democracies**, hybrid regimes and authoritarian states. Full liberal democracies share the features in the following list; flawed or partial democracies share most of these features but may be weak in one or two respects; hybrid regimes may have only some of these characteristics.

1. A written or unwritten **constitution**; that is, a set of laws which define the role, powers and structure of the different institutions that make up the state. It also makes clear in federal countries such as the USA, Nigeria, Germany, Switzerland, Belgium and Australia the relationship between the central or federal government and state, provincial or territorial governments.
2. An **executive** or **government** that makes, puts into action and reinforces law and social policy. It is usually headed by a president or prime minister who leads a cabinet made up of ministers who have been given responsibility and budgets to run large government departments. The executive exercises authority over most areas of the internal social life of a society, especially the economic, education, welfare and criminal justice systems as well as making foreign policy and maintaining diplomatic relationships with other states.
3. A **parliament or legislature** made up of elected representatives (which includes those of the ruling political party and those of opposition parties) who critically examine and debate the laws and policies introduced by the executive in order to make sure that it is not exceeding its powers and to make certain that such laws and policies take account of the rights of all social groups that make up society.

   Some legislatures have the legal authority to remove the executive if they feel it has exceeded its power or if a president or prime minister is accused of criminal offences such as treason or corruption, or of bringing the office into disrepute. In the USA, this legal process is known as 'impeachment'.

## Activity

*The USA's legislature is known collectively as Congress.*

Research how the legislature of the USA is organised.

4. A body of public officials or civil servants that are appointed on the basis of merit to manage the day-to-day affairs of the state, and who are answerable to elected officials such as ministers.
5. An **independent judiciary** – in the USA and many other societies, a **Supreme Court** exists which aims to protect constitutional rights and prevent governments from behaving illegally.
6. A guarantee to meet basic needs and to safeguard individual human rights and freedoms. Liberal democracies often take responsibility for meeting the basic needs of its most vulnerable citizens and social groups from the cradle to the grave. For example, they may provide education and free or subsidised healthcare. Many states also guarantee and defend the rights and freedoms of their citizens because such rights confer dignity on individual citizens and promote tolerance and social order. For example, liberal democracies generally support freedom of speech and expression. Criticism of the political system and politicians is actively encouraged so long as it is not **slanderous** or **libellous**. Moreover, in liberal democracies, all citizens, regardless of social background, have the right to run for elected public office.
7. Elections that are frequent, free and fair. For example, in the USA, elections for president occur every four years, although there is a maximum term of eight years imposed on successful candidates. In France, a new president is elected every five years after two rounds of voting.
8. **Universal suffrage** or the right to vote. Usually, all adults or a majority of them have the right to vote in elections unless they are legitimately banned from doing so because they are suffering from severe mental illness or are in prison.
9. A free and independent media. Every citizen has the right to obtain information or news, especially about government activity, from sources independent of government or interests that support the government.

## Partial and hybrid democracies

Held points to a number of countries which he describes as 'partial democracies'. These societies demonstrate some accountability to citizens via elections but may exercise some restrictions on their citizens. For example, they may deny women, homosexuals and ethnic minorities (especially migrant groups) human rights or curb the activities of trade unions or human rights organisations. In 2018, the EIU downgraded the USA to a partial democracy because it argued that free speech and an independent media and judiciary were under attack from the Trump administration. The American government's treatment of suspected Islamic terrorists who have been kept without trial for years at the Guantanamo Bay detention centre, and the 2018 separation of migrant children from their parents at the Mexican border and their confinement in cages, has also attracted global criticism of the USA's attitude towards human rights.

**Hybrid regimes** are nations in which irregularities in elections prevent them from being free and fair. Such countries may have regular elections but unfair pressure may be exerted on political opponents, and the media may be controlled by elites and therefore be biased in favour of the state or its leadership. Moreover, corruption and bribery of politicians and other public servants may be common, and some human rights may be violated. Russia is regarded by the EIU as a typical hybrid nation.

## Authoritarian political systems

In 1974, according to Held, a large number (68 per cent) of political systems worldwide were **authoritarian**. Authoritarianism refers to the principle of unquestioning submission to authority. In terms of a political system, 'authoritarian government' denotes any political system that concentrates power in the hands of a single leader or political party, or a small elite (or **oligarchy**) that is not constitutionally responsible to the mass of the people that make up a territory or nation. There are a number of variations on authoritarian political regimes, which we now explain.

## Fascism

Some notorious authoritarian political regimes have been organised around **fascist** principles – for example, Hitler's Germany and Mussolini's Italy in the 1930s and 1940s. Fascism is a totalitarian governmental system led by a 'supreme' leader or dictator (who often comes to power on the basis of force of personality or charisma and/or because they have managed to obtain the support of the military-industrial elite). Such leaders exercise complete power and often command blind loyalty and obedience from followers, allies and subordinates. Fascists often use coercion in the form of violence to forcibly suppress opposition and criticism. Opponents who pose a serious threat to the regime may be imprisoned without trial, and even executed, on fabricated political charges. Fascist regimes also emphasise an aggressive nationalism, often underpinned by a contempt for 'lesser' nations and ethnic groups and racism. Consequently, fascist governments in the past have engaged in ethnic cleansing of groups they believe to be inferior in breeding. For example, the Nazis systematically exterminated 6 million Jewish people (known as the 'Holocaust'). Finally, fascist regimes often organise, control and regiment all industry and commerce in service of the fascist state.

## Communism

A large number of authoritarian regimes which exercised totalitarian power in the 20th century were the direct and indirect result of the communist revolution that took place in Russia in 1917, which led to the setting up in 1922 of the communist state of the USSR (the Union of Soviet Socialist Republics). The USSR rejected liberal-democratic principles such as free elections or **pluralism** – the idea that a range of political parties should compete with one another for the votes of an electorate. Instead, this particular authoritarian state was based on five fundamental principles:

1. It was a one-party state in that the communist party was regarded as the only legitimate organisation that could propel the goals of the state forward. Individuals were expected by the party to commit themselves wholeheartedly to communist objectives. Consequently individual rights, such as freedom of speech and assembly, were rejected, while those who criticised the party, the state and the supreme leader were often exiled to work camps in Siberia or executed.
2. Power was concentrated in the hands of the leaders of the party – for example, in the 1920s Joseph Stalin managed, with the assistance of coercive institutions such as the secret police (KGB), to achieve absolute power, which he used to exterminate or exile his opponents within the party and crush any criticism and dissent. The death of Stalin in 1953 saw the communist leadership shift from the notion of **autocracy** (dictatorial rule by one person) to oligarchy (rule by an elite; in this case, the **Politburo** – the policy-making committee of the Soviet Communist Party).
3. **Propaganda** – biased or misleading information – was circulated widely and constantly repeated to convince the population of the USSR that the communist project was on track and working effectively.
4. A centralised '**command economy**' was put into place. This is where the state rather than the free market determines what goods should be produced or to what extent or at what speed industry should develop. For example, in the 1920s, Stalin instigated a massive agricultural programme, which resulted in the death of millions of peasants and, in the 1930s, an accelerated industrialisation programme, which resulted in both the modernisation and rapid urbanisation of Soviet society.
5. The export of communist ideas worldwide intended to kick-start communist revolutions around the world. This had some success – for example, North Korea and China installed communist regimes in 1948 and 1949 respectively, while other societies such as Cuba (1959), Somalia (1969), Yemen (1970), Congo (1970), Ethiopia (1974), Mozambique, Vietnam, Laos, Angola (all 1975) and Afghanistan (1978) declared themselves either socialist or Marxist republics.

The success of the Soviet army during World War II led to the Soviet occupation of much of Eastern Europe and the imposition of communism and puppet communist leaders, controlled by the USSR, on occupied Eastern European countries such as Poland, East Germany, Czechoslovakia, Hungary, Romania and Albania.

However, in 2018, only five authoritarian regimes based on communist principles remain worldwide – China,

North Korea, Vietnam, Cuba and Laos. Between 1989 and 1992, most of the communist regimes of Eastern Europe collapsed and their governments adopted universal suffrage and free elections. The Soviet Union fragmented into 15 independent nation-states, most of which abandoned the one-party system and adopted democracy.

### Contemporary Marxist regimes

The communist regimes that continue to exist today have shifted away from pure communist ideals. For example, China has survived as a 'communist' nation-state to become the leading economic power in the world because in the 1990s the Chinese leadership abandoned the notion that the state should exclusively command and shape the future direction of the economy. Private enterprise was encouraged and the Chinese leadership surrendered some of their economic controls to the 'natural' processes of the free market. As a result, China has been described as a '**market-Leninist**' system. However, political and social controls were not surrendered. The Chinese Communist Party continues to exert considerable social control over the Chinese people in the form of censorship of the media, and particularly over Chinese people's access to and use of non-Chinese websites and social media platforms. China is still a one-party state and President Xi has recently been appointed president for life.

### Military dictatorships

Some authoritarian states originate in military coups or takeovers. Huntington (1991) observed that between 1950 and 1975 a significant number of countries, especially in Latin America and Africa, experienced military rule after **coups d'état**, which often used force to remove democratically elected leaders. These military forms of political rule produced autocratic or oligarchic rulers in countries as diverse as Spain, Portugal, Greece, Argentina, Chile, Brazil, Zaire, Iraq, Pakistan and Myanmar.

### Apartheid

Some authoritarian states have been based on racial segregation. The **apartheid** system – a system of institutionalised racial segregation – shaped the political system of South Africa between 1948 and 1994. In this system, the White minority imposed strict controls over the majority Black population.

### Theocracies

Some authoritarian states are **theocracies** – that is, they are ruled by people and/or laws considered to have divine authority. For example, Saudi Arabia is an absolute monarchy underpinned by Islamic theology. Since 1932, Saudi Arabia has been ruled by the House of Saud. The power of the king is inherited and regarded as legitimate because it is accepted by the people that his power is divinely ordained (that is, it comes directly from God). Moreover, both the power of the king and the constitution of Saudi Arabia are based on the Qur'an and the support of **Wahhabi** religious clerics and scholars – a strict form of Sunni Islam which forbids the promotion of religions other than Islam. Other theocracies include Afghanistan, the Islamic Republic of Iran, Sudan, Yemen and Mauritania.

#### Activity

*The Vatican City is an authoritarian state.*

Consider the reasons why the Vatican City is technically an authoritarian state.

### Liberal democracies and authoritarian states today

Held claims that the number of liberal democracies, whether full, partial or hybrid, increased greatly across the world in the 19th and 20th centuries. In 2018, the EIU estimated that of the 167 countries in the world, 19 qualified as full democracies with a further 57 (including the USA) qualifying as flawed or partial democracies. Forty-six per cent of countries worldwide can be called 'liberal-democratic'. In addition, the EIU identified 39 countries as hybrid-democratic (23 per cent), while 52 countries were deemed authoritarian (31 per cent). This means that liberal-democratic principles can be found in most societies around the world.

Held observes, then, that there has been a significant decline in the number of authoritarian states but that there is no guarantee that authoritarian states will eventually convert to liberal democracy. Held argues that liberal democracies are often resisted by ruling elites and often only emerge after a period in which the struggles of working-class, ethnic groups and civil rights activists are violently suppressed.

## The nation-state

It is impossible to discuss the role of liberal democracy without identifying and describing its basic unit – the nation-state. Steger (2017) argues that, over the past two centuries, humans have organised their political differences as follows:

- They tend to identify with a particular geographical location or territory in which they and their ancestors have physically lived since time immemorial. This territory may take on the status of nation-state when other surrounding territories recognise and respect the validity and legitimacy of borders differentiating land as belonging to other ethnic groups, tribes and so on.
- Nation-states exercise **sovereignty**. This means that other nation-states recognise that they have the right to govern themselves, to impose their authority, controls and laws on people within a particular bordered territory without direct interference from other nation-states.
- Nation-states are **bureaucratic** – in order to be effective at governing their citizens, they develop a system of rational rules and regulations, a clear hierarchy of authority and a specialised division of labour. A non-elected well-educated bureaucratic class of managers and professionals (civil servants) administrates the day-to-day running of the nation-state.
- Identification with such a nation-state may invoke pride in a shared history and a powerful sense of belonging in the form of **patriotism** – being proud of your country for what it does – and **nationalism** – being proud of your country no matter what it does.
- Relationships with other nation-states are an important feature of most nation-states. Most have established diplomatic relations with other nation-states worldwide in order to peacefully resolve problems that might arise between them and to safeguard their citizens when travelling abroad.

### Activity

Most of us belong to a nation-state which is committed to protecting us when we travel to other nation-states. What symbols of your nationhood do you (or other citizens) carry with you to other countries? How would you seek help from your nation-state if you ran into trouble abroad?

- Nation-states usually monopolise any powers of coercion. In other words, the state supervises policing and the judicial system. It also maintains an armed force in the shape of an army, navy or air force in order to protect its interests and security from either internal threats (such as terrorism or uprisings) or external threats (for example, invasion).
- Nation-states often attempt to manage their economies in order to maintain employment, inflation, the price of basic necessities, and therefore living standards, to preserve the value of their currency, to control taxation, interest rates, public spending and to reduce the national debt and to maintain a certain level of trade with other nation-states. Some nation-states will be very hands-on in terms of managing their economies, while others may prefer minimal intervention.
- People in nation-states organise themselves politically in order to protect their right to occupy that territory. Most territories have tended to adopt liberal-democratic means of doing this. However, as we have already seen, authoritarian systems and autocratic leaders may be welcomed in some parts of the world.
- Citizens in nation-states subscribe to a collective identity based on an artificial division between the 'domestic' – the familiar 'we' who have lived on this land for generations and have constructed a nation-state to reflect that fact – and the unfamiliar 'foreign' 'them' – potential invaders and threats such as migrants.
- Steger, therefore, observes that modern nation-states are both psychological and physical manifestations. People live within real borders but what is just as important is the sense of **existential security** – the feeling that the state will protect the interests of both ourselves and future generations and the sense of historical continuity that produces strong feelings of **social integration** and solidarity. In other words, the concept of nation-state is successful when people feel psychologically committed to it. This psychological commitment is nurtured, says Steger, by social institutions such

as the media and sport, usually with state support, which demonise 'outsiders' so that citizens are encouraged to believe in the superiority of their own nation and cultural way of life. Steger argues that this **demonisation** of others often supplies the mental energy required for mass warfare.

## Human rights

There are a number of slightly differing definitions of human rights. Generally, human rights are moral principles or norms that describe certain standards of human behaviour seen to be worth protecting by both domestic and international laws. However, there is little agreement on what constitutes such rights or principles. The literature on human rights suggests there exist three broad approaches: entitlement, equality or a combination of the two.

**'Entitlement'** focuses on those positive economic and welfare rights to which some sociologists believe citizens should be entitled. For example, Frank Bealey and Allan Johnson (1999) suggest that any list of human rights should include the right to life or survival and the right to property. J.A. Ferguson (1986) argues that if nation-states have the resources, it is desirable that they protect their citizens from hunger and that they should guarantee them a minimum standard of living, as well as free education (thus guaranteeing a level of literacy and numeracy) and healthcare for all.

An **'equality'** approach is organised around the concept of equality before the law and is focused on the notion that the state may deliberately deprive some groups of the rights that the majority take for granted because the state disapproves of their political or religious beliefs. Some groups may be deprived of the same rights or opportunities as the majority because they have inherited ascribed characteristics such as gender, race, ethnicity or tribe. Moreover, some groups may be defined as 'deviant' by the state because of their sexuality. Francis Fukuyama (2018) suggests that there are three fundamental sets of rights brought together in the 'equality' approach to human rights:

a) **Civil rights** – the rights that people have in a society to equal treatment and equal opportunities, whatever their race, sex, or religion.

b) **Religious rights** – being able to express one's religious beliefs and follow particular religious practices free from persecution and state controls.

c) **Political rights** – to be able to express political opinions which may be in opposition to or critical of the government in power. Particular freedoms are seen as essential to the health of nation-states that practise liberal democracy. These include freedom of speech, the freedom to lawfully and peacefully assemble in public, in order to criticise other political points of view or to protest or demonstrate against those in power. Other political freedoms include the right to form opposition parties or to go on strike.

Many authoritarian states fail to guarantee these rights for their citizens. The evidence collected by organisations such as Amnesty International suggests that some authoritarian states routinely engage in persecution, discrimination, imprisonment without trial, torture, assassination and summary executions of political opponents and critics.

In addition to Fukuyama's civil, religious and political categories of human rights, we could add another category – **social rights** – which might include the following freedoms:

- not to be forced into slavery
- not to be forced into marriage
- not to be forced to become a child soldier
- not to be forcibly trafficked into the global sex trade
- to be free from being victims of war crimes such as mass rape and kidnappings.

Two examples of international **non-governmental organisations** that aim to monitor, highlight and prevent such future abuses are Amnesty International and Human Rights Watch. The website of Amnesty International UK states that:

*Human rights are the fundamental rights and freedoms that belong to every single one of us, anywhere in the world. Human rights apply no matter where you are from, what you believe in, or how you choose to live your life. Human rights can never be taken away, but they can sometimes be restricted – for example if a person breaks the law, or in the interests of national security. These rights and freedoms are based on values like dignity, fairness, equality, respect and independence. But human rights are not just abstract concepts – they are defined and protected by law.*

Some approaches to human rights combine the 'entitlement' and 'equality' approaches. The United Nations Universal Declaration of Human Rights (UDHR) is a good example of this. It highlights 30 rights and freedoms, including the right to asylum, the right to freedom from torture, the right to free speech and the right to education.

## Activity

Research and choose one or two human rights from the UN's declaration and design a colourful poster that advertises why such rights are a 'good' thing.

## The critique of universal definitions of human rights

Jeffrey Haynes (2008) argues that few human rights have universal application. He observes that, while (nearly) everyone would agree that it is wrong to kill people without justification or let them starve wilfully, it is doubtful that all nation-states could guarantee their citizens the right, for example, to a house, jobs, paid holidays and clean water. He observes that all these things are highly desirable but questions whether they are 'rights' and points out that, sometimes through no fault of their own, many less industrialised societies lack the economic means to provide such rights to all their citizens.

Haynes also points out that the successful provision of human rights depends on too many factors which are beyond the control of weak or poor nation-states. Examples include: unfair terms of world trade, which mean that such societies do not receive a fair price for their raw materials and **cash crops**; the power of Western transnationals to corrupt those in power in less industrialised societies; and the presence of armed conflicts such as civil wars (often encouraged by other more powerful nation-states and transnationals in order to gain control over scarce raw resources such as blood diamonds, coltan and uranium). Consequently, it has been suggested by Stanley Cohen (2007) that definitions of human rights should be extended so that they are truly global and cover the activities of the richer Western nations and **transnational companies**. Examples might include:

- the right to be treated as an equal partner in world trade
- the right to receive a fair market price for any raw materials and cash crops produced for sale on the world market
- the right for workers in the less industrialised world to be paid a fair wage for their labour
- the right of children to a childhood rather than being exploited by transnational companies for their labour in sweat shops and factories

## Individualistic and collectivistic conceptions of human rights

Haynes observes that a major problem inherent in the definitions of human rights used by the UNDHR or organisations such as Amnesty International is that they are based on 'individualistic' conceptions of human rights which originate in Western philosophy. However, in contrast there also exist 'collectivistic' notions of human rights which may justify the 'harsh' treatment of some individuals and groups in the name of the 'collective good'. Michael Sodaro (2004) notes that 'abuses' in the name of the common good might include violation of freedom of speech and right to vote, the arrest and torture of political dissidents, mass atrocities committed in times of civil war or unrest, religious and ethnic persecution and the abuse and repression of women.

Haynes argues that Asian value systems stress collective rights and that individualistic Western-orientated human rights are 'culturally alien' to Asian elites because Asian countries have cultures and histories that reflect the importance of the community. These collective rights supposedly reflect a range of 'desirable' socio-political values and rights. Various Asian nation-states, particularly China, Singapore, Malaysia and Indonesia and the Philippines, have long claimed that the suppression of individualistic human rights such as freedom of speech and control over the media and the internet was a necessary price to pay for strong and continuous economic growth and rising living standards. However, critics of this view, such as Ken Christie and Denny Roy (2001) argued that this is an attempt to justify and perpetuate authoritarian government. As Haynes argues, 'collective rights are a cloak for authoritarian and erratic rule, reflecting the narrow political interest of those in power, not the collective concerns of society. Such governments are often illiberal democracies – characterised by a mix of democracy, liberalism, capitalism, oligarchy and corruption'. Haynes notes that China has attempted to justify its violations of human rights using this collectivist argument. For example, every year, many Chinese citizens (reported to number in the thousands) are executed under a legal system which Haynes argues is both corrupt and over-secretive. As the rest of the world moves towards the abolition of the death penalty, China has actually extended its use. Most of those executed according to Amnesty International come from poor and marginalised groups. The Chinese have particularly targeted the Muslim Uighur ethnic group and those belonging to the Falun Gong religion.

Haynes observes that the collectivist justification for the suppression of individualistic human rights has recently weakened because many Asian societies, with the exception of China, have experienced an economic downturn and decline in living standards. Randall Peerenboom (2007) argues optimistically that China will eventually adopt an individualistic concept of political and human rights and a greater degree of democratic accountability. Haynes agrees, and concludes that the present tension between Western individualistic and Asian collectivistic conceptions of human rights is the product of social progress – it simply reflects the difference between modernisation and tradition.

## Evaluating definitions of human rights

The debate about what constitute human rights is a heated one. Some sociologists, especially those from non-Western societies, claim that definitions and categories are notoriously subjective and ethnocentric because such definitions are dominated by Western cultural experience. Moreover, Westerners often characterise non-Western cultures as backward and inferior for not following Western standards regarding human rights.

Haynes (2008) observes that there exists a vigorous debate about the cultural relativity of human rights. Abdullahi Ahmed An-Na'im (2001) accepts that human rights are rights that are due to all human beings by virtue of their humanity, and that groups should not be deprived of such rights because of their race, national origin, culture, religion, language or gender. However, he questions whether such rights are truly universal – that is, relevant or applicable to every culture.

Gustavo Esteva (1992) rejects the idea that there exists universal agreement about what should constitute a list of human rights. As a postmodernist thinker, Esteva claims that we live in a '**pluriverse**' rather than a universe. This means that there are countless cultural ways in which people live in relation to others, and as such the human rights record of nation-states in the less industrialised world cannot be judged by Western individualistic standards. They can only be judged by the standards of similar cultures and societies.

Esteva promotes the idea of **cultural relativity**. This is the idea that, because different cultures have differing reference points, it is not appropriate to judge all societies according to one universal standard. For example, the experience of being brought up and living in a Western society prevents Westerners from making objective judgements and assessments about other cultures.

Esteva argues that the debate about human rights, what the modern nation-state should look like and how its leaders should behave is all too often shaped by Western culture.

Wolfgang Sachs (2009) argues that Western attempts to shape a universal definition of human rights is hypocritical because Western societies regularly engage in human rights abuses but imply that these 'abuses' are less important than those practised by less industrialised nation-states in Asia and Africa. For example, many states of the USA still practise the death penalty and US prisons contain a disproportionate number of Black inmates when compared to the percentage of the US population that is Black. Other critics argue that if the USA wishes to shape universal standards on human rights, it needs to seriously tackle its own human rights issues such as: the disproportionate number of unarmed Black people who are being shot dead by the police, which inspired the 'Black Lives Matter' movement; and the sexual abuse of women by powerful men, which inspired the 'MeToo' and 'Time'sUp' movements.

### Activity

Make a list of the 'rights' that you believe should be included in an index of human rights that the state must protect.

## Critique of the cultural relativity argument

Cultural relativists are probably correct to point out that human rights are not perfect in the West, and specific issues still need to be addressed and rectified. The continuing incarceration without trial of Islamist terrorist suspects by the USA and the use of torture techniques such as waterboarding are obvious examples of human rights abuse carried out by and in the West. However, the cultural relativity argument suffers from two major weaknesses.

1. It ignores the fact that 193 nation-states have voluntarily joined the United Nations (UN). Only three nation-states – the Vatican City, Palestine and Kosovo – are not members (the latter two because their sovereign status is not recognised by some UN members and they have been

consequently 'blocked' from membership). In 1948, the UN launched the UDHR. This cannot be described as a Western product because it has been extensively renegotiated and revised with input from a range of Western and non-Western societies. This renegotiation actually led to some of the original rights, such as the right to property, being dropped from the UDHR. It also led to the adoption of the principle that it might be necessary to set aside or suspend individual rights in the national interest, especially when countries are at war. Moreover, most UN members have signed up to the International Court of Justice (ICJ or World Court), which settles legal disputes between UN members. However, both China and the USA have refused to accept the legal rulings of the ICJ in recent years.

As Haynes argues, the fact that the vast majority of countries around the world have signed up to the UN, UDHR and ICJ weakens the cultural relativist argument. Nation-states that have agreed to abide by the UDHR and the judgements of the ICJ cannot claim the right to pick and choose human rights, enforcing the ones they like and ignoring those they do not.

## Activity

*The International Court of Justice, which is the principal judicial organ of the United Nations (UN).*

Research the type of issues that are dealt with by the International Court of Justice.

2. The cultural relativity argument sees everything as a Western construct, but this has not proved to be very pragmatic in helping nation-states to identify what counts as a human right or as abuse of those rights.

## Key terms

**Liberal democracy** A form of nation-state in which people have the right to vote their leaders in and out of power.

**Representative democracy** A type of democracy founded on the principle of elected officials representing a group of people.

**Full democracy** Nations where civil liberties and basic political freedoms are not only respected, but also reinforced by a political culture conducive to the thriving of democratic principles.

**Partial or flawed democracies** Governments which demonstrate some accountability to the people but which may restrict the activities of some minority groups.

**Constitution** A body of fundamental principles or established precedents according to which a state or other organisation is acknowledged to be governed.

**Executive/government** The branch of a government responsible for putting decisions or laws into effect.

**Legislature/parliament** A governing body that makes laws and can also amend or repeal them.

**Independent judiciary** Judges and courts which are free of influence from other branches of government or private interests.

**Supreme Court** The highest judicial court in a country or state.

**Slanderous** Making a false spoken statement damaging to a person's reputation.

**Libellous** Making a false written statement damaging to a person's reputation.

**Universal suffrage** The right of almost all adults to vote in political elections.

**Hybrid regimes** States in which governments are elected but in which no opposition parties are allowed or the media are controlled by elites or in which political corruption is rife.

**Authoritarian states** A form of government characterised by strong central power and limited political or individual freedoms.

**Oligarchy** Rule by a few.

**Fascist** An extreme right-wing movement which is anti-democratic and believes in rule by a totalitarian one-party state.

**Pluralism** A condition or system in which a multiplicity of competing political parties coexist.

**Autocracy** Dictatorship or a system of government by one person with absolute power.

**Politburo** The principal policy-making committee of a communist party.

**Propaganda** Information, especially of a biased or misleading nature, used to promote a political cause or point of view.

**Command economy** A system where the government, rather than the free market, determines how the economy should be planned and managed. It is a key feature of any communist society.

**Market-Leninist** Slang for the Chinese way of managing the economy – a mixture of a central planned economy with the tolerance of some free market capitalism.

**Coup d'état** The sudden, often violent and undemocratic overthrow of a government, often by the military.

**Apartheid** An official system of racial segregation administered by the White minority government of South Africa between 1948 and 1994.

**Theocracy** A system of government in which priests, ayatollahs or a divinely ordained ruler govern in the name of God or a god.

**Wahhabi** A strictly orthodox Sunni Muslim sect which is still the predominant religious force in Saudi Arabia.

**Sovereignty** The authority of a state to govern itself or another state.

**Bureaucratic** A system of government in which most of the important decisions are taken by state officials or civil servants rather than by elected politicians.

**Patriotism** National loyalty or vigorous support for one's country.

**Nationalism** Extreme form of patriotism marked by a feeling of superiority over other countries.

**Existential security** The feeling that survival is secure enough that it can be taken for granted.

**Social integration** The process during which newcomers or minorities are incorporated into the social structure of the host society.

**Demonisation** Negative stereotyping of a particular social group.

**Entitlement** With regard to human rights, the idea that the state should provide its people with basic rights – for example, the right to education.

**Equality** With regard to human rights, the idea that all citizens, regardless of social background, should have the right to be treated equally.

**Civil rights** The rights of citizens to political and social freedom and equality.

**Religious rights** The freedom to exercise particular religious beliefs and practices without persecution or to change religious beliefs and practices.

**Political rights** The right to vote for any political party without fear of discrimination.

**Social rights** Another term for socio-economic rights such as the right to an education or an adequate standard of living or justice.

**Non-government organisations (NGOs)** Any organisation or agency that is not financed by government or which works outside state control.

**Cash crops** A crop produced for its commercial value, to be exported rather than for domestic use by the grower – for example, tea, coffee, cocoa.

**Transnational companies (TNCs)** Multinational companies which produce, market and sell products across the world.

**Pluriverse** An idea associated with Esteva – he claims that there is no such thing as universal human experience. Instead, he argues that there are countless cultural ways in which people live in relation to others.

**Cultural relativity** The idea that, because different cultures have differing reference points, it is not appropriate to judge all societies according to one universal standard.

## Summary

1. The world has experienced political globalisation. Most countries in the world are nation-states that practise liberal or representative democracy.
2. However, not all nation-states are full democracies. A substantial minority are partial or hybrid democracies, because they lack some of the features necessary to qualify as proper democracies.
3. About a third of nation-states are authoritarian or totalitarian regimes which deny their people the right to vote in free elections. These regimes are ruled by either communist, military or theocratic autocrats or oligarchies.

4. Most citizens of the world belong to specific independent nation-states which exercise sovereignty over given physical territories. However, such states are becoming increasingly interconnected and inter-dependent because of the processes of political, economic and ecological globalisation.
5. Most nation-states are committed to protecting the human rights of their citizens, although there is no overall agreement on how rights should be defined.

# Unit 8.3.2 Global social movements and attempts to oppose globalisation

Elizabeth Bennett (2012) defines global social movements (GSMs) as 'networks that collaborate across borders to advance thematically similar agendas throughout the world'. She argues that GSMs have consequently become powerful actors in global governance. David Held et al. argue that such GSMs are increasingly important in a globalised world because liberal-democratic nation-states are struggling to cope with the consequences of globalisation, particularly with the ecological-environmental crisis, and the dislocation and potential conflict associated with global migration.

Held et al. suggest that there have been three sociological reactions to these crises and threats:

1. Liberal internationalists argue that nation-states and non-government global organisations such as the United Nations (UN) and the World Trade Organization (WTO) need to be reformed, because at the moment they favour global processes which are creating problems for the poor and powerless in both more and less industrialised societies.
2. Radical critics stress the need for the creation of alternative mechanisms of global, social, economic and political organisation. This radical approach foresees a major role for GSMs based on the idea of equality, common good and harmony with the natural environment. It argues that such movements can act as a '**politics of resistance**' and have the potential to empower ordinary citizens in both more and less industrialised societies. Radicals argue that GSMs can encourage a sense of belonging to a global community. The hope is that membership of such movements will result in people developing a global consciousness that will motivate them to form '**communities of fate**'. These will challenge individualism and other negative aspects of globalisation so that ordinary citizens can take back some control over their own lives from these global forces.
3. The **cosmopolitan** approach takes a more positive approach to globalisation. It argues that the nation-state is a thing of the past and that people need to realise that they are now citizens of the world. This rather optimistic approach suggests that most of us are capable of successfully negotiating a path between the global and the local or between the modern and the traditional, to become hybridised global citizens taking the best from the local and the global.

## Defining social movements

In order to understand the nature of GSMs, Cohen and Kennedy (2000) argue that it is important to understand how social movements differ from conventional political organisations such as political parties, pressure groups and trade unions.

John Wilson (1973) defines a social movement as a conscious, collective and organised attempt to bring about or to resist large-scale change in the social order by non-institutionalised means. He observes that social movements often comprise both 'heroes and clowns, fanatics and fools...animated by the injustice and anxieties they see around them'. Members of such movements often see themselves as on a crusade against the evils of society.

Paul Byrne (1997) claimed that social movements have unique features in that:

- They often act in unpredictable ways.
- They are seen as irrational because members are not acting in their own self-interest. They are **altruistic** – working for the common good.
- They are often seen or interpreted as unreasonable because members may not feel constrained by law. They may feel justified in engaging in anti-social or illegal action.
- They look disorganised because they do not display the classic features of organisations – hierarchies, bureaucracies and formality. The activities of their members may seem emotional rather than objective.

Cyrus Zirakzadeh (2007) observes that members of social movements come from a very broad range of social backgrounds. They are comfortable with using disruptive tactics that bring them into confrontation with the agents of social control such as the police, because they are consciously committed to replacing traditional ways of doing things with radical change.

### Activity

What sort of 'disruptive tactics' might social movements use, and in what ways might these be successful?

## Global social movements

Cohen and Kennedy argue that most global social movements evolved between the 1960s and 1990s. They argue that the social movements visible in the 1960s were internationalist in that they maintained links with other social movements abroad., Most of these social movements focused on '**emancipatory politics**' – issues that reach beyond the boundaries of a particular nation-state such as women's rights, international capitalism, civil rights, anti-war, racism and environmental issues.

Another source of social movements, particularly in the 1960s, were the counter-cultures or student protest movements which emerged in both the USA and Europe in 1968. These movements were mainly focused on protesting the USA's military presence in Vietnam. For example, in 1968, serious protests mainly led by student demonstrators broke out against the Vietnam War in Paris, London, Berlin and Tokyo as well as across the USA. In the 1970s and 1980s, student social movements also focused on rejecting the authority and materialism they associated with their parents' generation and supporting nuclear disarmament. They often questioned the moral authority of the capitalist system.

*Police fire tear gas to control student riots in Paris, 1968.*

According to Cohen and Kennedy, social movements became global in the late 1990s for five broad reasons:

1. The spread of higher education in many more industrialised societies enabled people to become more knowledgeable about science and technology. They became more aware that they were living in what Ulrich Beck calls 'risk societies' – that industry, science and technology were increasing risks and threats to the eco-systems in which they lived and even the future of humanity and the planet. Many responded to their fears about the threats posed to the environment by nuclear technology, chemical, nuclear and biological weaponry and genetically modified crops by getting involved in non-governmental organisations (NGOs) such as Friends of the Earth and Greenpeace.

2. The 1990s saw the emergence of new forms of communication technology, particularly satellite television, the internet and personal laptop computers. Manjunath Pendakur and Roma Harris (2002) argue that the development of the internet and laptop computers enabled small, traditionally powerless groups to become 'self-creative' social movements. It particularly gave them the ability to produce and circulate their own literature which challenged the versions of reality issued by the more powerful groups that were suppressing or exploiting them. It also meant that atrocities committed against powerless groups could be communicated almost immediately.

   The internet, in particular, was probably the reason why global social movements became so popular in the late 1990s. This was because, as a public sphere that anybody could access at no or little cost, it provided those interested in global issues the opportunity to access a wide range of information and alternative interpretations and viewpoints, which were unlikely to be found in the conventional mainstream media.

   Michael Itzoe (1995) observes that in the 1990s the internet was 'a loose and anarchic confederation of millions of users around the world who communicated in perhaps the freest forum of speech in history'. It was particularly useful in establishing what the neo-Marxist Castells (1996) calls the '**network society**' (see Unit 8.2.1 for a more detailed discussion of this).

   Castells argues that in late-modern capitalist society the emergence of this network society transformed the nature of communication. Information which had once been the exclusive resource of the powerful and which had previously flowed top-down, now flowed horizontally – many to many rather than from a few to the many. The networked society placed power in the hands of the people and gave voice to groups such as the poor, the politically repressed, women, ethnic minorities, the LGBT community and oppressed groups in other countries who might otherwise have gone unheard.

These technological developments meant that global networks evolved – made up of loose alliances between **anarchists**, socialists, feminists, environmentalists and anti-poverty campaigners – who were able to compile and share online information about the effects of globalisation on the economies of developing nations, particularly in Africa, which could be quickly distributed to both the global media, and used to challenge the status quo. These global networks eventually united into what became known as the anti-globalisation movement.

Mark Engler (2008) notes that the existence of this movement is disputed by some sociologists because it includes such a diverse range of groups subscribing to a selection of sometimes contradictory ideological views. For example, it includes trade unionists, environmentalists, anarchists, land rights and **indigenous rights** activists, organisations promoting human rights and **sustainable development**, opponents of privatisation, and anti-sweat-shop campaigners. However, Engler argues that these groups do constitute a movement because they share the view that the policies of corporate globalisation have exacerbated global poverty and increased global inequality. Moreover, despite their ideological differences, these groups annually gather to coordinate policy and action. The World Social Forum serves as a site for activist networking and for the coordination of campaigns which target transnational corporations. They have also mobilised anti-war rallies against military intervention in Iraq and Afghanistan and protests outside the meetings of global institutions such as the World Trade Organization, the International Monetary Fund, the World Bank and the G7 (previously G8, a gathering of leaders of the seven most economically powerful nation-states).

3. The impact of the anti-globalisation movement in the 1990s was made more effective by the decision of many NGOs to line up with and support the aims of the anti-globalisation movement. In the 1980s, many NGOs were becoming frustrated at the lack of progress they were making in terms of improving human rights and eradicating poverty and debt. They realised that they lacked the power to influence nation-states, who often ignored their demands for change. In the 1990s, several NGOs, including Oxfam, Action Aid, Amnesty International, Friends of the Earth and Greenpeace, aligned themselves with the anti-globalisation movement. These NGOs gave the movement both political and moral legitimacy and the NGOs' research departments were able to provide the movement with facts that helped them to mobilise resources, campaigns and protests more effectively.

## Activity

*Greenpeace* Arctic Sunrise *ship protesting against Arctic oil production.*

Research the range of issues, activities and campaigns that the following groups are involved in: Friends of the Earth, Greenpeace, Amnesty International, Oxfam and the World Social Forum. Are these global or localised issues?

4. However, the digital revolution that occurred post-2000 symbolised by the rapid spread of social media has probably been the biggest influence on the growing influence of global social movements, and especially the anti-globalisation sector. Most social movements maintain their own websites, which allow them to campaign and influence public opinion on the specific issue they have formed around, and to put pressure on nation-states through, for example, online

petitions. Such websites also act as a recruiting tool. Furthermore, hacker groups affiliated to the anti-globalisation movement (known as 'hacktivists'), such as Anonymous, have defaced corporate and government websites and engaged in virtual sabotage such as web-sit-ins (sending so much information to a site so that it crashes), email bombing, and information theft, especially computer code theft.

## Activity

'Global social movements have encouraged ordinary people to believe that they can have influence over global issues'. Evaluate this point of view.

Moreover, the development of social media platforms and apps in the last 10 years means that images of war crimes or atrocities can be uploaded to media organisations and global subscribers in real time, thus mobilising effective support and putting pressure on the international political community to criticise or to take action in the form of sanctions against nation-states guilty of abusing human rights. This has led to some sociologists claiming that social media are powerful tools of social change – for example, that Twitter and Facebook played a major role in the Arab Spring movement between 2010 and 2014 and which led to the fall of authoritarian regimes in Tunisia, Egypt and Libya.

## Contemporary issues: Twitter as a revolutionary tool of social change

*Occupy protesters outside the Reichstag in Berlin.*

Murthy (2013) empirically investigated the impact of Twitter on political change (see also Unit 6.3.2). He claims that Twitter, which has 149 million users worldwide, has proved extremely useful as a coordinator of street protests and that it also played a significant role in attracting support to Occupy – an international socio-political movement against social and economic inequality and the lack of 'real democracy' around the world. In 2011, Occupy campaigners literally occupied areas in 951 cities across 82 countries. For example, the movement engaged in a high-profile occupation of the financial centre of New York – Wall Street.

Murthy also argues that Twitter played an important role in the Arab Spring movements which spread across the Middle East and North Africa between 2011 and 2012. First, he argues that Twitter was particularly effective in the Egyptian protests that ousted President Mubarak in 2012, because it enabled a mass movement of people to go out onto the streets (although Murthy notes that high unemployment, persistent poverty and police brutality were probably the main motivations for people protesting in the streets). Murthy also notes that both the internet and Twitter were regarded by the Egyptian authorities as so threatening in their dissemination of activist information that they were shut down for a week by the government in January 2011. Second, Murthy argues that Twitter helped to bring international attention to what was going on by acting as a valuable news source for international journalists.

He concludes that, 'even if tweets did not bring feet to Egyptian streets, they helped to facilitate a diverse global network of individuals who participated in a wide-ranging set of mobilisation efforts from the retweeters in Starbucks to those sending letters to their Congresspeople/Ministers or participating in activist movements both online and offline'.

Murthy argues that Twitter as a communications medium has the potential to shape many aspects of people's social, political and economic lives. However, not all media sociologists agree. Radio Free Europe's Golnaz Esfandiari (2010) has reviewed the role of social media in the coordination of street protests in Iran in 2009. Western journalists were allegedly astounded at the sudden influx of information coming out of Iran via Twitter, which was unusual in the light of the media blackout ordered by the Iranian government. This prompted Western journalists to dub the protests the 'Twitter Revolution'. However, Esfandiari claims that opposition activists rarely used Twitter and that they preferred to use text messages, email and blogs. He argues that most Twitter posts were probably planted by foreign intelligence agencies, particularly the American CIA. He supports this argument by pointing out that most Twitter posts were in English rather than Farsi. Esfandiari observes that 'no one seemed to wonder why people trying to coordinate protests in Iran would be writing in any language other than Farsi'.

Source: The Twitter Devolution' 08/06/2010, https://foreignpolicy.com/2010/06/08/the-twitter-devolution/.

## Questions

1. Analyse the role of Twitter in mobilising and coordinating protest movements in Iran and during the Arab Spring.
2. Using information from this source and the section on social movements, assess the idea that the internet, social media and the social network society are good for liberal democracies.

5. Zsuzsa Hegedus (1989) suggests that the media attention that the anti-globalisation movement received in its early form resulted in a mental shift among young people as they realised that their localised concerns were inextricably linked to wider global structures and problems. In other words, what threatens or concerns one person wherever they are in the world equally threatens everyone else in the long term. Hegedus claims that the anti-globalisation movement led to a 'planetization of understanding' that 'virtually everything needed to be radically rethought' (p. 299 of Cohen and Kennedy, 2000). He observed that supporters of the anti-globalisation movement were often very personally committed to a collective future at a local, national and planetary level. In other words, they believe that solutions are only meaningful if they involve joint struggles.

   Moreover, as our cultural, media and economic life has become globalised and interconnected, it is now possible for individuals who are conscious of global inequality because of their involvement with the anti-globalisation movement to engage with and influence the behaviour of transnational companies – for example, via ethical or green consumerism or by boycotting goods produced made by companies which have acquired a poor global reputation.

## Contemporary issues: Anti-globalisation movements

*Make Poverty History march, Edinburgh, Scotland.*

Cohen and Kennedy argue that social movements such as the anti-globalisation movement may be more effective in bringing about social and global change than nation-states because:

- They do not promote narrow territorial or national interests. They are not constrained by patriotism or nationalism.
- They are not slowed down by the formality of diplomacy.
- They are not responsible for the problems they are attempting to resolve.
- They generally attract lots of public support, especially from the young and educated, as well as the disadvantaged and the poor.
- They are in touch with ordinary people.
- They are not weighed down by bureaucracy and regulations.
- They have diverse memberships and can mobilise support at many levels.

However, Cohen and Kennedy also identify several factors that may inhibit the activities of social movements. These include:

- They often have limited funds.
- They may have to engage in stunts in order to attract media attention.
- People living in other parts of the world may interpret their activities as patronising.
- Cultural and language barriers may impede their effectiveness.

## Questions

1. Consider the list of advantages of social movements over nation-states listed by Cohen and Kennedy and, after class discussion, rank them in terms of importance.
2. Why might people living in other societies and cultures regard the activities of social movements as patronising, especially with regard to human rights?

## The critique of global social movements

Most of the criticism focused on global social movements has focused on their use of digital technology and especially the idea that such technology would democratise society. Marxists, for example, argue that this technology is concentrated in the hands of a very small number of capitalist transnational corporations and individuals who exert greater power and influence than any individual consumer or even network of anti-globalists. Political elite power-holders, such as government departments and agencies, and the security services, have also seen the power of new media delivery systems and have constructed sophisticated and elaborate websites to make sure their view of the world dominates the internet. The ex-CIA analyst Edward Snowden claimed in 2015 that the British security services have the technology to access private information stored on people's smartphones. Moreover, authoritarian states such as China and Iran have built firewalls to prevent their populations accessing the internet and viewing subversive material that criticises their leaders.

Keen (2008) is very critical of the democratic potential of the internet, which he claims is actually chaotic in practice. He claims that it has no governing moral code and that it is a place where truth is selective and frequently subject to change. Four criticisms can be made of the idea that social media are sources of political literacy and that they have inspired the growth of social movements that aim to bring about radical social and political change:

- Keen believes that the internet has actually replaced genuine knowledge with the 'wisdom of the crowd', which dangerously blurs the lines between fact and opinion and between informed argument and blustering speculation/gossip.
- Nick Rochlin (2017) believes that the ubiquity of social media means that many societies have now entered into a **post-truth** era in which facts and evidence have been replaced by personal belief and emotion. He argues that the nature of news, and what people accept as news, is also shifting toward a belief-and emotion-based market. The truth of the story no longer matters. What matters is that the story falls in line with what a person wants to hear. Facts are now often written off as '**fake news**'; that is, news that is seen to attack a person's pre-existing beliefs.
- Social networking sites and blogs do not contribute to the democratic process in any way because they are merely a means for narcissistic self-broadcasting. Keen claims they exist purely for individuals to indulge in shameless self-promotion and to promote conspiracy theories.
- User-generated sites such as Wikipedia are open to abuse and bias, and are consequently unreliable as sources of information.

## Key terms

**Politics of resistance** A form of collective civil disobedience aimed at opposing the effects of economic, political and ecological globalisation.

**Communities of fate** Protest movements, such as environmentalism, in which members attempt to shape their own futures through active participation and dialogue.

**Cosmopolitan** An ideology which states that all human beings belong to a single global community.

**Altruistic** Working selflessly for the good of the community rather than for oneself.

**Emancipatory politics** Movements that are concerned above all with liberating individuals and groups from constraints that adversely affect their life chances.

**Network society** The social, political, economic and cultural changes caused by the spread of networked, digital information and communications technologies.

**Anarchists** People who rebel against any authority, established order or any ruling power.

**Indigenous rights** The rights of people who inhabited a particular territory pre-colonialism.

**Sustainable development** Economic development that is conducted without depletion of natural resources.

**Post-truth** Circumstances in which objective facts are less influential in shaping public opinion than appeals to emotion and personal belief.

**Fake news** False information or propaganda published under the guise of being real, true news.

## Summary

1. Political, economic and ecological globalisation have had negative effects that have motivated citizens of the world to organise themselves into social movements to resist such processes in order to take back control over their lives.
2. These social movements have become increasingly globalised because of the development of digital technology, which has led to the emergence of a networked society in which information can be quickly disseminated and which coordinates global protest campaigns against the effects of globalisation and the activities of its agents.
3. Some sociologists see a networked society as good for global democracy, because it has supposedly been at the forefront of anti-global movements such as Occupy, Make Poverty History and the World Social Forum. Some see it as playing a central role in the Arab Spring movement, too.
4. Global social movements are seen as responsible for raising the planetary consciousness of individuals and for encouraging actions such as ethical consumerism and consumer boycotts.
5. However, critics of the network society claim that it has led to the emergence of fake news, the promotion of the idea that truth and knowledge are relative concepts and a blurring of the line between fact and fiction.

# Unit 8.3.3 Debates about the role of the nation-state in tackling global social and environmental problems

It has become very apparent over the past 30 years that a number of global problems have appeared which are a threat to the future of humanity or, at the very least, to the law and order many of us take for granted. Examples include global networks of crime and terror, the global movement of capital and labour (in the form of migration) and global climate change. The appearance of these global problems has raised the issue of whether nation-states have the power and resources to resolve these problems. This unit examines whether the democratic nation-state is capable of dealing with the social problems blamed by many people on economic globalisation.

## Threats to the liberal-democratic nation state

Many commentators have expressed concern that liberal democratic nation-states are either in a state of crisis or in threat of being transformed into illiberal or flawed democracies. Some experts predict that these illiberal democracies may even abandon all pretence of democracy in the near future and become authoritarian regimes and reverse civil and human rights laws.

John Gray (2018) argues that the liberal-democratic nation-state is in particular danger from the rise of **populism** in both the USA and Europe. He observes that populist leaders and political parties such as President Trump in the USA, Viktor Orban in Hungary and the Five-Star Movement in Italy have experienced great electoral success in recent years.

Populism has a number of distinctive features:

- Cas Mudde and Cristobal Kaltwasser (2017) define populism as the idea that society is separated into two groups at odds with one another – that is, the people or workers versus a 'crooked or corrupt elitist establishment'. Ben Moffitt (2017) observes that populist leaders claim to represent the unified 'will of the people' and, in so doing, they present the enemy of the people as the liberal political **elite** that has governed those societies for generations. Populists often imply that if you are not with the people, you must be against them.
- Populism tends to be on the 'right' of the political spectrum because one of its central aims is '**nativism**' and nationalism – that is, they claim that they are protecting the economic, cultural and religious traditions and interests of a native-born population against immigrants.
- It involves the maintenance of a state of constant crisis which can only be resolved by populist leaders presenting themselves to the people as 'strong men' who sometimes have to use authoritarian methods with reluctance.
- Nadia Urbinati (2014) argues that populist content is 'made of negatives' – whether it is anti-politics, anti-intellectualism, anti-elite. For example, in Europe, it is often presented as anti-EU.
- Populist leaders are extremely versatile. They are quicker than established leaders to react to ordinary people's fears, but this often results in '**irresponsible bidding**'. In order to attract popular support, they make radical promises to change things which are popular in the short term but probably unfeasible or impractical in the long term.

Michael Sandel (2018) suggests that one of the 'negatives' that populist leaders highlight is globalisation, which he argues has created the conditions for populism. Sandel argues that the liberal governing elite of capitalist nation-states have failed to deal with five problems caused by globalisation:

1. Ordinary people have experienced first-hand rising inequalities in income and wealth. They can see that economic globalisation seems to financially benefit only those at the very top of society. For example, there was resentment that banks were not 'punished' for the 2008 global financial crisis that resulted in many governments introducing austerity measures which had a disproportionate effect on the poorest sections of societies. Large sections of society feel aggrieved because they feel that the global economy and culture has left them behind.
2. The free trade agreements and free movement of labour associated with economic globalisation may have also contributed to growing economic inequality because local workers see these as threatening local jobs and stagnating wages. Workers who believe that their country cares more for cheap goods and labour than the job prospects of their own people often feel betrayed.
3. Sandel claims that the leaders of liberal-democratic nation-states need to understand that global markets are not neutral instruments for defining the common good. Rather, they tend to benefit the few at the expense of the many. Globalisation has produced industrial decline both in the USA and Europe, and high levels of unemployment, poverty and, most importantly, loss of social esteem, uncertainty and humiliation for many.
4. Economic globalisation has also exposed the empty promises of Western capitalist society, especially the view that such societies are meritocratic and that, if people are willing to work hard, they will experience upward social mobility and material rewards. However, the evidence is clear – Americans born to poor parents now tend to remain poor as adults.
5. Those at the bottom of society may feel aggrieved, because they sense that the global system is rigged against them. They consequently see those who have benefited from globalisation as having cheated their way to the top.

Sandel argues that nation-states need to rethink how globalisation is managed, because the growing inequality in wealth and income that is resulting from it is creating a volatile brew of anger and resentment. The victims of globalisation are increasingly attracted to populist politicians who feed off people's sense of injustice by promising to restore a country's global reputation (for example, President Putin promises the Russian people that he will reverse the indignities that Russia has supposedly experienced since the 1990s, while President Trump has promised to make 'America great again'). Sandel suggests that these victims need to be compensated; otherwise, the people of liberal democracies may be attracted to populist politicians and show willingness to exchange liberal democracy for more authoritarian or illiberal-democratic forms of government. Authoritarian forms of government also have the side-effect of increasing nationalism and xenophobia (hatred of foreigners and especially migrants), which often results in an increase in hate crimes and human rights abuses.

David Runciman (2018) observes that illiberal democracies are not '**open societies**' because authoritarian leaders exercise control over the flow of information and the media. Another global social problem that has been identified as a potential threat to the liberal-democratic nation-state is something that Michiko Kakutani (2018) calls '**truth decay**'. She argues that democracy depends on two related principles:

- the reality of experience (being able to distinguish between fact and fiction), and
- standards of thought (being able to distinguish between what is true or false).

Kakutani claims that we now live in a world in which people today are more susceptible to political manipulation. Political leaders, especially those who display populist and autocratic tendencies, frequently demonstrate contempt for facts and experts. They promote emotion over reason. Kakutani claims that the global world has entered a post-truth era in which fake news, alternative facts and relativism are regarded as more valid than reliably collected evidence. She notes that even history has been undermined by truth decay. For example, she observes that there are literally thousands of social media posts and blogs that deny that the Holocaust ever happened. There are concerns, too, that media transnationals such as Facebook are illegally gathering personal data from social media sites and selling this data onto populist movements so that they can target susceptible voters with advertisements and social media campaigns that seek to 'persuade' users to support their cause.

Kakutani argues that around the world waves of populism and fundamentalism are actively using untruths to elevate fear and anger over reasoned debate. This has the effect of eroding democracy and replacing expertise with the 'wisdom' of the crowd. Tom Nichols (2017) argues that there now exists a wilful hostility towards established knowledge, with people aggressively arguing that 'every opinion on any is as good as every other'. **Relativism** and ignorance, argues Nichols, are now fashionable. Naomi Oreskes and Erik Conway (2010) argue that Western societies have seen the emergence of 'merchants of doubt', which aim to give minority views more credence than they deserve. Eva Wiseman (2018) observes that relativity in the media often means dragging a learned expert down to the level of the opinions of the rest of us in order to give the impression of reasoned debate.

## Contemporary issues: Truth decay

*Big Brother is watching you, a still from the 1956 film of George Orwell's novel.*

Kakutani points out that authoritarian regimes throughout history have 'co-opted everyday language in an effort to control how people communicate... to deny the existence of external reality and safeguard the infallibility of autocrats and oligarchies'. She quotes Hannah Arendt (1951), who said that 'The ideal subject of totalitarian rule is not the convinced Nazi or the convinced communist, but people for whom the distinction between fact and fiction and between true and false no longer exist.' Kakutani concludes that 'lies are told to assert power over truth itself and without truth democracy is hobbled'. She claims that this is a chilling description of the political and cultural landscape that we inhabit today – 'a world in which fake news and lies are pumped out in industrial volume by Russian troll factories, emitted in an endless stream from the mouth and Twitter feed of the President of the USA and sent flying across the world through social media accounts at lightning speed'.

Source: Adapted from 'The Death of Truth: How We Gave Up on Facts and Ended Up with Trump' by Michiko Kakutani, *Guardian*, 14/07/2018.

## Questions

1. Who is the ideal subject of totalitarian rule according to Arendt?
2. Identify three reasons why Kakutani is pessimistic about the future of democracy.
3. Why are people today more susceptible to political manipulation? Give reasons for your answer.

# Debates about the role of the nation-state in tackling global environmental problems

Globalisation, or at least the globalisation of industrial production, has had a number of environmental effects. These **ecological** effects of globalisation are now scientifically recognised as potentially life-threatening for life on the planet (although some continue to assert that climate change is fake news). As Steger observes, it has become virtually impossible to ignore the fact that people everywhere on the planet are linked to each other through the air that they breathe, the climate they depend on, the food they eat and the water they drink. Steger notes that 'despite this obvious lesson of interdependence, our planet's ecosystems are subjected to continuous human assault'.

## The consequences of ecological globalisation

Environmental disasters which occur in one place (for example, the accidents at nuclear power plants: Chernobyl in the Ukraine in 1986 and Fukushima, Japan, in 2011) had a global impact because they dispersed radioactive material across the world.

Most environmental global problems are not caused by a single event but by a multiplicity of human activities across the world which don't respect national borders and therefore impact on everyone. Steger observes that in the last few decades the scale, speed and depth of the earth's environmental decline has been unprecedented. Examples of this global decline include:

- A worldwide reduction in biodiversity, particularly in plant and animal species. Entire species of mammals, insects, marine life and birds are experiencing mass extinction. Some experts fear that up to 50 per cent of all current plant and animal species will have disappeared by 2100.
- A sharp loss is occurring in natural resources, such as fertile land because of overuse (which is leading to **desertification**), the destruction of rainforests (which safely process potentially dangerous gases such as carbon dioxide as well as providing much of our oxygen) and the decline of drinking water because of drought and water's overuse by industry. There are fears that future wars and conflicts may result from competition for such scarce resources.
- Global poisoning of the global biosphere (the atmosphere, the climate, the oceans and the seas) is occurring daily as manufacturing industry worldwide pumps polluting gases such as carbon dioxide into the skies, as hazardous waste such as plastic, chemicals and human waste are dumped untreated into rivers, landfill sites and the sea, and as oil companies continue to take risks that result in disastrous oil spills (for example, in 2010, a BP oil platform – Deepwater Horizon – exploded in the Gulf of Mexico and fouled more than 1300 miles of coastline, killing vast swathes of seabirds and sea creatures). BP pleaded guilty in the US federal court in 2012 on negligence, pollution and manslaughter charges and agreed to pay $4.5 billion in fines.
- Worldwide climate change, particularly global warming (rising global temperatures) is having catastrophic consequences in terms of extreme weather events such as wildfires, hurricanes, storms, floods, droughts and rising sea levels.

## Activity

Design a poster which documents the range of ecological problems that threatens the future existence of the planet and humanity.

## Explanations for ecological globalisation

1. Cultures shape how people view their natural environment. Pre-industrial societies tend to emphasise the interdependence of all living things, and the view that there exists a delicate balance between human wants and ecological needs. Consequently, such cultures believe that nature should be treated with respect. In contrast,

industrial cultures see the environment as a 'resource' to be used instrumentally to fulfil human needs and wants. Nature is something to be tamed and conquered for industrial purposes and profit.

2. The idea that nature is a resource to be exploited is linked to the cultural values of consumerism and materialism. These actively encourage workers and citizens to see the chief value of life as the limitless accumulation of material goods.

   This relentless consumption of material goods is particularly evident in Western countries. For example, the USA only makes up 6 per cent of the world's population but consumes one-quarter of the world's energy resources. In contrast, India, which has 16 per cent of the world's population, only consumes 3 per cent of the world's energy. Beck (1992) claimed that modern societies are '**risk societies**' in that modern consumption has turned consumers into potential victims of ecological globalisation through what he calls the '**boomerang effect**'. For example, the lead in petrol often turns up in the lungs of children or in the breastmilk consumed by babies in distant cities.

## Activity

Consider how our demand for the latest technology – for example, smartphone – may be increasing the risk to the world's eco-systems. Consider, for example, the following:

- The raw materials that comprise a smartphone – coltan is a very important component. Where does this come from? Where is it mined? Are there human and environmental costs involved in its extraction?
- How are the millions of smartphones, made obsolete by new technology, disposed of?
- Do obsolete smartphones contain 'threats' to the environment or to the health of those involved in their disposal?

3. Consumption of the world's natural resources increased as less industrialised nations have industrialised. Demand for consumer goods soared as the urban populations of countries such as India and China dramatically increased, which meant more strain on land and food resources and a greater reliance on oil and petroleum.

It is unlikely that nation-states acting alone can protect their citizens from being victims of climate change, atmospheric pollution and so on. Most nation-states are generally limited in their efforts to protect the biosphere, because most environmental problems are transnational or global in nature. They originate beyond the borders of most nation-states. Individual nation-states cannot control the natural conditions (for example, winds and tides) that transport gases, toxic poisons, plastics, radioactivity and human wastes into their atmospheres, rivers, coastlines and water supplies.

Moreover, no nation-state is going to attempt to tackle these global problems alone, because such an attempt is likely to prove costly and wasteful (especially if their neighbours are failing to take similar action).

The impotence of nation-states has led to the emergence of the global social movement of environmentalism, which aims to raise global consciousness of the threats and dangers of ignoring how society and human behaviour are negatively impacting on the future of the planet and humanity. This social movement has generally been led by non-governmental organisations (NGOs) such as Greenpeace and Friends of the Earth.

This movement seeks to transform the world by fundamentally changing the way people think about it. It aims to educate global citizens in an attempt to change individual and group behaviour, by challenging the idea that the earth is an inexhaustible resource and that humanity can only fulfil itself through the consumption of material goods. Environmentalism, as a global social movement and ideology, claims to represent the interests of all humanity and is committed to achieving positive change through direct collective action. It tries to do so, for example, by directly confronting transnationals or governments that are damaging the environment to highlight the extent of the problem, and also through the encouragement of more individualised actions such as ethical consumerism, the use of renewable forms of energy such as wind and solar power, and recycling.

However, the impact of this social movement has been undermined by the fact that the media often present aspects of the green movement such as veganism and animal rights activists as odd, eccentric and even extremist, especially those which have aligned themselves with the anti-globalisation movement. Some of the goals of environmentalists have been dismissed as too utopian, in that they argue that cultures need to become more self-sufficient and less dependent on manufacturing industry or carbon-based energy.

Most attempts to combat the threat posed by the globalisation of problems such as global warming have been led by the United Nations Environment Programme (UNEP) which has encouraged its member states to take action and to set targets to cut greenhouse gas emissions in order to manage climate change and global warming. Summit meetings in Montreal (1987) and Copenhagen (1992) were successful in phasing out chemicals called CFCs, which were destroying the ozone layer in the earth's atmosphere. The UN Framework on Climate Change summit in Paris (2015) was moderately successful, in that the nation-states that took part:

- committed themselves to slowing the rise of global temperatures
- pledged to limit the amount of greenhouses gases emitted by human activity to the same levels that trees, soils and oceans can naturally absorb, at some point between 2050 and 2100
- to review each other's contribution to cutting these emissions every five years.

However, this multi-nation-state approach has run into a number of problems:

**a)** The world's two biggest economic powers and sources of global pollution – China and the USA – have proven unwilling to reduce their carbon emissions, because they see such environmental controls as threatening their economic growth and the living standards of their citizens.

**b)** Even if all countries agreed to abide by the Paris agreement, there exists no international law to effectively reinforce the agreement and no universally agreed sanctions that could be used by the global community to punish those nation-states that break it.

**c)** Poor countries regard the agreement as unfair (and consequently are more likely to breach it) because they rightly point out it is the over-consumption of the world's resources by the richer nations that has caused the bulk of the environmental problems that the world is currently experiencing. They also argue that the only way they can pull their people out of poverty is by developing manufacturing industry or by clearing land for cash crops – both strategies which damage or destroy eco-systems. Consequently, the richer nation-states agreed in Paris to financially assist the efforts of poorer countries to switch to cleaner forms of renewable energy.

**d)** Powerful social forces outside nation-states, made up of transnational corporations who deal in carbon-based energy sources such as the oil and chemical industry, have strongly lobbied against the Paris agreement. In 2017, President Trump announced that he was withdrawing the USA from it.

**e)** Kakutani suggests that both nation-states who support the need for climate change and the environmentalist social movement have been handicapped in these post-truth times by fake science, which denies the existence of climate change, and by relativists who insist that equivalent attention should be given to scientists and politicians who deny global warming despite the weight of evidence supporting the former over the latter. Kakutani calls these climate change deniers the 'merchants of doubt' and observes that they are composed of right-wing think-tanks who represent the fossil-fuel industry. She argues that they have been very successful in sowing confusion and doubt about climate change and creating the conditions in which governments can justify inaction.

In conclusion, political globalisation has been ineffective in controlling and managing the threats and dangers to the planet and humanity posed by ecological globalisation. Runciman (2018) argues that the threat of environmental disaster paralyses the nation-state rather than galvanising it. He observes that 'entropy replaces explosive change'. Peter Christoff and Robyn Eckersley (2013) claim that problems such as global warming and climate change are unlikely to be seriously tackled while global capitalism continues to be dominated and shaped by the ideology of neoliberalism, which views nature as a market resource to be exploited for profit.

Finally, some critics of this view claim that current environmental problems, which in many ways are global in scale and impact, might not be linked causally to the wider processes of globalisation. For example, the rapid industrialisation, population growth and urbanisation of countries such as China, India and Russia, and the unrelenting development of unregulated capitalism in general, are much more the drivers of current ecological problems than globalisation itself.

## Key terms

**Populism** A range of political approaches or movements critical of ruling elites and which emphasises the will of the people.

**Elite** The richest, most powerful, best-educated or best-trained group in a society.

**Nativism** The policy of protecting the interests of native-born or established inhabitants against those of immigrants.

**Irresponsible bidding** With regard to populism, making promises to the people that are unlikely to be kept.

**Open society** A society in which information freely and truthfully flows without censorship.

**Truth decay** The blurring of lines between opinion and fact that sees all experience and beliefs as being as important as expertise based on evidence. It often results in disagreement about what constitutes 'truth'.

**Relativism** The postmodern idea that knowledge, truth and morality exist in relation to culture, historical context, and even personal opinion and experience, and consequently cannot be absolute or unquestionable.

**Ecological** Relating to the environment.

**Desertification** The process by which fertile land becomes desert, typically as a result of drought, deforestation or inappropriate agriculture.

**Risk society** According to Beck, the technology associated with late-capitalist society has brought about many benefits in terms of consumer goods but it has also brought about negative effects – for example, in terms of a wide range of risks to both the environment and climate.

**Boomerang effect** A type of manufactured risk – for example, toxic materials used in the manufacturing process may find their way into the food chain and affect the health of future generations.

## Summary

1. Representative democracy is under threat from populist political movements.
2. Populism is fuelled by the side-effects of economic globalisation, specifically the inequalities in income and wealth, mass unemployment, stagnation of wages and the humiliation and lack of self-esteem experienced by its victims, who see globalisation as benefiting the few at the expense of the many.
3. Populist politicians manipulate their populations via truth decay. They promote emotion over reason, fiction over facts and fake news over expertise and evidence.
4. Ecological globalisation has led to a range of environmental problems that is threatening the future of the planet and humanity.
5. Single nation-states do not have the power or resources to single-handedly deal with the global environmental crisis.
6. Most nation-states have signed up to United Nations initiatives to tackle the most pressing environmental problems, such as carbon emissions and global warming, although China and the USA have generally failed to cooperate fully.
7. A global environmentalist movement has emerged led by non-governmental organisations (NGOs) such as Greenpeace to raise public consciousness of the dangers of ecological globalisation.

# END-OF-PART QUESTIONS

**0 1** Describe two types of environmental problems that some sociologists claim are caused by globalisation. **[4 marks]**

**0 2** Explain one strength and one limitation of authoritarian states. **[6 marks]**

**0 3** Explain two reasons why economic globalisation has contributed to the rise of populist politicians and parties. **[8 marks]**

# SECTION B
# CONTEMPORARY ISSUES

## Contents


| | | |
|---|---|---|
| **Part 4** | **Globalisation, poverty and inequality** | **519** |
| **Part 5** | **Globalisation and migration** | **534** |
| **Part 6** | **Globalisation and crime** | **559** |


Three of the key concepts are particularly relevant in this section.

First, *inequality and opportunity*. Global inequality is on the rise and takes many forms – for example, inequalities can be seen across societies in access to education, literacy, income, poverty and health. Some countries are characterised by immense wealth, whilst other countries regularly suffer utter destitution. Migration is also very much linked to *inequality and opportunity* in that the majority of migrants are poor and aspire to settle in a country which they hope will provide them and their children with a better life in terms of educational and employment opportunities. This key concept is also important when considering global crime. The poor, wherever they live in the world, are most often the victims of global crime. Global crime is also stratified according to wealth and poverty in that criminal commodities and services tend to originate in the poorest areas of the world in order to meet demand from the more economically developed Western nations.

Second, *power, control and resistance.* Many transnational organisations aim to improve economic and social well-being and reduce inequality. However, some critics suggest that some of these transnational organisations merely reinforce global inequality because they primarily aim to protect the economies of the most economically developed countries (**MEDCs**) from harm. These criticisms have highlighted the need for non-government transnational organisations such as charities, pressure groups and global digital networks to challenge global inequality. Migration is also linked to the concepts of *power, control and resistance* in that many migrants are fleeing war, civil conflict, repression and their persecution by more powerful groups. This key concept is also central to the analysis of global crime and the difficulties of establishing international laws and policing such laws.

Third, *structure and human agency*. While most migration is voluntary, some is forced. If the alternative to migration is death from starvation and disease, famine and natural disaster, or torture and death because a person is deemed a 'threat' by the state, then the decision to leave is actually structured by events or powers beyond the individual's control. Feminist perspectives on crime also focus on the concept of *structure and human agency*. Many feminists claim that patriarchal assumptions are embedded in the organisation of societies and may be responsible for gender inequalities in criminal behaviour. However, some feminists suggest that the taken-for-granted binary distinction between male offenders and female victims may be over-simplistic. Recent research suggests that global crime needs to be investigated from the perspective of female victims in order to ascertain how much of their experience is the product of social factors beyond their control and how much choice or agency they actually exert over their experience of global crime.

Part 4 considers global poverty and inequalities, focusing on how globalisation impacts on life changes in developing countries, particularly in relation to education, income and health, and how transnational organisations attempt to tackle global inequalities. It concludes by considering two sociological explanations for global inequalities.

Part 5 examines global migration, in particular reasons for global migration and its consequences. It also explores sociological theories about who benefits from global migration.

Part 6 looks at global crime. It identifies types of global crimes and considers sociological explanations. It also looks at the difficulties of policing and prosecuting global crime.

# PART 4 GLOBALISATION, POVERTY AND INEQUALITY

## Contents


| | | |
|---|---|---|
| Unit 8.4.1 | **The impact of globalisation on life chances in less industrialised countries, in relation to education, income and health** | 519 |
| Unit 8.4.2 | **The role of transnational organisations in tackling global inequalities** | 522 |
| Unit 8.4.3 | **Sociological explanations for global inequalities** | 528 |


This part focuses on global inequality. This takes many forms but the main focus will be on education, income, poverty and health. Global inequality is on the rise but at vastly different rates across the world. The nation-states of the world exist in a hierarchy of affluence that ranges from utter destitution in the least economically developed countries (**LEDCs**) to immense wealth in the most economically developed countries (MEDCs). For example, in 2014, the richest 85 people in the world – who mainly reside in MEDCs – shared a combined wealth equal to the poorest 3.5 billion people on the planet – who mainly live in LEDCs. Sociologists working in the field of global development have focused on measuring inequality and progress towards 'development' (although there is a great deal of disagreement among experts how this should be defined and measured). Most agree that global inequality will be eradicated when all countries worldwide experience similar levels of economic and social well-being.

The second unit focuses on transnational organisations that aim to bring such economic and social well-being about. Some of these organisations are alliances of nation-states, such as the United Nations, in which the MEDCs have committed themselves to assisting the LEDCs onto the path towards development. However, critics suggest that some of these transnational organisations merely reinforce global inequality because they primarily aim to protect the economies of MEDCs from harm.

The third unit focuses on sociological explanations for global inequality. There are two broad schools of thought. Modernisation theory, closely related to functionalist theory, argues that global inequality is largely self-inflicted and is caused by fundamental weaknesses in the organisation and value systems of LEDCs. In contrast, Marxists such as Andre Gunder Frank (1979) argue that the global capitalist system, dominated by MEDCs, has intentionally exploited LEDCs and deliberately kept them in a state of under-development.

## Unit 8.4.1 The impact of globalisation on life chances in less industrialised countries, in relation to education, income and health

Most of the world's income and wealth is concentrated in the more economically developed countries (MEDCs), which, with the exception of Japan, Australia and New Zealand, are overwhelmingly situated in the West. Most of the extreme poverty found in the world is concentrated in the least economically developed societies (LEDCs). Absolute poverty is the daily norm in such societies, as are high rates of child malnutrition, high child mortality rates and low life expectancy for adults. There are an estimated 60 countries that have experienced little, if any, economic growth in the past 20 years. These countries are mainly located in sub-Saharan Africa (for example, Niger and Ethiopia), Central Asia (for example, Afghanistan) and South Asia (for example, Bangladesh) and are home to 1 billion people. This lack of growth has had a very negative impact on these countries' ability to provide basic education and healthcare. Consequently, high illiteracy rates and infant mortality rates are the norm in these societies.

## Global education inequalities

The evidence regarding global education is not positive. A United Nations Educational Scientific and Cultural Organisation (UNESCO) report on **literacy** published in 2017 stated that that 750 million adults in 2016 – two-thirds of whom are women – were illiterate. 102 million of this illiterate population were aged between 15 and 24 years old.

UNESCO observes that Southern Asia is home to almost one-half of the global illiterate population (49 per cent). In addition, 27 per cent of all illiterate adults live in sub-Saharan Africa, 10 per cent in Eastern and South-Eastern Asia, 9 per cent in Northern Africa and Western Asia, and about 4 per cent in Latin America and the Caribbean. Less than 2 per cent of the global illiterate population live in the remaining regions combined (Central Asia, Europe and Northern America, and Oceania).

With regard to the gender gap, UNESCO notes that in Europe and Northern America, Eastern and South-Eastern Asia, and Latin America and the Caribbean, there is no or little difference between male and female adult literacy rates. On the other hand, there are relatively large gender gaps to the disadvantage of females in Northern Africa, Southern Asia, and sub-Saharan Africa. However, among young people, gender gaps in literacy skills are generally smaller and improving more quickly over time.

### Activity

1. List three possible reasons why female children are more likely to be illiterate or less likely to be educated compared with male children.
2. Think of two reasons why the gender gap has got smaller in the present generation of young people.

African countries have the highest adult illiteracy rates in the world – for example, 73 per cent of the population of South Sudan is illiterate. The only country that lies outside the African continent with comparable illiteracy is Afghanistan, which has an illiteracy rate of 71.9 per cent.

Official statistics suggest that China's literacy rate has rapidly improved since 1990. For example, in 2010, 95 per cent of China's population could read and write, although this still means that an estimated 54 million people aged 15 and older were unable to read or write a simple sentence. China has also dramatically reduced the gap between male and female literacy. In 1990, this was 87 per cent for men and only 68 per cent for women. However, by 2010 women's literacy had improved to 98 per cent for adult men compared with 93 per cent for women. Among young people, the gender gap has narrowed considerably: 99.7 per cent for males and 99.6 per cent for females. According to UNESCO, several other developing countries in Asia have mirrored China's improvement, including Thailand (with a 96 per cent literacy rate), the Philippines (95 per cent) and Indonesia (93 per cent).

UNESCO argues that literacy statistics often obscure differences in wealth and poverty. The Brookings Institute (2015) estimates that if education is measured by average levels of attainment – how much children have learned and how long they have spent in school – then African countries are about 100 years behind countries in North America and Europe. Furthermore, it found that the education levels of the adult workforce in the USA and Europe measured by average numbers of years of school is double that of workers in many African countries.

However, there are a number of other trends which suggest that some Western societies actually lag behind Asian countries with regard to certain aspects of education. For example, the 2016 Trends in International Maths and Science Study (TIMSS) report concluded that Singapore, Hong Kong, South Korea and Japan dominate international rankings for maths and science and are well ahead of Western countries such as the UK and USA.

### Activity

*Students in many Asian countries excel in maths and science.*

Can you think of any explanations for why Asian children are better at maths and science than Western children?

## Global income inequalities

According to the 2018 World Inequality Report compiled by Facundo Alvaredo, Thomas Piketty et al., income inequality has increased rapidly in North America and Asia, grown moderately in Europe, and stabilised at an extremely high level in the Middle East, sub-Saharan Africa and Brazil since 1980. The poorest half of the global population has seen some income growth but this has been matched by the income growth experienced by the top 0.1 per cent of the world's population.

In 2015, the World Bank announced that, for the first time, the proportion of the world's population living in extreme poverty had fallen to below 10 per cent. This decline has occurred because of increased employment opportunities brought about by globalisation, especially the creation of millions of new, more productive jobs, mostly in Asia. More people in the less industrialised world have jobs now than ever before, and those jobs, despite being low-paid (compared with wages in the more industrialised world), provide a better standard of living than **subsistence** agricultural work. However, despite this good news, the World Bank estimated that 768 million people worldwide were living in extreme poverty in 2017.

### Activity

*Favela (slum) de Rocinha in Rio de Janeiro, Brazil. The world's most populous favela.*

Identify three reasons why the global number of those living in extreme poverty has recently fallen to below 10 per cent.

However, jobs in the less industrialised world are vulnerable to the negative side of globalisation, especially global economic downturns. Economic crises starting in a single country often become global and can have a devastating effect on labour markets in both the industrialised and less industrialised worlds. For example, the 2008 global banking crisis, which originated in the USA, initiated a crisis that resulted in massive global unemployment. For example, China lost between 20 million and 36 million jobs, particularly among migrants working in factories manufacturing products that were to be exported to the USA and Europe.

## Global health inequalities

In the wealthy industrialised countries, the main causes of death are the so-called '**diseases of affluence**' – cancer, strokes and heart disease – mainly caused by 'excessive' lifestyles: too much fatty food, obesity, alcohol and smoking, for example. In contrast, people in the less industrialised world are more likely to die of '**diseases of poverty**' – preventable and treatable diseases – caused by lack of access to amenities that Western populations take for granted, such as nutritional diets, clean water, vaccination and maternal care.

A number of major inequalities in health between the MEDCs and LEDCs can be observed:

- In 2010, in some parts of sub-Saharan Africa, premature adult death rates were nearly four times higher than those experienced in Western European countries. There are 21 African countries in which average life expectancy is below 60 years. The lowest life expectancy of all is found in Sierra Leone, where it is only 50 years. Asian life expectancy too has soared in recent years. For example, Japan tops the world's life expectancy league table list, with its citizens living to 83.7 years (males 80.5 and females 86.8). Another major global inequality in health can be observed by looking at **infant mortality rates**. The World Health Organization (WHO) estimates that 5.6 million children under the age of 5 years died in 2016, mainly in Africa. About 45 per cent of these deaths were linked to **malnutrition**. WHO statistics suggest that 52 million children worldwide suffer from malnutrition. Malnutrition severely weakens children's resistance to infections such as measles, diphtheria and tuberculosis. According to WHO, 250 000 children died of tuberculosis in 2016, mostly in LEDCs. According to UNICEF, approximately 1300 young children die every day from diarrhoea in poorer countries (480 000 children a year), despite the availability of simple effective treatment.
- Malaria is a major cause of death, particularly in Africa. For example, 100 000 people in Nigeria lost their lives to this disease in 2017. Children

under the age of 2 and pregnant women are particularly at risk. Catherine West (2018) observes that malaria traps people in poverty, prevents children from attending school and costs countries in Africa about $10.3 billion a year in terms of lost working hours and cost of treatment.

## Activity

Research the reasons why in recent years there have been improvements in global life expectancy. Pay special attention to malaria and HIV/AIDS.

## Key terms

**MEDCs** The most economically developed or richest countries in the world.

**LEDCs** The least economically developed or poorest countries in the world.

**Literacy** The ability to read and write.

**Subsistence** Supporting oneself at a minimal level, in order to survive.

**Diseases of affluence** Life-threatening conditions caused by wealthy or rich lifestyles.

**Diseases of poverty** Life-threatening diseases caused by malnutrition and lack of access to clean water and sanitation.

**Infant mortality rates** Death rates experienced by children aged 5 years and under.

**Malnutrition** Not having enough to eat or not eating enough of the 'right' things.

## Summary

1. Significant global inequalities exist in income, access to school, literacy levels, infant mortality rates and life expectancy between MEDCs and LEDCs, especially those situated in Africa.
2. Females are more likely to experience these inequalities compared with males in LEDCs.

# Unit 8.4.2 The role of transnational organisations in tackling global inequalities

This unit will focus on three sets of international non-governmental organisations (NGOs), known as transnational organisations, which aim to tackle global inequality. The first set is composed of alliances of nation-states such as the United Nations (UN), the European Union and the G7. Second, many countries are also members of transnational trade organisations that aim to set out the rules for world trade such as the World Trade Organization (WTO) or the World Bank and International Monetary Fund (IMF), which aim to promote economic growth and to reduce global inequalities such as poverty.

Finally, in addition to these global alliances and networks of nation-states, there are non-government transnational organisations working with and within LEDCs to tackle and alleviate poverty and to improve educational and health facilities. These include formal confederations and international charities such as Oxfam, which work with partners and local communities in over 90 countries to mobilise the power of people in LEDCs against poverty. In addition to charities, there also exists a globalised network of activists held together by a digital communication grid, known as the anti-globalisation movement (AGM).

## Alliances of nation-states

Alliances of nation-states include the United Nations (UN), the European Union and the G7.

### The United Nations

The United Nations (UN) was set up in 1945. It is a coalition of 193 sovereign nation-states, including both MEDCs and LEDCs, all of which have equal representation in the UN General Assembly. The UN Charter states that membership is open to all peace-loving states which accept and are willing to carry out the obligations contained in the Charter, particularly those aimed at tackling global inequalities.

The UN has a number of agencies working within LEDCs, including WHO, UNESCO and the UN International Children's Emergency Fund (UNICEF). The UN is committed to reducing global inequalities. For example, in 2000, the UN published a number of **Millennium Development Goals (MDGs),** which aim to reduce certain global inequalities by 2030. These included achieving universal primary education, promoting gender equality and empowering women, reducing child mortality, improving maternal health, and combating HIV/AIDS, malaria and other diseases. The richer members of the UN countries agree to support poorer UN members to achieve these MDGs through the provision of aid, the reduction of debt and the formation of fairer trade relationships.

However, critics of the MDGs argue that they do not go far enough in demanding greater **accountability** from those who govern less industrialised nations. They argue that goals need to be added that protect basic human rights, religious tolerance and political freedom, and especially the right to vote in democratic and free elections.

## Activity

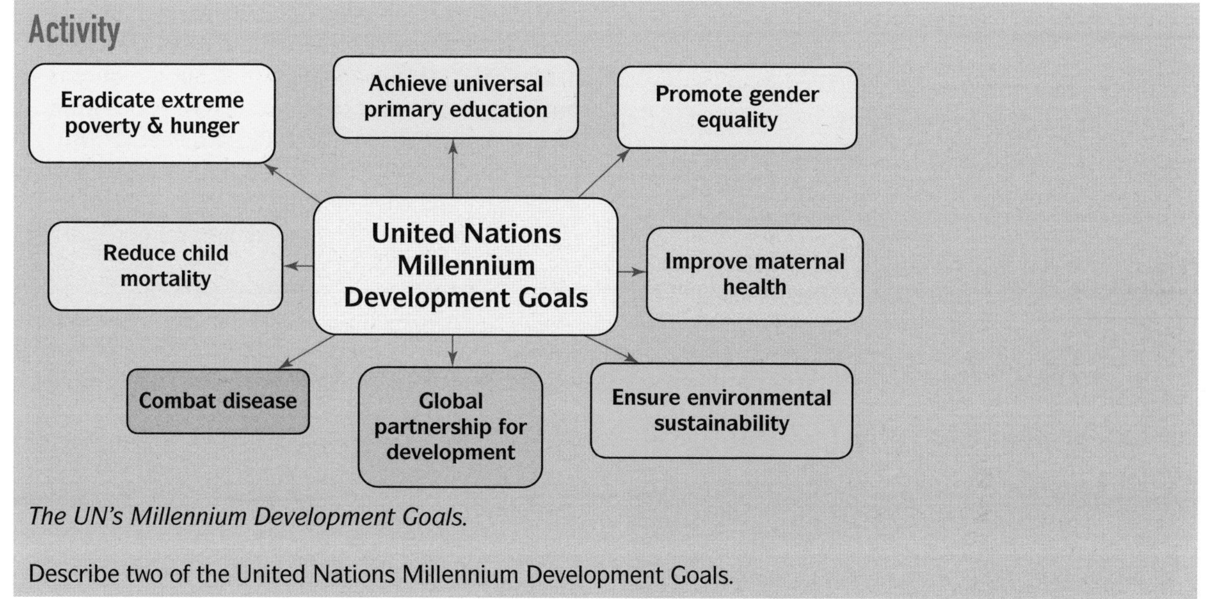


*The UN's Millennium Development Goals.*

Describe two of the United Nations Millennium Development Goals.

In 2015, the UN claimed that a billion people living in extreme poverty, defined as living on $1 or less a day, had been lifted out of poverty (a fall of 50 per cent) since 1990 in Asia, Latin America and Africa. The UN also reaffirmed its commitment to eradicate extreme poverty by 2030.

### The European Union (EU)

The European Union (EU) is a political and economic union of 28 European states (this will reduce to 27 when the UK exits in 2019). The EU is also committed to tackling global inequalities. For example, in 2013 the EU spent 56.5 billion euros on giving assistance to LEDCs outside of the EU. This aid is regularly audited and assessed to prevent corruption by local elites. According to the EU, developing countries have a strong say in how EU aid is spent, as do non-governmental organisations (NGOs), such as international charities, trade unions, human rights groups and environmental organisations.

### The G7

The Group of Seven (G7) refers to a group of highly industrialised nations – France, Germany, Italy, the UK, Japan, the US and Canada. These MEDCs are the seven largest advanced economies in the world and represent more than 62 per cent of global net wealth. The leaders of the G7 hold an annual summit in order to discuss and tackle global issues such as global economic inequality, trade, aid and debt, global security, climate change and terrorism. Recent summits have been marred by protests organised by the anti-globalisation movement (AGM), which sees the G7 as partly responsible for global inequalities. The AGM argue that the G7 is primarily motivated by its need to protect its dominance of world trade and therefore the MEDCs' disproportionate share of the world's wealth. The AGM points out that the G7 is not democratic or accountable for the decisions it makes, which often ignore the interests of the LEDCs.

## Transnational organisations

In addition to the UN, the EU and G7, there also exist transnational organisations, which aim to manage and regulate global trade as well as global financial and monetary systems. These include the WTO, the World Bank and the IMF.

## The World Trade Organization (WTO)

In 1947, the General Agreement on Tariffs and Trade (GATT) was signed by the Western powers to govern global trade and to reduce trade barriers and competition between nations. In 1994, the World Trade Organization (WTO) was set up to replace GATT. It currently has 161 member states. The WTO has taken over and extended the GATT agreements on global trade in goods, as well as negotiating a new GATT – which covers global services such as telecommunications, banking and investment, transport, education, health and the environment.

However, Ha-Joon Chang (2008) has criticised the free-trade agenda of the WTO because he claims that the global trade rules they have set down are unfair and biased against the LEDCs and are the main cause of the global inequalities that exist today. This is because the WTO pressures poorer countries to open up their economies to Western banks and transnational companies (TNCs), and to abandon **tariffs** (taxes) on imports from the West. However, under GATT, MEDCs are allowed to impose **quotas** restricting the import of manufactured goods from the less industrialised world. Richard Peet (2009) argues that the WTO has rigged trade rules in favour of the West and consequently the WTO is a rich man's club dominated by the **neoliberal** free market philosophy of the MEDCs.

### Contemporary issues: The World Trade Organization – Amrita Narlikar, Martin Daunton and Robert Stern (2014)

*Protesters demonstrate against the WTO in Hong Kong in 2005.*

Narlikar et al. (2014) observe that, for such a small organisation, the WTO arouses a surprising degree of popular interest, emotions and drama. NGOs have frequently staged massive anti-WTO demonstrations. It is now rare that high-level meetings of the WTO do not attract angry mobs. The WTO might be loved by neoliberal thinkers but it is detested by many.

The WTO is committed to the concept of free trade. It believes that unlimited competition in the free market is the best way to organise an economy because it allegedly forces both sellers and buyers to perform with maximum efficiency. Government intervention is viewed as harmful because it reduces competition. The WTO is consequently committed to removing obstacles to free trade wherever they may exist.

However, Chang and others argue that WTO policy is biased in favour of Western governments and TNCs. Chang argues that Western governments are using the WTO to say to the rest of the world 'Do as we say, not as we do.' He suggests that MEDCs developed and became wealthy as a result of the sorts of interventionist policies rejected by the WTO. Narlikar et al. also argue that the MEDCs have historically been reluctant to reduce trade barriers and quick to raise them.

Some sociologists claim that the WTO has hidden goals that are more to do with assisting the economic success of the MEDCs and TNCs. Critics claim that WTO decision-making is dominated by MEDCs. Critics also claim that the WTO sees trade as more important than values such as human rights, the environment, workers' rights, gender and the eradication of poverty.

#### Questions

1. Visit the website of the WTO (www. wto.org/) and note down the aims and objectives – 'what we do' – of the organisation.
2. Explain why the WTO is 'loved by neoliberal thinkers'.
3. In your opinion, why is the WTO blamed for global inequalities?

### The World Bank and International Monetary Fund (IMF)

The World Bank is an international financial institution that provides loans to countries of the world for **capital projects**. It also aims to achieve two related goals – reducing the numbers in extreme poverty to less than 3 per cent of the world's population, and sharing prosperity by encouraging economic growth in LEDC countries – which it is hoping to achieve by 2030.

Another similar transnational organisation is the International Monetary Fund (IMF), to which most nation-states (with the exception of North Korea and Cuba) belong. The IMF has two main goals. First, it aims to ensure the stability of the international monetary and financial system. Second, it helps to resolve economic crises, and works with its member countries to promote economic growth and to alleviate poverty. Increasingly the IMF specialises in short-term loans to less industrialised countries whose economies are weak or in trouble because of debt or because of a decline in the value of their commodity exports to the West.

However, critics claim that both the World Bank and IMF are dominated by neoliberal policy makers who favour richer Western countries at the expense of poorer countries. Both agencies have been criticised by Joseph Stiglitz (2017), as agents of the neoliberal WTO. Peet actually refers to the WTO, IMF and World Bank as the 'unholy trinity' and suggests that they exist to strong-arm poorer countries into accepting neoliberal political policies in return for economic assistance. Chang argues that the World Bank and IMF present themselves as 'good Samaritans' whose only motive is to assist LEDCs. However, he argues that they are actually 'bad Samaritans' because their motives are essentially selfish. Chang argues that the real point of the WTO, IMF and World Bank is to create an environment in the poorer nation-states that is friendly to TNC goods, investment and the exploitation of their labour force. He argues that conditions for granting loans to LEDCs are often politically biased in the sense that the IMF will only lend the money if the LEDC agrees to cut public spending on health, education and pensions and to freeze wages (thus increasing global inequalities) and to open up its domestic markets to TNCs. Ankie Hoogvelt (2001) observes that those LEDCs that comply with these neoliberal demands are rewarded with IMF and World Bank support, while those that do not are refused help. Stiglitz concludes that the IMF and World Bank undermine democracy because they are unelected bureaucrats. He concludes that IMF/World Bank policies simply do not work. Despite decades of IMF and World Bank 'help', Africa, for example, is probably worse off in terms of income and wealth than it was 40 years ago.

## The role of local and transnational NGOs

Julie Fisher (1998) notes that the globalisation of capitalism has led to a decline in the power of the state especially in the developing world and this has produced a growing number of groups known collectively as 'non-governmental organisations' (NGOs). These have taken on an enormously diverse range of activities, including promoting human rights and social justice, protesting against environmental degradation and so on. In the view of some observers, the rise in influence of these NGOs constitutes a 'quiet revolution' in that they reflect and constitute a '**civil society**' that has the potential to wield power and influence comparable to the nation-state.

### Charities

Many NGOs are global charities, such as Oxfam, Save the Children, the Red Cross, Catholic Agency For Overseas Development (CAFOD) and so on, which respond to a range of needs in the developing world. These NGOs are funded in two main ways: through public donation (made possible through campaigning, lobbying and advertising), and official aid funds from government, the EU and the UN. This official funding is based on the fact that NGOs are often the experts on the ground and in the field. They are more in tune with the needs of local people in the less industrialised world because they often work closely with local community associations to reduce global inequalities by identifying and responding to local needs and to bring about beneficial change in infrastructure, education and health. Michael Edwards (2014) identifies four key functions of NGOs.

(a) To improve local situations – when NGOs such as Christian Aid first got involved in the less industrialised world, their focus was very much on providing 'basic needs' – that is, lifting the poor, especially children, out of poverty and helping to improve diet, access to clean water, shelter, vaccination and so on. However, most NGOs today aim to help local people attain '**social well-being**' too; for example, the right to be healthy and to live into old age, the right for both sexes to be educated and so on.

(b) To respond to emergencies and disasters – the larger NGOs often have the infrastructure, contacts and so on to be able to respond quickly when disasters such as tsunamis, earthquakes or volcanic eruptions hit the less industrialised world. They are usually on the front-line when responding to man-made disasters – for example, in refugee camps for those fleeing war or persecution.

(c) To hold powerful TNCs such as the WTO to account – Edwards argues that NGOs should monitor the activities of the WTO, the World Bank, the G7 and the IMF, as well as Western governments and TNCs, to make them accountable for their decisions and actions in the less industrialised world, especially if these undermine local social well-being, human rights or the environment.

(d) To mobilise public opinion and, if necessary, protest – Edwards argues it is important for NGOs to mobilise support from all sections of society, both in LEDCs and MEDCs. He argues that NGOs should focus on educating the Western public about the causes of global inequality so there is more public engagement with the issues.

## Evaluating NGOs

In sociological terms, there seem to be mixed feelings about the effectiveness of NGO activity.

- Some sociologists view them as positive agencies for change because they are unencumbered and untainted by politics or greed. In this sense, NGOs are idealised as organisations populated by those who simply want to help others. Philip McMichael (2016) notes that NGOs are seen as having greater 'diversity, credibility and creativity' than official organisations such as the World Bank. They are seen as implementing 'just development' based on 'equity, democracy and social justice'. The fact that many NGOs are not burdened with large bureaucracies means that they are relatively flexible, innovative in their thinking and practice and fairly efficient at identifying local needs.
- It is often assumed that NGOs are self-funding and that their ability to operate in the less industrialised world is financed by public donations. Edwards and David Hulme (1996) point out that many NGOs are actually financed by Western governments and international agencies such as the EU and UN. In other words, many NGOs are contractors who are working on behalf of their clients or funders. However, this can arouse suspicion of NGO activities. Edwards and Hulme observed that in India this led to NGOs with foreign connections sometimes being regarded as anti-nationalist agents of capitalism and the promoters of Western political and cultural values.
- Edwards and Hulme claim that mainstream NGOs have increasingly distanced themselves from groups such as the AGM, which challenge the existing neoliberal power structure. They argue that NGOs have failed to bring about changes in the neoliberal systems and structures that perpetuate global inequality.
- The 21st century has also seen an examination of the motives of those who lead NGOs. Edwards argues that NGOs should be 'working themselves out of a job'. In other words, if they were successful, they would no longer be needed. However, the reality is that NGOs have grown fat on development and consequently funds have increasingly been channelled into administrative costs as NGOs have become overly bureaucratic. NGOs are often not democratic and are rarely accountable for their actions. This has led to the accusation by critics such as Graham Hancock (1994) that NGO leaders are 'lords of poverty' and have a vested interest in the poverty of LEDCs. It is this poverty that ensures their high salaries and job security.

## The anti-globalisation movement

In addition to NGOs, there is a loose affiliation of organisations that constitutes a **social movement** known as the 'anti-globalisation movement' (AGM). This shares common concerns about the way the world economy favours Western interests and the way that trade and neoliberal economic interests are favoured over the human rights of people in LEDCs. This protest movement is not actually against globalisation but rather its negative consequences, which the AGM believes cause global inequalities, and which generally benefits MEDC economies at the expense of LEDCs. This **grassroots** movement is presently centred around five well-organised and active international campaigns:

- opposing the WTO
- reforming the World Bank and IMF
- calling for the cancellation of debt owed by LEDCs
- insisting that TNCs act responsibly and ethically – for example, by paying their fair share of taxes
- opposing environmental degradation.

According to Arturo Escobar (2008), the AGM has enthused ordinary people, especially young people, who have ethical concerns with the way global capitalism operates (and particularly the ways in which it encourages and sustains global inequalities, debt, subsistence wages and child labour in the developing world) and wish to voice these concerns. Many young people who actively protested on the streets at WTO or G7 conferences did so because they were convinced that Western governments are colluding with global corporations. Naomi Klein (2001) argues that what unites all these people is their desire for a citizen-centred alternative to the power that neoliberal capitalism exerts over their everyday lives.

The AGM therefore empowers ordinary people by providing a global network in which they can engage in levels of protest that suit their situation. This may include attending Live Aid concerts, boycotting goods that are produced by environmentally unfriendly methods or by regimes with poor human rights records, or signing petitions for the Making Poverty History movement. Alternatively, it may include committing oneself to full-blown street protests and criminal anti-corporate behaviour such as vandalising the stores of those seen to be global corporate 'villains'. Escobar concludes that the main achievement of AGMs has been the raising of public awareness of the consequences of unfettered global capitalism and of the fact that alternative ways of seeing and practising development do exist.

## Activity

*Nelson Mandela speaks at a Make Poverty History event in central London in February 2005.*

'Non-government organisations have been very effective in reducing global inequalities'. Evaluate this view.

## Conclusions

It is difficult to come to any firm conclusions about NGOs because, as Edwards notes, there is such variation and diversity within the NGO sector that it is very difficult for sociologists to work out their impact at the local, national and global level. They differ from one another considerably in terms of their functions, goals, organisational structures and memberships. This makes it difficult to generalise about their success or failure.

However, Edwards and Hulme argue that NGOs have to engage more with the AGM. This may be uncomfortable for them considering the source of their funding, but it will function to give those without a voice in the less industrialised world membership of a civil society that can powerfully highlight the negative consequences of the globalisation process – for example, inequalities in wealth and income, education and health for poorer countries. They also argue that the AGM and NGO lobbying now means that commitment to human rights is regarded by the general public as a basic principle of development. The AGM, too, has kept the spotlight on the need for reform of transnational agencies such as the World Bank and WTO, as well as issues such as inequalities in terms of trade. However, on a negative note, Edwards points out that, despite 70 years of NGO activity in the less industrialised world, the main causes of inequality in this part of the world remain unchallenged.

## Key terms

**Millennium Development Goals** A set of international goals relating to economic and social well-being established by the United Nations. They are thought to be achievable by 2030.

**Accountability** Taking responsibility for decisions that have been made.

**Tariffs** A tax or duty to be paid on particular imports or exports.

**Quotas** An official limit set on the number of products that can be imported into a country.

**Neoliberal** A set of economic ideas that stresses that trade should be free of government intervention and totally reliant on market forces and unlimited and unregulated competition so that buyers and sellers perform with maximum efficiency.

**Capital project** A project that requires substantial investment to improve or replace an aspect of a country's infrastructure – for example, an airport.

**Civil society** Refers to the notion that citizens of a society may act together in a common cause – for instance, in order to right a wrong. Civil society may oppose governments, for example, on austerity cuts.

**Social well-being** A feeling of belonging or social inclusion based on feeling happy, safe, comfortable and psychologically healthy.

**Social movement** A type of group action that empowers ordinary and oppressed people and aims to challenge or resist the decisions and actions of more powerful groups.

**Grassroots** The ordinary people who are regarded as the main body of an organisation's membership.

## Summary

1. There are three main types of transnational organisations which wield political power. The most formidable are those which are made up of nation-states such as the UN, EU and G7, which aim to preserve global security and peace. They are also committed to reducing global inequalities.
2. Other types of transnational organisations are those formed by a collection of nation-states to regulate trade between countries, such as WTO, the World Bank and IMF. However, these organisations have been accused of worsening global inequalities.
3. In addition, non-governmental organisations such as charities aim to reduce global inequalities in the least economically developed parts of the world.
4. Social movements such as the anti-globalisation movement are also transnational in character and have been instrumental in raising global consciousness about the extent and causes of global inequalities.

# Unit 8.4.3 Sociological explanations for global inequalities

This unit will examine the two sociological explanations for global inequalities. First, modernisation theory argues that LEDC poverty is largely self-inflicted. Sociologists from this school of thought, who are mainly American, claim that both the structure and cultures of societies that experience inequality are inherently flawed and that if global inequalities are to be reduced, such countries need to adopt Western norms and values. In contrast, Marxism or 'dependency theory' rejects the view that the problems of LEDCs are essentially internal. Rather, Marxists argue that global capitalism is responsible for global inequality in much the same way that capitalism in specific societies is responsible for class inequalities. Dependency theory argues that MEDCs, especially European and US capitalism, have exploited the LEDCs in much the same way that the bourgeoisie has exploited the labour power of the working classes in their own societies. This exploitation has both an historical and contemporary character, as this unit will outline.

## Modernisation theory

Modernisation theory sets out to identify what internal economic and cultural conditions were supposedly preventing poorer countries from modernising. Walt Rostow (1971) claimed that LEDCs were held back by 'traditional beliefs and values' and these needed to be replaced with Western cultural values and practices.

Other modernisation theory sociologists such as Talcott Parsons (1966) argued that global inequalities can be eradicated if cultural barriers in poorer societies are overcome. Parsons, in particular, was very critical of traditional societies because he believed they were too attached to old-fashioned customs, rituals, practices and institutions and therefore unwilling to entertain social change. Parsons saw modernisation impeded by the following traditional values:

(a) Religious values that stress patriarchy – these particularly prevent intelligent and skilled women from competing equally with men.

(b) **Particularism** – people are judged and allocated tasks on the basis of family relationships rather than ability. This undermines the motivation and innovation required to try new roles and ways of doing things.

(c) **Fatalism** – people in poverty often subscribe to the view that things will never change. This may mean that people may passively accept their lot rather than actively seek to change society for the better.

(d) **Collectivism** – people may not be motivated to change their material circumstances because they defer to group pressure and put their membership of a social group before self-interest.

Parsons argued that these traditional ways of thinking and practices are the enemy of progress. He believed that people in undeveloped societies need to develop an '**entrepreneurial spirit**' if economic growth is to be achieved and this could only happen if people in these societies became more receptive to Western values such as **meritocracy**, **universalism** and individualism. Parsons claimed that traditional institutions stifled the individual initiative, **free enterprise** and the risk-taking necessary for societies to develop and modernise.

Some modernisation theorists claim that global inequalities are entirely caused by the alleged substandard quality of the culture of less advanced societies. For example, David Landes (1998) suggests that Europeans are more rational, ordered, diligent, productive, literate and inventive than non-Europeans. Furthermore, he argues that Europeans subscribe to an 'advanced' value system organised around democracy, freedom of speech, property rights, the rule of law and a work ethic that encourages hard work and the thrifty use of both time and money. Niall Ferguson (2011) agrees with this analysis when he argues that Europe and the USA developed six 'killer apps' – the ability to compete, a scientific approach to problem-solving, a respect for property rights, medicine, consumerism and a work ethic – that produced their economic and material success. The implication of such analysis is that less industrialised societies need to do the same.

### Activity

Design a 'Modernisation theory' poster which identifies the specific institutions and values which are supposedly holding up the progress of LEDCs and bringing about global inequalities.

### Evaluating modernisation theory

(1) Jeffrey Sachs (2005) is critical of this modernisation argument because it fails to acknowledge the true cause of inequality – lack of resources. Sachs argues that people in poorer countries often lack **human capital** (good health, nutrition and skills), **infrastructure** (facilities such as roads or digital technology), capital (money) and **public institutional capital** (services) through no fault of their own.

(2) Critics claim that modernisation theory is clearly ethnocentric and condescendingly biased because it argues that Western forms of civilisation are technically and morally superior and that the cultures of less industrialised societies are deficient in important respects. It often dismisses such cultures as 'backward' if they insist on retaining some elements of traditional culture and belief and/or if they apply fundamentalist religious principles to the organisation of their society.

However, Chris Edwards (1992) suggests that the traditional and modern can actually be successfully combined. He argues that the economic success of Asian economies such as South Korea, Singapore and China is due to a successful combination of traditional religious values and practices with Western rational thinking and practices. Religions in these societies have encouraged the emergence of a moral and authoritarian political leadership that demands sacrifice, obedience and hard work from its population in return for prosperity. This has paved the way for an acceptance of Western economic and cultural practices, such as widespread respect for meritocratic education for both males and females, commitment to hard work at school and in the workplace, discipline, innovation and ambition.

(3) Modernisation theory generally ignores the **'crisis of modernism'**, which is apparent in the Western industrialised world. For example, despite **affluence**, inequalities in the distribution of income and wealth in the West may be fuelling social problems such as poverty, homelessness, and high rates of crime, drug abuse and suicide.

While modernisation theory has been very unpopular, one aspect that appears to be true is that, in order to reduce global inequality, sociologists need to understand culture. While modernisation theorists are critical of traditional culture (seeing it as an obstacle to development), postmodernists celebrate culture and argue that it is more important than economics in encouraging social change.

### Activity

Describe two internal reasons why some societies experience inequality, according to modernisation theory.

## Marxist dependency theory

The Marxist sociologist Frank (1979) rejected the modernisation theory argument that global inequalities are caused by the 'deficient' cultures of poorer nation-states. In contrast, Frank argued that global inequalities are caused by external social forces over which poorer nation-states have little or no control. In particular, he argued that global capitalism has deliberately and systematically under-developed the economies of poorer countries in order to benefit the economies of the richer nations. This capitalist exploitation has resulted in poorer nations being left in a state of dependency on Western nation-states. Therefore, Frank's theory is known as dependency theory.

Activity

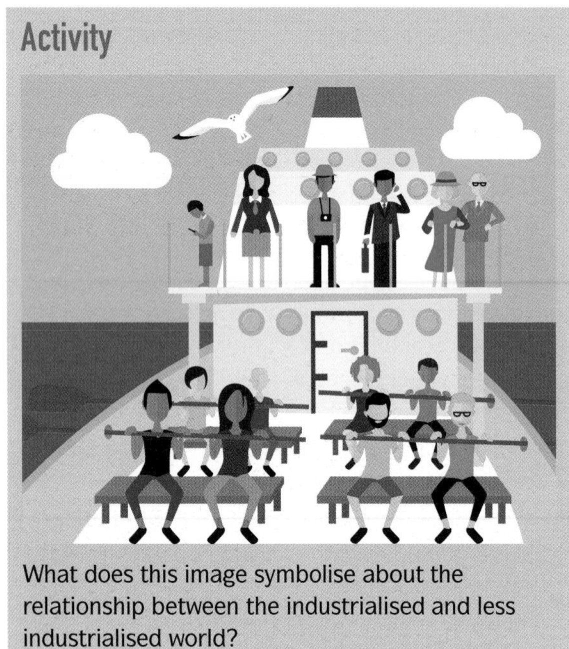

What does this image symbolise about the relationship between the industrialised and less industrialised world?

## The world capitalist system

Frank argued that, since the 16th century, there has existed a world capitalist system organised in a similar fashion to the unequal and exploitative economic or class relationships that make up the internal organisation of capitalist societies. This world capitalist system is organised as an interlocking chain. At one end of the chain is the powerful and wealthy 'metropolis' made up of the MEDCs. At the other end of the chain are the undeveloped 'satellite', or LEDCs. The relationship between the core and the periphery is based on exploitation. The metropolis exploits the cheap labour, materials and cash crops of the satellite countries, with the cooperation of their ruling elites, because it has greater military power and wealth and because it controls the terms of world trade. This exploitation has resulted in an accumulation of wealth in the West, and in stagnation, destitution and inequalities in income, education and health in the less industrialised world. Frank argued that the West has a vested interest in making sure that global inequalities continue relatively undisturbed and that less industrialised societies remain economically weak and reliant on the West.

## Historical forms of exploitation – slavery and colonialism

Frank argued that global inequalities were first established through the use of both slavery and colonialism. Over a 200-year period (1650 to 1850), the **triangular slave trade** shipped approximately 9 million Africans aged between 15 and 35 across the Atlantic to work as an exceptionally cheap form of labour on cotton, sugar and tobacco plantations in America and the West Indies that were owned mainly by British settlers. This generated tremendous profits for both the British slave-traders and the plantation owners that were largely invested in industrial production (factories) in the West.

Activity

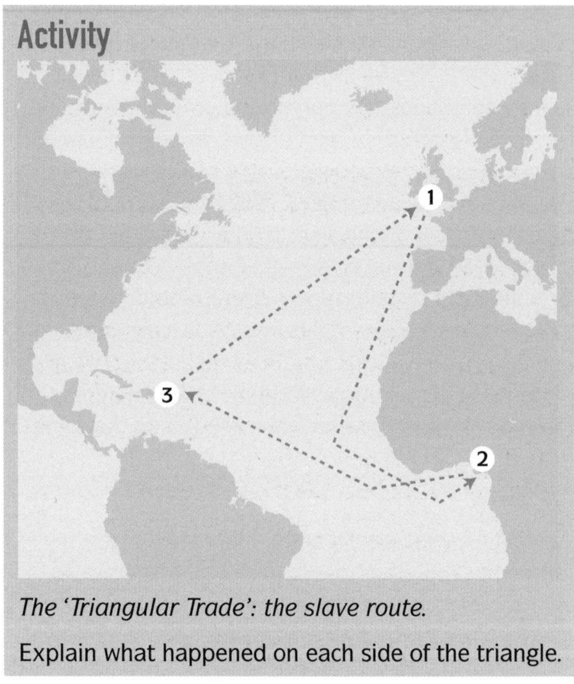


*The 'Triangular Trade': the slave route.*

Explain what happened on each side of the triangle.

Furthermore, **imperialism** and **colonialism** locked much of Africa, Asia and Central and South America even further into an exploitative relationship with the capitalist West. During the period 1650 to 1900, using their superior naval and military technology, European powers, with Britain at the fore, were able to conquer and colonise many parts of the world. The principal result of this European rule was the creation of a global economy in which the colonies were primarily exploited for their cheap food, raw materials and labour. Local industries were either destroyed or undermined by cheap imported manufactured goods from the West.

## Neo-colonialism

Many former colonies may have achieved political independence today as nation-states, but dependency theory argues that their exploitation continues via **neo-colonialism**. Frank argued that these new forms of colonialism are more subtle but are equally as destructive as slavery and colonialism. Frank identified three main types of neo-colonialism:

**Terms of world trade** The terms of world trade are dominated by Western markets and needs. This means that many poor countries do not get a fair price for their raw materials, cash crops or manufactured goods.

**TNCs** Western TNCs are frequently criticised for exploiting LEDCs. Klein (2008) claims that TNCs often exercise power without responsibility, while Joel Bakan (2005) describes TNCs as 'institutional psychopaths'. He claims that they are programmed to exploit and dehumanise people for profit. For example, the sweat-shop conditions of transnational factories in developing countries have been criticised by Klein for their use of child labour, hazardous working conditions and exploitative rates of pay. Shell in Nigeria and RTZ in Angola have exploited natural resources with ruthlessness and indifference. Indigenous people have had their land forcibly seized and, despite international protests, have been removed at gunpoint from their homelands by local elites working on behalf of these TNCs.

**Aid** **Aid** is another means by which Western countries can exploit the less industrialised world because it inevitably leads to such countries being in debt to Western governments and banks. Aid is also only handed out to poorer countries with strings attached. For example, the recipient country may only be allowed to spend that aid on products from the donor country. Kenan Malik (2018) observes that the richer nations often use aid as a weapon to promote their own products and political interests. Half of all international aid from rich nations to poor nations is **'tied aid',** which means that recipient countries must use it to buy goods and services from the donor nation. For example, close to 80 per cent of the money distributed to LEDCs by the US Agency for International Development (USAID) goes directly to American transnationals. In other words, USAID puts 'America first'.

A 2014 report by the US Congressional Research Service concluded that 'aid can act as both carrot and stick and is a means of influencing events, solving specific problems and projecting US values'. Since 9/11, aid has become a vital instrument in the war on terror. Moreover, EU aid to LEDCs in Africa has become increasingly dependent on those countries curbing illegal migration to Europe. In other words, as Malik notes, 'aid is, at best, a kind of bribe, at worst a form of blackmail'.

Malik also points out that a high proportion of aid from MEDCs to LEDCs is in the form of loans, which cripple the latter through the accumulation of debt. Many MEDCs receive more in interest payments from recipient countries than they give in aid. Critics of aid therefore argue than an aid programme that works for the economies of MEDCs is incompatible with aid that helps the poorest.

### Activity

*A textile factory producing jeans for export to a Western discounter.*

Explain, and illustrate with examples, two types of neo-colonialism.

## Assessing dependency theory

### Strengths

Hoogvelt (2001) argues that dependency theory was a major influence on the political ideologies of many less industrialised countries in the 1960s and 1970s. She notes that political leaders, particularly in Africa, used the principles of dependency theory to argue for 'development as liberation' from Western exploitation. Political and social movements in Africa in this period consequently stressed nationalism, self-reliance and breaking away from MEDCs as a means of countering neo-colonialism. These strategies were practised in Venezuela under Hugo Chavez from 1999 until his death in 2013 and in present-day Ecuador.

The experience of Cuba, which experienced a Marxist revolution in 1959, suggests that a socialist model of development can resist dependency and produce positive benefits. Despite decades of enforced isolationism (until 2015, the USA imposed a trade embargo on Cuba that made it extremely difficult for Cuba to export its goods), Cuba ranks among the top 5 per cent of 125 developing countries in terms of adult literacy rates, infant and maternal mortality rates and life expectancy.

### Activity

Another important Marxist explanation of global inequality is provided by the world systems theory of Wallerstein, who appears in Unit 8.1.3. Make notes on Wallerstein's theory, including strengths and weaknesses.

#### Criticisms

However, dependency theory has been criticised for several reasons:

1. 'Dependency' is an extremely difficult concept to operationalise and, therefore, test or measure empirically.
2. Frank painted the relationship between rich nation-states and LEDCs as always exploitative, but some commentators have suggested that this is over-simplistic. For example, Canada, China and the UK are also very dependent upon US trade. However, it is doubtful whether these relationships are exploitative because the health of the US economy depends on maintaining positive trade relationships with all these countries. In other words, the interconnectedness of the global economy means that capitalist economies are often interdependent. In other words, the USA needs Canada, China and the UK as much as they need the USA.
3. John Goldthorpe (1975) argues that it is incorrect to assume that colonialism, TNCs and aid are simply exploitative and that they have brought no benefits to the less industrialised world. He argues that the British brought much-needed infrastructure to their colonies in the form of railways, roads, telecommunications, port facilities and **urbanisation**. Moreover, they provided people with wage labour and organised land use to make it more efficient. Moreover, he argues that countries such as Afghanistan and Ethiopia, which remained free from long-term colonisation, face severe problems of poverty and inequality today because they lack the infrastructure provided by the colonial powers.
4. Economic historians such as Robert C Allen (2011) argue that a fundamental weakness of dependency theory is that it offers no realistic alternative to capitalism or solutions to global inequality. It is also a fact that capitalism as an economic system has brought tangible benefits to all parts of the world, for example it has raised the standard of living of the bulk of the poor. The credibility of neo-Marxist dependency theory was further undermined by the collapse of the East European communist bloc in the 1990s and the apparent conversion of China to entrepreneurial capitalism in the last decade. Conditions in North Korea – the country that adheres most strictly to communist principles – do not make alternatives to capitalism appealing.

### Activity

'Global inequalities are caused by the failure of poor countries to modernise'. Evaluate this view.

## The post-development perspective

Post-development thinkers argue that sociologists need to view global inequality from the perspective of those who live in LEDCs. For example, Marshall Sahlins (1997) and Majid Rahnema (1997) argue that it is often assumed that people who lack material possessions are in poverty and consequently unhappy. However, they argue that, although people in the less industrialised world may have few material possessions, this does not mean that they see themselves as poor. They may actually be happy, because they belong to a supportive community, live a simple spiritual life, are attuned to their environment and have the love of their family. They argue that the view that poverty inevitably leads to unhappiness is a Western social construction.

Raff Carmen (1996) argues that Western approaches to development often imply that inequality is the fault of the victim. He argues that this is demeaning and dehumanising because the poor of the LEDCs often end up internalising the myth that they are incapable, incompetent and the problem. Thomas Sankara (1988) argued that consequently their minds end up being colonised with the idea that they should be dependent and that they should look to the West for direction. Eduardo Galeano (1992) succinctly summarised this self-fulfilling prophecy consequence as 'they train you to be paralysed, then they sell you crutches'.

## Key terms

**Particularism** Treating a person as a unique individual because they are loved as a member of a particular family.

**Fatalism** The belief that events are fixed in advance and problems are simply inevitable so that human beings are powerless to change them.

**Collectivism** The idea that the individual is subordinate to the larger group to which they belong.

**Entrepreneurial spirit** The ambition and drive to run a successful business.

**Meritocratic** Giving people status or rewards because of what they achieve, rather than because of their wealth or social position.

**Universalism** An idea underpinned by equality of opportunity that people should be judged by the same standards – for example, through the taking of exams.

**Free enterprise** An economic system in which private business operates in competition and is largely free of state control.

**Human capital** The skills, knowledge and experience possessed by an individual or population, viewed in terms of their value or cost to an organisation or country.

**Infrastructure** The basic physical and organisational structures and facilities (for example, buildings, roads, power supplies) needed for the operation of a society or enterprise.

**Public institutional capital** Public services provided by the state – for example, education, healthcare, pensions, social care.

**Crisis of modernism** The unique social problems associated with modern societies – for example, high suicide and crime rates, poor mental health.

**Affluence** The state of having a very good standard of living or wealth.

**Triangular slave trade** A historical term for the slave trade that was organised between three regions – Africa, the Americas and Europe.

**Imperialism** Rule by an empire – for example, the British Empire.

**Colonialism** Practice by which a powerful country or an empire directly controls less powerful countries through force and uses their resources to increase its own power and wealth.

**Neo-colonialism** A modern version of capitalist exploitation in which rich countries benefit from the terms of world trade, transnational investment in the economies of poor countries and aid that is tied to economic or political interests.

**Aid** Financial help, usually provided by rich countries to poorer countries. It can come in the form of grants (which do not need to be paid back), tied aid or loans with interest.

**Tied aid** Foreign aid that must be spent in the country providing the aid (the donor country).

**Urbanisation** An increase in population in cities and towns versus rural areas.

## Summary

1. There are two contrasting sociological explanations for global inequalities.
2. Modernisation theory claims that global inequalities are the result of faulty value systems and particularly the failure of some societies to abandon traditional ways of thinking and cultural practices and to adopt modern or Western values and norms. According to this theory, the failure of LEDCs to progress reflects the backwardness of both their leaders and people.
3. The Marxist-influenced dependency theory argues that global inequalities have been nurtured for hundreds of years by a global capitalist system that encouraged both the slave trade – which took valuable human resources, especially from African nations – and imperial powers like Britain to engage in colonialism. The profits from both slavery and colonialism benefited Western economies at the expense of those LEDCs that were colonised.
4. Dependency theory argues that global capitalism continues to exploit poorer countries today. Terms of world trade favour Western economies, and poorer societies consequently do not get a fair price for their raw materials or cash crops. Western transnational corporations also benefit from the cheap labour available in the LEDCs. Finally, aid that is supposed to alleviate and lift countries out of poverty often benefits the donor at the expense of the recipient.

# END-OF-PART QUESTIONS

**0 1** Describe two types of global health inequality **[4 marks]**

**0 2** Describe two forms of historical exploitation that led to some societies, especially in Africa, experiencing severe global inequalities. **[6 marks]**

**0 3** Explain two reasons why transnational trade organisations such as the World Trade Organization and the World Bank have been accused of increasing global inequalities. **[8 marks]**

# PART 5 GLOBALISATION AND MIGRATION

## Contents

**Unit 8.5.1** **The causes of global migration** **534**

**Unit 8.5.2** **The consequences of global migration** **541**

**Unit 8.5.3** **Debates about who benefits from migration** **551**

As many sociologists have observed, people throughout history have moved from place to place, within particular regions as well as across the world, either individually or as a part of a mass movement of other migrants.

The first unit of this part focuses on the causes of global migration – in particular, the forms it takes and why it happens. The second unit specifically focuses on the consequences of global migration. For example, it examines how migration affects the culture of the host country. Does it, for example, undermine, dilute or threaten the culture of the host culture, therefore creating tension and hostility as some populist politicians and media outlets argue, or does it actually enrich these countries? Some sociologists have expressed concern that global migration may be having a destabilising effect on both Western economies and political systems and that some nation-states may undergo social change and evolve or develop into authoritarian illiberal democracies as a result. The third unit will explore sociological theories about who benefits from global migration.

## Unit 8.5.1 The causes of global migration

This unit aims to examine the origins of global migration. Global migration is not a modern phenomenon. As Bernadette Hanlon and Thomas Vicino (2014) point out, 'throughout history, human populations have moved from place to place. As hunters, gatherers and **nomads**, we have moved in search of food and shelter. Fleeing famine, natural disasters and potential aggression from other humans, we sought out new territories'. However, there are signs that global migration has intensified in recent years because of economic globalisation.

This unit also examines the reasons why global migration occurs by analysing why some individuals and social groups may be pushed out of the societies in which they are born. It also explores the 'pull' factors associated with some Western countries. What is it that is so attractive in these countries that thousands of people believe that it is worth spending their life savings and putting themselves and their families at such great risk and danger travelling great distances across war zones, inhospitable terrain and treacherous seas?

### Demography and migration

Sociologists are interested in **demography** – the study of population change – and how this is affected by birth, death, life expectancy and migration. The indigenous populations of MEDCs such as the UK and Japan are shrinking because **birth rates** are not exceeding or keeping pace with death rates. They are also ageing, because **fertility rates** have also fallen. Women are having fewer children and consequently elderly people are starting to outnumber younger people. Both these trends – shrinkage and ageing – will severely impact on the economies of society as they experience a shortage of young, fit and healthy workers. Migration is, therefore, important to make up for this potential shortage.

Stephen Castles (2007) defines global or international migration as 'a social phenomenon that crosses national borders and affects two or more nation-states'. The UN defines a **migrant** as a person who resides outside of their country of origin for a period of at least one year.

Immigration refers to the influx of **non-indigenous** people into a host country or nation-state in which they do not possess citizenship. After a period of residence, immigration may involve becoming a naturalised citizen of the host country. For example, a Mexican who has lived in the USA for 10 years may apply for American citizenship. This involves taking tests in reading, writing and speaking English as well as a civics test which covers important US history and government topics. Applicants also have to undergo an interview. If successful, the applicant has to swear a public Oath of Allegiance to the United States and will be issued with a Permanent Resident Card and Certificate of Naturalization. Once a person becomes a US citizen, they have the following rights and responsibilities: they have the right to live in the USA, they have the right to vote in federal elections, they are expected to be loyal to and support the US Constitution, and they have the opportunity to bring family members to the USA.

### Activity

*Making the Oath of Allegiance at a naturalisation ceremony in Miami Beach, Florida.*

Why do you think immigrants must swear a public Oath of Allegiance to the United States in order to gain American citizenship?

**Net migration** refers to the difference between the number of **immigrants** (people coming into a country) and the number of **emigrants** (people leaving a country) throughout the year. When more people enter a country as immigrants, the result is a positive net migration rate, meaning that more people are entering than leaving a country. A negative net migration rate means that more people are leaving than entering the area. For example, in 2016, there were 500 000 more immigrants to Germany than emigrants (1.865 million arrived, while 1.365 million left). In 2015, net migration in Germany was a great deal higher (1.15 million migrants entered Germany while only 135 000 people left).

The UN estimates that, in 2010, 214 million people or 3.1 per cent of the world's population were living outside the country in which they were born. The majority – 128 million, or 60 per cent of global migrants – lived in North America, Australia, Japan, New Zealand and Europe. The remaining 86 million lived in LEDCs – especially those found in Africa, Asia (excluding Japan), Latin America and the Caribbean. Hanlon and Vicino observe that most global migration tends to be from LEDCs to MEDCs – in other words, those from poor societies aim to emigrate to the more **affluent** Western societies.

## The reliability of migration statistics

Hanlon and Vicino suggest that the official statistics on global migration may be unreliable because different societies define migrants in different ways. For example, the US government collects data on its 'foreign-born' population but includes in this group those who have achieved US-citizen status. In contrast, statistics collected by the EU excludes all those who have become **naturalised**. It is also very difficult to estimate the numbers of undocumented or illegal migrants that are in a country at any given time, because these largely avoid contact with the authorities. There is always going to be a '**hidden iceberg**' of unrecorded migrants.

## Voluntary migration

Voluntary migrants move to other countries out of choice, usually because the economic conditions and living standards that they experience in their country of origin are not as desirable as those found in other countries. For example, there may be high rates of unemployment in their mother country. They may be frequently under-employed or wages may rarely rise above subsistence levels. Consequently, much migration, whether it is permanent or temporary, legally documented or not, is **labour migration**. It involves people looking for work or better economic conditions or being actively sought by employers in the destination countries. These economic or labour migrants may fall into several categories:

**High-skilled migrants** This group includes engineers, doctors, IT experts, teachers, scientists, researchers, academics, technocrats from governments and NGOs, graduates and skilled entrepreneurs. The majority of these types of workers migrate from less industrialised countries to work in the USA, Europe and the Middle East because their countries of birth lack the public or private infrastructure that might employ them, and because more affluent countries can offer them both high wages and benefits, such as health insurance and pensions, as well as greater career opportunities.

Many MEDC countries have adapted their immigration policies and laws in order to attract and accommodate these skilled migrants (who normally have little trouble obtaining visas and work permits) and to encourage them to take up citizenship. This type of migration is not equally weighted between MEDCs and LEDCs. Only a minority of skilled professionals migrate from MEDCs to LEDCs, mainly to work in the development sector or on NGO projects.

**Undocumented low-skilled and unskilled migrants** These migrants tend to face official obstacles with regard to migration. Consequently, those migrants who enter a country without the required legal documentation, or who are in possession of forged documents, or who over-stay their visas or work permits, tend to be low-skilled or unskilled labour migrants. In 2014, it was estimated that there were 11 million undocumented or unauthorised immigrants in the USA. In 2018, the BBC stated that it is not entirely clear how many illegal immigrants there are in the UK, although estimates range from 300 000 to over 1 million.

**Temporary labour migrants** Not all migration is permanent. Immigration may involve working temporarily as a foreign worker on a short-term contract and then returning to one's country of origin. Some migrants engage in '**circular migration**' – a process by which people migrate to another country to work on a specific project, return to their country of origin and then migrate again to do a similar job in another country altogether. For example, a Sri Lankan construction worker may travel to Qatar to work on the football stadiums required for the 2022 FIFA World Cup and then move on to to work on building projects in Dubai. The ease of global transit and the demand for particular skills by some countries means that circular migration is more possible today compared with the past, especially for those with professional qualifications. The number of temporary labour migrants is about three times greater than the number of permanent labour migrants. However, most temporary labour migrants return to their country of origin within five years.

## Activity

*Construction workers from Sri Lanka in front of the hotel The Torch and the Khalifa International Stadium in Doha, Qatar.*

Write brief notes to summarise the different types of labour migration.

**Educational migrants** A person may move to another country temporarily to go to school, college or university. For example, according to the UK Council for International Student Affairs (UKCISA), there were 442 000 non-UK students studying in the UK in 2016–17. One-third of these were from China (95 000), while 18 000 students came from USA, 16 000 from Malaysia, nearly 17 000 from Hong Kong and over 12 000 from Nigeria.

**Expatriates** Some people may emigrate to another country in order to retire, to take advantage of the climate for health reasons or because they want the rich experience of living elsewhere. British expatriates living in Europe tend to be older than the average labour migrant. For example, it is estimated that 240 000 British expats live in Dubai, 310 000 live in Spain and 190 000 live in France. The term 'expatriate' is extremely loaded because it is mainly used to describe educated, rich professionals working abroad, while those in less privileged positions — for example, a maid in the Gulf States or a construction worker in Asia — are deemed foreign workers or migrant workers. The classification matters, because such language can in some cases be used as a political tool to dehumanise migrants and promote fears about immigration.

### Activity

Why are words like 'expatriates', 'immigrants' and 'illegal' loaded with bias? How does such bias influence the debate about migration?

## Involuntary migration

Some groups of migrants are forced by the actions of others or by some event over which they exercise no control to leave their country of birth. This group can be divided into:

**Refugees** The UN defines a refugee as someone who has a realistic fear of being persecuted by the government of the country from which they originate for reasons of race, religion, nationality, membership of a particular social group or political opinion. This fear has led them to **flight migration** to another country. They are unable or unwilling to return to their home country because they fear for their life or their freedom.

**Asylum seekers** An **asylum seeker** is someone who claims to be a refugee but whose claim has not yet been evaluated and processed. This person has applied for asylum, sanctuary or protection in a nation-state other than the one in which they were born or raised on the grounds that returning to his or her country would lead to persecution, death or imprisonment on account of race, religion, nationality or **proscribed** political beliefs. Not every asylum seeker will be recognised as a refugee, but every refugee is initially an asylum seeker.

**Environmental migrants** These are people who leave the country of their birth because of environmental problems associated with climate change. This group tends to live in rural areas but may be forced to involuntarily migrate because of disastrous long-term ecological events such as drought, desertification, famine, or sudden natural disasters such as landslides, volcanic eruptions, tsunami and earthquakes.

### Activity

*A prototype of the US–Mexico border wall near the Otay Mesa Port of Entry, San Diego, California.*

President Trump has announced plans to build a wall between the USA and Mexico to keep out illegal migrants. Make a list of the arguments for and against the success of this idea.

**Victims of human trafficking** Clandestine migration into Mexico from other Central American countries such as Guatemala and El Salvador, and across the border from Mexico into the USA, is very common but not easy. Migrants need to avoid detection by the authorities, but once in Mexico they also need to navigate a long, difficult and dangerous walk through the Sonoran Desert and the crossing of the Rio Grande. A total of 2413 migrants died between 1990 and 2013 attempting the journey through the Sonoran Desert. Migrants, therefore, voluntarily pay guides known as **'coyotes'** between $5,000 and $10,000 each to guide them across the desert to the border.

There is also evidence that organised criminal gangs in the Balkans are coercing and enslaving vulnerable groups such as women and children. Traffickers often take advantage of poverty, lack of prospects and hope for a better future by tricking and luring their victims into other countries. Evidence collected by Europol (2018) suggests that this is a highly profitable criminal trade. It is also very sophisticated, because it often involves the skilled forgery of official documents such as visas and passports as well as the bribery and corruption of state officials working in customs, immigration and police. Victims of the traffickers may be transported (often in lorries and shipping containers) and smuggled across international borders against their will, to be exploited in other countries as forced prostitutes, labourers, domestic servants and beggars. Some may be forced into marriage or criminality. Upon arrival in other countries, trafficking victims are often coerced into dependence through **debt bondage**, violence or drugs. They are often kept in a state of semi-imprisonment (for example, they may have their passports confiscated and be kept in locked or barred accommodation).

Kevin Bales and Zoe Trodd (2009) estimate that there are 27 million slaves worldwide, mainly women and children who have been forced into manual labour and prostitution by human-trafficking gangs.

A Human Rights Watch 2004 report on the treatment of foreign workers in Saudi Arabia found that, although slavery had been abolished in the kingdom in 1962, migrant workers in Saudi Arabia suffer extreme forms of labour exploitation that often resemble slavery-like conditions. The overwhelming majority of these migrants are low-paid workers from Asia, particularly India, Bangladesh and the Philippines and Africa.

### Summary

In summary, then, global migration refers to the mostly voluntary, but sometimes involuntary, movement of individuals or groups of people (who share particular social characteristics – socio-economic status, race, ethnicity, religion and nationality) from a country (in which they were probably born and in which they and their extended kin have lived for generations) to another country, in which they settle down either temporarily (before returning home eventually) or permanently as naturalised citizens of their adopted country.

## Reasons for migration

Factors influencing migration can be divided into push factors (that 'push' people away from their country) and pull factors (that 'pull' people towards another country).

### Push factors influencing migration

Particular social factors or influences beyond the individual's control may push people out of particular societies and coerce them to leave their place of origin to become migrants. These **push factors** include:

- **Subsistence poverty.**
- Low wages and living standards.
- **Existential insecurity** – this concept essentially means that people in these parts of the world do not know whether they and their children will be alive tomorrow, next week or next year. Life is full of risk because of factors such as diseases of poverty, lack of infrastructure such as a basic health service and child vaccination, frequent natural disasters such as earthquakes and flooding and war.
- Lack of job opportunities.
- Political or religious persecution – for example, there is evidence that, since 2014, the government of Myanmar has been engaged in the ethnic cleansing of a minority Muslim tribe, the Rohingya. A total of 700 000 members of this tribe have migrated across the border into Bangladesh to escape the violence perpetrated on them by the Myanmar army.
- War – migration into Europe since 2010 has mainly been made up of Syrians fleeing the civil war and people from Iraq and Afghanistan fleeing religious conflict.

### Pull factors influencing migration

**Pull factors** are mainly economic, and include:

- *Western demand for skills, labour and services* – This factor was particularly important post-World War II, when European societies experienced a shortage of labour because of casualties incurred during wartime and required migrant labour to revitalise their economies and for reconstruction. In receiving countries, there is an ever-growing demand for low-status, low-skilled and low-paid jobs, especially in the service and domestic sectors.
- *Better employment opportunities and pay* – Graduates, academics and particularly health professionals such as doctors and nurses from LEDCs may migrate to MEDCs because they are attracted by educational, research and job opportunities. The wages paid by American, Middle Eastern and European employers are likely to be higher than those in their countries of origin.
- *Political freedom* – migrants who might face arrest as **dissidents** in their home country may be attracted by the liberalism of Western liberal democracies that protect freedom of speech, movement and protest.
- *Education* – migrants may be attracted by the quality and reputation of universities in the USA and Europe, as well as the educational qualifications on offer. In 2007, more than a quarter of immigrants

came to the UK for this reason. Many leave after completing their education.

- *Liberal immigration policies and open borders* – migrants may be attracted by countries which have open-border immigration policies. For example, the EU's **Schengen Agreement** is a 1985 treaty which led to the creation of Europe's Schengen Area, in which internal border checks have largely been abolished. These relatively relaxed border controls have been blamed by some anti-EU politicians for the migrant crisis beginning in 2015 that saw hundreds of thousands of migrants from Africa and the Middle East attempting to enter Europe.
- *Family reunion* – many people migrate to join partners, family members or friends. Martell (2010) refers to this as **chain migration**. The United States, for example, has a much more liberal family-oriented migration policy than other Western countries. Martell observes that about 70 per cent of documented migration into the USA is family chain migration. In contrast, only 14 per cent of documented migration is labour migration, while only 12 per cent of migrants officially enter the USA for humanitarian reasons (that is, people being granted asylum).
- *Social support networks* – migration may be made easier, and less costly and risky, if social networks facilitated by digital communication exist between groups who have already settled in another country and their friends, extended kin and others situated in their country of origin. These networks may act as a pull factor because they facilitate transnational movement by providing economic, social, political, religious and moral supports for migrants. They can help with the integration of migrants by assisting their search for jobs and housing as well as providing emotional, social, community, financial, political and legal support when needed. This social network can, therefore, help reduce the risks and costs associated with global migration.

## Global labour patterns

The UN's International Migration Report (2017) observes the following patterns with regard to global migration and labour:

1. Over 60 per cent of all international migrants live in Asia (80 million) or Europe (78 million). Northern America hosted the third largest number of international migrants (58 million), followed by Africa (25 million), Latin America and the Caribbean (10 million) and Oceania (8 million).
2. In 2017, two-thirds (67 per cent) of all international migrants were living in just 20 countries. The largest number of international migrants (50 million) resided in the United States of America. Saudi Arabia, Germany and the Russian Federation hosted the second, third and fourth largest numbers of migrants worldwide (around 12 million each), followed by UK, with nearly 9 million.
3. Some MEDCs, especially Canada and Australia, have perfected a system of selective immigration linked to their economic, manpower and immigration departments and are intent on finding particular types of skilled or professional workers – for example, dentists, doctors or radiographers. These countries want skills, youth, good health, education and lack of dependants. Equally welcomed are business migrants who bring wealth and possibly jobs with them.
4. Most international migrants move from lower- to higher-wage labour markets, which explains why the MEDCs, with 16 per cent of the world's workers, have over 60 per cent of the world's migrants. For example, the average monthly salary for a Mexican worker employed in the United States at the end of 2016 was $1870, which is six times higher than the average wage in Mexico of $291 a month.
5. Most migrants move from the rural regions of LEDCs to urban centres, particularly big cities in the MEDCs.
6. The majority of migrants are in low-status, low-skilled and low-paid factory jobs. This means that migrants tend to earn lower wages than local workers, although they tend to do the work that local workers are unwilling to do. In the USA, Hispanic migrants make up 27 per cent of the American construction workforce and 23 per cent of the agricultural workforce. A great deal of the latter work is seasonal. In Europe, there is some evidence that refugees are often over-qualified for the type of zero-hour contract and minimum wage jobs available to them. Migrants to the EU often do not get recognition for qualifications gained in their home countries. For example, in 2016 an EU research paper concluded that 71 per cent of refugees in Germany are over-qualified for the work they do. Similar research in the Republic of Ireland found that migrant workers were more educated than their Irish counterparts.

7. Migration often involves **counter-migration**. There is both inflow and outflow, especially in MEDCs. Some Western professionals may choose to work for NGOs in less developed countries or to become **expatriates** because they have previously enjoyed high wage levels and have accumulated savings. It is, therefore, important to consider net migration when looking at labour patterns.
8. Globally, about half of the world's migrants have been women for the past four decades. The migration of women is mostly unrelated to career advancement and skill acquisition. Evidence suggests that a significant number of migrant women possess skills and qualifications often not recognised or unneeded in the types of work that they perform. Migration for women workers often involves **de-skilling**. For example, many Filipino women with college degrees work in domestic service or the entertainment industry.

*Filipino domestic helpers socialising on their Sunday day off in Hong Kong, 2007.*

## Tourism

The UN World Tourism Organisation (UNWTO) claims that growth in global migration and tourism are two of the most significant expressions of globalisation. Migration makes important social and economic contributions to destination countries, culturally enriching their societies, enhancing tourism products and providing labour for the travel, tourism, hospitality and catering sectors. Migration in itself is also a clear generator of tourism demand, with the increasingly two-way flow of expatriates visiting their countries of origin and, in turn, their relatives and friends visiting relations based in new host countries. Nuno Carlos and Muhammad Shahbaz (2012) see tourism as a type of temporary international migration. They argue that immigration promotes tourism because tourism is a facilitator of immigration. For example, David Simpson's (2010) study of the relationship between migration and tourism found that a large percentage of international tourist arrivals into Australia were people visiting friends and relatives who had migrated and settled down as permanent residents. Moreover, a large number of outgoing tourists were returning to their countries of origin to visit friends and relatives. The rapid expansion of Australia as an exporter of education services, with over half a million international students, was also a driver of tourism.

### Key terms

**Nomad** A person or group that wanders from place to place.

**Demography** The sociological study of statistics relating to births, fertility, death and migration in order to study population change.

**Birth rate** The number of live births per 1000 of the population per year.

**Fertility rate** The number of live births per 1000 women between the ages of 15 and 44 years.

**Migrant** A person who moves from one place to another, usually to find work or better living conditions.

**Non-indigenous** (also non-native or foreign-born) Originating outside of a particular nation-state.

**Net migration** The difference between the number of immigrants (people coming into an area) and the number of emigrants (people leaving an area).

**Immigrant** An incomer into a society from another country.

**Emigrant** A person who leaves their own country in order to settle permanently or temporarily in another.

**Affluent** Economically well-off or rich.

**Naturalised** To confer the rights of a citizen or national on a foreigner or migrant.

**Hidden iceberg** A metaphor which refers to the small perceptible part of a much larger situation or problem that remains hidden.

**Labour migration** Moving abroad to work.

**Circular migration** A repetitive movement of a migrant worker between home and a range of host areas, typically for the purpose of employment.

**Flight migration** Fleeing a country because of persecution.

**Asylum seeker** A person who has left their home country as a political refugee and is seeking sanctuary and protection in another.

**Proscribed** To forbid, usually by law.

**Coyotes** Mexican guides who lead illegal migrants across Mexico into the USA for a fee.

**Debt bondage** When a person is forced to work to pay off a debt which may originate in the fee paid to people smugglers for being trafficked.

**Indigenous** Native to a particular country.

**Push factors** Social factors, often beyond the control of the individual, that may force a person and their family to leave their country of origin.

**Subsistence poverty** Having, earning or growing just enough to survive.

**Existential insecurity** Anxiety associated with mortality. The feeling that you are at risk from various factors over which you have little or no control.

**Pull factors** Social factors that might encourage you to move to another society – for example, better job opportunities, higher pay.

**Dissident** A person who opposes a government, especially an authoritarian one.

**Schengen Agreement** A European treaty that encourages the maintenance of open borders and the free movement of workers.

**Chain migration** A type of migration in which migrants who have settled in another country eventually bring over their extended kin.

**Counter-migration** Migration in the opposite direction.

**Expatriates** People who live outside their native country.

**De-skilling** A reduction in the skill a worker requires to do a particular job, especially compared with past working conditions. It is often caused by automation.

## Summary

1. Global migration is important because many societies have ageing populations. Natural birth rates are not keeping pace with death rates. Migrant workers are necessary for economic reasons to replace retiring and dying workers.
2. Twenty-first-century global migration is mainly motivated by push factors (escaping from situations such as poverty, war and persecution – conditions which are largely beyond the individual's control) or pull factors (other countries look attractive in terms of job opportunities, pay and standard of living).
3. Most global migration takes the form of people moving from poorer countries in Africa and Asia to richer countries in the West.
4. Some Western countries are keen to attract highly skilled and educated migrants from LEDCs and offer naturalisation as a motivation.
5. However, most global migration is made up of unskilled migrants who enter either the USA or Europe illegally and without official documentation.
6. Only 3 per cent of the world's population are migrants living outside their country.
7. There is a close relationship between tourism and global migration.

# Unit 8.5.2 The consequences of global migration

This unit considers both the positive and negative consequences of global migration. We begin by looking at the economic consequences of migration both for the receiving and sending societies and for individual migrants. We also explore the political consequences of mass global migration for liberal-democratic nation-states.

Finally, we examine how the economic, political and cultural consequences of global migration impact on the daily lives of migrants and their experience of living in new societies.

## The economic consequences of global migration

Held and McGrew (2007) argue that in the absence of large-scale migration several European economies would have run into very significant labour market and economic problems for three reasons:

1. Post-World War II, many European societies experienced a significant shortage of labour power,

especially in some sections of the manufacturing and service sectors which demanded semi-skilled and unskilled labour. European governments actively sought out such labour from the less industrialised world, especially in those countries which were ex-colonies. The period of the 1950s to 1970s saw a significant mass migration of such workers and their families from countries in Asia and Africa into European cities to take up essential low-skilled jobs. Often workers in the receiving countries did not want to do this work – for example, shift work in heavy industry such as iron and steel, repetitive work in textile mills and cleaning jobs in city office blocks.

2. The birth and fertility rates of many European societies fell dramatically during the course of the 20th century to the extent that the number of children being born was not keeping pace with the number of workers lost to death and retirement.
3. Many European nations as well as the USA and Japan are experiencing an ageing population as life expectancy increases. First, this is potentially a problem in its own right, because it can be costly in two respects. Those who have retired are paid a state pension out of taxation but the burden of this is falling disproportionately on a shrinking number of younger workers. Global migration is important because it can add to the number of workers who are being taxed, therefore relieving this disproportionate burden on native-born taxpayers. Second, an ageing population is likely to incur great future costs to the state, which has to provide health and social care for its elderly population. Global migration is beneficial because migrants pay tax, which helps finance these sectors. Moreover, global migrants can take up those jobs in health and social care sectors that home-grown workers may be reluctant to take on.

   However, an alternative argument from some economists is that employing migrant labour was convenient rather than necessary; migrant workers were cheaper to employ than the alternative, which would have been more capital investment in automation and improved productivity.

Held and McGrew, therefore, argue that global migration can economically compensate for these demographic problems because migrants earn income that is taxed and they are also more willing than home-grown workers (who tend to occupy the higher-paid skilled jobs) to carry out low-status work essential to the smooth running of both society and the economy.

## Activity

Design a promotional poster or advertisement aimed at convincing both a sending country and a receiving country of the merits of migration.

## The economic consequences of global migration for the receiving country

Critics of global migration have argued that global migration has the negative effect of depressing local wages and raising unemployment among home-grown workers because more workers are chasing the same number of jobs. However, the findings of the many studies of the effects of migration on wages and employment levels do not support this view for three reasons:

(a) Timothy Hatton and Jeffrey Williamson (2005) observe that labour-migrants tend to go where there are vacancies rather than compete with indigenous workers for jobs.

(b) Most highly skilled labour-migrants take on jobs in the receiving countries where there is a shortage of skilled home-grown workers (especially in the health or IT sectors). For example, migrants make up 22 per cent of nurses in the UK.

(c) George Borjas (2004) points out that migration might have a harmful effect on the employment opportunities and pay levels of home-grown workers if migrants were competing for the same low-skilled, low-status jobs. However, migrants usually take up those low-paid casual jobs shunned by indigenous workers, such as seasonal physically demanding agricultural work, shift work in so-called dirty or hazardous industries and insecure temporary work such as cleaning, catering, the social care of the elderly, fast-food production and delivery driving found in the **gig economy**.

If wage levels do fall in some industries in which migrants can be found, this is often the doing of employers rather than migrants, because some employers cynically use migration as a means of deterring home-grown workers from demanding higher rates of pay or better working conditions. Employers may threaten to make home-grown workers redundant if they do not passively accept the wage levels offered. Employers may feel confident in adopting such tactics to socially control their present workforce because they know that they will find migrant workers willing to accept the lower wage.

Migrant wages can actually boost the economy of a receiving country because:

**(a)** their income is taxed and contributes towards public services

**(b)** they spend their wages on goods and services within the country in which they have settled.

In the USA, the Congress Commission on Immigration Reform (1997) concluded that, overall, immigration into the USA had a positive effect on the US economy for three reasons. First, migrants made a significant tax contribution to the US economy. Second, migrants mainly spent their spare cash on US goods. Third, immigrants were generally paid less than the value of the goods and services they produced. A British Home Office study (2001) also concluded that migration was good for the UK because immigrants often created new businesses and jobs, paid taxes, spent their wages on British goods and services and were willing to do the jobs that British workers were reluctant to do.

## The economic consequences of global migration for the migrants' country of origin

With regard to the economic benefits for the migrants' country of origin, there is some evidence that migration results in a reduction of unemployment and therefore less spending on welfare in those countries. However, Hanlon and Vicino observe that a negative economic consequence of migration is that some receiving nations do not recognise the educational or professional qualifications issued by sending societies. This can produce wasteful **under-employment** in which talented and well-qualified migrants are forced to take semi-skilled and unskilled work in receiving societies – for example, working as cleaners, security guards and taxi drivers to support their families. It is argued that the internationalisation of education and qualifications may eventually solve this problem, although this argument fails to take account that such international education may only be available to children from the most affluent or elite families in the sending societies.

An important economic aspect of global migration is the value of **remittances**. Remittances are cross-border transfers of money from workers in one country back to their country of origin – often through payments to family members. Many migrant workers are seasonal workers, but large numbers work for extended periods of time, and even those who have settled in a host country and gained the right to citizenship continue to transfer money back to extended families in their country of origin.

It was estimated by the World Bank in 2014 that around 80 per cent of all global remittances went to less industrialised countries – that is, $436 billion out of a total of $583 billion, which is around double the amount of global development aid. India, China, the Philippines, Mexico and Nigeria, in particular, economically benefit from remittances sent home by migrants.

Hanlon and Vicino argue that remittances have four distinct economic advantages for less industrialised nations:

- They contribute to the alleviation of poverty. For example, Khalid Koser (2007) observes that in Lesotho 80 per cent of rural household incomes come from remittances.
- In households receiving remittances from abroad, children are less likely to drop out of school.
- The health of children tends to be better in households receiving remittances. Average birth weight in these households tends to be higher, too.
- When remittances are sent home in the form of cash, they supply the economy of less industrialised nations with much-needed foreign currency. This is useful because some natural resources, particularly oil, can only be bought on the international market using US dollars.

However, Hanlon and Vicino also observe that remittances from relatives abroad can contribute to inequalities within a developing society, as well. For example, Donald Terry and Stephen Wilson (2005) found that 80 per cent of Mexican households receiving money from abroad could afford to buy their own home compared with only 30 per cent of households who did not receive remittances. Hanlon and Vicino also argue that family pressure to send money home can be so intense that this can lead some migrants into illegal activity such as prostitution and criminality.

## The brain drain

Some economists and sociologists note that global migration often has the economic side-effect that sending societies lose their most talented and educated citizens and thereby lose the potential return on their investment in the education and training of this group of workers. The evidence suggests that receiving countries, particularly those in Europe, the Middle East and the USA economically benefit from this brain drain. For example, Peter Stalker (2008) estimates that 1.5 million skilled migrants work and live in Western Europe, the USA, Japan and Australia, while sending countries such as Haiti, Sierra Leone, Ghana and the UK are those most likely to lose accomplished and skilled workers to other societies.

There are signs that the developmental progress of poorer countries may be impeded by this **brain drain**, especially with regard to education and healthcare. For example, Koser found that only 50 out of the 600 doctors trained in Zambia since 2010 are actually practising medicine in Zambia. Moreover, there are more Malawian doctors practising medicine in the city of Manchester in England than there are in Malawi. There is evidence that global migration worsens global inequalities. The WHO recommends that countries should have 20 doctors per 100 000 people. However, 37 out of 47 sub-Saharan nations are unable to achieve this target because of the global migration of their health professionals. Similarly, Kevin O'Neill (2003) observes that Taiwan and India are losing thousands of skilled IT experts to Silicon Valley companies in the USA (although these workers do eventually return to their country of origin).

However, in conclusion, Julian Simon (1989) argued that if we consider both the sending and the receiving countries as part of the same world, the overall effect of migration on the average standard of living of the world's people is positive. The main reason for this is that migrants go from situations where they are unproductive to ones in which they become more productive.

### Activity

How might you evaluate Simon's view that migrants go from situations in which they are unproductive to ones in which they become more productive? Do you think this is equally true of men and women?

## The political consequences of global migration

Martell (2010) argues that sociologists need to examine the political consequences of global migration because political debate about migration, especially in the USA and Europe, is being increasingly interpreted by political leaders, parties and voters as more about immigration than emigration. It is often socially constructed as a social problem that can only be resolved by bringing in stricter social controls. There is some concern that these controls may eventually involve the infringement of the human rights by nation-states of both migrants and their own citizens.

Held, too, argues that global migration has implications for the autonomy and sovereignty of nation-states. He argues that the flow of illegal and undocumented migrants into both the USA and Europe demonstrates the limited ability of many nation-states to secure their own borders. He notes that even those states which have extended border surveillance by building fences and checkpoints have been unable to stem the flow of illegal migrants.

### The 'clash of civilisations'

Hanlon and Vicino argue that, in the contemporary world, the group of migrants most likely to be typically represented and perceived as a potential aggressor and threat to the national security of receiving countries by the leaders of European countries and their populist opponents are Muslims. Some commentators have even gone as far as suggesting that there exists a fundamental clash of cultures or civilisations between Christian Europe and the Islamic world.

Douglas Murray (2018) is typical of this approach. He criticises liberal-democratic nation-states for denying or diminishing the problems that come with sudden large increases in immigration when the migrants come from Islamic cultures. The most important fact about the European migrant crisis, Murray claims, is that it involves an encounter between Islam with a 'faithless' or secular Europe. He argues that the unwanted outcome of this encounter or clash of civilisations will be the **Islamisation** of the continent (because the birth rate of Muslim migrants is significantly higher than that of Europeans), and the end of European civilisation. However, Murray's thesis (which is shared by many European far-right nationalist groups and some populist politicians, notably the Prime Minister of Hungary, Viktor Orbán) is criticised by Gray (2018), who argues that Murray is selective in his use of facts because it is not only Europe that shuts out Muslims. Gray points out that many Muslim countries do so, too. For example, Saudi Arabia has built a 600-mile-long fence along its border with Iraq and there are similar barriers between Turkey and Syria, and Iran and Pakistan. Gray believes that an Islamised Europe is a fantasy, because Islam itself is too divided – it contains so many different strands – to unite against Christian Europe.

Huntington (2004) has applied this clash of civilisations thesis to the USA. He claims that the USA is likely to experience a 'loss of national identity' if it fails to slow down migration from Mexico. He argues that Hispanic culture is a threat to Anglo-American identity and culture and that, if current trends continue (especially with regard to Mexicans' higher birth rate), Americans of Hispanic descent who speak Spanish as their first language will eventually outnumber English-speaking Americans in many parts of the USA.

Gray points out that global migration is mainly the product of war, environmental collapse and globalisation rather than a concerted effort by particular cultures to dominate other cultures. In particular, Gray argues that the rapid global movement of capital and production has destroyed livelihoods, resulted in uneven global development and global inequality. This has given migrants the incentive to seek opportunities in richer countries. However, they may not be welcomed, especially by poorer people in such receiving societies who may be facing the same global pressures and inequalities.

## Immigration control as securitisation

Although in 2016 only 2 per cent of the world's population lived outside its country of origin, immigration control has become the central issue in the most advanced nations. Many governments seek to restrict population flows, especially those originating in the poorer countries of the global South.

Many European countries have reacted to migration from outside the EU by introducing tighter immigration and security controls. Some European countries are now beginning to oppose EU rules on open borders. For example, the so-called Visegrád Group of Eastern European countries – Hungary, Poland, the Czech Republic and Slovakia – have made it very clear that the optimum number of migrants from non-EU states that they intend to welcome in 2018 is zero, while Austria and Italy are taking steps to deport migrants from non-EU states who have already arrived. In Germany, the interior minister threatened to close the country's borders in 2018.

Many countries worldwide have attempted to securitise their borders against these perceived external threats by enhancing and increasing the powers of their police and immigration services. Some have upped or tightened their visa requirements and made due process of the law more difficult for asylum seekers. For example, President Trump has threatened to build a wall between the USA and Mexico and given substantial funding to the US Immigration and Customs Enforcement (ICE) to remove illegal migrants from the USA. In the UK, there is evidence that the UK government in 2016 set out to create a '**hostile environment**' for migrants in which both skilled and unskilled migrants were threatened with deportation. There is also evidence of greater civil rights abuses of migrants – for example, the separation of children from their parents on the Mexican border by the ICE in the USA attracted a great deal of global condemnation.

*Migrant children eating a meal at the homestead temporary shelter for unaccompanied minors in Florida.*

## Global migration and the rise of populism and authoritarianism

Gray (2016) suggests that the EU faces a **'trilemma'** that it cannot resolve which is made up of open borders, liberal democracy and highly developed **welfare states**. He claims that these three things are not sustainable at the same time. He points out that it was relatively easy for pre-1914 Europe to be borderless because democracy was limited and welfare systems had not been established. However, he argues that once people are given the democratic vote, they resist open borders because they fear the effects of immigration on the costs of their welfare and healthcare systems and wage levels. In reaction to these anxieties, they demand more say in the overall direction of their society and, in particular, they demand limits on immigration. If their protests are ignored by mainstream politicians, they may tend to turn to authoritarian leaders and illiberal democracy as a form of protest.

Consequently, Gray argues that the European model of social democracy is in danger of becoming extinct. Tony Judt (2012) argued that democracy works best in small **homogeneous** countries where issues of trust and mutual suspicion rarely arise. A willingness to pay for other people's services and benefits rests on the understanding that they in turn will do likewise for you and your children because they are like you and see the world as you do. In contrast, where immigration and visible minorities have altered the demography of a country, we typically find suspicion of others and a loss of enthusiasm for the institutions of the welfare state. Voters flock to far-right fringe parties who often flirt with nationalist ideas. As has been demonstrated in Hungary, Poland and Turkey, and even the USA, populist politicians and leaders aim to make their power secure by promising to restore national pride by changing the constitution, limiting the independence of the judiciary and controlling or threatening the media. Gray argues that the number of illiberal democracies may increase in Europe as a result of these trends.

## Contemporary issues: Migration as a consequence of the Syrian civil war

*The ruins of Homs.*

A recent challenging problem is the increasing trans-border migration flows into Europe that have come about as a result of the Syrian civil war which erupted in 2011 and has resulted in 250 000 deaths in the past five years. By 2016, 6 million Syrians out of a total population of 23 million had been internally displaced, while 5 million had fled the country in search of personal safety and economic opportunity. Most ended up in neighbouring countries such as Turkey and Lebanon. However, hundreds of thousands of Syrians have undertaken the dangerous crossing of the Mediterranean from Turkey to Greece hoping to find refuge in the EU. Many have died in the attempt. Once in Greece, they have embarked on a long arduous journey on foot and by train across Eastern Europe to Western Europe, especially to Germany, France and Sweden. The EU appealed to its member countries to take in quotas of Syrians. Germany, in particular, set an example by accepting over 1 million refugees from Syria, Iraq and Afghanistan. However, some EU countries have refused to abide by this EU request to take in refugees. For example, Austria closed its borders, while Hungary erected border fences. Italy, too, has refused to allow NGO boats that have rescued refugees from sinking vessels in the Mediterranean to dock in Italian ports. However, there is some evidence of cultural strain and inter-ethnic tensions in host countries, as indigenous populations see these migrants as outsiders who are draining their country's economic resources.

The Syrian refugee crisis has revealed the inadequacy of the EU's current immigration arrangements based on national preferences. The Schengen Agreement that provided for open borders among EU core countries lacks the robustness and comprehensiveness required for coping with hundreds of thousands of refugees. As policy differences between member states became more pronounced, some member states withdrew from the agreement and reinstated systematic border controls. Others placed arbitrary limits on the number of refugees they were willing to process and refused to consider a more coordinated approach. The EU faced a predicament that suggested deep divisions exist over migration policy among member states.

### Questions

1. What percentage of the Syrian population has left Syria because of the civil war?
2. What is the Schengen Agreement and how ideally should it have benefited migration?
3. How has the 'migrant crisis' threatened the unity of the EU?

The politics of global migration has become toxic because migration has been linked by some populist politicians with the terror attacks carried out in Paris, Nice and Brussels in 2015 and 2016. The political debate about global migration is now focused on the inadequacy of national borders and security routines to protect the populations of host or receiving countries from this threat.

## The social consequences of global migration

Global migration has had significant economic and political effects for nation-states, but what are its social consequences on the everyday social life of people attempting to make a new life for themselves in countries which may 'fear' their presence?

On a positive note, many migrants from poorer parts of the world have escaped from poverty, under-employment and persecution. They have made new lives for both themselves and their children, and the evidence suggests that if they have become naturalised citizens in the country in which they have settled, they have access to the same rights, opportunities and existential security taken for granted by the host population.

However, it is also important to understand that the decision to migrate has both economic and psychological costs for the individual. For example, leaving family and friends behind is not easy, and becoming a 'stranger in a strange land' can be extremely stressful. Douglas Massey (2003) argues that this stress of migration can be alleviated if a social network of migrants, former migrants and non-migrants exists in both the origin and destination societies and connects old and new migrants to one another. This network can facilitate the process of settlement and the formation of migrant communities by offering social capital in the form of social, cultural and religious support and ties. Moreover, migrants can draw on such networks for business and employment opportunities. Such networks are also an important aspect of chain migration because, as John and Leatrice MacDonald (1974) argue, through such networks prospective migrants learn of opportunities and often have initial accommodation and employment arranged by previous migrants already settled in the host country.

### Global migration, demonisation, fear and moral panic

There is some evidence that the news media of receiving countries have negatively represented immigrants as a social problem and consequently a common news **representation** is the idea that global migration is posing a threat to the safety and security of those who live in a host society. Moral panics have, therefore, been constructed around:

**Migrants** Journalists often present global migration as a 'threat' especially by exaggerating and overestimating the extent and scale of migration. News stories rarely mention the fact that 97.5 per cent of the world's population live in the country of their birth. Representations of migrants are often both xenophobic and racist in popular newspapers. They are perceived as a threat in terms of their 'numbers'. Sensationalist headlines claim they are 'flooding' in or that a tsunami of immigrants is about to be unleashed on Europe. Editorials often compare migrants to vermin such as rats and cockroaches. A study of UK newspapers by Heaven Crawley, Simon McMahon and Katharine Jones (2016) found that migrants were often presented as a threat because of the supposed impact they have on the supply of **scarce resources** such as jobs, housing and welfare and health services. Moreover, their study found that migrants were rarely given a voice in such stories. For example, migrant voices were only referenced in 15 per cent of articles on migration and even then migration was framed as a 'threat' and migrants as actual or potential 'villains'. The authors conclude that 'the absence of migrant voices as sources in the media can deprive the audience of a complex or nuanced understanding of migration issues. It can also have negative consequences for migrant integration and for the personal well-being and security of migrants and their sense of belonging. This, in turn, can undermine the extent to which migrants feel that they belong in British society, even when they have been living in the UK for a long time.'

**Refugees and asylum seekers** These are often portrayed by the media as coming to Europe to take advantage of Europe's supposedly generous health and welfare systems. However, research by Corrado Giulietti (2014) found that decisions to migrate are not made on the basis of the relative generosity of the receiving nation's social benefits. Research by the Information Centre about Asylums and Refugees (2004) observed that newspapers across Europe have constructed an image of migrants as a problem or threat to the identity and cohesion of European societies. This sensationalist approach results in the demonisation of migrants and refugees by whipping up a **moral panic** – a public frenzy of fear and animosity towards all migrants which turns them into '**folk devils**' and in turn fuels racism, hostility and **hate crimes.**

**Muslims** Muslims in particular are often portrayed by the media as the 'enemy within'. Elizabeth Poole (2002) argues that, even before 9/11, Islam was often demonised and distorted by the Western media and presented as a threat to Western values. Media representations of Islam have, therefore, long been predominantly negative. Consequently Muslims have been homogenised (despite **intra-Islamic** differences in interpretation of theology, values and lifestyles) by Western journalists as 'backward, irrational, unchanging fundamentalist, **misogynist** (who would be) manipulative in the use of their faith for political and personal gain'. Moreover, it is often implied that most Muslims are potential terrorists. These negative media representations of Muslims fuel **Islamophobia** – a generalised hatred or dislike of Muslim migrants. Michele Tribalet (2011) studied Muslim Arabs in France, who have been particularly criticised for rejecting Western values by the French media and nationalist politicians in the aftermath of the terrorist attacks in Paris, Nice and on the office of the French satirical magazine *Charlie Hebdo*. However, Tribalet found that this migrant community was in fact well assimilated into French society. She found that the majority of Muslims in France were not fundamentalists, nor were they supporters of radical **jihadism**. Many Arab households spoke French in the home. There had also been a decline in traditional arranged marriages in favour of intermarriage.

There is evidence that such distorted media representations may be partially responsible for the increase in racist hate crimes across Europe, especially violent attacks on migrants and Muslim communities. These representations may also assist in the promotion of extreme forms of nationalism and electoral support for populist anti-immigration and anti-Muslim movements such as Britain First and the English Defence League in the UK, the Northern League and Five Star in Italy, Fidesz and Jobbik in Hungary, Pegida in Germany and the National Rally in France.

Anthony Smith (1990) argued that it is not immigration that is the problem, but the reception of immigrants by the host population, media and politicians that has stirred up racial hatred, intolerance and violence. This reception has encouraged negative interpretations and misinformation (about migrants abusing welfare systems or committing crime). Furthermore, the positive effects of migration are deliberately neglected or ignored by the mainstream media, as are the facts that most migrants in Europe and the USA are in work, are not claiming benefits and are making significant positive contributions to the economies of receiving societies. There is no evidence that immigration has increased the crime rate of any receiving country, contrary to media misinformation.

### Activity

'Global migration has produced major social anxieties and problems in Western societies.' Evaluate this view.

## The cultural consequences of global migration

Martell points out that migrants do more than work. He argues that societies are plural cultural entities that are always in a state of change and that migration is an important aspect of this change. Migration contributes positively to the cultures of receiving societies because the culture of migrants is often dynamic and rich in diversity. The culture of receiving countries, especially its cuisine, music, fashion, values, film and media is often enhanced by migration, which produces cultural pluralism and hybridity and therefore new forms of consumption and lifestyle.

In the course of hybridisation, cultures often generate new forms and make new connections with one another. For example, hybridisation may involve the blending of, say, language. In some US states in which the numbers of Hispanic people are growing, people may speak 'Spanglish' – a combination of Spanish and English. In many West African countries, people mix French with local languages to create a hybrid unique to that part of the world.

Music is another part of a country's culture that can be mixed with other cultures. For example, Korean musicians have combined local music with European-style pop music to create K-pop, while US musicians from Hispanic social backgrounds such as Jennifer Lopez (J-Lo), Shakira, Gloria Estefan, The Mavericks and Ricky Martin have mixed Cuban and flamenco rhythms with US country, rhythm and blues and soul to create unique hybrid new genres. Artists such as Shakira and J-Lo also incorporate Spanish into their American songs to bring a little bit of diversity to the USA.

## Activity

*Colombian singer Shakira, Hollywood, USA, 2011.*

Stars such as Shakira may genuinely want to encourage diversity and hybridisation, but do you think that the music transnationals that manufacture their products are motivated by the same goals? What economic factors are more likely to influence the music industry?

Douglas Bourn (2008) argues that young people living in societies in which migration and cultural hybridity are the norm are the social group most likely to be open to the idea of adopting a global identity, because their economic position is more vulnerable to the risks associated with economic globalisation. They are also more likely to be involved in digital global networks such as social media platforms and to identify with the anti-globalisation movement's rejection of global inequality. They are, therefore, more likely to use global media to develop a global identity through which they can express themselves. This global identity may at some stage go beyond and replace local or national identity as they come to recognise that all cultures have equal value. Those who subscribe to a global identity are likely to believe that consequently their loyalty should lie with *all* human beings, that people whatever their country of origin have common goals and that a diversity of cultures and ethnicities actually complement one another rather than being inherently divisive.

## Contemporary issues: Małgorzata Martynuska – Cultural Hybridity in the USA exemplified by Tex-Mex cuisine

*Tex-Mex cuisine.*

When new immigrants arrive in the USA, the processes of acculturation, hybridisation and transculturation begin. Global migration has a large impact not only on the lives of migrants who travel to another culture but also on the host culture itself.

For example, Mexican food is itself a fusion that combined the elements of indigenous Aztec and Spanish culinary traditions. As Mexicans migrated into the USA, it influenced American regional cuisine, creating the hybrid food cultures known as Tex-Mex, produced in the Mexican-Texas borderlands, and now marketed by American corporations and carried around the globe.

Tex-Mex dishes such as beef tacos, enchiladas, burritos and tostadas are a particularly popular feature of US cuisine. Tex-Mex recipes have been more Americanised to include more animal protein, especially more meat. The fast-food 'taco' was inspired by Mexican American street vendors and appropriated by an American food corporation called Taco Bell, which came up with the idea of the 'taco shell' – a pre-fried tortilla that could be easily filled with stuffing and served fast so the customers did not need to wait long. This way of preparation distanced that particular type of Mexican food from its ethnic roots.

## Questions

1. Identify three cultural influences that are hybridised within Tex-Mex food.
2. In what ways has Tex-Mex food become part of the American way of life?
3. In what ways has Tex-Mex food become globalised?

Source: Małgorzata Martynuska (2017), Cultural Hybridity in the USA exemplified by Tex-Mex cuisine (*International Review of Social Research* 2017; 7(2): 90–98)

## Activity

'Global migration has positive consequences for both sending and host societies.' Evaluate this view.

## Key terms

**Gig economy** A labour market characterised by insecure temporary jobs and low pay as opposed to permanent jobs.

**Under-employment** Not having enough paid work or not doing work that makes full use of a worker's skills and abilities.

**Remittances** A sum of money sent from migrants back to kin in their home country.

**Brain drain** The emigration of highly trained or qualified people from a particular country.

**Islamisation** The process of bringing someone or something under the influence of Islam or under Islamic rule.

**Hostile environment** A set of administrative and legislative practices employed by the British government, aimed at making life for migrants who wished to stay in the UK as difficult as possible.

**Trilemma** A difficult choice between three options.

**Welfare state** A system whereby the state undertakes to protect the health and well-being of its citizens, especially those in financial or social need, by means of grants, pensions and other benefits.

**Homogeneous** Of the same kind or very alike.

**Representation** The way that the media portray particular social groups such as women, ethnic minorities or young people.

**Scarce resources** The limited availability of particular social things such as jobs, goods, housing and so on which people may be competing for.

**Moral panic** An instance of public anxiety or alarm in response to a problem regarded as threatening the moral standards of society, usually created by newspapers and other forms of media.

**Folk devils** A person, social group or thing perceived to be a threat to society or a social problem.

**Hate crimes** A crime motivated by racial, sexual or other prejudice, typically one involving violence.

**Intra-Islamic** Differences of interpretation of holy texts that exist within Islam. For example, Islam is made up of dozens of sects that reflect these differences.

**Misogynist** A person who dislikes, despises or is strongly prejudiced against women.

**Islamophobia** Dislike of or prejudice against Islam or Muslims, especially as a political force.

**Jihadism** Someone who sees violent struggle as necessary to eradicate obstacles to restoring God's rule on earth.

## Summary

1. Despite fears that global labour-migration might have negative consequences for receiving countries, most experts agree that global migration is necessary and actually has a positive impact on the economies of receiving societies.
2. However, global migration may have an unfortunate consequence for the economies of sending societies in that they often experience a brain drain of talented individuals. This may be one reason why they have not developed to the same degree as European societies.
3. Nevertheless, there is evidence that remittances sent home by migrants to their extended kin make a significant contribution to the economies of sending societies, and to lifting families out of poverty.
4. There are signs that global migration, especially undocumented migration, from the Middle East and Africa, has been negatively greeted by European populations, who are reacting to their concerns and fears by voting for populist politicians and nationalist far-right political parties that are promising to tighten up immigration controls.
5. There is evidence that media representations of migrants, refugees and Muslims in both Europe and the USA may be responsible for an upsurge in racism, Islamophobia and hate crime directed against migrant populations.
6. Some sociologists argue that global migration can contribute to the richness and diversity of culture by producing hybridised versions of cuisine, music and other cultural products.
7. Global migration may also be contributing to the emergence of a global identity among the young that promotes equality and tolerance of difference.

# Unit 8.5.3 Debates about who benefits from migration

There are a number of sociological perspectives that focus on migration. Functionalist theory has had a significant influence on assimilation theory, which suggests that both migrants and the societies in which they settle can benefit from global migration if they are willing to fully immerse themselves into the culture of the host society. However, critics argue that a multicultural approach would allow all sections of society to benefit from cultural pluralism and diversity.

Neoliberalists argue that global migration has potentially positive economic, political and cultural benefits for both receiving and sending societies alike. They argue that the free market in labour, capital and products is the most efficient way to bring about economic growth and to facilitate movement in labour as well as trade in goods and services.

Marxist sociologists argue that global migration only benefits the capitalist class and the core countries at the centre of the global capitalist system.

Interactionists argue that sociologists need to examine how migration is experienced and interpreted by migrants themselves. Finally, postmodernists focus on how global migration may be producing new forms of hybrid or global culture.

## Assimilation theory

Assimilation theory is highly influenced by functionalism (see Unit 2.2.1), which depicts host societies such as Britain and USA as stable, homogeneous and orderly societies with a high degree of **consensus** over values and norms. This consensus is potentially disturbed by global migration, which results in the arrival of migrant 'strangers' who subscribe to different cultural values and who have the potential to clash with the host population over the distribution of scarce resources such as jobs and housing.

Hanlon and Vicino (2014) claim that assimilation has been particularly successful in the USA, which is a relatively new country that has been mainly populated by migrants. They describe assimilation as a process of fusion in which migrant persons and groups acquire the memory, sense and attitudes of the host population and are incorporated into a common cultural life. Over time, these migrants become part of mainstream life and culture. They achieve cultural solidarity, which is sufficient to maintain a common national existence. This may be achieved in a variety of ways – for example, by learning the language and adopting the norms of the host population, in the USA, by celebrating Thanksgiving and Independence Day.

## Activity

*An ethnically diverse business team in the USA.*

What makes assimilation successful in the USA? What might be obstacles to this process?

Milton Gordon (1981) sees assimilation as occurring in three stages:

1. **Acculturation** – adopting the language and customs of the host society.
2. **Structural assimilation** – migrants become integrated into education and the economy. They experience economic success and upward mobility.
3. Intermarriage.

Herbert Gans (1997) observed that assimilation unfolds over generations and that the pace might vary, especially if the dominant culture constructs social obstacles – for example, **segregation** and the **Jim Crow laws** in the southern states of the USA.

### The critique of assimilation theory

Some critics argue that assimilation is both **ethnocentric** and racist. It heavily implies that the host culture is somehow richer and more dynamic than migrant culture and controversially suggests that migrants should forget or abandon altogether their previous way of life. **Cultural pluralists** point out that migrant culture can have a very positive effect in enriching the host culture, because the process of acculturation cuts both ways (see the Contemporary issues box about Tex-Mex cuisine in Unit 8.5.2) and can result in a culturally rich hybrid mix.

*Notting Hill Carnival in London, UK.*

## The multiculturalist approach

The assumption that progress towards racial harmony requires assimilation ignores other possible forms of coexistence. Consequently, some sociologists have promoted an alternative approach – **multiculturalism.** This is the belief that the best way to promote social integration in an ethnically diverse society is for the state to provide some level of public recognition and support for ethnic minorities to maintain and express their distinct identities and practices, rather than expect them to abandon these and assimilate into the culture of the ethnic majority.

Mehlman Petrzela (2013) observes that multiculturalism recognises the equal worth of various groups rather than insisting that all defer to the dominant culture. It also signals a commitment by the state to equally ensure the civil rights of all migrant groups. It acknowledges and accepts their unique ethnic identities and accepts and tolerates any differences that exist between migrants and the host population.

However, in recent years there are signs that states are retreating from multiculturalism, because it is believed that some migrant groups are not committed to social solidarity or cohesion. Critics believe it has led to nativism or divisive tribalism, the celebration of difference and as such is a threat to national identity and solidarity. Some countries, notably France, have resorted instead to **secular** assimilation by banning the wearing of religious symbols in public places and banning the wearing of the hijab in schools.

### Activity

Research the reasons why France has banned the wearing of religious symbols.

## Structuralist approaches to global migration

Structuralist critics have pointed out that **institutional racism** may be the cause of cultural conflict between migrants and host populations. There is a good deal of evidence that suggests that racist prejudices and practices are embedded in the structural organisation of society and its social institutions. It is these structural inequalities and deficiencies which are the main causes of any conflict between migrants and their hosts. Anthony Heath and Sin Yi Cheung (2007) found that non-European migrants to the USA and Europe experienced an 'ethnic penalty' in that that second-generation Whites experienced better employment opportunities and higher pay rates than second-generation non-Europeans. Similarly, Marxists are critical of multiculturalism because it fails to address these structural inequalities. As Will Kymlicka (2012) observes, 'even if all Britons enjoy Jamaican steel drum music or Indian samosas, this would do nothing to address the real problems facing Caribbean and South Asian communities in Britain – problems of unemployment, poor educational outcomes, residential segregation, poor English language skills and political marginalization'.

However, critics of institutional racism claim that those who argue in favour of institutional racism fail to explain ethnic variations in educational achievement, employment and unemployment, social mobility and arrest rates. For example, some non-European migrants into Europe, notably Chinese and Indians, actually achieve better sets of educational qualifications than their indigenous peers. Moreover, this argument fails to explain why Black males are more likely to be arrested than Black females.

Michael Collins (2015) claims that multiculturalism has led to the emergence of a 'race relations industry' which is self-perpetuating. He argues that racism in its truest form has actually diminished but racism has been reinvented by the multiculturalism industry as institutional racism in order to justify a billion-dollar industry that employs thousands of academics, civil servants, consultants and human rights lawyers.

## The neoliberal approach to global migration

Neoliberals argue in favour of open migration because the free movement of labour supposedly enhances the effectiveness of free market capitalism. The EU's open border policy is very influenced by neoliberalism, which encourages the withdrawal of state control and restrictions over certain forms of external and internal migration. However, such free movement of labour has attracted criticism from both the right and left of the political spectrum. For example, Yascha Mounk (2018) claims that neoliberalism's promotion of global migration has had three negative global effects. First, it has resulted in the stagnation of average living standards for the majority of Western workers. Second, those born and raised in receiving countries feel that their whole way of life is under threat from migrants, as it has slowly transformed **mono-ethnic** countries into multicultural societies. Third, the rise of social media allows populist politicians to manipulate and widely communicate the fears of those disaffected by global migration.

## The New Right – clash of civilisation theory

**Conservative** sociologists such as Huntington have criticised neoliberals because they believe that open borders and global migration have resulted in a clash of civilisations, especially in Europe between the religious ideologies of Christianity and Islam.

However, Huntington has been accused of stereotyping all Muslims and for failing to see that fundamentalists are only a tiny minority of a complex Islamic world in which there are more differences than similarities. Yuval Noah Harari (2018) believes that Huntington overstates the differences between the Western and Islamic worlds. He argues that there are more similarities between the West and Islam, and claims that 'when it comes to the practical stuff – how to build a state, an economy, a hospital or a bomb – almost all of us belong to the same civilisation'. He observes that humanity will continue to have huge arguments and bitter conflicts but these are unlikely to isolate us from one another, and, although humanity is far from constituting a harmonious community, we are all members of a single rowdy global civilisation.

## Feminism

Feminists argue that studies of migration are often **malestream** in that they assume that males make up the bulk of migrants, that the male takes the lead in migration and that female members of the family follow later. However, Hanlon and Vicino observe that the number of females migrating for economic reasons is on the rise, and that in some regions, especially North America and Europe, female migration is more likely than male migration. For example, in 2005, 65 per cent of those who emigrated out of the Philippines, and about 79 per cent of Indonesian migrants, were female. Many of these migrated to the Gulf states in order to meet demands for domestic labour.

Women are now more likely to migrate independently of men. They are also more likely to be professional labour-migrants or international students rather than family dependants of male migrants.

Feminists observe that female migrants are particularly vulnerable to exploitation and irregular employment. They have highlighted the fact that much of the demand for female migration is coming from the global service economy and, in particular, the sex industry.

Females are also more likely than males to be refugees. They may be fleeing their country of origin because of gender-based forms of persecution such as rape (which is often perpetrated by soldiers), domestic violence, forced marriage, honour killings and so on. The UN High Commission of Refugees (UNHCR) now recognises the unique difficulties faced by refugee women and has set up specific 'Women at Risk' programmes.

### Activity

*A female refugee and her child outside a UNHCR tent on the island of Kos, Greece, 2015.*

In your opinion, why might forms of persecution specifically aimed at women require special UNHCR attention compared with the persecution of males? Think about concepts such as **stigmatisation**, shame and low self-esteem when considering your answer.

Feminists argue that female migrants are often handicapped by the immigration policies of receiving countries, which classify them as dependants of men. Their family role is emphasised at the expense of their role in the labour market. This often results in their failure to obtain work permits and their entry into the low-skilled and low-paid informal gig economy.

Finally, Nicola Mai and Russell King (2009) found that some female migration may be motivated by the fact that some countries – for example, Uganda and Tanzania – persecute and imprison people with an LGBT identity.

## Marxist approaches to global migration

Wallerstein (2011) argues that global migration is closely linked to the history and development of the modern capitalist world economy in which Western core countries are engaged in a neo-colonial form of exploitation of the resources and labour power of **periphery** countries, which are often ex-colonies (see Unit 8.2.2). Wallerstein argues that the countries at the centre of this capitalist global economy have deliberately under-developed the periphery countries, therefore creating the conditions of poverty and global inequality, which are the main drivers or push factors of global migration. For example, Massey (2003) argues that the introduction of capitalist intensive farming techniques or **agribusiness** resulted in people being forced off land they and their families had occupied for generations, thus creating unemployment and the impetus for migration.

Moreover, global migration, especially to the USA, has strengthened the position of this nation-state as the centre of the world capitalist economy. However, this came at a tremendous human cost, as the native-born population was subjected to **genocide** because they were interpreted by migrants from Europe as an 'obstacle to progress'.

Stephen Castles and Godula Kosack (1985) argue that global migrants that settle in capitalist societies are part and parcel of the proletariat, but argue that they are deliberately treated in a discriminatory way by the capitalist class for three reasons:

1. **Legitimisation** – Castles and Kosack argue that the capitalist class deliberately encourages racism in order to justify the low pay and precarious working conditions of migrant workers. Consequently, such workers are seen as second-class citizens undeserving of the same rights as White workers because they are often undocumented and presented by the media as a threat to indigenous workers. This ideology is beneficial to capitalism because employers profit from the exploitation of cheap migrant labour.
2. **Divide and rule** – They also argue that anti-migrant feeling benefits employers because it divides the proletariat. There is some evidence that indigenous workforces fear losing their jobs to the cheaper labour of migrant workers. Employers often play on these fears during pay negotiations to prevent indigenous workers from demanding higher wages or going on strike.
3. **Scapegoating** – When a society is troubled by severe social and economic problems, then widespread frustration, aggression and demands for radical change can result. However, instead of directing this anger at the capitalist class or economic system, indigenous workers are encouraged by racist ideology and agents such as the mass media to blame relatively vulnerable groups such as migrants for unemployment, declining living standards and growing inequality. Migrants become the scapegoats for the social and economic mismanagement of capitalism. This process benefits the wealthy and powerful capitalist class because it protects them from direct criticism and reduces pressure for radical change.

However, Castles and Kosack have been criticised for their economic reductionism – that is, for seeing social class as more important than other forms of status inequality. For example, the apartheid system that dominated South Africa between 1948 and 1994 was not the product of capitalism.

Furthermore, not all ethnic minorities end up in manual labour as the neo-Marxist Robert Miles (2003) acknowledges. He observes that some highly skilled migrants are economically successful and are part of the middle classes. These migrants, many of whom have set up businesses, may see their interests lying with capitalism. For example, in 2015, it was estimated by the Global Entrepreneurship Monitor (GEM) that migrants to the UK were three times more likely to be entrepreneurial than people born in Britain. The GEM found that 15.4 per cent of migrants to the UK had launched a business, compared with only 5.3 per cent of lifelong UK residents launching companies. It is also estimated that there are currently over 5000 Muslim millionaires in Britain. In 2016, *Forbes* magazine announced that, of the 400 richest Americans, a record 42 were migrants from 21 countries.

However, Miles observes that, because of institutional racism, the ethnicity of migrants may make it difficult for the most successful migrants to be fully accepted by the indigenous capitalist class. Miles, therefore, argues that they probably exist as a **racialised class fraction** within the middle class. They objectively occupy the same economic position as the home-grown wealthy, but they may subjectively be regarded by the indigenous capitalist class as having less social status because of their ethnicity or migrant status.

## Weberian explanations

The work of Max Weber (1864–1920) has had a significant influence on explanations for inequality for racial discrimination and inequality. Like Marx, he saw modern societies as characterised by a class struggle for income and wealth. However, he also noted that modern societies are characterised by status inequality. Status and power are usually in the hands of powerful status groups, thereby making it difficult for those with less status such as migrants to compete equally for scarce resources such as jobs and housing. Migrants, therefore, suffer from status inequality as well as class inequality. This status inequality can clearly be seen in the dual-labour market theory of R.D. Barron and G.M. Norris (1976).

## The dual-labour market theory

Barron and Norris claim that two labour markets exist in capitalist societies:

- *the primary labour sector* – this is characterised by secure, well-paid jobs, with long-term promotion prospects and is mainly dominated by home-grown workers
- *the secondary labour sector* – this is characterised by low-paid, unskilled and insecure jobs. Migrants are more likely to be found in this secondary sector. Michael Piore (1979) observes that private industries actively recruit foreign workers especially for the low-skilled and low-paid jobs in this sector that indigenous workers are unwilling to do.

However, Gans observes that many labour-migrants in the USA have experienced economic assimilation and over time have moved from the secondary labour sector into the primary sector. Research by Ken Wilson and Alejandro Portes (1980) suggests that the dual-labour market theory may be too static in its divide between primary and secondary jobs. They found that many recent Cuban migrants to Miami in the USA were economically better off than previous generations of Cuban migrants who were generally employed in secondary labour market jobs. The new migrants were entrepreneurial in the sense that they set up businesses providing services designed specifically for the Cuban community. Hanlon and Vicino observe that the labour market is at its most segregated in global cities such as London and New York. Consequently, migrants to these cities are likely to work in low-skilled service jobs which exist largely to support the lifestyle of indigenous professionals working in the knowledge and financial sectors of the economy, which tend to be concentrated in the centre of these cities – for example, Wall Street. These secondary jobs include domestic servants, nannies, taxi drivers, janitors, cleaners, hairdressers, waitresses, security guards and gardeners and so on.

*Little Havana Gamboa Barber Shop in Miami, Florida.*

## Interactionist approaches to migration

Interactionist approaches to migration focus on **agency**, particularly the push and pull factors that might motivate a person to embark upon a highly dangerous and potentially life-threatening journey across the world. Massey (2003) has examined migration networks, which he describes as sets of interpersonal ties that connect potential migrants with actual migrants who are already settled elsewhere. Anita Bocker (1994) found evidence that migrants who have successfully settled in other societies function as '**bridgeheads**', reducing the risks as well as material and psychological costs of subsequent migration. Such networks provide social capital – contacts that can advise on successful routes, guides, transportation, arranging residence papers, finding jobs and a place to live, and even finding a potential marriage partner.

Massey argues that the decision to migrate involves the potential migrant weighing up the potential costs (for example, the risk of death and leaving family, children and friends behind) against the potential benefits (for example, lifting oneself or one's family via remittances out of poverty). However, Massey notes that this cost–benefit model assumes that potential migrants have access to all available information needed to make rational choices. This is unlikely to be the case. Migrants often only have limited and often contradictory information. This may explain why global migration is such a hazardous business and why, despite the fact that most poor people in the least economically developed countries want to escape poverty, the poorest generally do not migrate.

## Postmodernist approaches

Postmodernists tend to focus on 'culture and identity' issues rather than issues such as inequality.

Hein de Haas (2008) argues that postmodernist perspectives on global migration are increasingly focused on the increased possibilities for migrants and their families to live transnationally and to adopt **transnational identities**. This is because of the advances in digital technology that make it possible for migrants to develop links with their societies of origin via the internet and especially social media sites, mobile phones and satellite television, and to remit money through globalised banking systems or informal channels. This increasingly enables migrants and their families to foster double loyalties, to travel back and forth, to relate to people, and to work and do business simultaneously in distant places. In other words, there is increasing scope for migrants and their families to pursue transnational livelihoods.

De Haas observes that sociologists have long assumed that migrants' integration into host societies would coincide with a gradual loosening of ties with their societies of origin. However, it has become increasingly clear that many migrant groups maintain strong transnational ties over sustained periods. Migrants' engagement with their origin country is not conditional on their return, but can be sustained through digital networks, tourism and circular migration. De Haas argues that transnational ties can eventually become transgenerational as the children of migrants come to qualitatively value and maintain ties to their parents' country of origin.

Yasmin Abdel-Magied (2013) claims that the children of migrants are more likely to subscribe to a global or transnational identity and to see themselves as global citizens. She argues that the extent of global migration that exists today means there is a level of cross-cultural pollination that has not been seen before in history. Migrants and their children have greater choice and freedom now to create and mould a globalised form of identity. She observes that global identity is likely to weaken national, ethnic and religious forms of identity. She also speculates that such global identities are almost certainly likely to be hybridised identities.

## Conclusions

Global migration has a long history. Moreover, it is a complex process that has profoundly affected the social, economic, political and cultural aspects of both sending and receiving societies. Migrants have come from all corners of the world and brought with them particular ways of thinking and new ways of life which have fundamentally transformed societies and contributed to a smaller, more connected global world.

### Activity

'Global migration benefits both sending and receiving societies.' Evaluate this view.

### Key terms

**Consensus** Common agreement.

**Acculturation** The process of adopting the cultural traits or social patterns of another group.

**Structural assimilation** The incorporation into society of a migrant group so that it has equal access to education, jobs and all social institutions.

**Segregation** The action or state of setting someone or something apart from others, often on the grounds of race or ethnicity.

**Jim Crow laws** State and local laws that enforced racial segregation in the Southern United States.

**Ethnocentric** Judging or evaluating other cultures according to the standards of one's own culture.

**Cultural pluralists** Those who believe that smaller groups within a larger society should be encouraged to maintain their unique cultural identities.

**Secular** Not having any connection with religion.

**Institutional racism** Racial prejudice or discrimination that has become established as normal behaviour within a society or organisation.

**Mono-ethnic** The dominance of a single ethnic group in terms of numbers.

**Conservative** A person, social group or political party that is averse to change and holds traditional values.

**Malestream** Research based on a masculine perspective, which often in consequence renders invisible the feminine or feminist perspective.

**Stigmatisation** A form of negative judgemental labelling that sets a person or group apart as a problem or threat to others.

**Periphery** On the edge or margins of a group or particular activity.

**Agribusiness** Agriculture conducted on intensive industrial principles using technology and intensive labour.

**Genocide** The deliberate killing of a large group of people, especially those of a particular nation or ethnic group.

**Legitimisation** To justify something by making it legal or socially acceptable.

**Divide and rule** The policy of maintaining control over one's subordinates or opponents by encouraging dissent between them, thereby preventing them from uniting in opposition.

**Scapegoating** The process of attaching blame (usually to a visible but powerless group).

**Racialised class fraction** An ethnic or migrant group that is objectively part of a particular social class but subjectively is not accepted by the majority of that class because of racial prejudice.

**Agency** Free will or choice to behave in a particular way.

**Bridgeheads** A foothold or position established in another society.

**Transnational identity** An identity associated with international migrants that is shaped by globalisation or by membership of two or more societies.

## Summary

1. Assimilation theory argues that both migrants and the societies in which they settle can benefit from migration so long as migrants fully integrate into the receiving society.
2. Multicultural theory claims assimilation theory is ethnocentric. Multiculturalists argue that migrant groups should retain their culture and recognise that they can make a rich cultural contribution to receiving societies.
3. However, multiculturalism has been criticised as a threat to both the social solidarity and national identity of European societies.
4. Structuralists argue that both assimilation and multiculturalism were weakened by the presence of racism, which they claim is structurally embedded into the organisation of many receiving societies.
5. Neoliberals argue that the free movement of labour is good for capitalism. However, there is evidence that it has caused great resentment among workers in the EU who feel it is threatening both their livelihoods and whole way of life.
6. New Right sociologists believe that global migration has brought about a cultural collision between Western and Islamic civilisations.
7. Feminists argue that global migration often involves the forced migration or trafficking of females for sexual purposes.
8. Marxists argue that global migration only benefits the global capitalist economy and the elite few who profit from it.
9. Marxists also observe that migrant workers are deliberately treated in a discriminatory fashion in order to divide and rule the proletariat.
10. The dual-labour market theory argues that global migration mainly benefits those in high-status jobs in the primary labour sector who are serviced by the migrant labour of the secondary labour market.
11. Interactionists focus on agency – the reasons why people choose to migrate and how they assess the costs and benefits of migration. They highlight the role of social networks and social capital in the decision to migrate.
12. Postmodernists argue that a global or transnational identity may emerge from global migration.

# END-OF-PART QUESTIONS

| 0 | 1 | Describe two pull factors that might encourage global migration. **[4 marks]**

| 0 | 2 | Explain one strength and one limitation of migration for sending societies. **[6 marks]**

| 0 | 3 | Explain two reasons why some sociologists are critical of global migration. **[8 marks]**

# PART 6 GLOBALISATION AND CRIME

## Contents


| | | |
|---|---|---|
| **Unit 8.6.1** | **Reasons for the emergence of global crime** | **559** |
| **Unit 8.6.2** | **Sociological explanations for global crime and who benefits** | **569** |
| **Unit 8.6.3** | **Policing and prosecuting global crime** | **576** |


As the world economy has globalised, so has its illegal and criminal counterpart. Global criminals have adopted new technologies, adapted horizontal networks of communication and transportation that are difficult to trace and stop, and diversified their activities. The result has been an unparalleled level of international crime coordinated by powerful individuals who plan and manage the illicit activities of the criminal cartels and gangs responsible for the illegal distribution of illicit products and services across the world. However, this criminal world economy is a complex world that often overlaps with the legitimate world of commerce and politics. Consequently, sociologists who study crime – criminologists – argue that it is also important when examining global crime to study carefully the activities of so-called legitimate individuals and organisations, especially transnational corporations and the nation-state, because their actions may also stray into the unlawful. Bakan (2005), for example, argues that corporate culture forces decent people who work for corporations to do indecent illegal things. The quest for profit means that everything and anything is legitimate in pursuit of that goal – for example, using child labour, setting up sweat shops, bribing government officials, despoiling the environment and evading tax.

However, any examination of global crime must also involve scrutiny of the activities of nation-states, and their political and military elites, because many of these have also committed global crime – for example, politicians may be guilty of corruption – taking massive bribes from transnationals in return for arms contracts or in return for handing out licences to drill for oil or to mine for precious raw materials.

The first unit focuses on identifying types of global crimes and the reasons for their emergence. The second unit explores sociological explanations for global crime by asking who benefits. The third unit examines why it is difficult to establish international laws and why it is seemingly even tougher to police such laws and punish global criminals so that they are sufficiently deterred from offending again.

## Unit 8.6.1 Reasons for the emergence of global crime

This unit focuses on identifying types of global crimes and the reasons for their emergence.

### The rise of globalised crime

The United Nations Office on Drugs and Crime (UNODC) observed in 2010 that global governance had failed to keep pace with economic globalisation. Consequently, as unprecedented openness in trade, finance, travel and communication created economic growth and well-being, it also gave rise to massive opportunities for criminals to make their business prosper. As a result, organised crime has diversified, gone global, and consequently 'illicit goods are sourced from one continent, trafficked across another, and marketed in a third. Mafias are today truly a transnational problem: a threat to security, especially in poor and conflict-ridden countries. Crime is fuelling corruption, infiltrating business and politics, and hindering development'.

Global crime, sometimes known as transnational crime or 'crimes without frontiers', can be understood as crime that takes place across the borders of two or more countries. Tom Obokata and Brian Payne (2018) observe that transnational crime has been a part of international relations and international trade for quite some time, but that, as societies and individuals have become more connected to one another, globalisation has enabled criminal networks to establish themselves in many different countries.

The scale of global crime has increased significantly in recent years. Until the 1970s, most crime was fairly localised – it mainly took place within national borders and local criminals rarely had international contact with criminals outside of their borders. However, today, organised criminal gangs are increasingly part of a wider global network of criminality. This is partly because global migration is blurring the usual distinction between the local and the international. The British National Crime Agency reported in 2018 that a large number of foreign nationals were heavily involved in the illegal drugs trade in the UK, some of whom were utilising cultural and family ties to the countries that drugs come from or which they travel through. Such ties made it easier for them to take major roles in the trade.

Cohen and Kennedy (2000) observe that, while tourism is the largest legitimate sector of the global economy, global crime is much more profitable. In 2010, both the United Nations and Castells estimated that global organised crime was worth $1.3 trillion per year. Misha Glenny (2009) refers to the flow of capital and profit generated by global crime as the '**shadow economy**' and estimates that this accounts for 15 per cent of the value of wealth generated by countries across the world.

The global criminal economy has a number of features mirroring the global capitalist economy. Glenny observes that organised crime in a globalising world operates in the same way as any other business:

- It has **zones of production**, such as Afghanistan and Pakistan in which opium poppies are cultivated, and Peru and Bolivia in which coca-leaves are harvested. These crops are processed in Colombia and Mexico into cocaine, and in Turkey into heroin.
- It has **zones of distribution** – for example, organised **cartels** in Colombia (particularly gangs in Medellin and Cali) control the distribution of cocaine via containerisation into Europe (usually after making alliances with Russian, Balkan and other organised European gangs). In Mexico, conflict between drug-trafficking syndicates led by the likes of Joaquin 'El Chapo' Guzman, and aiming to take control of the extremely lucrative cross-border routes into the USA, has resulted in the death or disappearance of over 200 000 people since 2006. Jamaica is an important staging post for smuggling cocaine into the UK and Europe via **drug mules** recruited by the **Yardie** gangs allied to the Colombian and Mexican cartels.

## Activity

*El Chapo headed Mexico's most powerful criminal organisation – the Sinaloa Cartel – until his capture in 2016.*

In which ways does the global criminal economy mirror the global capitalist economy?

- It has **zones of consumption**, such as the European Union, Japan and the USA. Many global criminal networks have developed to feed a demand from the affluent West for drugs and prostitution.

Castells argues that globalisation resulted in the development of physical, digital and financial networks that cut across national borders and which led to knowledge as well as goods and people moving quickly, easily and cheaply across the world. The sum of these changes is the development of a global criminal or 'shadow' economy in which there exist complex interconnections between a range of criminal networks in a variety of countries, including the US, Italian and Russian mafias, Colombian, Mexican and Turkish drug cartels, the Italian **Camorra**, and Chinese **triads**. These criminal networks operate transnationally because globalisation reduces risk and increases profit. Although global in scope, they are also often organised along national, regional or ethnic lines. For example, there are close links between triads based in China and the Chinese **diaspora**. The Russian mafia similarly maintains strong links with the Russian diaspora in the USA and Europe.

## Contemporary issues: Globalised crime in Russia

According to Glenny, the globalisation of crime was particularly facilitated by the development of Russian criminal networks, which emerged after the collapse of communism post-1990. As state assets were privatised, some Russian politicians, civil servants and generals collaborated with organised criminal networks from other countries to buy up roubles (Russian currency) before dumping them on world currency markets in order to slash the value of the currency. This enabled them to buy up the former assets of the USSR (such as gas and oilfields, hotels and land) at bargain prices. Substantial parts of the gold reserves of the Soviet state were stolen and taken abroad and used by Russian gangsters and oligarchs to fund the purchase of privatised assets. Corrupt politicians were bribed to ease this process. Glenny argues that, as a result, politics and business have merged in Russia with both home-based and international Russian gangsters. This has occurred to the extent that recent CIA files leaked by WikiLeaks indicate that the US government refers to Russia as a 'mafia state' and suggests that President Putin has become extremely wealthy – possibly the richest man in the world – as a result of him turning a blind eye to his gangster friends.

### Questions

1. How did the political, military and business worlds in Russia overlap post-communism with the criminal world?
2. Why do you think CIA files refer to Russia as a 'mafia state'?

## Types of globalised crime

The UNODC has identified a massive growth in a number of forms of global crimes.

### Trafficking and dealing in drugs, particularly cocaine and heroin

Cohen and Kennedy observe that this is the most lucrative of all global crimes but profits depend on the fact that there is a massive demand for illegal substances in Europe and the USA, and a 'pitiful' need to continue to grow drugs by farmers in the supplier countries because they would otherwise descend into abject poverty. Clare Hargreaves (1992) argues that the USA consumes more cocaine than any other industrialised country. In the 1990s, she found that Americans spent $110 million a year on drugs ($28 million was spent on cocaine). This was double the profits of the top 500 companies in the USA put together.

Drug cartels are the criminal equivalent of transnational companies. The success of this extremely profitable criminal enterprise depends on the efficacy of their subsidiary operations, which look after stages of the global process: the actual growing of the crops (opium poppies and coca-leaf); the transportation of the crop to processing centres in other parts of the world (where it is turned into the 'product' using sophisticated and hazardous scientific techniques); the smuggling of the product across international borders; the dilution of the pure product into high-value merchandise for consumption by individuals; the making of alliances with domestic gangs in order to distribute the product; the marketing and sale to customers; and the laundering of the 'dirty' money earned on the streets into 'clean' money that can be invested in legitimate projects such as the construction industry and real estate. This is a complex business that involves huge investment and sophisticated logistics but generates huge profits if successful. For example, in 1989, the Colombian narco-kingpin, Pablo Escobar, was estimated by *Forbes* magazine to be worth $3 billion when his Medellin cartel controlled about 80 per cent of the global cocaine market.

However, a disturbing by-product of this global drug trade are the thousands of deaths every year – these deaths include addicts but also the thousands of people killed in drug turf wars. (In Juarez, a city on the border between Mexico and the USA, nearly 15 000 people were murdered by drug cartels in 2011.)

## Activity

*Before he was killed by the Colombian army, Escobar, as head of the Medellin drug cartel, was estimated to be earning $420 million a week from the distribution of cocaine.*

How many different negative effects of the drug trade can you think of (consider effects on drug addicts, drug dealers, drug smugglers and so on).

Cohen and Kennedy argue that, given its social and economic importance to a number of countries, the drug trade also serves to corrupt the political process. In their view, in countries such as Colombia, Bolivia, Pakistan, Afghanistan, Somalia, Jamaica and Russia, the distinction between crime, politics and banking is so fine that 'players can barely tell the difference'.

### Human trafficking

The trafficking of children and women is big business. Gangs based in Serbia, Bulgaria, Romania and Albania are thought to be mainly responsible for illegally smuggling approximately half a million females a year into Western Europe. The **modus operandi** of these gangs is to set up job agencies which claim that they can obtain legitimate well-paid jobs and work permits for young educated women as nannies and au pairs in Western European countries in return for the women paying the agency a cash fee. However, evidence from UNODC suggests that, when such women turned up for meetings with the agencies, gang members would drug and rape them, take their passports and put them to work as **forced prostitutes** in brothels across Europe, particularly in Germany, the Netherlands, Belgium and Scandinavia. The UN has also highlighted the role of Chinese and Vietnamese gangs in the kidnap of girls in order to cater for Westerners who travel to countries such as Thailand and the Philippines for the purpose of '**sex tourism**'.

*Modern slavery.*

Cohen and Kennedy observe that, in both Thailand and the Philippines, sex tourism is one of the biggest earners of **foreign exchange**. The forced prostitutes (many of whom have been sold by their parents to 'flesh merchants') to work out of brothels advertised as part of sex tourism packages. The gangs and middlemen who control the supply of women and manage the brothels pocket most of the girls' earnings.

Cohen and Kennedy also observe that 'sex tourism shades into the **mail order bride** business'. Potential husbands arrive on package tours to examine 'the goods'. Young girls and women who are desperate to get out of poverty and to financially help their family often 'agree' to marry Western men considerably older than themselves.

## Smuggling of migrants

Since 2010, people-trafficking gangs operating out of North Africa and Turkey have been heavily involved in the illegal smuggling of undocumented migrants (many of whom were escaping extreme poverty, civil war in Syria and persecution) into Europe via Greece, Italy and Spain, in return for large fees. The crossing across the Mediterranean can be extremely dangerous and many hundreds of refugees – men, women and children – have drowned as boats have capsized (see also Unit 8.5.1).

## Arms trafficking to illegal regimes, guerrilla groups and terrorists

According to a 2018 report by Europol, weapons trafficking is almost exclusively a supplementary rather than a primary source of income for the small number of organised criminal groups involved. Most groups enter the weapons-trafficking business through other criminal activity, which may offer contacts, knowledge of existing routes and infrastructure related to the smuggling of weapons, explosives, chemical, biological, radiological and nuclear materials (particularly from the former Soviet republics). However, a potential major global concern is the increasing likelihood that these criminal networks may supply terrorist groups with firearms, ammunition and explosives.

Research by Judith Aldridge (2017) found that the **dark web/dark net** is a major facilitator of the illegal sales of firearms, weapons and explosives and a source of digital guides on how to construct bombs and weapons.

Transparency International, an international non-governmental organisation which aims to combat global corruption, estimates that the global cost of corruption in the legal defence sector or arms trade amounts to at least $20 billion (£12.6 billion) a year – the total sum pledged by the (then) G8 countries in 2009 to fight world hunger. Andrew Feinstein (2012) estimates that corruption in the form of bribes paid to politicians, civil servants, senior army, navy and air force officers and middlemen while engaged in the legal trading of arms between arms-exporting nations such as the UK and USA, and arms-importing countries such as Saudi Arabia, Pakistan and South Africa, accounts for around 40 per cent of all corruption in world trade.

## Counterfeiting and smuggling

In 2016, a joint report by the OECD and EUIPO concluded that imports of counterfeit and pirated goods, especially of designer goods and labels, are worth nearly half a trillion dollars a year, or around 2.5 per cent of global imports, with US, Italian and French luxury brands the hardest hit. A range of products is faked or counterfeited from handbags and perfumes to machine parts and chemicals. Most fake goods originate in middle income or LEDCs, with China the top producer. The smuggling of counterfeits could not be successful without port officials, customs officials and local police officers being open to bribery.

### Activity

*Luxury brands such as Gucci and Rolex are often copied by counterfeiting and sold on the streets in Europe's capital cities.*

Why do you think that counterfeiting is a crime (consider impacts on both companies and consumers)?

Another aspect of smuggling is the global trade in luxury cars, particularly models by Audi, BMW, Lexus and Mercedes-Benz, which are mainly stolen by triad gangs in the West and containerised and sold to buyers in China, the Philippines and Russia.

## Maritime piracy

Piracy is a violent, acquisitive crime. It is transnational because a ship is considered the sovereign territory of the nation whose flag it flies. Piracy is organised because commandeering a ship at sea requires considerable planning and some specialised expertise. Most piracy at sea takes place off the coast of Somalia, especially in the Gulf of Aden. In 2009, more than half of global piracy attacks were ascribed to Somali pirates. Most attacks involve the hijacking of a vessel such as an oil tanker and threatening the captain and crew until a ransom is paid. In 2008, the average ransom was estimated at between $500,000 and $2 million.

## Corporate crime and money laundering

**Money laundering** is the process of creating the appearance that large amounts of money obtained from criminal activity, such as drug trafficking or terrorist activity, originated from a legitimate source. The money from the illicit activity is considered dirty, and the process 'launders' the money to make it seem as though it was 'cleanly' earned through legitimate activities.

There is no doubt that global crime could not exist on the scale that it does without the cooperation of financial corporations such as international banks and the powerful financiers who run them. For example, a number of mainstream banks have recently been heavily fined by the US authorities for allowing Mexican drug cartels to set up accounts in which they have deposited profits from their global drug deals. In 2017, it was reported that Azerbaijan's ruling elite operated a secret $2.9 billion (£2.2 billion) scheme to launder money through a network of British corporations.

Oliver Bullough (2018) refers to the shadow financial sector that is responsible for money laundering and other illegal financial services such as tax evasion as 'Moneyland'. He observes that the global rich, including global gangsters and cartel chiefs, move their money, their children, their assets and themselves wherever they wish, picking and choosing which countries' laws they wish to live by. Bullough argues that Britain is at the centre of Moneyland. He agrees with the conclusion of Roberto Saviano, expert on the mafia, who calls Britain 'the most corrupt country in the World'. Bullough cites a report by Deutsche Bank in 2015 that claimed that $125 billion of 'flight capital' (money moved abroad by 'anxious' owners who have often acquired the money via corruption and crime) had entered the British economy 'without anyone noticing'. For example, it was alleged by the US Senate Committee that Omar Bongo (president of Gabon from 1967 to 2009) has channelled $130 million through Citibank. Bullough claims that London overflows with lawyers, bankers, accountants, estate agents, public relations advisers, luxury-goods sellers, restaurateurs and art dealers who make their living servicing criminals.

Bullough argues that globalisation means that Moneyland keeps shifting its shape. The latest fashion, especially for Russian and Chinese elites, some of whom have made their money from global crime, is to buy passports or **residency** from countries such as Cyprus, Israel and Malta. The latter has reportedly raised over $3 billion from passport sales (Bullough, 2018).

## Corruption

In general, corruption is a form of dishonesty or criminal activity undertaken by a person or global corporation entrusted with a position of authority, often to acquire financial benefit. The World Bank considers corruption to be the major challenge to its twin goals of ending extreme poverty by 2030 and boosting shared prosperity for the poorest 40 per cent of people in developing countries. It estimates that global businesses and individuals pay an estimated $1.5 trillion in bribes every year. This is equivalent to about 2 per cent of global wealth and 10 times the value of overseas development assistance. The World Bank concludes that the poor pay the highest percentage of their income in bribes. For example, in Paraguay, the poor spend 12.6 per cent of their income on bribes, while high-income households only pay 6.4 per cent. Most importantly, corruption undermines the relationship between the state and its citizens.

### Activity

What sort of ways might corruption undermine the relationship between a state and its citizens?

## Cybercrime

'Cybercrime' has been used to describe a wide range of offences, including offences against computer data and systems (such as 'hacking'), computer-related forgery and fraud (such as 'phishing'), content offences (such as disseminating child pornography) and copyright offences (such as the dissemination of pirated content). It has evolved from the mischievous one-upmanship of cyber-vandals or **hacktivists** to a range of sophisticated profit-making criminal enterprises in a remarkably short period of time. The internet has facilitated a number of traditional organised crime activities but our collective dependence on it has also created a number of new criminal opportunities such as **identity theft**. Some analysts have estimated losses to cybercrime to be as much as $1 trillion in 2008, although this figure is hotly contested.

Glenny has expressed concern about the role of the dark net in the spread of global crime. This is an encrypted network of untraceable online activity and approximately 30 000 hidden and anonymous websites hosted by a software known as 'Tor'. Nikita Malik (2018) claims that the dark net is being used by extremists and terrorists to plot future attacks, raise funds and recruit new followers. Terrorist organisations and individuals are evading security services and intelligence agencies by 'hiding in the shadows' of the dark net, using encrypted messaging services, to communicate and anonymous **cryptocurrencies** such as bitcoin to generate funds.

## Terrorism

Tamara Makarenko (2004) argues that terrorism is increasingly a global crime for several reasons. First, terror organisations that share a particular creed and ideology (for example, Islamist jihadists), but which are based on different continents – for example, in Europe and Syria (IS), Somalia (El Shabaab), Afghanistan (al-Qaeda) and Nigeria (Boko Haram) – share information, personnel and resources and sometimes coordinate global attacks. There is also evidence that terrorist groups from Ireland, Spain, Japan and Palestine cooperated with each other in the 1970s. Second, terrorist attacks can occur anywhere in the world. Third, the victims of terrorist attacks, especially if they occur in global cosmopolitan cities such as London, Paris and New York, are often global tourists. Fourth, many terrorist groups rely on other global criminal networks, particularly drugs, for funding. Finally, although fundamentalist groups such as al-Qaeda and ISIS are committed to a return to traditional or fundamentalist religious values, they rely on modern global media, especially the internet, to make their case and to radicalise and recruit young Muslims to their cause.

## Crimes against the environment – green crimes

Green crime is a form of global crime because the planet is a single eco-system in which human beings, other species and the environment are interconnected and inter-dependent. Green harms are global in character because they do not respect national borders. Pollution and waste – for example, plastic produced by China, the USA and Europe – is carried via the atmosphere or the ocean currents across the world. Harm done to other species or aspects of the environment, such as the air, drinking water supplies, the ocean and the rainforest, impact negatively on the quality and future of human life wherever it is in the world. For example, radioactive fallout from the Chernobyl nuclear reactor disaster of 1986 spread thousands of miles across Europe.

Nigel South (2014) classifies green crime into primary crimes and secondary crimes. Primary crimes are the direct result of the destruction and degradation of the planet's resources and include:

- crimes of air pollution, such as industrial carbon and greenhouse gas emissions
- crimes of deforestation, such as illegal logging
- crimes of species decline and animal rights
- crimes of freshwater and marine pollution, such as oil spillages.

The UNODC has highlighted two important aspects of green crime which seem to be on the increase. First, the natural resources of the LEDCs such as oil, diamonds, gold or other valuable metals and ores are being misappropriated and illegally trafficked by individuals, governments and TNCs. However, the UNODC also points out that the biological resources of some countries, especially threatened animal species, timber and fish, are also being stolen and illegally trafficked. In particular, exotic animal products such as rhino horns and tiger skins command high prices due to strong global demand, especially from Asia. The UNODC points out that many wild species are harvested in South-East Asia for traditional medicine, food and decor products, as well as being captured for the pet trade.

South identifies secondary green crimes as those which involve flouting existing laws and regulations – for example:

- dumping toxic waste, particularly in the developing world
- breaches of health and safety rules, causing disasters such as Chernobyl (1986) and the Union Carbide chemical factory disaster in Bhopal, India (1984)

- offloading products such as pharmaceuticals and pesticides onto LEDC markets after they have been banned on health and safety grounds in the West.

## Activity

'Global crime takes several forms.' Evaluate this view.

## Corporate crime

Corporate crimes are committed by the owners, executives, directors and managers of large companies, not necessarily for personal gain (although they may financially benefit in the long run). These offences aim to maximise profit or to artificially inflate a company's share price on the stock exchange. Corporate crimes tend to be global especially if the company is a TNC that operates in several countries across the world; for example, its manufacturing plants may be based in multiple global locations and it may advertise and sell its products worldwide. Alleged corporate wrongdoing involving multinational companies can be very difficult to prosecute. Examples of controversial disasters involving multinational companies include the following:

- Companies putting their workforces and local populations at risk because they have failed to abide by local health and safety laws relating to environmental pollution or taken shortcuts in safety measures which have resulted in death or exposure to toxic substances that may shorten life expectancy. For example in 1984 a gas leak at the American company Union Carbide's chemical plant at Bhopal, India, resulted in the deaths of hundreds of local people living near the plant. In 2001, Nike were accused by Global Exchange, a pressure group that monitors the activities of TNCs, of exploiting child labour in Central American sweat shops that had been contracted to produce their sportswear and trainers. Another example was the collapse in 2013 of Rana Plaza, a structurally unsound building in Dhaka, Bangladesh. The building housed factories producing goods for many multinational corporations, including Walmart, Monsoon, Accessorize and Primark. In the tragedy, 1129 people died and over 2000 were injured. Several owners of the sweat shops producing goods for TNCs have been charged with murder. The disaster has forced TNCs to promise that contracts will only be placed with employers who can guarantee safe working conditions.

*Bangladeshi people gather as rescuers look for survivors and victims at the site of the Rana Plaza building which collapsed in Dhaka.*

- The evidence suggests that global corporations involved in the manufacture and distribution of products such as cigarettes and pesticides concealed their carcinogenic properties from global consumers for many years.
- TNCs may create environmental hazards. For example, in 2006, the chemical TNC Trafigura were accused of hiring a local company in the West African country Ivory Coast (Côte d'Ivoire) to illegally dump their toxic waste. This scandal only became public after dozens of children fell ill after playing at the dump site. However, it proved difficult to prosecute Trafigura for this environmental harm because the company refused to disclose the contents of the toxic waste, which hampered both the clean-up and the medical response. In 2007, Trafigura agreed to pay the Côte d'Ivoire government a settlement of $200 million that granted the company immunity from prosecution. In 2008, the Dutch courts found Trafigura guilty of illegally exporting waste from the Netherlands and fined it 1 million euros but, according to a 2016 report by Amnesty International, Dutch prosecutors decided not to prosecute Trafigura for the illegal dumping because they found it too difficult to coordinate with the Côte d'Ivoire government. Many of those affected are still waiting for an adequate remedy and justice.
- Vincenzo Ruggiero and South (2013) have documented environmental disasters they believe to be caused by global corporations attempting to minimise costs and to maximise profits. In particular, they highlight the oil spills associated with BP in Canada's Prudhoe Bay in 2006 and the Deepwater Horizon rig explosion in the Gulf of Mexico in 2010.

*Dark clouds fill the sky as clean-up crews conduct controlled burns of oil gathered from the surface of the Gulf of Mexico following the BP Deepwater Horizon oil spill disaster.*

- There is evidence that global arms corporations have corrupted politicians and government officials all around the world by paying them huge bribes in order to win contracts. In 2008, the Organisation for Economic Co-operation and Development expressed its disappointment and serious concern at the UK's continued failure to address deficiencies in its laws on bribery of foreign public officials and on corporate liability for foreign bribery.
- Some global companies have actually been involved in the illegal overthrow of democratically elected governments in Iran (1953), Guatemala (1954) and Chile (1974).
- Many global banking corporations have been suspected of being involved in money laundering of the proceeds of criminal activities such as drugs, corruption and prostitution. For example, in 2018, the Danske Bank was revealed to have thousands of suspicious customers responsible for about $234 billion of transactions over a nine-year period. The scandal was truly global in that it involved 32 currencies, companies from Cyprus, the British Virgin Islands and the Seychelles. Customers were traced to Russia, the Ukraine and Azerbaijan. The US Department of Justice investigation is ongoing.
- Global corporations are often accused of tax evasion. The Panama Papers (2016) and the Paradise Papers (2017) were leaked documents that showed widespread illegal tax evasion by global corporations and wealthy individuals.

### Activity

Global corporations such as Amazon, Starbucks and Vodafone have been accused of using off-shore tax havens to avoid paying their fair share of taxes on sales in countries around the world in which they make tremendous profits. Some neoliberal critics point out that tax *evasion* is the illegal evasion of taxes by individuals, corporations and trusts, whereas tax *avoidance* is the legal use of tax laws to reduce one's tax burden. However, some radical criminologists believe tax avoidance should be seen as a crime because it involves the abuse of power, denied to most citizens, by hiding true earnings or profits from the tax authorities.

List reasons for and against tax avoidance, and debate whether it ought to be criminalised.

## Reasons for the emergence of global crime

There are several reasons why crime has become a global phenomenon.

### Cheaper air travel, container transport and tourism

The development of cheap travel has made it more profitable and easier to smuggle illegal products such as drugs across borders. In particular, the invention and introduction of container shipping made a great contribution to the globalisation of trade. According to Martin Parker (2012), the container has particularly facilitated the activities of global criminals such as pirates, drug and people traffickers and criminal syndicates engaged in counterfeiting and smuggling luxury goods and cars. New information and digital communication technologies such as the internet, email and the cheap availability of mobile burner phones have made it easier for international criminals and terrorists to communicate with one another.

### The deregulation of global markets

This process, which mainly occurred from the 1980s onwards, was encouraged by neoliberals and global organisations such as the World Bank. It means that it is relatively easy to set up anonymous shell companies (whose owners are almost impossible to trace through official channels) in off-shore tax havens to move profits and launder cash around the world.

Many small countries, particularly the British Virgin Islands, the Bahamas, the Cayman Islands, Panama and Costa Rica, have set themselves up as tax havens in order to generate foreign earnings. These countries offer foreign individuals and businesses little or no tax liability in a politically and economically stable environment. They pride themselves on asking no questions about the source of the cash that is deposited in their country and often refuse to reveal any information about their clients to foreign governments, police forces or tax authorities. For example, drug money, in particular, is often used to set up 'ghost' or shell companies in these tax havens. These companies do not produce anything but 'magically' make profits that can be transferred to legitimate mainstream banks.

## The digitalisation of the global financial market

The world banking system now operates 24 hours a day, 7 days a week. This means that money can be transferred instantaneously and anonymously to the bank accounts of shell companies in off-shore tax havens. This has particularly facilitated the laundering of money earned from criminal activity.

## Migration, war and conflict

War in particular parts of the world, and the misery and poverty that it leaves in its wake, has fuelled a demand for migration to more prosperous parts of the world. This has resulted in the emergence of people-trafficking gangs which offer transport to a seemingly more affluent West at a cost of several thousand dollars.

## Poverty

Economic deprivation is probably the major reason why global crime has developed.

Evidence suggests that poverty also shapes the supply and demand of global drugs. For example, in the developing world, war and poverty have led to some farmers having to abandon conventional crops. In Afghanistan and north-west Pakistan, farmers were 'encouraged' by war-lords to plant opium poppies.

In South America, similar economic pressures have 'forced' farmers to grow coca plants. For example, the decision by multinational companies in the 1970s such as Heinz, Coca-Cola and Pepsi to switch from using tin cans to aluminium cans decimated the tin industry of Bolivia and created massive unemployment in that country. Unemployed tin miners in Bolivia were forced back to the land to survive. Many turned to farming coca-leaves, because the cartels were willing to pay a greater price for this crop than farmers could get at local markets for growing maize.

With regard to the demand for drugs, particularly heroin, the de-industrialisation of Western societies led to the decline of manufacturing industry, long-term unemployment and severe economic deprivation in inner-city areas in both the USA and UK. Studies of long-term drug addicts, especially users of heroin and crack, suggest that the low self-esteem, boredom and humiliation experienced by those with little opportunity to work may be a significant factor influencing their decision to use hard drugs, usually as an alternative way to fill up their time or to help them forget about the hardship they are experiencing. For example, evidence from a study conducted by Amy Bohnert (2009) suggests that heroin and cannabis are being consumed mainly by young adults living in lower socio-economic urban neighbourhoods in the USA.

## Public and official indifference

It can be argued that a grey area exists in some societies between the legal and the illegal, and this has probably contributed to public indifference and some official reluctance to take immediate action against global crime. For example, the taking of bribes in some societies, especially poorer ones, is a fairly routine and normal practice. In Western societies, deliberate tax evasion (which is an illegal offence) may actually be admired.

### Activity

Evaluate the relationship between global crime and poverty.

### Key terms

**Shadow economy** Illegal or criminal economic activity which exists alongside a country's official economy – for example, the black market.

**Zones of production** Areas of the less industrialised world in which crops are grown that are later processed into cannabis resin, heroin or cocaine.

**Zones of distribution** Areas of the world which are the launch-point or staging posts for the distribution of illegal goods into the West.

**Cartel** An organisation of criminals who associate in order to grow or manufacture, process and distribute illegal goods, especially drugs such as heroin and cocaine.

**Drug mules** People who are paid to smuggle drugs across borders, usually inside their bodies.

**Yardie** A member of a Jamaican gang of criminals.

**Zones of consumption** The mainly Western market for illicit goods and services.

**Camorra** A type of mafia that operates mainly in Naples, Italy.

**Triads** Chinese-organised criminal gangs.

**Diaspora** People from a particular nation or ethnic community that are scattered across the world – for example, people of Jewish ancestry can be found in most countries around the world.

**Modus operandi** A particular way or method of doing something.

**Forced prostitution** Sexual slavery that takes place as a result of coercion by a third party.

**Sex tourism** The organisation of holidays with the purpose of taking advantage of the lack of restrictions imposed on sexual activity and prostitution by some foreign countries.

**Foreign exchange** The exchange of currencies – the US dollar is especially valued by poor countries, because oil can only be bought on the oil market using this currency.

**Mail order bride** A woman who lists herself in a catalogue and is selected by a man for marriage.

**Dark net/dark web** A computer network with encrypted and restricted access that is used chiefly for illegal peer-to-peer file sharing.

**Money laundering** The concealment of the origins of illegally obtained money, typically by means of transfers involving foreign banks or legitimate businesses.

**Residency** The official right granted by a government to live in its country although the person who is given residence may not necessarily have citizenship.

**Hacktivist** A person who gains unauthorised access to computer files or networks in order to further social or political ends.

**Identity theft** The fraudulent practice of stealing another person's name and personal information from information stored on the Web.

**Cryptocurrency** A digital currency such as bitcoin in which encryption techniques are used to regulate the generation of units of currency and verify the transfer of funds, operating independently of a central bank.

## Summary

1. Global crime is a huge problem, as illustrated by the fact that its total value is equivalent to 15 per cent of the world's wealth.
2. Most of the goods and services produced by the criminal economy originate in the poorer, less industrialised world but are consumed in the developed Western world.
3. The most lucrative of all global crimes is the production and trafficking of heroin and cocaine.
4. There is considerable overlap between global criminality and the activities of TNCs and nation-states.
5. The activities of TNCs often stray into the illicit sector in their pursuit of profit.
6. Most of the technology associated with globalisation, especially digitalisation and containerisation, has benefited global crime gangs.
7. There is a strong relationship between poverty and global crime.

# Unit 8.6.2 Sociological explanations for global crime and who benefits

This unit will examine sociological explanations for global crime, particularly in regard to who benefits from it. The focus will be on Marxist and feminist perspectives.

## Marxist perspectives

Marxists believe that global crime is inevitable because global capitalism is **criminogenic** – which means that crime is a natural outcome of the values and norms that people are socialised into by capitalism and their everyday experiences of that economic system.

Marxists argue that global capitalism strongly encourages people to believe in a free market ideology, known as neoliberalism, that suggests that status and success can only be truly measured or achieved via the acquisition of wealth and consumer goods. This neoliberal ideology may encourage both individuals and businesses to adopt immoral, selfish and illegal practices to compete with one another in order to make money and to achieve material success. Consequently, self-interest and the pursuit of profit and wealth may put pressure on all social classes, wherever they are situated in the global capitalist economy, to commit criminal acts without conscience or regardless of the costs to others.

Marxists also point out that the criminogenic effects of capitalism are often made worse by the structural inequalities embedded in the organisation of global capitalism.

The overall outcomes of global capitalism are two cultures:

- a 'culture of greed' dominated by the successful 'few' who control the majority of the world's wealth and who move in the same circles as those who have made their money directly from crime and who may, from time to time, knowingly or unknowingly, enter into business arrangements with these criminals
- a 'culture of failure' made up of the mass of workers or citizens whose main life experiences are shaped by the structural inequalities embedded in the organisation of capitalism such as low pay, unemployment, existential insecurity and poverty, which may lead to feelings such as **alienation**, humiliation, powerlessness, disaffection and envy. Some of these workers may view committing crime or becoming addicted to drugs as a form of rational compensation for the daily misery of inequality.

The Marxist criminologist Ian Taylor (1998) argued that the development of capitalism is the main driver for the globalisation of crime. The privatisation of state assets (see the Contemporary issues box Russia in Unit 8.6.1), the influence of neoliberal organisations such as the World Bank that led to the deregulation of the rules, regulations and laws governing the import–export of goods across the world and the promotion of the free market are features of the capitalist world economy (see discussion of Wallerstein in Unit 8.1.3). These features have created the conditions conducive to the growth and benefit of both transnational and local crime by elites and working-class offenders alike.

## The capitalist world economy

This can be illustrated in a number of ways:

**Neo-colonialism** Wallerstein (1983) argues that the global capitalist class, who are mainly situated in the core countries of the global capitalist economy, contribute to global crime by practising neo-colonialism. There are three types of neo-colonialist practice which benefit Western economies and the profits of TNCs but which damage the economy of poor countries:

- The core countries ensure that the terms of world trade favour their manufactured products at the expense of the cash crops (for example, tea, coffee, maize, cotton, fruit and vegetables) and raw materials (for example, tin, copper) that are often the main sources of income for LEDCs. The value of manufactured goods is generally stable, but the value of raw materials and cash crops often fluctuates because of speculation on stock markets and changes in public taste. Consequently, if Western demand for Bolivian tin or coal falls, then Bolivian mines shut down and miners are forced to turn to growing crops. However, the choice of crop may be determined by local markets. It may be less profitable to grow legitimate crops such as maize if global drug cartels are offering farmers higher returns for growing marijuana and coca. It is thought that farmers in countries currently dependent on revenue from their sugar crop, such as Jamaica and Barbados, may be tempted to switch to illicit crops if Western demand for sugar continues to fall because of Western health concerns about sugar intake.
- Global capitalism and cheap international transport and communication systems have allowed TNCs to shift production to developing countries especially in South Asia (for example, Bangladesh and Malaysia), where production costs are low (both in terms of taxes and the cost of labour) and where there is greater potential for maximising profit. This has led to some TNCs breaking laws in low-income countries, especially those relating to the health and safety of their workers. Often such companies also commit environmental or green offences such as exposing local populations to toxic pollutants, destroying local eco-systems by engaging in

**deforestation** and open-cast mining, recruiting and paying local warlords to use violence to force native people off land required by the TNC, or by polluting local **water tables** and wells with chemicals and **carcinogenic** waste.

- International aid in theory is supposed to assist an LEDC to develop by financing much-needed infrastructure such as transport and communication systems, education and healthcare, such as vaccination programmes. However, aid often 'disappears' and is misappropriated by a local **kleptocracy**. Additionally, aid often drags LEDCs into debt. Funds generated by the export of cash crops and raw materials often have to be diverted into debt repayments. LEDC governments may, therefore, be tempted to turn a blind eye to drug production because they know this brings in much-needed foreign exchange. The USA has actually attempted to convince South American countries such as Bolivia, Peru and Colombia to destroy drug crops (with the assistance of US armed forces) in return for economic aid.

### Deregulation of the world's financial sector

Marxists point out that economic globalisation means that global criminals and the legitimate super-rich now have the ability to move large amounts of money around the world because of the **deregulation** of the world's financial sector. The lack of global control on the digital transfer of money enables a whole range of financial crimes, from tax evasion and insider trading to defrauding transnational organisations such as the European Union out of grant and subsidy money. Estimates put losses from the EU at around $7 billion per year. In addition, lack of regulations, according to Bullough (2018), has given the super-rich the freedom to loot their own countries and transfer billions of illegally acquired cash to off-shore banks.

Marxists highlight the fact that deregulation and the existence of secretive tax havens have increased the opportunities for organised crime to launder the profits from illegal activities (such as drugs production and distribution) and to place this 'cleaned-up money' in **shell companies**, supposedly engaged in legal activities (such as gambling machines, hotel construction and import–export). The reluctance of conventional mainstream banks to ask questions about the origin of such funds also enables drug cartels to launder their profits safely.

## Activity

*The Panama Papers exposed the existence of a corrupt off-shore world of tax havens engaged in illegal tax evasion and money laundering.*

Research what the Panama Papers revealed.

### Economic depression in the USA and Europe

Global economic recession in the 1970s and the decision by some TNCs to shift their manufacturing to the less industrialised world had the effect of bringing about severe economic depression in both the USA and Europe. Unemployment and urban poverty dramatically increased. There is evidence that Western crime rates also steeply increased in the West in the period 1975–95 as sections of, for example, the American urban poor in the former industrial heartlands of Chicago, Detroit, Baltimore and Philadelphia became addicted to crack cocaine. In Europe, particularly the UK, the evidence similarly showed a close relationship between long-term unemployed youth and heroin addiction.

## Crime: the local and the global

Although globalisation often led to the development of international and transnational criminal organisations, localised forms of criminal organisation continued to be important. Marxist sociologists Dick Hobbs and Colin Dunningham (1998) studied criminal networks in the north-east of England and found that most crime in this region involved networks of interconnected local criminals who worked together from time to time rather than well-integrated and permanent gangs. They concluded that criminal activity, especially in the field of drugs, is best summed up by the term 'glocalisation'; that is, some successful criminals have established international contacts with global gangs originating in Colombia, Jamaica, Turkey, Pakistan and Holland. Sometimes this contact is facilitated by family contacts, especially in urban areas with high concentrations of migrants and minority ethnic groups.

These domestic gangs were, therefore, to some extent involved in international drug smuggling (although most responsibility for this lay with the global networks), but most of their domestic criminal activity was focused on the distribution and sale of drugs on the streets. For example, one criminal entrepreneur in the study 'Dave Peters' made so much money that he ended up living on the Costa del Sol, from where he ran a shipping business and a chain of clubs throughout Europe. However, he maintained strong contacts with his home town in England and owned a warehouse which he distributed stolen goods from. His operations were glocal in the sense that he was dependent on global networks to transport his drugs overland from Turkey to Britain, but he also depended on localised British networks to distribute his drugs across the British mainland.

Hobbs and Dunningham conclude that the most successful local criminals who dealt in drugs were immersed in a glocalised system. They maintained international contacts in order to ensure supply, but their main body of business was concerned with local distribution and the defence, using force if necessary, of their control of the local drug market against any competing gangs that might attempt to muscle in.

It is also important to understand that the extent of local crime within a particular society depends on the effectiveness of global crime networks and trade routes. For example, a great deal of domestic crime in Western societies is committed by heroin addicts, who need to consistently 'earn' a particular 'income' on a daily basis in order to maintain their supply and feed their drug habit. Heroin addicts, therefore, have to commit crime on a daily basis in order to maintain their supply. Some police forces in Britain estimate that up to 80 per cent of property crime (for example, theft, street robbery, burglary and shoplifting) in particular cities is committed by a hard core of 100 or so heroin addicts. If the global flow of heroin across a particular route is disrupted by a successful police operation or by conflict between global gangs, the domestic demand for heroin may outstrip the supply, therefore forcing the price of heroin to rise. Such price rises are likely to result in an increase in domestic crime as heroin addicts step up their criminal activities in order to meet the new price.

### Activity

'A great deal of global crime originates in the least economically industrialised countries of the world because such countries are deliberately kept in a state of poverty by Western capitalist interests.' Evaluate this view.

## Feminist perspectives

Michele Burman and Loraine Gelsthorpe (2017) observe that one of the most significant and influential contributions of feminism to criminology has been the generation of extensive research into violence against women, particularly in the context of globalisation. Feminist research has been instrumental in revealing the global nature of violence against women. Examples include research conducted by Aisha Gill et al. (2014) on honour killing in India and by Bulent Diken and Carsten Bagge Laustsen (2005) on the use of rape as a weapon in war. Burman and Gelsthorpe conclude that 'this significant body of scholarship has exposed some of the most prevalent and devastating forms of harmful behaviour committed against women and girls, whilst also broadening and deepening understandings and definitions of what counts as "crime"'.

Cohen and Kennedy (2000) argue that females living in the least economically developed societies are more likely to be exploited, and to be victims of global crimes such as forced prostitution and slavery, than Western women because:

- They are more likely to live in poverty. Diane Pearce (1978) coined the phrase 'the feminisation of poverty' to illustrate that women wherever they are in the world have always experienced more poverty than men.
- They are less likely to be well-educated.
- They do not enjoy the freedom of movement experienced by males, because they are likely to be restricted to the domestic sphere of the home and family.
- Patriarchal social relations (which often originate in religious, cultural and family traditions) reduce their freedom to make their own choices and consequently result in vulnerability and dependency on men.
- They are likely to lack political power and influence.

Feminists who have examined the experience of women in the less economically developed world have suggested that feminist priorities in this world are justifiably very different to those of feminists in the West, who see patriarchy as the cause of all their problems. However, for women in LEDCs, patriarchy is just one aspect of inequality that has to be confronted alongside other injustices that they experience on a daily basis.

## Activity

*Women demonstrating for women's and Dalit (untouchable) rights in Bangalore, India.*

What other 'injustices', in addition to those related to patriarchy, do you think females might experience in the less industrialised world? Think about issues such as ethnicity, caste and age.

Burman and Gelsthorpe argue that feminist analysis is increasingly focusing on the relationship between inequalities, powerlessness, victimisation and justice in a global context. For example, they observe that past studies of human trafficking have tended to take a malestream approach and consequently have downplayed the role of women as human traffickers. However, the United Nations Office on Drugs and Crime (UNODC) estimates, that nearly 30 per cent of traffickers are female and that half of all detected trafficking victims are female, and that the number of victims who are young girls is on the increase.

Feminist research has drawn attention to the difficulty in distinguishing between female offenders and victims of global crime. For example, Liz Hales and Gelsthorpe (2012) found that the number of foreign women in British prisons doubled between 1999 and 2009. Their research found female prisoners who were migrants from countries such as Nigeria and Vietnam. Most have been imprisoned for crimes relating to theft, drugs or false documentation. However, when Hales and Gelsthorpe interviewed these migrant women, they argued that the authorities blurred the distinction between 'criminal' and 'victim'. Many of the women had actually been held captive in slavery-like conditions, forced to work as prostitutes or in drug factories – sometimes for years. Furthermore, some had been systematically raped and beaten and their passports withheld by criminal gangs. Similar research by Maria De Angelis (2016) found that if women cooperated with the traffickers in order to avoid violence, this was often seen by official agencies such as the police as criminal collaboration and consequently they were no longer looked upon as victims.

Thanh-Dam Truong (2015) argues that there are competing feminist interpretations of human trafficking. Global feminism views human trafficking as a form of male violence against women which is reflective of a universal patriarchal oppression. In contrast, international feminism emphasises the political differences between nation-states and suggests that patriarchy takes a particular form depending on the specific cultural context of each nation-state. In other words, the patriarchy experienced by women in Myanmar may differ from that experienced in Vietnam because the cultures of these two countries differ. Intersectional feminism argues that patriarchy is only one social factor that exists alongside other important sources of inequality and oppression, such as age, family, nationality, regional and tribal identity, and socio-economic factors such as wealth and poverty. Feminists today are, therefore, likely to see patriarchal culture as only one of many negative influences on the experience of women that might lead to them being trafficked across borders into prostitution. Moreover, research by Laura Augustin (2007) suggests that not all young migrant women who are trafficked for sex purposes should be seen as victims, because her research found this categorisation was not shared by all the women who took part in her research. In other words, feminists such as Augustin argue that criminologists must examine the motives of the so-called migrant 'victims' themselves, who may view 'trafficking' as a 'necessary evil' in order to support the families or children they have left behind.

## Activity

On the basis of these studies, what is the problem with assuming that most global criminality is committed by males?

Other feminists have asked other important questions to illustrate the simplicity of categorising women as either 'offender' or 'victims', such as:

- Are the women who become perpetrators of human trafficking one-time victims?
- Are women subjected to duress or blackmail when participating in trafficking?

Saskia Sassen (2003) argues that feminism needs to examine the 'trafficking–migration' relationship. She has suggested that women's experience of human trafficking is best understood in the context of a 'feminisation of survival'. She argues that households and sometimes whole communities are often dependent on the labour and remittances of migrant women who have been trafficked for sex or domestic labour.

## Contemporary issues: Karl Thompson: Globalisation and modern slavery

Thompson (2017) observes that a good deal of contemporary feminism focuses on how the global sex industry now constitutes a modern form of slavery.

One of the main contributing factors to the increase in human trafficking is the widespread oppression of women in their countries of origin. Often females who belong to minority groups or who are members of lower socio-economic groups or castes are more vulnerable to trafficking, because these females are subjected to male controls. For example, in Thailand, UNODC has documented the sale by fathers of female children to gangs involved in organising sex tourism. Females are powerless to resist because traditional culture, particularly religious value systems, ascribe subordinate characteristics to them and place males in positions of authority. Moreover, the breakdown of society and the rule of law in regions characterised by armed conflict often results in displaced females becoming vulnerable to promises made by human traffickers of a better life in the West.

Feminist research has found that many women in poor societies are often lured into slavery by organised global gangs that promise them legitimate employment as maids, nannies or secretaries in Western Europe or the USA. Upon arrival, these women are often subjected to violence or the threat of it and told they have to work out a 'debt', supposedly based on the cost of their illegal transportation. The gangs often take away their official documentation such as passports, keep the women under lock and key, and force them into prostitution. If they do manage to escape captivity, they are unlikely to inform the authorities, because they either fear deportation back to their country of origin or because they fear for the safety of their families back home.

Radical feminists such as Sassen point out that physical violence against women and their female children condoned by traditional cultures poses a significant threat to the health and safety of migrant women and their female children, even after they have settled in a receiving society. In 2013, the WHO sponsored the first widespread study of global data on violence against women, and found that it constitutes a global health problem of epidemic proportions and that intimate partner violence is the most common form of global violence against women. There is also evidence that global migration has been accompanied by the importation of attitudes and practices that continue to subject migrant women and their female children to cruel, inhumane and degrading treatment such as domestic violence, female genital mutilation, honour killings and **infanticide**.

Source: adapted from https://revisesociology.com/2017/04/10/radical-feminism-globalization-gender-development/.

### Questions

1. Why can human trafficking be described as a modern form of slavery?
2. What sorts of degrading treatment might female migrants and their female children be subjected to even after they have settled in another country?

## Beck and risk society

One of the most influential theoretical approaches to understanding green crime is provided by the sociologist Beck and his idea of *Risk Society* (1992). Beck suggested that economic growth in more affluent countries has meant that the risks which result from a lack of resources (such as the risk of poverty) have declined, and science and technology have allowed humans to overcome many risks from the natural environment. For example, physical defences can provide against floods. However, human activity has created new risks such as the risks of nuclear contamination, toxins in the environment and environmental damage caused by pollution of various types. Many of these risks result from economic growth – for example, the way that growth has led to the increased use of motor cars. In the past, lower social classes tend to be most at risk from misfortunes, but many of the risks created by humans affect all social groups equally. For example, all classes are affected by a nuclear disaster. In *World at Risk* (2009), Beck suggested that there is more global awareness of the risks with increased publicity. Beck saw the harm done to the environment as integral to the development of **late-modern society**, in which humans attempt to control the world through the use of science and technology. The problem is that, in solving one set of problems, humans often create other problems. For example, nuclear energy could be used to counteract climate change, but it creates the risk of nuclear disaster (such as that at Chernobyl) as well as the problem of the disposal of nuclear waste.

Beck has been criticised for suggesting that all classes are equally vulnerable to human-made risks. For example, Philip Sutton (2015) points out that richer people can afford to live in parts of the world which are least affected by environmental damage. However, Sutton praises Beck for highlighting some of the environmental harm which comes from the legal use of technology.

### Key terms

**Criminogenic** Something, usually an environment or value system, that causes crime or encourages criminal behaviour. Marxists believe that capitalism does this.

**Alienation** Feeling unconnected or separated from the people around you or the work that you do.

**Deforestation** The action of clearing a wide area of trees.

**Water table** The level below ground that is saturated with water and often the origin of the supply of fresh drinking water.

**Carcinogenic** Cancer-causing.

**Kleptocracy** Corrupt leaders that use their power to exploit the people and natural resources of their own territory in order to extend their personal wealth and political powers.

**Deregulation** The removal of regulations or legal restrictions.

**Shell company** A company or corporation that exists only on paper and has no office or employees. It may have a bank account in which laundered money may be deposited.

**Infanticide** The killing of babies, usually at birth.

**Late-modern society** A term used by Giddens to describe global societies which he sees as exhibiting features that indicate a continuation of modernity rather than constituting a new type of postmodern society.

### Summary

1. Marxists believe that global criminality is caused by the criminogenic conditions and values of capitalism.
2. Poverty in the LEDCs is partly caused by neo-colonialism.
3. Poverty, in particular, is a major reason why people in LEDCs are motivated to grow and distribute illegal crops.
4. The Western market for the drugs produced by global drug gangs is dominated by those who have been most affected by Western multinationals' decision to transfer their manufacturing operations to the developing world – the urban poor, the long-term unemployed and the never-employed unemployed.
5. Feminists argue that global criminality, particularly human trafficking into the global sex industry, often involves the exploitation of females.
6. However, some feminists claim that it is too simple to view women who have been trafficked as victims.

# Unit 8.6.3 Policing and prosecuting global crime

Many of the challenges facing the nation-state today are no longer local or regional in nature because globalisation has produced transnational problems such as undocumented mass migration, environmental degradation, terrorism and armed conflict, which have produced in their wake a range of global crimes. Some of these crimes are the product of organised criminal gangs or cartels, whose members, in terms of drug and sex trafficking, the smuggling of counterfeit goods and money laundering, simply behave as if territorial laws and borders do not exist. Other crimes, especially environmental crimes, are committed by TNCs whose economic power and therefore influence is often greater than the countries in which they operate. In addition to green crime, such corporations may openly flaunt localised laws relating to working conditions in their factories, health and safety and financial and tax regulations.

All of these global crimes have produced a new challenge for both sociologists and the nation-state. Sociologists are interested in how nation-states seek to adapt their local forms of social control and punishment to address globally produced problems.

## Policing global crime

Katja Franko (2017) observes that, throughout much of their history, 'criminal justice and criminal law have been inherently territorial and tied to individual nation-states'. Consequently, policing and justice have traditionally focused on disputes between domestic citizens. However, the emergence of global crime has challenged the ability of the nation-state to protect its citizens and to ensure that justice is served if citizens fall victim to global criminality. Moreover, it can no longer be assumed that criminals who are caught and put on trial are the citizens of the prosecuting state. For example, the number of foreign prisoners in most Western European countries is well above 20 per cent. In Switzerland, it is 73.8 per cent and it is 60.4 per cent in Greece. As Franko argues, 'contemporary penal regimes process not only nationally marginalized populations, but increasingly also populations of what might be termed global outcasts'.

However, Franko argues that it should not be assumed that nation-states are impotent when it comes to dealing with global criminals. She points out that, although it may look like mafias and organised crime groups operate seamlessly across national borders and have a trans-border reach, they are still heavily embedded in local contexts and are therefore subject to local policing and justice.

With regard to the fact that these organised criminal gangs operate transnationally, 192 nation-states have formed Interpol. This is an international criminal police organisation which has been set up to facilitate cooperation between national police forces. It is mainly tasked with assisting the law enforcement agencies of individual nation-states in combating all forms of transnational crime and terrorism and providing those nation-states with the information and evidence necessary to secure successful prosecution of global criminals within their own borders. Interpol does not actually employ its own police officers with powers of arrest. Rather, it coordinates with the police in particular nation-states and all investigations and arrests are carried out by the police officers of the nation-state in which the criminal resides in accordance with their national laws. Additionally, although Interpol does not issue arrest warrants, a member country may request Interpol to issue a Red Notice (an international alert for a wanted person) on the basis of a valid national arrest warrant, but the arrest itself is carried out by the regular police of the nation-state.

However, Interpol has been criticised for allowing itself to be used for political purposes, because some authoritarian regimes have used it to issue Red Notices to track down political opponents and dissidents that have fled abroad in fear of their lives. For example, in 2013, the Russian secret service – the FSB – demanded that Interpol issue a Red Notice to help locate Bill Browder – an American businessman very critical of President Putin – so that he could be arrested and extradited. Chandima Withanaarachchi, a Sri Lankan blogger who exposes government corruption and human rights abuses, is also the subject of an Interpol Red Notice.

Interpol's ability to assist with the arrest of criminals is sometimes obstructed by nation-states that refuse to cooperate. For example, Julian Assange, the founder of WikiLeaks, an international non-profit organisation that has published secret CIA files, was accused in 2010 of rape by the Swedish authorities. In 2012, Assange took refuge in the Ecuadorian

Embassy in London, where he remains at the time of writing, because he suspects that the rape allegation is a contrived excuse to extradite him to the USA on espionage charges. Similarly, the CIA **whistle-blower** Edward Snowden sought asylum in Russia after the FBI issued a Red Notice for his arrest on charges of treason after he revealed that the CIA was collecting personal information on millions of innocent American citizens without any probable cause or search warrant.

## Activity

*Julian Assange on the balcony of the Ecuadorian Embassy in London, where he claims asylum.*

Research whether your national police force has recently worked with Interpol or other national police forces.

In addition to Interpol, in 1998 the EU founded Europol, which is tasked with promoting cooperation between the police forces of member states. Europol mainly acts as an intelligence agency in the fight against international crime, particularly drug trafficking, sex trafficking, modern slavery, cyber-crime, counterfeiting and terrorism. However, it is also capable of gathering information on crime beyond Europe, because it has entered into several international agreements with police forces across the world, such as the FBI in the USA. Like Interpol, Europol and its officials do not have executive powers. This means that they do not have powers of arrest and cannot carry out investigations without the approval of national police forces. In contrast to Interpol, Europol is politically accountable and dependent for its budget on the EU's Justice and Home Affairs Council (JHA).

In addition to being involved in networks such as Interpol and Europol, national police forces may enter into voluntary pacts with other national police forces to target specific global problems. For example, in 2015, police officers in Oslo, Norway, cooperated with their Romanian counterparts in efforts to control the migration associated with sex trafficking.

## Global crime and state sovereignty

Many critics of globalisation are concerned that it erodes state power and consequently that the setting up of transnational organisations to fight global crime contributes to the decline of the nation-state. However, Peter Andreas (2015) argues that global crime, especially the smuggling of cocaine across the Mexican-American border by the narco-cartels, has actually empowered the American state and policing agencies such as the CIA, FBI, the Drugs Enforcement Agency (DEA), Immigration, Customs Enforcement (ICE) and the Alcohol, Tobacco, Firearms and Explosives bureau (ATF). These agents of the American state have had millions of dollars pumped into them and their powers increased in order to slow down the flow of illegal immigrants and narcotics over the border from Mexico into the USA.

## Corporate crime

It is a fact that criminal justice systems, wherever they are located in the world, spend most of their time and energy prosecuting criminals who come from marginalised social backgrounds and who have committed conventional crimes such as murder, robbery and theft. It is a universal trend that rich and powerful individuals and corporations are rarely prosecuted and criminalised for those crimes committed by TNCs as part of their quest for profits. There are a number of reasons for this:

- Many TNCs are economically more powerful than some nation-states and can 'threaten' to withdraw their much-needed investment if the authorities threaten them with prosecution.
- Many TNCs and wealthy individuals can 'buy' their way out of trouble by corrupting local officials such as civil servants, police officers and judges with bribes.
- Marxists argue that the law in many nation-states is socially constructed in an ambiguous way when it comes to the activities of TNCs, so that if they behave in ways that cause harm, their offences are categorised as 'civil' rather than 'criminal'. Consequently, state agencies with limited powers

are responsible for dealing with such offences rather than the criminal justice system. Such agencies may have the power to fine corporations but they do not have the power to send corporate executives to prison. It is rare in most countries (although the USA has made progress in this area in recent years) for corporate executives to be prosecuted and imprisoned for, say, corporate manslaughter or environmental destruction.

- Even if corporations are pursued by the criminal justice system, local police forces are often handicapped by lack of funding, manpower and expertise. Corporate crime by its very nature can involve intricate and often impenetrable practices which ordinary people (who sit on juries) are unlikely to understand. Furthermore, the police themselves often lack the type of experts required to understand the intricacies of corporate crime – for example, specialists in **forensic accounting** or computer hacking who can track the trail of money that may be involved in illegal tax evasion, money laundering or the financing of terrorism.
- There is some evidence that official investigations into corporate crime can also face political interference. In 2007, British Aerospace Systems (BAE) paid bribes totalling £1 billion to a Saudi prince to ensure an arms contract with Saudi Arabia. However, this corruption went unprosecuted because the British government decided that 'the wider public interest' outweighed the need to maintain the rule of law. According to a *Guardian* newspaper investigation, prosecutors in the UK were told to abandon the proposed prosecution of both British and Saudi businessmen because this would cause serious damage to UK/Saudi security, intelligence and diplomatic cooperation. In 2010, BAE accepted guilt and agreed to pay civil penalties of $400 million in the USA and £30 million in the UK to settle corruption allegations against it relating to Tanzania and Saudi Arabia. However, the Campaign Against Arms Trade expressed disappointment that nobody was prosecuted in the criminal courts for these offences.

### Activity

'Global crime is weakening the nation-state.' Evaluate this view.

Western governments claim to be keen to be cracking down on corporate crime and especially tax-dodging. In 2014, they agreed on the Common Reporting Standard (CRS). This means that many rich countries now automatically swap information about assets belonging to each other's residents in their banks. It has had some success. For example, it has decimated some ancient European tax havens, such as Switzerland and Jersey. However, Bullough (2018) argues that there are gaping holes in the CRS because it does nothing for most poor countries because rich countries do not share information with them. Furthermore, the USA regularly demands information on Americans who bank abroad yet refuses to divulge the equivalent information on foreigners who bank in the US. Bullough argues that the USA has bullied the rest of the world into scrapping financial secrecy but has not applied the same standards to itself.

## Environmental crimes

Paddy Hillyard and Steve Tombs (2017) argue that many criminologists have long recognised and struggled with the inherent limitations of state-based definitions of crime, which are often criticised as 'artificial'. Rob White (2014), for example, argues that, if a particular action 'harms' the physical environment and the human and other living creatures within it, it should be defined as 'criminal' even if no law has been broken. White's approach is sometimes referred to as '**transgressive criminology**' because it oversteps or transgresses the boundaries of traditional criminology.

However, one of the biggest problems with regard to the policing and enforcement of 'offences' associated with environmental destruction or degradation is that there are no international laws or global agencies with the power to pursue so-called green criminals, whether these are individuals, TNCs or nation-states. Most laws relating to environmental harms are local. These can be ignored by powerful economic organisations such as transnationals. Local officials and politicians can be bribed by powerful interests so that they turn a 'blind eye' to the violation of such local laws.

Another problem is that international agreements made at international conferences about the state of the global environment, and which set targets on carbon emissions, climate change and so on – such as Kyoto (1997), Paris (2016) and Chatham House (2018) – are voluntary and not legally binding. Countries can ignore such agreements or withdraw from them. The USA, for example, has made it very clear that it does not intend to abide by the Paris protocols.

White believes that local laws and, therefore, definitions of crime are both insufficient and ineffective for dealing with environmental harms for two reasons:

- Threats to the environment are increasingly global rather than local in nature. For example, environmental disasters such as Chernobyl do not respect international borders – a problem created in one locality can have significant global effects.
- These global harms are often the result of global interests such as TNCs rather than local institutions who only have their own economic interests at heart.

White is very critical of nation-states such as China and the USA as well as transnational capitalist corporations which take an '**anthropocentric**' view of environmental harms. This means that they see such harms as a necessary part of human progress, profitability, economic growth and the highly materialist lifestyles that their citizens demand. Consequently, these nation-states and TNCs use their considerable power to make sure that environmental harms are not taken seriously or defined as unacceptable. They block all attempts to introduce international laws aimed at minimising environmental harm or at punishing those responsible for such harms.

White argues that an anthropocentric view of the environment should be abandoned in favour of an '**eco-centric**' view of environmental harms that highlights the inter-dependent relationship that exists between humans and their environment or eco-system. From this perspective, environmental harm will eventually lead to major harm to humankind. In the long term, these environmental harms have the potential to lead to the extinction of the human race if they are not addressed by punishing those responsible.

Hillyard and Tombs observe the emergence of a new sociological discipline known as **zemiology** (which originates from the Greek word for 'harm', *zemia*). Zemiology focuses on social harms which may not be technically illegal according to local or international laws but which nevertheless are harmful in the long term to the survival of humanity and the planet. Zemiologists believe that all actions, and especially those relating to the environment, should be judged entirely in terms of harm rather than in terms of law.

The emergence of this zemiological approach is extremely important because nation-states cannot agree on what should constitute green crime. International law is inadequate – most agreements on carbon emissions and climate change are voluntary. There is no agreement on what sanctions can be enforced if a country refuses or fails to abide by these agreements. There is no global agency that has the power to police green crime. Governments, especially in the developing world, are generally reluctant to rein in the harms done by global corporations because they are too dependent on the income generated from them in the form of taxation.

Reece Walters (2010) argues that it is useful to use the term 'eco-crime' (rather than 'environmental crime' or 'green crime') to identify actions or omissions which threaten long-term sustainability of life on earth or even the extinction of human and nonhuman life. They are essentially crimes against nature rather than just crimes against individual humans or other species. However, Walters also includes actions in the category of eco-crime which harm the well-being of humans or other species without threatening long-term sustainability. These types of offence may cause illness, pain, suffering, poverty or shorter life expectancy to humans, or damage other species (including plants as well as animals).

### Activity

*Oil spill clean-up.*

'Green crime should be defined as any deliberate harm to the natural environment and the creatures that live within it.' Evaluate this view.

## Conclusions

Global crime faces a number of problems in terms of policing and prosecution. The first problem is detection. Global crime differs from crime committed in local vicinities. Victims of local crimes tend to know that they have been assaulted, burgled or stolen from. As Hazell Croall (2011) notes, domestic crime usually involves 'blood on the streets'. Victims feel victimised and can consequently report that experience to their local police force, who can usually quite easily identify which law has been broken. In contrast, the victims of global crime are not so visible for a number of reasons. For example, other law-abiding citizens may not agree that heroin addicts or members of gangs killed in territorial disputes over drug dealing are victims. Moreover, many victims of global crimes such as counterfeiting or computer identity theft are unlikely to realise that they are victims. Similarly, financial or environmental crimes committed by TNCs or corrupt politicians and state officials have indirect victims rather than direct victims. For example, a worker may have to pay a greater proportion of their wages in tax because wealthy individuals and companies are engaged in legal or illegal tax avoidance/evasion. People are generally unaware that the air they breathe or that the water they drink may be polluted in some way. However, ordinary workers and citizens are unlikely to know this, because both TNCs and governments have the power and ability to conceal their crimes and so evade police attention and prosecution. For example, oil companies may fund research that argues convincingly against the idea that climate change is occurring. In summary, there is a hidden iceberg of global crime – it is difficult to estimate precisely how much of it exists. This, of course, also means that there is no accurate way of estimating the true value of such crime. Sociologists working in this field are over-reliant on secondary official sources such as Interpol and Europol, which may exaggerate the problem in order to justify extra funding.

The second problem is that, even if such crimes are detected, domestic police forces lack the resources – funding and specialised expertise – to investigate global crime. Moreover, governments often put pressure on local police forces to drop investigations into powerful interests such as other governments or wealthy corporations. Third, the power of those who commit global crimes and their primary commitment to profit means that they feel that they can neglect or even ignore compliance with local laws, unlike the bulk of ordinary citizens. Fourth, the lack of any comprehensive system of international law governing the wide range of global crimes and potential environmental harms that exist serves to weaken the attempts by local law agencies to deal with crimes that often go well beyond their borders. Finally, both the UN and the EU have failed to support local law enforcement in that both Europol and Interpol are fairly toothless bodies. Moreover, there is also a need for an International Criminal Court (ICC) organised along the lines of the current ICC (which only deals with war crimes) that has the power to extradite and prosecute those who run international criminal cartels, global corporations and the corrupt politicians and bureaucrats involved in the complex business of global crime.

## Key terms

**Whistle-blower** A person who informs on a person or organisation regarded as engaging in an unlawful or immoral activity.

**Forensic accounting** The use of accounting skills to investigate fraud or embezzlement and to analyse financial information for use in legal proceedings.

**Transgressive criminology** Criminologists who are interested in a broader definition of crime – activities that cause harm – rather than strictly activities that are against the law.

**Anthropocentric** Regarding humankind as the central or most important element of existence, especially as opposed to God or animals.

**Eco-centric** The view or belief that the rights and needs of humans are not more important than those of other living things.

**Zemiology** The study of social harms.

## Summary

1. Global crimes are mainly prosecuted by national police forces because, although global criminal networks operate across national borders, a great deal of their criminal activity is carried out within localised contexts.
2. The pursuit of global criminals by state police forces is supported by transnational non-government policing organisations such as Interpol and Europol.
3. Corporate crime is probably under-reported and less likely to be prosecuted compared with crime committed by ordinary individuals. This is because corporations wield great economic power that often enables them to avoid prosecution.
4. Corporate crimes are frequently categorised as civil rather than criminal offences and are immensely complex to understand.

5. Many harms done to the environment are not technically crimes or covered by international law. Criminologists who specialise in green crime argue that, if something is harmful to humanity or the eco-system in which humans and other forms of life live, it should be defined as criminal.

# END-OF-PART QUESTIONS

0 1 Describe two types of global crime carried out by transnational corporations. **[4 marks]**

0 2 Explain one strength and one limitation of using international laws to police environmental crime. **[6 marks]**

0 3 Explain two reasons why Marxists claim that global crime is criminogenic. **[8 marks]**

# EXAM-STYLE PRACTICE QUESTIONS

0 1 'Globalisation has led to cultural convergence.' Evaluate this view. **[35 marks]**

0 2 'Dependency theory exaggerates the influence of industrialised countries in the development process.' Evaluate this view. **[35 marks]**

# 9 PREPARING FOR EXAMINATIONS

In this chapter, you will explore a range of sample responses to the exam-style practice questions included at the end of Chapters 2 to 8 of this book. These responses and the activities around them are designed to help you to reflect upon and improve your own writing.

Exam-style questions and sample answers have been written by the authors. References to assessment and/or assessment preparation are the publisher's interpretation of the syllabus requirements and may not fully reflect the approach of Cambridge Assessment International Education. Cambridge International recommends that teachers consider using a range of teaching and learning resources in preparing learners for assessment, based on their own professional judgement of their students' needs.

# Socialisation and identity

To make the best use of this section, you should have already completed your own responses to the exam-style questions at the end of Chapter 2. Now look at the sample responses to Q1–4 below. As you read the shorter responses and the supporting comments, decide what mark your own response(s) deserve. Identify anything you could do to improve your responses. As you read the longer responses and the supporting comments, decide whether your own response is closer to the level of the 'competent' answer or the 'strong' answer. Identify any ways in which your own response could be improved, using the commentaries on the sample responses as guidance.

0 1 Describe two factors that might influence a person's social identity. **[4 marks]**

**Response**

*Social class may influence a person's social identity. This can be the social class that a person is born into, their attitudes and their wealth or income. These affect the way that a person sees themselves as well as the way others see them. It has an important influence on their life chances and the consumer goods they can afford to purchase as a way of expressing their identity.*

*Gender can influence a person's social identity. Socially constructed ideas about what it means to be a man or a woman vary from culture to culture but patriarchal ideology is universal, which means that men generally have more power in society compared to women. Gender can influence which roles people play and the choices available to them.*

## Comments

Two relevant factors (social class and gender) are identified for 2 marks; the way that each factor may influence a person's social identity is described accurately for a further 2 marks.

**Mark 4/4**

0 2a Explain two reasons why people usually conform to social expectations. **[8 marks]**

**Response**

1. *People usually conform to social expectations due to positive sanctions that are used by agencies of control to reward and reinforce the conformity of individuals who accept that complying with the rules brings about a social exchange that benefits themselves and their community. For example, conformity and working hard usually results in a pay rise and the opportunity thereby to have a better lifestyle in material terms.*
2. *Another reason people conform to social expectations is that social control agencies can also use negative sanctions or punishments. For example, if you do not conform to laws, you may be sent to prison.*

## Comments

Two reasons why people usually conform to social expectations are identified (2 marks). The first reason is explained and uses appropriate sociological material to support the answer and to show with the example of a pay rise why rewards might encourage a person to conform to social expectations. The second reason is less well developed and lacks reference to sociological material that explains why a punishment such as going to prison might encourage a person to conform to social expectations. For example, the answer might have referred to the loss of status and the stigma of going to prison as a relevant sociological explanation for why the threat of this particular punishment might encourage conformity.

**Mark 6/8**

**0 2b** Explain one strength and one limitation of the view that individual behaviour is shaped by the social structure. **[6 marks]**

## Response

*The view that individual behaviour is shaped by the social structure helps us to understand social conformity. Both functionalist and Marxist theory supports this view. Functionalists claim that institutions such as the family and education work together to ensure that young people are taught the norms and values on which the social structure is based. Marxist sociologists also see social structure dominating individual behaviour, though they argue that it is the requirements of the economic system specifically that exercise this controlling influence over people's thoughts and actions. The idea that individual behaviour is determined by the social structure is a strength because it helps us to understand why there are often similarities in the way individuals behave and why social interaction mostly takes place in an orderly way rather than being chaotic.*

*One limitation of this view is that it tries to explain conformity and non-conformity entirely in terms of the influence of social structure. The fact that people mostly accept social norms and values is seen as evidence that the institutions underpinning the social structure have been effective in shaping individual behaviour. Likewise, people who act contrary to social expectations are seen as lacking adequate exposure to these institutional influences (not attending school, for example). This is a limitation in the argument that individual behaviour is shaped by the social structure, as people may actively choose to reject social norms and values; their non-conformist behaviour is not necessarily the result of inadequate exposure to institutional influences. Nor should we assume that people who conform to social norms and values do so because they have been taught this is the right thing to do (it may have more to do with self-interest or apathy and/or a sense of being powerless to challenge the status quo, for example).*

### Comments

One acceptable strength is identified (the ability to explain similarities in individual behaviour) for 1 mark; how structures may influence behaviour is explained through reference to the role of the family and education in the socialisation process for the second mark. The final sentence provides a clear reason why the focus on the influence of structure in shaping individual behaviour is a strength and so the third mark is also merited.

One acceptable limitation is identified (the response tries to explain conformity and non-conformity entirely in terms of the influence of social structure) for 1 mark; the way that functionalist theory relies on exposure to institutional influences (socialisation effectively) to explain conformity and non-conformity is demonstrated in the second and third sentence for the second mark. The final sentence provides a clear reason why relying on the concept of social structure to explain individual behaviour is a limitation and so the third mark is also merited.

**Mark 6/6**

**0 3a** 'The role of socialisation in shaping human behaviour has been exaggerated.'

Explain this view. **[10 marks]**

## Competent answer

*Structural theories such as Marxists and Functionalists have been criticised for assuming that the people just accept social forces as a result of socialisation. Interactionists argue that human behaviour is a product of individual interactions and meanings. For example, interactionists claim that crimes are only criminal because we label it that way. Becker argues that actually, people commit deviant acts as part of a bigger process based on*

Although interactionists would add that society provides a menu of meanings from which the individual draws in making sense of the social world. Action is guided by social meanings rather than the individual having free choice in how they behave.

*decisions that a person makes. For example, people do not become criminals overnight, becoming a criminal is a process, and people have individual agency in that process. Once a person commits a crime, they can decide if they are going to commit another crime, or not. If they do commit a crime they may allow the label of criminal to become their master status, which means that is how they see themselves essentially – as a criminal. This is a form of self-fulfilling prophecy, or accepting and living up to the label.*

*The role of socialisation may also have been exaggerated as people behave the way they do due to innate or inborn biological factors. This is known as the nature vs nurture debate. Sociologists argue that people behave the way they do due to social factors, whereas others such as biologists claim that in fact, things like gender roles are connected to our biology. Functionalists claim for example that gender roles in the family are based around women giving birth and men being breadwinners because they do not give birth.*

Good to show awareness of non-sociological explanations for human behaviour in answering the question.

## Comments

The answer rightly uses the interactionist perspective as a way of illustrating how the role of socialisation in shaping human behaviour may have been exaggerated in other (structural) sociological perspectives. However, the interactionist critique of structural theories of socialisation could have been more clearly expressed and is inaccurate in some respects. There is a useful, but brief reference to the nature versus nurture debate.

**Mark 6/10**

### Strong answer

*All sociological theories assume that society is overwhelmingly the main influence on human behaviour. For structural theories (functionalism, Marxism), the socialisation process more or less ensures that people conform to social norms and values. Interactionists allow more scope for free will and personal choice in understanding human behaviour, though in this perspective it is still the process of interacting with each other in society (socialisation) that provides the main context for understanding how people act and think.*

*However, the importance of nature as an influence on human behaviour may have been underestimated in these sociological accounts. Sociobiologists such as Morris (1968) argue that it is not socialisation that shapes behaviour, rather it is biology that shapes human behaviour, due to the fact that sharing culture is based on the innate or genetic need to continue the life of the social group over time. They claim that human biology and behaviour are permanently linked. One example of this argument comes from the sociobiologists Lionel Tiger and Robin Fox, who argued that gender roles were biologically determined and as a result, any attempt to interfere with what they saw as the 'fixed' nature of masculine and feminine behaviour, was bound to end in failure. For example, they would argue this is why girls choose 'female' subjects at school such as Health and Social Care, which are an extension of the caregiving maternal role, while boys opt for typically 'male' subjects such as science and maths. Furthermore, some neuroscientists and psychologists such as Baron-Cohen argue that the female brain is genetically hard-wired for empathy while the male brain is hard-wired for understanding and building systems. This all suggests that sociological arguments that socialisation shapes human behaviour are problematic and exaggerated.*

A useful conclusion that is well supported by the preceding analysis.

## Comments

This answer provides a sustained account of arguments from sociobiologists and psychologists questioning the importance of socialisation in explaining human behaviour. Different contributors to the debate are mentioned and their ideas are accurately and succinctly described.

**Mark 10/10**

0 3b 'The role of socialisation in shaping human behaviour has been exaggerated.'

Using sociological material, give one argument against this view. **[6 marks]**

**Response**

*The functionalist Durkheim argues that socialisation is essential in shaping human behaviour. He carried out research into suicide rates using a comparative experiment. He argues that suicide rates differ in different societies because social forces control people's behaviour, not biological, innate factors. In fact he claims that the more integrated people are by things like religion (an agency of socialisation), the less likely they are to commit suicide. Durkheim claimed that his research proves that social forces are essential in shaping people's behaviour, rather than individual psychological or biological reasons for committing suicide.*

Good use of an example of socialisation to support the argument that is presented.

## Comments

This answer makes good use of Durkheim's own attempt to prove that socialisation is a key factor in shaping human behaviour. The relevance of Durkheim's study of suicide in this respect is made very clear in the answer.

**Mark 6/6**

**0 4** Evaluate the view that social control serves the interests of the ruling class. **[26 marks]**

## Competent answer

*Marxists take the view that social control is negative and increases the gap between the rich and the poor in society. The working class are socially controlled by feeling the system is fair rather than really understanding how much they are being exploited. The ruling class are led to believe that they are in control and they use their views to rule over the working class. The ruling class create the rules, laws and control people's behaviour. Althusser argues that social control takes two forms in capitalist society, repressive state apparatus which involves the police and the use of force, and then ideological state apparatus which is the way the working class are encouraged to 'love the system' rather than challenge it. Marxists argue that because of this social control, people will not speak to each other and realise how oppressed they are and this prevents a revolution happening. Marxists believe that the only way for society to be run more fairly is through communist society.*

*Functionalists argue that social control is a positive thing. They claim that social control makes sure that people are properly integrated into society's norms and values. Durkheim argues that if social control is not occurring then anomie will appear, which is a state of confusion where people do not know what the difference between right and wrong is.*

This paragraph lacks a clear explanation of how the functionalist view differs from the Marxist view; the differences are left somewhat implicit.

*Feminists argue that social control serves the interests of men not capitalism. Feminists such as Oakley show how in the family, men continue to expect women to take on a 'dual burden' which means that even though they work, they also have to keep doing the housework and that they do this because they are socially controlled.*

*Interactionists argue that actually social control is not happening and that people chose to behave the way they do through individual choice. They believe that people attach meanings to behaviour and decide for themselves how to behave rather than being socially controlled through social structures.*

This statement exaggerates the extent to which interactionists believe that people are free to choose how they behave.

*In conclusion, social control does operate to maintain the interests of capitalism, as there are massive inequalities in society, with the rich getting richer and the poor growing poorer. However feminists are right to say that actually women are far more socially controlled than men.*

### Comments

The response includes some useful contrasts between the Marxist theory of social control and other sociological perspectives on the subject, including the functionalists, feminists and interactionists. However, the assessment relies on general views about the nature of social control rather than focusing specifically on the issue of whether social control serves the interests of the ruling class.

**Mark 15/26**

### Strong answer

*According to Sailsbury (2018) there are structural and agency-based explanations of social control. Structural theorists claim that there are social forces which act on people and encourage them to behave in particular ways. Marxists claim that social control is linked to the perpetuation of the capitalist system; functionalists claim that social control plays a much more positive role in maintaining society. Interpretivists on the other hand, disagree and argue that people have individual agency and that social control is not so important. This essay will explore a range of ways that social control works according to different perspectives.*

*As suggested above, the macro, conflict, structural theory of Marxism emerged in response to emergence of capitalism which is a society where there are two socioeconomic classes known as the bourgeoisie who own the means of production (factories etc.) and the working class who are exploited by the bourgeoisie for their wage labour in order to make profit. So social control is about keeping the rich, rich and the poor, poor. This results in a conflict between the two social classes. Marxists such as Althusser claim that the ruling class need to use Repressive state apparatus such as the police as well as Ideological state apparatus such as the ideas in the family of 'love' and 'support' to prevent the working class from questioning the full extent of their exploitation. The working class are blind to their oppression and social control, which is known as false class consciousness. Marxists such as Gramsci say that the bourgeoisie also socially control the working class through imposing ruling class ideas onto the proletariat – known as hegemony. In fact, not all working class people feel oppressed or socially controlled and there are opportunities for social mobility in some cases. However, as the top wealthiest 5% own 80% of all wealth in the UK, it would seem that social class really does continue to support capitalism, with its ideology of pursuit of property, greed and profit.*

A balanced, considered assessment of the Marxist theory at the end of the paragraph.

*In some ways similar to Marxists, feminists also offer a conflict structural view of social control, but they are critical of Marxists who they see as ignoring the way women are exploited within a society characterised by patriarchal ideology. Radical feminists such as Millet argue that in order for patterns of social control to be changed, massive changes need to occur in society. Liberal feminists such as Somerville claim that progress is being made, both with changes in the law and changes in attitudes. The recent Equal Pay Audit highlights the fact that women continue to be paid significantly less than men which proves that social control of women, by men, or patriarchy, continues to be a real issue in society, even though girls outperform boys in education. Interpretivists such as Weber disagree with the view that social control supports capitalism, as they believe individuals*

There was an opportunity here to consider whether men can be seen as a ruling class, with women as the exploited and oppressed grouping.

*have agency and are not passive. They claim that in fact, individuals to some extent shape their own position in society and that other factors apart from social class may lead them to act in particular ways.*

*In conclusion, social control does appear to support capitalism as there is evidence that huge economic inequalities continue to exist in societies all over the world today. Moreover, the legal system in western societies is largely focused on the protection of private property, which in turn serves the interests of capitalism and the property owning ruling class. Governments rarely take actions that oppose the interests of the rich and powerful; indeed, it can be argued that a lot of government sanctions and controls are designed to support capitalism and the free market economy.*

A well-reasoned conclusion, with a number of points offered to support the main argument that social control appears to support ruling-class interests.

### Comments

The account of the Marxist theory of social control is well constructed with reference to relevant thinkers and concepts. Some attempt is made to assess whether or not social control serves the interests of the ruling class. Different perspectives on the role of social control are also noted, including the feminist view, which is very well summarised.

**Mark 23/26**

| 0 | 5 | Evaluate the view that people are free to choose their social identities today. **[26 marks]**

You might want to answer this question yourself and then use the checklist that follows to review your answer. Compare your work to a partner's. Identify strengths in the answers and also consider how they could be improved.

The following is a list of qualities that would be found in a 'strong' answer:

- Shows understanding of the key terms in the question.
- Identifies the main issues raised by the question.
- Explains the view expressed in the question using relevant sociological concepts, theories and arguments.
- Uses evidence and references to sociological studies to support key points, where appropriate.
- Considers the view expressed in the question from different angles, analysing arguments and evidence for and against.
- Presents the sociological material used (concepts, theories, arguments) in a clear and logical way that is easy to understand.
- Draws conclusions about which arguments and/or evidence in response to the question is most convincing; reasons why those conclusions have been reached should also be given.
- Includes a concluding paragraph that summarises the main arguments and ideas expressed in the answer and, ideally, also contributes a final point that secures the case made in responding to the question.

## Research methods

To make the best use of this section, you should have already completed your own responses to the exam-style questions at the end of Chapter 3. Now look at the sample responses to Q1–4 below. As you read the shorter responses and the supporting comments, decide what mark your own response(s) deserve. Identify anything you could do to improve your responses. As you read the longer responses and the supporting comments, decide whether your own response is closer to the level of the 'competent' answer or the 'strong' answer. Identify any ways in which your own response could be improved, using the commentaries on the sample responses as guidance.

**0 1** Describe two types of sampling method. **[4 marks]**

**Response**

*Snowball sampling: the researcher finds one appropriate person for their study and then gains their trust until that participant recommends other suitable participants. This is often used when there is no sampling frame available e.g. a study on gang members, as there is no publicly-available list of gang members.*

*Random sampling: this is basically 'picking names out of a hat'. The researcher uses a sampling frame, and each person on that list has an equal chance of being chosen.*

## Comments

Two types of sampling method are identified for 2 marks; each sampling method is described accurately for a further 2 marks.

**Mark 4/4**

**0 2a** Explain two reasons why laboratory experiments are rarely used in sociological research. **[8 marks]**

**Response**

1. *Laboratory experiments are not popular with sociologists (especially interpretivists) as they do not create valid data. This means the data are not true and accurate reflections of how people behave in real life. This is because an artificial environment is created when conducting laboratory experiments, and according to interpretivists, people act in response to their perception of their current situation. Therefore this means that participants will not be acting naturally as they're not in a natural environment when participating in a laboratory experiment.*
2. *Laboratory experiments are often not used in sociological research as sociologists are wary of the experimental effect. Laboratory experiments are usually carried out in an overt way, gaining informed consent to ensure it fits ethical guidelines. This means the participants know their behaviour is being recorded and analysed by the experimenter, so they change their behaviour: the Hawthorne Effect. This also reduces the validity of the results.*

## Comments

Two reasons why laboratory experiments are rarely used in sociological research are identified (2 marks). Each reason is explained (2 marks) and appropriate sociological material is used to support each reason (2 marks). The appropriate sociological material supporting the first reason includes the reference to the interpretivist view that 'people act in response to their perception of their current situation'. The second reason is supported with appropriate sociological material through the reference to the need to gain informed consent and follow ethical guidelines; also, the reference to the Hawthorne Effect. The first reason is fully developed, with the final sentence showing how the sociological material used supports the point about laboratory experiments failing to generate valid data. The second reason fails to explain why 'knowing their behaviour is being recorded' might lead the study group to change their behaviour, and for this reason only 3 marks are awarded for the second part of the answer. The first part of the answer is fully developed and gains 4 marks.

**Mark 7/8**

**0 2b** Explain one strength and one limitation of questionnaires. **[6 marks]**

**Response**

*Strength: it is relatively easy to reach a large sample spread across a large geographical area with questionnaires. This is because the method is not face-to-face, like interviews or observation. The researcher simply posts the written questions to as many participants as they wish, anywhere in the world. This means it is cheaper than paying the researcher's travel expenses necessary with other methods, and is often possible to reach a bigger and wider-ranging sample.*

*Limitation: questionnaires often have a low response rate as the researcher is not there in person to encourage people to complete it. They are often seen as 'junk mail' and thrown away. This means the results may not be representative as many of the original sample did not participate: often only people with lots of time on their hands bother to reply (e.g. elderly, retired people), as opposed to busy working people.*

## Comments

One acceptable strength is identified (ability to research a large sample) for 1 mark; the reason why questionnaires are effective in researching a large sample is explained (ease of posting to a large number of participants) for the second mark. However, the answer fails to explain why the ease of researching a large sample might be viewed as a strength. The third mark could have been given had the answer mentioned, for example, the ability to identify social trends reliably, which is more likely to be achieved by using a large and/or wide-ranging sample.

One acceptable limitation is identified (low response rate) for 1 mark; the reason why a questionnaire might have a low response rate is explained (because they may be seen as junk mail) for the second mark. The reason why a low response rate might prove to be a limitation is explained (it might undermine the representativeness of the original sample if only certain types of people reply) for the third mark.

**Mark 5/6**

**0 3a** 'Qualitative research data lack validity.'
Explain this view. **[10 marks]**

## Competent answer

*Qualitative data are information in word-form, whereas quantitative data are information in number-form. Quantitative data come from methods like questionnaires and structured interviews, and some sociologists say this is more reliable than qualitative. Qualitative data are gathered from methods such as observation and unstructured interviews. So qualitative data tend to be more detailed, and are often said to be more valid. However qualitative research data are not always valid as people sometimes lie in interviews. This may be because they're embarrassed. For example, when Barker studied the Unification Church (the Moonies) by carrying out observation, interviews and questionnaires, the sect members might have been embarrassed to admit their real reasons for joining.*

*Also, people may act differently if they know they're being researched. This is called the Hawthorne Effect. This may be because they want to impress the observer, or play up like children in secondary schools often do if they know*

This sentence tells us nothing about the subject of the question, which is qualitative data and the concept of validity; the sentence lacks relevance to the question, therefore.

In this part of the answer, it would have been better to explain what validity means and why qualitative research methods are effective in producing detailed (in-depth) data.

*an adult is watching them. Or they may show off in group interviews, or be shy and not show their real personality. When teachers are observed as part of an inspection they often change their behaviour. Or they may behave differently depending on what the researcher looks like or acts like.*

## Comments

Compared to the 'strong' answer, this answer is less focused. The description of quantitative data in the second sentence lacks relevance to the question and was unnecessary. Qualitative data are correctly linked to methods such as observation and unstructured interviews. However, the point that follows about people sometimes lying in interviews is not specific to unstructured interviews; it could apply to all interviews, including those which are designed to collect quantitative data. The concept of the Hawthorne Effect is explained quite well in the second paragraph, but reference to a relevant study would have helped support this part of the answer.

**Mark 6/10**

### Strong answer

*Research is said to be high in validity if it presents a true and accurate picture of what is being studied. Interpretivists claim that qualitative data are high in validity as they give an in-depth understanding of those being studied. However, there are some reasons why qualitative research methods can result in data lacking in validity.*

*Firstly, there is the issue of how the researcher might affect the participants, leading them to change their behaviour and not showing a true/accurate representation of their normal lives. This is a common disadvantage of carrying out overt observations, and is known as the Hawthorne Effect. For example, when Whyte observed an Italian-American gang in Boston, he was open with Doc (the gang leader and gatekeeper) about his true intentions, and Doc later admitted that he started to think before acting as he was concerned about how Whyte would question it. Therefore Doc was acting differently, and Whyte was not finding out about how Doc behaved normally, so the data were not fully valid.*

Good use of an example from a sociological study to show why the validity of data collected using qualitative research might be questioned.

*There is another issue with qualitative methods like unstructured interviews. In these interviews, the interviewer often spends a long time with the interviewee and builds up a trusting rapport with them. Whilst this might help the participants to feel more comfortable and give more detailed/truthful answers, the researcher may be less objective as they start to feel like a friend to the participant and view them in a very positive light. For example, Oakley spent about 30 hours with each woman in her 'From Here to Maternity' study, and admitted she was not impartial. Also, interviewees may say what they think the interviewer wants to hear (known as socially desirable answers) as they care about what their new 'friend' thinks of them.*

Good use of a relevant sociological term ('socially desirable answers') to demonstrate knowledge of a potential limitation with unstructured interviews that might affect the validity of the data collected.

## Comments

The answer opens with an accurate definition of the term 'validity'. Several reasons why qualitative research data may lack validity are then explored. Good use is made of relevant concepts (Hawthorne Effect, objective, socially desirable answers) in developing the answer. References to studies (Whyte, Oakley) help to support key points. While this answer could be further developed (for example, there was scope to add a few comments about the positivist critique of qualitative research data), it does cover enough relevant points in sufficient detail (concepts, studies, links to methods) to merit a high mark.

**Mark 9/10**

**0 3b** 'Qualitative research data lack validity.'

Using sociological material, give one argument against this view. **[6 marks]**

### Strong answer

*Interpretivists may argue that qualitative data do NOT lack validity because qualitative research methods allow the sociologist to build a good rapport with the participants. For example, participant observation allows the researcher to spend an extended period of time with the group they're studying, and this helps them to gain their trust e.g. James Patrick spent 4 months studying a Glasgow Gang. When a good rapport is built, it usually means that people 'open-up' more, and tell or show the sociologist more about their life. This means that the sociologist is able to build a true and accurate picture of those they're studying, which means the data are high in validity. While there is a danger that the researcher may lose objectivity by becoming too close to the study group, trained sociologists know to guard against this happening and they usually adopt special techniques to help ensure they remain objective throughout the research study.*

## Comments

The answer explains clearly the connection between gaining the trust of participants in qualitative research and the ability to collect data that are high in validity. The potential objection that researchers in participant observation studies may lose objectivity is addressed directly and answered.

**Mark 6/6**

**0 4** Evaluate the use of structured interviews in sociological research. **[26 marks]**

### Competent answer

*Structured interviews are when an interviewer asks a set of questions to someone, in the same way each time. For example, they are often used by market researchers who stop the public on the High Street. This is a good method because it is easy but not all sociologists agree, like those who would prefer valid data.*

*Structured interviews are good because they are cheap and quick as the researcher only has to read out a list of questions and write down the answers. You do not need to have much skill to be able to do that. This means you can have lots of participants. However they are not as cheap or quick as questionnaires. Once a questionnaire is written*

An attempt to define the term 'structured interviews', but the comment 'in the same way each time' is a rather vague description that reveals little about the distinctive features of the structured approach in interviewing.

A useful comparison with another research method, which helps to demonstrate analysis and evaluation skills.

*it can be emailed out to as many people as you want at the touch of a button. Interviews are better than questionnaires though as you actually get to meet the participants. It is necessary to convince people to be interviewed in the first place, but most people would probably be more willing to be asked questions than observed and put into an experiment.*

*Structured interviews can take time to prepare as the questions have to be written in advance, so the preparation is not as easy as unstructured interviews. However, the questions can be simple, closed questions like 'Are you married?'. Observation doesn't need any preparation at all, once you've found a group to study, you just observe them. Questionnaires need some preparation as you have to design the questionnaire. However laboratory experiments take a lot of planning and setting up.*

This is a rather simplistic view of research based on observation; all research methods take some preparation and require a range of skills on the part of the researcher.

*You tend to get lots of data from structured interviews because you can interview a lot of people as each one doesn't take long. This is called a large sample, and the sociologist can try to get people from all backgrounds involved to create results that are representative of society. Interviews are also good because you can try to be friendly to get the participants to trust you: this is called a good rapport. This is one reason why interpretivists like interviews, although they don't really use structured interviews as the questions are too inflexible and interpretivists like to find out lots of detail. This might be why Venkatesh chose to use participant observation instead when he was a 'Gang Leader for a Day'.*

*Overall, structured interviews are useful but do have quite a lot of disadvantages so not all sociologists would use them, and you can't achieve verstehen from them.*

While this is a relevant evaluative point, it needs to be supported with an explanation of what verstehen means and why structured interviews fail to achieve verstehen.

## Comments

Understanding of the term 'structured interviews' is demonstrated in the first paragraph, but the definition lacks detail and could be more precise. The language used is inexact in places. For example, the final sentence of the first paragraph refers to structured interviews being 'a good method because it is easy'; the response needed to explain in what way the method is easy and why this might make it a good method. Some relevant contrasts are drawn with other research methods, such as questionnaires in paragraph two and observation in paragraph three. However, the analysis lacks depth and some sweeping statements are made, such as 'observation doesn't need any preparation at all' and 'interpretivists like to find out lots of detail' (the point here is that positivists may also favour research data that are detailed, albeit 'detailed' in terms of the quantitative data produced). There are some links to relevant concepts, theory and studies in the answer, but not to the same extent as the 'strong' answer.

**Mark 16/26**

## Strong answer

*Structured interviews are when the researcher asks a list of prepared questions (known as an 'interview schedule') to the participants, usually in a face-to-face setting. They're often quite formal and don't allow for much flexibility. It is a common method but has both pros and cons.*

A clear and accurate definition of the term 'structured interviews', demonstrating good knowledge and understanding of the topic.

*Firstly, there is the issue of interviewer bias: when the participant's answers are influenced by the researcher's ethnicity, gender, social class, age, etc. So participants may give socially desirable answers: saying what they think the researcher wants to hear. For example, when Young and Willmott carried out their telephone interviews with working class families in London in the 1950s and 1970s, the wives they spoke to may not have felt able to be honest about how much housework their husbands did. This is because both sociologists were male, so the wives might not have felt comfortable criticising their husbands to another man. However, unstructured interviews are more affected by interviewer bias. This is because in a structured interview, the interviewer simply reads out the questions and records the answers. So it is far less 'chatty' and less friendly than an unstructured interview where the participants may want to please the researcher as they have built up a good relationship with them.*

Good use of a relevant sociological term, which demonstrates interpretation and application skills.

This point demonstrates analysis and evaluation skills in relation to the question.

*Ethically speaking, structured interviews are a good choice. This is because the researcher is there to fully explain the research to the participants, and gain their informed consent. The researcher can also judge body language to know when the questions are too sensitive and stop the interview if it seems to be upsetting them, and give the participants the 'right to withdraw'. Therefore it is better than methods such as covert observation. However, as the questions are fixed, it is not possible to change them to suit the participant. This is why many sociologists choose unstructured interviews instead to research sensitive topics. For example Dobash and Dobash researched 'Violence Against Wives' and would have needed to approach the questioning sensitively to avoid causing further upset to the domestic violence victims who they interviewed. Unstructured interviews are better in this sense as the researcher often spends longer with each participant, building a good rapport, and tailoring the questions to suit each individual participant.*

It is often helpful to consider ethical issues, alongside practical and theoretical issues, when considering the strengths and limitations of a particular research method or approach.

*Positivists would be more likely to use structured interviews than interpretivists, as they should create more reliable data than unstructured interviews. For example, in an interview about religion, the interviewer will ask standardised questions to every participant e.g. 'do you regularly go to a place of worship?'. The researcher can then come up with quantitative results such as '63% of the sample regularly go to a place of worship'. As the yes/no answers are clear-cut and not open to interpretation,*

A good link to a relevant theoretical perspective, again demonstrating interpretation and application skills.

*this means the results would be the same if another researcher carried out the same study, so this makes the results reliable. This is not true of unstructured interviews which tend to use more open questions, and where each interview is different. However, interpretivists would criticise structured interviews for not creating very valid data. This is because the interview schedule restricts both the interviewer and interviewee: the interviewer has to stick to the prepared questions, and the interviewee is usually only asked simple, closed questions, leaving little opportunity to explain themselves. Therefore the answers are superficial and cannot be said to be a full, true explanation of the meanings and motives behind the participants' thoughts and actions, meaning verstehen (true, deep understanding) is not achieved.*

A helpful point in evaluating the use of structured interviews in sociological research, with a good link to the concept of verstehen.

*To conclude, structured interviews are useful in studying relatively large samples, and if the sociologist wishes to create quantitative data. However, there are better methods for sociologists who want to gain a deep understanding. As with all research methods, time and funding permitting, using structured interviews alongside one or more other methods (methodological pluralism) will lead to more thorough and valid conclusions.*

## Comments

'Strong' answers are well-focused on the question and this response is no exception. A clear and accurate definition of the term 'structured interviews' is provided in the opening paragraph. Several strengths and limitations of structured interviews are identified and each is explained in appropriate detail, using references to relevant concepts and studies to emphasise the key points. Appropriately for a 'strong' answer, the analysis is measured and thoughtful: note, for example, how the strengths and limitations of structured interviews are shown to be relative to other research methods, such as unstructured interviews or covert participant observation. The analysis is also sustained; a range of considerations is covered, including the practical, ethical, and theoretical dimensions that are relevant when making judgements about research methods. Good links are made to the theoretical perspectives: positivism and interpretivism. There is also a well-formulated conclusion that demonstrates a balanced understanding of the circumstances under which the use of structured interviews in sociological research may or may not be useful.

**Mark 24/26**

0 5 Evaluate the view that sociological research should be value free. **[26 marks]**

You might want to answer this question yourself and then use the checklist that follows to review your answer. Compare your work to a partner's. Identify strengths in the answers and also consider how they could be improved.

The following is a list of qualities that would be found in a 'strong' answer:

- Shows understanding of the key terms in the question.
- Identifies the main issues raised by the question.
- Explains the view expressed in the question using relevant sociological concepts, theories and arguments.

- Uses evidence and references to sociological studies to support key points, where appropriate.
- Considers the view expressed in the question from different angles, analysing arguments and evidence for and against.
- Presents the sociological material used (concepts, theories, arguments) in a clear and logical way that is easy to understand.
- Draws conclusions about which arguments and/or evidence in response to the question is most convincing; reasons why those conclusions have been reached should also be given.
- Includes a concluding paragraph that summarises the main arguments and ideas expressed in the answer and, ideally, also contributes a final point that secures the case made in responding to the question.

# The family

To make the best use of this section, you should have already completed your own responses to the exam-style questions at the end of Chapter 4. Now look at the sample responses to Q1–4 below. As you read the shorter responses and the supporting comments, decide what mark your own response(s) deserve. Identify anything you could do to improve your responses. As you read the longer responses and the supporting comments, decide whether your own response is closer to the level of the 'competent' answer or the 'strong' answer. Identify any ways in which your own response could be improved, using the commentaries on the sample responses as guidance.

**0 1** Describe two types of family structure. **[4 marks]**

**Response**

- *Nuclear family: this consists of a married, heterosexual couple and their biological or adopted child/ren.*
- *Single parent family: this consists of just one parent/adult, usually the mother, and her child/ren.*

## Comments

Two types of family structure are identified (nuclear family and single parent family) for 2 marks, and both the main features of each family type are described accurately for a further 2 marks.

**Mark 4/4**

**0 2a** Explain two ways in which government policies may influence family life. **[8 marks]**

**Response**

*Government policies may influence family life by encouraging family diversity e.g. the UK Divorce Reform Act, 1969. After the introduction of this the divorce rate increased four-fold, and this was because it became easier to get divorced as the law changed divorce so you could get divorced due to 'irretrievable breakdown'. Therefore this meant you could get divorced just because the relationship had broken down, not due to something shameful like having an affair. This meant that family life was influenced as far more couples got divorced, and lots more children therefore lived in single parent families or with remarriage, reconstituted families. However the New Right disapprove of this as they believe the single parent families lead to more delinquent boys as they have not had a father at home to discipline them.*

A very clear and full explanation of how the change in the divorce law influenced family life.

The point in this sentence is irrelevant to the question, as it tells us nothing about how government policies may influence family life.

*Government policies may influence family life by encouraging marriage. For example, in the UK the Married Couples' Allowance, 2015. This allowed married couples to give part of their tax allowance to their husband/wife. However, you have to be married and one partner has to have no earnings or very low earnings, so this benefits married couples who have a 'stay-at-home mum' or one who only works a few part-time hours. Feminists would disapprove of this as it therefore encourages people to live in traditional nuclear families, with the woman being financially dependent and playing the expressive role, and the husband having much more power and playing the instrumental (breadwinner) role. This means that this government policy has influenced family life by encouraging traditional family structures and discouraging women working or couples not marrying.*

## Comments

Two ways in which government policies may influence family life are identified. The precise way in which the government policy in each case influences family life is explained clearly and fully.

**Mark 8/8**

| 0 | 2b | Explain one strength and one limitation of the Marxist view that the family is an agency of social control. **[6 marks]**

**Response**

- *A strength of the Marxist view that the family is an agency of social control is that other sociological theories agree that this is the case. For example, radical feminists agree that family is an agency of social control as it controls women, wives particularly. Marxists like Engels have a similar view, and Engels goes as far to say that the family puts women in the position of 'domestic slaves'. Also, Functionalists agree with Marxists that the family is the first and most important agency of socialisation, and by teaching us our norms and values, it controls our behaviour: this is social control.*
- *A limitation of the Marxist view that the family is an agency of social control is that it may be outdated, as we are now living in a time of greater family diversity. It is no longer the case that almost all people are living in traditional nuclear families and passing on capitalist values, many families in fact teach their children to oppose the government and the rich. For example, a significant number of children are growing up in single parent families where the parent does not work. So these children might not be socialised into the norm of working for a living in low-paid jobs which is what helps to keep the bourgeoisie rich and powerful according to Marxists.*

## Comments

The answer identifies one strength and one limitation of the Marxist view that the family is an agency of social control. The strength and the limitation are both well explained, with good development of each point.

**Mark 6/6**

**0 3a** 'Family diversity is the norm in most societies today.' Explain this view. **[10 marks]**

## Competent answer

*Rapoport and Rapoport say there are five types of family diversity: cultural, life-stage, organisational, generational and social class. For example there is cultural diversity in the family types in Britain as African-Caribbean people are more likely to be matrifocal families. And there's also generational diversity as the older generation think people should live in nuclear families, and younger people live in cohabiting couples more often. Also life stage diversity as most people are born into nuclear families but at some point will not live in a nuclear family, like when they are old and may live in a single person household as they've been widowed. In fact, only about a fifth of households in Britain contain nuclear families.*

*Demographic trends have changed in society. The birth rate is much lower than it was 100 years ago and so is the death rate, which means families are more likely to be beanpole nowadays. This means a family with lots of generations, but not many people in each generation. On average, British families have 1–2 children nowadays, whereas in the past they would have many more. This is partly due to more women working. There are also more widows as life expectancy has increased to approximately 80 years old and many of these people live on their own. Therefore people live in lots of different family and household types.*

Rather than providing an example of family diversity that would help answer the question, the point in this sentence suggests that most families are beanpole today and so it contradicts the idea of family diversity being the norm. Be careful to avoid making contradictory points in an answer.

### Comments

The answer includes some well-chosen examples of family diversity. It would have been helpful to support this material with a clear definition of what sociologists mean by 'family diversity'. Some information is provided about diversity in non-family household types (the reference to widows, for example), which is not directly relevant to the question. To strengthen your answer, more examples of family diversity might have been offered and/or more reasons given as to why there may be a move from the nuclear family norm to family diversity today.

**Mark 5/10**

## Strong answer

*Postmodernists believe that family diversity is the norm in most societies today, as people now have more choice. Beck and Gernsheim call this 'individualisation' which means that people no longer follow traditional norms, but make their own decisions. Postmodernists believe that many of the traditional structures in society have fragmented, or broken down, such as religion. This means that there are no longer such strong structures controlling us. One example of this is living with a boyfriend or girlfriend when not married to them: cohabitation. It used to be seen as a sin ('living in sin') whereas nowadays it is very common and socially acceptable to cohabit either before getting married or instead of getting married. This means there are now more cohabiting couples and less nuclear families than in the past. However these relationships are more likely to break down than nuclear families, which leads to more family diversity. This is one reason why family diversity is the norm in society today.*

*Liberal feminists also believe that family diversity is the norm in most societies today, and say this is because there has been a 'march of progress' due to legal changes making society more equal. One example of this is divorce, which use to be more expensive and difficult, so less people were willing to get divorced. Whereas now the divorce rate is much higher and, in the UK, this is partly because of the Divorce Reform Act, 1971, which made it much cheaper and easier to get divorced. Therefore more divorces means there are less nuclear families and more single parent families, singletons and reconstituted families, which means there is more family diversity. Liberal feminists are very pleased that family diversity is the norm today as they believe this means that more women are escaping patriarchal nuclear families.*

Be wary of over-generalising in answers. While cohabitation may be socially acceptable in some cultures, there are many cultures where living together outside of marriage is still seen as unacceptable.

Here it would have been helpful to include some figures, or a reference to studies, to support the claim that relationships based on cohabitation are more likely to break down than relationships based on marriage in the nuclear family.

## Comments

This answer makes some helpful links between different sociological perspectives (postmodernists and liberal feminists) and the concept of family diversity. Several examples of family diversity are mentioned and some attempt is made to explain why family diversity may be increasing. The idea that the nuclear family was once viewed as the norm in modern industrial societies is hinted at, but the answer could have been developed by being clearer on this point.

**Mark 8/10**

**0 3b** 'Family diversity is the norm in most societies today.'

Using sociological material, give one argument against this view. **[6 marks]**

### Strong answer

*It is not true that family diversity is the norm in all societies, or all ethnic groups in all societies. For example, divorce rates are still low in many Asian ethnic groups. Additionally, in many Muslim countries, such as Libya, divorce is still seen as shameful and a sin, and is uncommon. It is expected that most people will get married and stay married, and therefore most people live in nuclear or extended families, and other family types like single parent families and reconstituted families are rare. This is partly because secularisation has not happened to the same extent in these cultures as it seems to have done in, for example, white British society, so religion is still strong and therefore marriage is the norm and divorce is a sin. It would also be frowned upon to cohabit, or live in a same-sex relationship. This means most people live in nuclear or extended families, so there isn't much family diversity in much of the Asian and Muslim parts of the world.*

## Comments

The answer demonstrates that there are many societies today where family diversity is not the norm. Well-chosen examples are used to support the argument.

**Mark 6/6**

**0 4** Evaluate the view that the family is a patriarchal institution. **[26 marks]**

## Competent answer

*A patriarchal institution is one where men control women. Feminists think all sorts of things in society are patriarchal, such as the media, schools and the government. Sociologists are divided over whether the family is patriarchal.*

*Feminists believe the family is patriarchal as men benefit more. Women do a lot more housework and childcare. Wives tend to do the cleaning, cooking and looking after children and sometimes they have jobs too. Men have jobs and do less at home although they often do the gardening and put the rubbish out. Women also look after the family's emotions, so feminists say wives do the 'triple shift'. Functionalists call this the instrumental and expressive roles and say it is equal and fair, but feminists say it is not equal or fair. However this is not true of all families as some men are 'househusbands' and some families pay for a cleaner. In a lot of families both parents work and the children go to nursery or sometimes grandparents look after them. Also there are now things like washing machines, dishwashers and microwaves.*

*Functionalists say the family is not patriarchal as it is fair because both the husband and wife have jobs to do for the family. Men earn money and women do the housework and look after children. Also postmodernists say we can now choose whether to live in a family (or we could live alone or in a couple or with friends), and if we do choose to live in a family we can choose how it works. So some parents share the childcare by both working part-time. Other couples both work full time but pay for a nanny and a cleaner so don't do the domestic work themselves. There are now fewer nuclear families and more single-parent families, step-families and even same-sex families, so not all families are nuclear. This is partly because divorce rates have gone up a lot and also because a lot of people choose to live with their boyfriend or girlfriend instead of getting married to them. For example 40% of marriages in the UK end in divorce. Families also differ between cultures, for example there are lots of extended families in Asian cultures, and in these families the younger women do most of the housework, whereas the grandmothers tend to be cared for by their sons' wives and don't help as much.*

*Another reason why men might have more power in the family is that they generally earn more. This means they are kind of like the boss of the family, and can tell everyone how to spend the money. Therefore they have more power over decisions like whether to go on holiday, and where to. Wives are usually left to make the boring, everyday decisions like what to have for*

The link to feminist theory is particularly relevant in answering the question, as the concept of patriarchy in sociology has its basis in the writings of feminist theorists.

This is a well-made evaluative point, demonstrating the ability to think critically about the issues raised by the question.

The answer makes relevant contrasts between feminist and functionalist views of the family. Contrasting different theories is a good way of constructing an evaluative answer.

*dinner however. In many families, the mum chooses what the children wear, what goes in their packed lunch, chooses birthday cards etc, whereas dad often doesn't make any of these everyday decisions.*

*Overall it seems like not all families are patriarchal, so that is an overgeneralisation. It depends on whether you believe the functionalist, postmodernist or feminist argument.*

## Comments

There is an attempt to define the term 'patriarchal institution', but the definition lacks depth and precision. Good use is made of some feminist ideas about patriarchy and a useful contrast is made with the functionalist view of the family. Some reasons why men may have more power than women within the family are explored, but the analysis lacks references to studies and research evidence. This answer could have been improved by setting out more clearly what is meant by a patriarchal institution and showing more precisely how the family may operate in a patriarchal way.

**Mark 16/26**

### Strong answer

*Feminists would argue that the family is a patriarchal institution, meaning men have power over women. However, postmodernists believe that families are now less patriarchal, and functionalists believe that families are fair as men and women both have their own roles, although those roles are different to each other.*

*Radical feminists believe that the traditional nuclear family is used as a form of social control by men: suppressing women, and socialising the next generation of girls to accept patriarchy. For example Bernard (1982) argues all marriages contain two marriages: his and hers. By this she means that marriage benefits men far more e.g. married men have better life expectancy and health, yet married women experience worse mental health compared to married men or single women. One reason for this may be that married women suffer the 'dual burden' according to Oakley, responsible for two jobs; paid work and housework. Statistics support this globally, with women often doing considerably more hours of housework a week than men. Girls grow up seeing this as the norm: that women serve men. However, this is assuming that all families are traditional nuclear ones, which is less true in many Western societies nowadays. Postmodernists Beck and Beck-Gernsheim argue that we're less constrained by traditional norms now: individualization. One effect of this is that there are more 'families of choice': including people as family who aren't related or close friends of parents may act as 'aunts' and 'uncles'. Therefore it can be argued that families are not patriarchal as it is possible for each individual to choose who is in their family, meaning the power lies with each individual.*

High-quality answers often include references to the ideas and/or research findings of particular sociologists, so the reference here to Bernard's work (and to Oakley later in the paragraph) is well made.

*However, radical feminists use evidence of how common domestic violence is to argue that families are patriarchal. Dobash and Dobash studied found ¼ women will experience domestic violence. Radical feminists believe this is because men hold more power in marriage than wives, and therefore women are safer outside of marriage. Dunne supports this by arguing that there are ingrained gender scripts in nuclear families: norms about what wives and husbands do. These gender scripts are absent in same-sex couples where there is no patriarchy and a more equal balance of power. However, liberal feminists believe that patriarchy in families has reduced as there has been a march of progress in society. This means that things have improved for women, as they now have more choice in whether to marry or stay married, and therefore escape the patriarchal nuclear family. This is partly as divorce has become easier due to legal changes, and is also more socially acceptable. Though it must be remembered that in some cultures girls and women are forced to marry and stay married: patriarchal families at their most extreme. E.g. Niger has the highest rate of forced child marriage in the world, with ¾ of girls aged under 18-years in forced marriages. Therefore it could be argued that the family is still highly patriarchal within some cultures.*

Good use of statistical evidence here. Statistics from research studies are a good way to support key arguments and analytical points in an answer.

The danger of over-generalising is avoided here by noting that the situation may differ between cultures. Try to avoid creating the impression that all societies/ cultures are the same; usually, there will be important contrasts between societies that are worth noting in your answers.

*As well as women suffering the dual burden and domestic violence due to family life, Edgell argues that in families decision-making is not split fairly. This is because men tend to hold more power when it comes to the most important decisions, such as buying a house. This may be because men generally earn more than women, so believe they have the 'right' to decide how it is spent. Women are more likely to work part-time or not at all, as they stay at home to care for children. This therefore suggests that families are patriarchal as men hold more power in decision-making. However, not all families include a man so it is not possible for all families to be patriarchal. For example, there were 12 million single-parent families in the USA in 2017, and over 80% of single-parent families worldwide are headed by women. It is also common in African-Caribbean culture for women to shun men, forming matrifocal families, as men are seen as unreliable and a burden. Therefore single parent families are not patriarchal.*

*In conclusion, it seems the weight of the evidence suggests that nuclear families are patriarchal as men often hold more power, usually by being the higher earner and the key decision-maker. However, it is crucial to note that family diversity has increased globally, and some of the newer family types are not patriarchal. For example, the increase in dual-career families in which a woman's earnings as just as important to a couple's living standards as the earnings of her husband. Such as in China, 7% of married people live in DINK families – dual income, no kids.*

## Comments

The main strength of this answer is the impressive way in which it evaluates a range of arguments and evidence around the claim that the family is a patriarchal institution. A good combination of theory, research findings and the ideas of individual thinkers is used to develop the analysis. Different societies/cultures are taken into account when drawing wider conclusions about the relationship between the family and patriarchy.

**Mark 26/26**

0 5 Evaluate the view that family life is harmful for many people. **[26 marks]**

You might want to answer this question yourself and then use the checklist that follows to review your answer. Compare your work to a partner's. Identify strengths in the answers and also consider how they could be improved.

The following is a list of qualities that would be found in a 'strong' answer:

- Shows understanding of the key terms in the question.
- Identifies the main issues raised by the question.
- Explains the view expressed in the question using relevant sociological concepts, theories and arguments.
- Uses evidence and references to sociological studies to support key points, where appropriate.
- Considers the view expressed in the question from different angles, analysing arguments and evidence for and against.
- Presents the sociological material used (concepts, theories, arguments) in a clear and logical way that is easy to understand.
- Draws conclusions about which arguments and/or evidence in response to the question is most convincing; reasons why those conclusions have been reached should also be given.
- Includes a concluding paragraph that summarises the main arguments and ideas expressed in the answer and, ideally, also contributes a final point that secures the case made in responding to the question.

# Education

To make the best use of this section, you should have already completed your own responses to the exam-style questions at the end of Chapter 5. Now look at the sample responses to Q1–4 below. As you read the shorter responses and the supporting comments, decide what mark your own response(s) deserve. Identify anything you could do to improve your responses. As you read the longer responses and the supporting comments, decide whether your own response is closer to the level of the 'competent' answer or the 'strong' answer. Identify any ways in which your own response could be improved, using the commentaries on the sample responses as guidance.

0 1 Describe two examples of student subcultures. **[4 marks]**

### Response

*Anti-school subcultures: These are groups of students who tend to be badly behaved at school and do not focus on working hard to get good grades, but would rather be the 'class clown' and mess around to impress their peers. For example, the working class 'Lads' studied by Willis.*

*Ethnic group subcultures: Such as African-Caribbean boys in the British education system. Sewell says they are labelled by teachers 'troublemakers', and this may cause the boys to group together in response to the teacher racism, and behave badly (a self-fulfilling prophecy).*

## Comments

Two examples of student subcultures are identified for 2 marks. Each example is described accurately for a further 2 marks.

**Mark 4/4**

**0 2** Explain two ways in which education may contribute to social solidarity. **[8 marks]**

### Response

1. *By teaching all children the same norms and values, Durkheim argued that education can promote social solidarity by being a key institution of secondary socialisation. For example, all British schools now have to teach five 'British values' identified by the government, including 'democracy', 'rule of law' and 'respect and tolerance'. This means that the students realise that they are part of a collective, British society, something much larger than themselves from which they and the rest of the community benefit. Similarly, American students make the 'pledge of allegiance' at the start of the school day, promising their allegiance to the American flag.*
2. *By being a 'society in miniature', school is able to promote social solidarity. This is different to the family, where children are treated as individuals e.g. they do not have to stick to strict timetables or wear a uniform. Parsons believes families have 'particularistic values' whereas school is the same as society as it has 'universalistic standards' where everyone is treated the same. This means education prepares children for adulthood by being a bridge between the family and society, partly by showing students that they have to follow rules. This leads to adults following laws just like they followed school rules, which therefore contributes to social solidarity.*

## Comments

Two ways in which education may contribute to social solidarity are identified and both are explained in adequate detail. Relevant sociological material is used and it is clear in each case how that material supports the explanation.

**Mark 8/8**

**0 3** 'Educational systems in modern industrial societies are meritocratic.'
Using sociological material, give two arguments against this view. **[12 marks]**

### Competent answer

*Marxists believe that schools are deliberately not meritocratic so that the middle class can continue to be powerful. They do this by making sure working class students fail, such as the 'Lads' studied by Willis. Whereas middle class students are favoured by the education system so get good results, leading to good jobs, and more power in society. For example most teachers are middle class and use middle class words when they speak. This is also true of exams and textbooks. This is deliberate because the middle class want the working class to do factory jobs. Marxists think that our economy is capitalist and this must be changed to a communist one to make society fair.*

A stronger response might include an explanation of how the education system ensures that working-class students fail.

This sentence adds nothing to the answer and could have been omitted.

*The government has had to make social policies called compensatory education because the education system is not meritocratic. So in Britain they brought in things like Sure Start as poor children need extra help before they start school. Also Education Action Zones so that schools in poor areas get extra funding. This shows that not all schools are equally good, so education is not a 'fair playing field'. If education was meritocratic these would not be needed. Also, governments keep changing the education system which they wouldn't do if it was perfect.*

The idea of compensatory education and what it aims to achieve could be better explained here.

## Comments

Two arguments against the idea that education systems are meritocratic are identified, but the explanations offered lack some coherence and detail. For example, a fuller account might have been offered of the mechanisms through which the education system favours middle-class students. The reference to teachers using middle-class words when they speak is rather vague and doesn't really explain why this might disadvantage working-class students. The points about compensatory education lack clarity; for example, there needed to be more explanation of why the existence of Education Action Zones shows that not all schools are equally good.

**Mark 7/12**

### Strong answer

*If education was meritocratic, there wouldn't be significant attainment gaps between different ethnic groups. E.g. in Britain Chinese and Indian students have the highest attainment and those from Pakistani and Black Caribbean backgrounds have the lowest. This may be because not all ethnic groups have equal opportunities (which is a key feature of meritocratic systems) to gain high grades, partly due to teacher labelling when dividing students into sets and streams. Gillborn and Youdell argue that schools 'sacrifice' Black Caribbean students in order to ensure that the school achieves good results and therefore a good position on league tables. This is because Black Caribbean students were assumed to be less intelligent and put in lower sets where they did not receive the more experienced teachers and as much teacher support/effort as those in the higher sets did: they were 'systematically neglected'. Therefore education systems in modern industrial societies are not meritocratic as not all students are treated equally and given the same attention and expectations from teachers to do well.*

There was an opportunity here to use relevant statistical data to show the extent to which Chinese and Indian students have higher attainment levels than students from Pakistani and Black Caribbean backgrounds.

A well-chosen reference to a relevant study, demonstrating good interpretation and application skills.

*A meritocratic system is one in which those who succeed do so due to their individual merit. Therefore if education systems in modern industrial societies (e.g. China, Germany, USA) were meritocratic, educational success would not be caused by a student's social class, but by their individual talents/effort. However, middle class students tend to do significantly better. This might be because they are more likely to be able to afford to go to a private school, or live in an area with better-performing schools (where house prices are higher). Bourdieu calls this economic capital, whereas the working class suffers from material deprivation, so can't afford things like private tutors to enable them to do better at school. Marxists like Bowles and Gintis would agree that educational attainment is related to social class rather than to talent, so education is not meritocratic. They believe the education system disguises this with its myth of meritocracy, and that the working classes are in a false consciousness as they cannot see that education is designed to benefit the middle class and socialise the working class into being docile, obedient workers.*

There was an opportunity here to explain how the education system contributes to the 'myth of meritocracy'; for example, comprehensive schools in the UK contribute to the idea that all students are treated equally by being non-selective in their student intake and by offering the same curriculum to all students. In practice, however, comprehensive schools have been found to treat students unequally due to streaming and teacher labelling of students.

## Comments

Two arguments against the idea that education systems are meritocratic are described clearly and accurately. Each argument is supported with references to relevant sociologists and good use is made of appropriate concepts such as labelling, teacher expectations, material deprivation and false consciousness. Some use of statistical evidence to confirm the extent to which there are differences in attainment levels between the social groups mentioned (ethnic groups, social class groups) would have added to the high quality of the response.

**Mark 10/12**

| 0 | 4 | Evaluate the view that intelligence is the most important factor determining how well a child performs at school. **[26 marks]**

### Competent answer

*Not all students or schools get equally good results, and the general public seems to think this is because some people are more intelligent than others. But sociologists think there are lots of reasons.*

*Some people have a higher intelligence than others, this is tested by using IQ tests. For example, the test to get into grammar schools is an IQ test. You have to do things like predict which shape would come next in a sequence. Richer children do better on this so therefore this would suggest they have a higher IQ. This could be why they do better at school. Not everyone believes that IQ tests work well though.*

This paragraph provides quite a good summary of the case for intelligence being a key factor in educational achievement. However, the point in the final sentence is under-developed and no explanation is provided for the supposed limitations of IQ tests.

*Some sociologists believe that wealth determines how well you do at school (Marxists think this is something the ruling class have done deliberately). This is because rich children can afford revision guides and tutors, so have the best chance of doing well in their exams. They can also afford to live in nice, big houses in good areas, and also have a good diet. Whereas poor children can't and this is called material deprivation. So they often don't have a good diet and live in cramped houses in areas with bad schools. So it doesn't matter how clever they are if their school is bad.*

Relevant use of an appropriate concept, demonstrating sound interpretation and application skills.

*Poor children also have cultural deprivation. This means they don't have the right norms and values to do well at school. For example Sugarman says they have the subcultural values like fatalism and collectivism. Fatalism is when you believe that fate controls your life. Collectivism is when you put your friends and family before yourself. They often don't like school, and are naughty. This is also the same for some ethnicities that don't do well at school, and also boys (girls normally work harder). Whereas middle class children have stricter parents who push them more.*

A reference to a relevant source; there was scope to include more references to thinkers and studies in the response.

*However, schools and the government offer lots of things to help poorer students, like not making them pay for school trips or school dinners. Private schools even let some poor children go there free of charge. And some working class parents are very pushy as they don't want their children to fail at school like they did. Some poor students do really well and some rich students do really badly so that must be because they're more/less intelligent.*

An interesting point that demonstrates skill in analysis.

*Overall it is clear that intelligence does determine how well a child does at school, but so does how rich you are.*

## Comments

The possibility that intelligence influences educational achievement is considered and supported with some sound analytical points. Some social factors that might influence educational performance are also mentioned and there are appropriate references to relevant concepts such as material deprivation and cultural deprivation. The discussion overall lacks depth and there is a shortage of references to relevant thinkers and studies. There is no mention of the difficulties of defining intelligence and measuring its impact on educational performance. Nor does the response consider that hard work and good behaviour at school may be more important determinants of educational success than intelligence on its own.

**Mark 17/26**

## Strong answer

*Most sociologists believe social factors (e.g. social class), rather than intelligence, determine how well a child performs a school. However, there is some evidence to suggest that intelligence plays a key role too.*

The opening sentence provides a neat summary of the debate that is to follow.

*Some say that lower IQ levels in the working class are to blame for these students doing worse at school. For example, Jensen, who believes that 60–80% of intelligence comes from genetics, and the rest from the environment in which we live. This suggests that the working class is passing down lower levels of intelligence to their children, resulting in them persistently doing worse at school. However, cultural deprivation theorists do not agree. They argue that the working class is not less intelligent, but has a different culture to the middle class one used in schools. Bernstein says that teachers, textbooks and exam papers all use an elaborated speech code that middle class families are socialised into from birth by their families. So middle class students are not more intelligent, they are simply more familiar with the language used in schools, so school is easier. For example, they understand what an exam question is asking. Whereas a working class student may have the same level of knowledge about the topic that the exam question is asking about, but as they use a restricted speech code, they do not realise that this knowledge would win them marks.*

This would be a good opportunity to mention some of the difficulties in defining intelligence and measuring how much influence it has on educational attainment.

*Furthermore, it may not be actual intelligence that determines how well a child does at school, but how intelligent the teachers perceive students to be. Many sociological studies have suggested that teachers quickly label students based on their social class, ethnicity and gender. Liu and Xie studied the '4 + 1' (4 boys and 1 girl) who were performing badly in a Chinese school. They were poor and labelled as deviant and low ability by teachers, and the label became a self-fulfilling prophecy. This was supported by a field experiment carried out by Rosenthal and Jacobson, where they gave teachers false IQ results for their classes. At the end of the year, the students that had been randomly labelled with high IQ had made more progress than their peers. This shows how teacher expectations can affect how well a child does more than their actual intelligence.*

This point is neatly summarised, demonstrating a good understanding of the topic.

Good use of studies to support the main point of the paragraph.

*Finally, a child's chance of educational success may be more affected by the level of interest their parents show in their education than their intelligence. Douglas found that working class parents are less likely to attend Parents' Evenings, show ambition for their children and encourage their children to work hard at school. They also don't have the cultural capital to get their children into better schools, such as the knowledge and confidence to appeal if their child does not get into their first choice. Therefore middle class children are 'pushed' more by their parents to succeed, and also have the economic capital to pay for things such as private tuition/schools which can improve the results of even lower intelligence children.*

There was an opportunity to challenge this view of working-class parents by noting that these parents may be just as ambitious for their children as middle-class parents; they simply lack the knowledge and skills to support their children in the learning process effectively.

*Overall most of the evidence points towards intelligence having some effect on how well a child does, but it is not the biggest influence. Social class and wealth (and other characteristics such as ethnicity) seems to have a bigger impact, as even if a child is very intelligent, if they go to an underperforming school with a big anti-school subculture, the teachers are unlikely to be able to teach lessons in enough depth for students to gain top grades.*

The conclusion demonstrates good analysis and evaluation skills, providing a persuasive summary of why intelligence may not be the biggest influence on educational achievement.

### Comments

Some support is offered for the argument that intelligence is the main factor influencing educational achievement. The weaknesses in the arguments of thinkers such as Jensen who see intelligence as the key factor might have been explored more directly. Instead, the case for the importance of intelligence is contrasted with the opposing view that social factors are a more significant influence on educational achievement. Several well-chosen examples are used to illustrate how various social factors (teacher expectations, parental contribution, income and wealth) may influence how well children perform at school. There is a plausible conclusion that demonstrates good analysis and evaluation skills.

**Mark 22/26**

## The media

To make the best use of this section, you should have already completed your own responses to the exam-style questions at the end of Chapter 6. Now look at the sample responses to Q1 below. As you read the responses and the supporting comments, decide whether your own response is closer to the level of the 'competent' answer or the 'strong' answer. Identify any ways in which your own response could be improved, using the commentaries on the sample responses as guidance.

0 1 'Pluralist theory is mistaken in claiming that the media reflect a wide range of different interests in society.' Evaluate this view. **[35 marks]**

### Competent answer

*There are some who argue that the media reflect the views and needs of everyone in society fairly. These are known as pluralists. Pluralists believe that the media reflect everyone's views equally and in a fair way. On the other hand, there are others who disagree, for example Marxists who say that the media are not fair and instead they push the ideas of capitalism.*

*Pluralists are very optimistic. They think that if people have a strong set of views about an issue it will appear in the media. The media include the news, films, adverts and so on. Therefore, the media actually represent everyone in democracy. Dahl argues that even groups such as trade unions get the chance to express their views in the media. They ignore the fact that the media are run by the very rich at the top of society. For example, Rupert Murdoch who owns a large proportion of world media. They also ignore the fact that often the editors of newspapers are trying to push their right-wing views. For example, the Daily Mail editor Paul Dacre was very much a supporter of Brexit and this must have influenced people to vote for Brexit in 2016. People do not have to buy the Daily Mail, they chose to buy it and so Pluralists argue that this means that people decide what they want to read. If people wanted to read more about poor people's problems, they will buy more of that media and then the media will produce more of that type of media and so on. According to pluralists, media owners do not have time to think about what they are producing, they will just do whatever they*

This claim might have been supported with relevant statistical evidence about who owns the media.

*think the people will want. Marxists do not agree; they argue that the media owners are only interested in what will sell because they are businesses trying to make profit and in fact they are not interested in trying to help the poor or those at the bottom of society.*

Good, direct contrasting of the pluralist and Marxist perspectives.

*Marxists say that the media try to make people forget about the problems in society. They claim that the media actually support capitalist ideas because of this. For example, the media will not choose news that shows how bad things are for the poor. They will not report as much on stories which show how banks have been fraudulent so that people do not realise how unfair capitalism is. Miliband argued that the media reflect the views of the rich and not the poor. Some Marxists say that actually even groups such as women and the disabled are also ignored by the media and that the media are all about supporting the right-wing government, trying to make it look good and fair. Marxists make the point that the very rich, the elite or people like Murdoch are only interested in their own profit and use advertising to convince people the world is fair and equal even though it is not. Therefore, the media only reflect the interests of the rich, the elite in society.*

Relevant use of examples to illustrate the Marxist viewpoint.

*So, pluralists are wrong if they think that the media reflect the interests of everyone because they do not. Sometimes there are stories about the problems with society however and people might be more aware today of 'fake news'.*

## Comments

The account of pluralist theory is sound, though it might have been more detailed. Some good points are made about the Marxist perspective and how it differs from the pluralist theory. However, the response lacks a good, overall understanding of the Marxist theory and there is no mention of relevant concepts such as Ideological State Apparatus, false consciousness, gatekeepers, ideology, hegemony, media distortion and bias, and the manufacture of news. The opportunity to mention other perspectives on the media, such as the feminist and postmodernist viewpoints, was missed.

**Mark 19/35**

### Strong answer

*Pluralist theories of the media claim that in democratic societies power of the media is shared by a number of groups whose views vary and reflect the different parts of societies. Dahl for example claims that no one group is represented more than any other. Pluralists claim that a sharing and representative media is reflected across all forms of media platforms today such as the television, social media and films. They also argue that the people who control the media are the public themselves, the consumers of the media. These people are consumers or stakeholders in the media. Pluralists argue that the public have agency and choice in which types of media they engage with or consume. For example, if someone feels that they do not like one type of media representation, they can choose another, and if enough people feel this, then the media outlet will close down or change in response. Whale sums this up by saying 'it is readers who determine the character of the newspapers' (1977). Therefore, the people with the power to ensure their interests are reflected lies with the public.*

An accurate summary of the pluralist theory serves as a good starting point for the discussion that follows.

*Marxists totally disagree with this view, claiming that the media are run by the ruling classes to maintain their power and to prevent any questioning or challenging to the capitalist ideology that is central to society. So, they definitely argue that pluralist theories are mistaken – the media reflect the interests of the ruling class who impose their views and ideas onto the working class, a process that some Marxists refer to as hegemony. It must be noted however that Marx himself wrote a long time ago, well before the emergence of the media in all its forms today. However more recently others have developed his ideas and applied them to today's society. There are the traditional Marxist views such as Milliband who argue that the dominant media form part of the 'ruling class ideology' which encourage the working class to accept their low position and to not question the ways that they are exploited known as false class consciousness, for example, using the media to blame the working class for problems in society, directing attention away from the real causes of inequality such as tax evasion by the rich. This is called 'freedom of the press' which according to Milliband is really a myth, because in practice the media are owned by an increasingly small ruling class elite, the 'press barons' who do not reflect the views of the working class. In fact, Milliband claims that the media are hostile to any form of news that is Left Wing. Neo Marxists however challenge these views and argue that other forms of inequality beyond social class such as gender, ethnicity and age are also unaddressed by the ruling class media elite. Neo Marxists such as Gramsci claim that the media operate on a logic of profit, each media outlet trying to see their products with capitalist ideology so that the media become part of the 'cultural hegemony' that all major institutions reflect. Going further, Neo Marxist Harvey claims that the media promote neo-liberal ideas which reject notions of equality and justice and promote the privatisation of society. Other Neo Marxists Herman and Chomsky claim that the news filters reality so that it is a sort of concentrated version of capitalist ideas including advertising, selective evidence, biased stories which support the ruling class elite and a promotion of ruling class political ideas. They claim that this means the media promote ruling class propaganda.*

Good knowledge of different strands of Marxist theory demonstrated.

*Pluralists are therefore mistaken in their views; Marxist views show how today the media represent only neoliberal views. Editors generally promote right wing political views that in turn support their pursuit of profit. People who are disadvantaged are not generally successful in getting the sort of media that they want, that reflects their interests. However, there may be a strong case for suggesting that the new media provide outlets for a range of different groups to communicate with each other and spread their messages to wider audiences; arguably, the ruling class have less control over the new media than the traditional media.*

Balanced analysis looking at relevant issues from different angles.

## Comments

The response demonstrates a good understanding of the pluralist theory of the media. That theory is critically assessed through contrasts with the Marxist theory of the media. There is also a final paragraph that offers some deeper reflections on who controls the media. The response could have been even stronger had relevant evidence been used to support key conclusions, such as the claim that newspaper editors generally promote right-wing political views or that the media promote the privatisation of society.

**Mark 26/35**

**0 2** 'The uses and gratification model of media effects has more strengths than limitations.' Evaluate this view. **[35 marks]**

You might want to answer this question yourself and then use the checklist that follows to review your answer. Compare your work to a partner's. Identify strengths in the answers and also consider how they could be improved.

The following is a list of qualities that would be found in a 'strong' answer:

- Shows understanding of the key terms in the question.
- Identifies the main issues raised by the question.
- Explains the view expressed in the question using relevant sociological concepts, theories and arguments.
- Uses evidence and references to sociological studies to support key points, where appropriate.
- Considers the view expressed in the question from different angles, analysing arguments and evidence for and against.
- Presents the sociological material used (concepts, theories, arguments) in a clear and logical way that is easy to understand.
- Draws conclusions about which arguments and/or evidence in response to the question is most convincing; reasons why those conclusions have been reached should also be given.
- Includes a concluding paragraph that summarises the main arguments and ideas expressed in the answer and, ideally, also contributes a final point that secures the case made in responding to the question.

# Religion

To make the best use of this section, you should have already completed your own responses to the exam-style questions at the end of Chapter 7. Now look at the sample responses to Q1 below. As you read the responses and the supporting comments, decide whether your own response is closer to the level of the 'competent' answer or the 'strong' answer. Identify any ways in which your own response could be improved, using the commentaries on the sample responses as guidance.

| 0 | 1 | 'The arguments against the secularisation thesis are stronger than the arguments for.' Evaluate this view. **[35 marks]**

## Competent answer

*Secularisation refers to the process in which religion is becoming less important. There is a range of arguments and evidence which suggests religion remains important and also evidence to suggest it is in decline.*

*Early sociologists predicted that religion would become less important. But today some traditional religions are growing and that is because there is so much change in a postmodern world. This makes people feel insecure and want to turn to religion for comfort. For example, in Latin America Pentacostalism is growing and that is because people like the rules and traditional values it provides. On the other hand, many people no longer attend church in the UK, it is only 5% of the population. This means that secularisation is definitely happening.*

Good use of relevant examples from different countries.

*In terms of affiliation, people often like to think they are religious even if they don't go to church. Davie calls this 'vicarious religion'. This means that secularisation may not be happening. Also, the fact that there are lots more fundamentalist groups such as IS in Syria suggests that people are becoming more keen to be even more strictly religious today. But these groups are not everywhere. In America religion remains important even if Christianity is not practised as much, politics is full of religious ideas such as the New Christian Right.*

*Hinduism is growing because Hindus have a higher fertility rate, so this is evidence that secularisation is not occurring. However today there are less people attending church schools in the UK and the government in the UK are not very keen to talk about religion. This is called religious disengagement, and this shows that secularisation is happening.*

*New Age movements and new religious movements are growing so it might be that religion is changing and not declining. For example, in the Kendal Project, Heelas found that people, especially middle-class women like doing things like New Age movements. For example, going to Yoga. This might mean that people are still believing in some sort of spirituality but not actually going to church. In the Kendal project, people were really*

Good use of a relevant study.

*not going to church very much at all. Even though people are going to New Age movements they are not going in the same numbers as they used to go to church.*

*New religious movements have also grown, and these are strict, like sects and denominations where people get given rules, such as The Unification Church where people feel more settled because they have their religion to give them answers. Sects and Denominations are growing around the world and help people when they migrate. More people migrating means more religion because Bruce says they need religion for Cultural Defence and Cultural transition.*

*In conclusion, it is not very clear if secularisation is happening or not because it depends on how you measure religion. There are some new forms of religion which are really difficult to measure, but we do know that the traditional church is not so popular today in the UK. It really depends on where you are in the world.*

## Comments

Some well-chosen examples are used to support the arguments in this response and different religions are considered. There are a few references to relevant concepts, such as religious disengagement and cultural defence, but there was scope to include more concepts and also references to sociologists who have contributed to the secularisation debate. Assessment is offered at various points, but it lacks depth and only vague conclusions are drawn.

**Mark 20/35**

### Strong answer

*The secularisation thesis is the claim that there is an ongoing process by which religion is declining in importance. This claim is affected by how you choose to define and operationalise, or measure religion. Wilson (1966) provided a definition of secularisation, 'the process whereby religious thinking, practices and institutions lose social significance.' There are arguments and evidence for and against secularisation which vary from place to place and within different religious organisations. Stark and Bainbridge (1987) claim, that the secularisation process is occurring in traditional religions, but at the same time there is a regrowth of new forms of religion, therefore the secularisation process will never be fully complete.*

Good use of a relevant link to methodological issues.

*Davie claims that the secularisation process reached its peak in the 1970s, and that we have since been in a process of resacralisation (becoming sacred again) as well as seeing a revival of religious beliefs. Today 80%*

Good use of a relevant concept. Strong responses to the essay questions often include references to several appropriate concepts, as well as links to theories and studies.

*of the world's population claim an affiliation to a religion. Certainly, if we look at the growth of traditional religions such as Islam, which the Pew Research Centre predicts by 2050 is set to be larger globally (in terms of participants and membership) than Christianity. However, this is due to population growth in Muslim populations that have a higher fertility rate than Christian populations. There has also been a massive growth of denominational forms of Christianity. Bruce argues that due to rapid social changes and migration, people now need religion in their lives for practical purposes, cultural transition (to help them settle into a new area) and cultural defence (to maintain a particular ethnic identity in a new or hostile place).*

*Furthermore there is evidence to suggest that religion is playing an increasing role in social and political life, with the election of Trump as American President (who represents many of the beliefs of the New Christian Right). Also in terms of the relationship between religion and the state, Casanova (1994) supports the view that disengagement is not happening everywhere. He believes that recent history shows that there has been some decline in religious beliefs and practices in parts of Europe, this has not been the case in other parts of the world. Furthermore, Davie claims that today people are increasingly practising privatised religion, where they are religious but do not necessarily attend a place of worship. This makes it much harder to measure religiosity. This links to postmodern ideas about 'spiritual shopping' (Hervieu-Léger).*

*Finally, there is evidence that there are growing number of new forms of religions such as new religious movements and New Age movements that suggest that religion is changing to suit people's needs today for self fulfilment and a 'sacred canopy' in an increasingly uncertain and changing world. For example, the growth of scientology, a New Age movement which promises career success and fulfilment.*

Statistical data might be used here to illustrate the growing number of new forms of religion.

*However, the founding fathers of sociology such as Marx and Durkheim claimed that secularisation would occur. Marx in fact predicted that religion would disappear when communism occurred. Comte, an early sociologist, claimed that as science and scientific, rational thinking grew, they would replace religious thinking. The interpretivist Weber claimed that religion would decline due to the rise of modernity – according to him modernity and religion cannot exist at the same time. Bruce claims, like Weber, that it was particular Protestant beliefs that led to secularisation. However, Bruce claims it was also other changes that were happening in wider society that along with Protestantism created the conditions for secularisation. Some of the strongest evidence for secularisation is from church attendance in Britain and perhaps USA (although not as much). The USA is more ethnically diverse than the UK, although both countries have a majority of Christian based religions, there has been an increase in alternative religions partly as a result of high levels of immigration in recent years in both countries.*

*In conclusion, some claim that secularisation will occur as part of the globalisation and westernisation of the world. Bruce (2011) argues that secularisation will happen in western societies and that the process is irreversible. However, others such as Kepel (1994) disagree, using evidence of the growth of some forms of traditional religions among some groups in the west and beyond. In fact, some claim that secularisation among some groups has led to a desire among other groups to protect and extend religious belief, such as fundamentalist groups. Therefore, secularisation is not occurring to the extent suggested by the founding fathers, on a global level.*

## Comments

The answer demonstrates a sound understanding of the secularisation thesis. A wide range of material is used to discuss the arguments for and against the thesis. The response is analytical throughout and is supported with useful references to relevant concepts, thinkers and examples. The issues raised by the question are rightly considered in an international perspective, with reflections offered on the position of religion in different societies, as well as the impact of globalisation across the world. A thoughtful and well-supported conclusion is provided.

**Mark 29/35**

0 2 'The extent to which religious organisations are patriarchal has been exaggerated.' Evaluate this view. **[35 marks]**

You might want to answer this question yourself and then use the checklist that follows to review your answer. Compare your work to a partner's. Identify strengths in the answers and also consider how they could be improved.

The following is a list of qualities that would be found in a 'strong' answer:

- Shows understanding of the key terms in the question.
- Identifies the main issues raised by the question.
- Explains the view expressed in the question using relevant sociological concepts, theories and arguments.
- Uses evidence and references to sociological studies to support key points, where appropriate.
- Considers the view expressed in the question from different angles, analysing arguments and evidence for and against.
- Presents the sociological material used (concepts, theories, arguments) in a clear and logical way that is easy to understand.
- Draws conclusions about which arguments and/or evidence in response to the question is most convincing; reasons why those conclusions have been reached should also be given.
- Includes a concluding paragraph that summarises the main arguments and ideas expressed in the answer and, ideally, also contributes a final point that secures the case made in responding to the question.

## Globalisation

To make the best use of this section, you should have already completed your own responses to the exam-style questions at the end of Chapter 8. Now look at the sample responses to Q1 below. As you read the responses and the supporting comments, decide whether your own response is closer to the level of the 'competent' answer or the 'strong' answer. Identify any ways in which your own response could be improved, using the commentaries on the sample responses as guidance.

| 0 | 1 | 'Globalisation has led to cultural convergence.' Evaluate this view. **[35 marks]**

### Competent answer

*Globalisation means that the world is becoming more interconnected over time. For example, more ideas are being shared around the world through increased availability of the internet and we can travel more easily. Some sociologists claim that this means that people are sharing cultural ideas and becoming more similar (cultural convergence) and other sociologists argue that this means people feel they want to keep their identity different and unique.*

*One example of cultural convergence comes from the way that European and American companies can be found all over the world. These are called Transnational Corporations. If you go for a meal in China for example, you might be able to buy the same drink such as Coca-Cola as in America or anywhere else. This means that people no longer have 'local' cultural practices. The same goes with more secular ideas and practices, as the internet is 80% written in English, it reflects British and American ideas which tend to be more secular or liberal. There are some who worry that this means that local practices are going to be lost. Some people see this as a form of cultural imperialism. Marxists would argue that western companies spreading about the world mean that capitalist ideas are also spreading and that this is a real problem as capitalism means the workers are exploited globally. It also means that people are moving towards a more capitalist culture all over the world.*

A well-chosen example that helps to illustrate the meaning of 'cultural convergence'.

Here, it would have been helpful to provide an explanation and/or example of what is meant by 'capitalist culture'.

*Postmodernists say that globalisation may have a different effect and it might lead to people hearing about new and different ideas so that there are a lot of different cultures to choose from. For example there are lots more religions to choose from today because you can find them on the internet. Many New Age movements such as scientology are based on the internet and as such people can experience new forms of cultural ideas like religion without having to leave their homes. You can also travel and learn about new cultures, and there is more migration than ever which means that there are more cultural practices. Postmodernists would see cultural diversity as a key feature of society today, not cultural convergence. Bruce argues that as people move from one place to another they reinforce their cultural identity which is known as cultural defence. This suggests that globalisation does not lead to culture becoming the same. There are also examples of where two different cultural practices such as types of food from different cultures come together to form a new form of food which is known as hybrid. This is evidence of new forms of cultural diversity rather than cultural convergence. Another thing about postmodern global society is that people are more individualist which means that they can have quite complex identities based on their own choices rather than what they feel they should do. This suggests that people will pick and choose their own individual identity rather than accept the culture that everyone else has.*

Good use of the concept of cultural defence to develop an evaluative point.

The answer ends rather abruptly and lacks a well-formed conclusion.

## Comments

Some appropriate examples are used to illustrate the possible links between globalisation and cultural convergence. There is an attempt to define what is meant by globalisation, but it lacks detail. Some evaluative points are offered, mainly through reference to the postmodernist theory. However, the key points in the evaluation might have been stated more clearly and supported with a wider range of examples and/or more links to relevant sociological concepts and theories.

**Mark 21/35**

### Strong answer

*Globalisation is the process by which the world is becoming a smaller place, time and distance are becoming compressed. There are those who claim that the process is leading to cultural convergence, which means that people's way of life is becoming more homogenous or similar, while others claim there is evidence to suggest the opposite is the case, that cultures are becoming more different or divergent.*

*Evidence for cultural homogeneity comes from the technological advances that have allowed for the spread of global culture through the growth of transnational corporations. Products and brands such as McDonald's, Coca-Cola and Disney are found all over the world today, especially concentrated in more developed areas. This is possible not just through new forms of technology, advertising and media but also as a result of increasingly effective transport methods. Marxists such as Castells argue that cultural convergence is a result of the spread of capitalist ideologies. For example, the spread of ideas such as the pursuit of profit, individualism and consumerism. Once exposed to this set of ideas, societies are changed irreversibly. Castells argues that globalisation of western Capitalist values leads to the development of new forms of capitalist identities.*

*An example of this kind of homogenisation is through the work of Ritzer who claims that a process of 'McDonaldization' is happening. This is where the principles of a company like McDonald's is present in various ways in many societies. Ritzer claims that cultural homogenisation is part of a wider process of rationalisation, which means that traditional rules are being replaced by logical, consistent rules. In McDonald's, all tasks are judged on efficiency, predictability and control through the use of technology. Ritzer sees the McDonaldization and homogenisation of societies as a threat to the customs of society as a whole.*

Good use of examples to illustrate how cultural convergence may be occurring.

*Another example of the homogenisation of culture is body image. According to Bates (2011) the westernised view of thin women as beautiful is spreading to cultures where previously larger women were beautiful leading to some women feeling a real pressure to conform to western ideals.*

*On the other hand, increased access to cross-cultural ideas and transport has meant people are more able to access a wider range of choices when it comes to cultural practices. This is known as the cosmopolitan view, supported by Giddens, who claims that as a result of globalisation, culture is becoming less rigid and open to more debate. For example, in terms of beliefs, today more and more people are selecting alternative forms of religion, and pluralism is now a feature of religious beliefs all over the world. In fact, according to postmodernists such as Hervieu-Léger, today people can be 'spiritual shoppers' picking and choosing from a wide range of religious beliefs. This has led others to believe that western secular ideas are spreading and becoming more universal resulting in homogenisation.*

A clear summary of an alternative view to cultural convergence.

*There have also been new forms of cultural practice emerging as a result of globalisation, where two or more existing cultures combine to produce a new hybrid form. For example, in London, Johal and Bains describe an emergent hybrid identity based on a mixture of British and Asian cultures, known as 'Braisian'. These are third generation British Asians who at home act Asian and in the public domain act British.*

*In conclusion there are a wide range of ways in which in fact globalisation leads to cultural divergence rather than convergence. One contemporary example of this can be seen through the process of glocalisation where although people are aware of global changes in culture, they are transforming global themes to suit local practices.*

The answer includes a conclusion that summarises the main arguments put forward in response to the question.

## Comments

The connection between globalisation and cultural convergence is explained clearly, using some well-chosen examples and references to appropriate thinkers. Assessment is provided by outlining an alternative view to cultural convergence. There was scope to engage with the idea of cultural convergence more directly by, for example, questioning how far capitalist consumerism and ideals have spread in less industrialised societies or noting that even among Western industrialised societies there remain considerable differences in national and regional cultures between countries.

**Mark 28/35**

| 0 | 2 | 'Dependency theory exaggerates the influence of industrialised countries in the development process'. Evaluate this view. **[35 marks]**

You might want to answer this question yourself and then use the checklist that follows to review your answer. Compare your work to a partner's. Identify strengths in the answers and also consider how they could be improved.

The following is a list of qualities that would be found in a 'strong' answer:

- Shows understanding of the key terms in the question.
- Identifies the main issues raised by the question.
- Explains the view expressed in the question using relevant sociological concepts, theories and arguments.
- Uses evidence and references to sociological studies to support key points, where appropriate.
- Considers the view expressed in the question from different angles, analysing arguments and evidence for and against.
- Presents the sociological material used (concepts, theories, arguments) in a clear and logical way that is easy to understand.
- Draws conclusions about which arguments and/or evidence in response to the question are most convincing; reasons why those conclusions have been reached should also be given.
- Includes a concluding paragraph that summarises the main arguments and ideas expressed in the answer and, ideally, also contributes a final point that secures the case made in responding to the question.

# GLOSSARY OF KEY TERMS

## Chapter 1 Introduction

**Appropriation** Dishonest and unethical seizure of value or profit by the capitalist class of something produced by the labouring class.

**Authority** The power or right to give orders, make decisions and enforce obedience. It normally derives from a legal source.

**Biological analogy** The human body resembles society in that, as an effective totality, it is the sum of all its parts working together to ensure good health.

**Black Lives Matter** An international activist movement, originating in the African-American community, that campaigns against violence and systemic racism towards Black people.

**Bourgeois ideology** A set of ideas that originates with the capitalist class which attempts to convince members of society that inequality is a natural or normal outcome and that those who succeed or fail in the capitalist system deserve to do so.

**Bourgeoisie** The socio-economic group that owns the means of production and is responsible for the organisation of capitalism.

**Capitalism** An economic and political system in which a country's trade and industry are controlled by private owners for profit.

**Charismatic personality** Somebody with a compelling personality who has the ability to influence the behaviour of others.

**Coercion** The action or practice of persuading someone to do something by using force or threats.

**Collective consciousness** A shared set of cultural beliefs, values, norms and morality which function to unite society.

**Conflict** Disagreement or clash of interest.

**Conspicuous consumption** Expenditure on, and consumption of, luxuries on a lavish scale in an attempt to enhance one's prestige.

**Consumerism** The preoccupation of society with the acquisition of consumer goods.

**Consumption** Consumers spending money on commodities/goods (shopping).

**Cultural capital** The social, intellectual and cultural assets of a person that contribute to their educational success or social mobility, for example, knowing how to 'dress for success'.

**Cultural zombies** Workers who have been convinced by bourgeois ideology that they are responsible for their own fate and that they should uncritically accept their social position.

**Culture** The way of life of a particular group or society.

**Development** Improvement in the social and economic conditions of life of a society or people.

**Dramaturgical approach** The idea that people's day-to-day lives can be understood as resembling performers in action on a theatre stage.

**Ethnocentrism** A tendency to see the experience of others in terms of one's own culture. It often involves making unconscious negative judgements, because people assume that their cultural experience is 'normal' and all other experiences are 'abnormal'.

**False class consciousness** Being unaware that socio-economic position is caused by the organisation of the capitalist system.

**Front** The way we present ourselves in any given social situation to create specific impressions in the mind of others.

**Gender inequality** Refers to inequalities in wealth, pay, political power, access to certain types of jobs, and in the distribution of domestic tasks such as childcare and housework.

**Globalisation** The process through which the world is becoming increasingly interconnected as a result of increased trade and cultural exchange.

**High modernity** The later stages of modern societies identified by Beck, associated with manufactured risks to the ecology of the planet and high levels of individualisation.

**Human agency** The power people have to think for themselves and act in ways that shape their experiences and way of life.

**Impression management** The conscious or subconscious process in which people attempt to influence the perceptions of other people about a person, object or event.

**Individualisation** A social feature of late or postmodernity which encourages members of society to put the interests of themselves before the interests of the wider social group. It encourages selfishness rather than selflessness.

**Individualism** Being free from external pressures such as tradition and duty and being able to pursue one's own interests (sometimes at the expense of others).

**Inequality** The uneven distribution of resources so that some people have more benefits and opportunities than others in a society.

**Infrastructure** The economic system.

**Intersectionality** The acknowledgement that middle-class White women are not as exploited or as unequal as women from working-class and ethnic minority backgrounds, who may be held back by poverty, racism and religion.

**Labelling theory** The idea that people come to identify and behave in ways that reflect how more powerful others label or stereotype them.

**Labour power** The effort, skill and hours which a worker puts into the manufacture of a product.

**Late capitalism** A term used by Marxists to describe the later stages of modern capitalist society, especially capitalism's ability to exploit new global markets and to create new forms of labour in order to generate profit.

**Late modernity** A term used by Giddens to describe the later stages of modern society, which he claims is characterised by globalisation and reflexivity.

**Liquid modernity** A term used by Bauman to describe the later stages of modernity, which he sees as characterised by uncertainty.

**Manufactured risks** The risks produced by consumer demand for more consumer goods and the inability of capitalism to manufacture goods without risking the environment (for example, through pollution).

**Means of production** The resources required to manufacture a product; for example, capital for investment, raw materials, machinery and so on.

**Meta-narratives** Grand theories which aim to explain society and human behaviour.

**Modernity** A period in history or a type of society that is characterised by the use of advanced technology, belief in science, innovation and economic progress.

**Monopoly** The exclusive possession or control of the supply of, or trade in, a commodity or service.

**Narcissism** Extreme selfishness, with a grandiose view of one's own talents and a craving for admiration.

**Nation-states** A sovereign state of which most of the citizens or subjects are united by factors which define a nation, such as language, possession of a territory with borders and/or common descent.

**New Age religion** A type of religion which aims to help people find spiritual fulfilment through practices such as meditation, healing and self-discovery.

**New social movements** Political movements, which are often radical, global in reach and disproportionately supported by young people and coordinated online.

**Oligopoly** A state of limited competition, in which a market is shared by a very small number of producers or sellers.

**Opportunity** The number of desirable options available to an individual or group in a particular society.

**Over-deterministic** Believing that everything that happens could not happen in any other way.

**Patriarchy** Male domination of society and the social institutions that comprise it.

**Post-industrial** A stage in a society's development when the service sector of the economy generates more wealth than the industrial or manufacturing sector of the economy.

**Post-truth** A situation in which expert opinion and facts are less influential in shaping public attitudes than emotion, faith and personal belief.

**Power** The ability to direct or influence the behaviour of others.

**Proletariat** The labouring or working class.

**Reflexivity** The state of being able to examine one's own feelings, reactions and motives for acting and being able to adjust one's behaviour or identity accordingly.

**Relativism** The view that there is no such thing as absolute truth and that all opinions and experiences have validity.

**Resistance** Individual or group opposition to social control.

**Risk society** Beck's idea that technology used by capitalist societies has many negative consequences for humankind in terms of pollution, new diseases and environmental destruction.

**Self-fulfilling prophecy** This involves the application of a false definition or label to a person which makes a prediction about future behaviour. This labelling results in a new behaviour which confirms the initial label or prophecy.

**Self-religions** New Age religions which claim to improve self.

**Semiology** Sometimes called 'semiotics', this is the sociological study of signs and symbols. Sociologists have used it to study the content of media, for example, some feminists argue that the frequent use by journalists of the word 'girls' instead of 'women' symbolises patriarchal subordination.

**Social actors** Term used by social action theories to describe people or individuals who freely enter into interaction with others.

**Social capital** The collective value of all social networks (the value of knowing influential people), and the obligations that arise from these networks to do things for each other (for example, to return a favour).

**Social change** The transition from one form of social arrangement, or type of society, to another.

**Social class inequality** Inequalities in income and wealth, political power, life chances, levels of education, health and so on between the richest and poorest groups in capitalist society.

**Social control** The ways in which our behaviour, thoughts and appearance are regulated by the norms, rules and laws of society.

**Social exchange theory** A sociological theory which explains social order and stability as a consequence of negotiated exchanges between social actors. Interaction involves transactions between individuals that result in mutual value being exchanged. For example, if a group of people agree to abide by the law, the whole community benefits.

**Social identity** A person's sense of who they are based on their group membership.

**Social integration** Fitting into society.

**Social meanings** When we interpret the actions of others, we apply meaning to that action and respond accordingly.

**Social relations of production** The relationship between employers and workers.

**Social solidarity** A feeling of community or social belonging which results in feeling a bond with others.

**Social structure** The system of social institutions and patterned relations between large social groups.

**Socialisation** The processes through which people learn about the norms, rules and laws of society.

**Status** Social standing or the prestige attached to particular social roles.

**Superstructure** All of the cultural and social institutions that function to transmit capitalist ideology, especially the idea that the existence of wealth and poverty are justified.

**Surplus value** The excess of value produced by the labour of workers over the wages they are paid.

**Symbol** A thing that represents or stands for something else, especially a material object representing something abstract. For example, language in the form of writing is symbolic of spoken sounds. The word 'cat' is symbolic of a general group of domesticated pet, whereas the word 'Siamese' is symbolic of a particular breed of cat.

**Symbolic interaction** A social action theory that claims that identity is developed through interaction with others. A key feature of such interaction is the process of interpreting the symbolic behaviour of others, for example, their facial expression and body language.

**Traditional society** A type of society based on an agricultural economy where behaviour is regulated by largely unchanging customs and beliefs.

**Value consensus** Common or shared agreement.

## Chapter 2 Socialisation and identity

**Agency** Free will or the ability to choose particular courses of action.

**Anarchy** A state of disorder due to absence or non-recognition of authority or agencies of social control.

**Anomie** According to Durkheim – a state of normlessness or moral uncertainty in which the social rules of behaviour are not clearly drawn, therefore making people more prone to deviance.

**Artefacts** Material objects such as flags or monuments and buildings or cultural products such as sport, music and national dishes which have symbolic meaning for members of particular societies.

**Beliefs** Ideas that members of society hold to be true.

**Bonding social capital** The sharing of information or resources that may create opportunities for jobs or mutual help.

**Bridging social capital** Social and political alliances or networks that increase the potential for social change.

**Caste system** A religious and ascribed system of stratification mainly found in India and Indian communities abroad that categorises people into five status groups, which determine their occupation and the Hindu concept of religious purity.

**Class consciousness** A Marxist concept that relates to awareness of one's place in a system of social class, especially as it relates to the class struggle.

**Collectivism** The practice or principle of giving a group priority over each individual with in it.

**Conflict theories** Theories such as Marxism and feminism which see societies as characterised by conflict between social classes or between men and women.

**Conformity** Abiding by or complying with social norms, rules and laws.

**Conscience** Refers to the moral sense of right and wrong introduced to children from a very young age during the socialisation process which aims to deter deviant behaviour by setting off feelings of guilt if the child thinks about doing wrong.

**Consensual policing** The power of the police to fulfil their functions and duties is dependent on public approval of their existence, actions and behaviour and on their ability to secure and maintain public respect.

**Consensus theory** A type of structuralist approach which sees society as characterised by agreement and order; for example, functionalism.

**Control by consent** Persuading a social group that they should obey rules because they will benefit from them in the long term.

**Cost-benefit analysis** A process that involves members of society rationally weighing up the benefit of, say, obeying the law against the costs of not doing so or of rejecting the need for law altogether.

**Cultural amnesia** The collective loss of memory.

**Cultural appropriation** This involves members of a dominant culture taking cultural artefacts from a marginalised group without permission, and usually with little respect for or knowledge about that culture.

**Custom** A regular pattern of behaviour that is accepted as a routine norm in a particular society; for example, shaking hands when greeting someone.

**Dalit** The non-caste of 'untouchables' who occupy the lowest social rung of the Indian caste system and who do the dirtiest jobs.

**Decadence** Spiritual emptiness.

**Deferred gratification** The ability to forego or postpone gratification or pleasure now by making the decision to gain greater rewards later – say, by saving for the future or studying for a degree.

**Demonisation** The social practice of treating some groups as if they were 'social problems' or a threat to those who belong to mainstream law-abiding society.

**Deviance** Behaviour that is regarded as either offensive or odd to a social group or society and is therefore regarded as requiring some form of formal or informal regulation.

**Fatalism** The belief that all events are predetermined and inevitable, and that we are powerless and incapable of bringing about social change.

**Fat-shaming** The action or practice of humiliating someone judged to be fat or overweight by making mocking or critical comments about their size.

**Feral children** Children who have been deprived of interaction with other humans because they have been abandoned into the wild (and, in some cases, allegedly raised by animals) or kept in isolation.

**Folk culture** A type of culture which stems from the experiences, customs, traditions and beliefs of rural communities such as the peasantry or tribes that make up part of a wider culture, and which is passed down by word-of-mouth.

**Formal social control** Sanctions enforced by official agencies such as government in reaction to the breaking of written formal rules.

**Free will** The power to make decisions or choices that are not shaped by social forces beyond the control of the individual.

**Fundamentalism** A very conservative version of religion which believes that God's word and religious texts are infallible and need to be interpreted literally.

**Gender role socialisation** The process of learning behaviour that is culturally expected from males and females.

**Gender roles** The social expectations that underpin what is expected of a boy/man and a girl/woman in any given society.

**Gig economy** A labour market characterised by the prevalence of short-term contracts or freelance work as opposed to permanent jobs.

**Global risks** Globalisation has increased people's risk of being victims of global warming, terrorism, crime and so on.

**Globalisation** The trend of increasing interaction between societies and people worldwide due to advances in transportation and digital communications.

**Glocalisation** A trend which sees global actors flexibly altering their global brands so that they suit the needs of and respect local cultures. Local cultures may take aspects of a global product and adapt it so that it appeals to local consumers.

**Hegemonic** Culturally dominant.

**Hegemonic femininity** A version of feminine identity which stresses that females are subordinate and their 'natural' roles should be confined to the spheres of motherhood and the home.

**Hegemonic masculinity** A version of masculine identity which defines a 'real man' in terms of toughness, emotional hardness and the power to provide for his family.

**Hidden curriculum** The unwritten, unofficial, and often unintended lessons, values and attitudes that encourage conformity that students allegedly learn in classrooms and schools.

**High culture** Cultural products, such as art and literature, that are regarded as rare, unique and the product of exceptional talent.

**Humanist approach** A micro or 'bottom-up' approach which is interested in how social reality is 'interpreted' by individuals during their everyday interaction with others.

**Hybridised identity** A form of identity that is constructed by combining aspects of two or more cultures.

**Identity** The qualities, beliefs, personality, looks and/or expressions that constitute both how you see yourself and how other people may see or judge you.

**Ideological** Based on untrue information, propagated by a powerful group, aimed at justifying and legitimating some type of inequality.

**Ideological power** Dominating culture or ideas.

**Imitation** Children copying the actions of significant role models in their lives, especially their parents.

**Informal social controls** The negative reaction of friends, relatives and peers to deviance that encourages conformity to the informal rules employed by such groups.

**Jati** The caste system.

**Law** A rule or system of rules which a society agrees to follow and which regulate the behaviour of all. The role of the police and the courts is to enforce those rules by arresting those who break them and to impose punishments if found guilty of doing so.

**Macro approaches** A top-down approach which is mainly interested in how society or aspects of it influence individual actions.

**Mass or popular culture** Cultural artefacts such as pop music or Hollywood blockbusters that are mass produced for mass consumption.

**Mechanical solidarity** The sense of togetherness in a society that arises when people perform similar work and share similar experiences, customs, values and beliefs. Such societies view society as more important than the individual.

**Middle class** Those occupations that require a professional qualification or who manage capitalism on behalf of the capitalist class. This group tends to be highly rewarded in terms of income and status.

**Misogyny** Hatred of women.

**Nature versus nurture debate** The debate as to whether human behaviour is the product of innate biological influences such as instinct or genetics or whether it is the product of environmental influences such as social upbringing or the quality of socialisation.

**Negative sanctions** Punishments aimed at deterring deviance.

**Norms** The rules that govern what behaviour is normal in any given social situation.

**Organic solidarity** A type of system in which community ties are loose because people are exposed to a greater range of ideas, which encourages individualism and less moral certainty.

**Peer group** A group of people of approximately the same age, status and interests.

**Populism** A system of ideas that claims to support the will of the people.

**Positive sanctions** Rewards which encourage conformity.

**Positivist** A scientific approach which aims to document the impact of social forces on human behaviour by collecting large-scale data using sociological methods which are regarded as highly reliable and objective.

**Precariat** People whose employment and income are insecure, especially when considered as a class.

**Present-day orientation** A view likely to be held by members of the precariat, whose members may believe that people should live for today and that there is little hope for the future because of their experience of job insecurity.

**Primary socialisation** The process of learning that occurs in the family when parents teach children the language, attitudes, values, norms and ethics of the culture in which they live so that they grow up to be citizens and workers who conform to what society expects of them.

**Relativity of culture** The idea that what constitutes culture differs across time periods, societies and even between social groups living in the same society.

**Reproductive rights** The right of women to control their own bodies.

**Role** The behaviour that is expected from those who occupy a particular status.

**Role models** Significant others who are respected by those with less status (such as children) and whose behaviour sets an example to be imitated.

**Sampling frame** A list of people who might take part in a sociological study.

**Sanctions** A negative sanction is a threatened penalty for disobeying a law or rule. A positive sanction may take the form of approval or a reward.

**Satipatthana** A Buddhist concept that stresses mindfulness or awareness of others.

**Secondary socialisation** The process of social learning that is in addition to that which occurs in the family. Agents of secondary socialisation include formal education systems, religion, the workplace, and the media.

**Secular** Not subject to religious routines or rules.

**Self** This is composed of two parts; the 'I' is how people see themselves, while the 'me' is how we present ourselves when interacting with others.

**Social class** A socio-economic status and identity which is hierarchically organised on the basis of occupation, wealth, income and life chances.

**Social closure** Exclusionary practices employed by wealthy high-status groups to protect their monopoly and ownership of both wealth and property, so preventing other groups from becoming members of their class.

**Social construct/construction** A belief, characteristic or set of behaviours and assumptions that is produced or manufactured by the actions of those who constitute society or powerful social groups.

**Social construction** An interactionist concept that refers to behaviour that is thought to be natural but is actually the product of cultural expectations and processes.

**Social controls** Regulations and rules which aim to reinforce 'ideal' behaviour and to ensure conformity. Failure to abide by social controls may result in public punishment.

**Social exchange** Interaction and negotiation between individuals that involves maximum benefit and minimum cost for mutual or reciprocal benefit.

**Social mores** Values, often influenced by religion, which set out the moral principles and rules of societies; for example, that sexual relationships should only be conducted in the moral context of marriage.

**Social pressure** Influence exerted on an individual or group by a more or equally powerful person or group. The influence might take the form of rational argument, persuasion or coercion (threats, violence and so on). For example, a peer group may exert social pressure on an adolescent to behave in an anti-social manner.

**Social stratification** A system of social ranking, usually based on wealth, income, race, education and power.

**Social structure** The social organisation of society.

**Socialisation** The process of social learning that occurs in the period from birth to death in which individuals acquire and absorb the cultural values and norms of the society in which they live.

**Socialism** A left-wing political ideology or set of beliefs that states all people are equal and should enjoy equal opportunities with regard to access to education, qualifications, jobs and wealth creation.

**Society** A community of people who share a common territory and culture and consequently interact with one another daily.

**Spectacular youth subculture** Highly visible groups of young people who commit themselves to a certain 'shocking' look in terms of hairstyle, dress codes and so on, and whose behaviour is often interpreted by the older generation and the media as 'threatening' the moral order or stability of society.

**Structuralist theories** Theories such as functionalism, Marxism and feminism which claim people's actions are the product of the ways their societies are organised or structured.

**Structuration** A theory of society invented by Giddens which argues that human behaviour is caused by a combination of structure and agency.

**Subculture** A distinct group that exists within a wider society. A subculture has a very distinct and separate identity, for example, in terms of the way they dress or behave – that stands out from mainstream culture.

**Super-rich/uber-wealthy** An expression used to describe the richest 1 per cent of billionaires and multi-millionaires.

**Symbiotic** Inter-dependent.

**Symbolisation** A process found in some news reporting of social groups in which journalists identify key features of particular groups, especially young people, so that they can be avoided by others or be easily identified and targeted by the police.

**Toxic masculinity** A consequence of hegemonic masculinity in that males may suffer from depression or suicidal thoughts because they believe they cannot publicly display emotion or vulnerability. It may also be expressed through violence and misogyny.

**Unskilled class/underclass** Values, often influenced by religion, which set out the moral principles and rules of societies; for example, that sexual relationships should only be conducted in the moral context of marriage.

**Upper class** The social group that has the highest status in society. This status is often inherited. It is often called the 'ruling class'.

**Value system** A collection of values, norms, traditions and customs agreed upon and shared by a social group or society.

**Values** General guidelines about how members of society should behave. Values generally shape norms of behaviour. For example, many societies value marriage.

**Voluntarism** The idea that human action is voluntary rather than imposed externally by social forces beyond the individual's control. Voluntarists as represented by social action theories believe that social behaviour is the result of people having free will and the ability to choose how to act.

**Xenophobic** Fear or hatred of foreigners such as refugees or migrants.

## Chapter 3 Research methods

**Audience analysis** Examining how audiences respond to and interpret documentary material.

**Bias** Error or distortion in the data arising from the way evidence is collected or interpreted.

**Case study** A study of a particular instance of something.

**Closed questions** Questions in which the range of responses is fixed by the researcher.

**Closed system** A system in which all the variables can be controlled.

**Coded** Answers are classified into various categories.

**Correlation** A statistical link between two or more variables or factors.

**Covert observation** Observation-based research in which the observer's true identity and the purpose of their study are hidden from participants.

**Data** Information that a researcher draws on and/or generates during a study.

**Deductive approach** Starting with a theory and using evidence to test that theory.

**Digital content** Information such as social media that is distributed via the internet.

**Ethical** Relating to moral principles that state what is right and wrong.

**Ethical guidelines** Guidance provided by social science organisations and universities on how to conduct morally acceptable research, covering issues such as informed consent and confidentiality.

**Ethical issue** A concern with morals and how to conduct morally acceptable research.

**Ethnography** The study of the way of life of a group of people in order to understand their world from their perspective.

**Experimental effect** Any unintended impact of the experiment on participants.

**Experimenter bias** The unintended effect of the experimenter on a participant.

**Falsification** Looking for evidence to disprove a theory.

**Feminist methodology** A methodology designed to reflect feminist ideals and values.

**Field experiment** An experiment conducted in everyday social settings.

**Focus group** A group discussion about one particular theme or topic guided by a moderator; it explores how participants interact and respond to each other's views.

**Formal content analysis** Counting how often particular words, phrases and images occur.

**Gatekeeper** The person or group in a particular setting such as a school with responsibility for allowing (or otherwise) a researcher to undertake research in that site.

**Generalisation** A statement based on a relatively small group which is then applied to a larger group.

**Grounded theory** Starting from 'concrete data' and building upwards to theory.

**Group interview** A type of interview covering a range of themes or topics; the researcher questions and collects data from several people at once.

**Hawthorne effect** Changes in participants' behaviour resulting from an awareness that they are taking part in an experiment.

**Historical documents** Documents from the past.

**Hypothesis** A testable statement about the relationship between two or more variables.

**Inductive approach** Starting with evidence and developing a theory from that evidence.

**Informed consent** The participant only agrees to participate in the research once the sociologist has explained fully what the research is about and why it is being undertaken.

**Interpretivism** An approach that explores people's lived experiences and the meanings they attach to their actions. It favours qualitative data.

**Interview bias** The effect of the interview situation itself on a participant's responses.

**Interviewer bias** The effect of the interviewer on a research participant's answers.

**Key informant** A member of the group being studied who provides important information and often sponsors the researcher.

**Laboratory experiment** An experiment conducted in a specially designed setting.

**Life history** A case study of an individual's life.

**Longitudinal study** A study of the same group of people over time.

**Meta-narratives** Grand stories which claim to explain things.

**Methodological pluralism** The use of a plurality or range of research methods, including both quantitative and qualitative methods.

**Methodology** A theory about how research should proceed.

**Mixed-methods approaches** Using more than one method in a research project, often combining both qualitative and quantitative techniques.

**Moderator** An interviewer who guides focus group discussions.

**Non-directive interviewing** An interviewing technique that seeks to avoid leading participants to answer in particular ways.

**Non-participant observation** An observation-based study in which the researcher does not join those they are studying.

**Normal science** Science which operates within an established paradigm.

**Objectivity** A value-free, impartial, unbiased view.

**Observation schedule** Instructions which tell the observer what to look for and how to record it.

**Observer effect** This occurs in an observation-based study when the observer's known presence changes the behaviour of the people being studied.

**Official statistics** Numerical data produced by government departments and agencies.

**Open system** A system in which it is impossible to control all the variables.

**Open-ended/open questions** Questions which allow the respondent to answer in their own words.

**Operationalise** Translate abstract concepts into a form that can be measured.

**Overt observation** Open research in which the observer's true identity and the purpose of their research are revealed to participants.

**Paradigm** A framework of concepts and theories which states how the natural world operates.

**Participant observation** A qualitative method in which the researcher gathers data by joining a group and taking part in its activities.

**Personal documents** Letters, diaries, notes and photographs.

**Pilot study** A small-scale study to check the suitability of the methods to be used in the main study.

**Population** The group under study from which a sample is selected.

**Positivism** An approach based partly on the methods used in the natural sciences. It favours quantitative data.

**Primary data** New information produced by the researcher during the research process.

**Qualitative data** All data (such as quotations from interview participants) that is not in numerical form.

**Quantitative data** Information in the form of statistics.

**Quota sampling** A type of stratified sampling in which selection from the strata is not random.

**Random sampling** A sampling technique in which every member of the sampling frame has a known chance of being selected.

**Rapport** A friendly, trusting and understanding relationship.

**Realist view** An approach which assumes that events in both the natural and social worlds are produced by underlying structures and mechanisms.

**Reflexivity** In the context of research, reflecting on yourself, looking back at your research, and examining how your values and background might have influenced your findings.

**Relativism** The idea that all knowledge is relative to time, place, culture and the individual.

**Reliability** Data are reliable when different researchers using the same methods obtain the same results.

**Replication** Repeating an experiment or research study under the same conditions.

**Representative sample** A subgroup that is typical of its population.

**Research ethics committees** Bodies in universities that scrutinise research proposals.

**Research methods** Techniques for collecting data such as interviews or questionnaires.

**Research participants** The people who researchers study.

**Response rate** The percentage of the sample that participates in the research.

**Sample** A subgroup of research participants from the larger group to be studied.

**Sample attrition** The reduction in the size of the original sample over time.

**Sampling frame** A list of members of the research population.

**Sampling technique** A procedure (such as snowball or stratified random sampling) used to obtain a sample.

**Sampling unit** A member of the research population such as a household or a student.

**Scientific revolution** The overthrow of an established paradigm by a new paradigm.

**Secondary data** Pre-existing information used by the researcher.

**Self-completion questionnaire** A questionnaire that the respondent fills in.

**Semiology** The analysis of signs.

**Semiotic analysis** The study of signs and symbols and how they combine to create meaning.

**Semi-structured interview** Similar to a structured interview, but the interviewer probes with additional questions.

**Simple random sampling** A technique in which all members of the sampling frame have an equal chance of being selected.

**Snowball sampling** A technique in which members of the sample select each other.

**Social desirability effect** Bias resulting from a research participant's desire to reflect in their responses what is generally seen as the right way to behave.

**Social facts** The institutions, norms and values of society.

**Social survey** Systematic collection of the same type of data from a fairly large number of people.

**Stratified random sampling** A technique in which the population is divided into strata and the sample is randomly drawn from each stratum. It attempts to reflect particular characteristics, such as age and gender, of the population.

**Structured interview** A questionnaire which the interviewer read outs and fills in.

**Structured/systematic observation** An observation-based study which usually employs an observation schedule to generate quantitative data.

**Subjectivity** A personal view based on an individual's values and beliefs.

**Textual analysis** Examining how the words and phrases chosen encourage a particular reading of a document.

**Thematic analysis** Interpreting the meanings, motives and ideologies that underlie documents.

**Trend** The general direction in which statistics on something (such as the divorce rate) change or move over time.

**Triangulation** A way of cross-checking the validity of research findings by, for example, using mixed methods.

**Unstructured interview** An interview with few, if any, pre-set questions, though researchers usually have certain topics they wish to cover.

**Unstructured observation** An observation-based study that produces a detailed description of behaviour as seen by the researcher.

**Validity** Data are valid if they represent a true or accurate measurement.

**Value free** Objective, impartial and unbiased.

**Variables** Factors that affect behaviour. Variables can vary, for example, temperature can increase or decrease.

**Verstehen** As used by Weber, an approach for interpreting the meanings and motives that direct individual action. It involves understanding research participants' situations as they themselves understand them.

**Victim surveys** Surveys that ask respondents whether they have been victims of particular crimes during a specified period and, if so, whether they reported them to the police.

**Volunteer sample** A sample in which members of the sample are self-selected.

## Chapter 4 The family

**Arranged marriage** A type of marriage organised or arranged by the parents of the couple and/or matchmakers.

**Age patriarchy** A system of inequalities caused primarily by age differences and especially the idea that adults, particularly the heads of households, know what is best for children.

**Alienation** A concept which Marxists in particular suggest is now becoming a common characteristic of how workers feel about their jobs. Alienation refers to the lack of satisfaction, identification and control that workers experience on a daily basis and the fact that they work merely for a wage.

**Ascription/ascribed role** A role assigned at birth over which an individual has little choice or say. For example, members of a royal family inherit a role. In patriarchal societies, females involuntarily occupy a subordinate role.

**Baby strike** A call by radical feminists for women to refuse to have babies, claiming that motherhood is the biggest obstacle to women's progress and that it reinforces patriarchy.

**Basic and irreducible functions** The two crucial functions performed by the nuclear family in modern capitalist societies: the primary socialisation of children, and the stabilisation of adult personalities.

**Beanpole family** A four-generational type of family that has few extended kin such as aunts, uncles and cousins.

**Bigamy** The state of being married to two people at the same time. It is a criminal offence in Western societies.

**Bi-nuclear family** Children of divorced or separated couples often belong to two nuclear families because their natural parents have remarried or are cohabiting with a new partner.

**Blended family** A variation on the reconstituted family that includes, in addition to step-children, the natural children of the remarried couple.

**Boomerang family** Families in which children leave home, but because of circumstances beyond their control they are forced to return to live with their parents as young adults.

**Canalisation** A component of gender role socialisation where parents lead or channel their children's interests and activities to gender-appropriate areas. For example, toys are often classified as suitable for either boys or girls.

**Chaos of love** Beck believes that marriage is potentially a battleground, because the institution of marriage demands compromise and selflessness but people often look out for their own interests first.

**Child abuse** Physical maltreatment or sexual molestation of a child.

**Child-centredness** The notion that the child should be the focus of attention. Child-centred families see raising children as the most important component of family life.

**Child-free** The decision usually taken in conjunction with a partner not to have children.

**Childlessness** The state of not having children. This may be voluntary or involuntary.

**Chore wars** The conflict that results between a couple about who should be responsible for domestic labour.

**Civil rights** The rights of citizens to political and social freedom and equality.

**Class diversity** Refers to how social class, especially wealth and poverty, may shape family living arrangements and the opportunities for a quality childhood.

**Cohabitation** The state of living together and having an intimate relationship without being married.

**Commune** A type of cooperative household made up of mainly unrelated people who agree to share work, possessions and religious or social objectives.

**Concerted cultivation** A type of middle-class socialisation of children which aims to develop or encourage cultured behaviour and knowledge, such as knowledge of art, history, literature and so on, which may be advantageous in educational contexts.

**Conflict** A clash of interests that can cause inequality.

**Conjugal roles** The roles played by a male and female partner in marriage or in a cohabiting relationship.

**Consensual** All involved agree willingly.

**Conspicuous consumption** Expenditure on, or consumption of, luxuries on a lavish scale in an attempt to enhance one's prestige.

**Consumerism** The act of shopping for consumer items or commodities.

**Consumption** Refers to the spending of money on goods and services. A successful economy needs to competitively market its goods and services in ways that attract consumers to spend their cash on them.

**Consumption as compensation** The idea that parents buy their children consumer items to compensate for not spending quality time with them.

**Co-parenting** When a separated, divorced or unmarried couple share the duties of parenting, for example, a child may spend part of a week living with one parent and the rest of the week living with the other.

**Crisis of masculinity** The idea that men are more likely to suffer from anxiety and depression because their traditional roles as breadwinner and head of household are fast disappearing.

**Cult of the individual** An idea very similar to Beck's concept of individualisation. It refers to the increasing trend to put ourselves before others and a desire not to live or mix with others, therefore the trend towards living in single person households.

**Cultural diversity** Refers to how families might differ in organisation across different societies and across ethnic and religious groups within the same society.

**Cultural hegemony** Domination or rule maintained through ideological or cultural means.

**Decentring of conjugal relationships** A radical feminist idea that rejects the idea that the most important relationship a woman has is with a man. Radical feminists believe that women can have the same quality family relationships with other women and/or gay men.

**Dependency culture** According to New Right sociologists, a way of life characterised by dependency on state benefits.

**Digital feminism** Feminists, who mainly belong to the millennial generation, who challenge sexism and misogyny using online digital sites such as Twitter and Facebook and by setting up internet websites such as Everydaysexism.com.

**DINK families** 'Dual income, no kids'. A term which refers to a couple who both earn an income and do not (yet) have children.

**Dispersed extended family** Extended kin (grandparents, aunts, uncles and cousins) who normally live in geographically scattered nuclear families but who feel a sense of duty and obligation to provide mutual support and assistance to each other in times of need or to get together on symbolic occasions such as Christmas.

**Divorce** The legal dissolution of a marriage by a court or other competent body.

**Domestic diversity** Differences of internal arrangements of families. For example, in some families the mother has a career and goes out to work. In others, the mother stays at home full-time, and in a rare number of families the father stays at home as a full-time carer.

**Domestic division of labour** The way that men and women divide up housework and childcare between themselves.

**Domestic labour** Unpaid labour – housework, childcare and so on – carried out within the home, often by women.

**Domestic violence** Violence, usually committed by the male spouse on his female partner and/or his children.

**Dowry system** Refers to the cash and property that the bride's family gives to the bridegroom, his parents, or his relatives as a condition of the marriage.

**Dual burden** Another term for the second shift.

**Dual income/dual career nuclear families** A family in which both adults have a career and in which the wage of each partner makes a significant contribution to the lifestyle of the family.

**Dual-career/income families** Families in which both adult partners pursue a career and in which each contribute income that is important to the family's standard of living.

**Dual-heritage children** The children of interethnic marriages.

**Egalitarian** The principle that all people are equal and deserve equal rights and opportunities.

**Emotion work** The idea that women are responsible for the emotional health and well-being of family members.

**Emotional participation** Sharing one's feelings, experiences and emotions, particularly within an intimate relationship or family context.

**Empirical** Based on experience or observation.

**Empty nest families** Households in which only the parents remain once their grown-up children have left home.

**Empty-shell marriage** A loveless marriage in which husband and wife stay together for financial or religious reasons or for the sake of the children, but essentially lead separate lives in the same house.

**Epistemological** Relating to how knowledge of a given subject is obtained.

**Ethnocentric** Judging other cultures according to preconceptions originating in the standards and customs of one's own culture.

**Ethnocentrism** Judging one's own cultural experience to be 'better' than that of other cultures.

**Ethnographic** Sociological research which studies social groups in their own environment going about their everyday business.

**Expressive leader** The role of nurturer of children, primarily responsible for the primary socialisation of children, and emotional caretaker. According to Parsons, females have a 'natural' empathy for this role.

**Extended family** A unit consisting of the nuclear family plus other kin who may live under the same roof or in close proximity so that contact is regular and frequent.

**Failure to launch generation** Children who for a variety of reasons have not been able to leave home and therefore still live with their parents despite being adults.

**False needs** According to Marxism, the logic of capitalism as expressed through advertising is to sell as many commodities to consumers as possible. This often involves 'persuading' consumers to indulge in false wants or needs, that is, to buy commodities that are not essential and not built to last.

**Falsely conscious** A way of thinking that prevents a person from perceiving the true nature of their social or economic situation.

**Families of choice** An idea which suggests that members of our family are who we choose them to be – for example, we might regard close friends as symbolic family members, as well as cats and dogs.

**Femicide** The murder of females.

**Fictive kin** Normally, close friends of the family, particularly parents, who have been given the honorary title of 'uncle' or 'aunt'.

**Fidelity** Faithfulness, usually in a relationship.

**Filial piety** A Confucian belief that children should have a great respect for their elders, especially parents and grandparents.

**First wave of feminism** Ideas that appeared in the 18th and 19th century that challenged male domination of the family and eventually led to women being allowed to vote.

**Forced marriage** A marriage in which one or more of the parties is married without his or her consent or against his or her will.

**Fourth wave of feminism** Type of feminism, particularly the digital feminism practised by millennials.

**Gender binary** The classification of sex and gender into two distinct, opposite and disconnected forms of masculine and feminine.

**Gender bound** The idea that men and women are culturally obligated to perform certain tasks – for example, that men provide for their families and women are emotional caretakers.

**Gender scripts** The idea that male and female behaviour is performed according to cultural expectations about masculinity and femininity.

**Genderquake** A radical change in attitudes compared with previous generations, so radical that it symbolises a seismic (earthquake-type) upheaval.

**Geographical mobility** Refers to people and families physically moving across the country, usually in search of work or education.

**Girl power** A media-invented term which claimed that females wielded cultural power in the 1990s because they imitated role models such as Madonna.

**Glass ceiling** The unseen, yet unbreachable, barrier that keeps women from rising to the upper rungs of the corporate ladder, regardless of their qualifications or achievements.

**Hetero-norm** The idea that relationships should be heterosexual.

**'Honour'-related murders** The murder of a girl or woman by a family member for an actual or assumed sexual or behavioural transgression, including adultery, sexual intercourse or pregnancy outside marriage, or even for being raped.

**Household** This includes all those who live under the same roof or occupy the same dwelling. These people need not be necessarily related.

**Ideology** A set of ideas which most people believe to be true but which in fact are myths or misrepresentations. They are usually encouraged by powerful groups because such ideas tend to justify and legitimate the power and wealth of those groups.

**Ideology of the family** A set of dominant ideas and beliefs which have the effect of instructing members of society about how families and the roles within them should be organised.

**In vitro fertilisation** A medical procedure whereby an egg is fertilised by sperm in a test tube or elsewhere outside the body.

**Individualisation** A concept associated with Beck that refers to a dominant ideology that stresses freedom from obligation or community pressure and gives people the freedom to look out for themselves first and foremost.

**Infantilisation** To reduce something to a childish state or condition.

**Institutional sexism** Ideas and practices that may be consciously or unconsciously embedded in the regulations and actions of an organisation such as a school or police force.

**Instrumental leader** The role of economic provider or breadwinner for the nuclear family. Parsons claimed that this is usually the role of the male.

**Inter-ethnic marriage** Marriages that take place between people who are from different racial or ethnic groups.

**Intersectional feminism** A critique of liberal and radical feminism which implied that the experience of patriarchy was the same for all women. Black and Asian feminists, and Marxist feminists pointed out that gender often interacts or intersects with social class, race and patriarchy to produce unique experiences of patriarchy.

**Irretrievable breakdown** When both spouses agree that the marriage is over and that there is no hope that it will be ever revived.

**Isolated nuclear family** A family that is self-contained and which has little contact with extended kin.

**Kibbutz** A type of commune or household found in Israel (plural 'kibbutzim').

**Kinship** Relationship between people who are related to each other by blood, marriage or adoption.

**Ladettes** A term used by the media in the 1990s to describe young women who used their leisure time to act in the same way as men.

**Leftover women** A term used in China to describe women who are still not married by the age of 27. They are seen to be 'left on the shelf'.

**LGBT community** A loose grouping of lesbian, gay, bisexual, and transgender organisations, and subcultures, united by a common culture and social movements. These communities generally celebrate pride, diversity, individuality and sexuality.

**Liberal feminism** A collection of feminist sociologists who highlighted gender inequality in areas such as education and put pressure on governments to challenge it by introducing equal rights and opportunities legislation and social policies.

**Liberate** To free somebody from oppression or exploitation.

**Life-course** The stages that all human beings go through during their life, covering birth to death.

**Living apart together (LAT)** A modern household set-up in which a couple who are romantically involved make the decision to maintain separate households rather than move in together.

**Loss of functions** The functionalist idea that the multi-functional extended family of the pre-industrial era lost many of its functions after the industrial revolution.

**Malestream** A concept developed by feminist theorists to describe the situation when male sociologists carry out research which either ignores or neglects women's experience and/ or focuses on a masculine perspective and then assumes that the findings can be applied to women as well.

**Manipulation** A component of gender role socialisation in which parents encourage behaviour which is culturally acceptable for boys or girls but discourage behaviour that might be interpreted as not fitting cultural norms.

**March of progress** The idea that features of contemporary life are an improvement on how they were previously organised.

**Marriage rate** The number of marriages per 1000 people per year.

**Matriarchal** A society or community dominated by women – the opposite to patriarchal.

**Matrifocal** A society or culture based on the mother as the head of the family or household.

**Millennial feminists** Feminists who were born in the late 1980s and who in the early 21st century were in their 20s and early 30s. This generation, especially if it has experienced higher education, is thought to be highly politicised. Surveys suggest that they see females as equal to males and consequently they are less likely to tolerate inequality, sexism and misogyny and more likely than previous generations to challenge patriarchal processes.

**Misogyny** "Dislike of, contempt for, or ingrained prejudice against women."

**Monogamy** The state of only being married to one person at any one time.

**Motherhood penalty** Craig claims that motherhood often means that women have more responsibility for domestic labour and less time for leisure.

**Multi-functional** Performing lots of functions, such as the pre-industrial family.

**Neo-conventional family** Chester's term for the modern form of nuclear family. According to Chester, most of us will live as a child or adult in this type of family at some point in our lives.

**Nuclear family** A unit that comprises mother, father and children, natural or adopted.

**Organisational diversity** Differences in the size or organisation of families. Extended families are obviously larger than nuclear families, which in turn are larger than one-parent families.

**Partnership penalty** An idea associated with Craig. She claims that the decision of a couple to live together or marry benefits the male but penalises the female, in that she ends up responsible for the bulk of domestic labour.

**Personal communities** A network of close friends and kin (even pets) that a person might regard as closest to them.

**Personal life** Smart believes that, rather than study families, sociologists should study how individuals negotiate their way through their personal lives. By doing this, we can see that a vast range of people beyond immediate kin play important roles in our lives.

**Perverse incentive** An incentive that results in unintended negative consequences; for example, females may find it advantageous to get pregnant and bring up a child alone rather than get married, because state benefits are generous.

**Pester power** The ability of children to pressurise their parents into buying them products, especially items advertised in the media.

**Polyandry** A type of polygamy in which a woman can marry more than one husband. It is quite rare compared with polygyny.

**Polygamy** A cultural norm which allows spouses to have more than one husband or wife.

**Polygyny** A type of polygamy in which a man can marry more than one woman or can be married to a set of co-wives.

**Post-feminism** A 1990s trend that suggested that females no longer had any need for second-wave feminism because they now had girl power. Many critics saw it as a media construction and as reflecting a male backlash against radical feminism.

**Power-feminism** Another term for post-feminism.

**Private patriarchy** A type of male domination found exclusively in the home, family and in personal relationships.

**Public patriarchy** Institutionalised forms of sexual prejudice and discrimination found across a range of social institutions, including government, education and the law.

**Radical feminism** A group of feminists who attempted to explain gender inequality by constructing structural theories that saw patriarchy as a complex inter-dependent social system. The theory was often seen as men-hating because it is hyper-critical of what it saw as male exploitation and oppression of women.

**Radical psychiatry** A school of psychiatric thought that believes psychiatric problems are caused by alienation brought about by the intensity of family relationships.

**Reconstituted family** Also called a step-family – a family unit where one or both parents have children from a previous relationship but have combined to form a new family.

**Remarriage** The act of marrying again after experiencing a divorce.

**Renaissance children** Middle-class children possessing lots of cultural capital that is, knowledge valued by schools and universities.

**Reproductive rights** The right of females to control their own bodies; for example, the right of women to decide whether they want to have children or be child-free, when to have children and how many children to have.

**Same-sex marriage** Also known as gay marriage – the marriage of same-sex couples recognised by law as having the same status and rights as marriage of opposite-sex couples.

**Sandwich carers** Refers to those looking after young children at the same time as caring for older parents. It can also be used much more broadly to describe a variety of multiple caring responsibilities for people in different generations.

**Second shift** The idea that married women have two jobs and consequently no leisure time. They spend their day in paid work but still do most of the unpaid labour in the home.

**Second wave of feminism** Liberal, radical and Marxist feminist ideas that appeared in the 1960s and 1970s, often collectively known as the 'women's liberation movement'.

**Secularisation** A general decline in religious belief in God and religious practices such as regularly going to church.

**Separation** Informal separation occurs when spouses live apart, but do not pursue formal separation or divorce.

**Serial monogamy** The practice of engaging in a succession of monogamous cohabiting relationships or marriages.

**Sexualisation of children** The idea that children are growing up too quickly because the media are introducing them to adult themes such as sex far too early in their development.

**Single-parent families** Families with children under age 18 headed by a parent who is widowed or divorced and who has not remarried, or by a parent who has never married.

**Single-person households** A person living alone.

**Sociability** The quality of liking to meet and spend time with other people.

**Social blurring** The idea that the distinction between children and adults is beginning to disappear as children aspire to behave like adults and as adults treat children as their equals.

**Social construction** A term used by social action theories to indicate that some social processes are the product or invention of society, dominant social groups or cultural norms.

**Socialist/Marxist feminism** A type of feminism that argued that gender inequality was linked to class inequality. Both were seen to be the product of capitalism – for example, capitalist employers profit from women's unpaid domestic labour.

**Stabilisation of adult personality** An irreducible function of the nuclear family according to Parsons, in which the male worker's immersion in his family supposedly relieves him of the pressures of work and contemporary society, just as a warm bath soothes and relaxes the body.

**Stigma** A negative label or a mark of disgrace associated with a particular circumstance, quality or person.

**Structural differentiation** The emergence of specialised agencies which gradually took over many of the functions of the pre-industrial extended family.

**Suffrage** The right to vote.

**Surrogacy** The process in which a woman agrees to bear a child on behalf of another woman, either from her own egg fertilised by the other woman's partner, or from the implantation in her uterus of a fertilised egg from the other woman.

**Symmetrical family** A type of nuclear family identified by Young and Willmott in which husband and wife supposedly share domestic labour, decision-making and leisure time.

**Synergistic** The interaction or cooperation of two individuals, such as grandparents and grandchildren, which produces a combined effect greater than the sum of their separate effects.

**Test-tube babies** Children who are the product of reproductive technology such as in vitro fertilisation or artificial insemination because their parents cannot conceive naturally for medical reasons.

**Theoretical imperialism** The insistence that one particular type of experience should take precedence over all other experiences. Radical feminism was accused of this by intersectional feminists for implying that all women experienced patriarchal control in the same way.

**Third wave of feminism** Refers to two unrelated forms of feminism that appeared about the same time (1980s/1990s) – intersectional feminism and post-feminism.

**Time-budget study** A type of social survey which asks respondents to estimate the amount of time they spend on a particular task.

**Toxic masculinity** A type of masculinity which exhibits negative traits such as violence, sexual aggression and an inability or reluctance to express emotions because of a belief that it is weak to do so.

**Transphobia** Refers to a range of negative attitudes, feelings, actions or hate crimes toward transgender or transsexual people.

**Triple shift** The idea that women have three pressures on their time – paid work, unpaid domestic labour and emotion work.

**Triple systems theory** A feminist theory of patriarchy associated with Walby which argues that there are three crucial influences on a woman's experience of inequality and oppression – gender, social class and ethnicity.

**Underclass** The lowest social stratum in a country or community, consisting of the poor and unemployed. The New Right claim that members of the underclass are most likely to be welfare-dependent and criminal.

**Unit of consumption** The family is the main unit of consumption in capitalist society because agents of capitalism such as advertisers and the media promote consumer items in such a way that they are specifically aimed at encouraging family members to buy them.

**Urbanisation** The process of people who had previously lived in the countryside moving to the towns and cities, usually to find work in factories, mills and so on.

**Vertical extended family** Families composed of three generations that may live under the same roof or in very close proximity who are in frequent daily contact.

**Voluntary childlessness** Consciously and voluntarily choosing not to have children. It should be distinguished from the state of not being able to have children for medical or biological reasons.

**Welfare state** A system whereby the state undertakes to protect the health and well-being of its citizens, especially those in financial or social need, by means of grants, pensions and other benefits.

**Welfare-dependent** The New Right claim that some individuals are no longer capable of taking responsibility for themselves because they have grown too dependent on state benefits. They are no longer motivated to seek work.

**Workhouse** A British public or charitable institution in which the poor, especially children, the elderly and the sick and disabled, received somewhere to live in return for work. Most poor people feared being sent to the workhouse because it was a humiliating and shameful experience.

## Chapter 5 Education

**Ability groups** Groups in which students are placed on the basis of their perceived ability.

**Absolute mobility** The total amount of social mobility in a society.

**Achieved status** Status or positions in society that are

earned on the basis of individual talents or merit.

**Alienation** A feeling of being cut off from and unable to find satisfaction from work.

**Anti-school culture** Student subculture which rejects the norms and values of the school.

**Ascribed status** Status or positions in society that are fixed at birth and unchanging over time, including hereditary titles linked to family background (for example, King or Princess) or the status of a daughter or son within a family.

**Attainment gap** A difference in achievements between groups which is based, for example, on class, gender or ethnicity.

**Banding** Placing students in a band containing two or more classes, which may be regrouped for different subjects.

**Branch campus** A campus which is a branch of the main university.

**Capital** In Marxist terms, wealth derived from ownership of the means of production. Bourdieu broadened this to include the main social, cultural and symbolic resources as well as economic resources that determine people's position in society.

**Collectivism** Emphasis on the group rather than the individual.

**Commodity** Something that can be bought and sold.

**Compensatory education** Making up for, or compensating for, the supposed deficiencies of so-called culturally deprived groups.

**Conversion** The process by which one form of capital reinforces another.

**Correspondence theory** A theory that states that there is a similarity between two things.

**Counter-school culture** A school-based subculture whose members reject the norms and values of the school and replace them with anti-school norms and values.

**Creaming** Selecting students who appear most likely to succeed for entry to educational institutions.

**Crisis of masculinity** The idea that males see their traditional masculine identity as under threat today.

**Cultural capital** The manners, tastes, interests and language of the 'dominant classes' which can be translated into wealth, income, power and prestige.

**Cultural deprivation theory** The idea that certain groups are deprived of, or deficient in, things seen as necessary for high educational attainment.

**Cultural reproduction** The transmission of cultural norms, values and experiences between the generations.

**Differential educational attainment** The different attainment levels of different groups of children, for example, class, gender and ethnic groups.

**Economic capital** Financial resources in the form of income and wealth.

**Educational Priority Areas** Programmes of compensatory education in parts of England.

**Educational triage** The division of students into three groups in terms of their expected GCSE grades.

**Elaborated code** Speech in which meanings are made explicit and spelled out.

**Elimination** The elimination of members of the working class from higher levels of education.

**Equality of opportunity** A system in which every person has an equal chance of success.

**Ethnocentric** Evaluating one's own culture or ethnic group as superior to others.

**Ethnocentrism** The belief that one's own culture or ethnic group is superior to others.

**Extra-curricular activities** Activities undertaken outside lessons at school such as clubs and debating societies, or hobbies undertaken outside school such as yoga or dance.

**False class consciousness** A false picture of society that disguises the exploitation of the subject class (the proletariat in capitalist societies).

**Fatalism** Accepting a situation rather than making efforts to improve it.

**Formal curriculum** The stated knowledge and skills which students are expected to acquire.

**Globalisation** The process by which societies, cultures and economies become increasingly interconnected.

**Habitus** The dispositions, expectations, attitudes and values held by particular groups.

**Hegemonic masculinity** The dominant and pervasive view of masculinity.

**Hidden curriculum** The messages schools transmit which are not part of the standard taught curriculum and which are largely hidden from teachers and students.

**Ideological State Apparatuses** Institutions, including the education system, that transmit ruling-class ideology.

**Immediate gratification** Focusing on the pleasures of the moment rather than putting them off for future reward.

**Individualisation** An emphasis on the individual, on self-construction, self-reliance and self-sufficiency.

**Institutional racism** Racial prejudice and discrimination that form part of the taken-for-granted assumptions and operations of institutions.

**Interactionism** A sociological theory which examines interaction between members of small social groups.

**Intergenerational mobility** Movement up or down between the strata or layers of society as measured between the generations of a family.

**Intersectionality** The idea that factors such as class, gender and ethnicity interact and combine to shape people's identities and experiences.

**Intragenerational mobility** An individual's movement up or down between the strata or layers of society over the course of their life.

**IQ** Intelligence quotient – a score based on a test designed to measure a person's intelligence.

**Label** A definition of a person placed on them by others.

**Life chances** An individual's chances of achieving positive or negative outcomes – relating, for example, to education, health and housing – as they progress through life.

**Marketisation** The process in which organisations compete in the market.

**Material deprivation** A lack of material resources.

**Meritocratic** Description of a system in which a person's position is based on merit – for example, talent and hard work – rather than on their social origins, ethnicity or gender.

**Mixed-ability groups** Groups in which students are randomly placed or intentionally mixed in terms of their perceived ability.

**Moral panic** A widespread panic that something is morally wrong.

**Multinational education businesses** Private education companies which have branches in two or more countries.

**Particularistic meanings** Meanings that are tied to a particular social context and not readily available to outsiders.

**Particularistic standards** Standards that apply to particular people, for example, to particular children in families.

**Patriarchal ideology** The idea that male dominance in society is reasonable and acceptable.

**Performativity** How well an individual or organisation performs.

**Positive discrimination** Treating a particular group more favourably than others.

**Present-time orientation** A focus on the present rather than the future.

**Primary socialisation** The earliest and probably the most important part of the socialisation process, usually within families.

**Privatise** Move from state to private ownership.

**Project Head Start** A programme of pre-school compensatory education in the USA.

**Pupil subculture** The distinctive norms and values of a particular group of students.

**Relative mobility** The comparative chances of people from different class backgrounds reaching particular positions in the social structure.

**Repressive State Apparatuses** Institutions, such as the army and the police, that keep the subject class in its place.

**Restricted code** A kind of shorthand speech in which meanings are not spelled out.

**Role allocation** A system of allocating people to roles which best suit their aptitudes and capabilities.

**Ruling-class ideology** A system of ideas that justify the position of the ruling class (the bourgeoisie in capitalist societies).

**Second modernity** A new phase of modernity characterised by risk, uncertainty and individualisation.

**Secondary socialisation** The socialisation that takes place during later life, for example, within schools and workplaces.

**Self-concept** An individual's picture or view of themselves.

**Self-fulfilling prophecy** A tendency for the way people are labelled to shape their actions.

**Setting** Placing students in an ability group for particular subjects.

**Shop-floor culture** The culture of low-skill workers which has similarities to the counter-school culture.

**Sites of ideological struggle** Places where there are conflicts based on different beliefs and values.

**Social capital** A social network that can be used as a resource.

**Social reproduction** The reproduction of social inequality from one generation to the next.

**Social solidarity** This involves a commitment to society, a sense of belonging, and a feeling that the social unit is more important than the individual.

**Social stratification** The way that society is structured or divided into hierarchical layers or strata, with the most privileged at the top and the least privileged at the bottom. Examples include caste and social class.

**Specialised division of labour** A labour force with a large number of specialised occupations.

**Stratification system** The way a society is structured or divided into hierarchical strata or layers, with the most privileged group at the top and the least favoured at the bottom.

**Streaming** Placing students in a particular group for all subjects. The whole class becomes an ability group.

**Subculture** The distinctive norms and values of a particular social group.

**Symbolic capital** Honour, prestige and reputation.

**Universalistic meanings** Meanings that are not tied to a particular context or situation.

**Universalistic standards** Standards that apply to everybody – for example, to all college students or to all employees in the workplace.

**Value consensus** Agreement about the main values of society.

**Vocationalism** Education and training designed to prepare young people for employment and to teach work skills to meet the needs of industry.

## Chapter 6 The media

**Affirmative action** Action designed to compensate for past discrimination through the use of quotas, for example.

**Agenda-setting** The role of news media in shaping the public's opinion of what the important issues are facing society and how they should be understood.

**American Dream** The belief that anyone who works hard enough and has the necessary talent can reach the top of the ladder in the USA.

**Anecdotal evidence** Evidence collected in a casual or informal manner and relying heavily, or entirely, on personal testimony.

**Atomised mass** A view of the media audience as made up of a very large number of people who lack relationships with others.

**Austerity** The policy, adopted by right-wing governments in a number of countries following the 2008 financial crisis, of cutting welfare expenditure and public services.

**Authoritarian regime** A political system that concentrates political power in an authority not responsible to the people.

**Autocracy** A political regime in which power is concentrated in the hands of one individual – common in authoritarian regimes.

**Avatars** In computing, an avatar is the graphical representation of the user or the user's alter ego or character in a virtual reality setting.

**Blackface** The use of make-up to darken the skin.

**Bling** Cheap and showy jewellery.

**Capitalism** A system for organising the production, distribution and exchange of goods and services based on private ownership and the profit motive.

**Chavs** An insulting word for people, particularly young people, whose way of dressing, speaking and behaving is thought to show their lack of education and their low social class.

**Citizen journalists** Members of the general public who collect and disseminate news over the internet.

**Collapse of communism** A series of events between 1989 and 1991 that led to the fall of communist regimes in Eastern Europe and the Soviet Union and led other communist regimes (such as China and Cuba) to introduce elements of capitalism into their previously socialist organisation of the economy.

**Collective intelligence** The notion that people working together collaboratively can produce an outcome that is superior to that produced by people working alone.

**Conspicuous consumption** The purchase and display of expensive items in order to demonstrate one's wealth.

**Copycat violence** Violence which mimics an earlier violent episode.

**Criminogenic** Generating or causing crime.

**Cross-media ownership** The ownership of different kinds of media organisations by a single company.

**Cultural hegemony** Rule or domination achieved by persuading people that values, beliefs and ideas that serve the interests of a dominant class are 'common-sense'.

**Democratic regime** A political system in which power is ultimately held by the people.

**Desensitisation** An effect which dampens the emotional impact of something which would otherwise be distressing, such as viewing violent behaviour.

**Deviancy amplification** A social process in which actions intended to reduce deviance have the opposite effect.

**Deviancy amplification spiral** A vicious circle in which attempts to control deviance feed back on themselves, producing increased deviance.

**Digital activism** The use of new information and communication technologies in social and political campaigning.

**Digital natives** People who have grown up since birth with digital technology.

**Disinhibition effect** An effect which reduces the power of in-built barriers to acting in a deviant or criminal way.

**Editorial independence** The idea that editors should be able to make decisions without interference from the owners of media outlets.

**Epistemology** The branch of philosophy concerned with studying the grounds of knowledge – that is, the basis on which someone can claim to know that something is true.

**Eve teasing** A euphemism used in South Asia to refer to sexual harassment of women and girls.

**False consciousness** A view of the world which is mistaken.

**Fantasy crime wave** An imaginary increase in crime.

**Flawed democracies** Nations where elections are fair and free, and basic civil liberties are honoured, but which may have significant democratic failings in other respects.

**Folk devils** People belonging to a deviant subculture who are seen as a threat to society.

**Gatekeepers** Individuals or organisations that control the flow of information reaching the general public.

**Gender dysphoria** A condition where a person experiences discomfort or distress because there is a mismatch between their biological sex and gender identity.

**Gender segregation** Organisational structures which separate boys and girls/men and women.

**Glass ceiling** An invisible barrier making it difficult for women to achieve top positions in society.

**Hard news** News stories that focus on politics, economics, war and crime; in contrast to 'soft news', which focuses on human interest stories.

**Homophobia** The irrational fear or hatred of people who are sexually attracted to the same sex.

**Hybrid regime** A political system which combines elements of democracy with authoritarianism.

**Hyper-connectivity** The state of being constantly connected to others through a variety of digital platforms such as mobile phones, tablets and computers.

**Hyperreality** The reality created by a media-saturated society where it is no longer possible to separate representations of reality from reality.

**Impression management** Efforts to control how other people see us.

**Interpretative frameworks/frames** Ways in which the news media interpret the events that they report.

**Irony** Saying the opposite of what you mean. For example saying, 'Well, that's brilliant!' when what you a mean is that it's dreadful.

**Judiciary** The branch of the state which interprets and applies the law.

**Labelling theory** A theory of deviance drawing upon symbolic interactionism and pluralism.

**Media conglomerates** Media corporations that are made up of a number of different, seemingly unrelated businesses.

**Media plurality** The situation where there is a range of agencies owning and providing media content.

**Media sensationalism** The use of exaggeration or distortion to represent people or events in ways which will provoke a strong emotional reaction in the audience.

**Meritocratic** Relating to a society or organisation in which success or failure is based on merit, defined as effort plus ability.

**Messages** In the context of studies of the media, 'messages' is a generic term for anything the media transmits. It could be a newspaper story, a movie, a television programme, a tweet, an email or any of a wide variety of other types of message.

**Misogynistic** Reflecting hatred of, contempt for, or ingrained prejudice against girls and women.

**Moral entrepreneurs** People who make moral judgements and seek to bring about social change in line with these judgements.

**Moral panic** Widespread public concern about a particular group or activity that is seen as a threat to society.

**Multiculturalism** A social policy in which the co-existence of different ethnic groups is accepted without pressure for ethnic minorities to assimilate into the majority culture.

**Narrowcasting** Transmitting media messages to a specific segment of the audience (in contrast to broadcasting).

**Neo-conservative governments** Governments that embrace right-wing ideas as set out above.

**News values** Journalists' ideas about what is and is not newsworthy.

**Non-governmental organisation** A non-profit organisation that operates independently of any government.

**Online grooming** Using digital technology to build an emotional connection with a child to gain their trust for the purposes of sexual abuse, sexual exploitation or trafficking.

**'Other'** 'Othering' involves persuading people that certain individuals or groups are unlike themselves and undeserving of their respect or concern.

**Participatory culture** A participatory culture is a culture with relatively low barriers to artistic expression and civic engagement, strong support for creating and sharing one's creations, and some type of informal mentorship whereby what is known by the most experienced is passed along to novices.

**Pastiche** A composition in literature, music or painting made up of bits of other works or imitations of another's style.

**Pathological** Causing social sickness.

**Phenotypical** Relating to visible biological characteristics.

**Picket line** A boundary established by workers on strike, especially at the entrance to their place of work, which other workers are asked not to cross.

**Pluralist theories** Theories which argue that power and influence in democratic societies is spread out across a variety of competing interest groups.

**Polysemic** Having many possible meanings.

**Prescient** Knowing or correctly suggesting what will happen in the future.

**Press barons** Wealthy owners of newspapers who are considered to have too much influence.

**Primary definers** Individuals or organisations to whom journalists turn first to comment on the events they report.

**Racialised** Identified as belonging to a racial group.

**Right-wing populism** A political strategy that involves support for traditional morality, a strong state and laissez-faire capitalism combined with anti-immigrant and nationalistic rhetoric, and which claims to speak up for the ordinary person against the elite (therefore, 'populist').

**Ruling-class ideology** The set of ideas and beliefs which justify the dominant position of the capitalist class.

**Scapegoated** Blamed for problems not of their making.

**Sexism, racism, ageism and classism** Belief systems which suggest that certain groups – men, white people, middle-aged people and upper classes – are inherently superior to others.

**Shop stewards** Trades union members elected as representatives of a 'shop' (or department) in dealings with the management.

**Simulacra** (singular 'simulacrum') Signs (words, images and so on) which no longer bear any connection to the real world.

**Simulations** Copies of reality.

**'Skivers and strivers'** Terms used by Conservative politicians in the UK to divide the working class by suggesting that some were lazy ('skivers') while others were hard-working ('strivers').

**Social construct** A feature of a society which appears to be a natural or given phenomenon, but which is actually a product of social processes.

**Social democracy** A left-wing political philosophy which supports government intervention in capitalist societies in order to protect the general welfare of citizens.

**Social stratification** The ordering of society into layers with different amounts of wealth, status and power.

**State-sponsored trolling** Where governments employ people to manipulate online discussions in ways which promote the interests of those governments, both home and abroad.

**Stereotypes** Shared preconceptions, often of a negative kind, about the characteristics of a social group which assume that all members of the group are alike.

**Technological convergence** In the context of ICT, refers to the combination of two or more technologies in a single device.

**Tech-savvy** Someone who is knowledgeable about, and skilled in, the use of modern technology, especially computers.

**The internet and World Wide Web** These terms are often used as if they refer to the same thing. Strictly speaking, they do not. The internet is a massive network of computer networks (a networking infrastructure) begun in the 1960s that connects millions of computers and other digital devices together globally. The Web (or World Wide Web), on the other hand, is the system of webpages and sites that is accessed via the internet. It was developed in the late 1980s by Tim Berners Lee.

**Transnational corporations (TNCs)** Companies that operate across national boundaries.

**Underclass** A social category or group existing beneath the class structure of a society.

**Welfare state** All those services provided by the state intended to maintain the well-being of its citizens.

**Xenophobia** Hatred or fear of foreigners.

## Chapter 7 Religion

**Accommodation** Adapting religious beliefs in response to a changed environment.

**Affiliation** A sense of belonging to a religious organisation.

**Age** The length of time a person has lived.

**Apostasy** Abandoning a set of religious beliefs in a hostile environment.

**Artefacts** Things produced by the research process (for example, resulting from a technical error) that do not exist in the phenomenon being studied.

**Ascetic** An austere and self-disciplined lifestyle that does not involve indulging in any of life's pleasures.

**Attitude to risk** The extent to which individuals are willing to expose themselves to social practices, beliefs and situations that carry a possibility of danger.

**Audience cults** Cults that do not require much commitment from followers and involve little face-to-face interaction.

**Belief system** A set of ideas held by individuals or groups that help them to interpret and make sense of the world.

**Beliefs** Ideas or convictions that individuals or groups hold to be true even when they are not based on evidence.

**Calling** The vocation, position in society or particular way of life that some individuals believe they are called to by God.

**Chain of memory** The way that memories (including religious beliefs) are passed down from one generation to the next.

**Church** The dominant religious organisation in a society, which is associated with Christian worship and usually claims a monopoly of the religious truth.

**Client cults** Cults that offer services (courses or rituals) to their followers but require little commitment.

**Closed belief system** A set of ideas that is not open to testing or criticism, so its beliefs tend not to change. Religion and magic are seen as examples of closed belief systems. Religion, for instance, is based on faith rather than on the testing of evidence.

**Cohort** A group of people born in a particular time period.

**Congregational domain** The site of conventional religious organisations where congregations meet together to pray in a consecrated place of religious worship.

**Conservative force** A factor such as religion or the mass media that inhibits social, economic or political change.

**Cult** To Wallis, a cult is a relatively small organisation with beliefs that are considered deviant by most people but which coexists with other belief systems in society.

**Cult movements** Cults that involve followers/believers fully and act as full religious organisations.

**Cultural defence** An ethnic group using religion to reinforce and maintain ethnic identity and pride.

**Cultural imperialism** The practice of imposing a culture, viewpoint or civilisation on people in another, less powerful country.

**Cultural transition** An ethnic group using religion to cope with social change and migration.

**Denomination** A religious organisation that has broken away from the main religious organisation in a society and accepts the legitimacy of other religious organisations.

**Differential socialisation** The contrasting ways in which females and males are brought up within and outside the family.

**Diffuse** Spread across a wide area or among a range of people.

**Disengagement** The withdrawal of churches from wider society because of their declining influence on other institutions, particularly politics and the legal system.

**Egalitarianism** The tendency towards becoming more equal.

**Elect** The people chosen by God to be saved and destined to go to heaven.

**Enlightenment** The period from the 17th century in Europe that emphasised reason, was sceptical about belief systems such as religion and put its faith in natural science and progress.

**Evangelicalism** A movement within Protestant Christianity that is seen as conservative in its support of traditional values.

**Exclusive definitions (of religion)** Narrow definitions that include traditional religions but exclude other belief systems.

**Functional definitions (of religion)** Definitions that focus on the functions or roles of religion – what religion does rather than what it is.

**Fundamentalism** A form of religion whose adherents want to return to what they see as the core doctrines of the faith as set out in sacred texts such as the Bible or the Qur'an. Christian fundamentalists, for example, adopt a literal interpretation of biblical accounts of miracles and the Creation.

**Fundamentalist beliefs** A set of religious beliefs that advocates returning to the 'fundamental' original teachings of a particular religion.

**Fuzzy fidelity** A vague belief that there may be some sort of religious or spiritual force without any adherence to specific religious belief.

**Globalisation** Involves all parts of the world becoming increasingly interconnected, so that national boundaries – in some respects, at least – become less important.

**Goddess religion** Religion that honours the 'divine feminine', the female side of the divine.

**Holistic milieu** The varied settings in which New Age spirituality is promoted and practised, including groups and therapy sessions.

**Ideology** A set of dominant ideas in society that distort reality and serve the interests of a particular group, such as men or the ruling class.

**Inclusive definitions (of religion)** Broad definitions that include traditional religions and other belief systems such as nationalism, communism and humanism.

**Individual sphere** The sphere of social life concerned with individual identity.

**Individualism** The process whereby individuals focused more on their own personal ideas and thoughts than on conforming to social expectations.

**Knowledge claims** Information or statements (for example, claims about what the world is like) that a particular individual, group or belief system such as science holds to be true but which are nonetheless open to debate.

**Liberal feminists** Those who believe that gender equality is possible within existing social structures, with changes in attitudes, laws and social policies.

**Liberal Western values** A set of ideas which focus on individualism and choice as well as rights.

**Liberation theology** A movement of radical Roman Catholic priests in Latin America, dating to the 1960s, who promote political change, fight oppression and support the poor.

**Marginal groups** Members of groups outside the mainstream of social life, who often feel that they are not receiving the prestige and/or economic rewards they deserve.

**Mechanism of social control** A means by which individuals are persuaded to conform to the rules in society.

**Membership** The way some participants of religion have joined their church.

**Meta-narratives** Large-scale singular explanations of society.

**Modern Western society** The period approximately between 1850 and 1980s when many societies became industrialised and when structural differentiation occurred.

**Modernisation** The process of moving from traditional society to a modern developed society.

**New Age** A term for a wide range of broadly spiritual beliefs and practices that emphasise the discovery of spirituality within the self. People seek spiritual experiences, inner peace or growth through, for example, meditation, crystal healing and/or aromatherapy.

**New Age movements** Diverse and loosely organised groups that became popular in the 1970s and 1980s, within which people seek spiritual experiences focusing primarily on the development of the self. They are sometimes viewed as a subset of new religious movements. Examples include est, Heaven's Gate and Dianic Wicca.

**New Christian Right** A term originating in the USA to describe Christian groups with links to the right-wing Republican Party. They have conservative views on social issues and want religious culture to be central in public life.

**New religious movements** Religious/spiritual organisations and movements such as Seventh-Day Adventists, the Unification Church and Pentecostalism that are of relatively modern origin and are in some form of opposition to (or differentiation from) longer-established, more powerful religious organisations such as the Roman Catholic Church.

**Open belief system** A set of ideas that makes knowledge claims based on the testing of evidence. Consequently, its beliefs develop over time. Science is seen as an open belief system that tests evidence through observation and experimentation.

**Participation** The various ways in which people are involved with a religion – for example, attending services.

**Patriarchy** A pattern/structure of male dominance and control.

**Period effect** The effects of being born in a particular era on social beliefs and practices.

**Predestination** The belief that God has predetermined whether people will be saved or damned after they die.

**Primary institutions** Institutions associated with work and politics.

**Private sphere** The social world inside families involving personal relationships.

**Privatised religion** Religion of significance to the individual but which has relatively little connection to religious institutions and little or no importance in wider society.

**Protestant ethic** Weber used this term to refer to the value that Calvinists placed on the importance of thrift, abstaining from pleasure and the duty to work hard in one's calling.

**Public sphere** The social world outside the family and personal life.

**Radical feminists** Those who believe that society is dominated by men and the only way to improve the position of women is via radical changes in society.

**Rational choice theory** An approach that assumes most people are naturally religious, that religious belief is based on rational choices and that religion meets individuals' needs.

**Rationalisation** A process in which people calculate the most efficient means to achieve given objectives rather than relying on faith or tradition to guide their actions.

**Re-enchantment** The process by which people re-engage with spirituality.

**Relative deprivation** This refers to subjectively perceived deprivation – the feeling of having less than others.

**Religion** Often defined narrowly as a belief system related to supernatural beings or divine forces. However, there are several ways of defining religion including substantive, functional and social constructionist approaches.

**Religiosity** The quality of being religious, linked to beliefs and values.

**Religious revival** The idea that spiritual and religious ideas and practices are going through a period of growth as people re-engage with the same or new forms of belief systems.

**Renewed vigour** An increase in the intensity of religious feelings in response to perceived hostility.

**Resacralisation** The process by which interest in and belief in the sacred is revived.

**Rituals** Religious practices or ceremonies comprising a set of actions that are carried out in an established order.

**Sacralisation** The process of becoming sacred.

**Schisms** Splits in religious organisations to form separate groups.

**Secondary institutions** Institutions associated with caring for others, such as the family and religion.

**Sect** A relatively small religious organisation which is in conflict with other belief systems in a society.

**Secularisation** A process involving a decline in the social significance of religion.

**Self-spirituality** The practice of searching for spirituality inside oneself.

**Social constructionist approach (to defining religion)** Rather than trying to provide a single definition, this approach focuses on how religion is used in daily life.

**Social differentiation** There are many different groups in society, such as age, gender and class.

**Societalisation** The process by which close-knit local communities lose power to larger towns and cities or bureaucratic states.

**Spirit of capitalism** The essence of capitalism involving the single-minded pursuit of profit as an end in itself.

**Spiritual individualism** Religion in which individuals follow their own spiritual path rather than following the teachings of a particular religious leader or religious institution.

**Spiritual revolution** Radical change in the nature of spirituality, moving from the congregational domain to the holistic milieu.

**Spiritual shopping** The idea that people relate to religion as consumers, and that they select and consume various forms of religion, sometimes multiple forms at the same time.

**Structural differentiation** The process by which institutions become separated and specialised.

**Structural location** The position of different social groups within the social structure – for example, the greater involvement of men in full-time paid employment than women.

**Substantive definitions (of religion)** Definitions that focus on the substance or content of religion – what religion is rather than what it does.

**The sacred and the profane** Durkheim's distinction between things that are set apart and inspire reverential attitudes among followers (the sacred) and ordinary, everyday things (the profane).

**The secularisation thesis** The theory or hypothesis that religion is having less influence on people's lives.

**Theodicy of disprivilege** Weber's concept for a set of ideas which explain inequalities using religious beliefs. A theodicy is a religious explanation or justification; disprivilege is a lack of material success and social status.

**Theodicy of good fortune** A religious explanation for suffering which claims that wealth and worldly success are indicators of virtue.

**Theodicy of misfortune** A religious explanation for suffering which claims that wealth and worldly success are indicators of evil.

**Totemism** A form of religion practised by the Australian Aboriginal peoples in which a sacred totem (usually a plant or animal) symbolises the clan.

**Truth claims** Statements or ideas that particular individuals, groups or belief systems (such as religions) hold to be true, and which are not open to debate.

**World-accommodating new religious movements** Religious movements of relatively recent origin that hold strong religious beliefs but reject mainstream religious doctrine. Nevertheless, they allow members to have conventional lives outside their religious practice.

**World-affirming new religious movements** Religious movements that developed from the 1960s onwards; they are positive about mainstream society, and their religious practices tend to encourage or facilitate social and economic success.

**World-rejecting new religious movements** Religious movements that developed from the 1960s onwards and are hostile to the social world outside the movement.

## Chapter 8 Globalisation

**Accountability** Taking responsibility for decisions that have been made.

**Acculturation** The process of adopting the cultural traits or social patterns of another group.

**Affluence** The state of having a very good standard of living or wealth.

**Affluent** Economically well-off or rich.

**Agency** Free will or choice to behave in a particular way.

**Agribusiness** Agriculture conducted on intensive industrial principles using technology and intensive labour.

**Aid** Financial help, usually provided by rich countries to poorer countries. It can come in the form of grants (which do not need to be paid back), tied aid or loans with interest.

**Alienation** Feeling unconnected or separated from the people around you or the work that you do.

**Altruistic** Working selflessly for the good of the community rather than for oneself.

**Americanisation** The dominance of American cultural products such as Hollywood films or rap music.

**Anarchists** People who rebel against any authority, established order or any ruling power.

**Anthropocentric** Regarding humankind as the central or most important element of existence, especially as opposed to God or animals.

**Anti-globalisation movement** A disparate collection of interest groups that feel that the problems of the group they represent have been brought about by global processes. The movement often uses global social media to coordinate and unify its protests against globalisation at events where world leaders meet.

**Apartheid** An official system of racial segregation administered by the White minority government of South Africa between 1948 and 1994.

**Assimilation** The process in which an ethnic group subculture is absorbed into a wider culture. It involves ethnic groups either voluntarily or being forced to give up traditional aspects of their culture. The culture of the minority group comes to resemble that of the majority group.

**Asylum seeker** A person who has left their home country as a political refugee and is seeking sanctuary and protection in another.

**Authoritarian states** A form of government characterised by strong central power and limited political or individual freedoms.

**Autocracy** Dictatorship or a system of government by one person with absolute power.

**Birth rate** The number of live births per 1000 of the population per year.

**Bonding social capital** The sharing of information or resources that may create opportunities for jobs or mutual help.

**Boomerang effect** A type of manufactured risk – for example, toxic materials used in the manufacturing process may find their way into the food chain and affect the health of future generations.

**Brain drain** The emigration of highly trained or qualified people from a particular country.

**BRIC** An acronym for the fast-growing economies of Brazil, Russia, India and China.

**Bridgeheads** A foothold or position established in another society.

**Bridging social capital** Social and political alliances or networks that increase the potential for social change.

**Bureaucratic** A system of government in which most of the important decisions are taken by state officials or civil servants rather than by elected politicians.

**Camorra** A type of mafia that operates mainly in Naples, Italy.

**Capital project** A project that requires substantial investment to improve or replace an aspect of a country's infrastructure – for example, an airport.

**Carcinogenic** Cancer-causing.

**Cartel** An organisation of criminals who associate in order to grow or manufacture, process and distribute illegal goods, especially drugs such as heroin and cocaine.

**Cash crops** A crop produced for its commercial value, to be exported rather than for domestic use by the grower – for example, tea, coffee, cocoa.

**Chain migration** A type of migration in which migrants who have settled in another country eventually bring over their extended kin.

**Circular migration** A repetitive movement of a migrant worker between home and a range of host areas, typically for the purpose of employment.

**Civil rights** The rights of citizens to political and social freedom and equality.

**Civil society** Refers to the notion that citizens of a society may act together in a common cause – for instance, in order to right a wrong. Civil society may oppose governments, for example, on austerity cuts.

**Collectivism** The idea that the individual is subordinate to the larger group to which they belong.

**Colonialism** Practice by which a powerful country or an empire directly controls less powerful countries through force and uses their resources to increase its own power and wealth.

**Command economy** A system where the government, rather than the free market, determines how the economy should be planned and managed. It is a key feature of any communist society.

**Commodification** Applying an economic value to a range of human activities.

**Communities of fate** Protest movements, such as environmentalism, in which members attempt to shape their own futures through active participation and dialogue.

**Conglomerates** A corporation composed of a collection of companies which have been brought together by mergers and takeovers.

**Consensus** Common agreement.

**Conservative** A person, social group or political party that is averse to change and holds traditional values.

**Constitution** A body of fundamental principles or established precedents according to which a state or other organisation is acknowledged to be governed.

**Cosmopolitan** An ideology which states that all human beings belong to a single global community.

**Counter-Migration** Migration in the opposite direction.

**Coup d'état** The sudden, often violent and undemocratic overthrow of a government, often by the military.

**Coyotes** Mexican guides who lead illegal migrants across Mexico into the USA for a fee.

**Creolisation** A hybrid mix of different cultures – for example, see Miller's work on how Trinidadian people use Facebook as 'Fasbook'.

**Criminogenic** Something, usually an environment or value system, that causes crime or encourages criminal behaviour. Marxists believe that capitalism does this.

**Crisis of modernism** The unique social problems associated with modern societies – for example, high suicide and crime rates, poor mental health.

**Cryptocurrency** A digital currency such as bitcoin in which encryption techniques are used to regulate the generation of units of currency and verify the transfer of funds, operating independently of a central bank.

**Cultural convergence** The process by which different cultures become very similar or the same.

**Cultural defence** In a racist or hostile society, ethnic minority groups may use aspects of their religion as a way of defending their culture if it is under threat.

**Cultural divergence** The process by which cultures become different from one another or even come into conflict with one another.

**Cultural imperialism** The process and practice of promoting one culture over another. Many sociologists see it as the consequence of the ubiquity of Western and especially American cultural products.

**Cultural pluralists** Those who believe that smaller groups within a larger society should be encouraged to maintain their unique cultural identities.

**Cultural relativity** The idea that, because different cultures have differing reference points, it is not appropriate to judge all societies according to one universal standard.

**Dark net/dark web** A computer network with encrypted and restricted access that is used chiefly for illegal peer-to-peer file sharing.

**Debt bondage** When a person is forced to work to pay off a debt which may originate in the fee paid to people smugglers for being trafficked.

**Deforestation** The action of clearing a wide area of trees.

**Demography** The sociological study of statistics relating to births, fertility, death and migration in order to study population change.

**Demonisation** Negative stereotyping of a particular social group.

**Deregulation** The removal of regulations or legal restrictions.

**Desertification** The process by which fertile land becomes desert, typically as a result of drought, deforestation or inappropriate agriculture.

**De-skilling** A reduction in the skill a worker requires to do a particular job, especially compared with past working conditions. It is often caused by automation.

**Diaspora** People from a particular nation or ethnic community that are scattered across the world – for example, people of Jewish ancestry can be found in most countries around the world.

**Digital underclass** People who are so disadvantaged that they cannot afford access to digital technology such as smartphones, laptops and broadband, ownership of which many people take for granted.

**Diseases of affluence** Life-threatening conditions caused by wealthy or rich lifestyles.

**Diseases of poverty** Life-threatening diseases caused by malnutrition and lack of access to clean water and sanitation.

**Dissident** A person who opposes a government, especially an authoritarian one.

**Divide and rule** The policy of maintaining control over one's subordinates or opponents by encouraging dissent between them, thereby preventing them from uniting in opposition.

**Drug mules** People who are paid to smuggle drugs across borders, usually inside their bodies.

**Eco-centric** The view or belief that the rights and needs of humans are not more important than those of other living things.

**Ecological** Relating to the environment.

**Elite** The richest, most powerful, best-educated or best-trained group in a society.

**Emancipatory politics** Movements that are concerned above all with liberating individuals and groups from constraints that adversely affect their life chances.

**Emigrant** A person who leaves their own country in order to settle permanently or temporarily in another.

**Empathetic** Demonstrating the ability to understand and share the feelings of others.

**Entitlement** With regard to human rights, the idea that the state should provide its people with basic rights – for example, the right to education.

**Entrepreneurial spirit** The ambition and drive to run a successful business.

**Equality** With regard to human rights, the idea that all citizens, regardless of social background, should have the right to be treated equally.

**Ethnocentric** Judging or evaluating other cultures according to the standards of one's own culture.

**Executive/government** The branch of a government responsible for putting decisions or laws into effect.

**Existential insecurity** Anxiety associated with mortality. The feeling that you are at risk from various factors over which you have little or no control.

**Existential security** The feeling that survival is secure enough that it can be taken for granted.

**Expatriates** People who live outside their native country.

**Fake news** False information or propaganda published under the guise of being real, true news.

**Fascist** An extreme right-wing movement which is anti-democratic and believes in rule by a totalitarian one-party state.

**Fatalism** The belief that events are fixed in advance and problems are simply inevitable so that human beings are powerless to change them.

**Fertility rate** The number of live births per 1000 women between the ages of 15 and 44 years.

**Flight migration** Fleeing a country because of persecution.

**Folk devils** A person, social group or thing perceived to be a threat to society or a social problem.

**Forced prostitution** Sexual slavery that takes place as a result of coercion by a third party.

**Foreign exchange** The exchange of currencies – the US dollar is especially valued by poor countries, because oil can only be bought on the oil market using this currency.

**Forensic accounting** The use of accounting skills to investigate fraud or embezzlement and to analyse financial information for use in legal proceedings.

**Free enterprise** An economic system in which private business operates in competition and is largely free of state control.

**Full democracy** Nations where civil liberties and basic political freedoms are not only respected, but also reinforced by a political culture conducive to the thriving of democratic principles.

**Fundamentalism** A form of a religion, especially Islam or Protestant Christianity, that believes in and acts upon a literal interpretation of holy texts.

**Fundamentalist** A strict, literal interpretation of scripture in a religion.

**Genocide** The deliberate killing of a large group of people, especially those of a particular nation or ethnic group.

**Gig economy** A labour market characterised by insecure temporary jobs and low pay as opposed to permanent jobs.

**Global imagining** People's growing consciousness that they share a common global culture or that they share common interests with their neighbours in the global village.

**Globalisation** The trend of increasing interaction between societies and individuals on a worldwide scale due to advances in transportation and communication technology.

**Globalists** Sociologists who believe that globalisation has had significant and real effects on the world, although they may disagree as to whether these effects are positive or negative.

**Globality** A social condition characterised by tight economic, political, cultural and environmental interconnectedness and flows underpinned by technological innovation that have rendered most national borders and boundaries irrelevant.

**Glocalisation** A combination of the words 'globalisation' and 'localisation', used to describe a product or service that is developed and distributed globally, but is also adjusted to accommodate the user or consumer in a local market. The term is also used more generally as a hybrid fusing of the global and local, as in 'Bollywood'.

**Grassroots** The ordinary people who are regarded as the main body of an organisation's membership.

**Hacktivist** A person who gains unauthorised access to computer files or networks in order to further social or political ends.

**Hate crimes** A crime motivated by racial, sexual or other prejudice, typically one involving violence.

**Hidden iceberg** A metaphor which refers to the small perceptible part of a much larger situation or problem that remains hidden.

**Homogeneous** Of the same kind or very alike.

**Homogenisation** The process of being or becoming the same.

**Hostile environment** A set of administrative and legislative practices employed by the British government, aimed at making life for migrants who wished to stay in the UK as difficult as possible.

**Human capital** The skills, knowledge and experience possessed by an individual or population, viewed in terms of their value or cost to an organisation or country.

**Hybrid regimes** States in which governments are elected but in which no opposition parties are allowed or the media are controlled by elites or in which political corruption is rife.

**Hyper-globalists** Sociologists who are optimistic and positive about the effects of globalisation.

**Identity performance** A type of impression management in which a person presents a particular version of themselves for public consumption – for example, on a social media site – in order to manage other people's opinion about them.

**Identity theft** The fraudulent practice of stealing another person's name and personal information from information stored on the Web.

**Immigrant** An incomer into a society from another country.

**Imperialism** Rule by an empire – for example, the British Empire.

**Independent judiciary** Judges and courts which are free of influence from other branches of government or private interests.

**Indigenisation** The action or process of bringing something under the control, dominance, or influence of the people native to an area.

**Indigenous** Native to a particular country.

**Indigenous rights** The rights of people who inhabited a particular territory pre-colonialism.

**Infant mortality rates** Death rates experienced by children aged five years and under.

**Infanticide** The killing of babies, usually at birth.

**Infrastructure** The basic physical and organisational structures and facilities (for example, buildings, roads, power supplies) needed for the operation of a society or enterprise.

**Institutional racism** Racial prejudice or discrimination that has become established as normal behaviour within a society or organisation.

**Intra-Islamic** Differences of interpretation of holy texts that exist within Islam. For example, Islam is made up of dozens of sects that reflect these differences.

**Irresponsible bidding** With regard to populism, making promises to the people that are unlikely to be kept.

**Islamisation** The process of bringing someone or something under the influence of Islam or under Islamic rule.

**Islamophobia** Dislike of or prejudice against Islam or Muslims, especially as a political force.

**Jihadism** Someone who sees violent struggle as necessary to eradicate obstacles to restoring God's rule on earth.

**Jim Crow laws** State and local laws that enforced racial segregation in the Southern United States.

**Kleptocracy** Corrupt leaders that use their power to exploit the people and natural resources of their own territory in order to extend their personal wealth and political powers.

**Labour migration** Moving abroad to work.

**Late-modern society** A term used by Giddens to describe global societies which he sees as exhibiting features that indicate a continuation of modernity rather than constituting a new type of postmodern society.

**LEDCs** The least economically developed or poorest countries in the world.

**Legislature/parliament** A governing body that makes laws and can also amend or repeal them.

**Legitimisation** To justify something by making it legal or socially acceptable.

**Libellous** Making a false written statement damaging to a person's reputation.

**Liberal democracy** A form of nation-state in which people have the right to vote their leaders in and out of power.

**Literacy** The ability to read and write.

**Macro-level** Processes that happen at a societal or structural level.

**Mail order bride** A woman who lists herself in a catalogue and is selected by a man for marriage.

**Malestream** Research based on a masculine perspective, which often in consequence renders invisible the feminine or feminist perspective.

**Malnutrition** Not having enough to eat or not eating enough of the 'right' things.

**Market-Leninist** Slang for the Chinese way of managing the economy – a mixture of a central planned economy with the tolerance of some free market capitalism.

**Mass self-communication** A type of communication in which a user selects the group of people symbolised by a website or online community that they want to communicate with and directs their message appropriately.

**McWorld** A term used to indicate a particular standardisation of production techniques inspired by the McDonald's fast-food chain and seen to epitomise globalisation.

**MEDCs** The most economically developed or richest countries in the world.

**Meritocratic** Giving people status or rewards because of what they achieve, rather than because of their wealth or social position.

**Micro-aggression** Indirect, subtle or unintentional discrimination against members of a marginalised group – for example, giving disapproving looks.

**Micro-level** Processes that occur at the level of individuals.

**Migrant** A person who moves from one place to another, usually to find work or better living conditions.

**Millennium Development Goals** A set of international goals relating to economic and social well-being established by the United Nations. They are thought to be achievable by 2030.

**Misogynist** A person who dislikes, despises or is strongly prejudiced against women.

**Modus operandi** A particular way or method of doing something.

**Money laundering** The concealment of the origins of illegally obtained money, typically by means of transfers involving foreign banks or legitimate businesses.

**Mono-ethnic** The dominance of a single ethnic group in terms of numbers.

**Moral panic** An instance of public anxiety or alarm in response to a problem regarded as threatening the moral standards of society, usually created by newspapers and other forms of media.

**Multiculturalism** The presence of, or support and respect for, the presence of several distinct cultural or ethnic groups within a society.

**Narcissism** Self-obsession.

**Nationalism** Extreme form of patriotism marked by a feeling of superiority over other countries.

**Nativism** The policy of protecting the interests of native-born or established inhabitants against those of immigrants.

**Naturalised** To confer the rights of a citizen or national on a foreigner or migrant.

**Neo-colonialism** A modern version of capitalist exploitation in which rich countries benefit from the terms of world trade, transnational investment in the economies of poor countries and aid that is tied to economic or political interests.

**Neoliberal** A set of economic ideas that stresses that trade should be free of government intervention and totally reliant on market forces and unlimited and unregulated competition so that buyers and sellers perform with maximum efficiency.

**Net migration** The difference between the number of immigrants (people coming into an area) and the number of emigrants (people leaving an area).

**Network society** The social, political, economic and cultural changes caused by the spread of networked, digital information and communications technologies.

**Networked global society** The idea that people sat at their computers are technologically linked to a global network of hundreds of thousands of others and consequently are potentially able to bring about economic, social and political change.

**Nomad** A person or group that wanders from place to place.

**Non-government organisations (NGOs)** Any organisation or agency that is not financed by government or which works outside state control.

**Non-indigenous** (also non-native or foreign-born) Originating outside of a particular nation-state.

**Oligarchy** Rule by a few.

**Open society** A society in which information freely and truthfully flows without censorship.

**Othering** Viewing another person as different or inferior or alien compared with oneself. A form of stereotyping based on ignorance.

**Outgoing** In terms of personality, someone who is sociable and easy to talk to.

**Partial or flawed democracies** Governments which demonstrate some accountability to the people but which may restrict the activities of some minority groups.

**Particularism** Treating a person as a unique individual because they are loved as a member of a particular family.

**Patriotism** National loyalty or vigorous support for one's country.

**Periphery** On the edge or margins of a group or particular activity.

**Pluralism** A condition or system in which a multiplicity of competing political parties coexist.

**Pluriverse** "An idea associated with Esteva – he claims that there is no such thing as universal human experience. Instead, he argues that there are countless cultural ways in which people live in relation to others."

**Politburo** The principal policy-making committee of a communist party.

**Political rights** The right to vote for any political party without fear of discrimination.

**Politics of resistance** A form of collective civil disobedience aimed at opposing the effects of economic, political and ecological globalisation.

**Populism** A range of political approaches or movements critical of ruling elites and which emphasises the will of the people.

**Post-familial family** A type of family that spends its leisure time online or playing with digital devices rather than actively spending it in each other's company. Parents today, for example, often Facebook their children to tell them to come downstairs for their meals.

**Post-truth** Circumstances in which objective facts are less influential in shaping public opinion than appeals to emotion and personal belief.

**Propaganda** Information, especially of a biased or misleading nature, used to promote a political cause or point of view.

**Proscribed** To forbid, usually by law.

**Proto-communities** An early form of community. Often used to describe online communities that have not been established or in place for very long.

**Public institutional capital** Public services provided by the state – for example, education, healthcare, pensions, social care.

**Pull factors** Social factors that might encourage you to move to another society – for example, better job opportunities, higher pay.

**Push factors** Social factors, often beyond the control of the individual, that may force a person and their family to leave their country of origin.

**Quotas** An official limit set on the number of products that can be imported into a country.

**Racialised class fraction** An ethnic or migrant group that is objectively part of a particular social class but subjectively is not accepted by the majority of that class because of racial prejudice.

**Relativism** The postmodern idea that knowledge, truth and morality exist in relation to culture, historical context, and even personal opinion and experience, and consequently cannot be absolute or unquestionable.

**Religious rights** The freedom to exercise particular religious beliefs and practices without persecution or to change religious beliefs and practices.

**Remittances** A sum of money sent from migrants back to kin in their home country.

**Representation** The way that the media portray particular social groups such as women, ethnic minorities or young people.

**Representative democracy** A type of democracy founded on the principle of elected officials representing a group of people.

**Residency** The official right granted by a government to live in its country although the person who is given residence may not necessarily have citizenship.

**Reverse cultural flow** It is often assumed that the cultural flow of ideas and cultural products is from the West to other parts of the world. However, Western culture has also been heavily influenced by a cultural flow from the East in the form of religion, diet, exercise regimes and so on.

**Risk society** According to Beck, the technology associated with late-capitalist society has brought about many benefits in terms of consumer goods but it has also brought about negative effects – for example, in terms of a wide range of risks to both the environment and climate.

**Scapegoating** The process of attaching blame (usually to a visible but powerless group).

**Scarce resources** The limited availability of particular social things such as jobs, goods, housing and so on which people may be competing for.

**Schengen Agreement** A European treaty that encourages the maintenance of open borders and the free movement of workers.

**Secular** Not having any connection with religion.

**Segregation** The action or state of setting someone or something apart from others, often on the grounds of race or ethnicity.

**Sex tourism** The organisation of holidays with the purpose of taking advantage of the lack of restrictions imposed on sexual activity and prostitution by some foreign countries.

**Shadow economy** Illegal or criminal economic activity which exists alongside a country's official economy – for example, the black market.

**Shell company** A company or corporation that exists only on paper and has no office or employees. It may have a bank account in which laundered money may be deposited.

**Slanderous** Making a false spoken statement damaging to a person's reputation.

**Social capital** The collective value of all social networks (the value of knowing influential people), and the obligations that arise from these networks to do things for each other (for example, to return a favour).

**Social integration** The process during which newcomers or minorities are incorporated into the social structure of the host society.

**Social media apps** Digital applications that are designed to allow people to share digital content quickly, efficiently, and in real time.

**Social movement** A type of group action that empowers ordinary and oppressed people and aims to challenge or resist the decisions and actions of more powerful groups.

**Social rights** Another term for socio-economic rights such as the right to an education or an adequate standard of living or justice.

**Social well-being** A feeling of belonging or social inclusion based on feeling happy, safe, comfortable and psychologically healthy.

**Sovereignty** The authority of a state to govern itself or another state.

**Space–time compression** A term invented by David Harvey that refers to a set of processes that impact time and space that is, they cause the relative distances between places as measured in terms of travel time or cost to shrink so that the world seems to be a much smaller place.

**Stigmatisation** A form of negative judgemental labelling that sets a person or group apart as a problem or threat to others.

**Structural assimilation** The incorporation into society of a migrant group so that it has equal access to education, jobs and all social institutions.

**Subsistence** Supporting oneself at a minimal level, in order to survive.

**Subsistence poverty** Having, earning or growing just enough to survive.

**Supreme Court** The highest judicial court in a country or state.

**Sustainable development** Economic development that is conducted without depletion of natural resources.

**Symbolic annihilation of women** A term invented by Tuchman that suggests that media representations of women rarely report their achievements or, if they do, tend to trivialise and devalue them. Women are often reduced in the media to being wives and girlfriends of men.

**Tariffs** A tax or duty to be paid on particular imports or exports.

**Theocracy** A system of government in which priests, ayatollahs or a divinely ordained ruler govern in the name of God or a god.

**Tied aid** Foreign aid that must be spent in the country providing the aid (the donor country).

**Transgressive criminology** Criminologists who are interested in a broader definition of crime – activities that cause harm – rather than strictly activities that are against the law.

**Transnational companies (TNCs)** Multinational companies which produce, market and sell products across the world.

**Transnational identity** An identity associated with international migrants that is shaped by globalisation or by membership of two or more societies.

**Transworld instantaneity** Scholte defines this as global connections that move anywhere across the planet in no time. For instance, digital technology can connect people at the same time wherever they are located in the world using devices.

**Transworld simultaneity** Scholte defines this as global connections that extend across the planet at the same time. For instance, people in lots of places doing the same thing, such as young people drinking Coca-Cola as a lifestyle choice.

**Triads** Chinese-organised criminal gangs.

**Triangular slave trade** A historical term for the slave trade that was organised between three regions – Africa, the Americas and Europe.

**Trilemma** A difficult choice between three options.

**Truth decay** The blurring of lines between opinion and fact that sees all experience and beliefs as being as important as expertise based on evidence. It often results in disagreement about what constitutes 'truth'.

**Under-employment** Not having enough paid work or not doing work that makes full use of a worker's skills and abilities.

**Universal suffrage** The right of almost all adults to vote in political elections.

**Universalism** An idea underpinned by equality of opportunity that people should be judged by the same standards – for example, through the taking of exams.

**Urbanisation** An increase in population in cities and towns versus rural areas.

**Virtual communities** An online community that only meets in cyberspace.

**Wahhabi** A strictly orthodox Sunni Muslim sect which is still the predominant religious force in Saudi Arabia.

**Water table** The level below ground that is saturated with water and often the origin of the supply of fresh drinking water.

**Welfare state** A system whereby the state undertakes to protect the health and well-being of its citizens, especially those in financial or social need, by means of grants, pensions and other benefits.

**Westernisation** The process whereby cultures adopt American or European ways of thinking or cultural practices.

**Whistle-blower** A person who informs on a person or organisation regarded as engaging in an unlawful or immoral activity.

**Xenophobia** Fear or hatred of foreigners often expressed through open or subtle forms of hostility and aggression.

**Yardie** A member of a Jamaican gang of criminals.

**Zemiology** The study of social harms.

**Zones of consumption** The mainly Western market for illicit goods and services.

**Zones of distribution** Areas of the world which are the launch-point or staging posts for the distribution of illegal goods into the West.

**Zones of production** Areas of the less industrialised world in which crops are grown that are later processed into cannabis resin, heroin or cocaine.

# REFERENCES

## Chapter 1


Anderson, B. and Willer, D. (1981) *Networks, Exchange, and Coercion: The Elementary Theory and Its Applications*, Elsevier Science Ltd, NY.

Bauman, Z. (2000) *Liquid Modernity*, Polity Press, Cambridge.

Blau, P. (1986) *Exchange and Power in Social Life*, Transaction Publishers, New Brunswick.

Blumer, H. (1962/1992) *Symbolic Interactionism: Perspective and Method*, University of California Press, Berkeley, CA.

Bull, J. (2017) *Post-Truth: How B******* Conquered the World*, Biteback Publishing, London.

Crenshaw, K. (1989) 'Demarginalizing the Intersection of Race and Sex: A Black Feminist Critique of Antidiscrimination Doctrine, Feminist Theory and Antiracist Politics', *University of Chicago Legal Forum*, no. 1, article 8.

Durkheim, É. (1893) *The Division of Labour in Society*, in R. A. Jones, *Émile Durkheim: An Introduction to Four Major* Works (1986) Sage Publications, Inc., CA.

Eddo-Lodge, R. (2018) *Why I'm No Longer Talking to White People About Race*, Bloomsbury Publishing, London.

Firati, F. and Venkatesh, A. (1995) 'Liberatory Postmodernism and the Reenchantment of Consumption', *Journal of Consumer Research*, vol. 22, no. 3.

Foster, J.B. (2014) *The Theory of Monopoly Capitalism: An Elaboration of Marxian Political Economy*, Monthly Review Press, NY.

Giddens, A. and Pierson, C. (1998) *Conversations with Anthony Giddens: Making Sense of Modernity*, Polity Press, Cambridge.

Goffman, E. (1990) *The Presentation of Self in Everyday Life*, Penguin, London.

Gramsci, A. (2005) *Selections from the Prison Notebooks of Antonio Gramsci*, Lawrence & Wishart Ltd, London.

Habermas, J. (1984) *The Theory of Communicative Action: Reason and the Rationalization of Society*, Beacon Press, Boston.

Homans, G. (1961) *Social Behavior: Its Elementary Forms*, Harcourt, Brace & World, NY.

Lyotard, J-F. (1984) *The Postmodern Condition: A Report on Knowledge*, Manchester University Press, Manchester.

McChesney, R. (2013) *Digital Disconnect: How Capitalism is Turning the Internet Against Democracy*, The New Press, NY.

Mead, G. H. (1934/2015) *Mind, Self and Society: The Definitive Edition*, University of Chicago Press, Chicago.

Molm, L. (1997) *Coercive Power in Social Exchange*, Cambridge University Press, Cambridge.

Morales, B (2017) 'Western Feminism's Ethnocentric Ideals and Lack of Intersectionality in Itself are not Qualifications to Define Women as a Whole', *Medium*, 8 February.

Moreton-Robinson, A (2000) *Talkin' Up to the White Woman: Indigenous Women and Feminism*, University of Queensland Press, St Lucia, Queensland.

Mythen, G. (2004) *Ulrich Beck: A Critical Introduction to the Risk Society*, Pluto Press, London.

Oxfam International (2018) 'Reward Work, Not Wealth', © Oxfam International.

Strinati, D. (2004) *An Introduction to Theories of Popular Culture*, 2nd edn, Routledge, London.

Wrong, D. (1961) 'The oversocialized conception of man in modern Sociology', *American Sociological Review*, vol. 26, no. 2.

Zanetti, L. and Carr, A. (1999) 'Exaggerating the Dialectic: Postmodernism's "New Individualism" and the Detrimental Effects on Citizenship', *Administrative Theory and Praxis*, vol. 21, no. 2.


## Chapter 2


Adams, J. T. (1931) *The Epic of America*, Greenwood Press, CA.

Akumu, P. (2018) 'Ugandan women kneeling in deference is cultural – it's also humiliating', *The Guardian*, 21 January.

An-Na'im, A. (1992) *Human Rights in Cross-Cultural Perspectives: Quest for Consensus*, University of Pennsylvania, PA.

Bandura, A. (1963) 'Behavior theory and indemnificatory learning', *American Journal of Orthopsychiatry*, vol. 33.

Banyard, K. (2011) *The Equality Illusion: The Truth about Women and Men Today*, Faber & Faber, London.

Baron-Cohen, S. (2012) *The Essential Difference: Men, Women and the Extreme Male Brain*, Penguin, London.

Bauman, Z. (1992) *Intimations of Postmodernity*, Routledge, London.

Baumeister, R. (1986) *Identity: Cultural Change and the Struggle for Self*, Oxford University Press, Oxford.

Becker, H. (1995) *Making the Grade: The Academic Side of College Life*, Transaction Publishers, New Brunswick.

Bellin, E. (2004) 'The Robustness of Authoritarianism in the Middle East: Exceptionalism in Comparative Perspective' *Comparative Politics*, vol. 36, no. 2.

Bradley, H. (1996) *Fractured Identities: Changing Patterns of Inequality*, Polity Press, Cambridge.

Brady, E. (2018) 'Is this woman too much a man?', *USA Today*, 8th May.

Byanyima, W. (2018) quoted in P. Akumu, 'Ugandan women kneeling in deference is cultural – it's also humiliating', *The Guardian*, 21 January.

Candland, D. (1996) *Feral Children and Clever Animals: Reflections on Human Nature*, Oxford University Press, Oxford.

Carroll, J. (2009) *Practicing Catholic*, Houghton Mifflin Harcourt, NY.

Cochrane, A. and Pain, K. (2000) 'A Globalizing Society?' in D. Held (ed.) *A Globalizing World?: Culture, Economics and Politics*, Routledge, London.

Cohen, S. (1973) *Folk Devils and Moral Panics*, Routledge, Oxford.

Connell, R. (1987) *Gender and Power: Society, the Person and Sexual Politics*, Polity Press, Cambridge.

Cooley, C. (1998) *On Self and Social Organization*, University of Chicago Press, Chicago.

Corrigan, P. (1979) *Schooling the Smash Street Kids*, Macmillan, London.

Cote, J. (2000) *Arrested Adulthood: The Changing Nature of Maturity and Identity*, New York University Press, NY.

Credit Suisse (2016) 'The *Global Wealth Report 2016', Credit Suisse Research Institute.*

Doughty, C. (2018) *From Here to Eternity: Traveling the World to Find the Good Death*, W. W. Norton & Company, NY.

Durrant, J. and Ensom, R. (2012) 'Physical punishment of children: Lessons from 20 years of research', *Canadian Medical Association Journal*, vol. 184, no. 12.

Egan, D. (2013) 'How Do Online Social Networking Sites Affect the Shaping of the Social Self In Late Modernity? The Case of Facebook', Thesis, *Maynooth University*, Co Kildare.

Elias, N. (1978) *The Civilizing Process*, Wiley-Blackwell, London.

Featherstone, M. and Hepworth, M. (1991) 'The Mask of Ageing and the postmodern life-course', in M. Featherstone, M. Hepworth and B. S. Turner (eds) *The Body: Social Process and Cultural Theory*, Sage Publications, Ltd., CA.

Fine, C. (2011) *Delusions of Gender: The Real Science Behind Sex Differences*, Icon Books, London.

Friedman, J. (2017) *Yes Means Yes: Visions of Female Sexual Power and a World without Rape*, Seal Press, Berkeley, CA.

Giddens, A. (1997) *Sociology*, 3rd edn, Polity Press, Cambridge.

(1999) *Runaway World: How Globalization is Reshaping Our Lives*, Profile Books, London.

Gordon, M. et al. (2013) 'Culture Influence on the Perception of the Body Language by Arab and Malay Students', *International Journal of Applied Linguistics & English Literature*, vol. 2, no. 6.

Haralambos, M. and Holborn, M. (2013) *Sociology: Themes and Perspectives*, 7th edn, Collins, London.

Hervieu-Léger, D. (2000) *Religion as a Chain of Memory*, Polity Press, Cambridge.

Hitchings, H. (2013) *Sorry! The English and Their Manners*, John Murray, London.

Jacobs, J. (1961) *The Death and Life of Great American Cities*, Random House, NY.

Jacobson, J. (2015) *Islam in Transition: Religion and Identity among British Pakistani Youth*, Routledge, London.

James, C. L. R. (1963) *Beyond a Boundary*, Hutchinson, London.

Jencks, C. (1993) *Culture*, Routledge, London.

Johnson, D. and Johnson, J. (2018) 'Social Stratification in India', *Center For Global Education*, asiasociety.org.

Krockow, E. et al. (2018) 'Are some cultures less trusting than others?', *The Conversation*, 31 January.

Kuczynski, L. (2012) *Handbook of Dynamics in Parent-Child Relations*, SAGE Publications, Inc., CA.

Kwok S. Y. C. L., Chai, W and He, X. (2013) 'Child abuse and suicidal ideation among adolescents in China', *Child Abuse & Neglect*, vol. 37, no. 11.

Lewis, C. S. (1952) *Mere Christianity*, HarperCollins, London.

Loh Kok Wah, F. and Ojendal, J. (2004) *Southeast Asian Responses to Globalization: Restructuring Governance and Deepening Democracy*, NIAS Press, Copenhagen.

Mac an Ghaill, M. (2004) *The Making of Men: Masculinities, Sexualities and Schooling*, Open University Press, Buckingham.

Martell, L. (2010) *The Sociology of Globalization*, Polity Press, Cambridge.

Matlak, M. (2014) 'The Crisis of Masculinity in the Economic Crisis Context', *Procedia: Social and Behavioral Sciences*, vol. 140.

McKay, D. (2016) *An Archipelago of Care: Filipino Migrants and Global Networks*, Indiana University Press, Bloomington, 2016.

McLaughlin, S. (2017) 'Facebook and the presentation of self: a structure versus agency approach', *Sociology Review*, vol. 26, no. 4

Mead, G. H. (1934/2015) *[see chapter 1 refs]*

Messerschmidt, J. (2018) *Hegemonic Masculinity: Formulation, Reformulation, and Amplification*, Rowman & Littlefield Publishers, Maryland.

Miller, D. (2011) *Tales From Facebook*, Polity Press, Cambridge.

Morgan, D. (1996) *Family Connections: An Introduction to Family Studies*, Polity Press, Cambridge.

Morris, D. (1968) *The Naked Ape*, McGraw-Hill, NY.

Oakley, A. (1972) *Sex, Gender and Society*, Maurice Temple Smith, London.

Orth, U., Trzesniewski, K. and Robins, R. (2010) 'Self-Esteem Development From Young Adulthood to Old Age: A Cohort-Sequential Longitudinal Study', *Journal of Personality and Social Psychology*, vol. 98, no. 4.

Pakulski, J. and Waters, M. (1996) *The Death of Class*, SAGE Publications, Inc., CA.

Pew Centre 2014 research on Americas bearing arms, in C. Shultz (2014) 'More Americans Are Pro-Gun than Pro-Gun Control', *Smithsonian.com*, 11 December.

Piaget, J. (2001) *The Language and Thought of the Child*, Routledge, London.

Plantilla, J. (1996) '*National Human Rights Institutions and Human Rights Education*', paper submitted at the Preliminary Meeting on National Human Rights Commissions held on March 13-16 in Hong Kong by the Asian Human Rights Commission.

Postman, N. (1985) *Amusing Ourselves to Death: Public Discourse in the Age of Show Business*, Penguin, NY.

Redfern, C. and Aune, K. (2013) *Reclaiming the F Word: Feminism Today*, Zed Books, London.

Roberts, R. et al. (1999) 'The Structure of Ethnic Identity of Young Adolescents from Diverse Ethnocultural Groups', *The Journal of Early Adolescence*, vol. 19, no. 3.

Salisbury, J. (2018) 'Sociological theory revisited', *Sociology Review*, vol. 27, no. 4.

Sandbrook, D. (2012) *Mad as Hell: The Crisis of the 1970s and the Rise of the Populist Right*, Anchor Books, NY.

Sandset, T. (2012) *Color as Matter: Narratives of Race, Ethnicity, and the Deployment of Color*, Master Thesis, Dissertation, University of Oslo, Oslo.

Schoppe-Sullivan, S. et al. (2017) 'What Are Men Doing While Women Perform Extra Unpaid Labor? Leisure and Specialization at the Transition to Parenthood', *Sex Roles*, vol. 78, no. 4.

Sharpe, S. (1990) *Voices From Home: Girls Talk About Their Families*, Virago Upstarts, London.

Shils, E. and Grosby, S. (1997) *The Virtue of Civility: Selected Essays on Liberalism, Tradition, and Civil Society*, Liberty Fund Inc., Indianapolis.

Standing, G. (2016) *The Precariat: The New Dangerous Class*, Bloomsbury Academic, London.

Stephens, J. (2017) 'Toxic masculinity is everywhere. It's up to us men to fix this', *The Guardian*, 23 October.

Strinati, D. (1995) *An Introduction to Theories of Popular Culture*, Routledge, London and NY.

Suzman, J. (2018) 'Automation may bring the realisation that we're not hard-wired to work', *New Statesman*, 8 January.

Tarde, G. (1903) *The Laws of Imitation*, Henry Holt and Company, NY.

Thompson, K. (2017) 'The Hidden Curriculum and School Ethos' revisesociology.com.

Tiger, L. and Fox, R. (1971) *The Imperial Animal*, Holt, Reinhart & Winston, NY.

Tunstall, J. (1983) *The Media in Britain*, Constable, London.

Twenge, J. (2014) *Generation Me: Why Today's Young Americans Are More Confident, Assertive, Entitled – And More Miserable Than Ever Before*, Atria Books, NY.

Valentine, G. (2003) 'Boundary Crossings: Transitions from Childhood to Adulthood', *Children's Geographies*, vol. 1, no. 1.

Vauclair, C-M. et al. (2017) 'Income inequality and fear of crime across the European region', *European Journal of Criminology*, vol. 14, no. 2.

Walter, N. (1999) *The New Feminism*, Virago, London.

Wells, K. (2009 1st edn, 2014 2nd edn) *Childhood in a Global Perspective*, Polity Press, Cambridge.

Wilkinson, H. (1994) *No Turning Back: Generations and the Genderquake*, Demos, London.

Wilkinson, R. and Pickett, K. (2018) The *Inner Level: How More Equal Societies Reduce Stress, Restore Sanity and Improve Everyone's Wellbeing*, Allen Lane, London.

Willis, P. (1977) *Learning to Labour: How Working Class Kids Get Working Class Jobs*, Columbia University Press, NY.

Wolf, N. (1990) *The Beauty Myth*, Vintage, London.

Wooldridge, A. and Micklethwait, J. (2010) *God is Back: How the Global Rise of Faith is Changing the World*, Penguin, London.

Young, J. (1971*) The Drugtakers*, HarperCollins, London.

# Chapter 3

Ali, S. (2011) 'Visual analysis', in C. Seale (ed.) *Researching Society and Culture*, Sage, London.

Atkinson, J. M. (1978) *Discovering Suicide*, Macmillan, London.

Ayodele, J. O. (2015) 'Crime-reporting practices among market women in Oyo, Nigeria', *SAGE Open*, April-June.

Becker, H. S. (1970) *Sociological Work*, Transaction Publishers, New Brunswick.

Behnke, S. (2009) 'A classic study, revisited', *Monitor on Psychology*, vol. 40, no. 5.

Bhaskar, R. (1978) *A Realist Theory of Science*, 2nd edn, Harvester, Hassocks.

Bryman, A. (2016) *Social Research Methods*, 5th edn, Oxford University Press, Oxford.

Comte, A. (1986) *The Positive Philosophy*, Bell & Sons, London.

Critchfield, R. (1978) *Look to Suffering, Look to Joy*, American Universities Field Staff, Hanover, NH.

Douglas, J. D. (1967) *The Social Meanings of Suicide*, Princeton University Press, NJ.

Durkheim, É. (1938, orig. 1895) *The Rules of Sociological Method*, Free Press, NY.

(1970, orig. 1897) *Suicide: A Study in Sociology*, Routledge, London.

Edwards, R. and Holland, J. (2013) *What is Qualitative Interviewing?* Bloomsbury, London.

Fielding, N. (1993) 'Ethnography' in N. Gilbert (ed.) *Researching Social Life*, Sage, London.

Francis, B. (2000) *Boys, Girls and Achievement: Addressing the Classroom Issues*, RoutledgeFalmer, London.

Geertz, C. (1973) *The Interpretation of Cultures*, Basic Books, NY.

Glasgow University Media Group (1976) *Bad news*, Routledge & Kegan Paul, London.

Global Media Monitoring Project (2015) highlights of findings, whomakesthenews.org.

Global School-based Student Health Survey (GSHS) (2011), www.who.int.

Goffman, E. (1968) *Asylums*, Penguin, Harmondsworth.

Gouldner, A. W. (1975) *For Sociology*, Penguin, Harmondsworth.

Griffin, J. H. (1960) *Black Like Me*, Signet, NY.

Grogan, S. and Richards, H. (2002) 'Body image: focus groups with boys and men', *Men and Masculinities*, vol. 4, no. 3.

Harvey, D. (2014) *Seventeen Contradictions and the End of Capitalism*, Profile Books, London.

(2010) *The Enigma of Capital and the Crises of Capitalism*, Profile Books, London.

Harvey, D. and Slatin, G. (1975) 'The relationship between child's SES and teacher expectations: a test of the middle-class bias hypothesis', *Social Forces*, vol. 54, no. 1.

Heelas, P., Woodhead, L., Seel, B., Tusting, K. and Szerszynski, B. (2005) *The Spiritual Revolution: Why Religion is Giving Way to Spirituality*, Blackwell, Oxford.

Hite, S. (1994) *The Hite Report on the Family: Growing up under Patriarchy*, Grove Press, NY.

HMIC (2014) *Crime-recording: Making the Victim Count*, HMIC, London.

Hobbs, D. (1988) *Doing the Business*, Oxford University Press, Oxford.

Hollis, M. E. (2014) 'Assessing the experiences of female and minority police officers: Observations from an ethnographic researcher', in K. Lumsden and A. Winter (eds) *Reflexivity in Criminological Research*, Palgrave Macmillan, Basingstoke.

Homan, R. (1991) *The Ethics of Social Research*, Longman, London.

International Sociological Association's (2001) Code of Ethics, *International Sociological Association*.

Klineberg, O. (1971) 'Race and IQ', *The Unesco Courier*, November.

Kuhn, T. S. (1962) *The Structure of Scientific Revolutions*, University of Chicago Press, Chicago.

Lakatos, I. and Musgrave (eds) *Criticism and the Growth of Knowledge*, Cambridge University Press, Cambridge.

Lewis, O. (1951) *Life in a Mexican Village: Tepoztlan Restudied*, University of Illinois Press, Urbana, IL.

Liu, L. and Xie, A. (2017) 'Muddling through school life: an ethnographic study of the subculture of "deviant" students in China', *International Studies in Sociology of Education*, vol. 26, no. 2.

Lyotard, J-F. (1984) *[see chapter 1 refs]*

May, T. (2001) *Social research: Issues, methods and process*, 3rd edn, Open University Press, Maidenhead.

Mies, M. (1993) 'Towards a methodology for feminist research', in M. Hammersley (ed.) *Social Research: Philosophy, Politics and Practice*, Sage, London.

Milgram, S. (1963) 'A behavioural study of obedience', *Journal of Abnormal and Social Psychology*, vol. 67, no. 4.

Morley, L. and Lussier, K. (2009) 'Intersecting poverty and participation in higher education in Ghana and Tanzania', *International Studies in Sociology of Education*, vol. 19, no. 2.

Morgan, D. (2006) 'Focus groups' in P. Jupp (ed.) *The Sage Dictionary of Social Research Methods*, Sage, London.

ONS (2016) 'Statistical Bulletin: Crime in England and Wales: year ending June 2016', *Office for National Statistics*, 20 October.

Otis, E. M. (2016) 'Bridgework: Globalization, Gender, and Service Labor at a Luxury Hotel', *Gender and Society*, vol. 30, no. 6.

Parker, M. (2000) *Organisational Culture and Identity*, Sage, London.

Pawson, R. (1989) 'Methodology' in M. Haralambos (ed.) *Developments in Sociology*, vol. 5, Causeway Press, Ormskirk.

(1995) 'Methods of content/ document/ media analysis' in M. Haralambos (ed.) *Developments in Sociology*, vol. 11, Causeway Press, Ormskirk.

Popper, K. R (1979) *Objective Knowledge: An Evolutionary Approach*, Clarendon Press, Oxford.

(1959) *The Logic of Scientific Discovery*, Hutchinson, London.

Redfield, R. (1930) *Tepoztlan: A Mexican Village*, University of Chicago Press, Chicago.

*Research Ethics Guidebook* (2017) Institute of Education, University of London, London.

Riddell, S. I. (1992) *Gender and the Politics of the Curriculum*, Routledge, London.

Ruwanpura, K. N. (2015) 'The weakest link? Unions, freedom of association and ethical codes: A case study from a factory setting in Sri Lanka', *Ethnography*, vol. 16, no. 1.

Sayer, A. (1992) *Method in Social Science: A Realist Approach*, Routledge, London.

Scott, J. (1990) *Matter of Record: Documentary Sources in Social Research*, Polity Press, Cambridge.

Seale, C. (2012) 'Sampling' in C. Seale (ed.) *Researching Society and Culture*, Sage, London.

Silverman, D. (2013) *Doing Qualitative Research*, 4th edn, Sage, London.

(2015) *Interpreting Qualitative Data*, 5th edn, Sage, London.

Sissons, M. (1970) *The Psychology of Social Class*, Open University Press, Milton Keynes.

Smith, J., Gilford, S. and O'Sullivan, A. (1998) *The Family Background of Homeless Young People*, Family Policy Studies Centre, London.

Stands in Timber, J. and Liberty, M. (1967) *Cheyenne Memories*, Yale University Press, CT.

Stanley, L. (2010) 'To the letter: Thomas and Znaniecki's *The Polish Peasant* and writing a life, sociologically speaking', *Life Writing*, vol. 7.

Sullivan, A. (2007) 'Cultural Capital, Cultural Knowledge and Ability', *Sociological Research*, vol. 12, no. 6.

Swedberg, R. (2011) 'Theorising in sociology and social science: Turning to the context of discovery', *Springer Science + Business Media*, 12 November.

Thomas, W. I. and Znaniecki, F. (1919) *The Polish Peasant in Europe and America*, University of Chicago Press, Chicago.

Venkatesh, S. (2009) *Gang Leader for a Day*, Penguin, London.

Walford, G. (1993) 'Researching the City Technology College Kingshurst' in R. Burgess (ed.) *Research Methods*, Nelson, London.

Weber, M. (1947) *The Theory of Social and Economic Organisation*, Oxford University Press, NY.

Whyte, W. F. (1955) *Street Corner Society*, 2nd edn, University of Chicago Press, Chicago.

Williams, J. A. Jr (1971) 'Interviewer-respondent interaction', B. J. Franklin and H. W. Osborne (eds) *Research Methods: Issues and Insights*, Wadsworth Publishing Co Inc.

## Chapter 4

Abbott, P., Wallace, C. and Tyler, M. (2005) *An Introduction to Sociology: Feminist Perspectives*, 3rd edn, Routledge, London.

Ansley, F. (1972) quoted in J. Bernard (1976) *The Future of Marriage*, Penguin, Harmondsworth.

Arfini, L. (2016) 'Significant shift in the concept of mother and father in the last 100 years', *Trinity News*, 27 May.

Ariès, P. (1962) *Centuries of Childhood*, Penguin, Harmondsworth.

Barrett, M. and McIntosh, M. (1980) 'The "Family Wage": Some Problems for Socialists and Feminists', *Capital and Class*, vol. 4, no. 2.

BBC News Online (2014), 'Who cleans up in the Chore Wars?', 19 September.

Beck, U. (1992) *Risk Society: Towards a New Modernity*, Sage, London and NY.

Beck, U. and Beck-Gernsheim, E. (2001) *Individualization: Institutionalized Individualism and its Social and Political Consequences*, Sage Publications Ltd., London.

Ben-Galim, D. and Silim, A. (2013) 'The Sandwich Generation: Older Women Balancing Work and Care', *IPPR*, London, 25 August.

Benston, M. (1972) 'The political economy of women's liberation', in N. Glazer-Malbin and H. Y. Waehrer (eds) *Women in a Man-Made World*, Rand McNally College Publishing Company, Chicago.

Bernard, J. (1982) *The Future of Marriage*, Bantam Books, NY.

Beynon, H. (1984) *Working for Ford*, 2nd edn, Penguin, Harmondsworth.

Bittman, M. and Pixley, J. (1997) *The Double Life of the Family*, Allen & Unwin, Crows Nest, NSW.

Brannen, J. (2003) 'The age of beanpole families', *Sociology Review*, vol. 13, no. 1.

Brooks, D. (2001) 'The Organization Kid', *The Atlantic*, April.

Brownmiller, S. (1975) *Against Our Will: Men, Women and Rape*, Penguin, Harmondsworth.

Budgeon, S. (2011) *Third Wave Feminism and the Politics of Gender in Late Modernity*, Palgrave Macmillan, Basingstoke.

Burghes, L., Clarke, L. and Cronin, N. (1997) *Fathers and Fatherhood in Britain*, Family Policy Studies Centre, Oxford.

Burton, L. and Bengtson, V. (1985) 'Black Grandmothers: Issues of Timing and Continuity of Roles' in V. Bengtson and J. F. Robertson (eds) *Grandparenthood*, Sage, Beverley Hills, CA.

Butler, C. (1995) 'Religion and gender: Young Muslim women in Britain', *Sociology Review*, vol. 4, no. 3.

Butler, J. (2006) *Gender Trouble*, Routledge, Abingdon.

Cameron, F. (2018) 'Conversations in my Kitchen', *The Observer magazine*, August.

Campbell, B. (2014) 'Why we need a new women's revolution', *The Guardian*, 25 May.

Carrington, C. (1999) *No Place Like Home: Relationships and Family Life Among Lesbians and Gay Men*, University of Chicago Press, Chicago.

Chambers, D. (2012) *A Sociology of Family Life*, Polity Press, Cambridge.

Chapman, T. (2004) *Gender and Domestic Life: Changing Practices in Families and Households*, Palgrave Macmillan, Basingstoke.

Cheal, D. (2002) *Sociology of Family Life*, Palgrave Macmillan, Basingstoke.

Chester, R. (1985) 'The Rise of the Neo-Conventional Family', *New Society*, 9 May.

Clarke, J. (2009) 'Histories of Childhood' in D. Wyse (ed.) *Childhood Studies: An Introduction*, John Wiley & Sons, NJ.

Corsaro, W. A. (2011) *The Sociology of Childhood*, London: Sage Publications Inc., London.

Corse, S. M. and Silva, J. M. (2013) 'Intimate Inequalities: Love and Work in a Post-Industrial Landscape', paper presented at the American Sociological Association Annual Meeting, NY.

Craig, L. (2007) 'Is There Really a "Second Shift', and If So, Who Does It? A Time-Diary Investigation', *Feminist Review*, vol. 86, no. 1.

Crompton, R. (2006) *Employment and the Family. The Reconfiguration of Work and Family Life in Contemporary Societies*, Cambridge University Press, Cambridge.

Cunningham, H. (2006) *The Invention of Childhood*, BBC Books, London.

De'Ath, E. and Slater, D. (1992) *Parenting Threads, Caring for Children when Couples Part*, Stepfamily Publications, London.

Del Boca, D. (2014) 'Italian campaigners call for housewives to be paid a salary', *The Guardian*, 7 March.

Delamont, S. (2001) *Changing Women, Unchanged Men*, Open University Press, Buckingham.

Delphy, C. and Leonard, D. (1992) *Familiar Exploitation: A New Analysis of Marriage in Contemporary Western Societies*, Polity Press, Cambridge.

Dobash, R. E. and Dobash, R. (1979) *Violence against Wives: A Case against the Patriarchy Violence Against Wives*, Free Press, NY.

Duncan, S. et al. (2014) 'Living Apart Together: uncoupling intimacy and co-residence', *The Sociology Teacher*, vol. 3, no. 1.

Duncombe, J. and Marsden, D. (1995) 'Women's "triple shift": paid employment, domestic labour and "emotion work"', *Sociology Review*, vol. 4, no. 4.

Dunne, G. (1997) *Lesbian Lifestyles: Women's Work and the Politics of Sexuality*, Macmillan, Basingstoke.

Dworkin, A. (1974) *Woman Hating*, Penguin, NY.

Edgell, S. (1980) *Middle-class Couples: A Study of Segregation, Domination and Inequality in Marriage*, George Allen & Unwin, London.

Ellwood, W. (1982) 'Two Steps Forward, One Step Back', *New Internationalist*, 1 December.

Evans, J. and Chandler, J. (2006) 'To Buy or not to Buy: Family Dynamics and Children's Consumption', *Sociological Research Online*, vol. 11, no. 2.

Fairbairns, Z. (1988) 'Wages for Housework', *New Internationalist*, Issue 181, 5 March.

Fine, C. (2011) *[see chapter 2 refs]*

(2017) *Testosterone Rex: Unmaking the Myths of Our Gendered Minds*, Icon Books, London.

Firestone, S. (1970) *The Dialectic of Sex: The Case for Feminist Revolution*, Women's Press, London.

Fletcher, R. (1988) *The Shaking of the Foundations: Family and Society*, Routledge, London.

Ford, R. and Millar, J. (1998) *Private Lives and Public Responses*, Policy Studies Institute, London.

Friedan, B. (1963/2010) *The Feminine Mystique*, Penguin Modern Classics, Harmondsworth.

Gabb, J. (2008) *Researching Intimacy in Families*, Palgrave Macmillan, Basingstoke.

Gavron, H. (1966) *The Captive Wife: Conflicts of Housebound Mothers*, Routledge & Kegan Paul, London.

Ghuman, P. A. S. (2003) *Double Loyalties: South Asian Adolescents in the West*, University of Wales Press, Cardiff.

Giddens, A. (1991) *The Consequences of Modernity*, Polity Press, Cambridge.

(1992) *The Transformation of Intimacy: Sexuality, Love and Eroticism in Modern Societies*, Stanford University Press, Stanford.

Gillespie, R. (2003) 'Childfree and Feminine: Understanding the Gender Identity of Voluntarily Childless Women', *Gender and Society*, vol. 17, no. 1.

Gillis, S. and Munford, R. (2004) 'Genealogies and Generations: the politics and praxis of third wave feminism', *Women's History* Review, vol. 13, no. 2.

Gimenez, M. and Collins, J. (1990) *Work Without Wages: Comparative Studies of Domestic Labor and Self-Employment*, State University of New York Press, NY.

Gough, K. (1973) *The Origin of the Family*, New Hogtown Press, Toronto.

Gray, A. (2006) 'The Time Economy of Parenting', *Sociological Research Online*, vol. 11, no. 3.

Greer, G. (1970/2006) *The Female Eunuch*, Harper Perennial, London.

(2000) *The Whole Woman*, Anchor Books, NY.

Gubernskaya, Z. (2008) 'Attitudes toward Cohabitation in 28 Countries: Does Marital Status Matter?', University of California, CA.

Guo, D. (2017) 'Well educated, single women in their late 20s are called "leftover women" in China', *Quartz*, 3 July.

Hakim, C. (2000) *Key Issues in Women's Work: Female Heterogeneity and the Polarisation of Women's Employment*, Athlone Press, London.

(2010) 'Erotic Capital', *European Sociological Review*, vol. 26, no. 5.

Hardill, I. et al. (1997) 'Who Decides What? Decision Making in Dual-Career Households', *Work, Employment & Society*, vol. 11, no. 2.

Hareven, T. K. (2000) *Families, History and Social Change: Life Course and Cross-Cultural Perspectives*, Perseus Books, NY.

Hart, N. (1976) *When Marriage Ends*, Tavistock, London.

Hauari, H. and Hollingworth, K. (2009) 'Understanding fathering: masculinity, diversity and change', *Joseph Rowntree Foundation*, 18 September.

Healey, J. and Yarrow, S. (1997) *Family Matters: Parents Living with Children in Old Age*, Policy Press, Bristol.

Heywood, C. (2001) *A history of childhood: Children and childhood in the west from medieval to modern times*, Policy Press, Bristol.

(2018) *Childhood in Modern Europe*, Cambridge University Press, Cambridge.

Higgins, C. (2018) 'The Age of Patriarchy: How an unfashionable idea became a rallying cry for feminism today', *The Guardian*, 22 June.

Hillman, M., Adams, J., Whitelegg, J. (1990) *One False Move... A Study of Children's Independent Mobility*, PSI Publishing, London.

Hinkley, T. et al. (2014) 'Early Childhood Electronic Media Use as a Predictor of Poorer Well-being: A Prospective Cohort Study', *JAMA Pediatrics*, vol. 168, no. 5.

Hochschild, A. (2003) *The Managed Heart: The Commercialisation of Human Feeling*, 2nd edn, University of California Press, Berkeley, CA.

hooks, b. (1981) *Ain't I A Woman?*, South End Press, Boston, MA.

James, A. and Prout, A. (1997) *Constructing and Reconstructing Childhood: Contemporary Issues in the Sociological Study of Childhood*, RoutledgeFalmer, London.

Jefferis, B., Power, C. and Hertzman, C. (2002) 'Birth weight, childhood socioeconomic environment, and cognitive development in the 1958 British birth cohort study', *BMJ*, vol. 325, no. 305.

Jessel, J. et al. (2011) 'Different spaces: Learning and literacy with children and their grandparents in east London homes', *Linguistics and Education*, vol. 22, no. 1.

Klinenberg, E. (2014) *Going Solo*, Gerald Duckworth & Co Ltd, London.

Kuo, L. (2018) 'Too smart, too successful: Mongolia's superwomen struggle to find husbands', *The Guardian*, 24 June.

Laing, R. D. (1971) *The Politics of the Family and Other Essays*, Tavistock Publications, London.

Lareau, A. (2011) *Unequal Childhoods: Class, Race, and Family Life, With an Update a Decade Later*, University of California Press, Berkley, CA.

Layard, R. and Dunn, J. (2009) *A Good Childhood: Searching for Values in a Competitive Age*, Penguin, London.

Leach, E. (1967) *A Runaway World? The Reith Lectures 1967*, BBC Books, London.

Leclerc-Madlala, S. (2002) 'Youth, HIV/AIDS and the importance of sexual culture and context in Social Dynamics', *A Journal of African Studies*, vol. 28, no. 1.

Leighton, G. (1992) '"Wives and Husbands" Labour Market Participation and Household Resource Distribution in the Context of Middle-class Male Unemployment', in S. Arber and N. Gilbert (eds) *Women and Working Lives: Divisions and Change*, Palgrave Macmillan, Basingstoke.

Leonard, M. (2000) 'Back to the Future? The Domestic Division of Labour', *Sociology Review*, vol. 10 no. 2.

Levin, I. (2004) 'Living Apart Together: A New Family Form', *Current Sociology*, vol. 52, no. 2.

Lewis, J. and Haskey, J. (2006) 'Living-apart-together in Britain: context and meaning', *International Journal of Law in Context*, vol. 2, no. 1.

Livingstone, S. (2009) *Children and the Internet: Great Expectations, Challenging Realities*, Polity Press, Cambridge.

Loscocco, K. and Walzer, S. (2013) 'Gender and the Culture of Heterosexual Marriage in the United States', *Journal of Family Theory & Review*, vol. 5, no. 1.

Marcuse, H. (1964) *One-Dimensional Man: Studies In the Ideology of Advanced Industrial Society*, Beacon Press, Boston.

Martin, W. (2013) *Stepmonster: A New Look at Why Real Stepmothers Think, Feel, and Act the Way We Do*, CreateSpace Independent Publishing Platform, CA.

Mbagaya, C. (2010) 'Child maltreatment in Kenya, Zambia, and the Netherlands: a cross-cultural comparison of prevalence, psychopathological sequelae, and mediation by PTSS', *Center for Child and Family Studies*, Faculty of Social and Behavioural Sciences, Leiden University, Leiden.

McHale, S., Crouter, A. C. and Whiteman, S. D. (2003) 'The Family Contexts of Gender Development in Childhood and Adolescence', *Social Development*, vol. 12, no. 1.

McRobbie, A. (2000) *Feminism and Youth Culture*, Palgrave Macmillan, Basingstoke.

Miller, T. (2010) *Making Sense of Fatherhood*, Cambridge University Press, Cambridge.

Millett, K. (1970) *Sexual Politics*, Virago Press, London.

Mirza, H. S. (1997) *Black British Feminism: A Reader*, Routledge, London.

Morgan, D. (1996) *[see chapter 2 refs]*

(2011) *Rethinking Family Practices*, Palgrave Macmillan, Basingstoke.

Morgan, P. (2007) *The War Between the State and the Family: How Government Divides and Impoverishes*, London: The Institute of Economic Affairs, London.

Morrow, V. (1998) *Understanding Families: Children's Perspectives*, National Children's Bureau.

Murdock, G. P. (1949) *Social Structure*, Macmillan, NY.

Murray, C. (1994) *Underclass: The Crisis Deepens*, IEA Health and Welfare Unit, London.

Ní Bhrolchain, M. and Beaujouan, E. (2011) 'Cohabitation and marriage in Britain since the 1970s', *Population Trends*, vol. 145, no. 145.

Ntshangase, N. (2017) 'One man, four wives: The new hit reality TV show', *BBC Trending*, 5 June.

Oakley, A. (1972) *[see chapter 2 refs]*

(1974) *The Sociology of Housework*, Pantheon Books, NY.

(1985) *Subject Women*, Fontana Press, Glasgow.

ONS (2012) 'Marriages in England and Wales (Provisional): 2012', Office for National Statistics.

ONS (2015) 'Marriages in England and Wales: 2015 (Provisional)', Office for National Statistics.

Oyserman, D., Radin, N. and Benn, R. (1993) 'Dynamics in a three-generational family: Teens, grandparents, and babies', *Developmental Psychology*, vol. 29, no. 3.

Paglia, C. (1990) *Sexual Personae*, Yale University Press, CT.

Pahl, R. and Spencer, L. (2001) *Rethinking Friendship: Personal Communities and Social Cohesion*, ESRC Report.

Park, K. (2005) 'Choosing childlessness: Weber's typology of action and motives of the voluntarily childless', *Sociological Inquiry*, vol. 75, no. 3.

Parsons, T. (1965) 'The normal American family', in S. M. Farber (ed.) *Man and Civilization: the Family's Search for Survival*, McGraw-Hill, NY.

Pearson, J., Hunter, A. G., Ensminger, M. E. and Kellam, S. G. (1990) 'Black Grandmothers in Multigenerational Households: Diversity In Family Structure and Parenting Involvement in the Woodlawn Community', *Child Development*, vol. 61, no. 2.

Phillips, M. (1997) 'All Must Have Prizes', *British Journal of Educational Studies*, vol. 45, no. 3.

Pollock, L. (1983) *Forgotten Children*, Blackwell, Oxford.

Postman, N. (1994) *The Disappearance of Childhood*, Delacorte Press, NY.

Pugh, A. (2002) 'From "Compensation" to "Childhood Wonder": Why Parents Buy', *Center for Working Families*, University of California, Berkeley, CA.

Pullinger, J. (2014) *Sociological Thinking: A New Introduction*, Cambridge Academic, Cambridge.

Purdy, L. (1997) *Reproducing Persons: Issues in Feminist Bioethics*, Cornell University Press, NY.

Rapoport, R., Fogarty, M., Rapoport, R. and Aldgate, J. (1982) *Families in Britain*, Routledge & Kegan Paul, London.

Rector, R. (2014) 'How Welfare Undermines Marriage and What to Do About It', *The Heritage Foundation*, November 17.

Redfern, C. and Aune, K. (2013) *[see chapter 2 refs]*

Regnerus, M. (2017) 'Cheap Sex and the Decline of Marriage', *The Wall Street Journal*, September 29.

Risman, B. (1986) 'Can Men "Mother"? Life as a Single Father', *Family Relations*, vol. 35, no. 1.

Roseneil, S. (2013) *Beyond Citizenship?: Feminism and the Transformation of Belonging*, Palgrave MacMillan, Basingstoke.

Ross, N., Hill, M., Sweeting, H. and Cunningham-Burley, S. (2005) *Grandparents and Teen Grandchildren: Exploring Intergenerational Relationships*, Centre for Research on Families and Relationships, Edinburgh.

Rutter, J. and Evans, B. (2011) 'Listening to Grandparents: Informal Childcare Research Paper 1', *Family and Daycare Trust*.

Salway, S. et al. (2009) 'Understanding the experiences of Asian fathers in Britain', *Joseph Rowntree Foundation*, 18 September.

Sharpe, S. (1976) *Just Like a Girl*, 2nd edn, Penguin, Harmondsworth.

Shaw, A. (2000) *Kinship and Continuity: Pakistani Families in Britain*, Routledge, London.

Singer, P. W. (2006) *Children at War*, University of California Press, Berkeley, CA.

Smart, C. (2007) *Personal Life*, Polity Press, Cambridge.

Somerville, J. (2000) *Feminism and the Family: Politics and Society in the USA and UK*, Palgrave Macmillan, Basingstoke.

Starkweather, K. E and Hames, R. (2012) 'A Survey of Non-Classical Polyandry', *Human Nature*, vol. 23, no. 2.

Statham, J. (2011) 'Grandparents providing childcare: Briefing Paper', *Childhood Wellbeing Research Centre*, Working Paper no. 10.

Stephens, J. (2017) *[see chapter 2 refs]*

Stoltenborgh, M. et al. (2011) 'A Global Perspective on Child Sexual Abuse: Meta-Analysis of Prevalence Around the World', *Child Maltreatment*, vol. 16, no. 2.

Taylor, Y. (2011) 'Intersectional dialogues - a politics of possibility?', *Feminism and Psychology*, vol. 21, no. 2.

Thornes, B. and Collard, J. (1979) *Who divorces?*, Routledge & Kegan Paul, London.

Tong, R. (2017) *Feminist Thought: A More Comprehensive Introduction*, Routledge, London.

Treas, J. and Dotti Sani, G. (2016) 'Today's parents spend more time with their kids than moms and dads did 50 years ago', *UCI News*, September 28.

Turnbull, C. M. (1987) *The Mountain People*, Touchstone, NY.

Tuttle, L. (1986) *The Encyclopedia of Feminism*, Arrow Books, London.

UNICEF, (2015) 'A Profile of Child Marriage in Africa', UNICEF.

Valentine, G. (1999) '"Oh please Mum. Oh please Dad". Negotiating children's spatial boundaries', In L. McKie et al. (eds) *Gender, Power and the Household*, Macmillan, Basingstoke.

Van Rompaey, V. and Roe, K. (2001) '"The Home as a Multimedia Environment: Families" Conception of Space and the Introduction of Information and Communication Technologies in the Home', *Communications*, vol. 26, no. 4.

Venning, A. and Walters, G. (2018) 'Men have more leisure time than women, but whose fault is that? Our husband and wife "discuss"', *Daily Telegraph*, 10 January.

Vincent, C. and Ball, S. (2007) '"Making Up" the Middle Class Child: Families, Activities and Class Dispositions', *Sociology*, vol. 41, no. 6.

Walby, S. (1990) *Theorizing Patriarchy*, John Wiley & Sons, NJ.

Wallander, E. quoted in P. Paul (2001) 'Childless by choice', *American Demographics*, vol. 23, nos. 45–50.

Warin, J., Solomon, Y., Lewis, C. and Langford, W. (1999) *Fathers, Work and Family Life*, Family Policy Studies Centre, London.

Watanabe, M. (2014) 'What is patriarchy (and how does it hurt us all?)' *everyday feminism*, November 24.

Wells, K. (2009) *[see chapter 2 refs]*

Wilkinson, H. (1994) *[see chapter 2 refs]*

Wilson, A. (1980) 'The Infancy of the History of Childhood: An Appraisal of Philippe Aries', *History and Theory*, vol. 19, no. 2.

Wolf, N. (1990) *[see chapter 2 refs]*

Wollstonecraft, M. (1792/2015) *A Vindication of the Rights of Women*, Penguin Vintage Classics, Harmondsworth.

WorldVision (2015) 'Building a Better World for Children: Child Well-Being Summary Report 2015', *World Vision*.

Young, M. and Willmott, P. (1957) *Family and Kinship in East London*, Penguin, London.

(1973) *The Symmetrical Family*, Pantheon Books, NY.

Zaretsky, E. (1976) *Capitalism, the Family and Personal Life*, Pluto Press, London.

# Chapter 5


Abraham, J. (1995) *Divide and School: Gender and Class Dynamics in Comprehensive Education*, RoutledgeFalmer, London.

Abrantes, P. and Abrantes, M. (2014) 'Gendering Social Mobility: a comparative perspective on the nexus of education and class across Europe', *Gender and Education*, vol. 26, no. 4.

Acker, J. (1973) 'Women and social stratification: a case of intellectual sexism', *The American Journal of Sociology*, vol. 78, no. 4.

Allan, A. J. (2010) 'Picturing success: young femininities and the (im)possibilities of academic achievement in selective, single-sex schooling', *International Studies in Sociology of Education*, vol. 20, no. 1.

Althusser, L. (1972) 'Ideology and ideological state apparatus: notes towards an investigation' in B. R. Cosin (ed.) *Education, Structure and Society*, Penguin, Harmondsworth.

Archer, L. (2003) *Race, Masculinity and Schooling: Muslim Boys and Education*, Open University Press, Maidenhead.

Archer, L. and Francis, B. (2007) *Understanding Minority Ethnic Achievement: Race, Gender, Class and 'Success'*, Routledge, London.

Arnot, M. (2004) 'Male working-class identities and social justice: a reconsideration of Paul Willis's *Learning to Labour* in light of contemporary research' in N. Dolby and G. Dimitriadis with P. Willis (eds) *Learning to Labour in New Times*, RoutledgeFalmer, London.

Apple, M. W. (1997) 'What postmodernists forget: cultural capital and official knowledge', in A. H. Halsey, H. Lauder, P. Brown and A. Wells (eds) *Education, Culture, Economy, Society*, Oxford University Press, Oxford.

Ball, S. (1988) 'Education: the search for inequality', *Social Studies Review*, vol. 4, no. 2.

Ball, S. J. (2003) *Class Strategies and the Education Market: The Middle Classes and Social Advantage*, RoutledgeFalmer, London.

(2012) *Global Education Inc. New Policy Networks and the Neo-Liberal Imaginary*, Routledge, London.

(2013) *The Education Debate*, 2nd edn, The Policy Press, Bristol.

Ball, S. J. Bowe, R. and Gewirtz, S. (1994) 'Market forces and parental choice' in S. Tomlinson (ed.) *Educational Reform and its Consequences*, IPPR/Rivers Oram Press, London.

Ballantine, J. H. and Spade, J. Z. (2001 3rd edn, 2015 5th edn) *Schools and Society: A Sociological Approach to Education*, SAGE Publications, Inc., CA.

Basit, T. M. (2013) 'Educational capital as a catalyst for upward social mobility amongst British Asians: a three generational analysis', *British Educational Research Journal*, vol. 39, no. 4.

BBC News Online (2016), PISA Results 2016, 9 December.

Beck, U. (1992) *[see chapter 4 refs]*

Becker, H. S. (1970) *[see chapter 3 refs]*

Bennett, T. et al. (2009) *Culture, Class, Distinction*, Routledge, Abingdon.

Bernstein, B. (1961) 'Social class and linguistic development: a theory of social learning' in A.H. Halsey, J. Floud, and C.A. Anderson, *Education, Economy and Society*, Free Press, NY.

(1970) 'A socio-linguistic approach to social learning' in P. Worsley (ed.) *Modern Sociology: Introductory Readings*, Penguin, Harmondsworth.

Bernstein, B. (1971) 'On the Classification and Framing of Educational Knowledge' in Young, M. F. D (ed.) *Knowledge and Control: New Directions in the Sociology of Education*, Collier-Macmillan Publishers, London.

Blackstone, T. and Mortimore, J. (1994) 'Cultural factors in child-rearing and attitudes to education' in B. Moon and A.S. Mayes (eds) *Teaching and Learning in the Secondary School*, Routledge, London.

Blanden, J., Gregg, P. and Machin, S. (2005) 'Intergenerational Mobility in Europe and North America: A Report Supported by the Sutton Trust', *Centre for Economic Performance*.

Bourdieu, P. (1971) 'Systems of education and systems of thought' in M. F. D. Young (ed.) *Knowledge and Control*. Collier-Macmillan Publishers, London.

(1974) 'Cultural reproduction and social reproduction' in R. Brown (ed.) *Knowledge, Education and Cultural Change*, Tavistock, London.

(1976) 'The school as a conservative force: scholastic and cultural inequalities' in R. Dale, G. Esland and M. MacDonald (eds) *Schooling and Capitalism: A Sociological Reader*, Routledge & Kegan Paul, London.

(1984) *Distinction: A Social Critique of the Judgement of Taste*, Routledge & Kegan Paul, London.

(1986) 'The forms of capital' in J. G. Richardson (ed.) *Handbook of Theory and Research for the Sociology of Education*, Greenwood Press, NY.

Bourdieu, P. and Passeron, J. (1977) *Reproduction in Education, Society and Culture*, Sage, London.

Bowles, S. (1976) 'Unequal Education and the Reproduction of Labour Power', R. Dale, G. Esland and M. MacDonald (eds) *Schooling and Capitalism*, Routledge & Kegan Paul, London.

Bowles, S. and Gintis, H. (1976) *Schooling in Capitalist America*, Routledge & Kegan Paul, London.

Brown, P. (2013) 'Education, opportunity and the prospects for social mobility', *British Journal of Sociology of Education*, vol. 34, nos. 5–6.

Brown, P. and Lauder, H. (2006) 'Globalization, knowledge and the myth of the magnet economy', in H. Lauder, P. Brown, J. Dillabough, and A.H. Halsey, *Education, Globalization, and Social Change*, Oxford University Press, Oxford.

Carr, W. and Hartnett, A. (1996) *Education and the Struggle for Democracy*, Open University Press, Buckingham.

Cicourel, A. V. and Kitsuse, J. I. (1963) *The Educational Decision-Makers*, Bobbs-Merill, Indianapolis.

Cingano, F. (2014) 'Trends in income inequality and its impact on economic growth', *OECD Social, Employment and Migration Working Papers*, No. 163.

Clark, I. (2016) 'A Qualitative Analytic Case Study of Subliminal Gender Bias in Japanese ELTs'. *SAGE Open*. July–September 2016.

Coffield, F. and Williamson, B. (2011) *From Exam Factories to Communities of Discovery: The Democratic Route*, Institute of Education, University of London, London.

Colquhoun, R. (1976) 'Values, socialisation and achievement' in J. Beck et al. (eds) *Worlds Apart: Readings for a Sociology of Education*, Collier-Macmillan, London.

Connolly, P. (1998) *Racism, Gender Identities and Young Children*, Routledge, London.

David, M. E. (2016) *A Feminist Manifesto for Education*, Polity Press, Cambridge.

Davis, K and Moore, W. E. (1967, first published 1945) 'Some principles of stratification' in R. Bendix and S. M. Lipset (eds) *Class, Status and Power*, 2nd edn, Routledge & Kegan Paul, London.

Douglas, J. W. B. (1964) *The Home and the School: A Study of Ability and Attainment in the Primary School*, Macgibbon & Kee, London.

Douglas, J. W. B., Ross, J. M. and Simpson, H. R. (1970) *Natural Symbols*, Barrie & Jenkins, London.

Durkheim, É. (1961) *Moral Education*, Free Press, Glencoe.

Elliott, G. (2009) *Althusser: The Detour of Theory*, Haymarket Books, Chicago.

Eysenck, H. (1971) *Race, Intelligence and Education*, Temple Smith, London.

Foster, S. and Nicholls, J. (2008) 'America in World War II: An Analysis of History Textbooks from England, Japan, Sweden, and the United States', in J. H. Ballantine and J. Z. Spade (2008) *Schools and Society. A sociological approach to education*, 3rd edn, SAGE Publications, Inc., CA.

Francis, B. (2000) *[see chapter 3 refs]*

Francis, B. and Skelton, C. (2005) *Reassessing Gender and Achievement: Questioning Contemporary Key Debates*, Routledge, Abingdon.

Fuller, M. (1984) 'Black girls in a London comprehensive school' in M. Hammersley and P. Woods (eds) *Life in School, the Sociology of Pupil Culture*, Open University Press, Milton Keynes.

Gamoran, A. (2010) 'Tracking and inequality: new directions for research and practice', in M. W. Apple, S. J. Ball and L.A. Gandin (eds) *The Routledge International Handbook of the Sociology of Education*, Routledge, London.

Gardner, H. (1999) *Intelligence Reframed: Multiple Intelligences for the 21st Century*, Basic Books, NY.

Garrod, J. (2004) 'The education gender gap', *Sociology Review*, vol. 13, no. 4.

Gewirtz, S. (2001) 'Cloning the Blairs: New Labour's programme for the resocialisation of working-class parents', *Journal of Education Policy*, vol. 16, no. 4.

Gewirtz, S. and Cribb, A. (2009) *Understanding Education*, Polity Press, Cambridge.

Giddens, A. and Sutton, P. W. (2017) *Sociology*, 8th edn, Polity Press, Cambridge.

Gillborn, D. and Youdell, D. (2000) *Rationing Education: Policy, Practice, Reform and Equity*, Open University Press, Buckingham.

(2001) 'The new IQism: intelligence, "ability" and the rationing of education' in J. Demaine (ed.) *Sociology of Education Today*, Palgrave, Basingstoke.

Giroux, H. (1984) 'Ideology, agency and the process of schooling' in L. Barton and S. Walker (eds) *Social Crisis and Educational Research*, Croom Helm, London.

(2011) *On Critical Pedagogy (Critical Pedagogy Today)*, Bloomsbury, London.

Goldthorpe, J. H. (1980) *Social Mobility and Class Structure in Modern Britain*, Clarendon Press, Oxford.

Gorard, S. and Smith, E. (2004) 'What is 'underachievement' at school?' *School Leadership and Management*, vol. 24, no 2.

Gordon, L. (1984) 'Paul Willis - education, cultural production and social reproduction', *British Journal of Sociology of Education*, vol. 5, no. 2.

Green, A. (1997) *Education, Globalization and the Nation State*, Macmillan, London.

Gurney, E. (2017) 'Choosing schools, choosing selves: exploring the influence of parental identity and biography on the school choice process in Delhi, India', *International Studies in Sociology of Education*, vol. 26, no. 1.

Hallam, S. and Parsons, S. (2014) 'Streaming six-year-olds by ability only benefits the brightest', *The Conversation*, 25 September.

Halsey, A. H., Floud, J. and Anderson, C. A. (1961) *Education, Economy and Society*, Free Press, NY.

Hargreaves, A. (1982) 'Resistance and relative autonomy theories: problems of distortion and incoherence in recent Marxist analyses of education', *British Journal of Sociology of Education*, vol. 3, no. 2.

Henderson, P. (1976) 'Class structure and the concept of intelligence', in R. Dale, G. Esland and M. MacDonald (eds) *Schooling and Capitalism: A Sociological Reader*, Routledge & Kegan Paul, London.

Herrnstein, R. J. and Murray, C. (1994) *The Bell Curve: Intelligence and Class Structure in American Life*, Free Press, London.

Hirsch, D. (2007) 'Experiences of Poverty and Educational Disadvantage', *Joseph Rowntree Foundation*, 7 September.

Huisman, J. and Smits, J. (2015) 'Keeping children in school: Effects of household and context characteristics on school dropout in 363 districts of 30 developing countries', *SAGE Open*, October-December.

Hyman, H. H. (1967) 'The value systems of different classes' in R. Bendix and S. M. Lipset (eds) *Class, Status, and Power*, 2nd edn, Routledge & Kegan Paul, London.

Illich, I. (1971) *Deschooling Society*, Calder and Boyars, London.

Ireson, J., Hallam, S. and Hurley, C. (2001) *Ability Groupings in the Secondary School: Effects on Key Stage 4*, Institute of Education, University of London, London.

Islam, K. M. M and Asadullah, M. N. (2018) 'Gender stereotypes and education: A comparative content analysis of Malaysian, Indonesian, Pakistani and Bangladeshi school textbooks', *PLOS* ONE, vol. 13, no. 1.

Jackson, C. (2006) *Lads and Ladettes in School: Gender and a Fear of Failure*, Open University Press, Maidenhead.

Jamal, A. (2016) 'Why He Won't Send His Daughter to School—Barriers to Girls' Education in Northwest Pakistan: A Qualitative Delphi Study of Pashtun Men', *SAGE Open*, July–September.

Jensen, A. R. (1973) *Educational Differences*, Methuen, London.

(1972) *Genetics and Education*, Harper & Row, NY.

Karabel, J. and Halsey, A. H. (1977) *Power and Ideology in Education*, Oxford University Press, Oxford.

Keddie, N. (1973) *Tinker, Tailor... The Myth of Cultural Deprivation*, Penguin, Harmondsworth.

Klineberg, O. (1971) *[see chapter 3 refs]*

Labov, W. (1973) 'The logic of nonstandard English' in N. Keddie (ed.) *Tinker, Tailor... The Myth of Cultural Deprivation*, Penguin, Harmondsworth.

Lauder, H., Brown, P., Dillabough, J. and Halsey, A. H. (2006) *Education, Globalisation, and Social Change*, Oxford University Press, Oxford.

Lauder, H., Hughes, D. et al. (1999) *Trading in Futures: Why Markets in Education Don't Work*, Open University Press, Buckingham.

La Valle, I., Arthur, S., Millward, C., Scott, J. and Clayden, M. (2002) *Happy families? Atypical work and its influence on family life*, The Policy Press, Bristol.

Lee, J. F. K. and Collins, P. (2010) 'Construction of gender: a comparison of Australian and Hong Kong English language textbooks', *Journal of Gender Studies*, vol. 19, no. 2.

Let Toys Be Toys (2016) Annual Survey, 15 December.

Levin, H. M. and Belfield, C. R. (2006) 'The marketplace in education' in Lauder et al. (eds) *Education, Globalisation and Social Change*, Oxford University Press, Oxford.

Licht, B. G. and Dweck, C. S. (1987) 'Some differences in achievement orientations' in M. Arnot and G. Weiner (eds) *Gender under Scrutiny*, Hutchinson, London.

Liu, L. and Xie, A. (2017) *[see chapter 3 refs]*

Lobban, G. (1974) 'Data report on British reading schemes', *Times Educational Supplement*, 1 March.

Lupton, R. (2004) *Schools in Disadvantaged Areas: Recognising Context and Raising Quality*, London School of Economics and Political Science, London.

Lyotard, J-F. (1984) *[see chapter 1 refs]*

Mac an Ghaill, M. (1994) *[see chapter 2 refs]*

Mackintosh, N. J. (2011) *IQ and Human Intelligence*, Oxford University Press, Oxford.

Mathis, W. (2013) *Moving Beyond Tracking*, The National Education Policy Center, University of Colorado, Boulder.

McDougall, J. and Trotman, D. (2009) '"Doing theory" on education', in S. Warren (ed.) *An Introduction to Education Studies. Continuum International Publishing Group*, London.

Millett, K. (1970) *[see chapter 4 refs]*

Mirza, H. (1992) *Young, Female and Black*, Routledge, London.

Mitsos, E. and Browne, K. (1998) 'Gender differences in education: the underachievement of boys', *Sociology Review*, vol. 8, no. 1.

Modood, T. (2004) 'Capitals, ethnic identity and educational qualifications', *Cultural Trends*, vol. 13, no. 2.

Moore, R. (2004) *Education and Society*, Polity Press, Cambridge.

Morley, L. and Lussier, K. (2009) *[see chapter 3 refs]*

Murdoch, S. (2007) *IQ: How Psychology Hijacked Intelligence*, John Wiley and Sons, NJ.

Neves, T., Ferraz, H. and Nata, G. (2017) 'Social inequality in access to higher education: grade inflation in private schools and the ineffectiveness of compensatory education', *International Studies in Sociology of Education*, vol. 26, no. 2.

Norman, F., Turner, S., Granados, J., Schwarez, H., Green, H. and Harris, J. (1988) 'Look, Jane, look: anti-sexist initiatives in primary schools', in G. Weiner (ed.) *Just a Bunch of Girls*, Open University Press, Milton Keynes.

Organisation for Economic Cooperation and Development, (2017) *Education at a Glance 2017: OECD Indicators*, OECD Publishing, Paris.

(2010) *Going for Growth*, OECD Publishing, Paris.

(2016) *Gender gap In education*, OECD Publishing, Paris.

(1996) *The Knowledge-Based Economy*, OECD Publishing, Paris.

Parsons, T. (1951) *The Social System*, Free Press, NY.

(1961) 'The school class as a social system', in A. H. Halsey, J. Floud, and C.A. Anderson (eds) *Education, Economy and Society*, Free Press, NY.

Plomin, R., DeFries, J. C., Knopik, V. S. and Neiderhiser, J. M. (2013) *Behavioral Genetics*, 6th edn, Worth Publishers, NY.

Rampino, T. and Taylor, M. (2013) *Gender Differences in Educational Aspirations and Attitudes*, Institute for Social and Economic Research.

(2015) 'The education gender gap', *Sociology Review*, vol. 24, no. 4.

Randall, G. J. (1987) 'Gender differences in pupil-teacher interaction in workshops and laboratories', in M. Arnot and G. Weiner (eds) *Gender and the Politics of Schooling*, HarperCollins, London.

Rangel, C. and Lleras, C. (2010) 'Educational inequality in Colombia: family background, school quality and student achievement in Cartagena', *International Studies in Sociology of Education*, vol. 20, no. 4.

Ranson, S. (1996) 'Markets or democracy for education', in J. Ahier, B. Cosin and M. Hales (eds) *Diversity and Change*, Routledge, London.

Reay, D. (2001) '"Spice Girls", "Nice Girls", "Girlies" and "Tomboys": gender discourses, girls' cultures and femininities in the primary classroom', *Gender and Education*, vol. 13, no. 2.

Reay, D., David, M.E. and Ball, S. J. (2005) *Degrees of Choice: Class, Race, Gender and Higher Education*, Trentham Books, Stoke-on-Trent.

Reid, I. (1996) 'Education and Inequality', *Sociology Review*, vol. 6, no. 2.

Reynolds, K. (1991) 'Feminist thinking on education', *Social Studies Review*, vol. 6, no. 4.

Rikowski, G. (2002) 'Globalisation and education: a paper prepared for the House of Lords Select Committee on Economic Affairs, Inquiry in the Global Economy', *Report of the House of Lords Select Committee on Economic Affairs.*

(2005) 'In the dentist's chair: a response to Richard Hatcher's critique of *Habituation of the Nation* - Part One', *Flow of Ideas.*

Rist, R. (1970) 'Student social class and teacher expectations: the self-fulfilling prophecy in ghetto education', *Harvard Educational Review*, vol. 40.

Robertson, S. L. (2008) '"Producing" Knowledge Economies: The World Bank, the KAM, Education and Development, by the Centre for Globalisation, Education and Societies', University of Bristol, Bristol.

Rosen, H. (1974) *Language and Class*, 3rd edn, Falling Wall Press, Bristol.

Rosenthal, R. and Jacobson, L. (1968) *Pygmalion in the Classroom*, Holt, Rinehart & Winston, NY.

Saunders, P. (1995) 'Might Britain be a Meritocracy?', *Sociology*, vol. 29, no. 1.

(1996) 'Unequal But Fair? A Study of Class Barriers in Britain', *Civitas Choice in Welfare*, no. 2.

Savage, M. (2015) *Social Class in the 21st Century*, Penguin Random House, London.

Scott, J. (2005) 'Social Mobility: Occupational Snakes and Ladders', *Sociology Review*, vol. 26, no. 2.

Sewell, T. (1997) *Black Masculinities and Schooling*, Trentham Books, Stoke-on-Trent.

(2008) 'Racism is not the problem', *The Guardian*, 5 September.

Shain, F. (2010) 'Refusing to integrate: Asian girls and the experience of schooling' in C. Jackson, C. Paechter and E. Renold (eds) *Girls and Education 3–16: Continuing Concerns, New Agendas*, Open University Press, Maidenhead.

Sharpe, S. (1976 1st edn, 1994 2nd edn) *[see chapter 4 refs]*

Skelton, A. (1997) 'Studying hidden curricula: developing a perspective in the light of postmodern insights', *Curriculum Studies*, vol. 5, no. 2.

Smith, E. (2003a) 'Failing Boys and Moral Panics: Perspectives on the Underachievement Debate', *British Journal of Educational Studies*, vol. 51, no. 3.

(2003b) 'Understanding Underachievement: an investigation into the differential attainment of secondary school pupils', *British Journal of Sociology of Education*, vol. 24, no. 5.

Smith, T. and Noble, M. (1995) *Education Divides: Poverty and Schooling in the 1990s*, CPAG, London.

Spender, D. (1982) *Invisible Women: the Schooling Scandal*, Writer and Readers Publishing, London.

Spicer, A. (2016) 'The knowledge economy is a myth. We don't need more universities to feed it', *The Guardian*, 18 May.

Stanworth, M. (1983) *Gender and Schooling*, Hutchinson, London.

Strand, S. (2015) *Ethnicity, Deprivation and Educational Achievement at Age 16 in England: Trends Over Time*, Department for Education, London.

Sugarman, B. (1970) 'Social class, values and behaviour in schools' in M. Craft (ed.) *Family, Class and Education*, Longman, London.

Sullivan, A. (2001) 'Cultural capital and educational attainment', *Sociology*, vol. 35, no. 4.

(2002) 'Bourdieu and education: how useful is Bourdieu's theory for researchers? *The Netherlands' Journal of Social Sciences*, vol. 38, no. 2.

Swartz, D. L. (2003) 'From correspondence to contradiction and change: *Schooling in Capitalist America* revisited', *Sociological Forum*, vol. 18, no. 1.

Tāboas-Pais, M. I. and Rey-Cao, A. (2015) 'Racial representation in physical education textbooks for secondary schools: image content and perceptions held by students', *SAGE Open*, Jan-March.

Tikly, L., Haynes, J., Caballero, C., Hill, J. and Gillborn, D. (2006) 'Evaluation of Aiming High: African Caribbean Achievement Project', *DFES Research Report RR801*.

Torrance, H. (2006) 'Globalising empiricism: what, if anything, can be learned from international comparisons of educational achievement?' in H. Lauder et al. (eds) *Education, Globalisation and Social Change*, Oxford University Press, Oxford.

Usher, R. and Edwards, R. (1994) *Postmodernism and Education*, Routledge, London.

Vernon, P. E. (1969) *Intelligence and Cultural Environment*, Methuen, London.

Waldfogel, J. and Washbrook, E. (2010) 'Low Income and Early Cognitive Development in the U.K', *Sutton Trust*, 1 February.

Ward, M. R. M. (2015) *From Labouring to Learning: Working-Class Masculinities, Education and De-industrialisation*, Palgrave Macmillan, Basingstoke.

Whitty, G. (2002) *Making Sense of Education Policy*, Sage, London.

Wiliam, D. (2016) 'Wales Pisa Results: Little will be Learned', *BBC News Online*, 4 December.

Willis, P. (1977) *[see chapter 2 refs]*

Woolf, A. (2002) *Does Education Matter? Myths About Education and Economic Growth*, Penguin, Harmondsworth.

Young, M. F. D. (1971a) 'Introduction' in Young, M. F. D. (ed.) *Knowledge and Control*, Collier-Macmillan Publishers, London.

(1971b) 'An approach to the study of curricula as socially organised knowledge', in *Knowledge and Control*.

(1973) 'Curricula and the Social Organisation of Knowledge', in R. Brown, (ed.) *Knowledge, Education and Cultural Change*, Tavistock Publications, London.

# Chapter 6

Agbetu, T. (2006) 'Institutional Racism and the British media', *Ligali*, 28 January.

Age Concern (2000) 'How ageist is Britain?' www.ageconcern.org.uk.

Akinti, P. (2003) 'Captivate us', *The Guardian*, 21 February.

Bânyai, F., Zsila, A., Király, O., Maraz, A., Elekes, Z., Griffiths, M. D. et al. (2017) 'Problematic Social Media Use: Results from a Large-Scale Nationally Representative Adolescent Sample', *PLoS ONE*, vol. 12, no. 1.

Baker, G. (2017) 'Great Firewall of China closes loopholes', rsf.org, 9 October, 2017.

Bandura, A. (1963) 'Influences of model's reinforcement contingency on the acquisition of imitative responses', *Journal of Personality and Social Psychology*, vol. 1.

Bauerlein, M. (2009) *The Dumbest Generation: How the Digital Age Stupefies Young Americans and Jeopardizes Our Future*, Tarcher, NY.

Baumberg, B., Bell, K. and Gaffney, D. (2012) 'Benefits stigma in Britain', www.turn2us.org.uk.

Blumler, J. G. and McQuail, D. (1968) *Television in Politics: Its Uses and Influence*, Faber and Faber, London.

Carothers, T. (2015) 'Why Technology Hasn't Delivered More Democracy', *Foreign Policy*, 3 June.

Charlton, T., Gunter, B. and Hannan, A. (2000) *Broadcast Television Effects in a Remote Community*, Lawrence Erlbaum, NJ.

Cohen, S. (1972) *[see chapter 2 refs]*

Connell, R. W. (1995) *Masculinities*, Polity Press, Cambridge.

Cumberbatch, G. (2004) 'Video Violence: Villain or Victim?' *Report for the Video Standards Council*.

Curtis, M. (2017) *Web of Deceit*, Vintage, London.

Dahl, R. A. (1961) *Who Governs?* Yale University Press, CT.

Davies, T. (2016) 'Understanding the radicalisation of young British Muslims', *Sociology Review*, vol. 26, no. 2.

Doherty, B. (2015) 'Call me illegal: The semantic struggle over seeking asylum in Australia', *Reuters Institute for the Study of Journalism*, University of Oxford, Oxford.

Earl, J. and Kimport, K. (2011) *Digitally Enabled Social Change: Activism in the Internet Age*, MIT Press, London.

Fedrick, L. (2012) 'Racialisation and Caste in India', *Centre for Ethnicity and Racism Studies*, Working Paper, Mapping Global Racisms Project, University of Leeds, Leeds.

Ferguson, M. (1983) *Forever Feminine: Women's Magazines and the Cult of Femininity*, Heinemann, London.

Galtung, J, and Ruge, M. H. (1970) 'The Structure of Foreign News', in J. Tunstall (ed.) *Media Sociology: A Reader*, Constable, London.

Gauntlett, D. (2008) *Media, Gender and Identity: An Introduction*, 2nd edn, Routledge, London.

Gerbner, G. and Gross, L. (1976) 'Living with television: The violence profile', *Journal of Communication*, vol. 26.

Glasgow University Media Group (1976) *[see chapter 3 refs]*

(1980) *More Bad News*, Routledge & Kegan Paul, London.

(1982) *Really Bad News*, Writers and Readers Cooperative, London.

Goldberg, S. (2018) 'For Decades, Our Coverage Was Racist. To Rise Above Our Past, We Must Acknowledge It', *National Geographic*, April.

Goode, E. and Ben-Yehuda, N. (1994) *Moral Panics: The Social Construction of Deviance*, Blackwell, Oxford.

Government Office for Science (2013) *Future Identities: Changing identities in the UK: the next 10 years*, HMSO, London.

Hall, S. (1973) *Encoding and Decoding in the Television Discourse*, C.C.C.S. University of Birmingham, Birmingham.

Harvey, D. (2005) *A Brief History of Neoliberalism*, Oxford University Press, Oxford.

Hern, A. (2018) 'Face hooked: Social Media's addictive secrets' *The Guardian*, 24 January.

Herman, E. S. and Chomsky, N. (1988) *Manufacturing Consent – The Political Economy of the Mass Media*, Pantheon Books, NY.

Hill, A. (2002) 'Big Brother: The Real Audience', *Television and New Media*, vol. 3, no. 3.

Hollinsworth, D. (2005) '"My Island Home": Riot and Resistance in Media Representations of Aboriginality', *Social Alternatives*, vol. 24, no. 1.

Holsten, H. H. (2018) 'How does social media affect your well-being?' *ScienceNordic*, 7 March.

Idris, I. and Sudbury-Riley, L. (2016) 'The Representation of Older Adults in Malaysian Advertising', *The International Journal of Aging and Society*, vol. 6 no. 3.

Information Centre about Asylum and Refugees (2005) *Key Issues: Public Opinion on Asylum and Refugee Issues*.

Jenkins, H. (2006) *Convergence Culture: Where Old and New Media Collide*, New York University Press, NY.

Jensen, M. (2016) 'Digital Convergence: Global trends in broadband and broadcast media concentration', *Association for Progressive Communications*, 18 March.

Jones, O. (2011) *Chavs: The Demonisation of the Working Class*, Verso, London.

Joyce, M. (2013) 'Beyond cyber-optimism and cyber-pessimism', *Pragati*, 26 April.

Just The Women (2012) *A Joint Report by Eaves, End Violence Against Women Coalition, Equality Now and OBJECT.*

Katz, E. and Lazarsfeld, P. (1955) *Personal Influence*, Free Press, NY.

Keen, A. (2008) *The Cult of the Amateur*, Nicholas Brealey, London.

Kitzinger, J. (1999) 'A sociology of media power: key issues in audience reception research', in G. Philo (ed.) *Message Received*, Longman, Harlow.

Lee, M. M., Carpenter, B. and Meyers, L. S. (2007) 'Representations of older adults in television adverts', *Journal of Ageing Studies*, vol. 21.

Livesey, C. (2014) *Sociology*, Cambridge University Press, Cambridge.

Livingstone, S., Blum-Ross, A., Pavlick, J. and Ólafsson, K. (2018) 'Parenting for a Digital Future: Survey Report 1', LSE Department of Media and Communications.

Lull, J. (1995) *Media, Communication, Culture: A Global Approach*, Columbia University Press, NY.

MacDowall, A. and Van der Zee, B. (2017) 'Politics and money put double squeeze on free press', *The Guardian*, 1 December.

Madianou, M. and Miller, D. (2011) *Migration and New Media: Transnational Families and Polymedia*, Routledge, London.

Martin, G. (2015) 'Stop the boats! Moral panic in Australia over asylum Seekers', *Continuum*, vol. 29, no. 3.

Martinson, J., Cochrane, K., Ryan, S., Corrigan, T. and Bawdon, F. (2012) 'Seen but Not Heard: How Women Make Front Page News', *Women in Journalism*.

McCabe, B. A. and Martin, G. M. (2005) *School Violence, the Media and Criminal Justice Responses*, Peter Lang, NY.

McChesney, R. W. (2001) 'Global media, neoliberalism and imperialism', *Monthly Review*, vol. 52, no. 10.

(2013) *[see chapter 1 refs]*

McKendrick, J. H., Sinclair, S., Irwin, A., O'Donnell, H., Scott, G. and Dobbie, L. (2008) 'The Media: Poverty and Public Opinion in the UK', *Joseph Rowntree Foundation*, 10 September.

McNamara, J. R. (2006) *Media and Male Identity: The Making and Remaking of Men*, Palgrave, Basingstoke.

McRobbie, A. and Thornton, S. (1995) 'Rethinking "moral panic" for multi-mediated social worlds', *British Journal of Sociology*, vol. 46.

Meadows, M. (2004) 'Media Images of Indigenous Affairs in Australia', in J. Leigh and E. Loo (eds) *Outer Limits: A Reader in Communication Across Cultures*, Language Australia, Melbourne.

Miliband, R. (1973) *The State in Capitalist Society*, Quartet, London.

Milner, C., Van Norman, K. and Milner, J. (2012) 'The Media's Portrayal of Ageing in Global Population Ageing: Peril or Promise?' *Global Agenda Council on Ageing Society and World Economic Forum.*

Moore, K., Mason, P. and Lewis, J. (2008) *Images of Islam in the UK: The Representation of British Muslims in the National Print News Media 2000–2008*, Cardiff School of Journalism, Media and Cultural Studies and Channel 4 Dispatches.

Morley, D. (1980) *The Nationwide Audience*, British Film Institute, London.

Murthy, D. (2013) *Twitter*, Polity Press, Cambridge.

NCB (2008) 'Media Portrayal of Young People – impact and influences', www.open.ac.uk.

Negroponte, N. (2008) *Being Digital*, Alfred A. Knopf, NY.

Newman, D. (2006) *The Architecture of Stratification: Social Class and Inequality*, Sage, London.

Newson, E. (1994) *Video Violence and the Protection of Children*, Report of the Home Affairs Committee, HMSO, London.

O'Hara, M. (2018) 'Let's Tell the Truth About Poverty – And Stop This Assault on Welfare, *The Guardian*, 21 February.

Orttung, R. and Walker, C. (2014) 'Authoritarian regimes retool their media-control strategy', *The Washington Post*, 10 January.

Pearson, G. (1983) *Hooligan: A History of Respectable Fears*, Macmillan, London.

Philo, G. (2001) 'Media effects and the active audience', *Sociology Review*, vol. 10, no. 3.

(2012) 'The media and the global banking crisis', *Sociology Review*, vol. 21, no. 3.

Philo, G. and Beattie, L. (1999) 'Race, migration and media' in G. Philo (ed.) *Message Received: Glasgow Media Group Research 1993–1998*, Longman, London.

Philo, G. and Berry, M. (2004) *Bad News from Israel*, Pluto Press, London.

Philo, G. and Miller, D. (2001) *Market Killing: What the Free Market Does and What Social Scientists Can Do About It*, Longman, Harlow.

Powell, C. (2017) *#MeToo Goes Global and Crosses Multiple Boundaries*, blog post, 14 December.

Prensky, M. (2001) 'Digital Natives, Digital Immigrants', *On the Horizon*, vol. 9, no. 5.

Prieler, M., Ivanov, A. and Hagiwara, S. (2017) 'The Representation of Older People in E. Asian TV adverts', *International Journal of Ageing and Human Development*, vol. 85, no. 1.

Rajendran, T. (2018) 'Time's up Mister Bond: why new ideas of identity mean the next 007 should be black, bisexual – or even a woman', *The Conversation*, 13 April.

Reiner, R. (2010) 'Media made criminality: the representation of crime in the mass media' in M. Maguire, R. Morgan and R. Reiner (eds) *The Oxford Handbook of Criminology*, 4th edn, Oxford University Press, Oxford.

Rhodes, R. (2000) 'The media violence myth', *New York Times*, 17 September.

Robinson, W. I. (2004) *A Theory of Global Capitalism: Production, Class and State in a Transnational World*, Baltimore, John Hopkins University Press.

Rose, S. and Rose, H. (2005) 'Why we should give up on race', *The Guardian*, 4 March.

Simon, J. (2017) 'Introduction' to *Attacks on the Press: The New Face of Censorship*, Committee to Protect Journalists, NY.

Sittichai, R. and Smith, P. K. (2015) 'Bullying in South-East Asian countries: A review', *Aggression and Violent Behavior*, vol. 23.

Spencer-Thomas, O. (2008) 'What is newsworthy?', Available at www.owenspencer-thomas.com.

Stier, S. (2015) 'Democracy, autocracy and the news: the impact of regime type on media freedom', *Democratization*, vol. 22, no. 7.

Sveinsson, K. P. (2008) 'A Tale of Two Englands: "Race" and Violent Crime in the Press', Runnymede Trust, London.

Tebbel, C. (2000) *The Body Snatchers: How the Media Shapes Women*, Finch Publishing, NSW.

The Commission on Older Women (2013) Interim Report, www.policyforum.labour.org.uk.

Turkle, S. (1995) *Life on the Screen: Identity in the Age of the Internet*, Simon and Schuster, NY.

Ul Huda, A. R. and Ali, R. (2015) 'Portrayal of Women in Pakistani Media', *International Journal of Academic Research and Reflection*, vol. 3, no. 1.

UNESCO (2018) *World Trends in Freedom of Expression and Media Development: Global Report 2017/2018*, Paris.

*University News* (2017) 'Bollywood Needs to Rethink Dalit Representation, Media Scholar Says', *Birmingham City University*, 8 August.

Walby, S. (2011) *The Future of Feminism*, Polity Press, Cambridge.

Watson, J. (2008) *Media Communication: An Introduction to the Theory and Process*, 3rd edn, Palgrave, Basingstoke.

Wayne, M. (2007) 'The media and young people – hyping up the new folk devils', *Socialist Worker*, 22 September.

Whale, J. (1977) *The Politics of the Media*, Fontana, London.

Wilkins, L. (1967) *Social Deviance*, Tavistock, London.

Wilkinson, H. (1994) *[see chapter 2 refs]*

Wolf, N. (1990) *[see chapter 2 refs]*

Wood, J. (1996) 'Repeatable pleasures: notes on young people's use of video' in D. Buckingham (ed.) *Reading Audiences: Young People and the Media*, Manchester University Press, Manchester.

Young, J. (1971) *[see chapter 2 refs]*

(2007) *The Vertigo of Late Modernity*, SAGE Publications, London.

# Chapter 7

Aldridge, A. (2007) *Religion in the Contemporary World: A Sociological Introduction*, 2nd edn, Polity Press, Cambridge.

Almond, G. A., Scott Appleby, R. and Sivan, E. (2003) *Strong Religion: The Rise of Fundamentalisms around the World*, The University of Chicago Press, Chicago.

Anderson, A. H. (2014) *An Introduction to Pentecostalism*, 2nd edn, Cambridge University Press, Cambridge.

Armstrong, K. (1993) *Muhammad*, Harper One, San Francisco.

Badawi, L. (1994) 'Islam', in J. Holm and J. Bowker (eds) *Women in Religion*, Pinter Press, University of Virginia.

Bainbridge, W. S. (2009) 'Science and Religion', in P. B. Clarke (ed.) *The Oxford Handbook of the Sociology of Religion*, Oxford University Press, Oxford.

Beckford, J. A. (2003) *Social Theory and Religion*, Cambridge University Press, Cambridge.

Bird, J. (1999) *Investigating Religion*, Collins, London.

Bottomore, T. B. and Rubel, M. (1963) *Karl Marx: Selected Writings in Sociology and Social Philosophy*, Penguin, Harmondsworth.

Brierley, P. (2006) *Pulling Out of the Nose Dive: A Contemporary Picture of Churchgoing*, Christian Research, London.

Bruce, S. (1988) *The Rise and Fall of the New Christian Right: Conservative Protestant Politics in America, 1978-1988*, Clarendon Press, Oxford.

(1995) *Religion in Modern Britain*, Oxford University Press, Oxford.

(1996) *Religion in the Modern World: From Cathedrals to Cults*, Oxford University Press, Oxford.

(2000) *Fundamentalism*, Polity Press, Cambridge.

(2002) *God is Dead*, Blackwell, Oxford.

(2003) *Politics and Religion*, Polity Press, Cambridge.

(2011) *Secularization*, Oxford University Press, Oxford.

Brusco, E. (1996) *The Reformation of Machisimo: Evangelical Conversion and Gender in Colombia*, University of Texas Press, TX.

Burkimsher, M. (2008) 'Young people: are they less religious than older people and are they less religious than they used to be?' University of Geneva, Switzerland at the 5th Lausanne Researchers' Conference, Melbourne.

Casanova, J. (1994) *Public Religions in the Modern World*, University Chicago Press, Chicago.

(2003) 'Religion, European Secular Identities and European integration' paper presented at Mellon Sawyer Seminar, Cornell University, October 7.

Christiano, K. J., Swatos, W. H. and Kivisto, P. (2008) *Sociology of Religion: Contemporary Developments*, 2nd edn, Rowman and Littlefield Publishers Inc, Lanham, Maryland.

Chryssides, G. (1994) 'Britain's changing faiths: adaptation in a new environment', in G. Parsons (ed.) *The Growth of Religious Diversity in Britain*, Routledge, London.

Daly, M. (1973) *Beyond God the Father*, Beacon Press, London.

Davie, G. (1994) *Religion in Britain since 1945: Believing without Belonging*, Oxford, Blackwell.

(2002) 'Praying alone: Church-going in Britain and social capital', *Journal for Contemporary Religion*, vol. 17, no. 3.

(2007) *The Sociology of Religion*, Sage, London.

Dawkins, R. (2006) *The God Delusion*, Bantam Press, London.

Dawson, A. (2011) *Sociology of Religion*, SCM Press, London.

De Beauvoir, S. (1953) *The Second Sex*, London Press, London.

Dunlop, S. and Ward, P. (2014) 'Narrated photography: Visual representations of the sacred among young Polish migrants in England', *Fieldwork in Religion*, vol. 9, no. 1.

Durkheim, É. (1961) *The Elementary Forms of Religious Life*, Collier Books, NY.

Drane, J. (1999) *What is the New Age still saying to the Church?*, Marshall Pickering, London.

Eller, C. (1993) *Living in the Lap of the Goddess*, Crossroad Press, NY.

El Sadaawi, N. (1980) *The Hidden Face of Eve: Women in the Arab World*, Zed Press, London.

Faith Survey (2015) 'Christianity in the UK'. Available online at faithsurvey.co.uk.

Faiola, A. and Kirchner, S. (2017) 'In Germany, a new 'feminist' Islam is hoping to make a mark' Washington Post, 17 June.

Gerth, H. H and Mills, C. W. (1954) *From Max Weber, Essays in Sociology*, Routledge, London.

Giddens, A. and Sutton, P. W. (2013 8th edn, 2017 7th edn) *Sociology*, Polity Press, Cambridge.

Gillat-Ray, S. (2010) *Muslims in Britain: An Introduction*, Cambridge University Press, Cambridge.

Hamilton, M. (2001) *The Sociology of Religion*, 2nd edn, Routledge, London.

Heelas, P. (1996) 'De-traditionalisation of religion and self: the New Age and postmodernity', in K. Flanagan and P. Jupp (eds) *Postmodernity, Sociology and Religion*, Macmillan, Basingstoke.

(2015) 'Religion and Sources of Significance: The Dawning of a Secular Age?' in Martin Holborn (ed.) *Contemporary Sociology*, Polity Press, Cambridge. Sourced to 'The spirit of things unseen: beliefs in post-religious Britain', *Theos Think Tank*, available online.

Heelas, P., Woodhead, L., Seel, B., Tusting, K. and Szerszynski, B. (2005) *[see chapter 3 refs]*

Hervieu-Leger, D. (2000) *[see chapter 2 refs]*

Horton, R. (1993) *Patterns of Thought in Africa and the West: Essays on Magic, Religion and Science*, Cambridge University Press, Cambridge.

Holm, J. (1994) *Women in Religion*, Pinter Press, University of Virginia.

Hunt, S. (2004) *Religion in Everyday Life*, Routledge, Oxford.

International Panel on Social Progress, Chapter 16 (2016). Available online at www.ipsp.org.

Humanists UK website.

Kautsky, K. (1953) *Foundations of Christianity*, Russell, NY.

Kendall Project. Available online at www.lancaster.ac.uk.

Kepel, G. (1994) *The Revenge of God: The Resurgence of Islam, Christianity and Judaism in the Modern World*, Pennsylvania State University Press.

Kuhn, T. S. (1962) *[see chapter 3 refs]*

Lynch, M. (1983) *Art and Artefact in Laboratory Science*, Routledge & Kegan Paul, London.

Lyon, D. (2000) *Postmodernity*, 2nd edn, University of Minnesota Press.

Lyotard, J-F. (1984) *[see chapter 1 refs]*

(1979) 'Conversazione con Lyotard, Interview with Gianfranco Baruchello', vol. 30, no. 300.

McGuire, M. B. (2002) *Religion: The Social Context*, 5th edn, Wadsworth, Belmont, CA.

Maclean, R. (2017) 'Eat, pray, live: the Lagos megachurches building their very own cities', *The Guardian*, 11 September.

Maduro, O. (1982) *Religion and Social Conflicts*, Orbis Books, NY.

Marshall, G. (1982) *In Search of the Spirit of Capitalism: Max Weber and the Protestant Ethic Thesis*, Hutchinson, London.

Martin, D. (1969) 'Towards a General Theory of Secularization', *European Journal of Sociology*, vol. 10.

(2013) 'Pentecostalism: An alternative form of modernity and modernization?', in R.W. Hefner (ed.) *Global Pentecostalism in the 21st Century*, Indiana University Press, Indiana.

Marx, K. (1844) 'A contribution to the critique of Hegel's philosophy of right', *Deutsch-Franzosische Jahrbucker*, 7 & 10 February, Paris.

Miller, A. S. and Hoffman, J. P. (1995) 'Risk and religion: an explanation of gender differences in religion', *Journal for the Scientific Study of Religion*, vol. 34, no. 1.

National Centre for Social Research (2016) *British Social Attitudes Survey*, 33.

Nelson, G. K. (1986) 'Religion', in M. Haralambos (ed.) *Developments in Sociology*, vol. 2, Causeway Press, Ormskirk.

ONS (2011) 'What does the Census tell us about religion in 2011?', *Office for National Statistics*, 16 May.

Paden, W. E. (2009) 'Reappraising Durkheim for the study and teaching of religion', in P. Clarke (ed.) *The Oxford Handbook of the Sociology of Religion*, Oxford University Press, Oxford.

Palmer, S. (2008) *Women in New Religious Movements* in *The Oxford Handbook of New*

*Religious Movements*, J. R Lewis, Oxford University Press, Oxford.

Parsons, T. (1937) *The Structure of Social Action*, McGraw-Hill, NY.

(1964) *Essays in Sociological Theory*, Free Press, NY.

(1965) 'Religious perspectives in sociology and social psychology', in W. A. Lessa and E. Z. Vogt (eds) *Reader in Comparative Religion: an Anthropological Approach*, 2nd edn, Harper & Row, NY.

Pew Research Center (2016) 'The Gender Gap in Religion around the World', *Pew Forum*, March 22.

Popper, K. R. (1959, 2002) *The Logic of Scientific Discovery*, Hutchinson/Routledge, London.

(1974) *Objective Knowledge: an Evolutionary Approach*, Clarendon Press, Oxford.

Pryce, K. (1979) *Endless Pressure*, Penguin, Harmondsworth.

Rinaldo, R. (2010) 'The Islamic revival and women's political subjectivity in Indonesia', *Women's Studies International Forum*, vol. 33, no. 4.

Shih, F. (2010) 'Chinese "bad death" practices in Taiwan: maidens and modernity', *Mortality* vol. 15, no. 2.

Sombart, W. (1907) *Luxury and Capitalism*, University of Michigan Press, Ann Arbor.

Stark, R. and Bainbridge, W. A. (1985) *The Future of Religion*, University of California Press, Berkeley, CA.

(1987) *A Theory of Religion*, Bern, NY.

The Religious Literacy Project. 'Pentecostalism in Brazil', *Harvard Divinity School*.

Turner, B. (2005) 'The Sociology of Religion', in C. Calhoun, C. Rojek and B. Turner (eds) *The SAGE Handbook of Sociology*, Sage Publications Ltd, London.

Voas, D. and Crockett, A. (2005) 'Religion in Britain: neither believing nor belonging', *Sociology*, vol. 39, no. 1.

Voas, D. (2009) 'The Rise and Fall of Fuzzy Fidelity in Europe' *European Sociological Review*, vol. 25, no. 2.

Wallis, R. (1976) *The Road to Total Freedom: A Sociological Analysis of Scientology*, Heinemann, London.

(1984) *The Elementary Forms of the New Religious Life*, Routledge & Kegan Paul, London.

Watson, H. (1994) 'Women and the Veil: Personal Responses to Global Process', in A. Ahmed and H. Donnan, *Islam, Globalization and Postmodernity*, Routledge, London.

Weber, M. (1958) *The Protestant Ethic and the Spirit of Capitalism*, Charles Scribner's Sons, NY.

(1963) *The Sociology of Religion*, Beacon Press, Boston, MA.

Wilson, B. R. (1966) *Religion in a Secular Society*, C.A. Watts, London.

(1970) *Religious Sects: A Sociological Study*, McGraw Hill, NY.

(1994) *Apostates and New Religious Movements*, Freedom Publishing, LA.

Woodhead, L. (2005) 'Gendering secularisation theory', *Kvinder, Køn og Forskning (Women, Gender and Research; Denmark)* vol. 1.

(2007) 'Why So Many Women in Holistic Spirituality?' in K. Flanagan and P. Jupp (eds) *The Sociology of Spirituality*, Ahsgate, Aldershot.

World Values Survey website.

Wright, A. (1994) 'An approach to Jewish feminist theology', in S. Sheridan (ed.) *Hear our voice: Women Rabbis tell their stories*. London, SCM Press.

Woolgar, S. (1988) *Science: The Very Idea*, Tavistock, London.

Yinger, J. M. (1970) *The Scientific Study of Religion*, Routledge, London.

York, M. (2004) *Historical Dictionary of New Age Movements*, Scarecrow Press, NY.

# Chapter 8

Abdel-Magied, Y. (2013) 'UNAOC, 5th Global Forum, Vienna 2013 – Key Note Statement', *United Nations Alliance of* Civilizations, February 27.

Albrow, M. (1987) 'Editorial: Sociology for One World', *International Sociology*, vol. 2, no. 1.

Aldridge, J. (2017) 'Behind the Curtain: The illicit trade of firearms, explosives and ammunition on the dark web', *RAND Corporation*, CA.

Allen, R. C. (2011) *Global Economic History: A Very Short Introduction*, Oxford University Press, Oxford.

Andreas, P. (2015) 'International Politics and the Illicit Global Economy', *Perspectives on Politics*, vol. 13, no. 3.

An-Na'im, A. (2001) 'Human Rights in the Arab World: A Regional Perspective', *Human Rights Quarterly*, vol. 23, no. 3.

Arendt, H. (1951) *The Origins of Totalitarianism*, Schoken Books, NY.

Augustin, L. (2007) *Sex at the margins: Migration, Labour Markets and the Rescue Industry*, Zed Books, NY.

Bakan, J. (1995, 2005) *The Corporation: The Pathological Pursuit of Profit and Power*, Constable, London.

Bales, K. and Trodd, Z. (2009) *Modern Slavery: The Secret World of 27 Million People*, One World, Oxford.

Banks, J. A. (2017) *Citizenship Education and Global Migration: Implications for Theory, Research, and Teaching*, American Educational Research Association, Washington DC.

Barber, B. and Schulz, A. (ed.) (1995) *Jihad Vs. McWorld: How the Planet Is Both Falling Apart and Coming Together and What This Means for Democracy*, Times Books, NY.

(2003) *Jihad Vs McWorld: Terrorism's Challenge to Democracy*, 2nd edn, Corgi, London.

(2007) *Consumed: How Markets Corrupt Children, Infantilize Adults, and Swallow Citizens Whole*, W. W. Norton & Company, NY.

Bargh, J. A. and McKenna, K. Y. A. (2004) 'The Internet and Social Life', *Annual Review of Psychology*, vol. 55.

Barron, R. D. and Norris, G. N. (1976) in D. Leonard and S. Allen (eds) *Sexual Divisions and the Dual Labour Market in Sexual Divisions Revisited*, St. Martin's Press, NY.

Bauman, Z. (2007) *Liquid Times: Living in an Age of Uncertainty*, Polity Press, Cambridge.

Bealey, F. and Johnson, A. G. (1999) *The Blackwell Dictionary of Political Science: A User's Guide to Its Terms*, Blackwell, Oxford.

Beck, U. (1992) 'From Industrial Society to the Risk Society: Questions of Survival, Social Structure and Ecological Enlightenment', *Theory, Culture and Society*, vol. 9, no. 1.

(2009) *World at Risk*, 2nd edn, Polity Press, Cambridge.

Beckford, J. (2002) *Migration and Religion*, Edward Elgar Publishing, Cheltenham.

Bennett, E. (2012) 'Global Social Movements in Global Governance', *Globalization*, vol. 9, no. 6.

Bergesen, A. (1990) 'Turning world-system theory on its head', in M. Featherstone (ed.) *Global Culture: Rationalism, Globalisation and Modernity*, Sage, London.

Bocker, A. (1994) 'Chain migration over legally closed borders: settled immigrants as bridgeheads and gatekeepers', *Netherlands' Journal of Social Sciences*, vol. 30, no. 2.

Bohnert A. et al. (2009) 'A Social Network Perspective on Heroin and Cocaine Use Among Adults: Evidence of Bidirectional Influences, US National Library of Medicine', *Addiction*, vol. 104, no. 7.

Borjas, G. J. (2004) 'Increasing the Supply of Labour Through Immigration: Measuring the Impact on Native-born Workers', *Center for Immigration Studies*, 1 April.

Bourn, D. (2008) 'Young people, identity and living in a global society', *Policy & Practice A Development Education Review*, Centre for Global Education, no. 7.

Boyd, D. (2014) *It's Complicated: The Social Lives of Networked Teens*, Polity Press, Cambridge.

British Home Office study (2001) referenced in D. Coleman and R. Rowthorn (2004) 'The Economic Effects of Immigration into the United Kingdom', *Population and Development Review*, vol. 30, no. 4.

Brookings Institute (2015) 'Why Wait 100 Years? Bridging the Gap in Global Education', 10 June.

Bruce, S. (2002) *[see chapter 7 refs]*

Bullough, O. (2018) *Moneyland: Why Thieves And Crooks Now Rule The World And How To Take It Back*, Profile Books, London.

Burman, M. and Gelsthorpe, L. (2017) 'Feminist criminology: inequalities, powerlessness and justice' in A. Liebling, S. Maruna and L. McAra (eds) *The Oxford Handbook of Criminology*, 6th edn, Oxford University Press, Oxford.

Byrne, P. (1997) *Social Movements in Britain*, Routledge, London.

Carlos, N. and Shahbaz, M. (2012) 'Migration and Tourism Demand', *Theoretical and Applied Economics*, vol. 19, no. 2.

Carmen, R. (1996) *Autonomous Development: Humanising the Landscape*, Zed Books, London.

Castells, M. (1996) *The Rise of the Network Society*, Blackwell, Oxford.

(2009) *The Rise of the Network Society: Information Age: Economy, Society, and Culture*, Wiley-Blackwell, NJ.

Castles, S. (2007) 'Twenty-First-Century Migration as a Challenge to Sociology', *Journal of Ethnic and Migration Studies*, vol. 33, no. 3.

Castles, S. and Kosack, G. (1985) *Immigrant Workers and Class Structure in Western Europe*, 2nd edn, Oxford University Press, Oxford.

Chang, H-J. (2008) *Bad Samaritans: The Guilty Secrets of Rich Nations and the Threat to Global Prosperity*, Random House Business, London.

Christie, K. and Roy, D. (2001) *The Politics of Human Rights in East Asia*, Pluto Press, London.

Christoff, P. and Eckersley, R. (2013) *Globalization and the Environment*, Rowman & Littlefield Publishers, Lanham.

Chua, A. (2018) *Political Tribes: Group Instinct and the Fate of Nations*, Bloomsbury Publishing, London.

Clammer, J. (2014) 'Globalization, New Religions and the Contemporary Re-Imagining of Japanese Identity', *Global Ethnographic* 2.

Cochrane, A. and Pain, K. (2000) *[see chapter 2 refs]*

Cochrane, K. (2013) 'The fourth wave of feminism: meet the rebel women', *The Guardian*, 10 December.

Cohen, R. and Kennedy, P. (2012) *Global Sociology*, 2nd edn, Palgrave Macmillan, Basingstoke.

Cohen, S. (2007) 'Interview with Stan Cohen conducted by Laurie Taylor' in D. Downes (ed.) *Crime, social control and human rights: from moral panics to states of denial: essays in honour of Stanley Cohen*, Willan Publishing, Milton.

Collins, M. (2015) 'Why we should question the term "institutional racism"', *The Independent*, 19 March.

Congress Commission on Immigration Reform (1997).

Conway, E. M. and Oreskes, E. (2010) *Merchants of Doubt: How a Handful of Scientists Obscured the Truth on Issues from Tobacco Smoke to Global Warming*, Bloomsbury Press, NY.

Crawley, H., McMahon, S. and Jones, K. (2016) 'Victims and Villains: Migrant Voices in the British Media', *Centre for Trust*, Peace and Social Relations, Coventry.

Croall, H. (2011) *Crime and Society in Britain*, Pearson Education, Harlow.

De Angelis, M. (2016) *Human Trafficking: Women's Stories of Agency*, Cambridge Scholars Publishing, Lady Stephenson Library, Newcastle Upon Tyne.

de Haas, H. (2008) *'Migration and development: A theoretical perspective'*, IMI Working Paper 9, International Migration Institute, Oxford.

Diken, B. and Laustsen, C. B. (2005) 'Becoming Abject: Rape as a Weapon of War', *Body and Society*, vol. 11, no. 1.

Edwards, C. (1992) 'Industrialisation in South Korea' in T. Hewitt, H. Johnson and D. Wield (eds) *Industrialism and Development*, Oxford University Press, Oxford.

Edwards, M. (2014) *Civil Society*, 3rd edn, Polity Press, Cambridge.

Edwards, M. and Hulme, D. (1996) *Beyond the Magic Bullet: NGO Performance and Accountability in the Post-Cold War World,* Lynne Rienner Publishers, CO.

Ellwood, W. (2015) *Globalization: Buying & Selling the World*, 4th edn, New Internationalist, Ottowa.

Engler, M. (2008) *How to Rule the World: The Coming Battle Over the Global Economy*, Nation Books, NY.

Escobar, A. (2008) *Territories of Difference: Place, Movements, Life, Redes*, Duke University Press, Durham, NC.

Esfandiari, G. (2010) cited by J. Keller (2010) 'Evaluating Iran's Twitter Revolution', *The Atlantic*, 18 June. Original source: Esfandiari, G. (2010) 'The Twitter Devolution', *Foreign Policy*, June 8.

Esteva, G. (1992) 'Development' in W. Sachs (ed.) *The Development Dictionary: A Guide to Knowledge as Power*, Zed Books, London.

Feinstein, A. (2012) *The Shadow World: Inside the Global Arms Trade*, Penguin, London.

Ferguson, J. A. (1986) *'The Third World' in Foreign Policy and Human Rights*, Cambridge University Press, Cambridge.

Ferguson, N. (2011) *Civilization: The Six Killer Apps of Western Power*, Penguin, London.

Fisher, J. (1998) *Nongovernments: NGOs and the Political Redevelopment of the Third World*, Kumarian Press, West Hartford.

Frank, A. G. (1979) *Dependent Accumulation and Underdevelopment* Basingstoke: Palgrave Macmillan, London.

Franko, K. (2017) 'Criminology, punishment and the state in a globalized society' in A. Liebling, S. Maruna and L. McAra (eds) *The Oxford Handbook of Criminology*, 6th edn, Oxford University Press, Oxford.

Friedman, T. (2000) *The Lexus and the Olive Tree*, HarperCollins, London. Quoted in Hoo-Chang (2008) *Bad Samaritans: The Guilty Secrets of Rich Nations and the Threat to Global Prosperity*.

Fuchs, C. (1st edn 2013, 2nd edn 2017) *Social Media: A Critical Introduction*, 2[nd] edn, Sage, London.

Fukuyama, F. (2018) *Identity: Contemporary Identity Politics and the Struggle for Recognition*, Profile Books, London.

Galeano, E. (1992) 'Open Veins of Latin America', *Monthly Review*, vol. 25, no. 4.

Gans, H. (1997) 'Toward a Reconciliation of "Assimilation" and "Pluralism": The Interplay of Acculturation and Ethnic Retention', *The International Migration Review*, vol. 31, no. 4.

Gardner, H. and Davis, K. (2014) *The App Generation: How Today's Youth Navigate Identity, Intimacy and Imagination in a Digital World*, Yale University Press, CT.

Gessen, M. (2017) *The Future is History: How Totalitarianism Reclaimed Russia*, Granta Books, London.

Giddens, A. (1999) *[see chapter 2 refs]*

(1996) 'Globalization Excerpts from a Keynote Address at the UNRISD Conference on Globalization and Citizenship', *United Nations Research Institute for Social Development*, 1 December.

Gill, A., Strange, C. and Roberts, K. (2014) *Honour Killing and Violence*, Palgrave Macmillan, London.

Giulietti, C., Wahba, J. and Zenou, Y. (2014) 'Strong Versus Weak Ties in Migration', Discussion Paper No. 8089, *Institute for the Study of Labor* (IZA).

Glenny, M. (2009) *McMafia: Seriously Organised Crime*, Vintage, London.

Goldthorpe, J. E. (1975) *The Sociology of the Third World: Disparity and Involvement*, Cambridge University Press, London and NY.

Gordon, M. M. (1981) *America as a Multicultural Society*, American Academy of Political and Social Science, PA.

Gottschalk, S. (2010) 'The Presentation of Avatars in Second Life: Self and Interaction in Social Virtual Spaces', *Symbolic Interaction*, vol. 33, no. 4.

Gray, J. (2016) 'The age of hyper-terrorism', *New Statesman*, 5 April.

(2018) 'How deep is the decline of the West?', *New Statesman*, 25 July.

(2018) 'Identity politics and the threat to democracy', *New Statesman*, 26 September.

Hales, L. and Gelsthorpe, L. (2012) *The Criminalisation of Migrant Women*, Institute of Criminology, University of Cambridge, Cambridge.

Hancock, G. (1994) *Lords of Poverty*, Atlantic Monthly Press, NY.

Hanlon, B. and Vicino, T. (2014) *Global Migration: The Basics*, Routledge, London.

Harari, Y. N. (2018) *21 Lessons for the 21st Century*, Jonathon Cape, London.

Hargreaves, C. (1992) *Snowfields: The War on Cocaine in the Andes*, Zed Books, London.

Harvey, D. (1990) *The Condition of Postmodernity: An Enquiry into the Origins of Cultural Change*, Wiley-Blackwell, Oxford.

(2011) *The Enigma of Capital: And the Crises of Capitalism*, Profile Books, London.

Hatton, T. J. and Williamson, J. (2005) *Global Migration and the World Economy: Two Centuries of Policy and Performance*, MIT Press, Cambridge MA.

Haynes, J. (2008) *Development Studies*, Polity Press, Cambridge.

Heath, A. and Cheung, S-Y. (2007) *Unequal Chances: Ethnic Minorities in Western Labour Markets*, Oxford University Press for the British Academy, Oxford.

Hegedus, Z. (1989) 'Social Movements and Social Change in Self-creative Society: New Civil Initiatives in the International Arena', *International Sociology*, vol. 4, no. 1.

Held, D. (2006) *Models of Democracy*, 3rd edn, Stanford University Press, CA.

(2010) *The Cosmopolitanism Reader*, Polity Press, Cambridge.

Held, D., McGrew, A., Goldblatt, D. and Perraton, J. (2007) *Global Transformations: Politics, Economics, Culture*, Polity Press, Cambridge.

Helpser, E. (2017) 'The Social Relativity of Digital Exclusion: Applying Relative Deprivation Theory to Digital Inequalities', *Communications Theory*, vol. 27, no. 3.

Hillyard, P. and Tombs, S. (2017) 'Social harm and zemiology' in A. Liebling, S. Maruna and L. McAra (eds) *The Oxford Handbook of Criminology*, 6th edn. Oxford University Press, Oxford.

Hirsch, A. (2018) *Brit(ish): On Race, Identity and Belonging*, Jonathan Cape, London.

Hirst, P. and Thompson, G. (2009) *Globalization in Question*, 3[rd] edn, Polity Press, Cambridge.

Hobbs, D. and Dunningham, C. (1998) 'Glocal organized crime: context and pretext' in V. Ruggiero, N. South and I. Taylor (eds) *The New European Criminology*, Routledge, London.

Home Affairs Committee (2011) 'Forced marriage', *Parliament*, 17 May.

Hoogvelt, A. (2001) *Globalisation and the Post-Colonial World*, 2nd edn, Palgrave Macmillan, Basingstoke.

Huntington, S. (1991) *The Third Wave: Democratization in the Late Twentieth Century*, University of Oklahoma Press, Norman, OK and London.

(2002) *The Clash Of Civilizations: And The Remaking Of World Order*, reissue edn, Simon & Schuster UK, London.

(2004) *Who Are We? The Challenges to America's National Identity*, Simon & Schuster, NY.

ICAR (2004) Information Centre about Asylum Seekers and Refugees, *Media Image, Community Impact*. April. Information Centre on Asylum seekers and Refugees. Kings College, London.

Ignatieff, M. (2017) *The Ordinary Virtues: Moral Order in a Divided World*, Harvard University Press, MA.

Itzoe, M. (1995) *A Regulatory Scheme for Cyberporn*, December 7. Cited online by R. Feldman (1996) at osaka.law.miami.edu.

Judt, T. and Snydner, T. (2012) *Thinking the Twentieth Century*, Penguin, NY.

Kakutani, M. (2018) *The Death of Truth: Notes on Falsehood in the Age of Trump*, Tim Duggan Books, NY.

Kaye, F. referenced in S. Ahmed (2017) 'Little House on the Prairie and its contested political legacy', *New Statesman*, 1 December.

Keen, A. (2008) *[see chapter 6 refs]*

(2015) *The Internet is Not the Answer*, Atlantic Books, London.

Klein, N. (2001) *No Logo*, Flamingo, London.

(2008) *The Shock Doctrine: The Rise of Disaster Capitalism*, Penguin, London.

Koser, K. (2007) *International Migration: A Very Short Introduction*, Oxford University Press, Oxford.

Kundera, M. (2004) *Testaments Betrayed*, Faber & Faber, London.

Kymlicka, W. (2012) *Multiculturalism: Success, Failure, and the Future*, Migration Policy Institute, Washington D.C.

Landes, D. (1998) *The Wealth and Poverty of Nations*, Little Brown and Company, London.

Levinson, M. (2016) *The Box: How the Shipping Container Made the World Smaller and the World Economy Bigger*, Princeton University Press, NJ.

Levy, A. (2006) *Women and the Rise of Raunch Culture: Woman and the Rise of Raunch Culture*, Simon and Schuster, London.

Lewis, H. (2018) 'Two decades after Anita Hill, the promise of #MeToo is that women can stop paying a "creep tax"', *New Statesman*, 26 September.

Llosa, M. V. (2000) 'The Culture of Liberty', *Foreign Policy*, vol. 5.

MacDonald, J. S. and MacDonald, L. D. (1964) 'Chain Migration, Ethnic Neighbourhood Formation and Social Networks', *The Millbank Memorial Fund Quarterly*, vol. 42, no. 1.

Mai, N. and King, R. (2009) 'Love, Sexuality and Migration: Mapping the Issue(s)', *Mobilities*, vol. 4, no. 3.

Makarenko, T. (2004) 'The Crime–Terror Continuum: Tracing the Interplay between Transnational Organised Crime and Terrorism', *Global Crime*, vol. 6, no. 1.

Malik, K. (2018) 'As a system, foreign aid is a fraud and does nothing for inequality', *The Guardian*, 2 September.

Malik, N. (2018) *Terror in the Dark: How Terrorists Use Encryption, the Darknet and Cryptocurrencies*, The Henry Jackson Society, London.

Martell, L. (2010) *[see chapter 2 refs]*

Martynuska, M. (2017) 'Cultural Hybridity in the USA exemplified by Tex-Mex cuisine', *International Review of Social Research*, vol. 7, no. 2.

Massey, D. S. (2003) *Patterns and Processes of International Migration in the 21[st] Century*, Paper presented at the Conference on African Migration in Comparative Perspective, Johannesburg, South Africa, June 4 to June 7.

McChesney, R. (2008) *The Political Economy of Media: Enduring Issues, Emerging Dilemmas*, Monthly Review Press, New York.

McMichael, P. (2016) *Development and Social Change: A Global Perspective*, 6th edn, SAGE Publications, Inc., CA.

Miles, R. (2003) *Racism After 'Race Relations'*, Routledge, London.

Miller, D. (2011) *[see chapter 2 refs]*

Moffitt, B. (2017) *The Global Rise of Populism: Performance, Political Style, and Representation*, Stanford University Press, CA.

Mounk, Y. (2018) *The People vs. Democracy: Why Our Freedom Is in Danger and How to Save It*, Harvard University Press, MA.

Mudde, C. and Kaltwasser, C. (2017) *Populism: A Very Short Introduction*, Oxford University Press, Oxford.

Murray, D. (2018) *The Strange Death of Europe: Immigration, Identity, Islam*, Bloomsbury Continuum, London.

Murthy, D. (1st edn 2013, 2nd edn 2018) *[see chapter 6 refs]*

Narlikar, A., Daunton, M. and Stern, R. (2014) *The Oxford Handbook on The World Trade Organization*, Oxford University Press, Oxford.

Nichols, T. (2017) *The Death of Expertise: The Campaign Against Established Knowledge and Why it Matters*, Oxford University Press, NY.

O'Neill, J. (2001) 'Building Better Global Economic BRICs', *Goldman Sachs*, Global Economics Paper no. 66, 30 November.

O'Neill, K. (2003) 'Brain Drain and Gain: The Case of Taiwan', *Migration Policy Institute*, September 1.

Obokata, T. and Payne, B. (2018) *Transnational Organised Crime: A Comparative Analysis*, Routledge, London.

Parekh, S. and Wilcox, S. (2014) 'Feminist Perspectives on Globalization', *Stanford Encyclopaedia of Philosophy*, May 6.

Parker, M. (2012) 'Containerisation: Moving Things and Boxing Ideas', *Mobilities*, vol. 8, no. 3.

Parsons, T. (1966) *Societies: Evolutionary and comparative perspectives*, Prentice-Hall, Englewood Cliffs, N.J.

Pearce, D. (1978) 'The Feminization of Poverty: Women, Work, and Welfare', *Urban and Social Change Review*, vol. 11, no. 1.

Peet, R. (2009) *Unholy Trinity: The IMF, World Bank and WTO*, 2nd edn, Zed Books, London.

Pendakur, M. and Harris, R. (2002) *Citizenship and Participation in the Information Age*, 2nd edn, Garamond Press, Ontario.

Peerenboom, R. (2007) *China Modernizes: Threat to the West or Model for the Rest?* Oxford University Press, NY.

Petrzela, N. (2013) 'Multiculturalism', in I. Ness (ed.) *The Encyclopedia of Global Human Migration*, Wiley-Blackwell, NJ.

Pick, A. (2011) 'The Nation State; An Essay'. Available online at www.thenationstate.co.uk.

Piore, M. (1979) *Birds of Passage: Migrant Labor and Industrial Societies*, Cambridge University Press, Cambridge.

Poole, E. (2002) *Reporting Islam: Media Representations of British Muslims*, I. B. Tauris, London.

Rahnema, M. (1997) *The Post-Development Reader*, Zed Books, London.

Ritzer, G. (1993) *The McDonaldization of Society*, Pine Forge Press, Thousand Oaks, CA.

Robertson, R. (1992) *Globalization: Social Theory and Global Culture*, Sage, London.

(1995) 'Glocalization: Time–space and homogeneity–heterogeneity', in M. Featherstone, S. Lash and R. Robertson (eds) *Global Modernities*, Sage, London.

Rochlin, N. (2017) 'Fake news: belief in post-truth', *Lib HiTech*, vol. 35, no. 3.

Rostow, W. W. (1971) *The Stages of Economic Growth*, Cambridge University Press, Cambridge.

Ruggerio, V. and South, N. (2013) 'Toxic State-Corporate Crimes, Neo-liberalism and Green Criminology: The Hazards and Legacies of the Oil, Chemical and Mineral Industries', *International Journal for Crime, Justice and Social Democracy*, vol. 2, no. 2.

Runciman, D. (2018) *How Democracy Ends*, Profile Books, London.

Sachs, J. (2005) 'Why Aid Does Work', *BBC News*, 11 September.

Sahlins, M. (1997) 'The original affluent society' in M. Rahnema and V. Bawtree (eds) *The Post-Development Reader*, Zed Books, London.

Sandel, M. (2018) 'Populism, liberalism, and democracy', *Philosophy and Social Criticism*, vol. 44, no. 4.

Sankara, T. (1988) *Thomas Sankara Speaks: The Burkina Faso Revolution 1983–1987*, Pathfinder Press, NY.

Sassen, S. (2003) 'Global Cities and Survival Circuits', in B. Ehrenreich and A. Russell Hochschild (eds) *Global Woman: Nannies, Maids, and Sex Workers in the New Economy*, Granta Books, London.

Scholte, J-A. (2005) *Globalization: A Critical Introduction*, 2nd edn, Palgrave Macmillan, Basingstoke.

Seabrook, J. (2005) 'Globalization: a War on Local Cultures', *Sociology Review*, vol. 15, no. 2.

Segal, L. (2006) 'A Misguided Manifesto', *The Guardian*, 28 June.

Sen, A. (2002) 'Does globalization equal Westernisation?', *The Globalist*, 25 March.

Simon, J. (1989) *The Economic Consequences of Immigration*, Blackwell, Oxford.

Simpson, D. (2010) 'How does migration affect tourism flows?' Available online at www.cabi.org.

Smith, A. D. (1990) 'Towards a Global Culture', *Theory, Culture and Society*, vol. 7.

Sodaro, M. (2004) *Comparative Politics: A Global Introduction*, McGraw-Hill, NY.

South, N. (2014) 'Green Criminology: Reflections, Connections, Horizons', *International Journal for Crime, Justice and Social Democracy*, vol. 3, no. 2.

Stalker, P. (2008) *No-Nonsense Guide to International Migration*, New Internationalist, Oxford.

Steger, M. (2017) *Globalization: A Very Short Introduction*, 4th edn, Oxford University Press, Oxford.

Steven, P. (2004) *The No-Nonsense Guide to Global Media*, Verso, London.

Stiglitz, J. (2017) *Globalization and Its Discontents Revisited: Anti-Globalization in the Era of Trump*, Penguin, London.

Sutton, P. (2015) 'The environment: sociology at its [natural] limits' in M. Holborn, (ed.) *Contemporary Sociology*, Polity Press, Cambridge.

Taylor, I. (1998) *Crime and Political Economy*, Ashgate Publishing Limited, Farnham.

Terry, D. F and Wilson, S. R. (2005) *Beyond Small Change: Making Migrant Remittances Count*, Inter-American Development Bank, Washington D.C.

Thompson, K. (2017) 'Radical Feminism Applied to Globalisation, Gender and Development: Globalisation and Modern Slavery'. Available online at revisesociology.com

Tribalet, M. (2011) 'France, Islam and the banlieues: a debate on the place of Islam and class in the suburbs', *The Guardian*, 1 November.

Truong, T-D. (2015) 'Human Trafficking, Globalisation, and Transnational Feminist Responses' in R. Baksh and W. Harcourt (eds) *The Oxford Handbook of Transnational Feminist Movements*, Oxford Handbooks, Oxford University Press, Oxford.

Turkle, S. (2016) *Reclaiming Conversation: The Power of Talk in a Digital Age*, reprint edn, Penguin, NY.

Twenge, J. (2017) *iGen: Why Today's Super-Connected Kids Are Growing Up Less Rebellious, More Tolerant, Less Happy—and Completely Unprepared for Adulthood—and What That Means for the Rest of Us*, Atria Books, NY.

UN International Migration Report (2017) Department of Economic and Social Affairs, NY.

Urbinati, N. (2014) *Democracy Disfigured: Opinion, Truth, and the People*, Harvard University Press, Cambridge, MA.

Van Dijk, J. (2012) *The Network Society*, Sage Publications Ltd., London.

Wallerstein, I. (1983) *Historical Capitalism*, Verso, London.

(2011) *Historical Capitalism with Capitalist Civilization*, 3rd edn, Verso, London.

(2011) *The Modern World-System*, University of California Press, CA.

Walters, R. (2010) 'Eco-crime' in J. Muncie, D. Talbot and R. Walters (eds) *Crime: Local and Global*, Willan Publishing, Cullompton.

Wazir, B. (2018) 'Othering, micro-aggressions and subtle prejudice: growing up black and British', *New Statesman*, 18 February.

West, C. (2018) 'The UK is leading global efforts to eliminate tropical diseases', *The House Magazine*, 27 April.

White, R. (2014) *Green Criminology: An Introduction to the Study of Environmental Harm*, Routledge, London.

Wilson, J. (1973) *Introduction to Social Movements*, Basic Books, NY.

Wilson, K. L. and Portes, A. (1980) 'Immigrant Enclaves: An Analysis of the Labor Market Experiences of Cubans in Miami', *American Journal of Sociology*, vol. 86, no. 2.

Wiseman, E. (2018) '"Balance" isn't about dragging experts down to our level', *The Observer*, 12 August.

Wolfgang Sachs, W. (2009) *The Development Dictionary: A Guide to Knowledge as Power*, Zed Books, London and NJ.

World Inequality Report (2018), *World Inequality Lab*, compiled by Facundo Alvaredo, Thomas Piketty et al.

Zirakzadeh, C. (2007) *Social Movements in Politics: A Comparative Study*, Palgrave Macmillan, NY.

# INDEX


## A

ability groups, 295–6
absolute mobility, 252
abuse of women, 201
accommodation, 411
acculturation, 552
achieved status, 230
Adams, James Truslow, 27
affiliation, 444
affluence, 529
age identity
  adolescence or youth, 67–8
  childhood, 67
  middle age, 68
  old age, 68
  young adulthood, 68
ageism, 68
agency, 42, 556
agenda-setting, 342
age patriarchy, 210, 212
aid, 526
Akumu, Patience, 31
alienation, 154, 190, 233, 570
Althusser, Louis, 234
altruistic, 505
American culture values, 29
American Dream, 376
Americanisation, 492
anarchy, 50, 507
Anderson, Bo, 18
anecdotal evidence, 349
anomie, 51
antagonistic teachers, 302
'anthropocentric' view of environmental harms, 579
anti-globalisation movements (AGMs), 481, 507, 509–10, 526–7
apartheid system, 66, 498
apostasy, 411
appropriation, 10
Arab Spring, 436–7
Archer, Louise, 317–18
Arfini, Luca, 222
Ariès, Philippe, 203–5
Armstrong, Karen, 423
arranged marriage, 159
artefacts, 27, 403
ascetic, 431
ascribed roles, 148
ascribed status, 229
ascription, 147
assimilation, 486
asylum seekers, 547–8
atomised mass, 382
attainment gap, 246
audience analysis, 103
audience cults, 399
Aune, Kristine, 188
austerity, 343
authoritarianism, 27, 29
authoritarian political system, 496–9
authoritarian regime, 327–8
authority, 13
autocracy, 330, 497
avatars, 348
Ayodele, Johnson Oluwole, 122

## B

baby strike, 188
*Bad News*, 344
Bainbridge, William Sims, 399
banding, 296
Bandura, Albert, 36, 386
Barthes, Roland, 104
Basit, Themina, 304
Bauman, Zygmunt, 21
Baumeister, Roy, 35
beanpole family, 168, 220
Beaujouan, Éva, 161–2
Beck, Ulrich, 21, 575
Becker, Howard, 37, 127–8
Beckford, James, 395
beliefs, 26–7
belief systems, 394
Bellin, Eva, 27
Ben-Galim, Dalia, 220
Benston, Margaret, 190
Ben-Yehuda, Nachman, 387
Bernard, Jesse, 199
Bernstein, Basil, 282–4
Berry, Mike, 344
Bhrolchain, Máire Ní, 161–2
bias
  experimenter, 86
  interview, 84
  sources of, 136–7
Bible Belt, 39
bigamy, 157
binary, 63
bi-nuclear families, 173
biological analogy, 8
bi-racial member, 66
Bird, John, 410–11
Bittman, Michael, 199
Black community, police brutality towards, 14
Black identity, 66, 317
Black Lives Matter, 14
Black masculinities in school, 305–6
'Black Panther' movement, 64
Blanden, Jo, 254
Blau, Peter, 18
blended family, 166
'bling-dripping' thugs, 378
Blumer, Herbert, 15
Blumler, Jay, 382
'boat people' in Australia, 389
Boiz, 316
Bollywood, 72
bonding social capital, 50, 479
boomerang effect, 515
'boomerang' family, 171
Bourdieu, Pierre, 239–40, 265, 286–9
  idea of cultural capital, 304
bourgeois, 205
bourgeois ideology, 10
bourgeoisie, 9
Bowles, Samuel, 232–3, 249, 267
*Boys, Girls and Achievement* (Becky Francis), 134
Bradley, Harriett, 67
brain drain, 543–4
branch campuses, 237
Breen, Richard, 254
BRIC countries, 474
bridgeheads, 556
bridging social capital, 50, 479
Brown (2013), 255–6
Brownmiller, Susan, 198
Bruce (2000), 459
Bruce, Steve, 397, 411
bureaucratic, 499
Burghes, Louie, 224
Burt, Cyril, 271
Butler, Judith, 180–1
Byanyima, Winnie, 31

## C

canalisation, 182
capital, 239
capitalism, 9, 332
capitalist globalisation, 332–3
capitalist ideology, 154
capital projects, 525
Carr, Adrian, 20
Carroll, James, 27
cartels, 560
case studies, 112
chain of memory, 458
Chambers, Deborah, 159, 216, 223
Chandler, Joan, 216
chaos of love, 165
charismatic personality, 13
chavs, 378
Cheal, David, 151
child abuse, 154, 214
child-centredness, 206
child-free, 172
childhood
  adult or parental control over children, 212
  conventional or 'march of progress' approach to, 209
  feminist approach to, 213–14
  global experiences of, 212–13
  industrialisation and, 205–6
  New Right approach to, 209–10
  postmodernist approaches to, 216–17
  in pre-industrial society, 203–5
  religion and, 211–12
  sexualisation of, 210
  social action or interactionist approach to, 215–16
  social conflict approach to, 210–13
  social construction of, 203–9
  20th-century state and, 207–9
  working-class, 211
childhood socialisation, 36
  stages of, 35
Chomsky, Noam, 339
chore wars, 196
Christians, 302
Christian values, 30
church, 397
citizen journalists, 356
civil rights, 179, 500
clash of civilisations, 544–5
class subcultures, 280–2
client cults, 399
Clinton, Hillary, 101
closed belief systems, 402
closed system, 126–7
Cochrane, Allan, 71

coded questions, 82
coercion, 18
Coffield, Frank, 246
cohabitation, 161–2
  lesbian couples, 199
Cohen, Stan, 387–8
cohort study, 115, 412
collapse of communism, 333
collective consciousness, 8
collectivism, 281, 528
Collins, Jane, 190
colonialism, 530
command economy, 497
commodification of friendship and connectedness, 479
commodity, 237
communes, 145
communism, 497
communities of fate, 505
compensatory education, 285–6
Comte, Auguste, 2, 117–18
'concrete operational' phase, 35
conflict, 9, 164–5
conflict theories, 43
conformists, 305
Confucius, 29
conglomerates, 334, 465
congregational domain, 452
conjugal roles, 194
conscience, 35
consensual policing, 50
consensual social values, 146
consensus, 551
consensus theory, 43
Conservative sociologists, 553
conspicuous consumption, 20, 217, 377
constitution, 495
consumerism, 20, 216
consumption, 151
  as compensation, 217
  of goods, 20
content analysis
  limitations of, 103
  strengths of, 103
control, 25
control by consent, 44–5
conversion, 240
Cooley, Charles, 36
co-parenting model, 172
copycat violence, 386
correlation, 78
correspondence theory, 232
Corrigan, Paul, 38
Corsaro, William, 214
cosmopolitan approach to globalisation, 505
cost-benefit analysis, 50
Cote, James, 38
counter-school culture, 234–5
coups d'état, 498
covert observation, 92
Craig, Lyn, 196
creaming, 246
Crenshaw, Kimberlé, 14
creolisation, 488
crime statistics, 97
criminogenic, 569
crisis of masculinity, 61, 202, 314
crisis of modernism, 529
cross-media ownership, 334
crusaders, 302
cryptocurrencies, 565
cult movements, 399–400
cults, 174, 397, 455
cultural amnesia, 39
cultural appropriation, 72
cultural capital, 17, 239–40
cultural convergence, 484
cultural defence, 411, 459, 486–7
cultural deprivation theory, 280, 284–6
cultural divergence, 484–9
cultural diversity, 66
cultural globalisation, 470
cultural groups, 5
cultural hegemony, 188, 339
cultural imperialism, 427, 472
cultural markers, 68
cultural pluralists, 552
cultural relativity, 502
cultural transition, 411, 459
cultural zombies, 12
culture, 1, 26
  and beliefs, 26–7
  folk, 28–9
  high, 27–8
  and identity, 5–6, 8, 13–14
  language, 27
  norms, 30–1
  popular or mass, 27–8
  South-eastern Asian, 29
  symbolic cultural artefacts, 27
  value systems, 29–30
curriculum
  cultural capital and, 265
  culture and, 262
  economic demands and, 262–4
  ethnocentric, 268
  factors affecting curricula content, 261–4
  formal, 265–6
  gendered, 268–9
  gender influence on curriculum content, 264–5
  hidden, 267–8
  high- and low-status subjects, 261
customs, 33
cyberbullying, 217, 362–3
cyber-dependent crimes, 390
cyber-enabled crimes, 390

# D

Daly, Mary, 423
data
  primary, 76
  qualitative, 77
  quantitative, 77
  reliability of, 78
  secondary, 76
  sources of, 97–103
  validity of, 78
David, Miriam, 269
Davis, Kingsley, 230–2
death, attitudes and practices towards, 32
decentring of conjugal relationships, 173
deception, 109
deductive approach, 124
deforestation, 571
democratic regime, 327
demonisation, 500
demonised female, 47
denominations, 397
  Christian, 443
dependency culture, 170
deregulation, 571
desertification, 514
development, 2, 5
deviance, 33, 52
  as law-breaking, 33
  media and, 385–90
deviancy amplification, 387–90
deviant behaviour, 52
diffuse, 452
digital activism, 356–7
digital content, 100–1
  limitations of, 101
  strengths of, 101
digitalisation, 333
digital natives, 352
digital optimist view, 356–9
digital revolution, 333
digital social networking, 479–80
digital underclass, 481
DINK, 160
discourses, 66
diseases of affluence, 521
diseases of poverty, 521
disengagement, 444
disinhibition effect, 386
dispersed extended families, 167
domestic division of labour, 194
domestic labour, 194
domestic violence, 154, 201
Doughty, Caitlin, 32
Douglas, J.W.B., 281–2
dowry system, 193
dramaturgical approach to social action, 17
dual burden, 196
dual-career/income families, 160
dual-heritage children, 168
dual heritage identity, 66
dual-income or dual-career nuclear families, 168
dual-labour market theory, 555–6
Dunn, Judy, 216
Dunne, Gillian, 199
Durkheim, Émile, 2, 8, 50–1, 125
  account of religion, 414–16
  rules of sociological method, 118–19
  social facts, 118–19
  study of suicide, 119–20
  view on education, 228–9

# E

early-modern societies, 21
'eco-centric' view of environmental harms, 579
ecological globalisation, 514–16
economic capital, 239
Economist Intelligence Unit, 327
Eddo-Lodge, Reni, 14
education
  barriers to girls' education in North-West Pakistan, 311–12
  breadwinner identity and, 317–18
  in capitalist society, 232–3
  cultural capital and, 240
  cultural reproduction and, 239–40
  division of labour and, 229
  economic growth and, 242–3
  equal opportunity, meritocracy and, 241–2, 248–50
  functionalist view on, 228–32
  gender equality in, 263–4
  gender gap in, 309–10
  globalisation and, 237
  higher, 290–1
  ideological control and, 234
  influence of global capitalism in, 237
  marketisation of, 243
  Marxist views on, 232–8
  as a means to an end, 246

neoliberal perspectives, 244
school choice process in India, 243–4
school 'dropout' in developing countries, 250–1
social democratic and New Right views, 241–6
social mobility and, 252–7
social rules and, 229
value consensus and, 232
Education Action Zones (EAZs), 285–6
educational attainment
ability grouping and, 295–6
barriers to learning, 279–80
of boys, 312–15
class subcultures and, 280–1
cognitive development and, 278
cultural capital and, 286–7, 304
cultural explanations, 304–5
cultural factors and, 280–91
differential, 277
effect of private tuition and extra-curricular activities, 278–9
gender and, 307–15
habitus and, 287, 290–1
intelligence and, 275–6
interactionist perspectives on, 293–5
labelling of students and, 294–5
material factors and, 278–80
parental factors, 304
parental income and, 278
parental interest and, 281–2
relationship between ethnicity, subcultures and, 305–6
in schools in disadvantaged areas, 279
social class and, 292–9
speech patterns and, 282–4
teacher–pupil relationships and, 293
teachers' perceptions of students' social class and, 292–3
Educational Priority Areas (EPAs), 285
educational triage, 298–9
educational underachievement
boys' 'underachievement,' 315
consequences of, 250
Edwards, Richard, 260
Edwards, Rosalind, 88
elaborated code, 283
elect, 430
Elias, Norbert, 33
elimination, 288
elite, 512
emancipatory politics, 506
emotional participation, 199
emotion work, 198–9
empathetic person, 480
empirical, 174
'empty nest' family, 171
Engels, Friedrich, 153
Enlightenment, 402
entitlement, 500
entrepreneurial spirit, 529
epistemological shift, 174
epistemology, 349
equality, 500
equality of opportunity, 230, 241–2
ethnic cleansing, 66
ethnic identity, 64–6
ethnic revitalisation, 486
ethnocentric, 152, 552
ethnocentric curriculum, 266, 268
ethnocentrism, 14, 179, 268
ethnography, 112–15
limitations of, 115
in practice, 114
strengths of, 114
European Union (EU), 523
evangelical movement, 426, 435–6
Evans, Ben, 220
Evans, Julie, 216
Excellence in Cities (EiC), 285
exclusion, 18
executive, 495
existential security, 499
experimental effect, 86
experimenter bias, 86
experiments
field, 85
laboratory, 84
limitations of, 86–7
strengths of, 86
expressive leader, 150
extended family, 144, 147, 164
extra-curricular activities, 255
Eysenck, Hans, 273

## F

failure to launch generation, 173
Faith Girls, 319
fake news, 101, 346, 510
false class consciousness, 11–12, 232
false consciousness, 338, 340
falsely conscious workers, 154
false needs, 154
falsification, 124–5
families of choice, 173
family
conjugal roles in, 194–7
dark side of family relationships, 200–2
debates about gender equality in, 194–7
decision-making in, 197–8
definitions, 144–5
feminist theories of, 178–93
functionalist accounts of, 146–52
impact of life expectancy on, 218–22
Marxist accounts of, 153–5
Murdock's idea of, 146
family diversity
blended, 166
class diversity, 168
cultural diversity, 168
domestic diversity, 168
dominance of nuclear family and, 168
organisational diversity, 167
postmodernist perspectives on, 171–4
reconstituted families, 166
single parent families, 165–6
single-person households, 166
state and social policy and, 169–70
fantasy crime wave, 387
fascist principles, 497
fatalism, 281, 528
fatherhood, 223–4
fat-shaming, 47
Featherstone, Mike, 68
femicide, 201
feminine identity, 60–1
feminism, 13–14
digital form of, 180
ethnocentrism of, 14
first wave of, 178
fourth wave of, 180–1
impact of patriarchy, 14
intersectional, 14
liberal, 182–6
radical, 179, 186–90
relationship between subject choice and gender identity, 130
second wave of, 179
socialist or Marxist, 179, 190–3
sociology and, 181
third wave of, 179–80
Western, 14
women's movement and, 311
feminist methodology, 129
feminist spirituality, 423
feral or 'wild' children, 36
fictive kin, 172
fidelity, 146
field experiments, 85
filial piety, 221
Filipino caregivers, 48
Fine, Cordelia, 41
Firati, Fuat, 20
Firestone, Shulamith, 187–8
flawed democracies, 328
focus groups, 90–1
limitations of, 91
strengths of, 91
folk culture, 28–9
folk devils, 548
forced marriage, 159
forensic accounting, 578
formal agencies of social controls, 44–5
formal content analysis, 102
formal curriculum, 265–6
Foster, John Bellamy, 21
Foster, Stuart, 262
Fox, Robin, 41
frames, 342
Francis, Becky, 320–1
free enterprise, 529
free-trade, 469
free will, 43
full democracies, 495
functionalism, 8
functionalist theory of society, 8–9
fundamentalism, 426, 458–9, 484
fundamentalist beliefs, 407
funding in research, 137
fuzzy fidelity, 451

## G

Gabb, Jacqui, 198
Gang Girls, 303, 319
Gardner, Howard, 271–2
gatekeepers, 132, 341
Geeks, 316
Geertz, Clifford, 128
gender binary, 180
gender bound, 199
gender dysphoria, 362
gendered achievement
social changes and, 310–15
gendered classroom behaviour, 320–1
gendered curriculum, 268–9
gendered identities, 317
gendered toys, 308
gender inequality, 13
genderquake, 185
gender role socialisation, 33, 36
gender scripts, 199
gender socialisation
early, 307–8
educational attainment and, 307–10
in school, 308–9
subject choice and, 309
General Household Survey (GHS), 115

generalisations, 79, 109
genocide, 554
geographically mobile workforce, 147
Gewirtz, Sharon, 286
Ghuman, Paul. A. Singh, 211
Giddens, Anthony, 21, 26, 71, 201, 216, 223, 265
gig economy, 542
Gillborn, David, 293, 301–2
Gimenez, Martha, 190
Gintis, Herbert, 232–3, 249, 267
girl power, 180
Giroux, Henry, 267
glass ceiling, 192
global educational league tables, 245
global health inequalities, 521–2
global imagining, 464
global inequalities
  education, 520
  income, 521
  modernisation theory argument, 529–32
  post-development perspective, 532
  sociological explanations for, 528–9
globalisation, 2, 4, 485, 488
  causes of, 466
  cultural dimension of, 470–1
  definition of, 71, 464–6
  ecological, 514–16
  economic dimension of, 469
  education and, 237
  feminist theories of, 474–5
  globalist theories of, 472–4
  historical dimension of, 466
  impact on identity, 71–2, 478–82
  impact on life chances, 519–22
  macro-level, 465
  Marxist theories of, 474
  micro-level, 465
  moral dimension of, 471–2
  political or ideological dimension of, 471
  postmodernist perspective on, 489
  technological dimension of, 467–8
  transformationalist and postmodernist theories of, 475–6
globalised crime
  arms trafficking, 563
  corporate crimes, 564, 566–7, 577–8
  corruption, 564
  counterfeiting and smuggling, 563
  cybercrime, 564–5
  environmental crimes, 578–9
  feminist perspectives on, 572–4
  green crimes, 565–6
  maritime piracy, 563–4
  Marxist perspectives on, 569–72
  money laundering, 564
  policing and prosecuting, 576–7
  reasons for emergence of, 567–8
  rise of, 559–60
  in Russia, 561
  state sovereignty and, 577
  terrorism, 565
  trafficking and dealing in drugs, 561–3
globality, 464
global media landscape, 332–3
  broadcast media, 335
  global media access, 334–5
  internet and mobile, 335
  newspaper circulation, 335
  trends in, 334
Global Media Monitoring Project (GMMP), 102
global migration, 66
  assimilation theory to, 551–2
  benefits from, 551–7
  causes of, 534–40
  clash of civilisation theory and, 553–4
  as a consequence of the Syrian civil war, 546
  consequences of, 541–4
  cultural consequences of, 548–9
  economic consequences of, 541–4
  feminist approaches to, 554
  immigration control as securitisation, 545
  impact on lives of migrants, 549–50
  interactionist approaches to, 556
  Marxist approaches to, 554–5
  multiculturalist approaches to, 552
  neoliberal approach to, 553
  political consequences of, 544–7
  postmodernist approaches to, 556–7
  social consequences of, 547–8
  structuralist approaches to, 553
global network society, 468
global risks to identity, 72
global social movements (GSMs), 505–10
glocalisation, 72, 464
Goddess religion, 423
Goffman, Erving, 17, 92
Goldthorpe, John, 252
Goode, Erich, 387
Gordan, Marzieh, 30–1
Gouldner, Alvin W., 127
government, 495
Graeber, David, 21
Gramsci, Antonio, 12, 339
grandparents
  children's perceptions of, 221–2
  role and social position of, 220–1
grand theories, 129
grassroots movement, 526
Gray, Anne, 224
Greer, Germaine, 14, 187, 189
Gregg, Paul, 254
Griffin, John Howard, 92
Grosby, Steven, 50
grounded theory, 125
group interviews, 90
Group of Seven (G7), 523
Gubernskaya, Zoya, 161
Gurney, Eleanor, 243–4

## H

Habermas, Jurgen, 21
habitus, 240, 287, 290–1, 293
hacktivists, 564
Hakim, Catherine, 172
Harvey, Dale, 85, 87
Harvey, David, 339
hate crimes, 548
Hauari, Hanan, 224
Hawthorne effect, 86
Healthy, Happy, Holy Organization (3HO), 399
hegemonic definitions of femininity, 60
hegemonic masculinity, 61, 313
Henderson, Paul, 272
Hepworth, Mike, 68
Herman, Edward S., 339
Hern, Alex, 363
Herrnstein, Richard, 273–5
Hervieu-Léger, Danièle, 39, 458
hidden curriculum, 37, 232
  functionalist view of, 266–7
  Illich's account of, 268
  Marxist view of, 267
  radical view of, 267–8
high culture, 27–8
high modernity, 21
Hirst, Paul, 490
historical documents, 99
Hitchings, Henry, 30
Hobbes, Thomas, 4
Hobbs, Dick, 92
Hochschild, Arlie, 199
Hoffman, John P., 408
holistic milieu, 452
Holland, Janet, 88
Hollingworth, Katie, 224
Holocaust, 66
Homans, George, 17
homogeneous countries, 546
homogenisation, 484
homophobic attitudes and practices, 63
honour-related murders, 201
hostile environment, 545
household, 145
human agency, 6
human capital, 529
humanistic approach, 43
human rights, 500–3
Hunt, Stephen, 406
hybrid identities, 72
hybridisation, 488–9
hybridised popular culture, 6
hybrid regimes, 328, 496
hyper-connectivity, 359
hyper-globalists, 472–3
hyperreality, 348
hypodermic syringe model, 381–2
hypotheses, 80

## I

ideal pupil, 292–3
identity performance, 479
identity theft, 565
ideological device, 45
Ideological State Apparatuses, 234
ideology, 404
ideology of the family, 205
Illich, Ivan, 268
imitation, 36
immediate gratification, 281
impeachment, 495
imperialism, 530
impression management, 17, 362
inclusive definitions, 394–5
independent judiciary, 496
indigenisation, 475
indigenous rights, 507
individualisation, 21, 164–5, 312
individualism, 20, 442
inductive approach, 125
inequality, 3–4, 25
infantilisation, 68, 210
infant mortality rates, 521
informal agencies of social control, 45–9
  family as an agency of, 45–7
  media as agency of, 47–8
  peer group/friendship network as an agency of, 47
informed consent, 86, 109
infrastructure, 9–10, 529
innovators, 305
institutional racism, 302, 553
institutional sexism, 183
instrumental leader, 150
intelligence
  bodily kinesthetic, 272
  definition of, 271–2

educational achievement and, 275–6
environment and, 273–4
Gardner's theory of multiple, 271–2
heredity and, 273–4
ideology, power and, 272
interpersonal, 272
intrapersonal, 272
measuring, 272–3
musical, 272
spatial, 272
intelligence quotient (IQ), 272
interaction, 15
interactionism
dramaturgical approach, 17
evaluation of interactionist perspectives, 18–19
labelling theory, 15–17
social exchange theory, 17–18
symbolic, 15
interactionist perspective, 7–8
interactionists, 6
interactionist theories of society, 43
inter-ethnic marriages, 168
intergenerational mobility, 252
International Monetary Fund (IMF), 525
Internet and World Wide Web, 351
interpretative frameworks, 342
interpretivism, 79, 135
natural science methodology and, 127
qualitative research methods and, 119–22
intersectional feminists, 179
intersectionality, 14, 299
'intersex' identity, 64
interview bias, 84
intragenerational mobility, 252
intra-Islamic differences in interpretation of theology, 548
in vitro fertilisation, 173
Iranian revolution (1978–79), 436
irony, 347
irresponsible bidding, 512
Islamic cultures, 71
veiling, 426–7
Islamisation, 544
Islamophobia, 66, 548
isolated nuclear family, 147

## J

Jacobson, Jessica, 66
James, Allison, 215
Japanese values, 29–30
Jencks, Christopher, 26
Jensen, Arthur, 271
Jensen, Mike, 334
jihadism, 548
Jim Crow laws, 66, 552
judiciary, 327

## K

Keddie, Nell, 284–5
Kendal project, 452
key informant, 93
kibbutzim, 145
King, Reverend Martin Luther, 64
kinship, 144
kleptocracy, 571
Klineberg, Otto, 273
Klinenberg, Eric, 174
knowledge
educational, 260–1
postmodernism and, 259–61
power and, 261–2
social construction of, 259
knowledge claims of science, 401
knowledge economy, 262–4
Krockow, Eva, 29
Kuczynski, Leon, 35
Kuhn, Thomas, 125, 402
view of paradigms and scientific revolutions, 126
KwaZulu ceremony, 157
Kwok, Sylvia Y.C.L., 46

## L

labelling theory, 16–18, 387
laboratory experiments, 84
labour power, 10
ladettes, 180
Laing, R. D., 202
language, 27
late capitalism, 21
late-modern societies, 21, 575
Lauder, Hugh, 246
law, 33
Layard, Richard, 216
Leach, Edmund, 202
Leclerc-Madlala, Suzanne, 214
leftover women, 159
legislature, 495
legitimisation, 555
Leonard, Madeleine, 223
lesbian couples, 199
Lewis, C. S., 30
LGBT (lesbian, gay, bisexual and transgender) community, 180
libellous, 496
liberal chauvinists, 302
liberal democracies, 495–6
contemporary, 498–9
liberal feminism
perspectives on religion, 424–6
liberal feminists, 179
liberal Western values, 459
liberation theology, 433
life chances, 3, 249–50, 265
life-course analysis, 171–2
life expectancy
explanations for rates and rise in, 218–19
impact on family, 218–22
life history, 113
liquid modernity, 21
literacy, 520
living apart together (LAT) households, 173
Livingstone, Sonia, 217
Lombroso, Cesare, 52
longitudinal study, 115–16
looking glass self, 36
loss of functions, 150
loyalty, 29
Lull, James, 383
Lussier, Kattie, 299
Lynch, Michael, 403
Lyon, David, 457
Lyotard, Jean-François, 20, 260, 403–4, 457

## M

Machin, Stephen, 254
Mackintosh, Nicholas, 275–6
macro, 42, 52
magazine covers, 104
malestream, 554
malestream sociology, 129, 181
malnutrition, 521
manipulation, 182
manufactured risk, 21
march of progress, 209
marginal groups, 455
marital breakdown
explanations for increase in, 163–5
trends in, 163
types of, 163
marketisation, 243
market-Leninist system, 498
marriage
arranged, 159
bigamy, 157
feminist perspective, 160
forced, 159
global trends in, 159–61
Jesse Bernard's study of, 199
monogamy, 157
polyandry, 158
polygamy, 157
polygyny, 157–8
same-sex or gay, 157–9
serial monogamy, 157
women's feelings about, 198–9
marriage rate, 159
Martell, Luke, 72
Martin, Kimberly, 386
Marx, Karl, 9
behaviour of social classes, 10
critique of capitalism, 9
definition of surplus value, 10
existence of superstructure, 10–11
forensic analysis of capitalism, 9–11
portrayal of working-class people, 12
relationship between bourgeoisie and proletariat, 10
Marxism
accounts of religion, 404–6, 418–20
criticism of, 12
relationship between infrastructure and superstructure, 11
theory of society, 9–11
Marxist dependency theory, 529–32
masculine identity, 61
and social change, 61–4
mass self-communication, 478
material deprivation, 278
Mbagaya, Catherine, 214
McCabe, Gregory, 386
McChesney, Robert, 21, 492
McDonaldization, 491
McKay, Deirdre, 48
McKendrick, John, 378
McLaughlin, Sarah, 53
McQuail, Denis, 382
McWorld, 491
Mead, George Herbert, 36
Mead, Herbert, 15
means of production, 9
mechanical solidarity, 51
mechanism of social control, 419
media control
Marxist theories of, 338–40
neo-Marxist views and propaganda model, 339–40
pluralist theories of, 336–8
media effects
cultural effects model, 384–5
hypodermic syringe model, 381–2

'readings' or interpretations of media content, 384
reception analysis model, 383–4
two-step flow model, 382
uses and gratifications model, 382–3
media freedom
in authoritarian regimes, 329
censorship, 329–30
in democratic regimes, 330–2
indicators of, 327
masked political control, 329
Repression 2.0, 329
in Russia, 331
media messages, 337
media plurality, 330
media representations
of class and age, 376–80
cultural differences, 380
of gender, 366–71
of Muslims in the UK, 375
of old people, 379
of race and ethnicity, 371–6
of working class, 377–8
of youth in the UK, 378–9
media sensationalism, 342
media sources
limitations of, 102
strengths of, 101–2
media violence, 386–7
membership, 444
meritocracy, 233, 241–2, 376, 529
functionalist accounts of, 248
Marxist accounts of, 249
New Right accounts of, 248–9
social democratic views on, 249
meritocratic principles, 230
meta-narratives, 20, 129, 403
meteorology, 126
methodological pluralism, 122
methodology, 118
Micklethwait, John, 39
micro-aggressions, 486
Mies, Maria, 129
military dictatorships, 498
Millar, Jane, 170
millennial feminists, 180
Millennium Development Goals (MDGs), 522
Miller, Alan S., 408
Miller, Daniel, 30
Miller, David, 349
Miller, Tina, 223
Millett, Kate, 187–8
Mirza, Safia, 189
misogyny, 61, 180, 362, 548
mixed-ability groups, 296
moderator, 91
modernisation theory, 528–9
modernity, 5, 25
modern slavery, 574
mods, 388
Molm, Linda, 18
monogamy, 157
monopoly, 21
Moore, Wilbert E., 230–1
moral entrepreneurs, 388
Morales, Bri, 13
moral panic, 313, 342, 387–90, 548
Moreton-Robinson, Aileen, 14
Morgan, Patricia, 169
Morley, David, 383
Morley, Louise, 299
Morris, Desmond, 41
Morrow, Virginia, 215
motherhood, 222–3
motherhood penalty, 196
multiculturalism, 66, 378, 486, 552
multinational education businesses (MNEBs), 244
Murdoch, Stephen, 276
Murdoch Family Trust (MFT), 330
Murray, Charles, 273–5
Muslim identities, 317
Muslim migration, 548
Muslim societies, 31
cohabitation in, 161
customs, 33

## N

Naming Vocabulary Test, 278
narcissism, 20, 480
narrowcasting, 351
nationalism, 485, 499
nation-state, 20, 499–500
liberal-democratic, 511–13
nativism, 512
nature *versus* nurture debate, 40–1
neo-colonialism, 531, 570–1
neo-conservative governments, 330
neo-conventional family, 168
neoliberal free market, 524
neoliberalism, 333
Nepal Demographic and Health Survey (NDHS), 116
networked global society, 480
network society, 506
New Age, 20
beliefs, 400
movements, 407, 428, 452, 456
religion, 424
New Christian Right, 420
new media
challenges, 356–9
characteristics of, 351
crime and, 390
digital optimism *vs* digital pessimism, 353–5
digital optimist view, 360
digital pessimist view, 360–2
globalisation and digital divides, 352–3
impact of social identities and interpersonal relationships, 359–64
New religious movements, 398, 427, 456
New Right, 170
new social movements, 20
Newson, Elizabeth, 386
news production, 341–5
social manufacture of news, 341–2
sociological research on news, 342–5
news values, 341
Nicholls, Jason, 262
nomads, 534
'non-binary' gender identities, 64
non-conformist behaviour, 52
non-directive interview, 88
non-governmental organisations (NGOs), 326, 500
local and transnational, 525–6
non-participant observation
ethics and, 95
limitations of unstructured, 95–6
strengths of unstructured, 95
types of, 95
non-random sampling, 106–7
normal science, 125
norms, 30–1
nuclear family, 144

## O

Oakley, Ann, 36, 195
objectivity, 94
objectivity in research, 108
observation schedule, 95
observer effect, 94
official statistics
crime statistics, 97
limitations of, 98
police recorded crime (PRC), 97–8
strengths of, 98
victim surveys, 98
oligarchy, 496
oligopoly, 21
online grooming, 361
online identity, 478
open belief systems, 402
open societies, 513
open systems, 126–7
operationalised questionnaire, 81–2
opportunities, 3–4, 25
organic solidarity, 51
othering, 486
over-deterministic, 9
overt observation, 93
overt racists, 302
Oxford Mobility Study (OMS), 252–3

## P

Paglia, Camille, 180
Pain, Kathy, 71
Panama Papers, 340
panel study, 115
paradigm, 126
Paradise Papers, 340
Park, Kristin, 172
parliament, 495
Parsons, Talcott, 146–52
account of religion, 416–17
individual's educational attainments, 248
view on education, 229–30, 266
partial and hybrid democracies, 496
partial or flawed democracies, 495
participant observation, 91–4, 125
limitations of, 94–5
service sector in China, 93
strengths of, 94
particularism, 528
particularistic meanings, 283
particularistic standards, 229
partnership penalty, 196
pastiche, 347
patriarchal ideology, 269
patriarchy, 13–14, 187–8, 192, 422
patrimonialism, 27
patriotism, 499
Pawson, Ray, 102
Pearson, Geoffrey, 386
peer group, 38
Pentecostalism, 427–8, 432–3
performativity, 243
period effect, 412
personal communities, 172
personal documents
assessing, 99
ethics and documentary research, 99–100
limitations of, 100
strengths of, 100
personal life, 171–4
perverse incentive, 170
pessimistic globalists, 473

pester power, 216
Phillips, Melanie, 210
Philo, Greg, 344, 349
picket lines, 344
pilot studies, 108
Pixley, Jocelyn, 199
Plantilla, Jefferson, 29
play, 36
pluralism, 497
pluriverse, 502
police recorded crime (PRC), 97–8
Politburo, 497
political rights, 500
politics of resistance, 505
Pollock, Linda, 205
polyandry, 158
polygamy, 157
polygyny, 157–8
polysemic, 383
Popper, Karl, 124–5, 402
popular or mass culture, 27–8
population, 79
populism, 511
positive discrimination, 285
positivism, 78–9, 135
  Auguste Comte and, 117–18
  natural science methodology and, 124–5
positivist, 43
'post-familial' family, 480
post-feminists, 179
post-industrial economies, 20
post-industrial society, 5
Postman, Neil, 39, 210
postmodernism, 20–1
  belief systems, 403–4
  evaluation of, 21
  knowledge and, 259–61
  understanding of media, 347–9
  view of objectivity and research, 129
postmodernity, 5, 20, 25
post-racial identity, 66
post-truth era, 510
post-truth societies, 20
poverty, 3
power, 4, 18, 25
  knowledge and, 261–2
power-feminism, 180
predestination, 430
pre-modernity, 25
'preoperational' stage, 35
present-time orientation, 281
press barons, 338
primary data, 76
primary definers, 342
primary socialisation, 35–7, 229
  of children, 148
  family and, 35–6
  by others, 37
private patriarchy, 192
private sphere, 409
privatised education, 237
privatised religion, 457
probing, 88
profane, 415
Project Head Start, 285
proletariat, 10
propaganda, 497
Protestant ethic, 431
proto-communities, 480
Prout, Alan, 215
public institutional capital, 529
public patriarchy, 192
public sphere, 409
Purdy, Laura, 187

# Q

qualitative data, 77
qualitative research methods, 88–96
  interpretivism and, 119–22
quantitative data, 77
quantitative research methods, 80–7
  positivism and, 117–19
questionnaires, 80–3
  constructing, 81
  limitations of, 83
  operationalisation and coding, 81–2
  strengths of, 82–3
  types of questions, 80
questions
  closed, 80
  open-ended (or open), 80
quotas, 524
quota sampling, 106–7

# R

racialised class fraction, 555
racism in schools, 301–3
radical feminism, 179, 186–90
  evaluation of, 189–90
  perspectives on religion, 423–4
  role of ideology, 188–9
radical psychiatrist view of family, 202
random sampling, 106
Ranson, Stewart, 246
rapport, 88
rational choice theory, 417
rationalisation, 409
rationalism, 27
realism, 127
realist view of science, 126–7
rebel girls, 318–19
rebels, 306, 319
reconstituted families, 166
Redfern, Catherine, 188
re-enchantment, 457
reflexivity, 21, 129
reflexivity in research, 138
refugees, 547–8
Reid, Ivan, 268
relative deprivation, 455
relative mobility, 252
relative value, 29
relativism, 20, 129, 513
religion
  age differences in religiosity, 412–13
  belief systems and, 401–5
  as a change-promoting force, 430–2
  change-promoting or a change-inhibiting force, 424
  collective conscience and, 415
  conflict and, 437
  as a conservative force, 429–30
  ethnicity and, 410–12
  feminist perspectives on, 422–6
  functional definitions of, 394–5
  functionalist accounts of, 414–17
  inclusive and exclusive definitions of, 394–5
  Marxist accounts of, 404–6, 418–20
  measuring religious belief, 395–6
  in non-Protestant societies, 431
  patriarchy and gender inequality in, 426–8
  in postmodern global society, 457–8
  problems of meaning and, 417
  science and, 404
  secularisation and, 409
  social change and, 429–35
  social constructionist approaches, 395
  social control and, 419
  social groups and, 406–13
  social order and, 416
  substantive definitions of, 394
  truth claims of, 402
religiosity, 395
religious affiliation, 449–50
religious beliefs, 394
religious disengagement, 450
religious fundamentalism, 458–9
religious membership, 444, 447–8
religious movements, 435–7
religious organisation, types of, 396–7
religious participation, 444, 445–7
religious revival, 459–60
religious rights, 500
remarriages, 161
remittances, 543
renaissance children, 211
replication, 83
representation, 547
representative democracy, 495
representativeness in research, 109
representative sample, 79
Repression 2.0, 329
Repressive State Apparatuses, 234
reproductive rights, 61, 185
research data, 1
research ethics, 109–10
  anonymity and confidentiality, 109
  deception, 109
  informed consent, 109
  participants' privacy, 109
  protection from harm, 109
research ethics committee (REC), 109
research methods
  assessment of quality of, 108–9
  conduct of research, 108
  formulating research questions and hypotheses, 105
  interpretation of results, 108
  operationalisation of concepts, 108
  qualitative, 88–96
  quantitative, 80–7
  research strategy, 105
  samples, sampling frames and sampling techniques, 105–7
  stages of designing research, 105–9
residency, 564
resistance, 25
response rate, 82
restricted code, 283
retreatists, 306
reverse cultural flows, 489
Reynolds, Kate, 261
right-wing populism, 330
Rikowski, Glenn, 237–8
risk societies, 21, 515
rites of passage, 67
rituals, 394
Ritzer, George, 491
rockers, 388
Roe, Keith, 217
role allocation, 230
role models, 36
roles, 33
Rompaey, Veerle Van, 217
Ross, Nicola, 220

Roth, Kenneth, 332
ruling-class ideology, 232, 338
Rutter, Jill, 220

## S

sacralisation, 452
sacred, 414
Saint-Simon, Henri de, 2
Salisbury, Julian, 43
Salway, Sarah, 224
same-sex or gay marriage, 157–9
sample, 82
sample attrition, 116
sampling frame, 106
sampling technique, 106
sampling unit, 106
sanctions, 50
Sandbrook, Dominic, 39
sandwich carers, 219
Saunders, Peter, 248–9, 272, 274
scapegoating, 555
scarce resources, 547
sceptical globalism, 473–4
schisms, 441
Scholte, Jan Aarte, 493
science
  critical views of, 402–3
  Enlightenment and, 402
  knowledge claims of, 401
  laboratory-based studies of, 403
  postmodernism and, 403–4
  relationship between religion and, 404
scientific revolution, 126
Scott, John, 254
secondary data, 76
secondary socialisation, 37–9, 229
  college or university as an agency of, 37
  formal education and, 37–8
  media as agencies of, 39
  peer groups and friendship networks as agents of, 38
  religion as agent of, 39
  workplace as an agent of, 38
second modernity, 312
second shift, 196
sects, 397, 455
secular arrangements, 32
secular assimilation, 552
secularisation, 164, 409, 440–1, 452–3
  measures of, 444–7
  religious movements and, 451–3
secularisation thesis, 441–3
segregation, 552
self, 15, 43
self-completion questionnaires, 80
self-concept, 294
self-consciousness, 26
self-fulfilling prophecy, 15, 294–5
self-identity, 24
self-religions, 20
self-spirituality, 400
Semenya, Caster, 65
semiology, 103
semiotic analysis, 103
semi-structured interviews, 88
'sensorimotor' stage, 35
serial monogamy, 157
setting, 296, 303
Sewell, Tony, 305–6
sexualisation of childhood, 210
shadow economy, 560
Shain, Farzana, 303
shell companies, 571
Shils, Edward, 50
shop-floor culture, 235
shop stewards, 344, 384
Silim, Amna, 220
Simon, Joel, 329
simple random sampling, 106
simulacra, 348
simulations, 348
single parent families, 165–6
single-person households, 166
Sissons, Mary, 85
sites of ideological struggle, 233
skivers and strivers, 343
slanderous, 496
Slatin, Gerald, 85, 87
smacking, 46
Smart, Carol, 172, 174–5
snowball sampling, 107
sociability, 205
social action theory, 15, 18, 43, 215
social attitudes, changes in, 163–4
social behaviour, 2
social blurring, 210
social capital, 17, 239, 479
social change, 2, 5, 25, 455
  ethnic identity and, 66
  feminine identity and, 61
  masculine identity and, 61–4
social class
  researching interaction between strangers, 85
  teacher expectations and, 85
social construction of society, 41–2
social controls, 4, 44
  by consent, 44–5
  education as an important agency of, 45
  formal agencies of, 44–5
  informal agencies of, 45–9
  religion as agency of, 48–9
  workplace as agency of, 45
social democracy, 338
social desirability effect, 84
social differentiation, 441
social exchange, 50
social exchange theory, 17–18
social facts, 118–19
social identities, 5, 24
  age and, 67
  approaches to, 54–5
  construction of, 53
  ethnic identity and, 66
  ethnicity and, 64–6
  gender and, 60–4
  new media and, 359–64
  self-identity and, 53
  social class and, 55–60
  in UK, 360
social integration, 8, 499
socialisation, 5, 24, 35
  primary, 35–7
  secondary, 37–9
socialist or Marxist feminism, 179, 190–3
social learning theory, 36
  nature *versus* nurture debate, 40–1
social meanings, 15
social media
  effect on identity, 481
  growth of, 478
  use, 362–3
  women's identity and, 481–3
social mobility
  absolute, 252
  comparative studies of education and, 254–5
  defining, 252
  feminist approaches to, 256–7
  functionalist perspective, 255
  gendered, 257
  intergenerational mobility, 252
  intragenerational mobility, 252
  measuring, 252–3
  New Right or neoliberal approaches to, 256
  relative, 252
social mores and laws, 33
social movement, 526
social pressure, 50
social relations of production, 10
social reproduction, 240
social resistance, 4
social rights, 500
social solidarity, 8, 228
social status, 17
social stratification, 230
social structure, 12, 42
social survey, 80, 116
societalisation, 441
society, 24
sociological history of feminism, 178
sociological research, approaches to
  assessment, 138–9
  case studies, 112
  characteristics of researcher, 133
  cost and funding issues, 133
  ethical influences on, 133
  ethnography, 112–15
  longitudinal study, 115–16
  mixed-methods approaches, 122–3
  positivist/quantitative and interpretivist/ qualitative approaches, 117–22
  practical influences on, 132–3
  role of values in, 127–8
  social survey, 116
  sources of bias, 136–7
  subjects, 133
  theoretical influences on, 133–5
  time, 133
  topic and research questions, 133
Somerville, Jennifer, 189
South Asian students, 302–3
South-eastern Asian culture, 29
sovereignty, 499
space–time compression, 465
specialised division of labour, 229
specific value, 29
spectacular youth subcultures, 47
Spender, Dale, 264
Spicer, André, 264
spirit of capitalism, 431
spiritual individualism, 458
spiritual revolution, 452
spiritual shopping, 458
stabilisation of adult personality, 149
Stanworth, Michelle, 320–1
Stark, Rodney, 399
state-sponsored trolling, 330
Statham, June, 220
status, 13
status inequality, 13
Stephens, Jordan, 62, 202
Stier, Sebastian, 330
Stoltenborgh, Marije, 214
Strand, Steve, 304
stratification system, 253
stratified random sampling, 106
streaming, 295–7

Strinati, Dominic, 20
structural assimilation, 552
structural differentiation, 148, 441
structuralist theories of society, 42–3
structural perspective, 7–8
structured interviews
limitations of, 84
reasons for non-response, 83
strengths of, 83–4
structured observation, 95
4 + 1 students, 297–8
subculture, 47, 280–1
British Chinese students', 305
of deviant students in China, 297–8
female school, 318–19
gender and, 315–19
pupil, 297
subjectivity, 127
subordinate forms of masculinity, 63
sub-prime mortgage market, collapse of, 20
suffrage movement, 178
Sugarman, Barry, 281
Sullivan, Alice, 288–9
superstructure, 10–11
Supreme Court, 496
surrogacy, 173
Survivors, 319
sustainable development, 507
Sutton, Philip, 265
Suzman, James, 38
Swartz, David L., 233
symbol, 15
symbolic annihilation of women, 481
symbolic capital, 239
symbolic cultural artefacts, 27
symbolic interactionism, 15
symbolisation, 47
symmetrical family, 195
synergistic learning, 221
Syrian civil war, 546
systematic observation, 95

# T

Tarde, Gabriel, 36
tariffs (taxes), 524
tastes of dominant classes, 287–8
teachers' perceptions
of ethnicity, 302–3
gendered expectations, 320
of students' social class, 292–3
technological convergence, 351
terms of world trade, 531
test-tube baby, 173
textual analysis, 102–3
thematic analysis, 102
theocracies, 498
theodicy of disprivilege, 455
theodicy of good fortune, 406
theodicy of misfortune, 406
theoretical imperialism, 179
Thompson, Grahame, 490
Thompson, Karl, 37, 574
tied aid, 526
Tiger, Lionel, 41
time-budget studies, 196
Toraja, 32
totemism, 415
toxic masculinity, 61–2, 180, 201–2
transcendental Meditation (TM), 398
transgender identity, 63
transgressive criminology, 578
transnational companies (TNCs), 332, 501, 524–6, 531
transnational identities, 556
transnational organisations, 522–7
transphobic women, 180
transsexual identity, 63
transworld instantaneity, 493
transworld simultaneity, 493
triangular slave trade, 530
triangulation, 123
tricks of a trade, 38
trilemma, 545
triple shift, 198
triple systems theory, 192
Trump, Donald, 101
truth decay, 513
Tunstall, Jeremy, 39
Twenge, Jean, 39
Twitter, 357, 508–9

# U

underclass, 170, 378
under-employment, 543
United Nations (UN), 522–3
unit of consumption, 155
universalism, 529
universalistic, 283
universalistic standards, 229
Universal suffrage, 496
unstructured interviews
interview process, 88
limitations of, 89–90
strengths of, 88–9
unstructured observation, 95
urbanisation, 147
Usher, Robin, 260

# V

Valentine, Gill, 68, 215
value, 29–30
researchers', 137
value consensus, 8
value free, 118
variables, 84
Vauclair, Christin-Melanie, 68
Venkatesh, Alladi, 20
Vernon, Philip, 273
verstehen, 122
victim surveys, 98
*Violence Against Wives* (Rebecca Dobash and Russell Dobash), 184–5
virtual communities, 478
vocationalism, 244
voluntarist approach, 43
voluntary childlessness, 172
volunteer samples, 107

# W

Wages for Housework (WFH) campaign, 191
Wah, Francis Loh Kok, 29
Wahhabi religious clerics and scholars, 498
Walby, Sylvia, 192
Waldfogel, Jane, 278
Wallis, Roy, 396, 398–9, 407
Warin, Jo, 224
Washbrook, Elizabeth, 278
Watson, James, 383
Web 2.0, 351
Weber, Max, 13, 406, 430–2, 555
welfare-dependent 'problem' families, 170
welfare state, 206, 384, 545
Wenyu Chai, 46
Western cultures, 30
Western European societies, 39
Western IQ tests, 273
Westernisation, 490–3
Western societies
life chances of educational attainment, 249
rise in juvenile crime rates and anti-social behaviour in, 170
Western-style democracy, 27
whistle-blower, 577
Whitty, Geoff, 286
Wilkins, Leslie, 387
Wilkinson, Helen, 160
Willer, David, 18
Williamson, Bill, 246
Willis, Paul, 38, 234–6
*Learning to Labour*, 236
Wilson, Adrian, 205
Wolf, Naomi, 39, 180
Wollstonecraft, Mary, 178
Woodhead, Linda, 409–10
Wooldridge, Adrian, 39
Woolgar, Steve, 403
workhouse, 206
working-class masculinity, 235
world-accommodating new religious movements, 398–9
world-affirming new religious movements, 399
World Bank, 525
world capitalist system, 530
World Press Freedom Index, 326–7
world-rejecting new religious movements, 398
World Trade Organization (WTO), 524
Wrong, Dennis, 9, 12

# X

xenophobia, 485
Xuesong, 46

# Y

Youdell, Deborah, 293, 301–2
Young, Michael F.D., 259, 261–2

# Z

Zanetti, Lisa, 20
Zaretsky, Eli, 154–5
zemiology, 579
zones of consumption, 560
zones of distribution, 560
zones of production, 560
Zulu communities, 158

# PERMISSIONS ACKNOWLEDGEMENTS

The publishers gratefully acknowledge the permission granted to reproduce the copyright material in this book. Every effort has been made to trace copyright holders and to obtain their permission for the use of copyright material. The publishers will gladly receive any information enabling them to rectify any error or omission at the first opportunity.

**Images:** (l = left, r = right, t = top, b = bottom)

p. 1 Michele Burgess/Alamy Stock Photo, p. 2 Claudia Otte/Shutterstock, p. 3l Cryptographer/Shutterstock, p. 3r Matt Grant/Shutterstock, p. 4 John Roman Images/Shutterstock, p. 6 Rena Schild/Shutterstock, p. 8 Chanawat Phadwichit/Shutterstock, p. 16l Monkey Business Images/Shutterstock, p. 16r ESB Professional/Shutterstock, p. 17l Rido/Shutterstock, p. 17r Africa Studio/Shutterstock, pp. 24–25 BERENGERE CAVALIER/Alamy Stock Photo, p. 28t Everett Historical/Shutterstock, p. 28b Kobby Dagan/ Shutterstock, p. 30 Rawpixel.com/Shutterstock, p. 31 Kidsada Manchinda/ Shutterstock, p. 32l RubberBall/Alamy Stock Photo, p. 32r Dina Julayeva/ Shutterstock, p. 36 Kim Petersen/Alamy Stock Photo, p. 38 Monkey Business Images/Shutterstock, p. 46 © NSPCC Archive, p. 47 Olaf Schuelke/Alamy Stock Photo, p. 48 By Ian Miles-Flashpoint Pictures/Alamy Stock Photo, p. 54 Rachel Torres/Alamy Stock Photo, p. 57 Nestor Rizhniak/Shutterstock, p. 58 gualtiero boffi/Shutterstock, p. 62t © CALM, p. 62b WENN Rights Ltd/Alamy Stock Photo, p. 63 ZUMA Press, Inc./ Alamy Stock Photo, p. 64t CRS PHOTO/Shutterstock, p. 64b Ben Speck / Getty Images, p. 65 CP DC Press/Shutterstock, p. 68 Goncalo Diniz/Alamy Stock Photo, p. 69 CTK/Alamy Stock Photo, pp. 74–75 Stefan Dahl Langstrup/Alamy Stock Photo, p. 77 fstockfoto/Shutterstock, p. 78 Robyn Mackenzie/Shutterstock, p. 83 MAKI STUDIO/Alamy Stock Photo, p. 90 pixelheadphoto digitalskillets/Shutterstock, p. 93 View Stock/Alamy Stock Photo, p. 97 Larina Marina/Shutterstock, p. 99 World History Archive/ Alamy Stock Photo, p. 101 Tribune Content Agency LLC/Alamy Stock Photo, p. 102l fyv6561/Shutterstock, p. 102r Arterra Picture Library/ Alamy Stock Photo, p. 104 IZIS/Contributor/Getty Images, p. 106 Bakhtiar Zein/Shutterstock, p. 113 Yale University Press, p. 114 LAKRUWAN WANNIARACHCHI/Stringer/Getty, p. 118 michaeljung/Shutterstock, p. 122 imageBROKER/Alamy Stock Photo, p. 125 Mark Christopher Cooper/ Shutterstock, p. 127 Derek Meijer/Alamy Stock Photo, p. 135 Hero Images Inc./Alamy Stock Photo, pp. 142–143 Blend Images/Shutterstock, p. 144 Steve Speller/Alamy Stock Photo, p. 146 KPG_Payless/Shutterstock, p. 149l Pro Symbols/Shutterstock, p. 149r LightField Studios/Shutterstock, p. 152 NASA Photo/Alamy Stock Photo, p. 155 Helen Sessions/Alamy Stock Photo, p. 158t dpa picture alliance/Alamy Stock Photo, p. 160 Alex Segre/ Alamy Stock Photo, p. 167l Hero Images Inc./Alamy Stock Photo, p. 167r Kertu Saarits/Alamy Stock Photo, p. 177 Asiaselects/Alamy Stock Photo, p. 179 IanDagnall Computing/Alamy Stock Photo, p. 180 WENN Rights Ltd/ Alamy Stock Photo, p. 183l Marko Poplasen/Shutterstock, p. 183r Licensed under the Open Government Licence v3.0, p. 188 The Advertising Archive, p. 194 Trinity Mirror/Mirrorpix/Alamy Stock Photo, p. 195 xmee/ Shutterstock, p. 198 Olesya Kuznetsova/Shutterstock, p. 204 By Anthonius or Antoon Claeissins (www.weissgallery.com)[Public domain], via Wikimedia Commons, p. 206 chippix/Shutterstock, p. 207 pixelheadphoto digitalskillet/Shutterstock, p. 212 oliveromg/Shutterstock, p. 220 Monkey Business Images/Shutterstock, pp. 226–227 Caroline Penn/Alamy Stock Photo, p. 229 Hill Street Studios/Getty Images, p. 230 Chris Ryan/Getty Images, p. 231 Robert Kneschke/Shutterstock, p. 233l Jonathan Goldberg/ Alamy Stock Photo, p. 233r Monkey Business Images/Shutterstock, p. 235 Trinity Mirror/Mirrorpix/Alamy Stock Photo, p. 237 Middlesex University Press Release, p. 239 Igor Bulgarin/Shutterstock, p. 242 Prazis Images/ Shutterstock, p. 244 Robert Daemmrich Photography Inc/Getty Images, p. 245t flydragon/Shutterstock, p. 245b © World Bank, p. 248 Prazis Images/ Shutterstock, p. 250t Hindustan Times/Getty Images, p. 250b Hafizur_ rahman/Shutterstock, p. 255 begalphoto/Shutterstock, p. 256l Dima Sidelnikov/Shutterstock, p. 257 Rawpixel.com/Shutterstock, p. 260l Marcio Jose Bastos Silva/Shutterstock, p. 260r ProStockStudio/Shutterstock, p. 262 kaisayaShutterstock, p. 263 © FAWE 2017, p. 265 f11photo/ Shutterstock, p. 266 Patricia Dulasi/Shutterstock, p. 269 Solis Images/ Shutterstock, p. 270 Monkey Business Images/Shutterstock, p. 272 CP DC Press/Shutterstock, p. 273 Jirsak/Shutterstock, p. 275 wavebreakmedia/ Shutterstock, p. 276 lenetstan/Shutterstock, p. 279 Monkey Business Images/Shutterstock, p. 280 wong yu liang/Shutterstock, p. 282l milatas/ Shutterstock, p. 282r Monkey Business Images/Shutterstock, p. 286 © LBJ Library photo by Yoichi Okamoto, p. 287 Monkey Business Images/ Shutterstock, p. 290 MBI/Alamy Stock Photo, p. 293 Monkey Business Images/Shutterstock, p. 295 wavebreakmedia/Shutterstock, p. 296 milatas/Shutterstock, p. 298 TonyV3112/Shutterstock, p. 304 Flamingo Images/Shutterstock, p. 306 JGI/Tom Grill/Getty Images, p. 308 Glynsimages2013/Shutterstock, p. 309t Illustration from 5c More Sounds to Say by Harry Wingfield © Ladybird Books Ltd., 1965, p. 309b Grisha Bruev/Shutterstock, p. 311 Muhammed Furqan/Alamy Stock Photo, p. 312 Asier Romero/Shutterstock, p. 313 Jane Williams/Alamy Stock Photo, p. 317 rawpixel.com/Shutterstock, p. 321 Monkey Business Images/ Shutterstock, pp. 324–325 Anthony Brown/Alamy Stock Photo, p. 326 jeremy sutton-hibbert/Alamy Stock Photo, p. 337 kpzfoto/Alamy Stock Photo, p. 339 World History Archive/Alamy Stock Photo, p. 342 Lenscap/ Alamy Stock Photo, p. 346 The Photo Works/Alamy Stock Photo, p. 349 SFIO CRACHO/Shutterstock, p. 351 imageBROKER/Alamy Stock Photo, p. 353 Historic Collection/Alamy Stock Photo, p. 356 Barry Iverson/Alamy Stock Photo, p. 357 ZUMA Press, Inc./Alamy Stock Photo, p. 361 © Geric Cruz, p. 363 Mim Friday/Alamy Stock Photo, p. 365 Pictorial Press Ltd/ Alamy Stock Photo, p. 368 Hera Vintage Ads/Alamy Stock Photo, p. 370 Matthew Ashton/Contributor/Getty Images, p. 372 Kees Metselaar/Alamy Stock Photo, p. 373 Chronicle/Alamy Stock Photo, p. 377 Photo 12/Alamy Stock Photo, p. 378 Janine Wiedel Photolibrary/Alamy Stock Photo, p. 379 Eamonn M. McCormack/Stringer/Getty Images, p. 382 New York Daily News Archive/Contributor/Getty Images, p. 385 © www.turn2us.org.uk, p. 386 Everett Collection, Inc./Alamy Stock Photo, p. 388l Norman Potter/ Stringer/Getty Images, p. 388r Bentley Archive/Popperfoto/Contributor/ Getty Images, p. 389 Barcroft Media/Contributor/Getty Images, pp. 392–393 Mazur Travel/Shutterstock, p. 395 Vlad1988/Shutterstock, p. 398 Bloomsbury Photo inc./Alamy Stock Photo, p. 403 ProStockStudio/ Shutterstock, p. 404 Aphelleon/Shutterstock, p. 405 Pontino/Alamy Stock Photo, p. 407l Jim West/Alamy Stock Photo, p. 407r Paolo Bona/ Shutterstock, p. 408 CartoonMini/Shutterstock, p. 410l Nikki Zalewski/ Shutterstock, p. 410r IgorZh/Shutterstock, p. 411 cheng/Shutterstock, p. 415t Golden Shrimp/Shutterstock, p. 415b Penny Tweedie/Alamy Stock Photo, p. 416 Tanya Lapidus/Shutterstock, p. 419 Mary Evans Picture Library, p. 420 Baloncici/Shutterstock, p. 422 fredrisher/Shutterstock, p. 424 Chris Cooper-Smith/Alamy Stock Photo, p. 430 The Editorialist/Alamy Stock Photo, p. 431 By John Taylor (1578–1653) [Public domain], via Wikimedia Commons, p. 432 Mary Evans Picture Library, p. 433 Alf Ribeiro/Shutterstock, p. 434 vectorx2263/Shutterstock, p. 436 Mohamed Elsayyed/Shutterstock, p. 437 Everett Historical/Shutterstock, p. 439 robertharding/Alamy Stock Photo, p. 443 nodff /Shutterstock, p. 444 saravutpics/Shutterstock, p. 449 ariyo olasunkanmi/Shutterstock, p. 451t thomas koch/Shutterstock, p. 451b Humanists UK, p. 453 Philip Birtwistle/ Shutterstock, p. 456 Rawpixel.com/Shutterstock, p. 457 Phil Wills/Alamy Stock Photo, pp. 462–463 Yvette Cardozo/Alamy Stock Photo, p. 465 ITAR-TASS News Agency/Alamy Stock Photo, p. 468 kpzfoto/Alamy Stock Photo, p. 469 VanderWolf Images/Shutterstock, p. 470 ZUMA Press, Inc./ Alamy Stock Photo, p. 471 Maryna Shkvyria/Shutterstock, p. 473 David Wells/Alamy Stock Photo, p. 476 Peter Horree/Alamy Stock Photo, p. 480 Ollyy/Shutterstock, p. 482 Jeff Morgan 16/Alamy Stock Photo, p. 486 Contraband Collection/Alamy Stock Photo, p. 487 Granger Historical Picture Archive/Alamy Stock Photo, p. 491 ITAR-TASS News Agency/Alamy Stock Photo, p. 496 Tupungato/Shutterstock, p. 498 S-F/Shutterstock, p. 503 My Eyes4u/Shutterstock.com, p. 506 World History Archive/Alamy Stock Photo, p. 507 Arthur Greenberg/Alamy Stock Photo, p. 508 360b/ alamy Stock Photo, p. 509 GARY DOAK/Alamy Stock Photo, p. 513 AF archive/Alamy Stock Photo, p. 518 Sadik Gulec/Shutterstock, p. 520 Kirk Treakle/Alamy Stock Photo, p. 521 chris kolaczan/Shutterstock, p. 524 Ron Yue/Alamy Stock Photo, p. 527 Photofusion Picture Library/Alamy Stock Photo, p. 531 Joerg Boethling/Alamy Stock Photo, p. 535 JeffG/Alamy Stock Photo, p. 536 dpa picture alliance/Alamy Stock Photo, p. 537 CBP Photo/Alamy Stock Photo, p. 540 dbimages/Alamy Stock Photo, p. 545 Planetpix/Alamy Stock Photo, p. 546 Smallcreative/Shutterstock, p. 549t Paul Smith/Alamy Stock Photo, p. 549b stockcreations/Shutterstock, p. 552l Maksim Shmeljov/Shutterstock, p. 552r Tantse Manton/ Shutterstock, p. 554 Anthony JEAN/Alamy Stock Photo, p. 556 RosalreneBetancourt 9/Alamy Stock Photo, p. 560 Xinhua/Alamy Stock Photo, p. 561 Nikolay Gyngazov/Shutterstock, p. 562l GL Archive/Alamy Stock Photo, p. 562r Courtesy of The Home Office, p. 563 NothingIsEverything/Shutterstock, p. 566 Tansh/Alamy Stock Photo, p. 567 US Coast Guard Photo/Alamy Stock Photo, p. 571 ricochet64/Shutterstock, p. 573 Raj Singh/Alamy Stock Photo, p. 577 RichSTOCK/Alamy Stock Photo, p. 579 Tigergallery/Shutterstock, p. 582 Gábor Páll/Alamy Stock Photo.

Text: We are grateful to the following for permission to reproduce copyright material:

Extract on p.10 for the title 'Reward Work, Not Wealth', https://www.oxfam.org/en/research/reward-work-not-wealth. Reproduced with the permission of Oxfam, Oxfam House, John Smith Drive, Cowley, Oxford OX4 2JY, UK www.oxfam.org.uk. Oxfam does not necessarily endorse any text or activities that accompany the materials; Extracts on p.31 from 'Ugandan women kneeling in deference is cultural – it's also humiliating' by Patience Akumu, *The Guardian*, 21/01/2018, copyright © Guardian News & Media Ltd, 2019; An extract on p.37 from "The Hidden Curriculum and School Ethos" by Karl Thompson, 09/11/2017, https://revisesociology.com/2017/11/09/the-hidden-curriculum-and-school-ethos/. Reproduced with kind permission; An extract on p.53 from 'Facebook and the presentation of self: a structure versus agency approach' by Sarah McLaughlin, *Sociology Review*, Vol.26 (4), April 2017, p.10. Reproduced by permission of Philip Allan (for Hodder Education); An extract on p.62 adapted from 'Toxic masculinity is everywhere. It's up to us men to fix this' by Jordan Stephens, *The Guardian*, 23/10/2017, copyright © Guardian News & Media Ltd, 2019; An extract on p.65 from 'Is this woman too much a man?' by Erik Brady, *USA Today*, 08/05/2018, https://eu.usatoday.com/story/sports/columnist/erik-brady/2018/05/08/track-and-field-olympics-iaaf-ruling-caster-semenya/588443002/ copyright © 2018 Gannett-USA Today. All rights reserved. Used by permission and protected by the Copyright Laws of the United States. The printing, copying, redistribution, or retransmission of this Content without express written permission is prohibited; A table on p.80 from '2011 Global School based Student Health Survey Results', Mauritius Survey, Data location 44-44, Q21, WHO, www.who.in. Reproduced with permission; An extract on p.109 from *The International Sociological Association's Code of Ethics,* https://www.isa-sociology.org/en/about-isa/code-of-ethics/, copyright © ISA, International Sociological Association, 2018. Reproduced with permission; Extracts on pp.134, 320-321 from *Boys, Girls and Achievement: Addressing the Classroom Issues* by Becky Francis, Routledge-Falmer, 2000. Reproduced with permission from Taylor & Francis; An extract on p.167 from 'Too smart, too successful: Mongolia's superwomen struggle to find husbands' by Lily Kuo, *The Guardian*, 24/06/2018, copyright © Guardian News & Media Ltd, 2019; An extract on p.197 from 'Today's parents spend more time with their kids than moms and dads did 50 years ago' by Judith Treas and Giulia Dotti Sani, *UCI News*, 28/09/2016, https://news.uci.edu/2016/09/28/todays-parents-spend-more-time-with-their-kids-than-moms-and-dads-did-50-years-ago/. Reproduced with permission; An extract on p.198 from 'Women's "triple shift": paid employment, domestic labour and "emotion work"' by Jean Duncombe and Dennis Marsden, *Sociology Review*, Vol.4 (4), 1995, p106. Reproduced by permission of Philip Allan (for Hodder Education); Poetry and an extract on pp.234, 235 from *Learning to Labour: How working class kids get working class jobs* by Paul Willis, Columbia University Press, copyright © Paul Willis, 1977. Reproduced with permission from Taylor & Francis; An extract on p.263 from 'The Knowledge-Based Economy', Organisation for Economic Cooperation and Development, 1996, https://www.oecd.org/sti/sci-tech/1913021.pdf, source: OECD; An extract on pp.263-264 from http://fawe.org/home/our-programmes/interventions/science-mathematics-and-technology/, FAWE, Forum for African Women Educationalists. Reproduced with permission; Extracts on p.290 from *Class Strategies and the Education Market: The Middle Classes and Social Advantage* by Stephen J. Ball, 2003, p.168. Reproduced with permission from Taylor & Francis; Extracts on pp.297, 316-317 from *The Making of Men: Masculinities, Sexualities and Schooling* by Mac an Ghaill, M., Open University Press, 2004. Reproduced with permission; Extracts on pp.298, 301 and figure on p.299 from *Rationing Education: Policy, Practice, Reform and Equity* by Gillborn, D. and Youdell, D., Open University Press, 2000. Reproduced with permission; Figure on p.314 showing data from 'Percentage of 18- to 24-year-olds enrolled in degree-granting postsecondary institutions, by level of institution and sex and race/ethnicity of student: 1970 through 2015', in *Digest of Education Statistics, 52nd edition*, 2016 by Thomas D. Snyder, Cristobal de Brey and Sally A. Dillow, 2018, Table 302.60, (NCES 2017-094). National Center for Education Statistics, Institute of Education Sciences, U.S. Department of Education, Washington, DC; Text Box on p.331 'Predator of Press Freedom: Vladimir Putin', https://rsf.org/en/predator/vladimir-putin-0, copyright Reporters Sans Frontières /Reporters Without Borders. Reproduced with permission; Figure on p.333 'Percentage of global population accessing the internet from 2005 to 2017, by market maturity', Statista, https://www.statista.com/statistics/209096/share-of-internet-users-in-the-total-world-population-since-2006/. Reproduced with permission; An extract on p.343 adapted from 'Let's tell the truth about poverty – and stop this assault on welfare' by Mary O'Hara, *The Guardian*, 20/02/2018, copyright © Guardian News & Media Ltd, 2019; An extract on p.350 from 'Racism is not the problem' by Tony Sewell, *The Guardian*, 05/09/2008, copyright © Guardian News & Media Ltd, 2019; An extract on pp.357-358 adapted from *#MeToo Goes Global and Crossed Multiple Boundaries* by Catherine Powell, www.cfr.org, copyright © the Council on Foreign Relations, 2017. Reproduced with permission; An extract on p.361 abridged from *Migration and New Media: Transnational Families and Polymedia* by Mirca Madianou and Daniel Miller, Routledge, 2011. Funded by the Economic and Social Research Council (grant number RES-000-22-2266) and reproduced with kind permission; An extract on p.367 from "Women and the Media", http://beijing20.unwomen.org, copyright © UN Women, 2015. Reproduced with permission; An extract on p.373 from "For Decades, Our Coverage Was Racist. To Rise Above Our Past, We Must Acknowledge It" by Susan Goldberg, *National Geographic,* April 2018, https://www.nationalgeographic.com/. Reproduced with permission; An extract on pp.373-374 from "Bollywood needs to rethink Dalit representation, media scholar says", University News, 08/08/2017, Birmingham City University, https://www.bcu.ac.uk/news-events/news/bollywood-rethink-dalit. Reproduced with permission; Table on p.396 "Belief in God" from *British Social Attitudes Survey 33*, National Centre for Social Research, 2016, http://www.bsa.natcen.ac.uk. Reproduced with permission; Figure on p.447 and table on p.448 from 'UK Church Statistics No.3, 2018' edited by Peter Brierley, http://brierleyconsultancy.com. Reproduced with permission; An extract on p.462 from "Globalization Excerpts from a Keynote Address at the UNRISD Conference on Globalization and Citizenship", 01/12/1996 www.unrisd.org/unrisd/website/newsview.nsf/(httpNews)/3F2A5BF8EF7300D480256B750053C7EC. Reproduced with permission of the United Nations Research Institute for Social Development (UNRISD); Extracts on pp.464, 468, 477, 488, 514 from *Globalization: A Very Short Introduction* by Manfred Steger, 2017, Oxford University Press, copyright © Manfred B. Steger, 2017. Reproduced with permission of the Licensor through PLSClear; An extract on p.500 from https://www.amnesty.org.uk/what-are-human-rights, Amnesty International UK, copyright © amnesty.org.uk. Reproduced with permission; An extract on p.534 from *Global Migration: The Basics* by Bernadette Hanlon and Thomas Vicino, Routledge, 2014, p.1. Reproduced with permission from Taylor & Francis; and an extract on p.539 from *UN International Migration Report*, 2017, United Nations, Department of Economic and Social Affairs, Population Division. International Migration Report 2017: Highlights (ST/ESA/SER.A/404), https://www.un.org/development/desa/publications/international-migration-report-2017.html. Reproduced with permission.